THE ECONOMY TODAY
Ninth Edition

Bradley R. Schiller

American University

Boston   Burr Ridge, IL   Dubuque, IA   Madison, WI   New York   San Francisco   St. Louis
Bangkok   Bogotá   Caracas   Kuala Lumpur   Lisbon   London   Madrid   Mexico City
Milan   Montreal   New Delhi   Santiago   Seoul   Singapore   Sydney   Taipei   Toronto

McGraw-Hill Higher Education

*A Division of The **McGraw-Hill** Companies*

THE ECONOMY TODAY
Published by McGraw-Hill/Irwin, a business unit of The McGraw-Hill Companies, Inc., 1221 Avenue of the Americas, New York, NY, 10020. Copyright ' 2003, 2000, 1 997, 1994, 1991, 1989, 1986, 1983, 1980 by The McGraw-Hill Companies, Inc. All rights reserved. No part of this publication may be reproduced or distributed in any form or by any means, or stored in a database or retrieval system, without the prior written consent of The McGraw-Hill Companies, Inc., including, but not limited to, in any network or other electronic storage or transmission, or broadcast for distance learning. Some ancillaries, including electronic and print components, may not be available to customers outside the United States.

This book is printed on acid-free paper.

domestic   2 3 4 5 6 7 8 9 0 QWV/QWV 0 9 8 7 6 5 4 3 2
international 1 2 3 4 5 6 7 8 9 0 QWV/QWV 0 9 8 7 6 5 4 3 2

ISBN   0-07-286892-9

Publisher: *Gary Burke*
Executive sponsoring editor: *Paul Shensa*
Developmental editor: *Katie Crouch*
Marketing manager: *Martin D. Quinn*
Project manager: *Destiny Rynne*
Lead production supervisor: *Heather D. Burbridge*
Freelance design coordinator: *Laurie J. Entringer*
Producer, Media technology: *Melissa Kansa*
Lead supplement producer: *Becky Szura*
Photo research coordinator: *Jeremy Cheshareck*
Photo researcher: *Jennifer Blankenship*
Cover image: *© Comstock Inc.*
Interior design: *Ark Design*
Typeface: *10/12 Times New Roman*
Compositor: *Techbooks*
Printer: *Quebecor World Versailles Inc.*

Library of Congress Control Number: 2002100717

INTERNATIONAL EDITION ISBN 0-07-115114-1
Copyright ' 2003. Exclusive rights by The McGraw-Hill Companies, Inc. for manufacture and export. This book cannot be re-exported from the country to which it is sold by McGraw-Hill. The International Edition is not available in North America.

www.mhhe.com

REAL GROSS DOMESTIC PRODUCT IN CHAIN-WEIGHTED DOLLARS, 1929–2000 (1996 = 100)*

Year	GDP	Personal Consumption Expenditures Total	Gross Private Domestic Investment Total	Net Exports			Government Purchases					Percent Change from Prior Year GDP
				Net	Exports	Imports	Total	Federal			State and Local	
								Total	National Defense	Non-Defense		
1929	942	636	174	2	41	39	129	25	—	—	104	—
1930	858	596	122	0	34	34	139	28	—	—	111	−8.9
1931	792	574	100	−2	28	31	143	28	—	—	115	−7.7
1932	687	537	28	−2	22	25	138	27	—	—	108	−13.3
1933	673	513	30	−3	22	26	135	35	—	—	101	−2.1
1934	725	551	47	−1	25	26	150	45	—	—	94	7.7
1935	781	559	78	−8	27	35	156	46	—	—	113	7.7
1936	892	612	103	−5	29	34	182	72	—	—	109	14.2
1937	930	636	120	−2	36	38	174	67	—	—	112	4.3
1938	893	621	78	4	35	30	186	71	—	—	114	−4.0
1939	964	675	95	5	37	32	200	97	17	56	124	7.9
1940	1,039	687	139	9	43	33	207	87	45	54	119	7.8
1941	1,227	721	171	3	44	41	331	215	169	40	114	18.2
1942	1,473	721	93	−12	30	42	678	564	484	28	107	20.0
1943	1,766	742	61	−37	25	57	995	895	781	17	99	19.9
1944	1,915	769	67	−33	28	72	1,113	1,014	882	21	96	8.4
1945	1,838	819	94	−27	37	65	951	852	748	12	99	−4.0
1946	1,459	893	212	30	76	46	310	201	166	29	109	−20.8
1947	1,436	898	228	48	90	42	251	127	97	33	124	−1.5
1948	1,491	932	263	19	69	50	276	144	94	50	131	3.8
1949	1,497	953	214	19	68	48	308	160	105	54	147	.4
1950	1,627	1,002	296	3	60	57	326	167	125	41	159	8.7
1951	1,787	1,014	296	12	73	61	455	294	257	36	161	8.8
1952	1,863	1,059	323	2	71	68	536	372	326	45	164	4.3
1953	1,933	1,012	275	−8	79	76	561	389	329	60	172	3.7
1954	1,919	1,132	268	−2	71	73	521	335	288	47	174	−.7
1955	2,028	1,200	326	−6	77	83	506	307	267	40	198	5.6
1956	2,068	1,231	323	−1	89	89	509	303	266	37	205	2.0
1957	2,108	1,268	306	−2	97	95	533	316	279	37	217	1.8
1958	2,097	1,287	283	−19	84	78	546	312	265	46	234	−.5
1959	2,319	1,470	272	−34	72	106	661	395	325	65	260	7.2
1960	2,376	1,510	272	−21	87	108	661	380	322	58	275	2.5
1961	2,432	1,541	271	−19	88	107	693	395	332	63	298	2.3
1962	2,578	1,617	305	−26	93	119	735	423	345	78	306	6.0
1963	2,690	1,684	325	−22	100	122	752	425	338	82	322	4.3
1964	2,846	1,784	352	−15	114	129	767	418	323	95	344	5.8
1965	3,028	1,897	402	−26	116	142	791	424	321	98	367	6.4
1966	3,227	2,006	437	−40	124	164	862	466	362	99	391	6.6
1967	3,308	2,066	417	−49	127	176	927	504	404	100	418	2.5
1968	3,466	2,184	441	−78	136	202	956	514	415	95	442	4.8
1969	3,571	2,264	466	−70	143	213	952	493	391	98	459	3.0
1970	3,578	2,317	436	−64	159	223	931	456	354	98	471	.2
1971	3,697	2,405	485	−75	160	235	913	426	324	102	484	3.3
1972	3,898	2,550	543	−88	173	261	914	423	315	108	487	5.4
1973	4,123	2,675	606	−62	211	273	908	402	294	104	506	5.8
1974	4,099	2,653	561	−36	231	267	924	396	284	109	528	−.6
1975	4,084	2,710	462	−7	230	237	942	397	279	115	545	−.4
1976	4,311	2,868	555	−41	243	284	943	393	277	115	548	5.6
1977	4,511	2,992	639	−66	249	315	952	404	280	122	548	4.6
1978	4,760	3,124	713	−67	275	342	982	412	285	127	568	5.5
1979	4,912	3,203	735	−45	302	347	1,001	420	291	129	579	3.2
1980	4,900	3,193	655	+10	334	324	1,020	439	303	134	581	−.2
1981	5,021	3,236	715	+5	338	333	1,030	459	322	137	570	2.5
1982	4,919	3,275	615	−15	314	329	1,046	477	349	128	567	−2.0
1983	5,132	3,454	673	−64	306	370	1,081	506	371	135	575	4.3
1984	5,505	3,640	871	−129	332	461	1,118	525	395	129	593	7.3
1985	5,717	3,820	863	−149	341	490	1,190	560	423	137	629	3.8
1986	5,912	3,981	857	−165	366	531	1,255	586	445	141	669	3.4
1987	6,113	4,113	879	−156	408	564	1,292	597	450	146	695	3.4
1988	6,368	4,279	902	−112	473	585	1,307	586	446	138	721	4.2
1989	6,591	4,393	936	−79	529	608	1,343	594	443	150	749	3.5
1990	6,707	4,474	907	−56	575	632	1,387	606	443	163	781	1.8
1991	6,676	4,466	829	−15	613	629	1,403	604	438	166	798	−.5
1992	6,880	4,594	899	−19	651	670	1,410	595	417	177	815	3.0
1993	7,062	4,748	977	−59	672	731	1,398	572	394	177	827	2.7
1994	7,347	4,928	1,107	−86	732	819	1,400	551	375	175	848	4.0
1995	7,543	5,075	1,140	−78	808	886	1,406	536	361	174	869	2.7
1996	7,813	5,237	1,242	−89	874	963	1,421	531	357	174	890	3.6
1997	8,159	5,423	1,393	−113	981	1,094	1,455	529	347	181	925	4.4
1998	8,515	5,678	1,566	−221	1,003	1,224	1,486	526	341	185	959	4.4
1999	8,875	5,978	1,669	−322	1,033	1,355	1,536	540	348	191	995	4.2
2000	9,224	6,258	1,773	−399	1,133	1,532	1,573	546	349	197	1,026	5.0

*Years 1929–1958 approximated with constant 1992 prices.

ABOUT THE AUTHOR

Bradley R. Schiller has over three decades of experience teaching introductory economics at American University, the University of California (Berkeley and Santa Cruz), and the University of Maryland. He has given guest lectures at more than 100 colleges ranging from Fresno, California, to Istanbul, Turkey. Dr. Schiller's unique contribution to teaching is his ability to relate basic principles to current socioeconomic problems, institutions, and public policy decisions. This perspective is evident throughout *The Economy Today*.

Dr. Schiller derives this policy focus from his extensive experience as a Washington consultant. He has been a consultant to most major federal agencies, many congressional committees, and political candidates. In addition, he has evaluated scores of government programs and helped design others. His studies of discrimination, training programs, tax reform, pensions, welfare, Social Security, and lifetime wage patterns have appeared in both professional journals and popular media. Dr. Schiller is also a frequent commentator on economic policy for television, radio, and newspapers.

Dr. Schiller received his Ph.D. from Harvard in 1969. His B.A. degree, with great distinction, was completed at the University of California (Berkeley) in 1965. He is now a professor of economics in the School of Public Affairs at American University in Washington, D.C.

PREFACE

The terrorist attacks of September 11, 2001, increased the demand for economic education. In the immediate aftermath of those attacks, there was worldwide anxiety about the stability of the U.S. economy. Would the attacks topple the already-teetering U.S. economy into a deep and prolonged recession, dragging the world economy down with it? Or would the U.S. economy bounce back from the terrorists' "external shock" before much damage was done? Overnight, the field of economics attracted a larger and more attentive audience. That audience wants to know how the economy works, how global economies interact, and whether governments can assure economic security.

Can we deliver the goods? Can we explain how the pieces of the economy fit together? Can we identify the circumstances that justify government intervention in the marketplace? Can we explain how and why the Federal Reserve's lightning-fast injections of liquidity averted a financial meltdown in the aftermath of the terrorist attacks? Or why airport security might be a "public good" requiring government subsidy? Or why "saving Social Security" took a back seat to saving the economy in budget debates? Last, but far from least, can we convey all this information in a manner that students will actually absorb?

These are not small challenges. For nearly three decades I have been trying to meet these challenges in *The Economy Today*. My approach has been to deliver a focused, logically ordered introduction to economic principles. Rather than aspiring to encyclopedic coverage, *The Economy Today* strives to develop, illustrate, and review the core ideas of economic theory. To reinforce and enliven these concepts, *The Economy Today* teaches principles in a real-world context that students will recognize. Robinson Crusoe-type fables don't cut it with today's students. Nor do illustrations based on Aunt Gertrude's widget factory. As the accompanying *In the News* confirms, today's students want a slice of reality in their college courses.

The Economy Today has always delivered that slice and more, and the ninth edition is no exception. My Washington, D.C. base gives me a special advantage in illustrating how the real world challenges policymakers, in both macro principles (e.g. post-terrorist stabilization policy) and micro principles (e.g. anti-trust, energy regulation, Social Security). The real world is not confined to a few boxed inserts, but instead imbues the entire text. Students get the whole reality cake, not just a few crumbs. Experience has shown that teaching economics in such a pervasive real-world context awakens and sustains student interest in economic principles.

IN THE NEWS

Real World 101
Colleges Scramble to Serve Students Looking for Classes That Elucidate Current Events

Who knew that the University of Nebraska houses American academia's only Afghanistan studies center? Or that a top-notch geography department would put Southwest Texas State University in San Marcos on the map for CIA recruiters? Before September 11, such specialties attracted scant attention and few students. But the speed with which colleges nationwide have raced to accommodate the stampede of undergraduates suddenly interested in war-related subject areas has stunned even seasoned educators (and turned scores into celebrity-experts).

—Mary Lord

Source: *U.S. News & World Report,* November 5, 2001. Reprinted with permission. www.usnews.com

Analysis: Real-world events and issues spark student interest in academic courses. No text brings the real world into the economics course as much as *The Economy Today*.

The next few pages highlight the features that differentiate *The Economy Today* from other introductory texts. Over the years, some of those pioneering features have been copied by other texts. That suggests that competition still exists in the textbook market despite the mergers that have greatly reduced the number of publishers. In the spirit of that competition, *The Economy Today* keeps advancing pedagogical technology and updating content, staying ahead of the pack. I hope you and your students will profit from these efforts.

CENTRAL THEMES

Like no other text, *The Economy Today* is designed around four central themes that set the tone and content of the entire book.

Real-World Focus

The foremost motivating theme for *The Economy Today* is to understand the economy around us. In Chapter 2, students get a summary description of what the U.S. economy looks like and how it stacks up to other economies around the world. Students hear a lot about the inequality of U.S. incomes. But do they know that incomes are distributed far more equally in the United States than in Mexico, South Africa, or Brazil? (see World View, p.40) Chapter 2 establishes an empirical foundation for assessing economic performance. Business, consumer, global, and policy applications of economic principles are used throughout the text both to illustrate and reinforce basic principles. This is not an easy job. To do it successfully, the text must reflect the salient economic events and issues that captivate Main Street, Wall Street, Capitol Hill, and other world capitals. The issues range from terrorist "shocks," to the Microsoft antitrust case, to President Bush's rejection of the Kyoto treaty on global warming, to Social Security reform, to the demise of "dot.com" companies. Every chapter directly links basic economic principles to these headline-capturing issues, enlivening student interest and improving students' retention of the material.

Clean, Clear Theory

Despite the abundance of real-world applications, this is at heart a *principles* text, not a compendium of issues. Good theory and interesting applications are not mutually exclusive. This is a text that wants to *teach economics,* not just increase awareness of policy issues. To that end, *The Economy Today* provides a logically organized and uncluttered theoretical structure for macro, micro, and international theory. What distinguishes this text from others on the market is that it conveys this theory in a lively, student-friendly manner.

WHAT, HOW, and FOR WHOM

The core issues of WHAT, HOW, and FOR WHOM to produce are used as the links to connect economic principles with real-world issues. After the nature of these three core issues is discussed in Chapter 1, they become a foundation for organizing subsequent issues and applications. Chapter 2 gives students a graphic overview of how these issues have been resolved in the United States and other countries. In all subsequent chapters, prominent policy issues are explicitly discussed within the WHAT, HOW, and FOR WHOM context.

This emphasis on the three core issues is very different from approaches that emphasize a finite set of core principles or topical applications, approaches that are inherently subjective and necessarily incomplete. More importantly, any list of topical applications is ultimately just a collection of variants of the three core issues. The core issues of WHAT, HOW and FOR WHOM, not any particular set of their applications, are what command universal acceptance. It's far more important for students to recognize this core content than to memorize any particular list of applications.

Who Decides—Markets or Government?

This book also emphasizes the importance of the decision mechanisms we use to resolve the core issues. This is the "markets vs. government" debate. Should we let Adam Smith's "invisible hand" steer the economy, or should the government intervene to alter market outcomes? Should nations intervene to "protect" their currencies, or should they

PREFACE **vii**

let the financial markets alone set international exchanges rates? Rather than answering these questions, *The Economy Today* emphasizes the importance of decision mechanisms for our economic welfare. Right up front in Chapter 1, the potential for *market* failure as well as *government* failure is recognized. No panacea is offered, just a scientific way of thinking about how markets work and why we so often depend on them, yet at other times reject them.

DISTINCTIVE APPLICATIONS

In addition to the thematic elements that differentiate *The Economy Today* from its competitors, I have woven a set of applications into the text that further sets it apart.

In The News. Boxed applications taken from the front pages of *The Wall Street Journal, The Washington Post, The New York Times, Fortune, Business Week,* and other media are placed throughout the text. Four features make my *In the News* boxes distinctive. First, every one of them has a caption that ties the news story to key concepts. Second, every *In the News* box is referenced in the body of the text. Third, the *In the News* boxes are the subject of end-of-chapter discussion questions, problems in the *Student Problem Set,* and a designated subset of questions in the *Test Bank*. These three features make the *In the News* boxes an integral part of the learning process rather than just random add-ons. Finally, the 130 *In The News* boxes cover stories that will interest students, making the learning process a whole lot easier.

World Views. The 70 *World Views* boxes placed throughout the text offer global applications of key economic concepts. Like the domestic-oriented *In The News* boxes, all of the *World Views* are annotated with explanatory captions, referenced in the body of the text, and linked to the supplements as the subject of self-test, homework, and exam questions.

The Economy Tomorrow. Every chapter of the text ends with a future-looking application called *The Economy Tomorrow*. These sections challenge the student to apply the principles they have just learned to an ongoing or emerging policy issue. In Chapter 3, students are asked to decide whether the government should intervene to suppress price spikes in energy markets. In Chapter 9, the ability of the *Index of Leading Indicators* to foretell the future is assessed. In Chapter 12, students are asked whether the budget surplus should be used to "save" Social Security or put to other uses. In micro, the effects of B2B commerce on the evolution of market structures is considered (Chapter 21), as is the impact of competition on the (plunging) price of HDTVs (Chapter 23). In the international arena, the future role of the World Trade Organization is discussed. All of *The Economy Tomorrow* sections reinforce key concepts while emphasizing the urgency of their role in shaping the dimensions of our economic future.

Photos and Cartoons

The text presentation is occasionally enlivened with photos and cartoons that reflect basic concepts. The photos on page 39 are much more vivid testimony to the extremes of inequality than the data in Figure 2.6 (page 38). The contrasting photos of the original Apple I (page 498) and the iMac (page 507) underscore how the "animal spirits" of competitive markets spur innovation. Hopefully, that kind of photographic testimony will spark greater student interest in the mechanisms of income distribution. The cartoon on page 393 reminds students that economists are not all of the same mind. Every photo and cartoon is annotated and referenced in the body of the text. These visual features are an integral part of the presentation, not diversions.

DISTINCTIVE PEDAGOGY

My insistence on attaching explanatory captions to every photo, cartoon, and news box is representative of another differentiating feature of *The Economy Today*—user-friendly pedagogy. No matter how good the theoretical structure of a text is, it won't impress students unless it's taught in a user-friendly and productive way. That is why pedagogy has always been a central concern of this text.

Readability

The one adjective invariably used to describe *The Economy Today* is "readability." Professors often express a bit of shock when they realize that students actually enjoy reading the book. (Well, not as much as a Steven King novel, but a whole lot better than most textbooks they've had to plow through.) The writing style is lively and issue-focused. Unlike any other textbook on the market, every boxed feature, every graph, every table, and every cartoon is explained and analyzed. Because every feature is also referenced in the text, students actually learn the material rather than skipping over it.

Self Explanatory Graphs and Tables

Graphs are *completely* labeled, colorful, and positioned on background grids. Because students often enter the principles course as graph-phobics, graphs are frequently accompanied by synchronized tabular data. Every table is also annotated. This shouldn't be a product-differentiating feature but, sadly, it is. Putting a table in a textbook without an annotation is akin to writing a cluster of numbers on the board, then leaving the classroom without any explanation.

Reinforced Key Concepts

Key terms are defined in the margin when they first appear and, unlike in other texts, redefined as necessary in the margins of subsequent chapters. Website references are directly tied to the book's content, not hung on like ornaments. End-of-chapter discussion questions use tables, graphs, and boxed news stories from the text, reinforcing key concepts.

Student Problem Set

I firmly believe that students must *work* with key concepts in order to really learn them. Weekly homework assignments are *de rigueur* in my own classes. To facilitate homework assignments, I have prepared the *Student Problem Set* that includes built-in numerical and graphing problems that build on the tables, graphs, and boxed material in each chapter. Grids for drawing graphs are also provided. Each chapter's problem set is detachable and includes answer boxes that facilitate grading. (Answers are in the *Instructors Resource Manual*, in print or online.) The separately bound *Student Problem Set* come free with every new copy of *The Economy Today*.

Although the policy emphasis, uncluttered format, and student-friendly pedagogy help differentiate this book from others on the market, there are many other features of *The Economy Today* that make it stand out in macro, in micro, and in international economics.

DISTINCTIVE MACRO

The macro section of *The Economy Today* is well-known for its balanced presentation and for unique chapters. In addition, the AS/AD model is now separated from the Keynesian Cross, which gives instructors the freedom to cover the topics they want to include and easily exclude the ones they don't.

Balanced Macro Theory

This isn't a highly opinionated text. It doesn't assert that only long-run issues matter, or that monetary policy is the only effective lever of short-run stabilization. Rather, *The Economy Today* strives to offer students a *balanced* introduction to both short- and long-run macro concerns as well as an array of competing viewpoints. Keynes isn't dead, nor are supply-side policy options ignored. Instead, competing theories are presented in their best possible light, and then subjected to comparative scrutiny. This approach reflects my belief that students need to be exposed to a variety of perspectives if they're to understand the range and intensity of ongoing debates. One of my most cherished compliments is the question, "Which theory do you believe, Professor Schiller?" I'm not pushing any point of view, just core principles that will help students and instructors sort things out for themselves. The benefits of such an eclectic approach were strikingly evident in the aftermath of the September 11, 2001, terrorist attacks. Not only did policy discussion shift abruptly from long-run issues (e.g. productivity growth and "saving Social Security") to short-run issues (stabilizing the economy), but even Milton Friedman and Alan Greenspan endorsed countercyclical fiscal policy! Shouldn't students have a broad foundation of principles that enables them to follow these developments? *The Economy Today* offers such breadth of coverage.

Consistent AS/AD Framework

Too many textbooks still treat the aggregate supply/aggregate demand (AS/AD) framework as a separate theory. The AS/AD model is *not* a separate theory; it is just a convenient framework for illustrating macro theories in a world of changing prices. Keynes never said prices could not rise. So he would be surprised to see his macro theory of market instability confined to the "Keynesian Cross" framework. The full measure of Keynesian theory can be better illustrated in the AS/AD framework, without any loss of content (including multiplier effects). The same AS/AD *framework* can then be used to contrast competing short- and long-run theories of stabilization and growth.

The last few editions of *The Economy Today* have retained both the Keynesian Cross and AS/AD frameworks in the body of the text. This edition breaks away from that pattern. The core macro presentation is now exclusively rendered in the context of the AS/AD model. This greatly simplifies the presentation for students, who often got lost moving between the two models within one chapter. Since students have never encountered the Keynesian Cross model, they won't miss it in *The Economy Today*. For instructors who still want to use it, the Keynesian Cross is now contained in the appendix to Chapter 9. As that appendix explains, the two models are simply different paths for reaching the same conclusions. The advantage of the AS/AD framework is that it generates more useful policy guidelines in a world of changing price levels (see Figure 11.3, Figure 11.6, and Table 11.2, for examples).

Global Macro Constraints

The Economy Today incorporates not only the reality of changing price levels, but also the constraints of global linkages. The Fed's Board of Governors always looks over its shoulder at global markets when making decisions on domestic monetary policy. The impact of changing interest rates on the value of the dollar and global money flows is always discussed. Likewise, the effectiveness of fiscal-policy initiatives is always sensitive to potential export "leakage," and other trade effects. I have tried to convey a sense of how these global links constrain policy decisions and impacts in the "Global Macro" chapter. This unique chapter (18) is intended to introduce a dose of global reality into the macro course without delving into theories of trade or finance. It's a stand-alone chapter in the macro section. It is designed for instructors who sense the need to offer more of a global perspective in the macro course, but don't have time to delve into trade and finance theories.

Theory and Reality

The final chapter in the macro section serves two purposes. First, it brings together the various Keynesian, monetarist, supply-side, and growth theories into a convenient review format. No other text brings all the macro material into such a course-ending overview.

The second purpose of Chapter 19 is to examine why economic performance so often falls short of economic theory. This is a fun section, because it delves into the institutional and political constraints that shape and limit macro policy. Fiscal policy debates come alive when Republicans and Democrats start arguing over the size and content of anti-terrorism stimulus policy (see News, page 405). The chapter ends the macro course with the suggestion that the real world offers choices between *imperfect* markets and *imperfect* government intervention.

DISTINCTIVE MICRO

The micro section of *The Economy Today* focuses in on the performance of specific companies and government programs in order to showcase the principles of market structure, labor-market functioning, redistribution, and regulation.

Competitive Market Dynamics

The real power of the market originates in competitive forces that breed innovation in products and technology. Other texts treat the competitive firm as a lifeless agent buffeted by larger market forces, but this book provides very different coverage. *The Economy Today* is the only principles text that has two chapters on perfect competition: Chapter 22 on firm behavior and Chapter 23 on industry behavior. Chapter 23 traces the actual evolution of the computer industry from the 1976 Apple I (see photo, page 498) to the iMac (page 507). It gives students a real-world sense of how market structure changes over time and lets them see how dynamic, even revolutionary, competitive markets can be. The rise and fall of "dot.coms" and the ongoing plunge in HDTV prices reinforce the notion that competitive markets move with lightning speed to satisfy consumer demand.

(De)Regulation

Chapter 27 focuses on the (de)regulation of private industry. The chapter first examines the qualities of natural monopoly and the rationale for regulating its behavior. The trade-offs inherent in any regulatory strategy are highlighted in the review of the railroad, cable TV, airline, telephone, and electricity industries. The chapter ends with web exercises that encourage students to examine how federal (FDA) and state (power commission) regulation affects the prices of prescription drugs and electricity. As in so many areas, the choice between imperfect markets and imperfect regulation is emphasized.

Taxes and Transfers

The Economy Today offers parallel chapters on taxes and transfers. Chapters 33 and 34 emphasize the central trade-offs between equity and efficiency that plague tax and transfer policies. The varying distributional effects of specific taxes and transfers are highlighted. Examples are drawn from the Bush tax-cut packages of 2001, President Bush's own 2000 tax return (page 702), as well as the tax and benefit sides of Social Security. Taken together, the two chapters underscore the government's role in reshaping the market's answer to the FOR WHOM question.

Financial Markets

Chapter 32 emphasizes the *economic* rather than the institutional role of financial markets, a topic rarely found in competing texts. The stock and bond markets are viewed as arbiters of risk and mechanisms of resource allocation. The mechanisms of present value discounting are also covered. The chapter starts with the financing of Columbus' New World expedition and ends with a look at the role today's venture capitalists play in promoting growth and technology.

Real Companies, Real Products

Although real-world content is a general attribute of *The Economy Today*, the level of detail in the micro section is truly exceptional. Table 25.2 offers concentration ratios for specific *products* (e.g. video game machines), not the abstract industries (e.g. electronic equipment) that inhabit other texts. No other principles text provides such specific data, even though this is the kind of detail that students can relate to. The oligopoly chapter (25) reviews a slew of recent price-fixing cases (music CDs, laser eye surgery, auction houses) and mergers. The chapter on Monopolistic Competition (26) starts with an examination of Starbucks and ends with a look at the growing market for "branded" bottled waters. Students will recognize these names and absorb the principles of market structure. Football fans will gain a greater appreciation of labor-demand principles after examining the million-dollar paychecks of college football coaches.

DISTINCTIVE INTERNATIONAL

The global economy runs through every chapter of *The Economy Today*.

The most visible evidence of this globalism are in the 70 *World View* boxes that are distributed throughout the text. As noted earlier, these boxed illustrations offer specific global illustrations of basic principles. To facilitate their use, *every World View* has a brief caption that highlights the theoretical relevance of the example. The *Test Bank* and *Student Problem Set* also offer questions based on these *World Views*.

World Views

As noted earlier, Chapter 18 offers a unique global perspective on domestic macro policy. The Global Macro chapter is intended as a substitute for the traditional trade and finance chapters. It is designed for instructors who want to offer some international perspectives in the macro course but don't have time to cover trade and finance theory. In courses with more scope for international coverage, the global macro chapter can be used as a capstone to the more traditional chapters.

Global Macro

Consistent with the reality-based content of the entire text, the discussions of trade and finance theory go beyond basic principles to policy trade-offs and constraints. It's impossible to make sense of trade policy without recognizing the vested interests that battle trade principles. Chapter 35 and 36 emphasize that there are both winners and losers associated with every change in trade flows or exchange rates. Because vested interests are typically highly concentrated and well organized, they can often bend trade rules and flows to their advantage. Trade disputes over Mexican trucks, "dumped" steel, and sugar quotas help illustrate the realities of trade policy. The ongoing protest against the World Trade Organization is also assessed in terms of competing interests.

Vested Interests

DISTINCTIVE WEB SUPPORT

The ninth edition of *The Economy Today* continues to set the pace for web applications and support of the principles course.

A mini website directory is provided in each chapter's marginal WebNotes. These URLs aren't random picks; they were selected because they let students extend and update adjacent in-text discussions.

WebNotes

Internet addresses are also provided for most *In the News* and *World View* features. Professors and students can use these URLs to pursue policy issues in more depth.

URLs for Highlighted Material

The end of each chapter includes 2-4 Web Activities that send students to the web for data or issues to use in real-world applications of key concepts.

Web Activities

The Economy Today's website has been expanded to include even more features that both instructors and students will find engaging and instructive. The Online Learning Center has been completely reorganized so that the site is user-friendly and easy to navigate. Upon entering the website at www.mhhe.com/economics/schiller9, students and instructors will find three separate book covers: one for *The Economy Today,* one for *The Macro Economy Today,* and one for *The Micro Economy Today*. By clicking on the appropriate cover, users will link to a specific site for the version of the book they are using.

www.mhhe.com/ economics/schiller9

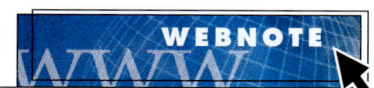

Visit the site dedicated to this text at www.mhhe.com/economics/schiller9.

Proceeding into the Student Center, students will find lots of brand-new interactive study material. Mark Maier of Glendale College has created two Web Activities per chapter and fifteen Web-Based Projects, unique to the site. In addition, Diane Keenan of Cerritos College has prepared fifteen self-grading multiple-choice questions per chapter, which are ideal for self-quizzing before a test. On top of all that, students have access to my periodic NewsFlashes, a User's Manual for the site, and links to Econ Graph Kit, DiscoverEcon, Economics on the Web, and Career Opportunities. They will also have the option of purchasing PowerWeb access with their book, which supplies them with three to five articles per week on the topics they are studying.

The password-protected Instructor Center includes some wonderful resources for instructors who want to include more interactive student activities in their courses. In addition to the downloadable *Instructor's Manual* and PowerPoints, Instructor's Notes are available for the Web-Based Projects and Web Activities to provide guidance for instructors who collect these assignments and grade them.

DiscoverEcon Software

The DiscoverEcon software, developed by Gerald Nelson of the University of Illinois at Urbana-Champaign, is an exciting complement to the text, featuring new learning opportunities for the students and easy integration into existing courses for the instructor. The software is like an interactive text: software chapters parallel text chapters, and software pages include specific page references to the text. New to this edition of DiscoverEcon are elements from the book such as WebNotes, chapter summaries, and end-of-chapter Web Activities; instructions on how to link your course website to a specific page of DiscoverEcon (in the *Instructor's Manual*); and students will now have the capacity to e-mail their quiz results directly to their instructor.

Opportunities for active learning abound. All chapters contain a multiple-choice quiz, essay questions with online links, and match-the-terms exercises. Interactive graphs, animated charts, and live tables let your students manipulate variables and study the outcomes. Links to the glossary and text references clarify key concepts, and Web-based exercises give students a direct link to the site in question. The software comes on a single CD that can be installed and run over a network, and is also available online, via a password code card supplied with new books or available for purchase separately. Link to DiscoverEcon online through the Schiller 9 website: www.mhhe.com/economics/schiller9.

WHAT'S NEW IN THE NINTH

To previous users of *The Economy Today,* all of its distinctive features have become familiar—and, hopefully, welcome. For those instructors already familiar with *The Economy Today,* the more urgent question is "What's new?" The answer is a *lot*. By way of brief summary, you may want to note the following:

Focus on AS/AD Framework

As described above, the Keynesian Cross diagrams have been moved to the appendix of Chapter 9, leaving the core presentation of Keynesian theory consistently in the aggregate supply/demand framework. This will simplify the discussion for students while preserving the core features of Keynesian theory. Chapter 9 has been retitled "Aggregate Demand" to convey its demand side focus.

More emphasis on AS/AD Shifts

Shifts of the aggregate demand and supply curve get more explicit emphasis as the causes and cures of short-run business cycles. This increased emphasis is particularly evident in Chapters 10 and 11 (for aggregate demand) and 16 (for aggregate supply).

Budget Surpluses

Although post-September 11 disaster assistance, the war against terrorism, and the 2001 recession decimated the FY2001-02 federal budget surplus, budget surpluses could persist for a decade or so. Chapter 12 devotes more space to the unique challenges that budget surpluses create while still drawing attention to the size and "burden" of the lingering national debt.

Terrorist Shocks

Naturally, the ninth edition also discusses the many ways the September 11 terrorist attacks affected the economy and policy decisions. Chapter 16 provides the perfect setting for viewing a terrorist attack as an "external shock" that shifts both aggregate supply and aggregate demand. The response to the attacks also highlights the importance of coordinating the many levers of economic policy, a central theme of Chapter 19. In micro, the new emphasis on air safety facilitates the use of airport security as another example of a classic *public good*.

The core market structure sequence (Chapters 22–26) is chock-full of new in-text examples that students will recognize (AOL Time Warner, America Online, Amazon.com, United Airlines, and, of course, the Microsoft anti-trust case). In keeping with evolving anti-trust policy, more emphasis is put on consumer welfare than impediments to competition per se.

Market Structures

In Chapter 27, the case study of interstate trucking has been deleted to make room for an expanded treatment of electricity deregulation. California's botched policy is the central case study, but a deregulation guide to every state is included (along with an enlightening web exercise).

Electricity Deregulation

The discussion of labor unions (Chapter 31) is enlivened with discussion of new unionization activities among university graduate assistants. By viewing universities as monopsonistic employers and graduate students as exploited labor, the text brings the essence of labor-management conflict back to life.

On-Campus Unions

Roughly 75 percent of the *In The News* and *World View* boxes have been updated with new articles and the most recent data.

***In The News* and *World View* Updates**

Aside from the boxed features, every other piece of economic data in the text has been updated. The in-text examples have been updated in every chapter as well, keeping *The Economy Today* as current as humanly possible.

Updates Everywhere

The *Student Problem Set* that used to reside at the very end of the text itself is now separately bound. More questions are included for each chapter, always with at least one graphing exercise. The separately bound Student Problem Set comes free with every new copy of the text. It can also be purchased separately for students relying on used textbooks.

Detached and Expanded Problem Set

NEW AND IMPROVED SUPPLEMENTS

Test Bank. Linda Wilson (University of Texas at Arlington) and Kevin Klein (Illinois College) expanded and updated the *Test Bank*. This team assures a high level of quality and consistency of the test questions and the greatest possible correlation with the content of the text as well as the *Study Guide,* which was also prepared by Linda and Kevin. All questions are coded according to level of difficulty and have a text-page reference where the student will find a discussion of the concept on which the question is based. The computerized *Test Bank* is available in Brownstone's Diploma 97, sophisticated test-making software that ensures maximum flexibility in test development, including the reconfiguration of graphing exercises. Both the print and computerized test banks will be offered in micro and macro versions, each of which contains over 3,000 questions.

Instructor Aids

PowerPoint Presentations. Anthony Zambelli of Cuyamaca College created new presentation slides for the ninth edition. Developed using Microsoft PowerPoint software, these slides are a step-by-step review of the key points in each of the book's 36 chapters. They are equally useful to the student at home or in the computer lab for review purposes. The more than 3,000 slides are offered in the split format for greatest convenience, and use animation to show students how graphs build and shift.

Overhead Transparencies. Over 200 of the text's key tables and graphs have been reproduced as full-color overhead transparency acetates.

Instructor's Resource Manual. Mark Maier of Glendale College has prepared the *Instructor's Resource Manual* as well as much of the original content for the website. This has allowed him to integrate the two in a way that will make online web resources easier than ever for instructors to use in class.

The *Instructor's Resource Manual* is available in book form or online, and includes chapter summaries and outlines, "lecture launchers" to stimulate class discussion, and photocopy ready media exercises to extend the analysis. It also includes a section that details common misconceptions regarding the material in a particular chapter; DiscoverEcon highlights; an annotated outline of the chapter; and answers to Questions for Discussion, Answers to The Student Problem Set, and Answers to Web Activities from the book.

News Flashes. As up-to-date as *The Economy Today* is, it can't foretell the future. As the future becomes the present, however, I write 2-page News Flashes describing major economic events and relating them to specific text references. These News Flashes provide good lecture material and can be copied for student use. Adopters of *The Economy Today* have the option of receiving News Flashes via fax or mail. They're also available on the Schiller website. Four to six News Flashes are sent to adopters each year. (Contact your local McGraw-Hill/Irwin sales representative to get on the mailing list.)

Student Aids

At the instructor's discretion, students have access to the News Flashes described above. In addition, the following supplements can facilitate learning.

Student Problem Set. The separately bound *Student Problem Set* is packaged with every new copy of *The Economy Today*. Each chapter has 5-8 numerical and graphing problems tied to the content of the text. Graphing grids are provided, as well as extra graphing paper and scratch paper. The answer blanks are formatted to facilitate grading and all answers are contained in the *Instructor's Resource Manual*. For convenience, the *Student Problem Set* is also perforated and 3-hole punched.

Study Guide. From a student's perspective, the most important supplement is the *Study Guide*. The new *Study Guide* has been completely updated by Linda Wilson (University of Texas at Arlington) and Kevin Klein (Illinois College). The *Study Guide* develops quantitative skills and the use of economic terminology, and enhances critical thinking capabilities. Each chapter includes a Quick Review which lists the key points in an easy-to-read bulleted format, Learning Objectives for the chapter, a crossword puzzle using Key Terms, ten True-False Questions with explanations, twenty Multiple-Choice Questions, Problems and Applications that relate directly back to the text, and Common Student Errors. Answers to all problems, exercises, and questions are provided at the end of each chapter.

ACKNOWLEDGMENTS

The ninth edition has been more of a team effort than most prior editions. I had a wonderful set of reviewers who scrutinized both the prior eighth edition and various drafts of this edition. My collaborators on the supplementary materials came through with a host of fresh ideas that reinvigorated the entire learning package. Linda Wilson and Kevin Klein added loads of new questions to the *Test Bank* and interesting new material in the *Study Guide*. They also tightened the links between these two supplements and the text itself. Mark Maier assumed full responsibility for the *Instructor's Resource Manual* and imbued it with some of the excitement and ingenuity he brings to his own classes. Diane Keenan and Mark together developed website content that will persuade more instructors to incorporate web resources into their courses. Tony Zambelli developed PowerPoint presentations that will help enliven classroom presentations. Jerry Nelson updated his exceptional DiscoverEcon tutorial software to retain its position as the student's best interactive support system.

Paul Shensa, who has been my economics editor for longer than I can remember, once again assembled the resources and talent to develop this edition. As development editor, Katie Crouch not only kept the production line moving, but even read and offered useful comments on the entire manuscript. Karen Minnich, the editorial assistant, also pitched in with ideas for *In The News* updates. Tara Straw, my research assistant at American University, was a critical source of data and news updates. The design team, led by Laurie Entringer, once again produced an open and engaging format. Destiny Rynne did an exceptional job as project manager, making sure all of the breaking news stories fit into the pages of *The Economy Today,* and getting the text on to campus in record time. I should probably also mention Gary Burke, Publisher, who pleads for the budget to pay for all of this production and for an occasional game in our recurring tennis matches. Finally, I hope to be eternally grateful to Marty Quinn, who is in charge of marketing this text for McGraw-Hill. His creative ideas and unflagging energy should put *The Economy Today* at the top of the sales chart.

As I noted earlier, the instructors who provided user surveys and critiques throughout the development process were wonderfully helpful and I want to recognize and thank them individually. Thanks to:

User Surveys

Glenn C. Ames, University of Georgia
Kaya Ford, NOVA Alexandria
William D. Goodman, Bluefield State College
Alan Gummerson, Florida International University
Steven Hickerson, Minnesota State University, Mankato
Jerry Ingram, University of Louisiana, Monroe
James A. Janke, Dakota State University
Hasan MacNeil, California State University—Chico
Christine Marston, University of Northern Colorado
Soloman Namala, Cerritos College
Taghi Ramin, William Paterson
Donald Renner, Minnesota State University—Mankato
John Romps, St. Anselm College
Rosemary Rossiter, Ohio University—Athens
Mike Sabet, Dakota State University
John Snead, Bluefield State University
Daniel A. Talley, Dakota State University
Michael Tansey, Rockhurst University
Joe Turek, Lynchburg College
Paul Watro, Jefferson Community College

Reviews

Rashid Al-Hmoud, Texas Tech University
C.J. Austermiller, Oakland Community College
Gilbert Becker, St. Anselm College
Suzanne R. Boyles, California State University, Fresno
Curtis Clark, Mountain View College
Ronald D. Elkins, Central Washington University
Michael Ellis, Texas Wesleyan University
Monica Escaleras, Florida International University
Robert Eyler, Sonoma State University
Monica Galizzi, University of Massachusetts—Lowell
Paul Graf, Pennsylvania State University
Robert Grafstein, University of Georgia
Dave Hickman, Frederick Community College
Edward Kaplan, NYC Technical College
Diane Keenan, Cerritos College
Kathy Kelly, University of Texas—Arlington
Norman Knaub, Pennsylvania State University—Altoona
Robert J. Lemke, Florida International University
Susan J. Linz, Michigan State University
Peter Lund, California State University, Sacramento
Robert Posatko, Shippensburg University
Henry D. Ryder, Gloucester County College

Dawn Saunders,
University of Vermont
Mary Ann Schulte,
Des Moines Area Community College—
Carroll Campus
Stephanie Seguino,
University of Vermont
Shahrokh Shahrokhi,
San Diego State University

Dorothy Siden,
Salem State College
Paul Swanson,
William Paterson University
Richard D. Wolff,
University of Massachusetts, Amherst
Ken Woodward,
Saddleback College
Virginia York,
Gulf Coast Community College

Finally, I'd like to thank all the professors and students who are going to use *The Economy Today* as an introduction to economics principles. I welcome any responses (even the bad ones) you'd like to pass on for future editions.

—Bradley R. Schiller

CONTENTS IN BRIEF

PREFACE vii

INTRO:
PART 1 BASIC CONCEPTS
CHAPTER 1 ECONOMICS: THE CORE ISSUES 1
Appendix: Using Graphs 21
CHAPTER 2 THE U.S. ECONOMY: A GLOBAL VIEW 26
CHAPTER 3 SUPPLY AND DEMAND 44
CHAPTER 4 THE PUBLIC SECTOR 69

MACRO:
PART 2 MEASURING MACRO OUTCOMES
CHAPTER 5 NATIONAL-INCOME ACCOUNTING 92
CHAPTER 6 UNEMPLOYMENT 112
CHAPTER 7 INFLATION 129

PART 3 CYCLICAL INSTABILITY
CHAPTER 8 THE BUSINESS CYCLE 150
CHAPTER 9 AGGREGATE DEMAND 174
Appendix: The Keynesian Cross 194
CHAPTER 10 SELF-ADJUSTMENT OR INSTABILITY? 198

PART 4 FISCAL POLICY OPTIONS
CHAPTER 11 FISCAL POLICY 218
CHAPTER 12 SURPLUSES, DEFICITS, AND DEBT 237

PART 5 MONETARY POLICY OPTIONS
CHAPTER 13 MONEY AND BANKS 262
CHAPTER 14 THE FEDERAL RESERVE SYSTEM 281
CHAPTER 15 MONETARY POLICY 298

PART 6 SUPPLY-SIDE OPTIONS

CHAPTER 16 SUPPLY-SIDE POLICY: SHORT-RUN OPTIONS 326

CHAPTER 17 GROWTH AND PRODUCTIVITY: LONG-RUN POSSIBILITIES 350

PART 7 POLICY CONSTRAINTS

CHAPTER 18 GLOBAL MACRO 370

CHAPTER 19 THEORY AND REALITY 386

MICRO:

PART 8 PRODUCT MARKETS: THE BASICS

CHAPTER 20 THE DEMAND FOR GOODS 412

Appendix: Indifference Curves 437

CHAPTER 21 THE COSTS OF PRODUCTION 444

PART 9 MARKET STRUCTURE

CHAPTER 22 THE COMPETITIVE FIRM 470

CHAPTER 23 COMPETITIVE MARKETS 493

CHAPTER 24 MONOPOLY 513

CHAPTER 25 OLIGOPOLY 535

CHAPTER 26 MONOPOLISTIC COMPETITION 561

PART 10 REGULATORY ISSUES

CHAPTER 27 (DE)REGULATION OF BUSINESS 574

CHAPTER 28 ENVIRONMENTAL PROTECTION 595

CHAPTER 29 THE FARM PROBLEM 615

PART 11 FACTOR MARKETS: BASIC THEORY

CHAPTER 30 THE LABOR MARKET 632

CHAPTER 31 LABOR UNIONS 655

CHAPTER 32 FINANCIAL MARKETS 673

PART 12 DISTRIBUTIONAL ISSUES

CHAPTER 33 TAXES: EQUITY VS. EFFICIENCY 694

CHAPTER 34 TRANSFER PAYMENTS: WELFARE AND SOCIAL SECURITY 712

PART 13 INTERNATIONAL ECONOMICS

CHAPTER 35 INTERNATIONAL TRADE 728

CHAPTER 36 INTERNATIONAL FINANCE 752

GLOSSARY G-1

INDEX I-1

CONTENTS

PREFACE v

PART 1 BASIC CONCEPTS

CHAPTER 1 ECONOMICS: THE CORE ISSUES 1

The Economy Is Us 3
Scarcity: The Core Problem 4
Production Possibilities 6
Basic Decisions 11
The Mechanisms of Choice 12
What Economics Is All About 15

Summary 20

Appendix: Using Graphs 21

WORLD VIEW:
Cloudy Days in Tomorrowland 2 • North Korea Says It Is Running Out of Food 9 • North Korea Expanding Missile Programs 9 • Index of Economic Freedom 14 • Farming, Capitalism Work Well In Cuba; Post-Soviet Food Crisis Called Over 16

IN THE NEWS:
Bush Seeking Defense Increase 18

THE ECONOMY TOMORROW:
To Intervene or Not? 19

CHAPTER 2 THE U.S. ECONOMY: A GLOBAL VIEW 26

What America Produces 26
How America Produces 33
For Whom America Produces 38

Summary 42

WORLD VIEW:
Comparative Output 27 • GDP Per Capita around the World 28 • The Education Gap between Rich and Poor Nations 34 • Income Share of the Rich 40

THE ECONOMY TOMORROW:
Levers of Change 41

CHAPTER 3 SUPPLY AND DEMAND 44

Market Participants 45
The Circular Flow 46
Demand 48
Supply 55
Equilibrium 57
Market Outcomes 62

Summary 67

WORLD VIEW:
Dining on the Downtick 63

IN THE NEWS:
PC Prices Fall with Demand 50 • Californians Pinched by Power Prices 58 • For Fans, What's 4 Nights for U2? 60 • Demand for Cipro Rising 63 • Federal Price Limits Backfire 66

THE ECONOMY TOMORROW:
Electric Shock: Energy-Price Spikes 64

CONTENTS xxiii

CHAPTER 4 THE PUBLIC SECTOR 69

Market Failure 70
Growth of Government 77
Taxation 80
Government Failure 84

Summary 89

> **THE ECONOMY TOMORROW:**
> Downsizing Government 87

> **WORLD VIEW:**
> Public-Sector Spending 79

> **IN THE NEWS:**
> Napster Gets Napped 72 • The Human Cost of Secondhand Smoke 74 • Big Lotteries' Real Losers 83 • Persistent Doubts about Government Waste 85 • Little Confidence in Government 88

PART 2 MEASURING MACRO OUTCOMES

CHAPTER 5 NATIONAL-INCOME ACCOUNTING 92

Measures of Output 93
The Uses of Output 102
Measures of Income 103
The Flow of Income 106

Summary 110

> **THE ECONOMY TOMORROW:**
> The Quality of Life 108

> **WORLD VIEW:**
> Global Inequalities 95

> **IN THE NEWS:**
> A Lot Going on under the Table 97 • America's Declining Social Health 109

CHAPTER 6 UNEMPLOYMENT 112

The Labor Force 113
Measuring Unemployment 115
The Human Costs 118
Defining Full Employment 120
The Historical Record 125

Summary 127

> **THE ECONOMY TOMORROW:**
> A Growing Skills Gap? 125

> **WORLD VIEW:**
> Europe's Unemployment Woes 119

> **IN THE NEWS:**
> Unemployment Benefits Not for Everyone 119 • Recession's Cost: Lives 121 • Unemployment Soars by 700,000 125 • What Lies in Store for Displaced Workers? 126

CONTENTS

WORLD VIEW:
Tortilla Price Hike Hits Mexico's Poorest 135 • Worldwide Inflation 143 • Sky-High Interest Rates South of the Border 145

IN THE NEWS:
Public Colleges' Tuition Rises 7.7% This Fall 132 • Ignoring Cell Phones Biases CPI Upward 142 • CPI Overstates Inflation, Senate Panel Says 146

WORLD VIEW:
Global Depression 155 • California Feels Asia's Pain 165 • Economy Expands, Barely 167 • Japan Sees Slight Drop in Its GDP 167 • China Reports 7.9% Growth 167

IN THE NEWS:
Market in Panic As Stocks Are Dumped in 12,894,600 Share Day; Bankers Halt It 151

WORLD VIEW:
Canada Forecasts Slower 2001 Growth, Citing U.S. "Spillover" 188

IN THE NEWS:
U.S. Consumer Confidence Drops to Seven-Year Low 183 • Falling Stocks Smash Nest Eggs 185 • Manufacturing-Output Slump Continues While Businesses Again Trim Inventories 187

CHAPTER 7 INFLATION 129

What Is Inflation? 130
Redistributive Effects of Inflation 131
Macro Consequences 136
Measuring Inflation 138
The Goal: Price Stability 140
The Historical Record 142
Causes of Inflation 144
Protective Mechanisms 144

Summary 147

THE ECONOMY TOMORROW:
The End of Inflation? 146

PART 3 CYCLICAL INSTABILITY

CHAPTER 8 THE BUSINESS CYCLE 150

Stable or Unstable? 151
Historical Cycles 153
A Model of the Macro Economy 157
Aggregate Demand and Supply 158
Competing Theories of Short-Run Instability 166
Long-Run Self-Adjustment 169

Summary 172

THE ECONOMY TOMORROW:
Macro Policy Options 170

CHAPTER 9 AGGREGATE DEMAND 174

Macro Equilibrium 174
Consumption 176
The Consumption Function 179
Investment 185
Government and Net Export Spending 188
Potential Macro Failure 189

Summary 193

Appendix: The Keynesian Cross 194

THE ECONOMY TOMORROW:
Looking for AD Shifts 192

CHAPTER 10 SELF-ADJUSTMENT OR INSTABILITY? 198

Leakages and Injections   198
The Multiplier Process   202
Macro Equilibrium Revisited   208
Adjustment to an Inflationary GDP Gap   211

Summary   214

THE ECONOMY TOMORROW:
Maintaining Consumer Confidence 213

WORLD VIEW:
U.S. Slowdown Helps Derail Asia 208 • Thrift Shift—The More the Japanese Save for a Rainy Day, the Gloomier It Gets 214

IN THE NEWS:
Small Businesses Hold Off on Big Purchases 203 • Terror's Aftermath: Layoffs 205 • Companies Begin Another Round of Job Cuts 207 • Harris Poll: Wiser but Unbowed 213

PART 4 FISCAL POLICY OPTIONS

CHAPTER 11 FISCAL POLICY 218

Taxes and Spending   218
Fiscal Stimulus   220
Fiscal Restraint   228
Fiscal Guidelines   232

Summary   235

THE ECONOMY TOMORROW:
The Concern for Content 233

WORLD VIEW:
China Races Its Spending Engines to Stave off Effects of Slowdown 224

IN THE NEWS:
Economy is Already Feeling the Impact of Federal Government's Spending Cuts 230 • Bush Seeks More Tax Cuts, Democrats Higher Spending 234

CHAPTER 12 SURPLUSES, DEFICITS, AND DEBT 237

Budget Effects of Fiscal Policy   237
Economic Effects of Deficits   245
Economic Effects of Surpluses   246
The Accumulation of Debt   246
Who Owns the Debt?   249
Burden of the Debt   251
External Debt   254
Deficit and Debt Limits   255

Summary   258

THE ECONOMY TOMORROW:
Saving Social Security 257

WORLD VIEW:
Budget Imbalances Common 240

IN THE NEWS:
Fiscal Policy in the Great Depression 244 • Tax Cut Shrinks Projected Surplus 247 • How the Surplus Could Vanish 256

PART 5 MONETARY POLICY OPTIONS

CHAPTER 13 MONEY AND BANKS 262

What is "Money"? 262
The Money Supply 263
Creation of Money 267
The Money Multiplier 273
Banks and the Circular Flow 276

Summary 279

> **THE ECONOMY TOMORROW:**
> When Banks Fail 277

> **WORLD VIEW:**
> The Cashless Society 263 • The Check Is Still in the Mail 264

> **IN THE NEWS:**
> Bank Reopens to Customers' Questions 278

CHAPTER 14 THE FEDERAL RESERVE SYSTEM 281

Structure of the Fed 281
Monetary Tools 283
Increasing the Money Supply 291
Decreasing the Money Supply 294

Summary 296

> **THE ECONOMY TOMORROW:**
> Is the Fed Losing Control? 294

> **WORLD VIEW:**
> Interest Rates Are Boosted Again in Europe 293 • Fighting Terror/Targeting Funds; Laws May Not Stop Flow of Terror Funds 295

> **IN THE NEWS:**
> Fed Cuts Deposit-Reserve Requirements 285 • Fed Again Reduces Key Rate 288 • Zero-Coupon Bonds 290

CHAPTER 15 MONETARY POLICY 298

The Money Market 299
Interest Rates and Spending 302
Policy Constraints 304
The Monetarist Perspective 309
The Concern for Content 315

Summary 321

> **THE ECONOMY TOMORROW:**
> Which Lever to Pull? 316

> **WORLD VIEW:**
> Why Japan Is Still Stuck 307 • Deflation Still Haunts the Bank of Japan 370

> **IN THE NEWS:**
> Why Mortgage Rates Aren't Falling 304 • Uneasy Banks May Tighten Loans, Stunt Recovery 305 • Vicious Cycle 308 • Monetarists Reject Focus on Lowering Rates 311 • "Not Worth a Continental": The U.S. Experience with Hyperinflation 312 • Money Is Free! 314

PART 6 SUPPLY-SIDE OPTIONS

CHAPTER 16 SUPPLY-SIDE POLICY: SHORT-RUN OPTIONS 326

Aggregate Supply 326
Shape of the AS Curve 327
Shifts of the AS Curve 330
Tax Incentives 334
Human Capital Investment 340
Deregulation 342
Easing Trade Barriers 344
Infrastructure Development 345
Expectations 346

Summary 348

> **WORLD VIEW:**
> Mitch Left Honduras a Republic without Bananas 332 • Border Could Open Soon to Mexican Truckers 345

> **IN THE NEWS:**
> The Misery Index 333 • Difficult Passage 334 • Congress Passes Tax-Cut Package 338 • Capital Gains Tax Reduction Is Considered 340 • Bush Signs Repeal of Ergonomics Rules 343

> **THE ECONOMY TOMORROW:**
> Rebuilding America 346

CHAPTER 17 GROWTH AND PRODUCTIVITY: LONG-RUN POSSIBILITIES 350

The Nature of Growth 351
Measures of Growth 352
Sources of Growth 357
Policy Levers 360

Summary 366

> **WORLD VIEW:**
> Comparative Investment and Growth 358 • Work Visas Are Allowing Washington to Sidestep Immigration Reform 361

> **IN THE NEWS:**
> The New Economy 353

> **THE ECONOMY TOMORROW:**
> Limitless Growth? 362

PART 7 POLICY CONSTRAINTS

CHAPTER 18 GLOBAL MACRO 370

International Trade 371
Trade Imbalances 375
International Finance 377
Capital Imbalances 378
Productivity and Competitiveness 380
Global Coordination 382

Summary 384

> **WORLD VIEW:**
> Tragedy Dashes Hope for Europe's Economy 371 • U.S. Growth Slows—and Foreign Economies Feel the Pain 374 • Oil Shocks 377 • Another Chink in the Economy's Armor 381 • U.S. Wants Europe, Japan to Ease Rates 383 • The Long History of Europe's Single Currency 384

> **THE ECONOMY TOMORROW:**
> A Global Currency? 383

CHAPTER 19 THEORY AND REALITY 386

Policy Levers 387
Idealized Uses 390
The Economic Record 393
Why Things Don't Always Work 395

Summary 409

> **WORLD VIEW:**
> Macro Performance in the 1990s 395 • Worldwide, Hope for Recovery Dims 400 • Japanese Tighten Belts 402

> **IN THE NEWS:**
> Finding a Fix for the Declining Economy 392 • Deficit-Cutting Wilts in Heat from Voters 396 • This Just In: Recession Ended 21 Months Ago 397 • Tough Calls in Economic Forecasting 398 • CBO's Flawed Forecasts 401 • The Path to a U.S. Budget 403 • Stimulus Package Stalled over Tax Breaks, Spending 405

> **THE ECONOMY TOMORROW:**
> Hands On or Hands Off? 406

PART 8 PRODUCT MARKETS: THE BASICS

CHAPTER 20 THE DEMAND FOR GOODS 412

Determinants of Demand 412
The Demand Curve 415
Price Elasticity 417
Price Elasticity and Total Revenue 423
Other Elasticities 425
Choosing among Products 430

Summary 435

Appendix: Indifference Curves 437

> **WORLD VIEW:**
> Cigarette Smuggling: A Lesson in Price Elasticity 422 • Where the Pitch is Loudest 434

> **IN THE NEWS:**
> Men vs. Women: How They Spend 413 • Dramatic Rise in Teenage Smoking 421 • Professor Becker Corrects President's Math 423 • Stung by the Economy, Americans Lose Their Appetite for Dining Out 428 • DVD Sales Are Soaring As Prices Drop 429 • Marketers Jump with Jordan's Return 433

> **THE ECONOMY TOMORROW:**
> Caveat Emptor 433

CHAPTER 21 THE COSTS OF PRODUCTION 444

The Production Function 444
Marginal Productivity 448
Resource Costs 449
Dollar Costs 451
Economic vs. Accounting Costs 459
Long-Run Costs 460
Economies of Scale 462

Summary 467

> **WORLD VIEW:**
> Number of Internet Sites Surges at End of Decade 466 • United States Gains Cost Advantage 466

> **IN THE NEWS:**
> GM, Isuzu Investing $320 Million to Build Advanced Diesel Engines for GM Pickups 461 • Funeral Giant Moves In on Small Rivals 463

> **THE ECONOMY TOMORROW:**
> Global Competitiveness and B2B Cost Savings 464

PART 9 MARKET STRUCTURE

CHAPTER 22 THE COMPETITIVE FIRM 470

The Profit Motive 470
Economic vs. Accounting Profits 471
Market Structure 475
The Nature of Perfect Competition 476
The Production Decision 477
Profit-Maximizing Rule 479
The Shutdown Decision 485
The Investment Decision 486
Determinants of Supply 487

Summary 491

> **IN THE NEWS:**
> Are Profits Bad 472 • Strawberry Fields Forever? 473 • T-Shirt Shop Owner's Lament: Too Many T-Shirt Shops 474 • Southern Farmers Hooked on New Cash Crop 483 • GM to Idle Cadillac Plant for Four Weeks 487 • EToys to Close Shop 487

> **THE ECONOMY TOMORROW:**
> E-Commerce Increasing Competition 490

CHAPTER 23 COMPETITIVE MARKETS 493

The Market Supply Curve 493
Competition at Work: Microcomputers 496
The Competitive Process 506

Summary 511

> **IN THE NEWS:**
> Whiskered Catfish Stir a New Trade Controversy 494 • Cost of Surfing the Internet Gets Cheaper As a Price War Flares 497 • IBM to Halt PCjr Output Next Month 506 • Price War Squeezes PC Makers 509 • Death Valley 510 • The Future of HDTV 511

> **THE ECONOMY TOMORROW:**
> HDTV for $500? 510

CHAPTER 24 MONOPOLY 513

Market Power 513
Market Power at Work: The Computer Market Revisited 517
A Comparative Perspective of Market Power 522
Pros and Cons of Market Power 526

Summary 533

> **WORLD VIEW:**
> Foxy Soviets Pelt The West 517 • New Competition May Mean Bad News for CNN 530

> **IN THE NEWS:**
> Concerts Becoming a Pricier Affair; Music Industry Consolidation Has Brought Higher Ticket Fees. Some Cry Foul 522 • Pepsi Takes Coke to Court 526 • Jury Rules Magnetek Unit Is Liable for Keeping Technology off Market 527 • Judge Says Microsoft Broke Antitrust Law 531

> **THE ECONOMY TOMORROW:**
> Microsoft: Bully or Genius? 530

CHAPTER 25 OLIGOPOLY 535

Market Structure 535
Oligopoly Behavior 539
The Kinked Demand Curve 543
Game Theory 545
Oligopoly vs. Competition 547
Coordination Problems 550
Barriers to Entry 553
Summary 559

> **THE ECONOMY TOMORROW:**
> Antitrust Guidelines 556

> **WORLD VIEW:**
> Putting Size in Global Perspective 539 • OPEC to Cut Oil Output by 1 Million Barrels 548

> **IN THE NEWS:**
> Pop Culture: RC Goes for the Youth Market 542 • Airlines Roll Back Fare Hike 545 • Coke and Pepsi May Call off Pricing Battle 546 • Charitable Conspiracy 551 • Behind the Screens 552 • New Airline Accuses Rivals of Predatory Pricing Tactics 553 • Frito-Lay Devours Snack-Food Business 554

CHAPTER 26 MONOPOLISTIC COMPETITION 561

Structure 561
Behavior 563
Summary 571

> **THE ECONOMY TOMORROW:**
> No Cease-Fire in Advertising Wars 568

> **WORLD VIEW:**
> The Best Global Brands 570

> **IN THE NEWS:**
> Water, Water Everywhere; Coke, Pepsi Unleash Flood of Ad Muscle 564 • Who Can Be Loyal to a Trash Bag? 564 • Computers: They're No Commodity 566 • The Cola Wars: It's Not All Taste 569 • A Closer Look at Prices 571

PART 10 REGULATORY ISSUES

CHAPTER 27 (DE)REGULATION OF BUSINESS 574

Antitrust vs. Regulation 574
Natural Monopoly 575
Regulatory Options 576
The Costs of Regulation 580
Deregulation in Practice 582
Summary 593

> **THE ECONOMY TOMORROW:**
> Deregulate Everything? 592

> **WORLD VIEW:**
> Demise of Telephone Monopolies 584

> **IN THE NEWS:**
> FCC: Nynex Padded Millions in Profits 579 • FCC Seeking More Money to Enforce New Cable Rules 580 • Competition in Local Phone Service Fails to Connect 585 • Flock of New Low-Fare Carriers Means Savings for Consumers 589 • California Consumers Can Choose Power Company 590 • Financial Woes Heating Up 591 • Power Check 592

CONTENTS xxxi

CHAPTER 28 ENVIRONMENTAL PROTECTION 595

The Environmental Threat 596
Pollution Damage 599
Market Incentives 599
Market Failure: External Costs 601
Regulatory Options 603
Balancing Benefits and Costs 609

Summary 613

THE ECONOMY TOMORROW:
The Greenhouse Threat 611

WORLD VIEW:
Guess Who Taxes Pollution Least 606 • Scientists Issue Dire Prediction on Warming 612

IN THE NEWS:
Dirty Air Can Shorten Your Life 597 • Beach Closings Linked to Pollution on Rise 598 • Auction: $156 to Emit a Ton of Pollutants 607 • Los Angeles Requires Recycling, Trash Separation 608 • Two Economists Question Benefit of Cleaning Up a Major Air Pollutant 610

CHAPTER 29 THE FARM PROBLEM 615

Destabilizing Forces 615
The First Farm Depression, 1920–1940 618
U.S. Farm Policy 619
The Second Farm Depression, 1980–1986 624

Summary 628

THE ECONOMY TOMORROW:
Farmers on the Dole 625

WORLD VIEW:
EU Farm Subsidies 623

IN THE NEWS:
Grain Prices Plowed Under 627

PART 11 FACTOR MARKETS: BASIC THEORY

CHAPTER 30 THE LABOR MARKET 632

Labor Supply 632
Market Supply 636
Labor Demand 637
A Firm's Hiring Decision 643
Market Equilibrium 646
Choosing among Inputs 648

Summary 653

THE ECONOMY TOMORROW:
Capping CEO Pay 650

WORLD VIEW:
In Moscow, 25,000 Apply for 630 Jobs at McDonald's 633 • Hardest Workers 635

IN THE NEWS:
MBA Grads Seek Challenge at Work, Not Just Big Bucks 634 • Majoring in Money 638 • Merit Pay for Priests 640 • Top Dollars, Top Coaches 644 • Wage Bill May Have Tax Breaks for Businesses 648 • What's a President Worth? 652

CHAPTER 31 LABOR UNIONS 655

The Labor Market 655
Labor Unions 657
The Potential Use of Power 657
The Extent of Union Power 661
Employer Power 663
Collective Bargaining 666
The Impact of Unions 668

Summary 671

WORLD VIEW:
Union Membership 662

IN THE NEWS:
What Autoworkers Won 658 • A Win for the Graduate(s) 663 • Free Agents in Sports: A Threat to Monopsony 664 • Caterpillar vs. the UAW 667

THE ECONOMY TOMORROW:
Merging to Survive 670

CHAPTER 32 FINANCIAL MARKETS 673

The Role of Financial Markets 673
The Present Value of Future Profits 675
The Stock Market 679
The Bond Market 686

Summary 690

IN THE NEWS:
Amazon.com's Stock Price 682 • Market Battered but Intact 684 • Venture Capital Falls 72 percent from Last Year 690

THE ECONOMY TOMORROW:
Venture Capitalists—Financing Tomorrow's Products 689

PART 12 DISTRIBUTIONAL ISSUES

CHAPTER 33 TAXES: EQUITY VS. EFFICIENCY 694

What is *Income*? 695
The Size Distribution of Income 695
The Federal Income Tax 697
Payroll, State, and Local Taxes 703
Taxes and Inequality 705
What is *Fair*? 706

Summary 710

WORLD VIEW:
Stones Keep England off '98 Tour to Avoid Tax 699

IN THE NEWS:
The President's Taxes 702 • Americans Like the Principle of a Flat Tax . . . But Not the Details 709

THE ECONOMY TOMORROW:
A Flat Tax? 708

CHAPTER 34 TRANSFER PAYMENTS: WELFARE AND SOCIAL SECURITY 712

Major Transfer Programs 712
Welfare Programs 715
Social Security 720

Summary 726

WORLD VIEW:
An Aging World 723

THE ECONOMY TODAY:
Privatize Social Security? 724

PART 13 INTERNATIONAL ECONOMICS

CHAPTER 35 INTERNATIONAL TRADE 728

U.S. Trade Patterns 728
Motivation to Trade 731
Pursuit of Comparative Advantage 736
Terms of Trade 737
Protectionist Pressures 739
Barriers to Trade 742

Summary 750

WORLD VIEW:
Export Ratios 730 • Ukraine Faces Wide Range of Steel Dumping Probes 741 • "Beggar-Thy-Neighbor" Policies in the 1930s 744 • Sugar Quota a Sour Deal 747 • House Acts to Block Mexican Trucks 747

IN THE NEWS:
Winning over Wine 739 • Farmers Stage Protests over Import of Products 742 • NAFTA Reallocates Labor: Comparative Advantage at Work 749

THE ECONOMY TOMORROW:
An Increasingly Global Market 748

CHAPTER 36 INTERNATIONAL FINANCE 752

Exchange Rates: The Global Link 752
Foreign-Exchange Markets 753
Market Dynamics 757
Resistance to Exchange-Rate Changes 760
Exchange-Rate Intervention 762

Summary 768

WORLD VIEW:
Foreign-Exchange Rates 756 • Money Crisis Pulling Asian Students Home 760 • Nobel Prize Was Nobler in October 761 • Brazil's Ills Distress Continent 768

IN THE NEWS:
Bush to Seek Protection for U.S. Steel Firms 761

THE ECONOMY TOMORROW:
Currency Bailouts 767

GLOSSARY G-1

INDEX I-1

CHAPTER 1

Economics: The Core Issues

In June 2001, Intel Corporation announced a research breakthrough that stunned the high-tech industry. The company's engineers had created a new transistor—the tiny part that regulates the flow of electricity on a silicon chip—that was just 20 billionths of a meter thick (about one-thousand the width of a human hair). The new transistors are so small that 1 billion of them can be packed onto a single chip. That's a gargantuan leap from the 42-million-transistor Pentium 4 chip that now dominates the market and light years away from the 2,300-transistor chip that powered IBM computers in 1972. What does all this have to do with you? For starters, it means that all electronic goods and services will be able to operate faster and with more options. In other words, the extraordinary array of goods we now confront in the marketplace will continue to expand and improve.

Maybe more isn't always better, but the history of humankind reveals a relentless quest for more and better output. To a large extent, the quest for more output has been driven by necessity. The world's population keeps growing, but the amount of land doesn't. That's why the English economist Thomas Malthus predicted in 1778 that the world would run out of food long before the nineteenth century ended. He didn't know that a few years later someone would invent the iron plow (1808), the reaper (1826), or the milking machine (1878). And Malthus had no conception of what biotechnology's "green revolution" might become and no clues at all about electronic circuits. So his prediction of global starvation turned out to be unduly pessimistic.

Although we've managed to increase global food output faster than the population has grown, we can't be complacent. The United Nations predicts that the world's population, now at 6 billion, will increase by another billion every 10 years. Even if we find ways for food output to keep pace, we can't be satisfied. Our future goals are much more ambitious. We want an ever higher standard of living, not just enough food on the table. No matter how fast our incomes grow, we always want more. The living standards earlier generations dreamed of we now take for granted. Today's luxuries—high-definition television, satellite phones, DVX-enhanced digital video—will most likely be viewed as necessities in a few years, but only if we keep squeezing more and more output out of available resources.

Ironically, some people fear we will do exactly that—and end up destroying the environment in the process. They foresee a Doomsday in which greenhouse gases generated by ever-rising production levels will overheat the earth, melt the solar icecaps, flood coastal areas, and destroy crops.

WORLD VIEW

Cloudy Days in Tomorrowland

We'd like to think all *our* predictions will prove right. But the highways of history are littered with wrong calls, false insights and bad guesses. Here's a sampler of twentieth-century futurology that flopped.

I confess that in 1901, I said to my brother Orville that man would not fly for 50 years . . . Ever since, I have distrusted myself and avoided all predictions.
— Wilbur Wright, *U.S. aviation pioneer, 1908*

I must confess that my imagination . . . refuses to see any sort of submarine doing anything but suffocating its crew and floundering at sea.
— H. G. Wells, *British novelist, 1901*

Airplanes are interesting toys but of no military value.
— Marshal Ferdinand Foch, *French military strategist and future World War I commander, 1911*

The horse is here to stay, but the automobile is only a novelty—a fad.
— *A president of the Michigan Savings Bank advising* Horace Rackham *(Henry Ford's lawyer) not to invest in the Ford Motor Co., 1903. Rackham ignored the advice, bought $5,000 worth of stock and sold it several years later for $12.5 million.*

Radio has no future.
— Lord Kelvin, *Scottish mathematician and physicist, former president of the Royal Society, 1897*

Everything that can be invented has been invented.
— Charles H. Duell, *U.S. commissioner of patents, 1899*

Who the hell wants to hear actors talk?
— Harry M. Warner, *Warner Brothers, 1927*

There is no reason for any individual to have a computer in their home.
— Kenneth Olsen, *president and founder of Digital Equipment Corp., 1977*

[Man will never reach the moon] regardless of all future scientific advances.
— Dr. Lee De Forest, *inventor of the Audion tube and a father of radio, February 25, 1967*

We don't like their sound. Groups of guitars are on the way out.
— Decca Records, *rejecting the Beatles, 1962*

What use could this company make of an electrical toy?
— *Western Union president* William Orton, *rejecting Alexander Graham Bell's offer to sell his struggling telephone company to Western Union for $100,000*

Computers in the future may . . . perhaps only weigh 1.5 tons.
— Popular Mechanics, *forecasting the development of computer technology, 1949*

Stocks have reached what looks like a permanently high plateau.
— Irving Fisher, *professor of economics, Yale University, October. 17, 1929*

[Television] won't be able to hold on to any market it captures after the first six months. People will soon get tired of staring at a plywood box every night.
— Darryl F. Zanuck, *head of 20th Century-Fox, 1946*

Source: *Newsweek*, January 27, 1997. Reprinted with permission. www.newsweek.com

Analysis: No one predicts the future well. But the economic choices we make today about the use of scarce resources will determine the kind of future we have.

Intel Corporation showcases its latest technology at www.intel.com/research/silicon.

economics: The study of how best to allocate scarce resources among competing uses.

As the accompanying World View illustrates, no one really knows how the future will unfold. Even some of history's greatest minds have made predictions that turned out to be ludicrous. In gazing into the future, however, we can be certain of some fundamental principles. The first principle is that resources will always be scarce, relative to our desires. Second, how we use those scarce resources will shape our future. If we use resources today to miniaturize electronic circuits, we'll be able to produce more and better products in the future. Likewise, if we build more factories and cyber networks today, we'll able to produce more output tomorrow. If we install more pollution controls in cars, power plants, and factories today, we'll even have cleaner air tomorrow.

The science of economics helps us frame these choices. In a nutshell, **economics is the study of how people use scarce resources.** How do you decide how much time to spend studying? How does Amazon.com decide how many workers to hire? How does Chrysler decide whether to use its factories to produce sports utility vehicles or sedans? What share of a nation's resources should be devoted to development of cyber networks, the delivery of healthcare services, or pollution control? In every instance alternative ways of using scarce labor, land, and building resources are available, and we have to choose one use over another.

In this first chapter we explore the nature of scarcity and the kinds of choices it forces us to make. As we'll see, *three core issues must be resolved:*

- *WHAT to produce with our limited resources.*
- *HOW to produce the goods and services we select.*
- *FOR WHOM goods and services are produced;* that is, who should get them.

We also have to decide who should answer these questions. Should the marketplace decide what gets produced and how and for whom? Or should the government dictate output choices, regulate production processes, and redistribute incomes? Should Microsoft decide what features get included in a computer's operating system, or should the government make that decision? Should private companies provide airport security or should the government assume that responsibility? Should interest rates be set by private banks alone, or should the government try to control interest rates? The battle over *who* should answer the core questions is often as contentious as the questions themselves.

THE ECONOMY IS US

To learn how the economy works, let's start with a simple truth: *The economy is us.* "The economy" is simply an abstraction referring to the grand sum of all our production and consumption activities. What we collectively produce is what the economy produces; what we collectively consume is what the economy consumes. In this sense, the concept of "the economy" is no more difficult than the concept of "the family." If someone tells you that the Jones family has an annual income of $42,000, you know that the reference is to the collective earnings of all the Joneses. Likewise, when someone reports that the nation's income is $10 trillion per year—as it now is—we should recognize that the reference is to the grand total of everyone's income. If we work fewer hours or get paid less, both family income *and* national income decline. The "meaningless statistics" (see accompanying cartoon) often cited in the news are just a summary of our collective market behavior.

The same relationship between individual behavior and aggregate behavior applies to specific outputs. If we as individuals insist on driving cars rather than taking pub-

"Meaningless statistics were up one-point-five per cent this month over last month."

Analysis: Many people think of economics as dull statistics. But economics is really about human behavior—how people decide to use scarce resources and how those decisions affect market outcomes.

lic transportation, the economy will produce millions of cars each year and consume vast quantities of oil. In a slightly different way, the economy produces billions of dollars of military hardware to satisfy our desire for national defense. In each case, the output of the economy reflects the collective behavior of the 280 million individuals who participate in the economy.

We may not always be happy with the output of the economy. But we can't ignore the link between individual action and collective outcomes. If the highways are clogged and the air is polluted as a consequence of our transportation choices, we can't blame someone else. If we're disturbed by the size of our military arsenal, we must still accept responsibility for our choices (or nonchoices, if we failed to vote). In either case, we continue to have the option of reallocating our resources. We can create a different outcome the next day, month, or year.

SCARCITY: THE CORE PROBLEM

Although we can change economic outcomes, we can't have everything we want. If you go to the mall with $20 in your pocket, you can only buy so much. The money in your pocket sets a *limit* to your spending.

The output of the entire economy is also limited. The limits in this case are set not by money but by the resources available for producing goods and services. Everyone wants more housing, new schools, better transit systems, and a new car; but even a country as rich as the United States can't produce everything people want. So, like every other nation, we have to grapple with the core problem of **scarcity**—the fact that there aren't enough resources available to satisfy all our desires.

scarcity: Lack of enough resources to satisfy all desired uses of those resources.

Factors of Production

factors of production: Resource inputs used to produce goods and services, such as land, labor, capital, and entrepreneurship.

The resources used to produce goods and services are called **factors of production.** The four basic factors of production are

- *Land*
- *Labor*
- *Capital*
- *Entrepreneurship*

These are the *inputs* needed to produce desired *outputs*. To produce this textbook, for example, we needed paper, printing presses, a building, and lots of labor. We also needed people with good ideas who could put it together. To produce the education you're getting in this class, we need not only a textbook but a classroom, a teacher, and a blackboard as well. Without factors of production, we simply can't produce anything.

Land. The first factor of production, land, refers not just to the ground but to all natural resources. Crude oil, water, air, and minerals are all included in our concept of "land."

Labor. Labor too has several dimensions. It's not simply a question of how many bodies there are; when we speak of labor as a factor of production, we refer to the skills and abilities to produce goods and services. Hence, both the quantity and the quality of human resources are included in the "labor" factor.

capital: Final goods produced for use in the production of other goods, e.g., equipment, structures.

Capital. The third factor of production is capital. In economics the term **capital** refers to final goods produced for use in further production. The residents of fishing villages in southern Thailand, for example, braid huge fishing nets. The sole purpose of these nets is to catch more fish. The nets themselves become a factor of production in obtaining the final goods (fish) that people desire. Thus, they're regarded as *capital*. Blast furnaces used to make steel and desks used to equip offices are also capital inputs.

Entrepreneurship. The more land, labor, and capital available, the greater the amount of potential output. A farmer with 10,000 acres, 12 employees, and six tractors can grow more crops than a farmer with half those resources. But there's no guarantee that he will. The farmer with fewer resources may have better ideas about what to plant, when to irrigate, or how to harvest the crops. *It's not just a matter of what resources you have but also of how well you use them.* This is where the fourth factor of production—**entrepreneurship**—comes in. The entrepreneur is the person who sees the opportunity for new or better products and brings together the resources needed for producing them. If it weren't for entrepreneurs, Thai fishermen would still be using sticks to catch fish. Without entrepreneurship, farmers would still be milking their cows by hand. If someone hadn't thought of a way to miniaturize electronic circuits, you wouldn't have a cell phone.

The role of entrepreneurs in economic progress is a key issue in the market versus government debate. The Austrian economist Joseph Schumpeter argued that free markets unleash the "animal spirits" of entrepreneurs, propelling innovation, technology, and growth. Critics of government regulation argue that government interference in the marketplace, however well intentioned, tends to stifle those very same animal spirits.

entrepreneurship: The assembling of resources to produce new or improved products and technologies.

Limits to Output

No matter how an economy is organized, there's a limit to how fast it can grow. The most evident limit is the amount of resources available for producing goods and services. These resource limits imply that we can't produce everything we want. Again, this is the core problem of scarcity—the fact that available resources are insufficient to satisfy all desired uses thereof.

Scarcity—the imbalance between our desires and available resources—forces us to make economic choices. When you've got only $20 in your pocket, the necessity for choice is obvious. Even $20 million might not buy everything you want. There are lots of different ways of spending money, and choices have to be made.

Your economics class also represents a decision about the use of scarce resources. The building space used for your economics class can't be used to show movies at the same time. Your professor can't lecture (produce education) and repair motorcycles simultaneously. Someone has made a decision about how these scarce resources (capital, labor) will be used.

Guns vs. Butter

One of the persistent choices about resource use entails defense spending. After the September 11, 2001 terrorist attacks on the World Trade Center and Pentagon, American citizens overwhelmingly favored an increase in military spending. But where were the extra resources going to come from? Any resources employed in national defense must be taken from other industries. The 1.4 million men and women already serving in the armed forces aren't available to build schools, program computers, or teach economics. Similarly, the land, labor, capital, and entrepreneurship devoted to producing military hardware aren't available for producing civilian goods. An *increase* in national defense would imply still more sacrifices of civilian goods and services. This is the "guns versus butter" dilemma that all nations confront.

After the end of the Cold War in 1989, the United States had chosen to produce far fewer "guns." The defense budget had declined from a high of 6.3 percent of total output in 1986 to only 3 percent in 2001. In the process, the armed forces had been cut by 500,000 men and women. These defense cutbacks freed up scarce resources that produced more civilian goods ("butter"). This is referred to as the "peace dividend" from military downsizing. The post-terrorist military buildup reversed part of that dividend.

To see how the share of output allocated to national defense has changed in recent decades, visit the Congressional Budget Office website at www.cbo.gov click on "Historical Budget Data" and search for "discretionary outlays."

Opportunity Costs

The changing peace dividend illustrates the significance of scarcity. *Every time we choose to use scarce resources in one way we give up the opportunity to use them in other ways.* If we build more weapons systems, we give up the opportunity to produce more civilian goods. The forgone civilian goods represent the **opportunity cost** of military output. The opportunity cost of any activity is the most desired goods or services forgone in order to make resources available for that activity. *Opportunity cost is what is given up in order to get something else.* Even a so-called free lunch has an opportunity cost (see cartoon). The resources used to produce the lunch could have been used to produce something else.

opportunity cost: The most desired goods or services that are forgone in order to obtain something else.

"There's no such thing as a free lunch."

Analysis: All goods and services have an opportunity cost. Even the resources used to produce a "free lunch" could have been used to produce something else.

Think about the cost of reading this book. That cost is not measured in dollars and cents. The true (economic) cost is, instead, measured in terms of some alternative activity. What would you like to be doing right now? The more time you spend reading this book, the less time you have available for that alternative use of your time. The opportunity cost of reading this text is the best alternative use of your scarce time. If you are missing your favorite TV show, we'd say that show is the opportunity cost of reading this book. It is what you gave up to do this assignment. Hopefully, the benefits you get from studying will outweigh that cost. Otherwise this wouldn't be the best way to use your scarce time.

PRODUCTION POSSIBILITIES

The opportunity costs implied by our every choice can be illustrated easily. Suppose the choice is between producing tennis shoes and assembling televisions. To keep things simple, assume that labor (workers) is the only factor of production needed to produce either good. Although other factors of production (land, machinery) are also needed in actual production, ignoring them for the moment does no harm. Let us assume further that we have a total of only 10 workers available per day to produce either shoes or televisions. Our initial problem is to determine the *limits* of output. How many shoes or televisions can be produced in a day with available resources?

Before going any further, notice how opportunity costs will affect the answer. If we use all 10 workers to produce shoes, no labor will be available to assemble televisions. In this case, forgone televisions would become the *opportunity cost* of a decision to employ all our resources in shoe production.

We still don't know how many shoes could be produced with 10 workers or exactly how many televisions would be forgone by such a decision. To get these answers, we need more details about the production processes involved—specifically, how many workers are required to stitch shoes or assemble televisions.

The Production Possibilities Curve

production possibilities: The alternative combinations of final goods and services that could be produced in a given time period with all available resources and technology.

Table 1.1 summarizes the hypothetical choices, or **production possibilities**, that we confront in this case. Row *A* of the table shows the consequences of a decision to produce shoes only. With 10 workers available and a labor requirement of 2 workers per shoe, we can stitch a maximum of five shoes per day. By so doing, however, we use all available workers, leaving none for TV assembly. If we want televisions, we have to cut back on shoe production; this is the essential choice we must make.

The remainder of Table 1.1 describes the full range of production choices. By cutting back shoe production from five to four shoes per day (row *B*), we reduce labor use from 10 workers to 8. That leaves 2 workers available for other uses.

TABLE 1.1
Production Possibilities Schedule

As long as resources are limited, their use entails an opportunity cost. In this case, resources (labor) used to stitch shoes can't be used for TV assembly at the same time. Hence, the forgone televisions are the opportunity cost of additional shoes. If all our resources were used to produce shoes (row A), no televisions could be assembled.

	Shoe Production					TV Assembly		
	Total Available Labor	Output of Shoes per Day	× Labor Needed per Shoe	= Total Labor Required for Shoes	Labor Not Used for Shoes	Potential Output of TVs per Day		Increase in TV Output
A	10	5	2	10	0	0		
B	10	4	2	8	2	2.0	>	2.0
C	10	3	2	6	4	3.0	>	1.0
D	10	2	2	4	6	3.8	>	0.8
E	10	1	2	2	8	4.5	>	0.7
F	10	0	2	0	10	5.0	>	0.5

If we employ these remaining 2 workers to assemble televisions, we can build two televisions a day. We would then end up with four shoes and two televisions per day. What's the opportunity cost of these two televisions? It's the one additional shoe (the fifth shoe) that we could have stitched but didn't.

As we proceed down the rows of Table 1.1, the nature of opportunity costs becomes apparent. Each additional television built implies the loss (opportunity cost) of shoe output. Likewise, every shoe stitched implies the loss of some TV output.

These trade-offs between TV assembly and shoe production are illustrated in the production possibilities curve of Figure 1.1. **Each point on the production possibilities curve depicts an alternative mix of output** that could be produced. In this case, each point represents a different combination of televisions and shoes that we could produce in a single day using all available resources (labor in this case).

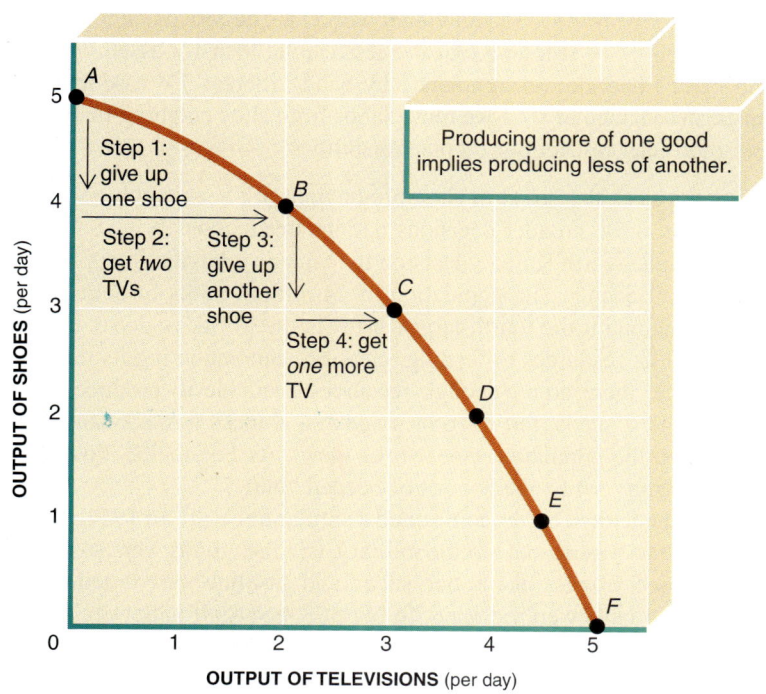

FIGURE 1.1
A Production Possibilities Curve

A production possibilities curve describes the various output combinations that could be produced in a given time period with available resources and technology. It represents a menu of output choices an economy confronts. Point B indicates that we could produce a *combination* of four shoes and two televisions per day. By producing one less shoe, we could assemble a third television, and thus move to point C. Points A, D, E, and F, illustrate still other output combinations that could be produced. This curve is a graphic illustration of the production possibilities schedule in Table 1.1.

Notice in particular how points *A* through *F* in Figure 1.1 represent the choices described in each row of Table 1.1. At point *A*, we're producing five shoes per day and no televisions. As we move down the curve from point *A* to point *B*, shoe production drops from five to four shoes per day while TV assembly increases from zero to two. In other words, we're giving up one shoe to get two televisions assembled. The opportunity cost of those televisions is one shoe that is given up. A production possibilities curve, then, is simply a graphic summary of production possibilities, as described in Table 1.1. It illustrates the alternative goods and services we could produce and the implied opportunity costs of each choice. In other words, *the production possibilities curve illustrates two essential principles:*

- *Scarce resources.* There's a limit to the amount we can produce in a given time period with available resources and technology.
- *Opportunity costs.* We can obtain additional quantities of any desired good only by reducing the potential production of another good.

Increasing Opportunity Costs

The shape of the production possibilities curve reflects another limitation on our choices. Notice how opportunity costs increase as we move along the production possibilities curve. When we cut shoe output from five shoes to four (step 1, Figure 1.1), we get two televisions (step 2). When we cut shoe production further, however (step 3), we get only one television per shoe given up (step 4). The opportunity cost of TV assembly is increasing. This process of increasing opportunity cost continues. By the time we give up the last shoe (row *F*), TV output increases by only 0.5: We get only half a television for the last shoe given up. These increases in opportunity cost are reflected in the outward bend of the production possibilities curve.

Why do opportunity costs increase? Mostly because it's difficult to move resources from one industry to another. It's easy to transform shoes to televisions on a blackboard. In the real world, however, resources don't adapt so easily. Workers who stitch shoes may not have the skills for TV assembly. As we continue to transfer labor from one industry to the other, we start getting fewer televisions for every shoe we give up. The difficulties entailed in transferring labor skills, capital, and entrepreneurship from one industry to another are so universal that we often speak of the *law* of *increasing opportunity cost.* This law says that we must give up ever-increasing quantities of other goods and services in order to get more of a particular good. The law isn't based solely on the limited versatility of individual workers. The *mix* of factor inputs makes a difference as well. Shoe stitching requires less capital than TV assembly. In a pinch, shoes could be stitched almost completely by hand, whereas TV assembly requires more sophisticated machinery. As we move labor from shoe stitching to TV assembly, available capital may restrict our output capabilities.

The Cost of North Korea's Military

The kind of opportunity costs that arise in shoe production or TV assembly takes on even greater significance in the broader decisions nations make about WHAT to produce. Consider, for example, North Korea's decision to maintain a large military. North Korea is a relatively small country: Its population of 24 million ranks fortieth in the world. Yet North Korea maintains the fourth-largest army in the world. To do so, it must allocate 14 percent of all its resources to feeding, clothing, and equipping its military forces. As a consequence, there aren't enough resources available to produce food. Without adequate machinery, seeds, fertilizer, or irrigation, Korea's farmers can't produce enough food to feed the population (see World View). As Figure 1.2 illustrates, the opportunity cost of "guns" in Korea is a lot of needed "butter."

During World War II, the United States confronted a similar trade-off. In 1944, nearly 40 percent of all U.S. output was devoted to the military. Civilian goods were so scarce that they had to be rationed. Staples like butter, sugar, and gasoline were doled out in small quantities. Even golf balls were rationed. In North Korea, golf balls would be a luxury even without a military buildup. As the share of North Korea's output devoted to the military increased, even basic food production became more difficult.

The International Institute for Strategic Studies compiles data on national military forces (www.isn.ethz.ch/iiss). To determine what percentage of a nation's population is in the armed forces, try the Central Intelligence Agency (www.odci.gov/cia/publications/factbook).

WORLD VIEW

North Korea Says It Is Running Out of Food

TOKYO, March 3 (Tuesday)—North Korea issued its most dire assessment yet of its food shortages on Monday, saying that a hungry population already living on starvation rations could run out of food in as little as two weeks.

The official state news agency reported that daily rations for most people had already been cut to seven ounces a day, far below what is generally considered necessary for survival. It said that even if that ration is cut in half, "the stock will run out in mid-March."

Because of North Korea's secretive nature, it is virtually impossible to know whether its statements about the shortages are accurate. If true, millions of people could be at immediate risk of famine and starvation.

—Kevin Sullivan
Washington Post, March 2, 1998.

North Korea Expanding Missile Programs

Despite international pressure to curtail its missile program, North Korea is building at least two new launch facilities for the medium-range Taepo Dong 1 and has stepped up production of short-range missiles, according to U.S. intelligence and diplomatic sources.

The projects, and a conclusion by U.S. intelligence agencies that North Korea intends to test-fire a second missile capable of striking Japan, are inflaming regional tensions, U.S. officials and Korea experts said.

—Dana Priest and Thomas W. Lippman
Washington Post, November 20, 1998, p. 1.

Source: © 1998 The Washington Post. Reprinted with permission. www.washingtonpost.com

Analysis: North Korea's inability to feed itself is partly due to maintaining its large army: Resources used for the military aren't available for producing food.

Russia confronted a similarly difficult trade-off. In September 2000, Russia decided it could no longer afford to devote such a large share of its resources to the military. It decided to shrink its armed forces by more than a fourth, releasing over 300,000 workers to produce civilian goods and services. As a result, Russia now has a smaller armed force than North Korea but also a lot more food. Figure 1.3 illustrates how other nations divide up available resources between military and civilian production. The $350 billion the United States now spends on national defense absorbs only 3 percent of total output. This made the opportunity costs of the post-terrorist military buildup less painful.

Not all of the choices on the production possibilities curve are equally desirable. They are, however, all *efficient*. Efficiency means squeezing *maximum* output out of available resources. Every point of the production possibilities curve satisfies this condition. Although the *mix* of output changes as we move around the production possibilities curve (Figures 1.1 and 1.2), at every point we are getting as much *total* output as physically possible. Since **efficiency** in production means simply "getting the most from

Efficiency

efficiency: Maximum output of a good from the resources used in production.

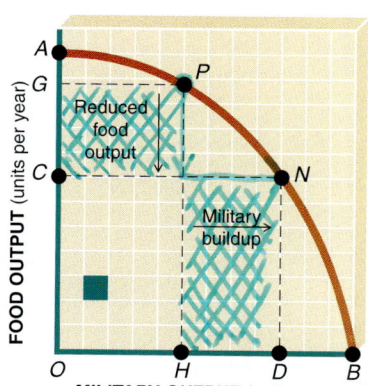

FIGURE 1.2
The Cost of an Army

North Korea devotes 14 percent of its output to the military. The opportunity cost of this decision is reduced output of food. As the military expands from *OH* to *OD,* food output drops from *OG* to *OC*.

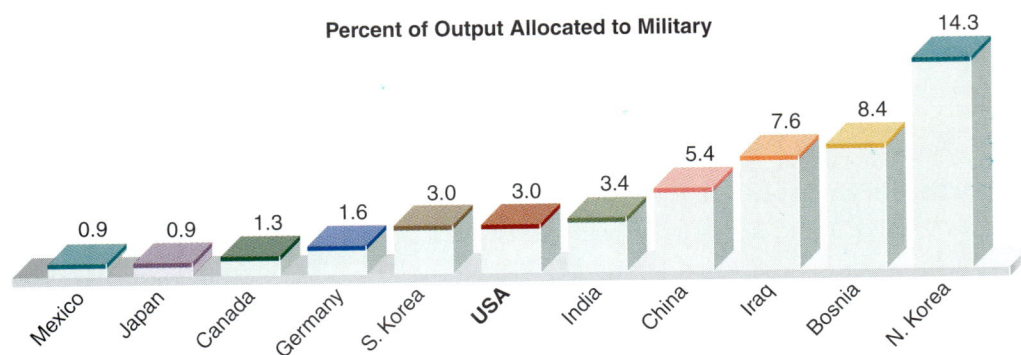

FIGURE 1.3
The Military Share of Output

The share of output allocated to the military is an indication of the opportunity cost of maintaining an army. North Korea has the highest cost, using 14 percent of its resources for military purposes. Although China and the United States have much larger armies their military *share* of output is much smaller.

Source: International Institute of Strategic Studies (1999 data).

Inefficiency

what you've got," every point on the production possibilities curve is efficient. At any point on the curve we are using all available resources in the best way we know how.

There's no guarantee, of course, that we'll always use resources so efficiently. *A production possibilities curve shows* potential *output, not necessarily* actual *output.* If we're inefficient, actual output will be less than that potential. This happens. In the real world, workers sometimes loaf on the job. Or they call in sick and go to a baseball game instead of working. Managers don't always give the clearest directions or stay in touch with advancing technology. Even students sometimes fail to put forth their best effort on homework assignments. This kind of slippage can prevent us from achieving maximum production. When that happens, we end up *inside* the production possibilities curve rather than *on* it.

Point Y in Figure 1.4 illustrates the consequences of inefficient production. At point Y, we're producing only three shoes and two televisions. This is less than our potential. We could assemble a third television without cutting back shoe production (point C). Or we could get an extra shoe without sacrificing any TV output (point B). Instead, we're producing *inside* the production possibilities curve at point Y. Such inefficiencies plagued centrally planned economies. Government-run factories guaranteed everyone a job regardless of how much output they produced. They became bloated bureaucracies; as much as 40 percent of the workers were superfluous. When communism collapsed, many of these factories were "privatized," that is, sold to private investors. The privatized companies were able to fire thousands of workers and *increase* output. Governments in Europe and Latin America have also sold off many of their state-owned enterprises in the hopes of increasing efficiency and reaching the production possibilities curve.

FIGURE 1.4
Points Inside and Outside the Curve

Points outside the production possibilities curve (point X) are unattainable with available resources and technology. Points inside the curve (point Y) represent the incomplete use of available resources. Only points on the production possibilities curve (A, B, C) represent maximum use of our production capabilities.

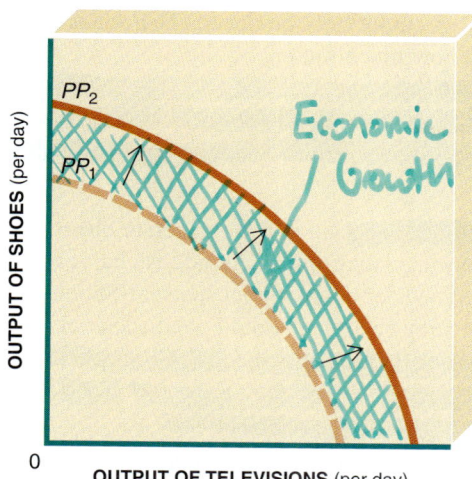

FIGURE 1.5

Growth: Increasing Production Possibilities

A production possibilities curve is based on *available* resources and technology. If more resources or better technology becomes available, production possibilities will increase. This economic growth is illustrated by the shift from PP_1 to PP_2.

PP_1 – Production possibility (Originally)
PP_2 – Production possibility w/ more resources or better technology

Countries may also end up inside their production possibilities curve if all available resources aren't used. In 1992, for example, as many as 10 million Americans were looking for work each week, but no one hired them. As a result, we were stuck *inside* the production possibilities curve, producing less output than we could have. A basic challenge for policymakers is to eliminate unemployment and keep the economy on its production possibilities curve. In 2000, the United States was much closer to this goal.

Unemployment

Figure 1.4 also illustrates an output mix that everyone would welcome. Point X lies *outside* the production possibilities curve. It suggests that we could get *more* goods than we're capable of producing! Unfortunately, point X is only a mirage: All output combinations that lie outside the production possibilities curve are unattainable with available resources and technology.

Things change, however. Over time, population increases and we get more labor. If we continue building factories and machinery, the stock of available capital will also increase. The *quality* of labor and capital will also increase if we train workers and pursue new technologies. Entrepreneurs may discover new products or better ways of producing old ones (e.g., Intel's latest chips). All these changes will increase potential output. This is illustrated in Figure 1.5 by the outward *shift* of the production possibilities curve. Before the appearance of new resources or better technology, our production possibilities were limited by the curve PP_1. **With more resources or better technology, our production possibilities increase.** This greater capacity to produce is represented by curve PP_2. This outward shift of the production possibilities curve is the essence of **economic growth**. With economic growth, countries can have more guns *and* more butter. Without economic growth, living standards decline as the population grows. This is the problem that plagues some of the world's poorest nations, where population increases every year but output often doesn't.

Economic Growth

economic growth: An increase in output (real GDP); an expansion of production possibilities.

BASIC DECISIONS

Production possibilities define the output choices that a nation confronts. From these choices every nation must make some basic decisions. As we noted at the beginning of this chapter, the three core economic questions are

- *WHAT to produce*
- *HOW to produce*
- *FOR WHOM to produce*

There are millions of points along a production possibilities curve, and each one represents a specific mix of output. We can choose only *one* of these points at any time.

WHAT

The point we choose determines what mix of output gets produced. That choice determines how many guns are produced, and how much butter.

The production possibilities curve doesn't tell us which mix of output is best; it just lays out a menu of available choices. It's up to us to pick out the one and only mix of output that will be produced at a given time. This WHAT decision is a basic decision every nation must make.

HOW

Decisions must also be made about HOW to produce. Should we generate electricity by burning coal, smashing atoms, or transforming solar power? Should we harvest ancient forests even if that destroys endangered owls or other animal species? Should we dump municipal and industrial waste into nearby rivers, or should we dispose of it in some other way? There are lots of different ways of producing goods and services, and someone has to make a decision about which production methods to use. The HOW decision is a question not just of efficiency but of social values as well.

FOR WHOM

After we've decided what to produce and how, we must address a third basic question: FOR WHOM? Who is going to get the output produced? Should everyone get an equal share? Should everyone wear the same clothes and drive identical cars? Should some people get to enjoy seven-course banquets while others forage in garbage cans for food scraps? How should the goods and services an economy produces be distributed? Are we satisfied with the way output is now distributed?

THE MECHANISMS OF CHOICE

Answers to the questions of WHAT, HOW, and FOR WHOM largely define an economy. But who formulates the answers? Who actually decides which goods are produced, what technologies are used, or how incomes are distributed?

The Invisible Hand of a Market Economy

Adam Smith had an answer back in 1776. In his classic work *The Wealth of Nations*, Smith said the "invisible hand" determines what gets produced, how, and for whom. The invisible hand he referred to wasn't a creature from a science fiction movie but, instead, a characterization of the way markets work.

Consider the decision about how many cars to produce in the United States. Who decides to produce over 6 million cars a year? There's no "auto czar" who dictates production. Not even General Motors can make such a decision. Instead, the *market* decides how many cars to produce. Millions of consumers signal their desire to have a car by browsing the Internet, visiting showrooms, and buying cars. Their purchases flash a green light to producers, who see the potential to earn more profits. To do so, they'll increase auto output. If consumers stop buying cars, profits will disappear. Producers will respond by reducing output, laying off workers, and even closing factories. These interactions between consumers and producers determine how many cars are produced.

Notice how the invisible hand moves us along the production possibilities curve. If consumers demand more cars, the mix of output will include more cars and less of other goods. If auto production is scaled back, the displaced autoworkers will end up producing other goods and services, which will change the mix of output in the opposite direction.

Adam Smith's invisible hand is now called the **market mechanism**. Notice that it doesn't require any direct contact between consumers and producers. Communication is indirect, transmitted by market prices and sales. Indeed, the essential feature of the market mechanism is the price signal. If you want something and have sufficient income, you can buy it. If enough people do the same thing, the total sales of that product will rise, and perhaps its price will as well. Producers, seeing sales and prices rise, will want to exploit this profit potential. To do so, they'll attempt to acquire a larger share of available resources and use it to produce the goods we desire. That's how the "invisible hand" works.

market mechanism: The use of market prices and sales to signal desired outputs (or resource allocations).

The market mechanism can also answer the HOW question. To maximize their profits, producers will seek to use the lowest-cost method of producing a good. By observing prices in the marketplace, they can identify the cheapest method and adopt it.

The market mechanism can also resolve the FOR WHOM question. A market distributes goods to the highest bidder. Individuals who are willing and able to pay the most for a good tend to get it in a pure market economy.

Adam Smith was so impressed with the ability of the market mechanism to answer the basic WHAT, HOW, and FOR WHOM questions that he urged government to "leave it alone" (**laissez faire**). In his view, the price signals and responses of the marketplace were likely to do a better job of allocating resources than any government could.

laissez faire: The doctrine of "leave it alone," of nonintervention by government in the market mechanism.

Government Intervention and Command Economies

The laissez-faire policy Adam Smith favored has always had its share of critics. Karl Marx emphasized how free markets tend to concentrate wealth and power in the hands of the few, at the expense of the many. As he saw it, unfettered markets permit the capitalists (those who own the machinery and factories) to enrich themselves while the proletariat (the workers) toil long hours for subsistence wages. Marx argued that the government not only had to intervene but had to *own* all the means of production—the factories, the machinery, the land—in order to avoid savage inequalities. In *Das Kapital* (1867) and the *Communist Manifesto* (1848), he laid the foundation for a communist state in which the government would be the master of economic outcomes.

The British economist John Maynard Keynes seemed to offer a less drastic solution. The market, he conceded, was pretty efficient in organizing production and building better mousetraps. However, individual producers and workers had no control over the broader economy. The cumulative actions of so many economic agents could easily tip the economy in the wrong direction. A completely unregulated market might veer off in one direction and then another as producers all rushed to increase output at the same time or throttled back production in a herdlike manner. The government, Keynes reasoned, could act like a pressure gauge, letting off excess steam or building it up as the economy needed. With the government maintaining overall balance in the economy, the market could live up to its performance expectations. While assuring a stable, full-employment environment, the government might also be able to redress excessive inequalities. In Keynes's view, government should play an active but not all-inclusive role in managing the economy.

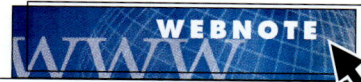

For more information on Smith, Malthus, Keynes, and Marx, visit the Federal Reserve Bank of San Francisco at www.frbsf.org/econedu and click on "Great Economists and Their Times" under "Publications and Resources."

Continuing Debates

These historical views shed perspective on today's political debates. The core of most debates is some variation of the WHAT, HOW, or FOR WHOM questions. Much of the debate is how these questions should be answered. Conservatives favor Adam Smith's laissez-faire approach, while liberals tend to think government intervention is likely to improve the answers. Conservatives resist workplace regulation, affirmative action, and minimum wages because such interventions might impair market efficiency. Liberals argue that such interventions temper the excesses of the market and promote both equity and efficiency.

The debate over how best to manage the economy is not unique to the United States. Countries around the world confront the same choice, between reliance on the market and reliance on the government. Few countries have ever relied exclusively on either one or the other to manage their economy. Even the former Soviet Union, where the government owned all the means of production and central planners dictated how they were to be used, made limited use of free markets. In Cuba, the government still manages the economy's resources but encourages farmers' markets and some private trade and investment. In Chile, the market has a much larger role in deciding what is produced, how it is produced, and who gets the resulting output.

To learn how the Heritage Foundation defines economic freedom, visit its website at www.heritage.org.

The World View below categorizes nations by the extent of their market reliance. Hong Kong scores high on this "Index of Economic Freedom" because its tax rates are relatively low, the public sector is comparatively small, and there are few restrictions on private investment or trade. By contrast, North Korea scores extremely low because the government owns all property, directly allocates resources, sets wages, and limits trade.

WORLD VIEW

Index of Economic Freedom

Hong Kong ranks number one among the world's nations in economic freedom. It achieves that status with low tax rates, free-trade policies, minimal government regulation, and secure property rights. These and other economic indicators place Hong Kong at the top of the Heritage Foundation's 2002 country rankings by the degree of "economic freedom." The "most free" and the "least free" (repressed) economies on the list of 155 countries are

Greatest Economic Freedom	Least Economic Freedom
Hong Kong	North Korea
Singapore	Iraq
New Zealand	Libya
Switzerland	Cuba
United States	Laos
Ireland	Iran
Luxembourg	Turkmenistan
Netherlands	Uzbekistan
Estonia	Belarus
	Zimbabwe

Source: Heritage Foundation, *2002 Index of Economic Freedom*, Washington, DC, 2002. www.heritage.org

Analysis: All nations must decide whether to rely on market signals or government directives to determine economic outcomes. Nations that rely the least on government intervention score highest on this Index of Economic Freedom.

The rankings shown in the World View are neither definitive nor stable. In 1989, Russia began a massive transformation from a state-controlled economy to a more market-oriented economy. Some of the former republics (e.g., Estonia) became relatively free, while others (e.g., Belarus) still rely on extensive government control of the economy. China has greatly expanded the role of private markets and Cuba is moving in the same direction in fits and starts.

In the United States, the changes have been less dramatic. The most notable shift was President Franklin Roosevelt's New Deal, which greatly expanded the government's role in the economy. In more recent times, the tug-of-war between laissez faire and government intervention has been much less decisive. Although President Reagan often said that "government *is* the problem," he hardly made a dent in government growth during the eight years of his presidency. Likewise, President Clinton's very different conviction that the government can *fix* problems, not cause them, had only minor effects on the size and scope of government activity. President George W. Bush has sought not only lower taxes but also less government regulation of HOW goods are produced.

A Mixed Economy

Even if President Bush got all the tax cuts and deregulation he wanted, the government would still play a large role in the U.S. economy. No one wants to rely exclusively on Adam Smith's invisible hand. Nor is anyone willing to have the economy steered exclusively by the highly visible hand of the government. The United States, like most nations, uses a combination of market signals and government directives to select economic outcomes. The resulting compromises are called **mixed economies**.

mixed economy: An economy that uses both market signals and government directives to allocate goods and resources.

The reluctance of countries around the world to rely exclusively on either market signals or government directives is due to the recognition that both mechanisms can and do fail on occasion. As we've seen, market signals are capable of answering the three core questions of WHAT, HOW, and FOR WHOM. But the answers may not be the best possible ones.

When market signals don't give the best possible answers to the WHAT, HOW, and FOR WHOM questions, we say that the market mechanism has *failed*. Specifically, **market failure** means that the invisible hand has failed to achieve the best possible outcomes. If the market fails, we end up with the wrong (*sub*optimal) mix of output, too much unemployment, polluted air, or an inequitable distribution of income.

In a market-driven economy, for example, producers will select production methods based on cost. Cost-driven production decisions, however, may lead a factory to spew pollution into the environment rather than to use cleaner but more expensive methods of production. The resulting pollution may be so bad that society ends up worse off as a result of the extra production. In such a case we may need government intervention to force better answers to the WHAT and HOW questions.

We could also let the market decide who gets to consume cigarettes. Anyone who had enough money to buy a pack of cigarettes would then be entitled to smoke. What if, however, children aren't experienced enough to balance the risks of smoking against the pleasures? What if nonsmokers are harmed by second-hand smoke? In this case as well, the market's answer to the FOR WHOM question might not be optimal.

Government intervention may move us closer to our economic goals. If so, the resulting mix of market signals and government directives would be an improvement over a purely market-driven economy. But government intervention may fail as well. **Government failure** occurs when government intervention fails to improve market outcomes or actually makes them worse.

The collapse of communism revealed how badly government directives can fail. But government failure also occurs in less spectacular ways. For example, the government may intervene to force an industry to clean up its pollution. The government's directives may impose such high costs that the industry closes factories and lays off workers. Some cutbacks in output might be appropriate, but they could also prove excessive. The government might also mandate pollution control technologies that are too expensive or even obsolete. None of this has to happen, but it might. If it does, government failure will have worsened economic outcomes.

The government might also fail if it interferes with the market's answer to the FOR WHOM question. For 30 years, socialist Cuba distributed goods by government directive, not market performance. Incomes were more equal, but uniformly low. To increase output and living standards, Cuba has turned to market incentives (see World View on the next page). As workers respond to these incentives, everyone may become better off—even while inequality increases.

Excessive taxes and transfer payments can also worsen economic outcomes. If the government raises taxes on the rich to pay welfare benefits for the poor, neither the rich nor the poor may see much purpose in working. In that case, the attempt to give everybody a "fair" share of the pie might end up shrinking the size of the pie. If that happened, society could end up worse off.

None of these failures has to occur, but they might. The challenge for society is to minimize failures by selecting the appropriate balance of market signals and government directives. This isn't an easy task. It requires that we know how markets work and why they sometimes fail. We also need to know what policy options the government has and how and when they might work.

WHAT ECONOMICS IS ALL ABOUT

Understanding how economies function is the basic purpose of studying economics. We seek to know how an economy is organized, how it behaves, and how successfully it achieves its basic objectives. Then, if we're lucky, we can discover better ways of attaining those same objectives.

Market Failure

market failure: An imperfection in the market mechanism that prevents optimal outcomes.

Government Failure

government failure: Government intervention that fails to improve economic outcomes.

Seeking Balance

WORLD VIEW

Farming, Capitalism Work Well in Cuba; Post-Soviet Food Crisis Called Over

There's a new revolution afoot in Cuba, a green revolution. We're talking veggies: bushels of beets, loads of lettuce, crates of cucumbers.

State-run farms are producing more vegetables than Cubans have seen in years. So many, in fact, that experts say the food crisis that began after the collapse of the Soviet Union is over.

One reason production is up: Farms are getting a dose of capitalism.

Field workers used to make the same wage no matter what they produced in a day. And if inspectors noticed that they were doing more than expected, they would even be penalized; their workload would be increased.

Now, the harder they work, the more money they make.

Wages for farmers range from 300 Cuban pesos ($13.64) to 800 pesos ($36.37) per month, up from 240 pesos ($10.90) in 1997, according to *Granma,* the newspaper of Cuba's Communist Party.

Workers, making an average of $12 a month in all industries, still have trouble putting food on the table. Red meat is out of reach for most Cubans. And soft drinks are a luxury for many.

But Cubans say food isn't as scarce as it was in 1993, when the island began to absorb the full impact of the collapse of its chief ally, the Soviet Union. That year, farms lost tens of millions of dollars. Inefficiency, low productivity, and high costs were to blame, experts say.

Last year, farms on the outskirts of Havana turned a profit for the first time in more than a decade, and they did it with fewer resources: less fuel, less fertilizer and fewer chemicals.

—Tracey Eaton

Source: *The Arizona Republic,* September 3, 2001. Reprinted with permission. www.arizonarepublic.com

Analysis: If the government distributes income without regard to work effort, people may not give their best effort. Market-based incomes increase inequality but also motivate higher productivity.

End vs. Means

Economists don't formulate an economy's objectives. Instead, they focus on the *means available for achieving given goals.* In 1978, for example, the U.S. Congress identified "full employment" as a major economic goal. Congress then directed future presidents (and their economic advisers) to formulate policies that would enable us to achieve full employment. The economist's job is to help design policies that will best achieve this and other economic goals.

Macro vs. Micro

The study of economics is typically divided into two parts: macroeconomics and microeconomics. Macroeconomics focuses on the behavior of an entire economy—the "big picture." In macroeconomics we worry about such national goals as full employment, control of inflation, and economic growth, without worrying about the well-being or behavior of specific individuals or groups. The essential concern of **macroeconomics** is to understand and improve the performance of the economy as a whole.

Microeconomics is concerned with the details of this big picture. In microeconomics we focus on the individuals, firms, and government agencies that actually compose the larger economy. Our interest here is in the behavior of individual economic actors. What are their goals? How can they best achieve these goals with their limited resources? How will they respond to various incentives and opportunities?

A primary concern of macroeconomics, for example, is to determine how much money, *in total,* consumers will spend on goods and services. In microeconomics, the focus is much narrower. In micro, attention is paid to purchases of *specific* goods and services rather than just aggregated totals. Macro likewise concerns itself with the level of *total* business investment, while micro examines how *individual* businesses make their investment decisions.

Although they operate at different levels of abstraction, macro and micro are intrinsically related. Macro (aggregate) outcomes depend on micro behavior, and micro (individual) behavior is affected by macro outcomes. One can't fully understand how an economy works until one understands how all the participants behave and why they

macroeconomics: The study of aggregate economic behavior, of the economy as a whole.

microeconomics: The study of individual behavior in the economy, of the components of the larger economy.

behave as they do. But just as you can drive a car without knowing how its engine is constructed, you can observe how an economy runs without completely disassembling it. In macroeconomics we observe that the car goes faster when the accelerator is depressed and that it slows when the brake is applied. That's all we need to know in most situations. At times, however, the car breaks down. When it does, we have to know something more about how the pedals work. This leads us into micro studies. How does each part work? Which ones can or should be fixed?

Our interest in microeconomics is motivated by more than our need to understand how the larger economy works. The "parts" of the economic engine are people. To the extent that we care about the welfare of individuals in society, we have a fundamental interest in microeconomic behavior and outcomes. In this regard, we examine how individual consumers and business firms seek to achieve specific goals in the marketplace. The goals aren't always related to output. Gary Becker won the 1992 Nobel Prize in economics for demonstrating how economic principles also affect decisions to marry, to have children, or to engage in criminal activities.

Theory vs. Reality

The distinction between macroeconomics and microeconomics is one of many simplifications we make in studying economic behavior. The economy is much too vast and complex to describe and explain in one course (or one lifetime). Accordingly, we focus on basic relationships, ignoring annoying detail. In so doing, we isolate basic principles of economic behavior and then use those principles to predict economic events and develop economic policies. This means that we formulate theories, or *models*, of economic behavior and then use those theories to evaluate and design economic policy.

Our model of consumer behavior assumes, for example, that people buy less of a good when its price rises. In reality, however, people *may* buy *more* of a good at increased prices, especially if those high prices create a certain snob appeal or if prices are expected to increase still further. In predicting consumer responses to price increases, we typically ignore such possibilities by *assuming* that the price of the good in question is the *only* thing that changes. This assumption of "other things remaining equal" (unchanged) (in Latin, ***ceteris paribus***) allows us to make straightforward predictions. If instead we described consumer responses to increased prices in any and all circumstances (allowing everything to change at once), every prediction would be accompanied by a book full of exceptions and qualifications. We'd look more like lawyers than economists.

ceteris paribus: The assumption of nothing else changing.

Although the assumption of *ceteris paribus* makes it easier to formulate economic theory and policy, it also increases the risk of error. If other things do change in significant ways, our predictions (and policies) may fail. But, like weather forecasters, we continue to make predictions, knowing that occasional failure is inevitable. In so doing, we're motivated by the conviction that it's better to be approximately right than to be dead wrong.

Politics. Politicians can't afford to be quite so complacent about economic predictions. Policy decisions must be made every day. And a politician's continued survival may depend on being more than approximately right. George H. Bush's loss in the 1992 election resulted in part from his repeated predictions that the economy was "turning around." When this optimistic forecast proved wrong, voters lost faith in President Bush's ability to direct the economy. Ironically, his son gained a critical advantage in the superclose 2000 presidential election because of another economic slowdown and a slumping stock market. Once again, voters sought a new economic policy team.

After he took office, President George W. Bush immediately sought to change the mix of output. Even before the September 11, 2001 terrorist attacks, he wanted more "guns," as reflected in added defense spending (see News). With the U.S. economy fully employed, the cost of those additional "guns" had to be less "butter." Was this the right choice? Economic theory can't really answer that question. The choice

Comparative data on the percentage of goods and services the various national governments provide is available from the Penn World Tables at www.pwt.econ.upenn.edu.

> **IN THE NEWS**
>
> ### Bush Seeking Defense Increase
> **'02 Budget Request Adds $18.4 Billion**
>
> The Bush administration said yesterday it will propose a 6 percent boost in its planned 2002 defense budget, an increase that contains new funds for missile defense, military pay and other benefits but is less than many senior officers had expected.
>
> The $18.4 billion addition, coming on top of previously announced increases, would raise next year's Pentagon budget to about $330 billion. That is roughly 10 percent more than this year's level but at least $10 billion less than the Joint Chiefs of Staff have said privately they believe is necessary.
>
> Administration officials described the increase as a temporary move that simply stabilizes the military while Defense Secretary Donald H. Rumsfeld plans far-reaching changes in strategy, weapons and troop structure. But by deferring the military's expectations, the administration may be setting up a brawl next year with Congress and the armed services.
>
> —Thomas E. Ricks
>
> Source: *Washington Post,* June 23, 2001. © 2001 The Washington Post. Reprinted with permission. www.washingtonpost.com

> **Analysis:** More military spending absorbs factors of production (land, labor, capital) that could be used to produce civilian goods. Choosing WHAT to produce is a basic economic issue.

between guns and butter is ultimately a political one—a decision that must take into account not only economic trade-offs (opportunity costs) but also social values. "Politics"—the balancing of competing interests—is an inevitable ingredient of economic policy.

Imperfect Knowledge. One last word of warning before you read further. Economics claims to be a science, in pursuit of basic truths. We want to understand and explain how the economy works without getting tangled up in subjective value judgments. This may be an impossible task. First, it's not clear where the truth lies. For more than 200 years economists have been arguing about what makes the economy tick. None of the competing theories has performed spectacularly well. Indeed, few economists have successfully predicted major economic events with any consistency. Even annual forecasts of inflation, unemployment, and output are regularly in error. Worse still, never-ending arguments about what caused a major economic event continue long after it occurs. In fact, economists are still arguing over the primary causes of the Great Depression of the 1930s!

In part, this enduring controversy reflects diverse sociopolitical views on the appropriate role of government. Some people think a big public sector is undesirable, even if it improves economic performance. But the controversy has even deeper roots. Major gaps in our understanding of the economy persist. We know how much of the economy works, but not all of it. We're adept at identifying all the forces at work, but not always successful in gauging their relative importance. In point of fact, we may *never* find an absolute truth, because the inner workings of the economy change over time. When economic behavior changes, our theories must be adapted.

In view of all these debates and uncertainties, don't expect to learn everything there is to know about the economy today in this text or course. Our goals are more modest. We want to develop a reasonable perspective on economic behavior, an understanding of basic principles. With this foundation, you should acquire a better view of how the economy works. Daily news reports on economic events should make more sense. Congressional debates on tax and budget policies should take on more meaning. You may even develop some insights that you can apply toward running a business or planning a career, or—if the Nobel prize-winning economist Gary Becker is right—developing a lasting marriage.

THE ECONOMY TOMORROW

When asked what they wish for, contestants at beauty contests often reply that they want "world peace," "a cure for AIDS," or the "elimination of poverty." Who could object to these goals? The serious question is how we'll achieve them, with or without the contestants' help.

The same can be said for our economic goals. Everyone wants full employment, low inflation, and a chicken in every pot. But how are we going to attain these goals? Should we rely on Adam Smith's invisible hand to lead us into the glow of the economy tomorrow? Or should the government intervene to be sure we get to the right destination? The fact that we live in a "mixed economy" doesn't relieve us of the decision about whether to intervene or not. The decision to intervene or not arises repeatedly, at both the micro and macro levels of the economy.

To Intervene or Not?

The 1998 antitrust suit against Microsoft brought the issue to the forefront of microeconomics. Microsoft has long proclaimed itself the world's premier innovator. So the company was appalled in 1998 when the U.S. Department of Justice accused Microsoft of suppressing innovation and harming consumers. A key issue was whether Microsoft could "bundle" its Internet browser with its Windows operating system. Microsoft asserted that by adding applications features to its operating system, it was offering a superior product. Essentially, Microsoft adopted a version of Adam Smith's argument as its central defense. Microsoft claimed that the *market,* not the *government,* should decide what computer products are produced and by whom. If Microsoft produced inferior products or charged excessive prices, the *market* would punish it with declining sales and profits. Since millions of consumers evidently were willing to buy Microsoft's products, the government should just "leave it alone."

Micro Intervention: The Microsoft Antitrust Case

For updates on the Microsoft case, see www.antitrust.org.

The Justice Department rejected that argument. It conceded that Microsoft produced a lot of good products. But it argued that Microsoft's near monopoly on operating systems gave it too much power to decide WHAT is produced. Even *better* products and prices would be available if more firms were able to compete. Government intervention was needed, the department claimed, to stop Microsoft from destroying potential competitors and restricting choices about WHAT to produce. In April 2000, a federal judge agreed. As a result of that guilty verdict, Microsoft was required to change some of its business practices.

The question of whether to intervene or not also arises at the macro level. Consider the level of interest rates. Changes in interest rates affect how much consumers end up paying for big-ticket items such as cars and houses that are financed with loans. High interest rates also raise the cost of your credit card balances and any student loans you might take out. For corporations, the interest rate may be a critical factor in deciding whether to invest in a new factory.

Macro Intervention: Fed Intervention

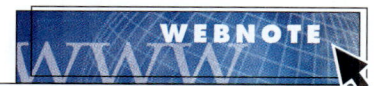

For more on the Fed's intervention, see www.federalreserve.gov.

The market is perfectly capable of determining the rates of interest. But the market's decision may not be consistent with our macro goals. If interest rates are too high, consumer and investor spending may decline, leaving output unsold and workers unemployed. If rates are too low, market participants may go on a spending spree that overheats the economy and causes inflation. Either outcome would represent macro failure.

To avert macro failure, the government regulates credit conditions. Specifically, the Federal Reserve (the central bank) tries to keep interest rates at the right level by regulating bank behavior. This gives the Fed enormous influence on macro outcomes. When the economy was booming in the mid-1990s, nearly everyone praised the Fed's intervention. When the Fed raised interest rates a bit too high and the economy slumped in 2000–01, however, critics were quick to charge that the Fed should have left the economy alone.

In these and all other cases the issue is always the same: Will government intervention *improve* economic outcomes or *worsen* them? As we observed earlier, both the market and the government may *fail* to move the economy in the right direction. Given these possibilities, the question of whether to intervene or not will be as pressing an issue in the economy tomorrow as it is in the economy today.

SUMMARY

- Scarcity is a basic fact of economic life. Factors of production (land, labor, capital, entrepreneurship) are scarce in relation to our desires for goods and services.
- All economic activity entails opportunity costs. Factors of production (resources) used to produce one output cannot simultaneously be used to produce something else. When we choose to produce one thing, we forsake the opportunity to produce some other good or service.
- A production possibilities curve illustrates the limits to production and the opportunity costs associated with different output combinations. It shows the alternative combinations of final goods and services that could be produced in a given period if all available resources and technology are used efficiently.
- The bent shape of the production possibilities curve reflects the law of increasing opportunity costs. This law states that increasing quantities of any good can be obtained only by sacrificing ever-increasing quantities of other goods.
- Inefficient or incomplete use of resources will fail to attain production possibilities. Additional resources or better technologies will expand them. This is the essence of economic growth.
- Every country must decide WHAT to produce, HOW to produce, and FOR WHOM to produce with its limited resources.
- The choices of WHAT, HOW, and FOR WHOM can be made by the market mechanism or by government directives. Most nations are mixed economies, using a combination of these two choice mechanisms.
- Market failure exists when market signals generate suboptimal outcomes. Government failure occurs when government intervention worsens economic outcomes. The challenge for economic theory and policy is to find the mix of market signals and government directives that best fulfills our social and economic goals.
- The study of economics focuses on the broad question of resource allocation. Macroeconomics is concerned with allocating the resources of an entire economy to achieve aggregate economic goals (e.g., full employment). Microeconomics focuses on the behavior and goals of individual market participants.

Key Terms

economics
scarcity
factors of production
capital
entrepreneurship
opportunity cost
production possibilities
efficiency
economic growth
market mechanism
laissez faire
mixed economy
market failure
government failure
macroeconomics
microeconomics
ceteris paribus

Questions for Discussion

1. What opportunity costs did you incur in reading this chapter? If you read four more chapters of this book today, would your opportunity cost (per chapter) increase? Explain.
2. How much time could you spend on homework in a day? How much do you spend? How do you decide?
3. What's the real cost of the food in the free lunch cartoon?
4. What is the opportunity cost of President Bush's proposed increase in defense spending (News, page 18)?
5. How might a nation's production possibilities be affected by the following?
   a. A decrease in taxes.
   b. An increase in government regulation.
   c. An increase in military spending.
   d. An increase in college tuition.
   e. Faster, more powerful electronic chips.
6. Markets reward individuals according to their output; communism rewards people according to their needs. How might these different systems affect work effort?

7. Why might efficiency increase when a company is privatized, that is, converted from government ownership to private ownership? Could efficiency decrease?
8. How does government intervention affect college admissions? Who would go to college in a completely private (market) college system?
9. Will the Cuban economy benefit from entrepreneurship and material incentives? (See World View, page 16.) Is there any downside to greater entrepreneurial freedom?

Web Activities

1. Log on to www.odci.gov/cia/publications/factbook/geos/kn.html and find the CIA's most recent estimate for GDP in North Korea. Based on the information found at this site, answer these questions.
   a. What is the value of North Korea's total output?
   b. How much more "butter" could North Korea produce if it reduced the military share of its output from 14 percent to 6 percent?
2. Log on to www.bea.doc.gov/bea/dn/nipaweb/Popular Tables.asp. Click on Table 1.1 for Gross Domestic Product and specify an information search for 1944–1946. Using the information you download, answer these questions.
   a. By how much did the military share of U.S. output decline between 1944 and 1946?
   b. By how much did the output of consumer goods increase?
3. What is your opportunity cost for attending college? First, estimate your annual college-related expenses, including tuition, books, supplies, and room and board if applicable. Since the major opportunity cost for most college students is forgone earnings, you'll need to find the median annual earnings for your age group at www.census.gov/hhes/www/income.html. Once you access this site, click on summary measure of income and find the median income for your age group. Add that figure to your estimated expenses to find your total opportunity cost for a year of college. Then, to reassure yourself that it's worth it, visit www.census.gov/ftp/pub/hhes/www/img/educate.gif.
4. Do economists have a sense of humor? Check it out at "Jokes about Economists and Economics" at netec.wustl.edu/JokEc.html.

THE ACCOMPANYING STUDENT PROBLEM SET CONTAINS NUMERICAL AND GRAPHING PROBLEMS FOR THIS CHAPTER

APPENDIX

USING GRAPHS

Economists like to draw graphs. In fact, we didn't even make it through the first chapter without a few graphs. This appendix looks more closely at the way graphs are drawn and used. The basic purpose of a graph is to illustrate a relationship between two *variables*. Consider, for example, the relationship between grades and studying. In general, we expect that additional hours of study time will lead to higher grades. Hence, we should be able to see a distinct relationship between hours of study time and grade-point average.

Suppose that we actually surveyed all the students taking this course with regard to their study time and grade-point averages. The resulting information can be compiled in a table such as Table A.1.

According to the table, students who don't study at all can expect an F in this course. To get a C, the average student apparently spends 8 hours a week studying. All those who study 16 hours a week end up with an A in the course.

These relationships between grades and studying can also be illustrated on a graph. Indeed, the whole purpose of a graph is to summarize numerical relationships.

TABLE A.1
Hypothetical Relationship of Grades to Study Time

Study Time (hours per week)	Grade-Point Average
16	4.0 (A)
14	3.5 (B+)
12	3.0 (B)
10	2.5 (C+)
8	2.0 (C)
6	1.5 (D+)
4	1.0 (D)
2	0.5 (F+)
0	0.0 (F)

We begin to construct a graph by drawing horizontal and vertical boundaries, as in Figure A.1. These boundaries are called the *axes* of the graph. On the vertical axis (often called the *Y* axis) we measure one of the variables; the other variable is measured on the horizontal axis (the *X* axis).

In this case, we shall measure the grade-point average on the vertical axis. We start at the *origin* (the intersection of the two axes) and count upward, letting the distance between horizontal lines represent half (0.5) a grade point. Each horizontal line is numbered, up to the maximum grade-point average of 4.0.

The number of hours each week spent doing homework is measured on the horizontal axis. We begin at the origin again, and count to the right. The *scale* (numbering) proceeds in increments of 1 hour, up to 20 hours per week.

When both axes have been labeled and measured, we can begin illustrating the relationship between study time and grades. Consider the typical student who does 8 hours of homework per week and has a 2.0 (C) grade-point average. We illustrate this relationship by first locating 8 hours on the horizontal axis. We then move up from that point a distance of 2.0 grade points, to point *M*. Point *M* tells us that 8 hours of study time per week is typically associated with a 2.0 grade-point average.

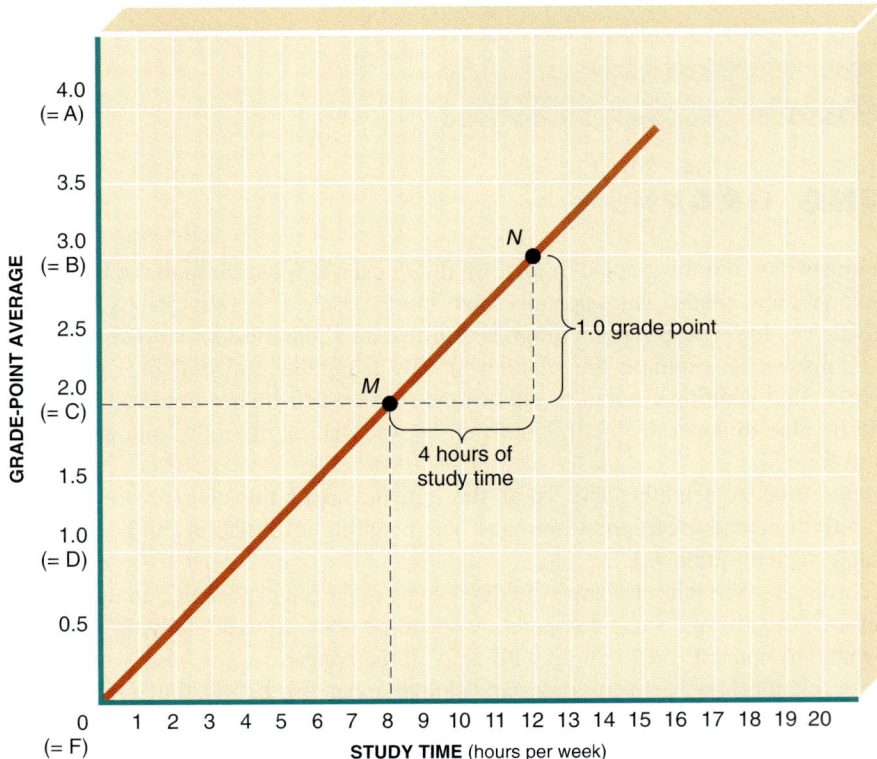

FIGURE A.1

The Relationship of Grades to Study Time

The upward (positive) slope of the curve indicates that additional studying is associated with higher grades. The average student (2.0, or C grade) studies 8 hours per week. This is indicated by point *M* on the graph.

The rest of the information in Table A.1 is drawn (or *plotted*) on the graph the same way. To illustrate the average grade for people who study 12 hours per week, we move upward from the number 12 on the horizontal axis until we reach the height of 3.0 on the vertical axis. At that intersection, we draw another point (point *N*).

Once we've plotted the various points describing the relationship of study time to grades, we may connect them with a line or curve. This line (curve) is our summary. In this case, the line slopes upward to the right—that is, it has a *positive* slope. This slope indicates that more hours of study time are associated with *higher* grades. Were higher grades associated with *less* study time, the curve in Figure A.1 would have a *negative* slope (downward from left to right).

Slopes

The upward slope of Figure A.1 tells us that higher grades are associated with increased amounts of study time. That same curve also tells us *by how much* grades tend to rise with study time. According to point *M* in Figure A.1, the average student studies 8 hours per week and earns a C (2.0 grade-point average). To earn a B (3.0 average), students apparently need to study an average of 12 hours per week (point *N*). Hence an increase of 4 hours of study time per week is associated with a 1-point increase in grade-point average. This relationship between *changes* in study time and *changes* in grade-point average is expressed by the steepness, or *slope,* of the graph.

The slope of any graph is calculated as

$$\text{Slope} = \frac{\text{vertical distance between two points}}{\text{horizontal distance between two points}}$$

In our example, the vertical distance between *M* and *N* represents a change in grade-point average. The horizontal distance between these two points represents the change in study time. Hence the slope of the graph between points *M* and *N* is equal to

$$\text{Slope} = \frac{3.0 \text{ grade} - 2.0 \text{ grade}}{12 \text{ hours} - 8 \text{ hours}} = \frac{1 \text{ grade point}}{4 \text{ hours}}$$

In other words, a 4-hour increase in study time (from 8 to 12 hours) is associated with a 1-point increase in grade-point average (see Figure A.1).

Shifts

The relationship between grades and studying illustrated in Figure A.1 isn't inevitable. It's simply a graphical illustration of student experiences, as revealed in our hypothetical survey. The relationship between study time and grades could be quite different.

Suppose that the university decided to raise grading standards, making it more difficult to achieve every grade other than an F. To achieve a C, a student now would need to study 12 hours per week, not just 8 (as in Figure A.1). Whereas students could previously expect to get a B by studying 12 hours per week, now they'd have to study 16 hours to get that grade.

Figure A.2 illustrates the new grading standards. Notice that the new curve lies to the right of the earlier curve. We say that the curve has *shifted* to reflect a change in the relationship between study time and grades. Point *R* indicates that 12 hours of study time now "produces" a C, not a B (point *N* on the old curve). Students who now study only 4 hours per week (point *S*) will fail. Under the old grading policy, they could have at least gotten a D. **When a curve shifts, the underlying relationship between the two variables has changed.**

A shift may also change the slope of the curve. In Figure A.2, the new grading curve is parallel to the old one; it therefore has the same slope. Under either the new grading policy or the old one, a 4-hour increase in study time leads to a 1-point increase in grades. Therefore, the slope of both curves in Figure A.2 is

$$\text{Slope} = \frac{\text{vertical change}}{\text{horizontal change}} = \frac{1}{4}$$

FIGURE A.2
A Shift

When a relationship between two variables changes, the entire curve *shifts*. In this case a tougher grading policy alters the relationship between study time and grades. To get a C, one must now study 12 hours per week (point R), not just 8 hours (point M).

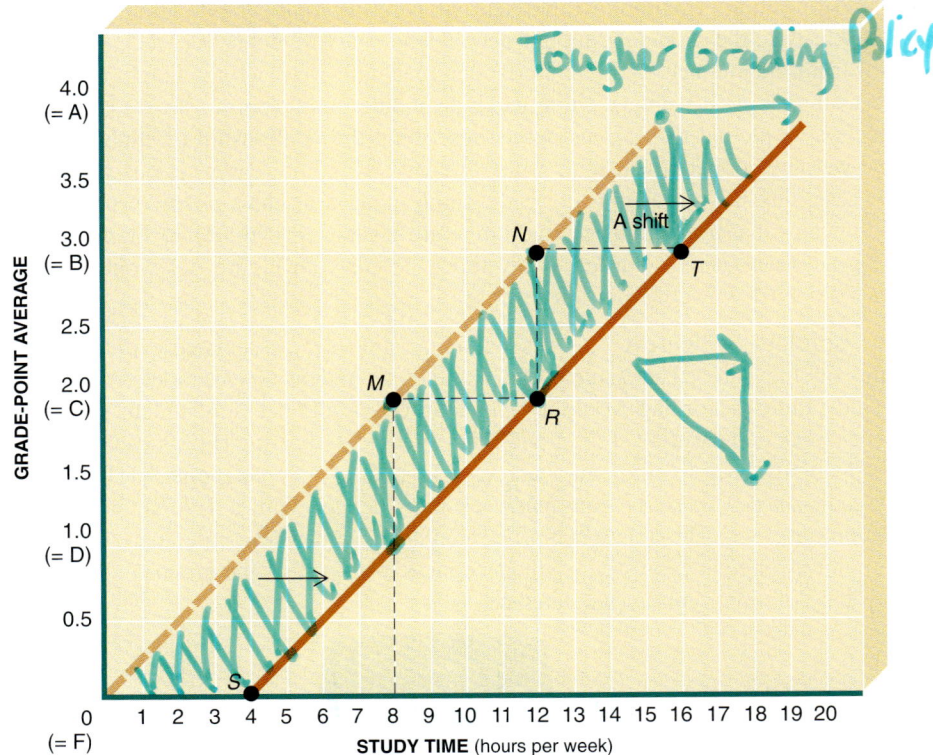

This too may change, however. Figure A.3 illustrates such a possibility. In this case, zero study time still results in an F. But now the payoff for additional studying is reduced. Now it takes 6 hours of study time to get a D (1.0 grade point), not 4 hours as before. Likewise, another 4 hours of study time (to a total of 10) raises the grade by only two-thirds of a point. It takes 6 hours to raise the grade a full point. The slope of the new line is therefore

$$\text{Slope} = \frac{\text{vertical change}}{\text{horizontal change}} = \frac{1}{6}$$

The new curve in Figure A.3 has a smaller slope than the original curve and so lies below it. What all this means is that it now takes a greater effort to *improve* your grade.

Linear vs. Nonlinear Curves

In Figures A.1–A.3 the relationship between grades and studying is represented by a straight line—that is, a *linear curve*. A distinguishing feature of linear curves is that they have the same (constant) slope throughout. In Figure A.1, it appears that *every* 4-hour increase in study time is associated with a 1-point increase in average grades. In Figure A.3, it appears that every 6-hour increase in study time leads to a 1-point increase in grades. But the relationship between studying and grades may not be linear. Higher grades may be more difficult to attain. You may be able to raise a C to a B by studying 4 hours more per week. But it may be harder to raise a B to an A. According to Figure A.4, it takes an additional 8 hours of studying to raise a B to an A. Thus the relationship between study time and grades is *nonlinear* in Figure A.4; the slope of the curve changes as study time increases. In this case, the slope decreases as study time increases. Grades continue to improve, but not so fast, as more and more time is devoted to homework. You may know the feeling.

Causation

Figure A.4 doesn't by itself guarantee that your grade-point average will rise if you study 4 more hours per week. In fact, the graph drawn in Figure A.4 doesn't prove that additional study ever results in higher grades. The graph is only a summary of empirical observations. It says nothing about cause and effect. It could be that students who study a lot are smarter to begin with. If so, then less able students might not get higher

FIGURE A.3
A Change in Slope

When a curve shifts, it may change its slope as well. In this case, a new grading policy makes each higher grade more difficult to reach. To raise a C to a B, for example, one must study 6 additional hours (compare points J and K). Earlier it took only 4 hours to move the grade scale up a full point. The slope of the line has declined from $0.25 (= 1 \div 4)$ to $0.17 (= 1 \div 6)$.

grades if they studied harder. In other words, the *cause* of higher grades is debatable. At best, the empirical relationship summarized in the graph may be used to support a particular theory (e.g., that it pays to study more). Graphs, like tables, charts, and other statistical media, rarely tell their own story; rather, they must be *interpreted* in terms of some underlying theory or expectation.

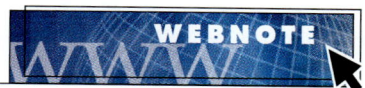

For online practice with graphs, visit "Math Skills for Introductory Economics" at syllabus.syr.edu/cid/graph/book.html.

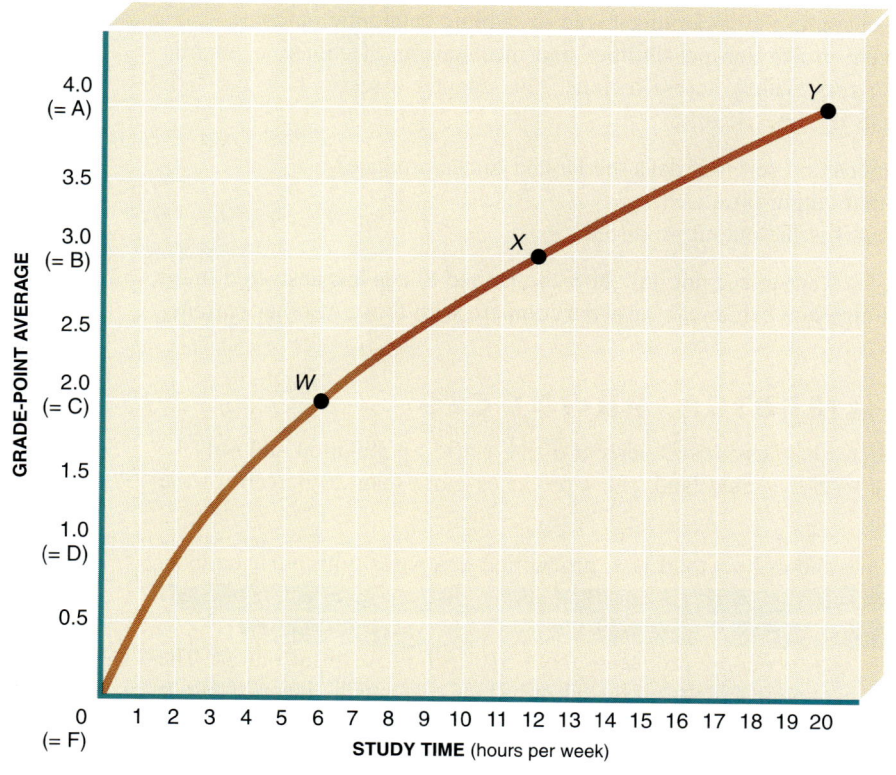

FIGURE A.4
A Nonlinear Relationship

Straight lines have a constant slope, implying a constant relationship between the two variables. But the relationship (and slope) may vary. In this case, it takes 6 extra hours of study to raise a C (point W) to a B (point X) but 8 extra hours to raise a B to an A (point Y). The slope decreases as we move up the curve.

CHAPTER 2

The U.S. Economy: A Global View

All nations must deal with the central economic questions of WHAT to produce, HOW to produce, and FOR WHOM to produce it. However, the nations of the world approach these issues with vastly different production possibilities. China, Canada, the United States, and Brazil each covers more than *3 million* acres of land. They have far greater production possibilities than Dominica, Tonga, Malta, or Lichtenstein, each of which has less than 500 acres of land. The population of China totals more than 1.3 billion people, five times that of the United States, and 25,000 times the population of Greenland. Obviously, these nations confront very different output choices.

In addition to varying production possibilities, the nations of the world use different mechanisms for deciding WHAT, HOW, and FOR WHOM to produce. Belarus, Romania, North Korea, and Cuba still rely heavily on central planning. By contrast, Singapore, New Zealand, Ireland, and the United States permit the market mechanism to play a dominant role in shaping economic outcomes.

With different production possibilities and mechanisms of choice, economic outcomes also vary widely across nations. This chapter assesses how the U.S. economy stacks up. Specifically,

- WHAT goods and services does the United States produce?
- HOW is that output produced?
- FOR WHOM is the output produced?

In each case, we want to see not only how the United States has answered these questions but also how America's answers compare with those of other nations.

WHAT AMERICA PRODUCES

The United States has less than 5 percent of the world's population and only 12 percent of the world's arable land, yet it produces more than 20 percent of the world's output.

The World View shows how total U.S. production compares with other nations. These comparisons are based on the total market value of all the goods and services a nation produces—what we call **gross domestic product (GDP)**.

In 2000, the U.S. economy produced about $10 trillion worth of output. The second-largest economy, China, produced only half that much. Japan came in third, with about 40 percent of U.S. output. Cuba, by contrast, produced only $1.6

GDP Comparisons

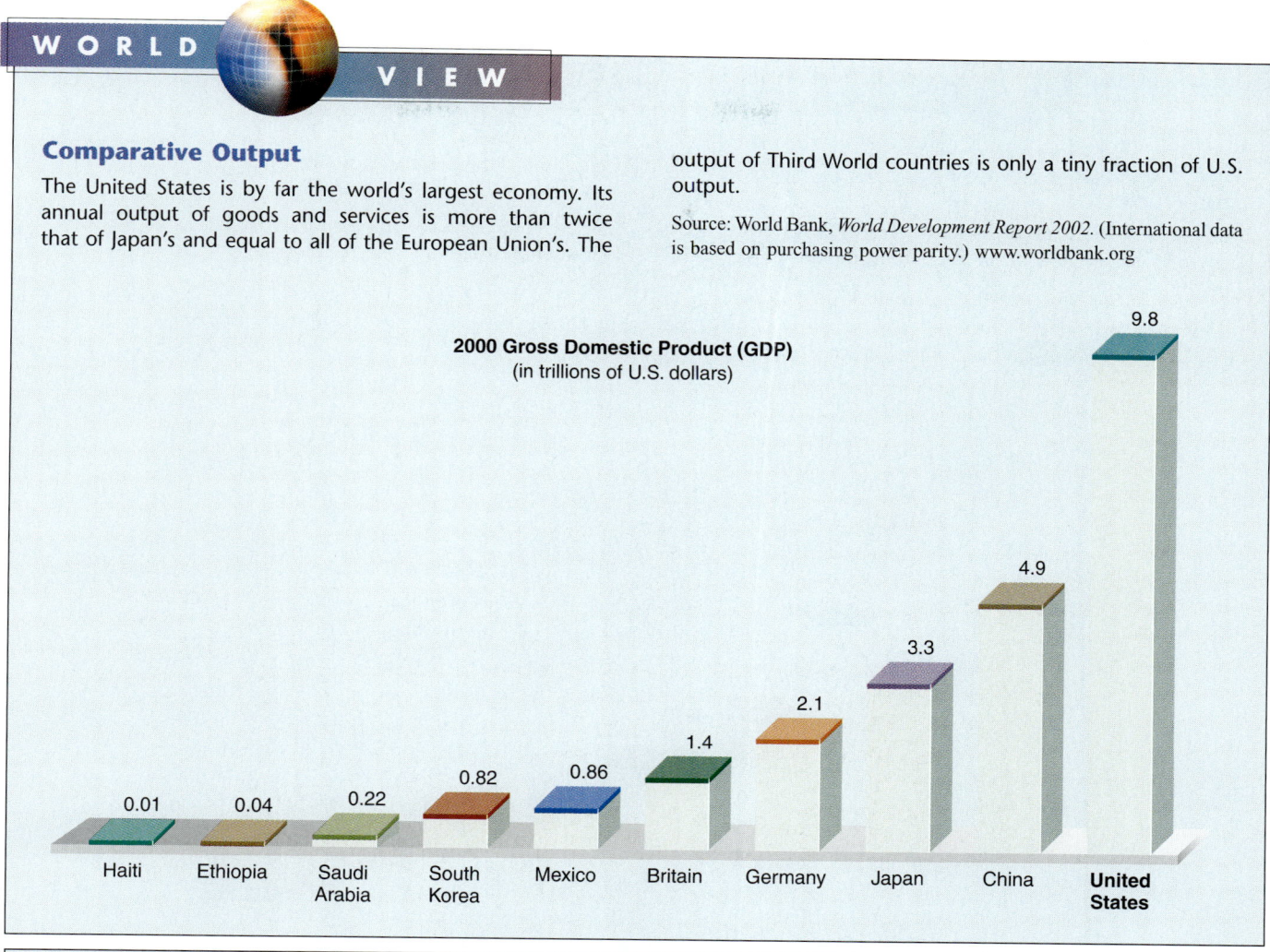

WORLD VIEW

Comparative Output

The United States is by far the world's largest economy. Its annual output of goods and services is more than twice that of Japan's and equal to all of the European Union's. The output of Third World countries is only a tiny fraction of U.S. output.

Source: World Bank, *World Development Report 2002*. (International data is based on purchasing power parity.) www.worldbank.org

2000 Gross Domestic Product (GDP)
(in trillions of U.S. dollars)

Country	GDP
Haiti	0.01
Ethiopia	0.04
Saudi Arabia	0.22
South Korea	0.82
Mexico	0.86
Britain	1.4
Germany	2.1
Japan	3.3
China	4.9
United States	9.8

Analysis: The market value of output (GDP) is a basic measure of an economy's size. The U.S. economy is far larger than any other and accounts for over one-fifth of the entire world's output.

billion of output, less than the state of South Dakota. Russia, which was once regarded as a superpower, produced only $1.1 trillion, about as much as New York state. The entire 15-member European Union produces less than the United States.

Per Capita GDP. What makes the U.S. share of world output so noteworthy is that with only 5 percent of the world's population, the United States produces far more output *per person* than other countries do. This people-based measure of economic performance is called **per capita GDP**. Per capita GDP is simply total output divided by total population. Per capita GDP doesn't tell us how much any specific person gets. Per capita GDP is an indicator of how much output the average person would get if all output were divided up evenly among the population.

In 2000, per capita GDP in the United States was more than $34,000—nearly five times as much as the average in the rest of the world. The following World View provides a global perspective on just how "rich" America is, as measured by the per capita production of goods and services. Some of the country-specific comparisons are startling. China, which has the world's second-largest GDP, also contains one-fifth of the

> **gross domestic product (GDP):** The total market value of all final goods and services produced within a nation's borders in a given time period.
>
> **per capita GDP:** The dollar value of GDP divided by total population; average GDP.

WORLD VIEW

GDP Per Capita around the World

The American standard of living is over five times higher than the world average. People in the poorest nations of the world (e.g., Haiti, Ethiopia) barely survive on per capita incomes that are a tiny fraction of U.S. standards.

Source: World Bank, *World Development Report 2002*. www.worldbank.org

Analysis: Per capita GDP is a measure of average living standards. Americans have access to far more goods and services than people in other nations do.

Data on the output of different nations are available from the Central Intelligence Agency at www.odci.gov/cia/publications/factbook.

economic growth: An increase in output (real GDP): an expansion of production possibilities.

world's population. Hence, China has such a relatively low per capita income that most of its citizens would be considered "poor" by official American standards. Yet people in other nations (e.g., Haiti, Ethiopia) don't even come close to that low standard. According to the World Bank, nearly half of the people on earth subsist on incomes of less than $2 a day. Seen in this context, it's easy to understand why the rest of the world envies (and sometimes resents) America's prosperity.

GDP Growth. What's even more startling about global comparisons is that the GDP gap between the United States and the world's poor nations keeps growing. The reason for that is **economic growth**. With few exceptions, U.S. output increases nearly every year. On average, U.S. output has grown by roughly 3 percent a year, nearly three times faster than population growth (1 percent). Hence, not only does *total* output keep rising, but *per capita* output keeps rising as well (see Figure 2.1).

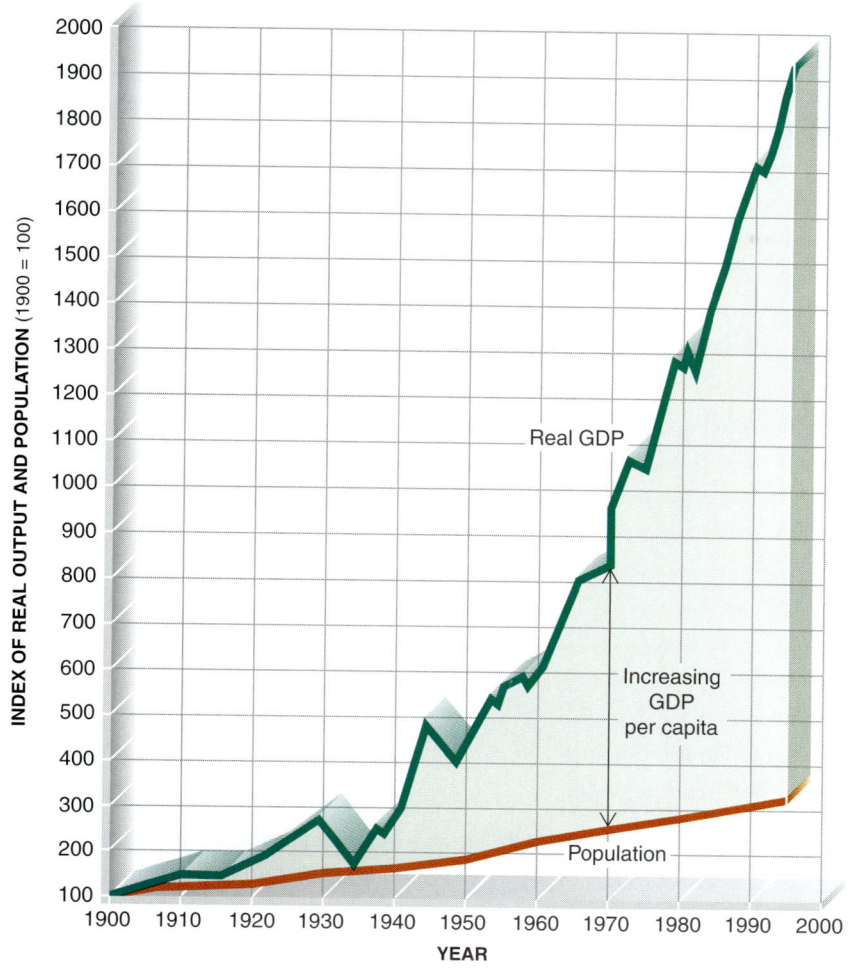

FIGURE 2.1
U.S. Output and Population Growth Since 1900

Over time, the growth of output in the United States has greatly exceeded population growth. As a consequence, GDP per capita has grown tremendously. GDP per capita was five times higher in 2000 than in 1900.

Source: U.S. Department of Labor.

Poor Nations. People in the world's poorest countries aren't so fortunate. China's economy has grown exceptionally fast in the last 20 years, propelling it to second place in the global GDP rankings. But in many other nations total output has actually *declined* year after year, further depressing living standards. Notice in Table 2.1, for example, what's been happening in Haiti. From 1990 to 2000, Haiti's output of goods and services (GDP) declined by an average of 0.6 percent a year. As a result, total Haitian output in 2000 was six percent *smaller* than in 1990. During those same years, the Haitian population kept growing—by over 2 percent a year. With *negative* economic growth and fast population growth, Haiti's per capita GDP fell below $1,200 a year. According to the United Nations, nearly two-thirds of Haiti's population was undernourished. To the average Haitian, America's prosperity looked more unattainable than ever. As Table 2.1 shows, even some poor nations that had *positive* GDP growth in the 1990s (e.g., Kenya, Venezuela) didn't grow fast enough to raise living standards. As a result, they fell even further behind America's (rising) level of prosperity.

The Mix of Output

Regardless of how much output a nation produces, the *mix* of output always includes both *goods* (such as cars, HDTVs, potatoes) and *services* (like this economics course, visits to a doctor, or a professional baseball game). A century ago, about two-thirds of U.S. output consisted of farm goods (37 percent), manufactured goods (22 percent), and mining (9 percent). Since then, over 25 *million* people have left the farms and sought jobs in other sectors. As a result, today's mix of output is reversed: **Nearly 75 percent of U.S. output consists of services, not goods.** According to the U.S. Bureau of Labor Statistics, that trend is increasing. Over 98 percent of future job growth will

TABLE 2.1
Growth Rates in Selected Countries, 1990–2000

The relationship between GDP growth and population growth is very different in rich and poor countries. The populations of rich countries are growing very slowly, and gains in per capita GDP are easily achieved. In the poorest countries, population is still increasing rapidly, making it difficult to raise living standards. Notice how per capita incomes are *declining* in many poor countries (such as Kenya, Venezuela, and Haiti).

	Average Growth Rate (1990–2000) of		
	GDP	Population	Per Capita GDP
High-income countries			
United States	3.4	1.2	2.2
Canada	2.9	1.0	1.9
France	1.7	0.4	1.3
Japan	1.3	0.3	1.0
Low-income countries			
China	10.3	1.1	9.2
India	6.0	1.8	4.2
Ethiopia	4.6	2.3	2.3
Nigeria	2.4	2.8	−0.4
Zimbabwe	2.4	2.2	0.2
Kenya	2.1	2.4	−0.3
Venezuela	1.6	2.1	−0.5
Haiti	−0.6	2.1	−2.7

Source: World Bank, *World Development Report, 2002.*

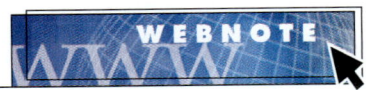

Data on the mix of output in different nations are compiled in the World Bank's annual World Development Report, available at www.worldbank.org.

be in service-producing industries such as health care, engineering, education, social services, and accounting. This trend will accelerate the change in the mix of output that has been under way for a long time (see Figure 2.2).

The *relative* decline in goods production (manufacturing, farming) doesn't mean that we're producing *fewer* goods today than in earlier decades. Quite the contrary. While some industries such as iron and steel have shrunk, others, such as chemicals, publishing, and telecommunications equipment, have grown tremendously. The result is that manufacturing output has increased fourfold since 1950. The same kind of thing has happened in the farm sector; where output keeps rising even though agriculture's *share* of total output has declined. It's just that output of *services* has increased so much faster.

Development Patterns. The transformation of the United States into a service economy is a reflection of our high incomes. In Ethiopia, where the most urgent concern is still to keep people from starving, over 50 percent of output comes from the farm

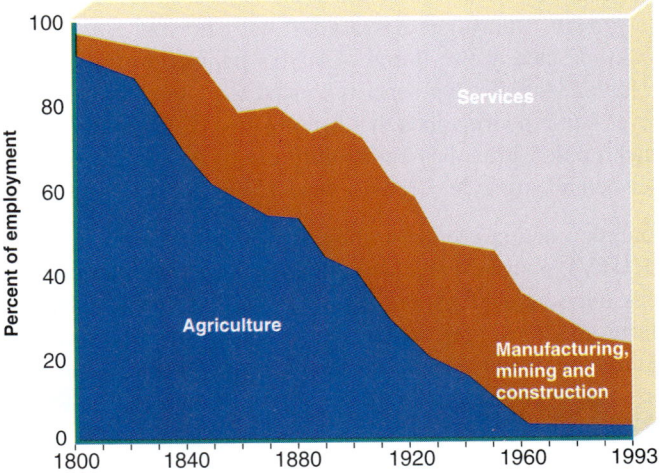

FIGURE 2.2
The Changing Mix of Output

Two hundred years ago, almost all U.S. output came from farms. Today, 75 percent of output consists of services, not farm or manufactured goods.

Source: US Department of Commerce.

sector. Poor people don't have enough income to buy dental services, vacations, or even an education, so the mix of output in poor countries is weighted toward goods, not services.

Today's Mix of Output

Services have become such a dominant share of the economy's output that we can say that *America is primarily a service economy and will become increasingly so in the future.* This generalization doesn't provide much detail, however, about exactly WHAT America produces. What kinds of services are being produced? Which goods?

We can develop a clearer picture of our answer to the WHAT question by examining the uses to which our output is put. *The four major uses of total output (GDP) are:*

- *Consumption*
- *Investment*
- *Government services*
- *Net exports*

Consumer Goods and Services. Most of America's output consists of consumer goods and services. This output includes everything from breakfast cereals (a good) to movie rentals (a service) and college education (another service)—anything and everything households buy for their own use. As Figure 2.3 illustrates, such consumption goods and services account for over two-thirds of all output.

Investment Goods and Services. Investment goods are a completely different type of output. *Investment goods are the plant, machinery, equipment, and structures that are produced for the business sector.* These investment goods are used to (1) replace worn-out equipment and factories, thus *maintaining* our production possibilities, and (2) increase and improve our stock of capital, thereby *expanding* our production possibilities.

Presently the United States devotes 18 percent of output to investment. The opportunity cost of building more plant and equipment is the extra consumer goods we could have produced instead. There's a payoff, however. New factories, buildings, and machinery allow us to produce *more* of all goods and services in the future.

Poor countries need capital investment desperately. Their incomes are so low, however, that they can't afford to cut back much on consumer goods. When Stalin wanted

investment: Expenditures on (production of) new plant, equipment, and structures (capital) in a given time period, plus changes in business inventories.

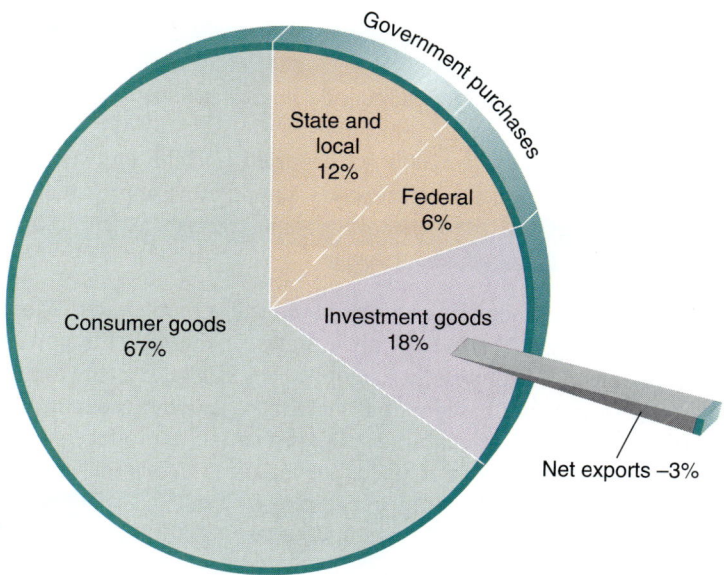

FIGURE 2.3
WHAT America Produces

Two-thirds of America's output consists of consumer goods and services. Investment (such as plant, equipment, buildings) claims about 18 percent of total output. The public sector gets nearly 18 percent. Although we export more than 11 percent of domestic output, we import an even larger share of goods and services; *net* exports are negative.

Source: *Economic Report of the President,* 2001.

32 BASIC CONCEPTS

to make Russia an industrial power, he cut output of consumer goods and forced Russian households to scrape by with meager supplies of food, clothing, and even shelter for decades. Today, most poor nations have to depend on foreign aid and other capital inflows to finance needed investment. Without more investment, they run the risk of continuing stagnation or even a decline of living standards.

Government Services. The third type of output included in GDP is government services. Federal, state, and local governments purchase resources to police the streets, teach classes, write laws, and build highways. The resources the government sector uses for these purposes are unavailable for either consumption or investment. At present, the production of government services absorbs roughly one-fifth of total U.S. output (see Figure 2.3).

Notice the emphasis again on the production of real goods and services. The federal government now *spends* about $2 trillion a year. Much of that spending, however, is in the form of income transfers, not resource purchases. **Income transfers are payments to individuals for which no direct service is provided.** Social Security benefits, welfare checks, food stamps, and unemployment benefits are all transfer payments. This spending is *not* part of our output of goods and services. *Only that part of federal spending used to acquire resources and produce services is counted in GDP.* Federal purchases (production) of goods and services account for only 6 percent of total output.

State and local governments are larger providers of public services. What state and local governments lack in size, they make up for in sheer numbers. In addition to the 50 state governments, there are 3000 counties, 18,000 cities, 17,000 townships, 21,000 school districts, and over 20,000 special districts. These are the government entities that build roads; provide schools, police, and firefighters; administer hospitals; and provide social services. The output of all these state and local governments accounts for roughly 11 percent of total GDP.

Net Exports. Finally, we should note that some of the goods and services we produce each year are used abroad rather than at home. In other words, we **export** some of our output to other countries.

International trade isn't a one-way street. While we export some of our own output, we also **import** goods and services from other countries. These imports may be used for consumption (sweaters from New Zealand, Japanese DVDs, travel), investment (German ball bearings, Lloyds of London insurance), or government (French radar screens). Theoretically, imports wouldn't affect the value of GDP since GDP includes only goods and services produced within a nation's borders. In practice, however, estimates of GDP are based on market *purchases,* not surveys of production. As a result, consumption, investment, and government purchases include imports as well as domestically produced goods. To get an accurate reading of *domestic* production, imports must be subtracted out.

Figure 2.4 summarizes America's trade. In 2000, we exported $773 billion worth of goods and another $296 billion of services. These exports amounted to approximately 11 percent of total output. We imported even more goods and services, however, and so ended up with negative **net exports** (a trade deficit).

Comparative Advantage

The motivation for this international trade originates in our quest for more output. Most of the goods we import could be produced in the United States. In fact, most imported goods have domestically produced substitutes, for example, cars, computers, and tomatoes. Our decision to import them is not based on our inability to produce them but on the efficiency of importing them. International trade allows a nation to produce goods in which it has a cost advantage and then trade them for imported goods in which it has a cost disadvantage. This principle of **comparative advantage** entails exporting goods with low opportunity cost and importing goods with high opportunity cost. In other words, international trade allows countries to produce and export what they do best and import goods they don't produce as efficiently.

---

income transfers: Payments to individuals for which no current goods or services are exchanged, e.g., Social Security, welfare, unemployment benefits.

exports: Goods and services sold to foreign buyers.

imports: Goods and services purchased from foreign sources.

net exports: The value of exports minus the value of imports.

comparative advantage: The ability of a country to produce a specific good at a lower opportunity cost than its trading partners.

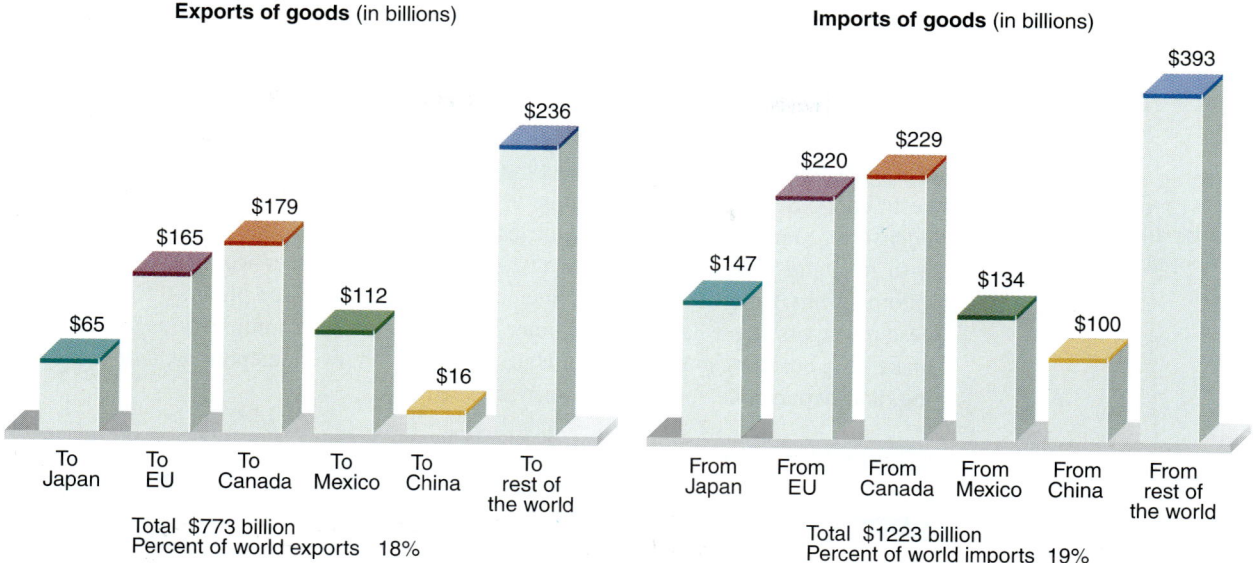

FIGURE 2.4
U.S. Exports and Imports

The United States is the world's largest exporter and importer. One third of all U.S. trade is with Canada and Mexico. The European Union, Japan, and China account for another third. In 2000, U.S. merchandise (goods) imports exceeded exports by $450 billion. This merchandise trade gap was partially offset by net *service* exports, leaving $369 billion of *net imports* (of goods and services).

Although all nations gain from international trade, smaller countries are most in need of specialization. With few resources, a small economy can't produce the whole array of goods and services consumers want. So they need to *specialize*—producing goods they can sell (export) in world markets. Saudi Arabia, for example, exports 40 percent of its total output, mostly in the form of crude oil. It then uses its export earnings to buy desired cars, engineering services, and food that it can't produce efficiently itself.

HOW AMERICA PRODUCES

All the goods and services included in gross domestic product are produced within the borders of the United States. The production process absorbs not only American-owned **factors of production** but also any foreign-owned land, labor, or capital used to produce goods or services in the United States. With the globalization of business ownership, its often difficult to even identify who owns which factors of production. It's easy, however, to observe where the factors of production are. So GDP focuses on geographical boundaries. Japanese investors may *own* the Honda factory in Ohio, but the cars *produced* there are part of U.S. output. By contrast, all the shoes produced at Nike's Malaysian factories are counted as part of that nation's GDP.

factors of production: Resource inputs used to produce goods and services, such as land, labor, capital, entrepreneurship.

A lot of people worry that the Nike factory in Malaysia is stealing U.S. jobs. Workers in Malaysia and other poor nations are willing to work for extremely low wages (recall that nearly half the world's population has incomes of less than $2 a day). But low foreign wages aren't as great a threat as they just appear. We also have to consider how much a worker *produces*. One reason wages are so low in the Third World is that workers produce so little. U.S. workers get paid an average of over $14 an hour because they *produce* so much.

Productivity

If the sheer number of workers was the decisive factor for a nation's output, China would have the world's largest economy. In reality, **productivity**—the amount of output a worker produces—is at least as important as the number of available workers. In fact, high productivity explains how the United States, with 280 million people,

productivity: Output per unit of input, such as output per labor-hour.

produces more goods and services than the combined output of China, India, Indonesia, and Brazil—nations with a combined population 10 times larger than the U.S!

Factors of Production

Capital Stock. The exceptional productivity of U.S. workers is due in large part to an abundance of capital. America has accumulated a massive stock of capital—over $10 trillion worth of machinery, factories, and buildings. As a result of all this prior investment, U.S. production tends to be very **capital-intensive.** The contrast with *labor-intensive* production in poorer-countries is striking. A Chinese farmer mostly works with his hands and crude implements, whereas a U.S. farmer works with computers, automated irrigation systems, and mechanized equipment (see photos). Russian business managers don't have the computer networks or telecommunications systems that make U.S. business so efficient. In Haiti and Ethiopia, even telephones, indoor plumbing, and dependable sources of power are scarce.

capital-intensive: Production processes that use a high ratio of capital to labor inputs.

Human Capital. Indoor plumbing and fiber-optic networks aren't the only kinds of capital a nation can accumulate. Human capital—the knowledge and skills workers possess—can also be accumulated. In the Stone Age, one's productive capacity was largely determined by physical strength and endurance. In today's economy, human capital is largely a product of education, training, and experience. Hence, a country can acquire more human capital even without more bodies.

human capital: The knowledge and skills possessed by the workforce.

Over time, the United States has invested heavily in human capital. In 1940, only 1 out of 20 young Americans graduated from college; today, over 30 percent of young people are college graduates. High school graduation rates have jumped from 38 percent to over 85 percent in the same time period. In the less developed countries, only 1 out of 2 youth ever *attend* high school, much less graduate (see World View). As a consequence, the United Nations estimates that 1 billion people—a sixth of humanity—are unable to read a book or even write their own names. Without even functional literacy,

WORLD VIEW

The Education Gap between Rich and Poor Nations

Virtually all Americans attend high school and roughly 85 percent graduate. In poor countries, relatively few workers attend high school and even fewer graduate. Half the workers in the world's poorest nations are illiterate.

Source: World Bank, *World Development Report, 2000/2001.* www.worldbank.org

Enrollment in secondary schools
(percent of school-age youth attending secondary schools)

Poor countries	Middle-income countries	High-income countries	United States
51%	71%	96%	96%

Analysis: The high productivity of the American economy is explained in part by the quality of its labor resources. Workers in poorer, less developed countries get much less education or training.

Analysis: An abundance of capital equipment and advanced technology make American farmers and workers far more productive than workers in poor nations.

such workers are doomed to low-productivity jobs. Despite low wages, they are not likely to "steal" many jobs from America's highly educated and trained workforce.

The huge output of the United States is thus explained not only by a wealth of resources but by their quality as well. **The high productivity of the U.S. economy results from using highly educated workers in capital-intensive production processes.**

Factor Mobility. Our continuing ability to produce the goods and services that consumers demand also depends on our agility in *reallocating* resources from one industry to another. Every year, some industries expand and others contract. Thousands of new firms are created each year and almost as many others disappear. In the process, land, labor, capital, and entrepreneurship move from one industry to another in response to changing demands and technology. In 1975, Federal Express, Compaq Computer, Staples, Oracle, and Amgen didn't even exist. Today these companies employ 200,000 people. These workers came from other firms and industries that weren't growing as fast.

Technological Advance. One of the forces that keeps shifting resources from one industry to another is continuing advances in technology. On the first page of this text we noted Intel's breakthrough in nanoelectronics. The discovery of new technology for microscopic miniaturization of electronic circuits expanded our production possibilities. In the process, the productivity of workers in the electronics industry will rise, as will per capita GDP. A similar phenomenon happened when the fax machine was invented. That discovery not only made communication a lot faster and easier. It also released thousands of workers from the courier (bike messenger) business. Those workers moved to new industries where their productivity was higher. *Whenever technology advances, an economy can produce more output with existing resources.*

Market Freedom. In assessing HOW goods are produced and economies grow, we must also take heed of the role the government plays. As we noted in Chapter 1, the amount of economic freedom varies greatly among the 200-plus nations of the world. Moreover, the Heritage Foundation has documented a positive relationship between the degree of economic freedom and economic growth (see Figure 2.5). Quite simply, when entrepreneurs are unfettered by regulation or high taxes, they are more likely to design and produce better mousetraps. When the government owns the factors of production, imposes high taxes, or tightly regulates output, there is little opportunity or incentive to design better products or pursue new technology.

Role of Government. Recognizing the productive value of economic freedom isn't tantamount to rejecting all government intervention. No one really advocates the complete abolition of government. On the contrary, the government plays a critical role in establishing a framework in which private businesses can operate.

Providing a Legal Framework. One of the most basic functions of government is to establish and enforce the rules of the game. In some bygone era maybe a person's word was sufficient to guarantee delivery or payment. Businesses today, however, rely

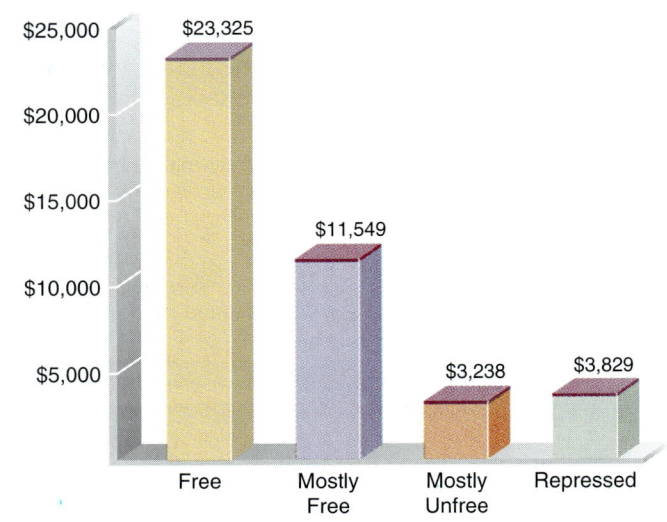

FIGURE 2.5
Economic Freedom and Per Capita GDP

The extent of economic freedom (market reliance) affects a nation's ability to grow. The Heritage Foundation shows that "repressed" (highly regulated and taxed) economies have much lower per capita GDPs than "free" (relatively unregulated, low-taxed) economies.

Source: Heritage Foundation, *2002 Index of Economic Freedom* (Washington, DC, 2002).

more on written contracts. The government gives legitimacy to contracts by establishing the rules for such pacts and by enforcing their provisions. In the absence of contractual rights, few companies would be willing to ship goods without prepayment (in cash). Even the incentive to write textbooks would disappear if government copyright laws didn't forbid unauthorized photocopying. By establishing ownership rights, contract rights, and other rules of the game, the government lays the foundation for market transactions.

Protecting the Environment. The government also intervenes in the market to protect the environment. The legal contract system is designed to protect the interests of a buyer and a seller who wish to do business. What if, however, the business they contract for harms third parties? How are the interests of persons who *aren't* party to the contract to be protected?

Numerous examples abound of how unregulated production may harm third parties. Earlier in the century, the steel mills around Pittsburgh blocked out the sun with clouds of sulfurous gases that spewed out of their furnaces. Local residents were harmed every time they inhaled. In the absence of government intervention, such side effects would be common. Decisions on how to produce would be based on costs alone, not on how the environment is affected. However, such **externalities**—spillover costs imposed on the broader community—affect our collective well-being. To reduce the external costs of production, the government limits air, water, and noise pollution and regulates environmental use.

externalities: Costs (or benefits) of a market activity borne by a third party.

In poor countries, environmental protection often gets much less priority. In Haiti, residents keep cutting down newly planted saplings, destroying any hope of reforestation. They need the firewood *now* and can't afford to take the long-run view of economic growth. The Brazilian rain forests that are critical to the earth's ecosystem suffer the same fate. In the Caspian Sea, people poach so many sturgeon that the entire caviar industry is on the verge of destruction. In all these cases, the unbridled pursuit of individual gain has damaged broader economic welfare. Some government regulation could both protect the environment and promote long-run growth.

Protecting Consumers. The government also uses its power to protect the interests of consumers. One way to do this is to prevent individual business firms from becoming too powerful. In the extreme case, a single firm might have a **monopoly** on the production of a specific good. As the sole producer of that good, a monopolist could dictate the price, the quality, and the quantity of the product. In such a situation, consumers would likely end up with the short end of the stick—paying too much for too little.

monopoly: A firm that produces the entire market supply of a particular good or service.

To protect consumers from monopoly exploitation, the government tries to prevent individual firms from dominating specific markets. Antitrust laws prohibit mergers or acquisitions that would threaten competition. The U.S. Department of Justice and the Federal Trade Commission also regulate pricing practices, advertising claims, and other behavior that might put consumers at an unfair disadvantage in product markets.

Government regulates the safety of many products. Consumers don't have enough expertise to assess the safety of various medicines, for example. If they rely on trial and error to determine drug safety, they might not get a second chance. To avoid this calamity, the government requires rigorous testing of new drugs, food additives, and other products.

Protecting Labor. The government also regulates how labor resources are used in the production process. In most poor nations, children are forced to start working at very early ages, often for minuscule wages. They often don't get the chance to go to school or to stay healthy. In Africa, 40 percent of children under age 14 works to survive or to help support their families. In the United States, child labor laws and compulsory schooling prevent minor children from being exploited. Government regulations also set standards for workplace safety, minimum wages, fringe benefits, and overtime provisions. After decades of bloody confrontations, the government also established the right of workers to organize and set rules for union-management relations. The introduction of unemployment insurance, Social Security, and disability insurance, and guarantees for private pension benefits also protect workers from the vagaries of the marketplace. These social benefits have profoundly affected how much people work, when they retire, and even how long they live.

Striking a Balance

All these government interventions are designed to change the way resources are used. Such interventions reflect the conviction that the market alone might not select the best possible way of producing goods and services. There's no guarantee, however, that government regulation of HOW goods are produced always makes us better off. Excessive regulation may inhibit production, raise product prices, and limit consumer choices. As noted in Chapter 1, *government* failure might replace *market* failure, leaving us no better off—possibly even worse off. This possibility underscores the importance of striking the right balance between market reliance and government regulation. The balance attained in the United States is surely not perfect, but it appears to be much more effective than the balances of regulation and free enterprise in most poor countries.

FOR WHOM AMERICA PRODUCES

As we've seen, America produces a huge quantity of output, using high-quality labor and capital resources. That leaves one basic question unanswered: FOR WHOM is all this output produced?

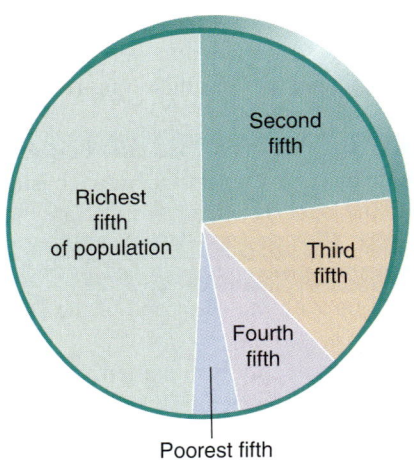

Income Quintile	2000 Income	Average Income	Share of Total Income (percent)
Lowest fifth	$0–18,000	$ 10,300	3.6
Second fifth	$18,000–33,000	$ 25,400	8.9
Third fifth	$33,000–52,300	$ 42,500	14.9
Fourth fifth	$52,300–82,000	$ 65,600	23.0
Highest fifth	above $82,000	$141,100	49.6

Source: U.S. Department of Commerce, Bureau of the Census (averages rounded to thousands of dollars).

FIGURE 2.6
The U.S. Distribution of Income

The richest fifth of U.S. households gets nearly half of all the income—a huge slice of the income pie. By contrast, the poorest fifth gets only a sliver.

How many goods and services one gets largely depends on how much income one has to spend. The U.S. economy uses the market mechanism to distribute most goods and services. Those who receive the most income get the most goods. This goes a long way toward explaining why millionaires live in mansions and homeless people seek shelter in abandoned cars. This is the kind of stark inequality that fueled Karl Marx's denunciation of capitalism. Even today, people wonder how some Americans can be so rich while others are so poor.

Figure 2.6 illustrates the actual distribution of income in the United States. For this illustration the entire population is sorted into five groups of equal size, ranked by

U.S. Income Distribution

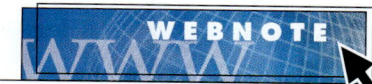

The most current data on the U.S. income distribution are available from the U.S. Bureau of the Census at www.census.gov/hhes/www/income.html.

Analysis: The market distributes income (and, in turn, goods and services) according to the resources an individual owns and how well they are used. If the resulting inequalities are too great, some redistribution via government intervention may be desired.

WORLD VIEW

Income Share of the Rich

Inequality tends to diminish as a country develops. In poor, developing nations, the richest tenth of the population typically gets 40 to 50 percent of all income. In developed countries, the richest tenth gets 20 to 35 percent of total income.

Source: World Bank, *World Development Report, 2002.* www.worldbank.org

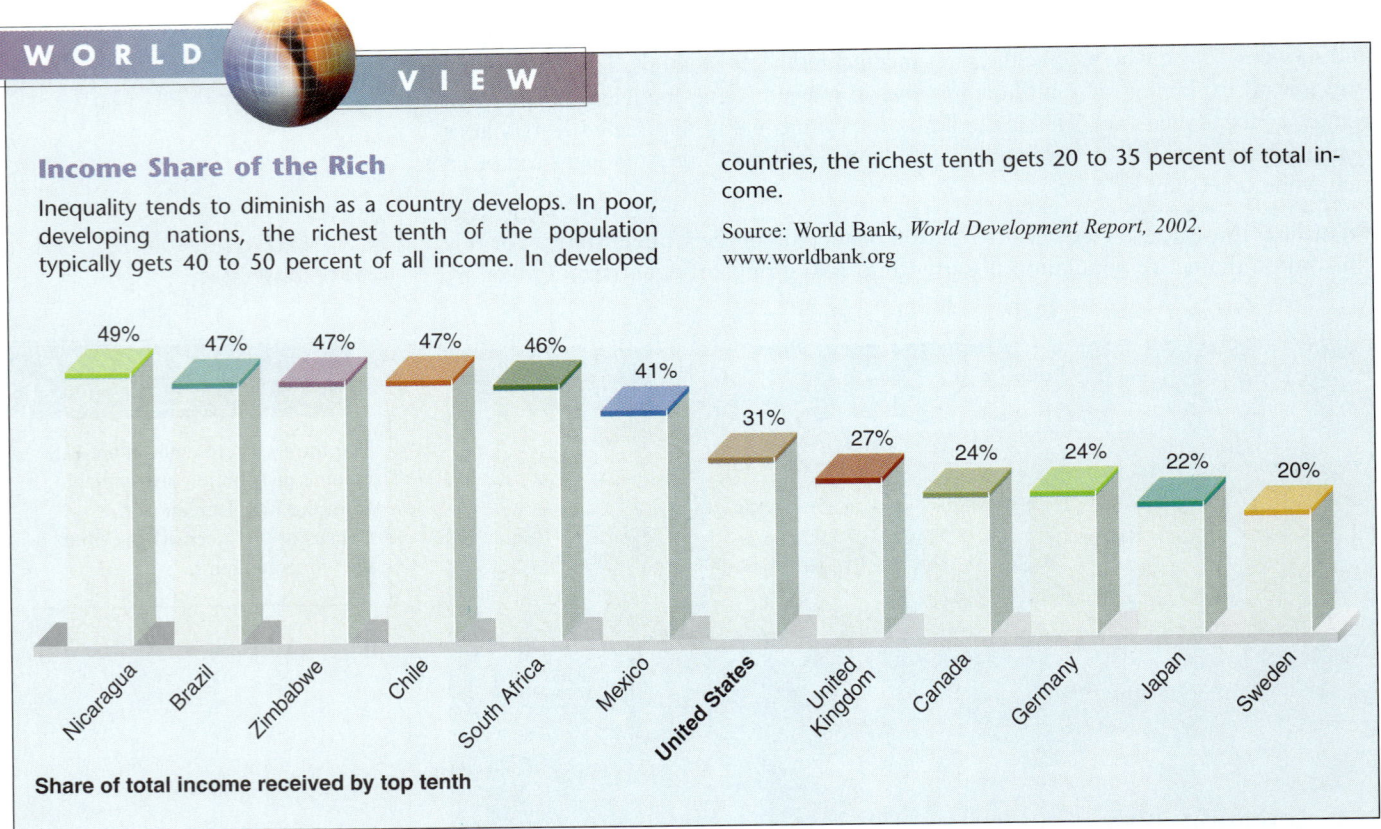

Share of total income received by top tenth

| Nicaragua | Brazil | Zimbabwe | Chile | South Africa | Mexico | United States | United Kingdom | Canada | Germany | Japan | Sweden |
| 49% | 47% | 47% | 47% | 46% | 41% | 31% | 27% | 24% | 24% | 22% | 20% |

Analysis: The FOR WHOM question is reflected in the distribution of income. Although the U.S. distribution is very unequal, inequalities loom even larger in most Third World countries.

---

income quintile: One-fifth of the population, rank-ordered by income (e.g., top fifth).

income. In this depiction, all the rich people are in the top **income quintile**; the poor are in the lowest quintile. To be in the top quintile in 2000, a household needed at least $82,000 of income. Households in the lowest quintile had incomes under $10,200.

The most striking feature of Figure 2.6 is how large a slice of the income pie rich people get: *The top 20 percent (quintile) of U.S. households gets nearly half of all U.S. income.* By contrast, the poorest 20 percent (quintile) of U.S. households gets only a sliver of the income pie—less than 4 percent. Those grossly unequal slices explain why 44 percent of all Americans believe the nation is divided into "haves" and "have nots" (June 2001, Pew Research Center Survey).

Global Inequality

As unequal as U.S. incomes are, income disparities are actually greater in many other countries. Ironically, income inequalities are often greatest in the poorest countries. In Brazil, Nicaragua, Zimbabwe, and South Africa, the richest *tenth* of the population has a far larger share of income than the richest 10 percent of Americans have. These and other comparisons of the FOR WHOM resolution are illustrated in the World View above.

Comparisons across countries would manifest even greater inequality. As we saw earlier, Third World GDP per capita is far below U.S. levels. As a consequence, even poor people in the United States receive far more goods and services than the average household in most low-income countries.

THE ECONOMY TOMORROW

 Global answers to the basic questions of WHAT, HOW, and FOR WHOM have been shaped by market forces and government intervention. Those answers aren't permanent, however. And the answers haven't always lived up to expectations. People everywhere want changes in the economy of tomorrow—more and better output, a cleaner environment, and less poverty. How will we achieve these goals?

Levers of Change

One central concern for the economy tomorrow is how fast incomes will grow. The prosperity that the United States enjoys today is the result of persistent growth in the nation's resources and productivity. The economic slowdown of 2000–01 reminded us, however, that continued fast growth isn't guaranteed. What can be done to accelerate growth in the economy tomorrow?

Income Stagnation?

Market Signals. To a large extent the pace of economic growth depends on a nation's willingness to invest—in human capital (via education and training), in physical capital (via new machinery), and in technology (via research and development). All of these investments require resources that could be used elsewhere, like producing consumer goods. Hence, growth prospects depend in part on consuming a smaller share of total output and devoting more resources to investment activities. U.S. households, however, have been unwilling to save much: In the 1990s, the average saving rate hovered close to zero. A big chunk of U.S. investments was financed by a steady inflow of foreign investment (e.g., Japanese car factories in Ohio). As aging Baby Boomers prepare to retire, they may start to save more, freeing up resources for investment.

Government Directives. Government intervention might help increase saving rates and investment. Tax breaks for 401(k) and IRA savings plans encourage people to save a larger share of their income. Tax breaks and student loans encourage more people to go to college (acquire more human capital). Likewise, various tax credits and deductions can encourage more research and development and more investment in physical capital (factories, office buildings, and so forth). Which of these interventions we choose depends on how well the market itself promotes investment and economic growth.

In the quest for faster income growth, we must also pay heed to HOW we produce. Stories about environmental spoilage and habitat destruction are all too familiar. Can we avoid environmental destruction in the economy tomorrow?

Environmental Destruction?

Market Signals. The market itself isn't bent on environmental destruction. On the contrary, advancing technology and rising incomes have made environmental protection both possible and desirable. Few poor countries can afford such luxuries. With increasing affluence, Americans demand not only more pristine environments but also expanded recreational opportunities. This creates market incentives for developing more environmentally sensitive communities. (Would there be so many wild animal parks if consumers weren't willing and able to pay admission?) Rising prices for increasingly scarce resources also create market incentives for conservation, recycling, and new development.

Government Directives. As noted earlier, the market's answers to the HOW question aren't likely to be completely satisfying. Consumers aren't willing to pay voluntarily for auto emissions controls that clean up the air other people breathe. Such controls were available in the market for years, but no one purchased them. The government had to *require* cars to be equipped with smog controls in order to get a better HOW answer. The challenge for tomorrow is to develop a set of government regulations, incentives, and prohibitions that will balance environmental concerns with the continuing quest for material advancement.

Widening Inequality? How much inequality will we accept in the economy tomorrow? Until now, the FOR WHOM question has been settled quite favorably for the rich. Moreover, it appears that inequalities are widening. What should we do?

Market Signals. The recent surge in inequality is largely due to changing demands for labor. The fastest-growing sectors of the economy have increased the demand for highly educated workers, especially those with advanced technical skills. Rising wages in these fields send a signal to prospective workers that they should stay in school longer and pursue technical training if needed. Rising wages for skilled workers also create a market incentive for employers to offer more training and to reorganize production. Even Kobe Bryant's multimillion-dollar paychecks affect human capital decisions. His success motivated thousands of other athletes to work harder, hoping to excel. Likewise, thousands of entrepreneurs are trying to figure out what new toy to create, knowing that consumers reward marketing success with enormous profits. If all incomes were equal, it's unlikely that medical students, athletes, entrepreneurs, or the average worker would strive so hard. *Market-driven inequalities are both a reward to productive achievement and an incentive to produce more.* If these market responses emerge, inequalities will diminish.

Government Directives. The market alone may not reduce inequalities quickly or adequately enough, however. The government might have to intervene to break down discriminatory barriers that block access to schools or jobs. Government training subsidies might also give the poor a boost up the economic ladder. The government might also use its tax and transfer policies to force a more even distribution of the nation's income.

The Outlook

The economy tomorrow will look different than the economy today. The mix of output, the methods of production, and the distribution of income change every day. Often the changes occur so slowly that they aren't noticed at first. Like glacier movements, however, the changes can be profound. The farm sector, for example, didn't disappear in a single year. But the exodus of thousands of farmers each year gradually transformed the WHAT, HOW, and FOR WHOM outcomes of the U.S. economy. Those outcomes will continue to change in response to market signals and future decisions about how and when the government should intervene. In deciding whether to intervene, the government must not only identify potential market failures but also avoid introducing government failure.

SUMMARY

- Answers to the core WHAT, HOW, and FOR WHOM questions vary greatly across nations. These differences reflect varying production possibilities, choice mechanisms, and values.
- Gross domestic product (GDP) is the basic measure of how much an economy produces. The United States produces over $10 trillion of output per year, more than one-fifth of the world's total. The U.S. GDP per capita is five times the world average.
- The high level of U.S. per capita GDP reflects the high productivity of U.S. workers. Abundant capital, education, technology, training, and management all contribute to high productivity. The relatively high degree of U.S. economic freedom (market reliance) is also an important cause of superior economic growth.
- Over 75 percent of U.S. output consists of services, including government services. This is a reversal of historical ratios and reflects the relatively high incomes in the United States. Poor nations produce much higher proportions of food and manufactured goods.
- Most of America's output consists of consumer goods and services. Investment goods account for only 18 percent of total output, and government purchases almost 20 percent.
- Incomes are distributed very unequally among households, with households in the highest income class

- (quintile) receiving over 10 times more income than low-income households. Incomes are even less equally distributed in many poor nations.
- Government intervenes in the economy to improve the market's answers to the WHAT, HOW, and FOR WHOM questions. The risk of government failure spurs debate over the right mix of market reliance and government regulation.
- The mix of output, production methods, and the income distribution continues to change. The WHAT, HOW, and FOR WHOM answers in tomorrow's economy will depend on the interplay of (changing) market signals and (changing) government policy.

Key Terms

gross domestic product (GDP)
per capita GDP
economic growth
investment
income transfers
exports
imports
net exports
comparative advantage
factors of production
productivity
capital intensive
human capital
externalities
monopoly
income quintile

Questions for Discussion

1. Americans already enjoy living standards that far exceed world averages. Do we have enough? Should we even try to produce more?
2. Why is per capita GDP so much higher in the United States than in Mexico?
3. Why do people suggest that the United States needs to devote more output to investment goods? Why not produce just consumption goods?
4. The U.S. farm population has shrunk by over 25 million people since 1900. Where did all the people go? Why did they move?
5. How might the following government interventions affect a nation's economic growth?
   a. Mandatory school attendance.
   b. High income taxes.
   c. Copyright and patent protection.
   d. Political corruption.
6. How many people are employed by your local or state government? What do they produce? What is the opportunity cost of that output?
7. Why should the government regulate how goods are produced? Can regulation ever be excessive?
8. Should the government try to equalize incomes more by raising taxes on the rich and giving more money to the poor? How might such redistribution affect total output and growth?
9. Do we need more or less government intervention to decide WHAT, HOW, and FOR WHOM? Provide specific examples.

WEB ACTIVITIES

1. Per capita GDP is only one measure of socioeconomic welfare. How does the United States compare to China, Mexico, and Haiti in terms of (*a*) life expectancy, (*b*) adult literacy, (*c*) child nutrition, and (*d*) access to sanitation? Construct a table based on Table 2 of Selected World Indicators at www.worldbank.org/wdr/2000/fullreport.html.
2. Compare the U.S. per capita GDP, as found at www.cia.gov/cia/publications/factbook, to that of China and Mexico. What are some possible explanations for the differences in per capita GDP?
3. How have the income shares of the richest and poorest quintiles changed in the last few years? Information to answer this question can be found at www.census.gov/hhes/www/income.html. Access the main report, then access Table C listed under Highlights. Look under shares of household income of quintiles for your answer.

ALERT! THE ACCOMPANYING STUDENT PROBLEM SET CONTAINS NUMERICAL AND GRAPHING PROBLEMS FOR THIS CHAPTER

CHAPTER 3

Supply and Demand

The lights went out in California in January 2001. With only minutes of warning, sections of high-tech Silicon Valley, San Francisco, the state capital of Sacramento, and a host of smaller cities went dark. Schools closed early, traffic signals malfunctioned, ATM machines shut down, and elevators abruptly stopped. "It's like we're living in Bosnia," said Michael Mischer, an Oakland, California, baker. "How could this happen?"[1]

California's governor, Gray Davis, had a ready answer. He said out-of-state power company "pirates" were gouging California residents with exorbitant prices they could not pay. As he saw it, the electricity crisis was just an example of market-driven greed. To resolve the crisis, the governor proposed stiff price controls, the state purchase of transmission lines, and state-ordered customer refunds from "profiteering" power companies. As he saw it, only the state government could keep the lights on.

Critics said the governor's explanation made for good politics but bad economics. Government intervention, not the market, was the cause of the electricity crisis, they said. Supply and demand were out of balance in California and only *higher* prices and *less* government intervention could keep the lights on. U.S. Treasury Secretary Paul O'Neill criticized the governor for trying "to defeat economics. . . I mean, you don't have to have an economics degree to understand that this is an unworkable situation." One of UC–Berkeley's Nobel-winning economists, Daniel McFadden, echoed that sentiment, blaming the state's "rigid regulation" for its energy woes. President Bush was equally adamant that "price controls will not solve the problem" and urged the state to rely more on the market than on state legislators to avoid future blackouts.

California's 2001 energy crisis is a classic illustration of why the choice between market reliance and government intervention is so critical and often so controversial. The goal in this chapter is to put that choice into a coherent framework. To do so, we'll focus on how unregulated markets work. How does the market mechanism decide WHAT to produce, HOW to produce, and FOR WHOM to produce? Specifically,

- What determines the price of a good or service?
- How does the price of a product affect its production and consumption?
- Why do prices and production levels often change?

[1] Rene Sanchez and William Booth, "California Forced to Turn the Lights Off," *Washington Post*, January 18, 2001, p. 1.

Once we've seen how unregulated markets work, we'll examine why people often seek government intervention and what effects that intervention might have. Hopefully, the lights won't go off before we finish.

MARKET PARTICIPANTS

A good way to start figuring out how markets work is to see who participates in them. The answer is simple: just about every person and institution on the planet. Domestically, over 280 million consumers, about 20 million business firms, and tens of thousands of government agencies participate directly in the U.S. economy. Millions of international buyers and sellers also participate in U.S. markets.

Maximizing Behavior

All these market participants come into the marketplace to satisfy specific goals. Consumers, for example, come with a limited amount of income to spend. Their objective is to buy the most desirable goods and services that their limited budgets will permit. We can't afford *everything* we want, so we must make *choices* about how to spend our scarce dollars. Our goal is to *maximize* the utility (satisfaction) we get from our available incomes.

Businesses also try to maximize in the marketplace. In their case, the quest is for maximum *profits*. Business profits are the difference between sales receipts and total costs. To maximize profits, business firms try to use resources efficiently in producing products that consumers desire.

The public sector also has maximizing goals. The purpose of government is to use available resources to serve public needs. The resources available for this purpose are limited too. Hence, local, state, and federal governments must use scarce resources carefully, striving to maximize the general welfare of society. International consumers and producers pursue these same goals when participating in our markets.

Market participants sometimes lose sight of their respective goals. Consumers sometimes buy impulsively and later wish they'd used their income more wisely. Likewise, a producer may take a two-hour lunch, even at the sacrifice of maximum profits. And elected officials sometimes put their personal interests ahead of the public's interest. In all sectors of the economy, however, *the basic goals of utility maximization, profit maximization, and welfare maximization explain most market activity.*

Specialization and Exchange

The notion that buying and selling goods and services in the market might maximize our well-being originates in two simple observations. First, most of us are incapable of producing everything we desire to consume. Second, even if we *could* produce all our own goods and services, it would still make sense to specialize, producing only one product and trading it for other desired goods and services.

Suppose you were capable of growing your own food, stitching your own clothes, building your own shelter, and even writing your own economics text. Even in this little Utopia, it would still make sense to decide how *best* to expend your limited time and energy and to rely on others to fill in the gaps. If you were *most* proficient at growing food, you would be best off spending your time farming. You could then exchange some of your food output for the clothes, shelter, and books you wanted. In the end, you'd be able to consume *more* goods than if you'd tried to make everything yourself.

Our economic interactions with others are thus necessitated by two constraints:

1. Our absolute inability as individuals to produce all the things we need or desire.
2. The limited amount of time, energy, and resources we have for producing those things we could make for ourselves.

Together, these constraints lead us to specialize and interact. Most of the interactions that result take place in the market.

THE CIRCULAR FLOW

Figure 3.1 summarizes the kinds of interactions that occur among market participants. Note first that the figure identifies four separate groups of participants. Domestically, the rectangle labeled "Consumers" includes all 280 million consumers in the United States. In the "Business firms" box are grouped all the domestic business enterprises that buy and sell goods and services. The third participant, "Governments," includes the many separate agencies of the federal government, as well as state and local governments. Figure 3.1 also illustrates the role of global actors.

The Two Markets

factor market: Any place where factors of production (e.g., land, labor, capital) are bought and sold.

The easiest way to keep track of all this market activity is to distinguish two basic markets. Figure 3.1 makes this distinction by portraying separate circles for product markets and factor markets. In **factor markets,** factors of production are exchanged. Market participants buy or sell land, labor, or capital that can be used in the production process. When you go looking for work, for example, you're making a factor of production—your labor—available to producers. The producers will hire you—purchase your services in the factor market—if you're offering the skills they need at a price they're willing to pay. The same kind of interaction occurs in factor markets when the government enlists workers into the armed services or when the Japanese buy farmland in Montana.

Interactions within factor markets are only half the story. At the end of a hard day's work, consumers go to the grocery store (or to a virtual store online) to buy desired goods and services—that is, to buy *products.* In this context, consumers again interact with business firms, this time purchasing goods and services those firms have produced. These interactions occur in **product markets.** Foreigners also participate in the

product market: Any place where finished goods and services (products) are bought and sold.

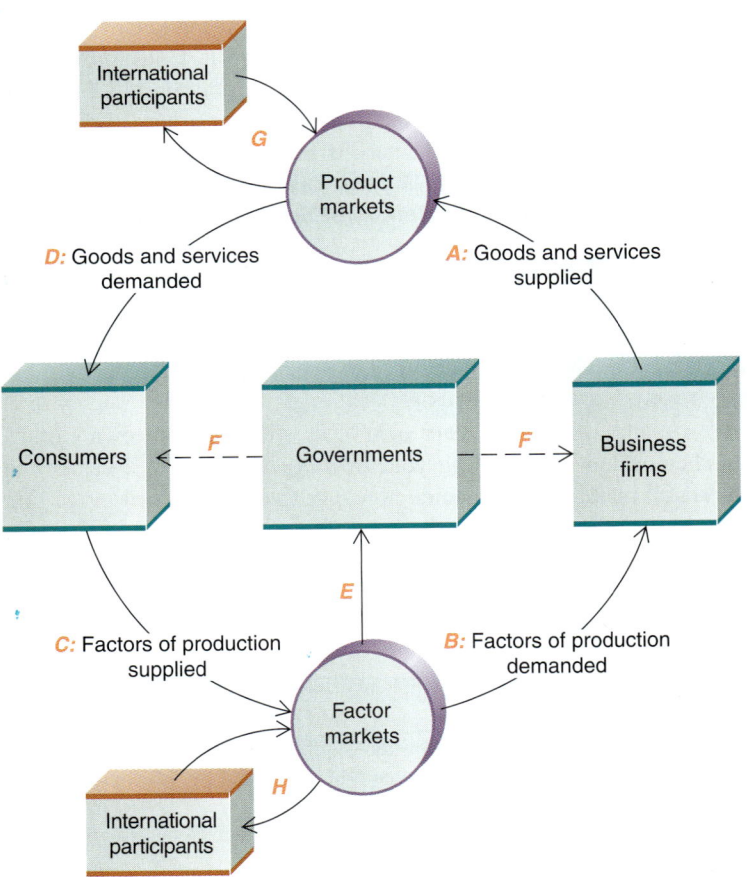

FIGURE 3.1
The Circular Flow

Business firms supply goods and services to product markets (point *A*) and purchase factors of production in factor markets (*B*). Individual consumers supply factors of production such as their own labor (*C*) and purchase final goods and services (*D*). Federal, state, and local governments acquire resources in factor markets (*E*) and provide services to both consumers and business (*F*). International participants also take part by supplying imports, purchasing exports (*G*), and buying and selling factors of production (*H*).

product market by supplying goods and services (imports) to the United States and buying some of our output (exports).

The government sector also supplies services. (e.g., education, national defense, highways.) In California, Governor Davis even wanted the state to supply electricity to households and businesses. Most government services aren't explicitly sold in product markets, however. Typically, they're delivered "free," without an explicit price (e.g., public elementary schools, highways). This doesn't mean government services are truly free, though. There's still an opportunity cost associated with every service the government provides. Consumers and businesses pay that cost indirectly through taxes rather than directly through market prices.

In Figure 3.1, the arrow connecting product markets to consumers (point *D*) emphasizes the fact that consumers, by definition, don't supply products. When individuals produce goods and services, they do so within the government or business sector. For instance, a doctor, a dentist, or an economic consultant functions in two sectors. When selling services in the market, this person is regarded as a "business"; when away from the office, he or she is regarded as a "consumer." This distinction is helpful in emphasizing that *the consumer is the final recipient of all goods and services produced.*

Locating Markets. Although we refer repeatedly to two kinds of markets in this book, it would be a little foolish to go off in search of the product and factor markets. Neither a factor market nor a product market is a single, identifiable structure. The term *market* simply refers to a place or situation where an economic exchange occurs—where a buyer and seller interact. The exchange may take place on the street, in a taxicab, over the phone, by mail, or in cyberspace. In some cases, the market used may in fact be quite distinguishable, as in the case of a retail store, the Chicago Commodity Exchange, or a state employment office. But whatever it looks like, a market exists wherever and whenever an exchange takes place.

Dollars and Exchange

Figure 3.1 provides a useful summary of market activities, but it neglects one critical element of market interactions: dollars. Each arrow in the figure actually has two dimensions. Consider again the arrow linking consumers to product markets: It's drawn in only one direction because consumers, by definition, don't provide goods and services directly to product markets. But they do provide something: dollars. If you want to obtain something from a product market, you must offer to pay for it (typically, with cash, check, or credit card). Consumers exchange dollars for goods and services in product markets.

The same kinds of exchange occur in factor markets. When you go to work, you exchange a factor of production (your labor) for income, typically a paycheck. Here again, the path connecting consumers to factor markets really goes in two directions: one of real resources, the other of dollars. Consumers receive wages, rent, and interest for the labor, land, and capital they bring to the factor markets. Indeed, nearly *every market transaction involves an exchange of dollars for goods (in product markets) or resources (in factor markets).* Money is thus critical in facilitating market exchanges and the specialization the exchanges permit.

Supply and Demand

In every market transaction there must be a buyer and a seller. The seller is on the **supply** side of the market; the buyer is on the **demand** side. As noted earlier, we *supply* resources to the market when we look for a job—that is, when we offer our labor in exchange for income. We *demand* goods when we shop in a supermarket—that is, when we're prepared to offer dollars in exchange for something to eat. Business firms may *supply* goods and services in product markets at the same time they're *demanding* factors of production in factor markets. Whether one is on the supply side or the demand side of any particular market transaction depends on the nature of the exchange, not on the people or institutions involved.

supply: The ability and willingness to sell (produce) specific quantities of a good at alternative prices in a given time period, *ceteris paribus.*

DEMAND

To get a sense of how the demand side of market transactions work, we'll focus first on a single consumer. Then we'll aggregate to illustrate *market* demand.

Individual Demand

We can begin to understand how market forces work by looking more closely at the behavior of a single market participant. Let us start with Tom, a senior at Clearview College. Tom has majored in everything from art history to government in his three years at Clearview. He didn't connect to any of those fields and is on the brink of academic dismissal. To make matters worse, his parents have threatened to cut him off financially unless he gets serious about his course work. By that, they mean he should enroll in courses that will lead to a job after graduation. Tom thinks he has found the perfect solution: web design. Everything associated with the Internet pays big bucks. Plus, the girls seem to think webbies are "cool." Or at least so Tom thinks. And his parents would definitely approve. So Tom has enrolled in web-design courses.

Unfortunately for Tom, he never developed computer skills. Until he got to Clearview College, he thought mastering Sony's latest alien-attack video game was the pinnacle of electronic wizardry. His parents had given him a wired iMac, but he used it only for surfing hot video sites. The concept of using his computer for course work, much less developing some web content, was completely foreign to him. To compound his problems, Tom didn't have a clue about "streaming," "interfacing," "animation," or the other concepts the web-design instructor outlined in the first lecture.

Given his circumstances, Tom was desperate to find someone who could tutor him in web design. But desperation is not enough to secure the services of a web architect. In a market-based economy, you must also be willing to *pay* for the things you want. Specifically, a demand exists only if someone is willing and able to pay for the good—that is, exchange dollars of a good or service in the marketplace. Is Tom willing and able to pay for the web-design tutoring he so obviously needs?

Let us assume that Tom has some income and is willing to spend some of it to get a tutor. Under these assumptions, we can claim that Tom is a participant in the *market* for web-design services.

But how much is Tom willing to pay? Surely, Tom is not prepared to exchange *all* his income for help in mastering web design. After all, Tom could use his income to buy more desirable goods and services. If he spent all his income on a web tutor, that help would have an extremely high **opportunity cost.** He would be giving up the opportunity to spend that income on other goods and services. He'd pass his web-design class but have little else. It doesn't sound like a good idea to Tom. Even though Tom says he would be willing to pay *anything* to pass the web-design course, he probably has lower prices in mind. Indeed, it would be more reasonable to assume that there are *limits* to the amount Tom is willing to pay for any given quantity of web-design tutoring. These limits will be determined by how much income Tom has to spend and how many other goods and services he must forsake in order to pay for a tutor.

Tom also knows that his grade in web design will depend in part on how much tutoring service he buys. He can pass the course with only few hours of design help. If he wants a better grade, however, the cost is going to escalate quickly.

Naturally, Tom wants it all: an A in web design and a ticket to higher-paying jobs. But here again the distinction between *desire* and *demand* is relevant. He may *desire* to master web design, but his actual proficiency will depend on how many hours of tutoring he is willing to *pay* for.

We assume, then, that when Tom starts looking for a web-design tutor he has in mind some sort of **demand schedule,** like that described in Figure 3.2. According to row *A* of this schedule, Tom is willing and able to buy only 1 hour of tutoring service per semester if he must pay $50 an hour. At such an outrageous price he will learn minimal skills and pass the course. Just the bare minimum is all Tom is willing to buy at that price.

---

demand: The ability and willingness to buy specific quantities of a good at alternative prices in a given time period, *ceteris paribus*.

opportunity cost: The most desired goods or services that are forgone in order to obtain something else.

demand schedule: A table showing the quantities of a good a consumer is willing and able to buy at alternative prices in a given time period, *ceteris paribus*.

CHAPTER 3: SUPPLY AND DEMAND   49

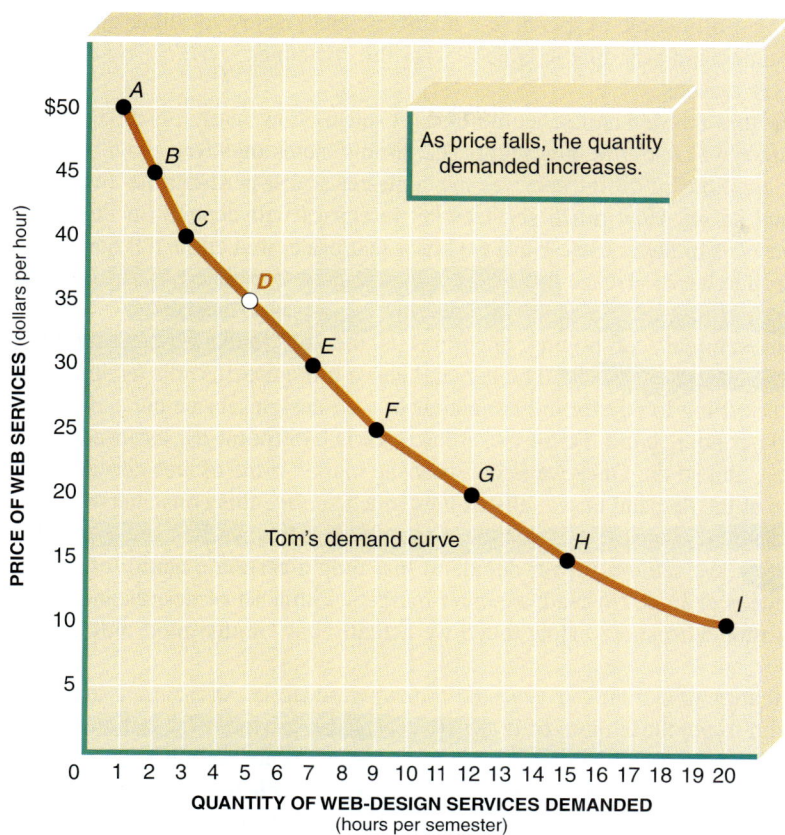

FIGURE 3.2
A Demand Schedule and Curve

A demand schedule indicates the quantities of a good a consumer is able and willing to buy at alternative prices (*ceteris paribus*). The demand schedule indicates that Tom would buy 5 hours of web-design services per semester if the price were $35 per hour (row *D*). If web services were less expensive (rows *E–I*), Tom would purchase a larger quantity.

A demand curve is a graphical illustration of a demand schedule. Each point on the curve refers to a specific quantity that will be demanded at a given price. If, for example, the price of web services were $35 per hour, this curve tells us the consumer would purchase 5 hours per semester (point *D*). If web services cost $30 per hour, 7 hours per semester would be demanded (point *E*). Each point on the curve corresponds to a row in the schedule.

	Tom's Demand Schedule	
	Price of Service (per hour)	Quantity of Service Demanded (hours per semester)
A	$50	1
B	45	2
C	40	3
D	35	5
E	30	7
F	25	9
G	20	12
H	15	15
I	10	20

At lower prices, Tom would behave differently. According to Figure 3.2, Tom would purchase more tutoring services if the price per hour were less. At lower prices, he would not have to give up so many other goods and services for each hour of technical help. The reduced opportunity costs implied by lower service prices increase the attractiveness of professional help. Indeed, we see from row *I* of the demand schedule that Tom is willing to purchase 20 hours per semester—the whole bag of design tricks—if the price of tutoring is as low as $10 per hour.

Notice that the demand schedule doesn't tell us anything about *why* this consumer is willing to pay specific prices for various amounts of tutoring. Tom's expressed willingness to pay for web-design tutoring may reflect a desperate need to finish a web-design course, a lot of income to spend, or a relatively small desire for other goods and services. All the demand schedule tells us is what the consumer is *willing and able* to buy, for whatever reasons.

Also observe that the demand schedule doesn't tell us how many hours of design help the consumer will *actually* buy. Figure 3.2 simply states that Tom is *willing and able* to pay for one hour of design services per semester at $50 per hour, for two hours at $45 each, and so on. How much services he purchases will depend on the actual price of web services in the market. Until we know that price, we cannot tell how much service will be purchased. Hence **"demand" is an expression of consumer buying intentions, of a willingness to buy, not a statement of actual purchases.**

A convenient summary of buying intentions is the **demand curve, a graphical illustration of the demand schedule**. The demand curve in Figure 3.2 tells us again that this consumer is willing to pay for only one hour of web-design service per semester if the price is $50 per hour (point *A*), for two if the price is $45 (point *B*), for three at $40 a hour (point *C*), and so on. Once we know what the market price of web service actually is, a glance at the demand curve tells us how much service this consumer will buy.

What the notion of *demand* emphasizes is that the amount we buy of a good depends on its price. We seldom if ever decide to buy only a certain quantity of a good at whatever price is charged. Instead, we enter markets with a set of desires and a limited amount of money to spend. How much we actually buy of any good will depend on its price.

A common feature of demand curves is their downward slope. As the price of a good falls, people tend to purchase more of it. In Figure 3.2 the quantity of web-tutorial services demanded increases (moves rightward along the horizontal axis) as the price per hour decreases (moves down the vertical axis). This inverse relationship between price and quantity is so common we refer to it as the **law of demand.** Compaq used this law to increase computer sales in 2000 (see News).

demand curve: A curve describing the quantities of a good a consumer is willing and able to buy at alternative prices in a given time period, *ceteris paribus*.

law of demand: The quantity of a good demanded in a given time period increases as its price falls, *ceteris paribus*.

IN THE NEWS

PC Prices Fall with Demand
Retailers Try to Minimize Losses with Big Rebates

Compaq Computer became the latest casualty of the weakening personal computer market, warning Tuesday that its fourth-quarter sales and profit will fall short of Wall Street's expectations.

The world's biggest PC maker blamed softening consumer and small-business demand—heightening expectations that PC makers may have to resort to price cuts to move excess inventory.

"We're seeing some of the biggest rebates we've ever seen in the PC industry," says Kevin Knox, a Gartner analyst in Stamford, Conn.

- Consumers can get rebates of $100 to $400 on PCs by Compaq, Hewlett-Packard and eMachines at Circuit City, Best Buy and other retailers.

If sales don't pick up, bigger rebates are likely in January, analysts say.
- In a typical holiday bargain at Circuit City, shoppers can snap up a Compaq Presario computer, originally priced at $1,099, for $649. . . .

Analysts say PC makers and retail chains have inventory backlogs of eight to 12 weeks. The industry likes to see a backlog of three to four weeks. . . .

Worldwide, fourth-quarter PC shipments will be up 20 percent over the same period a year ago, says market research firm IDC.

—Edward Iwata

Source: *USA Today*, December 13, 2000. © 2000 USA Today. Reprinted with permission. www.usatoday.com

Analysis: The law of demand predicted that Compaq would sell more computers if it reduced their price. That is exactly what happened.

The demand curve in Figure 3.2 has only two dimensions—quantity demanded (on the horizontal axis) and price (on the vertical axis). This seems to imply that the amount of computer services demanded depends only on the price of that service. This is surely not the case. A consumer's willingness and ability to buy a product at various prices depend on a variety of forces. **The determinants of market demand include**

- *Tastes* (desire for this and other goods).
- *Income* (of the consumer).
- *Other goods* (their availability and price).
- *Expectations* (for income, prices, tastes).
- *Number of buyers.*

Determinants of Demand

Tom's "taste" for web-design services has nothing to do with taste buds. *Taste* is just another word for desire. In this case Tom's taste for web-design services is clearly acquired. If he didn't have to pass a web-design course, he would have no desire for related services, and thus no demand. If he had no income, he couldn't *demand* any web-design services either, no matter how much he might *desire* them.

Other goods also affect the demand for web-design services. Their effect depends on whether they're *substitute* goods or *complementary* goods. A **substitute good** is one that might be purchased instead of web-design services. In Tom's simple world, pizza is a substitute for web services. If the price of pizza fell, Tom would buy more pizzas and cut back on his purchases of web services. When the price of a substitute good falls, the demand for web services declines.

A **complementary good** is one that's typically consumed with, rather than instead of, web services. If textbook prices or tuition increases, Tom might take fewer classes and demand *less* web-design assistance. In this case, a price increase for a complementary good causes the demand for web services to decline.

substitute goods: Goods that substitute for each other; when the price of good *x* rises, the demand for good *y* increases, *ceteris paribus*.

complementary goods: Goods frequently consumed in combination; when the price of good *x* rises, the demand for good *y* falls, *ceteris paribus*.

Expectations also play a role in consumer decisions. If Tom expected to flunk his web-design course anyway, he probably wouldn't waste any money getting tutorial help; his demand for such services would disappear. On the other hand, if he expects a web tutor to determine his college fate, he might be more willing to buy such services.

Ceteris Paribus

If demand is in fact such a multidimensional decision, how can we reduce it to only the two dimensions of price and quantity? In Chapter 1 we first encountered this *ceteris paribus* trick. To simplify their models of the world, economists focus on only one or two forces at a time and *assume* nothing else changes. We know a consumer's tastes, income, other goods, and expectations all affect the decision to buy web services. But we want to focus on the relationship between quantity demanded and price. That is, we want to know what *independent* influence price has on consumption decisions. To find out, we must isolate that one influence, price, and assume that the determinants of demand remain unchanged.

ceteris paribus: The assumption of nothing else changing.

The *ceteris paribus* assumption is not as farfetched as it may seem. People's tastes, income, and expectations do not change quickly. Also, the prices and availability of other goods don't change all that fast. Hence, a change in the *price* of a product may be the only factor that prompts a change in quantity demanded.

The ability to predict consumer responses to a price change is important. What would happen, for example, to enrollment at your school if tuition doubled? Must we guess? Or can we use demand curves to predict how the quantity of applications will change as the price of college goes up? **Demand curves show us how changes in market prices alter consumer behavior.** We used the demand curve in Figure 3.2 to predict how Tom's web-design ability would change at different tutorial prices.

Shifts in Demand

Although demand curves are useful in predicting consumer responses to market signals, they aren't infallible. The problem is that **the determinants of demand can and do change.** When they do, a specific demand curve may become obsolete. A **demand curve (schedule) is valid only so long as the underlying determinants of demand remain constant.** If the *ceteris paribus* assumption is violated—if tastes, income, other

shift in demand: A change in the quantity demanded at any (every) given price.

goods, or expectations change—the ability or willingness to buy will change. When this happens, the demand curve will **shift** to a new position.

Suppose, for example, that Tom won $1,000 in the state lottery. This increase in his income would greatly increase his ability to pay for tutoring services. Figure 3.3 shows the effect of this windfall on Tom's demand. The old demand curve, D_1, is no longer relevant. Tom's lottery winnings enable him to buy more web service at any price, as illustrated by the new demand curve, D_2. According to this new curve, lucky Tom is now willing and able to buy 12 hours per semester at the price of $35 per hour (point d_2). This is a large increase in demand; previously (before winning the lottery) he demanded only 5 hours at that price (point d_1).

With his higher income, Tom can buy more tutoring services at every price. Thus, *the entire demand curve shifts to the right when income goes up.* Figure 3.3 illustrates both the old (prelottery) and the new (postlottery) demand curves.

Income is only one of the basic determinants of demand. Changes in any of the other determinants of demand would also cause the demand curve to shift. Tom's taste for web-tutoring might increase dramatically, for example, if his parents promised to buy him a new car for passing web design. In that case, he might be willing to forgo other goods and spend more of his income on tutors. *An increase in taste (desire) also shifts the demand curve to the right.*

FIGURE 3.3
Shifts vs. Movements

A demand curve shows how a consumer responds to price changes. If the determinants of demand stay constant, the response is a *movement* along the curve to a new quantity demanded. In this case, the quantity demanded increases from 5 (point d_1), to 12 (point g_1), if price falls from $35 to $20 per hour.

If the determinants of demand change, the entire demand curve *shifts*. In this case, an increase in income increases demand. With more income, Tom is willing to buy 12 hours even at the initial price of $35 (point d_2).

	Price (per hour)	Quantity Demanded (hours per semester)	
		Initial Demand	After Increase in Income
A	$50	1	8
B	45	2	9
C	40	3	10
D	35	5	12
E	30	7	14
F	25	9	16
G	20	12	19
H	15	15	22
I	10	20	27

Pizza and Politics. A similar demand shift occurs at the White House when a political crisis erupts. On an average day, White House staffers order about $180 of pizzas from the nearby Domino's. When a crisis hits, however, staffers work well into the night and their demand for pizza soars. During the 1998 Clinton impeachment hearings, White House staffers ordered more than $1,000 of pizza per day!

It's important to distinguish shifts of the demand curve from movements along the demand curve. *Movements along a demand curve are a response to price changes for that good.* Such movements assume that determinants of demand are unchanged. By contrast, *shifts of the demand curve occur when the determinants of demand change.* When tastes, income, other goods, or expectations are altered, the basic relationship between price and quantity demanded is changed (shifts).

For convenience, movements along a demand curve and shifts of the demand curve have their own labels. Specifically, take care to distinguish

- *Changes in quantity demanded:* movements along a given demand curve, in response to price changes of that good.
- *Changes in demand:* shifts of the demand curve due to changes in tastes, income, other goods, or expectations.

Tom's behavior in the web-services market will change if either the price of web services changes (a movement) or the underlying determinants of his demand are altered (a shift). Notice in Figure 3.3 that he ends up buying 12 hours of web tutoring if either the price of web services falls or his income increases. Demand curves help us predict those market responses.

Whatever we say about demand for web-design tutoring on the part of one wannabe Web Master, we can also say about every student at Clearview College (or, for that matter, about all consumers). Some students have no interest in web design and aren't willing to pay for related services: They don't participate in the web-services market. Other students want such services but don't have enough income to pay for them: They too are excluded from the web-services market. A large number of students, however, not only have a need (or desire) for web services but also are willing and able to purchase such services.

What we start with in product markets, then, is many individual demand curves. Fortunately, it's possible to combine all the individual demand curves into a single **market demand.** The aggregation process is no more difficult than simple arithmetic. Suppose you would be willing to buy one hour of computer services per semester at a price of $80 per hour. George, who is also desperate to learn web design, would buy two at that price; and I would buy none, since my publisher (McGraw-Hill) creates a web page for me (try mhhe.com/economics/Schiller). What would our combined (market) demand for hours of design services be at that price? Clearly, our individual inclinations indicate that we would be willing to buy a total of three hours of design services per semester if the price were $80 per hour. Our combined willingness to buy—our collective market demand—is nothing more than the sum of our individual demands. The same kind of aggregation can be performed for all consumers, leading to a summary of the total market demand for a specific good or service. This *market demand is determined by the number of potential buyers and their respective tastes, incomes, other goods, and expectations.*

Figure 3.4 provides the basic market demand schedule for a situation in which only three consumers participate in the market. It illustrates the same market situation with demand curves. The three individuals who participate in the market demand for web services at Clearview College obviously differ greatly, as suggested by their respective demand schedules. Tom *has* to pass his web-design classes or confront college and parental rejection. He also has a nice allowance (income), so can afford to buy a lot of tutorial help. His demand schedule is portrayed in the first column of the table (and is

Movements vs. Shifts

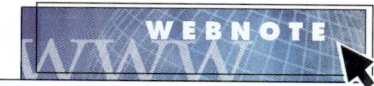

Priceline.com is an online service for buying airline tickets. To use it, you must specify the *highest* price you're willing to pay for air travel between two cities. In effect, you reveal your demand curve to Priceline. If they find a ticket that costs no more than the price you're willing and able to pay, you must buy it. Priceline makes a profit by matching demand and supply. Try it at www.priceline.com.

Market Demand

market demand: The total quantities of a good or service people are willing and able to buy at alternative prices in a given time period; the sum of individual demands.

The Market Demand Curve

54 BASIC CONCEPTS

FIGURE 3.4
Construction of the Market Demand Curve

Market demand represents the combined demands of all market participants. To determine the total quantity of web services demanded at any given price, we add the separate demands of the individual consumers. Row G of this schedule indicates that a total quantity of 39 hours per semester will be demanded at a price of $20 per hour. This same conclusion is reached by adding the individual demand curves, leading to point G on the market demand curve.

| | Price (per hour) | Quantity of Web Services Demanded (hours per semester) ||||| Market Demand |
		Tom	+ George	+ Lisa	+ Me	=	
A	$50	1	4	0	0		5
B	45	2	6	0	0		8
C	40	3	8	0	0		11
D	35	5	11	0	0		16
E	30	7	14	1	0		22
F	25	9	18	3	0		30
G	20	12	22	5	0		39
H	15	15	26	6	0		47
I	10	20	30	7	0		57

identical to the one we examined in Figure 3.2). George is also desperate to acquire some job skills and is willing to pay relatively high prices for web-design tutoring. His demand is summarized in the second column under Quantity Demanded in the table.

The third consumer in this market is Lisa. Lisa already knows the nuts and bolts of web design, so she doesn't have as desperate a need for tutorial services. She would like to upgrade her skills, however, especially in animation and e-commerce applications. But her limited budget precludes paying a lot for help. She will buy some technical support only if the price falls to $30 per hour. Should tutors cost less, she'd even buy quite a few hours of design services. Finally, there is my demand schedule (column 4 under Quantity Demanded), which confirms that I really don't participate in the web-services market.

The differing personalities and consumption habits of Tom, George, Lisa, and me are expressed in our individual demand schedules and associated curves in Figure 3.4. To determine the *market* demand for web services from this information, we simply add these four separate demands. The end result of this aggregation is, first, a *market* demand schedule and, second, the resultant *market* demand curve. These market summaries describe the various quantities of web service that Clearview College students are *willing and able* to purchase each semester at various prices.

How much web service will be purchased each semester? Knowing how much help Tom, George, Lisa, and I are willing to buy at various prices doesn't tell you how much we're actually going to purchase. To determine the actual consumption of web services, we have to know something about prices and supplies. Which of the many different prices illustrated in Figures 3.3 and 3.4 will actually prevail? How will that price be determined?

SUPPLY

To understand how the price of web services is established, we must also look at the other side of the market: the supply side. We need to know how many hours of design services people are willing and able to *sell* at various prices, that is, the **market supply.** As on the demand side, the *market supply* depends on the behavior of all the individuals willing and able to supply web services at some price.

Let's return to the Clearview campus for a moment. What we need to know now is how much tutorial web service people are willing and able to provide. Generally speaking, web-page design can be fun, but it can also be drudge work, especially when you're doing it for someone else. Software programs like PhotoShop, Flash, and Fireworks have made web-page design easier and more creative. But teaching someone else to design web pages is still work. So few people offer to supply web services just for the fun of it. Web designers do it for money. Specifically, they do it to earn income that they, in turn, can spend on goods and services they desire.

How much income must be offered to induce web designers to do a job depends on a variety of things. The *determinants of market supply* include

- *Technology*
- *Factor costs*
- *Other goods*
- *Taxes and subsidies*
- *Expectations*
- *Number of sellers*

The technology of web design, for example, is always getting easier and more creative. With a program like PageOut, for example, it's very easy to create a bread-and-butter web page. A continuous stream of new software programs (e.g., Fireworks, DreamWeaver) keeps stretching the possibilities for graphics, animation, interactivity, and content. These technological advances mean that web-design services can be supplied more quickly and cheaply. They also make *teaching* web design easier. As a result, they induce people to supply more web-design services at every price.

> **market supply:** The total quantities of a good that sellers are willing and able to sell at alternative prices in a given time period, *ceteris paribus*.

Determinants of Supply

WEBNOTE

Sellers of books and cars post asking prices for their products on the Internet. With the help of search engines such as amazon.com and junglee.com, consumers can locate the seller who's offering the lowest price. By examining a lot of offers, you could also construct a supply curve showing how the quantity supplied increases at higher prices.

How much web-design service is offered at any given price also depends on the cost of factors of production. If the software programs needed to create web pages are cheap (or, better yet, free), web designers can afford to charge lower prices. If the required software inputs are expensive, however, they will have to charge more money per hour for their services.

Other goods can also affect the willingness to supply web-design services. If you can make more income waiting tables than you can designing web pages, why would you even boot up the computer? As the prices paid for other goods and sevices change, they will influence people's decision about whether to offer web services.

In the real world, the decision to supply goods and services is also influenced by the long arm of Uncle Sam. Federal, state, and local governments impose taxes on income earned in the marketplace. When tax rates are high, people get to keep less of the income they earn. Some people may conclude that web design is no longer worth the hassle and withdraw from the market.

Expectations are also important on the supply side of the market. If web designers expect higher prices, lower costs, or reduced taxes, they may be more willing to learn new software programs. On the other hand, if they have poor expectations about the future, they may just sell their computers and find something else to do.

Finally, we note that the number of available web designers will affect the quantity of service offered for sale at various prices. If there are lots of willing web designers on campus, a large quantity of web service will be available.

All these considerations—factor costs, technology, expectations—affect the decision to offer web services and at what price. In general, we assume that web architects will be willing to provide more help if the per-hour price is high and less if the price is low. In other words, there is a **law of supply** that parallels the law of demand. On the supply side the law says that *larger quantities will be offered for sale at higher prices.* Here again, the laws rest on the *ceteris paribus* assumption: The quantity supplied increases at higher prices *if* the determinants of supply are constant. **Supply curves are upward-sloping to the right,** as in Figure 3.5. Note how the *quantity supplied* jumps from 39 hours (point *d*) to 130 hours (point *h*) when the price of web service doubles (from $20 to $40 per hour).

law of supply: The quantity of a good supplied in a given time period increases as its price increases, *ceteris paribus.*

Market Supply

Figure 3.5 also illustrates how market supply is constructed from the supply decisions of individual sellers. In this case, only three web masters are available. Ann is willing to provide a lot of design help at low prices, whereas Bob requires at least $20 an hour. Cory won't touch the keyboard for less than $40 an hour.

By adding the quantity each webhead is willing to offer at every price, we can construct the market supply curve. Notice in Figure 3.5, for example, how the quantity supplied to the market at $45 (point *i*) comes from the individual efforts of Ann (93 hours), Bob (33 hours), and Cory (14 hours). **The market supply curve is just a summary of the supply intentions of all producers.**

None of the points on the market supply curve (Figure 3.5) tells us how much web-design service is actually being sold on the Clearview campus. **Market supply is an expression of sellers' intentions—an offer to sell—not a statement of actual sales.** My next door neighbor may be willing to sell his 1994 Honda Civic for $8,000, but most likely he'll never find a buyer at that price. Nevertheless, his *willingness* to sell his car at that price is part of the *market supply* of used cars.

Shifts of Supply

As with demand, there's nothing sacred about any given set of supply intentions. Supply curves *shift* when the underlying determinants of supply change. Thus, we again distinguish

- **Changes in quantity supplied:** movements along a given supply curve.
- **Changes in supply:** shifts of the supply curve.

Our Latin friend *ceteris paribus* is once again the decisive factor. If the price of a product is the only variable changing, then we can **track changes in quantity supplied along**

FIGURE 3.5
Market Supply

The market supply curve indicates the *combined* sales intentions of all market participants. If the price of web services were $45 per hour (point *i*), the *total* quantity of services supplied would be 140 hours per semester. This quantity is determined by adding the supply decisions of all individual producers. In this case, Ann supplies 93 hours, Bob supplies 33, and Cory supplies the rest.

	Price (per hour)	Ann	Bob	Cory	Market
j	$50	94	35	19	148
i	45	93	33	14	140
h	40	90	30	10	130
g	35	86	28	0	114
f	30	78	12	0	90
e	25	53	9	0	62
d	20	32	7	0	39
c	15	20	0	0	20

Quantity of Web Services Supplied by Ann + Bob + Cory = Market

the supply curve. But if *ceteris paribus* is violated—if technology, factor costs, the profitability of producing other goods, tax rates, expectations, or the number of sellers change—then **changes in supply are illustrated by shifts of the supply curve.**

The News on the next page illustrates how supply shifts aggravated California's electricity crisis. Most of the electricity produced in California is generated at hydroelectric dams (40 percent) or gas-fired power plants (35 percent). In 2000–01, a near-record drought reduced water levels and hydroelectric capacity; the electricity supply curve shifted to the left. Higher prices for natural gas also raised factor costs for power plants. This meant power plants weren't as willing to sell electricity at existing prices. This caused another leftward supply shift. This double supply-side whammy caused wholesale electricity prices in California to jump sharply.

EQUILIBRIUM

The abrupt spike in California electricity prices offers some clues as to how the forces of supply and demand set, and change, market prices. To get a more detailed sense of how those forces work, we'll return to the mythical Clearview College web-services market for a moment. How did supply and demand resolve the WHAT, HOW, and FOR WHOM questions in that market?

Figure 3.6 helps answer that question by bringing together the market supply and demand curves we've already examined (Figures 3.4 and 3.5). When we put the two curves together, we see that *only one price and quantity are compatible with the existing intentions of both buyers and sellers.* This equilibrium occurs at the intersection of the two curves in Figure 3.6. Once it's established, web services will cost

IN THE NEWS

Californians Pinched by Power Prices

A year ago no one in California was talking about electricity prices. Now, power prices are the talk of the town in swank Malibu, the farm capital of Modesto, and the techno-savy suites of Silicon Valley. Not even escalating real estate prices can keep up with the torrid pace of electricity prices. A year ago, the wholesale price of electricity was so low that nobody gave it a second thought. Since then, the price has skyrocketed by over 1,000 percent—from 3 cents a kilowatt-hour to more than 40 cents. The Golden State's utilities are going bankrupt, and threats of statewide blackouts are real.

Energy analysts point to a low snowpack and a jump in natural gas prices to explain the energy price pinch. The second worst drought in California's history has left the state's vital hydroelectric system short of water. Plus sharply higher gas prices have increased the cost of gas-fired generators. These supply problems imply continuing energy-price woes for the state's 34 million residents and businesses.

—March, 2001

Analysis: When factor costs or availability worsen, the supply curve shifts to the left. Such leftward supply-curve shifts push prices up the market demand curve.

$20 per hour. At that **equilibrium price,** campus webheads will sell a total of 39 hours of tutoring per semester—the same amount that students wish to buy at that price. Those 39 hours of web-design service will be part of WHAT is produced.

Market Clearing

equilibrium price: The price at which the quantity of a good demanded in a given time period equals the quantity supplied.

An equilibrium doesn't imply that everyone is happy with the prevailing price or quantity. Notice in Figure 3.6, for example, that some students who want to buy web-design assistance services don't get any. These would-be buyers are arrayed along the demand curve *below* the equilibrium. Because the price they're *willing* to pay is less than the equilibrium price, they don't get any web-design help. The market's FOR WHOM answer includes only those students willing and able to pay the equilibrium price.

Likewise, some would-be sellers in the market don't sell as much service as they might like. These people are arrayed along the supply curve *above* the equilibrium. Because they insist on being paid a price higher than the equilibrium price, they don't actually sell anything.

Although not everyone gets full satisfaction from the market equilibrium, that unique outcome is efficient. The equilibrium price and quantity reflect a compromise between buyers and sellers. No other compromise yields a quantity demanded that's exactly equal to the quantity supplied.

The Invisible Hand. The equilibrium price isn't determined by any single individual. Rather, it's determined by the collective behavior of many buyers and sellers, each acting out his or her own demand or supply schedule. It's this kind of impersonal price determination that gave rise to Adam Smith's characterization of the market mecha-

FIGURE 3.6
Equilibrium Price

Only at equilibrium is the quantity demanded equal to the quantity supplied. In this case, the equilibrium price is $20 per hour, and 39 hours is the equilibrium quantity. At higher prices, a market surplus exists—the quantity supplied exceeds the quantity demanded. At prices below equilibrium, a market shortage exists.

The intersecton of the demand and supply curves in the graph represents equilibrium price and output in this market.

Price (per hour)	Quantity Supplied (hours per semester)		Quantity Demanded (hours per semester)
$50	148		5
45	140		8
40	130	market surplus	11
35	114		16
30	90		22
25	62		30
20	39	equilibrium	39
15	20	market shortage	47
10	10		57

nism as "the invisible hand." In attempting to explain how the **market mechanism** works, the famed eighteenth-century economist noted a certain feature of market prices. The market behaves as if some unseen force (the invisible hand) were examining each individual's supply or demand schedule and then selecting a price that assured an equilibrium. In practice, of course, the process of price determination isn't so mysterious: It's a simple process of trial and error.

Suppose for the moment that campus webheads believed their services could be sold for $25 per hour rather than the equilibrium price of $20 and offered it only at this higher price. From the demand and supply schedules depicted in Figure 3.6 we can foresee the consequences. At $25 per hour, campus webheads would be offering more tutoring services (point *y*) than Tom, George, and Lisa were willing to buy (point *x*) at that price. A **market surplus** of web services would exist in the sense that more tutoring was being offered for sale (supplied) than students cared to purchase at the available price.

As Figure 3.6 indicates, at a price of $25 per hour, a market surplus of 32 hours per semester exists. Under these circumstances, campus webheads would be spending many idle hours at their keyboards waiting for customers to appear. Their waiting will be in vain because the quantity of web tutoring demanded will not increase until the price

market mechanism: The use of market prices and sales to signal desired outputs (or resource allocations).

Surplus and Shortage

market surplus: The amount by which the quantity supplied exceeds the quantity demanded at a given price; excess supply.

of tutoring falls. That is the clear message of the demand curve. As would-be tutors get this message, they'll reduce their prices. This is the response the market mechanism signals.

As sellers' asking prices decline, the quantity demanded will increase. This concept is illustrated in Figure 3.6 by the movement along the demand curve from point *x* to lower prices and greater quantity demanded. As we move down the market demand curve, the *desire* for web-design help doesn't change, but the quantity people are *able and willing to buy* increases. When the price falls to $20 per hour, the quantity demanded will finally equal the quantity supplied. This is the *equilibrium* illustrated in Figure 3.6.

An Initial Shortage. A very different sequence of events would occur if a market shortage existed. Suppose someone were to spread the word that web-tutoring services were available at only $15 per page. Tom, George, and Lisa would be standing in line to get tutorial help, but campus web designers wouldn't be willing to supply the quantity desired at that price. As Figure 3.6 confirms, at $15 per hour, the quantity demanded (47 hours per semester) would greatly exceed the quantity supplied (20 hours per semester). In this situation, we may speak of a **market shortage,** that is, an excess of quantity demanded over quantity supplied. At a price of $15 an hour, the shortage amounts to 27 hours of tutoring services.

When a market shortage exists, not all consumer demands can be satisfied. Some people who are *willing* to buy web help at the going price ($15) won't be able to do so. To assure themselves of sufficient help, Tom, George, Lisa, or some other consumer may offer to pay a *higher* price, thus initiating a move up the demand curve in Figure 3.6. The higher prices offered will in turn induce other enterprising students to tutor more, thus ensuring an upward movement along the market supply curve. Thus, a higher price tends to evoke a greater quantity supplied, as reflected in the upward-sloping supply curve. Notice, again, that the *desire* to tutor web design hasn't changed; only the quantity supplied has responded to a change in price.

Self-Adjusting Prices. What we observe, then, is that whenever the market price is set above or below the equilibrium price, either a market surplus or a market shortage will emerge. To overcome a surplus or shortage, buyers and sellers will change

> **market shortage:** The amount by which the quantity demanded exceeds the quantity supplied at a given price; excess demand.

For Fans, What's 4 Nights for U2?

After an 80-hour ordeal—four nights stuffed in a car, three days breathing bus exhaust, scarfing Cokes and franks, running blocks for pit stops—the three University of Maryland seniors who camped out at RFK Stadium prevailed. They beat the scalpers to U2 concert tickets.

At 8 A.M. today they would be, if all went as planned, first in line at the RFK box office. By 9 A.M. the 52,000-seat stadium will sell out, predicted a Ticketmaster official.

"It's what you got to do to get good seats," said Crawford Conniff, 22, stretched out near the stadium among traffic island dandelions.

"We have unlimited time," said Mike Collins, 22. "If we had a job making 50 grand, we could pay $150 to scalpers."

Actually, $150 sounds cheap for the $28.50 face-value tickets. Today's ticket sale for the Aug. 15 concert, one of the summer's hottest, is likely to ignite an orgy of profiteering.

When the band played Los Angeles, scalpers scored up to $1,200 a ticket for prime seats. In Washington, as early as Tuesday, ticket brokers had stationed students, unemployed and even homeless people at ticket outlets to snap up hundreds of choice seats.

—Laura Blumenfeld

Source: *Washington Post,* April 25, 1992. © 1992 The Washington Post. Reprinted with permission. www.washingtonpost.com

Analysis: In equilibrium, everyone who is willing and able to pay the equilibrium price gets to see the show. If price is below equilibrium, the quantity demanded exceeds the quantity supplied, so only people willing and able to stand in line for tickets will get them initially.

their behavior. Webheads will have to compete for customers by reducing prices when a market surplus exists. If a shortage exists, buyers will compete for service by offering to pay higher prices. Only at the *equilibrium* price will no further adjustments be required.

Sometimes the market price is slow to adjust, and a disequilibrium persists, as is often the case with tickets to rock concerts, football games, and other events. People initially adjust their behavior by standing in ticket lines for hours, hoping to buy a ticket at the below-equilibrium price (see News). The tickets are typically resold ("scalped"), however, at prices closer to equilibrium.

Business firms can discover equilibrium prices by trial and error. If they find that consumer purchases aren't keeping up with production, they may conclude that their price is above the equilibrium price. They'll have to get rid of their accumulated inventory. To do so they'll have to lower their price (by a Grand End-of-Year Sale, perhaps). In the happy situation where consumer purchases are outpacing production, a firm might conclude that its price was a trifle too low and give it a nudge upward. In any case, the equilibrium price can be established after a few trials in the marketplace.

Changes in Equilibrium

No equilibrium price is permanent. The equilibrium price established in the Clearview College web-services market, for example, was the unique outcome of specific demand and supply schedules. Those schedules themselves were based on our assumption of *ceteris paribus*. We assumed that the "taste" (desire) for web-design assistance was given, as were consumers' incomes, the price and availability of other goods, and expectations. Any of these determinants of demand could change. When one does, the demand curve has to be redrawn. Such a shift of the demand curve will lead to a new equilibrium price and quantity. Indeed, *the equilibrium price will change whenever the supply or demand curve shifts.*

A Demand Shift. We can illustrate how equilibrium prices change by taking one last look at the Clearview College web-services market. Our original supply and demand curves, together with the resulting equilibrium (point E_1), are depicted in Figure 3.7. Now suppose that all the professors at Clearview begin requiring class-specific web pages from each student. The increased need (desire) for web-design ability will affect market demand. Tom, George, and Lisa are suddenly willing to buy more web tutoring at every price than they were before. That is, the *demand* for web services has increased. We can represent this increased demand by a rightward *shift* of the market demand curve, as illustrated in Figure 3.7a.

Note that the new demand curve intersects the (unchanged) market supply curve at a new price (point E_2), the equilibrium price is now $30 per hour. This new equilibrium price will persist until either the demand curve or the supply curve shifts again.

A Supply Shift. Figure 3.7b illustrates a *supply* shift. The decrease (leftward shift) in supply might occur if some on-campus webheads got sick. Or approaching exams might convince would-be tutors they have no time to spare. **Whenever supply decreases (shifts left), price tends to rise,** as in Figure 3.7b.

The rock band U2 learned about changing equilibriums the hard way. As the accompanying NEWS reported, ticket prices for the band's 1992 tour were below equilibrium, creating a *market shortage*. So U2 raised prices to as much as $52.50 a ticket for their 1997 tour—nearly double the 1992 price. By then, however, demand had shifted to the left, due to a lack of U2 hits and an increased number of competing concerts. By the time they got to their second city they were playing in stadiums with lots of empty seats. The apparent *market surplus* led critics to label the 1997 "Pop Mart" tour a disaster. For their 2001 "Elevation Tour", U2 offered "festival seating" for only $35.

Market outcomes shifted even more dramatically after the anthrax attacks on the U.S. mail in October 2001. Only one drug, Cipro, is approved to fight the deadly anthrax bacteria. When several people died from exposure to anthrax-laden mail, demand for Cipro soared (see NEWS on page 63). This demand shift created an immediate market shortage.

FIGURE 3.7
Changes in Equilibrium

If demand or supply change (shift), market equilibrium will change as well.

Demand shift. In (*a*), the rightward shift of the demand curve illustrates an increase in demand. When demand increases, the equilibrium price rises (from E_1 to E_2).

Supply shift. In (*b*), the leftward shift of the supply curve illustrates a decrease in supply. This raises the equilibrium price to E_3.

Demand and supply curves shift only when their underlying determinants change, that is, when *ceteris paribus* is violated.

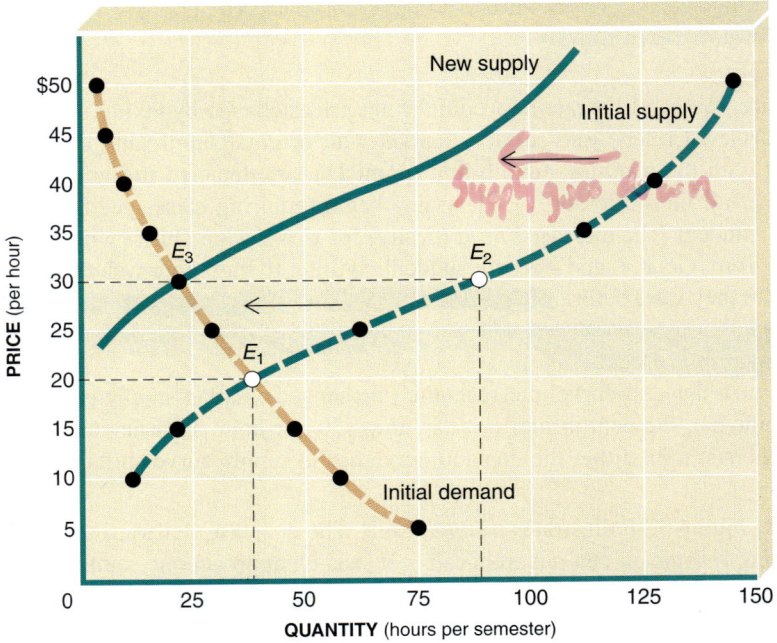

The accompanying World View shows how rapid price adjustments can alleviate market shortages and surpluses. In this unusual case, a restaurant continuously adjusts its prices to ensure that everything on the menu is ordered.

MARKET OUTCOMES

Notice how the market mechanism resolves the basic economic questions of WHAT, HOW, and FOR WHOM.

IN THE NEWS

Demand for Cipro Rising

NYC sees 62% increase in anti-anthrax prescriptions

Despite public health officials' admonitions against stockpiling drugs to protect against bioterrorism, new prescriptions for Cipro, the only drug approved to fight anthrax, in New York City have soared.

For the week ending Oct. 5, New York pharmacists filled 18,348 new prescriptions for the antibiotic, compared with just 11,313 for the same week in 2000, an increase of 62%, according to NDCHealth, a health-care information services company based in Atlanta.

Cipro, as well as a variety of other antibiotics, can prevent illness from anthrax exposure if taken before symptoms appear. Exposed individuals must take the drug for 60 days.

Still, Tommy Thompson, secretary of Health and Human Services, and other public health officials have urged Americans not to panic and hoard Cipro or other antibiotics. "You don't have to hoard antibiotics," Thompson said Friday at a briefing in which he announced a $643 million proposal to boost government stocks of antibiotics. "We're purchasing more."

Bayer, maker of Cipro, has said that it plans to reopen a German plant to meet increased demand for the drug.

—Rita Rubin

Source: *USA Today,* October 16, 2001, p. 40.

Analysis: When a determinant of demand (e.g., tastes, expectations) changes, the demand curve shifts. When this happens, the equilibrium price will change.

WHAT

The WHAT question refers to the amount of web tutorial services to include in society's mix of output. The answer at Clearview College was 39 hours of web services per semester. This decision wasn't reached in a referendum, but instead in the market equilibrium (Figure 3.6). In the same way but on a larger scale, millions of consumers and a handful of auto producers decide to include 6 million or so passenger cars in each

WORLD VIEW

Dining on the Downtick

Americans aren't the only consumers who fall for packaging. Since late January, Parisians (not to mention TV crews from around the world) have been drawn to 6 rue Feydeau to try La Connivence, a restaurant with a new gimmick. The name means "collusion," and yes, of course, La Connivence is a block away from the Bourse, the French stock exchange.

What's the gimmick? Just that the restaurant's prices fluctuate according to supply and demand. The more a dish is ordered, the higher its price. A dish that's ignored gets cheaper.

Customers tune in to the day's menu (couched in trading terms) on computer screens. Among a typical day's options: *forte baisse du haddock* ("precipitous drop in haddock"), *vif recul de la côte de boeuf* ("rapid decline in beef ribs"), *la brochette de lotte au plus bas* ("fish kabob hits bottom"). Then comes the major decision—whether to opt for the price that's listed when you order or to gamble that the price will have gone down by the time you finish your meal.

So far, only main dishes are open to speculation, but co-owners Pierre Guette, an ex-professor at a top French business school, and Jean-Paul Trastour, an ex-journalist at *Le Nouvel Observateur,* are adding wine to the risk list.

La Connivence is open for dinner, but the midday "session" (as the owners call it) is the one to catch. That's when the traders of Paris leave the floor to push their luck *à table.* But here, at least, the return on their $15 investment (the average price of a meal) is immediate—and usually good.

—Christina de Liagre

Source: *New York,* April 7, 1986. © 1986 K-III Magazine Corporation. All rights reserved. Reprinted with the permission of *New York* magazine. www.newyorkmag.com

Analysis: A market surplus signals that price is too high; a market shortage suggests that price is too low. This restaurant adjusts price until the quantity supplied equals the quantity demanded.

64 BASIC CONCEPTS

year's mix of output. Auto prices and quantities adjust until consumers buy the same quantity that auto manufacturers produce.

HOW

The market mechanism also determines HOW goods are produced. Profit-seeking producers will strive to produce web designs and automobiles in the most efficient way. They'll use market prices to decide not only WHAT to produce but also what resources to use in the production process. If new software simplifies web design—and is priced low enough—webheads will use it. Likewise, auto manufacturers will use robots rather than humans on the assembly line if robots reduce costs and increase profits.

FOR WHOM

Finally, the invisible hand of the market will determine who gets the goods produced. At Clearview College, who got web tutoring? Only those students who were willing and able to pay $20 per hour for that service. FOR WHOM are all those automobiles produced each year? The answer is the same: those consumers who are willing and able to pay the market price for a new car.

Optimal, Not Perfect

Not everyone is happy with these answers, of course. Tom would like to pay only $10 an hour for a tutor. And some of the Clearview students don't have enough income to buy any tutoring. They think it's unfair that they have to design their own web pages while richer students can have someone else do their design work for them. Students who can't afford cars are even less happy with the market's answer to the FOR WHOM question.

Although the outcomes of the marketplace aren't perfect, they're often optimal. Optimal outcomes are the best possible *given* our incomes and scarce resources. In other words, we expect the choices made in the marketplace to be the best possible choices for each participant. Why do we draw such a conclusion? Because Tom and George and everybody in our little Clearview College drama had (and continue to have) absolute freedom to make their own purchase and consumption decisions. And also because we assume that sooner or later they'll make the choices they find most satisfying. The results are *optimal* in the sense that everyone has done as well as she or he could, given their income and talents.

THE ECONOMY TOMORROW

Electric Shock: Energy-Price Spikes

The notion that markets generate optimal outcomes sounded absurd to Californians in 2000–01. As we noted earlier, wholesale energy prices jumped by over 1,000 percent in a single year. As Californians saw it, the only thing that protected them from these skyrocketing prices was government regulation. In 1996, the California legislature had set a ceiling on the *retail* price of electricity. The prices paid by consumers could *not* rise until at least 2002, no matter what happened to wholesale prices. As far as California's consumers were concerned, government intervention was their bulwark against the "price-gouging profiteers" that ruled the marketplace. Most of the state's residents welcomed Governor Gray Davis's January 2001 promises to keep cheap electricity flowing to the state's homes and businesses.

Equilibrium Pricing

As we've seen in this chapter, market prices aren't set by price-gouging profiteers. Sure, huge corporations, especially monopolies, can have a big influence on the market price of a good. But the equilibrium price must still reflect *both* sides of the market, that is, *supply* and demand. Furthermore, **an increase in the equilibrium price can result from an increase (rightward shift) in demand or a decrease (leftward shift) of supply.** Both shifts occurred in California.

Increased Demand

California's demand for electricity increases as its population grows and its economy expands. Abnormally cold winters or hot summers also increase the demand for electricity-driven heat and air conditioning. Between 1996 and 2001, the California economy grew by 29 percent. The winter of 2001 was colder than normal and the summer was a bit hotter than average. All these factors combined to shift the state's demand for electricity rightward as in Figure 3.8.

Decreased Supply

No new power plants or hydroelectric plants were built in California during the 1990s. The state managed to keep up with increased energy demand only by importing electricity from other states. With high-speed transmission lines, electricity can be shipped to California residents from power plants in Oregon, Idaho, and elsewhere. In 2001, however, several determinants of supply changed in adverse ways. Higher natural gas prices increased the cost of producing electricity in all states. Maintenance problems caused recurring shutdowns of California power plants. Low snowpacks reduced the power capacity of hydroelectric dams throughout the West. Market supply shifted to the left.

Disequilibrium Pricing

The consequences of a leftward supply shift and a rightward demand shift are evident in Figure 3.8; the equilibrium price of electricity skyrocketed. Residents of California didn't have to pay this higher price, however. Remember that the California legislature had put a **price ceiling** on retail electricity prices. By law, the retail price of electricity was stuck at 10 cents per kilowatt-hour, far below the new equilibrium price.

price ceiling: Upper limit imposed on the price of a good.

FIGURE 3.8
Price Ceilings Create Shortages

In 1996, the state of California set a price ceiling of 10 cents per kilowatt-hour. By 2001, however, demand had increased (to D_2) and supply had decreased (to S_2). At the ceiling price the quantity demanded (qd_c) exceeded the quantity supplied (qs_c), causing a market shortage and rolling blackouts. At the higher equilibrium (E_2) price there are no blackouts. Consumers reduce their energy consumption (to qe_2 from qd_c) and power companies increase electricity deliveries (to qe_2 from qs_c).

At first, Californians rejoiced at the low, government-set price. Then they learned the consequences of *dis*equilibrium pricing. At the ceiling price of 10 cents per kilowatt-hour, the quantity of electricity demanded (qd_c in Figure 3.8) exceeded that quantity supplied (qs_c). It was a classic case of *market shortage*. Because of the shortage, not everyone who was willing and able to pay the ceiling price (10 cents) could actually get the electricity they demanded. That's when the state had to resort to rolling blackouts. The blackouts left everyone with less electricity than they demanded. That experience helped convince Californians that price ceilings weren't as good as they appeared. In fact, **price ceilings have three predictable effects; they**

- *Increase the quantity demanded.*
- *Decrease the quantity supplied.*
- *Create a market shortage.*

Given the choice between no electricity and high-priced electricity, state residents changed their view of market pricing. They didn't welcome higher prices but recognized that **higher prices**

- *Reduce quantity demanded.*
- *Increase quantity supplied.*
- *Thereby alleviating market shortages.*

At the low, state-set price, consumers had no incentive to set air-conditioner thermostats higher, to set heater thermostats lower, or even turn off the lights and computer when they went out. At higher market prices, they'd think about those energy savings more often and reduce the quantity demanded. At the equilibrium price of E_2 in Figure 3.8, consumers are demanding (and using) less electricity than at qd_c. On the

Federal Price Limits Backfire

Some Generators Withhold Power rather than Abide by Rate Caps

Officials in California and Nevada, after months of lobbying for federal regulators to cap Western power prices, warned yesterday that the newly imposed limits have had the unintended consequence of increasing a threat of blackouts in the two states.

The warnings were issued as California came within minutes of rolling blackouts yesterday afternoon, and one day after the first-ever rolling blackouts in Las Vegas forced energy-hungry casinos to shut off fountains and reduce air conditioning.

The two states are asking the Federal Energy Regulatory Commission to take a closer look at the so-called price mitigation plan and come up with revisions that would deter power companies from withholding electricity during shortages. . . .

The crux of the problem is that price limits kick in during shortages, yet power companies say these caps force them to sell power at below-market rates during periods of high demand.

Some companies have responded by holding back power rather than face the expense of shipping electricity from state to state. Each mile that electricity must be transmitted adds to the overall cost.

"No one's going to pay for transmission if the cost is near the caps," said Gary Ackerman, executive director of the Western Power Trading Forum, an energy-industry association in Menlo Park.

Ackerman said several companies in his organization decided that there was no economic advantage to offering power in regional markets when price controls are in effect.

"This means individual regions like California or Las Vegas could end up not having enough," Ackerman said. "It increases the threat of blackouts."

— David Lazarus

Source: *San Francisco Chronicle*, July 4, 2001. Reprinted with permission. www.sfgate.com/news

Analysis: Price ceilings diminish the profitability of producing a good and so reduce the quantity supplied to the market. This may worsen market shortages.

supply side, higher market prices encourage both in-state and out-of-state power providers to increase power-generating capacity and even sell it to California utilities. Once California residents recognized the virtue of equilibrium pricing, they saw that government intervention (price ceilings) might have been as much to blame as "power-producing profiteers" for the state's blackouts. In April 2001, Governor Davis abandoned the 1996 price ceiling and moved closer to equilibrium pricing with a 26 percent increase in retail electricity prices.

Looming Battles of the Power Grid

Other states have been affected by California's electricity crisis. The continuing demand of California residents for out-of-state power (a substitute good) has increased demand and raised electricity prices in Oregon, Nevada, Idaho, and other states in the interconnected Western power grid. As their own electricity prices rise, consumers in those states are asking government to intervene. In 2001, they convinced the federal government (the Federal Energy Regulatory Commission) to impose price ceilings across the Western grid. As the accompanying News reports, however, those price ceilings backfired. Confronted with price limits and increased regulatory paperwork, power providers decided it made less sense to supply electricity to the price-controlled states, much less to add to power capacity.

As battles over access to energy sources continue, the patience of the public will be tested. As energy prices rise, the incentive to supply more electricity increases. But power plants can't be built overnight, and new energy sources won't appear instantly. It takes *time* for market supply and demand to adjust. The greatest risk for the economy tomorrow is that political impatience today may slow the market adjustments needed to bring energy markets into equilibrium.

SUMMARY

- Individual consumers, business firms, government agencies, and foreigners participate in the marketplace by offering to buy or sell goods and services, or factors of production. Participation is motivated by the desire to maximize utility (consumers), profits (business firms), or the general welfare (government agencies) from the limited resources each participant has.
- All interactions in the marketplace involve the exchange of either factors of production or finished products. Although the actual exchanges can occur anywhere, they take place in product markets or factor markets, depending on what is being exchanged.
- People willing and able to buy a particular good at some price are part of the market demand for that product. All those willing and able to sell that good at some price are part of the market supply. Total market demand or supply is the sum of individual demands or supplies.
- Supply and demand curves illustrate how the quantity demanded or supplied changes in response to a change in the price of that good, if nothing else changes (*ceteris paribus*). Demand curves slope downward; supply curves slope upward.
- Determinants of market demand include the number of potential buyers and their respective tastes (desires), incomes, other goods, and expectations. If any of these determinants change, the demand curve shifts. Movements along a demand curve are induced only by a change in the price of that good.
- Determinants of market supply include factor costs, technology, profitability of other goods, expectations, tax rates, and number of sellers. Supply shifts when these underlying determinants change.
- The quantity of goods or resources actually exchanged in each market depends on the behavior of all buyers and sellers, as summarized in market supply and demand curves. At the point where the two curves intersect, an equilibrium price—the price at which the quantity demanded equals the quantity supplied—is established.
- A distinctive feature of the equilibrium price and quantity is that it's the only price-quantity combination acceptable to buyers and sellers alike. At higher prices, sellers supply more than buyers are willing to purchase (a market surplus); at lower prices, the amount demanded exceeds the quantity supplied (a market shortage). Only the equilibrium price clears the market.
- Price ceilings are disequilibrium prices imposed on the marketplace. Such price controls create an imbalance between quantities demanded and supplied, resulting in market shortages.

Key Terms

factor market
product market
supply
demand
opportunity cost
demand schedule
demand curve

law of demand
substitute goods
complementary goods
ceteris paribus
shift in demand
market demand
market supply

law of supply
equilibrium price
market mechanism
market surplus
market shortage
price ceiling

Questions for Discussion

1. In our story of Tom, the student confronted with a web-design assignment, we emphasized the great urgency of his desire for web services. Many people would say that Tom had an "absolute need" for web help and therefore was ready to "pay anything" to get it. If this were true, what shape would his demand curve have? Why isn't this realistic?
2. With respect to the demand for college enrollment, which of the following would cause (1) a movement along the demand curve or (2) a shift of the demand curve?
   a. An increase in incomes.
   b. Lower tuition.
   c. More student loans.
   d. An increase in textbook prices.
3. Illustrate the market situation for the U2 concert (see page 60). Why didn't the concert promoters set an equilibrium price?
4. Which determinants of pizza demand change when the White House is in crisis?
5. Can you explain the practice of scalping tickets for major sporting events in terms of market shortages? How else might tickets be distributed?
6. How else besides higher prices could the 2001 market shortage in California's electricity market have been alleviated? Consider both demand- and supply-side options.
7. What would happen in the apple market if the government set a *minimum* price of $2.00 per apple? What might motivate such a policy?
8. The World View on page 63 describes the use of prices to achieve an equilibrium in the kitchen. What happens to the food at more traditional restaurants?
9. Is there a shortage of on-campus parking at your school? How might the shortage be resolved?
10. Do Internet price information services tend to raise or lower the price consumers pay for a product?

Web Activities

1. How has the average retail price of electricity in your state changed over the past 10 years? What are some possible explanations for this change? How does the price of electricity in your state compare to the national average? What are some possible explanations for the difference?

   To find information to answer this question, log on to www.energy.gov, click the button for Data and Prices, click the button for Current Energy Prices. Find the button for Fuel Price and navigate to the Retail Revenue for Electricity. Finally, click the button for Annual Average Revenue per Kilowatt-hour for Residential Sales by State, 1990–2000.
2. Go to an auction site such as eBay at www.ebay.com. Pick a product and track its current winning lowest bid price over one day. How does the price change as the time draws nearer to closing time? Draw a supply and demand diagram of the auction.
3. The New York Mercantile Exchange is a market in which buyers and sellers set prices for the promises to deliver various commodities in the future. After logging on to www.nymex.com, find a chart for electricity futures. Record these numbers, and explain why there is a spike in the futures price of electricity during the months of July and August.

 THE ACCOMPANYING STUDENT PROBLEM SET CONTAINS NUMERICAL AND GRAPHING PROBLEMS FOR THIS CHAPTER

CHAPTER 4

The Public Sector

The market has a keen ear for private wants, but a deaf ear for public needs.
—Robert Heilbroner

Markets do work: The interaction of supply and demand in product markets *does* generate goods and services. Likewise, the interaction of supply and demand in labor markets *does* yield jobs, wages, and a distribution of income. As we've observed, the market is capable of determining WHAT goods to produce, HOW, and FOR WHOM.

But are the market's answers good enough? Is the mix of output produced by unregulated markets the best possible mix? Will producers choose the production process that strikes a desirable balance between production and the environment? Will the market-generated distribution of income be fair enough? Will there be enough jobs for everyone who wants one?

We've already seen that the market's answers might not be the best. Monopoly power might constrain the mix of output, raise product prices, and grab too large a share of total income. Such situations call for antitrust action to regulate or dismantle market power. Other circumstances may also prevent the market from offering up the optimal mix of output, method of production, or distribution of income. Whenever that happens, government intervention may be needed to ensure better answers to the WHAT, HOW, and FOR WHOM questions.

This chapter identifies the circumstances under which government intervention is desirable. To this end, we answer the following questions:

- Under what circumstances do markets fail?
- How can government intervention help?
- How much government intervention is desirable?

As we'll see, there's substantial agreement about how and when markets fail to give us the best WHAT, HOW, and FOR WHOM answers. But there's much less agreement about whether government intervention improves the situation. Indeed, an overwhelming majority of Americans are ambivalent about government intervention. They want the government to "fix" the mix of output, protect the environment, and ensure an adequate level of income for everyone. But voters are equally quick to blame government meddling for many of our economic woes.

MARKET FAILURE

We can visualize the potential for government intervention by focusing on the WHAT question. Our goal here is to produce the best possible mix of output with existing resources. We illustrated this goal earlier with production possibilities curves. Figure 4.1 assumes that of all the possible combinations of output we could produce, the unique combination at point X represents the most desirable one. In other words, it's the **optimal mix of output**, the one that maximizes our collective social utility. We haven't yet figured out how to pinpoint that optimal mix; we're simply using the arbitrary point X in Figure 4.1 to represent that best-possible outcome.

Ideally, the **market mechanism** would lead us to point X. Price signals in the marketplace are supposed to move factors of production from one industry to another in response to consumer demands. If we demand more computers—offer to buy more at a given price—more resources (labor) will be allocated to computer manufacturing. Similarly, a fall in demand will encourage producers to stop making computers and offer their services in another industry. *Changes in market prices direct resources from one industry to another,* moving us along the perimeter of the production possibilities curve.

Where will the market mechanism take us? Will it move resources around until we end up at the optimal point X? Or will it leave us at another point on the production possibilities curve, with a *sub*optimal mix of output? (If point X is the *optimal*, or best-possible, mix, all other output mixes must be *sub*optimal.)

We use the term **market failure** to refer to situations where the market generates less than perfect (suboptimal) outcomes. If the invisible hand of the marketplace produces a mix of output that's different from the one society most desires, then it has failed. *Market failure implies that the forces of supply and demand haven't led us to the best point on the production possibilities curve.* Such a failure is illustrated by point M in Figure 4.1. Point M is assumed to be the mix of output generated by market forces. Notice that the market mix (M) doesn't represent the optimal mix, which is assumed to be at point X. The market in this case *fails;* we get the wrong answer to the WHAT question.

Market failure opens the door for government intervention. If the market can't do the job, we need some form of *nonmarket* force to get the right answers. In terms of Figure 4.1, we need something to change the mix of output—to move us from point M (the market mix of output) to point X (the optimal mix of output). Accordingly, *market failure establishes a basis for government intervention.* We look to the government to push market outcomes closer to the ideal.

optimal mix of output: The most desirable combination of output attainable with existing resources, technology, and social values.

market mechanism: The use of market prices and sales to signal desired outputs (or resource allocations).

market failure: An imperfection in the market mechanism that prevents optimal outcomes.

FIGURE 4.1
Market Failure

We can produce any mix of output on the production possibilities curve. Our goal is to produce the optimal (best possible) mix of output, as represented by point X. Market forces, however, might produce another combination, like point M. In that case, the market fails—it produces a suboptimal mix of output.

CHAPTER 4: THE PUBLIC SECTOR

Causes of Market Failure. Because market failure is the justification for government intervention, we need to know how and when market failure occurs. *The four specific sources of market failure are*

- *Public goods*
- *Externalities*
- *Market power*
- *Equity*

First we examine the nature of these problems and then we see why government intervention is called for in each case.

The market mechanism has the unique capability to signal consumer demands for various goods and services. By offering to pay higher or lower prices for some goods, we express our preferences about WHAT to produce. However, this mode of communication works efficiently only if the benefits of consuming a particular good are available only to the individuals who purchase that product.

Consider doughnuts, for example. When you eat a doughnut, you alone get the satisfaction from its sweet, greasy taste—that is, you derive a private benefit. No one else benefits from your consumption of a doughnut: The doughnut you purchase in the market is yours alone to consume; it's a **private good**. Accordingly, your decision to purchase the doughnut will be determined only by your anticipated satisfaction, your income, and your opportunity costs.

Public Goods

private good: A good or service whose consumption by one person excludes consumption by others.

No Exclusion. Most of the goods and services produced in the public sector are different from doughnuts—and not just because doughnuts look, taste, and smell different from "star wars" missile shields. When you buy a doughnut, you effectively exclude others from consumption of that product. If Dunkin' Donuts sells you a particular pastry, it can't supply the same pastry to someone else. If you devour it, no one else can. In this sense, the transaction and product are completely private.

The same exclusiveness is not characteristic of national defense. If you buy a missile defense system to thwart enemy attacks, there's no way you can exclude your neighbors from the protection your system provides. Either the missile shield deters would-be attackers or it doesn't. In the former case, both you and your neighbors survive happily ever after; in the latter case, we're all blown away together. In that sense, you and your neighbors consume the benefits of a missile shield *jointly*. National defense isn't a divisible service. There's no such thing as exclusive consumption here. The consumption of nuclear defenses is a communal feat, no matter who pays for them. Accordingly, national defense is regarded as a **public good** in the sense that *consumption of a public good by one person doesn't preclude consumption of the same good by another person*. By contrast, a doughnut is a private good because if I eat it, no one else can consume it.

public good: A good or service whose consumption by one person does not exclude consumption by others.

The Free-Rider Dilemma. The communal nature of public goods creates a dilemma. If you and I will *both* benefit from nuclear defenses, which one of us should buy the missile shield? I'd prefer that *you* buy it, thereby giving me protection at no direct cost. Hence, I may profess no desire for a missile shield, secretly hoping to take a **free ride** on your market purchase. Unfortunately, you too have an incentive to conceal your desire for national defenses. As a consequence, neither one of us may step forward to demand a missile shield in the marketplace. We'll both end up defenseless.

free rider: An individual who reaps direct benefits from someone else's purchase (consumption) of a public good.

Flood control is also a public good. No one in the valley wants to be flooded out. But each landowner knows that a flood-control dam will protect *all* the landowners, regardless of who pays. Either the entire valley is protected or no one is. Accordingly, individual farmers and landowners may say they don't *want* a dam and aren't willing to *pay* for it. Everyone is waiting and hoping that someone else will pay for flood control. In other words, everyone wants a *free ride*. Thus, if we leave it to market forces, no one will *demand* flood control and all the property in the valley will be washed away.

The difference between public goods and private goods rests on *technical considerations* not political philosophy. The central question is whether we have the technical capability to exclude nonpayers. In the case of national defense or flood control, we simply don't have that capability. Even city streets have the characteristics of public goods. Although theoretically we could restrict the use of streets to those who paid to use them, a tollgate on every corner would be exceedingly expensive and impractical. Here again, joint or public consumption appears to be the only feasible alternative. As the accompanying News on Napster emphasizes, the technical capability to exclude nonpayers is the key factor in identifying "public goods."

To the list of public goods we could add the administration of justice (including prisons), the regulation of commerce, the conduct of foreign relations, airport security, and even Fourth of July fireworks. These services—which cost tens of *billions* of dollars and employ thousands of workers—provide benefits to everyone, no matter who pays for them. In each instance it's impossible or prohibitively expensive to exclude nonpayers from the services provided.

Underproduction of Public Goods. The free riders associated with public goods upset the customary practice of paying for what you get. If I can get all the national defense, flood control, and laws I want without paying for them, I'm not about to complain. I'm perfectly happy to let you pay for the services while we all consume them. Of course, you may feel the same way. Why should you pay for these services if you can consume just as much of them when your neighbors foot the whole bill? It might seem selfish not to pay your share of the cost of providing public goods. But you'd be better off in a material sense if you spent your income on doughnuts, letting others pick up the tab for public services.

Because the familiar link between paying and consuming is broken, public goods can't be peddled in the supermarket. People are reluctant to buy what they can get free, a perfectly rational response for consumers who have limited incomes to spend. Hence, *if public goods were marketed like private goods, everyone would wait for someone else to pay.* The end result might be a total lack of public services. This is the kind of dilemma Robert Heilbroner had in mind when he spoke of the market's "deaf ear" (see quote at the beginning of this chapter).

IN THE NEWS

Napster Gets Napped

Shawn Fanning had a brilliant idea for getting more music: download it from friends' computers to the Internet. So he wrote software that enabled online file-sharing of audio files. This peer-to-peer (P2P) online distribution system became an overnight sensation: within a year's time, 38 million consumers were using Napster's software to acquire recorded music.

At first blush, Napster's service looked like a classic "public good." The service was free, and one person's consumption did not impede another person from consuming the same service. Moreover, the distribution system was configured in such a way that nonpayers could not be excluded from the service.

The definition of "*public good*" relies, however, on whether nonpayers *can* be excluded, not whether they *are* excluded. In other words, technology is critical in classifying goods as "public" or "private." In Napster's case, encryption technology that could exclude nonpayers was available, but the company had *chosen* not to use it. After being sued by major recording companies for copyright infringement, Napster sold out. In 2001, the company joined up with Bertelsmann (BMG Records) and reconfigured its software to exclude nonpayers. The pay-for-play concept flopped, however, when other companies (e.g. Kazaa) introduced new file-sharing technology. Napster went bankrupt in 2002.

Analysis: A product is a "public good" only if nonpayers *cannot* be excluded from its consumption. Napster had the technical ability to exclude nonpayers but initially chose not to do so.

FIGURE 4.2
Underproduction of Public Goods

Suppose point A represents the optimal mix of output, that is, the mix of private and public goods that maximizes society's welfare. Because consumers won't demand purely public goods in the marketplace, the price mechanism won't allocate so many resources to their production. Instead, the market will tend to produce a mix of output like point B, which includes fewer public goods (0R) than is optimal (0S).

The production possibilities curve in Figure 4.2 illustrates the dilemma created by public goods. Suppose that point A represents the optimal mix of private and public goods. It's the mix of goods and services we'd select if everyone's preferences were known and reflected in production decisions. The market mechanism won't lead us to point A, however, because the demand for public goods will be hidden. If we rely on the market, nearly everyone will withhold demand for public goods, waiting for a free ride to point A. As a result, we'll get a smaller quantity of public goods than we really want. The market mechanism will leave us at a mix of output like that at point B, with few, if any, public goods. Since point A is assumed to be optimal, point B must be *suboptimal* (inferior to point A). The market fails: We can't rely on the market mechanism to allocate resources to the production of public goods, no matter how much they might be desired.

Note that we're using the term "public good" in a different way then most people use it. To most people, the "public good" refers to any good or service the government produces. In economics, however, the meaning is much more restrictive. The term "public good" refers only to those nonexcludable goods and services that must be consumed jointly, both by those who pay for them and by those who don't. Public goods can be produced by either the government or the private sector. Private goods can be produced in either sector as well. The problem is that *the market tends to underproduce public goods and overproduce private goods*. If we want more public goods, we need a *nonmarket* force—government intervention—to get them. The government will have to force people to pay taxes, then use the tax revenues to pay for the production of national defense, flood control, and other public goods.

The free-rider problem associated with public goods is one justification for government intervention. It's not the only justification, however. Further grounds for intervention arise from the tendency of costs or benefits of some market activities to "spill over" onto third parties.

Your demand for a good reflects the amount of satisfaction you expect from its consumption. The price you're willing to pay acts as a market signal to producers of your preferences. Often, however, your consumption may affect others. The purchase of cigarettes, for example, expresses a smoker's demand for that good. But others may suffer from that consumption. In this case, smoke literally spills over onto other consumers, causing them discomfort and possibly even ill health (see News on the next page). Yet their loss isn't reflected in the market: The harm caused to nonsmokers is *external* to the market price of cigarettes.

The term **externalities** refers to all costs or benefits of a market activity borne by a third party, that is, by someone other than the immediate producer or consumer. *Whenever externalities are present, the preferences expressed in the marketplace won't be a complete measure of a good's value to society.* As a consequence, the

Externalities

externalities: Costs (or benefits) of a market activity borne by a third party; the difference between the social and private costs (benefits) of a market activity.

IN THE NEWS

The Human Cost of Secondhand Smoke

Estimated U.S. annual morbidity and mortality in nonsmokers from secondhand smoke:

DEVELOPMENTAL EFFECTS

Low birthweight	9,700–18,600 cases
Sudden infant death syndrome	1,900–2,700 deaths

RESPIRATORY EFFECTS IN CHILDREN

Middle ear infection	700,000–1.6 million visits to the doctor
Asthma induction	8,000–26,000 new cases
Asthma exacerbation	400,000–1 million children
Bronchitis or pneumonia*	150,000–300,000 cases
	7,500–15,000 hospitalizations
	136–212 deaths

CANCER

Lung cancer**	3,000 deaths

CARDIOVASCULAR EFFECTS

Ischemic heart disease	35,000–62,000 deaths

Source: California Environmental Protection Agency, *18 months and younger   **Estimates unavailable for nasal sinus cancer. *Washington Post*, September 29, 1997. © 1997 The Washington Post. Reprinted with permission. www.washingtonpost.com

Analysis: The health risks imposed on nonsmokers via "passive smoke" represent external costs. The market price of cigarettes doesn't reflect these costs.

---

market will fail to produce the right mix of output. Specifically, the market will underproduce goods that yield external benefits and overproduce those which generate external costs.

External Costs. Figure 4.3 shows how external costs cause the market to overproduce cigarettes. The market demand curve includes only the wishes of smokers, that is, people who are willing and able to purchase cigarettes. The forces of market demand and supply result in a market equilibrium at E_M in which q_M cigarettes are produced and consumed.

The well-being of *non*smokers isn't reflected in the market equilibrium at E_M. To take the *non*smoker's interests into account, we must subtract the external costs imposed on *them* from the value that *smokers* put on cigarettes. In general,

Social demand = market demand + externalities

In this case, the externality is a *cost,* so we must *subtract* the external cost from market demand to get a full accounting of social demand. The "social demand" curve in Figure 4.3 reflects this computation. To find this curve, we simply subtract the amount of external cost from every price on the market demand curve. What the *social* demand curve tells us is how much society would be willing and able to pay for cigarettes if the preferences of both smokers and nonsmokers were taken into account.

The social demand curve in Figure 4.3 creates a new equilibrium at q_o. This is the *optimal* quantity of cigarettes to produce (and consume). Yet the market alone would produce more than that (q_M). Government intervention may be needed to move the mix of output closer to society's optimal point.

The externalities associated with cigarette consumption have prompted many forms of government intervention, including mandatory health warnings on cigarette packaging, bans on advertising, and restrictions on locales where people may smoke.

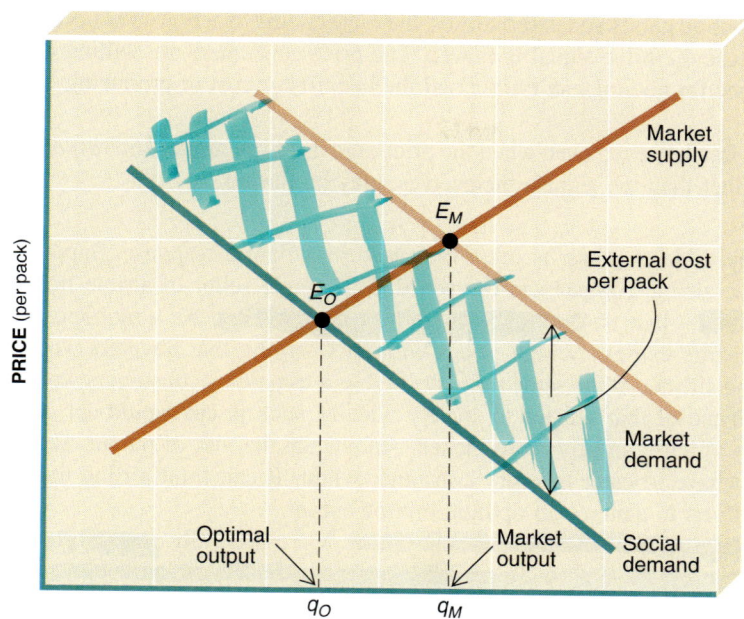

FIGURE 4.3
Externalities

The market responds to consumer demands, not externalities. Smokers demand q_M cigarettes. But external costs on nonsmokers imply that the *social* demand for cigarettes is less than (below) *market* demand. The socially optimal level of output is q_O, less than the market output q_M.

Courts have even determined that child custody decisions may be influenced by the smoking habits of the divorcing parents. All these interventions restrict the ability of individuals to maximize their personal utility in the marketplace. They're motivated by the recognition that the market mechanism responds only to the market demands of smokers and is unable to respond to nonmarketed externalities.

Externalities also exist in production. A power plant that burns high-sulfur coal damages the surrounding environment. Yet the damage inflicted on neighboring people, vegetation, and buildings is external to the cost calculations of the firm. Because the cost of such pollution is not reflected in the price of electricity, the firm will tend to produce more electricity (and pollution) than is socially desirable. To reduce this imbalance, the government has to step in and change market outcomes.

External Benefits. Externalities can also be beneficial. A product may generate external *benefits* rather than external *costs*. Your college is an example. The students who attend your school benefit directly from the education they receive. That's why they (and you) are willing to *pay* for tuition, books, and other services. The students in attendance aren't the only beneficiaries of this educational service, however. The research that a university conducts may yield benefits for a much broader community. The values and knowledge students acquire may also be shared with family, friends, and coworkers. These benefits would all be *external* to the market transaction between a paying student and the school. Positive externalities also arise from immunizations against infectious diseases.

If a product yields external benefits, the social demand is greater than the market demand. In this case, the social value of the good *exceeds* the market price (by the amount of external benefit). Accordingly, society wants *more* of the product than the market mechanism alone will produce at any given price. To get that additional output, the government may have to intervene with subsidies or other policies. We conclude then that **the market fails by**

- **Overproducing goods that have external costs.**
- **Underproducing goods that have external benefits.**

If externalities are present, the market won't produce the optimal mix of output. To get that optimal mix, we need government intervention.

Check out the pollution problems in your neighborhood at www.epa.gov/epahome/commsearch.htm.

Market Power

In the case of both public goods and externalities, the market fails to achieve the optimal mix of output because the price signal is flawed. The price consumers are willing and able to pay for a specific good doesn't reflect all the benefits or cost of producing that good.

The market may fail, however, even when the price signals are accurate. The *response* to price signals, rather than the signals themselves, may be flawed.

Restricted Supply. Market power is often the cause of a flawed response. Suppose there were only one airline company in the world. This single seller of airline travel would be a **monopoly**—that is, the only producer in that industry. As a monopolist, the airline could charge extremely high prices without worrying that travelers would flock to a competing airline. At the same time, the high prices paid by consumers would express the importance of that service to society. Ideally, such prices would act as a signal to producers to build and fly more planes—to change the mix of output. But a monopolist doesn't have to cater to every consumer whim. It can limit airline travel and obstruct our efforts to achieve an optimal mix of output.

Monopoly is the most severe form of **market power**. More generally, market power refers to any situation in which a single producer or consumer has the ability to alter the market price of a specific product. If the publisher (McGraw-Hill) charges a high price for this book, you'll have to pay the tab. McGraw-Hill has market power because there are relatively few economics textbooks and your professor has required you to use this one. You don't have power in the textbook market because your decision to buy or not won't alter the market price of this text. You're only one of the million students who are taking an introductory economics course this year.

The market power McGraw-Hill possesses is derived from the copyright on this text. No matter how profitable textbook sales might be, no one else is permitted to produce or sell this particular book. Patents are another common source of market power because they also preclude others from making or selling a specific product. Market power may also result from control of resources, restrictive production agreements, or efficiencies of large-scale production.

Whatever the source of market power, the direct consequence is that one or more producers attain discretionary power over the market's response to price signals. They may use that discretion to enrich themselves rather than to move the economy toward the optimal mix of output. In this case, the market will again fail to deliver the most desired goods and services.

The mandate for government intervention in this case is to prevent or dismantle concentrations of market power. That's the basic purpose of **antitrust** policy. Another option is to *regulate* market behavior. This was one of the goals of the antitrust case against Microsoft. The government was less interested in breaking Microsoft's near monopoly on operating systems than in changing the way Microsoft behaved.

In some cases, it may be economically efficient to have one large firm supply an entire market. Such a situation arises in **natural monopoly,** where a single firm can achieve economies of scale over the entire range of market output. Utility companies, local telephone service, subway systems, and cable all exhibit such scale (size) efficiencies. In these cases, a monopoly *structure* may be economically desirable. The government may have to regulate the *behavior* of a natural monopoly, however, to ensure that consumers get the benefits of that greater efficiency.

Inequity

Public goods, externalities, and market power all cause resource misallocations. Where these phenomena exist, the market mechanism will fail to produce the optimal mix of output.

Beyond the question of WHAT to produce, we're also concerned about FOR WHOM output is to be produced. The market answers this question by distributing a larger share of total output to those with the most income. Although this result may be efficient, it's not necessarily equitable. As we saw in Chapter 2, the market mechanism may enrich some people while leaving others to seek shelter in abandoned cars. If such outcomes

---

monopoly: A firm that produces the entire market supply of a particular good or service.

market power: The ability to alter the market price of a good or a service.

antitrust: Government intervention to alter market structure or prevent abuse of market power.

natural monopoly: An industry in which one firm can achieve economies of scale over the entire range of market supply.

violate our vision of equity, we may want the government to change the market-generated distribution of income.

Taxes and Transfers. The tax-and-transfer system is the principal mechanism for redistributing incomes. The idea here is to take some of the income away from those who have "too much" and give it to those whom the market has left with "too little." Taxes are levied to take back some of the income received from the market. Those tax revenues are then redistributed via transfer payments to those deemed needy, such as the poor, the aged, the unemployed. **Transfer payments** are income payments for which no goods or services are exchanged. They're used to bolster the incomes of those for whom the market itself provides too little.

Merit Goods. Often, our vision of what is "too little" is defined in terms of specific goods and services. There is a widespread consensus in the United States that everyone is entitled to some minimum levels of shelter, food, and health care. These are regarded as **merit goods,** in the same sense that everyone merits at least some minimum provision of such goods. When the market does not distribute that minimum provision, the government is called on to fill in the gaps. In this case, the income transfers take the form of *in-kind* transfers (e.g., Food Stamps, housing vouchers, Medicaid) rather than *cash* transfers (e.g., welfare checks, Social Security benefits).

Some people argue that we don't need the government to help the poor—that private charity alone will suffice. Unfortunately, private charity alone has never been adequate. One reason private charity doesn't suffice is the "free-rider" problem. If I contribute heavily to the poor, you benefit from safer streets (fewer muggers), a better environment (fewer slums and homeless people), and a clearer conscience (knowing fewer people are starving). In this sense, the relief of misery is a *public* good. Were I the only taxpayer to benefit substantially from the reduction of poverty, then charity would be a private affair. As long as income support substantially benefits the public at large, then income redistribution is a *public* good, for which public funding is appropriate. This is the *economic* rationale for public income-redistribution activities. To this rationale one can add such moral arguments as seem appropriate.

The micro failures of the marketplace imply that we're at the wrong point on the production possibilities curve or inequitably distributing the output produced. There's another basic question we've swept under the rug, however. How do we get to the production possibilities curve in the first place? To reach the curve, we must utilize all available resources and technology. Can we be confident that the invisible hand of the marketplace will use all our resources? Or will some people face **unemployment**—that is, be willing to work but unable to find a job?

And what about prices? Price signals are a critical feature of the market mechanism. But the validity of those signals depends on some stable measure of value. What good is a doubling of salary when the price of everything you buy doubles as well? Generally, rising prices will enrich people who own property and impoverish people who rent. That's why we strive to avoid **inflation**—a situation in which the *average* price level is increasing.

Historically, the marketplace has been wracked with bouts of both unemployment and inflation. These experiences have prompted calls for government intervention at the macro level. *The goal of macro intervention is to foster economic growth—to get us on the production possibilities curve (full employment), maintain a stable price level (price stability), and increase our capacity to produce (growth).*

GROWTH OF GOVERNMENT

The potential micro and macro failures of the marketplace provide specific justifications for government intervention. The question then turns to how well the activities of the public sector correspond to these implied mandates.

transfer payments: Payments to individuals for which no current goods or services are exchanged, like Social Security, welfare, unemployment benefits.

merit good: A food or service society deems everyone is entitled to some minimal quantity of.

Macro Instability

unemployment: The inability of labor-force participants to find jobs.

inflation: An increase in the average level of prices of goods and services.

Federal Growth

Until the 1930s the federal government's role was largely limited to national defense (a public good), enforcement of a common legal system (also a public good), and provision of postal service (equity). The Great Depression of the 1930s spawned a new range of government activities, including welfare and Social Security programs (equity), minimum wage laws and workplace standards (regulation), and massive public works (public goods and externalities). In the 1950s the federal government also assumed a greater role in maintaining macroeconomic stability (macro failure), protecting the environment (externalities), and safeguarding the public's health (externalities and equity).

These increasing responsibilities have greatly increased the size of the public sector. In 1902 the federal government employed fewer than 350,000 people and spent a mere $650 *million*. Today the federal government employs nearly 4 million people and spends roughly $2 *trillion* a year.

Direct Expenditure. Figure 4.4 summarizes the growth of the public sector since 1930. World War II caused a massive increase in the size of the federal government. Federal purchases of goods and services for the war accounted for over 40 percent of total output during the 1943–44 period. The federal share of total U.S. output fell abruptly after World War II, rose again during the Korean War (1950–53) and has declined slightly since then.

The decline in the federal share of total output is somewhat at odds with most people's perception of government growth. This discrepancy is explained by two phenomena. First, people see the *absolute* size of the government growing every year. But we're focusing here on the *relative* size of the public sector. Since the 1950s the public sector has grown more slowly than the private sector, slightly reducing its relative size. As the accompanying World View shows, other industrialized countries have significantly larger public sectors.

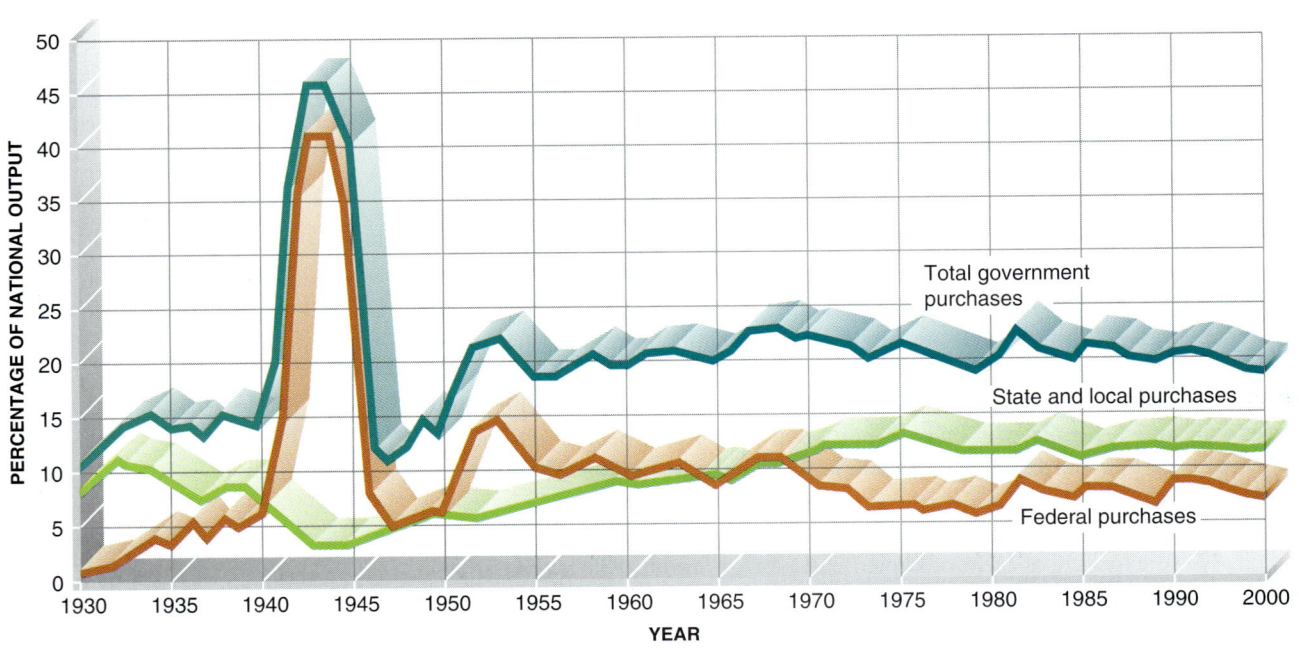

FIGURE 4.4
Government Growth

During World War II the public sector purchased nearly half of total U.S. output. Since the early 1950s the public-sector share of total output has declined to less than 20 percent. Within the public sector, however, there's been a major shift: State and local claims on resources have grown, while the federal share has declined significantly.

Source: *Economic Report of the President, 2001.*

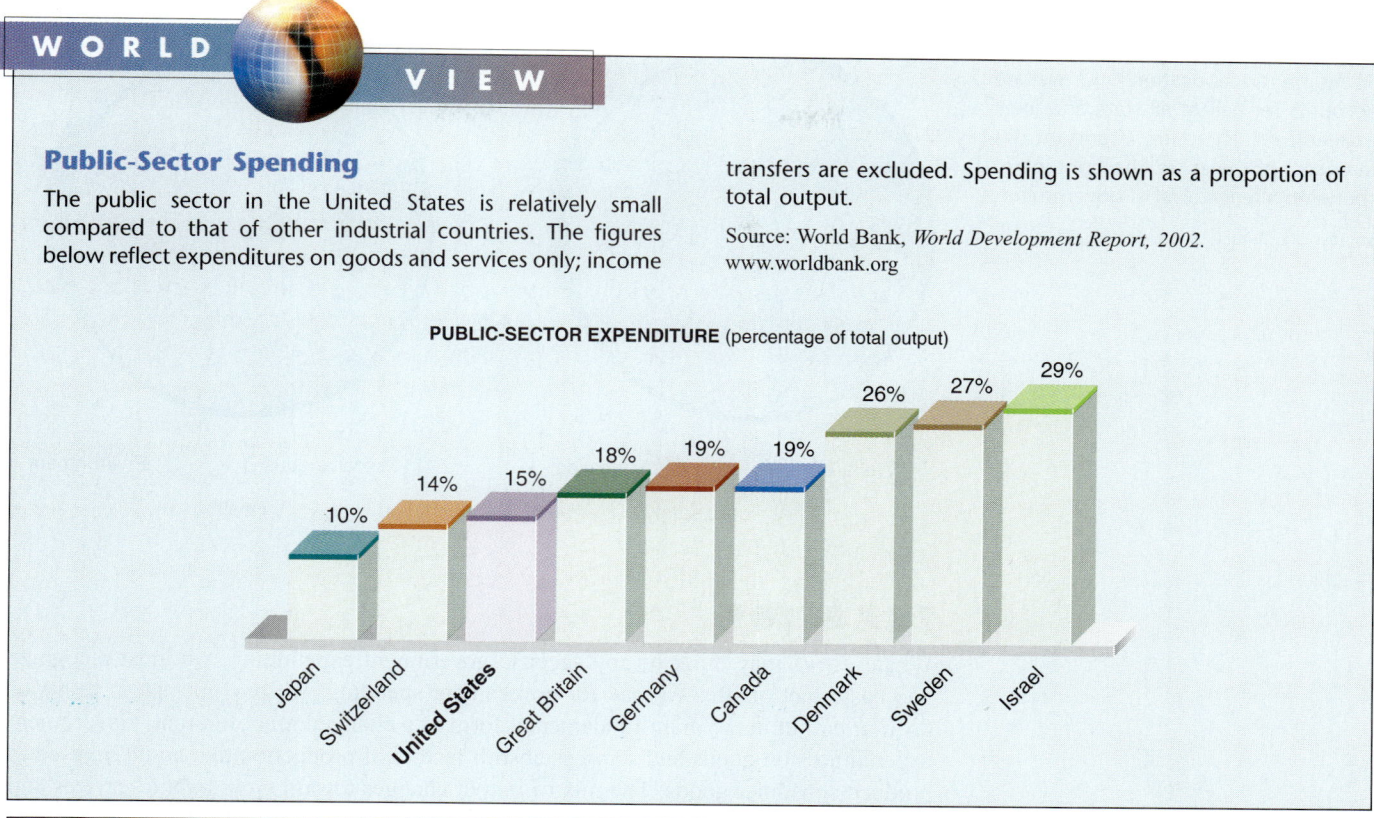

WORLD VIEW

Public-Sector Spending

The public sector in the United States is relatively small compared to that of other industrial countries. The figures below reflect expenditures on goods and services only; income transfers are excluded. Spending is shown as a proportion of total output.

Source: World Bank, *World Development Report, 2002*. www.worldbank.org

Analysis: The share of total output allocated to government services varies widely across nations. In the United States, the government share of output is relatively low.

Income Transfers. Figure 4.4 depicts only government spending on goods and services, not *all* public spending. Not included in our depiction of government growth is spending on income transfers. Direct expenditure on goods and services absorbs real resources, but income transfers don't. Hence, income transfers don't directly alter the mix of output. Their effect is primarily *distributional* (the FOR WHOM question), not *allocative* (the WHAT question). Were income transfers included, the relative size and growth of the federal government would be larger than Figure 4.4 depicts. This is because virtually all recent growth in federal expenditure has come from increased income transfers, not purchases of goods and services.

State and Local Growth

State and local spending on goods and services has followed a very different path than federal expenditure. Prior to World War II, state and local governments dominated public-sector spending. During the war, however, the share of total output going to state and local governments fell, hitting a low of 3 percent in that period (Figure 4.4).

State and local spending caught up with federal spending in the mid-1960s and has exceeded it ever since. Today more than 80,000 state and local government entities buy much more output than Uncle Sam and employ four times as many people.

Figure 4.5 is an overview of state and local budgets. Education is a huge expenditure at both levels of government. Most direct state spending is on colleges; most local spending is for elementary and secondary education. The fastest-growing areas for state expenditure are prisons (public safety) and welfare. At the local level, sewage and trash services are claiming an increasing share of budgets.

FIGURE 4.5
State and Local Spending

Spending on education and welfare accounts for half of all state and local expenditure. There are important differences, however, in the content of spending at each level of government.

Source: U.S. Bureau of the Census.

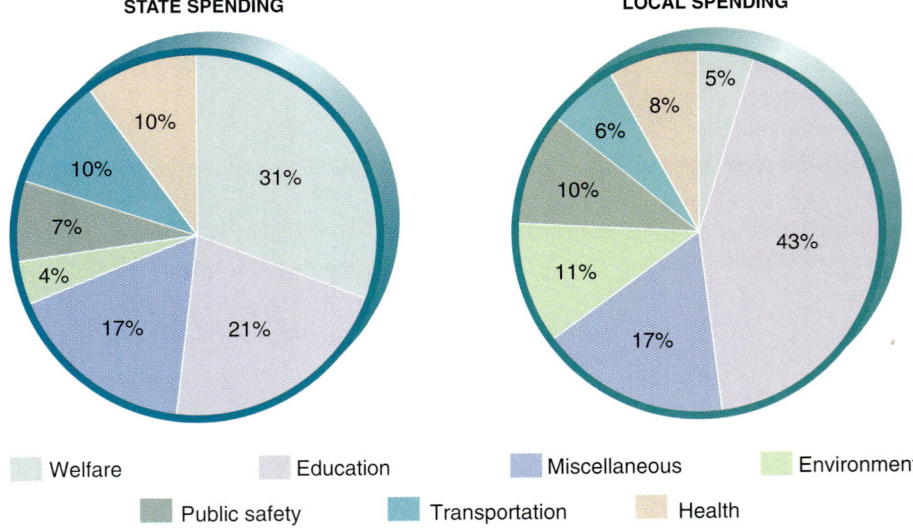

Welfare | Education | Miscellaneous | Environment
Public safety | Transportation | Health

TAXATION

Whatever we may think of any specific government expenditure, we must recognize one basic fact of life: We pay for government spending. We pay not just in terms of tax *dollars* but in the more fundamental form of a changed mix of output. Government expenditures on goods and services absorb factors of production that could be used to produce consumer goods. The mix of output changes toward *more* public services and *less* private goods and services. Resources used to produce missile shields or elementary schools simply aren't available to produce cars, houses, or restaurant meals. In real terms, the cost of government spending is measured by the private-sector output sacrificed when the government employs scarce factors of production.

The **opportunity costs** of public spending aren't always apparent. We don't directly hand over factors of production to the government. Instead, we give the government part of our income in the form of taxes. Those dollars are then used to buy factors of production or goods and services in the marketplace. Thus, **the primary function of taxes is to transfer command over resources (purchasing power) from the private sector to the public sector.** Although the government sometimes also borrows dollars to finance its purchases, taxes are the primary source of government revenues.

opportunity costs: The most desired goods or services that are forgone in order to obtain something else.

Federal Taxes

As recently as 1902, much of the revenue the federal government collected came from taxes imposed on alcoholic beverages. The federal government didn't have authority to collect income taxes. As a consequence, *total* federal revenue in 1902 was only $653 million.

Income Taxes. All that has changed. The Sixteenth Amendment to the U.S. Constitution, enacted in 1915, granted the federal government authority to collect income taxes. The government now collects over $1 *trillion* in that form alone. Although the federal government still collects taxes on alcoholic beverages, the individual income tax has become the largest single source of government revenue (see Figure 4.6).

progressive tax: A tax system in which tax rates rise as incomes rise.

In theory, the federal income tax is designed to be **progressive**—that is, to take a larger *fraction* of high incomes than of low incomes. In 2001, for example, a single person with less than $8,500 of income paid no federal income tax. A person with $8,500 to $15,000 was obligated to turn over 13 percent of each additional dollar of income to Uncle Sam. People with between $15,000 and $35,000 income confronted a 27 percent tax rate on their additional income. The marginal tax rate got as high as 38.6 percent for people earning more than $300,000 in income. Thus people with high incomes not only pay more taxes but also pay a larger *fraction* of their income in taxes.

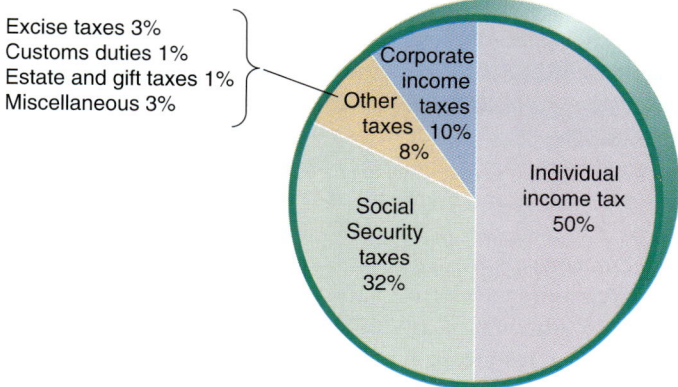

FIGURE 4.6
Federal Taxes

Taxes transfer purchasing power from the private sector to the public sector. The largest federal tax is the individual income tax. The second-largest source of federal revenue is the Social Security payroll tax.

Source: Office of Management and Budget, 2001 data.

Social Security Taxes. The second major source of federal revenue is the Social Security payroll tax. People now working transfer part of their earnings to retired workers by making "contributions" to Social Security. There's nothing voluntary about these "contributions"; they take the form of mandatory payroll deductions. In 2001, each worker paid 7.65 percent of his or her wages to Social Security and employers contributed an equal amount. As a consequence, the government collected more than $700 billion.

At first glance, the Social Security payroll tax looks like a **proportional tax,** that is, a tax that takes the *same* fraction of every taxpayer's income. But this isn't the case. The Social Security (FICA) tax isn't levied on every payroll dollar. Incomes above a certain ceiling (roughly $85,000 per year) aren't taxed. As a result, workers with really high salaries turn over a smaller fraction of their incomes to Social Security than do low-wage workers. This makes the Social Security payroll tax a **regressive tax.**

proportional tax: A tax that levies the same rate on every dollar of income.

regressive tax: A tax system in which tax rates fall as incomes rise.

Corporate Taxes. The federal government taxes the profits of corporations as well as the incomes of consumers. But there are far fewer corporations (less than 4 million) than consumers (280 million), and their profits are small in comparison to total consumer income. In 2001, the federal government collected only $200 billion in corporate income taxes, despite the fact that it imposed a tax rate of 34 percent on corporate profits.

The Office of Management and Budget's "A Citizen's Guide to the Federal Budget" provides convenient charts and data on federal revenues. See
www.whitehouse.gov/omb/budget
www.access.gpo.gov.su_docs
budget99 guide guide.html.

"I can't find anything wrong here, Mr. Truffle . . . you just seem to have too much left after taxes."

Analysis: Taxes are a financing mechanism that enable the government to purchase scarce resources. Higher taxes imply less private-sector purchases.

Excise Taxes. The last major source of federal revenue is excise taxes. Like the early taxes on whiskey, excise taxes are sales taxes imposed on specific goods and services. The federal government taxes not only liquor ($13.50 per gallon) but also gasoline (18.4 cents per gallon), cigarettes (39 cents per pack), telephone service (3 percent), and a variety of other goods and services. Such taxes not only discourage production and consumption of these goods—by raising their price and thereby reducing the quantity demanded—they also raise a substantial amount of revenue.

Current excise tax rates are available from the U.S. Bureau of Alcohol, Tobacco, and Firearms. See www.atf.treas.gov.

State and Local Revenues

Taxes. State and local governments also levy taxes on consumers and businesses. In general, cities depend heavily on property taxes, and state governments rely heavily on sales taxes (see Figure 4.7). Although nearly all states and many cities also impose income taxes, effective tax rates are so low (averaging less than 2 percent of personal income) that income tax revenues are much less than sales and property tax revenues.

Like the Social Security payroll tax, state and local taxes tend to be *regressive*—that is, they take a larger share of income from the poor than from the rich. Consider a 4 percent sales tax, for example. It might appear that a uniform tax rate like this would affect all consumers equally. But people with lower incomes tend to spend most of their income on goods and services. Thus, most of their income is subject to sales taxes. By contrast, a person with a high income can afford to save part of his or her income and thereby shelter it from sales taxes. A family that earns $40,000 and spends $30,000 of it on taxable goods and services, for example, pays $1,200 in sales taxes when the tax rate is 4 percent. In effect, then, they are handing over 3 percent of their *income* ($1,200 ÷ $40,000) to the state. By contrast, the family that makes only $12,000 and spends $11,500 of it for food, clothing, and shelter pays $460 in sales taxes in the same state. Their total tax is smaller, but it represents a much larger *share* (3.8 versus 3.0 percent) of their income.

Local property taxes are also regressive because poor people devote a larger portion of their incomes to housing costs. Property taxes directly affect housing costs. Hence, a larger share of a poor family's income is subject to property taxes. According to the Advisory Council on Intergovernmental Relations, a family earning $50,000 a year devotes only 2.5 percent of its income to property taxes, whereas a family earning $10,000 pays out 4.5 percent of its income in property taxes. State lotteries are also regressive, for the same reason (see News). Low-income players spend 1.4 percent of their incomes on lottery tickets while upper-income players devote only 0.1 percent of their income to lottery purchases.

The U.S. Census Bureau compiles the most comprehensive data on state and local government finances. For details visit www.census.gov/ftp/pub.

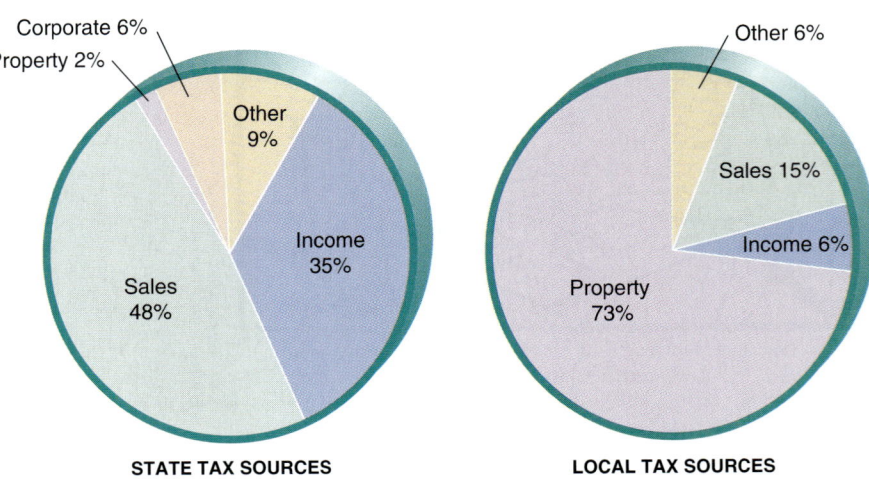

FIGURE 4.7
State and Local Tax Sources

State governments get half their tax revenue from sales taxes. By contrast, local governments depend heavily on property taxes.

Source: U.S. Department of Commerce 1998–99 data).

Federal Aid. Up until 1986, the federal government gave state and local governments some of its revenues for whatever purposes those entities desired. But such general revenue sharing was always small. Most grants to state and local governments are for specific purposes and included in the federal budget under the appropriate category. For example, the federal government spent $26 billion on natural resources and environment in 2001. But one-fifth of this amount was simply given to local communities for the construction of sewage treatment plants. The local governments actually purchased or built these plants; the federal government only provided the necessary revenue. Accordingly, the federal government maintained control over WHAT to produce, but local governments exercised some judgment on HOW to produce it.

This "strings-attached" nature of most federal aid is the distinguishing feature of **categorical grants**. Funds bestowed on state and local governments in the form of categorical grants have to be used for specific purposes. If a city government needs street lighting but federal grants are available only for sewage treatment or job training, the city must choose between one of the latter or do without federal aid. Categorical grants cannot be shifted from one use to another.

In 2001, the federal government gave over $300 billion to state and local governments in the form of categorical grants (including those for employment programs, Medicaid, schools, and highways). These federal grants accounted for about one-fifth of all state and local revenues.

categorical grants: Federal grants to state and local governments for specific expenditure purposes.

User Charges. The third major source of state and local revenues consists of **user charges**. The tuition that college students (or their parents) pay for attending a state university or community college is an all-too-familiar user charge. But tuition fees never cover the full costs of maintaining public colleges. Part of the costs of providing higher education are borne by all state taxpayers, whether or not they attend college. Public hospitals and highways are financed the same way, with users paying part of the costs directly and all taxpayers paying the remaining costs through state and local taxes. Hence, user charges aren't identical to market prices because they're not intended to cover the full costs of supplying a particular good.

user charge: Fee paid for the use of a public-sector good or service.

IN THE NEWS

Big Lotteries' Real Losers

The economy may be slowing, but Americans still seem to have plenty of money for gambling. During the two months leading up to this week's drawing for the multistate Powerball game's $295 million jackpot, 600 million tickets were sold and New Yorkers clogged the highways in search of a Powerball connection in Connecticut.

Gambling expansionists universally support betting in moderation only. But both the national gaming expansion and the lottery mania depend on repeat players for their growing success. Lotteries have collectively taken the name "the fool's tax" because the odds of winning are so small. The biggest players are disproportionately poor and uneducated. Everyone has heard the story about the unemployed ex-convict in need of back surgery who suddenly struck it rich on Powerball. For countless others facing financial straits, money squandered on losing tickets just made matters worse.

The top 20 percent of players, who spend an average of more than $4 on tickets each day, account for more than 80 percent of all sales. They are almost twice as likely as the average adult both to have dropped out of high school and to have a household income under $10,000. Surveys show that the higher the household income, the fewer the dollars spent annually on lottery tickets.

Source: *The New York Times*, August 29, 2001. Reprinted with permission. www.nytimes.com

Analysis: Poor people spend a larger percentage of their income on lottery tickets than do rich people. This makes lotteries a regressive source of government revenue.

GOVERNMENT FAILURE

Some government intervention in the marketplace is clearly desirable. The market mechanism can fail for a variety of reasons, leaving a laissez-faire economy short of its economic goals. But how much government intervention is desirable? Communist nations once thought that complete government control of production, consumption, and distribution decisions was the surest path to utopia. They learned the hard way that not only markets but governments as well can fail.

In this context, **government failure** means that government intervention fails to move us closer to our economic goals. In Figure 4.1, such a failure would mean that government intervention moved us from point *M* to a mix of output still further away from the optimal point *X*. Government failure would also exist if the distribution of income got worse, not better, as a result of government intervention. The government would also fail if the costs of government intervention exceeded the benefits of an improved output mix, cleaner production methods, or a fairer distribution of income.

government failure: Government intervention that fails to improve economic outcomes.

Perceptions of Waste

Taxpayers seem to have strong opinions about government failure. When asked whether the government "wastes" their tax dollars or uses them well, the overwhelming majority see waste in government (see News on "Persistent Doubts"). Moreover, perceptions of waste have increased along with the size of the public sector. The average taxpayer now believes that state governments waste 29 cents out of each dollar, while the federal government wastes 42 cents out of each tax dollar!

Government "waste" implies that the public sector isn't producing as many services as it could with the sources at its disposal. Such inefficiency implies that we're

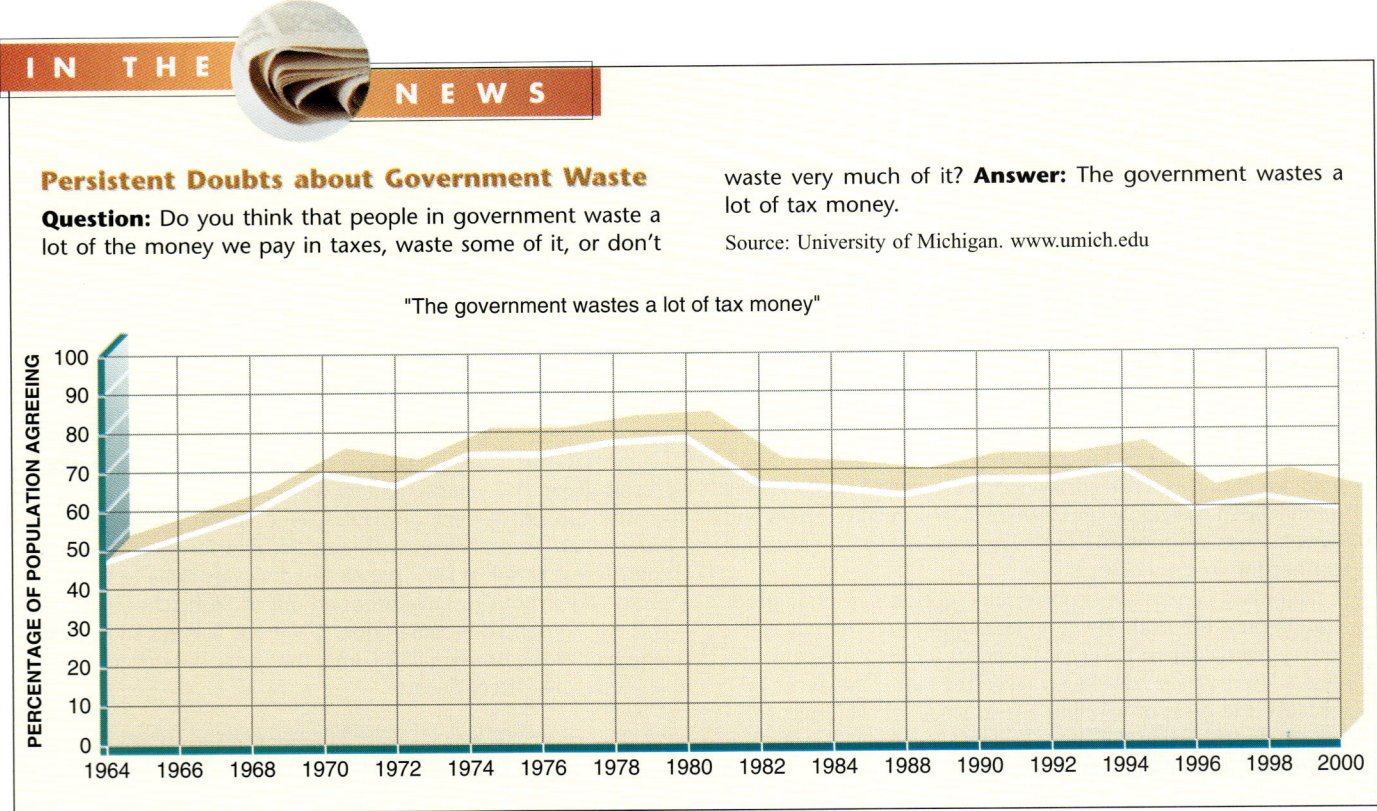

IN THE NEWS

Persistent Doubts about Government Waste

Question: Do you think that people in government waste a lot of the money we pay in taxes, waste some of it, or don't waste very much of it? **Answer:** The government wastes a lot of tax money.

Source: University of Michigan. www.umich.edu

"The government wastes a lot of tax money"

Analysis: Market failure justifies government intervention. If the government wastes resources, however, it too may fail to satisfy our economic goals.

producing somewhere *inside* our production possibilities curve rather than on it. If the government is wasting resources this way, we can't possibly be producing the optimal mix of output.

Even if the government weren't wasting resources, it might still be guilty of government failure. As important as efficiency in government may be, it begs the larger question of how many government services we really want. In reality, the issue of government waste encompasses two distinct questions:

- **Efficiency:** Are we getting as much service as we could from the resources we allocate to government?
- **Opportunity cost:** Are we giving up too many private-sector goods in order to get those services?

If the government is producing goods inefficiently, we end up *inside* the production possibilities curve, with less output than attainable. Even if the government is efficient, however, the *mix* of output may not be optimal. **Everything the government does entails an opportunity cost.** The more police officers or schoolteachers employed by the public sector, the fewer workers available to private producers and consumers. Similarly, the more computers, pencils, and paper consumed by government agencies, the fewer accessible to individuals and private companies.

When assessing government's role in the economy, then, we must consider not only what governments do but also what we give up to allow them to do it. The theory of public goods tells us only what activities are appropriate for government, not the proper *level* of such activity. National defense is clearly a proper function of the public sector. Not so clear, however, is how much the government should spend on tanks, aircraft carriers, and missile shields. The same is true of environmental protection or law enforcement.

The concept of opportunity costs puts a new perspective on the whole question of government size. Before we can decide how big is "too big," we must decide what we're willing to give up to support the public sector. A military force of 1.4 million men and women is "too big" from an economic perspective only if we value the forgone private production and consumption more highly than we value the added strength of our defenses. The government has gone "too far" if the highway it builds is less desired than the park and homes it implicitly replaced. In these and all cases, the assessment of bigness must come back to a comparison of what is given up with what is received. The assessment of government failure thus comes back to points on the production possibilities curve. Has the government moved us closer to the optimal mix of output or not?

This is a tough question to answer in the abstract. We can, however, use the concept of opportunity cost to assess the effectiveness of specific government interventions. From this perspective, additional public-sector activity is desirable only if the benefits from that activity exceed its opportunity costs. In other words, we compare the benefits of a public project to the value of the private goods given up to produce it. By performing this calculation repeatedly along the perimeter of the production possibilities curve, we could locate the optimal mix of output—the point at which no further increase in public-sector spending activity is desirable.

This same principle can be used to decide *which* goods to produce within the public sector. A public project is desirable only to the extent that it promises to yield some benefits (or utility). But all public projects involve opportunity costs. Hence, a project should be pursued only if its anticipated benefits exceeded the value of alternative resource uses. In this sense, the public sector confronts the same kind of dilemma we consumers have. There are hundreds of goods and services we'd *like* to have, but scarce resources require us to select only the best possible ones. That implies getting the highest possible ratio of benefits to costs.

Opportunity Cost

For more public opinion on the role of government, visit the University of Michigan's National Election Studies site at www.umich.edu/~nes/nesguide/gd-index.htm.

Cost-Benefit Analysis

Valuation Problems. Although the principles of benefit-cost analysis are simple enough, they're deceptive. How are we to measure the potential benefits of improved police services, for example? Should we estimate the number of robberies and murders prevented, calculate the worth of each, and add up the benefits? And how are we supposed to calculate the worth of a saved life? By a person's earnings? value of assets? number of friends? And what about the increased sense of security people have when they know the police are patrolling in their neighborhood? Should this be included in the benefit calculation? Some people will attach great value to this service; others will attach little. Whose values should be the standard?

When we're dealing with (private) market goods and services, we can gauge the benefits of a product by the amount of money consumers are willing to pay for it. This price signal isn't available for most public services, however, because of externalities and the nonexclusive nature of pure public goods (the free-rider problem). Hence, *the value (benefits) of public services must be estimated because they don't have (reliable) market prices*. This opens the door to endless political squabbles about how beneficial any particular government activity is.

The same problems arise in evaluating the government's efforts to redistribute incomes. Government transfer payments now go to retired workers, disabled people, veterans, farmers, sick people, students, pregnant women, unemployed people, poor people, and a long list of other recipients. To pay for all these transfers, the government must raise tax revenues. With so many people paying taxes and receiving transfer payments, the net effects on the distribution of income aren't easy to figure out. Yet we can't determine whether this government intervention is worth it until we know how the FOR WHOM answer was changed and what the tax-and-transfer effort cost us. Here again, there's at least a possibility of government failure.

Ballot Box Economics

In practice, we rely on political mechanisms, not cost-benefit calculations, to decide what to produce in the public sector and how to redistribute incomes. *Voting mechanisms substitute for the market mechanism in allocating resources to the public sector and deciding how to use them.* Some people have even suggested that the variety and volume of public goods are determined by the most votes, just as the variety and volume of private goods are determined by the most dollars. Thus, governments choose that level and mix of output (and related taxation) that seem to command the most votes.

Sometimes the link between the ballot box and output decisions is very clear and direct. State and local governments, for example, are often compelled to get voter approval before building another highway, school, housing project, or sewage plant. *Bond referenda* are direct requests by a government unit for the authority and purchasing power to expand the production of particular public goods. In 2000, for example, governments sought voter approval for $22 billion of new borrowing to finance public expenditure; over 70 percent of those requests were approved.

Although the direct link between bond referenda and spending decisions is important, it's more the exception than the rule. Bond referenda account for less than 1 percent of state and local expenditures (and none of federal expenditures). As a consequence, voter control of public spending is much less direct. Although federal agencies must receive authorization from Congress for all expenditures, consumers get a chance to elect new representatives only every two years. Much the same is true at state and local levels. Voters may be in a position to dictate the general level and pattern of public expenditures but have little direct influence on everyday output decisions. In this sense, the ballot box is a poor substitute for the market mechanism.

Even if the link between the ballot box and allocation decisions were stronger, the resulting mix of output might not be optimal. A democratic vote, for example, might yield a 51 percent majority for approval of new local highways. Should the highways then be built? The answer isn't obvious. After all, a large minority (49 percent) of the voters have stated that they don't want resources used this way. If we proceed to build

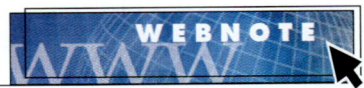

The National Conference of State Legislatures tracks bond referenda and other ballot issues. Visit them at www.ncsl.org to review recent ballots.

the highways, we'll make those people worse off. Even the voters who voted for the highways may end up worse off, depending on how the benefits and costs of the highway are distributed and what other opportunities exist. The basic dilemma is really twofold. *We don't know what the real demand for public services is, and votes alone don't reflect the intensity of individual demands.* Moreover, real-world decision making involves so many choices that a stable consensus is impossible.

Public-Choice Theory

In the midst of all this complexity and uncertainty, another factor may be decisive—namely, self-interest. In principle, government officials are supposed to serve the people. It doesn't take long, however, before officials realize that the public is indecisive about what it wants and takes very little interest in government's day-to-day activities. With such latitude, government officials can set their own agendas. Those agendas may give higher priority to personal advancement than to the needs of the public. Agency directors may foster new programs that enlarge their mandate, enhance their visibility, and increase their prestige or income. Members of Congress may likewise pursue legislative favors like tax breaks for supporters more diligently than they pursue the general public interest. In such cases, the probability of attaining the optimal mix of output declines.

The theory of **public choice** emphasizes the role of self-interest in public decision making. Public-choice theory essentially extends the analysis of market behavior to political behavior. Public officials are assumed to have specific personal goals (for example, power, recognition, wealth) that they'll pursue in office. *A central tenet of public-choice theory is that bureaucrats are just as selfish (utility maximizing) as everyone else.*

public choice: Theory of public-sector behavior emphasizing rational self-interest of decision makers and voters.

Public-choice theory provides a neat and simple explanation for public-sector decision making. But critics argue that the theory provides a woefully narrow view of public servants. Some people do selflessly pursue larger, public goals, such critics argue, and ideas can overwhelm self-interest. Steven Kelman of Harvard, for example, argues that narrow self-interest can't explain the War on Poverty of the 1960s, the tax revolt of the 1970s, or the deregulation movement of the 1980s. These tidal changes in public policy reflect the power of ideas, not simple self-interest.

Although self-interest can't provide a complete explanation of public decision making, it adds important perspectives on the policy process. James Buchanan of George Mason University (Virginia) won the 1986 Nobel Prize in economics for helping develop this public-choice perspective. It adds a personal dimension to the faceless mechanics of ballot box economics, cost-benefit analysis, and other "objective" mechanisms of public-sector decision making.

THE ECONOMY TOMORROW

Downsizing Government

The Great Depression of the 1930s devastated the world economy. For many people, it was compelling evidence that the market alone couldn't be trusted to answer the WHAT, HOW, and FOR WHOM questions. With unemployment, hunger, and homelessness at record levels, people everywhere turned to government for help. In the United States, Franklin Roosevelt's New Deal envisioned a more activist government, restoring full employment and assuring everyone some minimal level of economic security. In Eastern Europe, the Communist Party advanced the notion that outright government *control* of the economy was the only sure way to attain economic justice for all.

Confidence in the ability of government to resolve core economic issues continued to increase in the post–World War II era. Securing national defenses during the Cold War (1948–89) justified the maintenance of a large military establishment, both in the United States and elsewhere. The War on Poverty that began in the mid-1960s brought about a huge increase in government social programs and income transfers. As the U.S.

population has aged, the government's health care and retirement programs (e.g., Social Security, military and civilian government pensions) have grown rapidly. In each case, there was a political consensus that expanded public services would enhance society's welfare. That consensus helped grow *total* federal spending (including purchases and income transfers) from 17 percent of GDP in 1965 to over 23 percent in 1982.

Deficit Financing. President Reagan railed against the relentless growth of the federal government. To reverse that growth, he pushed a massive tax cut through Congress, hoping thereby to cut off the major source of government finances. But he couldn't convince Congress to reduce social-program spending, and he wanted more military spending. So the federal government kept growing, using *borrowed* money to replace the lost tax revenue.

Military Cutbacks. The end of the Cold War sparked a significant cutback in military outlays. Between 1991 and 1996, annual military spending declined by $54 *billion* a year. The size of the armed forces shrank by nearly 500,000 personnel. All these "guns" weren't converted to civilian "butter," however. As military spending declined in the 1990s, federal social spending continued to increase. As a result, the federal share of total output declined very slowly.

Nonmilitary Downsizing. Public opinion has not kept pace with the continued growth of federal programs. As we noted earlier, most taxpayers think the government wastes a lot of money. More to the point, a 2001 CBS news survey revealed that Americans are highly skeptical about the federal government's ability to fix things. As the accompanying News shows, only 3 percent of the population "always" trusts the government to do what is right. A lot of people now suspect government intervention *creates* more problems than it solves.

The increasing skepticism about government intervention has prompted a worldwide downsizing of the public sector. The downsizing has been most dramatic in the former communist nations, like the Soviet Union, where the mechanisms of central planning have been removed. In Europe and Latin America, the downsizing of government has

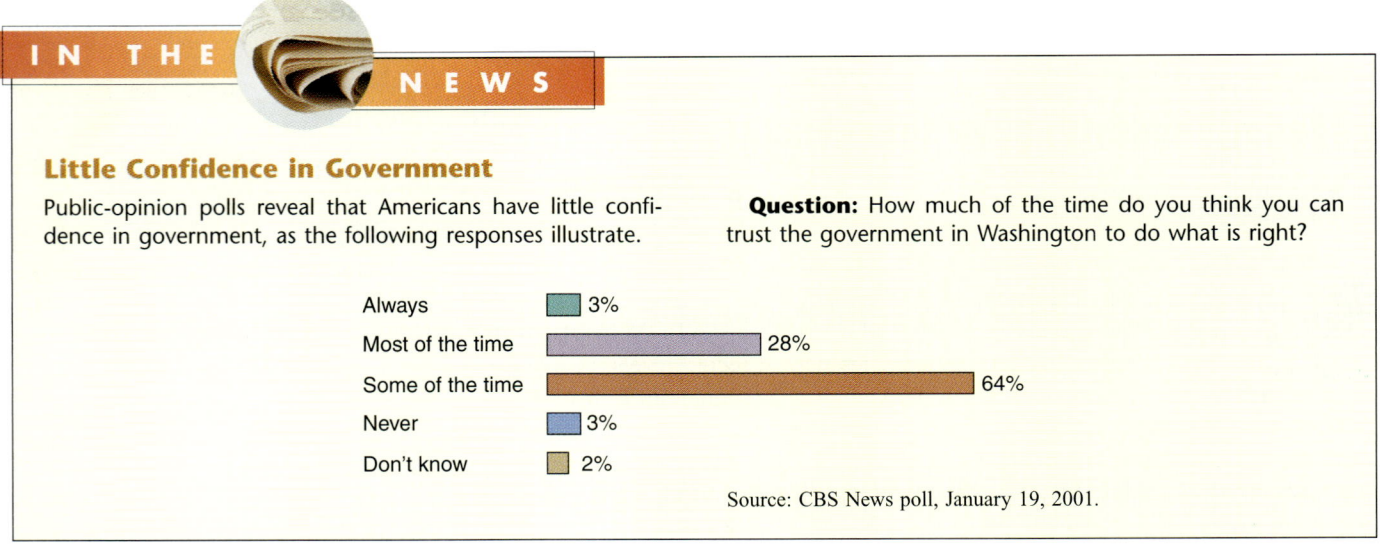

IN THE NEWS

Little Confidence in Government

Public-opinion polls reveal that Americans have little confidence in government, as the following responses illustrate.

Question: How much of the time do you think you can trust the government in Washington to do what is right?

Always	3%
Most of the time	28%
Some of the time	64%
Never	3%
Don't know	2%

Source: CBS News poll, January 19, 2001.

Analysis: In principle, governments intervene to remedy market failure. But the public has little confidence in government performance.

taken the form of privatization of government-owned industries such as railroads, airlines, and telephone service. In the United States, President George W. Bush has made the downsizing of government a policy priority. To achieve that goal, however, requires chipping away at specific programs. That's always the hard part. The war against terrorism that began in September 2001 made it impossible to reduce defense spending, leaving social spending the only target for budget cuts. Even desirable cutbacks in social spending, however, encounter the resistance of program beneficiaries and program bureaucrats. Few seasoned observers expect the government sector to shrink further in the economy tomorrow.

SUMMARY

- Government intervention in the marketplace is justified by market failure, that is, suboptimal market outcomes.
- The micro failures of the market originate in public goods, externalities, market power, and an inequitable distribution of income. These flaws deter the market from achieving the optimal mix of output or distribution of income.
- Public goods are those that can't be consumed exclusively; they're jointly consumed regardless of who pays. Because everyone seeks a free ride, no one demands public goods in the marketplace. Hence, the market underproduces public goods.
- Externalities are costs (or benefits) of a market transaction borne by a third party. Externalities create a divergence between social and private costs or benefits, causing suboptimal market outcomes. The market overproduces goods with external costs and underproduces goods with external benefits.
- Market power enables a producer to thwart market signals and maintain a suboptimal mix of output. Antitrust policy seeks to prevent or restrict market power. The government may also regulate the behavior of powerful firms.
- The market-generated distribution of income may be unfair. This inequity may prompt the government to intervene with taxes and transfer payments that redistribute incomes.
- The macro failures of the marketplace are reflected in unemployment and inflation. Government intervention is intended to achieve full employment and price stability.
- The federal government expanded greatly after 1930. More recent growth, however, has been in transfer payments, which now account for over half of federal expenditure.
- State and local governments purchase more output (14 percent of GDP) than the federal government (6 percent) and employ three times as many workers.
- Income and payroll taxes provide most federal revenues. States get most revenue from sales taxes; local governments rely on property taxes.
- Government failure occurs when intervention moves us away from rather than toward the optimal mix of ouput (or income). Failure may result from outright waste (operational inefficiency) or from a misallocation of resources. All government activity must be evaluated in terms of its opportunity cost, that is, the *private* goods and services forgone to make resources available to the public sector.
- Allocation decisions within the public sector may be based on benefit-cost analysis or votes. The self-interests of government agents may also affect decisions of when and how to intervene.

Key Terms

optimal mix of output
market mechanism
market failure
private good
public good
free rider
externalities
monopoly

market power
antitrust
natural monopoly
transfer payments
merit good
unemployment
inflation
opportunity cost

progressive tax
proportional tax
regressive tax
categorical grants
user charge
government failure
public choice

Questions for Discussion

1. Why should taxpayers subsidize public colleges and universities? What external benefits are generated by higher education?
2. If everyone seeks a free ride, what mix of output will be produced in Figure 4.2? Why would anyone voluntarily contribute to the purchase of public goods like flood control?
3. Could local fire departments be privately operated, with their services sold directly to customers? What problems would be involved in such a system?
4. Why might Fourth of July fireworks be considered a public good? Who should pay for them? What about airport security?
5. What is the specific market-failure justification for government spending on (*a*) public universities, (*b*) health care, (*c*) trash pickup, (*d*) highways, (*e*) police? Would a purely private economy produce any of these services?
6. Why should the well-being of nonsmokers affect the price and quantity of cigarettes produced?
7. The government now spends over $400 billion a year on Social Security benefits. Why don't we leave it to individuals to save for their own retirement?
8. No user fees are charged for Washington. D.C.'s public museums and exhibits. Should an entrance fee be levied?
9. Are subway fares progressive or regressive? How about highway tolls?
10. Should the government be downsized? Which functions should be cut back?

Web Activities

1. What nations in the world have the three largest public sectors as measured by total expenditures as a percentage of GDP? What nations have the smallest public sectors as measured in the same manner? You can find data to answer these questions in the World Bank's annual World Development Report at www.worldbank.org/wdr/. Look for "General govm't final cons. expenditure" in Table 3 (Economic Activity).
2. Find out about market power at www.antitrust.org. Choose one recent case to study. What is the source of market power in this case? What are the consequences for the U.S. economy? What is the proposed government intervention?
3. Data on state taxes and state expenditures are available at www.census.gov/govs/www/state.html. For your own state, find (*a*) the tax that generates the most revenue and (*b*) the largest expenditure category. How does your state compare with the total for all states? (See Figures 4.6 and 4.8 in the text.)

THE ACCOMPANYING STUDENT PROBLEM SET CONTAINS NUMERICAL AND GRAPHING PROBLEMS FOR THIS CHAPTER

PART 2

Measuring Macro Outcomes

Macroeconomics focuses on the performance of the entire economy rather than on the behavior of individual participants (a micro concern). The central concerns of macroeconomics are (1) the short-term business cycle and (2) long-term economic growth. In the long run, the focus is on expanding the economy's capacity to produce goods and services, thereby raising future living standards. In the short run, the emphasis is on fully using available capacity, thereby maximizing output and minimizing unemployment. Chapters 5 through 7 focus on the measurement tools used to gauge the nation's macroeconomic performance (both short-run and long-run). Also examined are the social and economic damage caused by unemployment and inflation.

CHAPTER 5

National-Income Accounting

A favorite cliché of policymakers in Washington is that government likes to tackle only those problems it can measure. Politicians need visible results. They want to be able to brag to their constituents about the miles of new highways built, the number of students who graduated, the number of families that left welfare, and the amount by which wages and income increased and unemployment declined. To do this, they must be able to measure economic outcomes.

The Great Depression of the 1930s was an object lesson in the need for better measures of economic performance. There were plenty of anecdotes about factories closing, farms failing, and people selling apples on the streets. But nobody knew the dimensions of the nation's economic meltdown until millions of workers had lost their jobs. The need for more timely information about the health of the national economy was evident. From that experience a commitment to **national-income accounting**—the measurement of aggregate economic activity—emerged. During the 1930s the economist Simon Kuznets (who later received a Nobel Prize for his work) and the U.S. Department of Commerce developed an accounting system that gauges the economy's health. That national-accounting system now churns out reams of data that are essential to tracking the economy's performance. They answer such questions as

- How much output is being produced? What is it being used for?
- How much income is being generated in the marketplace?
- What's happening to prices and wages?

It's tempting, of course, to ignore all these measurement questions, especially since they tend to be rather dull. But if we avoid measurement problems, we severely limit our ability to understand how the economy works or how well (or poorly) it's performing. We also limit our ability to design policies for improving economic performance.

National-income accounting also provides a useful perspective on the way the economy works. It shows how factor markets relate to product markets, how output relates to income, and how consumer spending and business investment relate to production. It also shows how the flow of taxes and government spending may alter economic outcomes.

MEASURES OF OUTPUT

The array of goods and services we produce is truly massive, including everything from professional baseball to guided-missile systems. All these things are part of our total output; the problem is to find a summary measure.

Itemizing the amount of each good or service produced each year won't solve our measurement problems. The resulting list would be so long that it would be both unwieldy and meaningless. We couldn't even add it up, since it would contain diverse goods measured in a variety of units, for example, packages, pounds, quarts. Nor could we compare one year's output to another's. Suppose that last year we produced 2 billion oranges, 2 million bicycles, and 700 rock concerts, whereas this year we produced 3 billion oranges, 4 million bicycles, and 600 rock concerts. Which year's output was larger? With more of some goods, but less of others, the answer isn't obvious.

To facilitate our accounting chores, we need some mechanism for organizing annual output data into a more manageable summary. The mechanism we use is prices. *Each good and service produced and brought to market has a price. That price serves as a measure of value for calculating total output.* Consider again the problem of determining how much output was produced this year and last. There's no obvious way to answer this question in physical terms alone. But once we know the price of each good, we can calculate the *value* of output produced in a given time period. The total dollar value of final output produced each year is called the **gross domestic product (GDP)**. GDP is simply the sum of all final goods and services produced for the market in a given time period, with each good or service valued at its market price.

Table 5.1 illustrates the use of prices to value total output in two hypothetical years. If oranges were 20 cents each last year and 2 billion oranges were produced, then the *value* of orange production last year was $400 million ($0.20 × 2 billion). In the same manner, we can determine that the value of bicycle production was $100 million and

national-income accounting: The measurement of aggregate economic activity, particularly national income and its components.

Gross Domestic Product

gross domestic product (GDP): The total market value of all final goods and services produced within a nation's borders in a given time period.

Output	Amount
a. Last Year's Output	
In physical terms:	
Oranges	2 billion
Bicycles	2 million
Rock concerts	700
Total	?
In monetary terms:	
2 billion oranges @ $0.20 each	$ 400 million
2 million bicycles @ $50 each	100 million
700 rock concerts @ $1 million each	700 million
Total	$1200 million
b. This Year's Output	
In physical terms:	
Oranges	3 billion
Bicycles	4 million
Rock concerts	600
Total	?
In monetary terms:	
3 billion oranges @ $0.20 each	$ 600 million
4 million bicycles @ $50 each	200 million
600 rock concerts @ $1 million each	600 million
Total	$1400 million

TABLE 5.1

The Measurement of Output
It's impossible to add up all output when output is counted in *physical* terms. Accordingly, total output is measured in *monetary* terms, with each good or service valued at its market price. GDP refers to the total market value of all goods and services produced in a given time period. According to the numbers in this table, the total *value* of the oranges, bicycles, and rock concerts produced last year was $1.2 billion.

the value of rock concerts was $700 million. By adding these figures, we can say that the value of last year's production—last year's GDP—was $1,200 million (Table 5.1*a*).

Now we're in a position to compare one year's output to another's. Table 5.1*b* shows that the use of prices enables us to say that the *value* of this year's output is $1,400 million. Hence, *total output* has increased from one year to the next. **The use of prices to value market output allows us to summarize output activity and to compare the output of one period with that of another.**

GDP vs. GNP. The concept of GDP is of relatively recent use in U.S. national-income accounts. Prior to 1992, most U.S. statistics focused on gross *national* product of G*N*P. **Gross *national* product refers to the output produced by American-owned factors of production regardless of where they're located.** **Gross *domestic* product refers to output produced within America's borders.** Thus, GNP would include some output from an Apple computer factory in Singapore but exclude some of the output produced by a Honda factory in Ohio. In an increasingly global economy, where factors of production and ownership move easily across international borders, the calculations of GNP became ever more complex. It also became a less dependable measure of the nation's economic health. **GDP is geographically focused, including all output produced within a nation's borders regardless of whose factors of production are used to produce it.** Apple's output in Singapore ends up in Singapore's GDP; the cars produced at Honda's Ohio plant are counted in America's GDP.

International Comparisons. The geographic focus of GDP facilitates international comparisons of economic activity. Is Japan's output as large as that of the United States? How could you tell? Japan produces a different mix of output than we do, making *quantity*-based comparisons difficult. We can compare the *value* of output produced in each country, however. The World View, "Comparative Output" in Chapter 2, shows that the value of America's GDP is nearly 2.5 times larger than Japan's.

GDP per Capita. International comparisons of total output are even more vivid in *per capita terms*. **GDP per capita relates the total value of annual output to the number of people who share that output; it refers to the average GDP per person.** In 2001, America's total GDP of $10 trillion was shared by 280 million citizens. Hence, our average, or *per capita,* GDP was nearly $36,000. By contrast, the average GDP for the entire world's inhabitants was only $7,500. In these terms, America's position as the richest country in the world clearly stands out.

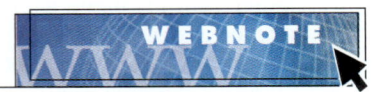

GDP per capita: Total GDP divided by total population; average GDP.

Statistical comparisons of GDP across nations are abstract and lifeless. They do, however, convey very real differences in the way people live. The accompanying World View examines some everyday realities of living in a poor nation, compared with a rich nation. Disparities in per capita GDP mean that people in low-income countries have little access to telephones, televisions, paved roads, or schools. They also die a lot younger than do people in rich countries.

But even the World View fails to fully convey how tough life is for people at the *bottom* of the income distribution in both poor and rich nations. Per capita GDP isn't a measure of what every citizen is getting. In the United States, millions of individuals have access to far more goods and services than our average per capita GDP, while millions of others must get by with much less. Although per capita GDP in Kuwait is three times larger than that of Brazil's, we can't conclude that the typical citizen of Kuwait is three times as well off as the typical Brazilian. The only thing these figures tell us is that the average Kuwaiti *could have* almost three times as many goods and services each year as the average Brazilian *if* GDP were distributed in the same way in both countries. **Measures of per capita GDP tell us nothing about the way GDP is actually distributed or used: they're only a statistical average.** When countries are quite similar in structure, institutions, and income distribution, however—or when historical comparisons are made within a country—per capita GDP can be viewed as a rough-and-ready measure of relative standards of living.

WEBNOTE

Global data on per capita incomes and other social indicators are available from the United Nations at www.un.org/depts/unsd/social/inc-eco.htm.

WORLD VIEW

Global Inequalities

The 2.5 billion residents of the world's low-income nations have comparatively few goods and services. Their average income (per capita GDP) is only $2,000 a year, a *fourteenth* of the average income in high-income nations such as the United States, Japan, and Germany. It's not just a colossal *income* disparity; it's also a disparity in the quality and even the duration of life. Some examples:

Source: World Bank, *World Development Report, 2000/2001* and 2002. www.worldbank.org

Analysis: Hidden behind dry statistical comparisons of per capita GDP lie very tangible and dramatic differences in the way people live. Low GDP per capita reflects a lot of deprivation.

Measurement Problems

Nonmarket Activities. Although the methods for calculating GDP and per capita GDP are straightforward, they do create a few problems. For one thing, our GDP measures exclude most goods and services that are *produced* but not *sold* in the market. This may appear to be a trivial point, but it isn't. Vast quantities of output never reach the market. For example, the homemaker who cleans, washes, gardens, shops, and cooks definitely contributes to the output of goods and services. Because she's not paid a market wage for these services, however, her efforts are excluded from the calculation.

of GDP. At the same time, we do count the efforts of those workers who sell identical homemaking services in the marketplace. This seeming contradiction is explained by the fact that a homemaker's services aren't sold in the market and therefore carry no explicit, market-determined value.

The exclusion of homemakers' services from the GDP accounts is particularly troublesome when we want to compare living standards over time or between countries. In the United States, for example, women have demonstrated an increasing tendency to hire domestic help and leave the house to find outside employment. As a result, much housework and child care that were previously excluded from GDP statistics (because they were unpaid family help) are now included (because they're done by paid help). In this respect, our historical GDP figures may exaggerate improvements in our standard of living.

Homemaking services aren't the only output excluded. If a friend helps you with your homework, the services never get into the GDP accounts. But if you hire a tutor or engage the services of a term paper-writing agency, the transaction becomes part of GDP. Here again, the problem is simply that we have no way to determine how much output was produced until it enters the market and is purchased.[1]

Unreported Income. The GDP statistics also fail to capture market activities that aren't reported to tax or census authorities. Many people work "off the books," getting paid in unreported cash. This so-called underground economy is motivated by tax avoidance and the need to conceal illegal activities. Although illegal activities capture most of the headlines, tax evasion on income earned in otherwise legal pursuits accounts for most of the underground economy. The Internal Revenue Service estimates that over two-thirds of underground income comes from legitimate wages, salaries, profits, interest, and pensions that simply aren't reported. As the accompanying News indicates, unreported income is particularly common in the service sector. People who mow lawns, clean houses, paint walls, or provide childcare services are apt to get paid in cash that isn't reported. The volume of such mundane transactions greatly exceeds the underground income generated by drug dealers, prostitutes, or gambling.

Value Added

Not every reported market transaction gets included at full value in GDP statistics. If it did, the same output would get counted over and over. The problem here is that the production of goods and services typically involves a series of distinct stages. Consider the production of a bagel, for example. For a bagel to reach Einstein's or some other bagel store, the farmer must grow some wheat, the miller must convert it to flour, and the baker must make bagels with it. Table 5.2 illustrates this chain of production.

Notice that each of the four stages of production depicted in Table 5.2 involves a separate market transaction. The farmer sells to the miller (stage 1), the miller to the baker (stage 2), the baker to the bagel store (stage 3), and finally, the store to the consumer. If we added up the separate value of each market transaction, we'd come to the conclusion that $1.75 of output had been produced. In fact, though, only one bagel has been produced, and it's worth only 75 cents. Hence, we should increase GDP—the value of output—only by 75 cents.

To get an accurate measure of GDP we must distinguish between *intermediate* goods and *final* goods. **Intermediate goods** are goods purchased for use as input in further stages of production. Final goods are the goods produced at the end of the production sequence, for use by consumers (or other market participants).

We can compute the value of *final* output in one of two ways. The easiest way would be to count only market transactions entailing final sales (stage 4 in Table 5.2). To do this, however, we'd have to know who purchased each good or service in order to know when we had reached the end of the process. Such a calculation would

intermediate goods: Goods or services purchased for use as input in the production of final goods or in services.

---

[1] The U.S. Commerce Department does, however, *estimate* the value of some nonmarket activities (e.g., food grown by farmers for their own consumption, the rental value of homeownership) and includes such estimates in GDP calculations.

TABLE 5.2
Value Added in Various Stages of Production

The value added at each stage of production represents a contribution to total output. Value added equals the market value of a product minus the cost of intermediate goods.

Stages of Production	Value of Transaction	Value Added
1. Farmer grows wheat, sells it to miller	$0.12	$0.12
2. Miller converts wheat to flour, sells it to baker	0.28	0.16
3. Baker bakes bagel, sells it to bagel store	0.60	0.32
4. Bagel store sells bagel to consumer	0.75	0.15
Total	$1.75	$0.75

also exclude any output produced in stages 1, 2, and 3 in Table 5.2 but not yet reflected in stage 4.

Another way to calculate GDP is to count only the **value added** at each stage of production. Consider the miller, for example. He doesn't really contribute $0.28 worth of production to total output, but only $0.16. The other $0.12 reflected in the price of his flour represents the contribution of the farmer who grew the wheat. By the same token, the baker *adds* only $0.32 to the value of output, as part of his output was purchased from the miller. By considering only the value *added* at each stage of production, we eliminate double counting. We don't count twice the *intermediate* goods and services that producers buy from other producers, which are then used as inputs. As Table 5.2 confirms, we can determine that value of final output by summing up the value added at each stage of production. (Note that $0.75 is also the price of a bagel.)

Although prices are a convenient measure of market value, they can also distort perceptions of real output. Imagine what would happen to our calculations of GDP if all

value added: The increase in the market value of a product that takes place at each stage of the production process.

Real vs. Nominal GDP

IN THE NEWS

A Lot Going On under the Table

- Percentage of households making untaxed or unmeasured "underground" purchases: 83
- Estimated unreported income per person in 2000, excluding illegal activities: $4,300
- Percentage of unreported income from wages and salaries: 18
- Percentage of unreported income from capital gains: 13
- Unreported income as a percentage of GDP: 12
- Taxes lost from unreported income in 2000: $195 billion

The underground economy—transactions that are untaxed or unaccounted for in GDP—involves a lot more than nannies and drug deals.

	Estimated Percentage of Services Supplied by the Underground Economy
Lawn maintenance	90
Domestic help	83
Child care	49
Home repair/improvements	34
Laundry/sewing services	25
Appliance repair	17
Car repairs	13
Haircuts/beauty service	8
Catering	8

Data from University of Michigan Institute for Social Research, U.S. Department of Labor.

Source: U.S. Internal Revenue Service. www.irs.gov

Analysis: GDP statistics include only the value of reported market transactions. Unreported transactions in the underground economy can't be counted and may therefore distort perceptions of economic activity.

98 MEASURING MACRO OUTCOMES

prices were to double from one year to the next. Suppose, for example, that the price of oranges, as shown in Table 5.1, rose from $0.20 to $0.40, the price of bicycles to $100, and the price of rock concerts to $2 million each. How would such price changes after this year's GDP? Obviously, the price increases would double the *value* of final output. Measured GDP would rise from $1,400 million to $2,800 million.

Such a rise in GDP doesn't reflect an increase in the *quantity* of goods and services available to us. We're still producing the same quantities shown in Table 5.1; only the prices of those goods have changed. Hence, changes in GDP brought about by changes in the price level can give us a distorted view of economic activity. Surely we wouldn't want to assert that our standard of living had improved just because price increases raised measured GDP from $1,400 million to $2,800 million.

To distinguish increases in the quantity of goods and services from increases in their prices, we must construct a measure of GDP that takes into account price-level changes. We do so by distinguishing between *real* GDP and *nominal* GDP. **Nominal GDP** is the value of final output measured in *current* prices, whereas **real GDP** is the value of output measured in *constant* prices. To calculate real GDP, we adjust the market value of goods and services for changing prices.

Note, for example, that in Table 5.1 prices are unchanged as we go from last year to this year. In this case, prices in the marketplace are constant, and interyear comparisons of prices are simple. But if all prices double, the comparison becomes more complicated. If all prices doubled from last year to this year, this year's nominal GDP would rise to $2,800 million. But these price increases wouldn't alter the quantity of goods produced. In other words, *real* GDP, valued at constant prices, would remain at $1,400 million. Thus, the distinction between nominal and real GDP is important whenever the price level changes.

Because the price level changes every year, both real and nominal GDP are regularly reported. Nominal GDP is computed simply by adding the current dollar value of production. Real GDP is computed by making an adjustment for changes in prices from year to year.

Consider the GDP statistics for 1999 and 2000, as displayed in Table 5.3. The first row shows nominal GDP in each year: nominal GDP increased by $664 billion between 1999 and 2000 (row 2). This 7 percent increase looks very impressive. However, some of that gain was fueled by higher prices, not increased output. Row 3 indicates that the price level rose by 2 percent during that same period.

Row 4 in Table 5.3 adjusts the GDP comparison for the change in prices. We deflate the 2000 nominal GDP by factoring out the 2 percent price increase. Simple division is all we need to compute *real* GDP in 2000 as being $9,767 billion. Hence, *real* GDP increased by only $469 billion in 2000 (row 5), not by the larger inflation-exaggerated amount in row 2.

Notice in Table 5.3 that in 1999 real and nominal GDP are identical because we're using that year as the basis of comparison. We're comparing performance in 2000 to that of the 1999 **base period**. Real GDP can be expressed in the prices of a particular

nominal GDP: The value of final output produced in a given period, measured in the prices of that period (current prices).

real GDP: The value of final output produced in a given period, adjusted for changing prices.

base period: The time period used for comparative analysis; the basis for indexing, for example, of price changes.

TABLE 5.3
Computing Real GDP
Real GDP is the inflation-adjusted value of nominal GDP. Between 1999 and 2000, nominal GDP increased by $664 billion (row 2). Some of this gain was due to rising prices (row 3). After adjusting for inflation, real GDP increased only by $469 billion (row 5).

	1999	2000
1. Nominal GDP (in billions)	$9,299	$9,963
2. Change in nominal GDP		+$664
3. Change in price level, 1999 to 2000		2.0%
4. Real GDP in 1999 dollars	$9,299	$9,767 $\left(=\dfrac{\$9,963}{1.02}\right)$
5. Change in real GDP		+$469

year; that year serves as the base for computing price-level and output changes. The general formula for computing real GDP is

$$\text{Real GDP in year } t = \frac{\text{nominal GDP in year } t}{\text{price index}}$$

The price index shows how average prices have changed between the base year and year t. Between 1999 and 2000, average prices rose 2 percent. This price-level change is indexed as 1.02. Thus, real GDP in 2000 is calculated as

$$\text{Real GDP in 2000 (1999 prices)} = \frac{\$9{,}963 \text{ billion}}{1.02} = \$9{,}767 \text{ billion}$$

This is the figure shown in row 4, Table 5.3.

The distinction between nominal and real GDP becomes critical when more distant years are compared. Between 1933 and 2000, for example, prices rose by 1,300 percent. Table 5.4 shows how such price-level changes can distort our views of how living

Find out how much real GDP fell per year during the Great Depression (1929–40) at www.bea.doc.gov/bea/dn/0898nip3/table1.htm.

TABLE 5.4

Real vs. Nominal GDP: An Historical View

Suppose we want to determine how much better off the average American was in 2000, as measured in terms of new goods and services, than people were during the Great Depression. To do this, we'd compare GDP per capita in 2000 with GDP per capita in 1933. The following data make that comparison.

	GDP	Population	Per Capita GDP
1933	$ 56 billion	126 million	$ 444
2000	9,963 billion	280 million	35,582

In 1933, the nation's GDP of $56 billion was shared by 126 million Americans, yielding a *per capita* GDP of $444. By contrast, GDP in 2000, was roughly 178 times larger, at $9,963 billion. This vastly larger GDP was shared by 280 million people, giving us a per capita GDP of $35,582. Hence, it would appear that our standard of living in 2000 was 80 times higher than the standard of 1933.

But this increase in *nominal* GDP vastly exaggerates our material well-being. The average price of goods and services—the *price level*—increased by 1,300 percent between 1933 and 2000. The goods and services you might have bought for $1 in 1933 cost $14 in 2000. In other words, we needed a lot more dollars in 2000 to buy any given combination of real goods and services.

To compare our *real* GDP in 2000 with the real GDP of 1933, we have to adjust for this tremendous jump in prices (inflation). We do so by measuring both years' output in terms of *constant* prices. Since prices went up, on average, fourteenfold between 1933 and 2000, we simply divide the 2000 *nominal* output by 14. The calculation is

$$\text{Real GDP in 2000 (1933 prices)} = \text{nominal 2000 GDP} \times \frac{\text{1933 price level}}{\text{2000 price level}}$$

By arbitrarily setting the level of prices in 1933 at 100 and noting that prices have increased fourteenfold since then, we can calculate

$$\text{Real GDP in 2000 (1933 prices)} = \$9{,}963 \text{ billion} \times \frac{100}{1{,}400}$$
$$= \$712 \text{ billion}$$

With a population of 280 million, this left us with real GDP per capita of $2,543 in 2000—as measured in 1933 dollars. This was more than nearly six times the *real* per capita GDP of the depression ($444), but not nearly so great an increase as comparisons of *nominal* GDP suggest.

100 MEASURING MACRO OUTCOMES

standards have changed since the Great Depression: In *nominal* terms, our per capita income has risen a whopping 80 times over; in *real* terms, however, the income gain is a much less spectacular six times over.

Figure 5.1 shows how nominal and real GDP have changed in the last 20 years. Real GDP is calculated here on the basis of the level of prices prevailing in 1996. (Note that real and nominal GDP are identical in that year.) The dollar value of output produced each year has risen considerably faster than the quantity of output, reflecting persistent increases in the price level—that is, **inflation**.

Notice in particular that continuing inflation tends to obscure the actual *declines* in real output. Real GDP actually declined in 1982 and 1991, though nominal GDP kept rising. Although the *value* of final output continued to rise in those years, the actual production of goods and services was falling; nominal and real GDP moved in opposite directions.

Chain-Weighted Price Adjustments. Although the distinction between real and nominal GDP is critical in measuring the nation's economic health, the procedure for making inflation adjustments isn't perfect. When we use the prices of a specific year as the base for computing real GDP, we're implicitly freezing *relative* prices

> **Inflation:** An increase in the average level of prices of goods and services.

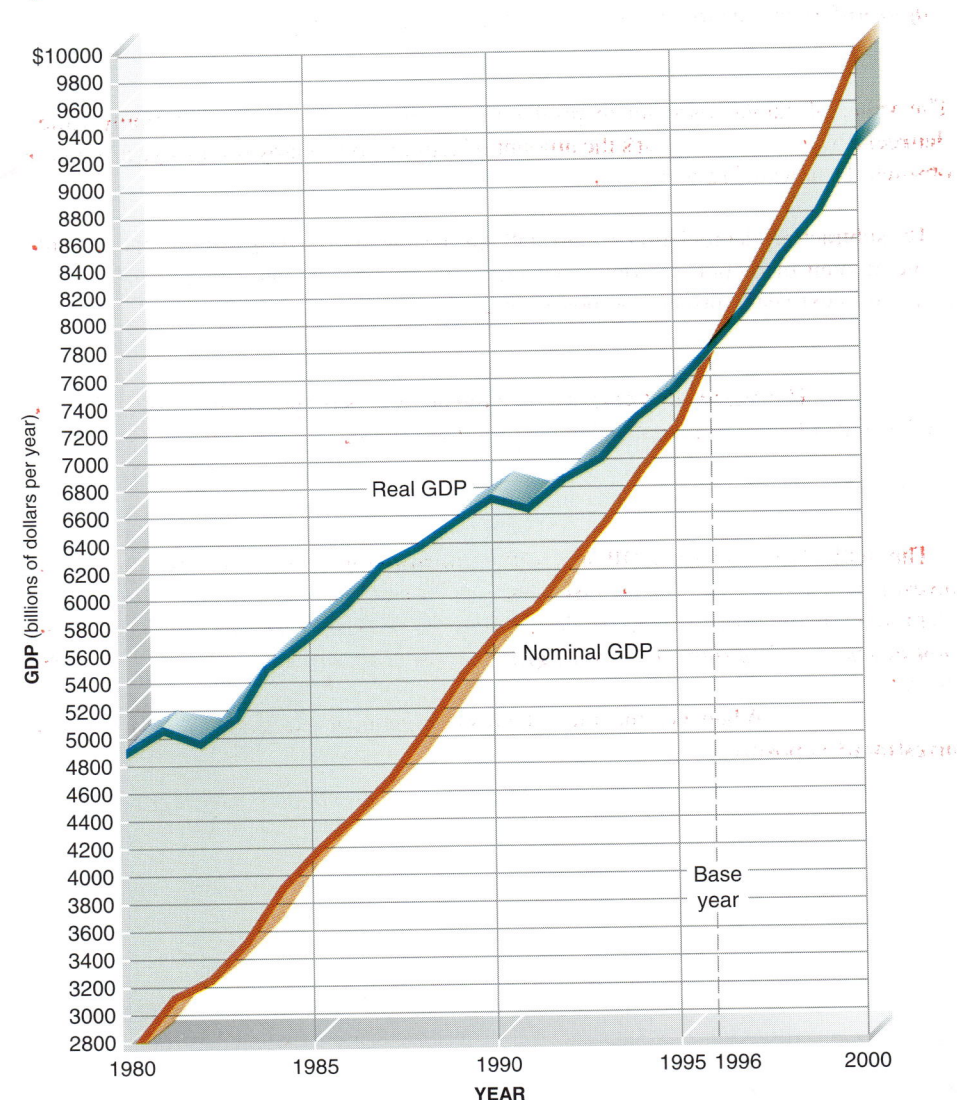

FIGURE 5.1
Changes in GDP: Nominal vs. Real

Increases in *nominal* GDP reflect higher prices as well as more output. Increases in *real* GDP reflect more output only. To measure these real changes, we must value each year's output in terms of common base prices. In this figure the reference year is 1996. Notice that *real* GDP declined in 1982 and 1991, although *nominal* GDP continued to rise. Nominal GDP rises faster than real GDP as a result of inflation.

Source: *Economic Report of the President, 2001.*

as well as *average* prices. Over time, however, relative prices can change markedly. Computer prices, for example, have fallen sharply in recent years in both absolute and relative terms. During the same period, unit sales of computers have increased by 20 to 25 percent a year. If we use the higher computer prices of 1996 to compute that sales growth, we'll greatly exaggerate the *value* of today's computer output. If we use today's prices, however, we'll underestimate the value of output in the period since 1996. To resolve this problem, the U.S. Department of Commerce uses a *chain-weighted* price index to compute real GDP. Instead of using the prices of a *single* base year to compute real GDP, chain-weighted indexes use a *moving average of price levels in consecutive years as an inflation adjustment*. When chain-weighted price adjustments are made, real GDP still refers to the inflation-adjusted value of GDP but isn't expressed in terms of the prices prevailing in any specific base year. All official estimates of real GDP are now based on chain-weighted price indexes.

Changes in real GDP from one year to the next tell us how much the economy's output is growing. Some of that growth, however, may come at the expense of future output. Recall that our **production possibilities** determine how much output we can produce. Those limits are, in turn, established by the availability of factors of production and technology. If we use up some of these resources to produce this year's output, future production possibilities may shrink. Next year we won't be able to produce as much output unless we replace factors of production we use this year.

We routinely use up plant and equipment (capital) in the production process. To maintain our production possibilities, therefore, we have to at least replace what we've used. The value of capital used up in producing goods and services is commonly called **depreciation**.[2] In principle, it's the amount of capital worn out by use in a year or made obsolete by advancing technology. In practice, the amount of capital depreciation is estimated by the U.S. Department of Commerce.

By subtracting depreciation from GDP we get **net domestic product (NDP)**. This is the amount of output we could consume without reducing our stock of capital and therewith next year's production possibilities.

The distinction between GDP and NDP has important implications for the mix of output. To maintain our production possibilities, we must at least replace the capital we consume. This means that at least some of each year's output must consist of newly produced plant and equipment—that is, **investment** goods. Indeed, our total production of new plant, equipment, and structures—that is, our gross investment—must at least match our depreciation. If we fail to allocate at least that much of our output to investment, our stock of capital and production possibilities will shrink.

The distinction between GDP and NDP is mirrored in a distinction between *gross* investment and *net* investment. **Gross investment** is positive as long as some new plant and equipment are being produced. But the stock of capital—the total collection of plant and equipment—won't grow unless gross investment exceeds depreciation. That is, the *flow* of new capital must exceed depreciation, or our *stock* of capital will decline. Whenever the rate of gross investment exceeds depreciation, net investment is positive.

Notice that net investment can be negative as well; in such situations we're wearing out plant and equipment faster than we're replacing it. When net investment is negative, our capital stock is shrinking. This was the situation during the period 1932–34 for the U.S. economy. Gross investment fell so sharply (see front endpaper of book) that it wasn't even replacing used-up machinery and structures. As a result, the economy's ability to produce goods and services declined.

If you want to see some great charts on GDP and other economic statistics, visit The Dismal Scientist website at www.economy.com/dismal/ or the Economist at http://www.economist.com/markets/indicators/index.cfm

Net Domestic Product

production possibilities: The alternative combinations of final goods and services that could be produced in a given time period with all available resources and technology.

depreciation: The consumption of capital in the production process; the wearing out of plant and equipment.

net domestic product (NDP): GDP less depreciation.

investment: Expenditures on (production of) new plant, equipment, and structures (capital) in a given time period, plus changes in business inventories.

gross investment: Total investment expenditure in a given time period.

net investment: Gross investment less depreciation.

---

[2]The terms *depreciation* and *capital consumption allowance* are used interchangeably. The depreciation charges firms commonly make, however, are determined in part by income tax regulations and thus may not accurately reflect the amount of capital consumed.

THE USES OF OUTPUT

The role of investment in maintaining or expanding our production possibilities helps focus attention on the uses to which GDP is put. It's not just the total value of annual output that matters, its also the use that we make of that output. **The GDP accounts also tell us what mix of output we've selected, that is, society's answer to the core issue of WHAT to produce.**

Consumption

The major uses of total output conform to the four sets of market participants we encountered in Chapter 2, namely, consumers, business firms, government, and foreigners. Those goods and services used by households are called *consumption goods* and range all the way from doughnuts to online computer services and include all goods and services households purchase in product markets. As we observed in Chapter 2, all this consumer spending claims two-thirds of our annual output (see Figure 2.3).

Investment

Investment goods represent another use of GDP. Investment goods are the plant, machinery, and equipment we produce. Net changes in business inventories and expenditures for residential construction are also counted as investment. To produce any of these investment goods, we must use scarce resources that could be used to produce something else. Resources used to produce buildings or machinery can't simultaneously be used to produce television sets or video disks (opportunity costs again). Investment spending claims more than a sixth of our total output.

Government Spending

The third major uses of GDP is the *public sector*. Federal, state, and local governments purchase resources to police the streets, teach classes, write laws, and build highways. The resources purchased by the government sector are unavailable for either consumption or investment purposes. At present, government spending on goods and services (*not* income transfers) claims less than one-fifth of total output.

Net Exports

Finally, remember that some of the goods and services we produce each year are used abroad rather than at home. That is, we **export** some of our output to other countries, for whatever use they care to make of it. Thus, GDP—the value of output produced—will be larger than the sum of our own consumption, investment, and government purchases to the extent that we succeed in exporting goods and services.

exports: Goods and services sold to international buyers.

We **import** goods and services as well. A flight to London on British Air is an imported service; a Jaguar is an imported good. These goods and services aren't part of America's GDP since they weren't produced within our borders (even though Jaguar is owned by Ford, the cars are produced in England). In principle, these imports never enter the GDP accounts. In practice, however, it's difficult to distinguish imports from domestic-made products, especially when goods include value added from both foreign and domestic producers. Over one-fifth of the 1995 Ford Contour, for example, consisted of parts manufactured in Japan, Mexico, Thailand, Britain, Spain, and Germany; final assembly took place in Kansas City. Should that car be counted as an "American" product or as an import? Rather than try to sort out all these products and parts, the U.S. Commerce Department simply subtracts the value of all imports from the value of total spending. Thus, exports are *added* to GDP and *imports* are subtracted. The difference between the two expenditure flows is called **net exports**.

imports: Goods and services purchased from international sources.

net exports: The value of exports minus the value of imports.

What we end up with is a simple method for computing GDP. **The value of GDP can be computed by adding up the expenditures of market participants.** Specifically, we note that

$$GDP = C + I + G + (X - IM)$$

where C = consumption expenditure
I = investment expenditure
G = government expenditure
X = exports
IM = imports

This approach to GDP accounting emphasizes the fact that all the output produced in the economy is claimed by someone. If we know who's buying our output, we know how much was produced and what uses were made of it.

MEASURES OF INCOME

There's another way of looking at GDP. Instead of looking at who's *buying* our output, we can look at who's *being paid* to produce it. Like markets themselves, GDP accounts have two sides: One side focuses on expenditure (the demand side), the other side focuses on income (the supply side).

We've already observed (see Figure 3.1) that every market transaction involves an *exchange* of dollars for a good or resource. Moreover, the *value* of each good or resource is measured by the amount of money exchanged for it (its market price). Hence, the total value of market incomes must equal the total value of final output, or GDP. In other words, one person's expenditure always represents another person's income.

Figure 5.2 illustrates the link between spending on output and incomes. This is a modified version of the circular flow we saw in Chapter 3. The spending that flows into the product market gets funneled into the factor market when resources are employed to produce the goods people want. The expenditure then flows into the hands of business owners, workers, landlords, and other resource owners. With the exception of sales taxes and depreciation, all spending on output becomes income to factors of production.

The equivalence of output and income isn't dependent on any magical qualities possessed by money. Were we to produce only one product—say, wheat—and pay everyone in bushels and pecks, total income would still equal total output. People couldn't receive in income more wheat than we produced. On the other hand, all the wheat produced would go to *someone*. Hence, one could say that the production possibilities of the economy define the limits to real income. The amount of income actually generated in any year depends on the production and expenditure decisions of consumers, firms, and government agencies.

Table 5.5 shows the actual flow of output and income in the U.S. economy during 2000. Total output is made up of the familiar components of GDP: consumption, investment, government goods and services, and net exports. The figures on the left side of Table 5.5 indicate that consumers spent $6,757 billion, businesses spent $1,833 billion on plant and equipment, governments spent $1,744 billion, and net imports were $371 billion. Our total output value (GDP) was thus nearly $10 trillion in 2000.

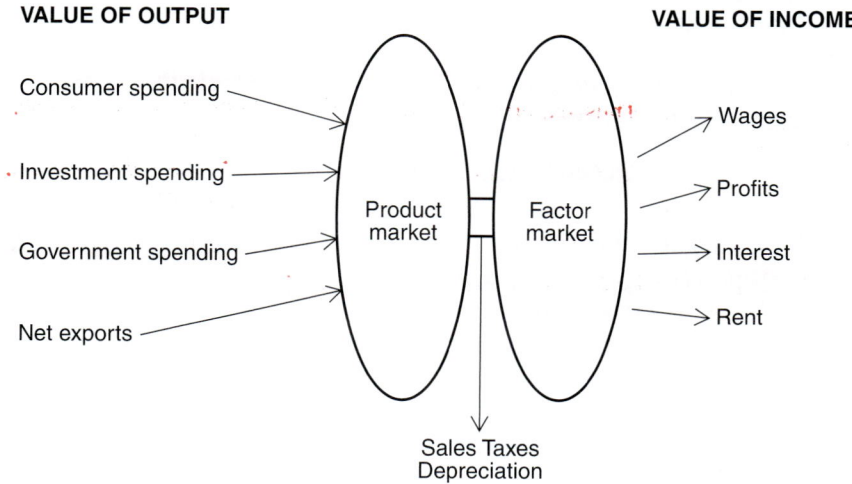

FIGURE 5.2

Output = Income

All the spending that establishes the value of output also determines the value of incomes. With minor exceptions, the market value of incomes must equal the market value of output.

TABLE 5.5
The Equivalence of Expenditure and Income (in billions of dollars)

The value of total expenditure must equal the value of total income. Why? Because every dollar spent on output becomes a dollar of income for someone.

Expenditure		Income	
Consumer goods and services	$6,757	Wages and salaries	$5,638
Investment in plant, equipment, and inventory	1,833	Corporate profits	946
		Proprietors' income	688
		Farm income	22
Government goods and services	1,744	Rents	140
		Interest	567
Exports	1,097	Sales taxes	770
Imports	(1,468)	Depreciation	1,257
		Less statistical discrepancy	(65)
Total value of output	$9,963	Total value of income	$9,963

Source: U.S. Department of Commerce (2000 data).

The right-hand side of Table 5.5 indicates who received the income generated from these markets transactions. Every dollar spent on goods and services provides income to someone. It may go to a worker (as wage or salary) or to a business firm (as profit and depreciation allowance). It may go to a landlord (as rent), to a lender (as interest), or to government (as sales or property tax). None of the dollars spent on goods and services disappears into thin air.

National Income

Although it may be exciting to know that we collectively received $10 trillion of income in 2000, it might be of more interest to know who actually got all that income. After all, in addition to the 280 million pairs of outstretched palms among us, millions of businesses and government agencies were also competing for those dollars and the goods and services they represent. By charting the flow of income through the economy, we can see FOR WHOM our output was produced.

Depreciation. Our annual income flow originated in product-market sales. Purchases of final goods and services create a flow of income to producers and, through them, to factors of production. But a major diversion of sales revenues occurs immediately, as a result of depreciation charges made by businesses. As we noted earlier, some of our capital resources are used up in the process of production. For the most part, these resources are owned by business firms that expect to be compensated for such investments. Accordingly, they regard some of the sales revenue generated in product markets as reimbursement for wear and tear on capital plant and equipment. They therefore subtract *depreciation charges* from gross revenues in calculating their incomes. Depreciation charges reduce GDP to the level of NDP before any income is available to current factors of production. As we saw earlier,

$$NDP = GDP - depreciation$$

Indirect Business Taxes. Another major diversion of the income flow occurs at its point of origin. When goods are sold in the marketplace, their purchase price is typically encumbered with some sort of sales tax. Thus, some of the revenue generated in product markets disappears before any factor of production gets a chance to claim it. These *indirect business taxes*, as they're called, aren't considered part of national income because they don't represent payment to factors of production. But they do account for a large part of the income spent in the marketplace.

Net Foreign Factor Income. Finally, we must remember that some of the income generated in product markets belongs to foreigners. Wages, interest, and profits paid to foreigners are not part of U.S. income. So we need to subtract that outflow.

Recall also that U.S. citizens own factors of production employed in other nations (e.g., a Ford plant in Mexico; a McDonald's outlet in Singapore). This creates an *inflow* of income to U.S. households. To make the transition of total U.S. output to total U.S. income, we must add back in the net inflow of foreign factor income.

Once depreciation charges and indirect business taxes are subtracted from GDP and net foreign factor income added, we're left with **national income (NI)**, which is the total income earned by U.S. factors of production. Thus,

NI = NDP − indirect business taxes + net foreign factor income

As Table 5.6 illustrates, our national income in 2000 was $8,002 billion, nearly $2 trillion less than GDP.

National income is the income earned not only by households (consumers) but also by corporations. Theoretically, all the income corporations receive represents income for their owners—the households who hold stock in the corporations. But the flow of income through corporations to stockholders is far from complete. First, corporations may pay taxes on their profits. Accordingly, some of the income received on behalf of a corporation's stockholders goes into the public treasury rather than into private bank accounts. Second, corporate managers typically find some urgent need for cash. As a result, part of the profits are retained by the corporation rather than passed on to the stockholders in the form of dividends. Accordingly, both *corporate taxes* and *retained earnings* must be subtracted from national income before we can determine how much income flows into the hands of consumers.

Still another deduction must be made for *Social Security taxes*. Nearly all people who earn a wage or salary are required by law to pay Social Security "contributions." In 2002, the Social Security tax rate for workers was 7.65 percent of the first $84,900 of earnings received in the year. Workers never see this income because it is withheld

national income (NI): Total income earned by current factors of production: GDP less depreciation and indirect business taxes, plus net foreign factor income.

Personal Income

Income Flow	Amount (in billions)
Gross domestic product (GDP)	$9,963
Less depreciation	(1,257)
Net domestic product (NDP)	8,706
Less indirect business taxes	(770)
Plus net foreign factor income	(4)
Less statistical discrepancy	70
National income (NI)	8,002
Less corporate taxes	(284)
Less retained earnings*	(244)
Less Social Security taxes	(827)
Plus transfer payments	1,068
Plus net interest	567
Personal income (PI)	8,282
Less personal taxes	(1,292)
Disposable income (DI)	6,990

*Retained earnings are net of inventory valuation changes and depreciation.
Source: U.S. Department of Commerce.

TABLE 5.6
The Flow of Income, 2000
The revenue generated from market transactions passes through many hands. Households end up with disposable income equal to about 70 percent of GDP, after depreciation and taxes are taken out and net interest and transfer payments are added back in. Disposable income is either spent (consumption) or saved by households.

personal income (PI): Income received by households before payment of personal taxes.

by employers and sent directly to the U.S. Treasury. Thus, the flow of national income is reduced considerably before it becomes **personal income (PI),** the amount of income received by households before payment of personal taxes.

Not all of our adjustments to national income are negative. Households receive income in the form of transfer payments from the public treasury. More than 45 million people receive monthly Social Security checks, for example, and another 20 million receive some form of public welfare. These income transfers represent income for the people who receive them. People also receive interest payments in excess of those they pay (largely because of interest payments on the government debt). This *net* interest is another source of personal income. Accordingly, our calculation of personal income is as follows:

- *National income* (= income earned by factors of production)
  less corporate taxes
  retained earnings
  Social Security taxes
  plus transfer payments
  net interest
- *Equals* **personal income** (= income received by households)

The total flow of income generated in production is significantly reduced before it gets into the hands of individual households. But we haven't yet reached the end of the reduction process. We have to set something aside for personal income taxes. To be sure we don't forget about our obligations, Uncle Sam and his state and local affiliates usually arrange to have their share taken off the top. Personal income taxes are withheld by the employer, who thus acts as a tax collector. Accordingly, to calculate **disposable income (DI),** which is the amount of income consumers may themselves spend (dispose of), we reduce personal income by the amount of personal taxes:

disposable income (DI): After-tax income of households; personal income less personal taxes.

$$\text{Disposable income} = \text{personal income} - \text{personal taxes}$$

Disposable income is the end of the accounting line. As Table 5.6 shows, households end up with roughly 70 percent of the revenues generated from final market sales (GDP). Once consumers get this disposable income in their hands, they face two choices. They may choose to *spend* their disposable income on consumer goods and services. Or they may choose to *save* it. These are the only two choices in GDP accounting. Saving, in this context, simply refers to disposable income that isn't spent on consumption. In the analysis of income and saving flows, we don't care whether savings are hidden under a mattress, deposited in the bank, or otherwise secured. All we want to know is whether disposable income is spent or not. Thus, all disposable income is, by definition, either consumed or saved; that is,

saving: That part of disposable income not spent on current consumption; disposable income less consumption.

$$\text{Disposable income} = \text{consumption} + \text{saving}$$

For the latest data on GDP and its components visit the Bureau of Economic Analysis at www.bea.doc.gov.

THE FLOW OF INCOME

Figure 5.3 summarizes the relationship between expenditure and income. The essential point again is that every dollar spent on goods and services flows into somebody's hands. Thus, *the dollar value of output will always equal the dollar value of income.* Specifically, total income (GDP) ends up distributed in the following way:

- To *households,* in the form of disposable income.
- To *business,* in the form of retained earnings and depreciation allowances.
- To *government,* in the form of taxes.

Income and Expenditure

The annual flow of income to households, businesses, and government is part of a continuing process. Households rarely stash their disposable income under the mattress;

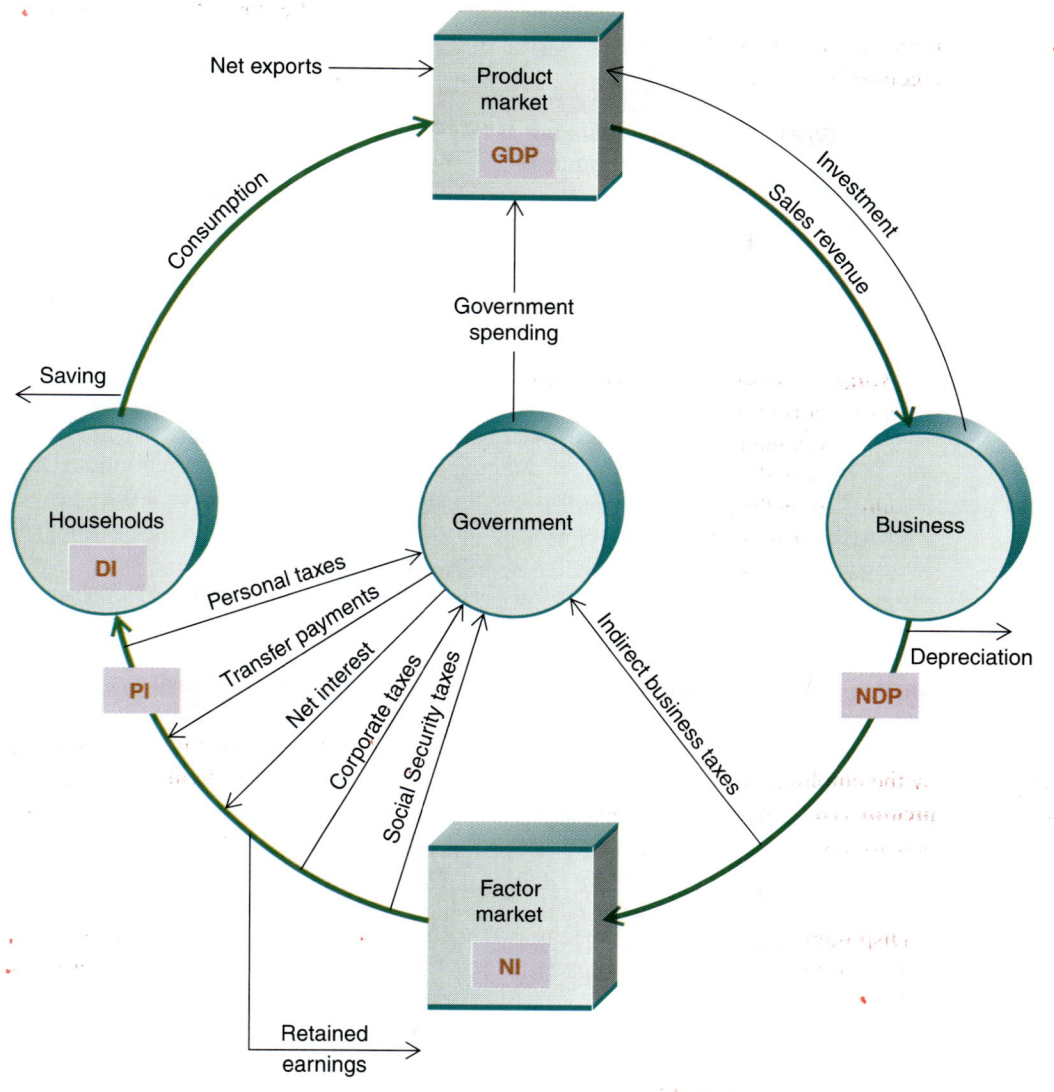

FIGURE 5.3
The Circular Flow of Spending and Income

GDP represents the dollar value of final output sold in the product market. The revenue stream flowing from GDP works its way through NDP, NI, and PI before reaching households in the form of smaller DI. DI is in turn either spent or saved by consumers. This consumption, plus investment, government spending, and net exports, continues the circular flow.

they spend most of it on consumption. This spending adds to GDP in the next round of activity, thereby helping to keep the flow of income moving.

Business firms also have a lot of purchasing power tied up in retained earnings and depreciation charges. This income, too, may be recycled—returned to the circular flow—in the form of business investment.

Even the income that flows into public treasuries finds its way back into the marketplace, as government agencies hire police officers, soldiers, and clerks, or they buy goods and services. Thus, **the flow of income that starts with GDP ultimately returns to the market in the form of new consumption (C), investment (I), and government purchases (G)**. A new GDP arises, and the flow starts all over. In later chapters we examine in detail these *expenditure* flows, with particular emphasis on their ability to keep the economy producing at its full potential.

THE ECONOMY TOMORROW

The Quality of Life

Money, money, money—it seems that's all we talk about. Why don't we talk about important things like beauty, virtue, or the quality of life? Will the economy of tomorrow be filled with a glut of products but devoid of real meaning? Do the GDP accounts—either the expenditure side or the income side—tell us anything we really want to know about the quality of life? If no, why should we bother to examine them?

Intangibles

All the economic measures discussed in this chapter are important indexes of individual and collective welfare; they tell us something about how well people are living. They don't, however, capture the completeness of the way in which we view the world or the totality of what makes our lives satisfying. A clear day, a sense of accomplishment, even a smile can do more for a person's sense of well-being than can favorable movements in the GDP accounts. Or, as John Kenneth Galbraith put it, "In a rational lifestyle, some people could find contentment working moderately and then sitting by the street—and talking, thinking, drawing, painting, scribbling, or making love in a suitably discreet way. None of these requires an expanding economy."[3]

The emphasis on economic outcomes arises not from ignorance of life's other meanings but from the visibility of the economic outcomes. We all realize that well-being arises from both material and intangible pleasures, but the intangibles tend to be elusive. It's not easy to gauge individual happiness, much less to ascertain the status of our collective satisfaction. We have to rely on measures we can see, touch, and count. As long as the material components of our environment bear some positive relation to our well-being, they at least serve a useful purpose.

In some situations, however, more physical output may actually worsen our collective welfare. If increased automobile production raises congestion and pollution levels, the rise in GDP occasioned by those additional cars is a misleading index of society's welfare. In such a case, the rise in GDP might actually mask a *decrease* in the well-being of the population. We might also wonder whether more casinos, more prisons, more telemarketing, more divorce litigation, and more Prozac—all of which contribute to GDP growth—are really valid measures of our well-being (see cartoon). Exclusive emphasis on measurable output would clearly be a mistake in many cases.

What is true of automobile production might also be true of other outputs. Increased development of urban areas may cause a loss of social welfare if that development occurs at the expense of space, trees, and tranquillity. Increased mechanization on the farm may raise agricultural output but isolate and uproot farmers. So, too, increased productivity in factories and offices might contribute to a sense of alienation. These ill effects of increased output needn't occur; but if they do, indexes of output tell us less about social or individual well-being.

Index of Well-Being

Researchers at Fordham University devised an alternative index of well-being. Their Index of Social Health includes a few economic parameters (such as unemployment and weekly earnings) but puts more emphasis on sociological behavior (such as child abuse and teen suicides). They claim that this broader view points to stagnation in societal well-being over the past two decades, even though GDP was rising (see News.)

Even if the Index of Social Health is a valid gauge of our collective well-being, we shouldn't conclude that the national-income accounts are useless or irrelevant. These points help underscore the fact that *social welfare* and *economic welfare* aren't synonymous. The GDP accounts tell us whether our economic welfare has increased,

---

[3]Cited in Leonard Silk, *Nixonomics*, 2d ed. (New York: Praeger, 1973), p. 163.

Analysis: GDP includes *everything* produced and sold in the product market, no matter how much each good or service contributes to our social well-being.

as measured by the value of goods and services produced. They don't tell us how highly we value additional goods and services relative to nonmarket phenomena. Nor do they even tell us whether important social costs were incurred in the process of production. These judgments must be made outside the market; they're social decisions.

Finally, note that any given level of GDP can encompass many combinations of output. Choosing WHAT to produce is still a critical question, even after the goal of *maximum* production has been established. The quality of life in the economy tomorrow will depend on what specific mix of goods and services we include in GDP.

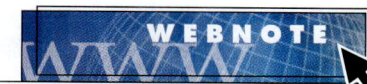

The United Nations has constructed a Human Development Index that offers a broader view of social well-being than GDP alone. For details and country rankings, visit www.undp.org. Also check the Genuine Progress Indicator at www.rprogress.org.

IN THE NEWS

America's Declining Social Health

National-income accounts are regularly reported and widely quoted. They do not, however, adequately reflect the nation's *social* performance. To measure more accurately the country's social health, a Fordham University team of social scientists has devised an Index of Social Health with 16 indicators, including infant mortality, drug abuse, health-insurance coverage, and poverty among the aged. According to this index, America's social health deteriorated sharply in the mid-1970s. The index of social health stayed flat in the 1980s and 1990s, despite a sustained rise in the nation's economy.

Source: Fordham Institute, *1998 Index of Social Health*, Tarrytown, NY.

Analysis: The national-income accounts emphasize material well-being. They are an important, but not complete, gauge of our societal welfare.

SUMMARY

- National-income accounting is the measurement of our annual output and income flows. The national-income accounts provide a basis for assessing our economic performance, designing public policy, and understanding how all the parts of the economy interact.
- The most comprehensive measure of our output is gross domestic product (GDP), the total market value of all final goods and services produced within a nation's borders during a given time period.
- In calculating GDP, we include only the value added at each stage of production. This procedure eliminates the possibility of the double counting that would result because business firms buy intermediate goods from other firms and include the associated costs in their selling price. For the most part, only marketed goods and services are included in GDP.
- To distinguish physical changes in output from monetary changes in its value, we compute both nominal and real GDP. Nominal GDP is the value of output expressed in *current* prices. Real GDP is the value of output expressed in *constant* prices (the prices of some *base* year).
- Each year some of our capital equipment is worn out in the process of production. Hence, GDP is larger than the amount of goods and services we could consume without reducing our production possibilities. The amount of capital used up each year is referred to as *depreciation*.
- By subtracting depreciation from GDP we derive net domestic product (NDP). The difference between NDP and GDP is also equal to the difference between *gross* investment—the sum of all our current plant and equipment expenditures—and *net* investment—the amount of investment over and above that required to replace wornout capital.
- All the income generated in market sales (GDP) is received by someone. The sequence of flows involved in this process is

    GDP
    less depreciation
    equals NDP
    less indirect business taxes
    plus net foreign factor income
    equals national income (NI)
    less corporate taxes,
        retained earnings, and
        Social Security taxes
    plus transfer payments and
        net interest
    equals personal income (PI)
    less personal income taxes
    equals disposable income (DI)

- The incomes received by households, business firms, and governments provide the purchasing power required to buy the nation's output. As that purchasing power is spent, further GDP is created and the circular flow continues.

Key Terms

national-income accounting
gross domestic product (GDP)
GDP per capita
intermediate goods
value added
nominal GDP
real GDP
base period

inflation
production possibilities
depreciation
net domestic product (NDP)
investment
gross investment
net investment

exports
imports
net exports
national income (NI)
personal income (PI)
disposable income (DI)
saving

Questions for Discussion

1. The manuscript for this book was typed by a friend. Had I hired a secretary to do the same job, GDP would have been higher, even though the amount of output would have been identical. Why is this? Does this make sense?
2. GDP in 1981 was $2.96 trillion. It grew to $3.07 trillion in 1982, yet the quantity of output actually decreased. How is this possible?
3. If gross investment is not large enough to replace the capital that depreciates in a particular year, is net investment greater or less than zero? What happens to our production possibilities?
4. Can we increase consumption in a given year without cutting back on either investment or government services? Under what conditions?

5. Why is it important to know how much output is being produced? Who uses such information?
6. How might the quality of life be adversely affected by an increase in GDP?
7. Is the Fordham Index of Social Health, discussed in The Economy Tomorrow, a better barometer of well-being than GDP? What are its relative advantages or disadvantages?

Web Activities

1. Access the U.S. Department of Commerce's Bureau of Economic Analysis at www.bea.doc.gov/bea/dn1.htm, and then access the most recent press release to find the dollar value of nominal GDP for the most recent quarter available. What was the GDP growth rate for that period? Break the number down into its four components: consumer spending, business investment, net exports, and government spending. Then estimate how much each component contributes to the overall growth rate. For example, if GDP has grown by 1 percent, how much of this growth can be attributed to the growth in consumer spending?
2. The United Nations Human Development Index (www.undp.org) ranks countries by GDP per capita and by "human development" based on health, education, and income. Access the most recent Human Development Index and find the U.S. ranking. Why isn't the U.S. ranked higher on this index? Where do we perform poorly? (*Hint:* Access the other reports and find the U.S. values for areas included in the Human Development Index.)
3. Graph the values of real and nominal GDP since 1990. What accounts for the difference in these two numbers? To find these numbers, log on to www.bea.doc.gov/bea/dn1.htm and access the most recent data on real and nominal GDP.

 ALERT! THE ACCOMPANYING STUDENT PROBLEM SET CONTAINS NUMERICAL AND GRAPHING PROBLEMS FOR THIS CHAPTER

Handwritten notes:

GDP − depreciation = ~~GDP~~ NDP − indirect business taxes + net foreign factor income = NI − corporate taxes − retained earnings − social security taxes + transfer payments and net interest = PI − personal income taxes = DI

GDP − Gross Domestic Product
~~GNP − Gross National Product~~
NI − National Income
PI − Personal Income
DI − Disposable Income

NDP − Net Domestic Product

CHAPTER 6

Unemployment

George H. had worked at the paper mill for 18 years. Now he was 37 years old, with a wife and three children. With his base salary of $38,200 and the performance bonus he received nearly every year, he was doing pretty well. He had his own home, two cars, company-paid health insurance for the family, and a growing nest egg in the company's pension plan. The H. family wasn't rich, but they were comfortable and secure.

Or so they thought. Overnight the H. family's comfort was shattered. Without warning, the paper mill was closed in February 1991. George H., along with 2,300 fellow workers, was permanently laid off. The weekly paychecks and the company-paid health insurance stopped immediately; the pension nest egg was in doubt. Within a few weeks, George H. was on the street looking for a new job—an experience he hadn't had since high school. The unemployment benefits the state provided didn't come close to paying the mortgage payment, groceries, insurance, and other necessities. And even those benefits soon ran out. The H. family quickly used up its savings, including the $5,000 they'd set aside for the children's college education.

George H. stayed unemployed for nearly two years. His wife found a part-time waitressing job, and his oldest son went to work rather than college. George himself ultimately found a warehousing job that paid only half as much as his previous job.

In the recession of 1990–91 nearly 2 *million* workers lost their jobs as companies "downsized," "restructured," or simply closed. Not all these displaced workers fared as badly as George H. and his family. But the job loss was a painful experience for every one of those displaced workers. That's the human side of an economic downturn.

The pain of joblessness is not confined to those who lose their jobs. In recessions, students discover that jobs are hard to find in the summer. In the recession of 2001, college graduates found out that jobs weren't waiting for them. No matter how good their grades were or how nice their résumés look, some graduates just didn't get any job offers. Those who did get job offers were dismayed when start dates were postponed—or the offer was rescinded. Even people with jobs feel some economic pain: Their paychecks shrink when hours or wages are scaled back.

In this chapter we take a closer look at the problem of unemployment, focusing on the following questions:

- When is a person "unemployed"?
- What are the costs of unemployment?
- What's an appropriate policy goal for "full employment"?

As we answer these questions, we'll develop a sense of why full employment is a major goal of macro policy and begin to see some of the obstacles we face in achieving it.

THE LABOR FORCE

To assess the dimensions of our unemployment problems, we first need to decide who wants a job. Millions of people are jobless, yet they're not part of our unemployment problem. Full-time students, young children playing with their toys, and older people living in retirement are all jobless. We don't expect them to be working, so we don't regard them as part of the unemployment problem. We're not concerned that *everybody* be put to work, only with ensuring jobs for all those persons who are ready and willing to work.

To distinguish between those people who want a job from those who don't, we separate the entire population into two distinct groups. One group consists of *labor-force participants;* the other group encompasses all *nonparticipants*.

The **labor force** includes everyone age 16 and older who is actually working plus all those who aren't working but are actively seeking employment. Individuals are also counted as employed in a particular week if their failure to work is due to vacation, illness, labor dispute (strike), or bad weather. All such persons are regarded as "with a job but not at work." Also, unpaid family members working in a family enterprise (farming, for example) are counted as employed. **People who are neither employed nor actively seeking work aren't counted as part of the labor force;** they're referred to as *nonparticipants*. As Figure 6.1 shows, only half the U.S. population participates in the labor force.

Note that our definition of labor-force participation excludes most household and volunteer activities. A woman who chooses to devote her energies to household responsibilities or to unpaid charity work isn't counted as part of the labor force, no

labor force: All persons age 16 and over who are either working for pay or actively seeking paid employment.

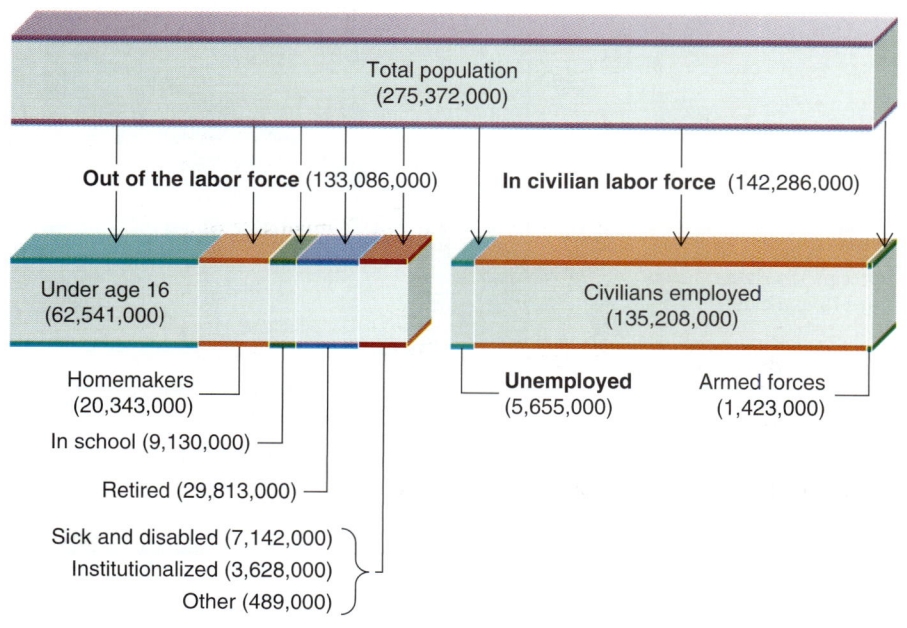

FIGURE 6.1
The Labor Force, 2000

Only half the total U.S. population participates in the civilian labor force. The rest of the population is too young, in school, at home, retired, or otherwise unavailable.

Unemployment statistics count only those participants who aren't currently working but are actively seeking paid employment. Nonparticipants are neither employed nor actively seeking employment.

Source: U.S. Bureau of Labor Statistics.

114 MEASURING MACRO OUTCOMES

matter how hard she works. Because she's neither in paid employment nor seeking such employment in the marketplace, she's regarded as outside the labor market (a nonparticipant). But if she decides to seek a paid job outside the home, we'd say that she's "entering the labor force." Students too are typically out of the labor force until they leave school. They "*enter*" the labor force when they go looking for a job, either during the summer or after graduation. People "*exit*" the labor force when they go back to school, return to household activities, go to prison, or retire. These entrants and exits keep changing the size and composition of the labor force.

Since 1960, the U.S. labor force has more than doubled in size. As Figure 6.2 indicates, this labor-force growth has come from two distinct sources: population growth and a rising **labor-force participation rate.** The U.S. population has increased by only 50 percent since 1960, just half as fast as the labor force. The difference is explained by the rapid increase in the labor-force participation of women. Notice in Figure 6.2 that only one out of three women participated in the labor force in 1950–60, whereas six out of ten now do so. The labor-force participation of men actually declined during the same period, even though it remains higher than that of women.

> **labor-force participation rate:** The percentage of the working-age population working or seeking employment.

Growth of Production Possibilities

The growth of the labor force has been an important source of the nation's economic growth. As we first saw in Chapter 1, the quantity of goods and services an economy can produce in any time period is limited by two factors:

- *Availability of factors of production.*
- *Our technological know-how.*

> **production possibilities:** The alternative combinations of final goods and services that could be produced in a given time period with all available resources and technology.

As the available labor force has grown, the nation's **production possibilities** curve has shifted outward, as in Figure 6.3. With those shifts has come an increased capacity for producing goods and services, the essence of long-run **economic growth.**

Institutional Constraints. We could grow the economy even faster if we used more labor and natural resources. But we've chosen to impose institutional constraints on resource exploitation. Child labor laws, for example, prohibit small children from working, no matter how much they or their parents yearn to contribute to total output. Yet we could produce more output this year if we put all those little bodies to work. In fact,

> **economic growth:** An increase in output (real GDP); an expansion of production possibilities.

FIGURE 6.2
A Growing Labor Force

The labor force expands as the population increases. A big increase in the participation rate of women has also added to labor-force growth.

Source: *Economic Report of the President, 2001.*

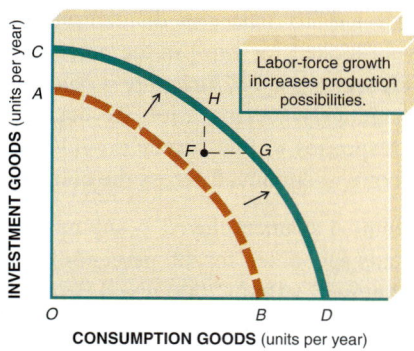

FIGURE 6.3
Labor-Force Growth

The amount of labor available for work—the *labor force*—is a prime determinant of a nation's production possibilities. As the labor force grows, so does the capacity to produce. To produce at capacity, however, the labor force must be fully employed. At point F, resources are unemployed.

we could produce a little more output this year if you were to put down this book and get a job. To the extent that small children, students, and others are precluded from working, both the size of our labor force (our *available* labor) and our potential output shrink.

Constraints are also imposed on the use of material resources and technology. We won't cut down all the forests this year and build everybody a wooden palace. We've collectively decided to preserve some natural habitat for owls and other endangered species. Therefore, the federal government limits each year's tree harvest on public lands. The federal government also restricts the use of nuclear technology. In both cases, the need for environmental protection constrains the use of resources or technology and limits annual output. These are *institutional* constraints on our productive capacity. Without such constraints, we could produce more output. Our production possibilities in any year therefore depend not only on what resources and technology are available but also on how we choose to restrict their use.

An expanding labor force not only increases our capacity to produce but also implies the need to keep creating new jobs. Even in the short run (with given resources and technology), we have to confront the issue of job availability.

We can't reach points beyond the production possibilities curve, but we can easily end up somewhere inside that curve, as at point F in Figure 6.3. When that happens, we're not producing at (short-run) capacity, and some available resources remain underused. **To make full use of available production capacity, the labor force must be fully employed.** If we fail to provide jobs for all labor-force participants, we end up with less than capacity output and the related problem of **unemployment.** As the labor force grows, the challenge of keeping all labor-force participants employed intensifies.

Okun's Law. Arthur Okun quantified the relationship between the production possibilities curve and unemployment. According to the original formulation of **Okun's Law,** each additional 1 percent of unemployment translated into a loss of 3 percent in real output. More recent estimates of Okun's Law put the ratio at about 1 to 2, largely due to the changing composition of both the labor force (more women and teenagers) and output (more services). Using that 2-to-1 ratio allows us to put a dollar value on the aggregate cost of unemployment. In 1992, high unemployment left us $240 billion short of our production possibilities. That output shortfall implied a loss of $920 of goods and services for every American.

MEASURING UNEMPLOYMENT

To determine how many people are actually unemployed, the U.S. Census Bureau surveys about 60,000 households each month. The Census interviewers first determine whether a person is employed—that is, worked for pay in the previous week (or didn't work due to illness, vacation, bad weather, or a labor strike). If the person isn't employed,

Unemployment

unemployment: The inability of labor-force participants to find jobs.

Okun's Law: 1 percent more unemployment is estimated to equal 2 percent less output.

The Unemployment Rate

unemployment rate: The proportion of the labor force that is unemployed.

Data on unemployment by race and gender from 1948 to the present are available from the Bureau of Labor Statistics at www.bls.gov.

he or she is either unemployed or out of the labor force. To make that distinction, the Census interviewers ask whether the person actively looked for work in the preceding four weeks. *If a person is not employed and actively seeking a job, he or she is counted as unemployed.* Individuals neither employed nor actively seeking a job are counted as outside the labor force (nonparticipants). The responses to this survey provide the basis for estimating the total number of people who are unemployed across the country.

In 2000, an average of 5.7 million persons were counted as unemployed in any month. As Figure 6.1 suggests, these unemployed individuals accounted for 4.0 percent of our total labor force. Accordingly, the average **unemployment rate** in 2000 was 4 percent.

$$\text{Unemployment rate} = \frac{\text{number of unemployed people}}{\text{labor force}}$$

The monthly unemployment figures indicate not only the total amount of unemployment in the economy but also which groups are suffering the greatest unemployment. Typically, teenagers just entering the labor market have the greatest difficulty finding (or keeping) jobs. They have no job experience and relatively few marketable skills. Employers are reluctant to hire them, especially if they must pay the federal minimum wage. As a consequence, teenage unemployment rates are typically three times higher than adult unemployment rates (see Figure 6.4).

Minority workers also experience above-average unemployment. Notice in Figure 6.4 that black and hispanic unemployment rates are much higher than white worker's unemployment rates.

FIGURE 6.4
Unemployment Isn't Experienced Equally by Race, Sex, or Education

Minority groups, teenagers, and less educated individuals experience higher rates of unemployment. Teenage unemployment rates are particularly high, especially for black and other minority youth.

Source: U.S. Department of Labor.

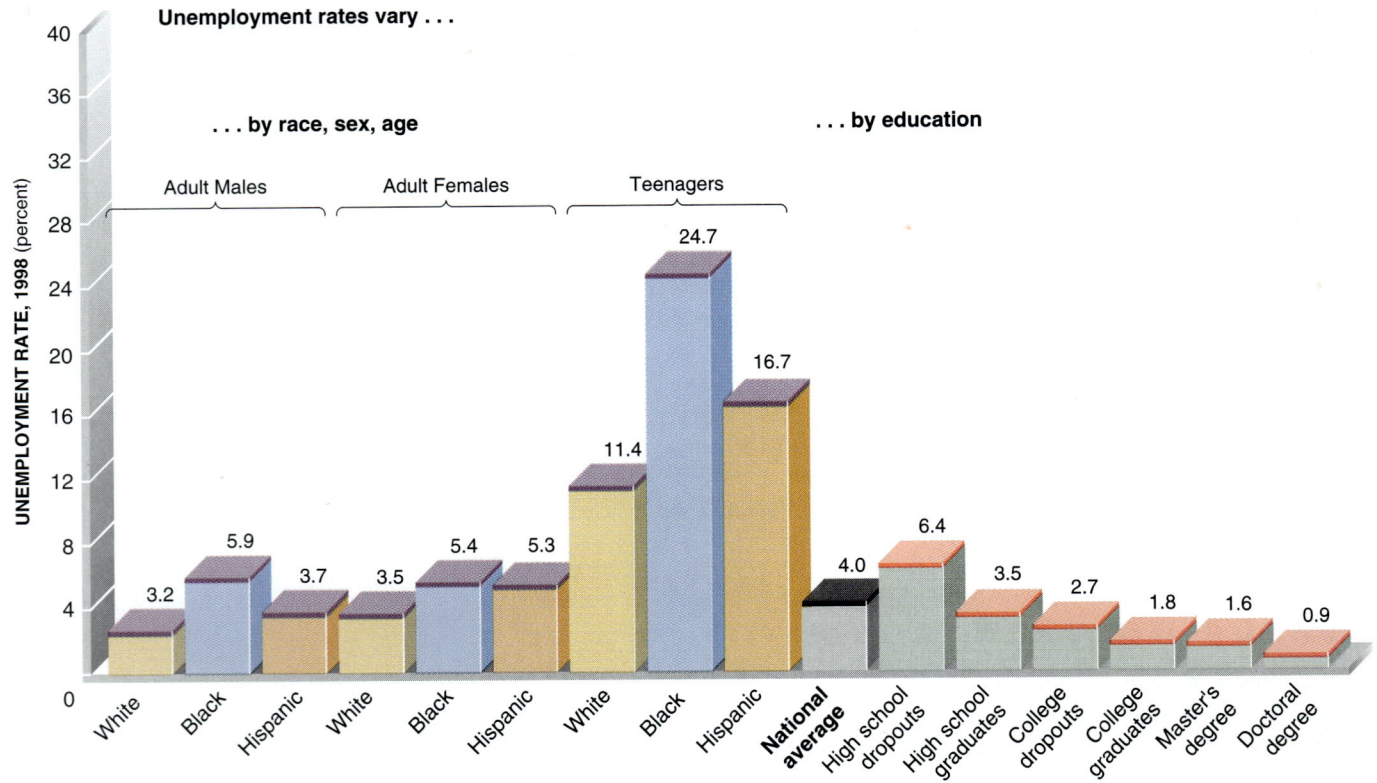

Education also affects the chances of being unemployed. If you graduate from college, your chances of being unemployed drop sharply, regardless of gender or race (Figure 6.4). Advancing technology and a shift to services from manufacturing have put a premium on better-educated workers. Very few people with master's or doctoral degrees stand in unemployment lines.

Although high school dropouts are more likely to be unemployed than college graduates, they don't *stay* unemployed. In fact, most people who become unemployed remain jobless for a relatively brief period of time. As Table 6.1 indicates, the median spell of unemployment in 2000 was six weeks. Less than one out of eight unemployed individuals had been jobless for as long as six months (27 weeks or longer). People who lose their jobs do find new ones. **When the economy is growing, both unemployment rates and the average duration of unemployment decline.** Recessions have the opposite effect—raising the costs of unemployment significantly.

The reason a person becomes unemployed also affects the length of time the person stays jobless. A person just entering the labor market might need more time to identify job openings and develop job contacts. By contrast, an autoworker laid off for a temporary plant closing can expect to return to work quickly. Figure 6.5 on the next page depicts these and other reasons for unemployment. In 2000, nearly half the unemployed were job losers (laid off or fired), and one in seven were job leavers (quit). The rest were new entrants (primarily teenagers) or reentrants (primarily mothers returning to the workforce). Like the duration of unemployment, the reasons for joblessness are very sensitive to economic conditions. In really bad years, most of the unemployed are job losers, and they remain out of work a long time.

Unemployment statistics don't tell the complete story about the human costs of a sluggish economy. When unemployment persists, job seekers become increasingly frustrated. After repeated rejections, job seekers often get so discouraged that they give up the search and turn to their families, friends, or public welfare for income support. When the Census Bureau interviewer asks whether they're actively seeking employment, such **discouraged workers** are apt to reply no. Yet they'd like to be working, and they'd probably be out looking for work if jobs prospects were better.

Discouraged workers aren't counted as part of our unemployment problem because they're technically out of the labor force. The Labor Department estimates that in 2000—a very good year for jobs—only 260,000 individuals fell into this uncounted class of discouraged workers. In years of high unemployment, this number jumps sharply.

Some people can't afford to be discouraged. Many people who become jobless have family responsibilities and bills to pay: They simply can't afford to drop out of the labor force. Instead, they're compelled to take some job—any job—just to keep body and soul together. The resultant job may be part-time or full-time and may pay very little.

The Duration of Unemployment

Reasons for Unemployment

Discouraged Workers

discouraged worker: An individual who isn't actively seeking employment but would look for or accept a job if one were available.

Underemployment

Duration	Percent of Unemployed
Less than 5 weeks	45.0
5 to 14 weeks	31.8
15 to 26 weeks	11.8
27 to 51 weeks	5.4
52 weeks or more	6.0

Source: U.S. Bureau of Labor Statistics (2000 data).

TABLE 6.1
Duration of Unemployment
The severity of unemployment depends on how long the spell of joblessness lasts. About one-third of unemployed workers return to work quickly, but many others remain unemployed for six months or longer.

FIGURE 6.5
Reasons for Unemployment

People become unemployed for various reasons. Less than half of the unemployed were job losers in 2000. Just as many were entering or reentering the labor market in search of a job. In recessions, the proportion of job losers shoots up.

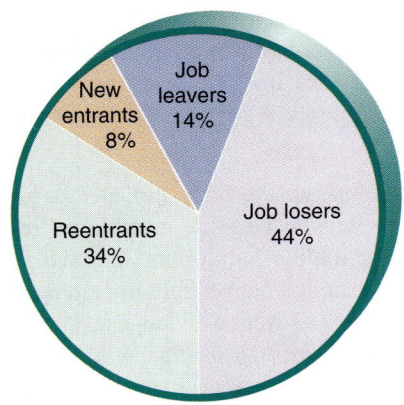

underemployment: People seeking full-time paid employment who work only part-time or are employed at jobs below their capability.

Nevertheless, any paid employment is sufficient to exclude the person from the count of the unemployed, though not from a condition of **underemployment**.

Underemployed workers represent labor resources that aren't being fully utilized. They're part of our unemployment problem, even if they're not officially counted as *unemployed*. In 2000, nearly 3 million workers were underemployed in the U.S. economy.

The Phantom Unemployed

Although discouraged and underemployed workers aren't counted in official unemployment statistics, some of the people who *are* counted probably shouldn't be. Many people report that they're actively seeking a job even when they have little interest in finding employment. To some extent, public policy actually encourages such behavior. For example, welfare recipients are often required to look for a job, even though some welfare mothers would prefer to spend all their time raising their children. Their resultant job search is likely to be perfunctory at best, including perhaps only one trip to the state employment office. Similarly, most states require people receiving unemployment benefits to provide evidence that they're looking for a job, even though some recipients may prefer a brief period of joblessness. Here again, reported unemployment may conceal labor-force nonparticipation. More generous benefits in European nations are thought to create similar problems (see the following World View).

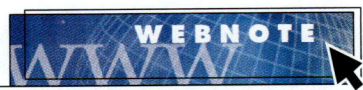

For the most recent data on unemployment in the United States, visit the U.S. Bureau of Labor Statistics at www.bls.gov.

THE HUMAN COSTS

Although our measures of unemployment aren't perfect, they're a reliable index to a serious macro problem. Unemployment statistics tell us that millions of people are jobless. That may be all right for a day or even a week, but if you need income to keep body and soul together, prolonged unemployment can hurt.

Compare unemployment rates of different countries at stats.bls.gov/fls

The most visible impact of unemployment on individuals is the loss of income associated with working. For workers who've been unemployed for long periods of time, such losses can spell financial disaster. Typically, an unemployed person must rely on a combination of savings, income from other family members, and government unemployment benefits for financial support. After these sources of support are exhausted (see News), public welfare is often the only legal support left.

Not all unemployed people experience such a financial disaster, of course. College students who fail to find summer employment are unlikely to end up on welfare the following semester. Similarly, teenagers and others looking for part-time employment won't suffer great economic losses from unemployment. Nevertheless, the experience of unemployment—of not being able to find a job when you want one—can still be painful. This sensation isn't easily forgotten, even after one has finally found employment.

WORLD VIEW

Europe's Unemployment Woes

Years of sluggish economic growth (low demand) raised unemployment rates in Europe to levels rarely seen in the United States. Generous unemployment benefits cushion the personal losses from joblessness, but they also discourage European workers from accepting new jobs (less supply).

Source: U.S. Department of Labor (2000 data). http://stats.bls.gov/fls

Country	Rate
United States	4.0
Japan	4.8
United Kingdom	5.5
Canada	5.8
Australia	6.6
Belgium	7.0
Germany	8.3
France	9.7
Italy	10.7
Spain	14.1

Analysis: Throughout the 1990s unemployment rates were significantly higher in Europe than in the United States. Analysts blame both sluggish economic growth and high unemployment benefits.

IN THE NEWS

Unemployment Benefits Not for Everyone

In 2000, over 7 million people collected unemployment benefits averaging $230 per week. But don't rush to the state unemployment office yet—not all unemployed people are eligible. To qualify for weekly unemployment benefits you must have worked a substantial length of time and earned some minimum amount of wages, both determined by your state. Furthermore, you must have a "good" reason for having lost your last job. Most states will not provide benefits to students (or their professors!) during summer vacations, to professional athletes in the off-season, or to individuals who quit their last jobs.

If you qualify for benefits, the amount of benefits you receive each week will depend on your previous wages. In most states the benefits are equal to about one-half of the previous weekly wage, up to a state-determined maximum. The maximum benefit in 2000 ranged from $190 in Mississippi to a high of $477 in Massachusetts.

Unemployment benefits are financed by a tax on employers and can continue for as long as 26 weeks. During periods of high unemployment, the duration of benefit eligibility may be extended another 13 weeks or more.

Source: U.S. Employment and Training Administration
www.workforcesecurity.doleta.gov

Analysis: Some of the income lost due to unemployment is replaced by unemployment insurance benefits. Not all unemployed persons are eligible, however, and the duration of benefits is limited.

It is difficult to measure all the intangible effects of unemployment on individual workers. Studies have shown, however, that joblessness causes more crime, more health problems, more divorces, and other problems (see News). Such findings underscore the notion that prolonged unemployment poses a real danger to many individuals. Like George H., the worker discussed at the beginning of this chapter, many unemployed workers simply can't cope with the resulting stress. Thomas Cottle, a lecturer at Harvard Medical School, stated the case more bluntly: "I'm now convinced that unemployment is *the* killer disease in this country—responsible for wife beating, infertility, and even tooth decay."

German psychiatrists have also observed that unemployment can be hazardous to your health. They estimate that the anxieties and other nervous disorders that accompany one year of unemployment can reduce life expectancy by as much as five years. In Japan, the suicide rate jumped by more than 50 percent in 1999 when the economy plunged into recession. In New Zealand, suicide rates are twice as high for unemployed workers than for employed ones.

There's an upside to these relationships as well. When the U.S. unemployment rate fell steadily in the late 1990s, so did crime rates, premarital births, divorce rates, and child abuse. Declining unemployment rates weren't the only cause of these trends, but they certainly helped.

DEFINING FULL EMPLOYMENT

In view of the economic and social losses associated with unemployment, it's not surprising that *full employment* is one of our basic macroeconomic goals. You may be surprised to learn, however, that "*full*" employment isn't the same thing as "*zero*" unemployment. There are in fact several reasons for regarding some degree of unemployment as inevitable and even desirable.

Seasonal Unemployment

seasonal unemployment: Unemployment due to seasonal changes in employment or labor supply.

Some joblessness is virtually inevitable as long as we continue to grow crops, build houses, or go skiing at certain seasons of the year. At the end of each such season, thousands of workers must go searching for new jobs, experiencing some **seasonal unemployment** in the process.

Seasonal fluctuations also arise on the supply side of the labor market. Teenage unemployment rates, for example, rise sharply in the summer as students look for temporary jobs. To avoid such unemployment completely, we'd either have to keep everyone in school or ensure that all students went immediately from the classroom to the workroom. Neither alternative is likely, much less desirable.[1]

Frictional Unemployment

There are other reasons for expecting a certain amount of unemployment. Many workers have sound financial or personal reasons for leaving one job to look for another. In the process of moving from one job to another, a person may well miss a few days or even weeks of work without any serious personal or social consequences. On the contrary, people who spend more time looking for work may find *better* jobs.

The same is true of students first entering the labor market. It's not likely that you'll find a job the moment you leave school. Nor should you necessarily take the first job offered. If you spend some time looking for work, you're more likely to find a job you like. The job-search period gives you an opportunity to find out what kinds of jobs are available, what skills they require, and what they pay. Accordingly, a brief period of job search may benefit labor market entrants and the larger economy. The

---

[1]Seasonal variations in employment and labor supply not only create some unemployment in the annual averages but also distort monthly comparisons. Unemployment rates are always higher in February (when farming and housing construction come to a virtual standstill) and June (when a mass of students go looking for summer jobs). The Labor Department adjusts monthly unemployment rates according to this seasonal pattern and reports "seasonally adjusted" unemployment rates for each month. Seasonal adjustments don't alter *annual* averages, however.

IN THE NEWS

Recession's Cost: Lives

The economy may be killing us.

A study out today says a poor economy in 30 selected cities is responsible for:

- 6.7% more murders—730 a year.
- 3.1% more deaths from stroke—1,386 annually.
- 5.6% more fatal heart disease—17,654 a year.

Another report blames the recession for 1,170 more suicides in the USA—up 3.9 percent.

The middle class was hurting before the recession, says University of Utah economist Mary Merva.

"We were already pushed to the limit," says Merva, who co-authored a study of unemployment in 30 big cities with 80 million people from 1976 to 1990.

"This could be the straw that breaks our back."

The study found that a 1 percentage point rise in unemployment meant more crime:

- Violent, up 3.4 percent.
- Nonviolent, up 2.4 percent.

"Stress can be directed inward, like smoking, drinking or having higher blood pressure," Merva says, "or outward like beating your wife, abusing your child."

Johns Hopkins University economist Harvey Brenner, author of a similar report, says a troubled economy breeds a sick society.

"Health and social well-being of the country is directly affected by the behavior of the economy," he says.

"When national economic decisions are made, health concerns should have a seat at the table."

—Robert Davis

Source: *USA Today*, October 16, 1992. © 1992 USA Today. Reprinted with permission. www.usatoday.com

Analysis: The cost of unemployment is not measured in lost wages alone. Prolonged unemployment also impairs health, social relationships, and productivity.

---

unemployment associated with these kinds of job searches is referred to as **frictional unemployment.**

Three factors distinguish frictional unemployment from other kinds of unemployment. First, enough jobs exist for those who are frictionally unemployed—that is, there's adequate *demand* for labor. Second, those individuals who are frictionally unemployed have the skills required for available jobs. Third, the period of job search will be relatively short. Under these conditions, frictional unemployment resembles an unconventional game of musical chairs. There are enough chairs of the right size for everyone, and people dance around them for only a brief period of time.

No one knows for sure just how much of our unemployment problem is frictional. Most economists agree, however, that friction alone is responsible for an unemployment rate of 2 to 3 percent. Accordingly, our definition of *"full employment"* should allow for at least this much unemployment.

For many job seekers, the period between jobs may drag on for months or even years because they don't have the skills that employers require. Imagine, for example, the predicament of steelworkers. During the 1980s, the steel industry contracted as consumers demanded fewer and lighter-weight cars and as construction of highways, bridges, and buildings slowed. In the process, over 300,000 steelworkers lost their jobs. Most of these workers had a decade or more of experience and substantial skill. But the skills they'd perfected were no longer in demand. They couldn't perform the jobs available in computer software, biotechnology, or other expanding industries. Although there were enough job vacancies in the labor market, the steelworkers couldn't fill them: These workers were victims of **structural unemployment.**

The same kind of structural displacement hit the defense industry in the 1990s. Cutbacks in national defense spending forced weapons manufactures, aerospace firms,

frictional unemployment: Brief periods of unemployment experienced by people moving between jobs or into the labor market.

Structural Unemployment

structural unemployment: Unemployment caused by a mismatch between the skills (or location) of job seekers and the requirements (or location) of available jobs.

and electronics companies to reduce output and lay off thousands of workers. The displaced workers soon discovered that their highly developed skills weren't immediately applicable in nondefense industries.

Teenagers from urban slums also suffer from structural unemployment. Most poor teenagers have an inadequate education, few job-related skills, and little work experience. From their perspective, almost all decent jobs are "out of reach." As a consequence, these teenagers, many of whom are from minority groups, remain unemployed far longer than can be explained by frictional forces.

Structural unemployment violates the second condition for frictional unemployment: that the job seekers can perform the available jobs. Structural unemployment is analogous to a musical chairs game in which there are enough chairs for everyone, but some of them are too small to sit on. It's a more serious concern than frictional unemployment and incompatible with any notion of full employment.

Cyclical Unemployment

cyclical unemployment: Unemployment attributable to a lack of job vacancies, that is, to an inadequate level of aggregate demand.

The fourth type of unemployment is **cyclical unemployment**—joblessness that occurs when there aren't simply enough jobs to go around. Cyclical unemployment exists when the number of workers demanded falls short of the number of persons supplied (in the labor force). This isn't a case of mobility between jobs (frictional unemployment) or even of job seekers' skills (structural unemployment). Rather, it's simply an inadequate level of demand for goods and services and thus for labor. Cyclical unemployment resembles the most familiar form of musical chairs, in which the number of chairs is always less than the number of players.

The Great Depression is the most striking example of cyclical unemployment. The dramatic increase in unemployment rates that began in 1930 (see Figure 6.6) wasn't due to any increase in friction or sudden decline in workers' skills. Instead, the high rates of unemployment that persisted for a *decade* were caused by a sudden decline in the market demand for goods and services. How do we know? Just notice what happened to our unemployment rate when the demand for military goods and services increased in 1941!

Slow Growth. Cyclical unemployment can emerge even when the economy is expanding. Keep in mind that the labor force is always growing, due to population growth and continuing immigration. If these additional labor-force participants are to find jobs,

FIGURE 6.6
The Unemployment Record

Unemployment rates reached record heights (25 percent) during the Great Depression. In more recent decades, the unemployment rate has varied from 4 percent in full-employment years to over 10 percent in recession years. Keeping the labor force fully employed is a primary macro policy goal.

Source: U.S. Department of Labor.

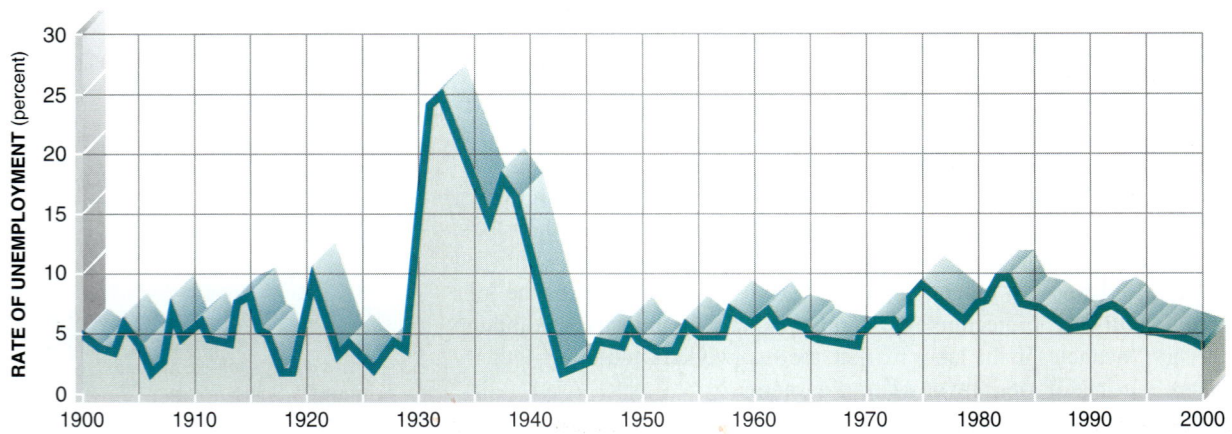

the economy must grow. Specifically, *the economy must grow at least as fast as the labor force to avoid cyclical unemployment.* When economic growth slows below this threshold, unemployment rates start to rise.

In later chapters we examine the causes of cyclical unemployment and explore some potential policy responses. At this point, however, we're just establishing some perspective on the goal of full employment. In the Employment Act of 1946, Congress committed the federal government to pursue a goal of "maximum" employment but didn't specify exactly what that rate was. Presumably, this meant avoiding as much cyclical and structural unemployment as possible while keeping frictional unemployment within reasonable bounds. As guidelines for public policy, these perspectives are admittedly vague.

The Full-Employment Goal

Inflationary Pressures. The first attempt to define *full employment* more precisely was undertaken in the early 1960s. At that time the Council of Economic Advisers (itself created by the Employment Act of 1946) decided that our proximity to full employment could be gauged by watching *prices*. As the economy approached its production possibilities, labor and other resources would become increasingly scarce. As market participants bid for these remaining resources, wages and prices would start to rise. Hence, *rising prices are a signal that employment is nearing capacity.*

After examining the relationship between unemployment and inflation, the Council of Economic Advisers decided to peg full employment at 4 percent unemployment. The unemployment rate could fall below 4 percent. If it did, however, price levels would begin to rise. Thus, 4 percent unemployment was regarded as an acceptable compromise of our employment and price goals.

Changes in Structural Unemployment. During the 1970s and early 1980s, this view of our full-employment potential was considered overly optimistic. Unemployment rates stayed far above 4 percent, even when the economy expanded. Moreover, inflation began to accelerate at higher levels of unemployment. Critics suggested that structural barriers to full employment had intensified, necessitating a redefinition of our full-employment goal. These structural barriers included the following:

- *More youth and women.* Between 1956 and 1979, the proportion of teenagers in the labor force increased from 6 percent to 9 percent. During the same period, the proportion of adult women in the labor force grew tremendously (see Figure 6.2). Many of these women were entering the labor force for the first time—or reentering it after long periods of homemaking. These trends increased frictional and structural unemployment.
- *Liberal transfer payments.* Higher benefits and easier rules for unemployment insurance, food stamps, welfare, and Social Security made unemployment less painful. As a result, critics suggested, more people were willing to stay unemployed rather than work.
- *Structural changes in demand.* Changes in consumer demand, technology, and trade shrank the markets in steel, textiles, autos, and other industries. The workers dislocated from these industries couldn't be absorbed fast enough in new high-tech and other service industries.

In view of these factors, the Council of Economic Advisers later raised the level of unemployment thought to be compatible with price stability. In 1983, the Reagan administration concluded that the "inflation-threshold" unemployment rate was between 6 and 7 percent (see cartoon on next page).

Declining Structural Pressures. The structural barriers that intensified inflationary pressures in the 1970s and early 1980s receded in the 1990s. The number of teenagers

full employment: The lowest rate of unemployment compatible with price stability; variously estimated at between 4 percent and 6 percent unemployment.

The "Natural" Rate of Unemployment

natural rate of unemployment: Long-term rate of unemployment determined by structural forces in labor and product markets.

Congressional Targets

To see the Fed's annual Humphrey-Hawkins report to Congress, go to www.federalreserve.gov/board-docs/hh.

declined by 3 million between 1981 and 1993. The upsurge in women's participation in the labor force also leveled off. High school and college attendance and graduation rates increased. All these structural changes made it easier to lower unemployment rates without increasing inflation. In 1991, the first Bush administration concluded that **full employment** was equivalent to 5.5 percent unemployment. In 1999, the Clinton administration suggested the full-employment threshold might have dropped even further, to 5.3 percent. In reality, the national unemployment rate stayed below even that benchmark for four years (Figure 6.6) without any upsurge in inflation.

The ambiguity about which rate of unemployment might trigger an upsurge in inflation has convinced some analysts to abandon the inflation-based concept of full employment. They prefer to specify a "natural" rate of unemployment that doesn't depend on inflation trends. In this view, the natural rate of unemployment consists of frictional and structural components only. It's the rate of unemployment that will prevail in the long run. In the short run, both the unemployment rate and the inflation rate may go up and down. However, the economy will tend to gravitate toward the long-run **natural rate of unemployment.**

Although the natural rate concept avoids specifying a short-term inflation trigger, it too is subject to debate. As we've seen, the *structural* determinants of unemployment (e.g., age and composition of the labor force) change over time. When structural forces change, the level of natural unemployment presumably changes as well.

Although most economists agree that an unemployment rate of 4 to 6 percent is consistent with either natural or full employment, Congress has set tougher goals for macro policy. According to the Full Employment and Balanced Growth Act of 1978 (commonly called the Humphrey-Hawkins Act), our national goal is to attain a 4 percent rate of unemployment. The act also requires a goal of 3 percent inflation. There was an escape clause, however. In the event that both goals couldn't be met, the president could set higher, provisional definitions of full employment.

"I don't *like* six-per-cent unemployment, either. But I can live with it."

Analysis: So-called full employment entails a compromise between employment and inflation goals. That compromise doesn't affect everyone equally.

IN THE NEWS

Unemployment Soars by 700,000

The U.S. jobless rate surged to 5.4 percent last month, the highest level in almost five years, as companies laid off hundreds of thousands of workers in the wake of the Sept. 11 terrorist attacks, the Labor Department reported yesterday.

The rate jumped from 4.9 percent in September, for the biggest monthly increase since the recession of 1980.

As the economy deteriorated, jobless rates rose significantly for every major demographic group—adult men and women, teens, whites, blacks and persons of Hispanic origin—as the ranks of the unemployed soared to 7.7 million from 7 million.

The number of people working part time, either because their workweeks were cut back or because they could not find full-time jobs, is also growing. Over the past two months, this group has increased by 1.1 million, to 4.5 million.

—John M. Berry

Source: *Washington Post*, November 3, 2001, p. 1. © 2001 The Washington Post. Reprinted with permission. www.washingtonpost.com

Analysis: A slowdown in economic growth causes the unemployment rate to rise—sometimes sharply.

THE HISTORICAL RECORD

Although there's some ambiguity about the specific definition of full employment, the historical record is littered with evident failures. Our greatest failure occurred during the Great Depression, when as much as one-fourth of the labor force was unemployed. As Figure 6.6 shows, unemployment rates were extraordinarily high throughout the 1930s.

Unemployment rates fell dramatically during World War II. In 1944, virtually anyone who was ready and willing to work quickly found a job: The civilian unemployment rate hit a rock-bottom 1.2 percent.

Since 1950, the unemployment rate has fluctuated from a low of 2.8 percent during the Korean War (1953) to a high of 10.8 percent during the 1981–82 recession. From 1982 to 1989 the unemployment rate receded, but it shot up again in the 1990–91 recession. As many as 10 million workers were unemployed at one time during that recession. Millions more experienced joblessness during the course of that economic downturn. During the last half of the 1990s the unemployment rate fell steadily and hit the low end of the full-employment range in 2000. Slow GDP growth in 2000–01 and the economic stall caused by the September 11, 2001 terrorist attacks, pushed the unemployment rate sharply higher in late 2001 (see News).

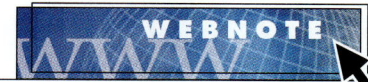

To get a more vivid image of the Great Depression than unemployment statistics provide, see the photo collection of the Farm Security Administration at memory.loc.gov/ammem/fsowhome.html.

THE ECONOMY TOMORROW

Our success in maintaining full employment in the economy of tomorrow will depend on both structural and cyclical forces. Of particular concern is the rapid pace of structural change in the U.S. economy. The blue collar manufacturing industries are receding as the economy becomes even more service-oriented. The U.S. Bureau of Labor Statistics estimates that **98 percent of all new jobs created in the next decade will be service jobs.** These new service jobs will be highly concentrated in computer hardware and software, health services, residential care, and personnel services (see Table 6.2).

The new jobs of the economy tomorrow will require increasing levels of education and skill. Workers with the requisite skills will enjoy high wages and experience little unemployment. Workers without the right skills, however, will find themselves out of

A Growing Skills Gap?

New Jobs

TABLE 6.2
Projected Employment Changes, 2000–2010

As the economy grows, some industries expand and others contract. These industry shifts will create structural unemployment problems, particularly for workers displaced from declining industries and labor market entrants with little education.

Industry	Change in Employment
Fastest growing	
Computer services	+86%
Health services	+68%
Residential care	+64%
Cable and pay TV services	+51%
Business services	+50%
Personnel supply services	+49%
Public warehousing	+45%
Water and sanitation services	+45%
Most rapidly declining	
Watches, clocks	−53%
Footwear, except rubber and plastic	−53%
Coal mining	−30%
Metal cans and shipping containers	−29%
Leather products	−28%
Railroad transportation	−26%
Private household services	−25%
Apparel	−25%

Source: U.S. Bureau of Labor Statistics.

step with a fast-changing market. This trend was already evident in the 1990s. The wage gap between college graduates and high school graduates has widened, and unemployment differentials have increased as well.

Old Skills The **skills gap** isn't confined to young workers first entering the labor market. Old-line industries are downsizing and restructuring in response to changing markets. In the

IN THE NEWS

What Lies in Store for Displaced Workers?

Nearly 2 million long-tenured workers lost their jobs in 1997–98 due to plant closings, slack work, or company restructuring. All of these tenured workers had held their jobs for at least three years, over a third had worked at their job more than ten years.

The 1997–98 cohort of displaced workers typically found a new job in 5 weeks time, but older and less educated workers spent months looking for work (see chart). One out of five workers withdrew from the labor force.

The displaced workers of 1997–98 were relatively lucky. A growing economy and declining national unemployment made it easier to find a new job. In a stagnant or contracting economy, the damage from job displacement is much greater.

Status in February 2000 of Workers Displaced in 1997–98

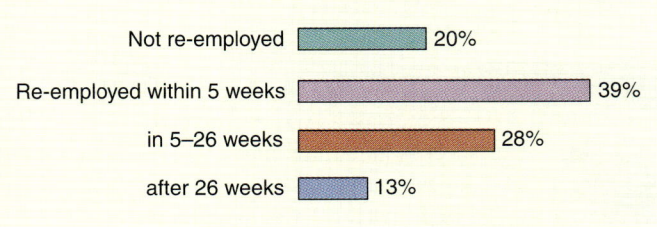

- Not re-employed: 20%
- Re-employed within 5 weeks: 39%
- in 5–26 weeks: 28%
- after 26 weeks: 13%

Source: Ryan T. Helwig, "Worker Displacement in a Strong Labor Market." *Monthly Labor Review,* June 2001, p. 13–28.

Analysis: Workers who lose their jobs in declining industries are likely to become structurally unemployed. They often remain unemployed for long periods and must often accept lower wages on a new job.

1980s, for example, the steel industry shed over 300,000 workers and the auto industry over 400,000 workers. In the next decade still more workers will lose jobs in these and other declining industries (see Table 6.2). The workers dislocated from these and other industries have solid work experience and skill, but *not* the skills required in today's economy. These dislocated workers, like the coal miners of earlier decades, increase structural employment. As revealed in the accompanying News, it was difficult for these dislocated workers to find new jobs. When they did, their wage on the new job was often less than their prior wage. **As the skills gap widens, structural unemployment increases.**

The employment challenge of the economy tomorrow is to reduce the structural unemployment that accompanies economic growth. This will require not only macroeconomic policies that keep *demand* increasing, but also education and training initiatives that narrow the skills gap on the *supply*-side of markets.

> **skills gap:** Gap between skills required for emerging jobs and the skills of workers.

SUMMARY

- To understand unemployment, we must distinguish the labor force from the larger population. Only people who are working (employed) or spend some time looking for a job (unemployed) are participants in the labor force. People neither working nor looking for work are outside the labor force.
- The size of the labor force affects production possibilities. As the labor force grows, so does the capacity to produce goods and services.
- Unemployment implies that we're producing inside the production possibilities curve rather than on it.
- The macroeconomic loss imposed by unemployment is reduced output of goods and services. Okun's Law suggests that 1 percentage point in unemployment is equivalent to a 2 percentage point decline in output.
- The human cost of unemployment includes not only financial losses but social, physical, and psychological costs as well.
- Unemployment is distributed unevenly; minorities, teenagers, and the less educated have much higher rates of unemployment. Also hurt are discouraged workers—those who've stopped looking for work at part-time or menial jobs because they can't find full-time jobs equal to their training or potential.
- There are four types of unemployment: seasonal, frictional, structural, and cyclical. Because some seasonal and frictional unemployment is inevitable and even desirable, full employment is not defined as zero unemployment. These considerations, plus fear of inflationary consequences, result in full employment being defined as an unemployment rate of 4 to 6 percent.
- The economy (output) must grow at least as fast as the labor force to keep the unemployment rate from rising.
- The natural rate of unemployment is based on frictional and structural forces, without reference to short-term price (inflation) pressures.
- Unemployment rates got as high as 25 percent in the 1930s. Since 1960, the unemployment rate has ranged from 3.4 to 10.8 percent.
- Our ability to achieve full employment in the future depends not only on increasing demand, but also on closing the skills gap. This necessitates more and better education and training activity.

Key Terms

labor force
labor-force participation rate
production possibilities
economic growth
unemployment
Okun's Law
unemployment rate
discouraged worker
underemployment
seasonal unemployment
frictional unemployment
structural unemployment
cyclical unemployment
full employment
natural rate of unemployment
skills gap

Questions for Discussion

1. Is it possible for unemployment rates to increase at the same time that the number of employed persons is increasing? How?
2. If more teenagers stay in school longer, what happens to (*a*) production possibilities? (*b*) unemployment rates?
3. What factors might explain (*a*) the rising labor-force participation rate of women and (*b*) the declining participation of men? (See Figure 6.2 for trends.)
4. Why might job (re)entrants have a harder time finding a job than job losers?
5. If the government guaranteed some income to all unemployed persons, how might the unemployment rate be affected? Who should get unemployment benefits? (See News page 119).
6. Can you identify three institutional constraints on the use of resources (factors of production)? What has motivated these constraints?
7. Why is frictional unemployment deemed desirable?
8. Why do people expect inflation to heat up when the unemployment rate approaches 4 percent?
9. What's the difference between "full" and "natural" employment rates?
10. Why is employment declining in the footwear and watch industries? Will workers displaced from these industries be able to get jobs in any of the fastest-growing occupations listed in Table 6.2? What, if anything, could the government do to help?

Web Activities

1. Find the unemployment rate for your own age group, your gender, and your race or ethnicity at the U.S. Bureau of Labor Statistics. You can find this data at www.bls.gov. Once you have accessed the site, find national employment and access the employment situation summary. Compare each rate with the overall U.S. unemployment rate. Using the types of unemployment described in the text of this chapter, explain why each unemployment rate differs from the overall unemployment rate.
2. What are the employment prospects in your chosen profession (or one that you might consider)? Find out at www.bls.gov/oco/ocoiab.htm. Look at the employment outlook. What factors will create jobs (or decrease the number of jobs) in this field?
3. Log into www.whitehouse.gov/fsbr/employment.html, and click on the chart for civilian labor force (supply).
    a. By how much has the labor force grown since 1989?
    b. Using the same source, click on the chart for unemployment. During that same period, has the number of people unemployed increased or decreased?
    c. Are these two numbers inconsistent?

THE ACCOMPANYING STUDENT PROBLEM SET CONTAINS NUMERICAL AND GRAPHING PROBLEMS FOR THIS CHAPTER

CHAPTER 7

Inflation

Germany set a record in 1923 that no other nation wants to beat. In that year, prices in Germany rose a *trillion* times over. Prices rose so fast that workers took "shopping breaks" to spend their twice-a-day paychecks before they became worthless. Menu prices in restaurants rose while people were still eating! Accumulated savings became worthless, as did outstanding loans. People needed sacks of currency to buy bread, butter, and other staples. With prices more than doubling every *day*, no one could afford to save, invest, lend money, or make long-term plans. In the frenzy of escalating prices, production of goods and services came to a halt, unemployment rose tenfold, and the German economy all but collapsed.

Hungary had a similar episode of runaway inflation in 1946, as did Japan. More recently, Russia, Bulgaria, Brazil, Zaire, Yugoslavia, Argentina, and Uruguay have all witnessed at least a tenfold jump in prices in a single year.

The United States has never experienced such a price frenzy. During the Revolutionary War, prices did double in one year, but that was a singular event. In the last decade, U.S. prices have risen just 1 to 4 percent a year. Despite this enviable record, Americans still *worry* a lot about inflation. In response to this anxiety, every president since Franklin Roosevelt has expressed a determination to keep prices from rising. In 1971, the Nixon administration took drastic action to stop inflation. With prices rising an average of only 3 percent, President Nixon imposed price controls on U.S. producers to keep prices from rising any faster. For 90 days all wages and prices were frozen by law—price increases were prohibited. For three more years, wage and price increases were limited by legal rules.

In 1990, U.S. prices were rising at a 6 percent clip—twice the pace that triggered the 1971–74 wage and price controls. Calling such price increases "unacceptable," Federal Reserve Chairman Alan Greenspan set a goal of *zero* percent inflation. In pursuit of that goal, the Fed slowed economic growth so much that the economy fell into a recession. The Fed did the same thing again in early 2000. With even less evidence of inflation, the Fed slowed the economy to the brink of another recession.

In later chapters we'll examine how the Fed and other policymakers slow the economy down or speed it up. Before looking at the levers of macro policy, however, we need to examine our policy goals. Why is inflation so feared? How much inflation is unacceptable? To get a handle on this basic issue, we'll ask and answer the following questions:

- What kind of price increases are referred to as *inflation*?
- Who is hurt (or helped) by inflation?
- What is an appropriate goal for *price stability*?

As we'll discover, inflation is a serious problem, but not for the reasons most people cite. We'll also see why deflation—falling prices—isn't as welcome as it might appear.

WHAT IS INFLATION?

Most people associate **inflation** with price increases on specific goods and services. The economy isn't necessarily experiencing an inflation, however, every time the price of a cup of coffee goes up. We must be careful to distinguish the phenomenon of inflation from price increases for specific goods. *Inflation is an increase in the average level of prices, not a change in any specific price.*

inflation: An increase in the average level of prices of goods and services.

The Average Price

Suppose you wanted to know the average price of fruit in the supermarket. Surely you wouldn't have much success in seeking out an average fruit—nobody would be quite sure what you had in mind. You might have some success, however, if you sought out the prices of apples, oranges, cherries, and peaches. Knowing the price of each kind of fruit, you could then compute the average price of fruit. The resultant figure wouldn't refer to any particular product but would convey a sense of how much a typical basket of fruit might cost. By repeating these calculations every day, you could then determine whether fruit prices, *on average,* were changing. On occasion, you might even notice that apple prices rose while orange prices fell, leaving the *average* price of fruit unchanged.

The same kinds of calculations are made to measure inflation in the entire economy. We first determine the average price of all output—the average price level—then look for changes in that average. A rise in the average price level is referred to as inflation.

The average price level may fall as well as rise. A decline in average prices—a **deflation**—occurs when price decreases on some goods and services outweigh price increases on all others. This happened in Japan in 1995, and again in 2000 (see World View "Worldwide Inflation," p. 143). Such deflations are rare, however: The United States has not experienced any general deflation since 1940.

deflation: A decrease in the average level of prices of goods and services.

Relative Prices vs. the Price Level

Because inflation and deflation are measured in terms of average price levels, it's possible for individual prices to rise or fall continuously without changing the average price level. We already noted, for example, that the price of apples can rise without increasing the average price of fruit, so long as the price of some other fruit, such as oranges, falls. In such circumstances, **relative prices** are changing, but not average prices. An increase in the relative price of apples, for example, simply means that apples have become more expensive in comparison with other fruits (or any other goods or services).

relative price: The price of one good in comparison with the price of other goods.

Changes in relative prices may occur in a period of stable average prices, or in periods of inflation or deflation. In fact, in an economy as vast as ours—in which literally millions of goods and services are exchanged in the factor and product markets—relative prices are always changing. Indeed, relative price changes are an essential ingredient of the market mechanism. Recall from Chapter 3 what happens when the market price of web-design services rises relative to other goods and services. This (relative) price rise alerts web architects (producers) to increase their output, cutting back on other production or leisure activities.

A general inflation—an increase in the average price level—doesn't perform this same market function. If all prices rise at the same rate, price increases for specific goods are of little value as market signals. In less extreme cases, when most but not all prices are rising, changes in relative prices do occur but aren't so immediately apparent. Table 7.1 reminds us that some prices do fall even during periods of general inflation.

TABLE 7.1
Prices That Have Fallen
Inflation refers to an increase in the *average* price level. It doesn't mean that *all* prices are rising. In fact, many prices fall, even during periods of general inflation.

Item	Early Price	2001 Price
Long-distance telephone call (per minute)	$ 6.90 (1915)	$ 0.07
Pocket electronic calculator	200.00 (1972)	5.90
Digital watch	2,000.00 (1972)	1.99
Polaroid camera (color)	150.00 (1963)	29.95
Pantyhose	2.16 (1967)	1.29
Ballpoint pen	0.89 (1965)	0.29
Transistor radio	55.00 (1967)	5.99
Videocassette recorder	1,500.00 (1977)	89.00
DVD player	800.00 (1997)	99.00
Laptop computer	3,500.00 (1986)	1,200.00
Airfare (New York–Paris)	490.00 (1958)	328.00
Microwave oven	400.00 (1972)	79.00
Contact lenses	275.00 (1972)	39.00
Television (19-inch, color)	469.00 (1980)	189.00
Compact disk player	1,000.00 (1985)	29.00

REDISTRIBUTIVE EFFECTS OF INFLATION

The distinction between relative and average prices helps us determine who's hurt by inflation—and who's helped. Popular opinion notwithstanding, it's simply not true that everyone is worse off when prices rise. ***Although inflation makes some people worse off, it makes other people better off.*** Some people even get rich when prices rise! The micro consequences of inflation are reflected in redistributions of income and wealth, not general declines in either measure of our economic welfare. These redistributions occur because people buy different combinations of goods and services, own different assets, and sell distinct goods or services (including labor). The impact of inflation on individuals therefore depends on how prices change for the goods and services each person actually buys or sells.

Price Effects

Price changes are the most visible consequence of inflation. If you've been paying tuition, you know how painful a price hike can be. Ten years ago, the average in-state tuition at public colleges and universities was $500 per year. Today the average in-state tuition exceeds $3,600 (see the News on the next page). At private universities, tuition has increased eightfold in the past 10 years, to over $17,000. You don't need a whole course in economics to figure out the implications of these tuition hikes. To stay in college, you (or your parents) must forgo increasing amounts of other goods and services. You end up being worse off since you can't buy as many goods and services as you could before tuition went up.

The effect of tuition increases on your economic welfare is reflected in the distinction between nominal income and real income. **Nominal income** is the amount of money you receive in a particular time period; it's measured in current dollars. **Real income**, by contrast, is the purchasing power of that money, as measured by the quantity of goods and services your dollars will buy. If the number of dollars you receive every year is always the same, your *nominal income* doesn't change—but your *real income* will rise or fall with price changes.

Suppose your parents agree to give you $6,000 a year while you're in school. Out of that $6,000 you must pay for your tuition, room and board, books, and everything else. The budget for your first year at school might look like this:

nominal income: The amount of money income received in a given time period, measured in current dollars.

real income: Income in constant dollars; nominal income adjusted for inflation.

IN THE NEWS

Public Colleges' Tuition Rises 7.7% This Fall

The price of higher education increased significantly this fall, particularly at public colleges and universities, where tuitions surged by 7.7 percent in a year, the College Board announced yesterday.

The tuition increases at four-year public colleges and universities were accompanied by a 6.6 percent increase in room-and-board charges. The increases were more than double the nation's inflation rate, which was about 2.6 percent for the year.

The tuition increases at public schools outstripped those at the nation's 1,730 private four-year colleges and universities, where tuition went up 5.5 percent this fall—an increase comparable to those in recent years. Room-and-board charges at private colleges increased 4.7 percent. . . .

Even with the recent increases, College Board officials said that higher education remained affordable for most Americans. The average annual tuition at a four-year public college or university is $3,754. Room-and-board charges at those schools average $5,254. At private four-year institutions, tuitions average $17,123 and room-and-board charges average $6,455.

At private two-year schools, tuitions averaged $7,953 this fall, while tuitions at two-year public schools averaged $1,738.

—Michael A. Fletcher

Source: *Washington Post*, October 24, 2001. © 2001 The Washington Post. Reprinted with permission. www.washingtonpost.com

Analysis: Tuition increases reduce the real income of students. How much you suffer from inflation depends on what happens to the prices of the products you purchase.

FIRST YEAR'S BUDGET	
Nominal income	$6,000
Consumption	
Tuition	$3,000
Room and board	2,000
Books	300
Everything else	700
Total	$6,000

After paying for all your essential expenses, you have $700 to spend on clothes, entertainment, or anything else you want. That's not exactly living high, but it's not poverty.

Now suppose tuition increases to $3,500 in your second year, while all other prices remain the same. What will happen to your nominal income? Nothing. Unless your parents take pity on you, you'll still be getting $6,000 a year. Your nominal income is unchanged. Your *real* income, however, will suffer. This is evident in the second year's budget:

SECOND YEAR'S BUDGET	
Nominal income	$6,000
Consumption	
Tuition	$3,500
Room and board	2,000
Books	300
Everything else	200
Total	$6,000

You now have to use more of your income to pay tuition. This means you have less income to spend on other things. Since room and board and books still cost $2,300 per year, there's only one place to cut: the category of "everything else." After tuition increases, you can spend only $200 per year on movies, clothes, pizzas, and dates—not $700, as in the "good old days." This $500 reduction in purchasing power represents a *real* income loss. Even though your *nominal* income is still $6,000, you have $500 less of "everything else" in your second year than you had in the first.

Although tuition hikes reduce the real income of students, nonstudents aren't hurt by such price increases. In fact, if tuition *doubled*, nonstudents really wouldn't care. They could continue to buy the same bundle of goods and services they'd been buying all along. Tuition increases reduce the real incomes only of people who go to college. Two basic lessons about inflation are to be learned from this sad story:

- ***Not all prices rise at the same rate during an inflation.*** In our example, tuition increased substantially while other prices remained steady. Hence, the "average" price increase wasn't representative of any particular good or service. Typically, some prices rise rapidly, others only modestly, and some actually fall.
- ***Not everyone suffers equally from inflation.*** This follows from our first observation. Those people who consume the goods and services that are rising faster in price bear a greater burden of inflation; their real incomes fall more. Other consumers bear a lesser burden, or even none at all, depending on how fast the prices rise for the goods they enjoy.

Table 7.2 illustrates some of the price changes that occurred in 2000. The average rate of inflation was only 3.4 percent. This was little solace to college students, however, who confronted tuition increases of 4.1 percent, and 7 percent price hikes on textbooks (sorry!). On the other hand, price reductions on video rentals and computers spared consumers of these products from the pain of the *average* inflation rate.

Income Effects

Even if all prices rose at the *same* rate, inflation would still redistribute income. The redistributive effects of inflation originate not only in *expenditure* patterns but also *income* patterns. Even if all *prices* were rising at the same rate, not all *incomes* would be keeping pace. In reality, some people's incomes rise faster than inflation while others' increase more slowly. Some people have fixed incomes that *don't* go up with inflation. Fixed-income groups include those retired people who depend primarily on private pensions and workers with multiyear contracts that fix wage rates at preinflation levels. Lenders (like banks) that have lent funds at fixed interest rates also suffer real income losses when price levels rise. They continue to receive interest payments fixed in *nominal* dollars that have increasingly less *real* value. All these market participants experience a declining share of real income (and output) in inflationary periods.

Not all market participants suffer a real income decline when prices rise. Some people's nominal income rises *faster* than average prices, thereby boosting their *real* incomes. Keep in mind that there are two sides to every market transaction. ***What looks like a price to a buyer looks like an income to a seller.*** If students all pay higher tuition, the university will take in more income. To the extent that the nominal incomes colleges receive increase faster than average prices, they actually *benefit* from inflation. They end up being able to buy *more* goods and services (including faculty, buildings, and library books) after a period of inflation than they could before. Their real income rises.

Prices That Rose (percent)		Prices That Fell (percent)	
Gasoline	+28.5	Coffee	−0.5
Lettuce	+9.5	Video rentals	−1.5
Airfares	+9.4	Women's dresses	−6.9
Textbooks	+7.0	Oranges	−14.7
Cable TV	+4.8	Computers	−23.2
College tuition	+4.1		
Average inflation rate: +3.4%			
Source: U.S. Bureau of Labor Statistics.			

TABLE 7.2
Price Changes in 2000
The average rate of inflation conceals substantial differences in the price changes of specific goods and services. The impact of inflation on individuals depends in part on which goods and services are consumed. People who buy goods whose prices are rising fastest lose more real income. In 2000, drivers and fliers were particularly hard-hit by inflation.

FIGURE 7.1
Nominal Wages and Prices

Inflation implies not only higher prices but higher incomes as well. Hence, inflation can't make *everyone* worse off. Wages trail behind prices when nonwage incomes (e.g., rents, profits) are rising faster, payroll taxes or fringe benefits are increasing, or productivity is rising more slowly. Wages rise faster than prices in the opposite circumstances.

Source: *Economic Report of the President, 2001.*

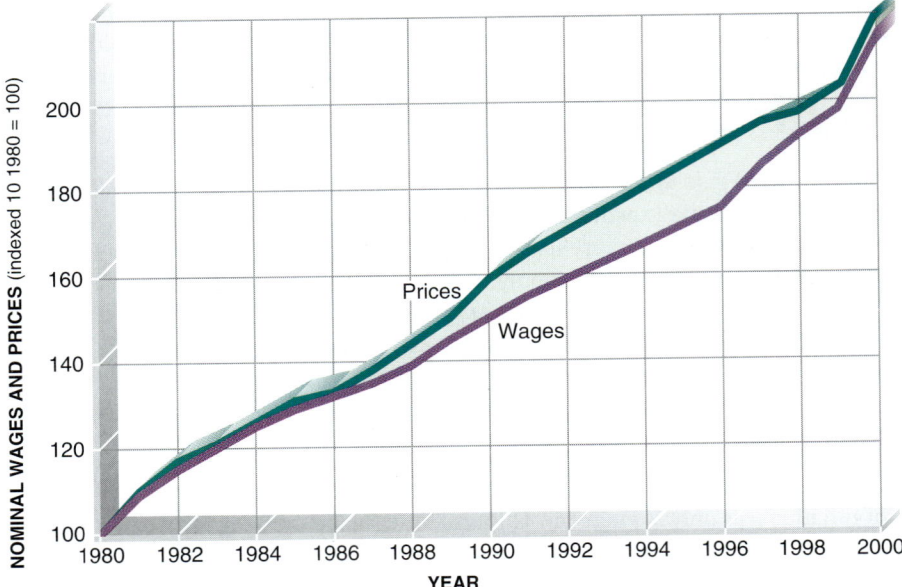

Once we recognize that nominal incomes and prices don't all increase at the same rate, it makes no sense to say that "inflation hurts everybody." **If prices are rising, incomes must be rising too.** In fact, on *average,* incomes rise just as fast as prices (see Figure 7.1). That fact is of little comfort, however, to those who end up losing real income in the inflation game.

Wealth Effects

Still more winners and losers of the inflation game are selected on the basis of the assets they hold. Suppose you deposit $100 in a savings account on January 1, where it earns 5 percent interest. At the end of the year you'll have more nominal wealth ($105) than you started with ($100). But what if all prices have doubled in the meantime? In that case, your $105 will buy you no more at the end of the year than $52.50 would have bought you at the beginning. Inflation in this case reduces the *real* value of your savings, and you end up worse off than those individuals who spent all their income earlier in the year!

Table 7.3 shows how the value of various assets have changed. Between 1991 and 2001, the average price level increased 32 percent. The average value of stocks, diamonds, and homes rose much faster than the price level, increasing the *real* value of those assets. Farm land prices rose too, but just a bit more than average prices. People who owned bonds, silver, and gold weren't so lucky; their *real* wealth declined.

TABLE 7.3
The Real Story of Wealth
Households hold their wealth in many different forms. As the value of various assets changes, so does a person's wealth. Between 1991 and 2001, inflation was very good to people who held stocks. By contrast, the real value of bonds, gold, and silver fell.

Asset	Change in Value, 1991–2001
Stocks	+250%
Diamonds	+71%
Oil	+66%
Housing	+56%
U.S. farmland	+49%
Average price level	+32%
Silver	+22%
Bonds	+20%
Stamps	−9%
Gold	−29%

WORLD VIEW

Tortilla Price Hike Hits Mexico's Poorest

MEXICO CITY—When the Mexican government ended its long-standing subsidy of tortillas on Jan. 1, the result was a five-day crash course in free-market economics and tortilla politics that left a bad taste in everyone's mouth.

For 25 years, the government has subsidized tortilla production and regulated the price of the popular corn-flour pancakes, which are to Mexicans what baguettes are to Parisians or rice is to the Chinese. But falling oil prices and pressure from international lenders have forced the government to cut spending. When the ax fell on tortilla subsidies, prices responded like a basketball released from the bottom of a swimming pool, more than doubling in some places.

The result has been an angry backlash, particularly among impoverished Mexicans who rely on the soft, chewy disks for half their daily diet.

"Tortillas are the most politically sensitive product in the Mexican economy, and that was why they were the last to be liberalized," said political commentator Sergio Sarmiento.

—John Ward Anderson

Source: *Washington Post*, January 12, 1999. © 1999 The Washington Post. Reprinted with permission. www.washingtonpost.com

Analysis: The redistributive effects of inflation can cause a political backlash. No one wants to pay higher prices.

By altering relative prices, incomes, and the real value of wealth, inflation turns out to be a mechanism for redistributing incomes and wealth. ***The redistributive mechanics of inflation include***

- ***Price effects.*** People who prefer goods and services that are increasing in price least quickly end up with a larger share of real income.
- ***Income effects.*** People whose nominal incomes rise faster than the rate of inflation end up with a larger share of total income.
- ***Wealth effects.*** People who own assets that are increasing in real value end up better off than others.

Redistributions

On the other hand, people whose nominal incomes don't keep pace with inflation end up with smaller shares of total output. The same thing is true of those who enjoy goods that are rising fastest in price or who hold assets that are declining in real value. In this sense, **inflation acts just like a tax, taking income or wealth from one group and giving it to another.** But we have no assurance that this particular tax will behave like Robin Hood, taking from the rich and giving to the poor. In reality, inflation often redistributes income in the opposite direction.

Because of its redistributive effects, inflation also increases social and economic tensions. Tensions—between labor and management, between government and the people, and among consumers—may overwhelm a society and its institutions. As Gardner Ackley of the University of Michigan observed, "A significant real cost of inflation is what it does to morale, to social coherence, and to people's attitudes toward each other." "This society," added Arthur Okun, "is built on implicit and explicit contracts. . . . They are linked to the idea that the dollar means something. If you cannot depend on the value of the dollar, this system is undermined. People will constantly feel they've been fooled and cheated."[1] This is how the middle class felt in Germany in 1923 and in China in 1948, when the value of their savings was wiped out by sudden and unanticipated inflation. A surge in prices also stirred social and political tensions in Russia as it moved from a price-controlled economy to a market-driven economy in the 1990s. A similar political backlash occurred in Mexico in 1999 when tortilla prices jumped (see World View). On a more personal level, psychotherapists report that

Social Tensions

---

[1] Quoted in *Business Week*, May 22, 1978, p. 118.

"inflation stress" leads to more frequent marital spats, pessimism, diminished self-confidence, and even sexual insecurity. Some people turn to crime as a way of solving the problem.

Money Illusion

Even those people whose nominal incomes keep up with inflation often feel oppressed by rising prices. People feel that they *deserve* any increases in wages they receive. When they later discover that their higher (nominal) wages don't buy any additional goods, they feel cheated. They feel worse off, even though they haven't suffered any actual loss of real income. This phenomenon is called **money illusion.** People suffering from money illusion are forever reminding us that they used to pay only $1 to see a movie or $8 for a textbook. What they forget is that nominal incomes were also a lot lower in the "good old days" than they are today.

money illusion: The use of nominal dollars rather than real dollars to gauge changes in one's income or wealth.

MACRO CONSEQUENCES

Although redistributions of income and wealth are the primary consequences of inflation, inflation has *macroeconomic* effects as well. Inflation can alter the rate and mix of output by changing consumption, work, saving, investment, and trade behavior.

Uncertainty

One of the most immediate consequences of inflation is uncertainty. When the average price level is changing significantly in either direction, economic decisions become more difficult. As the accompanying cartoon suggests, even something as simple as ordering a restaurant meal is more difficult if menu prices are changing (as they did during Germany's 1923 runaway inflation). Longer-term decisions are even more difficult. Should you commit yourself to four years of college, for example, if you aren't certain that you or your parents will be able to afford the full costs? In a period of stable prices you can be fairly certain of what a college education will cost. But if prices are rising, you can no longer be sure how large the bill will be. Under such circumstances, some individuals may decide not to enter college rather than risk the possibility of being driven out later by rising costs.

Price uncertainties affect production decisions as well. Imagine a firm that's considering building a new factory. Typically, the construction of a factory takes two years or more, including planning, site selection, and actual construction. If construction costs change rapidly, the firm may find that it's unable to complete the factory or to operate it profitably. Confronted with this added uncertainty, the firm may decide not to build a new plant in the first place.

WEBNOTE

To see how much the cost of college or any product will change at different inflation rates, use the CPI inflator provided by the Federal Reserve Bank of Minneapolis at woodrow.mpls.frb.fed.us/economy/calc/cpihome.html.

"DO I HAVE YOUR ASSURANCE THAT PRICES WILL NOT BE INCREASED BEFORE WE ARE SERVED?"

Analysis: The uncertainty caused by rising prices causes stress and may alter consumption and investment decisions.

Shortened Time Horizons

When market participants become less certain about the future, the economy is likely to suffer in the end. In general, *people shorten their time horizons in the face of inflation uncertainties.* If consumers and producers postpone or cancel their expenditure plans, the demand for goods and services will fall. Eventually our production of goods and services will fall as well, and we'll end up somewhere inside our production possibilities curve, with increased unemployment.

The effect of rising price levels on time horizons was dramatically illustrated during Germany's **hyperinflation** of the early 1920s. With prices doubling every *week*, German workers couldn't afford to wait until the end of the week to do their shopping. Instead, they were paid twice daily and given brief "shopping breaks" to make their essential purchases. In this case, the rate of expenditure on goods and services actually increased as a result of inflation, but the rate of production fell. The same kind of frenzy occurred in China during 1948 and 1949. The Nationalist Chinese yuan declined precipitously in value, and market participants rushed to spend their incomes as fast as they could. No one saved income or even tried to.

Hyperinflation also crippled the Russian economy during the period 1990–92. Prices rose by 200 percent in 1991 and by another 1,000 percent in 1992. These price increases rendered the Russian ruble nearly worthless. No one wanted to hold rubles or trade for them. Farmers preferred to hold potatoes rather than sell them. Producers of shoes and clothes likewise decided to hold rather than sell their products. The resulting contraction in supply caused a severe decline in Russian output.

hyperinflation: Inflation rate in excess of 200 percent, lasting at least one year.

Speculation

Inflation threatens not only to reduce the level of economic activity but to change its very nature. If you really expect prices to rise, it makes sense to buy goods and resources now for resale later. If prices rise fast enough, you can make a handsome profit. These are the kinds of thoughts that motivate people to buy houses, precious metals, commodities, and other assets. But such speculation, if carried too far, can detract from the production process. If speculative profits become too easy, few people will engage in production; instead, everyone will be buying and selling existing goods. People may even be encouraged to withhold resources from the production process, hoping to sell them later at higher prices, which is what Russian farmers were doing in 1991 when they withheld potatoes from the market. As such behavior becomes widespread, production declines and unemployment rises.

WEBNOTE

Want a "down-under" view of inflation? The Reserve Bank of New Zealand offers insights into the problems of inflation at www.rbnz.govt.nz/monopol/about/0053316.html.

Bracket Creep

Another reason that savings, investment, and work effort decline when prices rise is that taxes go up, too. Federal income tax rates are *progressive;* that is, tax rates are higher for larger incomes. The intent of these progressive rates is to redistribute income from rich to poor. However, inflation tends to increase *everyone's* income. In the process, people are pushed into higher tax brackets and confront higher tax rates. The process is referred to as **bracket creep.** In recent years, bracket creep has been limited by the inflation indexing of personal income tax rates and a reduction in the number of tax brackets. However, Social Security payroll taxes and most state and local taxes aren't indexed.

bracket creep: The movement of taxpayers into higher tax brackets (rates) as nominal incomes grow.

Although the public sector still reaps some gain from inflation, inflation stress tends to create a political backlash. Voters are quick to blame the government for inflation. If the administration doesn't put a stop to inflation, the voters will turn to someone who promises to do so.

Deflation Dangers

Ironically, a *falling* price level—a deflation—might not make people happy either. In fact, a falling price level can do the same kind of harm as a rising price level. When prices are falling, people on fixed incomes and long-term contracts gain more *real* income. Lenders win and creditors lose. People who hold cash or bonds win: Homeowners and stamp collectors lose. A deflation simply reverses the kinds of redistributions caused by inflation.

A falling price level also has similar macro consequences. Time horizons get shorter. Businesses are more reluctant to borrow money or to invest. People lose confidence in themselves and public institutions when declining price levels deflate their incomes and assets.

MEASURING INFLATION

In view of the macro and micro consequences of price-level changes, the measurement of inflation serves two purposes: to gauge the average rate of inflation and to identify its principal victims.

Consumer Price Index

The most common measure of inflation is the **Consumer Price Index (CPI).** As its name suggests, the CPI is a mechanism for measuring changes in the average price of consumer goods and services. It's analogous to the fruit price index we discussed earlier. The CPI doesn't refer to the price of any particular good but to the average price of all consumer goods.

Consumer Price Index (CPI): A measure (index) of changes in the average price of consumer goods and services.

By itself, the "average price" of consumer goods isn't a very useful number. But once we know the average price of consumer goods, we can observe whether that average rises—that is, whether inflation is occurring. By observing the extent to which prices increase, we can calculate the **inflation rate.**

inflation rate: The annual percentage rate of increase in the average price level.

We can get a better sense of how inflation is measured by observing how the CPI is constructed. The process begins by identifying a market basket of goods and services the typical consumer buys. For this purpose, the Bureau of Labor Statistics surveys a large sample of families every year to determine what goods and services consumers actually buy. Figure 7.2 summarizes the results of the 1999 survey, which reveal that 32.6 cents out of every consumer dollar is spent on housing (shelter, furnishings, and utilities), 13.6 cents on food, and another 19 cents on transportation. Only 5 cents of every consumer dollar is spent on entertainment.

Within these broad categories of expenditure, the Bureau of Labor Statistics itemizes specific goods and services. The details of the expenditure survey show, for example, that private expenditures for reading and education account for only 2 percent of the typical consumer's budget, less than is spent on alcoholic beverages and tobacco. It also shows that we spend 7 cents out of every dollar on fuel, to drive our cars (3.1 cents) and to heat and cool our houses (3.9 cents).

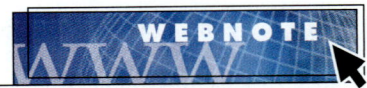

At the U.S. Bureau of Labor Statistics, www.bls.gov, you can find the CPI for the most recent month and the same month last year.

Once we know what the typical consumer buys, it's relatively easy to calculate the average price of a market basket. The Bureau of Labor Statistics actually goes shopping in 85 cities across the country, recording the prices of the 184 items that make up the typical market basket. Approximately 19,000 stores are visited, and 60,000 landlords, renters, and homeowners are surveyed—every month!

As a result of these massive, ongoing surveys, the Bureau of Labor Statistics can tell us what's happening to consumer prices. Suppose, for example, that the market basket cost $100 last year and that the same basket of goods and services cost $110 this year. On the basis of those two shopping trips, we could conclude that consumer prices had risen by 10 percent in one year.

In practice, the CPI is usually expressed in terms of what the market basket cost in a specific **base period.** The price level in the base period is arbitrarily designated as 100. In the case of the CPI, the average price level for the period 1982–84 is usually used as the base for computing price changes. Hence, the price index for that base period is set at 100. In January 2002, the CPI registered 179. In other words, it cost $179 in 2002 to buy the same market baskets that cost only $100 in the base period. Prices had increased by an average of 79 percent over that period. Each month the Bureau of Labor Statistics updates the CPI, telling us how the current cost of that same basket compares to its cost between 1982 and 1984.[2]

base period: The time period used for comparative analysis: the basis for indexing, for example, of price changes.

[2] Since January 1978, the Bureau of Labor Statistics has actually been computing two CPIs, one for urban wage earners and clerical workers and the second and larger one for all urban consumers (about 80 percent of the population). A third index, which uses rent rather than ownership costs of shelter, was introduced in 1983. The "urban/rental" index is most commonly cited.

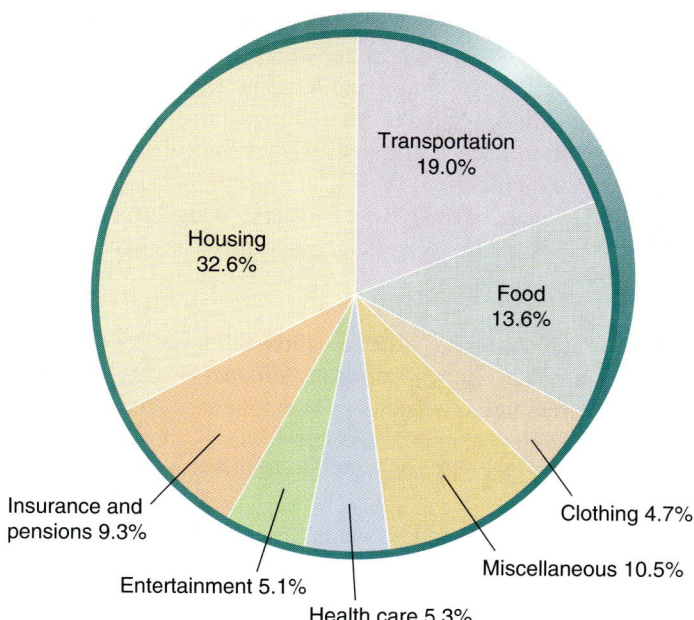

FIGURE 7.2
The Market Basket

To measure changes in average prices, we must first know what goods and services consumers buy. This diagram, based on consumer surveys, shows how the typical urban consumer spends each dollar. Housing, transportation, and food account for over two-thirds of consumer spending.

Source: U.S. Bureau of Labor Statistics (1999 data).

Table 7.4 illustrates how changes in the official CPI are computed. Notice that all price changes don't have the same impact on the inflation rate. Rather, *the effect of a specific price change on the inflation rate depends on the product's relative importance in consumer budgets.*

The U.S. Bureau of Labor Statistics updates the CPI and PPI every month. For the latest inflation data visit the bureau at stats.bls.gov/cpihome.htm. Click on "ppi-home" for an explanation of how the PPI and CPI differ.

> The Consumer Expenditure Survey of 1999 revealed that the average household spends 0.85 cent of every consumer dollar on college tuition. Households without college students don't pay any tuition, of course. And your family probably devotes *more* than 0.85 cent of each consumer dollar to tuition. On *average* however, 0.85 cent is the proportion of each dollar spent on tuition. This figure is the *item weight* of tuition in computing the CPI.
>
> The impact on the CPI of a price change for a specific good is calculated as follows:
>
> Item weight × percentage change in price of item = percentage change in CPI
>
> Suppose that tuition prices suddenly go up 20 percent. What impact will this single price increase have on the CPI? In this case, where tuition is the only price that increases, the impact on the CPI will be only 0.17 percent (0.0085 × 20) as illustrated below. Thus, a very large increase in the price of tuition (20 percent) has a tiny impact (0.17 percent) on the *average* price level.
>
> Housing, on the other hand, accounts for 32.6 percent of consumer expenditure. Thus if housing prices increase 20 percent, and housing is the only price that increases, the impact on the CPI will be 6.52 percent, as shown below.
>
> The relative importance of an item in consumer budgets—its item weight—is a key determinant of its inflationary impact.

Item	Item Weight	×	Price Increase for the Item	=	Impact on the CPI
College tuition	0.0085		20%		0.17%
Housing	0.326		20%		6.52%

TABLE 7.4
Computing Changes in the CPI
The impact of any price change on the average price level depends on the importance of an item in the typical consumer budget.

item weight: The percentage of total expenditure spent on a specific product; used to compute inflation indexes.

The relative importance of a product in consumer budgets is reflected in its **item weight,** which refers to the percentage of a typical consumer budget spent on the item. Table 7.4 shows the item weights for college tuition and housing. College tuition may loom very large in your personal budget, but less than 1 percent of *all* consumer expenditure is spent on college tuition. Hence, the item weight for college tuition in the *average* consumer budget is only 0.0085.

Housing costs absorb a far larger share of the typical consumer budget. As Table 7.4 shows, the item weight for housing is 0.326. Accordingly, rent increases have a much larger impact on the CPI than do tuition hikes.

Producer Price Indexes

In addition to the familiar Consumer Price Index, there are three Producer Price Indexes (PPIs). The PPIs keep track of average prices received by *producers*. One index includes crude materials, another covers intermediate goods, and the last covers finished goods. The three PPIs don't include all producer prices but primarily those in mining, manufacturing, and agriculture. Like the CPI, changes in the PPIs are identified in monthly surveys.

Over long periods of time, the PPIs and the CPI generally reflect the same rate of inflation. In the short run, however, the PPIs usually increase before the CPI, because it takes time for producers' price increases to be reflected in the prices that consumers pay. For this reason, the PPIs are watched closely as a clue to potential changes in consumer prices.

The GDP Deflator

GDP deflator: A price index that refers to all goods and services included in GDP.

The broadest price index is the GDP deflator. The GDP deflator covers all output, including consumer goods, investment goods, and government services. Unlike the CPI and PPIs, the **GDP deflator** isn't based on a fixed "basket" of goods or services. Rather, it allows the contents of the basket to change with people's consumption and investment patterns. The GDP deflator therefore isn't a pure measure of price change. Its value reflects both price changes and market responses to those price changes, as reflected in new expenditure patterns. Hence, the GDP deflator typically registers a lower inflation rate than the CPI.

Real vs. Nominal GDP. The GDP deflator is used to adjust nominal output values for changing price levels. Recall that **nominal GDP** refers to the *current*-dollar value of output, whereas **real GDP** denotes the *inflation-adjusted* value of output. These two measures of output are connected by the GDP deflator:

nominal GDP: The value of final output produced in a given period, measured in the prices of that period (current prices).

$$\text{Real GDP} = \frac{\text{nominal GDP}}{\text{GDP deflator}}$$

real GDP: The value of final output produced in a given period, adjusted for changing prices.

The nominal values of GDP were $10 trillion in 2000 and $5.7 trillion in 1990. However, the price level rose by 24 percent between those years. Hence, real GDP in 2000 in the base-period prices of 1990 was

$$\frac{\text{2000 real GDP}}{\text{(in 1990 prices)}} = \frac{\text{nominal GDP}}{\text{price deflator}} = \frac{\$10 \text{ trillion}}{\frac{124}{100}} = \frac{\$10 \text{ trillion}}{1.24} = \$8.06 \text{ trillion}$$

Changes in real GDP are a good measure of how output and living standards are changing. Nominal GDP statistics, by contrast, mix up output and price changes.

THE GOAL: PRICE STABILITY

In view of the inequities, anxieties, and real losses caused by inflation, it's not surprising that price stability is a major goal of economic policy. As we observed at the beginning of this chapter, every U.S. president since Franklin Roosevelt has decreed price stability to be a foremost policy goal. Unfortunately, few presidents (or their advisers) have stated exactly what they mean by "price stability." Do they mean *no* change in the average price level? Or is some upward creep in the price index acceptable?

A Numerical Goal

An explicit numerical goal for **price stability** was established for the first time in the Full Employment and Balanced Growth Act of 1978. According to that act, the goal of economic policy is to hold the rate of inflation under 3 percent.

Unemployment Concerns

Why did Congress choose 3 percent inflation rather than zero inflation as the benchmark for price stability? One reason was concern about unemployment. To keep prices from rising, the government might have to restrain spending in the economy. Such restraint could lead to cutbacks in production and an increase in joblessness. In other words, there might be a trade-off between declining inflation and rising unemployment. From this perspective, a little bit of inflation might be the "price" the economy has to pay to keep unemployment rates from rising.

Recall how the same kind of logic was used to define the goal of full employment. The fear there was that price pressures would increase as the economy approached its production possibilities. This suggested that some unemployment might be the "price" the economy has to pay for price stability. Accordingly, the goal of "full employment" was defined as the lowest rate of unemployment *consistent with stable prices*. The same kind of thinking is apparent here. The amount of inflation regarded as tolerable depends in part on the effect of anti-inflation strategies on unemployment rates. After reviewing our experiences with both unemployment and inflation, Congress concluded that 3 percent inflation was a safe target.

price stability: The absence of significant changes in the average price level; officially defined as a rate of inflation of less than 3 percent.

Quality Changes

The second argument for setting our price-stability goal above zero inflation relates to our measurement capabilities. The Consumer Price Index isn't a perfect measure of inflation. In essence, the CPI simply monitors the price of specific goods over time. Over time, however, the goods themselves change, too. Old products become better as a result of *quality improvements.* A projection TV set costs more today than a TV did in 1955, but today's television also delivers a bigger, clearer picture, in digital sound and color, and with a host of on-screen programming options. Hence, increases in the price of TV sets tend to exaggerate the true rate of inflation: Most of the higher price represents more product.

The same is true of automobiles. The best-selling car in 1958 (a Chevrolet Bel Air) had a list price of only $2,618. That makes a 2002 Ford Taurus look awfully expensive at $19,225. The quality of today's cars is much better, however. Improvements since 1958 include seat belts, air bags, variable-speed windshield wipers, electronic ignitions, rear-window defrosters, radial tires, antilock brakes, emergency flashers, remote-control mirrors, crash-resistant bodies, a doubling of fuel mileage, and a 100-fold decrease in exhaust pollutants. As a result, today's higher car prices also buy cars that are safer, cleaner, and more comfortable.

The U.S. Bureau of Labor Statistics does adjust the CPI for quality changes. Such adjustments inevitably entail subjective judgments, however. Critics are quick to complain that the CPI overstates inflation because quality improvements are undervalued.

New Products

The problem of measuring quality improvements is even more difficult in the case of new products. The computers and word processors used today didn't exist when the Census Bureau conducted its 1972–73 survey of consumer expenditure. The 1982–84 expenditure survey included those products but not still newer ones such as the cellular phone. As the News on the next page explains, the omission of cellular phones caused the CPI to overstate the rate of inflation. The consumer expenditure survey of 1993–95 included cell phones but not digital cameras, HDTVs, or DVD players—all of which have had declining prices. As a result, there's a significant (though unmeasured) element of error in the CPI insofar as it's intended to gauge changes in the average prices paid by consumers. The goal of 3 percent inflation allows for such errors.

IN THE NEWS

Ignoring Cell Phones Biases CPI Upward

Cellular telephones have been in commercial operation in the United States for 13 years. Beginning in Chicago in late 1983, and then at the Los Angeles Olympic Games in 1984, cellular telephone usage spread first to the top 30 Metropolitan Statistical Areas (MSAs), then to the other 300 or so MSAs, and finally to rural areas. At year-end 1996, there were over 40 million cellular subscribers in the United States. . . .

Yet the cellular telephone will not be included in the calculation of the Consumer Price Index (CPI) until 1998 or 1999. "This neglect of new goods leads to an upward bias in the CPI," NBER Research Associate Jerry Hausman concludes.

The CPI estimates that since 1988, telecommunications prices have increased by 8.5 percent, or 1.02 percent per year. A corrected index that includes cellular service decreased 1.28 percent per year since 1988, Hausman figures. "Thus, the bias in the BLS [Bureau of Labor Statistics] telecommunications services CPI equals approximately 2.3 percentage points per year."

Source: National Bureau of Economic Research, *NBER Digest*, June 1997. www.nber.org/digest

Analysis: Since the CPI tracks prices for a fixed basket of goods, it misses the effects of falling prices on new goods that appear between survey periods.

THE HISTORICAL RECORD

In the long view of history, the United States has done a good job of maintaining price stability. On closer inspection, however, our inflation performance is very uneven. Table 7.5 summarizes the long view, with data going back to 1800. The base period for pricing the market basket of goods is again 1982–84. Notice that the same market basket cost only $17 in 1800. Consumer prices increased 500 percent in 183 years. But also observe how frequently the price level *fell* in the 1800s and again in the 1930s. These recurrent deflations held down the long-run inflation rate. Because of these periodic deflations, average prices in 1945 were at the same level as in 1800!

Figure 7.3 provides a closer view of our more recent experience with inflation. In this figure we transform annual changes in the CPI into percentage rates of inflation. The CPI increased from 72.6 to 82.4 during 1980. This 9.8-point jump in the CPI translates into a 13.5 percent rate of inflation (9.8 ÷ 72.6 = 0.135). This inflation rate, represented by point A in Figure 7.3, was the highest in a generation. Since then, prices have continued to increase, but at much slower rates.

As the accompanying World View documents, the low rates of inflation the United States has experienced are far below the pace in other nations. In 2000, for example,

TABLE 7.5
Two Centuries of Price Changes
Before World War II, the average level of prices rose in some years and fell in others. Since 1945, prices have risen continuously. The Consumer Price Index has more than doubled since 1980.

Year	CPI	Year	CPI	Year	CPI	Year	CPI
1800	17.0	1900	8.3	1940	14.0	1980	82.4
1825	11.3	1915	10.1	1950	24.1	1982–84	100.0
1850	8.3	1920	20.0	1960	29.6	1990	130.5
1875	11.0	1930	16.7	1970	38.8	2000	172.8

Note: Data from 1915 forward reflect the official all-items Consumer Price Index, which used the pre-1983 measure of shelter costs. Estimated indexes for 1800 through 1900 are drawn from several sources.

Source: U.S. Bureau of Labor Statistics.

FIGURE 7.3
Annual Inflation Rates

During the 1920s and 1930s, consumer prices fell significantly, causing a general deflation. Since the Great Depression, however, average prices have risen almost every year. But even during this inflationary period, the annual rate of price increase has varied widely. In 1980, the rate of inflation was 13.5 percent (point A); in 1998, average prices rose only 1.6 percent (point B).

Source: U.S. Bureau of Labor Statistics.

Worldwide Inflation

In many countries prices rise at rates much higher than those in the United States. In 2000, the inflation rate in the Congo (Democratic Republic) was so high that prices rose 70 percent every *month*.

In the United States the inflation rate for the entire *year* was only 3.4 percent. In Japan, the price level actually *fell* by 0.6 percent. What are the implications of such wildly different inflation rates?

Country	Inflation Rate	Country	Inflation Rate
Congo	554	Venezuela	16
Angola	325	United States	3.4
Belarus	169	Canada	2.7
Ecuador	96	Germany	2.1
Turkey	55	Japan	−0.6
Russia	21		

Source: International Monetary Fund, *World Economic Outlook*, 2001. www.imf.org

Analysis: Although inflation is regarded as a major macro problem in the United States, American inflation rates are comparatively low. Many developing countries have extraordinarily fast price increases.

the U.S. inflation rate was less than Europe's and incomprehensibly high for consumers in the Congo, where prices rose 70 percent per *month*.

CAUSES OF INFLATION

The evident variation in year-to-year inflation rates requires explanation. So do the horrifying bouts of hyperinflation that have erupted in other nations at various times. What causes price levels to rise or fall?

In the most general terms, this is an easy question to answer. Recall that all market transactions entail two converging forces, namely, *demand* and *supply*. Accordingly, any explanation of changing price levels must be rooted in one of these two market forces.

Demand-Pull Inflation

Excessive pressure on the demand side of the economy is often the cause of inflation. Suppose the economy was already producing at capacity but that consumers were willing and able to buy even more goods. With accumulated savings or easy access to credit, consumers could end up trying to buy more output than the economy was producing. This would be a classic case of "too much money chasing too few goods." As consumers sought to acquire more goods, store shelves (inventory) would begin to empty. Seeing this, producers would begin raising prices. The end result would be a demand-driven rise in average prices, or demand-pull inflation.

Cost-Push Inflation

The pressure on prices could also originate on the supply side. When the Organization of Petroleum Exporting Countries (OPEC) abruptly increased oil prices in 2000–01, production costs increased in a broad array of industries. To cover these higher costs, producers raised output prices. When Hurricane Mitch devastated Honduras in 1998, it destroyed a huge portion of that country's production capacity, including its farm output. As market participants scurried for the remaining output, prices rose across the board.

Inflationary pressures could also originate in higher wages. If labor unions were able to abruptly push up wage rates, the costs of production would increase, putting pressure on product prices.

For current news stories on inflation, check out the Excite server www.excite.com. Search for "inflation."

PROTECTIVE MECHANISMS

Whatever the *causes* of inflation, market participants don't want to suffer the consequences. Even at a relatively low rate of inflation, the real value of money declines over time. If prices rise by an average of just 4 percent a year, the real value of $1,000 drops to $822 in five years and to only $676 in ten years (see Table 7.6). *Low rates of inflation don't have the drama of hyperinflation, but they still redistribute real wealth and income.*

COLAs

Market participants can protect themselves from inflation by *indexing* their nominal incomes, as is done with Social Security benefits, for example. In any year that the rate of inflation exceeds 3 percent, Social Security benefits go up *automatically* by the same percentage as the inflation rate. This **cost-of-living adjustment (COLA)** ensures that nominal benefits keep pace with the rising prices. Because of the COLA, much of the real income of retirees is protected (private pensions typically don't include COLAs).

Landlords often protect their real incomes with COLAs as well, by including in their leases provisions that automatically increase rents by the rate of inflation. COLAs are also common in labor union agreements, government transfer programs (like food stamps), and many other contracts. In every such case, *a COLA protects real income from inflation.*

cost-of-living adjustment (COLA): Automatic adjustments of nominal income to the rate of inflation.

ARMs

Cost-of-living adjustments have also become more common in loan agreements. As we noted before, debtors win and creditors lose when the price level rises. Suppose a loan

TABLE 7.6

Inflation's Impact, 2002–2012

In the past 20 years, the U.S. rate of inflation ranged from a low of 1 percent to a high of 13 percent. Does a range of 12 percentage points really make much difference? One way to find out is to see how a specific sum of money will shrink in real value in a decade.

Here's what would happen to the real value of $1,000 from January 1, 2002, to January 1, 2012, at different inflation rates. At 2 percent inflation, $1,000 held for 10 years would be worth $820. At 10 percent inflation that same $1,000 would buy only $386 worth of goods in the year 2012.

Year	\multicolumn{5}{c}{Annual Inflation Rate}
	2 Percent	4 Percent	6 Percent	8 Percent	10 Percent
2002	$1,000	$1,000	$1,000	$1,000	$1,000
2003	980	962	943	926	909
2004	961	925	890	857	826
2005	942	889	840	794	751
2006	924	855	792	735	683
2007	906	822	747	681	621
2008	888	790	705	630	564
2009	871	760	665	584	513
2010	853	731	627	540	467
2011	837	703	592	500	424
2012	820	676	558	463	386

requires interest payments equal to 5 percent of the amount (principal) borrowed. If the rate of inflation jumps to 7 percent, prices will be rising faster than interest is accumulating. Hence, the **real interest rate**—the inflation-adjusted rate of interest—will actually be negative. The interest payments made in future years will buy fewer goods than can be bought today.

The real rate of interest is calculated as

Real interest rate = nominal interest rate − anticipated rate of inflation

In this case, the nominal interest rate is 5 percent and inflation is 7 percent. Hence, the *real* rate of interest is *minus* 2 percent. The World View below illustrates how inflation can make even sky-high (nominal) interest rates look pretty mundane.

The distinction between real and nominal interest rates isn't too important if you're lending or borrowing money for just a couple of days. But the distinction is critical for long-term loans like home mortgages. Mortgage loans typically span a period of 25 to 30 years. If the inflation rate stays higher than the nominal interest rate during this period, the lender will end up with less *real* wealth than was initially lent.

To protect against such losses, the banking industry offers home loans, with adjustable interest rates. An **adjustable-rate mortgage (ARM)** stipulates an interest rate that

real interest rate: The nominal interest rate minus the anticipated inflation rate.

adjustable-rate mortgage (ARM): A mortgage (home loan) that adjusts the nominal interest rate to changing rates of inflation.

WORLD VIEW

Sky-High Interest Rates South of the Border

Fed up with those measly interest payments the bank pays on your hard-earned savings? Why not move your savings account to Ecuador, where banks were paying interest rates of 80 percent or more on savings accounts in 2000? That's right, 80 percent!

These sky-high interest rates look tempting, but there's a catch. The inflation rate in Ecuador in 2000 was 96 percent (see World View; p. 143.). So those high interest payments didn't keep up with rising prices. After inflation, savers had less buying power than when they first put money in the bank. The *real* interest rate—the nominal interest rate minus inflation was actually *negative*. That hardly justifies a trip to South America.

Source: International Monetary Fund
www.imf.org

Analysis: The appropriate measure of a return on savings is the *real* interest rate. The real rate equals the *nominal* rate minus anticipated inflation.

IN THE NEWS

CPI Overstates Inflation, Senate Panel Says

The government's most widely used inflation gauge, the consumer price index, will overstate future inflation by about one percentage point every year, according to a panel of five experts appointed by the Senate Finance Committee. . . .

The Congressional Budget Office has calculated that by shaving one percentage point off the cost-of-living increases in entitlement programs, the government would save the government about $140 billion a year by 2005. That would cut the projected budget deficit that year by about a third. . . .

In its interim report, the advisory committee estimated that the CPI now overstates the rise in living costs for the average household by somewhere from 0.7 percent to 2.0 percent each year, and has been doing so for at least the past 20 years.

—Steven Pearlstein

Source: *Washington Post*, September 15, 1995. © 1995 The Washington Post. Reprinted with permission. www.washingtonpost.com

Analysis: Changes in product quality and expenditure patterns may cause inflation to be overestimated. Any overstatement will increase federal outlays and reduce tax revenues because of inflation indexing.

---

changes during the term of the loan. A mortgage paying 5 percent interest in a stable (3 percent inflation) price environment may later require 9 percent interest if the inflation rate jumps to 7 percent. Such an adjustment would keep the real rate of interest at 2 percent.

The Cost of Mismeasurement

The proliferation of COLAs and ARMs has made the CPI a critical statistic in today's economy. The problem is simple: If the CPI goes up, so do government transfer payments, union wages, and nominal interest rates. Critics charge that the Bureau of Labor Statistics has persistently exaggerated the inflation rate by undervaluing quality improvements, new products, and changes in expenditure patterns. If the CPI overstates inflation by just one percentage point, the federal government loses $140 billion per year in increased outlays and reduced tax revenues (see News). In 1998, the CPI's market basket of goods and services was overhauled. The new index, based on 1993–95 expenditure patterns, includes more new products such as cell phones and new adjustments for quality improvements. As products continue to emerge and change, however, the CPI will remain an imperfect but highly useful measure of inflation.

THE ECONOMY TOMORROW

The End of Inflation?

The earth spins, the sun shines, prices rise: two generations have grown up believing that inflation is an unalterable fact of life. No wonder. A dollar today is worth only 13 cents in 1945 money; a pound is worth only 6p. Much of the damage was done in the 1970s and early 1980s, and much has improved since then. In the OECD countries inflation is now hovering around its 1960s level of 3–4 percent. That gives governments the best chance they have had for decades to kill it off and achieve price stability. Sadly, they may fluff it.

Historical Stability

Price stability is not as extraordinary as it sounds. It does not mean that all prices stay the same: some will fall, others rise, but the average price level remains constant. Anyway, inflation, in the sense of continuously rising prices, is historically the exception, not the rule. On the eve of the first world war, prices in Britain were on average no higher than at the time of the fire of London in 1666. . . . During those 250 years, the longest unbroken run of rising prices was six years. Since 1946, by contrast, prices in Britain have risen every year, and the same is true of virtually every other OECD country.

It is easy to say that double-digit inflation is bad, but harder to agree on the ideal rate. Should governments aim for 5 percent 3 percent, or 0 percent? Some claim that the extra benefits of zero inflation are tiny and would be outweighed by the short-term cost—lost output, lost jobs—of pushing inflation lower. A little bit of inflation, they say, acts like a lubricant, helping relative prices and wages to adjust more efficiently, since all wages and most prices are hard to cut in absolute terms. But a little inflation sounds like "a little drink" for an alcoholic. It can too easily accelerate. That is the lesson of the past 40 years—that and the fact that the economies with the lowest inflation have tended to be the ones with the least unemployment. Beyond the short term governments cannot choose to have a bit faster growth in exchange for a bit more inflation. The choice does not exist.

The Virtue of Zero

The rewards of reducing inflation from 5 percent to 0 percent may be smaller than those from crunching inflation from 5,000 percent to 5 percent, but they are still highly desirable. The best inflation rate is one that least affects the behaviour of companies, investors, shoppers and workers. That means zero, because anything higher interferes with the most fundamental function of prices—their ability to provide information about relative scarcities. If prices in general are rising by 5 percent a year, the fact that the price of one particular product rises by 8 percent goes largely unnoticed. Yet that product's relative 3 percent increase ought to attract the attention of potential new producers, and to encourage buyers to look elsewhere—in short, to set in train the changes that maximize economic efficiency. It would do that if the 3 percent rise was like a hillock in an otherwise flat landscape; but, in the mountains of generalized inflation, nobody notices a crag. Even with an annual inflation rate of 5 percent, the general price level doubles every 14 years, obscuring changes in relative prices.

Now imagine a world without inflation. Once it was believable, it would transform the way people behave. Companies would be confident about borrowing long-term money, and lenders confident about providing it. Real interest rates would fall. Firms would invest more because the probable pay-out would be clearer; the same would be true of individuals investing time and money on their education. Governments could budget for infrastructural projects, knowing that their plans would not be derailed by unexpected surges in prices. In general, everyone would think more about the long term because the long term would be easier to see.

Source: *The Economist,* January 22, 1992, p. 11. © 1992 The Economist Newspaper Group, Inc. Reprinted with permission. www.economist.com

SUMMARY

- Inflation is an increase in the average price level. Typically it's measured by changes in a price index such as the Consumer Price Index (CPI).
- At the micro level, inflation redistributes income by altering relative prices, income, and wealth. Because not all prices rise at the same rate and because not all people buy (and sell) the same goods or hold the same assets, inflation doesn't affect everyone equally. Some individuals actually gain from inflation, whereas others suffer a loss of real income or wealth.
- At the macro level, inflation threatens to reduce total output because it increases uncertainties about the future and thereby inhibits consumption and production decisions. Fear of rising prices can also stimulate spending, forcing the government to take restraining action that threatens full employment. Rising prices also encourage speculation and hoarding, which detract from productive activity.
- Fully anticipated inflation reduces the anxieties and real losses associated with rising prices. However, few people can foresee actual price patterns or make all the necessary adjustments in their market activity.
- The U.S. goal of price stability is defined as an inflation rate of less than 3 percent per year. This goal recognizes potential conflicts between zero inflation and full employment as well as the difficulties of measuring quality improvements and new products.
- From 1800 to 1945, prices both rose and fell, leaving the average price level unchanged. Since then, prices have risen nearly every year but at widely different rates.
- Inflation is caused by either excessive demand (demand-

pull inflation) or structural changes in supply (cost-push inflation).
- Cost-of-living adjustments (COLAs) and adjustable-rate mortgages (ARMs) help protect real incomes from inflation. Universal indexing, however, wouldn't eliminate inflationary redistributions of income and wealth.
- Worldwide inflation rates have diminished in recent years. Experience with inflation and changing patterns of asset ownership are creating political pressure for greater price stability.

Key Terms

inflation
deflation
relative price
nominal income
real income
money illusion
hyperinflation
bracket creep

Consumer Price Index (CPI)
inflation rate
base period
item weight
GDP deflator
nominal GDP

real GDP
price stability
cost-of-living adjustment (COLA)
real interest rate
adjustable-rate mortgage (ARM)

Questions for Discussion

1. Why would farmers rather store their output than sell it during periods of hyperinflation? How does this behavior affect prices?
2. In the German hyperinflation of the 1920s, how was production affected?
3. Whose real wealth (see Table 7.3) declined in the 1990s? Who else might have lost real income or wealth? Who gained as a result of inflation?
4. If *all* prices increased at the same rate (i.e., no *relative* price changes), would inflation have any redistributive effects?
5. Would it be advantageous to borrow money if you expected prices to rise? Would you want a fixed-rate loan or one with an adjustable interest rate?
6. Are people worse off when the price level rises as fast as their income? Why do people often feel worse off in such circumstances?
7. Identify two groups that benefit from deflation and two that lose.
8. Could demand-pull inflation occur before an economy was producing at capacity? How?
9. Why would anyone borrow money at 80 percent interest, as was the case in Ecuador in 2001? (See World View, "Sky-High Interest" (p. 145). Why would a bank lend money in that situation?

Web Activities

1. Log on to www.gallup.com/poll/topics/personal.asp. How do people rate the current state of the economy? How do they rate future prospect for the economy? What role do people's expectations about inflation play in their perception of future economic prospects?
2. Most nations have different rates of inflation. Log on to www.imf.org/external/pubs. Find the inflation rates for nations around the world in various tables in the most recent year. Who had the highest rate? Who had the lowest rate? Which nations had inflation in excess of 100 percent?
3. The cost of living varies between different areas of the country. If you earned $100,000 per year in Springfield, Illinois, and wanted to move to Washington, D.C., how much would you need in additional income for your cost of living to remain unchanged? To calculate this answer, log on to www2.homefair.com/calc/salcalc.html and use the salary calculator. What might explain the different costs, and how might they influence your decision to move there?

 THE ACCOMPANYING STUDENT PROBLEM SET CONTAINS NUMERICAL AND GRAPHING PROBLEMS FOR THIS CHAPTER

PART 3

Cyclical Instability

One of the central concerns of macroeconomics is the short-run business cycle—recurrent bouts of expansion and contraction of the nation's output. These cycles affect jobs, prices, economic growth, and international trade and financial balances. Chapters 8 through 10 focus on the nature of the business cycle and the market forces that might affect it.

CHAPTER 8

The Business Cycle

In 1929 it looked as though the sun would never set on the U.S. economy. For eight years in a row, the U.S. economy had been expanding rapidly. During the Roaring Twenties, the typical American family drove its first car, bought its first radio, and went to the movies for the first time. With factories running at capacity, virtually anyone who wanted to work found a job readily.

Everyone was optimistic. In his Acceptance Address in November 1928, President-elect Herbert Hoover echoed this optimism by declaring: "We in America today are nearer to the final triumph over poverty than ever before in the history of any land. . . . We shall soon with the help of God be in sight of the day when poverty will be banished from this nation."

The booming stock market seemed to confirm this optimistic outlook. Between 1921 and 1927 the stock market's value more than doubled, adding billions of dollars to the wealth of U.S. households and businesses. The stock market boom accelerated in 1927, causing stock prices to double again in less than two years. The roaring stock market made it look easy to get rich in America.

The party ended abruptly on October 24, 1929. On what came to be known as Black Thursday, the stock market crashed. In a few short hours, the market value of U.S. corporations tumbled, in the most frenzied selloff ever seen (see News). The next day President Hoover tried to assure America's stockholders that the economy was "on a sound and prosperous basis." But despite his assurances and the efforts of leading bankers to stem the decline, the stock market continued to plummet. The following Tuesday (October 29) the pace of selling quickened. By the end of the year, more than $40 billion of wealth had vanished in the Great Crash. Rich men became paupers overnight; ordinary families lost their savings, their homes, and even their lives.

The devastation was not confined to Wall Street. The financial flames engulfed the farms, the banks, and industry. Between 1930 and 1935, millions of rural families lost their farms. Automobile production fell from 4.5 million cars in 1929 to only 1.1 million in 1932. So many banks were forced to close that newly elected President Roosevelt had to declare a "bank holiday" in March 1933 to stem the outflow of cash to anxious depositors.

Throughout these years, the ranks of the unemployed continued to swell. In October 1929, only 3 percent of the workforce was unemployed. A year later the total was over 9 percent, and millions of additional workers were getting by on lower wages and shorter hours. But things got worse. By 1933, over one-fourth

IN THE NEWS

Market in Panic As Stocks Are Dumped in 12,894,600 Share Day; Bankers Halt It

Effect Is Felt on the Curb and throughout Nation—Financial District Goes Wild

The stock markets of the country tottered on the brink of panic yesterday as a prosperous people, gone suddenly hysterical with fear, attempted simultaneously to sell a record-breaking volume of securities for whatever they would bring.

The result was a financial nightmare, comparable to nothing ever before experienced in Wall Street. It rocked the financial district to its foundations, hopelessly overwhelmed its mechanical facilities, chilled its blood with terror.

In a society built largely on confidence, with real wealth expressed more or less inaccurately by pieces of paper, the entire fabric of economic stability threatened to come toppling down.

Into the frantic hands of a thousand brokers on the floor of the New York Stock Exchange poured the selling orders of the world. It was sell, sell, sell—hour after desperate hour until 1:30 P.M.

—Laurence Stern

Source: *The World*, October 25, 1929.

Analysis: Stock markets are a barometer of confidence in the economy. If people have doubts about the economy, they're less willing to hold stocks. The crash of 1929 mirrored and worsened consumer confidence.

---

of the labor force was unable to find work. People slept in the streets, scavenged for food, and sold apples on Wall Street.

The Great Depression seemed to last forever. In 1933, President Roosevelt lamented that one-third of the nation was ill-clothed, ill-housed, and ill-fed. Thousands of unemployed workers marched to the Capitol to demand jobs and aid. In 1938, nine years after Black Thursday, nearly 20 percent of the workforce was still idle.

The Great Depression shook not only the foundations of the world economy but also the self-confidence of the economics profession. No one had predicted the depression, and few could explain it. The ensuing search for explanations focused on three central questions:

- How stable is a market-driven economy?
- What forces cause instability?
- What, if anything, can the government do to promote steady economic growth?

The basic purpose of **macroeconomics** is to answer these questions—to *explain how and why economies grow and what causes the recurrent ups and downs of the economy that characterize the **business cycle**.* In this chapter we introduce the theoretical model economists use to describe and explain the short-run business cycle. We'll also preview some of the policy options the government might use to dampen those cycles.

macroeconomics: The study of aggregate economic behavior, of the economy as a whole.

business cycle: Alternating periods of economic growth and contraction.

STABLE OR UNSTABLE?

Prior to the 1930s, macro economists thought there could never be a Great Depression. The economic thinkers of the time asserted that a market-driven economy was inherently stable. There was no need for government intervention in the macro economy.

This **laissez-faire** view of macroeconomics seemed reasonable at the time. During the nineteenth century and the first 30 years of the twentieth, the U.S. economy experienced some bad years in which the nation's output declined and unemployment increased. But most of these episodes were relatively short-lived. The dominant feature of the Industrial Era was growth: an expanding economy, with more output, more jobs, and higher incomes nearly every year.

Classical Theory

laissez faire: The doctrine of "leave it alone," of nonintervention by government in the market mechanism.

A Self-Regulating Economy. In this environment, classical economists, as they later became known, propounded an optimistic view of the macro economy. *According to the classical view, the economy "self-adjusts" to deviations from its long-term growth trend.* Producers might occasionally reduce their output and throw people out of work, but these dislocations would cause little damage. If output declined and people lost their jobs, the internal forces of the marketplace would quickly restore prosperity. Economic downturns were viewed as temporary setbacks, not permanent problems.

The cornerstones of classical optimism were flexible prices and flexible wages. If producers couldn't sell all their output at current prices, they had two choices. They could reduce the rate of output and throw some people out of work, or they could reduce the price of their output, thereby stimulating an increase in the quantity demanded. According to the **law of demand,** price reductions cause an increase in unit sales. If prices fall far enough, all the output produced can be sold. Thus, flexible prices—prices that would drop when consumer demand slowed—virtually guaranteed that all output could be sold. No one would have to lose a job because of weak consumer demand.

Flexible prices had their counterpart in factor markets. If some workers were temporarily out of work, they'd compete for jobs by offering their services at lower wages. As wage rates declined, producers would find it profitable to hire more workers. Ultimately, flexible wages would ensure that everyone who wanted a job would have a job.

These optimistic views of the macro economy were summarized in Say's Law. **Say's Law**—named after the nineteenth-century economist Jean-Baptiste Say—decreed that "supply creates its own demand." Whatever was produced would be sold. All workers who sought employment would be hired. *Unsold goods and unemployed labor could emerge in this classical system, but both would disappear as soon as people had time to adjust prices and wages.* There could be no Great Depression—no protracted macro failure—in this classical view of the world.

Macro Failure. The Great Depression was a stunning blow to classical economists. At the onset of the depression, classical economists assured everyone that the setbacks in production and employment were temporary and would soon vanish. Andrew Mellon, Secretary of the U.S. Treasury, expressed this optimistic view in January 1930, just a few months after the stock market crash. Assessing the prospects for the year ahead, he said: "I see nothing . . . in the present situation that is either menacing or warrants pessimism. . . . I have every confidence that there will be a revival of activity in the spring and that during the coming year the country will make steady progress."[1] Merrill Lynch, one of the nation's largest brokerage houses, was urging that people should buy stocks. But the depression deepened. Indeed, unemployment grew and persisted *despite* falling prices and wages (see Figure 8.1). The classical self-adjustment mechanism simply didn't work.

The Keynesian Revolution

The Great Depression effectively destroyed the credibility of classical economic theory. As John Maynard Keynes pointed out in 1935, classical economists

> were apparently unmoved by the lack of correspondence between the results of their theory and the facts of observation:—a discrepancy which the ordinary man has not failed to observe. . . .
>
> The celebrated optimism of [classical] economic theory . . . is . . . to be traced, I think, to their having neglected to take account of the drag on prosperity which can be exercised by an insufficiency of effective demand. For there would obviously be a natural tendency towards the optimum employment of resources in a Society which was functioning after the manner of the classical postulates. It may well be that the classical theory represents the way in which we should like our Economy to behave. But to assume that it actually does so is to assume our difficulties away.[2]

---

[1] David A. Shannon, *The Great Depression* (Englewood Cliffs, NJ: Prentice Hall, 1960), p. 4.
[2] John Maynard Keynes, *The General Theory of Employment, Interest and Money* (London: Macmillan, 1936), pp. 33–34.

---

law of demand: The quantity of a good demanded in a given time period increases as its price falls, *ceteris paribus.*

Say's Law: Supply creates its own demand.

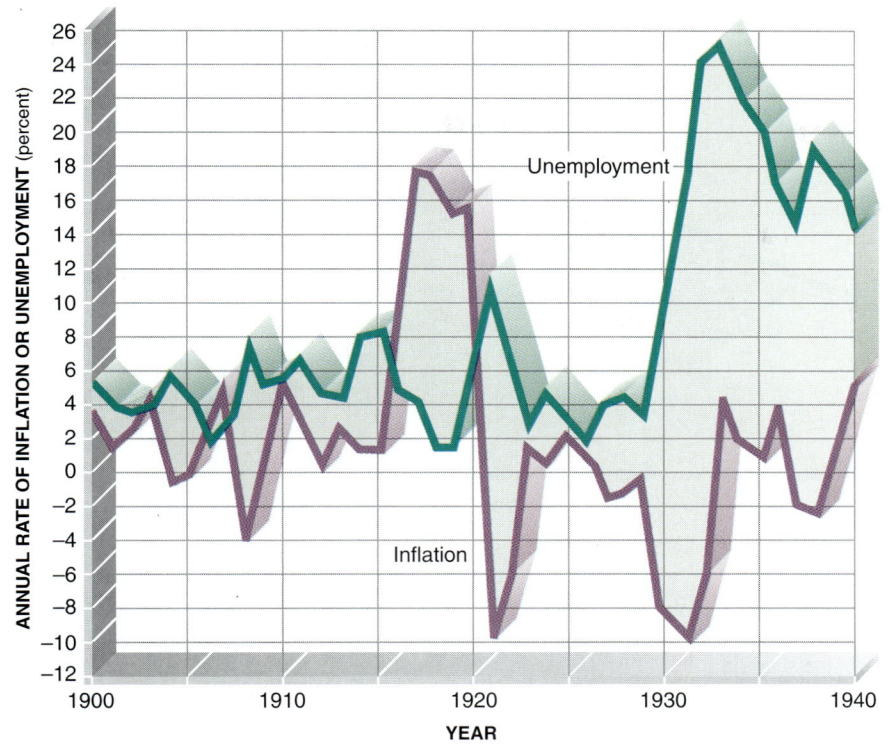

FIGURE 8.1

Inflation and Unemployment, 1900–1940

In the early 1900s, falling price levels (deflation) appeared to limit increases in unemployment. Periods of high unemployment also tended to be brief. These experiences were consistent with Say's Law.

In the 1930s, unemployment rates rose to unprecedented heights and stayed high for a decade. Falling wages and prices did not restore full employment. This macro failure prompted calls for new theories and policies to control the business cycle.

Source: U.S. Bureau of the Census, *The Statistics of the United States*, 1957.

Inherent Instability. Keynes went on to develop an alternative view of the macro economy. Whereas the classical economists viewed the economy as inherently stable, Keynes asserted that a market-driven economy is inherently unstable. Small disturbances in output, prices, or unemployment were likely to be magnified, not muted, by the invisible hand of the marketplace. The Great Depression was not a unique event, Keynes argued, but a calamity that would recur if we relied on the market mechanism to self-adjust.

Government Intervention. In Keynes' view, the inherent instability of the marketplace required government intervention. When the economy falters, we can't afford to wait for some assumed self-adjustment mechanism but must instead intervene to protect jobs and income. The government can do this by "priming the pump": buying more output, employing more people, providing more income transfers, and making more money available. When the economy overheats, the government must cool it down with higher taxes, spending reductions, and less money.

Keynes's denunciation of classical theory didn't end the macroeconomic debate. On the contrary, economists continue to wage fierce debates about the stability of the economy. Those debates fill the pages of the next few chapters. But before examining them, let's first take a quick look at the economy's actual performance.

HISTORICAL CYCLES

The upswings and downturns of the business cycle are gauged in terms of changes in total output. An economic upswing, or expansion, refers to an increase in the volume of goods and services produced. An economic downturn, or contraction, occurs when the total volume of production declines. Changes in employment typically mirror these changes in production.

Figure 8.2 depicts the stylized features of a business cycle. Over the long run, the output of the economy grows at roughly 3 percent per year. There's a lot of year-to-year

FIGURE 8.2
The Business Cycle

The model business cycle resembles a roller coaster. Output first climbs to a peak, then decreases. After hitting a trough, the economy recovers, with real GDP again increasing.

A central concern of macroeconomic theory is to determine whether a recurring business cycle exists, and if so, what are the forces that cause it.

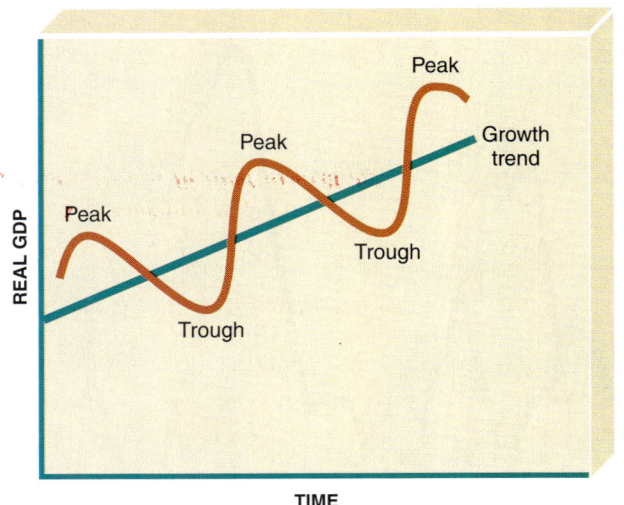

variation around this growth trend, however. The short-run cycle looks like a roller coaster, climbing steeply, then dropping from its peak. Once the trough is reached, the upswing starts again.

In reality, business cycles aren't as regular or as predictable as Figure 8.2 suggests. The U.S. economy has experienced recurrent upswings and downswings, but of widely varying length, intensity, and frequency.

Figure 8.3 illustrates the actual performance of the U.S. economy since 1929. Changes in total output are measured by changes in **real GDP**, the inflation-adjusted value of

real GDP: The value of final output produced in a given period, adjusted for changing prices.

FIGURE 8.3
The Business Cycle in U.S. History

From 1929 to 2001, real GDP increased at an average rate of 3 percent a year. But annual growth rates have departed widely from that average. Years of above-average growth seem to alternate with years of sluggish growth (*growth recessions*) and actual decreases in total output (*recessions*).

Source: U.S. Department of Commerce (2001).

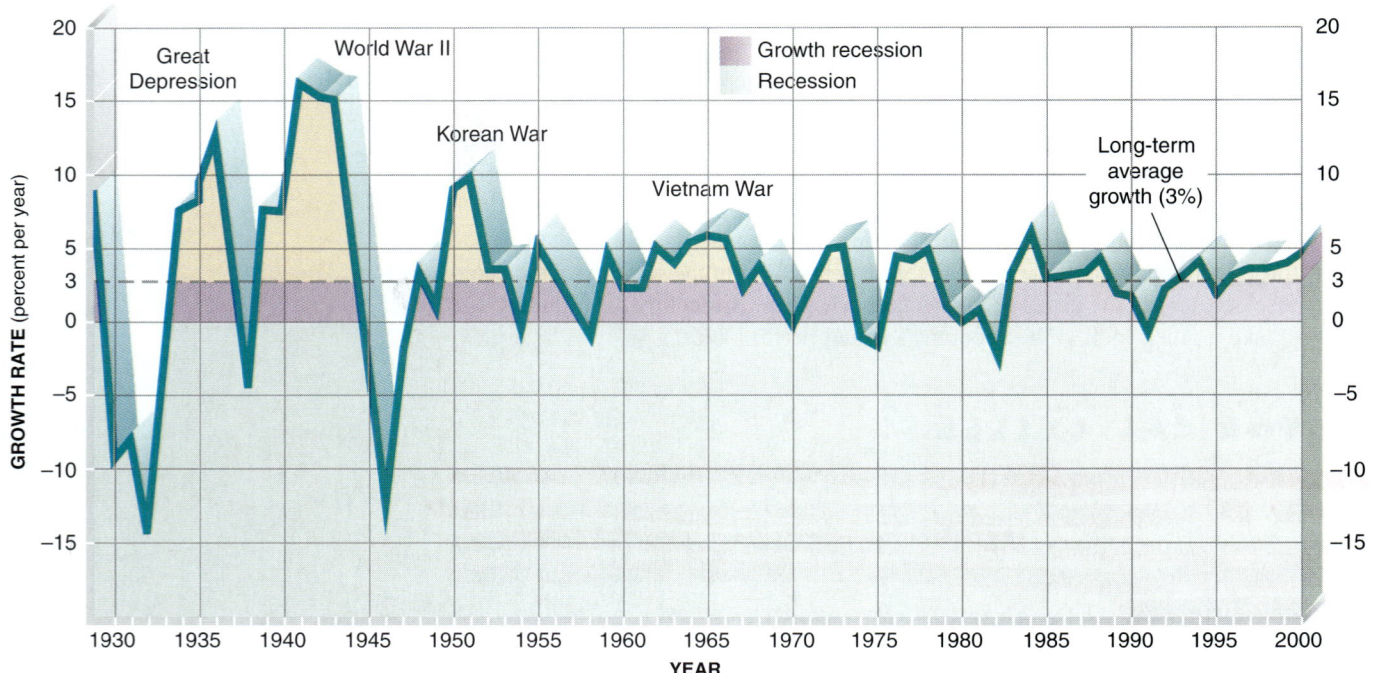

all goods and services produced. From a long-run view, the growth of real GDP has been impressive: Real GDP today is seven times larger than it was in 1929. Americans now consume a greater variety of goods and services, and in greater quantities, than earlier generations ever dreamed possible.

Our long-term success in raising living standards is clouded, however, by a spate of short-term macro setbacks. On closer inspection, the growth path of the U.S. economy isn't a smooth, rising trend but a series of steps, stumbles, and setbacks. This short-run instability is evident in Figure 8.3. The dashed line represents the long-term *average* growth rate of the U.S. economy. From 1929 through 2001, the U.S. economy expanded at an average rate of 3 percent per year. But Figure 8.3 clearly shows that we didn't grow so nicely every year. There were lots of years when real GDP grew by less than 3 percent. Worse still, there were many years of *negative* growth, with real GDP *declining* from one year to the next. These successive short-run contractions and expansions are the essence of the business cycle.

The most prolonged departure from our long-term growth path occurred during the Great Depression. Between 1929 and 1933, total U.S. output steadily declined. Notice in Figure 8.3 how the growth rate is negative in each of these years. During these four years of negative growth, real GDP contracted a total of nearly 30 percent. Investments in new plant and equipment virtually ceased. Economies around the world came to a grinding halt (see World View).

The U.S. economy rebounded in April 1933 and continued to expand for 3 years (see positive growth rates in Figure 8.3). By 1937, however, the rate of output was still below that of 1929. Then things got worse again. During 1938 and 1939 output again contracted and more people lost their jobs. At the end of the decade GDP per capita was lower than it had been in 1929.

World War II greatly increased the demand for goods and services and ended the Great Depression. During the war years, real GDP grew at unprecedented rates—almost 19 percent in a single year (1942). Virtually everyone was employed, either in the armed forces or in the factories. Throughout the war, America's productive capacity was strained to the limit.

The Great Depression

The National Archives provides a wealth of information on the Great Depression in the Hoover Presidential Library. Visit www.hoover.nara.gov. and click on "research/historical materials."

World War II

WORLD VIEW

Global Depression

The Great Depression wasn't confined to the U.S. economy. Most other countries suffered substantial losses of output and employment over a period of many years. Between 1929 and 1932, industrial production around the world fell 37 percent. The United States and Germany suffered the largest losses, while Spain and the Scandinavian countries lost only modest amounts of output.

Some countries escaped the ravages of the Great Depression altogether. The Soviet Union, largely insulated from Western economic structures, was in the midst of Stalin's forced industralization drive during the 1930s. China and Japan were also relatively isolated from world trade and finance and so suffered less damage from the depression.

Country	Decline in Industrial Output
Chile	−22%
France	−31
Germany	−47
Great Britain	−17
Japan	−2
Norway	−7
Spain	−12
United States	−46

Analysis: International trade and financial flows tie nations together. When the U.S. economy tumbled in the 1930s, other nations lost export sales. Such interactions made the Great Depression a worldwide calamity.

156 CYCLICAL INSTABILITY

The Postwar Years

recession: A decline in total output (real GDP) for two or more consecutive quarters.

In the postwar years, the U.S. economy resumed a pattern of alternating growth and contraction. The contracting periods are called *recessions*. Specifically, we use the term **recession** to mean a decline in real GDP that continues for at least two successive quarters. As Table 8.1 indicates, there have been 11 recessions since 1944. The most severe postwar recession occurred immediately after World War II ended. Sudden cutbacks in defense production caused GDP to decline sharply in 1945. That postwar recession was relatively brief, however. Pent-up demand for consumer goods and a surge in investment spending helped restore full employment. The Korean War (1950–53) further increased the demand for goods, accelerating economic growth.

The 1980s

The 1980s started with two recessions, the second lasting 16 months (July 1981–November 1982). Despite the onset of a second recession at midyear, the economy's total output actually increased in 1981. But the growth rate was so slow (1.9 percent) that few people noticed any improvement in their standard of living. Indeed, because output was growing more slowly than the labor force, the number of unemployed workers actually increased in 1981. These kinds of experiences are called **growth recessions**—the economy grows, but at a slower rate than the long-run (3 percent) average. Thus, a growth recession occurs when the economy expands too slowly. A recession occurs when real GDP actually contracts. A depression is an extremely deep and long recession—or when you don't even get socks for Christmas (see the cartoon).

growth recession: A period during which real GDP grows, but at a rate below the long-term trend of 3 percent.

In November 1982, the U.S. economy began an economic expansion that lasted over seven years. During that period, real GDP increased by over $1 trillion and nearly 20 million new jobs were created. It was the second-longest peacetime expansion in American history. As the expansion continued, however, the *rate* of economic growth diminished. By the end of the decade, economic growth had slowed to a crawl and another growth recession occurred.

The 1990s and 2000–

The 1990s started poorly as a result. The growth recession of 1989 became a full-blown recession in 1990. Beginning in July 1990, real GDP started declining. Although the recession officially ended eight months later (February 1991), subsequent growth was so slow that unemployment kept increasing. By the end of 1991, the recession had destroyed 2 million jobs and reduced total output by nearly 2 percent.

In 1992, the economy started to grow a bit faster, but unemployment rates stayed high for the entire year. The increase in output was so small that unemployment kept rising to a peak of 7.7 percent in June of that year. From 1992 through the middle of 2001, total output kept increasing. Growth of GDP once again created millions of new

TABLE 8.1
Business Slumps

The U.S. economy has experienced 13 business slumps since 1929. In the post–World War II period, these downturns have been much less severe. The typical recession lasts around 10 months. When will the next recession occur, and how long will it last?

Dates	Duration (months)	Percentage Decline in Real GDP	Peak Unemployment Rate
Aug. '29–Mar. '33	43	53.4%	24.9%
May '37–June '38	13	32.4	20.0
Feb. '45–Oct. '45	8	38.3	4.3
Nov. '48–Oct. '49	11	9.9	7.9
July '53–May '54	10	10.0	6.1
Aug. '57–Apr. '58	8	14.3	7.5
Apr. '60–Feb. '61	10	7.2	7.1
Dec. '69–Nov. '70	11	8.1	6.1
Nov. '73–Mar. '75	16	14.7	9.0
Jan. '80–July '80	6	8.7	7.6
July '81–Nov. '82	16	12.3	10.8
July '90–Feb. '91	8	2.2	6.5
Mar. '01–	?	?	?

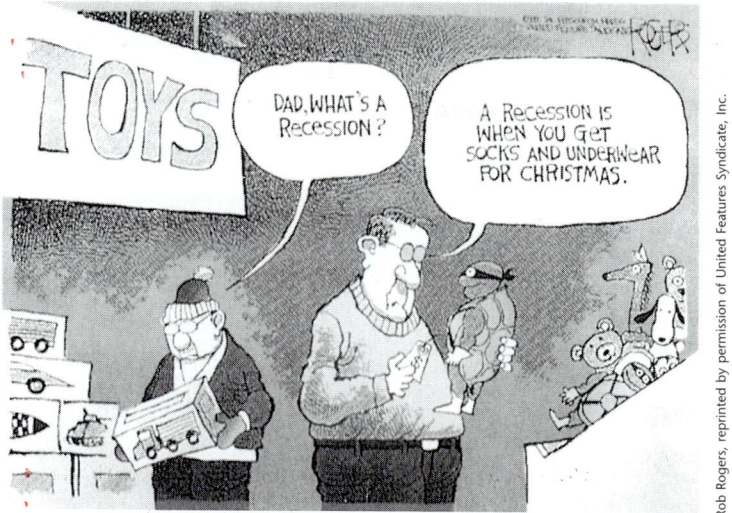

Analysis: Recessions occur when total output in the economy declines. In recessions, household income and spending fall.

jobs. In the fall of 2000, the national unemployment rate fell to 3.9 percent, the lowest in over three decades, and the economic expansion set a longevity record. Shortly thereafter, however, GDP growth slowed so much that the United States experienced another recession in 2001.

A MODEL OF THE MACRO ECONOMY

The bumpy growth record of the U.S. economy lends some validity to the notion of a recurring business cycle. Every decade seems to contain at least one boom or bust cycle. But the historical record doesn't really answer our key questions. Are business cycles *inevitable?* Can we do anything to control them? Keynes and the classical economists weren't debating whether business cycles occur but whether they're an appropriate target for government intervention. That debate continues.

To determine whether and how the government should try to control the business cycle, we first need to understand its origins. What causes the economy to expand or contract? What marketplace forces dampen (self-adjust) or magnify economic swings?

Figure 8.4 sets the stage for answering these questions with a broad view of how the macro economy works. This very basic macro model simply emphasizes that the performance of the economy depends on a finite set of determinants.

On the right side of Figure 8.4 the primary measures of macroeconomic performance are arrayed. These basic *macro outcomes include*

- *Output:* total value of goods and services produced (real GDP).
- *Jobs:* levels of employment and unemployment.
- *Prices:* average price of goods and services.
- *Growth:* year-to-year expansion in production capacity.
- *International balances:* international value of the dollar; trade and payments balances with other countries.

These macro outcomes define our economic welfare; we measure our economic well-being in terms of the value of output produced, number of jobs created, price stability, and rate of economic expansion. We also seek to maintain a certain balance in our international trade and financial relations. The economy's performance is rated by the "scores" on these five macro outcomes.

158 CYCLICAL INSTABILITY

FIGURE 8.4
The Macro Economy

The primary outcomes of the macro economy are output of goods and services, jobs, prices, economic growth, and international balances (trade, currency). These outcomes result from the interplay of internal market forces such as population growth, innovation, and spending patterns; external shocks such as wars, weather, and trade disruptions; and policy levers such as tax, budget, and regulatory decisions.

On the left side of Figure 8.4 the forces that affect macro outcomes are depicted. Three very broad forces are depicted; these **determinants of macro performance are**

- *Internal market forces:* population growth, spending behavior, invention and innovation, and the like.
- *External shocks:* wars, natural disasters, trade disruptions, and so on.
- *Policy levers:* tax policy, government spending, changes in the availability of money, and regulation, for example.

In the absence of external shocks or government policy, an economy would still function: It would still produce output, create jobs, develop prices, and maybe even grow. The U.S. economy operated with minimal government intervention for much of its history. Even today, many less developed countries operate in relative isolation from government or international events. In these situations, macro outcomes depend exclusively on internal market forces.

The crucial macro controversy is whether such pure, market-driven economies are inherently stable or unstable. Classical economists viewed internal market forces as self-stabilizing and saw no need for the box in Figure 8.4 labeled "Policy levers." Keynes argued that policy levers were both effective and necessary. Without such intervention, Keynes believed, the economy was doomed to bouts of repeated macro failure.

Modern economists hesitate to give policy intervention that great a role. Nearly all economists recognize that policy intervention affects macro outcomes. But there are great arguments about just how effective any policy lever is. Some economists even echo the classical notion that policy intervention may be either ineffective or, worse still, inherently destabilizing.

AGGREGATE DEMAND AND SUPPLY

To determine which views of economic performance are valid, we need to examine the inner workings of the macro economy. All Figure 8.4 tells us is that macro outcomes depend on certain identifiable forces. But the figure doesn't reveal *how* the determinants and outcomes are connected. What's in the mysterious circle labeled "Macro Economy" at the center of Figure 8.4?

When economists peer into the mechanics of the macro economy they see the forces of supply and demand at work. All the macro outcomes depicted in Figure 8.4 are the result of market transactions—an interaction between supply and demand. Hence, **any influence on macro outcomes must be transmitted through supply or demand.**

By conceptualizing the inner workings of the macro economy in supply and demand terms, economists have developed a remarkably simple model of how the economy works. To operationalize that model, however, we need to know more about the macroeconomic dimensions of supply and demand.

Economists use the term *aggregate demand* to refer to the collective behavior of all buyers in the marketplace. Specifically, **aggregate demand** refers to the various quantities of output (real GDP) that all people, taken together, are willing and able to buy at alternative price levels in a given period. Our view here encompasses the collective demand for *all* goods and services rather than the demand for any single good.

To understand the concept of aggregate demand better, imagine that everyone is paid on the same day. With their incomes in hand, people then enter the product market. The question becomes: How much output will people buy?

To answer this question, we have to know something about prices. If goods and services are cheap, people will be able to buy more with their available income. On the other hand, high prices will limit both the ability and willingness to purchase goods and services. Note that we're talking here about the *average* price level, not the price of any single good.

Figure 8.5 illustrates this simple relationship between average prices and real spending. The horizontal axis depicts the various quantities of (real) output that might be purchased. The vertical axis shows various price levels that might exist. *The aggregate demand curve illustrates how the real value of purchases varies with the average level of prices.* The downward slope of the aggregate demand curve suggests that with a given (constant) level of income, people will buy more goods and services at lower price levels. Why would this be the case? **Three separate reasons explain the downward slope of the aggregate demand curve:**

- *The real-balances effect.*
- *The foreign-trade effect.*
- *The interest-rate effect.*

Aggregate Demand

aggregate demand: The total quantity of output (real GDP) demanded at alternative price levels in a given time period, *ceteris paribus.*

FIGURE 8.5
Aggregate Demand

Aggregate demand refers to the total output (real GDP) demanded at alternative price levels, *ceteris paribus*. The vertical axis measures the average level of all prices rather than the price of a single good. Likewise, the horizontal axis refers to the real value of all goods and services, not the quantity of only one product.

The downward slope of the aggregate demand curve is due to the real-balances, foreign-trade, and interest-rate effects.

Real-Balances Effect. The most obvious explanation for the downward slope of the aggregate demand curve is that cheaper prices make dollars more valuable. Suppose you had $1,000 in your savings account. How much output could you buy with that savings balance? That depends on the price level. At current prices, you could buy $1,000 worth of output. But what if the price level rose? Then your $1,000 wouldn't stretch as far. *The real value of money is measured by how many goods and services each dollar will buy.* When the *real* value of your savings declines, your ability to purchase goods and services declines as well.

Suppose inflation pushes the price level up by 25 percent in a year. What will happen to the real value of your savings balance? At the end of the year, you'll have

$$\text{Real value of savings at year-end} = \frac{\text{savings balance}}{\frac{\text{price level at year-end}}{\text{price level at year-start}}}$$

$$= \frac{\$1,000}{\frac{125}{100}} = \frac{\$1,000}{1.25}$$

$$= \$800$$

In effect, inflation has wiped out a chunk of your purchasing power. At year's end, you can't buy as many goods and services as you could have at the beginning of the year. The quantity of output you demand will decrease. In Figure 8.5 this would be illustrated by a movement up the aggregate demand curve.

A declining price level (deflation) has the opposite effect. Specifically, lower price levels make you "richer": *The cash balances you hold in your pocket, in your bank account, or under your pillow are worth more when the price level falls.* As a result, you can buy *more* goods, even though your *nominal income* hasn't changed.

Lower price levels increase the purchasing power of other dollar-denominated assets as well. Bonds, for example, tend to rise in value when the price level falls. This may tempt consumers to use some of their bonds to buy goods and services. With greater real wealth, consumers might also decide to save less and spend more of their current income. In either case, the quantity of goods and services demanded at any given income level will increase. These real-balances effects create an inverse relationship between the price level and the real value of output demanded—that is, a downward-sloping aggregate demand curve.

Foreign-Trade Effect. The downward slope of the aggregate demand curve is reinforced by changes in imports and exports. Consumers have the option of buying either domestic or foreign goods. A decisive factor in choosing between them is their relative price. If the average price of U.S.-produced goods is rising, Americans may buy more imported goods and fewer domestically produced products. Conversely, falling price levels in the United States may convince consumers to buy more "Made in the USA" output and fewer imports.

International consumers are also swayed by relative price levels. When our price levels decline, overseas tourists flock to Disney World. Global consumers also buy more U.S. wheat, airplanes, and computers when our price levels decline. Conversely, the quantity of U.S. output demanded by international consumers declines when our price level rises. These changes in imports and exports contribute to the downward slope of the aggregate demand curve.

Interest-Rate Effect. Changes in the price level also affect the amount of money people need to borrow and so tend to affect interest rates. At lower price levels, consumer borrowing needs are smaller. As the demand for loans diminishes, interest rates tend to decline as well. This "cheaper" money stimulates more borrowing and loan-financed purchases. These interest-rate effects reinforce the downward slope of the aggregate demand curve, as illustrated in Figure 8.5.

Although lower price levels tend to increase the volume of output demanded, they have the opposite effect on the aggregate quantity supplied. As we observed, our production possibilities are defined by available resources and technology. Within those limits, however, producers must decide how much output they're *willing* to supply. Their supply decisions are influenced by changes in the price level.

Profit Effect. The primary motivation for supplying goods and services is the chance to earn a profit. Producers can earn a profit so long as the prices they receive for their output exceed the costs they pay in production. Hence, *changing price levels will affect the profitability of supplying goods*.

If the price level declines, profits tend to drop. In the short run, producers are saddled with some relatively constant costs like rent, interest payments, negotiated wages, and inputs already contracted for. If output prices fall, producers will be hard-pressed to pay these costs, much less earn a profit. Their response will be to reduce the rate of output.

Higher output prices have the opposite effect. Because many costs are relatively constant in the short run, higher prices for goods and services tend to widen profit margins. As profit margins widen, producers will want to produce and sell more goods. Thus, *we expect the rate of output to increase when the price level rises*. This expectation is reflected in the upward slope of the aggregate supply curve in Figure 8.6. **Aggregate supply** reflects the various quantities of real output that firms are willing and able to produce at alternative price levels, in a given time period.

Cost Effect. The upward slope of the aggregate supply curve is also explained by rising costs. The profit effect depends on some costs remaining constant when the average price level rises. Not all costs will remain constant, however. Producers may have to pay overtime wages, for example, to increase output, even if *base* wages are constant. Tight supplies of other inputs may also unleash cost increases. Such cost pressures tend to multiply as the rate of output increases. As time passes, even costs that initially stayed constant may start creeping upward.

All these cost pressures will make producing output more expensive. Producers will be willing to supply additional output only if prices rise at least as fast as costs.

Aggregate Supply

aggregate supply: The total quantity of output (real GDP) producers are willing and able to supply at alternative price levels in a given time period, *ceteris paribus*.

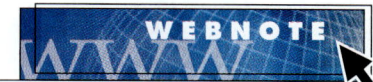

The slope of the aggregate supply curve depends in part on what producers pay for their inputs. Find out about producer prices at www.bls.gov.

FIGURE 8.6
Aggregate Supply

Aggregate supply is the real value of output (real GDP) producers are willing and able to bring to the market at alternative price levels, *ceteris paribus*. The upward slope of the aggregate supply curve reflects both profit effects (the lure of widening profit margins) and cost effects (increasing cost pressures).

162 CYCLICAL INSTABILITY

The upward slope of the aggregate supply curve in Figure 8.6 illustrates this cost effect. Notice how the aggregate supply curve is practically horizontal at low rates of aggregate output and then gets increasingly steeper. At high output levels the aggregate supply curve almost turns straight up. This changing slope reflects the fact that *cost pressures are minimal at low rates of output but intense as the economy approaches capacity.*

Macro Equilibrium

When all is said and done, what we end up with here is two rather conventional looking supply and demand curves. But these particular curves have special significance. Instead of describing the behavior of buyers and sellers in a single market (for example, the Clearview College web-services market in Chapter 3), aggregate supply and demand curves summarize the market activity of the whole (macro) economy. These curves tell us what *total* amount of goods and services will be supplied or demanded at various price levels.

These graphic summaries of buyer and seller behavior provide some important clues about the economy's performance. The most important clue is point E in Figure 8.7, where the aggregate demand and supply curves intersect. This is the only point at which the behavior of buyers and sellers is compatible. We know from the aggregate demand curve that people are willing and able to buy the quantity Q_E when the price level is at P_E. From the aggregate supply curve we know that businesses are prepared to sell quantity Q_E at the price level P_E. Hence, buyers and sellers are willing to trade exactly the same quantity (Q_E) at that price level. We call this situation **macro equilibrium**—the unique combination of prices and output compatible with both buyers and sellers' intentions.

To appreciate the significance of macro equilibrium, suppose that another price or output level existed. Imagine, for example, that prices were higher, at the level P_1 in Figure 8.7. How much output would people want to buy at that price level? How much would business want to produce and sell?

The aggregate demand curve tells us that people would want to buy only the quantity D_1 at the higher price level P_1. In contrast, business firms would want to sell a larger quantity, S_1. This is a *dis*equilibrium situation in which the intentions of buyers and sellers are incompatible. The aggregate *quantity supplied* (S_1) exceeds the aggregate *quantity demanded* (D_1). Accordingly, a lot of goods will remain unsold at price level P_1.

To sell these goods, producers will have to reduce their prices. As prices drop, producers will decrease the volume of goods sent to market. At the same time, the quan-

equilibrium (macro): The combination of price level and real output that is compatible with both aggregate demand and aggregate supply.

FIGURE 8.7
Macro Equilibrium

The aggregate demand and supply curves intersect at only one point (E). At that point, the price level (P_E) and output (Q_E) combination is compatible with both buyers' and sellers' intentions. The economy will gravitate to those equilibrium price (P_E) and output (Q_E) levels. At any other price level (e.g., P_1), the behavior of buyers and sellers is incompatible.

tities that consumers seek will increase. This adjustment process will continue until point E is reached and the quantities demanded and supplied are equal. At that point, the lower price level P_E will prevail.

The same kind of adjustment process would occur if a lower price level first existed. At lower prices, the aggregate quantity demanded would exceed the aggregate quantity supplied. The resulting shortages would permit sellers to raise their prices. As they did so, the aggregate quantity demanded would decrease, and the aggregate quantity supplied would increase. Eventually, we would return to point E, where the aggregate quantities demanded and supplied are equal. **Equilibrium is unique; it's the only price-output combination that is mutually compatible with aggregate supply and demand.** In terms of graphs, it's the only place the aggregate supply and demand curves intersect. At point E there's no reason for the level of output or prices to change. The behavior of buyers and sellers is compatible. By contrast, any other level of output or prices creates a disequilibrium that requires market adjustments. All other price and output combinations, therefore, are unstable. They won't last. Eventually, the economy will return to point E.

There are two potential problems with the macro equilibrium depicted in Figure 8.7. The *two potential problems with macro equilibrium are*:

- *Undesirability:* The price-output relationship at equilibrium may not satisfy our macroeconomic goals.
- *Instability:* Even if the designated macro equilibrium is optimal, it may be displaced by macro disturbances.

Macro Failures

Undesirability. The macro equilibrium depicted in Figure 8.7 is simply the intersection of two curves. All we know for sure is that people want to buy the same quantity of output that businesses want to sell at the price level P_E. This quantity (Q_E) may be more or less than our full-employment capacity. This contingency is illustrated in Figure 8.8. The output level Q_F represents our **full-employment GDP potential**. In this case, the equilibrium rate of output (Q_E) falls far short of capacity production. We've failed to achieve our goal of full employment.

Similar problems may arise from the equilibrium price level. Suppose that P^* represents the most desired price level. In Figure 8.8, we see that the equilibrium price

full-employment GDP: The total market value of final goods and services that could be produced in a given time period at full employment; potential GDP.

FIGURE 8.8
An Undesired Equilibrium

Equilibrium establishes only the level of prices and output that are compatible with both buyers' and sellers' intentions. These outcomes may not satisfy our policy goals. In this case, the equilibrium price level is too high (above P^*) and the equilibrium output rate falls short of full employment (Q_F).

164 CYCLICAL INSTABILITY

inflation: An increase in the average level of prices of goods and services.

level P_E exceeds P^*. If market behavior determines prices, the price level will rise above the desired level. The resulting increase in the average level of prices is what we call **inflation**.

It could be argued, of course, that our apparent macro failures are simply an artifact. We could have drawn the aggregate supply and demand curves to intersect at point F in Figure 8.8. At that intersection we'd be assured of both price stability and full employment. Why didn't we draw them there, instead of intersecting at point E?

On the graph we can draw curves anywhere we want. In the real world, however, only one set of aggregate supply and demand curves will correctly express buyers' and sellers' behavior. We must emphasize here that these "correct" curves may *not* intersect at point F, thus denying us price stability or full employment, or both. That is the kind of economic outcome illustrated in Figure 8.8.

Instability. Figure 8.8 is only the beginning of our macro worries. Suppose, just suppose, that the aggregate supply and demand curves actually intersected in the perfect spot. That is, imagine that macro equilibrium yielded the optimal levels of both employment and prices. If this happened, could we settle back and stop fretting about the state of the economy?

Unhappily, even a "perfect" macro equilibrium doesn't ensure a happy ending. The aggregate supply and demand curves aren't permanently locked into their respective positions. They can *shift*—and they will, whenever the behavior of buyers and sellers changes.

AS Shifts. Suppose the Organization of Petroleum Exporting Countries (OPEC) increased the price of oil, as it did in early 2001. These oil price hikes directly increased the cost of production in a wide range of U.S. industries, making producers less will-

FIGURE 8.9
Macro Disturbances

(a) **Aggregate supply** A decrease (leftward shift) of the aggregate supply (AS) curve tends to reduce real GDP and raise average prices. When supply shifts from AS_0 to AS_1, the equilibrium moves from F to G. Such a supply shift may result from higher import prices, changes in tax policy, or other events.

(b) **Aggregate demand** A decrease (leftward shift) in aggregate demand (AD) tends to reduce output and price levels. A fall in demand may be caused by decreased export demand, changes in expectations, taxes, or other events.

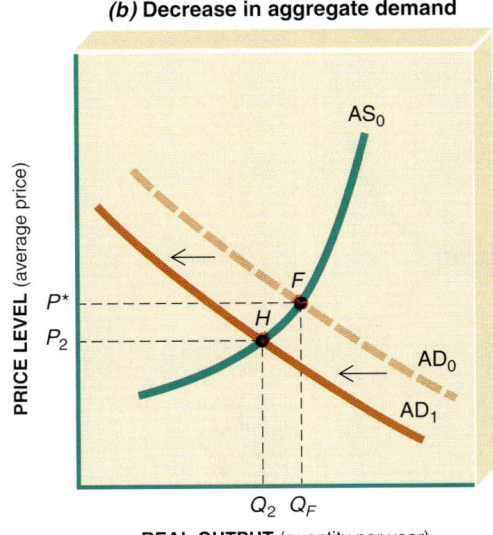

ing and able to supply goods at prevailing prices. Thus, the aggregate supply curve *shifted to the left,* as in Figure 8.9a.

The September 11, 2001 terrorist strikes against the World Trade Center and Pentagon also caused a leftward shift of aggregate supply. Physical destruction and fear of further terrorism kept some producers out of the market. Intensified security of transportation systems and buildings also increased the costs of supplying goods and services to the market.

The impact of a leftward supply shift on the economy is evident. Whereas macro equilibrium was originally located at the optimal point F, the new equilibrium is located at point G. At point G, less output is produced and prices are higher. Full employment and price stability have vanished before our eyes.

AD Shifts. A shift of the aggregate demand curve could do similar damage. Between 1997 and 1998, the currencies of Thailand, Indonesia, South Korea, and Malaysia collapsed, losing anywhere from 30 to 60 percent of their dollar value. As a consequence, Asian companies and consumers couldn't afford as many goods made in the United States. The quantity of real output (U.S. exports) they demanded at the price level P^* declined, causing the aggregate demand for U.S. output to shift to the left, as illustrated in Figure 8.9b. The leftward shift forced U.S. exporters to cut back production, increasing unemployment. As the World View relates, the West Coast suffered the most from this external shock.

Multiple Shifts. The situation gets even crazier when the aggregate supply and demand curves shift repeatedly in different directions. A leftward shift of the aggregate demand curve can cause a recession, as the rate of output falls. A later rightward shift of the aggregate demand curve can cause a recovery, with real GDP (and employment) again increasing. Shifts of the aggregate supply curve can cause similar upswings and downswings. Thus, *business cycles are likely to result from recurrent shifts of the aggregate supply and demand curves.*

WORLD VIEW

California Feels Asia's Pain

LOS ANGELES—The wave of Asian trade that lifted California to a $1 trillion gross state product last year—the USA's largest—is washing out again.

The ebb tide threatens to erode jobs and profits across the West Coast and casts a pall over the city that Port of Los Angeles Executive Director Larry Keller calls "the capital of the next century." Nowhere in the country is Asia's financial crisis more keenly felt.

Ships arriving from Asia fully loaded are departing 30 percent to 40 percent empty, southern California port officials say. Blue-chip companies, such as Intel, Microsoft and National Semiconductor—all big exporters to Asia—report reduced foreign sales demand.

Tourism is down, as many of the 1.5 million Japanese and South Koreans who normally visit California each year stay home. And farmers from the citrus groves of Ventura County to the beef and cotton belt of the San Joaquin Valley fear the potential double whammy of lost markets abroad worth hundreds of millions of dollars and depressed prices at home.

Smith Barney economist Kathryn Chin predicts Asia's problems could clip U.S. exports by $46 billion this year, deepening the estimated trade deficit to $193 billion, a record, and trimming gross domestic product by 0.7 percent. In California and the West, the proportionate damage is far greater. Chin says the Asian storm could slash the Western states' net exports by $14 billion, 1.2 percent of the region's gross product.

The Economic Policy Institute in Washington, D.C., says lost trade could trim 1 million jobs nationwide, led by 126,681 fewer jobs in California.

—Elliot Blair Smith

Source: *USA Today,* February 12, 1998. © 1998 USA Today. Reprinted with permission. www.usatoday.com

Analysis: A recession in Asia reduces the demand for U.S. exports. During 1997 and 1998, the "Asian flu" hit California particularly hard.

COMPETING THEORIES OF SHORT-RUN INSTABILITY

Figures 8.8 and 8.9 hardly inspire optimism about the macro economy. Figure 8.8 suggests that the odds of the market generating an equilibrium at full employment and price stability are about the same as finding a needle in a haystack. Figure 8.9 suggests that if we're lucky enough to find the needle, we'll probably drop it again. From this perspective, it appears that our worries about the business cycle are well founded.

The classical economists had no such worries. As we saw earlier, they believed that the economy would gravitate toward full employment. Keynes, on the other hand, worried that the macro equilibrium might start out badly and get worse in the absence of government intervention.

The AS/AD model doesn't really settle this controversy. It does, however, provide a convenient framework for comparing these and other theories about how the economy works. Essentially, *macro controversies focus on the shape of aggregate supply and demand curves and the potential to shift them.* With the right shape—or the correct shift—any desired equilibrium could be attained. As we'll see, there are differing views as to whether and how this happy outcome might come about. These differing views can be classified as demand-side explanations, supply-side explanations, or some combination of the two.

Demand-Side Theories

Keynesian Theory. Keynesian theory is the most prominent of the demand-side theories. Keynes argued that a deficiency of spending would tend to depress an economy. This deficiency might originate in consumer saving, inadequate business investment, or insufficient government spending. Whatever its origins, the lack of spending would leave goods unsold and production capacity unused. This contingency is illustrated by point E_1 in Figure 8.10a. Notice that the equilibrium at E_1 leaves the economy at Q_1, below its full-employment potential (Q_F). Thus, Keynes concluded that inadequate aggregate demand would cause persistently high unemployment.

Keynes developed his theory during the Great Depression, when the economy seemed to be stuck at a very low level of equilibrium output, far below full-employment GDP. The only way to end the depression, he argued, was for someone to start demanding

FIGURE 8.10
Demand-Side Theories

Inadequate demand may cause unemployment. In part (a), the demand AD_1 creates an equilibrium at E_1. The resulting output Q_1 falls short of full employment (Q_F).

In part (b), excessive aggregate demand causes inflation. The price level rises from P_0 to P_2 when aggregate demand expands to AD_2. Demand-side theories emphasize how inadequate or excessive AD can cause macro failures.

(a) Inadequate demand

(b) Excessive demand

more goods. He advocated a big hike in government spending to start the economy moving toward full employment. At the time his advice was largely ignored. When the United States mobilized for World War II, however, the sudden surge in government spending shifted the aggregate demand curve sharply to the right, restoring full employment (e.g., a reverse shift from AD_1 to AD_0 in Figure 8.10a). In times of peace, Keynes also advocated changing government taxes and spending to shift the aggregate demand curve in whatever direction is desired.

The accompanying World View contrasts GDP growth in the United States, Japan, and China in early 2001. Notice the role that aggregate demand plays in the stories. A decline in business spending is blamed for the U.S. slowdown and the Japanese recession. In China, an increase in consumer and government spending is credited for the spurt in real GDP. This is entirely consistent with Keynesian theory, which will be examined more closely in Chapters 9 through 11.

Monetary Theories. Another demand-side theory emphasizes the role of money in financing aggregate demand. Money and credit affect the ability and willingness of people to buy goods and services. If credit isn't available or is too expensive, consumers won't be able to buy as many cars, homes, or other expensive products. "Tight" money might also curtail business investment. In these circumstances, aggregate demand might prove to be inadequate, as illustrated in Figure 8.10a. In this case, an increase in the money supply may be required to shift the aggregate demand curve into the desired position.

WORLD VIEW

Economy Expands, Barely

The U.S. economy skirted the edge of a recession this spring as increases in consumer and government purchases narrowly offset the biggest drop in business spending in almost 20 years, the Commerce Department reported yesterday.

The economy grew in the second quarter at only a 0.7 percent annual rate, the smallest quarterly gain in eight years. After expanding more than 4 percent a year for several years, growth slowed abruptly in mid-2000 and over the past 12 months has averaged only a 1.3 percent annual rate.

—John M. Berry

Source: *Washington Post*, July 28, 2001. © 2001 The Washington Post. Reprinted with permission. www.washingtonpost.com

Japan Sees Slight Drop in Its GDP

TOKYO—Japan's economy contracted slightly in the first three months of this year, government data showed Monday, raising fears that the world's second-biggest economy is sinking into another recession.

Gross domestic product fell 0.2 percent in the three months ended March 31 from the previous quarter, seasonally adjusted, the government said today. Economists had expected the economy to expand 0.1 percent after growing 0.7 percent in the fourth quarter.

Business investment, the main source of economic growth the last two years, gave way in the first quarter, falling 1 percent from the fourth quarter, when it increased 6.7 percent. That was the first decline in three quarters.

—Ann Saphir and Neha Ku

Source: Bloomberg News, *Los Angeles Times*, June 11, 2001. Reprinted with permission. www.latimes.com

China Reports 7.9% Growth

SHANGHAI, July 17—China said today that its economy expanded 7.9 percent in the first six months of this year, exceeding the forecasts of many private experts and defying the global slowdown.

The State Statistical Bureau, which announced the increase, predicted that, in the absence of further deterioration in the economic outlook for the rest of the world, China's growth for the full year could top the government's target of 7 percent.

Analysts attribute the vigorous performance of China's economy to the strength of the nation's domestic market, with 1.3 billion consumers clamoring for new goods and services and the government providing an extra boost to demand by spending heavily on infrastructure and public works.

—Clay Chandler

Source: *Washington Post*, July 18, 2001. © 2001 The Washington Post. Reprinted with permission. www.washingtonpost.com

Analysis: Why do short-term growth rates vary across countries? In these stories, shifts of aggregate demand are emphasized, as in Figure 8.10.

Both the Keynesian and monetarist theories also regard aggregate demand as a prime suspect for inflationary problems. In Figure 8.10b, the curve AD_2 leads to an equilibrium at E_2. At first blush, that equilibrium looks desirable, as it offers more output (Q_2) than the full-employment threshold (Q_F). Notice, however, what's happening to prices: The price level rises from P_0 to P_2. Hence, excessive aggregate demand may cause inflation.

The more extreme monetary theories attribute all our macro successes and failures to management of the money supply. According to these *monetarist* theories, the economy will tend to stabilize at something like full-employment GDP. Thus, only the price level will be affected by changes in the money supply and resulting shifts of aggregate demand. We'll examine the basis for this view in a moment. At this juncture we simply note that both Keynesian and monetarist theories emphasize the potential of aggregate-demand shifts to alter some macro outcomes.

Supply-Side Theories

Figure 8.11 illustrates an entirely different explanation of the business cycle. Notice that the aggregate *supply* curve is on the move in Figure 8.11. The initial equilibrium is again at point E_0. This time, however, aggregate demand remains stationary, while aggregate supply shifts. The resulting decline of aggregate supply causes output and employment to decline (to Q_3 from Q_F).

Figure 8.11 tells us that aggregate supply may be responsible for downturns as well. Our failure to achieve full employment may result from the unwillingness of producers to provide more goods at existing prices. That unwillingness may originate in simple greed, in rising costs, in resource shortages, or in government taxes and regulation. Inadequate investment in infrastructure (e.g., roads, sewer systems) or skill training may also limit supply potential. Whatever the cause, if the aggregate supply curve is AS_1 rather than AS_0 full employment will not be achieved with the demand AD_0.

The inadequate supply illustrated in Figure 8.11 causes not only unemployment but inflation as well. At the equilibrium E_3, the price level has risen from P_0 to P_3. Hence, a decrease in aggregate supply can cause multiple macro problems. On the other hand, an increase—a rightward shift—in aggregate supply can move us closer to both our price-stability and full-employment goals. Chapter 16 examines the many ways of inducing such a shift.

Eclectic Explanations

Not everyone blames either the demand side or the supply side exclusively. The various macro theories tell us that both supply and demand can cause us to achieve or miss our policy goals. These theories also demonstrate how various shifts of the aggregate supply and demand curves can achieve any specific output or price level. One could also shift *both* the AS and AD curves to explain unemployment, inflation, or recurring business cycles. Such eclectic explanations of macro failure draw from both sides of the market.

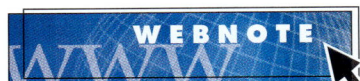

The U.S. Bureau of Economic Analysis compiles data on gross domestic product. Using data from its website at www.bea.doc.gov, determine the GDP growth rate for each of the last six quarters. What supply or demand shifts might explain recent quarterly fluctuations in real GDP?

FIGURE 8.11
Supply-Side Theories

Inadequate supply can keep the economy below its full-employment potential and cause prices to rise as well. AS_1 leads to output Q_3 and increases the price level from P_0 to P_3. Supply-side theories emphasize how AS shifts can worsen or improve macro outcomes.

LONG-RUN SELF-ADJUSTMENT

Some economists argue that these various theories of short-run instability aren't only confusing but also pointless. As they see it, what really matters is the *long*-run trend of the economy, not *short*-run fluctuations around those trends. In their view, month-to-month or quarter-to-quarter fluctuations in real output or prices are just statistical noise. The *long*-term path of output and prices is determined by more fundamental factors.

This emphasis on long-term outcomes is reminiscent of the classical theory: the view that the economy will self-adjust. A decrease in aggregate demand is only a *temporary* problem. Once producers and workers make the required price and wage adjustments, the economy will return to its long-run equilibrium growth path.

The monetarist theory we encountered a moment ago has a similar view of long-run stability. According to the monetarist theory, the supply of goods and services is determined by institutional factors such as the size of the labor force and technology. These factors determine a natural rate of output that's relatively immune to short-run fluctuations in aggregate demand. If this argument is valid, the long-run aggregate supply curve is vertical, not sloped.

Figure 8.12 illustrates the classical/monetarist view of long-run stability. The vertical long-run AS curve is anchored at the natural rate of output Q_N. The natural rate Q_N is itself determined by demographics, technology, market structure, and the institutional infrastructure of the economy.

If the long-run AS curve is really vertical, as the classical and monetarist theories assert, some startling conclusions follow. The most startling implication is that **aggregate-demand shifts affect prices but not output in the long run.** Notice in Figure 8.12 how the shift from AD_1 to AD_2 raises the price level but leaves output anchored at Q_N.

What has happened here? Didn't we suggest earlier that an increase in aggregate demand would spur producers to increase output? And aren't rising prices an extra incentive for doing so?

Monetarists concede that *short-run* price increases tend to widen profit margins. This profit effect is an incentive to increase the rate of output. In the *long run*, however,

FIGURE 8.12
The "Natural" Rate of Output

Monetarists and neoclassical theorists assert that the level of output is fixed at the natural rate Q_N by the size of the labor force, technology, and other institutional factors. As a result, fluctuations in aggregate demand affect the price level but not real output.

costs are likely to catch up with rising prices. Workers will demand higher wages, landlords will increase rents, and banks will charge higher interest rates as the price level rises. Hence, a rising price level has only a *temporary* profit effect on supply behavior. In the *long run,* cost effects will dominate. In the *long run,* a rising price level will be accompanied by rising costs, giving producers no special incentive to supply more output. Accordingly, output will revert to its natural rate Q_N.

Short- vs. Long-Run Perspectives

All this may well be true. But as Keynes pointed out, it's also true that "in the long run we are all dead." Whatever the long run may hold, it's in the short run that we must consume, invest, and find a job. However stable and predictable the long run might be, short-run variations in macro outcomes will determine how well we fare in any year. Moreover, *the short-run aggregate supply curve is likely to be upward-sloping,* as shown in our earlier graphs. This implies that both aggregate supply and aggregate demand influence short-run macro outcomes.

By distinguishing between short-run and long-run aggregate supply curves, competing economic theories achieve a standoff. Theories that highlight the necessity of policy intervention emphasize the importance of short-run macro outcomes. On the other hand, theories that emphasize the "natural" stability of the market point to the predictability of long-run outcomes. Even this fragile truce, however, is easily broken when the questions turn to the duration of the "short" run or the effectiveness of any particular policy option.

THE ECONOMY TOMORROW

Macro Policy Options

The aggregate supply-demand model is a convenient summary of how the macro economy works. The model raises more questions than it answers, however. We could draw the AS and AD curves—or shift them—to create any outcome we wanted. The real challenge for macro theory is to determine which curves (or shifts) best represent market reality. We'll spend a lot of time sifting through evidence and looking for the "correct" theory. At the outset of that quest, however, we might consider how the AS/AD model also helps define our macro policy options for the economy tomorrow.

Basic Policy Strategies

The basic choice between market-driven and government-directed behavior underlies all policy options. The aggregate supply-demand (AS/AD) framework adds a new dimension to this dichotomy. We can now identify *three distinct macro policy strategies:*

- *Shift the aggregate demand curve.* Find and use policy tools that stimulate or restrain total spending.
- *Shift the aggregate supply curve.* Find and implement policy levers that reduce the cost of production or otherwise stimulate more output at every price level.
- *Laissez faire.* If we can't identify or control the determinants of aggregate supply or demand, then we shouldn't interfere with the market.

The first two policy options entail government intervention. The third option, laissez faire, relies on market forces to self-adjust.

Specific Policy Options

All these policy strategies have been tried at one time or another.

Classical Approaches. The classical approach to economic policy embraced the laissez-faire perspective. Prior to the Great Depression, most economists were convinced that the economy would self-adjust to full employment. If the initial equilibrium rate of output were too low, the resulting imbalances would alter prices and wages, inducing changes in market behavior. The aggregate supply and demand curves would "naturally" shift, until they reached the intersection where full employment (Q_F) prevails.

Recent versions of the classical theory—dubbed the "new classical economics"—stress not only the market's "natural" ability to self-adjust to *long-run* equilibrium but also the inability of the government to improve *short-run* market outcomes. New classical economists point to the increasing ability of market participants to anticipate government policies and to take defensive actions that thwart them.

Fiscal Policy. The Great Depression cast serious doubt on the classical self-adjustment concept. According to Keynes's view, the economy would *not* self-adjust. Rather, it might stagnate until aggregate demand was forcibly shifted. An increase in government spending on goods and services might provide the necessary shift. Or a cut in taxes might be used to stimulate greater consumer and investor spending. These budgetary tools are the hallmark of fiscal policy. Specifically, **fiscal policy** is the use of government tax and spending powers to alter economic outcomes.

> **fiscal policy:** The use of government taxes and spending to alter macroeconomic outcomes.

Fiscal policy is an integral feature of modern economic policy. Every year the president and Congress debate the budget. They argue about whether the economy needs to be stimulated or restrained. They then argue about the level of spending or taxes required to ensure the desired outcome. This is the heart of fiscal policy.

Monetary Policy. The government budget doesn't get all the action. As suggested earlier, the amount of money in circulation may also affect macro equilibrium. If so, then the policy arsenal must include some levers to control the money supply. These are the province of monetary policy. **Monetary policy** refers to the use of money and credit controls to alter economic outcomes.

> **monetary policy:** The use of money and credit controls to influence macroeconomic outcomes.

The Federal Reserve (the "Fed") has direct control over monetary policy. The Fed is an independent regulatory body, charged with maintaining an "appropriate" supply of money. In practice, the Fed increases or decreases the money supply in accordance with its views of macro equilibrium.

Supply-Side Policy. Fiscal and monetary policies focus on the demand side of the market. Both are motivated by the conviction that appropriate shifts of the aggregate demand curve can bring about desired changes in output or price levels. **Supply-side policies** offer an alternative; they seek to shift the aggregate supply curve.

> **supply-side policy:** The use of tax incentives, (de)regulation, and other mechanisms to increase the ability and willingness to produce goods and services.

There are scores of supply-side levers. The most familiar are the tax cuts implemented by the Reagan administration in 1981. These tax cuts were designed to increase *supply,* not just demand (as does traditional fiscal policy). By reducing tax rates on wages and profits, the Reagan tax cuts sought to increase the willingness to supply goods at any given price level. The promise of greater after-tax income was the key incentive for the supply shift. President Clinton also embraced tax incentives but emphasized the long-term importance of infrastructure development and worker training in shifting the aggregate supply curve. After the terrorist attacks on September 11, 2001, President George W. Bush pushed Congress to give business tax breaks that would encourage increased investment in supply-side capacity.

Trade Policy. International trade and money flows offer yet another option for shifting aggregate supply and demand. A reduction in trade barriers makes imports cheaper and more available. This shifts the aggregate supply to the right, reducing price pressures at every output level. Changing the international value (exchange rate) of the dollar alters the relative price of U.S.-made goods, thereby shifting both aggregate demand and supply. Hence, trade policy is another tool in the macroeconomic toolbox.

Eclecticism. Few presidents commit themselves entirely to one macroeconomic strategy. Herbert Hoover, for example, was a fervent proponent of laissez faire. But even he was prepared to accelerate public works spending and income transfers to stop the Great Depression. Ironically, Franklin Roosevelt campaigned against these fiscal policies, arguing that such demand-side levers would unbalance the federal deficit. He later became a fervent believer in Keynesian-style fiscal policy.

Ronald Reagan was a champion of supply-side economics. But he also "primed the pump" with a huge increase in defense expenditures, a demand-side policy option. George H. Bush repeatedly expressed his confidence in the market's ability to self-adjust. But when the recession of 1990–91 began to cloud his reelection prospects, President Bush pushed for supply-side tax incentives and accelerated government spending. President Clinton emphasized the need for supply-side investments in human and physical capital to promote his "New Direction." He also relied on tax hikes and spending cuts (fiscal policy), however, to achieve his macroeconomic goals. For his part, President George W. Bush emphasized the importance of long-run strategies but pushed hard for short-run personal tax cuts when economic growth stalled and for business tax breaks and more government spending in the aftermath of the September 11, 2001 terrorist attacks.

In part, the eclectic use of policy options reflects a "do-whatever-it-takes-to-win" attitude on the part of politicians. But "politics" isn't the only explanation for the lack of clear-cut policy strategies. No economic theory has proved infallible. As we'll see, different theories provide important insights into how the economy works, but each falls short in explaining one or more of our economic problems. In these circumstances, policymakers are reluctant to put all their economic eggs in one basket. They prefer more "flexible" strategies. So we're likely to witness an eclectic mix of classical, fiscal, monetary, and supply-side policies in the economy tomorrow rather than single-minded adherence to any one theory.

SUMMARY

- The long-term growth rate of the U.S. economy is approximately 3 percent a year. But output doesn't increase 3 percent every year. In some years, real GDP grows much faster than that; in other years growth is slower. Sometimes total output actually declines.
- These short-run variations in GDP growth are a central focus of macroeconomics. Macro theory tries to explain the alternating periods of growth and contraction that characterize the business cycle; macro policy attempts to control the cycle.
- The primary outcomes of the macro economy are output, prices, jobs, and international balances. The outcomes result from the interplay of internal market forces, external shocks, and policy levers.
- All the influences on macro outcomes are transmitted through aggregate supply or aggregate demand. Aggregate supply and demand determine the equilibrium rate of output and prices. The economy will gravitate to that unique combination of output and price levels.
- Macro equilibrium may not be consistent with our nation's employment or price goals. Macro failure occurs when the economy's equilibrium isn't optimal.
- Macro equilibrium may be disturbed by changes in aggregate supply (AS) or aggregate demand (AD). Such changes are illustrated by shifts of the AS and AD curves, and they lead to a new equilibrium.
- Competing economic theories try to explain the shape and shifts of the aggregate supply and demand curves, thereby explaining the business cycle. Specific theories tend to emphasize demand or supply influences.
- In the long run the AS curve tends to be vertical, implying that changes in aggregate demand affect prices but not output. In the short run, however, the AS curve is sloped, making macro outcomes sensitive to both supply and demand.
- Macro policy options range from laissez faire (the classical approach) to various strategies for shifting either the aggregate demand curve or the aggregate supply curve.

Key Terms

- macroeconomics
- business cycle
- laissez faire
- law of demand
- Say's Law
- real GDP
- recession
- growth recession
- aggregate demand
- aggregate supply
- equilibrium (macro)
- full-employment GDP
- inflation
- fiscal policy
- monetary policy
- supply-side policy

Questions for Discussion

1. If business cycles were really inevitable, what purpose would macro policy serve?
2. What considerations might prompt consumers to demand fewer goods at current prices?
3. If equilibrium is compatible with both buyers' and sellers' intentions, how can it be undesirable?
4. The stock market plunge following the September 11, 2001, terrorist attacks greatly reduced the wealth of the average U.S. household. How might this have affected aggregate demand? Aggregate supply?
5. What exactly did Say mean when he said "supply creates its own demand"?
6. What's wrong with the Classical theory of self-adjustment? Why didn't sales and employment increase in 1929–33 in response to declining prices and wages (see Figure 8.1)?
7. What might have caused real GDP to decline so dramatically in (a) 1929 and (b) 1946 (see Figure 8.3)? What caused output to increase again in each case?
8. How would a sudden jump in U.S. prices affect (a) imports from Mexico, (b) exports to Mexico, and (c) U.S. aggregate demand?
9. Why might rising prices stimulate short-run production but have no effect on long-run production?
10. What factors might cause consumers to spend more of their income on goods and services, thereby shifting the AD curve rightward?

Web Activities

1. Draw two recent business cycles, from peak to trough, using data at www.nber.org/cycles.html. Label two peaks and troughs, and identify the number of months between them. Find the unemployment rate at each trough at ftp.bls.gov/pub/special.requests/lf/aat1.txt. Which recession was worse? Why? Are we currently in a recession? How can you tell?
2. Log into www.census.gov and click on the latest economic indicators button. Choose three economic indicators to examine (different indicators than described in questions 1). Explain what the trends in these indicators suggest about the current U.S. business cycle.
3. Using the data from the Organization for Economic Co-Operation and Development at www1.oecd.org/std/li1.htm, find out which country has experienced the longest recession in the last 10 years and which has enjoyed the greatest growth during the same period. Once you have accessed the site, click on "Statistics". Look for the information on peaks and troughs for each nation in the section titled "Turning points of the reference series." Using your knowledge of current events, was the first country's recession caused by reductions in aggregate supply, demand, or both? Was the second country's growth caused by increases in aggregate supply, demand, or both?

THE ACCOMPANYING STUDENT PROBLEM SET CONTAINS NUMERICAL AND GRAPHING PROBLEMS FOR THIS CHAPTER

CHAPTER 9

Aggregate Demand

Disaster struck much of the world with the Great Depression of the 1930s: In the United States alone, as many as 13 million people were out of work. They were capable people and eager to work. But no one would hire them. As sympathetic as employers might have been, they simply couldn't use any more workers. Consumers weren't buying the goods and services already being produced. Nor was anyone else: Business investment and exports were falling precipitously, and even government spending was declining. Confronted with this reality, employers kept cutting back on production and laying off workers. Not until the outbreak of World War II were enough jobs found for the "army of the unemployed," and most of these "jobs" were in the armed forces.

As noted in Chapter 8, the Great Depression was the springboard for the Keynesian approach to macro policy. John Maynard Keynes concluded that a market-driven economy could fall into a recessionary trap and not get out. The problem, as he saw it, lay on the *demand* side of product markets. If market participants were unwilling to buy all the output produced, full employment couldn't be achieved. Waiting for some alleged self-adjustment was fruitless, Keynes argued. Rather than wait forever—until, as Keynes put it, we're all "dead"—the government should intervene to boost total spending and get the economy back on track.

In this and the next two chapters we focus on the demand side of the macro economy. We start with the same questions Keynes posed:

- What are the components of aggregate demand?
- What determines the level of spending for each component?
- Will there be enough demand to maintain full employment?

MACRO EQUILIBRIUM

In Chapter 8 we got a bird's-eye view of how macro equilibrium is established. Producers have some notion of how much output they're willing and able to produce at various price levels. Likewise, consumers, businesses, governments, and foreign buyers have some notion of how much output they're willing and able to buy at different price levels. These forces of **aggregate demand** and **aggregate supply** confront each other in the marketplace. Eventually, buyers and sellers discover that only one price level and output combination is acceptable to *both* sides. This is the price-output combination we designate as **(macro) equilibrium.** At

FIGURE 9.1
Escaping a Recession

Aggregate demand (AD) might be insufficient to ensure full employment (Q_F), as illustrated by the intersection of AD_1 and the aggregate supply curve. The question is whether and how AD will increase—that is, *shift* rightward—say to AD_2. To answer these questions, the components or demand must be examined.

equilibrium, the aggregate quantity of goods demanded exactly equals the aggregate quantity supplied. In the absence of macro disturbances, the economy will gravitate toward equilibrium.

Figure 9.1 illustrates again this general view of macro equilibrium. In the figure, aggregate supply (AS) and demand (AD_1) establish an equilibrium at E_1. At this particular equilibrium, the value of real output is Q_E, significantly short of the economy's full-employment potential at Q_F. Accordingly, the economy depicted in Figure 9.1 is saddled with excessive unemployment.

All economists recognize that such a *short-run* macro failure is possible. We also realize that the unemployment problem depicted in Figure 9.1 would disappear if either the AD or AS curve shifted rightward. A central macro debate is over whether the curves *will* shift on their own (self-adjust). If not, the government might have to step in and do some heavy shifting.

The British economist John Maynard Keynes had a distinctive view of this macro failure. Keynes said deficient aggregate demand was likely to be the cause of high unemployment. Hence, the AD_1 curve is the culprit in Figure 9.1. Moreover, Keynes said a market-driven AD curve might not shift when needed. He feared that the AD curve could get stuck at AD_1, leaving the economy mired in recession. The market offered no automatic self-adjustment, as the classical economists had asserted. To get out of a recession, Keynes argued, the government would have to intervene and shift the AD curve rightward.

To assess the possibilities of such a macro failure, we need to examine the nature of aggregate demand more closely. Who's buying the output of the economy? What factors influence their purchase decisions?

We can best understand the nature of aggregate demand by breaking it down into its various components. *The four components of aggregate demand are*

- *Consumption (C)*
- *Investment (I)*
- *Government spending (G)*
- *Net exports (X − IM)*

How are spending decisions made in each of these sectors? What factors might *change* the level of spending, thereby *shifting* aggregate demand? Will any such shifts improve or worsen macro outcomes?

aggregate demand: The total quantity of output demanded at alternative price levels in a given time period, *ceteris paribus*.

The Desired Adjustment

aggregate supply: The total quantity of output producers are willing and able to supply at alternative price levels in a given time period, *ceteris paribus*.

equilibrium (macro): The combination of price level and real output that is compatible with both aggregate demand and aggregate supply.

Components of Aggregate Demand

CONSUMPTION

consumption: Expenditure by consumers on final goods and services.

Consider first the largest component of aggregate demand, namely, **consumption**. Consumption refers to expenditures by households (consumers) on final goods and services. As we observed in Chapter 2, *consumer expenditures account for two-thirds of total spending*. Hence, whatever factors alter consumer behavior are sure to have an impact on aggregate demand.

Income and Consumption

The aggregate demand curve asserts that the *real* value of output demanded depends on the price level. Keynes, however, argued that consumers don't really think in such terms. The typical consumer simply decides how much he or she is going to *spend*, in dollars. The most decisive influence on that spending decision is available income: Most consumers simply spend most of whatever income they have.

Figure 9.2 seems to confirm Keynes's view. Year after year, consumer spending has risen in tandem with income. Accordingly, if we know how much income consumers have, we should be able to predict roughly how much they'll spend on consumption.

disposable income: After-tax income of consumers; personal income less personal taxes.

Disposable income is the key concept here. As noted in Chapter 5, **disposable income** is the amount of income consumers actually take home after all taxes have been paid, transfers (e.g., Social Security benefits) have been received, and depreciation charges and retained earnings have been subtracted (see Table 5.6).

saving: That part of disposable income not spent on current consumption; disposable income less consumption.

What will consumers do with their disposable income? There are only two choices: They can either spend their disposable income on consumption, or they can save (not spend) it. At this point we don't care what form household **saving** might take (e.g., cash under the mattress, bank deposits, stock purchases); all we want to do is distinguish that share of disposable income spent on consumer goods and services from the remainder that is *not* spent. By definition, then, **all disposable income is either consumed (spent) or saved (not spent);** that is,

$$\text{Disposable income} = \text{consumption} + \text{saving}$$
$$(Y_D) \qquad\qquad (C) \qquad\quad (S)$$

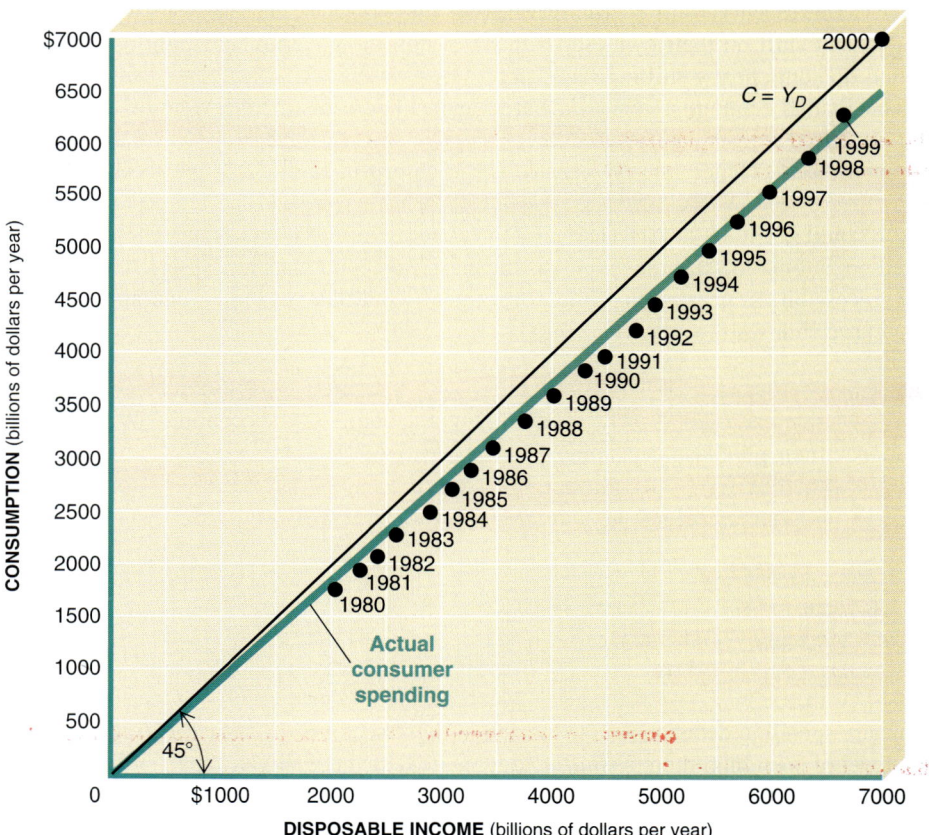

FIGURE 9.2
U.S. Consumption and Income

The points on the graph indicate the actual rates of U.S. disposable income and consumption for the years 1980–2000. By connecting these dots, we can approximate the long-term consumption function. Clearly, consumption rises with income. Indeed, consumers spend almost every extra dollar they receive.

What intrigued Keynes was that consumers might *not* spend all their income. This could leave aggregate demand short of its full-employment potential. This possibility led Keynes to take a closer look at the relationship of consumer spending to disposable income.

Keynes discovered two different ways of describing the consumption-income relationship. The first way focuses on the ratio of *total* consumption to *total* disposable income. The second method focuses on the relationship of *changes* in consumption to *changes* in disposable income.

The proportion of *total* disposable income spent on consumer goods and services is referred to as the **average propensity to consume (APC).** To determine the APC, we simply observe how much consumers spend in a given time period out of that period's disposable income. In 1999, for example, the disposable income of U.S. households amounted to $6,638 billion. Out of this amount, consumers spent $6,490 billion and saved only $148 billion. Accordingly, we may calculate the *average* propensity to consume as

$$\text{APC} = \frac{\text{total consumption}}{\text{total disposable income}} = \frac{C}{Y_D}$$

For 1999 this works out to

$$\text{APC} = \frac{\$6{,}490 \text{ billion}}{\$6{,}638 \text{ billion}} = 0.98$$

In other words, U.S. consumers spent just about every penny they received in 1999. Specifically, consumers spent, on average, 98 cents out of every dollar of income. Only 2 cents out of every disposable dollar was saved.

The relatively high APC in the United States distinguishes our consumer-oriented economy. In recent years, the U.S. APC has even *exceeded* 1.0, forcing U.S. households to finance some of their consumption with credit or past savings. In 2000, for example, the U.S. APC was 1.001; out of every $1,000 of disposable income they received, consumers spent $1,001.

If the APC can change from year to year, then consumers aren't spending the same fraction of every dollar received (the APC is just an average). This led Keynes to develop a second measure of consumption behavior, called the *marginal* propensity to consume. The **marginal propensity to consume (MPC)** tells us how much consumer expenditure will *change* in response to *changes* in disposable income. With the delta symbol, Δ, representing "change in," MPC can be written as

$$\text{MPC} = \frac{\text{change in consumption}}{\text{change in disposable income}} = \frac{\Delta C}{\Delta Y_D}$$

To calculate the marginal propensity to consume, we could ask how consumer spending in 1999 was affected by the *last* dollar of disposable income. That is, how did consumer spending change when disposable income increased from $6,637,999,999 to $6,638,000,000? If consumer spending increased by 80 cents when this last $1.00 was received, we'd calculate the *marginal* propensity to consume as

$$\text{MPC} = \frac{\Delta C}{\Delta Y_D} = \frac{\$0.80}{\$1.00} = 0.8$$

Notice that the MPC in this particular case (0.8) is lower than the APC (0.98). Suppose we had incorrectly assumed that consumers would always spend $0.98 of every dollar's income. Then we'd have expected the rate of consumer spending to rise by 98 cents as the last dollar was received. In fact, however, the rate of spending increased by only 80 cents. In other words, consumers responded to an *increase* in their income differently than past averages implied.

No one would be upset if our failure to distinguish the APC from the MPC led to an error of only $0.18 in forecasts of consumer spending. After all, the rate of consumer

Consumption vs. Saving

average propensity to consume (APC): Total consumption in a given period divided by total disposable income.

The Marginal Propensity to Consume

marginal propensity to consume (MPC): The fraction of each additional (marginal) dollar of disposable income spent on consumption; the change in consumption divided by the change in disposable income.

FIGURE 9.3
MPC and MPS

The marginal propensity to consume (MPC) tells us what portion of an extra dollar of income will be spent. The remaining portion will be saved. The MPC and MPS help us predict consumer behavior.

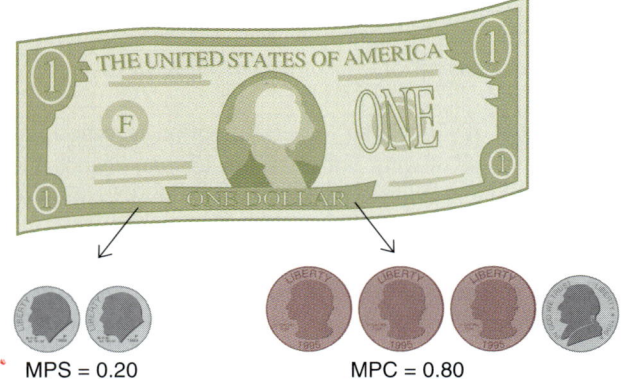

MPS = 0.20   MPC = 0.80

spending in the U.S. economy now exceeds $7 *trillion* per year! Policy decisions aren't calibrated in single dollars; typically, they involve *billion*-dollar changes in income. When we start playing with those sums—the actual focus of economic policymakers—the distinction between APC and MPC is significant.

The Marginal Propensity to Save

Once we know how much of their income consumers will spend, we also know how much they'll save. Remember that all **disposable income is, by definition, either consumed (spent on consumption) or saved.** Saving is just whatever income is left over after consumption expenditures. Accordingly, if the MPC is 0.80, then 20 cents of each additional dollar is being saved and 80 cents is being spent (see Figure 9.3). The **marginal propensity to save (MPS)**—the fraction of each additional dollar saved (that is, *not* spent)—is simply

$$MPS = 1 - MPC$$

marginal propensity to save (MPS): The fraction of each additional (marginal) dollar of disposable income not spent on consumption; 1 − MPC.

As Table 9.1 illustrates, if we know how much of their income consumers spend, we also know how much of it they save.

Go to the U.S. Bureau of Economic Activity (BEA) website at www.bea.doc.gov, and determine the rate of disposable income and consumer spending in the most recent two quarters. What was the APC in the most recent quarter? What was the MPC between the two quarters?

TABLE 9.1
Average and Marginal Propensities

MPC. The marginal propensity to consume (MPC) is the *change* in consumption that accompanies a *change* in disposable income; that is,

$$MPC = \frac{\Delta C}{\Delta Y_D}$$

APC. We may also be interested in the proportion of *total* disposable income that's spent on consumption. This is referred to as the *average* propensity to consume, and is computed:

$$APC = \frac{C}{Y_D}$$

MPS. The marginal propensity to *save* (MPS) is the fraction of each additional (marginal) dollar of disposable income *not* spent—that is, saved. This is summarized as

$$MPS = \frac{\Delta S}{\Delta Y_D}$$

MPS equals 1 − MPC, since every additional dollar is either spent (consumed) or not spent (saved).

APS. The average *propensity* to save equals $\frac{S}{Y_D}$.

THE CONSUMPTION FUNCTION

The MPC, MPS, APC, and APS are simply statistical measures of observed consumer behavior. What we really want to know is what drives these measures. If we know, then we'll be in a position to *predict* rather than just *observe* consumer behavior. This ability would be of immense value in anticipating and controlling short-run business cycles.

Keynes had several ideas about the determinants of consumption. Although he observed that consumer spending and income were highly correlated (Figure 9.2), he knew consumption wasn't *completely* determined by current income. In extreme cases, this is evident. People who have no income in a given period continue to consume goods and services. They finance their purchases by dipping into their savings accounts (past income) or using credit (future income) instead of spending current income. We also observe that people's spending sometimes *changes* even when income doesn't, suggesting that income isn't the *only* determinant of consumption. Other, *non*income determinants of consumption include

Autonomous Consumption

- **Expectations:** People who anticipate a pay raise, a tax refund, or a birthday check often start spending more money even before the extra income is received. Conversely, workers who anticipate being laid off tend to save more and spend less. Hence, *expectations* may alter consumer spending before income itself changes.
- **Wealth:** The amount of wealth an individual owns also affects a person's ability and willingness to consume. A homeowner may take out a home equity loan to buy a high definitive TV, a vacation, or a new car. In this case, consumer spending is being financed by wealth, not current income. *Changes* in wealth will also *change* consumer behavior. When the stock market rises, stockholders respond by saving less and spending more of their current income. This **wealth effect** was particularly evident in the late 1990s, when a persistent rise in the stock market helped fuel a consumption spree (and a negative savings rate).
- **Credit:** The availability of credit allows people to spend more than their current income. On the other hand, the need to repay past debts may limit current consumption. Here again, *changes* in credit availability or cost (interest rates) may alter consumer behavior.
- **Taxes:** Taxes are the link between total and disposable income. The tax cuts enacted in 2001 put more income into consumer hands immediately (via tax rebates) and left them with more income from future pay checks (via tax-rate cuts). These tax reductions stimulated more aggregate demand. Were income taxes to go up, disposable incomes and consumer spending would decline.
- **Price levels:** Rising price levels reduce the real value of money balances and may cause people to curtail spending. (This is the real-balances effect, which also helps explain aggregate demand.)

wealth effect: A change in consumer spending caused by a change in the value of owned assets.

Income-Dependent Consumption

In recognition of these many determinants of consumption, Keynes distinguished between two kinds of consumer spending: (1) spending *not* influenced by current income and (2) spending that *is* determined by current income. This simple categorization is summarized as

$$\text{Total consumption} = \text{autonomous consumption} + \text{income-dependent consumption}$$

where *autonomous* consumption refers to that consumption spending independent of current income. The level of autonomous spending depends instead on expectations, wealth, credit, taxes, price levels, and other nonincome influences.

These various determinants of consumption are summarized in an equation called the **consumption function**, which is written as

$$C = a + bY_D$$

consumption function: A mathematical relationship indicating the rate of desired consumer spending at various income levels.

where C = current consumption
a = autonomous consumption
b = marginal propensity to consume
Y_D = disposable income

At first blush, the consumption function is just a mathematical summary of consumer behavior. It has important *predictive* power, however: **The consumption function provides a precise basis for predicting how changes in income (Y_D) will affect consumer spending (C).** It also shows how changes in *non*income forces will affect consumer spending.

One Consumer's Behavior

To see how the consumption function works, consider the plight of Justin, a college freshman who has no income. How much will Justin spend? Obviously he must spend *something*, otherwise he'll starve to death. At a very low rate of income—in this case, zero—consumer spending depends less on current income than on basic survival needs, past savings, and credit. The *a* in the consumption function expresses this autonomous consumption: let's assume it's $50 per month. Thus, the monthly rate of consumption expenditure in this case is

$$C = \$50 + bY_D$$

Now suppose that Justin finds a job and begins earning $100 per month. Will his spending be affected? The $50 per month he'd been spending didn't buy much. Now that he's earning a little income, Justin will want to improve his lifestyle. That is, **we expect consumption to rise with income.** The marginal propensity to consume tells us how fast spending will rise.

Suppose Justin responds to the new-found income by increasing his consumption from $50 per month to $125. The *change* in his consumption is therefore $75. Dividing this *change* in his consumption ($75) by the *change* in income ($100) reveals that his marginal propensity to consume is 0.75.

Once we know the level of autonomous consumption ($50 per month) and the marginal propensity to consume (0.75), we can predict consumer behavior with uncanny accuracy. In this case, Justin's consumption function is

$$C = \$50 + 0.75Y_D$$

With these numerical values we can advance from simple *observation* (what he's spending now) to *prediction* (what he'll spend at different income levels). Figure 9.4 summarizes this predictive power.

We've already noted that Justin will spend $125 per month when his income is only $100. This observation is summarized in row *B* of the table in Figure 9.4 and by point *B* on the graph. Notice that his spending exceeds his income by $25 at this point. The other $25 is still being begged, borrowed, or withdrawn from savings. Without peering further into Justin's personal finances, we simply say that he's **dissaving** $25 per month. **Dissaving occurs whenever current consumption exceeds current income.** As the accompanying News suggests, dissaving is common in the United States, especially among younger people who are "livin' large."

dissaving: Consumption expenditure in excess of disposable income; a negative saving flow.

If Justin's income continues to rise, he'll stop dissaving at some point. Perhaps he'll even start saving enough to pay back all the people who have sustained him through these difficult months. Figure 9.4 shows just how and when this will occur.

The 45-Degree Line. The green line in Figure 9.4, with a 45-degree angle, represents all points where consumption and income are exactly equal ($C = Y_D$). Recall that Justin currently has an income of $100 per month. By moving up from the horizontal axis at $Y_D = \$100$, we see all the consumption possibilities he confronts. Were he to spend exactly $100 on consumption, he'd end up on the 45-degree line at point *G*. But we already know he doesn't stop there. Instead, he proceeds further, to point *B*. At point *B* the consumption function lies above the 45-degree line, so consumption exceeds income; dissaving is occurring.

CHAPTER 9: AGGREGATE DEMAND 181

IN THE NEWS

Livin' Large

Some 40% of Americans admit they live beyond their means. Seniors are the most likely to match their spending to their income, while young adults are most likely to overspend.

Source: *BusinessWeek*, August 27, 2001, p. 14.

SURVEY OF 1,010 ADULTS IN JANUARY, RELEASED JULY, 2001.

Data: Lutheran Brotherhood/Yankelovich Partners

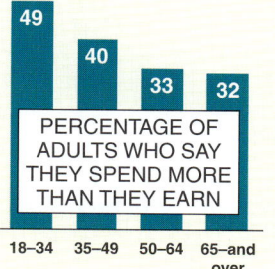

PERCENTAGE OF ADULTS WHO SAY THEY SPEND MORE THAN THEY EARN

Analysis: Dissaving occurs when consumer spending exceeds disposable income. Dissaving is financed with credit or prior savings.

	Disposable Income (Y_D)	Autonomous Consumption	+	Income Dependent Consumption	=	Total Consumption
A	$ 0	$50		$ 0		$ 50
B	100	50		75		125
C	200	50		150		200
D	300	50		225		275
E	400	50		300		350
F	500	50		375		425

FIGURE 9.4
Justin's Consumption Function

The rate of consumer spending (C) depends on disposable income (Y_D). The marginal propensity to consume indicates how much consumption will increase with each added dollar of income. In this case, when disposable income rises from $100 to $200, consumption increases by $75 (from point B to point C). The MPC = 0.75.

The consumption function can be expressed in an equation, a table, or a graph. Point B on the graph, for example, corresponds to row B in the table. Both indicate that this consumer desires to spend $125 per month when his income is $100 per month. The difference between income and consumption equals (dis)saving.

Observe, however, what happens when his disposable income rises to $200 per month (row C in the table in Figure 9.4). The upward slope of the consumption function (see graph) tells us that consumption spending continues to rise with income. In fact, *the slope of the consumption function equals the marginal propensity to consume*. In this case, we see that when income increases from $100 to $200, consumption rises from $125 (point B) to $200 (point C). Thus the *change* in consumption ($75) equals three-fourths of the *change* in income. The MPC is still 0.75.

Point C has further significance. At an income of $200 per month Justin is no longer dissaving but is now breaking even—that is, disposable income equals consumption, so saving equals zero. Notice that point C lies on the 45-degree line, where current consumption equals current income.

What would happen to spending if income increased still further? According to Figure 9.3, Justin will start *saving* once income exceeds $200 per month. To the right of point C, the consumption function always lies below the 45-degree line.

The Aggregate Consumption Function

Repeated studies of consumers suggest that there's nothing remarkable about Justin. The consumption function we've constructed for him can be used to depict all consumers simply by changing the numbers involved. Instead of dealing in hundreds of dollars per month, we now play with trillions of dollars per year. But the basic relationship is the same. This aggregate relationship between consumption spending and disposable income was already confirmed in Figure 9.2.

Shifts of the Consumption Function

Although the consumption function is a handy device for predicting consumer behavior, it's not infallible. People change their behavior. Neither autonomous consumption (the a in the consumption function) nor the marginal propensity to consume (the b in $C = a + bY_D$) is set in stone. Whenever one of these parameters changes, the entire consumption function *shifts* to a new position.

Consider first the value for a. We noted earlier that autonomous consumption depends on wealth, credit, expectations, taxes, and price levels. If any of these nonincome determinants changes, the value of the a in the consumption function will change as well.

Suppose consumers became more optimistic about the future, for whatever reason. Would their greater optimism prompt more spending? Probably so! Notice what happens to the consumption function when this happens. In Figure 9.5 the consumption function is initially at $C = a_1 + bY_D$. When consumer confidence increases, autonomous consumption rises to a_2. The new consumption function is therefore $C = a_2 + bY_D$. The consumption function has *shifted* upward; more consumption occurs at every rate of income.

FIGURE 9.5
Shift in the Consumption Function

Consumers' willingness to spend current income is affected by their confidence in the future. If consumers become more optimistic, autonomous consumption may increase from a_1 to a_2. This change will shift the entire consumption function upward.

FIGURE 9.6

Shifts vs. Movements: The 2001 Recession

Incomes declined and consumer confidence fell during the 2001 recession. The income decline prompted a movement along the initial consumption function from point *f* to point *g*. The fall in confidence shifted the entire consumption function downward (point *g* to point *h*); people spent less at every income level.

Were consumers to become more pessimistic, the consumption function would shift downward rather than upward. This is exactly what happened after the September 11, 2001, terrorist attacks on the World Trade Center and Pentagon (see Figure 9.6). People became fearful not only for their *physical* security, but for their *economic* security as well. Market disruptions and job layoffs added to the sense of insecurity. As a result, consumer confidence plunged in October 2001 (see News), shifting the consumption function downward.

Shifts of Aggregate Demand. Shifts of the consumption function are reflected in shifts of the aggregate demand curve. Consider again the October 2001 downward shift

IN THE NEWS

Consumer Confidence Drops to Seven-Year Low

Consumer confidence plunged this month to the lowest level in seven years, raising new concerns about whether consumers worried about their jobs and terrorist attacks may reduce their spending at a time when the U.S. economy is already faltering.

The Conference Board said yesterday that its confidence index fell to 85.5 this month, the lowest level since February 1994, from 97.0 in September. It was the fourth consecutive monthly decline.

"This is a very worrisome report, and what's worse is that by Friday morning it could be old news," said economist Oscar Gonzalez at John Hancock Financial Services in Boston, referring to the Friday release of the government's October unemployment report. If, as expected, the report shows a sharp rise in unemployment and decline in job growth, "it could be a crushing blow to confidence." "Having a job is probably the single biggest factor in consumers having confidence," Gonzalez said.

Analysts are keenly interested in consumers' attitudes because their spending accounts for two-thirds of the nation's economic output. Earlier this year, steady increases in consumer spending helped keep the economy growing despite big declines in business investment. Many economists now believe that the nation is slipping into recession and worry that a steep falloff in consumer spending could make it longer and more painful than otherwise.

—John M. Berry

Source: *Washington Post*, October 31, 2001. © 2001 The Washington Post. Reprinted with permission. www.washingtonpost.com

Analysis: Expectations of *future* income affect consumer spending. When consumer confidence in the future declines, autonomous spending drops and the consumption function shifts downward.

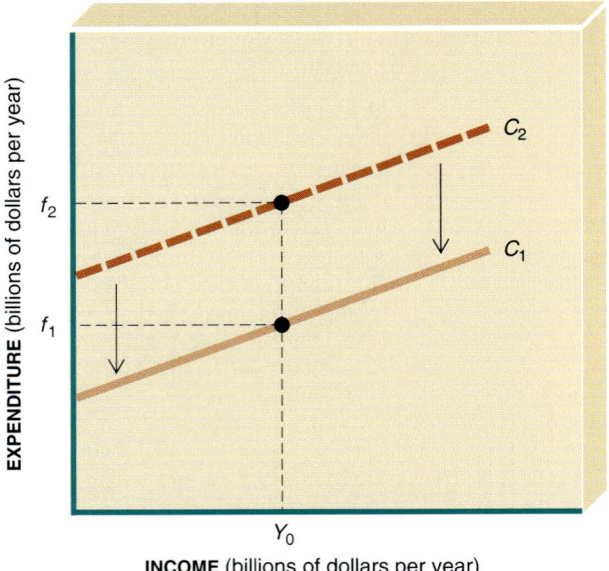

FIGURE 9.7
AD Effects of Consumption Shifts

A downward shift of the consumption function implies that households want to spend less of their income. Here consumption at the income level Y_D decreases from f_1 to f_2. This decreased expenditure is reflected in a leftward shift of the aggregate demand curve. At the initial price level P_1 consumers demanded Q_1 output. At that same price level, consumers now demand less output, Q_2 ($= f_1 - f_2$). (*Note:* Both income and the price level are being held constant here.)

of the consumption function. A decrease in consumer spending at any given income level implies a decrease in aggregate demand as well. Recall that the aggregate demand curve depicts how much real output will be demanded at various price levels, *with income held constant*. When the consumption function shifts downward, households spend less of their income. Hence, less real output is demanded at any given price level. To summarize,

- *A downward shift of the consumption function implies a leftward shift of the aggregate demand curve.*
- *An upward shift of the consumption function implies an increase (a rightward shift) in aggregate demand.*

These relationships are illustrated in Figure 9.7.

Shift Factors A change in consumer confidence is only one factor that might shift the aggregate demand curve. Shift factors include all nonincome (autonomous) determinants of consumption, including:

- *Changes in consumer confidence (expectations).*
- *Changes in wealth.*
- *Changes in credit conditions.*
- *Changes in tax policy.*

As we observed earlier, a change in the value of a household's assets (wealth) will alter autonomous consumption. The Council of Economic Advisers estimated that rising stock market prices added one percentage point to the average propensity to consume in 1997 and 1998.

The wealth effect turned negative, however, in 2000, when the stock market plunged (see News). With consumers spending less at every income level, aggregate demand fell (shifted leftward) in 2000–01 (Figure 9.7).

IN THE NEWS

Falling Stocks Smash Nest Eggs

"Wealth Effect" Has Gone Poof, and So Have Many Investors' Spending Plans

For a long time, the stock market was very good to Chuck Yanus—so good that he and his wife went out and bought themselves two Suzuki motorcycles for about $10,000 in cash.

The Yanus family felt so flush that when Honda introduced its new top-of-the-line Gold Wing touring bike (price tag: $17,000-plus) this year, the couple began making plans to give one to themselves for Christmas.

But then the markets plunged, vaporizing more than $2 trillion in stock value in the nine months since stocks peaked in March. The tech-heavy Nasdaq is down a stunning 36 percent this year and about 48 percent from its exhilarating high last spring. The Dow Jones industrial average, sober avatar of the Old Economy, is better, but not enough to avoid pain: It's down about 7 percent this year, after being up 25 percent last year.

Stock portfolios that gave investors thoughts of early retirement or made almost anything seem affordable were devastated.

"When you lop 25 percent off your bottom line, it makes you stop and think," says Yanus, 46, a district manager for Sun Microsystems in Syracuse, N.Y. Big-ticket items like the Gold Wing are out. "I said the hell with it, let's wait," Yanus says.

For many Americans like the Yanuses, the thrill is gone. The "wealth effect"—that giddy feeling of richness that consumers got as they watched the value of their portfolios and their homes soar—has been killed, or at least badly wounded, by the prolonged market decline.

Spending Spree May Be Over. Interviews with consumers around the country suggest that the market-driven shopping spree may be over. Many of the motorcycles, cars, houses, home renovations, big-screen TVs and other big-ticket purchases Americans would have made without hesitation a year or even six months ago are on hold.

—George Hager and Dina Temple-Raston

Source: *USA Today*, December 19, 2000. © 2001 USA Today. Reprinted with permission. www.usatoday.com

Analysis: The stock market plunge of 2000–01 reduced consumer wealth and autonomous consumption. This shifted the consumption function downward and the aggregate demand curve leftward.

The same emphasis on *change* applies to other shift factors. A *change* in tax rates or interest rates (credit conditions) is what *shifts* the consumption function up or down. These same changes therefore shift the aggregate demand curve left or right (Figure 9.7).

Shifts and Cycles

Shifts of aggregate demand can be a cause of macro instability. As we first observed in Chapter 8, recurrent shifts of aggregate demand may cause real output to alternately expand and contract, thereby giving rise to short-run business cycles. What we've observed here is that those aggregate demand shifts may originate in consumer behavior. Changes in consumer confidence, in wealth, or in credit conditions alter the rate of consumer spending. If consumer spending increases abruptly, demand-pull inflation may follow. If consumer spending slows abruptly, a recession may occur.

INVESTMENT

Although consumer spending can be unstable, the economy need not suffer every time the consumption function shifts. There are, after all, three other sources of aggregate demand: investment (I), government spending (G), and net exports ($X - IM$). These components of aggregate demand could potentially offset any shortfalls or instability in consumer spending. To assess this possibility, we will first examine how the level of investment is determined and how stable it is.

Determinants of Investment

As we observed in Chapter 5, investment spending accounts for roughly 18 percent of total output. That spending includes not only expenditures on new plant, equipment, and business software (all referred to as *fixed investment*) but also spending on inventories (called *inventory investment*). Residential construction is also counted in investment statistics because houses and apartment buildings continue to produce

186 CYCLICAL INSTABILITY

Investment: Expenditures on (production of) new plant, equipment, and structures (capital) in a given time period, plus changes in business inventories.

housing services for decades. All these forms of **investment** represent a demand for output.

Expectations. Expectations play a critical role in investment decisions. No firm wants to purchase new plant and equipment unless it is convinced people will later buy the output produced by that plant and that equipment. Nor do producers want to accumulate inventories of goods unless they expected consumers to eventually buy them. Thus, *favorable expectations of future sales are a necessary condition for investment spending.*

Interest Rates. A second determinant of investment spending is the rate of interest. Business firms typically borrow money in order to purchase plant and equipment. The higher the rate of interest, the costlier it is to invest. Accordingly, we anticipate a lower rate of investment spending when interest rates are high, more investment at lower rates, *ceteris paribus.*

Technology and Innovation. A third determinant of investment is changes in technology and innovation. When scientists learned how to miniaturize electronic circuitry, an entire new industry of electronic calculators, watches, and other goods sprang to life. In this case, the demand for investment goods shifted to the right as a result of improved miniaturized circuits and imaginative innovation (the use of the new technology in pocket calculators). More recently, technological advances and cost reductions have stimulated an investment spree in laptop computers, cellular phones, video conferencing, fiber-optic networks, and anything associated with the Internet.

The curve I_1, in Figure 9.8, depicts the general shape of the investment function. To find the rate of investment spending in this figure, we simply have to know the rate of interest. At an interest rate of 8 percent, for example, we expect to see $150 billion of investment (point A in Figure 9.8). At 6 percent interest, we'd expect $300 billion of investment (point B).

Shifts of Investment

These predictions about investment spending depend on a critical assumption; namely, that investor expectations are stable. In truth, that's a very tenuous assumption. While no one is entirely sure what shapes investor's expectations, experience shows that they are not as stable as the curve I_1 requires.

Altered Expectations. Business expectations are essentially a question of confidence in future sales. An upsurge in current consumer spending could raise investor expectations for future sales, shifting the investment function rightward (to I_2). New business software might induce a similar response. New business tax breaks might have

FIGURE 9.8
Investment Demand

The rate of desired investment depends on expectations, the rate of interest, and innovation. A *change* in expectations will *shift* the investment-demand curve. With given expectations, a change in the rate of interest will lead to *movements* along the existing investment-demand curve. In this case, an increase in investment beyond $150 billion per year (point A) may be caused by lower interest rates (point B) or improved expectations (point C). Keynes emphasized the role of investor expectations in maintaining full-employment spending.

IN THE NEWS

Manufacturing-Output Slump Continues While Businesses Again Trim Inventories

WASHINGTON—The manufacturing slump continued as output at factories, utilities and mines fell in April for the seventh straight month and capacity use dropped to its lowest level since 1991. . . .

Industrial production fell 0.3 percent in April, the Fed said, following a 0.1 percent drop in March. Capacity use also fell in April, to 78.5 percent from a revised 78.9 percent. . . .

In response to the slowing economy, businesses continued to draw down stocks of excess goods. The Commerce Department reported that business inventories fell 0.3 percent in March to a seasonally adjusted level of $1.21 trillion.

Inventories thinned even as businesses saw sales fall 0.3 percent in March to $888.3 billion, after a 0.4 percent drop in February. The inventory-to-sales ratio, which measures how many months it would take a firm to exhaust its inventory, was 1.37 in March.

—Rebecca Christie and Elizabeth Price

Source: *The Wall Street Journal*, May 15, 2001. Reprinted by permission of *The Wall Street Journal*. © 2001 Dow Jones & Company, Inc. All Rights Reserved Worldwide. www.wsj.com

Analysis: Business investment is based more on expected future sales than on current sales and income. When expectations for future sales growth diminish, investment spending on plant, equipment, and inventory drops.

---

the same effect. If any of these things happened, businesses would be more eager to invest. They'd borrow *more* money at any given interest rate (e.g., point C in Figure 9.8) and use it to buy more plant, equipment, and inventory.

Business expectations could worsen as well. The terrorist strikes of September 11, 2001 put a lot of investment plans on hold. A sudden drop in sales might also cause businesses to downgrade future growth prospects (see NEWS). A transportation strike or spike in oil prices might worsen sales expectations as well. These kinds of events will shift the investment function leftward, as to I_3 in Figure 9.8. **When investment spending declines, the aggregate demand curve shifts to the left.**

Empirical Instability. Figure 9.9 shows that unstable investment is more than just a theoretical threat to macro stability. What is depicted here are the quarter-to-quarter

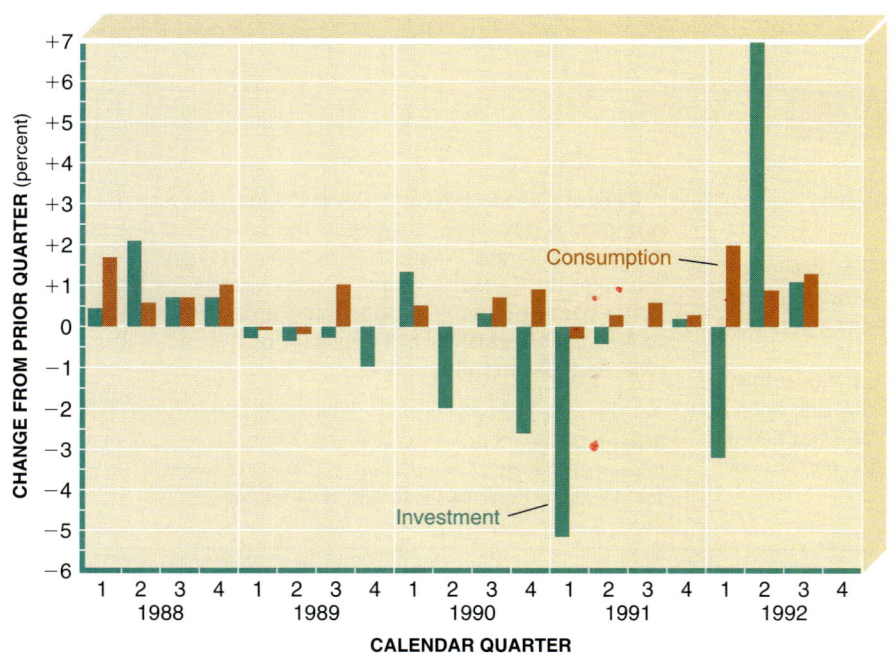

FIGURE 9.9
Volatile Investment Spending

Investment spending fluctuates more than consumption. Shown here are the quarter-to-quarter changes in the real rate of spending for fixed investment (excluding inventory changes) and total consumption. Notice the sharp drop in investment spending just prior to the recession that began in July 1990.

Source: *Economic Report of the President, 1993* (quarterly data seasonally adjusted).

188 CYCLICAL INSTABILITY

Check the U.S. Bureau of Economic Analysis (BEA) website at www.bea.doc.gov to see how much seasonally adjusted investment has varied in percentage terms over the past six quarters.

changes in both consumer spending and investor spending for the years 1988–92. Quarterly changes in *consumer* spending never exceeded 2 percent. However, *investment* spending plummeted by more than 5 percent in one quarter and jumped by 7 percent in another. Those abrupt changes in investment were a major cause of the 1990–91 recession and also an important source of subsequent recovery.

GOVERNMENT AND NET EXPORT SPENDING

The apparent instability of investment spending heightens rather than soothes anxiety about short-run macro instability. Together, consumption and investment account for roughly 80 percent of total output. As we have seen, the investment component of aggregate demand can be both uncertain and unstable. The consumption component of aggregate demand may shift abruptly as well. What about the other two sources of aggregate demand? What determines the level of government and net-export spending? How stable are they?

Government Spending

At present, the government sector (federal, state, and local) spends nearly $2 trillion on goods and services, all of which is part of aggregate demand (unlike income transfers, which are not). As we observed in Chapter 2, about two-thirds of this spending occurs at the state and local levels. That nonfederal spending is limited by tax receipts, because state and local governments typically confront legal limitations on borrowing money. As a consequence, state and local spending has a mild pro-cyclical component, with expenditure rising slightly as the economy (and tax receipts) expands and declining somewhat when the economy (and tax receipts) slumps.

Federal spending on goods and services is less dependent on current tax receipts. Decisions on defense spending, science, environmental protection, and health-care services are largely made independently of tax receipts. Hence, the level of federal spending on goods and services is not very cyclical. In fact, federal spending is often used to counter cyclical disruptions to aggregate demand, as we'll see in chapter 11. Income transfers (like unemployment insurance, welfare benefits, food stamps) also have a countercyclical pattern, but are not directly part of aggregate demand.

Net Exports

The fourth and final source of aggregate demand is net exports. Our gross exports depend on the spending behavior of foreign consumers and businesses. If foreign con-

Canada Forecasts Slower 2001 Growth, Citing U.S. "Spillover"

OTTAWA—Citing the impact of the slowing U.S. economy, the Bank of Canada lowered its forecast of gross domestic product growth this year to about 3 percent from a previous range of 3 percent to 4 percent.

In a revision of its monetary-policy report of last November. Canada's central bank said "the slowdown of the U.S. economy has been more abrupt than anticipated," and has had a "spillover effect" on Canada. More than 85 percent of Canadian exports go to the U.S.

Bank of Canada governor David Dodge said yesterday the economy is now likely to grow at the low end of the bank's 3–4 percent forecast made in November. The bank said that it estimates the Canadian economy grew last year by 5 percent.

The bank also said it expects total consumer price inflation to ease to an annual pace of 2 percent by the end of this year, reflecting declines in oil prices.

—Joel Baglole

Source: *The Wall Street Journal*, February 7, 2001. Reprinted by permission of *The Wall Street Journal*. © 2001 Dow Dones & Company, Inc. All Rights Reserved Worldwide. www.wsj.com

Analysis: Most Canadian exports go to the United States. So when the U.S. economy slows, Canada experiences a decline in export demand—a leftward shift in that country's aggregate demand.

sumers and investors behave like Americans, their demand for U.S. products will be subject to changes in *their* income, expectations, wealth, and other factors. In the Asian currency crisis of 1997–99, this was alarmingly evident: Once incomes in Asia began falling, U.S. exports to Asia of rice, corn, lumber, computers, and other goods and services fell sharply. So did the number of Asian students applying to U.S. colleges (a demand for U.S.-produced educational services). This decline in export spending represented a leftward shift of U.S. aggregate demand. The same kind of shift occurred in Canada's aggregate demand when the U.S. economy slowed in early 2001 (see World View).

Imports, too, can be unstable, and for the same reasons. Most U.S. imports are consumer goods and services. Imports, therefore, just get caught up in the ebb and flow of consumer spending. When consumer confidence slips or the stock market dips, import spending declines along with the rest of consumption (and investment). As a consequence, *net* exports can be both uncertain and unstable, creating further shifts of aggregate demand.

MACRO FAILURE

Once the potential instability of aggregate demand is recognized, the anxiety about macro instability begins to make sense. There is only one macro equilibrium at any one time—an equilibrium located at the intersection of the aggregate supply and demand curves. Keynes had two chief concerns about macro equilibrium, namely,

1. The market's macroequilibrium might not give us full employment or price stability.
2. Even if the market's macro equilibrium were perfectly positioned (i.e., with full employment and price stability), it might not last.

Figure 9.10a depicts the perfect macro equilibrium that everyone hopes for. Aggregate demand and aggregate supply intersect at E_1. At that macro equilibrium we get both full employment (Q_F) and price stability (P^*)—an ideal situation.

Undesired Equilibrium

Keynes didn't think such a perfect outcome was likely. Why should aggregate demand intersect with aggregate supply exactly at point E_1? As we've observed, consumers,

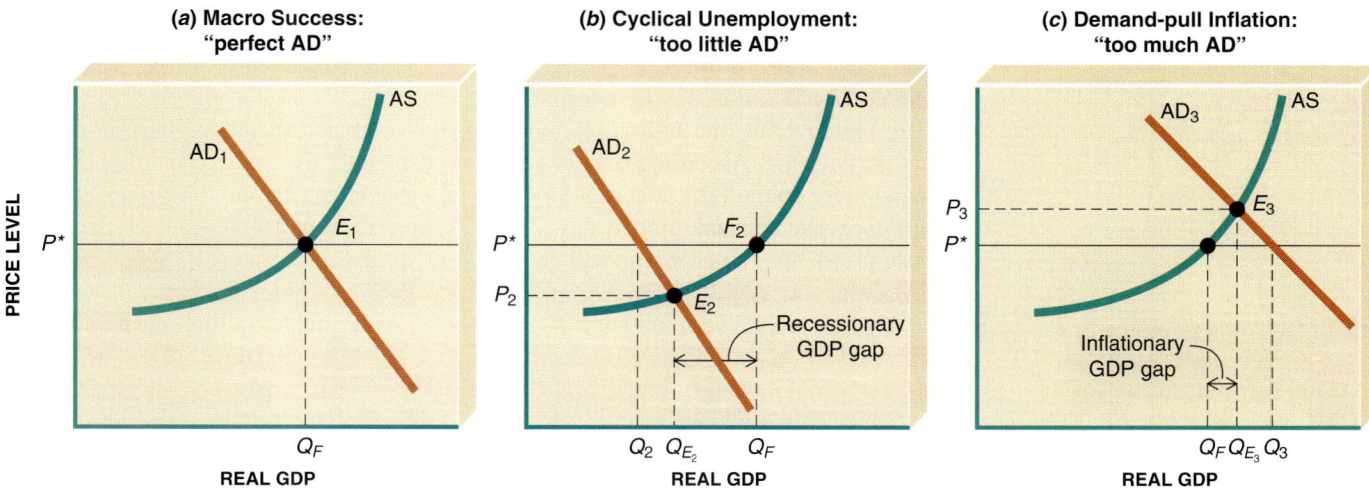

FIGURE 9.10
Macro Failures

Keynesian theory emphasizes that the combined spending decisions of consumers, investors, governments, and net exporters may not be compatible with the desired full employment (Q_F)–price stability (P^*) equilibrium (as they are in Figure a). Aggregate demand may be too small (Figure b) or too great (Figure c) causing cyclical unemployment (b) or demand-pull inflation (c). Worse yet, even a desirable macro equilibrium (a) may be upset by abrupt *shifts* of aggregate demand.

190 CYCLICAL INSTABILITY

investors, government, and foreigners make independent spending decisions, based on many influences. Why should all these decisions add up to just the right amount of aggregate demand? Keynes didn't think they would. Because market participants make independent spending decisions, there's no reason to expect that the sum of their expenditures will generate exactly the right amount of aggregate demand. Instead, there's a high likelihood that we'll confront an imbalance between desired spending and full-employment output levels—that is, too much or too little aggregate demand.

Recessionary GDP Gap. Figure 9.10b illustrates one of the undesired equilibriums that Keynes worried about. Full-employment GDP is still at Q_F and stable prices are at the level P^*. In this case, however, the rate of output demanded at price level P^* is only Q_2, far short of full-employment GDP (Q_F). How could this happen? Quite simple: The spending plans of consumers, investors, government, and export buyers don't generate enough aggregate demand at current (P^*) prices.

The economy depicted in Figure 9.10b is in trouble. At full employment, a lot more output would be produced than market participants would be willing to buy. As unsold inventories rose, production would get cut back, workers would get laid off, and prices would decline. Eventually, the economy would settle at F_2, where AD_2 and AS intersect. Equilibrium GDP would be equal to Q_{E2} and the equilibrium price level would be at P_2.

E_2 is clearly not a happy equilibrium. What particularly concerned Keynes was the **recessionary GDP gap,** the amount by which equilibrium GDP falls short of full-employment GDP. In Figure 9.10b, the recessionary GDP gap equals Q_F minus Q_{E2}. This gap represents unused productive capacity: lost GDP and unemployed workers. It is the breeding ground of **cyclical unemployment.**

Figure 9.11 illustrates this dilemma with more details on aggregate demand. The table depicts the demand for GDP at different price levels by consumers, investors, government, and net export buyers. Full-employment GDP is set at $10 trillion and the price level at 100. As is evident, however, the quantity of output demanded at that price level is only $8 trillion. This shortfall of aggregate demand will lead to output and price reductions, pushing the economy downward to equilibrium GDP, at point E. At that $AS = AD$ intersection, the *equilibrium* GDP is at $9 trillion, with a price level of 90. The recessionary GDP gap is therefore $1 trillion ($Q_F - Q_E$).

Inflationary GDP Gap. Aggregate demand won't always fall short of potential output. But Keynes saw it as a distinct possibility. He also realized that aggregate demand might even *exceed* the economy's full-employment/price stability capacity. This contingency is illustrated in Figure 9.10c.

In Figure 9.10c, the AD_3 curve represents the combined spending plans of all market participants. According to this aggregate demand curve, market participants demand more output (Q_3) at current prices than the economy can produce (Q_F). To meet this excessive demand, producers will use overtime shifts and strain capacity. This will push prices up. The economy will end up at the macro equilibrium E_3. At E_3 the price level is higher (inflation) and short-run output exceeds sustainable levels.

What we end up with in Figure 9.10c is another undesirable equilibrium. In this case we have an **inflationary GDP gap,** wherein equilibrium GDP (Q_{E3}) exceeds full-employment GDP (Q_F). This is a fertile breeding ground for **demand-pull inflation.**

The GDP gaps illustrated in Figure 9.10b and c are clearly troublesome. In a nutshell,

- *The goal is to produce at full employment, but*
- *Equilibrium GDP may be greater or less than full-employment GDP.*

Whenever equilibrium GDP differs from full-employment GDP, we confront a macro failure (unemployment or inflation).

Unstable Equilibrium

Things need not always work out so badly. Although Keynes thought it improbable, the spending plans of market participants *might* generate the perfect amount of aggregate demand, leaving the economy at the desired macro equilibrium depicted in Figure 9.10a.

---

full-employment GDP: The value of total output (real GDP) produced at full employment.

equilibrium GDP: The value of total output (real GDP) produced at macro equilibrium (AS = AD).

recessionary GDP gap: The amount of which equilibrium GDP falls short of full-employment GDP.

cyclical unemployment: Unemployment attributable to a lack of job vacancies; that is, to inadequate aggregate demand.

inflationary GDP gap: The amount by which equilibrium GDP exceeds full-employment GDP.

demand-pull inflation: An increase in the price level initiated by excessive aggregate demand.

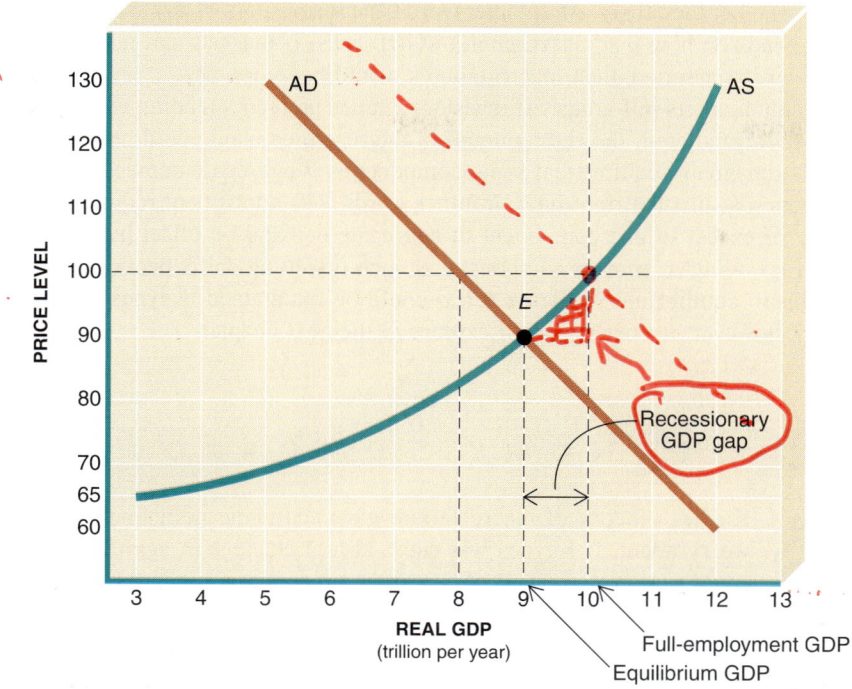

FIGURE 9.11
A Recessionary GDP Gap

The level of aggregate demand depends on the spending behavior of market participants. In this case, the level of GDP demanded at current prices ($P = 100$) ($8 trillion) is less than full-employment GDP ($10 trillion). This results in a lower equilibrium GDP ($9 trillion) and a recessionary GDP gap ($1 trillion). The price level also declines from 100 to 90.

Price Level	Real GDP Demanded (in $ trillions) by:				Aggregate Demand	Aggregate Supply
	Consumers	+ Investors	+ Government	+ Net Exports =		
130	3.0	0.25	1.5	0.25	5.0	12.0
120	3.5	0.50	1.5	0.50	6.0	11.5
110	4.0	0.75	1.5	0.75	7.0	11.0
100	4.5	1.00	1.5	1.0	8.0	10.0
90	5.0	1.25	1.5	1.25	9.0	9.0
80	5.5	1.50	1.5	1.50	10.0	7.0
70	6.0	1.75	1.5	1.75	11.0	5.0
60	6.5	2.0	1.5	2.0	12.0	3.0

In Figure 9.10a, equilibrium GDP equals full-employment GDP. Unfortunately, that happy outcome might not last. As we've observed, market participants may change their spending behavior abruptly. The stock market may boom or bust, shifting the consumption component of aggregate demand. Changed sales forecasts (expectations) may alter investment plans. Crises in foreign economies may disrupt export sales. A terrorist attack or outbreak of war may rock everybody's boat. Any of these events will cause the aggregate demand curve to shift. When this happens, the AD curve will get knocked out of its "perfect" position in Figure 9.10a, sending us to undesirable outcomes like 9.10b and 9.10c. Recurrent shifts of aggregate demand could even cause a **business cycle**.

Economies can get into macro trouble from the supply side of the market place as well, as we'll see later (Chapter 16). Keynes's emphasis on demand-side inadequacies serves as an early warning of potential macro failure, however. If aggregate demand is too little, too great, or too unstable, the economy will not reach and maintain the goals of full employment and price stability.

As we noted earlier, not everyone is as pessimistic as Keynes was about the prospects for macro bliss. The critical question is not whether undesirable outcomes might

business cycle: Alternating periods of economic growth and contraction.

Macro Failures

Self-Adjustment?

occur but whether they'll *persist*. In other words, the seriousness of any short-run macro failure depends on how markets *respond* to GDP gaps. If markets self-adjust, as classical economists asserted, then macro failures would be temporary.

How might markets self-adjust? If investors stepped up *their* spending whenever consumer spending faltered, the right amount of aggregate demand could be maintained. Such self-adjustment requires that some components of aggregate demand shift in the right direction at just the right time. In other words, self-adjustment requires that any instability or excess in one component of aggregate demand be offset by the level or change of spending in another component. If such offsetting shifts occurred, then the desired macro equilibrium in Figure 9.10a could be maintained. Keynes didn't think that likely, however, for reasons we'll explore in the next chapter.

THE ECONOMY TOMORROW

Looking for AD Shifts
The Index of Leading Indicators

Keynes's theory of macro failure gave economic policymakers a lot to worry about. If Keynes was right, abrupt changes in aggregate demand could ruin even the best of economic times. Even if he was wrong about the ability of the economy to self-adjust, sudden shifts of aggregate demand could cause a lot of temporary pain. To minimize such pain, policymakers need some way of peering into the future—to foresee coming shifts of aggregate demand. With such a crystal ball, they might be able to take defensive actions and keep the economy on track.

Market participants have developed all kinds of crystal balls for anticipating AD shifts. The Foundation for the Study of Cycles has identified 4,000 different crystal balls people use to foretell changes in spending. They include the ratio of used-car to new-car sales (it rises in economic downturns); the number of divorce petitions (it rises in bad times); animal population cycles (they peak just before economic downturns); and even the optimism/pessimism content of popular music (a reflection of consumer confidence).

TABLE 9.2
The Leading Economic Indicators
Everyone wants a crystal ball to foresee future economic events. In reality, forecasters must reckon with very crude predictors of the future. One of the most widely used predictors is the Index of Leading Economic Indicators, which includes 11 factors believed to predict economic activity three to six months in advance. Changes in the leading indicators are used to forecast changes in GDP.

The leading indicators rarely move in the same direction at the same time. They're weighted together to create the index. Up-and-down movements of the index are reported each month by the nonprofit Conference Board.

Indicator	Expected Impact
1. Average workweek	Hours worked per week typically increase when greater output and sales are expected.
2. Unemployment claims	Initial claims for unemployment benefits reflect changes in industry layoffs.
3. Delivery times	The longer it takes to deliver ordered goods, the greater the ratio of demand to supply.
4. Credit	Changes in business and consumer borrowing indicate potential purchasing power.
5. Materials prices	When producers step up production they buy more raw materials, pushing their prices higher.
6. Equipment orders	Orders for new equipment imply increased production capacity and higher anticipated sales.
7. Stock prices	Higher stock prices reflect expectations of greater sales and profits.
8. Money supply	Faster growth of the money supply implies a pickup in aggregate demand.
9. New orders	New orders for consumer goods trigger increases in production and employment.
10. Building permits	A permit represents the first step in housing construction.
11. Inventories	Companies build up inventory when they anticipate higher sales.

One of the most widely used crystal balls is the Index of Leading Indicators. What's appealing about that index is the plausible connection between its components and future spending. Equipment orders, for example, is one of the leading indicators (number 6 in Table 9.2). This seems eminently reasonable, since businesses don't order equipment unless they later plan to buy it. The same is true of building permits (indicator 10); people obtain permits only if they plan to build something. Hence, both indicators appear to be dependable signs of future investment.

Unfortunately, the Leading Indicators aren't a perfect crystal ball. Equipment orders are often canceled. Building plans get delayed or abandoned. Hence, shifts of aggregate demand still occur without warning. No crystal ball could predict a terrorist strike or the timing and magnitude of a natural disaster. Compared to other crystal balls, however, the Index of Leading Indicators has a pretty good track record—and a very big audience. It helps investors and policymakers foresee what the economy tomorrow might look like.

SUMMARY

- Macro failure occurs when the economy fails to achieve full employment and price stability.
- Too much or too little aggregate demand, relative to full employment, can cause macro failure. Too little aggregate demand causes cyclical unemployment; too much aggregate demand causes demand-pull inflation.
- Aggregate demand reflects the spending plans of consumers (C), investors (I), government (G), and foreign buyers (net exports = $X - IM$).
- Consumer spending is affected by nonincome (autonomous) factors and current income, as summarized in the consumption function: $C = a + bY_D$.
- Autonomous consumption (a) depends on wealth, expectations, taxes, credit, and price levels. Income-dependent consumption depends on the marginal propensity to consume (MPC), the b in the consumption function.
- Consumer saving is the difference between disposable income and consumption (that is, $S = Y_D - C$). All disposable income is either spent (C) or saved (S).
- The consumption function shifts up or down when autonomous influences such as wealth and expectations change. Shifts of the consumption function at a constant price level are reflected in shifts of the aggregate demand curve.
- Investment spending depends on interest rates, expectations for future sales, and innovation. Changes in expectations may abruptly alter investment spending.
- Government spending and net exports are influenced by a variety of cyclical and noncyclical factors and may also change abruptly.
- Even a "perfect" macro equilibrium may be upset by abrupt shifts of spending behavior. Recurrent shifts may cause a business cycle.

Key Terms

aggregate demand
aggregate supply
equilibrium (macro)
consumption
disposable income
saving
average propensity to consume (APC)
marginal propensity to consume (MPC)
marginal propensity to save (MPS)
wealth effect
consumption function
dissaving
investment
full-employment GDP
equilibrium GDP
recessionary GDP gap
cyclical unemployment
inflationary GDP gap
demand-pull inflation
business cycle

Questions for Discussion

1. What percentage of last month's income did you spend? How much more would you spend if you won a $1,000 lottery prize? Why might your average and marginal propensities to consume differ?
2. Why do rich people have a higher marginal propensity to save than poor people?
3. How do households dissave? Where do they get the money to finance their extra consumption? Can everyone dissave at the same time?

4. What events might change consumer confidence? (See News, page 183).
5. The News item on page 187 implies that business investment is affected by current sales. How might changes in current sales affect expectations or the rate of desired investment?
6. If state governments can't borrow money for noncapital expenditures, how will their level of spending be affected by (*a*) a recession. (*b*) an economic boom?
7. What factors influence the level of (*a*) U.S. exports to Mexico, (*b*) U.S. imports from Mexico?
8. Why wouldn't market participants always want to buy all the output produced?
9. If an inflationary GDP gap exists, what will happen to business inventories. How will producers respond?
10. How might a "perfect" macro equilibrium (Figure 9.10*a*) be affected by (*a*) a stock market crash, (*b*) the death of a president, (*c*) a recession in Canada, (*d*) a spike in oil prices?

Web Activities

1. Log on to www.bea.doc.gov/briefrm/tables/ebr1.htm. Record percentage changes in consumption, investment, government, and net exports for the last four quarters. Which changed the most? Which changed the least? Why?
2. Log on to www.census.gov and click on the latest economic indicators button. Are the indicators rising or falling during the past 12 months? What has happened to real GDP growth during the same period?
3. Log on to www.bea.doc.gov/briefrm/tables/ebr6.htm. Find data on the personal savings rate percentage. All other things remaining constant, what does the trend suggest is happening to current consumption spending? What impact does this have on the aggregate demand curve?

THE ACCOMPANYING STUDENT PROBLEM SET CONTAINS NUMERICAL AND GRAPHING PROBLEMS FOR THIS CHAPTER

APPENDIX

THE KEYNESIAN CROSS

The Keynesian analysis of aggregate demand clearly reveals the potential instability of the macro economy. As we've observed, a real GDP gap can cause either cyclical unemployment or demand-pull inflation. At the time Keynes developed his theory of instability, however, inflation was not a threat. In the Great Depression prices were *falling*. With unemployment rates reaching as high as 25 percent, no one worried that increased aggregate demand would push price levels up. The only concern was to get back to full employment.

Focus on Aggregate Expenditure

aggregate expenditure: The rate of total expenditure desired at alternative levels of income, *ceteris paribus*.

In that depressed economy, Keynes focused exclusively on the rate of *spending* in the economy, without distinguishing between real output and price levels. All he worried about is whether **aggregate expenditure**—the sum of consumer, investor, government, and net export buyers' spending plans—would be compatible with the dollar value of full-employment output.

For Keynes, the critical question was how much each group of market participants would spend at different levels of nominal *income*. As we saw earlier, Keynes showed that consumer spending directly varies with the level of income. That's why the consumption function in Figure 9.4 had *spending* on the vertical axis and nominal *income* on the horizontal axis.

Figure 9A.1 puts the consumption function into the larger context of the macro economy. In this figure, the focus is exclusively on *nominal* incomes and spending. Y_F in-

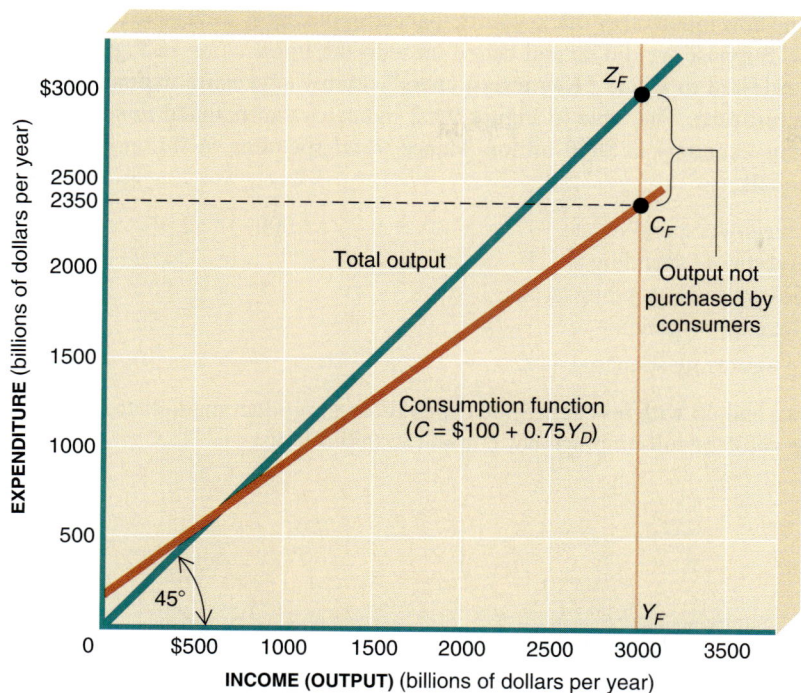

FIGURE 9A.1
The Consumption Shortfall

To determine how much output consumers will demand at full-employment output (Y_F), we refer to the consumption function. First locate full-employment output on the horizontal axis (at Y_F). Then move up until you reach the consumption function. In this case, the amount C_F (equal to $2,350 billion per year) will be demanded at full-employment output $3,000 billion per year). This leaves $650 billion of output not purchased by consumers.

dicates the dollar value of full-employment output at current prices. In this figure, $3,000 billion is assumed to be the value of Y_F. The 45-degree line shows all points where total spending equals total income.

The consumption function in Figure 9A.1 is the same one we used before, namely

$$C = \$100 + 0.75(Y_D)$$

Notice again that consumers *dissave* at lower income levels but *save* at higher income levels.

The Consumption Shortfall

What particularly worried Keynes was the level of intended consumption at full employment. At full employment, $3 trillion of income (output) is generated. But consumers plan to spend only

$$C = \$100 + 0.75(\$3{,}000 \text{ billion}) = \$2{,}350 \text{ billion}$$

and save the rest ($650 billion).[1] Were product-market sales totally dependent on consumers, this economy would be in trouble: Consumer spending falls short of full-employment output. In Figure 9A.1, this consumption shortfall is the vertical difference between points Z_F and C_F.

Nonconsumer Spending

The evident shortfall in consumer spending need not doom the economy to macro failure. There are other market participants, and their spending will add to aggregate expenditure. Keynes, however, emphasized that the spending decisions of investors, governments, and net export buyers are made independently. They *might* add up to just the right amount—or they might *not*.

---

[1] In principle, we first have to determine how much *disposable* income is generated by any given level of *total* income, then use the consumption function to determine how much consumption occurs. If Y_D is a constant percentage of Y, this two-step computation boils down to

$$Y_D = dY$$

where d = the share of total income received as disposable income, and

$$C = a + b(dY)$$
$$= a + (b \times d)Y$$

The term ($b \times d$) is the marginal propensity to consume out of *total* income.

196 CYCLICAL INSTABILITY

To determine how much other market participants might spend, we'd have to examine their behavior. Suppose we did so and ended up with the information in Figure 9A.2. Figure 9A.2, referred to as *the "Keynesian cross" relates aggregate expenditure to total income (output).* The table in Figure 9A.2 indicates that planned *non*consumer spending in this economy is $400 billion. Hence, *total* spending at full-employment output (Y_F) equals:

Consumer spending at	$Y_F = \$100 + 0.75(\$3,000) =$	$2,350
Investment spending at	Y_F =	150
Government spending at	Y_F =	200
Net export spending at	Y_F =	50
Aggregate spending at	Y_F =	$2,750

In this case, we end up with less aggregate expenditure in product markets ($2,750 billion) than the value of full-employment output ($3,000 billion).

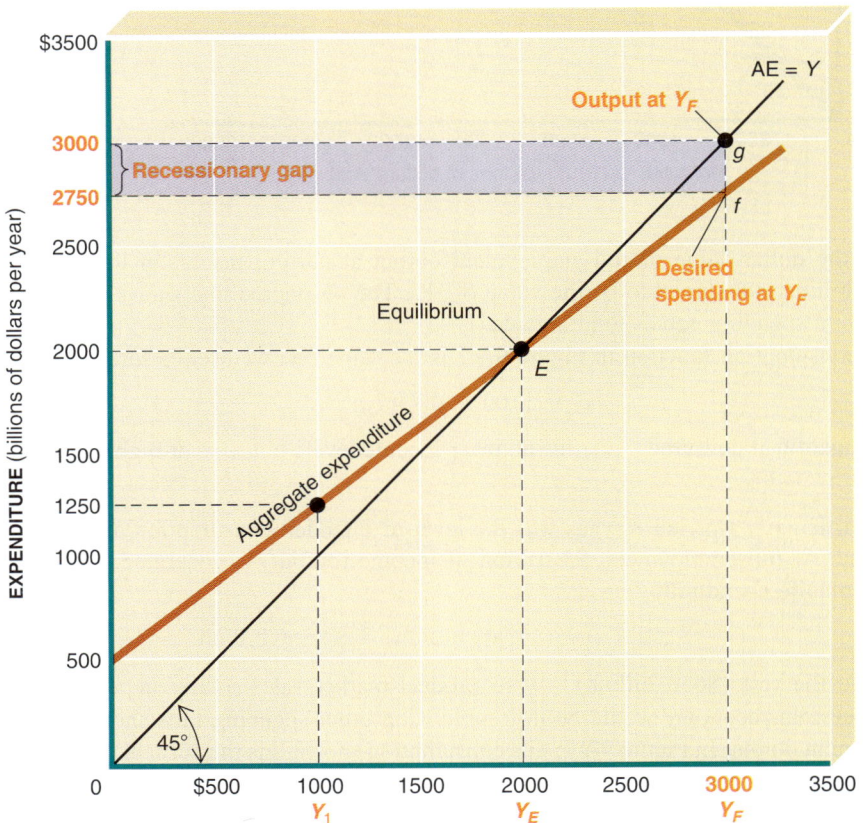

FIGURE 9A.2
Expenditure Equilibrium

There's only one rate of output at which desired expenditure equals the value of output. This expenditure equilibrium occurs at point E, where the aggregate expenditure and 45-degree lines intersect. At this equilibrium, $2,000 billion of output is produced and willingly purchased.

At full-employment output ($Y_F = \$3,000$), aggregate expenditure is only $2,750 billion. This spending shortfall leaves $250 billion of output unsold. The difference between full-employment output (point *g*) and desired spending at full employment (point *f*) is called the recessionary gap.

At Income (output) of	Consumers Desire to Spend	+	Investors Desire to Spend	+	Governments Desire to Spend	+	Net Export Spending	=	Aggregate Expenditure
$ 500	$ 475		$150		$200		$50		$ 875
1,000	850		150		200		50		1,250
1,500	1,225		150		200		50		1,625
2,000	1,600		150		200		50		2,000
2,500	1,975		150		200		50		2,375
3,000	2,350		150		200		50		2,750
3,500	2,725		150		200		50		3,125

The economy illustrated in Figure 9A.2 is in trouble. If full employment were achieved, it wouldn't last. At full employment, $3,000 billion of output would be produced. But only $2,750 of output would be sold. There isn't enough aggregate expenditure at current price levels to sustain full employment. As a result, $250 billion of unsold output piles up in warehouses and on store shelves. That unwanted inventory pileup is a harbinger of trouble.

The difference between full-employment output and desired spending at full employment is called a **recessionary gap.** Not enough output is willingly purchased at full employment to sustain the economy. Producers may react to the spending shortfall by cutting back on production and laying off workers.

recessionary gap: The amount by which aggregate spending at full employment falls short of full-employment output.

A Single Equilibrium. You might wonder whether the planned spending of market participants would ever be exactly equal to the value of output. It will, but not necessarily at the rate of output we seek.

Figure 9A.2 illustrates where this **expenditure equilibrium** exists. Recall the significance of the 45-degree line in that figure. The 45-degree line represents all points where expenditure *equals* income. At any point on this line there would be no difference between total spending and the value of output.

expenditure equilibrium: The rate of output at which desired spending equals the value of output.

The aggregate expenditure curve crosses the 45-degree line only once, at point E. At that point, therefore, desired spending is *exactly* equal to the value of output. In Figure 9A.2 this equilibrium occurs at an output rate of $2,000 billion. Notice in the accompanying table how much market participants desire to spend at that rate of output. We have

Consumer spending at $Y_E = \$100 + 0.75(\$2,000) = \$1,600$
Investment spending at Y_E $= 150$
Government spending at Y_E $= 200$
Net export spending at Y_E $= \underline{50}$
Aggregate spending at Y_E $= \$2,000$

At Y_E we have spending behavior that's completely compatible with the rate of production. At this equilibrium rate of output, no goods remain unsold. At that one rate of output where desired spending and the value of output are exactly equal, an expenditure equilibrium exists. At that equilibrium producers have no incentive to change the rate of output because they're selling everything they produce.

Unfortunately, the equilibrium depicted in Figure 9A.2 isn't the one we hoped to achieve. At Y_E the economy is well short of its full-employment goal (Y_F).

Macro Failure

The expenditure equilibrium won't always fall short of the economy's productive capacity. Indeed, market participants' spending desires could also *exceed* the economy's full-employment potential. This might happen if investors, the government, or foreigners wanted to buy more output or if the consumption function shifted upward. In such circumstances an **inflationary gap** would exist. An inflationary gap arises when market participants want to *spend more* income than can be produced at full employment. The resulting scramble for goods may start a bidding war that pushes price levels even higher. This would be another symptom of macro failure.

inflationary gap: The amount by which aggregate spending at full employment exceeds full-employment output.

The Keynesian analysis of aggregate *expenditure* looks remarkably similar to the Keynesian analysis of aggregate *demand*. In fact, it is: Both approaches lead to the same conclusions about macro instability. The key difference between the "old" (expenditure) analysis and the "new" (AD) analysis is the level of detail about macro outcomes. In the old aggregate-expenditure analysis, the focus was simply on total spending, the product of output and prices. In the newer AD analysis, the separate effects of macro instability on prices and real output are distinguished.[2] In a world where changes in both real output and price levels are important, the AD/AS framework is more useful.

Two Paths to the Same Conclusion

---

[2]This distinction is reflected in the differing definitions for the traditional *recessionary gap* (the *spending* shortfall at full-employment income) and the newer *recessionary GDP gap* (real output gap between full-employment GDP and equilibrium GDP).

CHAPTER 10

Self-Adjustment or Instability?

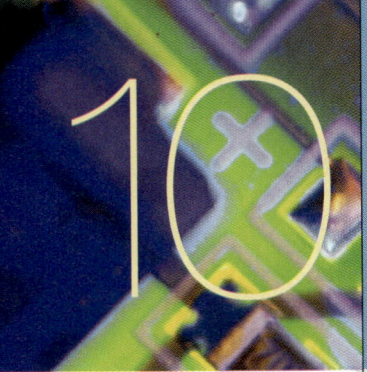

John Maynard Keynes took a dim view of a market-driven macro economy. He emphasized that (1) macro failure is likely to occur in such an economy, and worse yet, (2) macro failure isn't likely to go away. As noted earlier, the first prediction wasn't all that controversial. The classical economists had conceded the possibility of occasional recession or inflation. In their view, however, the economy would quickly self-adjust, restoring full employment and price stability. Keynes' second proposition challenged this view. The most distinctive, and frightening, proposition of Keynes's theory was that there'd be no automatic self-adjustment; the economy could stagnate in *persistent* unemployment or be subjected to *continuing* inflation.

President Herbert Hoover was a believer in the market's ability to self-adjust. So was President George H. Bush. As Hoover and Bush Sr. waited for the economy to self-adjust, however, they both lost their reelection bids. President George W. Bush wasn't willing to take that chance. As soon as he got elected, he pushed tax cuts through Congress that boosted consumer disposable incomes and helped bolster a sagging economy. After the terrorist attacks of September 11, 2001, he called for even greater government intervention.

These different presidential experiences don't resolve the self-adjustment debate; rather, they emphasize how important the debate is. In this chapter we'll focus on the *adjustment process,* that is, how markets *respond* to an undesirable equilibrium. We're especially concerned with the following questions:

- Why does anyone think the market might self-adjust (returning to a desired equilibrium)?
- Why might markets *not* self-adjust?
- Could market responses actually *worsen* macro outcomes?

LEAKAGES AND INJECTIONS

Chapter 9 demonstrated how the economy could end up at the wrong macro equilibrium—with too much or too little aggregate demand. Such an undesirable outcome might result from an initial imbalance between **aggregate demand** at the current price level and full-employment GDP. Or the economy could fall into trouble from a shift in aggregate demand that pushes the economy out of a desirable full-employment–price-stability equilibrium. Whatever the sequence of events might be, the bottom line is the same: Total spending doesn't match total output at the desired full-employment–price-stability level.

The Circular Flow. The circular flow of income illustrates both how such an undesirable outcome comes about and how it might be resolved. Recall that all income originates in product markets, where goods and services are sold. If the economy were producing at **full-employment GDP**, then enough income would be available to buy everything a fully employed economy produces. As we've seen, however, aggregate demand isn't so certain. It could happen that market participants opt *not* to spend all their income, leaving some goods unsold. Alternatively, they might try to buy *more* than full-employment output, pushing prices up.

To see how such imbalances might arise, Keynes distinguished *leakages* from the circular flow and *injections* into that flow, as illustrated in Figure 10.1.

As we observed in Chapter 9, consumers typically don't spend *all* the income they earn in product markets; they *save* some fraction of it. This is the first leak in the circular flow. Some income earned in product markets isn't being instantly converted into spending. This circular flow **leakage** creates the potential for a spending shortfall.

Suppose the economy were producing at full employment, with $3,000 billion of output at the current price level, indexed at $P = 100$. This initial output rate is marked by point F in Figure 10.2. Suppose further that *all* of the income generated in product markets went to consumers. In that case, would consumers *spend* enough to *maintain* full employment? We already observed in Chapter 9 that such an outcome is unlikely. Typically, consumers save a small fraction of their incomes.

If the consumption function were $C_F = \$100 \text{ billion} + 0.75Y$, consumers will spend only

$$C_F = \$100 \text{ billion} + 0.75(\$3,000 \text{ billion})$$
$$= \$2,350 \text{ billion}$$

aggregate demand (AD): The total quantity of output demanded at alternative price levels in a given time period, *ceteris paribus*.

full-employment GDP: The value of total output (real GDP) produced at full employment.

Consumer Saving

leakage: Income not spent directly on domestic output but instead diverted from the circular flow, for example, saving, imports, taxes.

FIGURE 10.1
Leakages and Injections

The income generated in production doesn't return completely to product markets in the form of consumer spending. Consumer saving, imports, taxes, and business saving all leak from the circular flow, reducing aggregate demand. If this leakage isn't offset, some of the output produced will remain unsold.

Business investment, government purchases of goods and services, and exports inject spending into the circular flow, adding to aggregate demand. The focus of macro concern is whether desired injections will offset desired leakage at full employment.

FIGURE 10.2
Leakage and AD

The disposable income consumers receive is only about 70 percent of total income (GDP), due to taxes and income held by businesses. Consumers also tend to save some of their disposable income and buy imported products. As a result of these leakages, consumers will demand less output at the current price level (P 100) than the economy produces at full-employment GDP (Q_F). In this case, consumers demand only $2,350 billion of output at the price level P 100 (point C_F) when $3,000 billion of output (income) is produced (point F).

at the current price level. This consumption behavior is illustrated in Figure 10.2 by the point C_F. Consumers would demand more real output with their current income if prices were to fall. Hence, the consumption component of aggregate demand slopes downward from point C_F. Our immediate concern, however, focuses on how much (real) output consumers will purchase at the current price level. At the price level $P100$ consumers choose to save $650 billion, leaving consumption ($2,350 billion) far short of full employment GDP ($3,000 billion).

The decision to save some fraction of household income isn't necessarily bad, but it does present a potential problem. Unless other market participants, such as business, government, and foreigners, buy this unsold output, goods will pile up on producer shelves. As undesired inventory accumulates, producers will reduce the rate of output and unemployment will rise.

Imports and Taxes

Saving isn't the only source of leakage. ***Imports also represent leakage from the circular flow.*** When consumers buy imported goods, their spending leaves (that is, leaks out of) the domestic circular flow and goes to foreign producers. As a consequence, income spent on imported goods and services is not part of the aggregate demand for domestic output.

In the real world, ***taxes are a form of leakage as well.*** A lot of revenue generated in market sales gets diverted into federal, state, and local government coffers. Sales taxes are taken out of the circular flow in product markets. Then payroll taxes and income taxes are taken out of wages. Households never get the chance to spend any of that income. They start with disposable income, which is much less than the total income generated in product markets. In 2000, disposable income was only $7 trillion while total income (GDP) was $10 trillion. Hence, consumers couldn't buy everything produced with their current incomes even if they saved nothing (which they did in 1999 and almost did in 2000 as well).

Business Saving

The business sector also keeps part of the income generated in product markets. Some revenue is set aside to cover the costs of maintaining, repairing, and replacing plant and equipment. The revenue held aside for these purposes is called a depreciation allowance. In addition, businesses tend to keep some part of total profit (retained earnings) for other business uses rather than turn all profits over to the business owners, for example, dividends to stockholders. The total value of depreciation allowances and retained earnings is called **gross business saving**. Whatever businesses save in these forms represents further leakage from the circular flow—income that doesn't automatically flow directly back into product markets.

gross business saving: Depreciation allowances and retained earnings.

Although leakage from the circular flow is a potential source of unemployment problems, we shouldn't conclude that the economy will sink as soon as consumers start saving some of their income, buy a few imports, or pay their taxes. Consumers aren't the only ones who buy goods and services in product markets; business firms and government agencies also contribute to total spending. So do international consumers who buy our exports. So before we run out into the streets screaming "The circular flow is leaking!" we need to look at what other market participants are doing.

Injections into the Circular Flow

The top half of Figure 10.1 completes the picture of the circular flow by depicting **injections** of new spending. When businesses buy plant and equipment, they add to the dollar value of product market sales. Government purchases and exports also inject spending into the product market. These *injections of investment, government, and export spending help offset leakage from saving, imports, and taxes*. As a result, there may be enough aggregate demand to maintain full employment at the current price level, even if consumers aren't spending every dollar of income.

injection: An addition of spending to the circular flow of income.

Self-Adjustment?

Classical economists assumed that injections of spending into the circular flow would always equal the outflowing leakage. Their optimism was largely based on investment behavior.

Flexible Interest Rates. Ignore all other injections and leakages for the moment and focus on just consumer saving and business investment (Figure 10.3). If consumer saving exceeds business investment, unspent income must be piling up somewhere (in bank accounts, for example). These unspent funds will be a tempting lure for business investors. In the classical view, businesses are always looking for funds to finance expansion or modernization. So they aren't likely to leave a pile of consumer savings sitting idle. Moreover, the banks and other institutions that are holding consumer savings will be eager to lend more funds as consumer savings piles up. To make more loans, they can lower the interest rate. As we observed in Chapter 9 (Figure 9.8), lower interest rates prompt businesses to borrow and invest more. Hence, *classical economists concluded that if interest rates fell far enough, business investment (injections) would equal consumer saving (leakage)*. From this perspective, any spending shortfall would soon be closed by this self-adjustment of leakage and injection flows. Aggregate demand would be maintained at full-employment GDP, because investment spending would soak up all consumer saving.

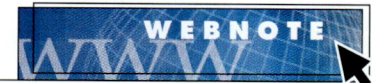

Check the U.S. Bureau of Economic Analysis (BEA) website at www.bea.doc.gov to see how much investment varied in the last year. Click on GDP Data, then Selected NIPA Tables.

Changing Expectations. Keynes argued that classical economists ignored the role of expectations in business investments. As Figure 9.8 illustrated, the level of investment *is* sensitive to interest rates. But the whole investment function *shifts* when business expectations change. Keynes thought it preposterous that investment spending

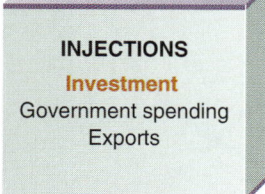

LEAKAGES	INJECTIONS
Consumer saving	Investment
Business saving	Government spending
Taxes	Exports
Imports	

FIGURE 10.3
Leakages and Injections

Macro stability depends on the balance between injections and leakages. Of these, consumer saving and business investment are the primary sources of (im)balance in a wholly private and closed economy. Hence the relationship between saving and investment reveals whether a market-driven economy will self-adjust to full employment and price stability.

would *increase* in response to *declining* sales. A decline in investment is more likely, Keynes argued.

Flexible Prices. There is another way the economy could self-adjust. Look at Figure 10.2 again. It says consumers will demand only $2,350 billion of output *at the current price level.* But what if prices *fell?* Then consumers would buy more output. In fact, if prices fell far enough, consumers might buy *all* the output produced at full employment. In Figure 10.2, the price level $P = 50$ elicits such a response.

Expectations (again). Keynes again chided the classical economists for their naiveté. Sure, a nationwide sale might prompt consumers to buy more goods and services. But how would businesses react? They had planned on selling Q_F amount of output at the price level $P = 100$. If prices must be cut in half to move their merchandise, businesses are likely to rethink their production and investment plans. Keynes argued that declining (retail) prices were likely to prompt investment cutbacks.

THE MULTIPLIER PROCESS

Keynes not only rejected the classical notion of self-adjustment, he also argued that things were likely to get *worse*, not better, once a spending shortfall emerged.

To understand Keynes's fears, imagine that the economy is initially at the desired full-employment GDP equilibrium, as represented again by point F in Figure 10.4. Included in that full-employment equilibrium GDP is

Consumption	= $2,350 billion
Investment	= 400 billion
Government	= 150 billion
Net exports	= 100 billion
Aggregate demand at current price level	= $3,000 billion

Everything looks good in this macro economy. This is pretty much how the U.S. economy looked from 1993 until early 2001.

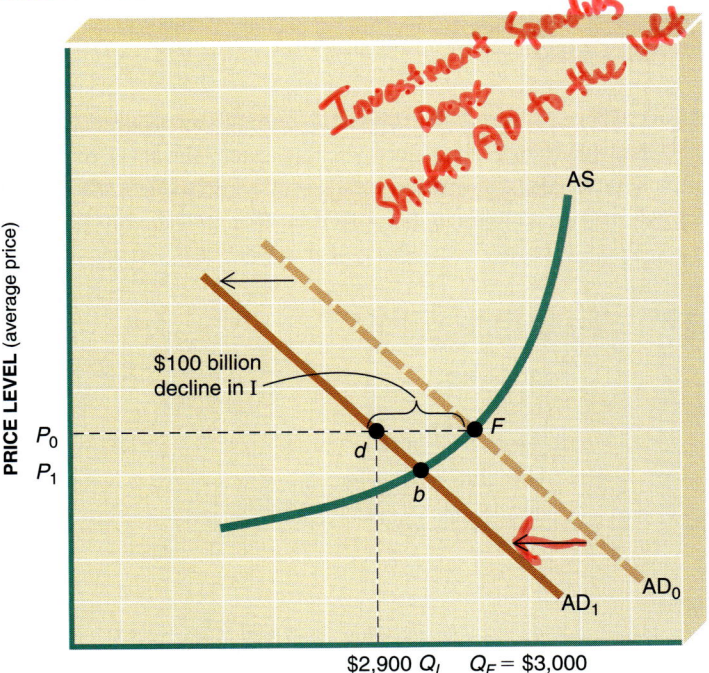

FIGURE 10.4
AD Shift

When investment spending drops, aggregate demand shifts to the left. In the short run, this causes output and the price level to fall. The initial equilibrium at F is pushed to a new equilibrium at point b.

A Decline in Investment

Now suppose that business expectations for future sales worsen. In early 2001, business forecasts of consumer spending were already declining. After the terrorist attacks of September 11, expectations fell even further. As expectations worsened, businesses cut back on investment spending (see NEWS).

Undesired Inventory. When business investment was cut back, unsold capital goods started piling up. Unsold trucks, office equipment, machinery, and airplanes quickly reached worrisome levels.

Ironically, this additional inventory is counted as part of investment spending. (Recall that our definition of investment spending includes changes in business inventories.) This additional inventory is clearly undesired, however, as producers had planned on selling these goods.

To keep track of these unwanted changes in investment, we **distinguish desired (or planned) investment from actual investment.** *Desired* investment represents purchases of new plant and equipment plus any *desired* changes in business inventories. By contrast, *actual* investment represents purchases of new plant and equipment plus *actual* changes in business inventories, desired or otherwise. In other words,

$$\text{Actual investment} = \text{desired investment} + \text{undesired investment}$$

At the Economics Briefing Room of the White House at www.whitehouse.gov/fsbr/output.html, find current data on output.

IN THE NEWS

Small Businesses Hold Off on Big Purchases
Capital Spending Helps Drive Economy, So Drop-off May Hurt

SAN FRANCISCO—Small companies are buying fewer trucks, computers and other big-ticket items—the capital purchases that could lift the U.S. economy.

About 28% of small firms plan big purchases, a major survey out Monday said. That's down from about 32% before the terrorist attacks.

Capital spending by small firms is critical. It helps them be more productive and boosts sales at big companies like Ford Motor and Dell Computer.

The USA's 5.6 million small employers account for about 26% of the estimated $1.4 trillion in annual company capital investments, says the National Federation of Independent Business (NFIB) trade group.

The survey of 582 firms was done last month by the NFIB. Nearly 60% of the firms were polled after Sept. 11.

Spending is down or flat for companies such as:

- Ball Volvo and GMC Trucks in Kahoka, Mo. Carla Ball's truck dealership needs to replace three aging parts delivery trucks. Cost: About $75,000.

  But Ball is waiting until pickup and truck sales improve. Many of her customers are haulers whose costs rose with fuel prices. That meant slower sales at Ball. No-interest automaker financing boosted sales somewhat—but not enough to make Ball confident about big purchases.

- Hire Standard Staffing, a temporary help firm in Washington, D.C. It could test 20 job applicants daily, instead of 15, if it added about $10,000 in computers. But customers have slowed or frozen hiring, pinching Hire Standard's growth.

  Owner Helen Hopkins won't borrow to buy equipment, even if interest rates fall to zero. She's focused on meeting payroll and paying telephone and insurance bills.

- Carey O'Donnell Public Relations Group in West Palm Beach, Fla. It planned to expand to handle two new clients. But since Sept. 11, one canceled a public relations campaign and the other deferred a decision.

  "Everything froze," owner Carey O'Donnell says.

  As a result, O'Donnell delayed buying about $5,000 in office equipment and will not add another employee to her current seven.

—Jim Hopkins

Source: *USA Today*, October 16, 2001. © 2001 USA Today. Reprinted with permission. www.usatoday.com

Analysis: Worsened sales expectations may cause a decline in investment spending that shifts the AD curve to the left, leading to pileups of unwanted inventory.

Falling Output and Prices. How are business firms likely to react when they see undesired inventory piling up on car lots and store shelves? They could regard the inventory pileup as a brief aberration and continue producing at full employment levels. But the inventory pileup might also set off sales alarms, causing business to alter their pricing, production, and investment plans. If that happens, they're likely to start cutting prices in an attempt to increase the rate of sales. Producers are also likely to reduce the rate of new output. Figure 10.4 illustrates these two responses. Assume for the sake of illustration that, investment spending (including inventory) declines by $100 billion at the existing price level P_C. This shifts the aggregate demand curve leftward from AD_0 to AD_1. If no other changes were to occur, the economy would gravitate toward a new **equilibrium GDP** at point b. At point b, the rate of output (Q_1) is less than the full-employment level (Q_F) and the price level has fallen from P_0 to P_1.

> **equilibrium GDP:** The value of total output (real GDP) produced at macro equilibrium (AS = AD).

Household Incomes

The decline in GDP depicted in Figure 10.4 isn't pretty. But Keynes warned that the picture would get uglier when *consumers* start feeling the impact of the production cutbacks.

So far we've treated the production cutbacks that accompany a GDP gap as a rather abstract problem. But the reality is that when production is cut back, people suffer. When producers decrease the rate of output, workers lose their jobs or face pay cuts, or both. Cutbacks in investment spending on September 2001 (prior NEWS) led to layoffs at Honeywell, Advanced Micro Devices, and other capital-equipment manufacturers (see News). An abrupt decline in travel caused even larger layoffs at airlines and aircraft manufacturers. As workers get laid off or have their wages cut, household incomes decline. Thus, *a reduction in investment spending implies a reduction in household incomes*.

Income-Dependent Consumption

We saw in Chapter 9 the kind of threat a reduction in household income poses. Those consumers who end up with less income won't be able to purchase as many goods and services as they did before. As a consequence, the total value of goods and services demanded will fall further, leading to still larger stocks of unsold goods, more job layoffs, and further reductions in income. It's this sequence of events—called the *multiplier process*—that makes a sudden decline in aggregate demand so frightening. What starts off as a relatively small spending shortfall quickly snowballs into a much larger problem.

We can see the multiplier process at work by watching what happens to the $100 billion decline in investment spending as it makes its way around the circular flow (Figure 10.5 on page 206). At first (step 1), the only thing that happens is that unsold goods appear (in the form of undesired inventories). Producers adjust to this problem by cutting back on production and laying off workers or reducing wages and prices (step 2). In either case, consumer income falls $100 billion per year shortly after the investment cutbacks occur (step 3).

How will consumers respond to this drop in disposable income? If disposable income falls, we expect consumer spending to drop as well. In fact, the consumption function tells us just how much spending will drop. The **marginal propensity to consume (MPC)** is the critical variable in this process. Since we've specified that $C = \$100 \text{ billion} + 0.75Y$, we anticipate that consumers will reduce their spending by $0.75 for every $1.00 of lost income. In the present example, the loss of $100 billion of annual income will induce consumers to reduce their rate of spending by $75 billion per year ($0.75 \times \$100$ billion). This drop in spending is illustrated by step 4 in Figure 10.5.

> **marginal propensity to consume (MPC):** The fraction of each additional (marginal) dollar of disposable income spent on consumption; the change in consumption divided by the change in disposable income.

The multiplier process doesn't stop here. A reduction in consumer spending quickly translates into more unsold output (step 5). As additional goods pile up on producers' shelves, we anticipate further cutbacks in production, employment, and disposable income (step 6).

As disposable incomes are further reduced by job layoffs and wage cuts (step 7), more reductions in consumer spending are sure to follow (step 8). Again the marginal

IN THE NEWS

Terror's Aftermath: Layoffs

Who knows how many of these might have come anyway? But since Sept. 11, companies have cut more than 160,000 jobs. Airlines were the hardest hit, but other industries were also affected. Here are some of the biggest.

COMPANY	CUTS	INDUSTRY
BOEING	30,000	Aerospace
AMERICAN AIRLINES	20,000	Airline
UNITED	20,000	Airline
DELTA	13,000	Airline
CONTINENTAL	12,000	Airline
STARWOOD HOTELS & RESORTS	12,000	Hotel
US AIRWAYS	11,000	Airline
NORTHWEST	10,000	Airline
BRITISH AIRWAYS	7,000	Airline
AIR CANADA	5,000	Airline
HONEYWELL INTERNATIONAL	3,800	Aerospace/Diversified materials
SWISSAIR	3,000	Airline
ALITALIA	2,500	Airline
TEXTRON	2,500	Aircraft manufacturing
EMC	2,400	Data storage
ADVANCED MICRO DEVICES	2,300	Microprocessors
AMERICA WEST	2,000	Airline
APPLIED MATERIALS	2,000	Semiconductors
MIDWAY	1,700	Airline
VIRGIN ATLANTIC	1,200	Airline

Source: *BusinessWeek*, October 8, 2001. Reprinted with permission. www.businessweek.com

Analysis: Cutbacks in production cause employee layoffs. The newly unemployed workers curtail *their* spending, causing sequential layoffs in other industries.

---

propensity to consume (MPC) tells us how large such reductions will be. With an MPC of 0.75, we may expect spending to fall by another $56.25 billion per year (0.75 × $75 billion).

The multiplier process continues to work until the reductions in income and sales become so small that no one's market behavior is significantly affected. We don't have to examine each step along the way because all the steps begin to look alike once we've gone around the circular flow a few times. We can foresee how large an impact the multiplier process will ultimately have. Each time the multiplier process works its way around the circular flow, the reduction in spending equals the previous drop in income multiplied by the MPC. Accordingly, by pressing a few keys on a calculator, we can produce a sequence of events like that depicted in Table 10.1 on the next page.

The impact of the multiplier is devastating. The ultimate reduction in real spending resulting from the initial drop in investment isn't $100 billion per year but $400 billion! Even if one is accustomed to thinking in terms of billions and trillions, this is a

The Multiplier

Do sports teams create multiplier effects for cities? Read about this at www.brook.edu/pub/review/summer97/noll.htm.

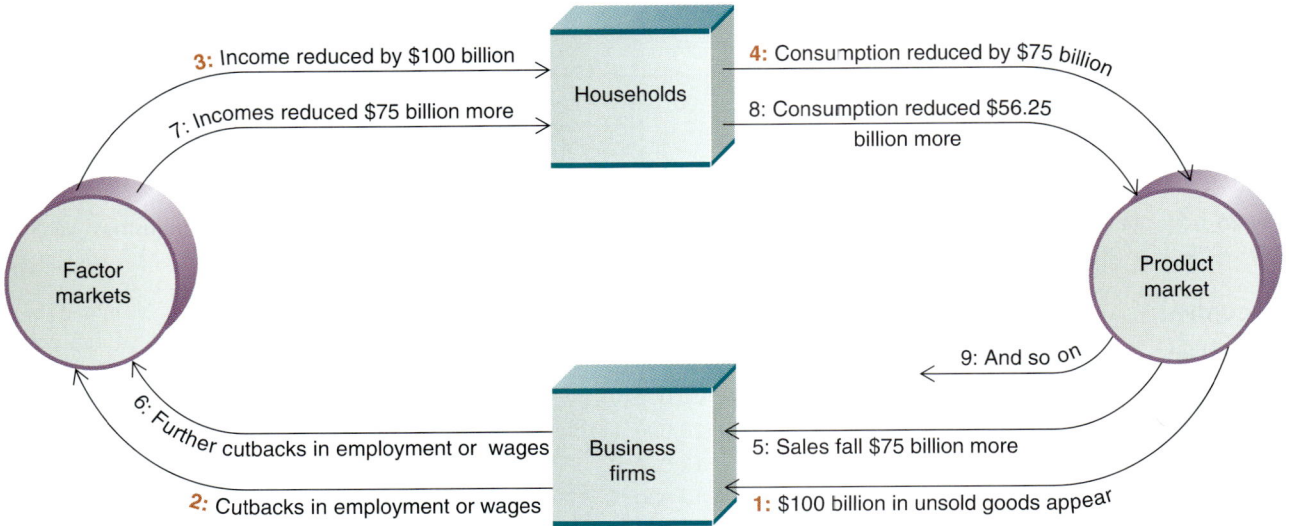

FIGURE 10.5
The Multiplier Process

A decline in investment (step 1) may lead to a cutback in production and income (step 2). A reduction in total income (step 3) will in turn lead to a reduction in consumer spending (step 4).

These additional cuts in spending cause a further decrease in income, leading to additional spending reductions, and so on. This sequence of adjustments is referred to as the *multiplier process*.

huge drop in demand. What the multiplier process demonstrates is that the dimensions of an initial spending gap greatly understate the severity of the economic dislocations that will follow in its wake. **The eventual decline in spending will be much larger than the initial (autonomous) decrease in aggregate demand.** This was evident in the recession of 2001, when layoffs snowballed from industry to industry (see News), ultimately leaving millions of people unemployed.

TABLE 10.1
The Multiplier Cycles

The circular flow of income implies that an initial change in income will lead to cumulative changes in consumer spending and income. Here, an initial income loss of $100 billion (first cycle) causes a cutback in consumer spending in the amount of $75 billion (second cycle). At each subsequent cycle, consumer spending drops by the amount MPC × prior change in income. Ultimately, total spending (and income) falls by $400 billion, or $1/(1 - \text{MPC}) \times$ initial change in spending.

Spending Cycles	Change in This Cycle's Spending and Income (billions per year)	Cumulative Decrease in Spending and Income (billions per year)
First cycle: recessionary gap emerges	$100.00	$100.00 } ΔI
Second cycle: consumption drops by MPC × $100	75.00	175.00
Third cycle: consumption drops by MPC × $75	56.25	231.25
Fourth cycle: consumption drops by MPC × $56.25	42.19	273.44
Fifth cycle: consumption drops by MPC × $42.19	31.64	305.08 } ΔC
Sixth cycle: consumption drops by MPC × $31.64	23.73	328.81
Seventh cycle: consumption drops by MPC × $23.73	17.80	346.61
Eighth cycle: consumption drops by MPC × $17.80	13.35	359.95
⋮	⋮	⋮
*n*th cycle and beyond		400.00

IN THE NEWS

Companies Begin Another Round of Job Cuts
Even More Layoffs Could Threaten if Recession Closes In

When it comes to layoffs, employers are finding once is not enough.

The ongoing economic downturn means companies that have already laid off workers are cutting again. For example:

- Compaq Computer last week reported that it was laying off about 4,000 additional workers. That's in addition to about 4,500 cuts earlier this year. . . .
- Even though 8,500 workers at Lucent Technologies have accepted an early retirement offer, CEO Henry Schacht said last week that the beleaguered company plans its third round of job cuts since January. . . .

The Murray Hill, N.J.–based company announced in January that it would eliminate 10,000 jobs and sell facilities employing an additional 6,000 workers as part of a restructuring and cost-cutting program.

- Santa Clara, Calif.–based Exodus Communications in June announced an unspecified number of layoffs. That follows the announcement in May that the web-hosting company would shed 675 positions, or about 15 percent of its workforce.
- Santa Clara–based equipment maker 3Com in May announced it was laying off 3,000 employees. That follows job cuts of about 1,200 in March.

This may just be the beginning of what's to come if the economy slides closer to a recession, some experts say.

—Stephanie Armour

Source: *USA Today*, July 17, 2001. © 2001 USA Today. Reprinted with permission. www.usatoday.com

Analysis: Few industries escape damage from a recession. Spending slowdowns spread from industry to industry in a multiplier-like way. Job layoffs reduce disposable income and consumption.

The ultimate impact of an AD shift on total spending can be determined by computing the change in income and consumption at each cycle of the circular flow, for an infinite number of cycles. This is the approach summarized in Table 10.1, with each row representing a spending cycle. The entire computation can be simplified considerably by using a single figure, the multiplier. The **multiplier** tells us the extent to which the rate of total spending will change in response to an initial change in the flow of expenditure. The multiplier summarizes the sequence of steps described in Table 10.1.[1] In its simplest form, the multiplier can be computed as:

$$\text{Multiplier} = \frac{1}{1 - \text{MPC}}$$

multiplier: The multiple by which an initial change in spending will alter total expenditure after an infinite number of spending cycles; $1/(1 - \text{MPC})$.

In our example, the initial change in spending occurs when investment drops by $100 billion per year at full-employment output ($3,000 billion per year). Table 10.1 indicates that this gap will lead to a $400 billion reduction in the rate of total spending at the current price level. Using the multiplier, we arrive at the same conclusion by observing that

$$\begin{aligned}
\text{Total change in spending} &= \text{multiplier} \times \text{initial change in aggregate spending} \\
&= \frac{1}{1 - \text{MPC}} \times \$100 \text{ billion per year} \\
&= \frac{1}{1 - 0.75} \times \$100 \text{ billion per year} \\
&= 4 \times \$100 \text{ billion per year} \\
&= \$400 \text{ billion per year}
\end{aligned}$$

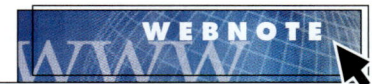

WEBNOTE

JWT Communications tracks ongoing layoffs. To see how widespread layoffs are in any time period, visit www.hrlive.com/layoff.

---

[1] The multiplier summarizes the geometric progression $1 + \text{MPC} + \text{MPC}^2 + \text{MPC}^3 + \ldots + \text{MPC}^n$, which equals $1/(1 - \text{MPC})$ when n becomes infinite.

WORLD VIEW

U.S. Slowdown Helps Derail Asia
High-Tech Firms Suffer Vicious Circle

SAN FRANCISCO—Waves from the U.S. high-tech and economic slump continue to crash onto Asian shores: Analysts fear the onset of a global recession and Japanese tech giant Fujitsu said Monday that it will cut 16,400 workers.

"The U.S. economy—especially the technology sector—was the primary locomotive for the export economies of Japan, Korea, Taiwan and Malaysia," says Sung Won Sohn, chief economist at Wells Fargo Bank. "Now that the bubble has burst here, it's having a devastating effect on Asia."

Among the dire signs:

- Fujitsu, the No. 2 maker of personal computers in Japan and a leading maker of flash-memory chips, will lay off 10 percent of its workers, including 5,000 employees in Japan and 11,400 employees at plants in Thailand, Vietnam and the Philippines. . . .
- The economy of Taiwan, a leading manufacturer and exporter of high-tech parts and goods, officially has entered a recession. In the first year-to-year drop in 26 years, Taiwan's gross domestic product plunged 2 percent in the second quarter from the same time last year, Taiwan's government said Friday. . . .
- When the U.S. economy started limping last year, Asia's economies were still dashing ahead at double-digit growth rates. Now, export-oriented Asia is expected to grow only 2 percent this year, with Japan's economy flat-lining. China predicts its huge economy will rise 8 percent this year. But analysts long skeptical of China's economic data say 4 percent to 6 percent is a more realistic figure. . . .

Like a boomerang, the economic chill in Asia is circling back and hurting the USA. Economists call it the "international-multiplier effect."

Cash-poor Asian nations can no longer buy high-tech goods and other products from U.S. companies, which also rely heavily on overseas trade.

—Edward Iwata

Source: *USA Today,* August 21, 2001. © 2001 USA Today. Reprinted with permission. www.usatoday.com

Analysis: Multiplier effects can spill over national borders. The 2001 economic slump in the United States reduced U.S. demand for Asian exports, setting off a sequence of spending cuts in Japan, Taiwan, and other Asian nations.

In other words, the cumulative decrease in total spending ($400 billion per year) resulting from a shortfall in aggregate demand gap at full employment is equal to the initial shortfall ($100 billion per year) multiplied by the multiplier (4). More generally, we may observe that the larger the fraction (MPC) of income respent in each round of the circular flow, the greater the impact of any autonomous change in spending on cumulative aggregate demand. The cumulative process of spending adjustments can also have worldwide effects. As the World View illustrates, Asia's economic growth slowed when the U.S. economy slumped in 2001.

MACRO EQUILIBRIUM REVISITED

The key features of the Keynesian adjustment process are

- Producers cut output and employment when output exceeds aggregate demand at the current price level (leakage exceeds injections).
- The resulting loss of income causes a decline in consumer spending.
- Declines in consumer spending lead to further production cutbacks, more lost income, and still less consumption.

Sequential AD Shifts

Figure 10.6 illustrates the ultimate impact of the multiplier process. Notice that the AD curve shifts *twice*. The first shift—from AD_0 to AD_1—represents the $100 billion drop in investment spending. As we saw earlier in Figure 10.4, this initial shift of aggregate demand will start the economy moving toward a new equilibrium at point *b*.

Along the way, however, the multiplier kicks in and things get worse. The decline in household income caused by investment cutbacks sets off the multiplier process,

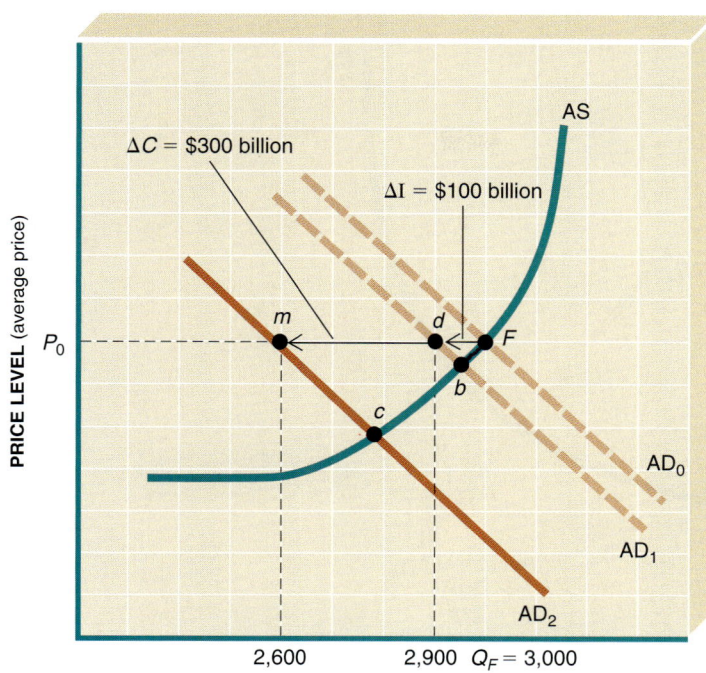

FIGURE 10.6
Multiplier Effects

A decline in investment spending reduces household income, setting off negative multiplier effects. Hence, the *initial* shift of AD_0 to AD_1 is followed by a *second* shift from of AD_1 to AD_2. The second shift represents reduced consumption.

Shift from AD_0 to AD_1 is less household income ∴ causing a second shift which is reduced consumption

causing a secondary shift of the AD curve. We measure these multiplier effects at the initial price level of P_0. With a marginal propensity to consume of 0.75, we've seen that induced consumption declines by $300 billion when autonomous investment declines by $100 billion. In Figure 10.6 this is illustrated by the *second* shift of the aggregate demand curve, from AD_1 to AD_2. Notice that the horizontal distance between AD_1 and AD_2 is $300 billion.

Although aggregate demand has fallen (shifted) by $400 billion, real output doesn't necessarily drop that much. **The impact of a shift in aggregate demand is reflected in both output and price changes.** This is evident in Figure 10.7, which is a close-up view of Figure 10.6. When AD shifts from AD_0 to AD_2 the macro equilibrium moved down the sloped AS curve to point c. At point c the new equilibrium output is Q_E and the new price level is P_E.

Recessionary GDP Gap. As long as the aggregate supply curve is upward-sloping, the shock of any AD shift will be spread across output and prices. In Figure 10.7, the net effect on real output is shown as the real GDP gap. **The recessionary GDP gap equals the difference between equilibrium real GDP (Q_E) and full-employment real GDP (Q_F).** It represents the amount by which the economy is underproducing during a recession. As we noted in Chapter 9, this is a classic case of **cyclical unemployment.**

Figure 10.7 not only illustrates how much output declines when AD falls but also provides an important clue about the difficulty of restoring full employment. Suppose the recessionary GDP gap were $200 billion, as illustrated in Figure 10.8. How much more AD would we need to get back to full employment?

Upward-Sloping AS. Suppose aggregate demand at the equilibrium price level (P'_E) were to increase by exactly $200 billion (including multiplier effects), as illustrated by the shift to AD_3. Would that get us back to full-employment output? Not according to Figure 10.8. **When AD increases, both output and prices go up.** Because the AS curve is upward-sloping, the $200 billion shift from AD_2 to AD_3 moves the new macro equi-

Price and Output Effects

recessionary GDP gap: The amount by which equilibrium GDP falls short of full-employment GDP.

cyclical unemployment: Unemployment attributable to a lack of job vacancies, that is, to an inadequate level of aggregate demand.

Short-Run Inflation-Unemployment Trade-Offs

FIGURE 10.7
Recessionary GDP Gap

The real GDP gap is the difference between equilibrium GDP (Q_E) and full-employment GDP (Q_F). It represents the lost output due to a recession.

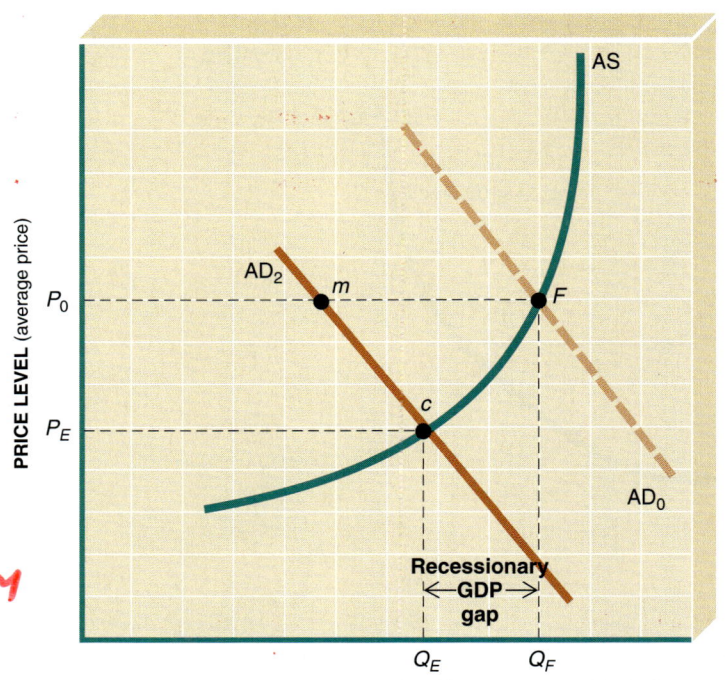

Handwritten notes:
Q_F - Full Employment GDP
Q_E - Equilibrium GDP

If $Q_F > Q_E$ a Recessionary gap occurs

librium to point *g* rather than point *f*. We'd like to get to point *f* with full employment and price stability. But as demand picks up, producers are likely to raise prices. This leads us up the AS curve to point *g*. At point *g*, we're still short of full employment and have experienced a bit of inflation (an increased price level). **So long as the short-run AS is upward-sloping, there's a trade-off between unemployment and inflation.** We can get lower rates of unemployment (more real output) only if we accept some inflation.

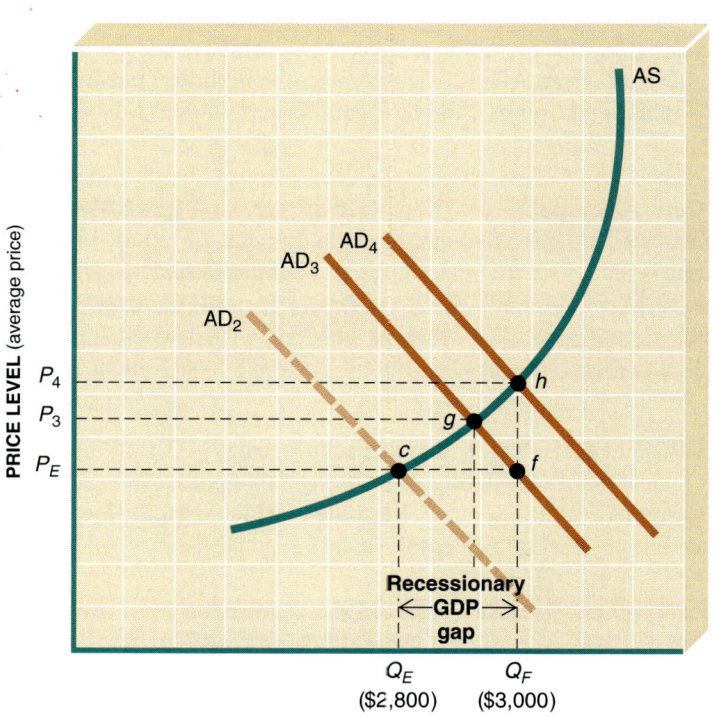

FIGURE 10.8
The Unemployment-Inflation Trade-Off

If the short-run AS curve is upward-sloping, an AD increase will raise output *and* prices. If AD increases by the amount of the recessionary GDP gap only (AD_2 to AD_3), full employment (Q_F) won't be reached. Macro equilibrium moves to point *g*, not point *f*.

CHAPTER 10: SELF-ADJUSTMENT OR INSTABILITY?

"Full" vs. "Natural" Unemployment. The short-term trade-off between unemployment and inflation is the basis for the definition of "full" employment. We don't define full employment as *zero* unemployment; we define it as the rate of unemployment *consistent with price stability*. As noted in Chapter 6, **full employment** is typically defined as a 4 to 6 percent rate of unemployment. What the upward-sloping AS curve tells us is that *the closer the economy gets to capacity output, the greater the risk of inflation.* To get back to full employment in Figure 10.8, aggregate demand would have to increase to AD_4, with the price level rising to P_4.

Not everyone accepts this notion of full employment. As we saw in Chapter 8, neoclassical and monetarist economists prefer to focus on *long*-run outcomes. In their view, the long-run AS curve is vertical (see Figure 8.12). In that long-run context, there's no unemployment-inflation trade-off: An AD shift doesn't change the "natural" (institutional) rate of unemployment but does alter the price level. We'll examine this argument in Chapters 16 and 17.

> **full employment:** The lowest rate of unemployment compatible with price stability; variously estimated at between 4 and 6 percent unemployment.

ADJUSTMENT TO AN INFLATIONARY GDP GAP

As we're observed, a sudden imbalance in spending flows can have a cumulative effect on macro outcomes that's larger than the initial imbalance. This multiplier process works both ways: Just as a *decrease* in investment (or any other injection) can send the economy into a recessionary tailspin, an *increase* in investment might initiate an inflationary spiral.

Figure 10.9 illustrates the consequences of a sudden jump in investment spending. We start out again in the happy equilibrium (point F), where full employment (Q_F) and price stability (P_0) prevail. Initial spending consists of

C = $2,350 billion   G = $150 billion
I = 400 billion   X − IM = $100 billion

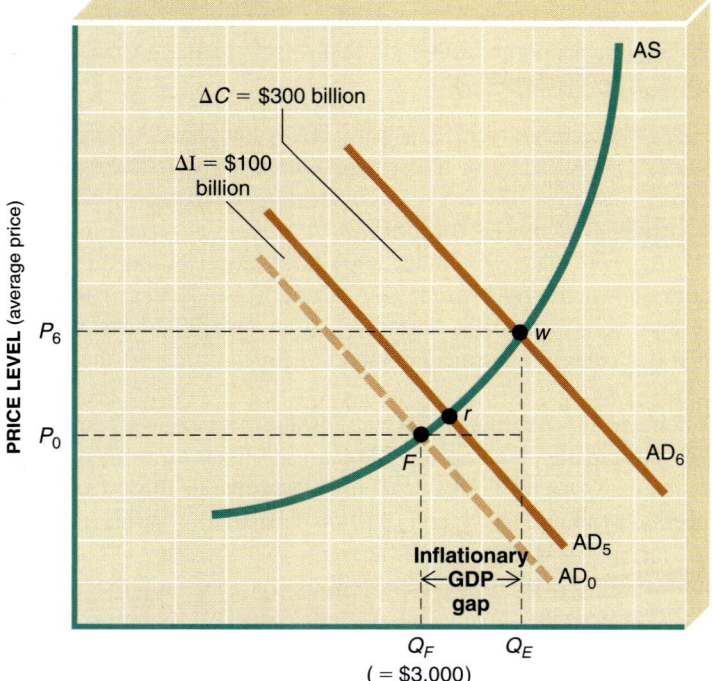

FIGURE 10.9
Demand-Pull Inflation

An increase in investment or other autonomous spending sets off multiplier effects shifting AD to the right. AD shifts to the right *twice*, first (AD_0 to AD_5) because of increased investment, then (AD_5 to AD_6) because of increased consumption. The increased AD moves the economy up the short-run AS curve, causing inflation.

212 CYCLICAL INSTABILITY

Increased Investment

Then investors suddenly decide to step up the rate of investment. Perhaps their expectations for future sales have risen. Maybe new technology has become available that compels firms to modernize their facilities. Whatever the reason, investors decide to raise the level of investment from $400 billion to $500 billion at the current price level (P_0). This change in investment spending shifts the aggregate demand curve from AD_0 to AD_5 (a horizontal shift of $100 billion).

Inventory Depletion. One of the first things you'll notice when AD shifts like this is that available inventories shrink. Investors can step up their *spending* more quickly than firms can increase their *production*. A lot of the increased investment demand will have to be satisfied from existing inventory. When this happens, *desired* investment (including desired inventory) will fall below actual investment. The decline in inventory is a signal to producers that it might be a good time to raise prices a bit. Thus, *inventory depletion is a warning sign of impending inflation.* As the economy moves up from point F to point r in Figure 10.9, that inflation starts to become visible.

Household Incomes

Whether or not prices start rising quickly, household incomes will get a boost from the increased investment. Producers will step up the rate of output to rebuild inventories and supply more investment goods, for example (equipment and structures). To do so, they'll hire more workers or extend working hours. The end result for workers will be fatter paychecks.

Induced Consumption

What will households do with these heftier paychecks? By now, you know what the consumer response to more income will be. The marginal propensity to consume prompts an increase in consumer spending. Eventually, consumer spending increases by a *multiple* of the income change. In this case, the consumption increase is $300 billion (see Table 10.1).

Figure 10.9 illustrates the secondary shift of AD caused by multiplier-induced consumption. Notice how the AD curve shifts a second time, from AD_5 to AD_6.

A New Equilibrium

The ultimate impact of the investment surge is reflected in the new equilibrium at point w. As before, the shift of AD has affected both real output and prices. Real output does increase beyond the full-employment level, but it does so only at the expense of accelerating inflation. This is a classic case of **demand-pull inflation**. The initial increase in investment was enough to kindle a little inflation. The multiplier effect worsened the problem by forcing the economy further along the ever-steeper AS curve. The **inflationary GDP gap** ends up as $Q_E - Q_F$.

demand-pull inflation: An increase in the price level initiated by excessive aggregate demand.

Booms and Busts

The Keynesian analysis of leakages, injections, and the multiplier paints a fairly grim picture of the prospects for macro stability. *The basic conclusion of the Keynesian analysis is that the economy is vulnerable to abrupt changes in spending behavior and won't self-adjust to a desired macro equilibrium.* A shift in aggregate demand can come from almost anywhere. The September 2001 terrorist attack on the World Trade Center shook both consumer and investor confidence. Businesses starting cutting back production even *before* inventories started piling up. Worsened *expectations* rather than rising inventories caused investment demand to shift, setting off the multiplier process.

inflationary GDP gap: The amount by which equilibrium GDP exceeds full-employment GDP.

When the aggregate demand curve shifts, macro equilibrium will be upset. Moreover, the responses of market participants to an abrupt AD shift are likely to worsen rather than improve market outcomes. As a result, the economy may gravitate toward an equilibrium of stagnant recession (point c in Figure 10.6) or persistent inflation (point w in Figure 10.9).

As Keynes saw it, the combination of alternating AD shifts and multiplier effects also causes recurring business cycles. A drop in consumer or business spending can set off a recessionary spiral of declining GDP and prices. A later increase in either consumer or business spending can set the ball rolling in the other direction. This may result in a series of economic booms and busts.

THE ECONOMY TOMORROW

 This chapter emphasized how a sudden change in investment might set off the multiplier process. Investors aren't the only potential culprits, however. A sudden change in government spending or exports could just as easily get the multiplier ball rolling. In fact, the whole process could originate with a change in *consumer* spending.

Recall the two components of consumption: *autonomous* consumption and *induced* consumption. These two components may be expressed as

$$C = a + bY$$

We've seen that autonomous consumption is influenced by *non*income factors, including consumer confidence. What's more, consumer confidence can change abruptly. When it does, the value of *a* in the consumption function will change and the consumption function itself will shift. A change in consumer confidence might also change the marginal propensity to consume, the *b* in the equation.

The reverberation of a change in consumer confidence will cause *two* shifts of the AD curve. The first shift will be due to the effect of changed consumer confidence on *autonomous* consumption. The second shift will result from the multiplier effects on *induced* consumption. This is exactly the kind of dilemma that prolonged the Japanese recession (see World View). As the outlook got gloomier, Japanese households decided to decrease autonomous consumption and reduce the marginal propensity to consume. Unfortunately, their attempt to save more and spend less worsened Japan's recession.

Because consumer spending vastly outweighs any other component of aggregate demand, the threat of abrupt changes in consumer behavior is serious. Although U.S. consumers have an optimistic bent (see News), an abrupt decline in consumer confidence

Maintaining Consumer Confidence

Consumer Confidence

The Official View: Always a Rosy Outlook

WORLD VIEW

Thrift Shift—The More the Japanese Save for a Rainy Day, the Gloomier It Gets

Stuffing Yen into the Drawer

A decade ago, when Japan was considered economically mighty and the U.S. was struggling, many economists agreed that a big reason for the disparity was savings: The thrifty Japanese had plenty to invest in their future, the wanton Americans too little.

Today, the average Japanese family puts away more than 13 percent of its income, the average American family 4 percent. Yet Japan is in the tank while the U.S. prospers.

Is saving no longer an economic virtue and profligacy no longer a vice? Did Benjamin Franklin get it all wrong? Maybe not—but it isn't as simple as Franklin's Poor Richard's Almanac made it seem:

An economy can save too much.

Japan is the first major developed country since World War II to confront the "paradox of thrift," the condition John Maynard Keynes worried about, where bad times lead individuals to save more, suppressing overall demand and making a country even worse off.

But these days, the pressing savings crisis is in Tokyo. Interest rates on bank deposits run below 1 percent, and still "households are saving too much," says Kengo Inoue, a Bank of Japan economist. "That's depressing demand and, over time, corporate investment." That, in turn, has become a drag on all of Asia.

So the Japanese government nudges its citizens to live it up. The Finance Ministry, concerned that families would simply tuck away a recent $500-a-household income-tax cut, launched a media blitz to advise people on how to spend the money.

—Jacob M. Schlesinger and David P. Hamilton

Source: *The Wall Street Journal,* July 2, 1998. Reprinted by permission of *The Wall Street Journal.* © 1998 Dow Jones & Company, Inc. All Rights Reserved Worldwide. www.wsj.com

Analysis: When Japanese consumers became more pessimistic about their economy, they started saving more and spending less. This shifted AD leftward and deepened the recession. Government officials urged them to spend more.

IN THE NEWS

Harris Poll: Wiser but Unbowed

How has the boom/bust economy of recent years affected Americans' perennial optimism? A *BusinessWeek*/Harris Poll of 1,022 adults, conducted July 20–25, found that most Americans believe the good times will return soon. Still, this outlook is tempered by a sense that the Brave New World of technology may not be quite the panacea it was once thought to be. Highlights of the poll:

Now, for the Turnaround

How optimistic or pessimistic are you that the U.S. can avoid a lengthy downturn marked by more large-scale job layoffs, further weakness in the stock market, and a decline in Americans' living standards?

Very optimistic	13%
Somewhat optimistic	50
Somewhat pessimistic	23%
Very pessimistic	8
Not sure/refused	7

The Future Is Ours

How confident are you that after the economic downturn ends, America can return to rapid economic growth, rising incomes, and good job opportunities?

Very confident	21%
Somewhat confident	55
Not very confident	17
Not at all confident	5
Not sure/refused	2

Source: *BusinessWeek*, August 27, 2001. Reprinted with permission. www.businessweek.com

Analysis: The willingness of consumers to keep spending depends on their outlook for the economy. U.S. consumers are relatively optimistic about future growth.

is always a possibility. Recognizing this, public officials strive to maintain consumer confidence in the economy tomorrow, even when such confidence might not be warranted. That's what Japanese officials were doing in 1998, described in the World View. That's also why President Hoover, bank officials, and major brokerage houses tried to assure the public in 1929 that the outlook was still rosy. (Look back at the first few pages of Chapter 8.) The "rosy outlook" is still the official perspective on the economy tomorrow. The White House is always upbeat about prospects for the economy. If it weren't—if it were even to hint at the possibility of a recession—consumer and investor confidence might wilt. Then the economy might turn ugly really fast.

SUMMARY

- The circular flow of income has offsetting leakages (consumer saving, taxes, business saving, imports) and injections (autonomous consumption, investment, government spending, exports).
- When desired injections equal leakage, the economy is in equilibrium.
- An imbalance of injections and leakages will cause the economy to expand or contract. An imbalance at full-employment GDP will cause cyclical unemployment or demand-pull inflation. How serious these problems become depends on how the market responds to the initial imbalance.
- Classical economists believed (changing) interest rates and price levels would equalize injections and leakages (especially consumer saving and investment), restoring full-employment equilibrium.
- Keynes showed that spending imbalances might actually *worsen* if consumer and investor expectations changed.
- An abrupt change in autonomous spending (injections) shifts the AD curve, setting off a sequential multiplier process that enlarges changes in equilibrium GDP.
- The multiplier itself is equal to $1/(1 - MPC)$. It indicates the cumulative change in demand that follows an initial (autonomous) disruption of spending flows.

- As long as the short-run aggregate supply curve slopes upward, AD shifts will affect both real output and prices.
- The recessionary GDP gap measures the amount by which equilibrium GDP falls short of full-employment GDP.
- Sudden changes in consumer confidence would destabilize the economy. To avoid this, policymakers always maintain a rosy outlook.

Key Terms

aggregate demand
full-employment GDP
leakage
gross business saving
injection

equilibrium GDP
marginal propensity to consume (MPC)
multiplier
recessionary GDP gap

cyclical unemployment
full employment
demand-pull inflation
inflationary GDP gap

Questions for Discussion

1. What factors might prompt the business sector to reduce planned investment spending?
2. Why wouldn't investment and saving flows at full employment always be equal?
3. When unwanted inventories pile up in retail stores, how is production affected? What are the steps in this process?
4. How can equilibrium output exceed full-employment output (as in Figure 10.9)?
5. How might the airline industry job losses described in the News feature on page 205 affect incomes in the clothing and travel industries?
6. Why would Asian economies stall when the U.S. economy slumps (World View, page 208)? How could the Asian economies self-adjust? Is that likely?
7. What forces might turn an economic bust into an economic boom?
   What forces might put an end to the boom?
8. What might trigger an abrupt decline in consumer spending?
9. What might get the international multiplier effect (World View, page 208) moving in the right direction?

Web Activities

1. How bad was the Great Depression in the United States? Check how long it lasted at www.nber.org/cycles.html. Find out how much real GDP and business investment fell at www.bea.doc.gov, and chart the unemployment rate for the period at www.bls.gov.
2. At the U.S. Congressional Budget Office, www.cbo.gov, find current economic projections. Look at the projections for the next three years' change in real output and the price level. How do they expect these statistics to change from the current level? Draw AD and AS curves to show what this office predicts will happen to the U.S. economy.
3. What happened to consumer confidence in the economy between 1988 and 1990? Log on to www.umich.edu/~nes/nesguide/toptable/tab4e_1.htm to see how many people think the economy got better during that time period. How does this help explain the economic downturn in the early 1990s? What happened to consumer confidence from 1992–98? Does this correspond to an expansion in the U.S. economy that you found in the chart at www.nber.org/cycles.html in web activity 1?

THE ACCOMPANYING STUDENT PROBLEM SET CONTAINS NUMERICAL AND GRAPHING PROBLEMS FOR THIS CHAPTER

PART 4

Fiscal Policy Options

The government's tax and spending activities influence economic outcomes. Keynesian theory emphasizes the inherent instability of a market economy and the necessity of using federal tax and spending power (fiscal policy) to stabilize the macro economy. Chapters 11 and 12 look closely at these issues.

CHAPTER 11

Fiscal Policy

The Keynesian theory of macro instability is practically a mandate for government intervention. From a Keynesian perspective, too little aggregate demand causes unemployment; too much aggregate demand causes inflation. Since the market itself won't correct these imbalances, the federal government must. Keynes concluded that the government must intervene to manage the level of aggregate demand. This implies increasing aggregate demand when it's deficient and decreasing aggregate demand when it's excessive.

This chapter examines some tools the federal government can use to alter macroeconomic outcomes. The questions we confront are

- Can government spending and tax policies help ensure full employment?
- What policy actions will help fight inflation?
- What are the risks of government intervention?

As we'll see, the government's tax and spending activities affect not only the *level* of output and prices but the *mix* of output as well.

TAXES AND SPENDING

Article I of the U.S. Constitution empowers Congress "to lay and collect taxes, duties, imposts and excises, to pay the debts and provide for the common defense and general welfare of the United States." Up until 1915, however, the federal government collected few taxes and spent little. In 1902, the federal government employed fewer than 350,000 people and spent a mere $650 million. Today, the federal government employs over 4 million people and spends more than $2 trillion a year.

Government Revenue

The tremendous expansion of the federal government started with the Sixteenth Amendment to the U.S. Constitution (1913); it extended the government's taxing power to *incomes*. Prior to that, most government revenue came from taxes on imports, whiskey, and tobacco. Once the federal government got the power to tax incomes, it had the revenue base to finance increased expenditure.

Today, the federal government collects over $2 trillion a year in tax revenues. Nearly half of that revenue comes from individual income taxes (see Figure 4.6). Social Security payroll taxes are the second-largest revenue sources, followed at a distance by corporate income taxes. The customs, whiskey, and tobacco taxes on which the federal government depended in 1902 now count for very little.

In 1902, federal government expenditures mirrored tax revenues: Both were very small. Today, things are very different. The federal government now spends virtually all of its much larger tax revenues. In some years Uncle Sam even borrows additional funds to pay for federal spending. In Chapter 12 we look at the implications of budget surpluses and deficits. In this chapter we focus on how government spending *directly* affects **aggregate demand**.

Purchases vs. Transfers. To understand how government spending affects aggregate demand, we must again distinguish between government *purchases* and *income transfers*. Government spending on defense, highways, and health care entail the purchase of goods and services in product markets; they're part of aggregate demand. By contrast, the government doesn't buy anything when it mails out Social Security checks. Those checks simply transfer income from taxpayers to retired workers. **Income transfers** don't become part of aggregate demand until the transfer recipients decide to spend that income.

As we observed in Chapter 4, less than half of all federal government spending entails the purchase of goods and services. The rest of federal spending is either an income transfer or an interest payment on the national debt.

The federal government's tax and spending powers give it a great deal of influence over aggregate demand. *The government can alter aggregate demand by*

- *Purchasing more or fewer goods and services.*
- *Raising or lowering taxes.*
- *Changing the level of income transfers.*

Fiscal policy entails the use of these various budget levers to influence macroeconomic outcomes. *From a macro perspective, the federal budget is a tool that can change aggregate demand and macroeconomic outcomes.* Figure 11.1 puts this tool into the framework of the basic AS/AD model.

Government Expenditure

aggregate demand: The total quantity of output demanded at alternative price levels in a given time period, *ceteris paribus*.

income transfers: Payments to individuals for which no current goods or services are exchanged, such as Social Security, welfare, unemployment benefits.

Fiscal Policy

fiscal policy: The use of government taxes and spending to alter macroeconomic outcomes.

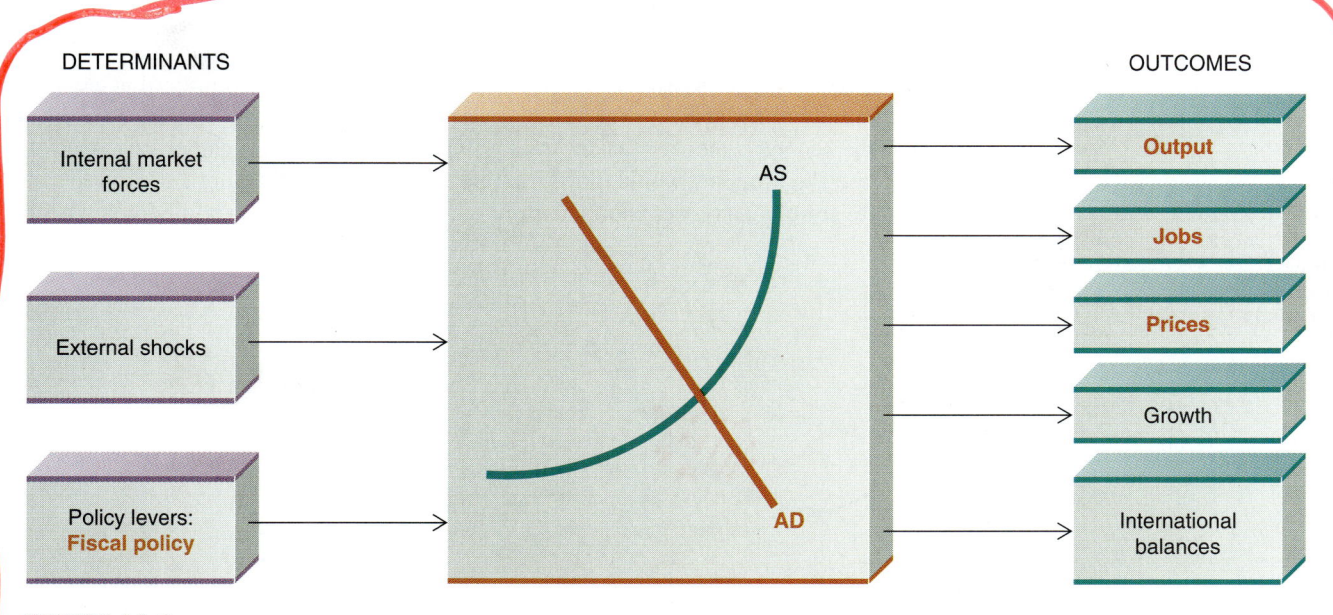

FIGURE 11.1
Fiscal Policy

Fiscal policy refers to the use of the government tax and spending powers to alter macro outcomes. Fiscal policy works principally through shifts of the aggregate demand curve.

equilibrium (macro): The combination of price level and real output that is compatible with both aggregate demand and aggregate supply.

recessionary GDP gap: The amount by which equilibrium GDP falls short of full-employment GDP.

Keynesian Strategy

fiscal stimulus: Tax cuts or spending hikes intended to increase (shift) aggregate demand.

The Fiscal Target

aggregate supply: The total quantity of output producers are willing and able to supply at alternative price levels in a given time period, *ceteris paribus*.

Although fiscal policy can be used to pursue any of our economic goals, we begin our study by exploring its potential to ensure full employment. We then look at its impact on inflation. Along the way we also observe the potential of fiscal policy to alter the mix of output and the distribution of income.

FISCAL STIMULUS

The basic premise of fiscal policy is that the market's short-run macro equilibrium may not be a desirable one. This is clearly the case in Figure 11.2. **Macro equilibrium** occurs at Q_E, where $5.6 trillion of output is being produced. Full-employment GDP occurs at Q_F, where the real value of output is $6 trillion. Accordingly, the economy depicted in Figure 11.2 confronts a **recessionary GDP gap** of $400 billion.

The Keynesian model of the adjustment process helps us not only understand how an economy can get into such trouble but also see how it might get out. Keynes emphasized how the aggregate demand curve *shifts* with changes in spending behavior. He also emphasized how new injections of spending into the circular flow multiply into much larger changes in total spending. From a Keynesian perspective, then, the way out of recession is obvious: Get someone to spend more on goods and services. Should desired spending increase, the aggregate demand curve would *shift* to the right, leading the economy out of recession. That additional spending impetus could come from increased government purchases or from tax cuts that induce increased consumption or investment. Such a **fiscal stimulus** might propel the economy out of recession.

Although the general strategy for Keynesian fiscal policy is clear, the scope of desired intervention isn't so evident. Two strategic policy questions must be addressed:

- By how much do we want to shift the AD curve to the right?
- How can we induce the desired shift?

At first glance, the size of the desired AD shift might seem obvious. If the GDP gap is $400 billion, why not just increase aggregate demand by that amount?

The Naive Keynesian Model. Keynes thought that policy might just work. The intent of the expansionary fiscal policy is to achieve full employment. In Figure 11.3, this goal would be attained at point *b*. When the AD curve shifts rightward by $400 billion, the new AD_2 curve in fact passes through point *b*, creating the possibility of achieving our full-employment goal.

Will the economy move so easily from point *a* to point *b*? Only under very special conditions. The economy would move from point *a* to point *b* in Figure 11.3 only if the **aggregate supply** curve were horizontal. In other words, we'd achieve full employment

FIGURE 11.2
The Policy Goal

If the economy is in a recessionary equilibrium like point *a*, the policy goal is to increase output to full employment (Q_F). Keynes urged the government to use its tax and spending powers to shift the AD curve rightward.

FIGURE 11.3
The AD Shortfall

If aggregate demand increased by the amount of the recessionary GDP gap, which is the shift from AD_1 to AD_2, equilibrium would occur at point c, leaving the economy short of full employment (Q_F). (Some of the increased demand pushes up prices instead of output.) To reach full-employment equilibrium (point d), the AD curve must shift to AD_3, thereby eliminating the entire AD shortfall. The AD shortfall—the horizontal distance between point a and point e—is the fiscal policy target for achieving full employment.

at the current price level (P_E) with the shift to AD_2 only if prices didn't rise when the economy expanded. This is the expectation of the naive Keynesian model. In fairness to Keynes, we must recall that he developed this approach during the Great Depression, when prices were *falling*. No one was worried that prices would rise if demand increased.

Price-Level Changes. Even in today's economy, prices may not rise every time aggregate demand increases. Over some ranges of real output, the AS curve may actually be horizontal. Eventually, however, we expect the AS curve to slope upward. When it does, any increase in aggregate demand affects both real output *and* prices. In those circumstances, an increase in aggregate demand doesn't translate dollar-for-dollar into increased real GDP. Instead, when the AD curve shifts to the right, the economy moves up the aggregate supply (AS) curve, not horizontally to the right. As a result both real output and the price level change.

Figure 11.3 illustrates the consequences of the upward-sloping aggregate supply curve. Suppose we actually increased aggregate demand by $400 billion, an amount equal to the initial GDP gap. When the aggregate demand curve shifts from AD_1 to AD_2, the economy moves to the macro equilibrium at point c, not to point b. As demand picks up, we expect cost pressures to increase, pushing the price level up the upward-sloping AS curve. At point c, the AS and AD_2 curves intersect, establishing a new equilibrium. At that equilibrium, the price level is higher than it was initially (P_E). Real output is higher as well but still short of the full-employment target (Q_F). Hence, the naive Keynesian policy fails to achieve full employment. To do better, we must recognize that shifting (increasing) aggregate demand by the amount of the GDP gap will achieve full employment only if the price level doesn't rise.

The AD Shortfall. Although the naive Keynesian approach doesn't work, we needn't forsake fiscal policy. Figure 11.3 simply tells us that the naive Keynesian policy prescription (increasing AD by the amount of the GDP gap) probably won't cure all our unemployment ills. It also suggests, however, that a *larger* dose of fiscal stimulus might just work. So long as the AS curve slopes upward, we must increase aggregate demand by more than the size of the recessionary GDP gap in order to achieve full employment.

AD shortfall: The amount of additional aggregate demand needed to achieve full employment after allowing for price-level changes.

Figure 11.3 illustrates this new policy target. The **AD shortfall** is the amount of additional aggregate demand needed to achieve full employment *after allowing for price-level changes*. Notice in Figure 11.3 that full employment (Q_F) is achieved only when the AD curve intersects the AS curve at point *d*. To get there, the aggregate demand curve must shift from AD_1 all the way to AD_3. That third aggregate demand curve passes through point *e* as well. Hence, aggregate demand must increase until it passes through point *e*. This *horizontal distance between point a and point e in Figure 11.3 measures the AD shortfall*. Aggregate demand must increase (shift) by the amount of the AD shortfall in order to achieve full employment. Thus, the AD shortfall is the fiscal target. In Figure 11.3, the AD shortfall amounts to $800 billion ($0.8 trillion). That's how much *additional* aggregate demand is required to reach full employment (Q_F).

Were we to increase AD by enough to attain full employment, it's apparent in Figure 11.3 that prices would increase as well. We'll examine this dilemma later; for the time being we focus on the policy options for increasing aggregate demand by the desired amount.

More Government Spending

The simplest way to shift aggregate demand is to increase government spending. If the government were to step up its purchases of tanks, highways, schools, and other goods, the increased spending would add directly to aggregate demand. This would shift the aggregate demand curve rightward, moving us closer to full employment. Hence, increased government spending is a form of fiscal stimulus.

Multiplier Effects. It isn't necessary for the government to make up the entire shortfall in aggregate demand. Suppose that the fiscal target was to increase aggregate demand by $800 billion, the AD shortfall illustrated in Figure 11.3. Were government spending to increase by that amount, the AD curve would actually shift *beyond* point *e* in Figure 11.3. In that case we'd quickly move from a situation of *inadequate* aggregate demand (point *a*) to a situation of *excessive* aggregate demand.

The origins of this apparent riddle lie in the circular flow of income. When the government buys more goods and services, it creates additional income for market participants. The recipients of this income will in turn spend it. Hence, each dollar gets spent and respent many times. This is the multiplier adjustment process we encountered in Chapter 10. As a result of this process, every dollar of new government spending has a multiplied impact on aggregate demand.

How much "bang" the economy gets for each government "buck" depends on the value of the **multiplier**. Specifically,

multiplier: The multiple by which an initial change in aggregate spending will alter total expenditure after an infinite number of spending cycles; 1/(1 − MPC).

$$\text{Total change in spending} = \text{multiplier} \times \text{new spending injection}$$

The multiplier adds a lot of punch to fiscal policy. Suppose that households have a marginal propensity to consume equal to 0.75. In this case, the multiplier would have a value of 4 and each dollar of new government expenditure would increase total expenditure by $4.

marginal propensity to consume (MPC): The fraction of each additional (marginal) dollar of disposable income spent on consumption; the change in consumption divided by the change in disposable income.

Figure 11.4 illustrates that leveraged impact of government spending. Aggregate demand shifts from AD_1 to AD_2 when the government buys an additional $200 billion of output. Multiplier effects then increase consumption spending by $600 billion. This additional consumption shifts aggregate demand further, to AD_3. Thus, the impact of fiscal stimulus on aggregate demand includes both the new government spending and all subsequent increases in consumer spending triggered by the additional government outlays. In Figure 11.4, the shift from AD_1 to AD_3 includes

AD_1 to AD_2: Shift due to $200 billion injection of new government spending.
AD_2 to AD_3: Shift due to multiplier-induced increase in consumption ($600 billion).

As a result of these initial and multiplier-induced shifts, aggregate demand at the current price level (P_E) increases by $800 billion. Thus,

$$\text{Increase (horizontal shift) in AD} = \text{multiplier} \times \text{fiscal stimulus}$$

FIGURE 11.4
Multiplier Effects

Fiscal stimulus will set off the multiplier process. As a result of this, aggregate demand will increase (shift) in two distinct steps: (1) the initial fiscal stimulus (AD_1 to AD_2) and (2) induced changes in consumption (AD_2 to AD_3). In this case, a $200 billion increase in government spending causes an $800 billion increase in aggregate demand at the *existing* price level.

This equation is identical to the one above but expressed in the terminology of fiscal policy. The "fiscal stimulus" is the "new spending injection" that sets the multiplier process in motion.

The Desired Stimulus. Multiplier effects make changes in government spending a powerful policy lever. The multiplier also increases the risk of error, however. Whereas too little fiscal stimulus may leave the economy in a recession, too much can rapidly lead to excessive spending and inflation. This was the dilemma President Bush confronted in his first year. He wanted a $1.6 trillion tax cut spread out over several years. Critics worried, however, that too much fiscal stimulus might accelerate inflation. A compromise of $1.35 trillion was struck in early 2001.

After the terrorist attacks of September 11, 2001, too *little,* not too much fiscal stimulus, was a greater risk. The attacks put an immediate damper on consumer and investor spending, widening the recessionary GDP gap. President Bush quickly asked Congress to approve more government spending and additional tax cuts to keep the economy growing.

Policy decisions would be a lot easier if we could anticipate such events. If we knew the exact dimensions of aggregate demand, as in Figure 11.3, we could easily calculate the required increase in the rate of government spending. The general formula for computing the *desired* stimulus is a simple rearrangement of the earlier formula:

$$\text{Desired fiscal stimulus} = \frac{\text{AD shortfall}}{\text{the multiplier}}$$

In the economy in Figure 11.3, we assumed the policy goal was to increase aggregate demand by the amount of the AD shortfall ($800 billion). Accordingly, we conclude that

$$\text{Desired fiscal stimulus} = \frac{\$800 \text{ billion}}{4}$$

$$= \$200 \text{ billion}$$

In other words, a $200 billion increase in government spending at the current price level would be enough fiscal stimulus to close the $800 billion AD shortfall and achieve full employment.

In practice, we rarely know the exact size of the shortfall in aggregate demand. The multiplier is also harder to calculate when taxes and imports enter the picture.

Tax Cuts

Nevertheless, the foregoing formula does provide a useful rule of thumb for determining how much fiscal stimulus is needed to achieve any desired increase in aggregate demand. Such calculations helped the Chinese government decide how much fiscal stimulus was needed in 2001 to keep its economy out of recession (see World View).

Although injections of government spending can close a GDP gap, increased government purchases aren't the only way to get there. The increased demand required to raise output and employment levels from Q_E to Q_F could emerge from increases in autonomous consumption or investment as well as from increased government spending. It could also come from abroad, in the form of increased demand for our exports. In other words, any Big Spender would help, whether from the public sector or the private sector. Of course, the reason we're initially at Q_E instead of Q_F in Figure 11.3 is that consumers, investors, and export buyers have chosen *not* to spend as much as required for full employment.

Consumer and investor decisions are subject to change. Moreover, fiscal policy can encourage such changes. Congress not only buys goods and services but also levies taxes. By lowering taxes, the government increases the **disposable income** of the private sector. This was the objective of the early Bush tax cuts, which gave all tax payers a rebate of $300–600 in the summer of 2001. By putting $38 billion more after-tax income into the hands of consumers, Congress hoped to stimulate (shift) the consumption component of aggregate demand.

To see what happened to real GDP in China after the 2001 fiscal stimulus, check out GDP data at the website of the China National Bureau of Statistics at http://english.peopledaily.com.cn

disposable income: After-tax income of consumers; personal income less personal taxes.

Taxes and Consumption. A tax cut directly increases the disposable income of consumers. The question here, however, is how a tax cut affects *spending*. By how much will consumption increase for every dollar of tax cuts?

The answer lies in the marginal propensity to consume. Consumers won't spend every dollar of tax cuts; they'll *save* some of the cut and spend the rest. The MPC tells us how the tax-cut dollar will be split between saving and spending. If the MPC is 0.75, consumers will spend $0.75 out of every tax-cut $1.00. In other words,

$$\text{Initial increase in consumption} = \text{MPC} \times \text{tax cut}$$

WORLD VIEW

China Races Its Spending Engines to Stave Off Effects of Slowdown

BEIJING—China's state spending is soaring to levels not seen since the Asian financial crisis, showing how Beijing is raising the stakes of its "borrow now, pay later" growth strategy as trading partners stumble.

China's fixed-asset investment reached $134 billion for the January–July period, up 18.4 percent from a year earlier. For July alone, that figure soared 20.4 percent from a year earlier, the National Bureau of Statistics announced. The bedrock of the government's deficit-spending program—infrastructure—accounted for slightly more than half the investment in the seven-month period.

Though China says its economy expanded 7.9 percent in the first half of the year, the global economic downturn is already weighing on the country, especially its export sector, a main driver of the economy.

To prevent a more significant slowdown, the government is again ramping up investment—a spending spree that mirrors increases in 1998, when China was shaken by the troubles of its neighbors. Like before, the government's goal is to improve the country's infrastructure while creating enough spillover wealth to trigger two domestic drivers: private investment and consumer spending.

— Peter Wonacott

Source: *The Wall Street Journal*, August 17, 2001. Reprinted by permission of *The Wall Street Journal*. © 2001 Dow Jones Company, Inc. All Rights Reserved Worldwide. www.wsj.com

---

Analysis: Fear of a pending decline in aggregate demand prompted China's government to increase government spending on roads, bridges, and telecom networks. The government hoped such a fiscal stimulus would "trigger" more consumer spending (multiplier effects).

If taxes were cut by $200 billion, the resulting spree would amount to

$$\text{Initial increase in consumption} = 0.75 \times \$200 \text{ billion}$$
$$= \$150 \text{ billion}$$

Hence, the effect of a tax cut that increases disposable incomes is to stimulate consumer spending. A tax cut therefore shifts the aggregate demand curve to the right.

The initial consumption spree induced by a tax cut starts the multiplier process in motion. The new consumer spending creates additional income for producers and workers, who will then use the additional income to increase their own consumption. This will propel us along the multiplier path already depicted in Figure 11.4. The cumulative change in total spending will be

$$\text{Cumulative change in spending} = \text{multiplier} \times \text{initial change in consumption}$$

In this case, the cumulative change is

$$\text{Cumulative change in spending} = \frac{1}{1 - \text{MPC}} \times \$150 \text{ billion}$$
$$= 4 \times \$150 \text{ billion}$$
$$= \$600 \text{ billion}$$

Here again we see that the multiplier increases the impact on aggregate demand of a fiscal policy stimulus. There's an important difference here, though. When we increased government spending by $200 billion, aggregate demand increased by $800 billion. When we cut taxes by $200 billion, however, aggregate demand increases by only $600 billion. Hence, a tax cut contains less fiscal stimulus than an increase in government spending of the same size.

The lesser stimulative power of tax cuts is explained by consumer saving. Only part of a tax cut gets spent. Consumers save the rest. This is evident in Figure 11.5 on the next page, which illustrates the successive rounds of the multiplier process. Notice that the tax cut is used to increase both consumption and saving, according to the MPC. Only that part of the tax cut that's used for consumption enters the circular flow as a spending injection. Hence, the initial spending injection is less than the size of the tax cuts. By contrast, every dollar of government purchases goes directly into the circular flow. Accordingly, tax cuts are less powerful than government purchases because the initial *spending* injection is smaller.

This doesn't mean we can't close the AD shortfall with a tax cut. It simply means that the desired tax cut must be larger than the required stimulus. It remains true that

$$\text{Desired fiscal stimulus} = \frac{\text{AD shortfall}}{\text{the multiplier}}$$

But now we're using increased consumption as the fiscal stimulus rather than increased government spending. Hence, we have to allow for the fact that the initial surge in consumption (the fiscal stimulus) will be *less* than the tax cut. Specifically,

$$\text{Initial consumption stimulus} = \text{MPC} \times \text{tax cut}$$

Hence, if we want to use a consumer tax cut to close a GDP gap, we have

$$\text{Desired tax cut} = \frac{\text{desired fiscal stimulus}}{\text{MPC}}$$

In the economy in Figure 11.3, we assumed that the desired stimulus is $200 billion and the MPC equals 0.75. Hence, the desired tax cut is

$$\text{Desired tax cut} = \frac{\$200 \text{ billion}}{0.75} = \$267 \text{ billion}$$

FIGURE 11.5
The Tax Cut Multiplier

Only part of a tax cut is used to increase consumption; the remainder is saved. Accordingly, the initial spending injection is less than the tax cut. This makes tax cuts less stimulative than government purchases of the same size.

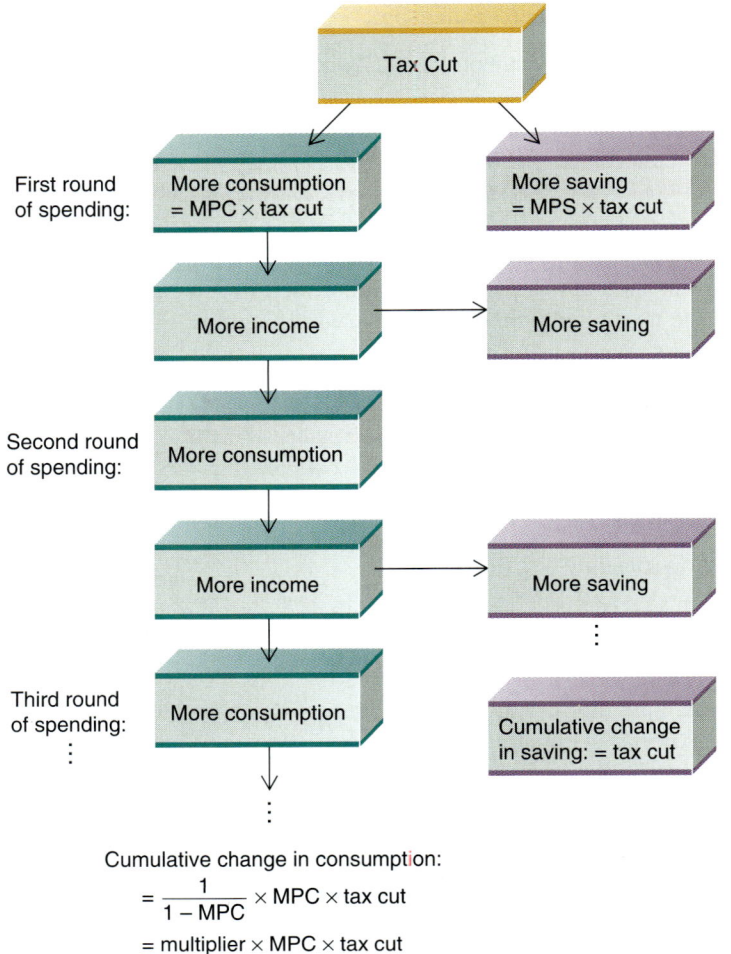

By cutting taxes $267 billion, we directly increase disposable income by the same amount. Consumers then increase their rate of spending $200 billion (0.75 × $267 billion); they save the remaining $67 billion. As the added spending enters the circular flow, it starts the multiplier process, ultimately increasing aggregate demand by $800 billion per year.

This comparison of government purchases and tax cuts clearly reveals their respective power. What we've demonstrated is that **a dollar of tax cuts is less stimulative than a dollar of government purchases.** This doesn't mean that tax cuts are undesirable, just that they need to be larger than the desired injection of spending. The News on page 228 shows that the 2001 tax cut was expected to boost both consumer spending and, as a result, real GDP growth.

The different effects of tax cuts and increased government spending have an important implication for government budgets. Because some of the power of a tax cut "leaks" into saving, tax increases don't "offset" government spending of equal value. This unexpected result is described in Table 11.1.

Taxes and Investment. A tax cut may also be an effective mechanism for increasing *investment* spending. As we observed in Chapter 9, investment decisions are guided by expectations of future profit. If a cut in corporate taxes raises potential after-tax profits, it should encourage additional investment. Once an increase in the rate of investment spending enters the circular flow, it has a multiplier effect on total spending like that which follows an initial change in consumer spending.

Different views of how the Bush tax cuts might affect spending, employment, and real GDP are available from the Heritage Foundation at www.heritage.org/library/cda/cda01-01.html and the Brookings Institution at www.brook.edu/comm/policybriefs/pb076/pb76.htm

TABLE 11.1
The Balanced Budget Multiplier
An increase in government spending paid for by a tax cut of equal size shifts aggregate demand. This box explains why.

> Many taxpayers and politicians demand that any new government spending be balanced with new taxes. Such balancing at the margin, it's asserted, will keep the budget deficit from rising, while avoiding further economic stimulus.
>
> However, changes in government spending (G) are more powerful than changes in taxes (T) or transfers. This implies that an increase in G apparently offset with an equal rise in T will actually increase aggregate demand.
>
> To see how this curious result comes about, suppose that the government decided to spend $50 billion per year on a new fleet of space shuttles and to pay for them by raising income taxes by the same amount. Thus
>
> $$\text{Change in } G = +\$50 \text{ billion per year}$$
> $$\text{Change in } T = +\$50 \text{ billion per year}$$
> $$\text{Change in budget balance} = 0$$
>
> How will this pay-as-you-go (balanced) budget initiative affect total spending?
>
> The increase in the rate of government spending represents a new injection of $50 billion. But households will have to reduce their consumption in order to pay the new taxes. The marginal propensity to consume (MPC) tells us how much consumption will be reduced when disposable income falls. The initial reduction in annual consumer spending equals MPC × 50 billion.
>
> The reduction in consumption is therefore less than the increase in government spending, implying a net increase in *aggregate* spending. The *initial* change in aggregate spending brought about by this balanced budget expenditure is
>
> Initial increase in government spending = $50 billion
> less Initial reduction in consumer spending = MPC × $50 billion
> Net initial change in total spending = (1 − MPC)$50 billion
>
> Like any other changes in the rate of spending, this initial increase in aggregate spending will start a multiplier process in motion. The *cumulative* change in expenditure will be much larger, as indicated by the multiplier. In this case, the cumulative (ultimate) change in total spending is
>
> $$\text{The multiplier} \times \text{initial change in spending per year} = \text{cumulative change in total spending}$$
>
> $$\frac{1}{1 - MPC} \times (1 - MPC)\$50 \text{ billion} = \$50 \text{ billion}$$
>
> Thus, the balanced budget multiplier is equal to 1. In this case, a $50 billion increase in annual government expenditure combined with an equivalent increase in taxes increases aggregate demand by $50 billion per year.

Tax cuts designed to stimulate consumption (C) and investment (I) have been used frequently. In 1963, President John F. Kennedy announced his intention to reduce taxes in order to stimulate the economy, citing that the marginal propensity to consume for the average U.S. family at that time appeared to be exceptionally high. His successor, Lyndon Johnson, concurred with Kennedy's reasoning. Johnson agreed to "shift emphasis sharply from expanding federal expenditure to boosting private consumer demand and business investment." He proceeded to cut personal and corporate taxes $11 billion. President Johnson proclaimed that "the $11 billion tax cut will challenge American businessmen, investors, and consumers to put their enlarged incomes to work in the private economy to expand output, investment, and jobs." He added, "I am confident that our private decision makers will rise to this challenge." They apparently did, because C + I increased $33 billion in 1963 and another $46 billion in 1965 (in part as a result of multiplier effects, of course).

The second-largest tax cut in history was initiated by President Ronald Reagan. In 1981, Congress cut personal taxes $250 billion over a three-year period and cut business

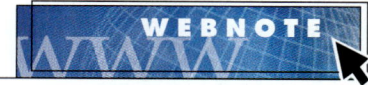

WEBNOTE

To follow the ups and downs of Federal income tax as a percentage of GDP, go to the Congressional Budget Office at www.cbo.gov and choose "Historical Budget Data."

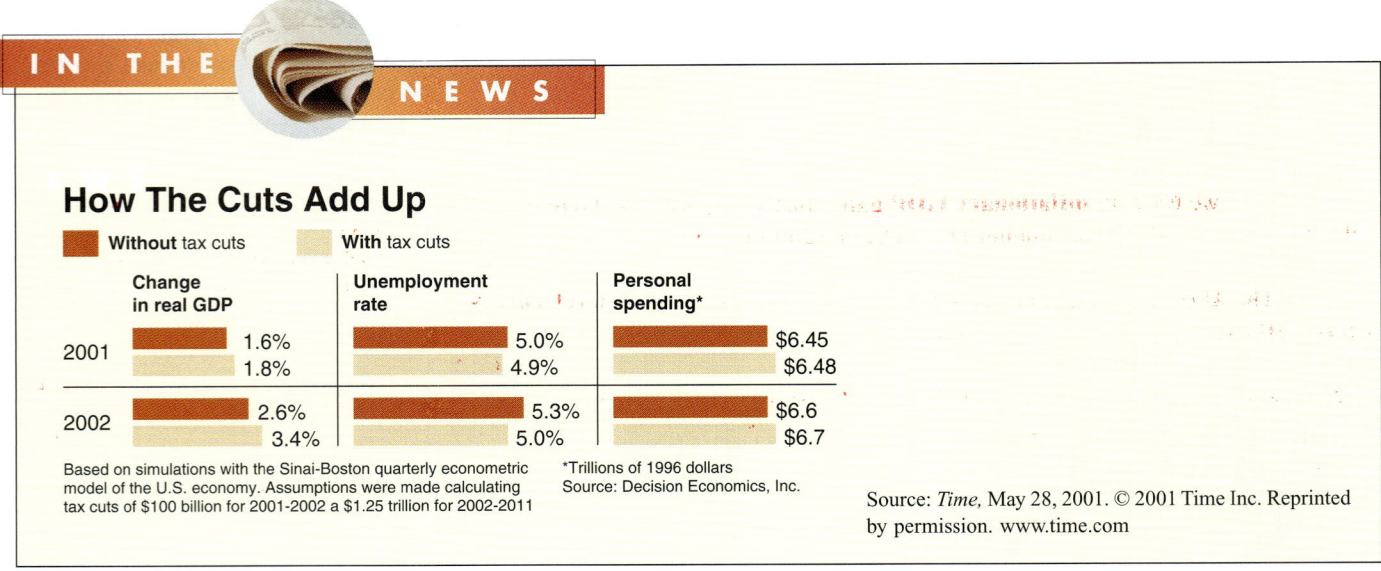

Analysis: The Bush tax cuts were a form of fiscal stimulus that boosted consumption (personal spending), increased real GDP growth, and reduced unemployment.

taxes another $70 billion. The resulting increase in disposable income stimulated consumer spending and helped push the economy out of the 1981–82 recession. When the economy slowed down at the end of the 1980s, President George H. Bush proposed to cut the capital gains tax, hoping to stimulate investment. President Clinton also embraced the notion of tax incentives for investment. He favored a tax credit for new investments in plant and equipment. If such credits increase the level of investment, multiplier effects will create additional jobs for many years.

Increased Transfers

A third fiscal policy option for stimulating the economy is to increase transfer payments. If Social Security recipients, welfare recipients, unemployment insurance beneficiaries, and veterans get larger benefit checks, they'll have more disposable income to spend. The resulting increase in consumption will boost aggregate demand.

Increased transfer payments don't, however, increase injections dollar-for-dollar. Here again, we have to recognize that consumers will save some of their additional transfer payments; only part (MPC) of the additional income will be injected into the spending stream. Hence, the initial fiscal stimulus of increased transfer payments is

Initial fiscal stimulus (injection) = MPC × increase in transfer payments.

This initial stimulus sets the multiplier in motion, shifting the aggregate demand curve further to the right.

FISCAL RESTRAINT

The objective of fiscal policy isn't always to increase aggregate demand. At times the economy is already expanding too fast and **fiscal restraint** is more appropriate. In these circumstances, policymakers are likely to be focused on inflation, not unemployment. Their objective will be to *reduce* aggregate demand, not to stimulate it.

fiscal restraint: Tax hikes or spending cuts intended to reduce (shift) aggregate demand.

The means available to the federal government for restraining aggregate demand emerge again from both sides of the budget. The difference here is that we use the budget tools in reverse. We now want to reduce government spending, increase taxes, or decrease transfer payments.

As before, our first task is to determine how much we want aggregate demand to fall. To determine this, we must consult Figure 11.6. The initial equilibrium in this case occurs at point E_1, where the AS and AD_1 curves intersect. At that equilibrium the unemployment rate falls below the rate consistent with full employment (Q_F) and we produce the output Q_1. The resulting strains on production push the price level to P_E, higher than we're willing to accept. Our goal is to maintain the price level at P_F, which is consistent with our notion of full employment *and* price stability.

In this case, we have an **inflationary GDP gap**—that is, equilibrium GDP exceeds full-employment GDP by the amount $Q_1 - Q_F$, or $200 billion. If we want to restore price stability (P_F), however, we need to reduce aggregate demand by *more* than this GDP gap. The **AD excess** takes into account potential changes in the price level. Observe that *the AD excess exceeds the inflationary GDP gap*. In Figure 11.6, the AD excess equals the horizontal distance from E_1 to point f, which amounts to $400 billion. This excess aggregate demand is our fiscal policy target. To restore price stability, we must shift the AD curve leftward until it passes through point f. The AD_2 curve does this. The shift to AD_2 moves the economy to a new equilibrium at E_2. At E_2 we have less output but also a lower price level (less inflation).

Knowing the dimensions of excess aggregate demand, we can compute the desired fiscal restraint as

$$\frac{\text{Desired}}{\text{fiscal restraint}} = \frac{\text{excess AD}}{\text{the multiplier}}$$

In other words, first we determine how far we want to shift the AD curve. Generally, the desired AD reduction will equal the excess AD. Then we compute how much government spending or taxes must be changed to achieve the desired shift, taking into account multiplier effects.

The first option to consider is budget cuts. By how much should we reduce government expenditure on goods and services? The answer is simple in this case: We first calculate the desired fiscal restraint, as computed above. Then we cut government expenditure by that amount.

The GDP gap in Figure 11.6 amounts to $200 billion ($Q_1 - Q_F$). If aggregate demand is reduced by that amount, however, some of the restraint will be dissipated in

The Fiscal Target

inflationary GDP gap: The amount by which equilibrium GDP exceeds full-employment GDP.

AD excess: The amount by which aggregate demand must be reduced to achieve full-employment equilibrium after allowing for price-level changes.

Budget Cuts

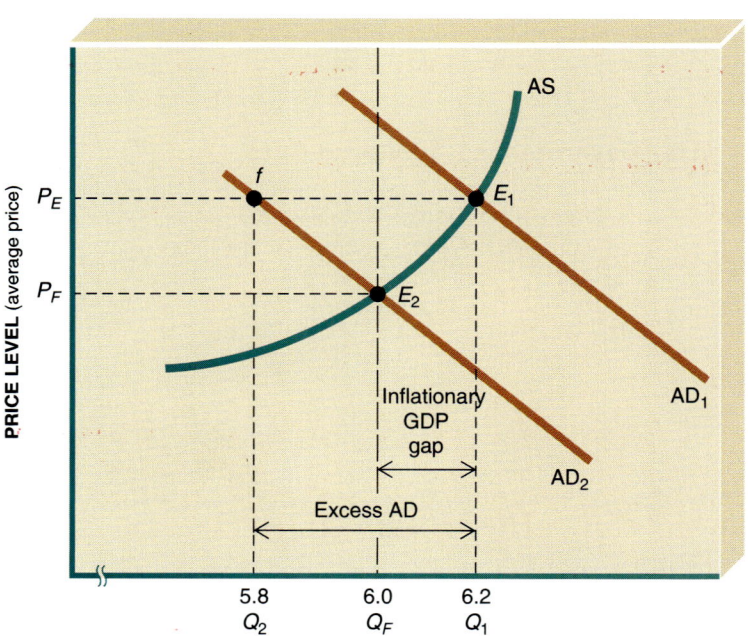

FIGURE 11.6
Excess Aggregate Demand

Too much aggregate demand (AD_1) causes the price level to rise (P_E) above its desired level (P_F). To restore price stability, the AD curve must shift leftward by the entire amount of the excess AD (here shown as $Q_1 - Q_2$). In this case, the excess AD amounts to $400 billion. If AD shifts by that much (from AD_1 to AD_2), the excess AD is eliminated and equilibrium moves from E_1 to E_2.

price-level reductions. To bring *equilibrium* GDP down to the full-employment (Q_F) level, even more of a spending reduction is needed. In this case, the excess AD amounts to $400 billion.

Budgets cuts of less than $400 billion will achieve the desired reduction in aggregate demand. If we assume a marginal propensity to consume of 0.75, the multiplier equals 4. In these circumstances, the desired fiscal restraint is

$$\text{Desired fiscal restraint} = \frac{\text{excess AD}}{\text{the multiplier}}$$

$$= \frac{\$400 \text{ billion}}{4}$$

$$= \$100 \text{ billion}$$

What would happen to aggregate demand if the federal government cut that much spending out of, say, the defense budget? Such a military cutback would throw a lot of aerospace employees out of work. Thousands of workers would get smaller paychecks, or perhaps none at all. These workers would be forced to cut back on their own spending, thereby reducing the consumption component of aggregate demand. Hence, aggregate demand would take two hits: first a cut in government spending, then induced cutbacks in consumer spending. The accompanying News feature highlights the impact of this multiplier process.

The marginal propensity to consume again reveals the power of the multiplier process. If the MPC is 0.75, the consumption of aerospace workers will drop by $75 billion when the government cutbacks reduce their income by $100 billion. (The rest of the income loss will be covered by a reduction in saving.)

From this point on the story should sound familiar. The $100 billion government cutback will ultimately reduce consumer spending by $300 billion. The total drop in spending is thus $400 billion. Like their mirror image, **budget cuts have a multiplied effect on aggregate demand.** The total impact is equal to

$$\text{Cumulative reduction in spending} = \text{multiplier} \times \text{initial budget cut (fiscal restraint)}$$

IN THE NEWS

Economy Is Already Feeling the Impact of Federal Government's Spending Cuts

WASHINGTON—Skeptical about the federal government's pledge to tighten its belt? Consider this: It already has, and that's one reason the economy is so sluggish.

Federal purchases of goods and services dropped 3.3 percent in 1992, the first decline in three years and the largest in almost 20. Behind the decline were huge defense cutbacks: These purchases tumbled more than 6.0 percent during the year.

But nondefense purchases are showing signs of shrinking, too. For two years in a row their rate of increase has slowed, and in the second quarter of this year they actually fell 1.8 percent. . . .

The economy has felt the pinch. Kurl Karl of the WEFA Group, economic consultants based in suburban Philadelphia, estimates that cuts in purchases by the federal government knocked as much as 0.5 percentage point off the gross domestic product last year, costing roughly 400,000 jobs, and will probably do the same in 1993.

"Government cuts in defense spending have definitely been a drag" on the economy, says Jim O'Sullivan, economist with Morgan Guaranty in New York.

— Lucinda Harper

Source: *The Wall Street Journal*, August 18, 1993. Reprinted by permission of *The Wall Street Journal*, © 1993 Dow Jones & Company, Inc. All Rights Reserved Worldwide. www.wsj.com

Analysis: Reductions in governmental spending on goods and services directly decrease aggregate demand. Multiplier effects induce additional cutbacks in consumption, further reducing aggregate demand.

This cumulative reduction in spending would eliminate excess aggregate demand. We conclude, then, that *the budget cuts should equal the size of the desired fiscal restraint.*

Tax increases can also be used to shift the aggregate demand curve to the left. The direct effect of a tax increase is a reduction in disposable income. People will pay the higher taxes by reducing their consumption *and* depleting their savings. The reduced consumption results in less aggregate demand. As consumers tighten their belts, they set off the multiplier process, leading to a much larger cumulative shift of aggregate demand.

Because people pay higher tax bills by reducing both consumption and saving (by MPC and MPS, respectively), *taxes must be increased more than a dollar to get a dollar of fiscal restraint*. This leads us to the following guideline:

$$\frac{\text{Desired increase}}{\text{in taxes}} = \frac{\text{desired fiscal restraint}}{\text{MPC}}$$

In other words, changes in taxes must always be larger than the desired change in leakages or injections. How much larger depends on the marginal propensity to consume. In this case

$$\frac{\text{Desired}}{\text{fiscal restraint}} = \frac{\text{excess AD}}{\text{the multiplier}}$$

$$= \frac{\$400 \text{ billion}}{4}$$

$$= \$100 \text{ billion}$$

Therefore, the appropriate tax increase is

$$\frac{\text{Desired}}{\text{tax hike}} = \frac{\$100 \text{ billion}}{\text{MPC}}$$

$$= \frac{\$100 \text{ billion}}{0.75}$$

$$= \$133 \text{ billion}$$

Were taxes increased by this amount, consumers would reduce their consumption by $100 billion (= 0.75 × $133 billion). This cutback in consumption would set off the multiplier, leading to a cumulative reduction in spending of $400 billion. In Figure 11.6, aggregate demand would shift from AD_1 to AD_3.

Tax increases have been used to "cool" the economy on several occasions. In 1968, for example, the economy was rapidly approaching full employment and Vietnam War expenditures were helping to drive up prices. Congress responded by imposing a 10 percent surtax (temporary additional tax) on income, which took more than $10 billion in purchasing power away from consumers. Resultant multiplier effects reduced spending in 1969 over $20 billion and thus helped restrain price pressures.

In 1982 there was great concern that the 1981 tax cuts had been excessive and that inflation was emerging. To reduce that inflationary pressure, Congress withdrew some of its earlier tax cuts, especially those designed to increase investment spending. The net effect of the Tax Equity and Fiscal Responsibility Act of 1982 was to increase taxes roughly $90 billion for the years 1983 to 1985. This shifted aggregate demand leftward, thus reducing price-level pressures.

Tax Hikes

The third option for fiscal restraint is to reduce transfer payments. *A cut in transfer payments works like a tax hike, reducing the disposable income of transfer recipients.* The appropriate size of the transfer cut can be computed exactly as the desired tax increase in the preceding formula.

Although transfer cuts have the same fiscal impact as a tax hike, they're seldom used. An outright cut in transfer payments has a direct and very visible impact on recipients, including the aged, the poor, the unemployed, and the disabled. Hence, this policy option smacks of "balancing the budget on the backs of the poor." In practice,

Reduced Transfers

232 FISCAL POLICY OPTIONS

absolute cuts in transfer payments are rarely proposed. Instead, this lever is sometimes used to reduce the rate of increase in transfer benefits. Then only *future* benefits are reduced, and not so visibly.

FISCAL GUIDELINES

A Primer: Simple Rules

The essence of fiscal policy entails deliberate shifting of the aggregate demand curve. The steps required to formulate fiscal policy are straightforward:

- *Specify the amount of the desired AD shift* (excess AD or AD shortfall).
- *Select the policy tools needed to induce the desired shift.*

As we've seen, the fiscal policy toolbox contains a variety of tools for managing aggregate demand. When the economy is in a slump, the government can stimulate the economy with more government purchases, tax cuts, or an increase in transfer payments. When the economy is overheated, the government can reduce inflationary pressures by reducing government purchases, raising taxes, and cutting transfer payments. Table 11.2 summarizes the policy options and the desired use of each.

A Warning: Crowding Out

The fiscal policy guidelines in Table 11.2 are a useful guide. However, they neglect a critical dimension of fiscal policy. Notice that we haven't said anything about how the government is going to *finance* its expenditures. Suppose the government wanted to stimulate the economy with a $50 billion increase in federal purchases. How would it pay for those purchases? If the government raised taxes for this purpose, the fiscal stimulus would be largely offset by resultant declines in consumption and investment. If, instead, the government *borrows* the money from the private sector, less credit may be available to finance consumption and investment, again creating an offsetting reduction in private demand. In either case, government spending may "crowd out" some private expenditure. If this happens, some of the intended fiscal stimulus may be offset by the **crowding out** of private expenditure. We examine this possibility further in Chapter 12 when we look at the budget deficits and surpluses that accompany fiscal policy.

crowding out: A reduction in private-sector borrowing (and spending) caused by increased government borrowing.

Time Lags

Another limitation on fiscal policy is *time*. In the real world it takes time to recognize that the economy is in trouble. A blip in the unemployment or inflation rate may not signal a trend. Before intervening, we may want to be more certain that a recessionary

---

TABLE 11.2
Fiscal Policy Primer
The goal of fiscal policy is to eliminate GDP gaps by shifting the AD curve rightward (to reduce unemployment) or leftward (to curb inflation). The desired shifts may be measured by the AD shortfall or the AD excess. In either case the desired fiscal initiative is equal to the desired shift divided by the multiplier. Once the size of the desired stimulus or restraint is known, the size of the appropriate policy options is easily calculated.

Fiscal Stimulus

$$\text{Desired fiscal stimulus} = \frac{\text{AD shortfall}}{\text{the multiplier}}$$

Policy Option	Amount
• Increase government purchases	desired fiscal stimulus
• Cut taxes	desired fiscal stimulus / MPC
• Increase transfers	desired fiscal stimulus / MPC

Fiscal Restraint

$$\text{Desired fiscal restraint} = \frac{\text{excess AD}}{\text{the multiplier}}$$

Policy Option	Amount
• Reduce government purchases	desired fiscal restraint
• Increase taxes	desired fiscal restraint / MPC
• Reduce transfer payments	desired fiscal restraint / MPC

or inflationary GDP gap is emerging. Then it will take time to develop a policy strategy and to get Congress to pass it. Once implemented, we'll have to wait for the many steps in the multiplier process to unfold. In the best of circumstances, the fiscal policy rescue may not arrive for quite a while. In the meantime, the very nature of our macro problems could change if the economy is hit with other internal or external shocks.

Before putting too much faith in fiscal policy, we should also remember who designs and implements tax and spending initiatives: the U.S. Congress. Once a tax or spending plan arrives at the Capitol, politics take over. However urgent fiscal restraint might be, members of Congress are reluctant to sacrifice any spending projects in their own districts. And if taxes are to be cut, they want *their* constituents to get the biggest tax savings. And no one in Congress wants a tax hike or spending cut *before* the election. This kind of pork barrel politics can alter the content and timing of fiscal policy. We'll examine the *politics* of fiscal policy further in Chapter 12.

Pork Barrel Politics

To review the latest budget data, go to the Congressional Budget Office at www.cbo.gov. CNN (www.cnn.com) is a good source for budget news.

THE ECONOMY TOMORROW

 The guidelines for fiscal policy don't say anything about how the government spends its revenue or whom it taxes. The important thing is that the right amount of spending take place at the right time. In other words, insofar as our stabilization objectives are concerned, the content of total spending is of secondary interest; the level of spending is the only thing that counts.

The Concern for Content

But it does matter, of course, whether federal expenditures are devoted to military hardware, urban transit systems, or tennis courts. Our economic goals include not only full employment and price stability but also a desirable mix of output, an equitable distribution of income, and adequate economic growth. These other goals are directly affected by the content of total spending. The relative emphasis on, and sometimes exclusive concern for, stabilization objectives—to the neglect of related GDP content—has been designated by Joan Robinson as the "second crisis of economic theory." She explains:

The "Second Crisis"

> The first crisis arose from the breakdown of a theory which could not account for the *level* of employment. The second crisis arises from a theory that cannot account for the *content* of employment.
>
> Keynes was arguing against the dominant orthodoxy which held that government expenditure could not increase employment. He had to prove, first of all, that it could. He had to show that an increase in investment will increase consumption—that more wages will be spent on more beer and boots whether the investment is useful or not. He had to show that the secondary increase in real income [the multiplier effect] is quite independent of the object of the primary outlay. Pay men to dig holes in the ground and fill them up again if you cannot do anything else.
>
> There was an enormous orthodox resistance to this idea. The whole weight of the argument had to be on this one obvious point.
>
> The war was a sharp lesson in Keynesism. Orthodoxy could not stand up any longer. Government accepted the responsibility to maintain a high and stable level of employment. Then economists took over Keynes and erected the new orthodoxy. Once the point had been established the question should have changed. Now that we all agree that government expenditure can maintain employment, we should argue about what the expenditure should be for. Keynes did not *want* anyone to dig holes and fill them.[1]

For a liberal viewpoint of the content of federal spending, go to the Center on Budget and Policy Priorities at www.cbpp.org. For a conservative perspective, go to the National Center for Policy Analysis at www.public-policy.org/~ncpa.

The alternatives to paying people for digging and filling holes in the ground are virtually endless. With $2 trillion to spend each year, the federal government has great

---

[1] From "The Second Crisis of Economic Theory," by Joan Robinson, *American Economic Review,* May 1972, p. 6. Used by permission of American Economic Association.

influence not only on short-run prices and employment but also on the mix of output, the distribution of income, and the prospects for long-run growth. In other words, fiscal policy helps shape the dimensions of the economy tomorrow.

Public vs. Private Spending

One of the most debated issues in fiscal policy is the balance between the public and private sectors. Critics of Keynesian theory object to its apparent endorsement of government growth. They fear that depending on government spending to stabilize the economy will lead to an ever-larger public sector. They attribute the growth of the government's GDP share (from 10 percent in 1930 to 18 percent today) to the big-government bias of Keynesian fiscal policy.

In principle, this big-government bias doesn't exist. Keynes never said government spending was the only lever of fiscal policy. Even in 1934 he advised President Roosevelt to pursue only *temporary* increases in government spending. As we've seen, tax policy can be used to alter consumer and investor spending as well. Hence, fiscal policy can just as easily focus on changing the level of *private*-sector spending as on changing *public*-sector spending. In 1934, however, business confidence was so low that tax-induced increases in investment seemed unlikely. In less desperate times, the choice of which fiscal tool to use is a political decision, not a Keynesian mandate. President Clinton favored increased government spending to stimulate the economy, whereas President George W. Bush has favored tax cuts that bolster private spending.

Output Mixes within Each Sector

In addition to choosing whether to increase public or private spending, fiscal policy must also consider the specific content of spending within each sector. Suppose we determine that stimulation of the private sector is preferable to additional government spending as a means of promoting full employment. We still have many choices. We could, for example, cut corporate taxes, cut individual taxes, reduce excise taxes, or increase Social Security benefits. Each alternative implies a different mix of consumption and investment and a different distribution of income. Congressional Democrats for example, characterized President George W. Bush's original 2001 tax-cut plan as a "fat cat's tax break." They objected that too much of the tax cuts went to high-income taxpayers. They wanted a smaller tax cut for the rich, more tax relief for the poor, and more government spending on social programs. After months of negotiation, they got

IN THE NEWS

Bush Seeks More Tax Cuts, Democrats Higher Spending

Economic Stimulus Package Sparks Debate over Size of Unemployment Help

WASHINGTON—President Bush and Democrats played tug-of-war over an economic stimulus package, as the administration insisted on more tax cuts and Democrats appealed for more direct spending.

Administration officials told congressional leaders that Mr. Bush wants the bulk of his proposed $60 billion to $75 billion package to go toward tax cuts. The rest would go to spending—much of it earmarked for a package of unemployment and health-care benefits for jobless workers.

Democratic leaders generally are comfortable with the size of the White House proposal but want to spend much more of it on worker benefits. Many Democrats also favor massive spending on bridges, road and other infrastructure to stimulate the economy rather than tax cuts, which they argue would go mostly to businesses and wealthy individuals.

—John D. McKinnon

Source: *The Wall Street Journal*, October 5, 2001. Reprinted by permission of The Wall Street Journal. © 2001 Dow Jones and Company, Inc. All Rights Reserved Worldwide. www.wsj.com

Analysis: Even when the need for fiscal stimulus is accepted, tough decisions still have to be made about whose taxes to cut, whose benefits to increase, or which programs to spend more on.

a compromise that altered both the mix of output and the distribution of income a bit more to their liking. The same kind of differences about the content of fiscal stimulus slowed the policy response to the September 11, 2001 terrorist attacks (see News).

SUMMARY

- The economy's short-run macro equilibrium may not coincide with full employment and price stability. Keynes advocated government intervention to shift the AD curve to a more desirable equilibrium.
- Fiscal policy refers to the use of the government's tax and spending powers to achieve desired macro outcomes. Options for fiscal stimulus include increasing government purchases, reducing taxes, and raising income transfers.
- Fiscal restraint may originate in reductions in government purchases, increases in taxes, or cuts in income transfers.
- Government purchases add directly to aggregate demand; taxes and transfers have an indirect effect by inducing changes in consumption and investment. This makes changes in government spending more powerful per dollar than changes in taxes or transfers.
- Fiscal policy initiatives have a multiplied impact on total spending and output. An increase in government spending, for example, will result in more disposable income, which will be used to finance further consumer spending.
- The objective of fiscal policy is to close GDP gaps. To do this, the aggregate demand curve must shift by more than the size of the GDP gap to compensate for changing price levels. The desired shift is equal to the aggregate demand shortfall (or excess).
- Changes in government spending and taxes alter the content of GDP and thus influence what to produce. Fiscal policy affects the relative size of the public and private sectors as well as the mix of output in each sector.

Key Terms

aggregate demand
income transfer
fiscal policy
equilibrium (macro)
recessionary GDP gap
fiscal stimulus

aggregate supply
AD shortfall
multiplier
marginal propensity to consume (MPC)
disposable income

fiscal restraint
inflationary GDP gap
AD excess
crowding out

Questions for Discussion

1. How can you tell if the economy is in equilibrium? How could you estimate the GDP gap?
2. Will an extra $20 billion per year spent on housing have the same impact on the economy as an extra $20 billion spent on interstate highways? Explain.
3. What happens to aggregate demand when transfer payments and the taxes to pay them both rise?
4. Why are the AD shortfall and AD excess larger than their respective GDP gaps? Are they ever the same size?
5. Will consumers always spend the same percentage of any tax cut? Why might they spend more or less than usual?
6. How does the slope of the AS curve affect the size of the AD shortfall? If the AS curve were horizontal, how large would the AD shortfall be in Figure 11.3?
7. According to the World View on page 224, what prompted China's fiscal stimulus (increased fixed-asset investment) in 2001? Had the government not intervened, what might have happened?
8. How quickly should Congress act to remedy an AD excess or shortfall? What are the risks of quick fiscal policy responses?
9. Why do critics charge that fiscal policy has a "big-government bias"?
10. In early 2001, congressional Democrats wanted a smaller tax cut and a bigger increase in government spending than President Bush proposed. If their policy had been adopted, what difference would it have made?

Web Activities

1. By how much has President Bush proposed to change the level of government spending during the next four years? Which is a larger portion of the proposed federal budget, discretionary or mandatory spending? Find information to answer this question at www.whitehouse.gov/omb/budget/fy2002/budiv_3.html.

2. Look at a summary of the Tax Relief Act of 2001 at www.whitehouse.gov/infocus/tax-relief. What was the purpose of that tax cut? Was the tax policy designed to be a countercyclical fiscal policy?

3. The U.S. federal budget is the focal point for debate on the role of government. Identify a liberal argument in favor of increased government spending at the Center on Budget and Policy Priorities at www.cbpp.org. Identify a conservative argument against increased government spending at the National Center for Policy Analysis at www.ncpa.org/pd/budget/budget.htm. For each side, give one possible counterargument to the position taken.

 THE ACCOMPANYING STUDENT PROBLEM SET CONTAINS NUMERICAL AND GRAPHING PROBLEMS FOR THIS CHAPTER

CHAPTER 12

Surpluses, Deficits, and Debt

The news was startling: Congress had actually balanced the federal budget. The year was 1998—a pivotal year in the history of the budget because it was the first year in a generation that the federal government had spent less money than it took in. In a White House ceremony celebrating that milestone, President Clinton hailed the budget *surplus* as one of his administration's greatest achievements. Newt Gingrich, then the Speaker of the U.S. House of Representatives, also lauded the surplus but asserted that the Republican-led Congress, not President Clinton, deserved credit for holding the line on government spending.

But the really amazing thing about the budget surplus was that hardly anyone outside Washington paid much attention. The financial markets didn't get excited, and the general public yawned at the news. How could this be? For decades the public had clamored for balanced budgets. Every year the "federal deficit" was cited in public opinion polls as one of the country's most urgent economic problems: 9 out of 10 Americans had even said they favored amending the Constitution to *require* Congress to balance the budget every year. In 1997, that proposal came within one vote of passing the U.S. Senate.

So why all the yawns? Did the public decide that Uncle Sam's budget balance wasn't really all that important? Were they disappointed that the economic landscape hadn't changed all that much when the budget surplus was attained? Had the evils of a budget deficit been exaggerated?

In this chapter we look closer at how government spending is *financed*. What happens to the budget balance when the budget is used as a policy lever to expand or contract the economy? What effect, if any, does a resulting deficit or surplus have on the economy? Should we applaud a surplus? Fear a deficit? To answer these questions we focus on three issues:

- How do deficits and surpluses arise?
- What harm (good) do deficits (surpluses) cause?
- Who will pay off the accumulated national debt?

As we'll see, the answers to these questions add another dimension to fiscal policy debates.

FISCAL POLICY OPTIONS

BUDGET EFFECTS OF FISCAL POLICY

Keynesian theory highlights the potential of **fiscal policy** to solve our macro problems. The guidelines are simple. Use fiscal stimulus—stepped-up government spending, tax cuts, increased transfers—to eliminate unemployment. Use fiscal restraint—less spending, tax hikes, reduced transfers—to keep inflation under control. From this perspective, the federal budget is a key policy lever for controlling the economy.

Use of the budget to stabilize the economy implies that federal expenditures and receipts won't always be equal. In a recession, for example, the government has sound reasons both to cut taxes and to increase its own spending. By reducing tax revenues and increasing expenditures simultaneously, however, the federal government will throw its budget out of balance. This practice is called **deficit spending,** a situation in which the government borrows funds to pay for spending that exceeds tax revenues. The size of the resulting **budget deficit** is equal to the difference between expenditures and receipts:

$$\text{Budget deficit} = \text{government spending} - \text{tax revenues} > 0$$

As Table 12.1 shows, the federal government had a budget deficit in 1997. In that year the government spent more than $1.6 trillion but had revenues of only $1.569 trillion, leaving a budget deficit of $22 billion.

Figure 12.1 shows that such deficit spending was the norm from 1970 to 1997. In fact, the deficit got as high as $290 billion one year (1992) and stayed above $100 billion for 15 years (1982–96). That 28-year string of deficits is what prompted taxpayers to demand that the federal government balance its budget. Against that string of deficits, the **budget surplus** of 1998 indeed looked like a stunning achievement.

By the time President George W. Bush took office, the budget surplus had grown to more than $200 billion per year. In the first eight months of his administration the most urgent budget issue was how to *use* large and growing surpluses. The economic slowdown and September 11 terrorist attacks made that question less urgent. In 2001, the budget surplus was cut nearly in half. Then a rapid military buildup and a sluggish economic recovery pushed the budget into deficit territory once again in FY 2002.

Keynesian View. From a Keynesian perspective there is nothing to fear from the reemergence of a budget deficit. Nor is a string of surpluses all that newsworthy. As far as Keynes was concerned, budget deficits and surpluses are just a routine byproduct of countercyclical fiscal policy (See World View on page 240). Deficits can easily arise when the government uses fiscal stimulus to increase aggregate demand, just as fiscal restraint may cause a budget surplus. As Keynes saw it, *the goal of macro policy is not to balance the budget but to balance the economy (at full employment).* If a budget deficit or surplus was needed to shift aggregate demand to the desired equilibrium, then so be it. In Keynes's view, a balanced budget would be appropriate only if all other injections and leakages were in balance and the economy was in full-employment equilibrium.

fiscal policy: The use of government taxes and spending to alter macroeconomic outcomes.

Budget Surpluses and Deficits

deficit spending: The use of borrowed funds to finance government expenditures that exceed tax revenues.

budget deficit: Amount by which government spending exceeds government revenue in a given time period.

budget surplus: An excess of government revenues over government expenditures in a given time period.

TABLE 12.1
Budget Deficits and Surpluses
Budget deficits arise when government outlays (spending) exceed revenues (receipts). When revenues exceed outlays, a budget surplus exists.

Budget Totals (in billions of dollars)	1997	1998	1999	2000	2001
Revenues	1,579	1,722	1,827	2,026	1,990
Outlays	−1,601	−1,653	−1,703	−1,789	−1,863
Surplus (deficit)	(22)	69	124	237	127

Source: Congressional Budget Office.

FIGURE 12.1
A String of Deficits

The federal government didn't achieve an annual budget surplus for 28 years. In the early 1980s, federal deficits increased dramatically and stayed high for years. These increased deficits resulted from both cyclical slowdowns and discretionary policies. Budget surpluses emerged in 1998, but vanished again in 2002.

Source: Congressional Budget Office.

Theory aside, budget analysts have concluded that Congress couldn't balance the federal budget every year even if it wanted to. Congress doesn't have as much control over spending and revenues as people assume. Hence, neither deficits nor surpluses are necessarily the result of fiscal policy decisions. To understand the limits of budget management, we have to take a closer look at how budget outlays and receipts are actually determined.

Discretionary vs. Automatic Spending

WORLD VIEW

Budget Imbalances Common

Although the U.S. budget deficits and surpluses receive the most attention, budget imbalances are a common feature of fiscal policy. As these figures reveal, many nations had budget surpluses in 2000; other countries had budget deficits.

BUDGET BALANCE (–) (percentage of GDP)
SURPLUS   DEFICIT

Australia, Austria, Belgium, Canada, France, Germany, Greece, Ireland, Japan, Netherlands, Sweden, Switzerland, United Kingdom, **United States**

Source: International Monetary Fund. www.imf.org

Analysis: To compare U.S. budget balances to those of other industrialized countries, we must adjust for differences in size by forming the *ratio* of deficits or surpluses to GDP. By this measure, U.S. budget imbalances haven't been that large.

---

fiscal year (FY): The 12-month period used for accounting purposes; begins October 1 for the federal government.

discretionary fiscal spending: Those elements of the federal budget not determined by past legislative or executive commitments.

fiscal restraint: Tax hikes or spending cuts intended to reduce (shift) aggregate demand.

fiscal stimulus: Tax cuts or spending hikes intended to increase (shift) aggregate demand.

At the beginning of each year, the president and Congress put together a budget blueprint for the next **fiscal year (FY)**. They don't start from scratch, however. Most budget line items reflect commitments made in earlier years. In FY 2001, for example, the federal budget included $430 billion in Social Security benefits. The FY 2001 budget also provided for $22 billion in veterans benefits, $205 billion for interest payments on the national debt, and many billions more for completion of projects begun in previous years. Short of repudiating all prior commitments, there's little that Congress or the president can do to alter these expenditures in any given year. *To a large extent, current revenues and expenditures are the result of decisions made in prior years.* In this sense, much of each year's budget is considered "*uncontrollable.*"

At present, uncontrollables account for roughly 80 percent of the federal budget. This leaves only 20 percent for **discretionary fiscal spending**—that is, spending decisions not "locked in" by prior legislative commitments. In recent years, rising interest payments and increasing entitlements (Social Security, Medicare, civil service pensions, etc.) have reduced the discretionary share of the budget even further. This doesn't mean that discretionary fiscal policy is no longer important; it simply means that the potential for *changing* budget outlays in any year is much smaller than it might first appear. Yet, the ability to *change* tax or spending levels is the force behind Keynesian fiscal policy. Recall that deliberate changes in government spending or taxes are the essence of **fiscal restraint and fiscal stimulus.** If most of the budget is uncontrollable, those policy levers are less effective.

Automatic Stabilizers. Most of the uncontrollable line items in the federal budget have another characteristic that directly affects budget deficits: their value *changes* with economic conditions. Consider unemployment insurance benefits. The unemployment insurance program, established in 1935, provides that persons who lose their jobs will receive some income (an average of $250 per week) from the government (see Chapter 6). The law establishes the *entitlement* to unemployment benefits but not the amount to be spent in any year. Each year's expenditure depends on how many workers lose their jobs and qualify for benefits. In 1991, for example, outlays for unemployment benefits increased by $8 billion. That increase in federal spending wasn't the result of any new policy decisions. Spending went up simply because more workers lost their jobs in the 1990–91 recession. The spending increase was *automatic,* not *discretionary.* The same thing happened in 2001.

Welfare benefits also increased by $5 billion in 1991. This increase in spending also occurred automatically in response to changing economic conditions. As more people lost jobs and used up their savings, they turned to welfare for help. They were *entitled* to welfare benefits according to eligibility rules already written; no new congressional or executive action was required to approve this increase in government spending.

Notice that outlays for unemployment compensation and welfare benefits increase when the economy goes into recession. This is exactly the kind of fiscal policy that Keynes advocated. The increase in **income transfers** helps offset the income losses due to recession. These increased transfers therefore act as **automatic stabilizers**—injecting new spending into the circular flow during economic contractions. Conversely, transfer payments decline when the economy is expanding and fewer people qualify for unemployment or welfare benefits. Hence, no one has to pull the fiscal policy lever to inject more or less entitlement spending into the circular flow; much of it happens automatically.

Automatic stabilizers also exist on the revenue side of the federal budget. Income taxes are an important stabilizer because they move up and down with the value of spending and output. As we've observed, if household incomes increase, a jump in consumer spending is likely to follow. The resultant multiplier effects might create some demand-pull inflation. The tax code lessens this inflationary pressure. When you get more income, you have to pay more taxes. Hence, income taxes siphon off some of the increased purchasing power that might have found its way to product markets. Progressive income taxes are particularly effective stabilizers, as they siphon off increasing proportions of purchasing power when incomes are rising and decreasing proportions when aggregate demand and output are falling.

Automatic stabilizers imply that policymakers don't have total control of each year's budget. In reality, *the size of the federal deficit or surplus is sensitive to expansion and contraction of the macro economy.*

Table 12.2 shows just how sensitive the budget is to cyclical forces. When the GDP growth rate falls by 1 percent, tax revenues decline by $30 billion. As the economy slows, people also turn to the government for additional income support: Unemployment benefits and other transfer payments increase by $10 billion. As a consequence, the budget surplus shrinks by $40 billion. This is exactly what happened in FY 2002: The recession that began in March 2001 shrank the budget surplus by roughly $100 billion (see News "How surplus could vanish on page 256)".

Inflation also affects the budget. Because Social Security benefits are automatically adjusted to inflation, federal outlays increase as the price level rises. This added expenditure is offset, however, by inflation-swollen tax receipts. Both Social Security payroll taxes and corporate profit taxes rise automatically with inflation. These offsetting expenditure and revenue effects almost cancel each other out: Table 12.2 shows that a one-point increase in the inflation rate *increases* the budget surplus by only $7 billion.

The most important implication of Table 12.2 is that neither the president nor the

income transfers: Payments to individuals for which no current goods or services are exchanged, such as Social Security, welfare, unemployment benefits.

automatic stabilizer: Federal expenditure or revenue item that automatically responds counter-cyclically to changes in national income, like unemployment benefits, income taxes.

Cyclical Deficits

TABLE 12.2
The Budget impact of Cyclical Forces (in 2002 dollars)
Changes in economic conditions alter federal revenue and spending. When GDP growth slows, tax revenues decline and income transfers increase. This shrinks the budget surplus.

Higher rates of inflation increase both outlays and revenues but not equally.

The cyclical balance reflects these budget impacts.

A. **Changes in Real GDP Growth**
   When the GDP growth rate decreases by one percentage point:
   1. Government spending (G) automatically increases for:
      Unemployment insurance benefits
      Food stamps
      Welfare benefits
      Social Security benefits
      Medicaid
      Total increase in outlays: +$10 billion
   2. Government tax revenues (T) automatically decline for:
      Individual income taxes
      Corporate income taxes
      Social Security payroll taxes:
      Total decline in revenues: −$30 billion
   3. **The surplus shrinks by $40 billion**

B. **Changes in Inflation**
   When the inflation rate increases by one percentage point:
   1. Government spending (G) automatically increases for:
      Indexed retirement and Social Security benefits
      Higher interest payments
      Total increase in outlays: +$29 billion
   2. Government tax revenues (T) automatically increase for:
      Corporate income taxes
      Social Security payroll taxes
      Total increase in revenues: +$36 billion
   3. **The surplus increases by $7 billion**

Source: Congressional Budget Office (first year effects).

Congress has complete control of the federal deficit. ***Actual budget deficits and surpluses may arise from economic conditions as well as policy.*** Perhaps no one learned this better than President Reagan. In 1980 he campaigned on a promise to balance the budget. The 1981–82 recession, however, caused the actual deficit to soar. The president later had to admit that actual deficits aren't solely the product of big spenders in Washington.

President George H. Bush explained the persistence of huge deficits during his presidency on the same basis. During the recession of 1990–91, the nation's unemployment rate jumped by more than two percentage points. That setback alone added roughly $84 billion to the federal deficit.

President Clinton had more luck with the deficit. Although he increased discretionary spending in his first two years, the annual budget deficit *shrank* by over $90 billion between 1993 and 1995. Most of the deficit reduction was due to automatic stabilizers that kicked in as GDP growth accelerated and the unemployment rate fell. As the economy continued to grow sharply, the unemployment rate fell to 4 percent. That surge in the economy affected the budget by increasing tax revenues, reducing income transfers, and propelling the 1998 budget into surplus. It was primarily the economy, not the president or the Congress, that produced the first budget surplus in a generation.

That part of the federal deficit attributable to cyclical disturbances (unemployment and inflation) is referred to as the **cyclical deficit.** As we've observed,

- *The cyclical deficit widens when GDP growth slows or inflation decreases.*
- *The cyclical deficit shrinks when GDP growth accelerates or inflation increases.*

If observed budget balances don't necessarily reflect fiscal policy decisions, how are

cyclical deficit: That portion of the budget balance attributable to short-run changes in economic conditions.

we to know whether fiscal policy is stimulative or restrictive? Clearly, some other indicator is needed.

To isolate the effects of fiscal policy, economists break down the actual budget balance into *cyclical* and *structural* components:

$$\begin{matrix} \text{Total budget} \\ \text{balance} \end{matrix} = \begin{matrix} \text{cyclical} \\ \text{balance} \end{matrix} + \begin{matrix} \text{structural} \\ \text{balance} \end{matrix}$$

The cyclical portion of the budget balance reflects the impact of the business cycle on federal tax revenues and spending. The **structural deficit** reflects fiscal policy decisions. Rather than comparing actual outlays to actual receipts, the structural deficit compares the outlays and receipts that would occur if the economy were at full employment.[1] This technique eliminates budget distortions caused by cyclical conditions. Any remaining changes in spending or outlays must be due to policy decisions. Hence, ***part of the deficit arises from cyclical changes in the economy; the rest is the result of discretionary fiscal policy.***

Table 12.3 shows how the total, cyclical, and structural balances have behaved in recent years. Consider what happened to the federal budget in 1990. In 1990 the federal deficit was $221 billion. In 1991 the deficit jumped to $269 billion. At first it appears that the government was trying to stimulate economic activity with expansionary fiscal policies. But this wasn't the case. The primary reason for the larger 1991 deficit was an abrupt halt in GDP growth. As the economy slipped into recession, the *cyclical* component shifted from a *surplus* of $8 billion in 1990 to a *deficit* of $46 billion in 1991. This $54 billion swing in the cyclical budget accounted for all the increase in the total budget deficit. By contrast, the *structural* deficit decreased by $6 billion, reflecting some *discretionary* fiscal restraint. (President George H. Bush was criticized for not doing more to end the recession.)

By distinguishing between the structural budget and the actual budget, we can evaluate fiscal policy more accurately. Only changes in the structural deficit are relevant. In fact, ***only changes in the structural budget balance measure the thrust of fiscal policy.*** By this measure we categorize fiscal policy in the following ways:

Structural Deficits

structural deficit: Federal revenues at full employment minus expenditures at full employment under prevailing fiscal policy.

For more historical data on cyclical and structural deficits, visit the U.S. Congressional Budget Office website at www.cbo.goy and look for "Historical Budget Data."

TABLE 12.3
Cyclical vs. Structural Budget Balances (in billions of dollars)
The budget balance includes both cyclical and structural components. Changes in the structural component result from policy changes; changes in the cyclical component result from changes in the economy. Between FY 1990 and FY 1991 the structural deficit shrank by $6 billion due to a small tax increase. The cyclical deficit widened by $54 billion, however, as the economy fell into a recession. As a result, the federal deficit increased by only $48 billion.

Fiscal Year	Budget Balance	=	Cyclical Component	+	Structural Component
1989	−152		+18		−170
1990	−221		+8		−229
1991	−269		−46		−223
1992	−290		−68		−222
1993	−255		−60		−195
1994	−203		−38		−165
1995	−164		−22		−142
1996	−108		−23		−85
1997	−22		+3		−25
1998	+69		+28		+41
1999	+124		+45		+79
2000	+237		+96		+141
2001	+127		+34		+93

Source: Congressional Budget Office. Miscellaneous adjustments included in structural deficit; December 2001 estimates for FY 2001.

---

[1] The structural deficit is also referred to as the "full-employment", "high-employment," or "standardized" deficit.

IN THE NEWS

Fiscal Policy in the Great Depression

In 1931 President Herbert Hoover observed, "Business depressions have been recurrent in the life of our country and are but transitory." Rather than proposing fiscal stimulus, Hoover complained that expansion of public-works programs had unbalanced the federal budget. In 1932 he proposed *cutbacks* in government spending and *higher* taxes. In his view, the "unquestioned balancing of the federal budget . . . is the first necessity of national stability and is the foundation of further recovery."

Franklin Roosevelt shared this view of fiscal policy. He criticized Hoover for not balancing the budget, and in 1933, warned Congress that "all public works must be considered from the point of view of the ability of the government treasury to pay for them."

As the accompanying figure shows, the budget deficit persisted throughout the Great Depression. But these deficits were the result of a declining economy, not stimulative fiscal policy. The structural deficit actually *decreased* from 1931 to 1933 (see figure), thereby restraining aggregate spending at a time when producers were desperate for increasing sales. Only when the structural deficit was expanded tremendously by spending during World War II did fiscal policy have a decidedly positive effect. Federal defense expenditures jumped from $2.2 billion in 1940 to $87.4 billion in 1994!

Source: Adapted from E. Cary Brown. "Fiscal Policy in the Thirties: A Reappraisal," *American Economic Review*, December 1956. Table 1. Used by permission of American Economic Association.

Analysis: From 1931 to 1933, the structural deficit decreased from $4.5 billion to a $2 billion *surplus*. This fiscal restraint reduced aggregate demand and deepened the Great Depression.

- ***Fiscal stimulus is measured by the increase in the structural deficit*** (or shrinkage in the structural surplus).
- ***Fiscal restraint is gauged by the decrease in the structural deficit*** (or increase in the structural surplus).

According to this measure, fiscal policy was actually restrictive during the Great Depression, when fiscal stimulus was desperately needed (see News). Both Presidents Hoover and Roosevelt thought the government should rein in its spending when tax revenues declined, so as to keep the federal budget balanced. It took years of economic devastation before the fiscal policy lever was reversed. Also notice in Table 12.3 the big jump in the structural surplus between 1999 and 2000. This $61 billion dose of fiscal restraint contributed to the recession of 2001.

ECONOMIC EFFECTS OF DEFICITS

No matter what the origins of budget deficits, most people are alarmed by them. Should they be? What are the *consequences* of budget deficits?

We've already encountered one potential consequence of deficit financing: *If the government borrows funds to finance deficits, the availability of funds for private-sector spending may be reduced.* This is the **crowding-out** problem first noted in Chapter 11. If crowding out occurs, the increase in government expenditure will be at least partially offset by reductions in consumption and investment.

If the economy were at full employment, crowding out would be inevitable. At full employment, we'd be on the production possibilities curve, using all available resources. As Figure 12.2 reminds us, additional government purchases can occur only if private-sector purchases are reduced. In real terms, *crowding out implies less private-sector output.*

Crowding out is complete only if the economy is at full employment. If the economy is in recession. it's possible to get more public-sector output (like highways, schools, defense) without cutbacks in private-sector output. This possibility is illustrated by the move from point *c* to point *b* in Figure 12.2.

What Figure 12.2 emphasizes is that *the risk of crowding out is greater the closer the economy is to full employment.* This implies that deficits are less appropriate at high levels of employment but more appropriate at low levels of employment.

Even if crowding out does occur, that doesn't mean that deficits are necessarily too big. Crowding out simply reminds us that there's an **opportunity cost** to government spending. We still have to decide whether the private-sector output crowded out by government expenditure is more or less desirable than the increased public-sector output. The deficits of the 1980s financed a substantial military buildup. Private investment spending stagnated, however. Hence, the deficits were desirable only if the resulting change in the mix of output was itself desired.

President Clinton agreed that deficit reduction was desirable. He also, however, defended government expenditure on education, training, and infrastructure as public "investment." He believed crowding out wasn't necessarily an unwelcome outcome, especially if government investments were well targeted. Public investments in education, health care, and transportation systems might even accelerate long-term economic growth.

Crowding Out

crowding out: A reduction in private-sector borrowing (and spending) caused by increased government borrowing.

Opportunity Cost

opportunity cost: The most desired goods or services that are forgone in order to obtain something else.

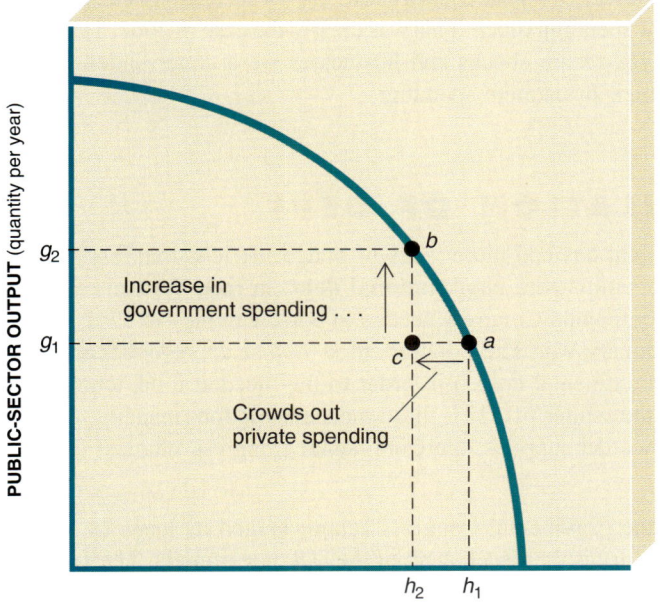

FIGURE 12.2
Crowding Out

If the economy is fully employed, an increase in public-sector expenditure (output) will reduce private-sector expenditure (output). In this case a deficit-financed increase in government expenditure moves the economy from point *a* to point *b*. In the process the quantity $h_1 - h_2$ of private-sector output is crowded out to make room for the increase in public-sector output (from g_1 to g_2). If the economy started at point *c*, however, with unemployed resources, crowding out need not occur.

ECONOMIC EFFECTS OF SURPLUSES

The economic effects of budget *surpluses* are the mirror image of those for deficits.

Crowding In

When the government takes in more revenue than it spends, it adds to leakage in the circular flow. But Uncle Sam doesn't hide the surplus under a mattress. And the sums involved (such as $237 billion in FY 2000) are too large to put in a bank. Were the government to buy corporate stock with the budget surplus, it would effectively be nationalizing private enterprises. So where does the surplus go?

There are really only four potential uses for a budget surplus, namely,

- *Spend it on goods and services.*
- *Cut taxes.*
- *Increase income transfers.*
- *Pay off old debt ("save it").*

The first three options effectively wipe out the surplus by changing budget outlays or receipts. There are important differences here, though. The first option—increased government spending—not only reduces the surplus but enlarges the public sector. Cutting taxes or increasing income transfers, by contrast, puts the money into the hands of consumers and enlarges the private sector. Whereas President Clinton favored more government spending, President George W. Bush insisted the government "give the money back to the people who paid the taxes." His $1.35 trillion tax cut wiped out about a fourth of the projected 2001–11 budget surplus (see News).

The fourth budget option is to use the surplus to pay off some of the debt accumulated from earlier deficits. This has a similar but less direct **crowding-in** effect. If Uncle Sam pays off some of his accumulated debt, households that were holding that debt (government bonds) will end up with more money. If they use that money to buy goods and services, then private-sector output will expand.

crowding in: An increase in private-sector borrowing (and spending) caused by decreased government borrowing.

Even people who haven't lent any money to Uncle Sam will benefit from the debt reduction. When the government reduces its level of borrowing, it takes pressure off market interest rates. As interest rates drop, consumers will be more willing and able to purchase big-ticket items such as cars, appliances, and houses, thus changing the mix of output in favor of private-sector production.

Cyclical Sensitivity

Like crowding out, the extent of crowding in depends on the state of the economy. In a recession, a surplus-induced decline in interest rates isn't likely to stimulate much spending. If consumer and investor confidence are low, even a surplus-financed tax cut might not lift private-sector spending much. This was clearly the case in 2001. Taxpayers were slow to spend their tax-rebate checks and businesses were unpersuaded by low interest rates to increase their investment spending.

THE ACCUMULATION OF DEBT

Because the U.S. government has had more years of budget deficits than budget surpluses, Uncle Sam has accumulated a large **national debt**. In fact, the United States started out in debt. The Continental Congress needed to borrow money in 1777 to continue fighting the Revolutionary War. The Congress tried to raise tax revenues and even printed new money (the Continental dollar) in order to buy needed food, tents, guns, and ammunition. But by the winter of 1777, these mechanisms for financing the war were failing. To acquire needed supplies, the Continental Congress plunged the new nation into debt.

national debt: Accumulated debt of the federal government.

Debt Creation

As with today's deficits, the Continental Congress acknowledged its loans by issuing bonds. Today the U.S. Treasury is the fiscal agent of the U.S. government. The Treasury collects tax revenues, signs checks for federal spending, and—when necessary—borrows funds to cover budget deficits. When the Treasury borrows funds, it issues

IN THE NEWS

Tax Cut Shrinks Projected Surplus

WASHINGTON – The new tax cut, coupled with falling corporate tax revenue, has gobbled up three-quarters of the projected federal budget surplus through 2004, a revised Congressional Budget Office estimate reveals.

As the surplus shrinks, budget experts from both parties now say Congress and President Bush will have to tap funds reserved for Medicare to pay for the spending increases they want for the fiscal year that begins in October. Dipping into Medicare is something lawmakers and the White House have vowed not to do.

The updated CBO forecast is a reversal from the steadily growing surpluses the budget office has reported for the past several years. Just last January, budget forecasters had expected the surplus—excluding funds reserved for Social Security and Medicare—to total a record $489 billion from 2001 through 2004. That number has shrunk to $127 billion.

The CBO attributes virtually all of the shrinking surplus to the 10-year, $1.35 trillion tax cut that Bush signed this month. It will lower the surplus by $310 billion through 2004. Falling corporate tax receipts will cost the Treasury $22 billion more over that period.

—Jonathan Weisman

Source: *USA Today*, June 27, 2001. © 2001 USA Today. Reprinted with permission. www.usatoday.com

Analysis: A tax cut reduces government revenues and shrinks the budget surplus (or widens the budget deficit). Such policy decisions are reflected in the structural component of the budget.

Treasury bonds; these are IOUs of the federal government. People buy bonds—lend money to the U.S. Treasury—because bonds pay interest and are a very safe haven for idle funds.

The total stock of all outstanding bonds represents the national debt. It's equal to the sum total of our accumulated deficits, less net repayments in years when a budget surplus existed. In other words, ***the national debt is a stock of IOUs created by annual deficit flows.*** Whenever there's a budget deficit, the national debt increases. In years when a budget surplus exists, the national debt can be pared down.

Treasury bonds: Promissory notes (IOUs) issued by the U.S. Treasury.

The United States began accumulating debt as soon as independence was declared. By 1783, the United States had borrowed over $8 million from France and $250,000 from Spain. Most of these funds were secretly obtained to help finance the Revolutionary War.

During the period 1790–1812, the United States often incurred debt but typically repaid it quickly. The War of 1812, however, caused a massive increase in the national debt. With neither a standing army nor an adequate source of tax revenues to acquire one, the U.S. government had to borrow money to repel the British. By 1816, the national debt was over $129 million. Although that figure seems tiny by today's standards, it amounted to 13 percent of national income in 1816.

Early History, 1776–1900

1835–1836: Debt-Free! After the War of 1812, the U.S. government used recurrent budget surpluses to repay its debt. These surpluses were so frequent that the U.S. government was completely out of debt by 1835. In 1835 and again in 1836, the government had neither national debt nor a budget deficit. The dilemma in those years was how to use the budget *surplus!* Since there was no accumulated debt, the option of using the surplus to reduce the debt didn't exist. In the end, Congress decided simply to distribute the surplus funds to the states. That was the last time the U.S. government was completely out of debt.

The Mexican-American War (1846–48) necessitated a sudden increase in federal spending. The deficits incurred to fight that war caused a fourfold increase in the debt. That debt was pared down the following decade. Then the Civil War (1861–65) broke out, and both sides needed debt financing. By the end of the Civil War, the North owed over $2.6 billion, or approximately half its national income. The South depended more heavily on newly printed Confederate currency to finance its side of the Civil War,

248 FISCAL POLICY OPTIONS

The Twentieth Century

relying on bond issues for only one-third of its financial needs. When the South lost, however, neither Confederate currency nor Confederate bonds had any value.[2]

The Spanish-American War (1898) also increased the national debt. But all prior debt was dwarfed by World War I, which increased the national debt from 3 percent of national income in 1917 to 41 percent at the war's end.

The national debt declined during the 1920s because the federal government was consistently spending less revenue than it took in. Budget surpluses disappeared quickly when the economy fell into the Great Depression, however, and the cyclical deficit widened (see News, page 244).

World War II. The most explosive jump in the national debt occurred during World War II, when the government had to mobilize all available resources. Rather than raise taxes to the fullest, the U.S. government restricted the availability of consumer goods. With consumer goods rationed, consumers had little choice but to increase their saving. Uncle Sam encouraged people to lend their idle funds to the U.S. Treasury by buying U.S. war bonds. The resulting bond purchases raised the national debt from 45 percent of GDP in 1940 to over 125 percent of GDP in 1946 (see Figure 12.3).

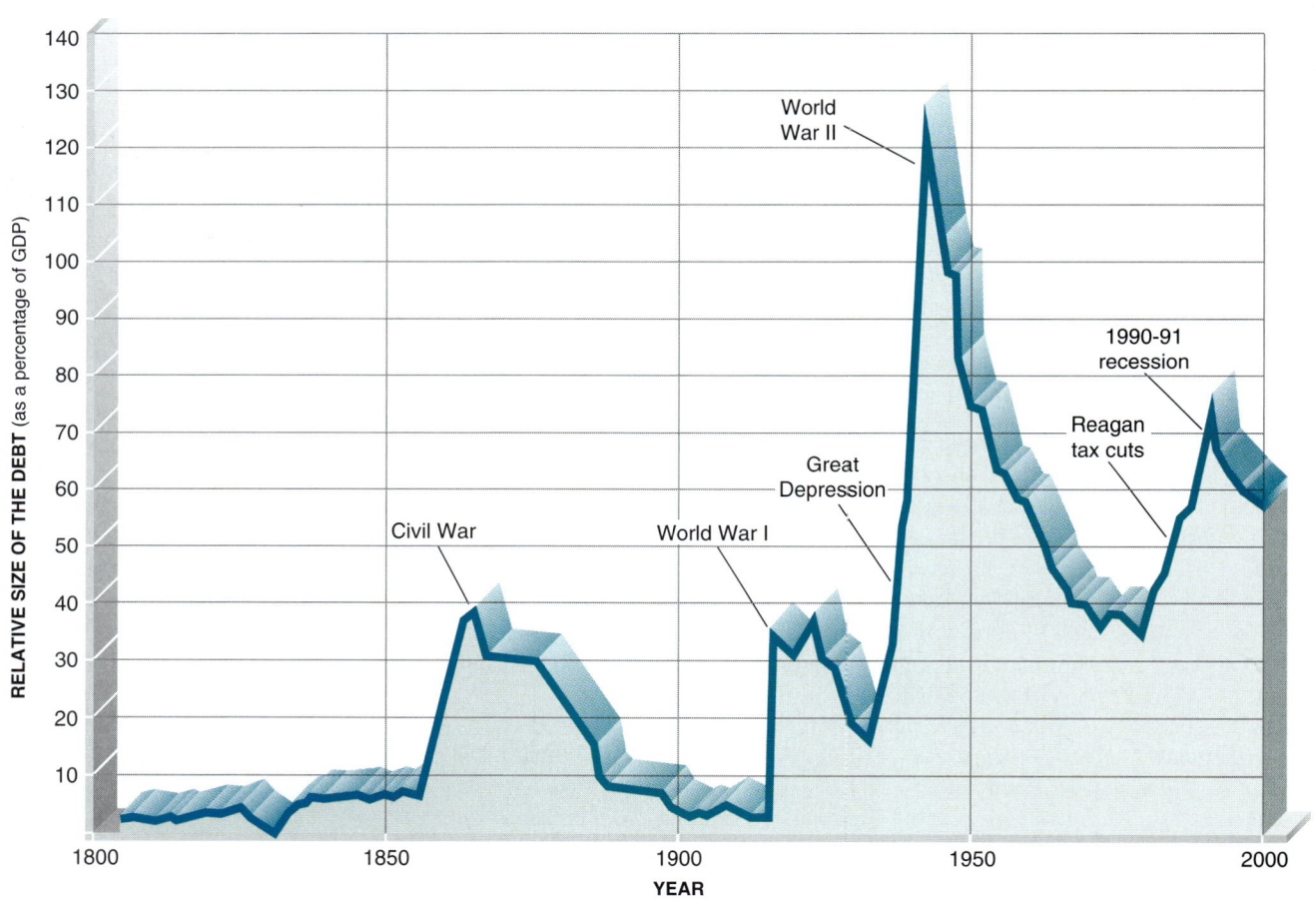

FIGURE 12.3
Historical View of the Debt/GDP Ratio

From 1790 to 1917, the national debt exceeded 10 percent of GDP only during the Civil War years. After 1917, however, the debt ratio grew sharply. World War I, the Great Depression, and World War II all caused major increases in the debt ratio. The tax cuts of 1981–84 and recession of 1990–91 caused further increases in the debt/GDP ratio.

Source: Office of Management and Budget.

[2]In anticipation of this situation, European leaders had forced the South to guarantee most of its loans with cotton. When the South was unable to repay its debts, these creditors could sell the cotton they had held as collateral. But most holders of Confederate bonds or currency received nothing.

TABLE 12.4
The National Debt

It took nearly a century for the national debt to reach $1 trillion. Then the debt tripled in a mere decade. By the end of 2000, the accumulated debt exceeded $5.6 trillion.

Year	Total Debt Outstanding (millions of dollars)	Year	Total Debt Outstanding (millions of dollars)
1791	75	1920	24,299
1800	83	1930	16,185
1810	53	1940	42,967
1816	127	1945	258,682
1820	91	1960	286,331
1835	0	1970	370,919
1850	63	1980	914,300
1865	2,678	1985	1,827,500
1890	1,122	1990	3,163,000
1900	1,263	1995	5,076,000
1915	1,191	2000	5,629,000

Source: Office of Management and Budget.

The 1980s. During the 1980s, the national debt jumped again—by nearly $2 *trillion*. This 10-year increase in the debt exceeded all the net debt accumulation since the country was founded. This time, however, the debt increase wasn't war-related. Instead, the debt explosion of the 1980s originated in recessions (1980–82 and 1990–91), massive tax cuts (1981–84), and increased defense spending. The recessions caused big jumps in the cyclical deficit while the Reagan tax cuts and military buildup caused the structural deficit to jump fourfold in only four years (1982–86). The combination of the cyclical and structural forces caused huge annual deficits that tripled the national debt in a single decade (Table 12.4).

The 1990s. The early 1990s continued the same trend. Discretionary federal spending increased sharply in the first two years of the George H. Bush administration. The federal government was also forced to bail out hundreds of failed savings and loan associations. Although taxes were raised a bit and military spending was cut back, the structural deficit was little changed. Then the recession of 1990–91 killed any chance of achieving smaller deficits. In only four years (1988–92) the national debt increased by another $1 trillion.

In 1993, the Clinton administration persuaded Congress to raise taxes, thereby reducing the structural deficit. Continuing recovery from the 1990–91 recession also reduced the cyclical deficit (see Table 12.3). Nevertheless, the budget deficits of 1993–96 pushed the national debt to over $5 trillion. After a couple of years of budget surplus, the accumulated debt still exceeded $5.6 trillion in 2002, which works out to nearly $20,000 of debt for every American citizen.

WHO OWNS THE DEBT?

To the average citizen, the accumulated national debt is both incomprehensible and frightening. Who can understand debts that are measured in *trillions* of dollars? Who can ever be expected to pay them?

The first thing to note about the national debt is that it represents not only a liability but an asset as well. When the U.S. Treasury borrows money, it issues bonds. Those bonds are a **liability** for the federal government since it must later repay the borrowed funds. But those same bonds are an **asset** to the people who hold them. Bondholders have a claim to future repayment. They can even convert that claim into cash by selling their bonds in the bond market. Therefore, ***national debt creates as much wealth***

WEBNOTE

The U.S. National Debt Clock tracks the debt. To see it, visit www.brillig.com/debt_clock or http://www.publicdebt.treas.gov/opd/opdpdodt.htm

Liabilities = Assets

liability: An obligation to make future payment; debt.

asset: Anything having exchange value in the marketplace; wealth.

(for bondholders) as liabilities (for the U.S. Treasury). Neither money nor any other form of wealth disappears when the government borrows money.

The fact that total bond assets equal total bond liabilities is of little consolation to taxpayers confronted with $5 trillion of national debt and worry when, if ever, they'll be able to repay it. The fear that either the U.S. government or its taxpayers will be "bankrupted" by the national debt always lurks in the shadows. How legitimate is that fear?

Ownership of the Debt

Figure 12.4 shows who owns the bonds the U.S. Treasury has issued. The largest bondholder is the U.S. government itself: *Federal agencies hold roughly 50 percent of all outstanding Treasury bonds.* The Federal Reserve System, an independent agency of the U.S. government, acquires Treasury bonds in its conduct of monetary policy (see Chapters 14 and 15). Other agencies of the U.S. government also purchase bonds. The Social Security Administration, for example, maintains a trust fund balance to cover any shortfall between monthly payroll tax receipts and retirement benefits. Most of that balance is held in the form of interest-bearing Treasury bonds. Thus, one arm of the federal government (the U.S. Treasury) owes another arm (the U.S. Social Security Administration) a significant part of the national debt. Because Social Security has been accumulating huge annual reserves in recent years, it's now the largest single holder of the national debt.

State and local governments hold another 8 percent of the national debt. This debt, too, arises when state and local governments use their own budget surpluses to purchase interest-bearing Treasury bonds.

The general public owns *directly* only about 6 percent of the national debt. This private wealth is in the form of familiar U.S. savings bonds or other types of Treasury bonds. Even more private wealth is held *indirectly*. As Figure 12.4 shows, 22 percent of the national debt is held by banks, insurance companies, money-market funds, corporations, and other institutions. All this wealth is ultimately owned by the people who have deposits at the bank or in money market funds, who own stock in corporations, or who are insured by companies that hold Treasury bonds. Thus, *U.S. households hold nearly 30 percent of the national debt, either directly or indirectly.*

internal debt: U.S. government debt (Treasury bonds) held by U.S. households and institutions.

All the debt held by U.S. households, institutions, and government entities is referred to as **internal debt**. As Figure 12.4 illustrates, 80 percent of the national debt is internal. In other words, we owe most of the national debt to ourselves.

The remaining 20 percent of the national debt is held by foreign banks, corporations, households, and governments. U.S. Treasury bonds are attractive to global participants because of their relative security, the interest they pay, and the general acceptability of dollar-denominated assets in world trade. All the bonds held by foreign households and institutions is referred to as **external debt**.

external debt: U.S. government debt (Treasury bonds) held by foreign households and institutions.

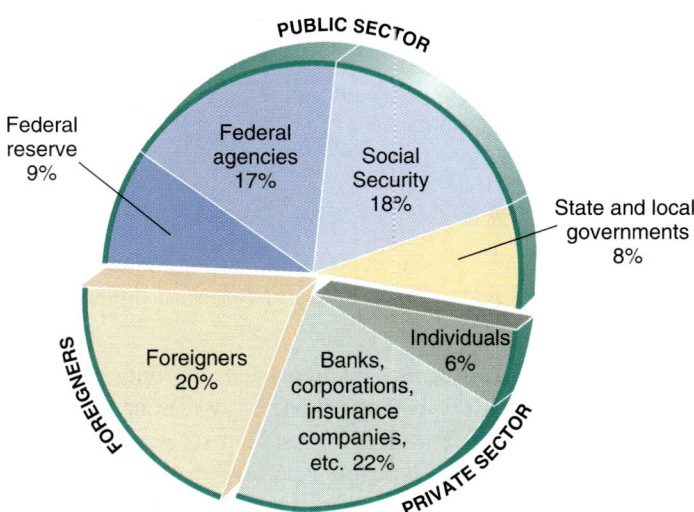

FIGURE 12.4
Debt Ownership

The bonds that create the national debt represent wealth that's owned by bondholders. Half of that wealth is held by the U.S. government itself. The private sector in the United States holds only 28 percent of the debt, and foreigners own about 20 percent.

Source: U.S. Treasury Department (2001 data).

BURDEN OF THE DEBT

It may be comforting to know that most of our national debt is owned internally, and much of it by the government itself. Figure 12.4 won't still the fears of most taxpayers, however, especially those who don't hold any Treasury bonds. From their perspective, the total debt still looks frightening.

How much of a "burden" the debt really represents isn't so evident. For nearly 30 years (1970–97), the federal government kept piling up more debt without apparent economic damage. As we saw earlier (Figure 12.3), deficits and debt stretched out over even longer periods in earlier decades.

How was the government able to pile debt upon debt? Quite simple: As debts have become due, the federal government has simply borrowed new funds to pay them off. New bonds have been issued to replace old bonds. This **refinancing** of the debt is a routine feature of the U.S. Treasury's debt management.

The ability of the U.S. Treasury to refinance its debt raises an intriguing question. What if the debt could be eternally refinanced? What if no one *ever* demanded to be paid off more than others were willing to lend Uncle Sam? Then the national debt would truly grow forever.

Two things are worrisome about this scenario. First, eternal refinancing seems like a chain letter that promises to make everyone rich. In this case, the chain requires that people hold ever-larger portions of their wealth in the form of Treasury bonds. People worry that the chain will be broken and that they'll be forced to repay all the outstanding debt. Parents worry that the scheme might break down in the next generation, unfairly burdening their own children or grandchildren (see cartoon).

Aside from its seeming implausibility, the notion of eternal refinancing seems to defy a basic maxim of economics, namely, that "there ain't no free lunch." Eternal refinancing makes it look as though government borrowing has no cost, as though federal spending financed by the national debt is really a free lunch.

There are two flaws in this way of thinking. The first relates to the interest charges that accompany debt. The second, and more important, oversight relates to the real economic costs of government activity.

Refinancing

refinancing: The issuance of new debt in payment of debt issued earlier.

"What's this I hear about you adults mortgaging my future?"

Analysis: The fear that present generations are passing the debt burden to future generations is exaggerated.

Debt Service

debt service: The interest required to be paid each year on outstanding debt.

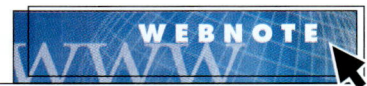

Find out about the U.S. Treasury government bills, notes, and bonds at www.publicdebt.treas.gov/of/ofaucrt.htm.

With over $5 trillion in accumulated debt, the U.S. government must make enormous interest payments every year. **Debt service** refers to these annual interest payments. In FY 2001, the U.S. Treasury paid over $200 billion in interest charges. These interest payments are a large and uncontrollable component of the federal budget. As such, they force the government to reduce outlays for other purposes or to finance a larger budget each year. In this respect, *interest payments restrict the government's ability to balance the budget or fund other public-sector activities.*

Although the debt-servicing requirements may pinch Uncle Sam's spending purse, the real economic consequences of interest payments are less evident. Who gets the interest payments? What economic resources are absorbed by those payments?

As noted, most of the nation's outstanding debt is internal—that is, owned by domestic households and institutions. Therefore, most interest payments are made to people and institutions within the United States. *Most debt servicing is simply a redistribution of income from taxpayers to bondholders.* In many cases, the taxpayer and bondholder are the same person. In all cases, however, the income that leaks from the circular flow in the form of taxes to pay for debt servicing returns to the circular flow as interest payments. Total income is unchanged. Thus, debt servicing may not have any direct effect on aggregate demand.

Debt servicing also has little impact on the real resources of the economy. The collection of additional taxes and the processing of interest payments require the use of some land, labor, and capital. But the value of the resources used for the processing of debt service is trivial—a tiny fraction of the interest payments themselves. This means that *interest payments themselves have virtually no direct opportunity cost.* The amount of goods and services available for other purposes is virtually unchanged as a result of debt servicing.

Opportunity Costs

If debt servicing absorbs few economic resources, can we conclude that the national debt really does represent a free lunch? Unfortunately not. But the concept of opportunity cost does provide a major clue about the true burden of the debt and who bears it.

Opportunity costs are incurred only when real resources (factors of production) are used. The amount of that cost is measured by the other goods and services that could have been produced with those resources, but weren't. As noted earlier, the *process* of debt servicing absorbs few resources and so has negligible opportunity cost. To understand the true burden of the national debt, we have to look at what that debt financed. *The true burden of the debt is the opportunity cost of the activities financed by the debt.* To assess that burden, we need to ask what the government did with the borrowed funds.

Government Purchases. Suppose Congress decides to upgrade our naval forces and borrows $10 billion for that purpose. What's the opportunity cost of that decision? The economic cost of the fleet upgrade is measured by the goods and services forgone in order to build more ships. The labor, land, and capital used to upgrade the fleet can't be used to produce something else. We give up the opportunity to produce another $10 billion worth of private goods and services when Congress upgrades the fleet.

The economic cost of the naval buildup is unaffected by the method of government finance. Whether the government borrows $10 billion or increases taxes by that amount, the forgone civilian output will still be $10 billion. *The opportunity cost of government purchases is the true burden of government activity, however financed.* The decision to finance such activity with debt rather than taxes doesn't materially alter that cost.

Transfer Payments. Suppose the government uses debt financing to pay for increased transfer payments rather than the purchase of real goods and services. What would be the burden of debt in this case?

Note first that transfer payments entail few real costs. Income transfers entail a redistribution of income from the taxpayer to the transfer recipient. The only direct costs of those transfer payments are the land, labor, and capital involved in the administrative process of making that transfer. Those direct costs are so trivial that they can be ignored. Whatever changes in output or prices occur because of transfer payments result from *indirect* behavioral responses. If taxpayers or transfer recipients respond to transfers by working, saving, or investing less, the economy may suffer. These important *indirect* effects must be distinguished from the *direct* cost of the transfers, which are minimal. As a result, the amount of income transferred isn't a meaningful measure of economic burden. Hence, the debt that originated in deficit-financed income transfers can't be viewed as a unique "burden" either.

The Real Trade-Offs

Although the national debt poses no special burden to the economy, the transactions it finances have a substantial impact on the basic questions of WHAT, HOW, and FOR WHOM to produce. The mix of output is influenced by how much deficit spending the government undertakes. The funds obtained by borrowing allow the federal government to bid for scarce resources. Private investors and consumers will have less access to loanable funds and be less able to acquire incomes or goods. The larger the deficit, the more the private sector gets squeezed. Hence, deficit financing allows the government to obtain more resources and change the mix of output. In general, ***deficit financing tends to change the mix of output in the direction of more public-sector goods.***

As noted earlier, the deficits of the 1980s helped finance a substantial military buildup. The same result could have been financed with higher taxes. Taxes are more visible and always unpopular, however. By borrowing rather than taxing, the federal government's claim on scarce resources is less apparent. Either financing method allows the public sector to expand at the expense of the private sector. This resource reallocation reveals the true burden of the debt: ***The burden of the debt is really the opportunity cost (crowding out) of deficit-financed government activity.*** How large that burden is depends on how many unemployed resources are available and the behavioral responses of consumers and investors to increased government activity.

Notice also *when* that cost is incurred. If the military is upgraded this year, then the opportunity cost is incurred this year. It's only while resources are actually being used by the military that we give up the opportunity to use them elsewhere. Opportunity costs are incurred at the time a government activity takes place, not when the resultant debt is paid. In other words, ***the primary burden of the debt is incurred when the debt-financed activity takes place.***

If the entire military buildup is completed this year, what costs are borne next year? None. The land, labor, and capital available next year can be used for whatever purposes are then desired. Once the military buildup is completed, no further resources are allocated to that purpose. The real costs of government projects can't be postponed until a later year. In other words, the real burden of the debt can't be passed on to future generations. On the contrary, future generations will benefit from the sacrifices made today to build ships, parks, highways, dams, and other public-sector projects. Future taxpayers will be able to *use* these projects without incurring the opportunity costs of their construction.

Economic Growth. Although future generations may benefit from current government spending, they may also be adversely affected by today's opportunity costs. Of particular concern is the possibility that government deficits might crowd out private investment. Investment is essential to enlarging our production possibilities and attaining higher living standards in the future. If federal deficits and debt-servicing requirements crowd our private investment, the rate of economic growth will slow, leaving future generations with less productive capacity than they would otherwise have. Thus, ***if debt-financed government spending crowds out private investment, future generations will bear some of the debt burden.*** Their burden will take the form of smaller-than-anticipated productive capacity.

optimal mix of output: The most desirable combination of output attainable with existing resources, technology, and social values.

There's no certainty that such crowding out will occur. Also, any reduction in private investment may be offset by public works (such as highways, schools, defense systems) that benefit future generations. So future generations may not suffer a net loss in welfare even if the national debt slows private investment and economic growth. From this perspective, *the whole debate about the burden of the debt is really an argument over the* **optimal mix of output.** If we permit more deficit spending, we're promoting more public-sector activity. On the other hand, limits on deficit financing curtail growth of the public sector. Battles over deficits and debts are a proxy for the more fundamental issue of private versus public spending.

Repayment. All this sounds a little too neat. Won't future generations have to pay interest on the debts we incur today? And might they even have to pay off some of the debt?

We've already observed that the collection of taxes and processing of interest payments absorb relatively few resources. Hence, the mechanisms of repayment entail little burden.

Notice also who *receives* future interest payments. When we die, we leave behind not only the national debt but also the bonds that represent ownership of that debt. Hence, future grandchildren will be both taxpayers *and* bondholders. If interest payments are made 30 years from today, only people who are alive and holding bonds at that time will receive interest payments. *Future interest payments entail a redistribution of income among taxpayers and bondholders living in the future.*

The same kind of redistribution occurs if and when our grandchildren decide to pay off the debt. Tax revenues will be used to pay off the debt. The debt payments will go to people then holding Treasury bonds. The entire redistribution will occur among people living in the future.

EXTERNAL DEBT

The nature of opportunity costs makes it difficult but not impossible to pass the debt burden on to future generations. The exception is the case of external debt.

No Crowding Out

When we borrow funds from abroad, we increase our ability to consume, invest, and finance government activity. In effect, other nations are lending us the income necessary to *import* more goods. If we can buy imports with borrowed funds (without offsetting exports), our real income will exceed our production possibilities. As Figure 12.5 illustrates, external borrowing allows us to enjoy a mix of output that lies *outside* our production possibilities curve. Specifically, *external financing allows us to get more public-sector goods without cutting back on private-sector production.* When we use external debt to finance government spending, we move from point *a* to point *d* in Figure 12.5. Imported goods and services eliminate the need to cut back on private-sector activity, a cutback that would otherwise force us to point *b* (see Figure 12.2). External financing eliminates this opportunity cost. The move from point *a* to point *d* reflects the additional imports financed by external debt.[3]

External financing appears to offer the proverbial free lunch. It would be a free lunch if foreign lenders were willing to accumulate U.S. Treasury bonds forever. They would then own stacks of paper (Treasury bonds), and we'd consume some of their output (our imports) each year. *As long as outsiders are willing to hold U.S. bonds, external*

---

[3] The imports needn't be public-sector goods. If enough consumer goods are imported to maintain private-sector activity at the rate h_1, the domestic resources idled by imports can be used to increase public-sector production.

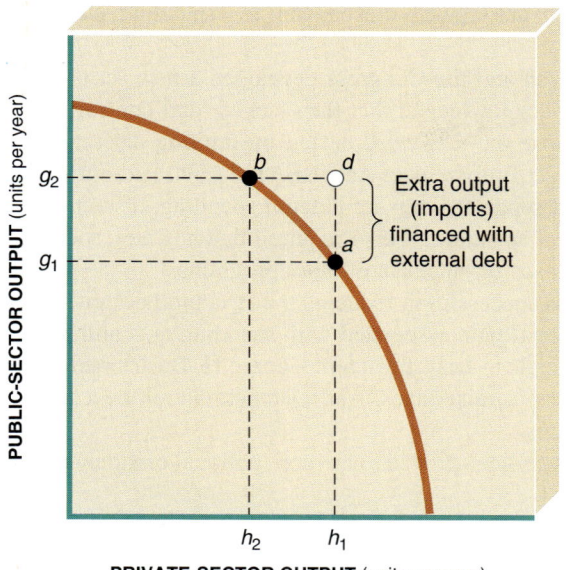

FIGURE 12.5
External Financing

A closed economy must forsake some private-sector output in order to increase public-sector output (see Figure 12.2). External financing temporarily eliminates that opportunity cost. Instead of having to move from *a* to *b*, external borrowing allows us to move from *a* to *d*. At point *d* we have more public output and no less private output.

financing imposes no real cost. No goods or services are given up to pay for the additional output received.

Foreign investors may not be willing to hold U.S. bonds indefinitely. At some point they'll want to collect their bills. To do this, they'll cash in (sell) their bonds, then use the proceeds to buy U.S. goods and services. When this happens, the United States will be *exporting* goods and services to pay off its debts. Recall that the external debt was used to acquire imported goods and services. Hence, *external debt must be repaid with exports of real goods and services.*

DEFICIT AND DEBT LIMITS

Although external and internal debts pose very different problems, most policy discussions overlook these distinctions. In policy debates, the aggregate size of the national debt is usually the only concern. The key policy questions are whether and how to limit or reduce the national debt.

The only way to stop the growth of the national debt is to eliminate the budget deficits that create debt. The first step in debt reduction, therefore, is a balanced annual budget. A balanced budget will at least stop the debt from growing further. **Deficit ceilings** are explicit limitations on the size of the annual budget deficit. A deficit ceiling of zero compels a balanced budget.

The Balanced Budget and Emergency Deficit Control Act of 1985—popularly referred to as the Gramm-Rudman-Hollings Act—was the first explicit attempt to force the federal budget into balance. The essence of the Gramm-Rudman Act was simple:

- First, it set a lower ceiling on each year's deficit, until budget balance was achieved.
- Second, it called for automatic cutbacks in spending if Congress failed to keep the deficit below the ceiling.

The original Gramm-Rudman law required Congress to pare the deficit from over $200 billion in FY 1985 to zero (a balanced budget) by 1991. But Congress wasn't willing to cut spending and increase taxes enough to meet those targets. And the

Repayment

Deficit Ceilings

deficit ceiling: An explicit, legislated limitation on the size of the budget deficit.

Supreme Court declared that the "automatic" mechanism for spending cuts was unconstitutional.

In 1990, President George H. Bush and the Congress developed a new set of rules for reducing the deficit. They first acknowledged that they lacked total control of the deficit. At best, Congress could close the *structural* deficit by limiting discretionary spending or raising taxes. The Budget Enforcement Act (BEA) of 1990 laid out a plan for doing exactly this. The BEA set separate limits on defense spending, discretionary domestic spending, and international spending. It also required that any new spending initiative be offset with increased taxes or cutbacks in other programs.

The Budget Enforcement Act was successful in reducing the structural deficit somewhat (see Table 12.1). But the political pain associated with spending cuts and higher taxes was too great for elected officials to bear. President George H. Bush's reelection bid was damaged by his willingness to raise taxes. And Democrats took heat for reducing the growth of social programs.

Soon thereafter, legislated deficit ceilings proved to be more political ornaments than binding budget mandates.

Debt Ceilings

debt ceiling: An explicit, legislated limit on the amount of outstanding national debt.

Explicit **debt ceilings** are another mechanism for forcing Congress to adopt specific fiscal policies. A debt ceiling can be used either to stop the accumulation of debt or to force the federal government to start *reducing* the accumulated national debt. In an era of budget surpluses, a declining debt ceiling can also force Congress to use some of the current surplus to pay off old debt (the fourth policy option on page 246). In 2001, several bills were introduced in the U.S. Congress for this purpose. In the end, however,

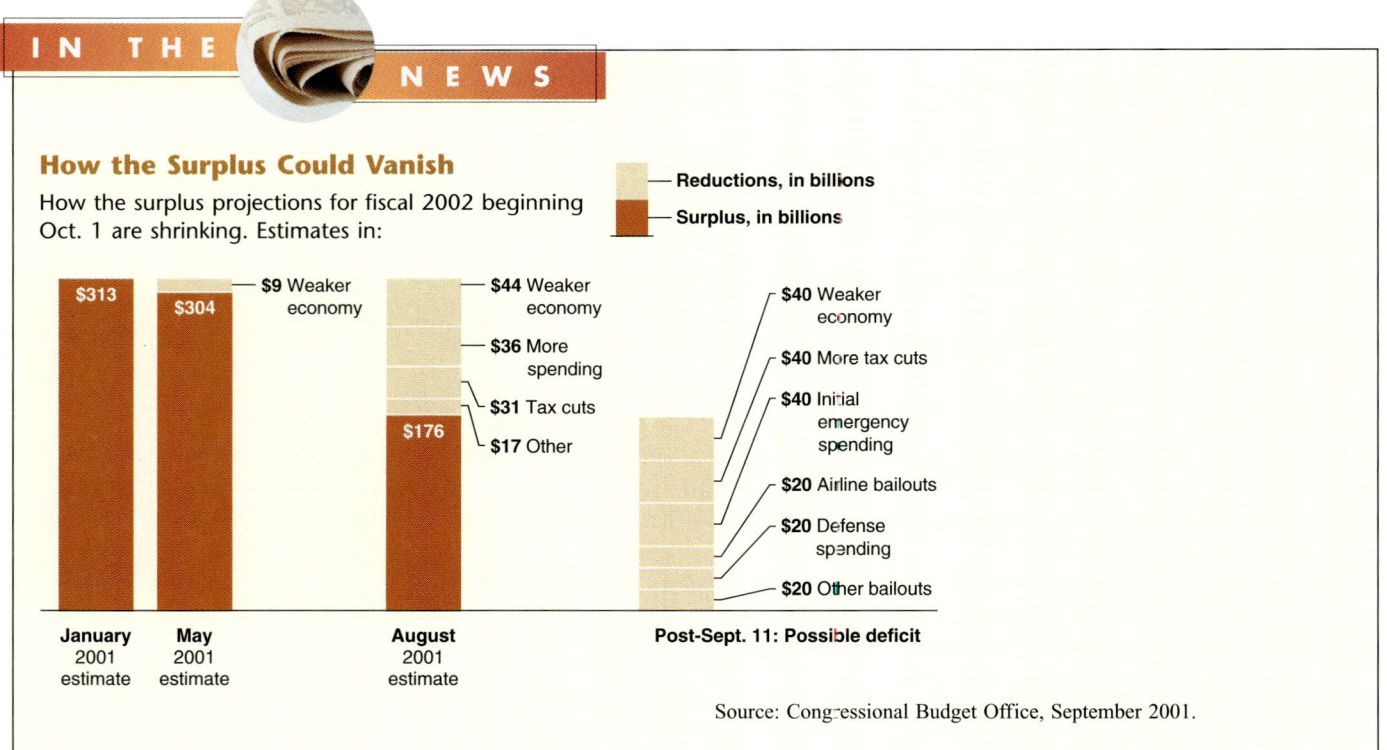

IN THE NEWS

How the Surplus Could Vanish

How the surplus projections for fiscal 2002 beginning Oct. 1 are shrinking. Estimates in:

- Reductions, in billions
- Surplus, in billions

January 2001 estimate: $313

May 2001 estimate: $304
- $9 Weaker economy

August 2001 estimate: $176
- $44 Weaker economy
- $36 More spending
- $31 Tax cuts
- $17 Other

Post-Sept. 11: Possible deficit
- $40 Weaker economy
- $40 More tax cuts
- $40 Initial emergency spending
- $20 Airline bailouts
- $20 Defense spending
- $20 Other bailouts

Source: Congressional Budget Office, September 2001.

Analysis: The size of a projected surplus depends on cyclical and structural forces. A tax cut (fiscal stimulus) and recession (cyclical setback) sharply reduced the FY 2001 budget surplus. Spending and tax-cut responses to the September 11, 2001 terrorist attacks, combined with a continuing recession, reduced the FY 2002 surplus even further.

President George W. Bush and congressional Democrats merely vowed to reduce the publicly held debt by the amount of the Social Security Trust Fund surplus. That would leave the *total* national debt unchanged but reduce the publicly held share of that debt. Even that vow was broken, however, when an abrupt slowdown of the economy and emergency spending in response to the September 11 terrorist attacks sharply reduced the size of projected surpluses (see News). *Like deficit ceilings, debt ceilings are really just political mechanisms for forging compromises on how best to use budget surpluses or deficits.*

For a discussion of deficits and deficit-reduction efforts, visit the U.S. Congressional Budget Office at www.cbo.gov.

THE ECONOMY TOMORROW

The Social Security Trust Fund has been a major source of funding for the federal government for over 20 years. Since 1985, the Trust Fund has collected more payroll (FICA) taxes each year than it has paid out in retirement benefits. As we noted already, all of those surpluses have been "invested" in Treasury securities, making the Social Security Trust Fund the U.S. Treasury's largest creditor. The Trust Fund now holds more than $1 trillion of Treasury securities and is still accumulating more. Between 2002 and 2014, the Trust Fund will acquire another $2 trillion in Treasury securities.

"Saving Social Security"

The persistent surpluses in the Social Security Trust Fund are largely the result of aging Baby Boomers. In the 15 years after World War II ended, birthrates soared. These Baby Boomers are now in their peak earning years (45–60) and paying lots of payroll taxes. This keeps the Social Security Trust Fund flush with cash.

Aging Baby Boomers

As we peer into the economy tomorrow, however, the fiscal outlook is not so bright. The Baby Boomers are fast approaching retirement age. When they do retire, the Baby Boomers will throw the budget of the Social Security Trust Fund out of whack. Today, there are 3.3 active (tax-paying) workers for every retiree. By 2015, that worker-retiree ratio will slip to 2.7. By 2030, there'll be only 2 workers for every retiree (see Table 12.5). By then, the Trust Fund payroll-tax collections will be a lot smaller than the benefit promises made to retired Baby Boomers.

In fact, the Trust Fund balance shifts from annual surpluses to annual deficits as soon as 2014. After that, Social Security will be able to pay promised benefits only if (1) the U.S. Treasury pays all interest due on bonds held by the Trust Fund and, ultimately, (2) the U.S. Treasury redeems the $3 trillion-plus of bonds the Trust Fund will then be holding. This is what scares aging Baby Boomers (and should worry you!).

Social Security Deficits

The Baby Boomers wonder where the Treasury is going to get the funds needed to repay the Social Security Trust Fund. There really aren't many options. *To pay back Social Security loans, the Congress will have to raise future taxes significantly or make substantial cuts in other (non–Social Security) programs.* Given the political pain of such options, Congress has chosen to "save Social Security" by merely paying off more of the *publicly held* debt.

Year	Workers per Beneficiary	Year	Workers per Beneficiary
1950	16.5	2000	3.4
1960	5.1	2015	2.7
1970	3.7	2030	2.0

Source: U.S. Social Security Administration.

TABLE 12.5
Changing Worker-Retiree Ratios
Fifty years ago there were over 16 tax-paying workers for every retiree. Today there are only 3.3, and the ratio slips below 3 when the Baby Boomers start retiring. This demographic change will convert Social Security surpluses into deficits, causing future budget problems.

FIGURE 12.6
Alternative Surplus Projections

Projections of future budget surpluses depend on the outlook for GDP growth. In the Congressional Budget Office's "optimistic" projections, GDP grows 3.4–3.5 percent a year. The "pessimist" outlook sees 2.0–2.3 percent growth; the middle "baseline" is 3.0 percent growth. All of these projections, made in January 2001, turned out to be overly optimistic.

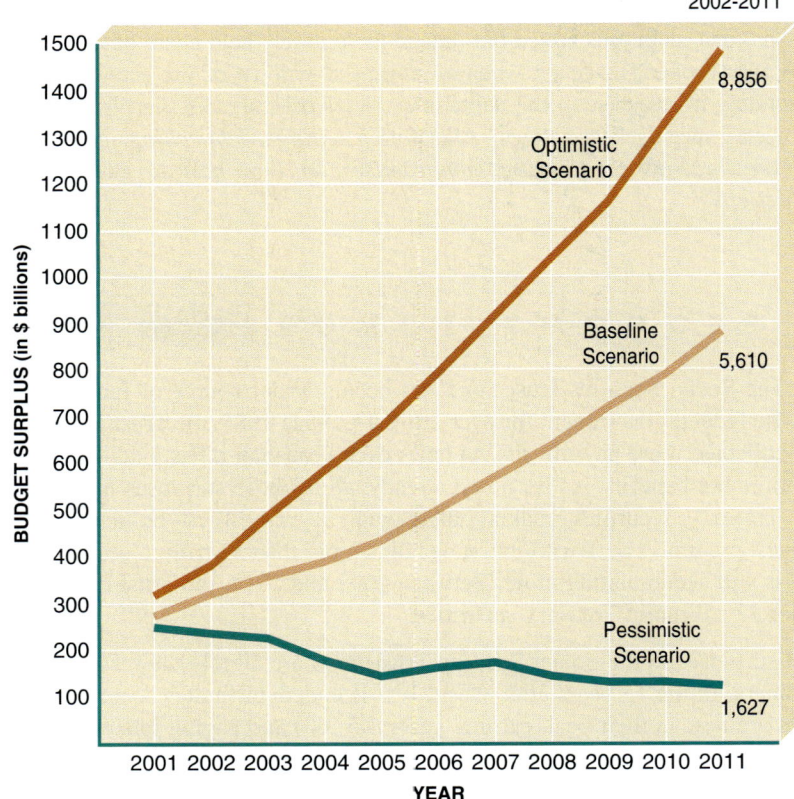

In doing so, the government hopes it will be easier to borrow more funds from the public later, when the Social Security surplus dries up. In the meantime, "saving Social Security" entails no more than accumulating more Treasury IOUs in the Social Security Trust Fund (what Congress calls the "*lock box*"). Paying back that debt will severely constrain discretionary fiscal policy in the economy tomorrow. If GDP growth (see Figure 12.6) slows, it will be even tougher to fund all promised Social Security benefits and existing non–Social Security programs.

SUMMARY

- Budget imbalances result from both discretionary fiscal policy (structural deficits and surpluses) and cyclical changes in the economy (cyclical deficits and surpluses).
- Fiscal restraint is measured by the reduction in the structural deficit; fiscal stimulus occurs when the structural deficit increases.
- Automatic stabilizers increase federal spending and reduce tax revenues during recessions. When the economy expands, they have the reverse effect, thereby shrinking the cyclical deficit.
- Deficit financing of government expenditure may crowd out private investment and consumption. The risk of crowding out increases as the economy approaches full employment. If investment becomes the opportunity cost of increased government spending, economic growth may slow.
- Crowding in refers to the increase in private-sector output made possible by a decline in government borrowing.
- Each year's deficit adds to the national debt. The national debt grew sporadically until World War II and then skyrocketed. A string of huge deficits in the 1980s and 1990s increased the national debt to over $5 trillion.
- Budget surpluses may be used to finance tax cuts or more government spending, or used to reduce accumulated national debt.
- Every dollar of national debt represents a dollar of assets to the people who hold U.S. Treasury bonds. Most U.S. bonds are held by government agencies, U.S. households, and U.S. banks, insurance companies, and other institutions.
- The real burden of the debt is the opportunity cost of the activities financed by the debt. That cost is borne at the

- time the deficit-financed activity takes place. The benefits of debt-financed activity may extend into the future.
- External debt permits the public sector to expand without reducing private-sector output. External debt also makes it possible to shift some of the real debt burden on to future generations.
- Deficit and debt ceilings are largely symbolic efforts to force consideration of real trade-offs, to restrain government spending, and to change the mix of output.
- The coming retirement of the Baby Boomers (born 1946–60) will transform Social Security surpluses into deficits, imposing severe constraints on future fiscal policy.

Key Terms

fiscal policy
deficit spending
budget deficit
budget surplus
fiscal year (FY)
discretionary fiscal spending
fiscal restraint
fiscal stimulus
income transfers

automatic stabilizer
cyclical deficit
structural deficit
crowding out
opportunity cost
crowding in
Treasury bonds
national debt
liability

asset
internal debt
external debt
refinancing
debt service
optimal mix of output
deficit ceiling
debt ceiling

Questions for Discussion

1. Who paid for the Revolutionary War? Did the deficit financing initiated by the Continental Congress pass the cost of the war on to future generations?
2. In what ways do future generations benefit from this generation's deficit spending? Cite three examples.
3. What's considered "too much" debt or "too large" a deficit? Are you able to provide any guidelines for deficit or debt ceilings?
4. If deficit spending "crowds out" some private investment, could future generations be worse off? If external financing eliminates crowding out, are future generations thereby protected?
5. A constitutional amendment has been proposed that would require Congress to balance the budget each year. Is it possible to balance the budget each year? Is it desirable?
6. What should the government do with a budget surplus?
7. By how much did defense spending increase in 1940 to 1944? (See back endpapers of this book.) What was crowded out?
8. How long would it take to pay off the national debt? How would the economy be affected?
9. Which of the following options do you favor for resolving future Social Security deficits? What are the advantages and disadvantages of each option? (a) cutting Social Security benefits, (b) raising payroll taxes, (c) cutting non–Social Security programs, (d) raising income taxes.

Web Activities

1. Summarize liberal and conservative views on a constitutional requirement to balance the federal budget. For the liberal position, go to www.epn.org. For the conservative position, go to www.concordcoalition.org or www.ncpa.org/pd/budget/budget-1.html.
2. What is the future of Social Security? Currently, Social Security is the largest holder of the national debt, a surplus that will increase and then fall as baby boomers retire. Visit the Cato Institute at www.socialsecurity.org/pubs/ssps/ssp-20es.html for a summary of the problem and what could be done. Is privatization of the Social Security System a good idea? Which solution makes the most sense?
3. Log on to www.whitehouse.gov/omb/budget/fy2002/budiv_3.html to find what the current projections are for a Social Security surplus (deficit) this fiscal year. How does this change in the next five years? What does this indicate about the future health of the Social Security System?

ALERT! THE ACCOMPANYING STUDENT PROBLEM SET CONTAINS NUMERICAL AND GRAPHING PROBLEMS FOR THIS CHAPTER

PART 5

Monetary Policy Options

Monetary policy tries to alter macro outcomes by managing the amount of money available in the economy. By changing the money supply and/or interest rates, monetary policy seeks to shift aggregate demand in the desired direction. Chapters 13 through 15 illustrate how this policy lever works.

CHAPTER 13

Money and Banks

Sophocles, the ancient Greek playwright, had very strong opinions about the role of money. As he saw it, "Of evils upon earth, the worst is money. It is money that sacks cities, and drives men forth from hearth and home; warps and seduces native intelligence, and breeds a habit of dishonesty."

In modern times, people may still be seduced by the lure of money and fashion their lives around its pursuit. Nevertheless, it's hard to imagine an economy functioning without money. Money affects not only morals and ideals but also the way an economy works.

This and the following two chapters examine the role of money in the economy today. We begin with a very simple question:

- What is money?

As we'll discover, money isn't exactly what you might think it is. There's a lot more money in the economy than there is cash. And there's a lot more income around than money. So money is something quite different from either cash or income. Once we've established the characteristics of money, we go on to ask:

- How is money created?
- What role do banks play in the circular flow of income and spending?

In Chapter 14 we look at how the Federal Reserve System controls the amount of money created. In Chapter 15 we look at the implications for monetary policy, another policy lever in our basic macro model.

WHAT IS "MONEY"?

To appreciate the significance of money for a modern economy, imagine for a moment that there were no such thing as money. How would you get something for breakfast? If you wanted eggs for breakfast, you'd have to tend your own chickens or go see Farmer Brown. But how would you pay Farmer Brown for his eggs? Without money, you'd have to offer him some goods or services that he could use. In other words, you'd have to engage in primitive **barter**—the direct exchange of one good for another—in order to get eggs for breakfast. You'd get those eggs only if Farmer Brown happened to want the particular goods or services you had to offer.

WORLD VIEW

The Cashless Society

Bartering Chokes Russian Economy

NARO-FOMINSK, RUSSIA—Natalya Karpova, a supervisor at a fabric factory here on the outskirts of Moscow, heard good news a couple of weeks ago. Three carloads of concrete utility poles had arrived at the train station.

This was a matter of utmost importance to Karpova, because her factory was a year behind on its electric bill and had no cash on hand. The electric company agreed to accept utility poles instead, but how to pay for utility poles with no rubles?

Simple. First, her factory shipped fabric 200 miles to a sewing factory in Nizhny Novgorod. In exchange for the fabric, that factory sewed shirts for the security guards who work at a nearby automobile manufacturer. In exchange for the shirts, the auto factory shipped a car and truck to a concrete plant. In exchange for the vehicles, the concrete plant delivered the poles to the electric company.

Thus did the Narfomsholk fabric factory pay for the power to run its dye machines.

But only for a while. "Now they want a steam shovel," said Karpova, with a little sigh.

This is how Karpova's factory and much of Russia's industry survives these days: barter. By some estimates, it accounts for almost three-fourths of all transactions.

Barter is poisoning the development of capitalism in Russia because it consumes huge amounts of time that would be better spent producing goods.

Many workers have no expectation of a real paycheck. Unpaid wages now amount to an estimated $11 billion. Instead of money, the workers are stuck with whatever the factory or farm is handing out, usually what it produces. The practice is so common now that only the more bizarre substitutes for wages draw notice, such as bras or coffins.

—Sharon LaFraniere

Source: *Washington Post*, September 3, 1998. © 1998, The Washington Post. Reprinted with permission. www.washingtonpost.com

Analysis: When the Russian ruble lost its value, people would no longer accept it in payment. Market transactions had to be bartered, a clumsy and inefficient process.

The use of money greatly simplifies market transactions. It's a lot easier to exchange money for eggs at the supermarket than to go into the country and barter with farmers every time you crave some eggs. Our ability to use money in market transactions, however, depends on the grocer's willingness to accept money as a *medium of exchange*. The grocer sells eggs for money only because he can use the same money to pay his help and buy the goods he himself desires. He too can exchange money for goods and services.

barter: The direct exchange of one good for another, without the use of money.

Without money, the process of acquiring goods and services would be much more difficult and time-consuming. This was evident when the value of the Russian ruble plummeted. Trading goods for Farmer Brown's eggs seems simple compared to the complicated barter deals Russian factories had to negotiate when paper money was no longer accepted (see World View). And Russian workers certainly would've preferred to be paid in cash rather than in bras and coffins.

THE MONEY SUPPLY

Although markets can't function well without money, they can get along without *dollars*. In the early days of colonial America, there were no U.S. dollars; a lot of business was conducted with Spanish and Portuguese gold coins. Later, people used Indian wampum, then tobacco, grain, fish, and furs as mediums of exchange. Throughout the colonies, gunpowder and bullets were frequently used for small change. These forms of money weren't as convenient as U.S. dollars, but they did the job.

This historical perspective on money highlights its essential characteristics. *Anything that serves all the following purposes can be thought of as money:*

- **Medium of exchange:** is accepted as payment for goods and services (and debts).
- **Store of value:** can be held for future purchases.
- **Standard of value:** serves as a yardstick for measuring the prices of goods and services.

Many Types of Money

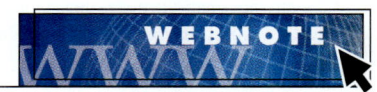

For a brief history of coins and to learn how coins are made, visit the U.S. mint at www.usmint.gov.

All the items used during the colonial days satisfied these conditions and were thus properly regarded as money.

After the colonies became an independent nation, the U.S. Constitution prohibited the federal government from issuing paper money. Money was instead issued by state-chartered banks. Between 1789 and 1865, over 30,000 different paper bills were issued by 1,600 banks in 34 states. People often preferred to get paid in gold, silver, or other commodities rather than in one of these uncertain currencies.

The first paper money the federal government issued consisted of $10 million worth of "greenbacks," printed in 1861 to finance the Civil War. The National Banking Act of 1863 gave the federal government permanent authority to issue money.

Modern Concepts

The "greenbacks" we carry around today aren't the only form of "money" we use. Most people realize this when they offer to pay for goods with a check rather than cash. People do distinguish between "cash" and "money," and for good reason. The "money" you have in a checking account can be used to buy goods and services or to pay debts, or it can be retained for future use. In these respects, your checking account balance is as much a part of your "money" as are the coins and dollars in your pocket or purse. You can access your balance by writing a check or using an ATM or debit card. As the World View documents, most U.S. households still prefer the old-fashioned method of writing a check. Checks are more convenient than cash because they eliminate trips to the bank. Checks are also safer: Lost or stolen cash is gone forever; checkbooks and credit cards are easily replaced at little or no cost. We might use checks even more frequently if everyone accepted them.

There's nothing unique about cash, then, insofar as the market is concerned. **Checking accounts can and do perform the same market functions as cash.** Accordingly, we must include checking account balances in our concept of **money**. The essence of money isn't its taste, color, or feel but, rather, its ability to purchase goods and services.

money: Anything generally accepted as a medium of exchange.

WORLD VIEW

The Check Is Still in the Mail

Checks Are King in the U.S. ...
Volume of transactions for various bill payment methods

PAYMENT METHOD	VOLUME (billions)	% OF TOTAL
Paper checks	65.0	75.0%
Credit cards	16.0	19.0
Electronic[1]	3.0	3.5
Debit cards	2.6	3.0
Wire transfers	0.1	0

[1]Mostly automatic deposit and automatic bill payer
Note: Figures may not add due to rounding

But Not Elsewhere
Percentage of non-check payment transactions per person

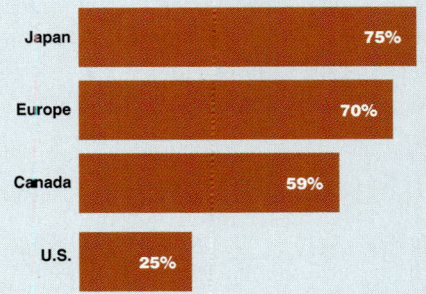

- Japan: 75%
- Europe: 70%
- Canada: 59%
- U.S.: 25%

Source: Bank for International Settlements

Source: *Wall Street Journal*, November 24, 1998. Reprinted by permission of The *Wall Street Journal*. © 1998, Dow Jones & Company, Inc. All Rights Reserved Worldwide. www.wsj.com

Analysis: Paper checks are still the preferred form of payment for U.S. households. Checks are also used to pay credit card balances.

Credit cards are another popular medium of exchange. People use credit cards for about one-third of all purchases over $100. This use is not sufficient, however, to qualify credit cards as a form of "money." Credit card balances must be paid by check or cash. The same holds true for balances in online electronic credit accounts ("e-cash"). Electronic purchases on the Internet or online services are ultimately paid by withdrawals from a bank account (by check or computer). Online payment mechanisms and credit cards are a payment *service,* not a final form of payment (credit card companies charge fees and interest for this service). The cards themselves are not a store of value, in contrast to cash or bank account balances.

The Diversity of Bank Accounts. To determine how much money is available to purchase goods and services, we need to count up all our coins and currency—as well as our bank account balances. This effort is complicated by the variety of bank accounts people have. In addition to simple no-interest checking accounts at full-service banks, people have bank accounts that pay interest, offer automatic transfers, require minimum holding periods, offer overdraft protection, or limit the number of checks that can be written. People also have "bank" accounts in credit unions, brokerage houses, and other nontraditional financial institutions.

Although all bank account balances can be spent, they're not all used the same way. People use regular checking accounts all the time to pay bills or make purchases. But consumers can't write checks on most savings accounts. And few people want to cash in a certificate of deposit just to go to the movies. Hence, *some bank accounts are better substitutes for cash than others.*

Several different measures of money have been developed to accommodate the diversity of bank accounts and other payment mechanisms. The narrowest definition of the **money supply** is designated **M1,** *which includes*

- *Currency in circulation*
- *Transactions account balances*
- *Traveler's checks*

As Figure 13.1 indicates, the largest component of this basic money supply (M1) is **transactions account** balances, which are the balances in bank accounts that are read-

M1: Cash and Transactions Accounts

money supply: (M1) Currency held by the public, plus balances in transactions accounts.

transactions account: A bank account that permits direct payment to a third party, for example, with a check.

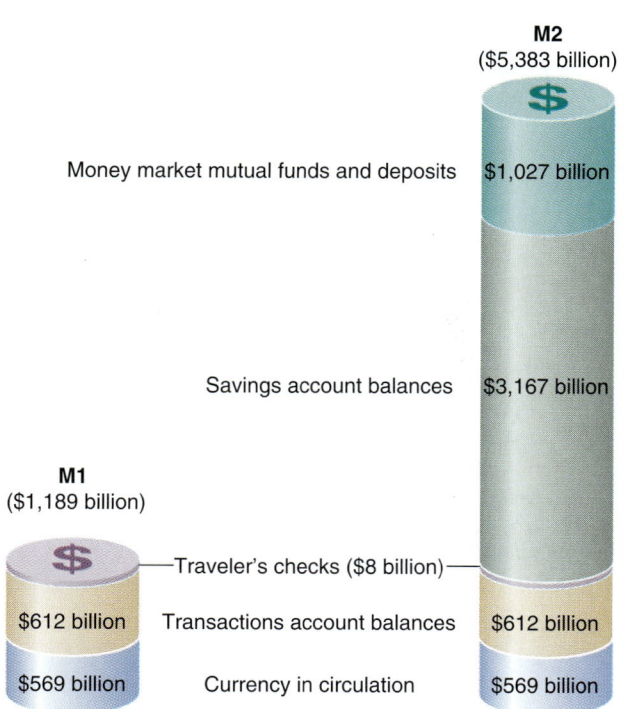

FIGURE 13.1

Composition of the Money Supply

Cash is a small part of the money supply. People also have easy access to transactions account balances and various savings account balances that are counted in measures of the money supply (M1 and M2). Because people hold so much money in money market mutual funds and savings (time-deposit) accounts, M2 is nearly five times larger than M1.

Source: Federal Reserve (September 2001 data).

ily accessed by check. Most people refer to these simply as "checking accounts." The term "transactions account" is broader, however, including NOW accounts, ATS accounts, credit union share drafts, and demand deposits at mutual savings banks. *The distinguishing feature of all transactions accounts is that they permit direct payment to a third party (by check or debit card),* without requiring a trip to the bank to make a special withdrawal. Because of this feature, transactions accounts are the readiest substitutes for cash in market transactions. Traveler's checks issued by nonbank firms such as American Express can also be used directly in market transactions, just like good old-fashioned cash.

Transactions accounts aren't the only substitute for cash. People can and do dip into savings accounts on occasion. People sometimes even cash in their certificates of deposit in order to buy something, despite the interest penalty associated with early withdrawal. And banks have made it easy to transfer funds from one type of account to another. Savings accounts can be transformed into transactions accounts with a phone call or computer instruction, such as automatic overdraft protection. As a result, *savings account balances are almost as good a substitute for cash as transactions account balances.*

Another popular way of holding money is to buy shares of money market mutual funds. Deposits into money market mutual funds are pooled and used to purchase interest-bearing securities such as Treasury bills. The interest rates paid on these funds are typically higher than those paid by banks. Moreover, the deposits made into the funds can often be withdrawn immediately, just like those in transactions accounts. When interest rates are high, deposits move out of regular transactions accounts into these money market mutual funds in order to earn a higher return.

Additional measures of the money supply have been constructed to account for the possibility of using savings account balances, money market mutual funds, and various other deposits to finance everyday spending. The most widely watched money measure is **M2**, which includes all of M1 *plus* balances in savings accounts, money market mutual funds, and some CDs ("time deposits"). As Figure 13.1 shows, M2 is nearly five times as large as M1. Table 13.1 summarizes the content of these and two other measures of money.

WEBNOTE

Everything you want to know about currency can be found at www.frbatlanta.org/publica/brochure/fundfac/money.htm.

M2 money supply: M1 plus balances in most savings accounts and money market mutual funds.

TABLE 13.1
Alternative Measures of the Money Supply
Measures of the money supply are intended to gauge the extent of purchasing power held by consumers. But the extent of purchasing power depends on how accessible assets are and how often people use them. The various money supply measures reflect variations in the liquidity and accessibility of assets.

Measure	Components
M1	Currency in circulation outside of bank vaults
	Demand deposits at commercial banks
	NOW and ATS accounts
	Credit union share drafts
	Demand deposits at mutual savings banks
	Traveler's checks (nonbank)
M2	M1 plus:
	Savings accounts
	Time deposits of less than $100,000
	Money market mutual funds
M3	M2 plus:
	Time deposits larger than $100,000
	Repurchase agreements
	Overnight Eurodollars
L	M3 plus other liquid assets, for example:
	Treasury bills
	U.S. savings bonds
	Bankers' acceptances
	Term Eurodollars
	Commercial paper

Our concern about the specific nature of money stems from our broader interest in **aggregate demand.** What we want to know is how much purchasing power consumers have, since this will affect their ability to purchase goods and services. What we've observed, however, is that money isn't so easily defined. How much spending power people have depends not only on the number of coins in their pockets but also on their willingness to write checks, make trips to the bank, or convert other assets into cash.

In an increasingly complex financial system, the core concept of "money" isn't easy to pin down. Nevertheless, the official measures of the money supply (particularly M1 and M2) are fairly reliable benchmarks for gauging how much purchasing power market participants have.

> **aggregate demand:** The total quantity of output demanded at alternative price levels in a given time period, *ceteris paribus*.

CREATION OF MONEY

Once we've decided what money is, we still have to explain where it comes from. Part of the explanation is simple. Currency must be printed. Some nations use private printers for this purpose, but all U.S. currency is printed by the Bureau of Engraving and Printing in Washington, D.C. Coins come from the U.S. mints located in Philadelphia and Denver. As we observed in Figure 13.1, however, currency is a small fraction of our total money supply. So we need to look elsewhere for the origins of most money. Specifically, where do all the transactions accounts come from? How do people acquire transactions deposits? How does the total amount of such deposits—and therefore the money supply of the economy—change?

Deposit Creation

Most people assume that all transactions account balances come from cash deposits. But this isn't the case. Direct deposits of paychecks, for example, are carried out by computer, not by the movement of cash (see cartoon). Moreover, the employer who issues the paycheck probably didn't make any cash deposits. It's more likely that she covered those paychecks with customers' checks that she deposited or with loans granted by the bank itself.

The ability of banks to lend money opens up a whole new set of possibilities for creating money. **When a bank lends someone money, it simply credits that individual's bank account.** The money appears in an account just as it would with a cash deposit. And the owner of the account is free to spend that money as with any positive balance. Hence, *in making a loan, a bank effectively creates money because transactions account balances are counted as part of the money supply.*

To understand the origins of our money supply then, we must recognize two basic principles:

Analysis: People see very little of their money—most deposits and loans are computer entries in the banking system.

268 MONETARY POLICY OPTIONS

- Transactions account balances are a large portion of the money supply.
- Banks can create transactions account balances by making loans.

> **deposit creation:** The creation of transactions deposits by bank lending.

The following two sections examine this process of **deposit creation** more closely. We determine how banks actually create deposits and what forces might limit the process of deposit creation.

Bank Regulation. Banks' deposit-creation activities are regulated by the government. The most important agency in this regard is the Federal Reserve System. "The Fed" puts limits on the amount of bank lending, thereby controlling the basic money supply. We'll discuss the structure and functions of the Fed in the next chapter; here we focus on the process of deposit creation itself.

A Monopoly Bank

Table 13.2 documents that there are thousands of banks, of various sorts, in the United States. To understand how banks create money, however, we'll simplify reality greatly. We'll assume for the moment that there's only one bank in town, University Bank. Imagine also that you've been saving some of your income by putting loose change into a piggy bank. Now, after months of saving, you break the bank and discover that your thrift has yielded $100. You immediately deposit this money in a new checking account at University Bank. How will this deposit affect the money supply?

Your initial deposit will have no immediate effect on the money supply. The coins in your piggy bank were already counted as part of the money supply (M1 and M2) because they represented cash held by the public. *When you deposit cash or coins in a bank, you're simply changing the composition of the money supply.* The public (you) now holds $100 less of coins but $100 more of transactions deposits. Accordingly,

TABLE 13.2
What Is a Bank?
The essential functions of a bank are to

- Accept deposits
- Offer drafts (check writing privileges)
- Make loans

In the United States, roughly 21,000 depository institutions fulfill these functions. These "banks" are typically classified into four general categories, even though most banks (and many other financial institutions) now offer similar services.

Type of Bank	Characteristics
Commercial banks	The nearly 9,000 commercial banks in the United States provide a full range of banking services, including savings ("time") and checking accounts and loans for all purposes. They hold nearly all demand deposits and nearly half of total savings deposits.
Savings and loan associations	Begun in 1831 as a mechanism for pooling the savings of a neighborhood in order to provide funds for home purchases, which is still the basic function of such banks. The nearly 550 S&Ls channel virtually all their savings deposits into home mortgages.
Mutual savings banks	Originally intended to serve very small savers (like the Boston Five Cents Savings Bank). They now use their deposits for a wider variety of purposes, including investment bonds and blue chip stocks. Almost all the 1,000 or so mutual savings banks are located in only five states: New York, Massachusetts, Connecticut, Pennsylvania, and New Jersey.
Credit unions	Cooperative societies formed by individuals bound together by some common tie, such as a common employer or labor union. Credit union members hold savings accounts and enjoy access to the pooled savings of all members. Most credit union loans are for consumer purchases. Although there are close to 11,000 credit unions in the United States, they hold less than 5 percent of total savings deposits.

no money is created by the demise of your piggy bank (the initial deposit). This accounting outcome is reflected in the following "T account" of University Bank and the composition of the money supply:

University Bank		Money Supply	
Assets	Liabilities	Cash held by the public	−$100
+$100 in coins	+$100 in deposits	Transactions deposits at bank	+$100
		Change in M	0

The T account shows that your coins are now held by University Bank. In exchange, the bank has credited your checking account $100. This balance is a liability for the bank since it must allow you to withdraw the deposit on demand.

The total money supply is unaffected by your cash deposit because two components of the money supply change in opposite directions (i.e., less cash, more bank deposits). This initial deposit is just the beginning of the money creation process, however. Banks aren't in business for your convenience; they're in business to earn a profit. To earn a profit on your deposit, University Bank will have to put your money to work. This means using your deposit as the basis for making a loan to someone who's willing to pay the bank interest for use of money. If the function of banks was merely to store money, they wouldn't pay interest on their accounts or offer free checking services. Instead, you'd have to pay them for these services. Banks pay you interest and offer free (or inexpensive) checking because they can use your money to make loans that earn interest.

The Initial Loan. Typically, a bank doesn't have much difficulty finding someone who wants to borrow money. Someone is always eager to borrow money. The question is: How much money can a bank lend? Can it lend your entire deposit? Or must University Bank keep some of your coins in reserve, in case you want to withdraw them?

To answer this question, suppose that University Bank decided to lend the entire $100 to Campus Radio. Campus Radio wants to buy a new antenna but doesn't have any money in its own checking account. To acquire the antenna, Campus Radio must take out a loan.

When University Bank agrees to lend Campus Radio $100, it does so by crediting the account of Campus Radio. Instead of giving Campus Radio $100 cash, University Bank simply adds $100 to Campus Radio's checking account balance. That is, the loan is made with a simple bookkeeping entry as follows:

University Bank		Money Supply	
Assets	Liabilities	Cash held by the public	no change
$100 in coins	$100 your account balance	Transactions deposits at bank	+$100
$100 in loans	$100 Campus Radio account	Change in M	+$100

This simple bookkeeping procedure is the key to creating money. When University Bank lends $100 to the Campus Radio account, it "creates" money. Keep in mind that transactions deposits are counted as part of the money supply. Once the $100 loan is credited to its account, Campus Radio can use this new money to purchase its desired antenna, without worrying that its check will bounce.

Or can it? Once University Bank grants a loan to Campus Radio, both you and Campus Radio have $100 in your checking accounts to spend. But the bank is holding only $100 of **reserves** (your coins). In other words, the increased account balance ob-

bank reserves: Assets held by a bank to fulfill its deposit obligations.

tained by Campus Radio doesn't limit your ability to write checks. There's been a net *increase* in the value of transactions deposits but no increase in bank reserves.

Secondary Deposits. What happens if Campus Radio actually spends the $100 on a new antenna? Won't this "use up all" the reserves held by the bank, endangering your check writing privileges? The answer is no.

Consider what happens when Atlas Antenna receives the check from Campus Radio. What will Atlas do with the check? Atlas could go to University Bank and exchange the check for $100 of cash (your coins). But Atlas may prefer to deposit the check in its own checking account at University Bank (still the only bank in town). This way, Atlas not only avoids the necessity of going to the bank (it can deposit the check by mail) but also keeps its money in a safe place. Should Atlas later want to spend the money, it can simply write a check. In the meantime, the bank continues to hold its entire reserves (your coins), and both you and Atlas have $100 to spend.

Fractional Reserves. Notice what's happened here. The money supply has increased by $100 as a result of deposit creation (the loan to Campus Radio). Moreover, the bank has been able to support $200 of transaction deposits (your account and either the Campus Radio or Atlas account) with only $100 of reserves (your coins). In other words, *bank reserves are only a fraction of total deposits.* In this case, University Bank's reserves (your $100 in coins) are only 50 percent of total deposits. Thus the bank's **reserve ratio** is 50 percent—that is,

reserve ratio: The ratio of a bank's reserves to its total transactions deposits.

$$\frac{\text{Reserve}}{\text{ratio}} = \frac{\text{bank reserves}}{\text{total deposits}}$$

The ability of University Bank to hold reserves that are only a fraction of total deposits results from two facts: (1) people use checks for most transactions, and (2) there's no other bank. Accordingly, reserves are rarely withdrawn from this monopoly bank. In fact, if people *never* withdrew their deposits and *all* transactions accounts were held at University Bank, University Bank wouldn't need *any* reserves. In this most unusual case, University Bank could make as many loans as it wanted. Every loan it made would increase the supply of money.

In reality, many banks are available, and people both withdraw cash from their accounts and write checks to people who have accounts in other banks. In addition, bank lending practices are regulated by the Federal Reserve System. *The Federal Reserve System requires banks to maintain some minimum reserve ratio.* This reserve requirement directly limits banks' ability to grant new loans.

Required Reserves. The potential impact of Federal Reserve requirements on bank lending can be readily seen. Suppose that the Federal Reserve imposed a minimum reserve requirement of 75 percent on University Bank. Such a requirement would prohibit University Bank from lending $100 to Campus Radio. That loan would result in $200 of deposits, supported by only $100 of reserves. The actual ratio of reserves to deposits would be 50 percent ($100 of reserves ÷ $200 of deposits), which would violate the Fed's assumed 75 percent reserve requirement. A 75 percent reserve requirement means that University Bank must hold **required reserves** equal to 75 percent of *total* deposits, including those created through loans.

required reserves: The minimum amount of reserves a bank is required to hold; equal to required reserve ratio times transactions deposits.

The bank's dilemma is evident in the following equation:

$$\frac{\text{Required}}{\text{reserves}} = \frac{\text{required reserve}}{\text{ratio}} \times \frac{\text{total}}{\text{deposits}}$$

To support $200 of total deposits, University Bank would need to satisfy this equation:

$$\frac{\text{Required}}{\text{reserves}} = 0.75 \times \$200 = \$150$$

But the bank has only $100 of reserves (your coins) and so would violate the reserve requirement if it increased total deposits to $200 by lending $100 to Campus Radio.

University Bank can still issue a loan to Campus Radio. But the loan must be less than $100 in order to keep the bank within the limits of the required reserve formula. Thus, *a minimum reserve requirement directly limits deposit-creation possibilities.* It's still true, however, as we'll now illustrate, that the banking system, taken as a whole, can create multiple loans (money) from a single deposit.

Table 13.3 illustrates the process of deposit creation in a multibank world with a required reserve ratio. In this case, we assume that legally required reserves must equal at least 20 percent of transactions deposits. Now when you deposit $100 in your checking account, University Bank must hold at least $20 as required reserves.[1]

A Multibank World

Excess Reserves. The remaining $80 the bank obtains from your deposit is regarded as **excess reserves**. These reserves are "excess" in that your bank is *required* to hold in reserve only $20 (equal to 20 percent of your initial $100 deposit):

excess reserves: Bank reserves in excess of required reserves.

$$\frac{\text{Excess}}{\text{reserves}} = \frac{\text{total}}{\text{reserves}} - \frac{\text{required}}{\text{reserves}}$$

The $80 of excess reserves isn't required and may be used to support additional loans. Hence, the bank can now lend $80. In view of the fact that banks earn profits (interest) by making loans, we assume that University Bank will try to use these excess reserves as soon as possible.

Find the most recent data on total bank reserves, borrowed reserves, excess reserves, and required reserves at the U.S. Federal Reserve: www.Federalreserve.gov/releases. Click on "Aggregate Reserves of Depository Institutions."

To keep track of the changes in reserves, deposit balances, and loans that occur in a multibank world we'll have to do some bookkeeping. For this purpose we'll again use the same balance sheet, or "T account," that banks themselves use. On the left side of the balance sheet, a bank lists all its assets. *Assets* are things the bank owns or is owed by others, including cash held in a bank's vaults, IOUs (loan obligations) from bank customers, reserve credits at the Federal Reserve (essentially the bank's own deposits at the central bank), and securities (bonds) the bank has purchased.

On the right side of the balance sheet a bank lists all its liabilities. *Liabilities* are things the bank owes to others. The largest liability is represented by the deposits of bank customers. The bank owes these deposits to its customers and must return them "on demand."

Table 13.3 also shows the use of balance sheets. Notice how the balance of University Bank now looks immediately after it receives your initial deposit (step 1, Table 13.3). Your deposit of coins is entered on both sides of University's balance sheet. On the left side, your deposit is regarded as an asset, because your piggy bank's coins have an immediate market value and can be used to pay off the bank's liabilities. The coins now appear as *reserves*. The reserves these coins represent are further divided into required reserves ($20, or 20 percent of your deposit) and excess reserves ($80).

On the right side of the balance sheet, the bank reminds itself that it has an obligation (liability) to return your deposit when you so demand. Thus, the bank's accounts balance, with assets and liabilities being equal. In fact, *a bank's books must always balance because all the bank's assets must belong to someone (its depositors or its owners).*

University Bank wants to do more than balance its books, however; it wants to earn profits. To do so, it will have to make loans—that is, put its excess reserves to work. Suppose that it lends $80 to Campus Radio.[2] As step 2, Table 13.3 illustrates, this loan alters both sides of University Bank's balance sheet. On the right-hand side, the bank creates a new transactions deposit for (credits the account of) Campus Radio; this item represents an additional liability (promise to pay). On the left-hand side of the balance sheet, two things happen. First, the bank notes that Campus Radio owes it $80 ("loans").

---

[1] The reserves themselves may be held in the form of cash in the bank's vault but are usually held as credits with one of the regional Federal Reserve banks.

[2] Because of the Fed's assumed minimum reserve requirement (20 percent), University Bank can now lend only $80 rather than $100, as before.

Second, the bank recognizes that it's now required to hold $36 in *required* reserves, in accordance with its higher level of transactions deposits ($180). (Recall we're assuming that required reserves are 20 percent of total transactions deposits.) Since its total reserves are still $100, $64 is left as *excess* reserves. Note again that ***excess reserves are reserves a bank isn't required to hold.***

Changes in the Money Supply. Before examining further changes in the balance sheet of University Bank, consider again what's happened to the economy's money supply during these first two steps. In the first step, you deposited $100 of cash in your checking account. This initial transaction didn't change the value of the money supply. Only the composition of the money supply (M1 or M2) was affected ($100 less cash held by the public, $100 more in transactions accounts).

Not until step 2—when the bank makes a loan—does all the excitement begin. In making a loan, the bank automatically increases the total money supply by $80. Why? Because someone (Campus Radio) now has more money (a transactions deposit) than it did before, *and no one else has any less.* And Campus Radio can use its money to buy goods and services, just like anybody else.

This second step is the heart of money creation. Money effectively appears out of thin air when a bank makes a loan. To understand how this works, you have to keep reminding yourself that money is more than the coins and currency we carry around. Transactions deposits are money too. Hence, ***the creation of transactions deposits via new loans is the same thing as creating money.***

More Deposit Creation. Suppose again that Campus Radio actually uses its $80 loan to buy an antenna. The rest of Table 13.3 illustrates how this additional transaction leads to further changes in balance sheets and the money supply.

In step 3, we see that when Campus Radio buys the $80 antenna, the balance in its checking account at University Bank drops to zero because it has spent all its money. As University Bank's liabilities fall (from $180 to $100), so does the level of its required reserves (from $36 to $20). (Note that required reserves are still 20 percent of its remaining transactions deposits.) But University Bank's excess reserves have disappeared completely! This disappearance reflects the fact that Atlas Antenna keeps *its* transactions account at another bank (Eternal Savings). When Atlas deposits the check it received from Campus Radio, Eternal Savings does two things: First it credits Atlas's account by $80. Second, it goes to University Bank to get the reserves that support the deposit.[3] The reserves later appear on the balance sheet of Eternal Savings as both required ($16) and excess ($64) reserves.

Observe that the money supply hasn't changed during step 3. The increase in the value of Atlas Antenna's transactions account balance exactly offsets the drop in the value of Campus Radio's transactions account. Ownership of the money supply is the only thing that has changed.

In step 4, Eternal Savings takes advantage of its newly acquired excess reserves by making a loan to Herman's Hardware. As before, the loan itself has two primary effects. First, it creates a transactions deposit of $64 for Herman's Hardware and thereby increases the money supply by the same amount. Second, it increases the required level of reserves at Eternal Savings. (To how much? Why?)

THE MONEY MULTIPLIER

By now it's perhaps obvious that the process of deposit creation won't come to an end quickly. On the contrary, it can continue indefinitely, just like the income multiplier process in Chapter 10. Indeed, people often refer to deposit creation as the money mul-

---

[3]In actuality, banks rarely "go" anywhere; such interbank reserve movements are handled by bank clearinghouses and regional Federal Reserve banks. The effect is the same, however. The nature and use of bank reserves are discussed more fully in Chapter 14.

Step 1: You deposit cash at University Bank. The deposit creates $100 of reserves, $20 of which are designated as required reserves.

University Bank

Assets		Liabilities	
Required reserves	$ 20	Your deposit	$100
Excess reserves	80		
Total	$100		100

Banking System

Change in Transactions Deposits	Change in M
+$100	$0

Step 2: The bank uses its excess reserves ($80) to make a loan to Campus Radio. Total deposits now equal $180. The money supply has increased.

University Bank

Assets		Liabilities	
Required reserves	$ 36	Your account	$100
Excess reserves	64	Campus Radio account	80
Loans	80		
Total	$180	Total	$180

Banking System

Δ Deposits	Δ M
+$ 80	+$ 80

Step 3: Campus Radio buys an antenna. This depletes Campus Radio's account but increases Atlas's balance. Eternal Savings gets $80 of reserves when the Campus Radio check clears.

University Bank

Assets		Liabilities	
Required reserves	$ 20	Your account	$100
Excess reserves	0	Campus Radio account	0
Loan	80		
Total	$100	Total	$100

Eternal Savings

Assets		Liabilities	
Required reserves	$16	Atlas Antenna account	$80
Excess reserves	64		
Total	$80	Total	$80

Banking System

Δ Deposits	Δ M
$0	$0

Step 4: Eternal Savings lends money to Herman's Hardware. Deposits, loans, and M all increase by $64.

University Bank

Assets		Liabilities	
Required reserves	$ 20	Your account	$100
Excess reserves	0	Campus Radio account	0
Loan	80		
Total	$100		$100

Eternal Savings

Assets		Liabilities	
Required reserves	$29	Atlas Antenna account	$ 80
Excess reserves	51	Herman's Hardware account	64
Loans	64		
	$144		$144

Banking System

Change in Transaction Deposits	Change in M
+$64	+$64

⋮

nth step: Some bank lends $1.00

| | | +1 | +1 |

Cumulative Change in Banking System

Bank Reserves	Transactions Deposits	Money Supply
+$100	+$500	+$400

TABLE 13.3
Deposit Creation
Excess reserves (step 1) are the basis of bank loans. When a bank uses its excess reserves to make a loan, it creates a deposit (step 2). When the loan is spent, a deposit will be made somewhere else (step 3). This new deposit creates additional excess reserves (step 3) that can be used for further loans (step 4, etc.). The process of deposit creation continues until the money supply has increased by a multiple of the initial deposit.

money multiplier: The number of deposit (loan) dollars that the banking system can create from $1 of excess reserves; equal to $1 \div$ required reserve ratio.

tiplier process, with the **money multiplier** expressed as the reciprocal of the required reserve ratio.[4] That is,

$$\text{Money multiplier} = \frac{1}{\text{required reserve ratio}}$$

Figure 13.2 illustrates the money multiplier process. When a new deposit enters the banking system, it creates both excess and required reserves. The required reserves represent leakage from the flow of money since they can't be used to create new loans. Excess reserves, on the other hand, can be used for new loans. Once those loans are made, they typically become transactions deposits elsewhere in the banking system. Then some additional leakage into required reserves occurs, and further loans are made. The process continues until all excess reserves have leaked into required reserves. Once excess reserves have completely disappeared, the total value of new loans will equal initial excess reserves multiplied by the money multiplier.

The potential of the money multiplier to create loans is summarized by the equation

$$\text{Excess reserves of banking system} \times \text{money multiplier} = \text{potential deposit creation}$$

Notice how the money multiplier worked in our previous example. The value of the money multiplier was equal to 5, since we assumed that the required reserve ratio was 0.20. Moreover, the initial level of excess reserves was $80, as a consequence of your original deposit (step 1). According to the money multiplier, then, the deposit-creation potential of the banking system was

$$\text{Excess reserves} (\$80) \times \text{money multiplier} (5) = \text{potential deposit creation} (\$400)$$

When all the banks fully utilized their excess reserves at each step of the money multiplier process, the ultimate increase in the money supply was in fact $400 (see the last row in Table 13.3).

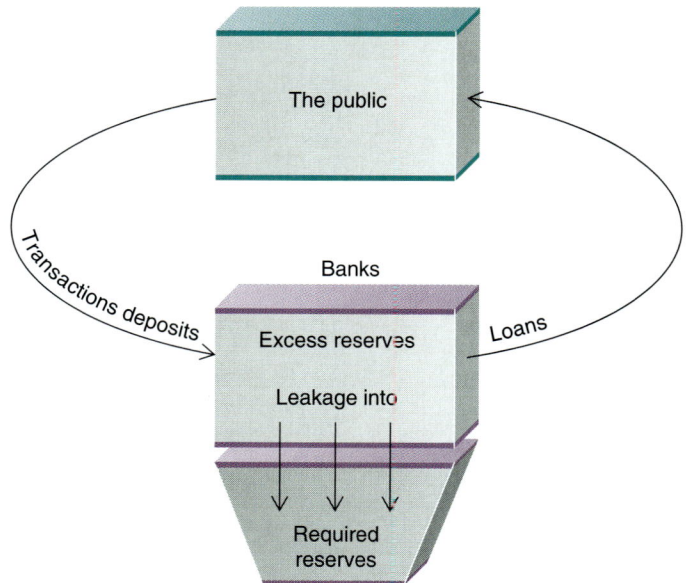

FIGURE 13.2
The Money Multiplier Process

Part of every new bank deposit leaks into required reserves. The rest—excess reserves—can be used to make loans. These loans, in turn, become deposits elsewhere. The process of money creation continues until all available reserves become required reserves.

[4]The money multiplier $(1/r)$ is the sum of the infinite geometric progression
$1 + (1-r) + (1-r)^2 + (1-r)^3 + \cdots + (1-r)^\infty$.

While you're struggling through Table 13.3, notice the critical role that excess reserves play in the process of deposit creation. A bank can make additional loans only if it has excess reserves. Without excess reserves, all of a bank's reserves are required, and no further liabilities (transactions deposits) can be created with new loans. On the other hand, a bank with excess reserves can make additional loans. In fact,

Excess Reserves as Lending Power

- *Each bank may lend an amount equal to its excess reserves and no more.*

As such loans enter the circular flow and become deposits elsewhere, they create new excess reserves and further lending capacity. As a consequence,

- *The entire banking system can increase the volume of loans by the amount of excess reserves multiplied by the money multiplier.*

By keeping track of excess reserves, then, we can gauge the lending capacity of any bank or, with the aid of the money multiplier, the entire banking system.

Table 13.4 summarizes the entire money multiplier process. In this case, we assume that all banks are initially "loaned up"—that is, without any excess reserves. The money

Required reserves = 0.20	Change in Transactions Deposits	Change in Total Reserves	Change in Required Reserves	Change in Excess Reserves	Change in Lending Capacity
If $100 in cash is deposited in Bank A, Bank A acquires	$100.00	$100.00	$20.00	$80.00	$80.00
If loan made and deposited elsewhere, Bank B acquires	80.00	80.00	16.00	64.00	64.00
If loan made and deposited elsewhere, Bank C acquires	64.00	64.00	12.80	51.20	51.20
If loan made and deposited elsewhere, Bank D acquires	51.20	51.20	10.24	40.96	40.96
If loan made and deposited elsewhere, Bank E acquires	40.96	40.96	8.19	32.77	32.77
If loan made and deposited elsewhere, Bank F acquires	32.77	32.77	6.55	26.27	26.22
If loan made and deposited elsewhere, Bank G acquires	26.22	26.22	5.24	20.98	20.98
. . .					
If loan made and deposited elsewhere, Bank Z acquires	0.38	0.38	0.08	0.30	0.30
Cumulative, through Bank Z	$498.80	$100.00	$99.76	$0.24	$398.80
. . .					
And if the process continues indefinitely	$500.00	$100.00	$100.00	$0.00	$400.00

A $100 cash deposit creates $400 of new lending capacity when the required reserve ratio is 0.20. Initial excess reserves are $80 (= $100 deposit − $20 required reserves). The money multiplier is 5(= 1 ÷ 0.20). New lending potential equals $400 (= $80 excess reserves × 5).

TABLE 13.4
The Money Multiplier at Work
The process of deposit creation continues as money passes through different banks in the form of multiple deposits and loans. At each step, excess reserves and new loans are created. The lending capacity of this system equals the money multiplier times excess reserves. In this case, initial excess reserves of $80 create the possibility of $400 of new loans when the reserve ratio is 0.20 (20 percent).

multiplier process begins when someone deposits $100 in cash into a transactions account at Bank A. If the required reserve ratio is 20 percent, this initial deposit creates $80 of excess reserves at Bank A while adding $100 to total transactions deposits.

If Bank A uses its newly acquired excess reserves to make a loan that ultimately ends up in Bank B, two things happen: Bank B acquires $64 in excess reserves (0.80 × $80), and total transactions deposits increase by another $80.

The money multiplier process continues with a series of loans and deposits. When the twenty-sixth loan is made (by bank Z), total loans grow by only $0.30 and transactions deposits by an equal amount. Should the process continue further, the *cumulative* change in loans will ultimately equal $400, that is, the money multiplier times initial excess reserves. The money supply will increase by the same amount.

BANKS AND THE CIRCULAR FLOW

The bookkeeping details of bank deposits and loans are rarely exciting and often confusing. But they do demonstrate convincingly that banks can create money. In that capacity, *banks perform two essential functions for the macro economy:*

- *Banks transfer money from savers to spenders by lending funds (reserves) held on deposit.*
- *The banking system creates additional money by making loans in excess of total reserves.*

In performing these two functions, banks change the size of the money supply—that is, the amount of purchasing power available for buying goods and services. Market participants may respond to these changes in the money supply by altering their spending behavior and shifting the aggregate demand curve.

Figure 13.3 is a simplified perspective on the role of banks in the circular flow. As before, income flows from product markets through business firms to factor markets and returns to consumers in the form of disposable income. Consumers spend most of their income but also save (don't spend) some of it.

FIGURE 13.3
Banks in the Circular Flow

Banks help transfer income from savers to spenders by using their deposits to make loans to business firms and consumers who want to spend more money than they have. By lending money, banks help maintain any desired rate of aggregate spending.

The leakage represented by consumer saving is a potential source of stabilization problems, particularly unemployment. If additional spending by business firms, foreigners, or governments doesn't compensate for consumer saving at full employment, a recessionary GDP gap will emerge, creating unemployment (see Chapters 9 and 10). Our interest here is in the role the banking system can play in encouraging such additional spending.

Financing Injections

Suppose for the moment that *all* consumer saving was deposited in piggy banks rather than depository institutions (banks) and that no one used checks. Under these circumstances, banks couldn't transfer money from savers to spenders by holding deposits and making loans.

In reality, a substantial portion of consumer saving *is* deposited in banks. These and other bank deposits can be used as the basis of loans, thereby returning purchasing power to the circular flow. In fact, the primary economic function of banks isn't to store money but to transfer purchasing power from savers to spenders. They do so by lending money to businesses for new plant and equipment, to consumers for new homes or cars, and to government entities that desire greater purchasing power. Moreover, because the banking system can make *multiple* loans from available reserves, banks don't have to receive all consumer saving in order to carry out their function. On the contrary, **the banking system can create any desired level of money supply if allowed to expand or reduce loan activity at will.**

There are three major constraints on the deposit creation of the banking system.

Constraints on Deposit Creation

Deposits. The first constraint is the willingness of consumers and businesses to continue using and accepting checks rather than cash in the marketplace. If people preferred to hold cash rather than checkbooks, banks wouldn't be able to acquire or maintain the reserves that are the foundation of bank lending activity.

Borrowers. The second constraint on deposit creation is the willingness of consumers, businesses, and governments to borrow the money that banks make available. The chain of events we've observed in deposit creation depends on the willingness of Campus Radio to borrow $80, of Herman's Hardware to borrow $64, and so on. If no one wanted to borrow any money, deposit creation would never begin. By the same reasoning, if all excess reserves aren't borrowed (lent), deposit creation won't live up to its theoretical potential.

Regulation. The third major constraint on deposit creation is the Federal Reserve System. As we've observed, the Fed may limit deposit creation by imposing reserve requirements. These and other tools of monetary policy are discussed in Chapter 14.

THE ECONOMY TOMORROW

When Banks Fail

The power of banks to create money originates in the *fractional reserve* system. As we've observed, a bank holds reserves that are a small fraction of its liabilities, implying that no bank could pay off its customers if they all sought to withdraw their deposits at one time.

Bank Panics

In earlier times, banks did experience occasional "runs" when depositors would rush to withdraw their funds. Such depositor runs usually began when word spread that a particular bank was running low on cash and might close. Depositor runs became self-fulfilling confirmation of a bank's insolvency. The resulting bank closing wiped out customer deposits, curtailed bank lending, and often pushed the economy into recession.

During the Great Depression there was widespread fear that the banking system would collapse. Borrowers weren't able to repay their loans and depositors were withdrawing more cash. As their reserves dwindled, banks' ability to create money evaporated. Suddenly, a chunk of money (bank deposits and loans) just disappeared. With little cash coming in and a lot of cash flowing out, banks quickly ran out of cash reserves and had to shut their doors. Between 1930 and 1933, over 9,000 banks failed. To prevent total collapse of the banking system, newly elected president Franklin Roosevelt declared a "bank holiday" that closed all the nation's banks for one week.

Deposit Insurance

Congress used that opportunity to create a deposit insurance that would protect customer deposits. The Federal Deposit Insurance Corporation (FDIC) and the Federal Savings and Loan Insurance Corporation (FSLIC) were created in 1933 and 1934 to ensure depositors that they'd get their money back even it their bank failed. The guarantee of insured deposits eliminated the motivation for deposit runs. If a bank closed, the federal government would step in and repay deposits.

The S&L Crisis

Federal deposit insurance provided a foundation for public confidence in the banking system. It didn't, however, ward off bank failures. In some respects, deposit insurance even contributed to bank failures. By insuring deposits, the federal government eliminated a major risk for bank customers. Depositors no longer had to concern themselves with the soundness of a bank's lending practices; their deposits were insured. This created the opportunity for bank owners to engage in riskier loans that had greater profit potential.

During the 1970s, accelerating inflation pushed interest rates up. To attract deposits, banks had to offer higher rates of interest on customer deposits. Many of their loans, however, were already set at lower interest rates. This was particularly true for savings and loan associations (S&Ls), which traditionally lent most of their funds in long-term home mortgages. Suddenly, they were stuck earning low interest rates on long-term mortgages while paying high interest rates on short-term deposits. This was a recipe for failure.

The woes of the S&Ls were exacerbated by increased competition from new financial institutions (like money market mutual funds) that enticed deposits away from S&Ls. Sharp downturns in oil prices and real estate also weakened borrowers' ability to repay their loans. These and other forces caused more than half the S&Ls that existed in 1970 to disappear by 1990. In 1988, more banks failed (200) than in any year since the Great Depression. The 1990–91 recession pushed still more banks into insolvency.

Bank Reopens to Customers' Questions

Worried customers streamed into a Superior Bank branch here Monday to find out if their money was safe three days after federal regulators seized the failed thrift.

Among the concerned customers was John Piotrowski, a Downers Grove management consultant, who had money stashed at the bank for his daughter's October wedding. "My wife almost fainted," when they heard about the bank's closure, he said.

The Office of Thrift Supervision closed Superior on Friday after federal regulators said the bank, based in suburban Oak Brook Terrace, was insolvent. The Federal Deposit Insurance Corp. was appointed the bank's receiver and reopened it Monday under the new name Superior Federal. Most customers who came to the Downers Grove branch on Monday got the good news that their money was safe because the FDIC insures accounts up to $100,000. However, accounts of more than $100,000 can be set up so they are FDIC insured, said David Barr, an FDIC spokesman.

—Deanna Bellandi

Source: Associated Press, July 31, 2001. Reprinted with permission. www.ap.org

Analysis: When a bank fails, the FDIC (or SAIF for savings banks) steps in to guarantee that deposited funds will be returned to depositors. The government then tries to sell the bank or its remaining assets (loans).

Bank Bailouts

The FSLIC and FDIC averted bank panics by paying off depositors in failed banks. So many S&Ls failed, however, that the FSLIC itself ran out of funds. Congress had to appropriate ever larger sums of money to bail out the banks. In 1992 alone, over $60 billion was spent on bank bailouts.

When the federal government steps in to pay insured deposits, it also assumes control of a failing bank (see News). The government then tries to arrange a merger or acquisition with a stronger bank. In the process, the federal government acquires some or all of the outstanding loans of the failed bank. The Resolution Trust Corporation (RTC) was created in 1989 to manage these loans. The RTC tried to collect outstanding loans or sell the properties (such as office buildings, shopping centers, homes) that were financed with those loans. Part of the huge outlays for bank bailouts in the early 1990s were offset by the proceeds from these RTC property sales.

Banks will continue to compete for deposits and loans in the economy tomorrow. They'll have the advantage of deposit insurance—provided by the FDIC and the renamed Savings Association Insurance Fund (SAIF)—in attracting new funds. Congress, however, has set more stringent requirements on the types of loans and investments banks can make. It has also forced bank owners to put more of their own funds at risk. The intent of these changes is to improve the financial stability of banks while assuring the public that their deposits are safe—even in banks with only fractional reserves.

SUMMARY

- In a market economy, money serves a critical function in facilitating exchanges and specialization, thus permitting increased output. *Money* refers to any medium that's generally accepted in exchange.
- Because people use bank account balances to buy goods and services, such balances are also regarded as money. The money supply M1 includes cash plus transactions account (checkable) deposits. M2 adds savings account balances and other deposits to form a broader measure of the money supply.
- Banks have the power to create money by making loans. In making loans, banks create new transactions deposits, which become part of the money supply.
- Banks' ability to make loans—create money—depends on their reserves. Only if a bank has excess reserves—reserves greater than those required by federal regulation—can it make new loans.
- As loans are spent, they create deposits elsewhere, making it possible for other banks to make additional loans.
- The money multiplier (1 ÷ required reserve ratio) indicates the total value of deposits that can be created by the banking system from excess reserves.
- The role of banks in creating money includes the transfer of money from savers to spenders as well as deposit creation in excess of deposit balances. Taken together, these two functions give banks direct control over the amount of purchasing power available in the marketplace.
- The deposit-creation potential of the banking system is limited by government regulation. It's also limited by the willingness of market participants to hold deposits or borrow money.
- When banks fail, the federal government (FDIC or SAIF) guarantees to pay deposits. To reduce bank failures, bank owners are now required to put more of their own assets at risk.

Key Terms

barter
money
money supply (M1, M2)
transactions account

aggregate demand
deposit creation
bank reserves
reserve ratio

required reserves
excess reserves
money multiplier

Questions for Discussion

1. How are an economy's production possibilities affected when workers are paid in bras and coffins rather than cash? (See World View, page 263, about bartering in Russia.)
2. What percentage of your monthly bills do you pay with (*a*) cash, (*b*) check, (*c*) credit card, and (*d*) automatic transfers. How do you pay off the credit card balance? How do your payment choices compare with the News summary on page 264? How does your use of cash compare with the composition of the money supply (Figure 13.1)?
3. If you can purchase airline tickets with online computer services, should your electronic account be counted in the money supply? Explain.
4. Does the fact that your bank keeps only a fraction of your account balance in reserve make you uncomfortable? Why don't people rush to the bank and retrieve their money? What would happen if they did?
5. If people never withdrew cash from banks, how much money could the banking system potentially create? Could this really happen? What might limit deposit creation in this case?
6. If all banks heeded Shakespeare's admonition "Neither a borrower nor a lender be," what would happen to the circular flow?
7. How does federal deposit insurance encourage greater risk taking by banks? Could the banking system function without government deposit insurance? How?
8. If Internet e-cash systems could make loans, how would the money supply be affected?

Web Activities

1. Find historical data for M1 and M2 at the Federal Reserve at www.federalreserve.gov/releases/h6/about.htm. During the past year, which measure of the money supply has increase the least? The most? Based on what you have learned about the difference between M1 and M2, what might explain why one type of money is increasing faster than the other?
2. Take the Money Challenge at the St. Louis Fed at www.stls.frb.org/education/econed3.html. Print your answers and bring them to class. Which question is most important for U.S. economic policy? Why?
3. Log on to www.federalreserve.gov/releases/h3/about.htm and access the latest release. (*a*) What is the latest level of required reserves? (*b*) Are banks keeping excess reserves?

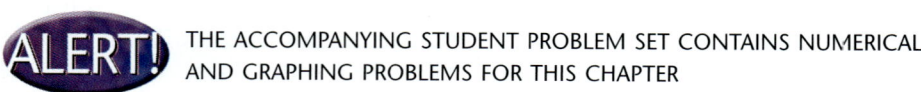

ALERT! THE ACCOMPANYING STUDENT PROBLEM SET CONTAINS NUMERICAL AND GRAPHING PROBLEMS FOR THIS CHAPTER

CHAPTER 14

The Federal Reserve System

We've seen how money is created. We've also gotten a few clues about how the government limits money creation and thus influences aggregate demand. This chapter examines the mechanics of government control more closely. The basic issues addressed are

- How does the government control the amount of money in the economy?
- Which government agency is responsible for exercising this control?
- How are banks and bond markets affected by the government's policies?

Most people have a ready answer for the first question. The popular view is that the government controls the amount of money in the economy by printing more or fewer dollar bills. But we've already observed that the concept of "money" isn't so simple. In Chapter 13 we demonstrated that banks, not the printing presses, create most of our money. In making loans, banks create transactions deposits that are counted as part of the money supply.

Because bank lending activities are the primary source of money, the ***government must regulate bank lending if it wants to control the amount of money in the economy.*** That's exactly what the Federal Reserve System does. The Federal Reserve System—the "Fed"—not only limits the volume of loans that the banking system can make from available reserves; it can also alter the amount of reserves banks hold.

The Federal Reserve System's control over the supply of money is the key mechanism of **monetary policy.** The potential of this policy lever to alter macro outcomes (unemployment, inflation, etc.) is examined in Chapter 15. For the time being, however, we focus on the *tools* of monetary policy.

STRUCTURE OF THE FED

In the absence of any government regulation, the supply of money would be determined by individual banks. Moreover, individual depositors would bear all the risks of bank failures. In fact, this is the way the banking system operated until 1914. The money supply was subject to abrupt changes, and consumers frequently lost their savings in recurrent bank failures.

A series of bank failures resulted in a severe financial panic in 1907. Millions of depositors lost their savings, and the economy was thrown into a tailspin. In the wake of this panic, a National Monetary Commission was established to ex-

monetary policy: The use of money and credit controls to influence macroeconomic outcomes.

amine ways of restructuring the banking system. The mandate of the commission was to find ways to avert recurrent financial crises. After five years of study, the commission recommended the creation of a Federal Reserve System. Congress accepted the commission's recommendations, and President Wilson signed the Federal Reserve Act in December 1913.

Federal Reserve Banks

The core of the Federal Reserve System consists of 12 Federal Reserve banks. Each bank acts as a central banker for the private banks in its region. In this role, the regional Fed banks perform the following services:

- *Clearing checks between private banks.* Suppose the Bank of America in San Francisco receives a deposit from one of its customers in the form of a share draft written on the New York State Employees Credit Union. The Bank of America doesn't have to go to New York to collect the cash or other reserves that support that draft. Instead, the Bank of America can deposit the draft (check) at its account with the Federal Reserve Bank of San Francisco. The Fed then collects from the credit union. This vital clearinghouse service saves the Bank of America and other private banks a great deal of time and expense in processing the 50 *billion* checks that are written every year.
- *Holding bank reserves.* Notice that the Fed's clearinghouse service was facilitated by the fact that the Bank of America and the New York Employees Credit Union had their own accounts at the Fed. As we noted in Chapter 13, banks are *required* to hold some minimum fraction of their deposits in reserve. Only a small amount of reserves is held as cash in a bank's vaults. The rest is held in reserve accounts at the regional Federal Reserve banks. These accounts at the Fed provide greater security and convenience for bank reserves and also enable the Fed to monitor the actual level of bank reserves.
- *Providing currency.* Before every major holiday there's a great demand for cash. People want some pocket money during holidays and know that it's difficult to cash checks on weekends or holidays, especially if they're going out of town. After the holiday is over, most of this cash is returned to the banks, typically by the stores, gas stations, and restaurants that benefited from holiday spending. Because banks hold very little cash in their vaults, they turn to the Fed to meet these sporadic cash demands. A private bank can simply call the regional Federal Reserve bank and order a supply of cash, to be delivered (by armored truck) before a weekend or holiday. The cash will be deducted from the bank's own account at the Fed. When all the cash comes back in after the holiday, the bank can reverse the process, sending the unneeded cash back to the Fed.
- *Providing loans.* The Federal Reserve banks may also loan reserves to private banks. This practice, called "discounting," is examined more closely in a moment.

The Board of Governors

At the top of the Federal Reserve System's organization chart (Figure 14.1) is the Board of Governors, which is responsible for setting monetary policy. The Board, located in Washington, D.C., consists of seven members (governors), appointed by the president of the United States and confirmed by the U.S. Senate. Board members are appointed for 14-year terms and can't be reappointed. Their exceptionally long appointments give the Fed governors a measure of political independence. They're not beholden to any elected official and will hold office longer than any president.

The intent of the Fed's independence is to keep control of the nation's money supply beyond the immediate reach of politicians (especially members of Congress, elected for two-year terms). The designers of the Fed system feared that political control of monetary policy would cause wild swings in the money supply and macro instability. Critics argue, however, that the Fed's independence makes it unresponsive to the majority will.

The president selects one of the governors to serve as chairman of the Board for four years. Alan Greenspan was first appointed as chairman by President Reagan, then

Who runs the Fed? Read profiles of the governors at www.federalreserve.gov/bios.

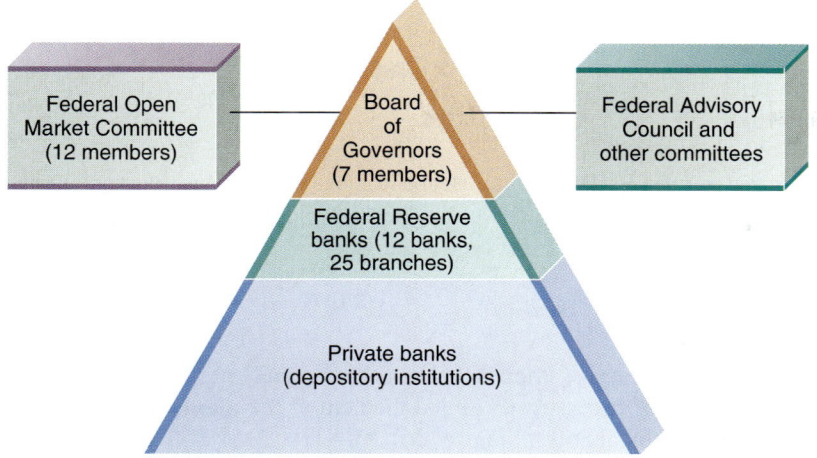

FIGURE 14.1
Structure of the Federal Reserve System

The Fed's broad policies are determined by the seven-member Board of Governors. The 12 Federal Reserve banks provide central banking services to individual banks in their respective regions. The Federal Open Market Committee directs Federal Reserve transactions in the money market. Various committees offer formal and informal advice to the Board of Governors.

reappointed for a four-year term by President George H. Bush in 1991, and twice reappointed by President Clinton (in 1996 and 2000). Chairman Greenspan is the primary spokesperson for Fed policy and reports to Congress every six months on the conduct of monetary policy.

A key arm of the Board is the Federal Open Market Committee (FOMC), which is responsible for the Fed's daily activity in financial markets. The FOMC plays a critical role in determining the level of reserves held by private banks. The membership of the FOMC includes all seven governors and 5 of the 12 regional Reserve bank presidents. The FOMC meets in Washington, D.C., every four or five weeks throughout the year to review the economy's performance. It decides whether the economy is growing fast enough (or too fast) and then adjusts monetary policy as needed.

MONETARY TOOLS

Our immediate interest isn't in the structure of the Federal Reserve but the way the Fed is able to alter the **money supply.** The Fed's control of the money supply is exercised by use of three policy instruments:

- Reserve requirements
- Discount rates
- Open market operations

We emphasized the need for banks to maintain some minimal level of reserves. As noted in Chapter 13, the Fed requires private banks to keep some stated fraction of their deposits "in reserve". These **required reserves** are held either in the form of actual vault cash or, more commonly, as credits (deposits) in the bank's "reserve account" at a regional Federal Reserve bank. ***By changing the reserve requirements, the Fed can directly alter the lending capacity of the banking system.***

Recall that the banking system's ability to make additional loans—create deposits—is determined by two factors: (1) the amount of excess reserves banks hold and (2) the money multiplier. Both factors are directly influenced by the Fed's required reserve ratio.

Suppose, for example, that banks hold $100 billion of deposits and total reserves of $30 billion. Assume too that the minimum reserve requirement is 20 percent. Under these circumstances, banks are holding more reserves than they have to. Recall that

$$\text{Required reserves} = \text{required reserves ratio} \times \text{total deposits}$$

The Federal Open Market Committee (FOMC)

money supply (M1): Currency held by the public, plus balances in transactions accounts.

M2 money supply: M1 plus balances in most savings accounts and money market mutual funds.

Reserve Requirements

required reserves: The minimum amount of reserves a bank is required to hold; equal to required reserve ratio times transactions deposits.

so, in this case

$$\text{Required reserves} = 0.20 \times \$100 \text{ billion}$$

$$= \$20 \text{ billion}$$

Banks are *required* to hold $20 billion in reserve to meet Federal Reserve regulations. They're actually holding $30 billion, however. The $10 billion difference between actual and required reserves is **excess reserves**—that is,

> **excess reserves:** Bank reserves in excess of required reserves.

$$\text{Excess reserves} = \text{total reserves} - \text{required reserves}$$

The existence of excess reserves implies that banks aren't fully utilizing their lending powers. With $10 billion of excess reserves and the help of the **money multiplier** the banks *could* lend an additional $50 billion.

> **money multiplier:** The number of deposit (loan) dollars that the banking system can create from $1 of excess reserves; equal to 1 ÷ required reserve ratio.

The potential for additional loans is calculated as

$$\text{Available lending capacity of banking system} = \text{excess reserves} \times \text{money multiplier}$$

or, in this case,

$$\$10 \text{ billion} \times \frac{1}{0.20} = \$50 \text{ billion of unused lending capacity}$$

That is, the banking system could create another $50 billion of money (transactions account balances) without any additional reserves.

A simple way to confirm this—and thereby check your arithmetic—is to note what would happen to total deposits if the banks actually made further loans. Total deposits would increase to $150 billion in this case (the initial $100 billion plus the new $50 billion), an amount that could be supported with $30 billion in reserves (20 percent of $150 billion).

But what if the Fed doesn't want the money supply to increase this much? Maybe prices are rising and the Fed wants to restrain rather than stimulate total spending in the economy. Under such circumstances, the Fed would want to restrict the availability of credit (loans). Does it have the power to do so? Can the Fed reduce the lending capacity of the banking system?

The answer to both questions is clearly yes. ***By raising the required reserve ratio, the Fed can immediately reduce the lending capacity of the banking system.***

Table 14.1 summarizes the impact of an increase in the required reserve ratio. In this case, the required reserve ratio is increased from 20 to 25 percent. Notice that this change in the reserve requirement has no effect on the amount of deposits in the banking system (row 1, Table 14.1) or the amount of total reserves (row 2). They remain at $100 billion and $30 billion, respectively. What the increased reserve requirement does

TABLE 14.1
The Impact of an Increased Reserve Requirement
An increase in the required reserve ratio reduces both excess reserves (row 4) and the money multiplier (row 5). As a consequence, changes in the reserve requirement have a substantial impact on the lending capacity of the banking system (row 6).

	Required Reserve Ratio	
	20 Percent	25 Percent
1. Total deposits	$100 billion	$100 billion
2. Total reserves	30 billion	30 billion
3. Required reserves	20 billion	25 billion
4. Excess reserves	10 billion	5 billion
5. Money multiplier	5	4
6. Unused lending capacity	$ 50 billion	$ 20 billion

affect is the way those reserves can be used. Before the increase, only $20 billion in reserves was *required,* leaving $10 billion of *excess* reserves. Now, however, banks are required to hold $25 billion (0.25 × $100 billion) in reserves, leaving them with only $5 billion in excess reserves. Thus an increase in the reserve requirement immediately reduces excess reserves, as illustrated in row 4, Table 14.1.

There's also a second effect. Notice what happens to the money multiplier (1 ÷ reserve ratio). Previously it was 5(1 ÷ 0.20); now it's only 4(1 ÷ 0.25). Consequently, a higher reserve requirement not only reduces excess reserves but diminishes their lending power as well.

A change in the reserve requirement, therefore, hits banks with a triple whammy. *A change in the reserve requirement causes a change in*

- *Excess reserves.*
- *The money multiplier.*
- *The lending capacity of the banking system.*

These changes lead to a sharp reduction in bank lending power. Whereas the banking system initially had the power to increase the volume of loans by $50 billion ($10 billion of excess reserves × 5), it now has only $20 billion ($5 million × 4) of unused lending capacity, as noted in the last row in Table 14.1

Changes in reserve requirements are a powerful weapon for altering the lending capacity of the banking system. The Fed uses this power sparingly, so as not to cause abrupt changes in the money supply and severe disruptions of banking activity. From 1970 to 1980, for example, reserve requirements were changed only twice, and then by only half a percentage point each time (for example, from 12.0 to 12.5 percent). The Fed cut the reserve requirement from 12 to 10 percent in 1992 to increase bank profits and encourage more lending (see News). Smaller banks have a lower reserve requirement (3 percent), which gives them a competitive advantage.

The Discount Rate

Banks have a tremendous incentive to maintain their reserves at or close to the minimum established by the Fed. Bank reserves held at the Fed earn no interest, but loans and bonds do. Hence, a profit-maximizing bank seeks to keep its excess reserves as low as possible, preferring to put its reserves to work. In fact, banks have demonstrated an uncanny ability to keep their reserves close to the minimum federal requirement. As Figure 14.2 illustrates, the only time banks held huge excess reserves was in the Great Depression of the 1930s. The banks didn't want to make any more loans and were fearful of panicky customers withdrawing their deposits.

IN THE NEWS

Fed Cuts Deposit-Reserve Requirements
Reduction Is the Latest Bid to Bolster Bank Profits and Encourage Lending

WASHINGTON—The Federal Reserve Board, in another attempt to shore up bank profits so bankers will be more willing to lend, reduced the fraction of deposits that must be held as reserves.

The Fed cut to 10 percent from 12 percent the percentage of checking account deposits that banks are required to hold as reserves. Because reserves must be in cash or in accounts that don't pay any interest, the change will add between $300 million and $600 million to bank industry profits.

—David Wessel

Source: *The Wall Street Journal,* February 19, 1992. Reprinted by permission of *The Wall Street Journal.* © 1992 Dow Jones & Company, Inc. All Rights Reserved Worldwide. www.wsj.com

Analysis: A reduction in the reserve requirement transforms some of the banking system's required reserves into excess reserves, thus increasing potential lending activity and profits. It also increases the size of the money multiplier.

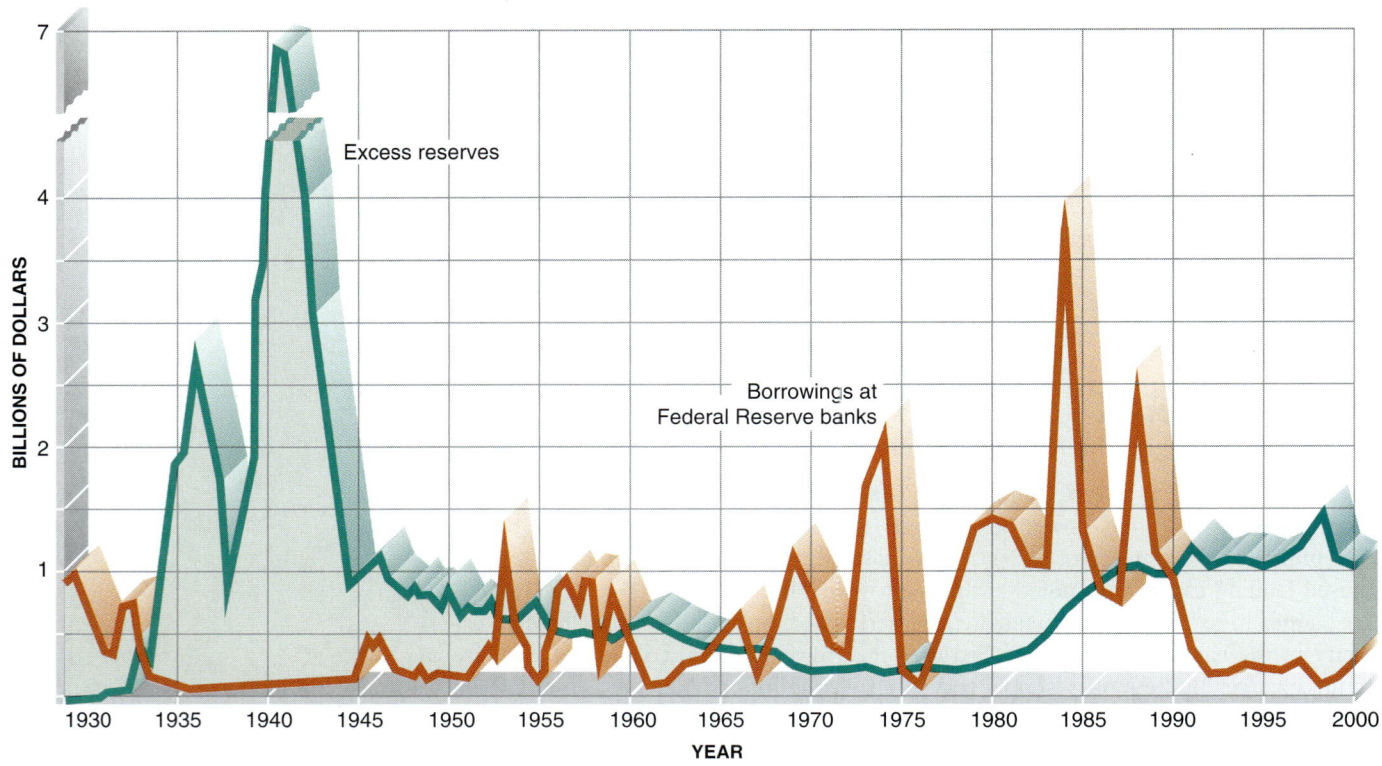

FIGURE 14.2
Excess Reserves and Borrowings

Excess reserves represent unused lending capacity. Hence, banks strive to keep excess reserves at a minimum. One exception to this practice occurred in the Great Depression, when banks were hesitant to make any loans. In trying to minimize excess reserves, banks occasionally fall short of required reserves. At such times they may borrow from other banks (the federal funds market), or they may borrow reserves from the Fed. Borrowing from the Fed is called "discounting."

WEBNOTE

The St. Louis Fed bank tracks bank reserves and borrowings; to update Figure 14.2, go to www.stls.frb.org/fred/data/reserves/borrow.

Because banks continually seek to keep excess reserves at a minimum, they run the risk of falling below reserve requirements. A large borrower may be a little slow in repaying a loan, or the rate of deposit withdrawals and transfers may exceed expectations. At such times, a bank may find that it doesn't have enough reserves to satisfy Fed requirements.

Banks could ensure continual compliance with reserve requirements by maintaining large amounts of excess reserves. But that's an unprofitable procedure, and a profit-maximizing bank will seek other alternatives.

The Federal Funds Market. A bank that finds itself short of reserves can turn to other banks for help. If a reserve-poor bank can borrow some reserves from a reserve-rich bank, it may be able to bridge its temporary deficit and satisfy the Fed. ***Reserves borrowed by one bank from another are referred to as "federal funds" and are lent for short periods, usually overnight.*** Although trips to the federal funds market—via telephone and computer—will usually satisfy Federal Reserve requirements, such trips aren't free. The lending bank will charge interest (the **federal funds rate**) on its interbank loan.[1] The use of the federal funds market to satisfy Federal Reserve requirements also depends on other banks having excess reserves to lend.

federal funds rate: The interest rate for interbank reserve loans.

---

[1] An overnight loan of $1 million at 6 percent interest (per year) costs $165 in interest charges plus any service fees that might be added. Banks make multimillion-dollar loans in the federal funds market.

Sale of Securities. Another option available to reserve-poor banks is the sale of securities. Banks use some of their excess reserves to buy government bonds, which pay interest. If a bank needs more reserves to satisfy federal regulations, it may sell these securities and deposit the proceeds at a regional Federal Reserve bank. Its reserve position is thereby increased. This option also involves distinct costs, however, both in forgone interest-earning opportunities and in the possibility of capital losses when the bond is offered for quick sale.

Discounting. A third option for avoiding a reserve shortage lies in the structure of the Federal Reserve System itself. The Fed not only establishes certain rules of behavior for banks but also functions as a central bank, or banker's bank. Banks maintain accounts with the regional Federal Reserve banks, much the way you and I maintain accounts with a local bank. Individual banks deposit and withdraw "reserve credits" from these accounts, just as we deposit and withdraw dollars. Should a bank find itself short of reserves, it can go to the Fed's "discount window" and borrow some reserves. This process is called **discounting.** Discounting means the Fed is lending reserves directly to private banks.[2]

The Fed's discounting operation provides private banks with an important source of reserves, but not without cost. The Fed too charges interest on the reserves it lends to banks, a rate of interest referred to as the **discount rate.**

The discount window is a mechanism for directly influencing the size of bank reserves. *By raising or lowering the discount rate, the Fed changes the cost of money for banks and therewith the incentive to borrow reserves.* At high discount rates, borrowing from the Fed is expensive. High discount rates also signal the Fed's desire to restrain the money supply and an accompanying reluctance to lend reserves. Low discount rates, on the other hand, make it profitable to acquire additional reserves and exploit one's lending capacity to the fullest. Low discount rates also indicate the Fed's willingness to support credit expansion. The accompanying News tells how the Fed reduced both the federal funds rate and the discount rate in August 2001 to encourage more borrowing and spending. After the September 11 attacks on the World Trade Center and Pentagon, the Fed reduced both rates again, and quite sharply.

Reserve requirements and discount window operations are important tools of monetary policy. But they don't come close to open market operations in day-to-day impact on the money supply. *Open market operations are the principal mechanism for directly altering the reserves of the banking system.* Since reserves are the lifeblood of the banking system, open market operations are of immediate and critical interest to private banks and the larger economy.

Portfolio Decisions. To appreciate the impact of open market operations, you have to think about the alternative uses for idle funds. Just about all of us have some idle funds, even if they amount to just a few dollars in our pocket or a minimal balance in our checking account. Other consumers and corporations have great amounts of idle funds, even millions of dollars at any time. Here we're concerned with what people decide to do with such funds.

People (and corporations) don't hold all their idle funds in transactions accounts or cash. Idle funds are also used to purchase stocks, build up savings account balances, and purchase bonds. These alternative uses of idle funds are attractive because they promise some additional income in the form of interest, dividends, or capital appreciation, such as higher stock prices. Deciding where to place idle funds is referred to as the **portfolio decision.**

discounting: Federal Reserve lending of reserves to private banks.

discount rate: The rate of interest the Federal Reserve charges for lending reserves to private banks.

Open Market Operations

portfolio decision: The choice of how (where) to hold idle funds.

---

[2]In the past banks had to present loan notes to the Fed in order to borrow reserves. The Fed "discounted" the notes by lending an amount equal to only a fraction of their face value. Although banks no longer have to present loans as collateral, the term "discounting" endures.

IN THE NEWS

Fed Again Reduces Key Rate

Federal Reserve officials, concerned about the uncertain outlook for the U.S. economy amid a global slowdown in growth, lowered their target for short-term interest rates yesterday for a seventh time this year and left the door open for more cuts if needed.

In announcing its decision, the Fed's top policymaking group, the Federal Open Market Committee, noted that U.S. consumer spending has held up recently "but business profits and capital spending continue to weaken and growth abroad is slowing, weighing on the U.S. economy."

The committee lowered the central bank's target for the federal funds rate, the interest rate financial institutions charge one another on overnight loans, by another quarter of a percentage point, to 3.5 percent. The key rate, which influences many other interest rates, including banks' prime lending rate, is now 3 percentage points lower than it was Jan. 1. ...

In a separate but related action, the Federal Reserve Board reduced the central bank's largely symbolic discount rate, the interest rate financial institutions pay when they borrow money from one of the 12 regional Federal Reserve banks, to 3 percent from 3.25 percent.

—John M. Berry

Source: *Washington Post*, August 22, 2001. © 2001 The Washington Post. Reprinted with permission. www.thewashingtonpost.com

Analysis: By reducing the federal funds and discount rates, the Fed encourages banks to borrow reserves and make more loans. Lower interest rates also encourage businesses and consumers to borrow and spend more.

Hold Money or Bonds? The Fed's open market operations focus on one of the portfolio choices people make: whether to deposit idle funds in bank accounts or purchase government bonds. The Fed attempts to influence this choice by making bonds more or less attractive, as circumstances warrant, thereby inducing people to move funds from banks to bond markets or vice versa. In the process, reserves either enter or leave the banking system, thereby altering the lending capacity of banks.

Figure 14.3 depicts the general nature of the Fed's open market operations. As we first observed in Chapter 13 (Figure 13.2), the process of deposit creation begins when people deposit money in the banking system. But people may also hold their assets in the form of bonds. The Fed's objective is to alter this portfolio decision by buying or selling bonds. *When the Fed buys bonds from the public, it increases the flow of deposits (reserves) to the banking system. Bond sales by the Fed reduce the flow.*

The Bond Market. To understand how open market operations work, let's look closer at the bond market. Not all of us buy and sell bonds, but a lot of consumers and corporations do: Daily volume in bond markets exceeds $500 billion. What's being exchanged in this market, and what influences decisions to buy or sell?

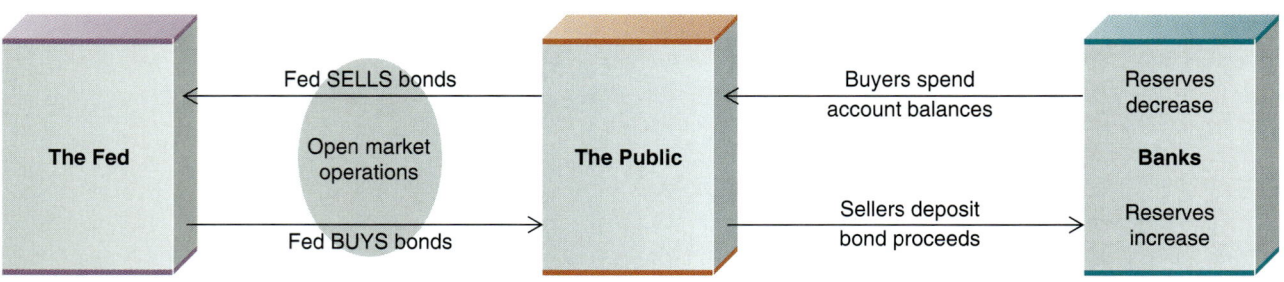

FIGURE 14.3
Open Market Operations

People may hold assets in the form of bank deposits (money) or bonds. When the Fed buys bonds from the public, it increases the flow of deposits (and reserves) to the banks. When the Fed sells bonds, it diminishes the flow of deposits and therewith the banks' capacity to lend (create money).

In our discussion thus far, we've portrayed banks as intermediaries between savers and spenders. Banks aren't the only mechanism available for transferring purchasing power from nonspenders to spenders. Funds are lent and borrowed in bond markets as well. In this case, a corporation may borrow money directly from consumers or other institutions. When it does so, it issues a bond as proof of its promise to repay the loan. A **bond** is simply a piece of paper certifying that someone has borrowed money and promises to pay it back at some future date. In other words, a bond is nothing more than an IOU. In the case of bond markets, however, the IOU is typically signed by a giant corporation or a government agency rather than a friend. It's therefore more widely accepted by lenders.

bond: A certificate acknowledging a debt and the amount of interest to be paid each year until repayment; an IOU.

Because most corporations and government agencies that borrow money in the bond market are well known and able to repay their debts, their bonds are actively traded. If I lend $1,000 to General Motors on a 10-year bond, for example, I don't have to wait 10 years to get my money back; I can resell the bond to someone else at any time. If I do, that person will collect the face value of the bond (plus interest) from GM when it's due. The actual purchase and sale of bonds take place in the bond market. Although a good deal of the action occurs on Wall Street in New York, the bond market has no unique location. Like other markets we've discussed, the bond market exists whenever and however bond buyers and sellers get together.

Bond Yields. People buy bonds because bonds pay interest. If you buy a General Motors bond, GM is obliged to pay you interest during the period of the loan. For example, an 8 percent 2015 GM bond in the amount of $1,000 states that GM will pay the bondholder $80 interest annually (8 percent of $1,000) until 2015. At that point the initial $1,000 loan will be repaid.

The current **yield** paid on a bond depends on the promised interest rate (8 percent in this case) and the actual purchase price of the bond. Specifically,

yield: The rate of return on a bond; the annual interest payment divided by the bond's price.

$$\text{Yield} = \frac{\text{annual interest payment}}{\text{price paid for bond}}$$

If you pay $1,000 for the bond, then the current yield is

$$\text{Yield} = \frac{\$80}{\$1,000} = 0.08, \text{ or } 8\%$$

which is the same as the interest rate printed on the face of the bond. But what if you pay only $900 for the bond? In this case, the interest rate paid by GM remains at 8 percent, but the *yield* jumps to

$$\text{Yield} = \frac{\$80}{\$900} = 0.089, \text{ or } 8.9\%$$

Buying a $1,000 bond for only $900 might seem like too good a bargain to be true. But bonds are often bought and sold at prices other than their face value (see News on the next page). In fact, *a principal objective of Federal Reserve open market activity is to alter the price of bonds, and therewith their yields.* By doing so, the Fed makes bonds a more or less attractive alternative to holding money.

Open Market Activity. The basic premise of open market activity is that participants in the bond market will respond to changes in bond prices and yields. As we've observed, *the less you pay for a bond, the higher its yield.* Accordingly, the Fed can induce people to buy bonds by offering to sell them at a lower price, for example, a $1,000, 8 percent bond for only $900. Similarly, the Fed can induce people to sell bonds by offering to buy them at higher prices. In either case, the Fed hopes to move reserves into or out of the banking system. In other words, **open market operations** entail the purchase and sale of government securities (bonds) for the purpose of altering the flow of reserves into and out of the banking system.

open market operations: Federal Reserve purchases and sales of government bonds for the purpose of altering bank reserves.

IN THE NEWS

Zero-Coupon Bonds

Conventional bonds make interest payments each year, often quarterly. However, some bonds pay no current interest. Because so-called zero-coupon bonds make no interest payments, they have a *current* yield of zero. In effect, a zero-coupon bond accumulates interest payments, paying them all at once when the bond comes due. The *yield* to *maturity* on such bonds is implied by the difference between the purchase price and the face value of the bond. A $1,000 "zero" due in 10 years, for example, might cost only $400 today. You lend $400 now and get back $1,000 in 10 years. The implied yield to maturity is approximately 9 percent.

Analysis: The yield (return) on a bond depends not only on annual interest payments but also on the difference between the price paid for the bond and its face (payoff) value.

Open Market Purchases. Suppose the Fed wants to increase the money supply and therefore desires to provide the banking system with additional reserves. To do so, it must persuade people to deposit a larger share of their financial assets in banks and hold less in other forms, particularly government bonds. *If the Fed offers to pay a higher price for bonds ("bids up bonds"), it will effectively lower bond yields and market interest rates.* The higher prices and lower yields will reduce the attractiveness of holding bonds. If the price offered by the Fed is high enough, people will sell some of their bonds to the Fed and deposit some or all of the proceeds of the sale in their bank accounts. This influx of money into bank accounts will directly increase bank reserves.

Figure 14.4 illustrates the dynamics of open market operations in more detail. When the Fed buys a bond from the public, it pays with a check written on itself. What will the bond seller do with the check? There really aren't any options. If the seller wants to use the proceeds of the bond sale, he or she will have to deposit the Fed check at a bank. The bank, in turn, deposits the check at a regional Federal Reserve bank, in exchange for a reserve credit. The bank's reserves are directly increased by the amount of the check. Thus, *by buying bonds, the Fed increases bank reserves.* These reserves can be used to expand the money supply still further, as banks put their newly acquired reserves to work making loans.

Open Market sales. Should the Fed desire to slow the growth in the money supply, it can reverse the whole process. Instead of offering to *buy* bonds, the Fed in this case will try to *sell* bonds. If the Fed "bids bonds down" (offers to sell them at low prices),

FIGURE 14.4
An Open Market Purchase

The Fed can increase bank reserves by buying government securities from the public. The Fed check used to buy securities (step 1) gets deposited in a private bank (step 2). The bank returns the check to the Fed (step 3), thereby obtaining additional reserves. To decrease bank reserves, the Fed would sell securities, thus reversing the flow of reserves.

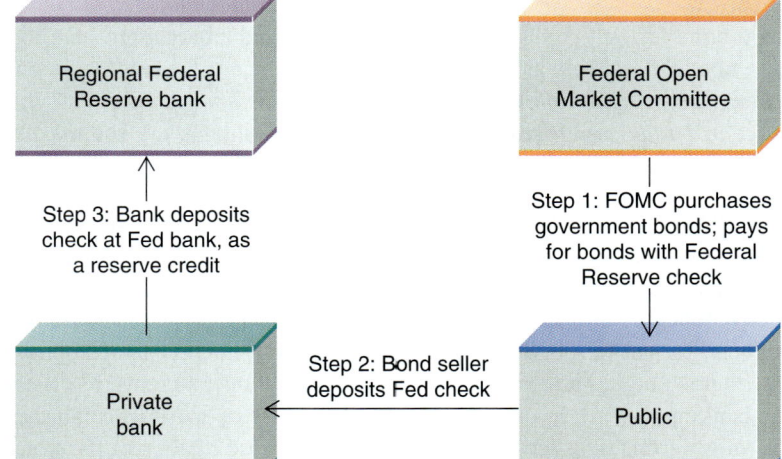

bond yields will rise. In response, individuals, corporations, and government agencies will convert some of their transactions deposits into bonds. When they do so, they write a check, paying the Fed for the bonds.[3] The Fed then returns the check to the depositor's bank, taking payment through a reduction in the bank's reserve account. The reserves of the banking system are thereby diminished, as is the capacity to make loans. Thus, *by selling bonds, the Fed reduces bank reserves.*

The Fed Funds Rate. A market signal of these changing reserve flows is provided by the federal funds rate. Recall that "fed funds" are excess reserves traded among banks. If the Fed pumps more reserves into the banking system (by buying bonds), the interest rate charged for overnight reserve loans—the federal funds rate—will decline. Conversely, if the Fed is reducing bank reserves (by selling bonds), the federal funds rate will increase. Hence, the federal funds rate is a highly visible signal of Federal Reserve open market operations. When Alan Greenspan reduced the federal funds rate *eleven times* in 2001, the Fed was underscoring the urgency of monetary stimulus to combat the recession and the after-effects of the September 11 terrorist attacks.

How has the federal funds rate changed in the past eight weeks? What does it signal about Federal Reserve activity? For data on the fed funds rate visit the Fed's website at www.federalreserve.gov.

Volume of Activity. To appreciate the significance of open market operations, you need a sense of magnitudes involved. The volume of trading in U.S. government securities exceeds $100 billion per day. The Fed alone owned over $500 billion worth of government securities at the beginning of 2002 and bought or sold enormous sums daily. Thus, open market operations involve tremendous amounts of money and, by implication, potential bank reserves. Each $1 of reserves represents something like $10 of potential lending capacity (via the money multiplier). Thus, open market operations can have a profound impact on the money supply.

INCREASING THE MONEY SUPPLY

The three major instruments of monetary policy are reserve requirements, discount rates, and open market operations. The Fed can use these levers individually or in combination to change the money supply. This section illustrates the use of each tool to attain a specific policy goal.

Suppose the policy goal is to increase the money supply from an assumed level of $340 billion to $400 billion. In surveying the nation's banks, the Fed discovers the facts shown in Table 14.2. On the basis of the facts presented in Table 14.2, it's evident that

- The banking system is "loaned up." Because excess reserves are zero (see row 5 in Table 14.2), there's no additional lending capacity.

Item	Amount
1. Cash held by public	$100 billion
2. Transactions deposits	240 billion
3. Total money supply (M1)	$340 billion
4. Required reserves	$ 60 billion
5. Excess reserves	0
6. Total reserves of banks	$ 60 billion
7. U.S. bonds held by public	$460 billion
8. Discount rate	7 percent

TABLE 14.2
How to Increase the Money Supply
The accompanying data depict a banking system that has $340 billion of money (M1) and no further lending capacity (excess reserves = 0). To enlarge M1 to $400 billion, the Fed can (1) lower the required reserve ratio, (2) reduce the discount rate, or (3) buy bonds held by the public.

---

[3] In actuality, the Fed deals directly with only 36 "primary" bond dealers. These intermediaries then trade with each other, "secondary" dealers, financial institutions, and individuals. These additional steps don't significantly alter the flow of funds depicted here.

- The required reserve ratio must be equal to 25 percent, because this is the current ratio of required reserves ($60 billion) to total deposits ($240 billion).

Accordingly, if the Fed wants to increase the money supply, it will have to pump additional reserves into the banking system or lower the reserve requirement. *To increase the money supply the Fed can*

- *Lower reserve requirements.*
- *Reduce the discount rate.*
- *Buy bonds.*

Lowering Reserve Requirements

Lowering the reserve requirements is an expedient way of increasing the lending capacity of the banking system. But by how much should the reserve requirement be reduced?

Recall that the Fed's policy objective is to increase the money supply from $340 billion to $400 billion, an increase of $60 billion. If the public isn't willing to hold any additional cash, this entire increase in money supply will have to take the form of added transactions deposits. In other words, total deposits will have to increase from $240 billion to $300 billion. These additional deposits will have to be *created* by the banks, in the form of new loans to consumers or business firms.

If the banking system is going to support $300 billion in transactions deposits with its *existing* reserves, the reserve requirement will have to be reduced from 25 percent; thus,

$$\frac{\text{Total reserves}}{\text{Desired level of deposits}} = \frac{\$60 \text{ billion}}{\$300 \text{ billion}} = 0.20$$

At the moment the Fed lowers the minimum reserve ratio to 0.20, *total* reserves won't change. The bank's potential lending power will change, however. Required reserves will drop to $48 billion (0.20 × $240 billion), and excess reserves will jump from zero to $12 billion. These new excess reserves imply an additional lending capacity:

$$\underset{(\$12 \text{ billion})}{\text{Excess reserves}} \times \underset{(5)}{\text{money multiplier}} = \underset{(\$60 \text{ billion})}{\text{unused lending capacity}}$$

If the banks succeed in putting all this new lending power to work—actually make $60 billion in new loans—the Fed's objective of increasing the money supply will be attained.

Lowering the Discount Rate

The second monetary tool available to the Fed is the discount rate. We assumed it was 7 percent initially (see row 8 in Table 14.2). If the Fed lowers this rate, it will become cheaper for banks to borrow reserves from the Fed. The banks will be more willing to borrow (cheaper) reserves so long as they can make additional loans to their own customers at higher interest rates. The profitability of discounting depends on the *difference* between the discount rate and the interest rate the bank charges its loan customers. The Fed increases this difference when it lowers the discount rate.

There's no way to calculate the appropriate discount rate without more detailed knowledge of the banking system's willingness to borrow reserves from the Fed. Nevertheless, we can determine how much reserves the banks *must* borrow if the Fed's money supply target is to be attained. The Fed's objective is to increase transactions deposits by $60 billion. If these deposits are to be created by the banks—and the reserve requirement is unchanged at 0.25—the banks will have to borrow an additional $15 billion of reserves ($60 billion divided by 4, the money multiplier).

Buying Bonds

The Fed can also get additional reserves into the banking system by buying U.S. bonds in the open market. As row 7 in Table 14.2 indicates, the public holds $460 billion in U.S. bonds, none of which are counted as part of the money supply. If the Fed can persuade people to sell some of these bonds, bank reserves will surely rise.

To achieve its money supply target, the Fed will offer to buy $15 billion of U.S. bonds. It will pay for these bonds with checks written on its own account at the Fed.

The people who sold the bonds will deposit these checks in their own transactions accounts. As they do so, they'll directly increase bank deposits and reserves by $15 billion.

Is $15 billion of open market purchases enough? Yes. The $15 billion is a direct addition to transactions deposits, and therefore to the money supply. The additional deposits bring in $15 billion of reserves, only $3.75 billion of which is required (0.25 × $15 billion). Hence, the new deposits bring in $11.25 billion of excess reserves, which themselves create an additional lending capacity:

For an inside view of how the Fed uses its policy tools, visit www.federalreserveeducation.org.

$$\underset{(\$11.25 \text{ billion})}{\text{Excess reserves}} \times \underset{(4)}{\text{money multiplier}} = \underset{(\$45 \text{ billion})}{\text{unused lending capacity}}$$

Thus, the $15 billion of open market purchases will eventually lead to a $60 billion increase in M1 as a consequence of both direct deposits ($15 billion) and subsequent loan activity ($45 billion).

Federal Funds Rate. When the Fed starts bidding up bonds, bond yields and market interest rates will start falling. So will the federal funds rate. This will give individual banks an incentive to borrow any excess reserves available, thereby accelerating deposit (loan) creation.

WORLD VIEW

Interest Rates Are Boosted Again in Europe

FRANKFURT—Citing inflation risks and the strongest economy in a decade, the European Central Bank yesterday lifted key interest rates a quarter point for the second time in six weeks—and most investors think more increases are in store.

The ECB, in a statement explaining the move, said a strong rise in oil prices and a falling euro are causing rises in the costs of imports and producer prices. These higher prices are in turn threatening consumer prices, the bank said.

"Economic conditions and prospects for the euro area appear to be better at present than at any time in the past decade," the ECB said in the statement. "At the same time, upside risks to price stability were seen as a reason for vigilance.

— G. Thomas Sims

Source: *The Wall Street Journal*, March 17, 2000. Reprinted by permission of *The Wall Street Journal*. © 2000 Dow Jones & Company, Inc. All Rights Reserved Worldwide. www.wsj.com

ECB Takes Action

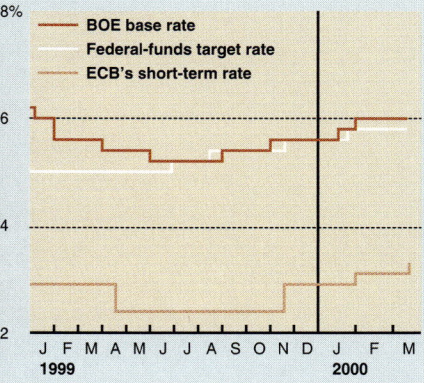

Analysis: Central banks boost interest rates and reduce money-supply growth when they want to restrain aggregate demand.

DECREASING THE MONEY SUPPLY

All the tools used to increase the money supply can also be used to decrease it. *To reduce the money supply, the Fed can*

- *Raise reserve requirements.*
- *Increase the discount rate.*
- *Sell bonds.*

On a week-to-week basis the Fed does occasionally seek to reduce the total amount of cash and transactions deposits held by the public. These are minor adjustments, however, to broader policies. A growing economy needs a steadily increasing supply of money to finance market exchanges. Hence, the Fed rarely seeks an outright reduction in the size of the money supply. What it does do is regulate the *rate of growth* in the money supply. When the Fed wants to slow the rate of consumer and investor spending, it restrains the *growth* of money and credit. Although many people talk about "reducing" the money supply, they're really talking about slowing its rate of growth. More immediately, they expect to see *rising* interest rates. To slow economic growth (and price inflation) in Europe, the European Central Bank pursued this sort of monetary restraint in early 2000 (see World View on the previous page).

THE ECONOMY TOMORROW

Is the Fed Losing Control?

The policy tools at the Fed's disposal imply tight control of the nation's money supply. By altering reserve requirements, discount rates, or open market purchases, the Fed apparently has the ability to increase or decrease the money supply at will. But the Fed's control is far from complete. The nature of "money," as well as our notion of what a "bank" is, keeps changing. As a result, the Fed has to run pretty fast just to stay in place.

Monetary Control Act

Before 1980, the Fed's control of the money supply wasn't only incomplete but actually weakening. The Fed didn't have authority over all banks. Only one-third of all commercial banks were members of the Federal Reserve System and subject to its regulations. All savings and loan associations and other savings banks remained outside the Federal Reserve System. These banks were subject to regulations of state banking commissions and other federal agencies but not to Federal Reserve requirements. As a consequence, a substantial quantity of money and near-money lay beyond the control of the Fed.

To increase the Fed's control of the money supply, Congress passed the Depository Institutions Deregulation and Monetary Control Act of 1980. Commonly referred to simply as the Monetary Control Act, that legislation subjected *all* commercial banks, S&Ls, savings banks, and most credit unions to Fed regulation. All depository institutions now have to satisfy new (and lower) Fed reserve requirements. All depository institutions also enjoy access to the Fed's discount window. These reforms (phased in over a period of seven years) obliterated the distinction between member and nonmember banks and greatly strengthened the Fed's control of the banking system.

Decline of Traditional Banks

Ironically, **as the Fed's control of the banks was increasing, the banks themselves were declining in importance.** Banks are part of a larger financial services industry that provides deposit, credit, and payment services. Many of these services are provided by financial institutions other than banks. These nonbank financial institutions have grown in importance while traditional banks have declined in number and importance.

Accepting and holding deposits is a core bank function. Consumers can also place idle funds in money market mutual funds (MMMF), however. MMMFs typically pay higher interest rates than traditional bank accounts and also permit limited check writing privileges. They thus serve as a potential substitute for traditional banks. Many brokerage houses also offer to hold idle cash in interest-earning accounts for their stock and bond customers.

Nonbanks are also competing against banks for loan business; 30 percent of all consumer loans are now made through credit cards. Banks themselves were once the primary source of credit cards. Now corporate giants like AT&T, GM, Sears, and American Airlines offer nonbank credit cards. Large corporations also offer loans to consumers who want to buy their products and even extend loans to unaffiliated businesses.

Insurance companies and pension funds also use their vast financial resources to make loans. The Teachers Insurance and Annuity Association (TIAA)—the pension fund for college professors—has lent over $10 billion directly to corporations. Many insurance companies provide long-term loans for commercial real estate.

Foreign banks, corporations, and pension funds may also extend credit to American businesses. They may also hold deposits of U.S. dollars abroad (for example, Eurodollars). As the accompanying World View illustrates, money—even terrorists' money—travels easily across national borders.

All this credit and deposit activity by global and nonbank institutions competes with traditional banks. And the nonbanks are winning the competition. In the past 20 years, the share of all financial institution assets held by banks has dropped from 37 percent to 27 percent, which means that banks are less important than they once were. This has made control of the money supply increasingly difficult.

Because of the difficulties in managing an increasingly globalized and electronic flow of funds, the Fed has shifted away from money-supply targets to interest rate targets. Although changes in the money supply and in interest rates are intrinsically related, in-

Focus on Fed Funds Rate, not Money Supply

WORLD VIEW

Fighting Terror/Targeting Funds; Laws May Not Stop Flow of Terror Funds

Congress is expected to approve legislation as early as today aimed at crippling the ability of terrorists to send money around the world. But law enforcement officials say that the increased globalization of electronic money transfer systems has made it easier than ever to move cash and avoid detection. . . .

The question, money laundering specialists say, is whether any unilateral action Congress takes can do much to stop the flow of dirty money across the world's borders. "The technology is changing all the time that makes it easier to transfer funds anonymously and to send money through five or six countries in one day," said William Schroeder, former director of the FBI's legal forfeiture division. "That makes it extremely difficult to connect people with money, to locate a money trail and follow it from person to person..."

Security cameras in Portland, Maine, captured pictures of suspected terrorists Muhammad Atta and Abdulaziz Alomari visiting two different ATMs on Sept. 10. Bank cash machines hardly qualify as cutting edge, but ATMs help criminals, according to the Treasury Department's Financial Crimes Enforcement Network, by allowing them "to wire funds into accounts in the United States from other nations and almost instantaneously and virtually anonymously to withdraw those funds."

Last year, federal prosecutors revealed that a husband-and-wife team with little more than a laptop computer and a license for what turned out to be a shell bank in Russia laundered more than $7 billion between 1996 and 1998. Using wire transfer software from the Bank of New York, the couple allegedly worked with the Russian mafia to send money from Moscow to New York to a series of offshore banks without tipping off regulators.

"If you know what you're doing, you can send money from the US to Spain to Cyprus to the Cayman Islands to Peru in a matter of minutes," said Schroeder.

—Scott Bernard Nelson

Source: *Boston Globe*, October 24, 2001. Reprinted with permission. search.boston.com/globe

Analysis: Nearly two-thirds of all U.S. currency circulates outside the United States, and over $1.5 trillion is transmitted by bank wire every day. This globalization of money makes it hard not only to track terrorists' money but also to control the domestic money supply.

terest rates are easier and faster to track. The Fed also has the financial power to change short-term interest rates through its massive open-market operations. If it chooses, the Fed can also offset abrupt changes in the flow of funds across national borders that might otherwise disrupt domestic interest rates. Last, but not least, the Fed recognizes that interest rates, not more obscure data on the money-supply or bank reserves, are the immediate concern in investment and "big-ticket" consumption decisions. As a result, the Fed will continue to use the federal funds rate as its primary barometer of monetary policy in the economy tomorrow.

SUMMARY

- The Federal Reserve System controls the nation's money supply by regulating the loan activity (deposit creation) of private banks (depository institutions).
- The core of the Federal Reserve System is the 12 regional Federal Reserve banks, which provide check-clearance, reserve deposit, and loan ("discounting") services to individual banks. Private banks are required to maintain minimum reserves on deposit at one of the regional Federal Reserve banks.
- The general policies of the Fed are set by its Board of Governors. The Board's chair is selected by the U.S. president and confirmed by the Senate. The chair serves as the chief spokesperson for monetary policy. The general policies of the Fed are carried out by the Federal Open Market Committee (FOMC), which directs open market sales and purchase of U.S. bonds.
- The Fed has three basic tools for changing the money supply. By altering the reserve requirement, the Fed can immediately change both the quantity of excess reserves in the banking system and the money multiplier, which limits banks' lending capacity. By altering discount rates (the rate of interest charged by the Fed for reserve borrowing), the Fed can also influence the amount of reserves maintained by banks. Finally, and most important, the Fed can increase or decrease the reserves of the banking system by buying or selling government bonds, that is, by engaging in open market operations.
- When the Fed buys bonds, it causes an increase in bank reserves (and lending capacity). When the Fed sells bonds, it induces a reduction in reserves (and lending capacity).
- The federal funds (interest) rate is a market signal of Fed open market activity and intentions.
- In the 1980s, the Fed gained greater control of the banking system. Global and nonbank institutions such as pension funds, insurance companies, and nonbank credit services have grown in importance, however, making control of the money supply more difficult.

Key Terms

monetary policy
money supply (M1, M2)
required reserves
excess reserves
money multiplier
federal funds rate
discounting
discount rate
portfolio decision
bond
yield
open market operations

Questions for Discussion

1. Why do banks want to maintain as little excess reserves as possible? Under what circumstances might banks want to hold excess reserves? (*Hint:* see Figure 14.2.)
2. Why do people hold bonds rather than larger savings account or checking account balances? Under what circumstances might they change their portfolios, moving their funds out of bonds into bank accounts?
3. What is the current price and yield of 30-year U.S. Treasury bonds? Of General Motors bonds? (Check the financial section of your daily newspaper.) What accounts for the difference?
4. Why did the European Central Bank raise interest rates in 2000? How did they expect consumers and businesses to respond? (See World View, page 293.)
5. Why might the Fed want to decrease the money supply?
6. Why would a zero-coupon bond (see News page 290) have a lower price than a bond paying annual interest?

7. In 2000–01, bond yields in Japan fell to less than 1.5 percent as the Bank of Japan bid up bond prices. Yet, relatively few people moved their assets out of bonds into banks. How might this failure of open-market operations be explained?

8. In 2001, the Fed reduced both the discount and federal fund rates dramatically. But bank loan volume didn't increase. What considerations might have constrained the market's response to Fed policy?

Web Activities

1. At www.federalreserve.gov/centralbanks.htm you'll find links to the home pages for the central banks of major industrialized countries. Visit the sites for two central banks other than ones in the United States. Find at least one difference between each foreign central bank and the U.S. Federal Reserve. Find at least one similarity.

2. Find the most recent testimony of the chairman of the Federal Reserve Board of Governor's at www.federalreserve.gov/boarddocs/hh. What does it indicate about the Fed's current monetary policy? What economic conditions is the Fed attempting to remedy or improve? Do you agree with current Fed policy?

 THE ACCOMPANYING STUDENT PROBLEM SET CONTAINS NUMERICAL AND GRAPHING PROBLEMS FOR THIS CHAPTER

CHAPTER 15

Monetary Policy

So what if the Federal Reserve System controls the nation's money supply? Why is this significant? Does it matter how much money is available?

Vladimir Lenin thought so. The first communist leader of the Soviet Union once remarked that the best way to destroy a society is to destroy its money. If a society's money became valueless, it would no longer be accepted in exchange for goods and services in product markets. People would have to resort to barter, and the economy's efficiency would be severely impaired. Adolf Hitler tried unsuccessfully to use this weapon against Great Britain during World War II. His plan was to counterfeit British currency, then drop it from planes flying over England. He believed that the sudden increase in the quantity of money, together with its suspect origins, would render the British pound valueless.

Even in peacetime, the quantity of money in circulation influences its value in the marketplace. Moreover, interest rates and access to credit (bank loans) are basic determinants of spending behavior. Consequently, control over the money supply implies an ability to influence macroeconomic outcomes.

But how much influence does the money supply have on macro performance? Specifically,

- What's the relationship between the money supply, interest rates, and aggregate demand?
- How can the Fed use its control of the money supply or interest rates to alter macro outcomes?
- How effective is monetary policy, compared to fiscal policy?

Economists offer very different answers to these questions. Some argue that changes in the money supply directly affect macro outcomes; others argue that the effects of such changes are indirect and less certain.

Paralleling these arguments about *how* **monetary policy** works are debates over the relative effectiveness of monetary and fiscal policy. Some economists argue that monetary policy is more effective than fiscal policy; others contend the reverse is true. This chapter examines these different views of money and assesses their implications for macro policy.

THE MONEY MARKET

The best place to learn how monetary policy works is the money *market*. You must abandon any mystical notions you may harbor about money and view it like any other commodity that's traded in the marketplace. Like other goods, there's a supply of money and a demand for money. Together they determine the "price" of money, or the **interest rate.**

At first glance, it may appear strange to call interest rates the price of money. But when you borrow money, the "price" you pay is measured by the interest rate you're charged. When interest rates are high, money is "expensive." When interest rates are low, money is "cheap."

Even people who don't borrow must contend with the price of money. Money, as we've seen, comes in many different forms. A common characteristic of all money is that it can be held as a store of value. People hold cash and maintain positive bank balances for this purpose. Most of the money in our common measures of **money supply (M1, M2)** is in the form of bank balances. There's an opportunity cost associated with such money balances, however. Money held in transactions accounts earns little or no interest. Money held in savings accounts and money market mutual funds does earn interest but usually at relatively low rates. By contrast, money used to buy bonds or stocks or to make loans is likely to earn a higher interest rate of return.

The Price of Money. The nature of the "price" of money should be apparent: People who hold *cash* are forgoing an opportunity to earn interest. So are people who hold money in checking accounts that pay no interest. In either case, *forgone interest is the opportunity cost (price) of money people choose to hold.* How high is that price? It's equal to the market rate of interest.

Money held in interest-paying bank accounts does earn some interest. In this case, the opportunity cost of holding money is the *difference* between the prevailing rate of interest and the rate paid on deposit balances. As is the case with cash and regular checking accounts, opportunity cost is measured by the forgone interest.

Once we recognize that money does have a price, we can easily formulate a demand for money. As is the case with all goods, the **demand for money** is a schedule (or curve) showing the quantity of money demanded at alternative prices (interest rates).

The decision to hold (demand) money balances is a **portfolio decision.** While at first glance it might seem irrational to hold money balances that pay little or no interest, there are many good reasons for doing so.

Transactions Demand. Even people who've mastered the principles of economics hold money. They do so because they want to buy goods and services. In order to transact business in product or factor markets, we need money in the form of either cash or a positive bank account balance. Debit cards and ATM cards don't work unless there's money in the bank. Payment by e-cash also requires a supporting bank balance. Even when we use credit cards, we're only postponing the date of payment by a few weeks or so. Accordingly, we recognize the existence of a basic **transactions demand for money.**

Precautionary Demand. Another reason people hold money is their fear of the proverbial rainy day. A sudden emergency may require money purchases over and above normal transactions needs. Moreover, such needs may arise when the banks are closed or in a community where one's checks aren't accepted. Also, future income is uncertain and may diminish unexpectedly. Therefore, people hold a bit more money (cash or bank account balances) than they anticipate spending. This **precautionary demand for money** is the extra money being held as a safeguard against the unexpected.

Speculative Demand. People also hold money for speculative purposes. Suppose you were interested in buying stocks or bonds but hadn't yet picked the right ones or

---

monetary policy: The use of money and credit controls to influence macroeconomic outcomes.

interest rate: The price paid for the use of money.

Money Balances

money supply (M1): Currency held by the public, plus balances in transactions accounts.

money supply (M2): M1 plus balances in most savings accounts and money market mutual funds.

The Demand for Money

demand for money: The quantities of money people are willing and able to hold at alternative interest rates, *ceteris paribus.*

portfolio decision: The choice of how (where) to hold idle funds.

transactions demand for money: Money held for the purpose of making everyday market purchases.

precautionary demand for money: Money held for unexpected market transactions or for emergencies.

speculative demand for money: Money held for speculative purposes, for later financial opportunities.

regarded their present prices as too high. In such circumstances, you might want to hold some money so that you could later buy a "hot" stock or bond at a price you think attractive. Thus, you'd be holding money in the hope that a better financial opportunity would later appear. In this sense, you'd be *speculating* with your money, forgoing present opportunities to earn interest in the hope of hitting a real jackpot later. These money balances represent a **speculative demand for money.**

The Market Demand Curve. These three motivations for holding money combine to create a *market demand* for money. The question is, what shape does this demand curve take? Does the quantity of money demanded decrease sharply as the rate of interest rises? Or do people tend to hold the same amount of money, regardless of its price?

People do cut down on their money balances when interest rates rise. At such times, the opportunity cost of holding money is simply too high. This explains why so many people move their money out of transactions deposits (M1) and into money market mutual funds (M2) when interest rates are extraordinarily high (for example, in 1980–82). Corporations are even more careful about managing their money when interest rates rise. Better money management requires watching checking account balances more closely and even making more frequent trips to the bank, but the opportunity costs are worth it.

Figure 15.1 illustrates the total market demand for money. Like nearly all demand curves, the market demand curve for money slopes downward. The downward slope indicates that *the quantity of money people are willing and able to hold (demand) increases as interest rates fall* (ceteris paribus).

Equilibrium

Once a money demand curve and a money supply curve are available, the action in money markets is easy to follow. Figure 15.1 summarizes this action. The money demand curve in Figure 15.1 reflects existing demands for holding money. The money supply curve is drawn at an arbitrary level of g_1. In practice, its position depends on

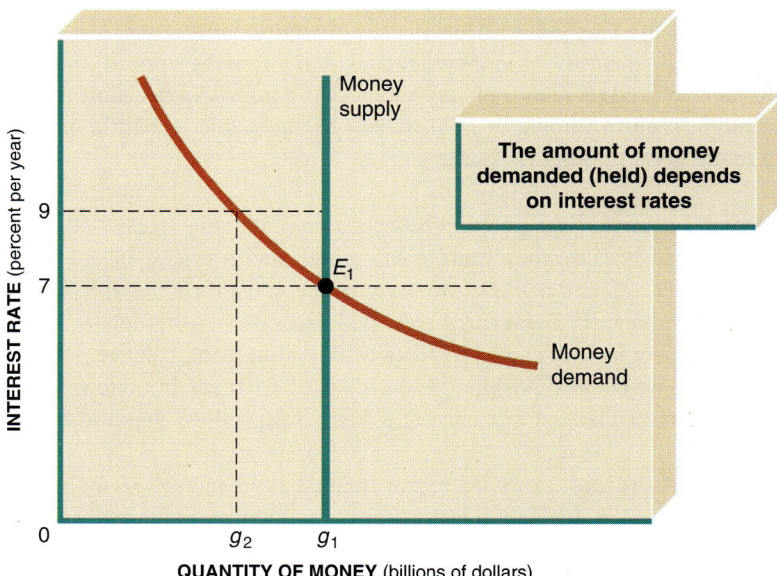

FIGURE 15.1
Money Market Equilibrium

All points on the market demand curve represent the quantity of money people are willing to hold at a specific interest rate. The equilibrium interest rate occurs at the intersection (E_1) of the money supply and money demand curves. At that rate of interest, people are willing to hold as much money as is available. At any other interest rate (for example, 9 percent), the quantity of money people are *willing* to hold won't equal the quantity available, and people will adjust their portfolios.

Federal Reserve policy (Chapter 14), the lending behavior of private banks, and the willingness of consumers and investors to borrow money.

The intersection of the money demand and money supply curves (E_1) establishes an **equilibrium rate of interest.** Only at this interest rate is the quantity of money supplied equal to the quantity demanded. In this case, we observe that an interest rate of 7 percent equates the desires of suppliers and demanders.

At any rate of interest other than 7 percent, the quantity of money demanded wouldn't equal the quantity supplied. Look at the imbalance that exists, for example, when the interest rate is 9 percent. At that rate, the quantity of money supplied (g_1 in Figure 15.1) exceeds the quantity demanded (g_2). All the money (g_1) must be held by someone, of course. But the demand curve indicates that people aren't *willing* to hold so much money at that interest rate (9 percent). People will adjust their portfolios by moving money out of cash and bank accounts into bonds or other assets that offer higher returns. This will tend to lower interest rates (recall that buying bonds tends to lower their yields). As interest rates drop, people are willing to hold more money. Ultimately we get to E_1, where the quantity of money demanded equals the quantity supplied. At that equilibrium, people are content with their portfolio choices.

equilibrium rate of interest: The interest rate at which the quantity of money demanded in a given time period equals the quantity of money supplied.

The equilibrium rate of interest is subject to change. As we saw in Chapter 14, the Federal Reserve System can alter the money supply through changes in reserve requirements, changes in the discount rate, or open market operations. By implication, then, *the Fed can alter the equilibrium rate of interest.*

Figure 15.2 illustrates the potential impact of monetary policy on the equilibrium rate of interest. Assume that the money supply is initially at g_1 and the equilibrium interest rate is 7 percent. The Fed then increases the money supply to g_3 by lowering the reserve requirement, reducing the discount rate, or, most likely, purchasing additional bonds in the open market. This expansionary monetary policy brings about a new equilibrium, at E_3. At this intersection, the market rate of interest is only 6 percent. Hence, by increasing the money supply, the Fed tends to lower the equilibrium rate of interest. To put the matter differently, people are *willing* to hold larger money balances only at lower interest rates.

Changing Interest Rates

FIGURE 15.2
Changing the Rate of Interest

Changes in the money supply tend to alter the equilibrium rate of interest. In this case, an increase in the money supply (from g_1 to g_3) lowers the equilibrium rate of interest (from 7 percent to 6 percent).

TABLE 15.1
The Hierarchy of Interest Rates
Interest rates reflect the risks and duration of loans. Because risks and loan terms vary greatly, dozens of different interest rates are available. Here are a few of the more common rates as of November 2001.

Interest Rate	Type of Loan	Rate
Discount rate	Reserves lent to banks by Fed	2.00%
Federal funds rate	Interbank reserves, overnight	2.55%
Prime rate	Bank loans to blue chip corporations	5.50%
Mortgage rate	Loans for house purchases; up to 30 years	6.56%
Auto loan	Financing of auto purchase	5.42%
Consumer installment credit	Loans for general purposes	13.25%
Credit cards	Financing of unpaid credit card purchases	14.60%

Source: Federal Reserve.

Were the Fed to reverse its policy and reduce the money supply, interest rates would rise. You can see this result in Figure 15.2 by observing the change in the rate of interest that occurs when the money supply *shrinks* from g_3 to g_1.

Federal Funds Rate. As we noted in Chapter 14, the most visible market signal of the Fed's activity is the **federal funds rate.** When the Fed injects or withdraws reserves from the banking system (via open market operations), the interest rate on interbank loans is most directly affected. Any change in the federal funds rate, moreover, is likely to affect a whole hierarchy of interest rates (see Table 15.1). *The federal funds rate reflects the cost of funds for banks.* When that cost decreases, banks respond by lowering the interest rates *they* charge to businesses (the prime rate), home buyers (the mortgage rate), and consumers (e.g., auto loans, installment credit, credit cards).

federal funds rate: The interest rate for interbank reserve loans.

INTEREST RATES AND SPENDING

A change in the interest rate isn't the end of this story. The ultimate objective of monetary policy is to alter macroeconomic outcomes: prices, output, employment. This requires a change in aggregate demand. Hence, the next question is how changes in interest rates affect consumer, investor, government, and net export spending.

Monetary Stimulus

Consider first a policy of monetary stimulus. The goal of monetary stimulus is to increase **aggregate demand.** A mechanism for doing so is lower interest rates.

aggregate demand: The total quantity of output demanded at alternative price levels in a given time period, *ceteris paribus.*

Investment. Will lower interest rates encourage spending? In Chapter 9 we observed that investment decisions are sensitive to the rate of interest. Specifically, we demonstrated that lower rates of interest reduce the cost of buying plant and equipment, making capital investment more profitable. Lower interest rates also reduce the opportunity cost of holding inventories. Accordingly, a lower rate of interest should result in a higher rate of desired investment spending, as shown by the movement down the investment-demand curve in Figure 15.3b.

Aggregate Demand. The increased investment brought about by lower interest rates represents an injection of new spending into the circular flow. That jump in spending will kick off multiplier effects and result in an even larger increase in aggregate demand. Figure 15.3c illustrates this increase by the rightward *shift* of the aggregate demand curve. Market participants, encouraged by lower interest rates, are now willing to buy more output at the prevailing price level.

Consumers too may change their behavior when interest rates fall. As interest rates fall, mortgage payments decline. Monthly payments on home equity and credit card balances may also decline. These lower interest changes can free up billions of consumer dollars. This increased net cash flow and lower interest rates may encourage

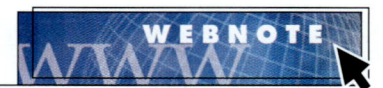

Compare the interest rates in Table 15.1 with today's rates at www.stls.frb.org.

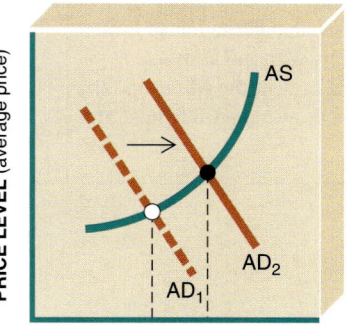

FIGURE 15.3
Monetary Stimulus

An increase in the money supply may reduce interest rates and encourage more investment. The increase in investment will trigger multiplier effects that increase aggregate demand by an even larger amount.

consumers to buy new cars, appliances, or other "big-ticket" items. State and local governments may also conclude that lower interest rates increase the desirability of bond-financed public works. All such responses would add to aggregate demand.

From this perspective, *the Fed's objective of stimulating the economy is achieved in three distinct steps:*

- *An increase in the money supply.*
- *A reduction in interest rates.*
- *An increase in aggregate demand.*

Quantitative Impact. Just how much stimulus can monetary policy create? According to Fed Chairman Alan Greenspan, the impact of monetary policy can be impressive:

$$\text{Greenspan's policy guide:} \quad \frac{1/10 \text{ point reduction in}}{\text{long-term interest rate}} = \frac{\$10 \text{ billion}}{\text{fiscal stimulus}}$$

By this rule of thumb, a full-point reduction in long-term interest rates would increase aggregate demand just as much as a $100 billion injection of new government spending. This is the kind of stimulus Greenspan was hoping for when the Fed cut interest rates repeatedly in 2001.

Like fiscal policy, monetary policy is a two-edged sword, at times seeking to increase aggregate demand and at other times trying to restrain it. When inflation threatens, the objective of monetary policy is to reduce the rate of total spending, which puts the Fed in the position of "leaning against the wind." If successful, the resulting reduction in spending will keep aggregate demand from increasing inflationary pressures.

Monetary Restraint

Higher Interest Rates. The mechanics of monetary policy designed to combat inflation are similar to those used to fight unemployment; only the direction is reversed. In this case, we seek to discourage spending by increasing the rate of interest. The Fed can push interest rates up by selling bonds, increasing the discount rate, or increasing the reserve requirement. All these actions reduce the money supply and help establish a new and higher equilibrium rate of interest.

The ultimate objective of a restrictive monetary policy is to reduce aggregate demand. For monetary restraint to succeed, spending behavior must be responsive to interest rates.

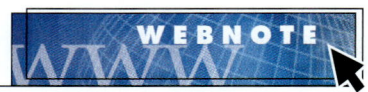

For an official explanation of monetary policy, with links to relevant data, visit the Minneapolis Fed at woodrow.mpls.frb.fed.us/info/policy.

Reduced Aggregate Demand. Figure 15.3 showed the impact of interest rates on investment and aggregate demand. If the interest rate rises from 6 to 7 percent, investment declines from I_2 to I_1 and aggregate demand shifts *leftward*. At higher rates of interest, many marginal investments will no longer be profitable. Likewise, many consumers will decide that they can't afford the higher monthly payments associated with increased interest rates; purchases of homes, cars, and household appliances will be postponed. State and local governments may also decide to cancel or postpone bond-financed projects. Thus, *monetary restraint is achieved with*

- *A decrease in the money supply.*
- *An increase in interest rates.*
- *A decrease in aggregate demand.*

The resulting leftward shift of the aggregate demand curve lessens inflationary pressures.

POLICY CONSTRAINTS

The mechanics of monetary policy are simple enough. They won't always work as well as we might hope, however. Several constraints can limit the Fed's ability to alter the money supply, interest rates, or aggregate demand.

Constraints on Monetary Stimulus

Short- vs. Long-Term Rates. One of the most visible constraints on monetary policy is the distinction between short-term interest rates and long-term interest rates. Greenspan's policy guide (previous page) focuses on changes in *long-term* rates like mortgages and installment loans. Yet, the Fed's open-market operations have the most direct effect on *short-term* rates (e.g., the overnight federal funds rate). As a consequence,

IN THE NEWS

Why Mortgage Rates Aren't Falling

Alan Greenspan Is Cutting Like Mad; but He Doesn't Control the Price of Long-Term Loans, Which Is Why Home Buyers Aren't Getting a Break

If you think that Alan Greenspan really controls interest rates, you haven't looked at the mortgage market lately. Uncle Alan has cut short-term interest rates by 2 percentage points so far this year, and may cut them again at Tuesday's Federal Reserve Board meeting. But the rate on 30-year mortgages—the most popular choice among home buyers—has barely budged. That rate averaged 7.22 percent last week, according to HSH Associates, only a freckle below the 7.31 percent it averaged for the first week of the year. (Fifteen-year rates, favored by refinancers, are down a bit more, to 6.73 from 6.94.) Greenspan started cutting rates on January 3.

Wait a minute. With the Fed cutting short-term rates like crazy, why haven't 30-year mortgages gotten cheaper? The answer is that modifier you probably skipped over: "short-term." The Fed controls *short-term* interest rates, but it doesn't control *long-term* rates. Most people blithely assume that long rates and short rates move in tandem—but they don't. And long-term rates are the key to what lenders charge for long-term, fixed-rate mortgages. "The Fed influences short-term rates to a very high degree, but it controls long-term rates to a lesser degree and sometimes not at all," says David Berson, chief economist of Fannie Mae, the nation's biggest supplier of mortgage money.

—Allan Sloan

Source: *Newsweek,* May 21, 2001, p. 46.

Analysis: Short-term interest rates like the federal funds rate are directly affected by Fed intervention, especially open-market operations. Long-term interest rates don't fluctuate as much, however.

the success of Fed intervention depends in part on how well changes in long-term interest rates mirror changes in short-term interest rates.

In 2001, the Fed reduced the federal funds rate by three full percentage points between January and September, the biggest reduction in short-term rates since 1994. Long-term rates fell much less, however. The interest rate on 30-year mortgages, for example, fell less than half a percentage point (see previous News).

Reluctant Lenders. There are several reasons why long-term rates might not closely mirror changes in short-term rates. The first potential constraint is the willingness of private banks to increase lending activity. The Fed can reduce the cost of funds to the banking system; the Fed can even reduce reserve requirements. But the money supply won't increase as much as expected unless banks lend more money.

If the banks instead choose to accumulate excess reserves, the money supply won't increase as much as intended. This happened in 2001, when the Fed was trying to stimulate the economy but banks were reluctant to increase their loan activity (see News). Banks were trying to shore up their own equity and were wary of making any new loans that might not get repaid in a weak economy. During the Great Depression banks also held onto their excess reserves instead of using them for new loans (recall Figure 14.2). In such cases, long-term rates stay relatively high even when short-term rates are falling.

Liquidity Trap. There are circumstances in which even *short-term* rates may not fall when the Fed wants them to. The possibility that interest rates may not respond to changes in the money supply is illustrated by the liquidity trap. When interest rates are low, the opportunity cost of holding money is cheap. At such times people may decide to hold all the money they can get, waiting for income-earning opportunities to improve. Bond prices, for example, may be high and their yields low. Buying bonds at

IN THE NEWS

Uneasy Banks May Tighten Loans, Stunt Recovery

Institutions Seeing More Write-Offs, Delinquencies

A rising tide of bad commercial loans could make banks more reluctant to lend and blunt the impact of the Federal Reserve's latest interest rate cut.

Banks earned a record $19.9 billion in the first quarter, but the proportion of commercial loans 90 days or more past due increased to 1.8 percent—a seven year high, according to a report released Wednesday by the Federal Deposit Insurance Corp.

In the same period, banks wrote off $7 billion in bad loans, up 38 percent from a year earlier.

The combination of higher write-offs and delinquent loans is worrisome, experts say. . . .

Banks will have to set aside more money as a reserve against loan losses, which will hurt their earnings.

More worrisome: Banks tend to reduce lending when write-offs rise. Even though the Fed's rate cuts could spur loan demand from corporate borrowers, companies could find loans harder to get, which could slow an economic recovery.

Last week, Fed Chief Alan Greenspan noted in a speech the increase in problem loans and urged banks not to choke off credit to healthy borrowers.

But about half of all banks have tightened their commercial loan standards this year, according to a survey released Wednesday by the Comptroller of the Currency, which regulates national banks. The most frequently cited reason was the economic outlook.

—Christine Dugas

Source: *USA Today*, June 23, 2001, p. 61.

Analysis: If banks are reluctant to make new loans in a depressed economy, new bank reserves created by the Fed won't bolster more spending.

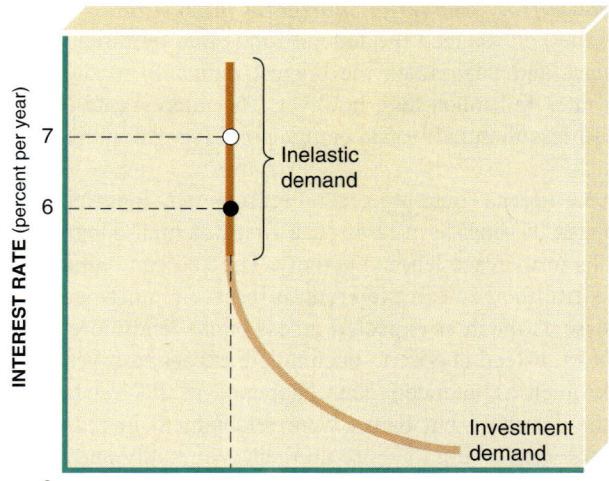

FIGURE 15.4
Constraints on Monetary Stimulus

(a) Liquidity trap If people are willing to hold unlimited amounts of money at the prevailing interest rate, increases in the money supply won't push interest rates lower. A liquidity trap—the horizontal segment of the money demand curve—prevents interest rates from falling.

(b) Inelastic Demand A lower interest rate won't always stimulate investment. If investors have unfavorable expectations for future sales, small reductions in interest rates may not alter their investment decisions. Here the rate of investment remains constant when the interest rate drops from 7 to 6 percent. This kind of situation blocks the second step in the Keynesian approach to monetary policy (see Figure 15.3b).

liquidity trap: The portion of the money demand curve that is horizontal; people are willing to hold unlimited amounts of money at some (low) interest rate.

such times entails the risk of capital losses (when bond prices fall) and little reward (since yields are low). Accordingly, market participants may decide just to hold any additional money the Fed supplies. At this juncture—a phenomenon Keynes called the **liquidity trap**—further expansion of the money supply has no effect on the rate of interest. The horizontal section of the money demand curve in Figure 15.4a portrays this situation.

What happens to interest rates when the initial equilibrium falls into this trap? Nothing at all. Notice that the equilibrium rate of interest doesn't fall when the money supply is increased from g_1 to g_2 (Figure 15.4a). People are willing to hold all that additional money without a reduction in the rate of interest. This is the behavior that neutralized Japan's monetary stimulus in 1999–2001 (see World View).

Low Expectations. Even if both short- and long-term interest rates do fall, we've no assurance that desired *spending* will increase as expected. Keynes put great emphasis on *expectations*. Recall that investment decisions are motivated not only by interest rates but by expectations as well. During a recession—when unemployment is high and the rate of spending low—corporations have little incentive to expand production capacity. With little expectation of future profit, investors are likely to be unimpressed by "cheap money" (low interest rates) and may decline to use the lending capacity that banks make available.

Investment demand that's slow to respond to the stimulus of cheap money is said to be *inelastic* because it won't expand. Consumers too are reluctant to borrow when current and future income prospects are uncertain or distinctly unfavorable. Accordingly, even if the Fed is successful in lowering interest rates, there's no assurance that lower interest rates will stimulate borrowing and spending. Such a reluctance to spend was evident early in 2001, even before the September 11 terrorist attacks. Although the Fed managed to push interest rates down to 20-year lows, investors and consumers preferred to pay off old debts rather than incur new ones (see News on the next page). The September 11 attacks made people even more reluctant to borrow and spend.

Monetary stimulus was even less effective in Japan in 1999–2001. When the Japanese central bank cut the discount rate from an extraordinary low $\frac{1}{2}$ percent to an unheard of $\frac{1}{4}$ percent, no one responded. In the lengthening recession Japanese consumers were trying to save more of their money and producer expectations were glum. So even *really* cheap loans didn't budge the aggregate demand curve.

The vertical portion of the investment demand curve in Figure 15.4 illustrates the possibility that investment spending may not respond to changes in the rate of interest. Notice that a reduction in the rate of interest from 7 percent to 6 percent doesn't increase investment spending. In this case, businesses are simply unwilling to invest any more funds. As a consequence, aggregate spending doesn't rise. The Fed's policy objective remains unfulfilled, even though the Fed has successfully lowered the rate of interest. Recall that the investment demand curve may also *shift* if expectations change. If expectations worsened, the investment demand curve would shift to the left and might result in even *less* investment at 6 percent interest (see Figure 15.4*b*).

Expectations. Expectations could also limit the effectiveness of monetary restraint. In pursuit of "tight" money, the Fed could drain bank reserves and force interest rates

Limits on Monetary Restraint

WORLD VIEW

Why Japan Is Stuck

Free Money Can't Budge the Economy

Decades from now, people may still be arguing over one of the most intriguing economic mysteries of the 1990s: How did a country as rich and sophisticated as Japan fall into a liquidity trap, a bizarre state of affairs in which even near-zero interest rates fail to get banks lending, businesses investing, consumers spending, and the real economy moving?

By any measure, Japan's economic crisis this decade has been a nightmare. A vortex of falling asset prices, banking crises, declining corporate profits, and rising government debt has sucked the economy down. After bumping along with a meager average growth rate of 1.5 percent between 1990 and 1997, Japan is now mired in an awful recession. On March 30, the government announced February's jobless rate had jumped to a record 4.6 percent, while household spending fell 5.7 percent in January, a 13-year low. . . .

Until recently it was barely credible that an advanced economy could face Japan's dilemma. True, academics once thought a lot about liquidity traps, which Depression-era economist John Maynard Keynes raised as a possibility in the 1930s. But interest in the issue waned in the inflationary postwar decades. And periodic recessions responded to the usual measures.

Blunt Tools. Then came the great Japanese recession. Today, the BOJ is virtually giving money away, and nobody wants it.

Japan has vast savings but no credit creation. Japan may have waited far too long to apply classic remedies. Fiscal and monetary tools become blunted once a depression psychology, such as Japan now suffers, sets in.

Japan has cut its official discount rate to 0.5 percent and short-term rates to nearly zero. Yet the economy isn't growing. Here's why:

Banks

Burdened by bad debts and short of capital, they aren't lending; instead, they are putting excess reserves in the bond market.

Companies

They have little incentive to borrow to finance new investment because industrial Japan is already saddled with excess capacity.

Consumers

They are so anxious that they are saving, not spending, even though bank deposits yield less than 1 percent.

Source: *Business Week*, April 12, 1999, p. 48.

Analysis: When consumers and businesses are very pessimistic, they are likely to hold more money rather than spend it. Such a liquidity trap blunts monetary stimulus.

IN THE NEWS

Vicious Cycle

Despite Rate Cuts, Mood in Boardrooms Is Darkening Further

WASHINGTON—Despite Wall Street's widespread hopes for an economic recovery in the second half of 2001, America's business leaders have adopted a decidedly gloomier view.

At companies across the nation, sales and earnings continue to fall below already-lowered expectations. Federal Reserve officials attempted to drive away that storm cloud yesterday by cutting interest rates by a quarter percentage point, their sixth rate cut in as many months. . . .

Fed officials, citing the risks of "economic weakness in the foreseeable future," sent a clear signal that they were poised to keep easing credit conditions through the summer.

The nation's businesses, meanwhile, have dealt with those same uncertainties by cutting spending, closing facilities and laying off workers—actions that, in turn, further dim the prospects for an imminent turnaround and complicate the Fed's job of keeping the economy out of the ditch. . . .

As corporate cutbacks ripple through the economy, they eventually reach consumers. After Alan White took a $125,000-a-year job last fall as marketing director for a division of Nortel Networks, his wife set her sights on buying an $18,000 silver Chrysler PT Cruiser. Even as the company went through a few waves of layoffs, earlier this year, Mr. White, who works for Nortel from his Alabama home, was spared.

In May, however, Nortel shut down the high-speed Internet-equipment business Mr. White worked for, which it had purchased just a year earlier. Nortel's first, selective layoffs seemed like the kind of retrenchments Mr. White had seen before. But the cuts that claimed his job were different, he says. "There was some shock. . . at the concept they would just dump the entire business, without selling it off or severely downsizing it." Now his family's new-car plans are on hold. Lower interest rates? He says they will mean little to him "unless I decide to buy something, and I'm not going to buy something until I have permanent employment."

That's partly why Fed officials say they are worried about "weak expansion of consumption," and why spending isn't growing at the pace that many store chains had expected, forcing a new wave of retrenchment in the retailing sector.

—Greg Ip

Source: *The Wall Street Journal*, June 28, 2001, p. 1.

Analysis: Interest rate cuts are supposed to stimulate investment and consumption. But gloomy expectations may deter people from borrowing and spending.

---

higher. Yet market participants might continue to borrow and spend if high expectations for rising sales and profits overwhelm high interest rates in investment decisions. Consumers too might believe that future incomes will be sufficient to cover larger debts and higher interest charges. Both groups might foresee accelerating inflation that would make even high interest rates look cheap in the future.

Global Money. Market participants might also tap global sources of money. If money gets too tight in domestic markets, business may borrow funds from foreign banks or institutions. GM, Disney, Exxon, and other multinational corporations can borrow funds from foreign subsidiaries, banks, and even bond markets. As we saw in Chapter 14, market participants can also secure funds from nonbank sources in the United States. These nonbank and global lenders make it harder for the Fed to restrain aggregate demand.

How Effective? In view of all these constraints on monetary policies, some observers have concluded that monetary policy is an undependable policy lever. Keynes, for example, emphasized that monetary policy wouldn't be very effective in ending a deep recession. He believed that the combination of reluctant bankers, the liquidity trap, and low expectations would render monetary stimulus ineffective. Using monetary policy to stimulate the economy in such circumstances would be akin to "pushing on a string." Alan Greenspan came to much the same conclusion in September 1992 when he said that further Fed stimulus would be ineffective in accelerating a recovery from the 1990–91 recession. He believed, however, that earlier cuts in interest rates would help stimulate spending once banks, investors, and consumers gained confidence in the economic out-

Analysis: Sometimes monetary stimulus doesn't get a stalled economy moving again.

look. The same kind of problem existing in 2001: The Fed's actions to reduce interest rates (11 times in as many months!) weren't enough to propel the economy forward (see cartoon). Market participants had to recover their confidence in the future before they would start spending "cheap" money.

The limitations on monetary restraint aren't considered as serious. The Fed has the power to reduce the money supply. If the money supply shrinks far enough, the rate of spending will have to slow down.

THE MONETARIST PERSPECTIVE

The Keynesian view of money emphasizes the role of interest rates in fulfilling the goals of monetary policy. *In the Keynesian model, changes in the money supply affect macro outcomes primarily through changes in interest rates.* The three-step sequence of (1) money supply change, (2) interest rate movement, and (3) aggregate demand shift makes monetary policy subject to several potential uncertainties. As we've seen, the economy doesn't always respond as expected to Fed policy.

An alternative view of monetary policy seizes on those occasional failures to offer another explanation of how the money supply affects macro outcomes. The so-called Monetarist school dismisses changes in short-term interest rates (e.g., the fed funds rate) as unpredictable and ineffective. They don't think real output levels are affected by monetary stimulus. As they see it, only the price level is affected by Fed policy, and then only by changes in the money supply. Monetarists conclude that monetary policy isn't an effective tool for fighting short-run business cycles, but it is a powerful tool for managing inflation.

Monetarists assert that the potential of monetary policy can be expressed in a simple equation called the **equation of exchange,** written as

$$MV = PQ$$

where M refers to the quantity of money in circulation and V to its **velocity** of circulation. Total spending in the economy is equal to the average price (P) of goods times the quantity (Q) of goods sold in a period. This spending is financed by the supply of money (M) times the velocity of its circulation (V).

Suppose, for example, that only two participants are in the market and that the money supply consists of one crisp $20 bill. What's the limit to total spending in this case? If you answer "$20," you haven't yet grasped the nature of the circular flow. Suppose I

The Equation of Exchange

equation of exchange: Money supply (M) times velocity of circulation (V) equals level of aggregate spending ($P \times Q$).

> **income velocity of money (V):** The number of times per year, on average, a dollar is used to purchase final goods and services; $PQ \div M$.

begin the circular flow by spending $20 on eggs, bacon, and a gallon of milk. The money I spend ends up in Farmer Brown's pocket because he is the only other market participant. Once in possession of the money, Farmer Brown may decide to satisfy his long-smoldering desire to learn something about economics and buy one of my books. If he acts on that decision, the $20 will return to me. At that point, both Farmer Brown and I have sold $20 worth of goods. Hence, $40 of total spending has been financed with one $20 bill.

As long as we keep using this $20 bill to buy goods and services from each other, we can continue to do business. Moreover, the faster we pass the money from hand to hand during any period of time, the greater the value of sales each of us can register. If the money is passed from hand to hand eight times, then I'll be able to sell $80 worth of textbooks and Farmer Brown will be able to sell $80 worth of produce during that period, for a total nominal output of $160. **The quantity of money in circulation and the velocity with which it travels (changes hands) in product markets will always be equal to the value of total spending and income (nominal GDP).** The relationship is summarized as

$$M \times V = P \times Q$$

In this case, the *equation of exchange* confirms that

$$\$20 \times 8 = \$160$$

The value of total sales for the year is $160.

Monetarists use the equation of exchange to simplify the explanation of how monetary policy works. There's no need, they argue, to follow the effects of changes in M through the money markets to interest rates and further to changes in total spending. The basic consequences of monetary policy are evident in the equation of exchange. The two sides of the equation of exchange must always be in balance. Hence, we can be absolutely certain that *if* **M increases, prices (P) or output (Q) must rise, or V must fall.**

The equation of exchange is an incontestable statement of how the money supply is related to macro outcomes. The equation itself, however, says nothing about *which* variables will respond to a change in the money supply. The *goal* of monetary policy is to change the macro outcomes on the right side of the equation. It's *possible*, however, that a change in M might be offset with a reverse change in V, leaving P and Q unaffected. Or it could happen that the *wrong* macro outcome is affected. Prices (P) might rise, for example, when we're trying to increase real output (Q).

Stable Velocity

Monetarists add some important assumptions to transform the equation of exchange from a simple identity to a behavioral *model* of macro performance. The first assumption is that the velocity of money (V) is stable. How fast people use their money balances depends on the institutional structure of money markets and people's habits. Neither the structure of money markets nor people's habits are likely to change when M is altered. Accordingly, an increase in M won't be offset by a reduction in V. Instead, the impact of an increased money supply will be transmitted to the right-hand side of the equation of exchange, which means that **total spending must rise if the money supply (M) grows and V is stable.**

Money Supply Focus

From a monetarist perspective, there's no need to trace the impacts of monetary policy through interest rate movements. The focus on interest rates is a uniquely Keynesian perspective. Monetarists claim that interest rate movements are secondary to the major thrust of monetary policy. **As monetarists see it, changes in the money supply must alter total spending, regardless of how interest rates move.**

A monetarist perspective leads to a wholly different strategy for the Fed. Because interest rates aren't part of the monetarist explanation of how monetary policy works, the Fed shouldn't try to manipulate interest rates (see News); instead, it should focus on the money supply itself. Monetarists also argue that the Fed can't really control in-

IN THE NEWS

Monetarists Reject Focus on Lowering Rates

A group of monetarist economists urged the . . . administration and the Federal Reserve yesterday to stop trying to encourage faster economic growth by insisting on lower interest rates.

The group, known as the Shadow Open Market Committee, said that the gross national product, adjusted for inflation, has grown during the past two years at a 2½ percent annual rate, only slightly less than its average for the last 100 years.

"Efforts to force interest rates lower, to depreciate the dollar and to stimulate the economy to head off protectionist (trade) legislation are based on the mistaken belief that we have learned how to stimulate now and prevent inflation later," the committee said in a statement issued after one of its semiannual meetings in New York. . . .

The Shadow Committee, headed by economists Allan H. Meltzer of Carnegie-Mellon University and Karl Brunner of the University of Rochester, was formed more than a decade ago to provide economic analysis and policy recommendations from a monetarist point of view.

—John M. Berry

Source: *Washington Post,* September 23, 1986, p. Cl. © 1986, The Washington Post. Reprinted with permission. www.washingtonpost.com

Analysis: Monetarists reject the notion that lower interest rates will necessarily stimulate aggregate demand. What matters is the supply of money, not the rate of interest.

---

terest rates well since they depend on both the supply of and the demand for money. What the Fed *can* control is the supply of money, and the equation of exchange clearly shows that money matters.

Some monetarists add yet another perspective to the equation of exchange. They assert that not only V but Q as well is stable. If this is true, then changes in the money supply (M) would affect only prices (P).

What does it mean for Q to be stable? The argument here is that the quantity of goods produced is primarily dependent on production capacity, labor market efficiency, and other "structural" forces. These structural forces establish a **"natural" rate of unemployment** that's fairly immune to short-run policy intervention. This is the *long-run* aggregate supply curve we first encountered in Chapter 8. From this perspective, there's no reason for producers to depart from this "natural" rate of output when the money supply increases. Producers are smart enough to know that both prices and costs will rise when spending increases. Hence, rising prices won't create any new profit incentives for increasing output. Firms will just continue producing at the "natural" rate with higher (nominal) prices and costs. As a result, increases in aggregate spending—whether financed by more M or faster V—aren't likely to alter real output levels. Q will stay constant.

If the quantity of real output is in fact stable, then P is the only thing that can change. Thus, **the most extreme monetarist perspective concludes that changes in the money supply affect prices only.** As the "simple economics" in the accompanying cartoon sug-

"Natural" Unemployment

natural rate of unemployment: long-term rate of unemployment determined by structural forces in labor and product markets.

Analysis: If the money supply shrinks (or its growth rate slows), price levels will rise less quickly.

gests, a decrease in *M* should directly reduce the price level. When *M increases,* total spending rises, but the higher nominal value of spending is completely absorbed by higher prices. In this view, monetary policy affects only the rate of inflation. This is the kind of money-driven inflation that bedeviled George Washington's army (see News).

Figure 15.5 illustrates the extreme monetarist argument in the context of aggregate supply and demand. The assertion that real output is fixed at the natural rate of unemployment is reflected in the vertical aggregate supply curve. With real output stuck at Q^*, any increase in aggregate demand directly raises the price level.

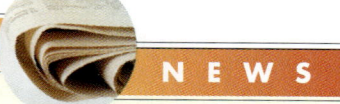

At first glance, the monetarist argument looks pretty slick. Keynesians worry about how the money supply affects interest rates, how interest rates affect spending, and how spending affects output. By contrast, monetarists point to a simple equation ($MV = PQ$) that produces straightforward responses to monetary policy.

There are fundamental differences between the two schools here, not only about how the economy works but also about how successful macro policy might be. To appreciate those differences, consider monetarist responses to inflationary and recessionary gaps.

Fighting Inflation. Consider again the options for fighting inflation. The objective of policy is to reduce aggregate spending. From a Keynesian perspective, the way to achieve this reduction is to shrink the money supply and drive up interest rates. But monetarists argue that nominal interest rates are already likely to be high. Furthermore, if an effective anti-inflation policy is adopted, interest rates will come *down,* not go up.

Real vs. Nominal Interest. To understand this monetarist conclusion, we have to distinguish between *nominal* interest rates and *real* ones. Nominal interest rates are the

IN THE NEWS

"Not Worth a Continental": The U.S. Experience with Hyperinflation

The government of the United States had no means to pay for the Revolutionary War. Specifically, the federal government had no power to levy taxes that might transfer resources from the private sector to the public sector. Instead, it could only request the states to levy taxes of their own and contribute them to the war effort. The states were not very responsive, however: state contributions accounted for only 6 percent of federal revenues during the war years.

To pay for needed weapons and soldiers, the federal government had only two other options, either (1) borrow money or (2) create new money. When loans proved to be inadequate, the Continental Congress started issuing new paper money—the "Continental" dollar—in 1775. By the end of 1779, Congress had authorized issuance of over $250 million in Continental dollars.

At first the paper money enabled George Washington's troops to acquire needed supplies, ammunition, and volunteers. But soon the flood of paper money inundated product markets. Wholesale prices of key commodities skyrocketed.

Commodity prices *doubled* in 1776, in 1777, and again in 1778. Then prices increased *tenfold* in the next two years.

Many farmers and storekeepers refused to sell goods to the army in exchange for Continental dollars. Rapid inflation had taught them that the paper money George Washington's troops offered was nearly worthless. The expression "not worth a Continental" became a popular reference to things of little value.

The states tried price controls and even empowered themselves to seize needed war supplies. But nothing could stop the inflation fueled by the explosive increase in the money supply. Fortunately, the war ended before the economy collapsed. After the war, the U.S. Congress established a new form of money, and in 1787 it empowered the federal government to levy taxes and mint gold and silver coins.

Source: Sidney Ratner, James H. Soltow, and Richard Sylla, *The Evolution of the American Economy.* © 1979 by Basic Books; 2nd ed., Macmillan, 1993. Reprinted by permission of the authors.

Analysis: Rapid expansion of the money supply will push the price level up. As inflation accelerates, money becomes less valuable.

FIGURE 15.5
The Monetarist View

Monetarists argue that the rate of real output is set by structural factors. Furthermore, firms aren't likely to be fooled into producing more just because prices are rising if costs are rising just as much. Hence, long-run aggregate supply remains at the "natural" level Q^*. Any increases in aggregate demand, therefore, raise the price level (inflation) but not output.

ones we actually see and pay. When a bank pays 5½ percent interest on your bank account, it's quoting (and paying) a nominal rate.

Real interest rates are never actually seen and rarely quoted. These are "inflation-adjusted" rates. Specifically, the **real interest rate** equals the nominal rate *minus* the anticipated rate of inflation; that is,

$$\text{Real interest rate} = \text{nominal interest rate} - \text{anticipated inflation rate}$$

real interest rate: The nominal rate of interest minus anticipated inflation rate.

Recall what inflation does to the purchasing power of the dollar: As inflation continues, each dollar purchases fewer goods and services. As a consequence, dollars borrowed today are of less real value when they're paid back later. The real rate of interest reflects this inflation adjustment.

Suppose you lend someone $100 at the beginning of the year, at 8 percent interest. You expect to get more back at the end of the year than you start with. That "more" you expect refers to *real* goods and services, not just dollar bills. Specifically, you anticipate that when the loan is repaid with interest at the end of the year, you'll be able to buy more goods and services than you could at the beginning. This expectation of a *real* gain is at least part of the reason for making a loan.

Your expected gain won't materialize, however, if all prices rise by 8 percent during the year. If the inflation rate is 8 percent, you'll discover that $108 buys you no more at the end of the year than $100 would have bought you at the beginning. Hence, you'd have given up the use of your money for an entire year without any real compensation. In such circumstances, the *real* rate of interest turns out to be zero; that is,

$$\text{Real interest rate} = 8\% \text{ nominal interest rate} - 8\% \text{ inflation rate}$$
$$= 0\%$$

The nominal rate of interest, then, really has two components: (1) the real rate of interest, and (2) an inflation adjustment. If the real rate of interest was 4 percent and an inflation rate of 9 percent was expected, the nominal rate of interest would be 13 percent. If inflationary expectations *improved*, the *nominal* interest rate would *fall*. This is evident in the rearranged formula:

$$\text{Nominal interest rate} = \text{real interest rate} + \text{anticipated rate of inflation}$$

If the real interest rate is 4 percent and anticipated inflation falls from 9 to 6 percent, the nominal interest rate would decline from 13 to 10 percent.

A central assumption of the monetarist perspective is that the real rate of interest is fairly stable. This is a critical point. *If the real rate of interest is stable, then changes in the nominal interest rate reflect only changes in anticipated inflation.* From this perspective, high nominal rates of interest are a symptom of inflation, not a cure. Indeed, high nominal rates may even look cheap if inflationary expectations are worsening faster than interest rates are rising (see News).

Consider the implications of all this for monetary policy. Suppose we want to close an inflationary GDP gap. Monetarists and Keynesians alike agree that a reduced money supply (*M*) will deflate total spending. But Keynesians rely on a "quick fix" of *higher* interest rates to slow consumption and investment spending. Monetarists, by contrast, assert that nominal interest rates will *fall* if the Fed tightens the money supply. Once market participants are convinced that the Fed is going to reduce money supply growth, inflationary expectations diminish. When inflationary expectations diminish, nominal interest rates will begin to fall.

To get a global view of how interest rates and inflation move together, visit Australia (their central bank) at www.rba.gov.au.

Short- vs. Long-Term Rates (again). The Monetarist argument is supported by the different movements of short-term and long-term interest rates. As we observed earlier, short-run rates (like the federal funds rate) are very responsive to Fed intervention. But long-term rates are much slower to respond. This suggests that banks and borrowers look beyond current economic conditions in making long-term financial commitments.

If the Fed is reducing money-supply growth, short-term rates may rise quickly. But long-term rates won't increase unless market participants expect inflation to worsen. Given the pivotal role of long-term rates in investment decisions, the Fed may have to stall GDP growth—even spark a recession—to restrain aggregate demand enough to stop prices from rising. Rather than take such risks, *monetarists advocate steady and predictable changes in the money supply.* Such a policy, they believe, would reduce uncertainties and thus stabilize both long-term interest rates and GDP growth.

IN THE NEWS

Money Is Free!

"Money's not tight, it's cheap. It's free!"

So says one of our most articulate friends along Wall Street. The point is that short-term interest rates, horrendous as they are, are below the short-term inflation rate, horrendous as it is. The August numbers showed a six-month inflation rate of 9.4 percent, for example, while six months earlier the prime interest rate was 8.0 percent. If you borrowed and paid back in cheaper dollars, you got your money for free.

We relate the quote because we have the impression a lot of folks in Washington don't realize how those of us out here in the real world look at these matters. In particular, the observation ought to be of interest to the Federal Reserve's Open Market Committee, which meets today to set money growth targets for both the next two months and the next year.

Out here in the real world, folks know free money when they see it. That is why interest rates will not go down, nor the dollar recover meaningfully, until inflation is reduced. And the longer the Fed delays in starting to curb money growth, the higher price the nation will have to pay before inflation is ultimately brought under control.

Source: *The Wall Street Journal.* Reprinted by permission of *The Wall Street Journal,* © 1978 Dow Jones & Company, Inc. All rights reserved worldwide. www.wsj.com

Analysis: Monetarists argue that changes in nominal interest rates have little effect on investment. In their view, *real* (inflation-adjusted) interest rates determine investment behavior.

Fighting Unemployment. The link between anticipated inflation and nominal interest rates also constrains expansionary monetary policy. The Keynesian cure for a recession is to expand M and lower interest rates. But monetarists fear that an increase in M will lead—via the equation of exchange—to higher P. If everyone believed this would happen, then an unexpectedly large increase in M would immediately raise people's inflationary expectations. Even if short-term interest rates fell, long-term interest rates might actually rise. This would defeat the purpose of monetary stimulus.

From a monetarist perspective, expansionary monetary policies aren't likely to lead us out of a recession (look again at the cartoon on p. 309). On the contrary, such policies might double our burden by heaping inflation on top of our unemployment woes. The rate of real output and employment is more dependent on structural characteristics of the economy than on changes in the money supply. All monetary policy should do is ensure a stable and predictable rate of growth in the money supply. Then people could concentrate on real production decisions without worrying so much about fluctuating prices.

THE CONCERN FOR CONTENT

Monetary policy, like fiscal policy, can affect more than just the *level* of total spending. We must give some consideration to the impact of Federal Reserve actions on the *content* of the GDP if we're going to be responsive to the "second crisis" of economic theory.[1]

The Mix of Output

Both Keynesians and monetarists agree that monetary policy will affect nominal interest rates. When interest rates change, not all spending decisions will be affected equally. Investment decisions that are highly sensitive to interest rates are more susceptible to monetary policy than others. The construction industry, especially the residential housing market, stands out in this respect. The sensitivity of housing costs to interest rate changes forces the construction industry to bear a disproportionate burden of restrictive monetary policy. Accordingly, when the Fed pursues a policy of tight money—high interest rates and limited lending capacity—it not only restrains total spending but reduces the share of housing in that spending. Utility industries, public works projects, and state and local finances are also disproportionately affected by monetary policy.

In addition to altering the content of demand and output, monetary policy affects the competitive structure of the market. When money is tight, banks must ration available credit among loan applicants. Large and powerful corporations aren't likely to run out of credit because banks will be hesitant to incur their displeasure and lose their business. Thus, General Motors and IBM stand a much better chance of obtaining tight money than does the corner grocery store. Moreover, if bank lending capacity becomes too small, GM and IBM can always resort to the bond market and borrow money directly from the public. Small businesses seldom have such an alternative.

Income Redistribution

Monetary policy also affects the distribution of income. When interest rates fall, borrowers pay smaller interest charges. On the other hand, lenders get smaller interest payments. Hence, a lower interest rate redistributes income from lenders to borrowers. When interest rates declined sharply in 2001, homeowners refinanced their mortgages and saved billions of dollars in interest payments. The decline in interest rates, however, *reduced* the income of retired persons, who depend heavily on interest payments from certificates of deposit, bonds, and other assets.

---

[1] See the quotation from Joan Robinson in Chapter 11, calling attention to the exclusive focus of economists on the *level* of economic activity (the "first crisis"), to the neglect of content (the "second crisis").

THE ECONOMY TOMORROW

Which Lever to Pull?

Our success in managing the macro economy of tomorrow depends on pulling the right policy levers at the right time. But which levers should be pulled? Keynesians and monetarists offer very different prescriptions for treating an ailing economy. Can we distill some usable policy guidelines from this discussion for policy decisions in the economy tomorrow?

The Policy Levers

The equation of exchange is a convenient summary of the differences between Keynesian and monetarist perspectives. There's no disagreement about the equation itself: aggregate spending ($M \times V$) must equal the value of total sales ($P \times Q$). *What Keynesians and monetarists argue about is which of the policy levers—M or V—is likely to be effective in altering aggregate spending.*

- *Monetarists* point to changes in the money supply (M) as the principal lever of macroeconomic policy. They assume V is reasonably stable.
- *Keynesian* fiscal policy *must* rely on changes in the velocity of money (V) because tax and expenditure policies have no direct impact on the money supply.

Crowding Out

The extreme monetarist position that *only* money matters is based on the assumption that the velocity of money (V) is constant. *If V is constant, changes in total spending can come about only through changes in the money supply.* There are no other policy levers on the left side of the equation of exchange.

Think about an increase in government spending designed to stimulate the economy. How does the government pay for this fiscal policy initiative? Monetarists argue that there are only two ways to pay for this increased expenditure (G): The government must either raise additional taxes or borrow more money. If the government raises taxes, the disposable income of consumers will be reduced, and private spending will fall. On the other hand, if the government borrows more money to pay for its expenditures, there will be less money available for loans to private consumers and investors. In either case, more government spending (G) implies less private spending (C or I). Thus, *increased G effectively* **"crowds out"** *some C or I, leaving total spending unchanged.* From this viewpoint, fiscal policy is ineffective; it can't even shift the aggregate demand curve. At best, fiscal policy can change the composition of demand and thus the mix of output. Only changes in M (monetary policy) can shift the aggregate demand curve.

Milton Friedman, formerly of the University of Chicago, champions the monetarist view with this argument:

> I believe that the state of the government budget matters; matters a great deal—for some things. The state of the government budget determines what fraction of the nation's income is spent through the government and what fraction is spent by individuals privately. The state of the government budget determines what the level of our taxes is, how much of our income we turn over to the government. The state of the government budget has a considerable effect on interest rates. If the federal government runs a large deficit, that means the government has to borrow in the market, which raises the demand for loanable funds and so tends to raise interest rates.
>
> If the government budget shifts to a surplus, that adds to the supply of loanable funds, which tends to lower interest rates. It was no surprise to those of us who stress money that enactment of the surtax was followed by a decline in interest rates. That's precisely what we had predicted and what our analysis leads us to predict. But—and I come to the main point—in my opinion, the state of the budget by itself has no significant effect on the course of nominal income, on inflation, on deflation, or on cyclical fluctuations.[2]

Keynesians reply that the alleged constant velocity of money is a monetarist's pipe dream. Some even argue that the velocity of money is so volatile that changes in V can

crowding out: A reduction in private-sector borrowing (and spending) caused by increased government borrowing.

---

[2] Milton Friedman and Walter W. Heller, *Monetary vs. Fiscal Policy* (New York: Norton, 1969). pp. 50–51.

TABLE 15.2
How Fiscal Policy Matters: Monetarist vs. Keynesian Views
Monetarists and Keynesians have very different views on the impact of fiscal policy. Monetarists assert that changes in government spending (G) and taxes (T) don't alter the velocity of money (V). As a result, fiscal policy alone can't alter total spending. Keynesians reject this view, arguing that V is changeable. They claim that tax cuts and increased government spending increase the velocity of money and so alter total spending.

Do Changes in G or T Affect:	Monetarist View	Keynesian View
1. Aggregate demand?	No (stable V causes crowding out)	Yes (V changes)
2. Prices?	No (aggregate demand not affected)	Maybe (if at capacity)
3. Real output?	No (aggregate demand not affected)	Yes (output responds to demand)
4. Nominal interest rates?	Yes (crowding out)	Maybe (may alter demand for money)
5. Real interest rates?	No (determined by real growth)	Yes (real growth and expectations may vary)

completely offset changes in M, leaving us with the proposition that money doesn't matter.

The liquidity trap illustrates the potential for V to change. Keynes argued that people tend to accumulate money balances—slow their rate of spending—during recessions. A slowdown in spending implies a reduction in the velocity of money. Indeed, in the extreme case of the liquidity trap, the velocity of money falls toward zero. Under these circumstances, changes in M (monetary policy) won't influence total spending. The velocity of money falls as rapidly as M increases. On the other hand, increased government spending (fiscal policy) can stimulate aggregate spending by putting idle money balances to work (thereby increasing V). Changes in fiscal policy will also influence consumer and investor expectations, and thereby further alter the rate of aggregate spending.

Tables 15.2 and 15.3 summarize these different perspectives on fiscal and monetary policy. The first table evaluates fiscal policy from both Keynesian and monetarist view-

How Fiscal Policy Works: Two Views

Do Changes in M Affect:	Monetarist View	Keynesian View
1. Aggregate demand?	Yes (V stable)	Maybe (V may change)
2. Prices?	Yes (V and Q stable)	Maybe (V and Q may change)
3. Real output?	No (rate of unemployment determined by structural forces)	Maybe (output responds to demand)
4. Nominal interest rates?	Yes (but direction unknown)	Maybe (liquidity trap)
5. Real interest rates?	No (depends on real growth)	Maybe (real growth may vary)

TABLE 15.3
How Money Matters: Monetarist vs. Keynesian Views
Because monetarists believe that V is stable, they assert that changes in the money supply (M) must alter total spending. But all the monetary impact is reflected in prices and nominal interest rates; *real* output and interest rates are unaffected.

Keynesians think that V is variable and thus that changes in M might *not* alter total spending. If monetary policy does alter aggregate spending, however, Keynesians expect all outcomes to be affected.

points. The central issue is whether and how a change in government spending (G) or taxes (T) will alter macroeconomic outcomes. Keynesians assert that aggregate demand will be affected as the velocity of money (V) changes. Monetarists say no, because they anticipate an unchanged V.

If aggregate demand isn't affected by a change in G or T, then fiscal policy won't affect prices (P) or real output (Q). Thus, monetarists conclude that fiscal policy isn't a viable tool for combating either inflation or unemployment. By contrast, Keynesians believe V will change and that output and prices will respond accordingly.

Insofar as interest rates are concerned, monetarists recognize that nominal interest rates will be affected (read Friedman's quote again) but *real* rates won't be because real interest rates depend on real output and growth, both of which are seen as immune to fiscal policy. Keynesians see less impact on nominal interest rates and more on real interest rates.

What all this boils down to is this: Fiscal policy, by itself, will be effective only if it can alter the velocity of money. **How well fiscal policy works depends on how much the velocity of money can be changed by government tax and spending decisions.**

How Monetary Policy Works: Two Views

Table 15.3 is a similar summary of monetary policy. This time the positions of monetarists and Keynesians are reversed, or nearly so. Monetarists say a change in M must alter total spending ($P \times Q$) because V is stable. Keynesians assert that V may vary, so they aren't convinced that monetary policy will always work. The heart of the controversy is again the velocity of money. Monetary policy works as long as V is stable, or at least predictable. **How well monetary policy works depends on how stable or predictable V is.**

Once the central role of velocity is understood, everything else falls into place. Monetarists assert that prices but not output will be directly affected by a change in M because the right-hand side of the equation of exchange contains only two variables (P and Q), and one of them (Q) is assumed unaffected by monetary policy. Keynesians, by contrast, aren't so sure prices will be affected by M or that real output won't be. It all depends on V and the responsiveness of P and Q to changes in aggregate spending.

Finally, monetarists predict that nominal interest rates will respond to changes in M, although they're not sure in what direction. It depends on how inflationary expectations adapt to changes in the money supply. Keynesian economists aren't so sure nominal interest rates will change but are sure about the direction if they do.

Is Velocity Stable?

Tables 15.2 and 15.3 highlight the velocity of money as a critical determinant of policy impact. The critical question appears to be whether V is stable or not. Why hasn't someone answered this simple question and resolved the debate over fiscal versus monetary policy?

Long-Run Stability. The velocity of money (V) turns out, in fact, to be quite stable over long periods of time. Over the past 30 years the velocity of money (M2) has averaged about 1.64, as Figure 15.6 illustrates. Moreover, the range of velocity has been fairly narrow, extending from a low of 1.56 in 1987 to a high of 2.05 in 1997. Monetarists conclude that the historical pattern justifies the assumption of a stable V.

Short-Run Instability. Keynesians reply that monetarists are farsighted and so fail to see significant short-run variations in V. The difference between a velocity of 1.56 and velocity of 2.05 translates into hundreds of billions of dollars in aggregate demand. Moreover, there's a pattern to short-run variations in V: Velocity tends to decline in recessions (see Figure 15.6). These are precisely the situations in which fiscal stimulus (increasing V) would be appropriate.

Money Supply Targets

The differing views of Keynesians and monetarists clearly lead to different conclusions about which policy lever to pull.

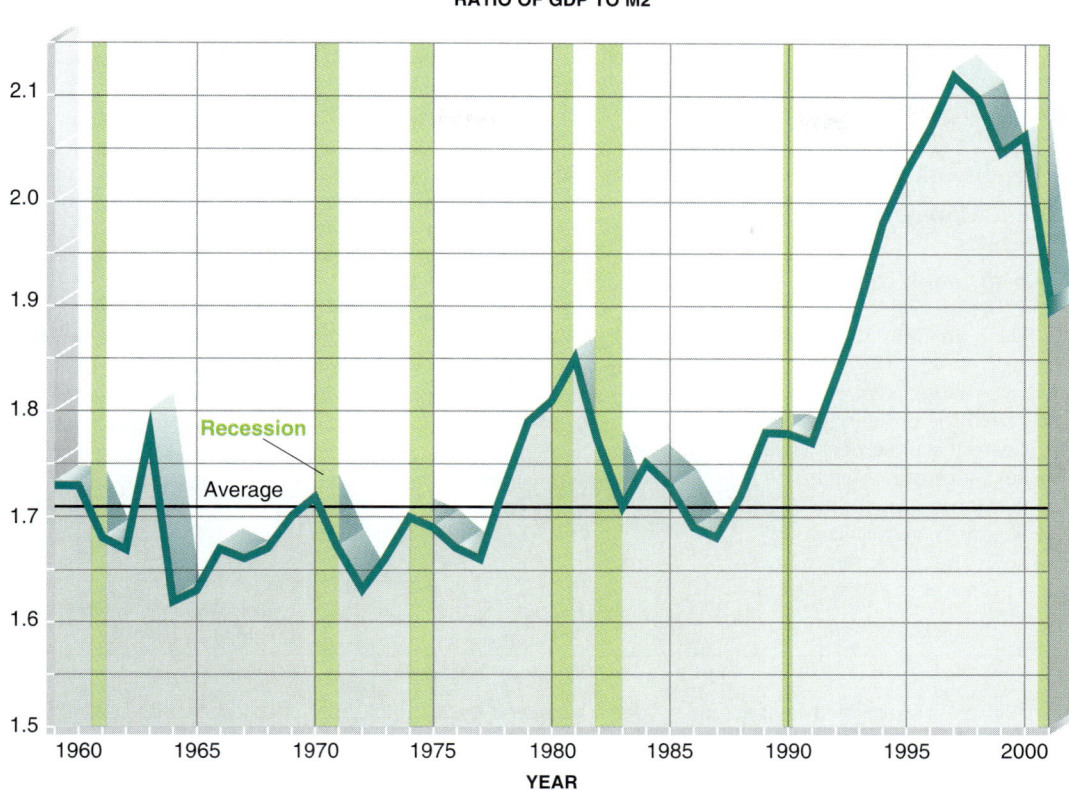

FIGURE 15.6
The Velocity of M2

The velocity of money (the ratio of GDP to M2) averages about 1.64. However, V appears to decline in recessions. Keynes urged the use of fiscal stimulus to boost V. Monetarists caution that short-run changes in V are too unpredictable.

Source: Federal Reserve

Monetarist Advice. The monetarists' policy advice to the Fed is straightforward. *Monetarists favor fixed money supply targets.* They believe that V is stable in the long run and unpredictable in the short run. Hence, the safest course of action is to focus on M. All the Fed has to do is announce its intention to increase the money supply by some fixed amount (such as 3 percent per year), then use its central banking powers to hit that money growth target. After rock-bottom interest rates failed to ignite the Japanese economy, the Bank of Japan decided to adopt the Monetarist approach in 2001 (see World View on the next page).

Keynesian Advice. *Keynesians reject fixed money supply targets,* favoring more flexibility in control of the money supply. In their view, a fixed money supply target would render monetary policy useless in combating cyclical swings of the economy. Keynesians prefer the risks of occasional policy errors to the straitjacket of a fixed money supply target. *Keynesians advocate targeting interest rates, not the money supply.* Keynesians also advocate liberal use of the fiscal policy lever.

The Fed's Eclecticism. For a brief period (1979–82) the Fed adopted the monetarists' policy of fixed money supply targets. On October 6, 1979, the chairman of the Fed (Paul Volcker) announced that the Fed would begin focusing on the money supply exclusively, without worrying about interest rates. The Fed's primary goal was to reduce inflation, which was then running at close to 14 percent a year. To slow the inflationary spiral, the Fed decided to limit sharply growth of the money supply.

Deflation Still Haunts the Bank of Japan
Critics Say Pledge to Raise a Money-Supply Target Hasn't Produced Results

TOKYO—The Japanese central bank, which had raised hopes it would try to reflate the nation's weak economy, again faces mounting criticism that it is failing to fight the demon of deflation.

The Bank of Japan said in March it would start aiming for a higher money supply, departing from the ordinary practice of targeting a key interest rate, to ease the price declines hammering Japanese companies. But since the March 19 announcement, economists note that Japan's key money-supply indicator has risen modestly, while prices are falling faster. . . .

Deflation is getting worse. The central bank said domestic wholesale prices fell 0.8 percent from a year earlier, dropping for the 10th month in a row.

The data put fresh pressure on central bank governor Masaru Hayami to do more to boost Japan's weakening economy. The bank's policy board meets Monday; most analysts expect it to ease credit in the next few months, but not right away.

In March, the bank unveiled a policy dubbed "quantitative easing," saying it would begin targeting increases in a part of the money supply—the reserve funds that private-sector banks keep at the Bank of Japan—starting with a boost to five trillion yen ($40.48 billion) from four trillion yen. The bank also said it would increase its outright purchases of long-term Japanese government bonds if necessary to top up the money supply.

—Michael Williams

Source: *The Wall Street Journal*, August 9, 2001, p. A9.

Analysis: When low (near zero) interest rates failed to spark an economy recovery, the Bank of Japan focused on increases in the money supply. Their goal was to keep the price level (*P*) from falling.

The Fed succeeded in reducing money supply growth and the inflationary spiral. But its tight-money policies sent interest rates soaring and pushed the economy into a deep recession (1981–82). Exactly three years after adopting the monetarist approach, the Fed abandoned it.

In place of a strict monetarist approach,[3] the Fed adopted an eclectic mixture of monetarist and Keynesian policies. For many years the Fed announced targets for money supply growth. But the targets were very broad and not very stable. At the beginning of 1986, for example, the Fed set a target of 3 to 8 percent growth for M1. That wide target gave it plenty of room to adjust to changing interest rates and cyclical changes. But the Fed actually missed the target by a mile—M1 increased by 15 percent in 1986. In explaining this mile-wide miss to Congress, Chairman Volcker emphasized pragmatism. "Success," he asserted, "will not be measured by whether or not we meet some preordained, arbitrary target: but by our macroeconomic performance." Since the economy was growing steadily in 1987, and inflation wasn't increasing, he concluded that monetary policy had been a success. He concluded his testimony by telling Congress that the Fed would no longer set targets for M1 but would instead keep an eye on broader money supply measures (M2 and M3; see Table 13.1) and interest rates. Nobel Laureate Paul Samuelson provided a glib explanation of this approach by noting that "God gave us two eyes so we can keep one on the money supply and the other on interest rates."

Fed watchers say that Alan Greenspan not only uses both eyes but also some personal radar to track the economy and formulate monetary policy. In early 1990, he refused to set a target for growth of the narrowly defined money supply (M1) and set very wide targets (3 to 7 percent) for broader measures of the money supply (M2). For 1993, the Fed set a very broad target range for M2 growth (2 to 6 percent). By midyear

---

[3]The Fed's policy of 1979–82 was not strict monetarism. Although the Fed emphasized money supply targets, it allowed the money supply to fluctuate much more than strict monetarists prescribed.

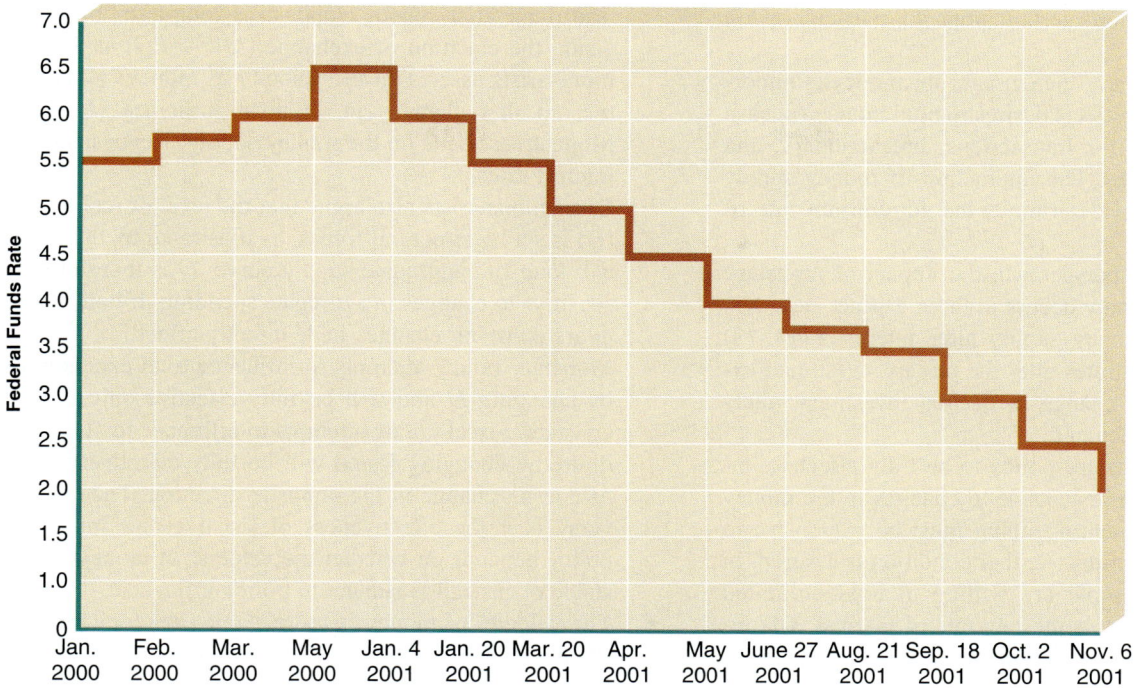

FIGURE 15.7
Policy Reversals

The Fed raised the federal funds rate sharply in 2000, hoping to engineer a "soft landing." The Fed then reversed course abruptly in 2001 when the economy slowed too much.

it was evident the Fed couldn't even hit that target. Rather than establish yet another target, however, the Fed chairman told Congress that M2 growth was an unreliable policy guide. A more eclectic mix of indicators—including several measures of both the money supply and interest rates—was more appropriate, Greenspan told Congress.

Focus on Federal Funds Rate. Since then, money-supply targets have all but been abandoned. For the last 8–10 years, the focus of Fed policy has been the federal funds rate. The Fed governors assess the state of the economy, then adjust the federal funds rate (via open-market operations) as they deem necessary. How do they decide how much of an adjustment is needed? As Alan Greenspan himself explained, "The Federal Reserve specializes in precision guesswork."

Precision guesswork seemed OK when the economy was booming. But many critics blamed the 1990–91 and 2000–01 recessions on excessive monetary restraint. The pattern of a rapidly rising federal funds rate in 2000 followed by an abrupt reversal in 2001 (see Figure 15.7) caused a lot of second-guessing about Fed policy. When people peer into the economy tomorrow, they wonder how much we should continue to rely on the Fed's "precision guesswork."

SUMMARY

- The essence of monetary policy lies in the Federal Reserve's control over the money supply. By altering the money supply, the Fed can determine the amount of purchasing power available.

- There are sharp disagreements about how monetary policy works. Keynesians argue that monetary policy works indirectly, through its effects on interest rates and spending. Monetarists assert that monetary policy has

more direct and more certain impacts, particularly on price levels.
- In the Keynesian view, the demand for money is important. This demand reflects desires to hold money (in cash or bank balances) for transactions, precautionary, and speculative purposes. The interaction of money supply and money demand determines the equilibrium rate of interest.
- From a Keynesian perspective, the impact of monetary policy on the economy occurs in three distinct steps. (1) Changes in the money supply alter interest rates. (2) Changes in interest rates alter the rate of investment expenditure. (3) The change in desired investment alters (shifts) aggregate demand.
- For Keynesian monetary policy to be fully effective, interest rates must be responsive to changes in the money supply, and investment spending must be responsive to changes in interest rates. Neither condition is assured. In a liquidity trap, people are willing to hold unlimited amounts of money at some low rate of interest. The interest rate won't fall below this level as the money supply increases. Also, investor expectations of sales and profits may override interest rate considerations in the investment decision.
- Fed policy has the most direct impact on short-term interest rates, particularly the overnight federal funds rate. Long-term rates are less responsive to open-market operations.
- The monetarist school emphasizes long-term linkages. Using the equation of exchange ($MV = PQ$) as a base, monetarists assert that the velocity of money (V) is stable, so that changes in M must influence ($P \times Q$). Monetarists focus on the money supply; Keynesians, on interest rates.
- Some monetarists also argue that the level of real output (Q) is set by structural forces, as illustrated by the vertical, long-run aggregate supply curve. Q is therefore insensitive to changes in aggregate spending. If both V and Q are constant, changes in M directly affect P.
- Monetary policy attempts to influence total expenditure by changing M and will be fully effective only if V is constant. Fiscal policy attempts to influence total expenditure by changing V and will be fully effective only if M doesn't change in the opposite direction. The controversy over the effectiveness of fiscal versus monetary policy depends on whether the velocity of money (V) is stable or instead is subject to policy influence.
- The velocity of money is more stable over long periods of time than over short periods. Keynesians conclude that this makes fiscal policy more powerful in the short run. Monetarists conclude that the unpredictability of short-run velocity makes *any* short-run policy risky.
- Fed policy has evolved from an emphasis on money-supply targets, to dual targeting of the money supply and interest rates, to a focus on short-term interest rates.

Key Terms

monetary policy
interest rate
money supply (M1, M2)
demand for money
portfolio decision
transactions demand for money
precautionary demand for money
speculative demand for money
equilibrium rate of interest
federal funds rate
aggregate demand
liquidity trap
equation of exchange
income velocity of money (V)
natural rate of unemployment
real interest rate
crowding out

Questions for Discussion

1. What proportions of your money balance are held for transactions, precautionary, and speculative purposes? Can you think of any other purposes for holding money?
2. Why do high interest rates so adversely affect the demand for housing and yet have so little influence on the demand for strawberries?
3. If the Federal Reserve banks mailed everyone a brand-new $100 bill, what would happen to prices, output, and income? Illustrate your answer by using the equation of exchange.
4. Can there be any inflation without an increase in the money supply? How?
5. How might the existence of multiplier effects increase the risk of inflation when interest rates are cut?
6. When prices started doubling (see News, page 312), why didn't the Continental Congress print even *more* money so Washington's army could continue to buy supplies? What brings an end to such "inflation financing"?
7. How can money be truly "free" if you have to pay interest on loans? (See News, page 314.)

8. Could long-term interest rates rise when short-term rates are falling? What would cause such a pattern?
9. If the Fed doesn't control mortgage rates (see News, page 304), who does?
10. Why were banks reluctant to use their lending capacity in 2001? (See News, page 305.) What did they do with their increased reserves?
11. How did the Bank of Japan hope to increase the money supply in 2001? (See World View, page 320.) If M did increase, would the economy necessarily recover?
12. In hindsight, why do you think the Fed raised interest rates so much in 2000 (see Figure 15.7)? How did that policy contribute to the 2001 recession? What would Monetarists have done in 2000–01?

Web Activities

1. By how much have the following interest rates changed in the last 12 months? (*a*) Federal funds, (*b*) 10-year Treasury bill, (*c*) 30-year mortgage rate. Why don't they all change by the same amount? Log on to www.economagic.com/popular.htm to find the rates.
2. Read the Fed's Beige Book summary of current economic conditions at www.federalreserve.gov/policy.htm. Click on Beige book and navigate to the most recent monthly report. What changes in monetary policy might the Fed use to improve the economy?
3. Log on to www.whitehouse.gov/fsbr/employment.html and find the current unemployment rate. Assume the full-employment unemployment rate is 4.3 percent. What open-market operations should the Fed initiate to help the economy reach its full-employment unemployment rate?

THE ACCOMPANYING STUDENT PROBLEM SET CONTAINS NUMERICAL AND GRAPHING PROBLEMS FOR THIS CHAPTER

PART 6

Supply-Side Options

Fiscal and monetary levers attempt to alter macro outcomes by managing aggregate demand. Supply-side policies focus on possibilities for shifting the aggregate *supply* curve instead. In the short run, any increase in aggregate supply promotes more output and less inflation. Supply-siders also emphasize how shifts of aggregate supply are critical to long-run economic growth. Chapter 16 focuses on short-run supply-side options; Chapter 17 takes the long-run view.

CHAPTER 16

Supply-Side Policy: Short-Run Options

Fiscal and monetary policies focus on the *demand* side of the macro economy. The basic premise of both approaches is that macro goals can be achieved by shifting the aggregate demand curve. The aggregate demand curve isn't the only game in town, however; there's an aggregate supply curve as well. Why not focus instead on possibilities for shifting the aggregate *supply* curve?

Any policies that alter the willingness or ability to supply goods at various price levels will shift the aggregate supply curve. This chapter identifies some of those policy options and examines how they affect macro outcomes. The focus is on two questions:

- How does the aggregate supply curve affect macro outcomes?
- How can the aggregate supply curve be shifted?

As we'll see, the aggregate supply curve plays a critical role in determining how difficult it is to achieve the goals of full employment and price stability.

AGGREGATE SUPPLY

The impetus for examining the supply side of the macro economy sprang up in the stagflation of the 1970s. **Stagflation** occurs when both unemployment *and* inflation increase at the same time. From 1973 to 1974, for example, consumer price inflation surged from 8.7 to 12.3 percent. At the same time, the unemployment rate jumped from 4.9 to 5.6 percent. How could this happen? *No shift of the aggregate demand curve can increase inflation and unemployment at the same time.* If aggregate demand increases (shifts right), the price level may rise but unemployment should decline with increased output. If aggregate demand decreases (shifts left), inflation should subside but unemployment increase. In other words, most demand-side theories predict that inflation and unemployment move in *opposite* directions in the short run. When this didn't happen, an alternative explanation was sought. The explanation was found on the supply side of the macro economy. Two critical clues were (1) the shape of the **aggregate supply** curve and (2) potential AS shifts.

SHAPE OF THE AS CURVE

As we've seen, the basic short-run objective of fiscal and monetary policy is to attain full employment and price stability. The strategy is to shift the aggregate demand curve to a more favorable position. Now the question turns to the *response* of producers to an aggregate demand shift. Will they increase real output? Raise prices? Or some combination of both?

The answer depends on the shape of the aggregate supply curve: *The response of producers to an AD shift is expressed in the slope and position of the aggregate supply curve.* Until now we've used a generally upward-sloping curve to depict aggregate supply, but we have to recognize that other supply responses are possible.

> **stagflation:** The simultaneous occurrence of substantial unemployment and inflation.
>
> **aggregate supply:** The total quantity of output producers are willing and able to supply at alternative price levels in a given time period, *ceteris paribus*.

Three Views of AS

Figure 16.1 illustrates three very different supply behaviors. Part (*a*) depicts what we've called the "naive" Keynesian view. Recall that Keynes was primarily concerned with the problem of unemployment. He didn't think there was much risk of inflation in the depths of a recession. He expected producers to increase output, not prices, when aggregate demand expanded. This expectation is illustrated by a *horizontal* AS curve. When fiscal or monetary stimulus shifts the AD curve rightward, output (Q) rises but not the price level (P). Only when capacity (Q^*) is reached do prices start rising abruptly.

The monetarist view of supply behavior is very different. In the most extreme monetarist view, real output remains at its "natural" rate, regardless of fiscal or monetary interventions. Rising prices don't entice producers to increase output because costs are likely to rise just as fast. They instead make output decisions based on more fundamental factors like technology and market size. The AS curve is *vertical* because output doesn't respond to changing price levels. (This is the long-run AS curve we first encountered in Chapter 8.) With a vertical AS curve, only prices can respond to a shift in aggregate demand. In Figure 16.1*b*, the AS curve is anchored at the natural rate of unemployment Q_N. When aggregate demand increases from AD_4 to AD_5, the price level (P) rises, but output (Q) is unchanged.

Figure 16.1*c* blends these Keynesian and monetarist perspectives into a hybrid AS curve. At low rates of output, the curve is nearly horizontal; at high rates of output, the AS curve becomes nearly vertical. In the broad middle of the AS curve, the curve slopes gently upward. In this area, shifts of aggregate demand affect *both* prices and output. The message of this hybrid AS curve is that the outcomes of fiscal and monetary policy depend on how close the economy is to full employment. *The closer we are to capacity, the greater the risk that fiscal or monetary stimulus will spill over into price inflation.*

The Inflation-Unemployment Trade-Off

Until now we've used the upward-sloping AS curve depicted in Figure 16.1*c* to characterize producer behavior. Because it allows for varying output/price responses at different levels of economic activity, the AS curve in Figure 16.1*c* is generally regarded as the most realistic for short-run outcomes. However, the upward-sloping section of the AS curve in Figure 16.1*c* has some disturbing implications. Because both prices and output respond to demand-side shifts, the economy can't attain both full employment and price stability at the same time—at least not with fiscal and monetary policies. Consider the simple geometry of policy stimulus and restraint.

Demand Stimulus. Monetary and fiscal stimulus shift the aggregate demand curve rightward. This demand-side effect is evident in all three graphs in Figure 16.1. However, *all rightward shifts of the aggregate demand curve increase both prices and output if the aggregate supply curve is upward-sloping.* This implies that fiscal and monetary efforts to reduce unemployment will also cause some inflation.

Demand Restraint. Monetary and fiscal restraint shift the aggregate demand curve leftward. *If the aggregate supply curve is upward-sloping, leftward shifts of the aggregate demand curve cause both prices and output to fall.* Therefore, fiscal and monetary efforts to reduce inflation will also increase unemployment.

FIGURE 16.1
Contrasting Views of Aggregate Supply

(*a*) **Keynesian AS** In the simple Keynesian model, the rate of output responds fully and automatically to increases in demand until full employment (Q^*) is reached. If demand increases from AD_1 to AD_2, equilibrium GDP will expand from Q_1 to Q^*, without any inflation. Inflation becomes a problem only if demand increases beyond capacity—to AD_3, for example.

(*b*) **Monetarist AS** Monetarists assert that changes in the money supply affect prices but not output. They regard aggregate supply as a fixed quantum, at the long-run, natural rate of unemployment (here noted as Q_N). Accordingly, a shift of demand (from AD_4 to AD_5) can affect only the price level (from P_4 to P_5).

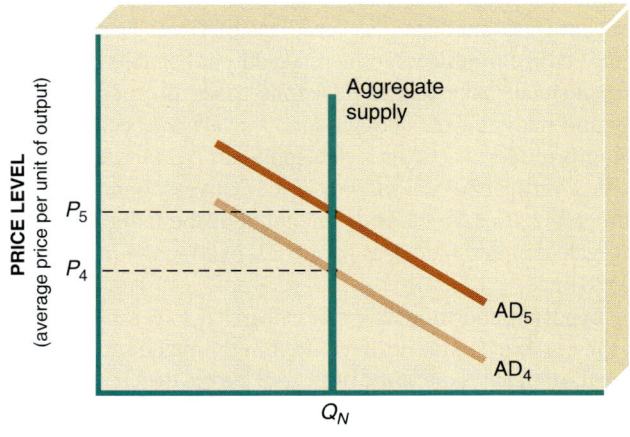

(*c*) **Hybrid AS** The consensus view incorporates Keynesian and monetarist perspectives but emphasizes the upward slope that dominates the middle of the AS curve. When demand increases, both price levels and the rate of output increase. Hence, the slope and position of the AS curve limit the effectiveness of fiscal and monetary policies.

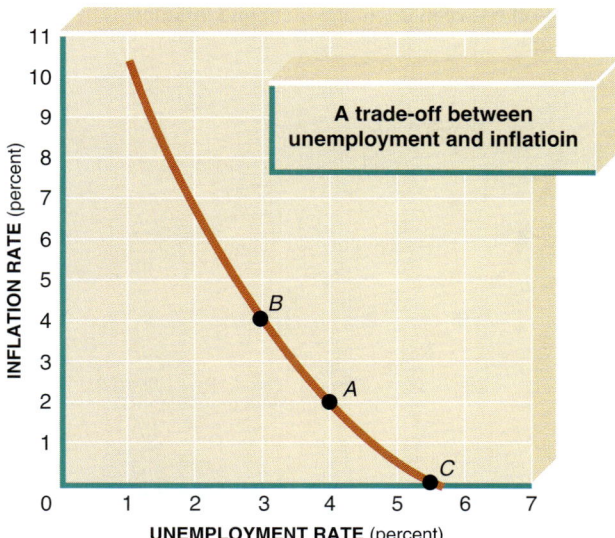

FIGURE 16.2
The Phillips Curve

The Phillips curve illustrates a trade-off between full employment and price stability. In the 1960s it appeared that efforts to reduce unemployment rates below 5.5 percent (point C) led to increasing rates of inflation (points A and B). Inflation threatened to reach unacceptable heights long before everyone was employed.

The Phillips Curve. The message of the upward-sloping aggregate supply curve is clear: *Demand-side policies alone can never succeed completely; they'll always cause some unwanted inflation or unemployment.*

Our macro track record provides ample evidence of this dilemma. Consider, for example, our experience with unemployment and inflation during the 1960s, as shown in Figure 16.2. This figure shows a **Phillips curve,** indicating that prices (*P*) generally started rising before the objective of expanded output (*Q*) had been completely attained. Inflation struck before full employment was reached.

The Phillips curve was developed by a New Zealand economist, Alban W. Phillips, to summarize the relationship between unemployment and inflation in England for the years 1826–1957.[1] The Phillips curve was raised from the status of an obscure graph to that of a policy issue by the discovery that the same kind of relationship apparently existed in other countries and at other times. Paul Samuelson and Robert Solow of the Massachusetts Institute of Technology were among the first to observe that the Phillips curve was a reasonable description of U.S. economic performance for the years 1900–60. For the post–World War II years in particular, Samuelson and Solow noted that an unemployment rate of 4 percent was likely to be accompanied by an inflation rate of approximately 2 percent. This relationship is expressed by point *A* in Figure 16.2. By contrast, lower rates of unemployment were associated with higher rates of inflation, as at point *B*. Alternatively, complete price stability appeared attainable only at the cost of an unemployment rate of 5.5 percent (point *C*). A seesaw kind of relationship existed between inflation and unemployment: When one went up, the other fell.

The trade-off between unemployment and inflation originates in the upward sloping AS curve. Figure 16.3*a* illustrates this point. Suppose the economy is initially at equilibrium *A*, with fairly stable prices but low output. When aggregate demand expands to AD$_2$, prices rise along with output, so we end up with higher inflation but less unemployment. This is also shown in Figure 16.3*b* by the move from point *a* to point *b* on the Phillips curve. The move from point *a* to point *b* indicates a decline in unemployment (more output) but an increase in inflation (higher price level). If demand is increased further, to AD$_3$, a still lower unemployment rate is achieved but at the cost of higher inflation (point *c*).

Phillips curve: An historical (inverse) relationship between the rate of unemployment and the rate of inflation; commonly expresses a trade-off between the two.

---

[1] A. W. Phillips. "The Relationship Between Unemployment and the Rate of Change of Money Wage Rates in the United Kingdom. 1826–1957." *Economica.* November 1958. Phillips's paper studied the relationship between unemployment and *wage* changes rather than *price* changes; most later formulations (and public policy) focus on prices.

SUPPLY-SIDE OPTIONS

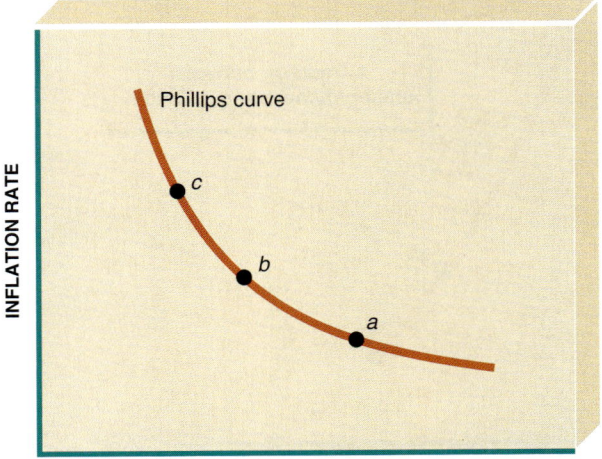

(a) Increases in aggregate demand cause...
(b) A trade-off between unemployment and inflation.

FIGURE 16.3
The Phillips Curve Trade-Off

If the aggregate supply curve slopes upward, increases in aggregate demand always cause both prices and output to rise. Thus, higher inflation becomes a cost of achieving lower unemployment. In (a), increased demand moves the economy from point A to point B. At B, unemployment is lower, but prices are higher. This trade-off is illustrated on the Phillips curve in (b). Each point on the Phillips curve represents a different AS/AD equilibrium from the graph on the left.

SHIFTS OF THE AS CURVE

The unemployment inflation trade-off implied by the upward-sloping AS curve is not etched in stone. Many economists argue that the economy can attain lower levels of unemployment *without* higher inflation. This certainly appeared to be the case in the 1990s: Unemployment rates fell sharply from 1992 to 2000 without any increase in inflation. How could this have happened? There's no AD shift in any of part of Figure 16.1 that would reduce both unemployment *and* inflation.

Rightward AS Shifts: All Good News

Only a rightward shift of the AS curve can reduce unemployment and inflation at the same time. When aggregate supply increases from AS_1 to AS_2 in Figure 16.4, macro equilibrium moves from E_1 to E_2. At E_2 real output is higher, so the unemployment rate must be lower. At E_2 the price level is also lower, indicating reduced inflation. Hence, a rightward shift of the AS curve offers the best of two worlds—something aggregate *demand* shifts (Figure 16.1) can't do.

Phillips Curve Shift. As we saw in Figure 16.3, the Phillips curve is a direct byproduct of the AS curve. Accordingly, *When the AS curve shifts, the Phillips curve shifts as well.* As Figure 16.5 illustrates, the Phillips curve shifts to the left, the opposite of the AS shift in Figure 16.4. No new information is conveyed here. The Phillips curve simply focuses more directly on the implied change in the unemployment-inflation trade-off. *When the Phillips curve shifts to the left, the unemployment-inflation trade-off eases.*

The Misery Index. To keep track of simultaneous changes in unemployment and inflation, Arthur Okun developed the "misery index"—a simple sum of the inflation and unemployment rates. As the News feature on page 333 illustrates, macro misery diminished substantially during the first Reagan administration (1981–84). President Clinton also benefited from a leftward shift of the Phillips curve through 1998, but saw the misery index climb in 1999–2000. President George W. Bush experienced a sharp increase in the misery index during the recession of 2001.

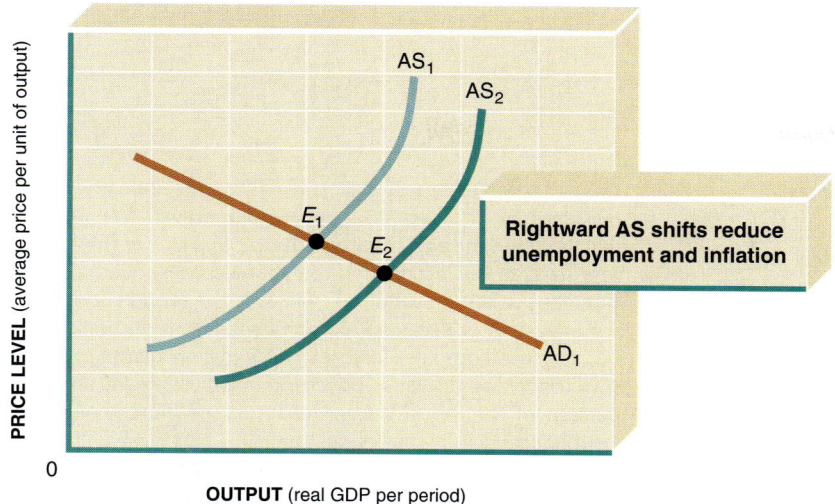

FIGURE 16.4
Shifts of Aggregate Supply

A rightward AS shift (AS$_1$ to AS$_2$) reduces both unemployment and inflation. A leftward shift has the opposite effect, creating stagflation.

Whereas rightward AS Shifts appear to be a dream come true, leftward AS shifts are a real nightmare. Imagine in Figure 16.4 that the AS shift is reversed, that is, from AS$_2$ to AS$_1$. What would happen? Output would decrease and prices would rise, exactly the kind of dilemma depicted in the cartoon on the next page. In other words, nothing would go in the right direction. This would be rampant stagflation.

A natural disaster can trigger a leftward shift of the AS curve, especially in smaller nations. In 1998, Hurricane Mitch struck Central America with a vengeance, killing upward of 10,000 people. In addition, Honduras' most important industry—bananas—was virtually wiped out, and even the banana trees themselves were destroyed (see World View). This supply-side shock diminished the capacity for future production.

In a large economy like that of the United States, leftward shifts of aggregate supply are less dramatic. When the Organization of Petroleum Exporting Countries (OPEC)

Leftward AS Shifts: All Bad News

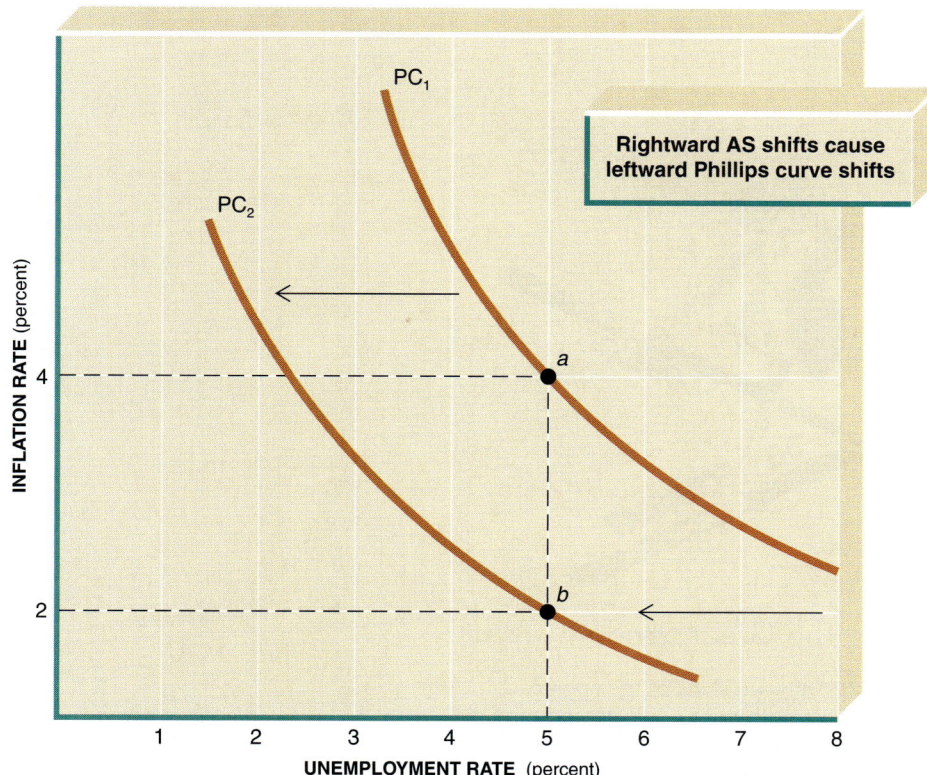

FIGURE 16.5
A Phillips Curve Shift

If the Phillips curve shifts leftward, the short-run unemployment inflation trade-off eases. With PC$_1$, 5 percent unemployment ignites 4 percent inflation (point *a*). With PC$_2$, 5 percent unemployment causes only 2 percent inflation (point *b*).

WORLD VIEW

Mitch Left Honduras a Republic without Bananas

LA CEIBITA, HONDURAS—Against all odds, Tropical Storm Mitch did not claim any lives among the 1,200 workers and residents of La Ceibita, a plantation town that is owned and managed by one of the largest private employers in Honduras, Cincinnati-based Chiquita Brands International. Throughout the country, flooding and landslides caused by Mitch killed perhaps 6,000 people, and another 4,000 in neighboring Nicaragua.

But the sense of relief felt by survivors such as Rodas, who has worked for Chiquita since he was 9, has largely been supplanted by worry about the future. Banana industry and government officials said that flooding destroyed not just the banana crop, but the plants themselves—in other words, virtually the entire banana industry in Honduras. The damage has already thrown thousands of people out of work and is expected to wipe out $255 million in annual banana exports over the next two years before the industry might begin to recover.

"This is by far the most devastating loss the industry has encountered in the last 25 years," said Steven Warshaw, Chiquita's president and chief operating officer. "We think all or close to all of our production of bananas is destroyed. . . ."

Chiquita officials in Honduras, which is the world's fourth-largest banana producer and exports about 6 billion bananas a year, said the company lost nearly 11 million plants on its 17,300 acres. Countrywide, government officials said, about 90 percent of the industry was destroyed, or more than 27 million plants.

The destruction was not confined to bananas, or to Honduras. Agriculture across Central America, where large portions of the impoverished populations rely on farming, was devastated by Mitch, which drowned crops with up to six feet of rain.

—John Ward Anderson

Source: *Washington Post*, November 19, 1998. © 1998 The Washington Post. Reprinted with permission. www.washingtonpost.com

Analysis: A natural disaster that destroys production capabilities shifts the aggregate supply curve to the left, which reduces output and raises price levels.

The Great Divide

Analysis: Leftward shifts of the aggregate supply curve push price levels up and output down. The remedy for such stagflation is a rightward shift of aggregate supply.

IN THE NEWS

The Misery Index

Unemployment is a problem and so is inflation. Being burdened with both problems at the same time is real misery.

The late Arthur Okun proposed measuring the extent of misery by adding together the inflation and unemployment rates. He called the sum of the two rates the "discomfort index". Political pundits quickly renamed it the "misery index".

In essence, the misery index is a measure of stagflation—the simultaneous occurrence of inflation and unemployment. In 1980, the misery index peaked at 19.6 percent as a result of high inflation (12.5 percent) as well as high unemployment (7.1 percent). Stagflation—and the misery it causes—has since receded markedly.

Source: *Economic Report of the President, 2001*.

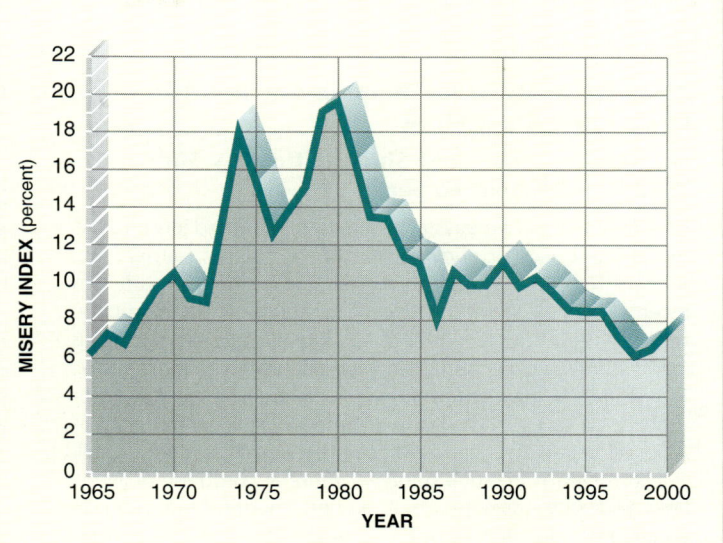

Analysis: Stagflation refers to the simultaneous occurrence of inflation and unemployment. The "misery index" combines both problems into a single measure of macro performance.

---

abruptly raised oil prices and limited exports to the United States, many industries experienced higher production costs and resource shortages, which reduced the ability and willingness to supply output at given price levels. The end result was an increase in both inflation and unemployment. This increase contributed to the big increase in macro misery during the years 1975–89, as depicted in the above News.

The September 11, 2001 terrorist attacks on the World Trade Center and Pentagon were another form of external shock. The attacks directly destroyed some production capacity (office space, telecommunications links, transportation links). But they took an even greater toll on the *willingness* to supply goods and services. In the aftermath of the attacks businesses, perceiving new risks to investment and production, held back from making new commitments. Increased security measures also made transporting goods more expensive (see News on the next page). All of these responses shifted the AS curve leftward and the Phillips curve rightward, adding to macro misery.

To update the misery index, retrieve data on unemployment and inflation from the U.S. Bureau of Labor Statistics at www.bls.gov.

From the supply side of macro markets, the appropriate response to negative external shocks is clear: shift the AS curve rightward. As the forgoing graphs have demonstrated, ***rightward shifts of the aggregate supply curve always generate desirable macro outcomes.*** The next question, of course, is how to shift the aggregate supply curve in the desired (rightward) direction. Supply-side economists look for clues among the forces that influence the supply-side response to changes in demand. Among those forces, the following policy options have been emphasized:

Policy Levers

- Tax incentives for saving, investment, and work.
- Human capital investment.
- Deregulation.
- Infrastructure development.

IN THE NEWS

Difficult Passage

After Terror Attacks, Shipping Goods Takes Longer and Costs More

For Trucks, Trains and Ships, Efficiency Suddenly Takes a Back Seat to Security

NEWARK, N.J.—Two days after terrorists slammed jets into the World Trade Center and the Pentagon, Quality Carriers Inc. rehired the $5,000-a-month night-shift security guard it had recently let go at its tankertruck terminal here. The company also paid two drivers a total of $1,200 to repark any vehicles loaded with chemicals in plain view and under security lights. To get in at night, the terminal's 52 drivers now must wait for supervisors to open the gate with new electronic gadgets.

For Quality Carriers, the country's biggest liquid-bulk trucker, there is no such thing anymore as a routine delivery. New York City police guarding against chemical or biological attacks now demand a copy of a driver's license and registration before allowing him to make his twice-daily delivery of fluorosilicic acid, a fluoridation agent, to a suburban water-treatment facility that serves the city.

"Our expenses are piling up," says Thomas Schofield, a regional vice president at the unit of Quality Distribution Inc. One example: $2,500 a week in lost driving time because of stepped-up scrutiny of the company's tankers at two oil refineries in New Jersey. From now on, Mr. Schofield says, the carrier is going to try to pass along most of the added costs to its customers.

The Sept. 11 terror attacks are wrenching the nation's freight-transportation system, which moved $9 trillion of cargo last year. The network of trucks, trains, planes and ships suddenly faces a slew of new costs, delays and demands that threaten to hobble an essential part of the already slumping U.S. economy.

—Daniel Machalaba and Rick Brooks

Source: *The Wall Street Journal,* September 27, 2001. Reprinted by permission of *The Wall Street Journal.* © 2001 Dow Jones & Company, Inc. All Rights Reserved Worldwide. www.wsj.com

Analysis: Increased security precautions after the September 11 terrorist attacks made transportation services more costly. This shifted the short-run AS curve leftward.

All these policies have the potential to change supply decisions *independently* of any changes in aggregate demand. If they're effective, they'll result in a rightward shift of the aggregate supply curve and an *improved* trade-off between unemployment and inflation.

TAX INCENTIVES

The most renowned supply-side policy option for improving the unemployment-inflation trade-off was the "supply-side" tax cuts of the early 1980s. Tax cuts are of course a staple of Keynesian economics. But tax cuts take on a whole new role on the supply side of the economy. ***In Keynesian economics, tax cuts are used to increase aggregate demand.*** By putting more disposable income in the hands of consumers, Keynesian economists seek to increase expenditure on goods and services. Output is expected to increase in response. From a Keynesian perspective, the form of the tax cut is not very important, as long as disposable income increases.

The supply side of the economy encourages a different view of taxes. Taxes not only alter disposable income but also affect the incentives to work and produce. High tax rates destroy the incentives to work and produce, so they end up reducing total output. Low tax rates, by contrast, allow people to keep more of what they earn and so stimulate greater output. ***The direct effects of taxes on the supply of goods are the concern of supply-side economists.*** Figure 16.6 shows the difference between demand side and supply-side perspectives on tax policy.

Marginal Tax Rates

Supply-side theory places special emphasis on *marginal* tax rates. The **marginal tax rate** is the tax rate imposed on the last (marginal) dollar of income received. In our progressive income tax system, marginal tax rates increase as more income is received.

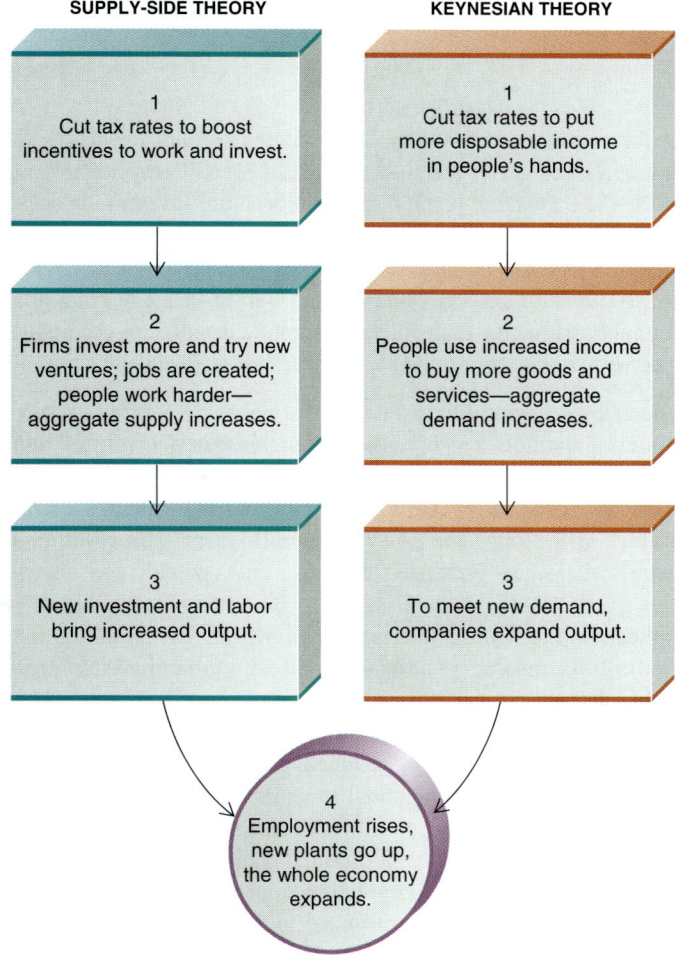

FIGURE 16.6
Two Theories for Getting the Economy Moving

Keynesians and supply-siders both advocate cutting taxes to reduce unemployment. But they have very different views on the kind of tax cuts required and the impact of any cuts enacted.

Uncle Sam takes a larger share out of each additional dollar earned. In 2000, the highest marginal tax rate on personal income was 39.6 percent. That top tax rate was far below the 91 percent rate that existed in 1944, but it was also a lot higher than the 12 percent tax rate imposed in 1914 (see Figure 16.7).

Does the marginal tax rate affect supply decisions? Will people work and invest as much when the marginal tax rate is 91 percent as when it is only 12 percent?

Labor Supply. The marginal tax rate influences the financial incentive to *increase* one's work. *If the marginal tax rate is high, there's less incentive to work more—* Uncle Sam will get most of the added income. Confronted with high marginal tax rates, workers may choose to stay home rather than work an extra shift. Families may decide that it doesn't pay to send both parents into the labor market. When marginal tax rates are low, by contrast, those extra work activities generate bigger increases in disposable income.

Entrepreneurship. Marginal tax rates affect not only labor-supply decisions but also decisions on whether to start or expand a business. Most small businesses are organized as sole proprietorships or partnerships and subject to *personal,* not *corporate,* tax rates. Hence, a decline in personal tax rates will affect the risk/reward balance for potential entrepreneurs. Columbia Business School professors William Gentry and Glenn Huber have demonstrated that progressive marginal tax rates discourage entry into self-employment. Syracuse professor Douglas Holtz-Eakin and Princeton

marginal tax rate: The tax rate imposed on the last (marginal) dollar of income.

economist Harvey Rosen have shown that the growth rate, investment, and employment of small businesses are also affected by marginal tax rates. As Holtz-Eakin concluded, "taxes matter."

Investment. Taxes matter for corporations too. Corporate entities account for nearly 90 percent of business output and 84 percent of business assets. Like small proprietorships, corporations, too, are motivated by after-tax profits. Hence, corporate **investment** decisions will be affected by corporate tax rates. If Uncle Sam imposes a high tax rate on corporate profits, the payoff to investors will be diminished. Potential investors may decide to consume their income or to purchase tax-free bonds rather than to invest in plant and equipment. If that happens, total investment will decline and output will suffer. Accordingly, *if high tax rates discourage investment, aggregate supply will be constrained.*

investment: Expenditures on (production of) new plant, equipment, and structures (capital) in a given time period, plus changes in business inventories.

Tax-Induced Supply Shifts

If tax rates affect supply decisions, then *changes* in tax rates will shift aggregate supply. Specifically, supply-siders conclude that *a reduction in marginal tax rates will shift the aggregate supply curve to the right.* The increased supply will come from three sources: more work effort, more entrepreneurship, and more investment. This increased willingness to produce will reduce the rate of unemployment. The additional output will also help reduce inflationary pressures. Thus we end up with less unemployment *and* less inflation.

From a supply-side perspective, the form of the tax cut is critical. For example, **tax rebates** are a one-time windfall to consumers and have no effect on marginal tax rates. As a consequence, disposable income rises, but not the incentives for work or production. Rebates directly affect only the demand side of the economy.

tax rebate: A lump-sum refund of taxes paid.

To stimulate aggregate *supply,* tax *rates* must be reduced, particularly at the margin. These cuts can take the form of reductions in personal income tax rates or reductions in the marginal tax rates imposed on businesses. In either case, the lower tax rates will give people a greater incentive to work, invest, and produce. This was the motivation for the Reagan tax cuts of 1981–84. Shifting the aggregate supply curve rightward was also the goal of President George W. Bush's 2001 proposal to cut the top marginal tax rate from 39.6 percent to 33 percent. Congress ultimately adopted a package of supply-side and demand-side incentives (see News on page 338). On the supply side it phased in a cut in the top marginal tax rate to 35 percent (see Figure 16.7). To shift aggregate demand, Congress also authorized $38 billion of tax rebates in 2001.

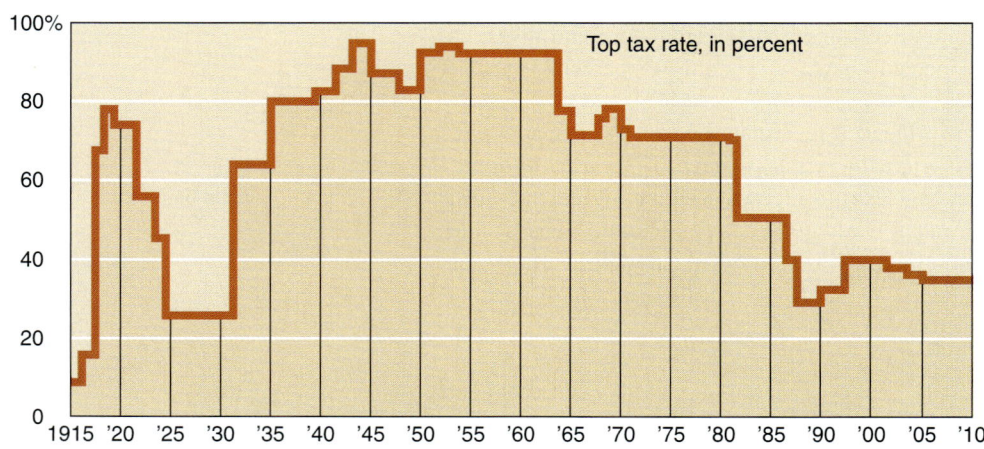

FIGURE 16.7
Changes in Marginal Tax Rates Since 1915

The top marginal tax rate on income has varied from a low of 12 percent to a high of 91 percent. Supply-side theory emphasizes how these varying tax rates affect work, investment, and production decisions, that is, aggregate supply.

Table 16.1 illustrates the distinction between Keynesian and supply-side tax cuts. Under both tax systems (*A* and *B*), a person earning $200 pays $80 in taxes before the tax cut and $60 after the tax cut. But under system *A*, the marginal tax rate is always 50 percent, which means that Uncle Sam is getting half of every dollar earned above $100. By contrast, system *B* imposes a marginal tax rate of only 30 percent—$0.30 of every dollar above $100 goes to the government. Under system *B*, people have a greater incentive to earn more than $100. Although both systems raise the same amount of taxes, system *B* offers greater incentives to work extra hours and produce more output.

Virtually all economists agree that tax rates influence people's decisions to work, invest, and produce. But the policy-relevant question is, *how much* influence do taxes have? Do reductions in the marginal tax rate shift the aggregate supply curve far to the right? Or are the resultant shifts quite small?

The response of labor and capital to a change in tax rates is summarized by the **tax elasticity of supply.** Like other elasticities, this one measures the proportional response of supplies to a change in price (in this case, a tax rate). Specifically, the tax elasticity of supply is the percentage change in quantity supplied divided by the percentage in tax rates, that is,

Tax Elasticity of Supply

tax elasticity of supply: The percentage change in quantity supplied divided by the percentage change in tax rates.

$$\text{Tax elasticity of supply} = \frac{\% \text{ change in quantity supplied}}{\% \text{ change in tax rate}}$$

Normally we expect quantity supplied to go up when tax rates go down. Elasticity (*E*) is therefore negative, although it's usually expressed in absolute terms (without the

TABLE 16.1
Average vs. Marginal Tax Rates

The same amount of taxes can be raised via two very different systems. Here a person earning $200 pays $80 in taxes under either system (*A* or *B*). Thus, the *average* tax rate (total tax ÷ total income) is the same in both cases ($80 ÷ $200 = 40%) But the *marginal* tax rates are very different. System *A* has a high marginal rate (50%), whereas system *B* has a low marginal tax rate (30%). System *B* provides a greater incentive for people to earn over $100.

		Initial Alternatives			
Tax System	Initial Tax Schedule	Tax on Income of $200	Tax Rate Average	Tax Rate Marginal	Disposable Income
A	$30 + 50% of income over $100	$80	40%	50%	$120
B	$50 + 30% of income over $100	$80	40%	30%	$120

The average tax rate could be cut to 30 percent under either system. Under both systems, the revised tax would be $60 and disposable income would be increased to $140. Keynesians would be happy with either form of tax cut. But supply-siders would favor system *B* because the lower marginal tax rate gives people more incentive to earn higher incomes.

		Alternative Forms of Tax Cut			
Tax System	Initial Tax Schedule	Tax on Income of $200	Tax Rate Average	Tax Rate Marginal	Disposable Income
A	$10 + 50% of income over $100	$60	30%	50%	$140
B	$30 + 30% of income over $100	$60	30%	30%	$140

IN THE NEWS

Congress Passes Tax Cut Package

The House and Senate gave final approval to a far-reaching package of tax breaks yesterday, handing President Bush a major victory on his top legislative priority at the close of a tumultuous week in which he and the Republicans lost control of the Senate.

The tax cut, the largest approved by Congress in two decades, provides for millions of refund checks of up to $600 apiece to be mailed to Americans this summer, and grants reductions in most tax rates, tax relief for married couples and parents of young children, and a repeal of the estate tax, though not until 2010.

All of these were priorities set out by the president, who welcomed the tax bill's passage after returning to the White House from Camp David. The plan "cuts income taxes for everyone who pays them. Nothing could be more profound, and nothing could be more fair," Bush said. . . .

The concept of issuing checks to provide immediate tax relief—and help stimulate the economy—was not in Bush's original plan and had not been included in either the House or Senate versions of the legislation; the House and Senate proposals had instead called for adjusting taxpayers' withholding tables.

But the administration, confronting claims from economists that adjusting the withholding tables would not provide a big enough economic boost and charges from Democrats that the tax cut was geared for the wealthy, pressed for including the refund checks in the final tax deal. . . .

The tax bill reduces the top rate from 39.6 percent to 35 percent by 2006, while the president had sought a 33 percent rate.

—Glenn Kessler and Juliet Eilperin

Source: *Washington Post*, May 27, 2001. © 2001 The Washington Post. Reprinted with permission. www.washingtonpost.com

Analysis: Tax cuts can focus on demand-side or supply-side incentives. The 2001 tax-cut package included both: tax rebates to stimulate demand and reductions in marginal tax rates to stimulate supply.

---

minus sign). The (absolute) value of E is typically greater than zero, since we expect *some* response to a tax cut. The policy issue boils down to the question of how large E actually is.

If the tax elasticity of supply were large enough, a tax cut might actually *increase* tax revenues. Suppose the tax elasticity were equal to 1.5. In that case a tax cut of 10 percent would cause output supplied to increase by 15 percent ($= 1.5 \times 10\%$). Such a large increase in the tax base (income) would result in *more* taxes being paid even though the tax *rate* was reduced. One of President Reagan's economic advisers, Arthur Laffer, actually thought such an outcome was possible. He predicted that tax revenues would increase after the Reagan supply-side tax cuts were made. In reality, the tax elasticity of supply turned out to be much smaller (around 0.15) and tax revenues fell substantially. The aggregate supply curve *did* shift to the right, but not very far, when marginal tax rates were cut.

The evidently low tax elasticity of supply helped President Clinton convince Congress to *increase* marginal tax rates in 1993. Although opponents objected that higher tax rates would reduce work and investment, the Clinton administration pointed out that any leftward shift of aggregate supply was likely to be small. President George W. Bush reversed that shift with the 2001–06 marginal tax-rate cuts.

Savings Incentives

saving: That part of disposable income not spent on current consumption; disposable income less consumption.

Supply side economists emphasize the importance of *long-run* responses to change tax incentives. On the demand side, an increase in income translates very quickly into increased spending. On the supply side, things don't happen so fast. It takes time to construct new plants and equipment. People are also slow to respond to new work and investment incentives. Hence, the full benefits of supply-side tax cuts—or the damage done by tax hikes—won't be immediately visible.

Of particular concern to supply-side economists is the rate of saving in the economy. Demand-side economists emphasize spending and tend to treat **saving** as a leakage problem. Supply-siders, by contrast, emphasize the importance of saving for financing investment and economic growth. At full employment, a greater volume of investment is possible only if the rate of consumption is cut back. In other words, additional investment requires additional saving. Hence, *supply-side economists favor tax incentives that encourage saving as well as greater tax incentives for investment.* This kind of perspective contrasts sharply with the Keynesian emphasis on stimulating consumption, as the accompanying cartoon emphasizes.

In the early 1980s, Congress greatly increased the incentives for saving. First, banks were permitted to increase the rate of interest paid on various types of savings accounts. Second, the tax on earned interest was reduced. Finally, new forms of tax-free savings were created, for example, Individual Retirement Accounts, or IRAs.

Despite these incentives, the U.S. savings rate declined during the 1980s. Household savings dropped from 6.2 percent of disposable income in 1981 to a low of 2.5 percent in 1987. Neither the tax incentive nor the high interest rates that prevailed in the early 1980s convinced Americans to save more.

The U.S. Bureau of Economic Analysis (BEA) maintains quarterly data on the personal saving rate of U.S. households. See "Economic Overview" at www.bea.doc.gov.

An alternative lever for shifting aggregate supply is to offer tax incentives for investment. The 1981 tax cuts focused on *personal* income tax rates. By contrast, President George H. Bush advocated cutting capital gains taxes. These are taxes levied on the increase in the value of property, such as land, buildings, and corporate stock, when it's sold. Lower capital gains taxes, Bush argued, would encourage people to start businesses or invest in them. As the News on the next page confirms, the push for a reduced capital gains tax resurfaced in early 2001.

President Clinton also emphasized the need for investment incentives. His very first proposal for stimulating the economy was a temporary investment tax credit. People who invested in new plant and equipment would receive a tax credit equal to 10 percent of their investment. In effect, Uncle Sam would pay for part of any new investment by collecting less taxes. Because the credit is available only to those who make new investments, it's a particularly efficient lever for shifting the aggregate supply curve. President Clinton withdrew the investment-credit proposal, however, when he decided that deficit reduction was a higher priority.

Investment Incentives

Find out *ways* to save taxes at www.irs.gov. Click on "Tax Info for You."

 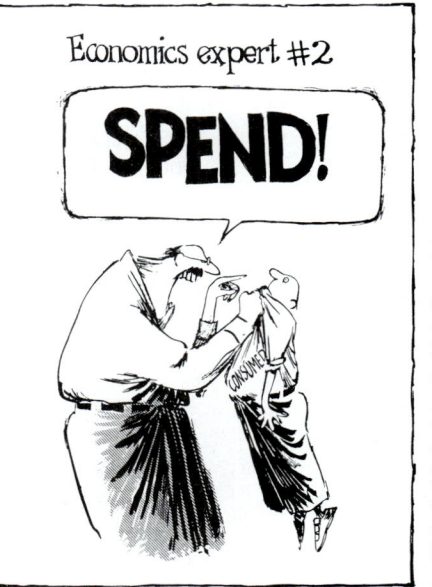

Analysis: In the short run, consumer saving may reduce aggregate demand. However, saving also finances increased investment, which is essential to long-run growth.

The business community sought similar tax credits in President George W. Bush's tax-cut package. But Bush cautioned that additional business tax breaks would make congressional passage of his tax proposal more difficult. After the September 11 terrorist attacks, however, this supply-side lever was pulled as well.

HUMAN CAPITAL INVESTMENT

A nation's ability to supply goods and services depends on its *human* capital as well as its *physical* capital. If the size of the labor force increased, more output could be produced in any given price level. Similarly, if the *quality* of the workforce were to increase, more output could be supplied at any given price level. In other words, increases in **human capital**—the skills and knowledge of the workforce—add to the nation's potential output.

human capital: The knowledge and skills possessed by the workforce.

Structural Unemployment

structural unemployment: Unemployment caused by a mismatch between the skills (or location) of job seekers and the requirements (or location) of available jobs.

A mismatch between the skills of the workforce and the requirements of new jobs is a major cause of the unemployment-inflation trade-off. When aggregate demand increases, employers want to hire more workers. But the available (unemployed) workers may not have the skills employers require. This is the essence of **structural unemployment.** The consequence is that employers can't increase output as fast as they'd like to. Prices, rather than output, increase.

The larger the skills gap between unemployed workers and the requirements of emerging jobs, the worse will be the Phillips curve trade-off. To improve the trade-off, the skills gap must be reduced. This is another supply-side imperative. ***Investments in human capital reduce structural unemployment and shift the aggregate supply curve rightward.***

Worker Training

The tax code is a policy tool for increasing human capital investment as well as physical capital investment. In this case tax credits are made available to employers who offer more worker training. Such credits reduce the employer's after-tax cost of training.

President Clinton proposed even stronger incentives for employer-based training. He wanted to *require* employers to spend at least 1.5 percent of their total payroll costs on training activities. Those employers who didn't provide training activities directly would

Capital Gains Tax Reduction Is Considered
Bush Team Weighs New Cut to Rev Up Flagging Economy

The Bush administration is edging toward supporting a cut in the capital gains tax as a way to stimulate the flagging economy that Republicans fear could lead to big Democratic gains in House elections next year, administration officials said yesterday.

The officials said the administration is debating whether to support the new tax cut as a preemptive strike against further deterioration of the economy or wait until mid-October to see whether economic indicators are still dropping. Continued economic weakness would make a rate reduction less vulnerable to likely Democratic attacks, they believe. . .

Conservatives have long contended that one of the most potent ways to promote economic growth is to cut the tax rate for capital gains—the profit made on an investment, such as real estate or stock, at the time it is sold.

The rate for most people is 20 percent. A proposal popular among Republican lawmakers would reduce the rate to 15 percent. Republicans argue that cutting the rate would eventually raise more money for the government by stimulating business activity.

—Mike Allen and Juliet Eilperin

Source: *Washington Post,* September 9, 2001. © 2001 The Washington Post. Reprinted with permission. www.washingtonpost.com

Analysis: Cuts in investment-related taxes encourage more investment spending and thus help increase aggregate demand.

have to pay an equivalent sum into a public training fund. This "play-or-pay" approach would force employers to invest in the human capital of their employees.

Although the "play-or-pay" concept is intriguing, it might actually shift the aggregate supply curve the *wrong* way. The *costs* of employing workers would rise in the short run as employers shelled out more money for training or taxes. Hence, the aggregate supply curve would shift *leftward* in the short run, worsening the unemployment-inflation trade-off. Only later might AS shift rightward, and then only to the extent that training actually improved **labor productivity.**

labor productivity: Amount of output produced by a worker in a given period of time; output per hour.

Education Spending

Another way to increase human capital is to expand and improve the efficacy of the education system. President George H. Bush encouraged local school systems to become more competitive. He suggested they experiment with vouchers that would allow students to attend the school of their choice. Schools would then have to offer services that attracted voucher-carrying students. Those schools that didn't compete successfully wouldn't have enough funds (vouchers) to continue.

President Clinton advocated a more conventional approach. He urged Congress to allocate more funds to the school system, particularly programs for preschoolers, like Head Start, and disadvantaged youth. He acknowledged the potential value of vouchers in increasing school quality but wanted to limit their use to public schools. If successful, these efforts will shift the aggregate supply curve rightward. They're more likely to develop human capital gradually, however, than to spur short-term economic growth.

President George W. Bush characterized himself as the "education President." He increased federal spending on education and improved tax incentives for college-savings accounts and tuition payments. Here again, however, any improvements in labor productivity are likely to emerge many years later. There is little potential for short-run AS shifts.

Affirmative Action

Lack of skills and experience aren't the only reasons it's sometimes hard to find the "right" workers. The mismatch between employed workers and jobs is often less a matter of skills than of race, gender, or age. In other words, discrimination can create an artificial barrier between job seekers and available job openings.

If discrimination tends to shift the aggregate supply curve leftward, then reducing discriminatory barriers should shift it to the right. Equal opportunity programs are thus a natural extension of a supply-side approach to macro policy. However, critics are also quick to point out the risks inherent in government regulation of hiring decisions. From a supply-side perspective, laws that forbid discrimination are welcome and should be enforced. But aggressive affirmative action programs that require employers to hire specific numbers of women or minority workers limit productive capabilities and can lead to excessive costs.

Transfer Payments

Welfare programs also discourage workers from taking available jobs. Unemployment and welfare benefits provide a source of income when a person isn't working. Although these **transfer payments** are motivated by humanitarian goals, they also inhibit labor supply. Transfer recipients must give up some or all of their welfare payments when they take a job, which makes working less attractive and therefore reduces the number of available workers. The net result is a leftward shift of the aggregate supply curve.

transfer payments: Payments to individuals for which no current goods or services are exchanged, like Social Security, welfare, unemployment benefits.

In 1996, Congress reformed the nation's core welfare program. The supply-side emphasis of that reform was manifest in the very title of the reform legislation: the Personal Responsibility and Work Opportunity Act. Congress set time limits on how long people can draw welfare benefits. The act also required recipients to engage in job-related activities like job search and training while still receiving benefits.

The 1986 reforms had a dramatic effect on recipient behavior. Nationally, over 5 million adults left welfare between 1996 and 2001. Over half of these ex-welfare recipients entered the labor force, thereby shifting the AS curve rightward.

Recognizing that income transfers reduce aggregate supply doesn't force us to eliminate all welfare programs. Welfare programs are also intended to serve important social needs. The AS/AD framework reminds us, however, that the structure of such programs will affect aggregate supply. With over 60 million Americans receiving income transfers, the effect on aggregate supply can be significant.

DEREGULATION

Government intervention affects the shape and position of the aggregate supply curve in other ways. The government intervenes directly in supply decisions by *regulating* employment and output behavior. In general, such regulations limit the flexibility of producers to respond to changes in demand. Government regulation also tends to raise production costs. The higher costs result not only from required changes in the production process but also from the expense of monitoring government regulations and filling out endless government forms. Thomas Hopkins, a Rochester Institute of Technology economist, estimates that the total costs of regulation exceed $700 billion a year. These added costs of production shift the aggregate supply curve to the left.

Factor Markets

Government intervention in factor markets increases the cost of supplying goods and services in many ways.

Minimum Wages. Minimum wage laws are one of the most familiar forms of factor-market regulation. The Fair Labor Standards Act of 1938 required employers to pay workers a minimum of 25 cents per hour. Over time, Congress has increased the coverage of that act and the minimum wage itself repeatedly (to $5.15 in 2001).

The goal of the minimum wage law is to ensure workers a decent standard of living. But the law has other effects as well. By prohibiting employers from using lower-paid workers, it limits the ability of employers to hire additional workers. Teenagers, for example, may not have enough skills or experience to merit the federal minimum wage. Employers may have to rely on more expensive workers rather than hire unemployed teenagers. In the absence of a minimum wage, employers would hire and train more teenagers and other low-skill workers. With minimum wage requirements, the costs of production increase.

Here again the issue is not whether minimum wage laws serve any social purposes but how they affect macro outcomes. By shifting the aggregate supply curve leftward, minimum wage laws make it more difficult to achieve full employment with stable prices.

Mandatory Benefits. Government-directed fringe benefits have the same kind of effect on aggregate supply. One of the first bills President Clinton signed into law was the Family and Medical Leave Act, which requires all businesses with 50 or more employees to grant leaves of absence for up to 12 weeks. The employer must continue to pay health benefits during such absences and must also incur the costs of recruiting and training temporary replacements. The General Accounting Office estimated this would add nearly $700 million per year to payroll costs. These added payroll costs add to the costs of production, making producers less willing to supply output at any given price level.

Occupational Health and Safety. Government regulation of factor markets extends beyond wages and benefits. The government also sets standards for workplace safety and health. The Occupational Safety and Health Administration (OSHA), for example, issued new rules in November 2000 to reduce and prevent ergonomic injuries at work. The rules would have required employers to redesign workplaces (assembly lines, computer workstations) to accommodate individual workers. The rules would have also required employers to pay higher health care costs and grant more injury-related leave. OSHA itself estimated that the new regulations would cost employers $4.5 billion a year. Employers said the ergonomics regulations would cost *far* more that—up to $125 billion a year. Concern over the implied upward shift of aggregate supply prompted Congress to rescind the new ergonomics rules in early 2001, before they took effect (see News). In scores of other cases, however, workplace regulation has raised production costs and constrained aggregate supply. Although all such regulations may improve workers' well-being, critics charge that the implied cost is too high.

The government's regulation of factor markets tends to raise production costs and inhibit supply. The same is true of regulations imposed directly on product markets, as the following examples illustrate.

Product Markets

Transportation Costs. At the federal level, various agencies regulate the output and prices of transportation services. Until 1984, the Civil Aeronautics Board (CAB) determined which routes airlines could fly and how much they could charge. The Interstate Commerce Commission (ICC) has had the same kind of power over trucking, interstate bus lines, and railroads. The routes, services, and prices for ships (in U.S. coastal waters and foreign commerce) have been established by the Federal Maritime Commission. In all these cases, the regulations constrained the ability of producers to respond to increases in demand. Existing producers couldn't increase output at will, and new producers were excluded from the market. Hence, the rate of output was kept too low and prices too high.

Similar problems continue to inflate intrastate trucking costs. All but eight states limit the routes, the loads, and the prices of intrastate trucking companies. These regulations promote inefficient transportation and protect producer profits. The net cost to the economy is at least $8 billion, or about $128 a year for a family of four.

Many cities and counties also limit the number of taxicabs and regulate their prices. The net effect of such regulation is to limit competition and drive up the cost of transportation.

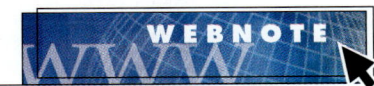

The Cato Institute, a conservative Washington, D.C., think tank, publishes lots of studies on regulatory costs; visit www.cato.org/research/ reglt-st.html.

Food and Drug Standards. The Food and Drug Administration (FDA) has a broad mandate to protect consumers from dangerous products. In fulfilling this responsibility, the FDA sets health standards for the content of specific foods. A hot dog, for example, can be labeled as such only if it contains specific mixtures of skeletal meat, pig lips,

Bush Signs Repeal of Ergonomics Rules

President Bush signed his first bill carrying national impact yesterday, repealing workplace safety regulations that he called "unduly burdensome and overly broad," and sending his administration to work on a business-friendlier substitute that is months or years away.

Republicans see the repeal, which was whisked through Congress, as a major step in diminishing the regulatory legacy of former president Bill Clinton. Speaking to female business leaders in the East Room, Bush praised Congress for beginning "a culture of accomplishment in Washington." . . .

The ergonomics regulations, which were 10 years in the making, would have taken effect in October. Labor Department officials said they have begun working on an alternative, which could include replacement regulations or voluntary guidelines. A third possibility is a new regulation written at the direction of Congress.

In the meantime, the Occupational Safety and Health Administration will continue to investigate complaints. "OSHA is still charged with ensuring a safe workplace," labor spokesman Stuart D. Roy said.

—Mike Allen

Source: *Washington Post*, March 21, 2001. © 2001 The Washington Post. Reprinted with permission. www.washingtonpost.com

Analysis: Workplace-safety regulations increase production costs and so shift the AS curve leftward. In this case, the implied shift was regarded as excessive.

snouts, and ears. By the same token, a milk chocolate bar is a milk chocolate bar, according to the FDA, only if it

> contains not less than 3.66 percent by weight of milk fat, not less than 12 percent by weight of milk solids, and not less than 10 percent by weight of chocolate liquor as calculated by subtracting from the weight of chocolate liquor used the weight of cacao fat therein and the weights therein of alkali and seasoning ingredients, if any, multiplying the remainder by 2.2, dividing the result by the weight of the finished milk chocolate, and multiplying the quotient by 100.

The FDA also sets standards for the testing of new drugs and evaluates the test results. In all three cases, the goal of regulation is to minimize health risks to consumers.

Like all regulation, however, the FDA standards entail real costs. The tests required for new drugs are expensive and time-consuming. Getting a new drug approved for sale can take years of effort and require a huge investment. The net results are that (1) fewer new drugs are brought to market and (2) those that do reach the market are more expensive than they would have been in the absence of regulation. In other words, the aggregate supply of goods is shifted to the left.

Other examples of government regulation are commonplace. The Environmental Protection Agency (EPA) regulates auto emissions, the discharge of industrial wastes, and water pollution. The U.S. Congress restricts foreign imports and raises their prices. The Federal Trade Commission (FTC) limits firms' freedom to increase their output or advertise their products.

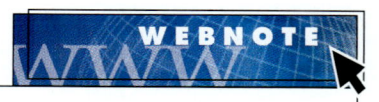

For the EPA's assessment of how its own regulations affect the U.S. economy, go to www.epa.gov. Click on "Browse EPA Topics," then choose "Economics."

Reducing Costs

Many—perhaps most—of these regulatory activities are beneficial. In fact, all were originally designed to serve specific public purposes. As a result of such regulation, we get safer drugs, cleaner air, and less deceptive advertising. We must also consider the costs involved, however. All regulatory activities impose direct and indirect costs. These costs must be compared to the benefits received. ***The basic contention of supply-side economists is that regulatory costs are now too high.*** To improve our economic performance, they assert, we must *deregulate* the production process, thereby shifting the aggregate supply curve to the right again.

EASING TRADE BARRIERS

Government regulation of international trade also influences the shape and position of aggregate supply. Trade flows affect both factor and product markers.

Factor Markets

In factor markers, U.S. producers buy raw materials, equipment parts, and components from foreign suppliers. Tariffs (taxes on imported goods) make such inputs more expensive, thereby increasing the cost of U.S. production. Regulations or quotas that make foreign inputs less accessible or more expensive similarly constrain the U.S. aggregate supply curve. The quota on imported sugar, for example, increases the cost of U.S.-produced soda, cookies, and candy. Just that one trade barrier has cost U.S. consumers over $2 billion in higher prices.

Product Markets

The same kind of trade barriers affect product markets directly. With completely unrestricted ("free") trade, foreign producers would be readily available to supply products to U.S. consumers. If U.S. producers were approaching capacity or incurring escalating cost pressures, foreign suppliers would act as a safety valve. By increasing the quantity of output available at any given price level, foreign suppliers help flatten out the aggregate supply curve.

Despite the success of the North American Free Trade Agreement (NAFTA) and the World Trade Organization (WTO) in reducing trade barriers, half of all U.S. imports are still subject to tariffs. Nontariff barriers (regulation, quotas, and so forth) also still constrain aggregate supply. This was evident in the 2001 battle over Mexican trucking. Although NAFTA authorized Mexican trucking companies to compete freely in the United

Border Could Open Soon to Mexican Truckers

Mexican truckers could soon be free to deliver their loads anywhere in the USA, the result of an arbitration ruling to be released today in a six-year trade dispute.

A five-member panel has ruled that the United States was bound by the North American Free Trade Agreement (NAFTA) to open its borders to Mexican trucks and was wrong to block them on safety grounds.

Under NAFTA, the U.S. agreed to give Mexican truckers access to Texas, New Mexico, Arizona and California by 1995 and to the entire USA by January 2000.

President Clinton, under pressure from organized labor, refused to open the border, citing safety concerns about Mexican vehicles.

As Texas governor and during his presidential campaign, President Bush called for the U.S. to open up to Mexican haulers. . . .

U.S. business groups have complained about high trucking costs, blamed on a shortage of drivers.

Donahue, a former trucking industry lobbyist, says the ruling will mean lower consumer costs from more efficient freight handling—and an increase in U.S. trucks traveling to the manufacturing corridor in northern Mexico.

—James Cox

Source: *USA Today*, February 7, 2001. © 2001 USA Today. Reprinted with permission. www.usatoday.com

Analysis: Trade barriers keep production costs high. Reducing trade barriers shifts the AS curve rightward.

States, U.S. labor unions (Teamsters) and trucking companies vigorously protested their entry, delaying the implied reduction in transportation costs (see World View).

Another global supply-side policy lever is immigration policy. Skill shortages in U.S. labor markets can be overcome with education and training. But even faster relief is available in the vast pool of foreign workers. In 2000, Congress increased the quota for software engineers and other high-tech workers by 70 percent, to 195,000 workers. The intent was to relieve the skill shortage in high-tech industries and with it, the cost pressures that were increasing the slope of the aggregate supply curve. Temporary visas for farm workers also help avert cost-push inflation in the farm sector. By regulating the flow of immigrant workers, Congress has the potential to alter the shape and position of the short-run AS curve.

Immigration

INFRASTRUCTURE DEVELOPMENT

Another way to reduce the costs of supplying goods and services is to improve the nation's **infrastructure**, that is, the transportation, communications, judicial, and other systems that bind the pieces of the economy into a coherent whole. The interstate

infrastructure: The transportation, communications, education, judicial, and other institutional systems that facilitate market exchanges.

"*I blame government, labor, business, and my ex-wife.*"

Analysis: Because many constraints on aggregate supply contribute to stagflation, it's hard to single out any one cause (or cure).

highway system, for example, enlarged the market for producers looking for new sales opportunities. Improved air traffic controls and larger airports have also made international markets and factors of production readily accessible. Without interstate highways and international airports, the process of supplying goods and services would be more localized and much more expensive.

It's easy to take infrastructure for granted until you have to make do without it. In recent years, U.S. producers have rushed into China, Russia, and Eastern Europe looking for new profit opportunities. What they discovered is that even simple communication is difficult where telephones are scarce and unreliable. In China, there are only nine telephones for every 100 people; Russia has 21. By contrast, the United States has 66 phones for every 100 people. Cars and taxicabs are almost as hard to locate in Russia or China, and conference facilities are primitive. There are few established clearinghouses for marketing information, and labor markets are fragmented and localized. Getting started sometimes requires doing everything from scratch.

Although the United States has a highly developed infrastructure, it too could be improved. There are roads and bridges to repair, more airports to be built, faster rail systems to construct, and space-age televideo networks to install. Spending on this kind of infrastructure will not only increase aggregate demand (fiscal stimulus) but also shift aggregate supply.

EXPECTATIONS

Last, but not least, we must again take expectations into account. Expectations play a crucial role not only in consumer expenditure decisions but in production and investment decisions as well. Hence, expectations will influence the shape of the short-run aggregate supply curve—the *willingness* and ability to supply output at various prices. If producers expect more "business-friendly" government policies (see News, page 343), they will be more willing to invest in new plant, equipment, and software. By contrast, the prospect of increasing government regulation or higher taxes deters investors from expanding production capacity. ***Because investment is always a bet on future economic conditions, expectations directly affect the shape of the AS curve.*** Hence, an improvement in expectations will shift the AS curve rightward. In the aftermath of the September 11, 2001 terrorist attacks rebuilding consumer and investor confidence was the most important task for both supply-side and demand-side policy.

THE ECONOMY TOMORROW

Rebuilding America

The output of the U.S. economy depends not only on *private* investment but on *public* investment as well. The infrastructure of transportation, communications, and environmental systems all affect the nation's production possibilities. As we look to the future, we have to wonder whether that infrastructure will satisfy the needs of the economy tomorrow. If it doesn't, it will become increasingly difficult and costly to increase output. Inadequate infrastructure would not only worsen short-term macro outcomes but also impair our ability to compete in world markets.

Declining Infrastructure Investment

The United States has over $2 trillion worth of public, nonmilitary infrastructure, including highways, bridges, sewage systems, buildings, hospitals, and schools. Like private capital (business plant, equipment, and structures), this *public* capital contributes to our production possibilities.

Investment in public infrastructure slowed down in the 1970s and 1980s. As Figure 16.8 shows, the rate of infrastructure investment peaked at around 3.5 percent of GDP in the mid-1960s. It then declined steadily to a low of about 0.5 percent of GDP in the early 1980s. As a result of this decline in spending, the United States has barely been

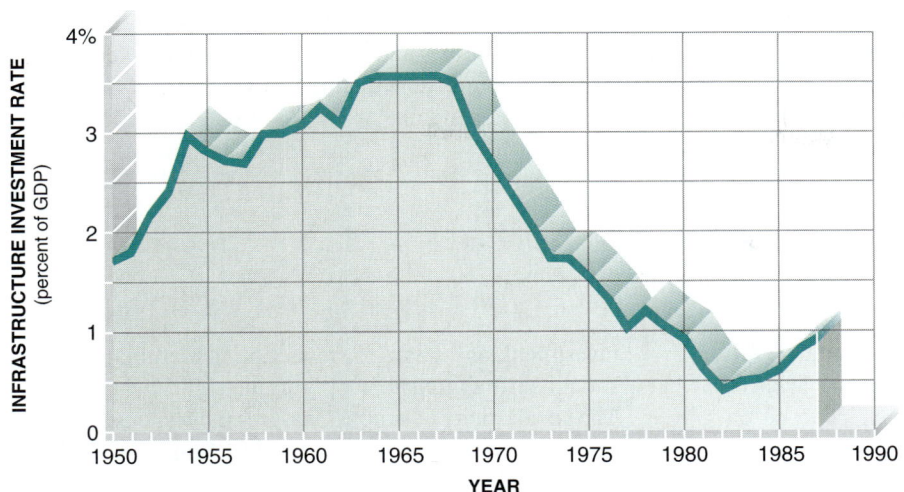

FIGURE 16.8
Declining Infrastructure Investment

Relative investments in civilian infrastructure dropped sharply in the 1970s and early 1980s. The investment ratio peaked at about 3.5 percent of GDP in the mid-1960s and plummeted to only 0.5 percent in 1981–82.

Source: David Alan Aschauer, "Infrastructure: America's Third Deficit." *Challenge,* March–April 1991. Reprinted with permission of publisher, M. E. Sharpe, Inc.

able to *maintain* existing infrastructure much less *expand* it. Studies by Alan Aschauer and others suggest that **declining infrastructure investment has reduced actual and potential output.** In other words, crumbling infrastructure has shifted the aggregate supply curve leftward.

Not everyone agrees that the nation's infrastructure is actually crumbling. Accident rates on the roads, rails, and in the air have been declining. Moreover, the quality of interstate roads—including the 155,000-mile National Highway system—has improved significantly since 1980. But everyone agrees that **the transportation system isn't keeping up with a growing economy.** Highway traffic is increasing at 2.5 percent a year, while airline passenger traffic is rising at closer to 4 percent a year. To accommodate this growth, we need more and better transportation systems.

The failure to expand the infrastructure could prove costly. The U.S. Department of Transportation estimates that people now spend nearly 800 *million* hours a year in traffic delays. If the nation's highways don't improve, those delays will skyrocket to 3.9 *billion* hours a year a decade from now. That's a lot of labor resources to leave idle. Moreover, cars stuck on congested highways waste a lot of gasoline: nearly 3 billion gallons a year.

Delays in air travel impose similar costs. The Federal Aviation Administration says air travel delays increase airline operating costs by over $2 billion a year and idle over $3 billion worth of passenger time. That time imposes a high opportunity cost in forgone business transactions and shortened vacations. Ultimately, all these costs are reflected in lower productivity, reduced output, and higher prices.

The Cost of Delay

To alleviate these constraints on aggregate supply, Congress voted to accelerate infrastructure spending. The Transportation Equity Act of 2000 raised federal spending to over $60 billion a year. Among the public investments:

The Rebuilding Process

- **Highways:** Highway construction and rehabilitation.
- **Air traffic control:** Modernization of the air traffic control system.
- **Weather service:** Modernization of the weather service (new satellites, a supercomputer).
- **Maglev trains:** Research on magnetically levitated ("maglev") trains that can travel at 300 miles per hour and are environmentally clean.
- **Smart cars and highways:** Research and testing of cars and highways outfitted with radar, monitors, and computers to reduce congestion and accidents.

Other legislation authorized more spending on sewage systems, access to space (for example, the space shuttle), modernization of the postal service, and construction of more hospitals, prisons, and other buildings. These infrastructure improvements increase aggregate supply, improving both short- and long-run economic outcomes. To keep track of such activity, the GDP accounts now distinguish government *investment* spending from government *consumption* spending.

SUMMARY

- Fiscal and monetary policies seek to attain full employment and price stability by altering the level of aggregate demand. Their success, however, depends on microeconomic responses, as reflected in the price and output decisions of market participants.
- The market's response to shifts in aggregate demand is reflected in the shape and position of the aggregate supply curve. If the curve slopes upward, a trade-off between unemployment and inflation exists. The Phillips curve illustrates the trade-off.
- If the aggregate supply curve shifts to the left, the trade-off between unemployment and inflation worsens. Stagflation—a combination of substantial inflation and unemployment—results. This is illustrated by rightward shifts of the Phillips curve.
- Supply-side policies attempt to alter price and output decisions directly. If successful, they'll shift the aggregate supply curve to the right. Such a shift implies less inflation *and* less unemployment.
- Marginal tax rates are a major concern of supply-side economists. High tax rates discourage extra work, investment, and saving. A reduction in marginal tax rates should shift aggregate supply to the right.
- The tax elasticity of supply measures the response of quantity supplied to changes in tax rates. Empirical evidence suggests that tax elasticity is low and that short-run shifts of the aggregate supply curve are therefore small.
- Investments in human capital increase productivity and therefore shift aggregate supply also. Workers' training and education enhancement are policy levers.
- Government regulation often raises the cost of production and limits output. Deregulation is intended to reduce costly restrictions on price and output behavior, thereby shifting aggregate supply to the right.
- Public infrastructure is part of the economy's capital resources. Investments in infrastructure (such as transportation systems) facilitate market exchanges and expand production possibilities.
- Trade barriers shift the AS curve leftward by raising the cost of imported imports and the price of imported products. Lowering trade barriers increases aggregate supply.

Key Terms

stagflation
aggregate supply
Phillips curve
marginal tax rate
investment
tax rebate
tax elasticity of supply
saving
human capital
structural unemployment
labor productivity
transfer payments
infrastructure

Questions for Discussion

1. Why might prices rise when aggregate demand increases? What factors might influence the extent of price inflation?
2. What were the unemployment and inflation rates last year? Where would they lie on Figure 16.5? Can you explain the implied shift from curve PC_2?
3. What were the demand-side incentives of the 2001 tax package? (See News, page 338.) What were the supply-side incentives?
4. Which of the following groups are likely to have the highest tax elasticity of labor supply? (*a*) college students, (*b*) single parents, (*c*) primary earners in two-parent families, (*d*) secondary earners in two-parent families. Why are there differences?
5. How is the aggregate supply curve affected by (*a*) minimum wage laws, (*b*) Social Security payroll taxes and retirement benefits?

6. OSHA predicted that its proposed ergonomics rules (News, page 343) would have cut repetitive-stress injuries by 50 percent. Was Congress correct in repealing those rules?
7. If all workplace-safety regulations both (*a*) improve workers well-being and (*b*) raise production costs, how should the line between "good" regulations and "bad" regulations be drawn?
8. How do each of the following infrastructure items affect aggregate supply? (*a*) highways, (*b*) schools, (*c*) sewage systems, (*d*) courts and prisons.
9. How would the volume and timing of a capital investments be affected by (*a*) a permanent cut in the capital-gains tax (see News, page 340), (*b*) a temporary 10-percent tax credit?
10. Why would Democrats oppose a capital gains tax cut that might invigorate a stalled economy? (See News, page 340.)
11. In the cartoon on page 339, which "expert" is the supply-sider?

Web Activities

1. Find the inflation rates and unemployment rates for each year since 1990 at www.bls.gov. Construct a Phillips curve for the 1990s. Do you see a pattern? Are the years since then on the same curve?
2. How much does the typical U.S. household pay in taxes? Compare the findings of a group that maintains federal taxes have gone up quickly (www.taxfoundation.org) with a group that maintains federal taxes haven't gone up quickly (www.cbpp.org). What policy recommendations does each group make based on its different reading of the data?

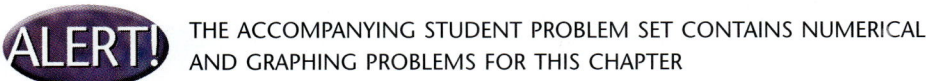

ALERT! THE ACCOMPANYING STUDENT PROBLEM SET CONTAINS NUMERICAL AND GRAPHING PROBLEMS FOR THIS CHAPTER

CHAPTER 17

Growth and Productivity: Long-Run Possibilities

> Economic growth is the fundamental determinant of the long-run success of any nation, the basic source of rising living standards, and the key to meeting the needs and desires of the American people.
>
> —*Economic Report of the President, 1992*

Imagine a world with no fax machines, no cellular phones, no satellite TV, and no digital sound. Such a world actually existed—and only 25 years ago! At the time, personal computers were still on the drawing board, and laptops weren't even envisioned. Websites were a place where spiders gathered, not locations in the Internet. Home video hadn't been seen, and no one had yet popped any microwave popcorn. Biotechnology hadn't yet produced any blockbuster drugs, and people wore the same pair of athletic shoes for a wide variety of sports.

New products are evidence of economic progress. Over time, we produce not only *more* goods and services but also *new* and *better* goods and services. In the process, we get richer: Our material living standards rise.

Rising living standards aren't inevitable, however. According to World Bank estimates, almost 3 *billion* people—nearly half the world's population—continue to live in abject poverty (with incomes of less than $2 per day). Worse still, living standards in many of the poorest countries have *fallen* in the last decade. Living standards also fell in Eastern Europe when communism collapsed and a painful transition to market economies began. Those living in the former Soviet bloc countries are counting on the power of free markets to jump-start their economies and raise living standards.

This chapter takes a longer-term view of economic performance. Chapters 8 to 16 were concerned with the business cycle—that is, *short-run* variations in output and prices. This chapter looks at the prospects for *long-run* growth and considers three questions:

- How important is economic growth?
- How does an economy grow?
- Is continued economic growth possible? Is it desirable?

We develop answers to these questions by first examining the nature of economic growth and then examining its sources and potential limits.

THE NATURE OF GROWTH

Economic growth refers to increases in the output of goods and services. But there are two distinct ways in which output increases, and they have very different implications for our economic welfare.

The easiest kind of growth comes from increased use of our productive capabilities. In any given year there's a limit to an economy's potential output. This limit is determined by the quantity of resources available and our technological know-how. We've illustrated these short-run limits with a **production possibilities** curve, as in Figure 17.1a. By using all our available resources and our best expertise, we can produce any combination of goods and services on the production possibilities curve.

We don't always take full advantage of our productive capacity. The economy often produces a mix of output that lies *inside* our production possibilities, like point *A* in Figure 17.1a. When this happens, a major *short-run* goal of macro policy is to achieve full employment—to move us from point *A* to some point on the production possibilities curve (such as point *B*). In the process, we produce more output.

Once we're fully utilizing our productive capacity, further increases in output are attainable only if we *expand* that capacity. To do so we have to *shift* the production possibilities curve outward as in Figure 17.1b. Such shifts imply an increase in *potential* GDP—that is, our productive capacity.

Over time, increases in capacity are critical. Short-run increases in the utilization of existing capacity can generate only modest increases in output. Even high unemployment rates, such as 7 percent, leave little room for increased output. **To achieve large and lasting increases in output we must push our production possibilities outward.** For this reason, economists often define **economic growth** in terms of changes in *potential* GDP.

The unique character of economic growth can also be illustrated with aggregate supply and demand curves. Figure 17.2 depicts both a sloped, *short-run* AS curve and a

Short-Run Changes in Capacity Utilization

production possibilities: The alternative combinations of final goods and services that could be produced in a given time period with all available resources and technology.

Long-Run Changes in Capacity

economic growth: An increase in output (real GDP); an expansion of production possibilities.

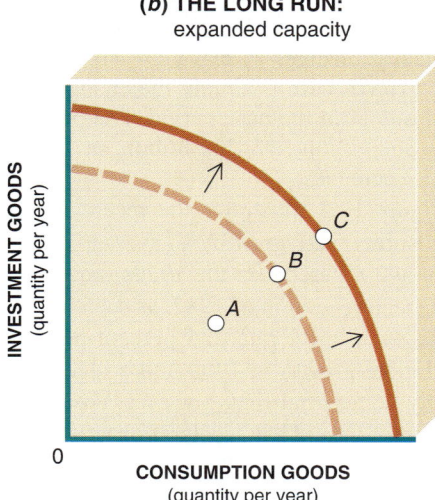

FIGURE 17.1
Two Types of Growth

Increases in output may result from increased use of existing capacity or from increases in that capacity itself. In part *a* the mix of output at point *A* doesn't make full use of production possibilities. Hence, we can get more output by employing more of our available resources or using them more efficiently. This is illustrated by point *B* (or any other point on the curve).

Once we're on the production possibilities curve, we can get more output only by *increasing* our productive capacity. This is illustrated by the outward *shift* of the production possibilities curve in part *b*.

FIGURE 17.2
Shifts of Long-Run Supply

Macro stabilization policies try to shift the aggregate demand curve (e.g., from AD_1 to AD_2) to achieve greater output and employment. The vertical long-run AS curve implies that these efforts will have no lasting impact on the natural rate of output, however. To achieve economic growth, the long-run aggregate supply curve must be shifted to the right (e.g., from $LRAS_1$ to $LRAS_2$)

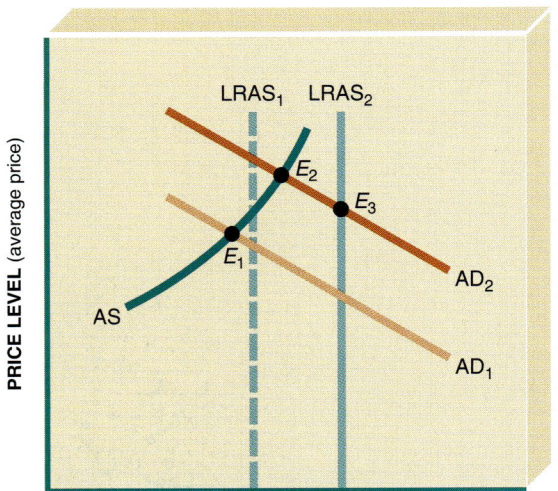

vertical, *long-run* AS curve. In the short run, macro stabilization policies try to shift the AD curve to a more desirable price-output equilibrium. Such demand-side policies are unlikely to change the country's long-run capacity to produce, however. At best they move the macro equilibrium to a more desirable point on the *short-run* AS curve (for example, from E_1 to E_2 in Figure 17.2).

Our productive capacity may increase nevertheless. If it does, the "natural" long-run AS curve will also shift. In this framework, *economic growth implies a rightward shift of the long-run aggregate supply curve.* Should that occur, the economy will be able to produce still more output with less inflationary pressure (e.g., as at E_3 in Figure 17.2).

Nominal vs. Real GDP

real GDP: The value of final output produced in a given period, adjusted for changing prices.

base period: The time period used for comparative analysis; the basis for indexing, e.g., of price changes.

Notice we refer to *real* GDP, not *nominal* GDP, in our concept of economic growth. Nominal GDP can rise even when the quantity of goods and services falls, as was the case in 1991. The total quantity of goods and services produced in 1991 was less than the quantity produced in 1990. Nevertheless, prices rose enough in 1991 to keep nominal GDP growing.

Real GDP refers to the actual quantity of goods and services produced. Real GDP avoids the distortions of inflation by adjusting for changing prices. By using 1992 prices as a **base period,** we observe that real GDP fell from $6139 billion in 1990 to only $6079 billion in 1991. Since then real GDP has increased substantially.

MEASURES OF GROWTH

The Growth Rate

growth rate: Percentage change in real output from one period to another.

Typically, changes in real GDP are expressed in percentage terms, as a growth *rate*. The **growth rate** is simply the change in real output between two periods divided by total output in the base period. The percentage decline in real output during 1991 was thus $60 billion ÷ $6139 billion, or 1 percent. By contrast, real output grew in 1992 by 2.7 percent.

The U.S. Bureau of Economic Analysis (BEA) maintains quarterly data on real GDP growth in their "overview of the U.S. economy" at www.bea.doc.gov.

Figure 17.3 illustrates the recent growth experience of the U.S. economy. In the 1960s, real GDP grew by an average of 4.1 percent per year. Economic growth slowed to only 2.8 percent in the 1970s, however, with actual output declines in three years. The steep recession of 1982, as seen in Figure 17.3, reduced GDP growth in the 1980s to an even lower rate: 2.5 percent per year. The 1990s started out even worse, with negligible growth in 1990 and a recession in 1991. The economy performed significantly better after that, however. From 1997 to 2000, real GDP grew by more than 4 percent a year. That acceleration of the growth rate was so impressive that observers began to talk about a "New Economy," in which faster growth would be the norm (see News).

FIGURE 17.3
Recent U.S. Growth Rates

Total output typically increases from one year to another. The focus of policy is on the growth *rate*, that is, how fast real GDP increases from one year to the next.

Source: *Economic Report of the President, 2001*.

The notion of a fast-growth New Economy was badly shaken in 2001. In the first quarter of 2001, GDP grew by only 1.3 percent and then by a miniscule 0.2 percent in the second quarter. In the third quarter (which included the Sept. 11 terrorist attacks), real GDP actually *declined* by 1.1 percent. Analysts fretted over whether the economy would ever get back on the "fast track" of 3.5–4.0 percent growth or would instead be saddled with years of more sluggish growth (2.0–2.5 percent)—or worse.

The New Economy

The U.S. economy today displays several exceptional features. The first is its strong rate of productivity growth. . . . A second is its unusually low levels of both inflation and unemployment. . . . A third is the disappearance of Federal budget deficits. . . . A fourth is the strength of the U.S. economy's performance relative to other industrial economies. . . . These developments reveal profound changes in economic trends that justify the term "New Economy."

Three interrelated factors lie behind these extraordinary economic gains: technological innovation, organizational changes in business, and public policy. . . . The interactions among these three factors have created a virtuous cycle in which developments in one area reinforce and stimulate developments in another. The result is an economic system in which the whole is greater than the sum of the parts. . . .

This Report defines the New Economy by the extraordinary gains in performance—including rapid productivity growth, rising incomes, low unemployment, and moderate inflation—that have resulted from this combination of virtually reinforcing advances in technologies, business practices, and economic policies.

Source: *Economic Report of the President, 2001*, pp. 22–23.

Analysis: The successes of the late 1990s spawned the hope of continuing rapid gains in productivity and GDP growth—a "new" economy. The recession of 2001, coupled with widespread "dot.com" failures, shed doubt on this concept.

The Exponential Process. At first blush, all the anxiety about growth rates seems a bit overblown. Indeed, the whole subject of economic growth looks rather dull when you discover that "big" gains in economic growth are measured in fractions of a percent. However, this initial impression isn't fair. First, even one year's "low" growth implies lost output. If we had just *maintained* output in 1991 at its 1990 level—that is, "achieved" a *zero* growth rate rather than a 1 percent decline—we would have had $60 billion more worth of goods and services, which works out to over $200 worth of goods and services per person. Lots of people would have liked that extra output. In today's $10 trillion economy, each 1 percent of economic growth is even more significant.

Second, economic growth is a *continuing* process. Gains made in one year accumulate in future years. It's like interest you earn at the bank: If you leave your money in the bank for several years, you begin to earn interest on your interest. Eventually you accumulate a nice little bankroll.

The process of economic growth works the same way. Each little shift of the production possibilities curve broadens the base for future GDP. As shifts accumulate over many years, the economy's productive capacity is greatly expanded. Ultimately we discover that those "little" differences in annual growth rates generate tremendous gains in GDP.

This cumulative process, whereby interest or growth is compounded from one year to the next, is called an "exponential process." At growth rates of 2.5 percent, GDP doubles in 28 years. With 3.5 percent growth, GDP doubles in only 20 years. In a single generation the *difference* between 2.5 percent growth and 3.5 percent growth amounts to $5 trillion of output a year. That *difference* is about half of this year's total output. From this longer-term perspective, the difference between 2.5 percent and 3.5 percent growth begins to look very meaningful.

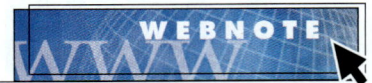

Find growth rates of various countries from the World Bank at www.worldbank.org/data. Click on "Data by Topic," then choose "Macroeconomics and Growth." Under "Economic Growth and Structure," click on "Growth of Output."

The exponential process looks even more meaningful when we translate it into *per capita* terms. We can do so by looking at GDP *per capita* rather than total GDP. **GDP per capita** is simply total output divided by total population. In 2000, the total output of the U.S. economy was $10 trillion. Since there were 280 million of us to share that output, GDP per capita was

GDP per Capita: A Measure of Living Standards

GDP per capita: Total GDP divided by total population; average GDP.

$$\text{GDP per capita (2000)} = \frac{\$10 \text{ trillion of output}}{280 \text{ million people}} = \$35{,}714$$

This does not mean that every man, woman, and child in the United States received $35,714 worth of goods and services in 2000; it simply indicates how much output was potentially available to the "average" person. GDP per capita is often used as a basic measure of our standard of living.

Growth in GDP per capita is attained only when the growth of output exceeds population growth. In the United States, this condition is usually achieved. Even when *total* GDP growth slowed in the 1970s and 1980s, *per capita* GDP kept rising because the U.S. population was growing by only 1 percent a year. Hence, even relatively slow economic growth of 2.5 percent a year was enough to keep raising living standards.

The developing nations of the Third World aren't so fortunate. Many of these countries bear both slower *economic* growth and faster *population* growth. They have a difficult time *maintaining* living standards, much less increasing them. Ethiopia, for example, is one of the poorest countries in the world, with GDP per capita of roughly $700 (see World View in Chapter 2, page 28). Yet its population continues to grow rapidly (2.8 percent per year), putting constant pressure on living standards. The population of Nigeria also grew by an average of 2.8 percent per year in the 1990s, while GDP grew at a slower rate of only 2.4 percent (see Table 2.1 on page 30). As a consequence, GDP per capita *declined* nearly 0.4 percent per year.

By comparison with these countries, the United States has been most fortunate. Our GDP per capita has more than doubled since 1970s, despite several recessions. This means that the average person today has twice as many goods and services as the average person had a generation ago.

TABLE 17.1
The Rule of 72

Net Growth Rate (percent)	Doubling Time (years)
0.0	Never
0.5	140
1.0	70
1.5	47
2.0	35
2.5	30
3.0	24
3.5	20
4.0	18

Small differences in annual growth rates cumulate into large differences in GDP. Shown here are the number of years it would take to double GDP per capita at various net growth rates. "Net" growth refers to the GDP growth rate minus the population growth rate.

Doubling times can be approximated by the "rule of 72." Seventy-two divided by the growth rate equals the number of years it takes to double.

What about the future? Will we continue to enjoy substantial gains in living standards? Many Americans harbor great doubts. A 2000 poll revealed that 15 percent of adults believe their children's living standards will be below today's level and another 36 percent believe future living standards will be no higher than today's. That would happen only if population growth outstrips or equals GDP growth. That seems most unlikely. Table 17.1 displays more optimistic scenarios in which GDP continues to grow faster than the population. If GDP *per capita* continues to grow at 2 percent per year—as it did in the 1990s—it will take 35 years to double our standard of living. If GDP per capita grows just half a percent faster, say, by 2.5 percent per year, our standard of living will double in only 30 years.

The potential increases in living standards depicted in Table 17.1 won't occur automatically. Someone is going to have to produce more output if we want GDP per capita to rise. One reason our living standard rose in the 1980s is that the labor force grew faster than the population. Those in the World War II baby boom had reached maturity and were entering the **labor force** in droves. At the same time, more women took jobs outside the home, a trend that continued into the 1990s. As a consequence, the **employment rate** increased significantly, as Figure 17.4 shows. With the number of workers growing faster than the population, GDP per capita was sure to rise.

GDP per Worker: A Measure of Productivity

labor force: All persons over age 16 who are either working for pay or actively seeking paid employment.

employment rate: The percentage of the adult population that is employed.

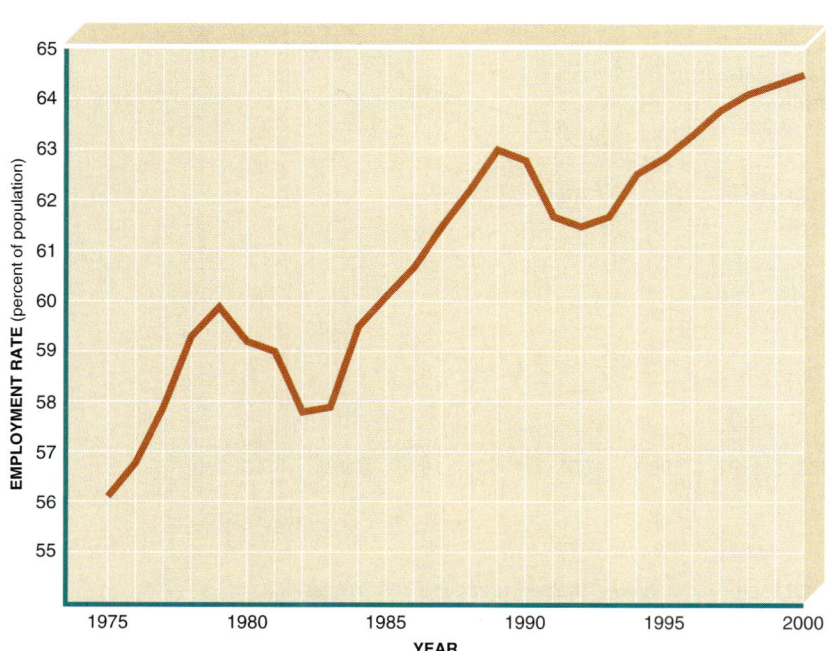

FIGURE 17.4
A Rising Employment Rate

The entry of Baby Boomers (born 1946–60) into the labor force and increased labor-force attachment of women caused the ratio of workers to total population (the employment rate) to rise. This boosted per capita GDP.

productivity: Output per unit of input, for example, output per labor-hour.

The U.S. Bureau of Labor Statistics (BLS) maintains quarterly data on labor productivity at www.bls.gov/data

The employment rate can't increase forever. At the limit, everyone would be in the labor market, and no further workers could be found. Further increases in GDP per capita could only come from increases in output *per worker*.

The most common measure of **productivity** is output per labor-hour, which is simply the ratio of total output to the number of hours worked. As noted earlier, total GDP in 2000 was $10 trillion. In that same year the labor force was employed for a total of 262 billion hours. Hence, the average worker's productivity was

$$\frac{\text{Labor}}{\text{productivity}} = \frac{\text{total output}}{\text{total labor-hours}}$$

$$= \frac{\$10 \text{ trillion}}{262 \text{ billion hours}}$$

$$= \$38 \text{ per hour}$$

The increase in our GDP per capita in recent decades is directly related to the higher productivity of the average U.S. worker. The average worker today produces twice as many goods and services than the average worker did in 1965.

The Productivity Turnaround. For economic growth to continue, the productivity of the average U.S. worker must rise still further. Will it? As Figure 17.5 reveals, productivity grew at an average pace of 1.4 percent from 1973 to 1995. Along the way,

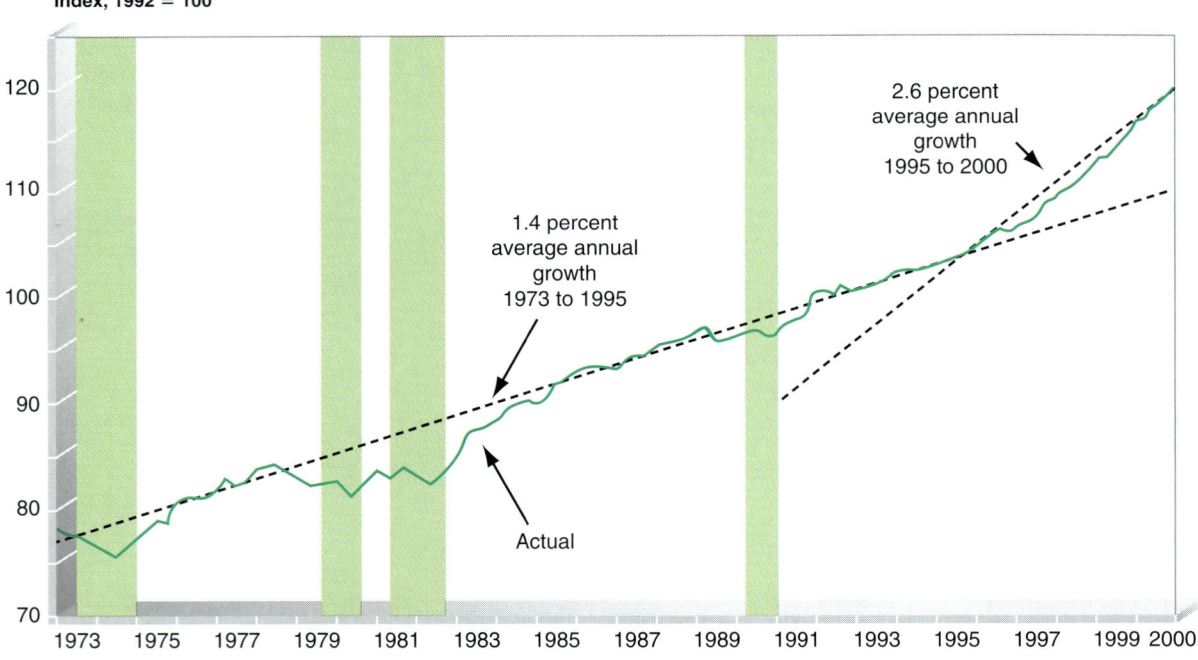

FIGURE 17.5
Productivity Gains

Increasing productivity (output per worker) is the critical factor in raising per capita GDP over time. Productivity advances slowed in 1978–84 but accelerated sharply in 1995–2000.

Note: Shaded areas indicate recessions.

Source: *U.S. Department of Commerce.*

however, there were many years (e.g., 1978–84) in which productivity advances slowed to a snail's pace. This productivity slowdown constrained GDP growth.

After 1995, productivity advances accelerated sharply, as seen in Figure 17.5. This productivity jump was so impressive that it raised hopes for a "New Economy" (see News, page 353), in which technological breakthroughs, better management, and enlightened public policy would keep both productivity and GDP growing at faster rates.

SOURCES OF GROWTH

The arithmetic of economic growth is simple. Future output growth depends on two factors:

$$\text{Growth rate of total output} = \text{Growth rate of labor force} + \text{Growth rate of productivity}$$

Accordingly, how fast GDP increases in the future depends on how fast the labor force grows and how fast productivity advances. Since the long-run growth of the labor force has stabilized at around 1.2 percent, the real uncertainty about future economic growth originates in the unpredictability of productivity advances. Will output per worker increase at the snail's pace of only 1 percent a year or at much faster rates of 2, 3, or even 4 percent per year?

To assess the potential for U.S. productivity gains, we need to examine the sources of productivity improvement. *The sources of productivity gains include*

- *Higher skills*—an increase in labor skills.
- *More capital*—an increase in the ratio of capital to labor.
- *Technological advance*—the development and use of better capital equipment and products.
- *Improved management*—better use of available resources in the production process.

Human-Capital Investment

Continuing advances in education and skills training have greatly increased the quality of U.S. labor. In 1950, less than 8 percent of all U.S. workers had completed college. Today, nearly 30 percent of the workforce has completed four years of college. There has also been a substantial increase in vocational training, both in the public sector and by private firms.

In the 1970s, these improvements in the quality of individual workers were offset by a change in the composition of the labor force. As we observed in Chapters 6 and 16, the proportion of teenagers and women in the labor force grew tremendously in the 1960s and 1970s. These Baby Boomers and their mothers contributed to higher output. Because teenagers and women (re)entering the labor market generally have less job experience than adult men, however, *average* productivity fell.

This phenomenon reversed itself in the 1990s, as the Baby Boomers reached their prime working years. The increased productivity of the workforce is not a reflection of the aging process itself. Rather, the gains in productivity reflect the greater **human-capital** investment associated with more schooling and more on-the-job learning.

human capital: The knowledge and skills possessed by the workforce.

Physical-Capital Investment

The knowledge and skills a worker brings to the job don't completely determine his or her productivity. A worker with no tools, no computers, and no machinery won't produce much even if she has a Ph.D. Similarly, a worker with outmoded equipment won't produce as much as an equally capable worker equipped with the newest machines and the best technology. From this perspective, *a primary determinant of labor productivity is the rate of capital investment.* In other words, improvements in output per *worker* depend in large part on increases in the quantity and quality of *capital* equipment (see World View).

The efforts of the average U.S. worker are presently augmented with over $100,000 of invested capital. This huge capital endowment is a prime source of high productivity.

WORLD VIEW

Comparative Investment and Growth

Investment in new plant and equipment is essential for economic growth. In general, countries that allocate a larger share of output to investment will grow more rapidly. In the 1990s, China had the highest growth rate and one of the highest investment rates.

Country	Investment as Percentage of GDP (average, 1990–1999)	Growth Rate of GDP (average, 1990–1999)
China	39	10.7
Thailand	36	4.7
Singapore	35	8.0
India	23	6.0
United States	18	3.3
Great Britain	17	2.5
South Africa	15	1.9

Source: World Bank.

Analysis: Investment increases production possibilities. Countries that devote a larger share of output to investment tend to grow faster.

To *increase* productivity, however, the quality and quantity of capital available to the average worker must continue to increase. That requires capital spending to increase faster than the labor force. With the labor force growing at 1.2 percent a year, that's not a hard standard to beat. How *much* faster capital investment grows is nevertheless a decisive factor in productivity gains. In the 1980s, investment growth was slow and erratic. In the 1990s, however, capital investment accelerated markedly. In 1996, 1997, 1998, 1999, and again in 2000, capital investment growth exceeded 10 percent a year. Investment in information technology (computers, software, and telecommunications equipment) was exceedingly robust, reaching growth rates as high as 25 percent. In the process, workers got "smarter," communications improved, and productivity jumped. The Council of Economic Advisers credited this boom in information-technology investment with nearly one-third of *all* the 1995–99 GDP growth.

Saving and Investment Rates. The dependence of productivity gains on capital investment puts a new perspective on consumption and saving. In the short run, the primary concern of macroeconomic policy is to balance aggregate demand and aggregate supply. In this context, savings are a form of leakage that requires offsetting injections of investment or government spending. From the longer-run perspective of economic growth, saving and investment take on added importance. ***Savings aren't just a form of leakage but a basic source of investment financing.*** If we use all our resources to produce consumer, export, and public-sector goods, there won't be any investment. In that case, we might not face a short-run stabilization problem—our productive capacity might be fully utilized—but we'd confront a long-run *growth* problem. Indeed, if we consumed our entire output, our productive capacity would actually shrink since we wouldn't even be replacing worn-out plant and equipment. We must have at least enough savings to finance **net investment.**

net investment: Gross investment less depreciation.

Household and Business Saving. Household saving rates in the United States have been notoriously low and falling since the early 1980s. In 2000, U.S. households actually *dis*saved—spending more on consumption than their disposable incomes. Despite the meager flow of household saving, investment growth actually accelerated in the late 1990s. Virtually all of that investment was financed with *business saving* and *foreign investment*. The retained earnings and depreciation allowances that create business savings generated a huge cash flow for investment in the 1990s.

Foreign Investment. In addition to this business-saving flow, foreign investors poured money into U.S. plant, equipment, software, and financial assets. These two income flows more than compensated for the virtual absence of household saving. Many people worry, though, that foreign investments may get diverted elsewhere and that business saving will drop when profits diminish. Then continued investment growth will be more dependent on a flow of funds from household saving.

The accumulation of more and better capital equipment does not itself guarantee higher productivity or faster GDP growth. The human factor is still critical: How well resources are organized and managed will affect the rate of growth. Hence, entrepreneurship and the quality of continuing management are also major determinants of economic growth.

Management Training

It's difficult to characterize differences in management techniques or to measure their effectiveness. However, much attention has been focused in recent years on the alleged shortsightedness of U.S. managers. The rumor is that U.S. firms focus too narrowly on short-term profits, neglecting long-term gains in productivity. They also emphasize quantity over quality of output. And they fail to include workers in key decisions, thus depriving themselves of important insights and goodwill. By contrast, firms in Japan and elsewhere concentrate on longer-term gains, quality control, and strong bonds between labor and management. As a consequence, Japanese firms enjoy remarkably good labor and customer relations, intense worker loyalty, and faster productivity gains.

If all these accusations about U.S. corporate management were true, the U.S. economy would surely be in a sorry state. At best, these contrasts between management practices serve as precautionary tales. The time horizons used for developing investment and production plans can affect long-run growth prospects. Management-labor relations can also materially affect productivity. Furthermore, management familiarity with *global* markets will affect a firm's ability to grow and prosper in both foreign and domestic markets. Corporations in the United States spend billions of dollars on management training to help keep company executives up to speed on these and other determinants of long-run productivity. Such investments in managerial talent are an important source of economic growth.

Research and Development

A fourth and vital source of productivity advance is research and development (R&D), a broad concept that includes scientific research, product development, innovations in production techniques, and the development of management improvements. R&D activity may be a specific, identifiable activity such as in a research lab, or it may be part of the process of learning by doing. In either case, the insights developed from R&D generally lead to new products and cheaper ways of producing them. Over time, R&D is credited with the greatest contributions to economic growth. In his study of U.S. growth during the period 1929–82, Edward Denison concluded that 26 percent of *total* growth was due to "advances in knowledge" (see Table 17.2).

The National Science Foundation tracks R&D spending. Visit www.nsf.gov. and click on "Science Statistics."

New Growth Theory. The evident contribution of "advances in knowledge" to economic growth has spawned a new perspective called "new growth theory." "Old growth theory," it is said, emphasized the importance of bricks and mortar, that is, saving and investing in new plant and equipment. By contrast, "new" growth theory emphasizes the importance of investing in ideas. Paul Romer, a Stanford economist, asserts that new ideas and the spread of knowledge are the primary engines of growth. Unfortunately, neither Romer nor anyone else is exactly sure how one spawns new ideas

TABLE 17.2
The Sources of U.S. Growth

From 1929 to 1982 total output grew by 3.2 percent annually. More than half of this growth was due to improvements in our technological and managerial capabilities. In the 1980s, productivity advances were even more important in increasing output. Such productivity improvements have shifted our production possibilities curve outward, increasing GDP per capita as well.

Source	Percentage Contribution to Output Growth
More inputs	
Additional labor	34
Additional capital	17
	51
Productivity advances	
Education of labor	13
Advances in knowledge	26
Improved resource allocation	8
Economies of scale	8
	55
Miscellaneous	−6
	100

Source: Edward F. Denison, *Trends in American Economic Growth*, 1929–1982 (Washington, D.C.: Brookings Institution, 1985).

or best disseminates knowledge. The only evident policy lever appears to be the support of research and development, a staple of "old" growth theory.

There's an important link between R&D and capital investment. As noted earlier, part of each year's gross investment compensates for the depreciation of existing plant and equipment. However, new machines are rarely identical to the ones they replace. When you get a new computer, you're not just *replacing* an old one; you're *upgrading* your computing capabilities with more memory, faster speed, and a lot of new features. Indeed, the availability of *better* technology is often the motive for such capital investment. The same kind of motivation spurs businesses to upgrade machines and structures. Hence, advances in technology and capital investment typically go hand in hand.

POLICY LEVERS

Once the sources of growth are known, policies for accelerating long-run economic growth can be developed. Although the pace of economic growth is primarily set by market forces, government policy may be able to affect that pace. Most of the policy options are distinctly *micro* in nature, although *macro* policy decisions are also important.

Governments at all levels already play a tremendous role in human-capital development by building, operating, and subsidizing schools. The quantity and quality of continuing investments in America's schools will have a major effect on future productivity. Government policy also plays an *indirect* role in schooling decisions by offering subsidized college loans.

Immigration policy is also a determinant of the nation's stock of human capital. At least 1 million immigrants enter the United States every year. As we noted in Chapter 16, Congress in 2000 increased the immigration quota for software engineers and other high-tech workers to 195,000 workers per year. This increased labor inflow not only relieved *short-run* wage and cost pressures but also enhanced the foundation for *long-run* growth. By regulating the number and skills of immigrants, the federal government can affect the size and quality of the U.S. labor force (see World View). Canada's immigration policy is designed explicitly to raise the skill level of its labor force, by awarding points for education, job skills, work experience and other productivity attributes.

Increasing Human-Capital Investment

The U.S. Immigration and Naturalization Service (INS) maintains a profile of immigrants, including their occupational skills. Visit www.ins.usdoj.gov/graphics/aboutins/statistics/index.htm.

WORLD VIEW

Work Visas Are Allowing Washington to Sidestep Immigration Reform

The inscription on the Statue of Liberty is quietly being rewritten: "Give me your tired, your poor, your huddled masses yearning to breathe free; I'll also take your skilled employees under the temporary visa program, H-1B."

The H-1B visa was established in 1990 to permit foreigners with a college degree or higher to work in the United States for a renewable three-year term for employers who petition on their behalf. In 1998, the program was expanded to allow 115,000 workers, up from 65,000, to enter the United States in fiscal years 1999 and 2000. Demand for H-1B visas by employers is high, particularly among high-technology companies.

Workers admitted under the H-1B program are not immigrants, but experts in the field expect that most of them will end up staying permanently in the United States.

In addition to workers with H-1B visas, hundreds of thousands of other foreigners are admitted to work temporarily in the United States under visa categories covering intracompany transfers, individuals with extraordinary ability, registered nurses and workers in nonprofit religious organizations. A fast-growing category is the Nafta TN visa, which offers an unlimited number of temporary visas for professional workers from Canada and soon Mexico.

In a new book, "Heaven's Door," George Borjas, a Harvard economist, proposes that the United States adopt a Canadian-style point system, in which applicants for visas are assigned points on the basis of characteristics like their ability to speak English, work-force skills, family ties, refugee status and ethnic diversity. Those whose total points exceed a certain threshold would be admitted.

—Alan B. Krueger

Source: *The New York Times,* May 25, 2000, © 2000 The New York Times Company. Reprinted with permission. www.nytimes.com

Analysis: Immigrant flows affect a nation's stock of human capital. Can or should immigrants be selected on the basis of human-capital traits?

As in the case of human capital, the possibilities for increasing physical-capital investment are also many and diverse.

Investment Incentives. The tax code is a mechanism for stimulating investment. Faster depreciation schedules, tax credits for new investments, and lower business tax rates all encourage increased investment in physical capital.

Savings Incentives. In principle, the government can also deepen the savings pool that finances investment. Here again, the tax code offers some policy levers. Tax preferences for Individual Retirement Accounts and other pension savings may increase the marginal propensity to save or at least redirect savings flows to longer-term investments. The Bush 2001 tax package (Chapter 11) included not only a *short-run* fiscal stimulus (e.g., tax rebates) but also enhanced incentives for *long-term* savings (retirement and college savings accounts).

Infrastructure Development. The government also directly affects the level of physical capital through its public works spending. As we observed in Chapter 16, the $2 trillion already invested in bridges, highways, airports, sewer systems, and other infrastructure is an important part of America's capital stock. In 2001, Congress contemplated a multiyear, $71 billion investment in high-speed rail lines. Investments of that sort reduce transportation and commuting costs, making more resources available for production.

Fiscal Responsibility. In addition to these many supply-side interventions, the government's *macro* policies also affect the rate of investment and growth. Of particular interest in this regard is the federal government's budget balance. As we've seen,

Increasing Physical-Capital Investment

See if you would qualify for Canadian immigration by completing the self-assessment worksheet provided by Canada's Department of Citizenship and Immigration @ www.cic.gc.ca/english

crowding out: A reduction in private-sector borrowing (and spending) caused by increased government borrowing.

crowding in: An increase in private-sector borrowing (and spending) caused by decreased government borrowing.

budget deficits may be a useful mechanism for attaining short-run macro stability. Those same deficits, however, may have negative long-run effects. If Uncle Sam borrows more funds from the national savings pool, other borrowers may end up with less. As we saw in Chapter 12, there's no guarantee that federal deficits will result in the **crowding out** of private investment. Let's recognize the risk of such an outcome, however. Hence, *fiscal and monetary policies must be evaluated in terms of their impact not only on (short-run) aggregate demand but also on long-run aggregate supply.*

In this regard, the transformation of federal budget deficits to budget surpluses after 1997 facilitated the **crowding in** of private investment. After 1997, more funds were available to private investors and at lower interest rates. This surely contributed to the accelerated growth of capital investment in 1996–2000.

Maintaining Stable Expectations

The position of the long-run AS curve also depends on a broader assessment of the economic outlook. Expectations are a critical factor in both consumption and investment behavior. People who expect to lose their job next year are unlikely to buy a new car or house this year. Likewise, if investors expect interest rates to jump next year, they may be less willing to initiate long-run capital projects.

A sense of political and economic stability is critical to any long-run current trend. Within that context, however, specific perceptions of government policy may also alter investment plans. Investors may look to the Fed for a sense of monetary stability. They may be looking for a greater commitment to long-run price stability than to short-run adjustments of aggregate demand. In the fiscal policy area the same kind of commitment to long-run fiscal discipline rather than to short-run stimulus may be sought. Such possibilities imply that macro policy must be sensitive to long-run expectations. It also implies that short-run goals may at times conflict with longer-run growth and investment objectives.

Institutional Context

Last, but not least, the prospects for economic growth depend on the institutional context of a nation's economy. We first encountered this proposition in Chapter 1. In the World View on page 14, nations were ranked on the basis of an Index of Freedom. Studies have shown how greater economic freedom—secure property rights, open trade, lower taxes, less regulation—typically fosters faster growth. In less regulated economies there's more scope for entrepreneurship and more opportunity to invest. Recognizing this, nations around the world, from India to China, to Russia, to Latin America, have deregulated industries, privatized state enterprises, and promoted more open trade and investment.

THE ECONOMY TOMORROW

Limitless Growth?

Suppose we pulled all the right policy levers and were able to keep the economy on a fast-paced growth track. Could the economy keep growing forever? Wouldn't we use up all available resources and ruin the environment in the process? How much long-term growth is really possible—or even desirable?

The Malthusian Formula for Destruction

The prospect of an eventual limit to economic growth originated in the eighteenth-century warnings of the Reverend Thomas Malthus. Malthus argued that continued economic growth was impossible because food production couldn't keep pace with population growth. His dire projections earned the economics profession its characterization as the "dismal science."

When Malthus first issued his warnings, in 1798, the population of England (including Wales) was about 9 million. Annual production of barley, oats, and related grains was approximately 162 million bushels, and wheat production was around 50 million bushels, just about enough to feed the English population (a little had to be imported from other countries). Although the relationship between food and population

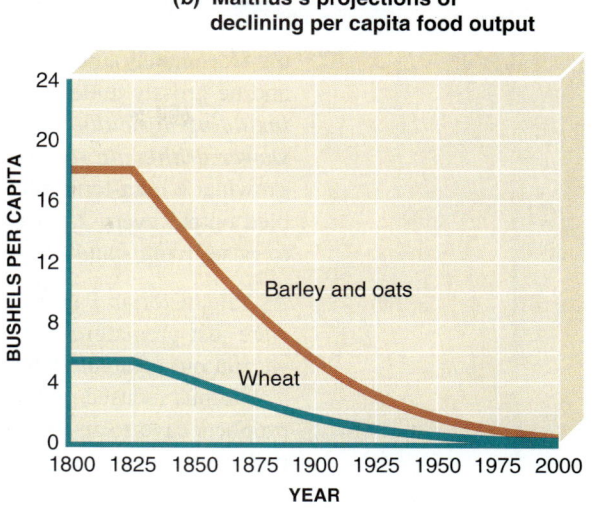

FIGURE 17.6
The Malthusian Doomsday

By projecting the growth rates of population and food output into the future, Malthus foresaw England's doomsday. At that time, the amount of available food per capita would be too small to sustain human life. Fortunately, Malthus overestimated population growth and underestimated productivity growth.

Source: Mathus' arithmetic applied to actual data for 1800 (see text).

was satisfactory in 1798, Malthus reasoned that starvation was not far off. First of all, he observed that "population, when unchecked, goes on doubling itself every 25 years, or increases in a geometrical ratio."[1] Thus, he foresaw the English population increasing to 36 million people by 1850, 144 million by 1900, and more than 1 billion by 1975, unless some social or natural restraints were imposed on population growth.

One natural population check that Malthus foresaw was a scarcity of food. England had only a limited amount of land available for cultivation and was already farming the most fertile tracts. Before long, all available land would be in use and only improvements in agricultural productivity (output per acre) could increase food supplies. Some productivity increases were possible, Malthus concluded, but "the means of subsistence, under circumstances the most favorable to human industry, could not possibly be made to increase faster than in an arithmetical ratio."[2]

With population increasing at a *geometric* rate and food supplies at an *arithmetic* rate, the eventual outcome is evident. Figure 17.6 illustrates how the difference between a **geometric growth** path and an **arithmetic growth** path ultimately leads to starvation. As Malthus calculated it, per capita wheat output would decline from 5.5 bushels in 1800 to only 1.7 bushels in 1900 (Figure 17.5b). This wasn't enough food to feed the English people. According to Malthus's projections, either England died off about 100 years ago or it has been maintained at the brink of starvation for more than a century only by recurrent plagues, wars, or the kind of "moral restraint" that's commonly associated with Victorian preachments.

Malthus's logic was impeccable. As long as population increased at a geometric rate while output increased at an arithmetic rate, England's doomsday was as certain as two plus two equals four. Malthus's error was not in his logic but in his empirical assumptions. He didn't know how fast output would increase over time, any more than we know whether people will be wearing electronic wings in the year 2203. He had to

Limits to Food Production

geometric growth: An increase in quantity by a constant proportion each year.

arithmetic growth: An increase in quantity by a constant amount each year.

---

[1] Thomas Malthus, *An Essay on the Principle of Population* (1798; reprint ed., Homewood, IL: Richard D. Irwin, 1963), p. 4.
[2] Ibid, p. 5.

make an educated guess about future productivity trends. He based his estimates on his own experiences at the very beginning of the Industrial Revolution. As it turned out (fortunately), he had no knowledge of the innovations that would change the world, and he grossly underestimated the rate at which productivity would increase. ***Output, including agricultural products, has increased at a geometric rate, not at the much slower arithmetic rate foreseen by Malthus.*** As we observed earlier, U.S. output has grown at a long-term rate of roughly 3 percent a year. This *geometric* growth has doubled output every 25 years or so. That rate of economic growth is more than enough to raise living standards for a population growing by only 1 percent a year.

Resource Constraints

As Yale historian Paul Kennedy has suggested, maybe Malthus's doomsday predictions were just premature, not wrong. Maybe growth will come to a screeching halt when we run out of arable land, water, oil, or some other vital resource.

Malthus focused on arable land as the ultimate resource constraint. Other doomsday prophets have focused on the supply of whale oil, coal, oil, potatoes and other "essential" resources. All such predictions ignore the role of markets in both promoting more efficient uses of scarce resources and finding substitutes for them. If, for example, the world were really running out of oil, what would happen to oil prices? Oil prices would rise substantially, prompting consumers to use oil more efficiently and prompting producers to develop alternative fuel sources. If productivity and the availability of substitutes increase fast enough, the price of "scarce" resources might actually fall rather than rise. This possibility prompted a famous "Doomsday bet" between University of Maryland business professor Julian Simon and Stanford ecologist Paul Ehrlich. In 1980, Paul Ehrlich identified five metals that he predicted would become so scarce as to slow economic growth. Simon wagered that the price of those metals would actually *decline* over the ensuing decade as productivity and available substitutes increased. In 1990, their prices had fallen, and Ehrlich paid Simon for the bet.

Environmental Destruction

The market's ability to circumvent resource constraints would seem to augur well for our future. Doomsayers warn, though, that other limits to growth will emerge, even in a world of "unlimited" resources and unending productivity advance. The villain this time is pollution. Over 20 years ago, Paul Ehrlich warned about this second problem:

> Attempts to increase food production further will tend to accelerate the deterioration of our environment, which in turn will eventually *reduce* the capacity of the Earth to produce food. It is not clear whether environmental decay has now gone so far as to be essentially irreversible; it is possible that the capacity of the planet to support human life has been permanently impaired. Such technological "successes" as automobiles, pesticides, and inorganic nitrogen fertilizers are major contributors to environmental deterioration.[3]

The "inevitability" of environmental destruction led G. Evelyn Hutchinson to conclude in 1970 that the limits of habitable existence on earth would be measured "in decades."[4]

It's not difficult for anyone with the basic five senses to comprehend the pollution problem. Pollution is as close these days as the air we breathe. Moreover, we can't fail to observe a distinct tendency for pollution levels to rise along with GDP and population expansion. If one projects such pollution trends into the future, things are bound to look pretty ugly.

Although pollution is universally acknowledged to be an important and annoying problem, we can't assume that the *rate* of pollution will continue unabated. On the contrary, the growing awareness of the pollution problem has already led to significant abatement-policy efforts. The Environmental Protection Agency (EPA), for example, is unquestionably a force working for cleaner air and water. Indeed, active policies to curb pollution are as familiar as auto-exhaust controls and DDT bans. A computer pro-

---

[3] Paul R. Ehrlich and Anne H. Ehrlich, *Population, Resources, Environment: Issues in Human Ecology,* 2nd ed. (San Francisco: W. H. Freeman, 1972), p. 442.
[4] Evelyn Hutchinson, "The Biosphere," *Scientific American,* September 1970, p. 53: Dennis L. Meadows et al., *The Limits to Growth* (New York: Universe Books, 1972), Chapter 4.

"And so, extrapolating from the best figures available, we see that current trends, unless dramatically reversed, will inevitably lead to a situation in which the sky will fall."

Analysis: Most doomsday predictions fail to recognize the possibilities for behavioral change—or the role of market incentives in encouraging it.

grammed 10 or 20 years ago to project present pollution levels wouldn't have foreseen these abatement efforts and would thus have overestimated current pollution levels.

This isn't to say that we have in any final way "solved" the pollution problem or that we're even doing the best job we possibly can. It simply says that geometric increases in pollution aren't inevitable. There's simply no compelling reason why we have to continue polluting the environment; if we stop, another doomsday can be averted. Julian Simon was so confident of our ability to do so that he offered another doomsday wager in 1996. He offered a $100,000 bet that by any measure human well-being will improve in the next decade.

Julian Simon may have been right that there are no limits to growth, at least none emanating from resource constraints or pollution thresholds. As Robert Solow summed up the issue:

> My real complaint about the Doomsday school [is that] it diverts attention from the really important things that can actually be done, step by step, to make things better. The end of the world *is* at hand—the earth, if you take the long view, will fall into the sun in a few billion years anyway, unless some other disaster happens first. In the meantime, I think we'd be better off passing a strong sulfur-emissions tax, or getting some Highway Trust Fund money allocated to mass transit, or building a humane and decent floor under family incomes, or overriding President Nixon's veto of a strong Water Quality Act, or reforming the tax system, or fending off starvation in Bengal—instead of worrying about the generalized "predicament of mankind."[5]

Karl Marx expressed these same thoughts nearly a century earlier. Marx chastised "the contemptible Malthus" for turning the attention of the working class away from what he regarded as the immediate problem of capitalist exploitation to some distant and ill-founded anxiety about "natural" disaster.[6]

The Possibility of Growth

Let's concede, then, that continued, perhaps even "limitless" growth is *possible*. Can we also agree that it's *desirable?* Those of us who commute on congested highways, worry about global warming, breathe foul air, and can't find a secluded camping site may raise a loud chorus of nos. But before reaching a conclusion let's at least determine what it is people don't like about the prospect of continued growth. Is it really

The Desirability of Growth

---

[5]Robert M. Solow. "Is the End of the World at Hand?" *Challenge,* March 1973, p. 50.
[6]Cited by John Maddox in *The Doomsday Syndrome* (New York: McGraw-Hill, 1972), pp. 40 and 45.

economic growth per se that people object to, or instead the specific ways GDP has grown in the past? To state the question this way may provoke a few second thoughts.

First of all, let's distinguish very clearly between economic growth and population growth. Congested neighborhoods, dining halls, and highways are the consequence of too many people, not of two many goods and services. Indeed, if we had *more* goods and services—if we had more houses and transit systems—much of the population congestion we now experience might be relieved. Maybe if we had enough resources to meet our existing demands *and* to build a solar-generated "new town" in the middle of Montana, people might move out of the crowded neighborhoods of Chicago and St. Louis. Well, probably not, but at least one thing is certain; with fewer goods and services, more people will have to share any given quantity of output.

Which brings us back to the really essential measure of growth, GDP per capita. Are there any serious grounds for desiring *less* GDP per capita, a reduced standard of living? And don't say yes just because you think we already have too many cars on our roads or calories in our bellies. That argument refers to the *mix* of output again and doesn't answer the question of whether or not we want *any* more goods or services per person. Increasing GDP per capita can take a million forms, including the educational services you're now consuming. The rejection of economic growth per se implies that none of those forms is desirable.

SUMMARY

- Economic growth refers to increases in real GDP. Short-run growth may result from increases in capacity utilization (like less unemployment). In the long run, however, growth requires increases in capacity itself—rightward shifts on the long-run aggregate supply curve.
- GDP per capita is a basic measure of living standards. GDP per worker is a basic measure of productivity.
- The rate of economic growth is set by the growth rate of the labor force *plus* the growth rate of output per worker (productivity). Over time, increases in productivity have been the primary cause of rising living standards.
- Productivity gains comes from many sources, including better labor quality, increased capital investment, research and development, improved management, and supportive government policies.
- Supply-side policies increase both the short- and long-run capacity to produce. Monetary and fiscal policies may also affect capital investment and thus the rate of economic growth.
- Productivity growth accelerated in 1995–2000 due to fast investment growth, especially in information technology. Sustaining rapid productivity gains is the critical challenge for long-run GDP growth.
- Recent U.S. investment growth has been financed with business saving, foreign investment, and the crowding in caused by reduced government borrowing. U.S. households save very little.
- The argument that there are identifiable and imminent limits to growth—perhaps even a cataclysmic doomsday—are founded on one of two concerns: (1) the depletion of resources and (2) pollution of the ecosystem.
- The general weakness of doomsday arguments is that they regard existing patterns of resource use or pollution as unalterable. As a consequence, they consistently underestimate the possibilities for technological advance or adaptation. Even optimistic projections of technological possibilities turn out to be pessimistic.
- Continued economic growth is desirable as long as it brings a higher standard of living for people and an increased ability to produce and consume socially desirable goods and services.

Key Terms

production possibilities
economic growth
real GDP
base period
growth rate

GDP per capita
labor force
employment rate
productivity
human capital

net investment
crowding out
crowding in
geometric growth
arithmetic growth

Questions for Discussion

1. In what specific ways (if any) does a college education increase a worker's productivity?
2. Why do productivity gains slow down in recessions? (See Figure 17.5.)
3. Why don't we consume all our current output instead of sacrificing some present consumption for investment?
4. Should we grant immigration rights based on potential contributions to economic growth as Canada does? (See World View, page 361.)
5. How would a growing federal budget surplus affect the prospects for long-run economic growth? Why might a growing surplus *not* be desirable?
6. Should fiscal policy encourage more consumption or more saving? Does it matter?
7. In 1866, Stanley Jevons predicted that economic growth would come to a halt when England ran out of coal, a doomsday that he reckoned would occur in the mid-1970s. How did we avert that projection?
8. Fertility rates in the United States have dropped so low that we're approaching zero population growth, a condition that France has maintained for decades. How will this affect our economic growth? Our standard of living?
9. Is limitless growth really possible? What forces do you think will be most important in slowing or halting economic growth?
10. Would you accept Julian Simon's second (1996) doomsday wager? What dimensions of human well-being might worsen in 10 years?

Web Activities

1. Research that is conducted at the World Bank focuses on economic growth. From the topic list at www.worldbank.org/research/projects.htm, choose a project that uses one of the terms identified in the book as a factor in economic growth. What does this abstract conclude about the relationship between this factor and economic growth?
2. Log on to www.bearstearns.com/ewatch/forindex.htm. What does Bear Stearns project for economic growth in the United States in the next 12 months? How does this compare to economic growth in the last 12 months? What are some likely explanations for these different growth rates?
3. Log on to www.bls.gov/data, and graph the change in labor productivity in the United States during the past 10 years. What is the exponential growth rate for that same time period? Why is this different than simply summing the consecutive quarters together? To find data to answer this question, access "Overall Most Requested Data" once you have logged on to www.bls.gov. Request output per hour of nonfarm business productivity.

THE ACCOMPANYING STUDENT PROBLEM SET CONTAINS NUMERICAL AND GRAPHING PROBLEMS FOR THIS CHAPTER

PART 7

Policy Constraints

Macro theories often provide conflicting advice about whether and how the government ought to intervene. To make matters worse, the information needed to make a decision is typically incomplete. Politics muddies the waters too by changing priorities and restricting the use of policy levers. Finally, there's the inescapable reality that everything changes at once—there's no *ceteris paribus* in the real world. Chapters 18 and 19 consider these constraints on policy development and implementation.

CHAPTER 18

Global Macro

> In this global economy there is no such thing as a purely domestic policy.
> —President Bill Clinton
> American University, February 26, 1993

Two years after making that statement, President Clinton got a crash course in global macroeconomics. The Mexican economy took a nosedive in 1995: Unemployment rose, prices skyrocketed, and the value of the Mexican peso plunged. President Clinton and his economic advisers quickly realized that this turn of events wasn't simply a Mexican problem. Mexico is one of America's largest export markets. If the Mexican economy sinks into a recession, Mexican consumers and businesses won't be able to buy so many U.S.-made goods. The U.S. economy would suffer export losses and related job losses.

The financial markets of Mexico and the United States are also linked. When the peso collapsed, many Mexicans rushed to convert their currency into U.S. dollars. As they moved assets into American banks, U.S. bank reserves increased. This capital inflow made the Fed's job of controlling the money supply that much more difficult.

There was no way the United States could seal off its economy from the Mexican crisis. So long as resources, goods, and money can move across national borders, countries are economically interdependent. Ironically, the 1993 North American Free Trade Agreement (NAFTA) had increased the interdependence between Mexico and the United States. Therefore, helping Mexico was also a way of helping the United States avert economic damage. This realization helped convince President Clinton to "bail out" Mexico with a multibillion-dollar loan. The U.S. Federal Reserve also helped control disruptions in currency flows and values.

The global economy got an even greater jolt when terrorists destroyed the World Trade Center in September 2001. The economic shock disrupted not only U.S. markets but global ones as well. As the accompanying World View relates, nations around the world worried that the economic shock to the U.S. economy would destabilize their economies too. If U.S. consumers and businesses curtailed their spending, export sales of other nations would decline. A *global* crisis, not just an

WORLD VIEW

Tragedy Dashes Hopes for Europe's Economy

The economic fallout doesn't stop at the U.S. border.

In the aftermath of last week's terror strikes, European companies say the uncertainty over what happens next will weigh on an already weak European economy for weeks, even months.

Economies around the world—including Japan, which has been struggling for years—had all been hoping to avoid recession this year, based on the prospect of the U.S. economy recovering. Those hopes are now gone.

Unease spells trouble for any economy: Businesses delay big orders; potential merger partners put their deal talks on ice; companies hold off on expansion plans; and consumers save rather than buy. "People won't be ordering big machines for a couple of million marks right now," said Diether Klingelnberg, whose company in Hueckeswagen, Germany, makes machine parts for the airline industry, among other sectors. "People want to wait and see what will happen.". . .

Baudouin Velge, chief economist of the Belgian Federation of Employers, a trade group representing 30,000 Belgian companies, figures, "The American economy will be hit by this for another six months," which delays the main boost Europe was counting on for its own recovery. The U.S. buys 22 percent of Europe's exports. Economists estimate a percentage-point drop in U.S. economic growth translates into a half-percentage point decline in European growth.

—Christopher Rhoads and G. Thomas Sims

Source: *The Wall Street Journal*, September 17, 2001. Reprinted by permission of *The Wall Street Journal*. © 2001 Dow Jones & Company, Inc. All rights reserved worldwide. www.wsj.com

Analysis: The flow of goods, labor, and money across national borders makes countries economically interdependent. A shock to the U.S. economy disrupts foreign economies as well, and vice versa.

American crisis, would ensue. Mindful of that possibility, the world's leaders quickly worked out a coordinated policy response.

This chapter explores this global interdependence. Of particular concern are the following questions:

- How does the U.S. economy interact with the rest of the world?
- How does the rest of the world affect U.S. macro outcomes?
- How does global interdependence limit macro policy options?

As we'll see, international transactions significantly affect U.S. economic performance and policy.

INTERNATIONAL TRADE

Japanese cars are the most visible reminders of America's global interdependence. American consumers purchase over 1 million cars from Japan each year and buy another million or so Toyotas, Nissans, Hondas, Mazdas, and Subarus produced in the United States. On the other side of the Pacific Ocean, Japanese autoworkers are apt to wear Levis, sip Coca-Cola, and grab a quick meal at McDonald's.

The motivations for international trade are explained at length in Chapter 35. Also discussed in Chapter 35 are the *microeconomic* demands for greater protection from "unfair" imports. What concerns us here is how such trade affects our domestic *macro* performance. Does trade help or hinder our efforts to attain full employment, price stability, and economic growth?

We first noticed in Chapter 9 that **imports** are a source of **leakage** in the circular flow. The income that U.S. consumers spend on Japanese cars *could* be spent in America. When that income instead leaks out of the circular flow, it limits domestic spending and related **multiplier** effects.

The basic macro model can be expanded easily to include this additional leakage. In a closed (no-trade) economy, total income and domestic spending are always equal—that is,

$$\text{Closed economy: } C + I + G = Y$$

Imports as Leakage

imports: Goods and services purchased from international sources.

leakage: Income not spent directly on domestic output but instead diverted from the circular flow, such as saving, imports, taxes.

multiplier: The multiple by which an initial change in aggregate spending will alter total expenditure after an infinite number of spending cycles.

marginal propensity to import (MPM): The fraction of each additional (marginal) dollar of disposable income spent on imports.

marginal propensity to save (MPS): The fraction of each additional (marginal) dollar of disposable income not spent on consumption; 1 − MPC.

When some goods are sold as exports and others can be purchased from abroad, however, this equality no longer holds. In an open economy, we have to take account of imports and exports: that is,

$$\text{Open economy: } C + I + G + X = Y + IM$$

where X refers to exports and IM to imports. *In an open economy, the combined spending of consumers, investors, and the government may not equal domestic output.* Total spending is augmented by the demand for exports, and the supply of goods is increased by imports.

Although imported goods may be desired, their availability complicates macro policy. Increases in aggregate spending are supposed to boost domestic output and employment. With imports, however, the link between spending and output is weakened. *Part of any increase in income will be spent on imports.* This fraction is called the **marginal propensity to import (MPM)**. Like its cousin, the **marginal propensity to save (MPS)**, the marginal propensity to import

- Reduces the initial impact on domestic demand of any income change.
- Reduces the size of the multiplier.

Table 18.1 illustrates the impact of imports on the Keynesian multiplier process. The process starts with an increase of $10 billion in new government spending. This injection directly adds $10 billion to consumer income (assuming an economy with no income taxes).

The successive panels of Table 18.1 illustrate the sequence of events that follows. In the closed economy, consumers have only two uses for their income: to spend it on domestic consumption ($B1$) or to save it ($B2$). We assume here the marginal propensity to save is 0.10. Hence consumers save $1 billion and spend the remaining $9 billion on domestic consumption.

In an open economy, consumers have an additional choice. They may spend their income on domestic goods ($B1$), save it ($B2$), *or* spend it on imported goods ($B3$). In Table 18.1 we assume that the marginal propensity to import is 0.10. Hence, consumers use their additional $10 billion of income the following way:

$8 billion spent on domestic consumption.
$1 billion saved.
$1 billion spent on imports.

TABLE 18.1
Imports as Leakage
Import leakage reduces the initial spending impact of autonomous changes in consumer income. Continuing import leakage reduces the size of the multiplier as well. In this case, the ultimate impact of added government spending is cut in half by import leakage: Aggregate demand increases by $50 billion rather than $100 billion in response to a $10 billion increase in government spending.

Action	Cumulative Change in Aggregate Demand	
	Closed Economy	Open Economy
A. Government spends additional $10 billion	+$10 billion	+$10 billion
B. Consumers use added $10 billion of income for:		
1. Domestic consumption	+$9 billion	+$8 billion
2. Saving (MPS = 0.1)	($1 billion)	($1 billion)
3. Imports (MPM = 0.1)	0	($1 billion)
C. Multiplier	$\frac{1}{\text{MPS}} = 10$	$\frac{1}{\text{MPS} + \text{MPM}} = 5$
D. Additional multiplier-induced consumption $= C \times B1$	+$90 billion	+$40 billion
E. Cumulative change $= A + D$	+$100 billion	+$50 billion

In the open economy, only $8 billion rather than $9 billion is initially spent on domestic consumption. Thus, *imports reduce the initial spending impact of added income.*

Import leakage continues through every round of the circular flow. As a consequence, *imports also reduce the value of the multiplier.* In this case, the multiplier is reduced from 10 to 5.

To see how this change in the multiplier comes about, note that *the value of the multiplier depends on the extent of leakage.* The most general form of the multiplier is

$$\text{Generalized multiplier} = \frac{1}{\text{leakage fraction}}$$

In a closed (no trade) and private (no taxes) economy, the multiplier takes the familiar Keynesian form:

$$\text{Closed economy multiplier (without taxes)} = \frac{1}{\text{MPS}}$$

In this case, consumer saving is the only form of leakage. Therefore, the marginal propensity to save (MPS) is the entire leakage fraction. In Table 18.1 the closed-economy multiplier is equal to 10 (see panel *C*).

Once we open the economy to trade, we have to contend with additional leakage. In an open economy, leakage results from the MPS *and* the MPM. Thus, the generalized multiplier becomes:

$$\text{Open economy multiplier (without taxes)} = \frac{1}{\text{MPS} + \text{MPM}}$$

Imports act just like saving leakage, decreasing the multiplier bang of each autonomous buck. In Table 18.1 (panel *C*),

$$\text{Open economy multiplier} = \frac{1}{\text{MPS} + \text{MPM}} = \frac{1}{0.1 + 0.1} = \frac{1}{0.2} = 5$$

The consequences of these different multipliers are striking. Panel *D* shows that additional consumption of $90 billion is induced in the closed economy. By comparison, the open economy generates only $40 billion of additional consumption.

The last panel of Table 18.1 summarizes the consequences for aggregate demand. The cumulative increase in aggregate demand is

$$\text{Cumulative change in aggregate demand} = \text{initial change in spending} \times \text{income multiplier}$$

In this example, the initial injection of spending is the $10 billion spent by the government. In the closed economy, this injection leads to a $100 billion increase in aggregate demand (panel *E*). In the open economy, the same injection increases aggregate demand only $50 billion! This end result is also illustrated in Figure 18.1, which shows how imports limit the shift of aggregate demand. The smaller shift that occurs in the open economy results in a smaller increase in equilibrium real GDP. In this sense *imports, by increasing leakage, reduce the impact of fiscal stimulus.* Notice in Figure 18.1 the much larger induced consumption in the closed economy. The fiscal stimulus shifts aggregate demand to AD_4 in the closed economy but only to AD_3 in the open economy. The end result is less of an increase in domestic output (and less inflationary pressure as well).

Global Stabilizer. The import leakage that reduces the effectiveness of fiscal stimulus can also act as an automatic stabilizer. This was particularly evident in early 2001. The slowdown in U.S. aggregate demand was heavily concentrated in high-tech

FIGURE 18.1
Imports Reduce Multiplier Effects

The amount of additional demand created by a fiscal stimulus depends on the marginal propensity to import. In a closed economy (MPM = 0) aggregate demand increases from AD_1 to AD_4. In an open economy (MPM > 0) imports limit spending on domestic goods, shifting aggregate demand only to AD_3.

sectors that are highly dependent on imported equipment and components; that is to say, industries with a very high marginal propensity to import. Hence, foreign producers absorbed a large share of the pain caused by the U.S. slowdown (see World View). In the absence of that safety valve, the U.S. economy would have suffered larger multiplier effects and a more severe slowdown.

WORLD VIEW

U.S. Growth Slows—and Foreign Economies Feel the Pain

But the Falloff in American Imports Is Limiting U.S. Weakness

If you want a vivid illustration of America's role in the global slowdown, consider that the U.S. buys up nearly one-fourth of the rest of the world's exports. And the growth rate of the volume of goods coming into the U.S. has swung from a 17 percent annual pace last autumn to a −5 percent pace currently. No wonder many economies abroad are struggling.

To an important extent, though, the rest of the world's pain is America's gain. True, the growing weakness in exports has been a considerable drag on the ailing manufacturing sector. But the dropoff in imports is acting like a shock absorber, because much of the fallout from weaker demand is being felt by foreign producers, not the U.S. economy. . . .

In this particular slowdown, the stabilizing influence of falling imports is especially large. That's because the slump is concentrated in business-sector cuts in capital spending and inventories, mainly for tech-equipment. About 36 percent of U.S. dollar outlays for capital goods goes to imports. For tech gear alone, imports account for about 16 percent. That means foreign companies—and countries—are absorbing a large share of the burden of dealing with U.S. corporate cutbacks. One case in point: Singapore is in recession mostly because its shipments to the U.S. of semiconductors and other tech components have plunged dramatically.

—James C. Cooper and Kathleen Madigan

Source: *BusinessWeek*, August 6, 2001, © 2001 The McGraw-Hill Companies, Inc. Reprinted with permission. www.businessweek.com

Analysis: Imports act as an automatic stabilizer by (1) absorbing some of lost sales in an economic downturn and (2) adding to aggregate supply as domestic capacity is approached.

International trade is a two-way street. Whereas we import goods and services from the rest of the world, other countries buy our **exports.** Thus, *export sales inject spending into our circular flow at the same time that imports cause leakage from it.*

Any changes in exports are regarded as autonomous, since export sales depend primarily on the income and spending behavior of foreigners. Hence, *a change in export demand causes a shift of the aggregate demand curve.* Like any other injection, an increase in export demand would set off a chain of multiplier effects. In other words, small changes in exports generate larger (multiplied) shifts of aggregate demand. This was a distinct risk for the U.S. economy in the 1997–98 Asian crisis: a reduction in American exports to Asia could have snowballed into very large job losses. When Japan fell into another recession in early 2001, U.S. exporters again lost sales and laid off workers.

TRADE IMBALANCES

With exports adding to aggregate spending, and imports subtracting from the circular flow, the net impact of international trade on the domestic economy comes down to a question of balance. *What counts is the difference between exports (injections) and imports (leakages).* If exports and imports were exactly equal, there would be no net stimulus or leakage from the rest of the world.

A convenient way of emphasizing the offsetting effects of exports and imports is to rearrange the income identity to

$$C + I + G + (X - IM) = Y$$

where $(X - IM)$ equals **net exports.**

If exports and imports were always equal, the term $(X - IM)$ would disappear and we could focus on domestic spending behavior. But why would we expect imports and exports to be equal? We now know that even *domestic* injections such as investment aren't likely to equal domestic leakages like saving. Indeed, the short-run macro stability problem arises because investment and saving decisions are made by different people and for very different reasons. There's no *a priori* reason to expect those outcomes to be identical.

The same problem affects international trade. Foreign decisions about how much to spend on American exports are made outside U.S. borders. Decisions in the United States about how much to spend on imports are made by American consumers, investors, and government agencies. Because these sets of shoppers are so isolated from one another, it seems unlikely that exports will ever equal imports. Instead, we have to expect a trade imbalance.

There are specific terms for characterizing trade imbalances. A U.S. **trade surplus** exists when America is exporting more goods and services than it's importing—that is, when net exports $(X - IM)$ are positive. When U.S. net exports are negative, imports exceed exports and the United States has a **trade deficit.** In 2000 the United States had a trade deficit of $369 billion. That deficit implies that U.S. consumers, investors, and government agencies were buying $369 billion more output in 2000 than American factories and offices were producing.

A trade deficit isn't all bad. After all, when imports exceed exports, we end up consuming more than we're producing. In effect, *a trade deficit permits domestic living standards to exceed domestic output.* It's almost like getting something for nothing—the proverbial free lunch. A trade deficit can also be an important safety valve for rising inflation pressures. In early 2000, the U.S. economy was producing at capacity and signs of demand-pull inflation were emerging (the Fed was raising interest rates). The ready availability of imported inputs and products helped keep inflation in check.

Trade deficits aren't always so beneficial. A trade deficit represents net leakage. That leakage may frustrate attempts to attain full employment. As we observed (Figure 18.1),

Exports as Injections

exports: Goods and services sold to foreign buyers.

net exports: The value of exports minus the value of imports: $(X - IM)$.

trade surplus: The amount by which the value of exports exceeds the value of imports in a given time period (positive net exports).

trade deficit: The amount by which the value of imports exceeds the value of exports in a given time period (negative net exports).

Macro Effects

To track changes in the U.S. trade balance, see the import and export data in "Balance of payments and related data" at the Bureau of Economic Analysis: www.bea.doc.gov.

crowding out: A reduction in private-sector borrowing (and spending) caused by increased government borrowing.

import leakage necessitates a larger fiscal injection to reach any particular spending goal. Larger injections may not be possible, especially if *budget* deficit concerns limit fiscal-policy initiatives.

Crowding Out Net Exports. One reason people worry about budget deficits is that increased government spending may supplant private investment and consumption. This is the **crowding-out** problem we first encountered in Chapter 12. It takes on a new dimension in an open economy. In an open economy, increased government purchases need not reduce private-sector spending—even at full employment! Increased imports can satisfy the increase in aggregate demand. Thus, in an open economy *an increase in imports can reduce domestic crowding out.*

The elbow room provided by imports relieves some of the worries about federal *budget* deficits. New concerns arise, however, about *trade* deficits. As imports increase, our net export position deteriorates. Hence, *in an open economy fiscal stimulus tends to crowd out net exports by boosting imports.* Indeed, any fiscal stimulus intended to boost domestic output will *worsen* the trade deficit. Consumers will spend some fraction of their additional income—the marginal propensity to import (MPM)—on imports. These added imports will widen the trade gap. Thus, *the objective of reducing the trade deficit may conflict with the goal of attaining full employment.*

A trade surplus can create similar problems. The additional spending implied by positive net exports may fuel inflationary pressures. If the economy is overheating, the policy objective is to restrain aggregate spending. But fiscal and monetary restraints don't directly affect the incomes, expectations, or tastes of foreign consumers. Foreign spending on U.S. goods may continue unabated, even as domestic monetary and fiscal restraint squeezes domestic consumers and investors. Indeed, domestic monetary and fiscal restraint will have to be harder, just to offset continuing export demand.

Worse yet, the trade surplus may grow in response to restrictive macro policies. Domestic consumers, squeezed by monetary and fiscal restraint, will reduce purchases of imported goods. On the other hand, if fiscal and monetary restraint reduces domestic inflation, foreigners may increase their export purchases. Here again, *trade goals and domestic macro goals may conflict.*

Foreign Perspectives

Who cares if our trade balance worsens? Why don't we just focus on our domestic macro equilibrium and ignore any trade imbalances that result? If we ignored trade imbalances, we wouldn't have a goal conflict and could achieve our domestic policy goals.

Unfortunately, our trading partners have their own policy objectives and may not be content to ignore our trade imbalances. *If the United States has a trade deficit, other countries must have a trade surplus.* This is simple arithmetic. Its implications are potentially worrisome, however. The rest of the world might not be happy about shipping us more output than they're getting in return. In real economic terms, they'd be picking up the tab for our "free lunch." Their exports would be financing a higher standard of living for us than our output alone permitted. At the same time, their living standards would be less than their output made possible. These disparities could cause tension. In addition, foreign nations might also be concerned about inflationary pressures of their own and so resist additional demand for their exports (our imports).

The whole notion of macro equilibrium gets much more complicated when we adopt these global views. From a global perspective, *we can't focus exclusively on domestic macro goals and ignore international repercussions.* If our trade balance upsets other economies, foreign nations may respond with their own macro and trade initiatives. These responses, in turn, would affect America's trade flows and so alter domestic outcomes. A *global* macro equilibrium would be attained only when no trading partner had reason to change macro or trade policy.

A Policy Constraint

From a macro perspective, our basic objective in both an open and a closed economy remains the same: to find the optimal balance of aggregate demand and aggregate supply. Trade flows may help or hinder this effort, depending on the timing, size, and source of the trade imbalance. Sudden *changes* in trade flows can create an external shock that upsets macro policy goals (see World View). All we know for certain is

- Imports and exports alter the levels of aggregate demand and aggregate supply.
- Trade flows may help or impede domestic macro policy attain its objectives.
- Macro policy decisions need to take account of international trade repercussions.

Thus, international trade adds an important new wrinkle to macro policy decision making.

INTERNATIONAL FINANCE

Our global interactions with the rest of the world are further complicated by international money flows. Money flows across international borders as easily as goods and services. In fact, money *must* move across borders to pay for imports and exports. In addition, people move money across borders to get bigger profits, higher interest rates, or more security. Like trade in goods and services, these international money flows alter macro outcomes and complicate macro decision making.

WORLD VIEW

Oil Shocks

In 1973, in 1979, and again in 2000, the Organization of Petroleum Exporting Countries (OPEC) sharply increased crude oil prices. The price of oil quadrupled in 1973 and doubled again in 1979. In early 2000, the price of oil jumped 50 percent. The resulting "shock" to macro equilibrium caused both higher unemployment and more inflation in oil-importing nations.

Inflationary Impact

An increase in the price of oil sets the stage for cost-push inflation. Industries using oil to fuel their machines or heat their furnaces are hit with an increase in production costs. These higher costs shift the aggregate *supply* curve to the left, as in the accompanying figure (AS_1 to AS_2).

Recessionary Impact

The leftward shift of the aggregate supply curve not only pushes the average price level up (to P_2) but also reduces output (to Q_2). In the United States, the 1973 reduction in total domestic output was aggravated by price controls on domestic oil and gas. As a consequence, many manufacturers were forced to shut down because they couldn't get the oil they were willing and able to purchase. Others shut down because higher fuel costs made continued production unprofitable.

Decreased Consumption

Although the most visible effects of oil shocks are inflation and shortages, the greatest threat often lies on the demand side

of product and factor markets. OPEC price boosts force consumers to spend more of their income on foreign oil imports. In 1973, the United States was spending approximately $10 billion a year on imported oil. After the OPEC price increase, our annual import bill suddenly jumped to $25 billion. This sudden increase in import leakage left consumers with less income to spend on domestic output. Thus, the aggregate *demand* curve shifted to the left, as from AD_1 to AD_2.

Analysis: Abrupt changes in the price or availability of imported goods will alter domestic output and spending. Such external shocks can worsen domestic inflation and unemployment.

Capital Inflows

In 2000, nearly $1 trillion of foreign capital flowed into the United States. A lot of this capital inflow was used to purchase U.S. bonds. The Treasury bonds were attractive to international investors for two reasons. First, real interest rates in the U.S. economy were relatively high, making them a more attractive investment than foreign bonds. Second, the U.S. economy looked more prosperous and more politically stable than many other places, making Treasury bonds appear more secure. Corporate bonds, stocks and other U.S. investments also looked attractive in early 2000, for much the same reasons. So people and institutions around the world moved some of their funds into U.S. markets, creating a tremendous capital inflow.

The profits of U.S. corporations operating abroad added to that capital inflow. When U.S. firms build plants abroad, they anticipate earning profits they can bring home. Over time, U.S. multinational firms have accumulated a sizable share of world markets, giving them a regular inflow of international profits. McDonald's, for example, operates more than 20,000 restaurants in 89 countries. Profits from its foreign outlets add to America's capital inflow.

Capital Outflows

Money flows out of the United States to the rest of the world for the same purposes. Most of the outflow is used to pay for U.S. imports (including foreign travel by U.S. citizens). In addition, U.S. investors may seek to invest in foreign countries and need to buy foreign land, labor, and capital. And U.S. households and institutions may be attracted to overseas *financial* investments, for example, foreign bonds or stocks. Some people simply want to keep their money in Swiss banks to avoid scrutiny or evade taxes. Finally, the U.S. government spends money in foreign countries to maintain American defenses, operate embassies, encourage economic development, and provide emergency relief. All these motivations cause a dollar outflow.

Part of the dollar outflow is also prompted by foreign investors and institutions. We already noted that a motivation for capital *inflows* is the desire for U.S.-based investments and profits. As interest and profits accumulate, foreign investors may want to retrieve some of their assets. Those repatriated interest and profit payments are part of the capital *outflows*. If the relative attractiveness of investments in the United States diminishes, even more foreign capital will flow out. When the U.S. stock market crashed in 2000–01, many foreign investors took their money and ran.

CAPITAL IMBALANCES

Like trade flows, capital flows won't always be balanced. At times, the outflow of dollars will exceed the inflow, and the United States will experience a **capital deficit.** At other times, the balance may be reversed, leaving the United States with a **capital surplus.** In 2000, the United States had a capital surplus of nearly $400 billion.

capital deficit: The amount by which the capital outflow exceeds the capital inflow in a given time period.

capital surplus: The amount by which the capital inflow exceeds the capital outflow in a given time period.

The huge capital surplus of 2000 is directly related to the huge trade deficit in that same year. When we import more than we export, we're effectively buying foreign goods and services on credit. The bulk of that credit is derived from the net inflow of foreign capital. The net inflow of money prompted by foreign investors creates a pool of funds that can be used to purchase foreign goods and services. If the capital inflow were smaller, our ability to purchase imports would be less, too. The reverse of this is true as well. If Americans weren't buying so many imports, foreigners wouldn't have as many dollars to invest in U.S. banks, corporations, and property. Thus, *capital imbalances are directly related to trade imbalances.*

Macro Effects

Capital imbalances are a problem for monetary policy. The essence of monetary policy is control of the money supply. When money is able to move across international borders at will, control of the money supply becomes more difficult.

Suppose inflationary forces are building and the Fed wants to reduce money supply growth. To do so, it might engage in open market operations, with the objective of net selling. By selling bonds, the Fed would seek to draw reserves out of the banking system and thereby slow money supply growth. The bond sales will also tend to raise in-

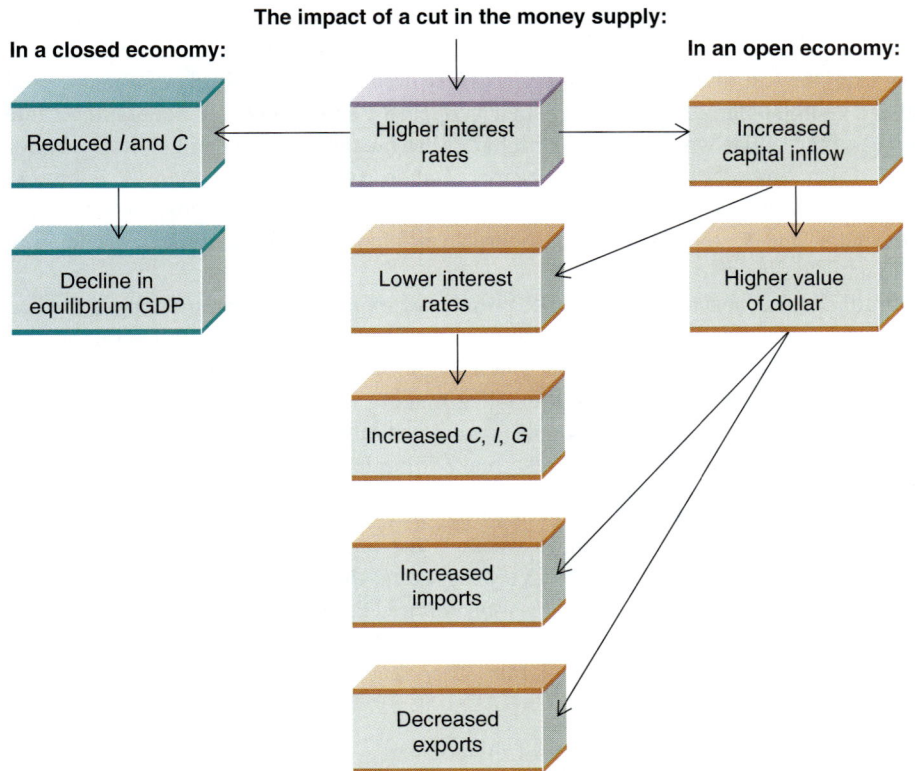

FIGURE 18.2
International Constraints on Monetary Policy

A reduction in the money supply is intended to reduce consumption and investment spending and thereby relieve inflationary pressures. If the money supply reduction increases domestic interest rates, however, it may trigger additional capital inflow. That increased capital inflow will frustrate monetary policy by increasing the money supply and holding down interest rates. The capital inflow will also tend to increase the value of the U.S. dollar and so widen the trade deficit.

terest rates and thus dampen both consumer and investor spending. This now-familiar sequence of events is illustrated on the left side of Figure 18.2.

The figure also illustrates how an open economy complicates monetary policy. The higher interest rates caused by the Fed's bond sales attract foreign investors. As the return on U.S. bonds increases, the inflow of foreign capital will accelerate. This will frustrate the Fed's goal of reducing money supply growth and tend to put downward pressure on domestic interest rates. The Fed will have to work harder (e.g., sell more bonds) to achieve any desired money supply target.

An important feature of Figure 18.2 is the box marked "higher value of dollar." When we purchase goods and services from foreign countries, we must exchange our dollars for foreign currency. The Japanese workers who make Toyotas, for example, are paid in yen. Their willingness to supply cars is based on how many yen, not dollars, they'll receive. Thus, we must first exchange dollars for yen before we can import Toyotas. When you travel abroad, you do these exchanges yourself, typically at banks, hotels, or special foreign exchange offices. When you stay at home and buy imported goods, someone else handles the exchange for you.

Whether you or some middleperson does the exchange is irrelevant. What matters is how many yen you get for your dollars. The more yen you get, the more Toyotas and other Japanese goods you're able to buy. In other words, *if the dollar's value in the world markets is high, imports are cheap.*

The dollar's value in international trade is reflected in the **exchange rate.** The exchange rate is simply the price (value) of one currency, measured in terms of another. The exchange rate prevailing at any time reflects the interplay of trade and capital flows and all their determinants. (Foreign exchange markets are examined in Chapter 36.) What matters here is that exchange rates *change,* often in response to monetary and fiscal policy.

Exchange Rates

exchange rate: The price of one country's currency expressed in terms of another's; the domestic price of a foreign currency.

In Figure 18.2. restrictive monetary policy causes domestic interest rates to rise. These higher interest rates make U.S. bonds more attractive and so increase capital inflow from the rest of the world. To buy Treasury bonds, however, foreign investors need dollars. As they clamor to exchange their yen, euros, and pounds for dollars, the value (price) of the dollar will increase. A higher dollar means that you can get more yen for every dollar. Imports thus become cheaper, and so Americans buy more of them. On the other hand, a stronger (more expensive) dollar makes U.S. exports costlier for foreign consumers, and so they buy fewer American products. The end result is a widening trade gap.

Similar global obstacles can impede policies of monetary stimulus. Suppose the Fed cut interest rates to stimulate aggregate demand. Those lower interest rates might start a capital outflow, as global investors sought higher returns elsewhere. This accelerated outflow would reduce the value of the dollar, making imports more expensive. The implied upward shift of aggregate supply would frustrate efforts to accelerate real GDP growth. The capital outflow would also make it harder to reduce interest rates.

Capital Flows—Another Policy Constraint

International capital flows add yet another complication to macro policy. The very existence of international capital flows weakens the Fed's ability to control the money supply. As the accompanying World View suggests, these global linkages were a significant policy constraint in 2001: the weakening U.S. dollar kept the Fed from offering more monetary stimulus. We conclude, then, that global money links create another policy headache: In addition to all our other macro worries, we now have to be concerned about

- The flow of capital into and out of the country.
- The effect of capital imbalances on domestic macro performance.
- How macro policy will affect international capital flows, exchange rates, and trade balances.

PRODUCTIVITY AND COMPETITIVENESS

The global dimensions of the economy add a whole new layer of complexity to macro policy. One might reasonably wonder whether international trade and finance is really worth all the trouble. Couldn't we get along just as well without the rest of the world?

Specialization

Perhaps. But we wouldn't be able to drink much coffee. Or spend summer vacations in Europe. Or buy Japanese cars and Mexican beer.

To decide whether international trade and finance is worth all the trouble, we have to consider how international exchanges affect our standard of living. One obvious advantage of trade is that it gives us access to goods and services we don't or can't produce at home, such as coffee, vacations abroad, bananas, and Italian shoes. These *imported goods and services broaden our consumption possibilities.*

Most of the goods and services we import *could* be produced at home. Cars and shoes are made in America as well as abroad, as is a small quantity of coffee and bananas (in Hawaii). Even more coffee and bananas *could* be produced in the United States if we invested enough in greenhouses that duplicated tropical conditions. Homegrown coffee and bananas would turn out to be terribly expensive, however, so we're better off importing them. This leaves domestic resources available for the production of other goods that we can more easily grow (corn), manufacture (computers), or build (houses). In other words, we're better off *specializing* in the production of things we do relatively well and *trading* with other nations for the rest of the goods and services we desire. This is the principle of **comparative advantage** we first encountered in Chapter 2. In essence, it recommends that we produce what we do best and trade with other nations for goods they produce best.

comparative advantage: The ability of a country to produce a specific good at a lower opportunity cost than its trading partners.

WORLD VIEW

Another Chink in the Economy's Armor
But If the Dollar's Down, Is the Bottom Near?

The dollar is too strong. That's what American steelmakers and other manufacturers who depend on selling their products overseas have complained all summer.

Not anymore. Since early July, the dollar is down 8 percent against the euro, its chief competitor. While that dip may be welcome among old-line exporters, it raises more serious questions about the health of the economy. That is because one key reason for the dollar's dip is that currency traders are beginning to concede that a rebound in the U.S. economy may be further off than expected. So they're selling greenbacks—literally taking their cash and betting that it will do better overseas.

The dollar's sudden weakness isn't all bad news. U.S. manufacturers such as General Motors and International Paper have pushed Treasury Secretary Paul O'Neill to talk down the dollar, figuring that a weaker currency will pump up the value of profit from overseas sales. That would shore up their earnings statements and, conceivably, their stock prices.

Weakling. The evidence on past efforts to boost the economy with a weak dollar is mixed at best. A policy launched in 1985 cut the currency's value by 40 percent, boosting exports, but was later cited by some economists as a cause of the October 1987 stock market crash. Some economists argue that a weak dollar assures one thing and one thing only: inflation. That's because a weaker dollar could prompt importers to boost prices to maintain profit margins, allowing domestic manufacturers to simply do the same, rather than focus on gaining market share.

The fear of inflation may have figured into the Fed's decision to hold off on a more dramatic move last week, some economists say.

—Noam Neusner

Source: *U.S. News & World Report*, September 3, 2001. Reprinted with permission. www.usnews.com

Dollar drop
The dollar is declining against the euro.
Euros per dollar

Analysis: The Fed may be reluctant to pursue a monetary stimulus if lower interest rates might spark a capital outflow, a weaker dollar, and higher import prices (inflation).

Specialization among countries increases world efficiency and output, making all nations richer.

Chapter 35 demonstrates the benefits of international specialization (the theory of comparative advantage). At this juncture we may note that the same principles that motivate *individuals* to specialize and then exchange their goods and services also motivate *nations* to specialize and then exchange their goods and services in international trade. In both cases, **productivity** and total output increase.

The increased output and productivity that specialization makes possible aren't the only benefits of international trade. ***Trade stimulates improvements in productivity.*** The presence of foreign producers keeps domestic producers on their toes. To compete in international markets, domestic producers must reduce costs and increase efficiency.

In recent years, America's huge trade deficits have provoked questions about the competitiveness of U.S. producers. The excess of imports over exports suggests to many people that America isn't producing goods of the quality and value that consumers demand. Productivity may have lagged in some U.S. industries. And other nations inevitably become more efficient in producing certain goods and services. But the trade gap isn't a general indictment of U.S. competitiveness.

As we've observed, international trade and capital flows are interrelated, and both are directly influenced by exchange rates. In the early 1980s, the relative attractiveness of America's capital markets led to a surge of capital inflows and a higher

> **productivity:** Output per unit of input, for example, output per labor-hour.

Competitiveness

The U.S. Bureau of Labor Statistics (BLS) assembles international comparisons of manufacturing productivity (also published in the *Monthly Labor Review*); visit www.bls.gov/fls

exchange rate for the U.S. dollar. Between 1981 and 1985, the world value of the U.S. dollar rose by 50 percent, which made all American goods more expensive in international markets. To *maintain* their prices in international markets, U.S. producers would have had to cut costs enough to offset that increase in the dollar's value. Although American productivity increased faster than foreign productivity in those years, few U.S. producers could stay ahead of the rising dollar. The resulting increase in the trade deficit was a product of the rising dollar, not of a decline in U.S. productivity. The same thing happened again during the period 1996–99, when the value of the dollar and the trade deficit both jumped. The same sequence was repeated in 2001.

Although a trade gap isn't necessarily evidence of declining competitiveness, it does draw policy attention to productivity issues. Productivity improvements are essential to economic growth and rising living standards. If a trade gap stimulates fiscal, monetary, and supply-side policies that foster productivity advances, then the economy may be better off as a result. By the same token, trade gaps remind us that policies that restrain productivity improvements (research, innovation, and investment) also have international consequences.

GLOBAL COORDINATION

As all countries begin to acknowledge the international dimensions of their economies, the desire for coordination grows. The coordination is pursued both through formal institutions and informal "understandings" among the major industrialized nations.

IMF

The most visible institution for global coordination is the International Monetary Fund (IMF). The IMF is sort of a bankers' United Nations. All nations contribute funds to the IMF, which then uses those funds to assist nations whose currency is in trouble. When Thailand devalued its currency (the baht) in July 1997, for example, the currencies of other Asian nations also plunged. As we noted earlier, this Asian crisis threatened U.S. exports as well as those of other nations. There was a distinct threat that the "Asian flu" would become a global contagion. To keep the Asian flu from spreading, the IMF lent more than $100 billion to Thailand, Korea, Indonesia, and other Asian nations. The IMF also loaned Brazil over $40 billion in 1998–99 and Argentina $22 billion in 2001 to avoid a "Latin flu" from spreading to other South American nations and the global economy.

Although the IMF often provides global "first aid," IMF assistance typically comes with strings attached, such as insisting that a debtor nation alter its domestic monetary fiscal or trade policies as a condition of an IMF bailout. Such intrusions into domestic macro policy are often resented, especially when they entail high political costs in the debtor nation (as in Argentina in 2001–02).

For a summary of IMF activities and recent bailouts, visit www.imf.org.

Group of Seven

The seven largest industrial countries (the United States, Japan, Canada, Germany, France, Italy, and Great Britain) attain a less formal mode of global coordination. The finance economic ministers of these nations meet periodically to assess the global outlook and coordinate macro policy. Although the Group of Seven (the G-7) has no formal apparatus for joint actions, any informal agreements it reaches can have a substantial effect on global trade and capital flow. Reaching agreement isn't always easy, however. In mid-2001, the Federal Reserve's attempts to stimulate the U.S. economy were frustrated by higher interest rates in Europe. Despite Fed pleas for greater monetary stimulus (see World View), the European Central Bank kept interest rates relatively high.

Global interests will never fully displace national policy priorities. However, even limited global coordination helps smooth out some of the rough spots of macro performance in an increasingly interdependent world.

WORLD VIEW

U.S. Wants Europe, Japan to Ease Rates
Moves Could Help Fortify Economies Overseas, Lift Dollar in Short Term

WASHINGTON—The Bush administration, hoping to see stronger economic growth overseas, wants Europe and Japan to follow the U.S. Federal Reserve's lead in easing monetary policy more aggressively.

U.S. officials hope the moves eventually will invigorate slack overseas markets for American companies. But they recognize that the more immediate effect is likely to be a stronger dollar that will make it tougher for American manufacturers to compete against foreign producers. Already, many companies complain that the strong dollar is hurting their exports at the same time that the weak euro is crimping profits from their European operations.

Unfazed by such concerns, a senior Bush administration official yesterday said the European Central Bank still "needs to ease up quite a bit," while Japan's financial authorities should combine expansion of that country's money supply with tough-minded economic reforms. . . .

On July 7, Mr. O'Neill will meet in Rome with his finance ministry counterparts from the other Group of Seven major industrialized nations. Treasury officials say that, while the secretary may push for enhanced growth, he won't press directly for rate cuts. "It's none of our business how they stimulate growth." Mr. O'Neill said yesterday. "It's entirely up to them."

But the U.S. is likely to find others around the table who think the ECB should do more to stimulate the economy.

The Italian and German governments—whose economies are among the worst-performing in the 12-nation euro area—are growing increasingly disgruntled with the central bank. The ECB has hardly budged on rates since the global slowdown began, cutting its key rate just a quarter point to 4.5 percent on May 10.

—Michael M. Phillips and Rebecca Quick

Source: *The Wall Street Journal*, June 28, 2001, p. A2. Reprinted by permission of *The Wall Street Journal*. © 2001 Dow Jones & Company, Inc. All rights reserved worldwide. www.wsj.com

Analysis: Global coordination of economic policies is limited by the different priorities of individual nations. In the absence of coordination, policy success is more difficult.

THE ECONOMY TOMORROW

A Global Currency?
The New Euro

On January 1, 1999, 11 European nations adopted a simple currency, the *euro*. That wasn't an easy or quick policy decision. As the accompanying World View notes, the quest for a common European currency began in the Middle Ages. The latest push for the euro began over 40 years ago. In view of this history, one has to wonder why a single European currency has been sought and why it has taken so long to attain.

The allure of a common currency is that it facilitates trade and capital flows across national borders. A common currency eliminates the uncertainties and added costs of diverse currencies. European businesses spent nearly $13 billion a year just on currency conversions. Exchange rate fluctuation also impeded cross-border business transactions, which is why the U.S. Congress created a national currency to replace the hundreds of state and private bank currencies that existed prior to 1863.

Macro Coordination

There's a huge difference, however, between creating a common *national* currency (the U.S. dollar) and a common *cross-national* currency like the euro. The 50 states that make up the United States share a common set of laws, monetary institutions, and government. The 11 nations of the European Union (EU) don't even share a common language, much less governmental authority. Accordingly, in creating a common currency, they agreed to submerge some national interests to broader European goals.

To maintain a common currency, nations must maintain common macro policies. Germany, for example, has been particularly vigilant about inflation, while Italy has given higher priority to reducing unemployment. As a result, Germany monetary policy tended to be tighter (more restrictive) than Italian monetary policy. When they adopted a common currency, Germany, Italy and the other 9 EU members had to find a middle

WORLD VIEW

The Long History of Europe's Single Currency

- **Middle Ages:** Feudal rulers frequently try to unify coins with trading partners.
- **1865–1927:** "Latin coin union" (France, Belgium, Italy, Switzerland, and Greece) undermined by policy rows.
- **1872–1924:** "Scandinavian coin union" (Sweden, Norway, and Denmark) works smoothly for a time but eroded by World War I.
- **1957:** European Community's founding Treaty of Rome provides for coordination of economic and monetary policies.
- **1970:** "Werner Plan" seeks to achieve monetary union by 1980, but is derailed by international oil crisis.
- **1972:** European nations link currencies in "snake" that limits fluctuations.
- **1979:** Founding of European Monetary System tying exchange rates.
- **1987:** Single European Act fixed objective of monetary union in a treaty for first time.
- **1989:** Delores Report outlines three-stage plan for monetary union.
- **1991:** EC heads of state agree in Maastricht, the Netherlands, to create a monetary union in 1997 or 1999.
- **1993:** After currency turmoil ejects Britain and Italy from exchange-rate mechanism, fluctuation bands are widened.
- **1994:** Founding of European Monetary Institute, forerunner of a European central bank.
- **1995:** EU governments agree they won't be able to meet the 1997 deadline.
- **1998:** Using 1997 data, EU rules which nations can participate in monetary union.
- **1999:** Parities of currencies are irrevocably fixed, European central bank takes over monetary policy.
- **2002:** Notes and coins in new currency issued to public; national currencies eliminated.

Source: *Deutsche Bank Research*. From *The Wall Street Journal*. December 13, 1995. Reprinted by permission of *The Wall Street Journal*, © 1995 Dow Jones & Company, Inc. All rights reserved worldwide. www.wsj.com. Updated by author 2002.

Analysis: The adoption of a common currency requires nations to give up control of monetary policy. Few countries are willing to do so.

ground for monetary policy. If unemployment or growth rates vary significantly across the 11 EU nations, such a middle ground may be politically difficult to maintain.

Recognizing these obstacles, the 11 EU nations initially hedged on their commitment to a common currency. Although the euro became the official currency of the 11 nations in 1999, each country maintained its own currency for three additional years. Euros did not circulate publicly until January 2002. And although the EU nations established a new European central bank, the central banks of the member nations still functioned for several years. Now the "trial marriage" is over, and the euro is the common currency of Europe, or at least most of Europe: Great Britain, Sweden, Denmark, and Switzerland opted to keep their national currencies. Submerging national priorities to the common interests of "Euroland" was viewed as too great a price to pay for greater cross-border efficiency. The challenge for the European Union now is to demonstrate that the benefits of global integration justify the loss of policy independence. If they succeed, more nations will adopt a common currency in the economy tomorrow.

Information on the euro and economic conditions in Euroland is posted at europa.eu.int.

SUMMARY

- The United States exports about 11 percent of total output and imports an even larger percentage. This international trade ties our macro performance to that of the rest of the world.
- Imports represent leakage from the circular flow and so tend to reduce equilibrium GDP. The marginal propensity to import also diminishes the multiplier impact of fiscal and monetary policies.
- Exports represent added spending on domestic output and so tend to increase equilibrium GDP. This added demand may conflict with restrictive macro policy objectives.

- Trade imbalances occur when exports and imports are unequal. Trade deficits imply that we're consuming more output than we're producing. Trade surpluses indicate the opposite.
- Fiscal stimulus increases imports and crowds out net exports. The resulting increase in the trade deficit may constrain policy options.
- Capital imbalances occur when capital inflows don't equal capital outflows. Capital surpluses help finance trade deficits but may also conflict with macro policy goals at home or abroad.
- International trade and capital flows place additional constraints on macro policy. Macro policy must both anticipate and respond to changes in trade and capital flows.
- The benefits of international trade and capital markets are the broadening of consumption possibilities and the enhanced productivity they promote. Productivity advances arise from specialization in production and from the competitive pressure of foreign producers and markets.
- In adopting a common currency, EU nations hope to broaden markets and accelerate productivity and growth. To maintain that currency, they may have to submerge some national priorities.

Key Terms

imports
leakage
multiplier
marginal propensity to import (MPM)
marginal propensity to save (MPS)
exports
net exports
trade deficit
trade deficit
crowding out
capital deficit
capital surplus
exchange rate
comparative advantage
productivity

Questions for Discussion

1. How is the U.S. economy affected by (*a*) a recession in Mexico, (*b*) simulative monetary policies in Mexico, (*c*) a drop in the value of the peso?
2. Suppose investors in other countries increased their purchases of U.S. corporate stock. How would this influx of capital affect the U.S. economy?
3. Why is it unrealistic to expect trade flows to be balanced?
4. Farmers in the United States export about one-third of their major crops. What would happen to U.S. farmers if foreign consumers stopped buying American food? What would happen to our macro equilibrium?
5. Japan imports most of the raw materials it uses in the production of finished goods. If the international prices of raw materials rose sharply, how would Japan's economy be affected? Would Japanese exports be affected?
6. How would a tax cut in the United States affect international capital and trade flows?
7. Why would the European Central Bank (ECB) need to be prodded into reducing interest rates (see World View, page 383)? What might have held the ECB back?
8. Who gains and who loses when the global value of the U.S. dollar rises?
9. Would a higher marginal propensity to import help or hinder domestic macro policy?

Web Activities

1. Log on to www.census.gov/indicator/www/ustrade.html. What is the current balance of trade for the United States? Has this balance been increasing or decreasing?
2. Log on to www.whitehouse.gov/fsbr/international.html, and find the statistics on U.S. international trade in goods and services. Graph the value of U.S. imports and GDP growth for the last two years. Based on these numbers, what is the implied marginal propensity to import (MPM)?
3. What comparative advantages does your state have? Check out your state's "trade map" at www.csis.org/nge/trade/ustrade.html. What are your state's major exports? Why do you think your state has a comparative advantage in those products? How much does your state export? What countries are the top export markets for your state?

ALERT! THE ACCOMPANYING STUDENT PROBLEM SET CONTAINS NUMERICAL AND GRAPHING PROBLEMS FOR THIS CHAPTER

CHAPTER 19

Theory and Reality

> There is no one solution. It isn't just a question of the budget. It isn't just the question of inflationary labor rates. It isn't just the question of sticky prices. It isn't just the question of what the Government does to keep prices up or to make regulations that tend to be inflationary. It isn't just the weather or just the drought.
>
> It is all these things. The interaction of these various factors is what is so terribly difficult for us to understand and, of course, what is so terribly difficult for us to deal with.
>
> —Former Secretary of the Treasury W. Michael Blumenthal

Macroeconomic theory is supposed to explain the business cycle and show policymakers how to control it. But something is obviously wrong. Despite our relative prosperity, we haven't consistently achieved the goals of full employment, price stability, and vigorous economic growth. All too often, either unemployment or inflation surges or economic growth slows down. No matter how hard we try to eliminate it, the business cycle seems to persist.

What accounts for this gap between the promises of economic theory and the reality of economic performance? Are the theories inadequate? Or is sound economic advice being ignored?

Many people blame the economists. They point to the conflicting advice of Keynesians, monetarists, and supply-siders and wonder what theory is supposed to be followed. If economists themselves can't agree, it is asked, why should anyone else listen to them?

Not surprisingly, economists see things a bit differently. First, they point out, the **business cycle** isn't as bad as it used to be. Since World War II, the economy has had many ups and downs, but none as severe as the Great Depression or earlier catastrophes. Second, economists complain that "politics" often takes precedence over good economic advice. Politicians are reluctant, for example, to raise taxes, cut spending, or slow money growth in order to control inflation. Their concern is winning the next election, not solving the country's economic problems.

When President Jimmy Carter was in office, he anguished over another problem: the complexity of economic decision making. In the real world, neither theory nor politics can keep up with all our economic goals. As President Carter observed: "We cannot concentrate just on inflation or just on unemployment or just on deficits in the federal budget or our international payments. Nor can we act in isolation from other countries. We must deal with all of these problems simultaneously and on a worldwide basis."

No president learned this lesson faster or more forcefully than George W. Bush. Just as he was putting the final touches on a bipartisan consensus on taxes, spending, and debt reduction, terrorists destroyed the World Trade Center and damaged the Pentagon. In response to those attacks, all major economic policy decisions had to be revised.

As if the burdens of a continuously changing world weren't enough, the president must also contend with sharply differing economic theories and advice, a slow and frequently hostile Congress, a massive and often unresponsive bureaucracy, and a complete lack of knowledge about the future.

This chapter confronts these and other frustrations of the real world head on. In so doing, we provide answers to the following questions:

- What's the ideal "package" of macro policies?
- How well does our macro performance live up to the promises of that package?
- What kinds of obstacles prevent us from doing better?

The answers to these questions may shed some light on a broader concern that has long troubled students and policymakers alike, namely, "If economists are so smart, why is the economy always in such a mess."

business cycle: Alternating periods of economic growth and contraction.

POLICY LEVERS

Table 19.1 summarizes the macroeconomic tools available to policymakers. Although this list is brief, we hardly need a reminder at this point of how powerful each instrument can be. Every one of these major policy instruments can significantly change our answers to the basic economic questions of WHAT, HOW, and FOR WHOM to produce.

The basic tools of **fiscal policy** are contained in the federal budget. Tax cuts are supposed to increase aggregate demand by putting more income in the hands of consumers and businesses. Tax increases are intended to curtail spending and reduce inflationary pressures. Table 19.2 summarizes some of the major tax changes of recent years.

The expenditure side of the federal budget is another fiscal policy tool. From a Keynesian perspective, increases in government spending raise aggregate demand and so encourage more production. A slowdown in government spending is supposed to restrain aggregate demand and lessen inflationary pressures.

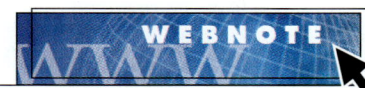

The Library of Congress maintains a summary of recent congressional tax legislation at thomas.loc.gov. Go to "Bill Summary and Status." Enter "taxes."

Fiscal Policy

fiscal policy: The use of government taxes and spending to alter macroeconomic outcomes.

Type of Policy	Policy Instruments
Fiscal	Tax cuts and increases
	Changes in government spending
Monetary	Open market operations
	Reserve requirements
	Discount rates
Supply-side	Tax incentives for investment and saving
	Deregulation
	Human-capital investment
	Infrastructure development
	Free trade
	Immigration

TABLE 19.1
The Policy Levers
Economic policymakers have access to a variety of policy instruments. The challenge is to choose the right tools at the right time. The mix of tools required may vary from problem to problem.

TABLE 19.2
Fiscal Policy Milestones

1986	Tax Reform Act	Major reduction in tax rates coupled with broadening of tax base
1990	Budget Enforcement Act	Limits set on discretionary spending; pay-as-you-go financing required for new initiatives
1993	Clinton "New Direction"	Tax increases and spending cuts to achieve $300 billion deficit reduction between 1994 and 1997
1994	Contract with America	Republican-led Congress cuts spending, sets seven-year target for balanced budget
1997	Balanced Budget Act, Taxpayer Relief Act	Package of tax cuts and spending cuts to balance budget by 2002
1998	Budget Surplus	Strong economy pushes budget into surplus
2001	Bush tax cuts	Immediate rebates plus multiyear rate cuts

automatic stabilizer: Federal expenditure or revenue item that automatically responds counter-cyclically to changes in national income—such as unemployment benefits, income taxes.

structural deficit: Federal revenues at full employment minus expenditures at full employment under prevailing fiscal policy.

fiscal stimulus: Tax cuts or spending hikes intended to increase (shift) aggregate demand.

fiscal restraint: Tax hikes or spending cuts intended to reduce (shift) aggregate demand.

Who Makes Fiscal Policy? As we first observed in Chapter 11, changes in taxes and government spending originate both in economic events and explicit policy decisions. When the economy slows, tax revenues decline, and government spending increases automatically. Conversely, when real GDP grows, tax revenues automatically rise, and government transfer payments decline. These **automatic stabilizers** are a basic countercyclical feature of the federal budget. They don't represent active fiscal policy. On the contrary, *fiscal policy refers to deliberate changes in tax or spending legislation.* These changes can be made only by the U.S. Congress. Every year the president proposes specific budget and tax changes, negotiates with Congress, then accepts or vetoes specific acts that Congress has passed. The resulting policy decisions represent "discretionary" fiscal policy. Those policy decisions expand or shrink the **structural deficit** and thus give the economy a shot of **fiscal stimulus** or **fiscal restraint**.

Monetary Policy

monetary policy: The use of money and credit controls to influence macroeconomic outcomes.

natural rate of unemployment: Long-term rate of unemployment determined by structural forces in labor and product markets.

The policy arsenal described in Table 19.1 also contains monetary tools. The tools of **monetary policy** include open market operations, discount rate changes, and reserve requirements.

As we saw in Chapter 15, there are disagreements over how these monetary tools should be used. Keynesians believe that interest rates are the critical policy lever. In their view, the money supply should be expanded or curtailed in order to achieve whatever interest rate is needed to shift aggregate demand. Monetarists, on the other hand, contend that the money supply itself is the critical policy lever and that it should be expanded at a steady and predictable rate. This policy, they believe, will ensure price stability and a **natural rate of unemployment.**

Who Makes Monetary Policy? Actual monetary policy decisions are made by the Federal Reserve's Board of Governors. Twice a year the Fed provides Congress with a broad overview of the economic outlook and monetary objectives. The Fed's assessment of the economy is updated each month at meetings of the Federal Open Market Committee (FOMC). The FOMC decides which monetary policy levers to pull.

Table 19.3 depicts milestones in recent monetary policy. Of particular interest is the October 1979 decision to adopt a pure monetarist approach. This involved an exclusive focus on the money supply, without regard for interest rates. After interest rates soared and the economy appeared on the brink of a depression, the Fed abandoned the monetarist approach and again began keeping an eye on both interest rates (the Keynesian focus) and the money supply.

Monetarists contend that the Fed never fully embraced their policy. The money supply grew at a very uneven pace in 1980, they argue, not at the steady, predictable rate

TABLE 19.3
Monetary Policy Milestones

October 1979	Fed adopts monetarist approach, focusing exclusively on money supply; interest rates soar
July 1982	Deep into recession, Fed votes to ease monetary restraint
October 1982	Fed abandons pure monetarist approach and expands money supply rapidly
May 1983	Fed reverses policy and begins slowing money supply growth
1985	Fed increases money supply with discount-rate cuts and open-market purchases
1987	Fed abandons money supply targets as policy guides; money supply growth decreases; discount rate increased
1989	Greenspan announces goal of "zero inflation," exercises more monetary restraint
1991	Deep in recession, the Fed begins to ease monetary restraint
1994	Fed slows M2 growth to 1 percent; raises federal funds rate by 3 percentage points as economy nears full employment
1995	Greenspan trumpets "soft landing" and eases monetary restraint
1998	Fed cuts interest rates to cushion U.S. economy from Asian crisis
1999–2000	Fed raises interest rates six times
2001	Fed cuts interest rates eleven times

that they demanded. Nevertheless, the policy shifts of 1979 and 1982 were distinctive and had dramatic effects.

A quick review of Table 19.3 reveals that such monetary policy reversals have been quite frequent. There were U-turns in monetary policy between 1982 and 1983, 1989 and 1991, 1998 and 1999, and again between 2000 and 2001.

Supply-side theory offers the third major set of policy tools. The focus of **supply-side policy** is to provide incentives to work, invest, and produce. Of particular concern are high tax rates and regulations that reduce supply incentives. Supply-siders argue that marginal tax rates and government regulation must be reduced in order to get more output without added inflation.

In the 1980s tax rates were reduced dramatically. The maximum marginal tax rate on individuals were cut from 70 to 50 percent in 1981, and then still further, to 28 percent, in 1987. The 1980s also witnessed major milestones in the deregulation of airlines, trucking, telephone service, and other industries (see Table 19.4).

Some of the momentum toward less regulation was reversed during the 1990s. New regulatory costs on business were created by the Americans with Disabilities Act, the 1990 amendments to the Clean Air Act, and the Family Leave Act of 1993. All three laws provide important benefits to workers or the environment. At the same time, however, they also make supplying goods and services more expensive.

The Clinton administration broadened supply-side efforts to include infrastructure development and increased investment in human capital (through education and skill training programs). These activities increase the capacity to produce and so shift the aggregate supply curve rightward. The Clinton administration also toughened environmental regulation, however, and sought legislation that would require employers to provide more training and fringe benefits (like health insurance), initiatives that shift the aggregate supply curve leftward. George W. Bush sought to reduce such regulations.

Who Makes Supply-Side Policy? Because tax rates are a basic tool of supply-side policy, fiscal and supply-side policies are often intertwined. When Congress changes the tax laws, it almost always alters marginal tax rates and thus changes production incentives. Notice, for example, that tax legislation appears in Table 19.4 as well as in Table 19.2. The Taxpayer Relief Act of 1997 not only changed total tax revenues (fiscal

Supply-Side Policy

supply-side policy: The use of tax incentives, (de)regulation, and other mechanisms to increase the ability and willingness to produce goods and services.

TABLE 19.4
Supply-Side Milestones

1990	Social Security Act amendments	Payroll tax increased to 7.65 percent
1990	Americans with Disabilities Act	Required employers to provide greater access for disabled individuals
1990	Immigration Act	Increased immigration, especially for high-skill workers
1990	Clean Air Act amendments	Increased pollution controls
1993	Rebuild America Program	Increased spending on infrastructure and human-capital investment
	Family Leave Act	Requires employers to provide unpaid leaves of absence for workers
	NAFTA	North American trade barriers lowered
1994	GATT renewed	World trade barriers lowered
1996	Telecommunications Act	Permits greater competition in cable and telephone industries
1996–1997	Minimum Wage Hike	Minimum wage jumps from $4.25 to $5.15 per hour
1996	Personal Responsibility and Work Opportunity Act	Requires more welfare recipients to work
1997	Taxpayer Relief Act	Created tuition tax credits, cut capital gains tax
1998	Workforce Investment Act	More funds for skill training
2000	Transportation Equity Act	New funding for highways, rails
2001	Bush tax cuts	Increased savings incentives; reduced marginal tax rates

policy) but also restructured production and investment-incentives (supply-side policy). The 2001 tax cuts also had both demand-side and supply-side provisions.

Supply-side and fiscal policies also interact on the outlay side of the budget. The Transportation Equity Act of 2000, for example, authorized accelerated public works spending (fiscal stimulus) on infrastructure development (increase in supply capacity). President Clinton's Rebuild America program also affected both aggregate demand and aggregate supply. *Deciding* **whether** *to increase spending is a fiscal policy decision; deciding* **how** *to spend available funds may entail supply-side policy.*

Regulatory policy is also fashioned by Congress. The president and executive agencies play a critical role in this supply-side area in the day-to-day decisions on how to interpret and enforce regulatory policies.

IDEALIZED USES

These fiscal, monetary, and supply-side tools are potentially powerful levers for controlling the economy. In principle, they can cure the excesses of the business cycle and promote faster economic growth. To see how, let's review their use in three distinct macroeconomic settings.

Case 1: Recession

When output and employment levels fall far short of the economy's full-employment potential, the mandate for public policy is clear. Aggregate demand must be increased so that producers can sell more goods, hire more workers, and move the economy toward its productive capacity. At such times the most urgent need is to get people back to work and close the **recessionary GDP gap.**

recessionary GDP gap: The amount by which equilibrium GDP falls short of full-employment GDP.

How can the government end a recession? Keynesians emphasize the need to increase aggregate demand by cutting taxes or boosting government spending. The resulting stimulus will set off a **multiplier** reaction. If the initial stimulus and multiplier are large enough, the recessionary GDP gap can be closed, propelling the economy to full employment.

Analysis: When the economy is flat on its back, it may need both monetary and fiscal stimulus.

multiplier: The multiple by which an initial change in aggregate spending will alter total expenditure after an infinite number of spending cycles; $1/(1 - MPC)$.

Modern Keynesians acknowledge that monetary policy might also help. Specifically, increases in the money supply may lower interest rates and thus give investment spending a further boost. To give the economy a really powerful stimulus, we might want to pull all these policy levers at the same time. That's what the government did in early 2001—using tax cuts, lower interest rates, and increased spending to jump start the economy (see cartoon and News).

Monetarists would proceed differently. First, they see no point in toying with the federal budget. In the pure monetarist model, changes in taxes or government spending may alter the mix of output but not its level. So long as the **velocity of money (V)** is constant, fiscal policy doesn't matter. In this view, the appropriate policy response to a recession is patience. As sales and output slow, interest rates decline, and new investment will be stimulated.

Supply-siders emphasize the need to improve production incentives. They urge cuts in marginal tax rates on investment and labor. They also look for ways to reduce government regulation. Finally, they urge that any increase in government spending (fiscal stimulus) focus on long-run capacity expansion such as infrastructure development.

velocity of money (V): The number of times per year, on average, that a dollar is used to purchase final goods and services; $PQ \div M$.

An overheated economy provides as clear a policy mandate as does a sluggish one. In this case, the immediate goal is to restrain aggregate demand until the rate of total expenditure is compatible with the productive capacity of the economy. This entails shifting the aggregate demand curve to the left in order to close the **inflationary GDP gap.** Keynesians would do this by raising taxes and cutting government spending. Keynesians would also see the desirability of increasing interest rates to curb investment spending.

Monetarists would simply cut the money supply. In their view, the short-run aggregate supply curve is unknown and unstable. The only predictable response is reflected in the vertical, long-run aggregate supply curve. According to this view, changes in the money supply alter prices, not output. Inflation is seen simply as "too much money chasing too few goods." Monetarists would turn off the money spigot. The Fed's job in this situation isn't only to reduce money supply growth but to convince market participants that a more cautious monetary policy will be continued. This was the intent of Chairman Greenspan's 1989 public commitment to zero inflation.

Supply-siders would point out that inflation implies both "too much money" and "not enough goods." They'd look at the supply side of the market for ways to expand productive capacity. In a highly inflationary setting, they'd propose more incentives to save. The additional savings would automatically reduce consumption while creating a larger pool of investable funds. Supply-siders would also cut taxes and regulations that raise production costs and lower import barriers that keep out cheaper foreign goods.

Case 2: Inflation

inflationary GDP gap: The amount by which equilibrium GDP exceeds full-employment GDP.

IN THE NEWS

Finding a Fix for the Declining Economy
Government's Options Include Spending, Cutting Rates and Taxes

WASHINGTON—With unemployment rising and the stock market slumping, politicians are nearing a panic, howling for the government to do *something* to stop the economic decline.

Of course, it isn't like policymakers have been sitting idly by. The Federal Reserve has cut interest rates seven times this year, while President Bush and Congress approved an emergency tax rebate. Those measures may well turn out to be sufficient to prevent a recession.

But with each passing day of scary data, patience inside the Beltway is wearing thin, especially for those folks running for re-election next year. Fed Chairman Alan Greenspan and his central-bank colleagues have a clear course: They will likely keep cutting interest rates. Here is a look at the more complex set of options facing the White House and Capitol Hill:

Q: Politics aside, does it really make economic sense to do anything?

A: Until recently, conventional wisdom told us no. The experts concluded that the wheels of government—outside the Fed—worked too slowly to give any short-term assistance, and by the time federal action kicked in, the economy would be recovering anyway, risking overstimulation. "I don't think the government really has the power to prevent recessions," says Murray Weidenbaum, who was chairman of President Reagan's Council of Economic Advisers.

Yet most economists—liberal and conservative alike—grudgingly admit that the answer may indeed be "yes," saying this year's tax rebate was well-timed, thus reviving interest in short-term measures.

Q: So what are the choices?

A: The most likely to succeed is fiscal stimulus—either spending increases or further tax cuts. That is, the federal government pumps more money into the economy. . . .

Q: If the government does end up accepting some fiscal stimulus, which is better, spending increases or tax cuts?

A: The case can be made that increasing spending makes more sense. The government can tweak outlays in a way to make sure every dollar gets spent. Tax cuts are less certain; recipients may stash some away. Indeed, some analysts think consumers are saving a good chunk of their rebates.

Yet spending has its own disadvantages. There can be long lags between congressional approval of a program and the time the money gets spent. And government spending, insulated from market forces, can be highly inefficient, diminishing its positive benefits. A decade of failed public-works-spending programs in Japan has done much to discredit the idea.

Q: What is the best kind of tax cut?

A: One that is likely to be spent quickly.

— Jacob M. Schlesinger

Source: *The Wall Street Journal,* September 11, 2001. Reprinted by permission of The Wall Street Journal. © 2001 Dow Jones & Company. All rights reserved worldwide. www.wsj.com

Analysis: The federal government has many policy levers at its disposal; they aren't certain to work as intended or on time, however.

Case 3: Stagflation

stagflation: The simultaneous occurrence of substantial unemployment and inflation.

Although serious inflations and recessions provide clear mandates for economic policy, there's a vast gray area between these extremes. Occasionally, the economy suffers from both inflation and unemployment at the same time, a condition called **stagflation.** In 1980, for example, the unemployment rate (7.1 percent) and the inflation rate (12.5 percent) were both too high. With an upward-sloping aggregate supply curve, the easy policy options were foreclosed. If aggregate demand were stimulated to reduce unemployment, the resultant pressure on prices might fuel the existing inflation. And if fiscal and monetary restraints were used to reduce inflationary pressures, unemployment might worsen. In such a situation, there are no simple solutions.

Knowing the causes of stagflation will help achieve the desired balance. If prices are rising before full employment is reached, some degree of structural unemployment is likely. An appropriate policy response might include more vocational training in skill-shortage areas as well as a redirection of aggregate demand toward labor-surplus sectors.

High tax rates or costly regulations might also contribute to stagflation. If either constraint exists, high prices (inflation) may not be a sufficient incentive for increased output. In this case, reductions in tax rates and regulation might help reduce both unemployment and inflation, which is the basic goal of supply-side policies.

Analysis: There are different theories about when and how the government should "fix" the economy. Policymakers must decide which advice to follow in specific situations.

Stagflation may also arise from a temporary contraction of aggregate supply that both reduces output and drives up prices. In this case, neither structural unemployment nor excessive demand is the culprit. Rather, an "external shock" (such as a natural disaster or a terrorist attack) or an abrupt change in world trade (such as an oil embargo) is likely to be the cause of the policy dilemma. Accordingly, none of our familiar policy tools is likely to provide a complete "cure." In most cases, the economy simply has to adjust to a temporary setback.

The apparently inexhaustible potential of public policy to alter the economy's performance has often generated optimistic expectations about the efficacy of fiscal, monetary, and supply-side tools. In the early 1960s, such optimism pervaded even the highest levels of government. Those were the days when prices were relatively stable, unemployment rates were falling, the economy was growing rapidly, and preparations were being made for the first trip into space. The potential of economic policy looked great indeed. It was also during the 1960s that a lot of people (mostly economists) spoke of the potential for **fine-tuning,** or altering economic outcomes to fit very exacting specifications. Flexible responses to changing market conditions, it was argued, could ensure fulfillment of our economic goals. The prescription was simple: When unemployment is the problem, simply give the economy a jolt of fiscal or monetary stimulus; when inflation is worrisome, simply tap on the fiscal or monetary brakes. To fulfill our goals for content and distribution, we simply pick the right target for stimulus or restraint. With a little attention and experience, the right speed could be found and the economy guided successfully down the road to prosperity. As the economic expansion of the 1990s stretched into the record books, the same kind of economic mastery was claimed. More that a few prominent economists claimed the business cycle was dead.

Fine-Tuning

fine-tuning: Adjustments in economic policy designed to counteract small changes in economic outcomes; continuous responses to changing economic conditions.

THE ECONOMIC RECORD

The economy's track record doesn't live up to these high expectations. To be sure, the economy has continued to grow and we've attained an impressive standard of living. We can't lose sight of the fact that our per capita income greatly exceeds the realities and even the expectations in most other countries of the world. Nevertheless, we must also recognize that our economic history is punctuated by periods of recession, high unemployment, inflation, and recurring concern for the distribution of income and mix of output.

The graphs in Figure 19.1 provide a quick summary of the gap between the theory and reality of economic policy. The Employment Act of 1946 committed the federal

FIGURE 19.1
The Economic Record

The Full Employment and Balanced Growth Act of 1978 established specific goals for unemployment (4 percent), inflation (3 percent), and economic growth (4 percent). We've rarely attained those goals, however, as these graphs illustrate. Measurement, design, and policy implementation problems help explain these shortcomings.

Source: *Economic Report of the President, 2001.*

government to macro stability. It's evident that we haven't kept that commitment. In the 1970s we rarely came close. Although we approached all three goals in the mid-1980s, our achievements were short-lived. Economic growth ground to a halt in 1989, and the economy slipped into yet another recession in 1990. Although inflation stayed low, unemployment rates jumped.

The economy performed very well again from 1992 until early 2000. After that, however, growth came to an abrupt halt again. With the economy teetering on recession, the unemployment rate started rising in mid-2000. Some of the people who had proclaimed the business cycle to be dead were out of work. Then the economy was hit by the external shock of a terrorist attack that suspended economic activity and shook investor and consumer confidence.

Looking back over the entire postwar period, the record includes nine years of outright recession (actual declines in output) and another 19 years of **growth recession** (growth of less than 3 percent). Moreover, the distribution of income in 2000 looked virtually identical to that of 1946, and nearly 30 million people were still officially counted as poor in the later year.

The economic performance of the United States was better than that of other Western nations in the 1990s. The economies of most countries didn't grow as fast as the U.S. economy in the 1990s. But, as the accompanying World View shows, some countries did a better job of restraining prices.

growth recession: A period during which real GDP grows, but at a rate below the long-term trend of 3 percent.

Macro Performance in the 1990s

The performance of the U.S. economy in the 1990s was better than most developed economies. Japan had the greatest success in restraining inflation (1.2 percent) but suffered from sluggish growth (1.5 percent per year). The United States grew faster and also experienced less unemployment than most European countries.

Performance (annual average percentage)	U.S.	Japan	Germany	United Kingdom	France	Italy	Canada
Real growth	2.4	1.5	2.4	1.6	1.8	1.4	1.8
Inflation	3.0	1.2	2.5	3.9	2.0	4.1	2.2
Unemployment	5.8	3.0	9.0	7.3	11.2	11.4	9.7

Source: International Monetary Fund. www.imf.org

Analysis: Macroeconomic performance varies a lot, both over time and across countries. In the 1990s, U.S. economic performance was above average on most measures.

When one looks at the specific policy initiatives of various administrations, the gap between theory and practice is even larger. The Fed's decision to reduce the money supply on repeated occasions during the Great Depression was colossally perverse. Only slightly less so was the Fed's decision to expand the money supply rapidly in 1978, despite evidence that inflationary pressures were already building up. During 1980–81 and again in 1989–90, the Fed slowed money supply growth much more and far longer than was justified. As a consequence, the economy suffered two consecutive recessions in the early 1980s and another one in the early 1990s. Pretty much the same sequence occured in 1999–2001.

On the fiscal side of the ledger, we must recall President Roosevelt's timid efforts to expand aggregate demand during the Great Depression. Also worth remembering is President Johnson's refusal to pay for the Vietnam War by either raising taxes or cutting nonmilitary expenditures. The resulting strain on the economy's capacity kindled inflationary pressures that lasted for years. For his part, President Carter increased labor costs (higher payroll taxes and minimum wages), farm prices, and government spending at a time when inflation was a foremost policy concern. President Reagan made his share of mistakes too, including the pursuit of deep budget cuts in the early stages of a recession. President George H. Bush ignored the recession for an entire year, believing that "self-adjustment" would ensure recovery. That mistake cost him his job.

President Clinton pushed through a tax increase in 1993 that helped subdue the recovery from the 1990–91 recession. He also caused the aggregate supply curve to shift upward by forcing employers to pay higher labor costs. President George W. Bush cut taxes and regulation to shift both aggregate supply and aggregate demand in the right direction. But his insistence on cutting the growth of federal spending in the midst of the 2001 recession was ill-timed (and ultimately reversed).

WHY THINGS DON'T ALWAYS WORK

There's plenty of blame to go around for all the blemishes on our economic record. Some people blame the Fed, others blame Congress, still others blame Japan or Mexico.

Some forces, however, constrain economic policy even when no one is specifically to blame. In this regard, we can distinguish *four obstacles to policy success:*

- *Goal conflicts*
- *Measurement problems*
- *Design problems*
- *Implementation problems*

Goal Conflicts

The first factor to take note of is potential conflicts in policy priorities. President Clinton had to confront this problem his first day in office. He had pledged to create new jobs by increasing public infrastructure spending and offering a middle-class tax cut. He had also promised to reduce the deficit, however. This created a clear goal conflict. In the end, President Clinton had to settle for a smaller increase in infrastructure spending and a tax *increase.* President George W. Bush confronted a similar problem. In the 2000 presidential campaign he had promised a big increase in federal spending on education. By the time he took office, however, the federal budget surplus was rapidly shrinking, and the goal of preserving the non–Social Security ("off budget") surplus took precedence.

These and other goal conflicts have their origin in the short-run trade-off between unemployment and inflation. Should we try to cure inflation, unemployment, or just a bit of both? Answers are likely to vary. Unemployed people put the highest priority on attaining full employment. Labor unions press for faster economic growth. Bankers, creditors, and people on fixed incomes demand an end to inflation.

This goal conflict is often institutionalized in the decision-making process. The Fed is traditionally viewed as the guardian of price stability. The president and Congress worry more about people's jobs and government programs, so they are less willing to raise taxes or cut spending.

Distributional goals may also conflict with macro objectives. Anti-inflationary policies may require cutbacks in programs for the poor, the elderly, or needy students. These cutbacks may be politically impossible (see News). Likewise, tight-money policies may be viewed as too great a burden for small businesses.

Deficit-Cutting Wilts in Heat from Voters
Entitlements Remain Mostly Off-Limits

In April, Sen. Pete V. Domenici (R-N.M.) suggested a plan for digging out of the massive federal deficit. His idea seemed modest on its face but was revolutionary by Washington standards.

Domenici proposed capping cost-of-living increases in entitlement programs, the automatic spending engines such as Medicaid, Medicare and federal retirement that are exempt from annual congressional review. . . .

Even before his proposal took shape, more than 3,000 New Mexico constituents sent him identical postcards opposing any effort to cap entitlement programs.

The National Council of Senior Citizens dubbed the plan "the most outrageous attack on the elderly we have seen in years." The Veterans of Foreign Wars expressed "shock and outrage." Milk producers accused Domenici of trying to balance the budget "on the back of farmers."

That was enough for the Senate, which voted 69 to 28 to reject the proposal.

—Eric Pianin

Source: *Washington Post*, August 4, 1992. © 1992 The Washington Post. Reprinted with permission. www.washingtonpost.com

Analysis: Changes in economic policy inevitably alter incomes and stir political opposition. Cuts in spending are particularly difficult to enact.

Although the policy levers in Table 19.1 are powerful, they can't grant all our wishes. Since we still live in a world of scarce resources, **all policy decisions entail opportunity costs,** which means that we'll always be confronted with trade-offs. The best we can hope for is a set of compromises that yields *optimal* outcomes, not ideal ones.

Measurement Problems

One reason firefighters are pretty successful in putting out fires before entire cities burn down is that fires are highly visible phenomena. But such visibility isn't characteristic of economic problems. An increase in the unemployment rate from 5 to 6 percent, for example, isn't the kind of thing you notice while crossing the street. Unless you work in the unemployment insurance office or lose your own job, the increase in unemployment isn't likely to attract your attention. The same is true of prices; small increases in product prices aren't likely to ring many alarms. Hence, both inflation and unemployment may worsen considerably before anyone takes serious notice. Were we as slow and ill-equipped to notice fires, whole neighborhoods would burn before someone rang the alarm.

Measurement problems are a very basic policy constraint. To formulate appropriate economic policy, we must first determine the nature of our problems. To do so, we must measure employment changes, output changes, price changes, and other macro outcomes. The old adage that governments are willing and able to solve only those problems they can measure is relevant here. Indeed, before the Great Depression, a fundamental constraint on public policy was the lack of statistics on what was happening in the economy. One lasting benefit of that experience is that we now try to keep informed on changing economic conditions. The information at hand, however, is always dated and incomplete. *At best, we know what was happening in the economy last month or last week.* The processes of data collection, assembly, and presentation take time, even in this age of high-speed computers. The average recession lasts about 11 months, but official data generally don't even confirm the existence of a recession until 8 months after a downturn starts! The recession of 1990–91 was no exception (see News).

Forecasts. In an ideal world, policymakers wouldn't just *respond* to economic problems but would also *anticipate* their occurrence. If an inflationary GDP gap is emerging, for example, we want to take immediate action to keep aggregate spending from increasing. That is, the successful firefighter not only responds to a fire but also looks for hazards that might start one.

Unfortunately, economic policymakers are again at a disadvantage. Their knowledge of future problems is even worse than their knowledge of current problems. *In designing policy, policymakers must depend on economic forecasts,* that is, informed guesses about what the economy will look like in future periods.

IN THE NEWS

This Just In: Recession Ended 21 Months Ago

WASHINGTON—Here's proof that economics is an inexact science. An official panel of economists determined today that the nation's ninth postwar recession ended a month before they realized it had started. And it took 21 months to sort all this out.

The dating committee of the National Bureau of Economic Research declared today that the recession had ended in March 1991—the month before it even announced there was a recession. The committee determined in April 1991 that the recession had begun in the previous July.

—Robert D. Hershey, Jr.

Source: *New York Times,* December 23, 1992. © 1992 The New York Times Company. Reprinted with permission. www.nytimes.com

Analysis: In the absence of timely information, today's policy decisions are inevitably based on yesterday's perceptions.

IN THE NEWS

Tough Calls in Economic Forecasting
Seers Often Peer into Cracked Crystal Balls

In presenting his annual economic outlook last Thursday, the chairman of President Clinton's Council of Economic Advisers was having nothing to do with all the recession talk going around.

"Let me be clear," Martin Baily said, "we don't think that we're going into recession."

The same message was delivered the next day by Clinton in a Rose Garden economic valedictory. Citing the predictions of 50 private forecasters known as the Blue Chip Consensus—"the experts who make a living doing this," as he put it—Clinton assured Americans that the economy would continue to grow this year at an annual rate of 2 percent to 3 percent.

What the president and his adviser failed to mention was that "the experts" have not predicted any of the nine recessions since the end of World War II. . . .

Allen Sinai of Decision Economics, a respected private forecaster, agreed. "Its probably only fair for forecasters to admit at times like this that we're simply not well equipped to predict turning points," he said. "A recession, by its nature, is a speculative call."

On first blush, such humility may seem at odds with the aura surrounding the modern day forecaster. Using high-speed computers and sophisticated models of the U.S. economy, they constantly revise their two-year predictions for everything from unemployment to business investment to long-term interest rates, expressed numerically to the first decimal point.

But according to the forecasters themselves, what may appear to be a precise science is a black art, one that is constantly confounded by the changing structure of the economy and the refusal of investors, consumers and business executives to behave as rationally and predictably in real life as they do in the economic models.

The reason we have trouble calling recessions is that all recessions are anomalies," said Joel Prakken, president of Macroeconomic Advisers of St. Louis, one of the nation's leading forecasting firms.

—Steven Peablstein

Source: *Washington Post*, January 15, 2001. © 2001 The Washington Post. Reprinted with permission. www.washingtonpost.com

Analysis: Even the most sophisticated computer models rely on basic assumptions about consumer and investor behavior. If the assumptions are wrong, the forecasts will likely be wrong as well (as they were in early 2001).

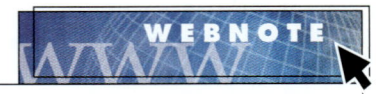

For an overview of the forecasting model the Congressional Budget Office uses, visit www.cbo.gov and search for the 2001 report, "Description of Economic Models."

Macro Models. Those guesses are often based on complex computer models of how the economy works. These models—referred to as *econometric macro models*—are mathematical summaries of the economy's performance. The models try to identify the key determinants of macro performance and then show what happens to macro outcomes when they change. As the accompanying News suggests, the apparent precision of such computer models may disguise "a black art."

An economist "feeds" the computer two essential inputs. One is a quantitative model of how the economy allegedly works. A Keynesian model, for example, includes equations that show multiplier spending responses to tax cuts. A monetarist model shows that tax cuts raise interest rates, not total spending ("crowding out"), and a supply-side model stipulates labor-supply and production responses. The computer can't tell which theory is right; it just predicts what it's programmed to see. In other words, the computer sees the world through the eyes of its economic master.

The second essential input in a computer forecast is the assumed values for critical variables. A Keynesian model, for example, must specify how large a multiplier to expect. All the computer does is carry out the required mathematical routines, once it's told that the multiplier is relevant and what its value is. It can't discern the true multiplier any better than it can pick the right theory.

Given the dependence of computers on the theories and perceptions of their economic masters, it's not surprising that computer forecasts often differ greatly. It's also not surprising that they're often wrong. Even policymakers who are familiar with both economic theory and computer models can make some pretty bad calls. In January 1990, Fed chairman Alan Greenspan assured Congress that the risk of a recession was as low as 20 percent. Although he said he "wouldn't bet the ranch" on such a low probability, he was confident that the odds of a recession were below 50 percent; five months after his testimony, the 1990–91 recession began.

Leading Indicators. Given the complexity of macro models, many people prefer to use simpler tools for divining the future. One of the most popular is the Index of Leading Economic Indicators. As noted in Chapter 9 (see Table 9.2, page 192), the Leading Indicators are things we can observe today that are logically linked to future production (e.g., orders for new equipment). Unfortunately, the logical sequence of events doesn't always unfold as anticipated. All too often, the links in the chain of Leading Indicators are broken by changing expectations and unanticipated events.

Crystal Balls. In view of the fragile foundations and spotty record of computer and index-based forecasts, many people shun them altogether, preferring to use their own "crystal balls." The Foundation for the Study of Cycles has identified 4,000 different crystal balls that people use to gauge the health of the economy, including the ratio of used-car to new-car sales (it rises in recession); the number of divorce petitions (it rises in bad times); animal population cycles (they peak just before economic downturns); and even the optimism/pessimism content of popular music (a reflection of consumer confidence). Corporate executives claim that such crystal balls are as valuable as professional economic forecasts. In a Gallup survey of CEOs, most respondents said economists' forecasts had little or no influence on company plans or policies. The head of one large company said, "I go out of my way to ignore them." The general public apparently shares this view, giving higher marks to the forecasts of sportswriters and weather forecasters than to those of economists.

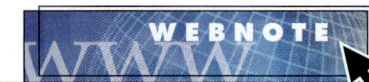

The Dismal Sciences company assembles economic forecasts and a broad array of economic statistics, along with user-friendly commentary. You can visit the company at www.dismal.com.

Economic forecasters defend themselves in two ways. First, they note that economic policy decisions are inevitably based on anticipated changes in the economy's performance. The decision to stimulate or restrain the economy can't be made by a flip of a coin; *someone* must try to foresee the future course of the economy. Second, forecasters claim that their quantitative approach is the only honest one. Because forecasting models require specific behavioral assumptions and estimates, they force people to spell out their versions of the future. Less rigorous ("gut feeling") approaches are too ambiguous and often inconsistent.

To review the latest forecasts of 50 noted economists, see the Blue Chip average at www.bluechippubs.com.

These are valid arguments. Still, one must be careful to distinguish the precision of computers from the inevitable uncertainties of their spoon-fed models. The basic law of the computer is GIGO: garbage in, garbage out. If the underlying models and assumptions are no good, the computer's forecasts won't be any better.

Policy and Forecasts. The task of forecasting the economic future is made still more complex by the interdependency of forecasts, policy decisions, and economic outcomes (see Figure 19.2). First, a forecast is made, based on current economic conditions, likely disturbances to the economy, and anticipated economic policy. These forecasts are then used to project likely budget deficits and other policy variables. Congress and the president react to these projections by revising fiscal, monetary, or supply-side policies. These changes, in turn, alter the basis for the initial forecasts.

This interdependence among forecasts, budget projections, and policy decisions was superbly illustrated in the early months of the George W. Bush presidency. At the beginning of 2001, both the White House and the Congress were forecasting enormous budget surpluses. The central policy debate focused on what to do with those surpluses. The Democrats wanted to spend the surplus; the Republicans wanted to give it back to households with larger tax cuts. As the debate dragged on, however, the weakening economy shrunk the surplus. In August 2001, the Congressional Budget Office (CBO) announced that the "on-budget" (non–Social Security) surplus it had forecast just seven months earlier had vanished. This forced both political parties to change their policy proposals. Protecting the vanishing surplus became the political priority. Spending proposals were scaled back, as were hopes of debt repayment.

FIGURE 19.2
The Mutual Dependence of Forecasts and Policy

Because tax revenues and government spending are sensitive to economic conditions, budget projections must rely on economic forecasts. The budget projections may alter policy decisions, however, and so change the basis for the initial forecasts. This interdependence between macro forecasts, budget projections, and policy decisions is virtually inevitable.

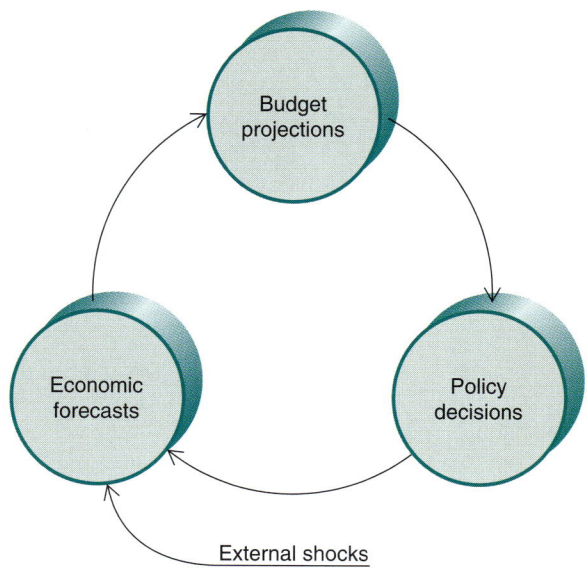

External Shocks. The CBO's forecasts of budget surpluses were already far wrong *before* the September 11, 2001, terrorist attack on the World Trade Center. That attack created an external shock that caused everyone to revise their economic forecasts. In the immediate aftermath of the attack, financial markets closed, air travel was suspended, sports events and concerts were canceled, businesses closed, and consumers stayed away from shopping malls. As a result, GDP declined, raising new fears of a global recession (see World View).

WORLD VIEW

Worldwide, Hope for Recovery Dims

Economic Shock in the U.S. May Trigger a Global Recession

The National Association for Business Economics was holding its annual meeting in the Marriott Hotel at the World Trade Center when disaster struck. "The chandeliers shook, we heard a concussive sound, and as we were herding out, we could see that one tower was burning," says Carl Tannenbaum, the chief economist of LaSalle Bank in Chicago, who was attending the meeting.

Just the day before, a panel of NABE economists had predicted slow growth, but no recession. That forecast was obsolete, however, the moment the first plane hit. In addition to destroying thousands of lives and billions of dollars in property, the terrorist attacks forced the shutdown of the financial markets, the temporary closure of U.S. businesses, and the grounding of air passenger and cargo traffic. Around the country, customers vanished from stores. With the U.S. already near zero growth, these impacts themselves are almost certain to tip the country into negative growth. "People are going to pause. And that pause is going to have a real impact on the third quarter and probably the fourth quarter," says Fred Poses, chairman and CEO of American Standard Companies.

A U.S. downturn will have repercussions all around the world. With Japan imploding economically, Asia in trouble, and Europe struggling, a recession in the U.S. would remove the last remaining source of demand from the global economy. "It's like throwing cold water on any prospects for a recovery," says Chang Il Hyung, senior vice-president of South Korea's Samsung Electronics Co., the world's largest memory chipmaker. With people around the globe watching the carnage in New York, consumer confidence and business investment could be hit everywhere. "Since the global economy is interwoven through trade and investment, all of us will be worse off," says Sung Won Sohn, chief economist at Wells Fargo & Co.

Source: *BusinessWeek*, September 24, 2001. © 2001 The McGraw-Hill Companies, Inc. Reprinted with permission. www.businessweek.com

Analysis: An external shock is by its very nature unanticipated. When it occurs, forecasts and policy decisions have to be revised.

The very nature of external *shocks* is that they are *unanticipated*. Hence, even if we knew enough about the economy to forecast "shockless" outcomes perfectly, an external shock could always disrupt the economy and ruin our forecasts. In reality, forecasting methods aren't even good enough to predict the behavior of a "shockless" economy with precision.

As the accompanying News reveals, the CBO's forecasting errors in 2001 were not an exception; they were the norm. When policymakers rely on such forecasts, they are likely to fail all too often.

Design Problems

Assume for the moment that we somehow are able to get a reliable forecast of where the economy is headed. The outlook, let's suppose, is bad. Now we're in the driver's seat to steer the economy past looming dangers. We need to chart our course—to design an economic plan. What action should we take? Which theory of macro behavior should guide us? How will the marketplace respond to any specific action we take?

Suppose, for example, that we adopt a Keynesian approach to ending a recession. Specifically, we cut income taxes to stimulate consumer spending. How do we know that consumers will respond as anticipated? In 1998, Japanese households used their tax cut to increase *savings* rather than consumption (see World View on the next page). In 2001, U.S. households were also slow to spend their tax rebates. When consumers don't respond as anticipated, the intended fiscal stimulus doesn't materialize. Such behavioral responses frustrate even the best-intentioned policy. The successful policymaker needs a very good crystal ball, one that will also foretell how market participants are going to respond to any specific actions taken.

For the latest CBO and Office of Management and Budget (OMB) macro forecasts, visit www.cbo.gov. Click on "Current Economic Projections."

Implementation Problems

Measurement and design problems can break the spirit of even the best policymaker (or the policymaker's economic advisers). Yet measurement and design problems are only part of the story. A good idea is of little value unless someone puts it to use. Accordingly, to understand fully why things go wrong, we must also consider the difficulties of *implementing* a well-designed policy.

Congressional Deliberations. Suppose that the president and his Council of Economic Advisers (perhaps in conjunction with the National Economic Council, the secretary of the Treasury, and the director of the Office of Management and Budget) decide that aggregate demand is slowing. A tax cut, they believe, is necessary to stimulate demand for goods and services. Can they simply go ahead and cut tax rates? No, because only the Congress can legislate tax changes. Once the president decides on the appropriate

CBO's Flawed Forecasts

Every year the Congressional Budget Office (CBO) forecasts the federal budget balance for the next five years. Those forecasts are rarely accurate. The typical CBO forecasting error for the *current* fiscal year amounts to 0.5 percent of GDP, or about $55 billion. Moreover, the errors widen for future years: For the *fifth* year out, CBO's forecasts typically miss the actual budget balance by a startling 3.1 percent of GDP. This implies that CBO's January 2001 forecast of the 2006 budget balance (a $505 billion surplus) will be off the mark by $412 billion!

Since 1981, CBO has both over- and underestimated federal budget balances. There has been a slightly pessimistic bias, however, especially in the boom years of 1992–2000. Forecasts from the president's Office of Management and Budget (OMB) haven't been any better.

Source: Congressional Budget Office, *The Budget and Economic Outlook, Fiscal Years 2002–2011.* www.cbo.gov

Analysis: The economic and budget forecasts that guide policy decisions are often flawed. This reduces the chances of policy success.

policy, he must ask Congress for authority to take the required action, which means a delay in implementing policy or possibly no policy at all.

At the very least, the president must convince Congress of the wisdom of his proposed policy. The tax proposal must work its way through separate committees of both the House of Representatives and the Senate, get on the congressional calendar, and be approved in each chamber. If there are important differences in Senate and House versions of the tax-cut legislation, they must be compromised in a joint conference. The modified proposal must then be returned to each chamber for approval (see News).

The same kind of process applies to the outlay side of the budget. Once the president has submitted his budget proposals (in January), Congress reviews them, then sets its own spending goals. After that, the budget is broken down into 13 different categories, and a separate appropriations bill is written for each one. These bills spell out in detail how much can be spent and for what purposes. Once Congress passes them, they go to the president for acceptance or veto.

Budget legislation requires Congress to finish these deliberations by October 1 (the beginning of the federal fiscal year), but Congress rarely meets this deadline. In most years, the budget debate continues well into the fiscal year. In some years, the budget debate isn't resolved until the fiscal year is nearly over! The final budget legislation is typically more than 1,000 pages long and so complex that few people understand all its dimensions.

Time Lags. This description of congressional activity isn't an outline for a civics course; rather, it's an important explanation of why economic policy isn't fully effective. *Even if the right policy is formulated to solve an emerging economic problem, there's no assurance that it will be implemented. And if it's implemented, there's no assurance that it will take effect at the right time.* Once of the most frightening prospects for economic policy is that a policy design intended to serve a specific problem will be im-

WORLD VIEW

Japanese Tighten Belts
Many Plan to Save, Not Spend, Tax Cut

CHIBA, Japan—The proof is not in the pudding. It's in the soy sauce.

Every day just about every Japanese person uses soy sauce, on rice and fish and chicken and in cooking. Yuzaburo Mogi, family patriarch of the famous Kikkoman brand, can tell by people's soy sauce-buying habits that his nation's economy is in deep trouble.

"Food companies are usually not hit by recession, but this time we are having trouble," said Mogi, whose family has been making soy sauce for more than 300 years. "People who usually buy expensive soy sauce are buying cheaper sauce. And people who bought our cheaper soy sauce are now buying other brands."

The declining soy sauce index is a useful indicator to explain why one of the world's richest countries is in so much trouble. The heart of why the economy is expected to shrink for the first time in a quarter-century is simple: People are spending less. . . .

Prime Minister Ryutaro Hashimoto aimed a $30 billion rescue effort directly at consumers last week. He proposed a tax cut that would give a typical household as much as $500 this year and again next year.

But housewives, retirees and salarymen in this Tokyo suburb are not impressed with Hashimoto's rescue. They said it will not move them to spend more.

In hours of discussions, they talked about why they started saving more: fear that more jobs will be lost and wages cut, distrust of the government's ability to correct structural problems in the economy and a growing feeling that if they do not look out for themselves, no one will.

—Mary Jordan and Kevin Sullivan

Source: *Washington Post,* April 14, 1998. © 1998 The Washington Post. Reprinted with permission. www.washingtonpost.com

Analysis: The success of macro policy depends on how market participants respond to policy initiatives. Japanese consumers didn't follow the Keynesian script.

Analysis: Fiscal policy decisions must be processed through lengthy administrative and congressional processes. This delays fiscal-policy responses to economic problems.

plemented much later, when economic conditions have changed. This isn't a remote danger. According to Christina Romer and Paul Romer, the Fed doesn't pull the monetary-stimulus lever until a recession is under way, and Congress is even slower in responding to an economic downturn. Indeed, a U.S. Treasury Department study concluded that almost every postwar fiscal stimulus package was enacted well after the end of the recession it was intended to cure!

Figure 19.3 is a schematic view of why macro policies don't always work as intended. There are always delays between the time a problem emerges and the time it's recognized. There are additional delays between recognition and response design, between design and implementation, and finally between implementation and impact. Not only may mistakes be made at each juncture, but even correct decisions may be overcome by changing economic conditions.

We can illustrate the processes in Figure 19.3 by considering how the income surtax of 1968 came about. The expansion of the Vietnam War in July 1965 added something

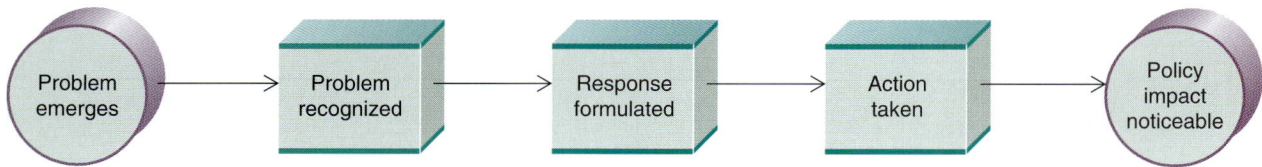

FIGURE 19.3
Policy Response: A Series of Time Lags

Even the best-intentioned economic policy can be frustrated by time lags. It takes time for a problem to be recognized, time to formulate a policy response, and still more time to implement that policy. By the time the policy begins to affect the economy, the underlying problem may have changed.

like $15 billion to aggregate demand at a time when the economy was already fully employed.[1] To offset resulting inflationary pressures, the president and Congress initiated some fiscal restraint, including the restoration of excise taxes on cars and telephones. Much stronger action was necessary, however. But President Lyndon Johnson insisted that the escalation of the war was temporary. From his perspective, the imposition of stronger fiscal restraints was tantamount to an admission that the war wouldn't be won quickly. Only after another 18 months of war did the administration propose further action. In January 1967, President Johnson called for a 6 percent surtax to correct the "imbalances created by the special pressures of Vietnam procurement." The problem that emerged in July 1965 wasn't recognized until 1966, and a response wasn't formulated until January 1967. Compounding these delays was the reluctance of Congress to help finance an undeclared war. Congress didn't take the requested action until June 1968. Thus, there was a three-year lag between the time the problem emerged and the policy response. In the interim, inflationary pressures worsened.

Politics vs. Economics. The delayed fiscal response to accelerated Vietnam expenditures also illustrates the very first barrier to policy implementation: *goal conflicts.* Just as the design of policy is compromised by conflicting interests, so too is the implementation of those designs. Especially noteworthy in this regard is the potential conflict of economic policy with political objectives. The conflict that existed between President Johnson's war objectives and his economic objectives is obvious. More generally, observers have noted that the president and Congress are reluctant to impose fiscal restraints (tax increases or budget cutbacks) in election years, regardless of economic circumstances. As the accompanying cartoon emphasizes, fiscal restraint is never popular.

The tendency of Congress to hold fiscal policy hostage to electoral concerns has created a pattern of short-run stops and starts—a kind of policy-induced business cycle. Indeed, some argue that the business cycle has been replaced with the political cycle: The economy is stimulated in the year of an election and then restrained in the postelection year. The conflict between the urgent need to get reelected and the necessity to manage the economy results in a seesaw kind of instability.

Even when the need for fiscal *stimulus* seems urgent—like after the September 11 terrorist attacks—politics can slow and distort the policy response. Two months after the attacks Republican and Democrat lawmakers were still far apart on how much fiscal stimulus to provide and what form the stimulus should take (see News). Critics feared that by the time Congress acted, the stimulus would be too late and possibly excessive.

In theory, the political independence of the Fed's Board of Governors provides some protection from ill-advised but politically advantageous policy initiatives. In practice, however, the Fed's relative obscurity and independence may backfire. The president and the Congress know that if they don't take effective action against inflation—by raising

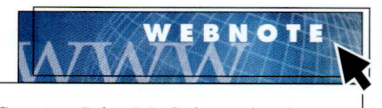

Senator John McCain maintains a list of political "pork" spending at www.senate.gov/~mccain/porkbar.htm

---
[1]This figure includes multiplier effects through the first quarter of 1966.

Analysis: Budget cuts are not popular with voters—even when economic conditions warrant fiscal restraint.

taxes or cutting government spending—the Fed can and will take stronger action to restrain aggregate demand. This is a classic case of having one's cake and eating it too. Elected officials win votes for not raising taxes or cutting some constituent's favorite spending program. They then take credit for any reduction in the rate of inflation brought about by Federal Reserve policies. To top it off, Congress and the president can also blame the Fed for driving up interest rates or starting a recession if monetary policy becomes too restrictive!

Finally, we must recognize that policy design is obstructed by a certain lack of will. Neither people on the street nor elected public officials focus constantly on economic goals and activities. Even students enrolled in economics courses have a hard time keeping their minds on the economy and its problems. The executive and legislative branches of government, for their part, are likely to focus on economic concerns only when eco-

IN THE NEWS

Stimulus Package Stalled over Tax Breaks, Spending

WASHINGTON—A multibilliondollar economic stimulus package aimed at energizing the faltering economy, helping the unemployed and giving low-income workers a tax rebate faces a stalemate in a deeply divided Senate this week.

Democrats and Republicans said Tuesday that bipartisan negotiations are needed if Congress is to find agreement on a bill that President Bush wants passed by the end of the month. But the two parties remain so far apart that they are only talking about talking, not actually working out a solution.

Democrats lack the votes to pass their $66.4 billion tax package and an additional $20 billion in domestic security spending that they want to attach. Republicans don't have enough votes for their alternative, either.

The problem for both sides: Passing anything in the Senate, controlled 50-49 by Democrats with one independent, requires consensus. Either side can invoke Senate rules that set a 60-vote hurdle, rather than a simple majority, for passage.

How does either side get there? "That's a good question," Sen. Daschle said. "Neither side has 60 votes at this point. So we know we've got to work together. . . ".

Adding to the disarray is a dispute over the Democrats' proposal to spend $20 billion more on homeland security, which Bush vowed to veto last week. Republicans say Democrats have simply dusted off old wish lists for public works and pork-barrel projects. And they say Democrats have even more spending cloaked in their tax bill, including $6 billion in farm aid that provides subsidies to bison ranchers.

"I thought this was going to be a stimulus package instead of a pork package," Lott said.

— William M. Welch

Source: *USA Today*, November 14, 2001. © 2001 USA Today. Reprinted with permission. www.usatoday.com

Analysis: Political disputes over the size and content of budget initiatives can slow and distort economic policy responses.

nomic problems become serious or voters demand action. Otherwise, policymakers are apt to be complacent about economic policy as long as economic performance is within a tolerable range of desired outcomes.

THE ECONOMY TOMORROW

Hands On or Hands Off?

In view of the goal conflicts and the measurement, design, and implementation problems that policymakers confront, it's less surprising that things sometimes go wrong than that things so often work out right. The maze of obstacles through which theory must pass before it becomes policy explains many economic disappointments. On this basis alone, we may conclude that ***consistent fine-tuning of the economy isn't compatible with either our design capabilities or our decision-making procedures.*** We have exhibited a strong capability to avoid major economic disruptions in the last four decades. We haven't, however, been able to make all the minor adjustments necessary to fulfill our goals completely. As Arthur Burns, former chairman of the Fed's Board of Governors, said:

> There has been much loose talk of "fine tuning" when the state of knowledge permits us to predict only within a fairly broad level the course of economic development and the results of policy actions.[2]

Hands Off Some critics of economic policy take this argument a few steps further. If fine-tuning isn't really possible, they say, we should abandon discretionary policies altogether and follow fixed rules for fiscal and monetary intervention.

As we saw in Chapter 15, pure monetarism would require the Fed to increase the money supply at a constant rate. Critics of fiscal policy would require the government to maintain balanced budgets, or at least to offset deficits in sluggish years with surpluses in years of high growth. Such rules would prevent policymakers from over- or understimulating the economy. Such rules would also add a dose of certainty to the economic outlook.

Milton Friedman has been one of the most persistent advocates of fixed policy rules. With discretionary authority, Friedman argues,

> the wrong decision is likely to be made in a large fraction of cases because the decision-makers are examining only a limited area and not taking into account the cumulative consequences of the policy as a whole. On the other hand, if a general rule is adopted for a group of cases as a bundle, the existence of that rule has favorable effects on people's attitudes and beliefs and expectations that would not follow even from the discretionary adoption of precisely the same policy on a series of separate occasions.[3]

The case for a hands-off policy stance is based on practical, not theoretical, arguments. ***Everyone agrees that flexible, discretionary policies could result in better economic performance. But Friedman and others argue that the practical requirements of monetary and fiscal management are too demanding and thus prone to failure.*** Moreover, required policies may be compromised by political pressures.

New Classical Economics. Monetarist critiques of discretionary policy are echoed by a new perspective referred to as new classical economics (NCE). Classical economists saw no need for discretionary macro policy. In their view, the private sector is inherently stable and government intervention serves no purpose. New classical economics reaches the same conclusion. As Robert Barro, a proponent of NCE, put it: "It is best for the government to provide a stable environment, and then mainly stay out of the way."[4] Barro

---

[2]*Newsweek,* August 27, 1973, p. 4.
[3]Milten Friedman, *Capitalism and Freedom* (Chicago: University of Chicago Press, 1962), p. 53.
[4]Robert Barro, "Don't Fool with Money, Cut Taxes," *The Wall Street Journal,* November 21, 1991, p. A14.

and other NCE economists based this laissez-faire conclusion on the intriguing notion of **rational expectations.** This notion contends that people make decisions on the basis of all available information, including the *future* effects of *current* government policy.

Suppose, for example, that the Fed decided to increase the money supply in order to boost output. If people had rational expectations, they'd anticipate that this money supply growth will fuel inflation. To protect themselves, they'd immediately demand higher prices and wages. As a result, the stimulative monetary policy would fail to boost real output. (Monetarists reach the same conclusion but for different reasons; for monetarists, the countervailing forces are technological and institutional rather than rational expectations.)

Discretionary fiscal policy could be equally ineffective. Suppose Congress accelerated government spending in an effort to boost aggregate demand. Monetarists contend that the accompanying increase in the deficit would push interest rates up and crowd out private investment and consumption. New classical economists again reach the same conclusion via a different route. They contend that people with rational expectations would anticipate that a larger deficit now will necessitate tax increases in later years. To prepare for later tax bills, consumers will reduce spending now, thereby saving more. This "rational" reduction in consumption will offset the increased government expenditure, thus rendering fiscal policy ineffective.

If the new classical economists are right, then the only policy that works is one that surprises people—one that consumers and investors don't anticipate. But a policy based on surprises isn't very practical. Accordingly, new classical economists conclude that minimal policy intervention is best. This conclusion provides yet another guideline for policy decisions (see Table 19.5 for a roster of competing theories).

> **rational expectations:** Hypothesis that people's spending decisions are based on all available information, including the anticipated effects of government intervention.

Keynesians	Keynesians believe that the private sector is inherently unstable and prone to stagnate at low levels of output and employment. They want the government to manage aggregate demand with changes in taxes and government's spending.
Modern ("neo") Keynesians	Post–World War II followers of Keynes worry about inflation as well as recession. They urge budgetary restraint to cool an overheated economy. They also use monetary policy to change interest rates.
Monetarists	The money supply is their only heavy hitter. By changing the money supply, they can raise or lower the price level. Pure monetarists shun active policy, believing that it destabilizes the otherwise stable private sector. Output and employment gravitate to their natural levels.
Supply-siders	Incentives to work, invest, and produce are the key to their plays. Cuts in marginal tax rates and government regulation are used to expand production capacity, thereby increasing output and reducing inflationary pressures.
New classical economists	They say fine-tuning won't work because once the private sector realizes what the government is doing, it will act to offset it. They also question the credibility of quick-fix promises. They favor steady, predictable policies.
Marxists	Marxists contend that the failures of the economy are inherent in its capitalist structure. The owners of capital won't strive for full employment or a more equitable income distribution. Workers, without any capital, have little incentive to excel. This team proposes starting a new game, with entirely different rules.

TABLE 19.5
Who's on First? Labeling Economists
It sometimes hard to tell who's on what side in economic debates. Although some economists are proud to wear the colors of monetarists, Keynesians, or other teams, many economists shun such allegiances. Indeed, economists are often accused of playing on one team one day and on another team the next, making it hard to tell which team is at bat. To simplify matters, this guide may be used for quick identification of the players. Closer observation is advised, however, before choosing up teams.

Hands On

Proponents of a hands-on policy strategy acknowledge the possibility of occasional blunders. They emphasize, however, the greater risks of doing nothing when the economy is faltering. Some proponents of the quick fix even turn the new classical economics argument on its head. Even the wrong policy, they argue, might be better than doing nothing if enough market participants believed that *change* implied *progress*. They cite the jump in consumer confidence that followed the election of Bill Clinton, who had emphasized the need for a *change* in policy but hadn't spelled out the details of that change. The surge in confidence itself stimulated consumer purchases, even before President Clinton took office. The same kind of response occurred after the September 11, 2001, terrorist attacks. Consumers were dazed and insecure. There was a serious risk that they would curtail spending if the government didn't *do something*. Details aside, they just wanted reassurance that someone was taking charge of events. Quick responses by the Fed (increasing the money supply), the Congress (authorizing more spending), and President Bush (mobilizing security and military forces) kept consumer confidence from plunging.

Just doing *something* isn't the purpose of a hands-on policy, of course. Policy activists believe that we have enough knowledge about how the economy works to pull the right policy levers most of the time. They also point to the historical record. Our economic track record may not be perfect, but the historical record of prices, employment, and growth has improved since active fiscal and monetary policies were adopted. Without flexibility in the money supply and the budget, they argue, the economy would be less stable and our economic goals would remain unfulfilled.

The historical evidence for discretionary policy is ambiguous. Victor Zarnowitz showed that the U.S. economy has been much more stable since 1946 than it was in earlier periods (1875–1918 and 1919–1945).[5] Recessions have gotten shorter and economic expansions longer. But a variety of factors—including a shift from manufacturing to services, a larger government sector, and automatic stabilizers—have contributed to this improved macro performance. The contribution of discretionary macro policy is less clear. It's easy to observe what actually happened but almost impossible to determine what would have occurred in other circumstances.

Finally, one must contend with the difficulties inherent in adhering to any fixed rules. How is the Fed, for example, supposed to maintain a steady rate of growth in the money supply? As we observed in Chapter 13, people move their funds back and forth between different kinds of "money." Also, the demand for money is subject to unpredictable shifts. To maintain a steady rate of growth in M2 or any other measure of money would require superhuman foresight and responses. As former Fed chairman Paul Volcker told Congress, it would be "exceedingly dangerous and in fact practically impossible to eliminate substantial elements of discretion in the conduct of Federal Reserve policy."

The same is true of fiscal policy. Government spending and taxes are directly influenced by changes in unemployment, inflation, interest rates, and growth. These automatic stabilizers make it virtually impossible to maintain any fixed rule for budget balancing. Moreover, if we eliminated the automatic stabilizers, we'd risk greater instability.

Modest Expectations

The clamor for fixed policy rules is more a rebuke of past policy than a viable policy alternative. We really have no choice but to pursue discretionary policies. Recognition of measurement, design, and implementation problems is important for an understanding of the way the economy functions. Even though it's impossible to reach all our goals, we can't abandon conscientious attempts to get as close as possible to goal fulfillment. If public policy can create a few more jobs, a better mix of output, a little more growth and price stability, or an improved distribution of income, those initiatives are worthwhile.

---

[5]Victor Zarnowitz, *Facts and Factors in the Recent Evolution of the Business Cycle in the United States* (Cambridge, MA: National Bureau of Economic Research, 1989).

SUMMARY

- The government possesses an array of macro policy levers, each of which can significantly alter economic outcomes. To end a recession, we can cut taxes, expand the money supply, or increase government spending. To curb inflation, we can reverse each of these policy levers. To overcome stagflation, we can combine fiscal and monetary levers with improved supply-side incentives.
- Although the potential of economic theory seems impressive, the economic record doesn't look as good. Persistent unemployment, recurring economic slowdowns, and nagging inflation suggest that the realities of policy making are more difficult than theory implies.
- To some extent, the failures of economic policy are a reflection of scarce resources and competing goals. Even when consensus exists, however, serious obstacles to effective economic policy remain. These obstacles include

  (a) Measurement problems. Our knowledge of economic performance is always dated and incomplete.
  (b) Design problems. We don't know exactly how the economy will respond to specific policies.
  (c) Implementation problems. It takes time for Congress and the president to agree on an appropriate plan of action. Moreover, political needs may take precedence over economic needs.

  For all these reasons, discretionary policy rarely lives up to its theoretical potential.
- Monetarists and new classical economists favor rules rather than discretionary macro policies. They argue that discretionary policies are unlikely to work and risk being wrong. Critics respond that discretionary policies are needed to cope with ever-changing economic circumstances.

Key Terms

business cycle
fiscal policy
automatic stabilizer
structural deficit
fiscal stimulus
fiscal restraint

monetary policy
natural rate of unemployment
supply-side policy
recessionary GDP gap
multiplier

velocity of money (V)
inflationary GDP gap
stagflation
fine-tuning
growth recession
rational expectations

Questions for Discussion

1. What policies would Keynesian, monetarists, and supply-siders advocate for (a) restraining inflation, (b) reducing unemployment?
2. Why do policymakers respond so slowly to economic problems?
3. If policymakers have instant data on the economy's performance, should they respond immediately? Why or why not?
4. Suppose it's an election year and aggregate demand is growing so fast that it threatens to set off an inflationary movement. Why might Congress and the president hesitate to cut back on government spending or raise taxes, as economic theory suggests is appropriate?
5. In his fiscal 2002 budget, President Bush proposed increases in defense spending while arguing for cutbacks in total spending. Should military spending be subject to macroeconomic constraints? What programs should be expanded or contracted to bring about needed changes in the budget? Is this feasible?
6. Prior to assuming office, President-elect Clinton pledged to propose a tax credit for new investment during the first months of his administration. How might such an announcement affect the timing of investment decisions?
7. Suppose the government proposes to cut taxes while maintaining the current level of government expenditures. To finance this deficit, it may either (a) sell bonds to the public or (b) print new money (via Federal Reserve cooperation). What are the likely effects of each of these alternatives on each of the following? Would Keynesians, monetarists, and supply-siders give the same answers?
   (a) Interest rates
   (b) Consumer spending
   (c) Business investment
   (d) Aggregate demand
8. Suppose the economy is slumping into recession and needs a fiscal policy boost. Voters, however, are opposed to larger federal deficits. What should policymakers do?
9. How were each of the following affected by the 2001 terrorist attack on the World Trade Center? (See World View, page 400.)
   (a) Federal tax revenues
   (b) Federal spending
   (c) U.S. imports
   (d) Short-run GDP growth
   (e) Long-run GDP growth
10. According to the News on page 392, why did Murray Weidenbaum conclude that the government can't prevent recessions? Is he right?

Web Activities

1. Identify forecasts for the current year's GDP growth at (*a*) the Congressional Budget Office, www.cbo.gov, (*b*) Office of Management and Budget, www.whitehouse.gov/omb, (*c*) private economists, www.forecasts.org/gdp.htm. Do these forecasts differ? If so, what accounts for the different forecasts?
2. Log on to the Congressional Budget Office site at www.whitehouse.gov/omb/budget/fy2002/budiv_3.html. What is the projected GDP and budget balance for five years from now? According to the News article on page 401, by how much is the forecast likely to be in error?
3. Debate continues today between supply-siders and new Keynesians. Identify one supply-side argument in papers from the Heritage Foundation at www.taxation.org. Identify one new Keynesian argument in articles available through the Electronic Policy network at www.epn.org (click on "Economic Policy").

THE ACCOMPANYING STUDENT PROBLEM SET CONTAINS NUMERICAL AND GRAPHING PROBLEMS FOR THIS CHAPTER

PART 8

Product Markets: The Basics

The prices and products we see every day emerge from decisions made by millions of individual consumers and firms. A primary objective of microeconomic theory is to explain how those decisions are made. How do consumers decide which products to buy and in what quantities? What does it cost business firms to produce the goods and services consumers demand? Chapters 20 and 21 address these issues.

CHAPTER 20

The Demand for Goods

After the September 2001 terrorist attacks on the World Trade Center and the Pentagon, few Americans wanted to board an airplane. When U.S. airports reopened a week later, hardly any passengers showed up. Most planes departed with very light loads. Despite pleas from political and business leaders, consumers refused to fly. Then the airlines reduced airfares—to *really* low levels. Two weeks after the terrorist attacks, roundtrip cross-country fares got as low as $118, with no advance purchase or minimum-stay requirements. Suddenly, air travel regained popularity. Within days after the fare cuts, travelers started filling up the planes again.

The experience of the airlines underscores the importance of *prices* in determining consumer behavior. Consumers "want," "need," and "just have to have" a vast array of goods and services. When decision time comes, however, product *prices* often dictate what consumers will actually buy. As we observed in Chapter 3, the quantity of a product *demanded* depends on its price. When the airlines cut airfares in late September 2001, consumers purchased a *lot* more tickets.

This chapter takes a closer look at how product prices affect consumer decisions. We focus on three related questions:

- How do we decide how much of any good to buy?
- How does a change in a product's price affect the quantity we purchase or the amount of money we spend on it?
- Why do we buy certain products but not others?

The law of demand (first encountered in Chapter 3) gives us some clues for answering these questions. But we need to look beyond that law to fashion more complete answers. We need to know what forces give demand curves their downward-sloping shape. We also need to know more about how to *use* demand curves to predict consumer behavior.

DETERMINANTS OF DEMAND

In seeking explanations for consumer behavior, we have to recognize that the field of economics doesn't have all the answers. But it does offer a unique perspective that sets it apart from other fields of study.

The Sociopsychiatric Explanation

Consider first the explanations of consumer behavior offered by other fields of study. Psychiatrists and psychologists have had a virtual field day formulating such explanations. Freud was among the first to describe us humans as bundles of subconscious (and unconscious) fears, complexes, and anxieties. From a Freudian perspective, we strive for ever higher levels of consumption to satisfy basic drives for security, sex, and ego gratifications. Like the most primitive of people, we clothe and adorn ourselves in ways that assert our identity and worth. We eat and smoke too much because we need the oral gratifications and security associated with mother's breast. Oversized homes and cars give us a source of warmth and security remembered from the womb. On the other hand, we often buy and consume some things we expressly don't desire, just to assert our rebellious feelings against our parents (or parent substitutes). In Freud's view, it's the constant interplay of these id, ego, and superego drives that motivates us to buy, buy, buy.

Sociologists offer additional explanations for our consumption behavior. Lloyd Warner and David Riesman, for example, noted our yearning to stand above the crowd, to receive recognition from the masses. For people with exceptional talents, such recognition may come easily. But for the ordinary person, recognition may depend on conspicuous consumption. A sleek car, a newer fashion, a more exotic vacation become expressions of identity that provoke recognition, even social acceptance. We strive for ever higher levels of consumption—not just to keep up with the Joneses but to surpass them.

Not *all* consumption is motivated by ego or status concerns, of course. Some food is consumed for the sake of self-preservation, some clothing worn for warmth, and some housing built for shelter. The typical U.S. consumer has more than enough income to satisfy these basic needs. In today's economy, most consumers also have *discretionary* income that can be used to satisfy psychological or sociological longings. Single women are able to spend a lot of money on clothes and pets, and men spend freely on entertainment, food, and drink (see News). Teenagers show off their affluence in purchases of electronic goods, cars, and clothes (see Figure 20.1).

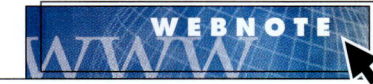

Each year the Bureau of Labor does another consumer expenditure survey. For the most recent data, visit www.bls.gov and first click on "Surveys and Programs" and then "prices and living conditions."

The Economic Explanation

Although psychiatrists and sociologists offer intriguing explanations for our consumption patterns, their explanations fall a bit short. Sociopsychiatric theories tell us why teenagers, men, and women *desire* certain goods and services. But they don't

Men vs. Women: How They Spend

Are men really different from women? If spending habits are any clue, males do differ from females. That's the conclusion one would draw from the latest Bureau of Labor Statistics (BLS) survey of consumer expenditure. Here's what BLS found out about the spending habits of young (under age 25) men and women who are living on their own:

Common Traits
- Young men have slightly more income to spend ($11,050) than do young women ($9,624). Both sexes go deep into debt, however, by spending $3,000–$4,000 more than their incomes.

- Neither sex spends much on charity, reading, or health care.

Distinctive Traits
- Young men spend 25 percent more at fast-food outlets, restaurants, and carryouts.
- Men spend twice as much on alcoholic beverages and smoking.
- Men spend twice as much as women do on television and stereo equipment.
- Young women spend a lot more money on clothing, personal care items and their pets.

Source: U.S. Bureau of Labor Statistics, 1998–1999, Consumer Expenditure Survey. www.bls.gov

Analysis: Consumer patterns vary by gender, age, and other characteristics. Economists try to isolate the common influences on consumer behavior.

FIGURE 20.1
Affluent Teenagers

Teenagers spend over $150 billion a year. Much of this spending is for cars, stereos, and other durables. The percentage of U.S. teenagers owning certain items is shown here.

Source: Teenage Research Unlimited (2000 data).

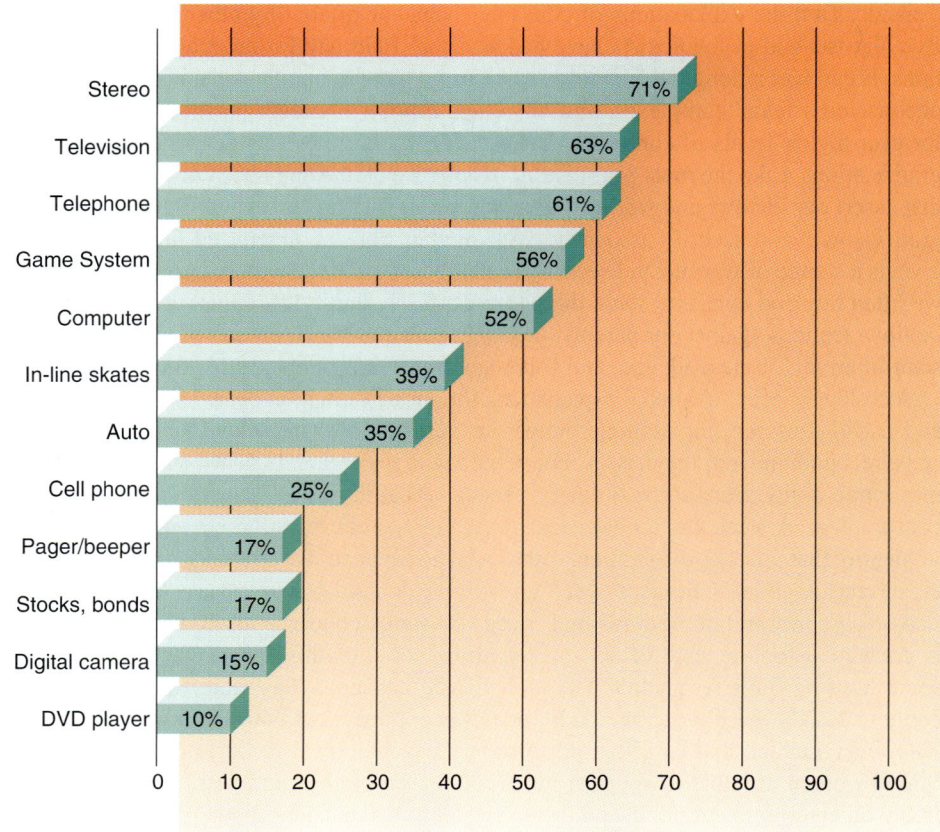

PERCENT OF TEENS OWNING PRODUCTS

explain which goods will actually be *purchased*. Desire is only the first step in the consumption process. To acquire goods and services, one must be willing and able to *pay* for one's wants. Producers won't give you their goods just to satisfy your Freudian desires. They want money in exchange for their goods. Hence, **prices and income are just as relevant to consumption decisions as are more basic desires and preferences.**

In explaining consumer behavior, economists focus on the *demand* for goods and services. As we observed in Chapter 3, **demand** entails the *willingness and ability to pay* for goods and services. To say that someone *demands* a particular good means that he or she will offer to *buy* it at some price(s). **An individual's demand for a specific product is determined by these four factors:**

- *Tastes* (desire for this and other goods).
- *Income* (of the consumer).
- *Expectations* (for income, prices, tastes).
- *Other goods* (their availability and prices).

Note again that desire (tastes) is only one determinant of demand. Other determinants of demand (income, expectations, and other goods) also influence whether a person will be willing and able to buy a certain good at a specific price.

The remainder of this chapter examines these determinants of demand. The objective is not only to explain consumer behavior but also to predict how consumption patterns change in response to *changes* in the price of a good or to *changes* in underlying tastes, income, prices or availability of other goods, or expectations.

demand: The willingness and ability to buy specific quantities of a good at alternative prices in a given time period, *ceteris paribus*.

THE DEMAND CURVE

The starting point for an economic analysis of demand is quite simple. Economists accept consumer tastes as the outcome of sociopsychiatric and cultural influences. They don't look beneath the surface to see how those tastes originated. Economists simply note the existence of certain tastes (desires) and then look to see how those tastes affect consumption decisions. The first observation is that the more pleasure a product gives us, the higher the price we'd be willing to pay for it. If the oral sensation of buttered popcorn at the movies really turns you on, you're likely to be willing to pay dearly for it. If, on the other hand, you have no great taste or desire for popcorn, the theater might have to give it away before you'd eat it.

Total vs. Marginal Utility. Economists use the term **utility** to refer to the expected pleasure, or satisfaction, obtained from goods and services. We also make an important distinction between total utility and marginal utility. **Total utility** refers to the amount of satisfaction obtained from your *entire* consumption of a product. By contrast, **marginal utility** refers to the amount of satisfaction you get from consuming the *last* (i.e., "marginal") unit of a product. More generally, note that

$$\frac{\text{Marginal utility}}{} = \frac{\text{change in total utility}}{\text{change in quantity}}$$

Diminishing Marginal Utility. The concepts of total and marginal utility explain not only why we buy popcorn at the movies but also why we stop eating it at some point. Even people who love popcorn (i.e., derive great *total* utility from it) don't eat endless quantities of it. Why not? Presumably because the thrill diminishes with each mouthful. The first box of popcorn may bring sensual gratification, but the second or third box is likely to bring a stomachache. We express this change in perceptions by noting that the *marginal* utility of the first box of popcorn is higher than the additional or *marginal* utility derived from the second box.

The behavior of popcorn connoisseurs isn't abnormal. As a rule, the amount of additional utility we obtain from a product declines as we continue to consume it. The third slice of pizza isn't as desirable as the first, the sixth beer not as satisfying as the fifth, and so forth. Indeed, this phenomenon of diminishing marginal utility is so nearly universal that economists have fashioned a law around it. This **law of diminishing marginal utility** states that each successive unit of a good consumed yields less *additional* utility.

The law of diminishing marginal utility does *not* say that we won't like the third box of popcorn, the second pizza slice, or the sixth beer; it just says we won't like them as much as the ones we've already consumed. Time is also important here: If the first pizza was eaten last year, the second pizza may now taste just as good. The law of diminishing marginal utility applies to short time periods.

Figure 20.2 illustrates how utility changes with the level of consumption. Notice that total utility continues to rise as we consume the first five boxes (ugh!) of popcorn. But total utility increases by smaller and smaller increments. Each successive step of the total utility curve in Figure 20.2 is a little smaller.

The height of each step of the total utility curve in Figure 20.2 represents *marginal* utility—the increments to total utility. *Marginal* utility is clearly diminishing. Nevertheless, because marginal utility is still *positive,* total utility is increasing. *As long as marginal utility is positive, total utility must be increasing* (note that the total utility curve is still rising for the fifth box of popcorn).

The situation changes with the sixth box of popcorn. According to Figure 20.2, the good sensations associated with popcorn consumption are completely forgotten by the time the sixth box arrives. Nausea and stomach cramps take over. Indeed, the sixth box is absolutely *distasteful,* as reflected in the downturn of *total* utility and the *negative* value for marginal utility. We were happier—in possession of more total utility—with

Utility Theory

utility: The pleasure or satisfaction obtained from a good or service.

total utility: The amount of satisfaction obtained from entire consumption of a product.

marginal utility: The change in total utility obtained by consuming one additional (marginal) unit of a good or service.

law of diminishing marginal utility: The marginal utility of a good declines as more of it is consumed in a given time period.

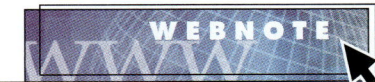

Do Americans have a taste for Jumbo Jacks? Go to facts at www.jackinthebox.com.

FIGURE 20.2
Total vs. Marginal Utility

The *total* utility derived from consuming a product comes from the *marginal* utilities of each successive unit. The total utility curve shows how each of the first five boxes of popcorn contributes to total utility. Note that each successive step is smaller. This reflects the law of diminishing marginal utility.

The sixth box of popcorn causes the total-utility steps to descend; the sixth box actually *reduces* total utility. This means that the sixth box has *negative* marginal utility.

The marginal utility curve (*b*) shows the change in total utility with each additional unit. It's derived from the total utility curve. Marginal utility here is positive but diminishing for the first five boxes.

only five boxes of popcorn. The sixth box—yielding *negative* marginal utility—reduces total satisfaction. This is the kind of sensation you'd probably experience if you ate six hamburgers (see cartoon).

Not every good ultimately reaches negative marginal utility. Yet the more general principle of diminishing marginal utility is experienced daily. That is, ***eventually additional quantities of a good yield increasingly smaller increments of satisfaction.***

Price and Quantity

Marginal utility is essentially a measure of how much we desire particular goods, our *taste*. But which ones will we buy? Clearly, we don't always buy the products we most desire. *Price* is often a problem. All too often we have to settle for goods that yield less marginal utility simply because they are available at a lower price. This explains why most people don't drive Porsches. Our desire ("taste") for a Porsche may be great, but its price is even greater. The challenge for most of us is to somehow reconcile our tastes with our bank balances.

In deciding whether to buy something, our immediate focus is typically on a single variable, namely *price*. Assume for the moment that a person's tastes, incomes, and expectations are set in stone, and that the prices of other goods are set as well. This is the **ceteris paribus** assumption we first encountered in Chapter 1. It doesn't mean that other influences on consumer behavior are unimportant. Rather, *ceteris paribus* simply allows us to focus on one variable at a time. In this case, we are focusing on price. What we want to know is how high a price a consumer is willing to pay for another unit of a product.

The concepts of marginal utility and *ceteris paribus* enable us to answer this question. The more marginal utility a product delivers, the more a consumer will be willing to pay for it. We also noted that marginal utility *diminishes* as increasing quantities of a product are consumed, suggesting that consumers willing to pay progressively *less* for additional quantities of a product. The moviegoer willing to pay 50 cents for that first

ceteris paribus: The assumption of nothing else changing.

Analysis: No matter how much we like a product, marginal utility is likely to diminish as we consume more of it. If marginal utility becomes *negative* (as here), total satisfaction will decrease.

mouth-watering ounce of buttered popcorn may not be willing to pay so much for a second or third ounce. The same is true for the second pizza, the sixth beer, and so forth. ***With given income, tastes, expectations, and prices of other goods and services, people are willing to buy additional quantities of a good only if its price falls.*** In other words, as the marginal utility of a good diminishes, so does our willingness to pay. This **law of demand** is illustrated in Figure 20.3 with the downward-sloping **demand curve.**

The law of demand and the law of diminishing marginal utility tell us nothing about why we crave popcorn or why our cravings subside. Those explanations are reserved for psychiatrists, sociologists, and physiologists. The laws of economics simply describe our market behavior.

PRICE ELASTICITY

The theory of demand helps explain consumer behavior. But it's not terribly helpful to the theater owner who's actually worried about popcorn sales. The general observation that popcorn sales decline when prices increase would be of little use. What the theater owner wants to know is *by how much* the quantity demanded would fall if the price were raised.

This is the same problem the airlines confronted after the September 2001 terrorist attacks. They knew more people would fly if airfares were reduced. But by *how much* did they have to cut fares to fill their planes again?

The central question in all these decisions is the response of quantity demanded to a change in price. ***The response of consumers to a change in price is measured by the price elasticity of demand.*** Specifically, the **price elasticity of demand** refers to

> **law of demand:** The quantity of a good demanded in a given time period increases as its price falls, *ceteris paribus.*

> **demand curve:** A curve describing the quantities of a good a consumer is willing and able to buy at alternative prices in a given period, *ceteris paribus.*

> **price elasticity of demand:** The percentage change in quantity demanded divided by the percentage change in price.

FIGURE 20.3
An Individual's Demand Schedule and Curve

Consumers are generally willing to buy larger quantities of a good at lower prices. This demand schedule illustrates the specific quantities demanded at alternative prices. If popcorn sold for 25 cents per ounce, this consumer would buy 12 ounces per show (row F). At higher prices, less popcorn would be purchased.

A downward-sloping demand curve expresses the law of demand: The quantity of a good demanded increases as its price falls. Notice that points A through J on the curve correspond to the rows of the demand schedule.

	Price (per ounce)	Quantity Demanded (ounces per show)
A	$0.50	1
B	0.45	2
C	0.40	4
D	0.35	6
E	0.30	9
F	0.25	12
G	0.20	16
H	0.15	20
I	0.10	25
J	0.05	30

the percentage change in quantity demanded divided by the percentage change in price—that is,

$$\text{Price elasticity } (E) = \frac{\% \text{ change in quantity demanded}}{\% \text{ change in price}}$$

What would the value of price elasticity be if air travel didn't change at all when price decreased by 5 percent? In that case the price elasticity of demand would be

$$E = \frac{\% \text{ change in quantity demanded}}{\% \text{ change in price}}$$

$$= \frac{0}{5} = 0$$

But is this realistic? According to the law of demand, the quantity demanded goes up when price goes down. So we'd expect *somebody* to buy more airline tickets if fares fell by 5 percent. In a large market like air travel, we don't expect *everybody* to jump on a plane when airfares are reduced. But if *some* consumers fly more, the percentage change in quantity demanded will be larger than zero. Indeed, **the law of demand implies that the price elasticity of demand will always be greater than zero.** Technically, the price elasticity of demand (E) would be a negative number since quantity demanded and price always move in opposite directions. For simplicity, however, E is typically expressed in absolute terms (without the minus sign). **The key question, then, is how much greater than zero E actually is.**

To get a feel for the dimensions of elasticity, let's return to the popcorn counter at the movies. We've already observed that at a price of 45 cents an ounce (point B in Figure 20.3), the average moviegoer demands 2 ounces of popcorn per show. At the lower price of 40 cents per ounce (point C), the quantity demanded jumps to 4 ounces per show.

We can summarize this response with the price elasticity of demand. To do so, we have to calculate the *percentage* changes in quantity and price. Consider the percentage change in quantity first. In this case, the change in quantity demanded is 4 ounces − 2 ounces = 2 ounces. The *percentage* change in quantity is therefore

$$\% \text{ change in quantity} = \frac{2}{q}$$

Computing Price Elasticity

The problem is to transform the denominator q into a number. Should we use the quantity of popcorn purchased *before* the price reduction, that is, $q_1 = 2$? Or should we use the quantity purchased *after* the price reduction, that is, $q_2 = 4$? The choice of denominator will have a big impact on the computed percentage change. To ensure consistency, economists prefer to use the *average* quantity in the denominator.[1] The average quantity is simply

$$\text{Average quantity} = \frac{q_1 + q_2}{2} = \frac{2 + 4}{2} = 3 \text{ ounces}$$

We can now complete the calculation of the percentage change in quantity demanded. It is

$$\frac{\% \text{ change in}}{\text{quantity demanded}} = \frac{\text{change in quantity}}{\text{average quantity}} = \frac{q_2 - q_1}{\frac{q_1 + q_2}{2}} = \frac{2}{3} = 0.667$$

Popcorn sales increased by an average of 67 percent when the price of popcorn was reduced from 45 cents to 40 cents per ounce.

The computation of the percentage change in price is similar. We first note that the price of popcorn fell by 5 cents (45¢ − 40¢) when we move from point B to point C on the demand curve (Figure 20.3). We then compute the *average* price of popcorn in this range of the demand curve as

$$\frac{\text{Average price}}{\text{of popcorn}} = \frac{p_1 + p_2}{2} = \frac{45 + 40}{2} = 42.5 \text{ cents}$$

This is our denominator in calculating the percentage price change. Using these numbers, we see that the absolute value of the percentage change is

$$\frac{\% \text{ change}}{\text{in price}} = \frac{\text{change in price}}{\text{average price}} = \frac{p_2 - p_1}{\frac{p_1 + p_2}{2}} = \frac{5}{42.5} = 0.118$$

The price of popcorn fell by 11.8 percent.

---

[1] This procedure is referred to as the *arc* (midpoint) elasticity of demand. If a single quantity (price) is used in the denominator, we refer to the *point* elasticity of demand.

Now we have all the information required to compute the price elasticity of demand. In this case,

$$E = \frac{\% \text{ change in demanded quantity}}{\% \text{ change in price}} = \frac{0.667}{0.118} = 5.65$$

What we get from all these calculations is a very useful number. It says that the consumer response to a price reduction will be extremely large. Specifically, the quantity of popcorn consumed will increase 5.65 times as fast as price falls. A 1 percent reduction in price brings about a 5.65 percent increase in purchases. The theater manager can therefore boost popcorn sales greatly by lowering price a little.

Elastic vs. Inelastic Demand. We characterize the demand for various goods in one of three ways: *elastic, inelastic,* or *unitary elastic.* If **E is larger than 1, demand is elastic.** Consumer response is large relative to the change in price.

If E is less than 1, we say demand is inelastic. *If demand is inelastic, consumers aren't very responsive to price changes.*

If E is equal to 1, demand is unitary elastic. In this case, the percentage change in quantity demanded is exactly equal to the percentage change in price.

Consider the case of smoking. Many smokers claim they'd "pay anything" for a cigarette after they've run out. But would they? Would they continue to smoke just as many cigarettes if prices doubled or tripled? If so, the demand curve would be vertical (as in Figure 20.4b) rather than downward sloping. Research suggests this is not the case: Higher cigarette prices *do* curb smoking. There is at least *some* elasticity in the demand for cigarettes. But the elasticity of demand is low; Table 20.1 indicates that the elasticity of cigarette demand is only 0.4.

Although the average adult smoker is not very responsive to changes in cigarette prices, teen smokers apparently are. As the accompanying News indicates, teen smoking drops by almost 7 percent when cigarette prices increase by 10 percent. Thus, the price elasticity of *teen* demand for smoking is

$$E = \frac{\text{percent drop in quantity demanded}}{\text{percent increase in price}} = \frac{7\%}{10\%} = 0.7$$

The American Cancer Society stages a Great American Smokeout every November. The society's goal is to help people, particularly teenagers, stop smoking. For statistics on smoking trends, visit www.cancer.org/smokeout/faq.html. Search for "Smoking."

FIGURE 20.4
Extremes of Elasticity

If demand were perfectly elastic ($E = \infty$), the demand curve would be *horizontal.* In that case, any increase in price (e.g., p_1 to p_2) would cause quantity demanded to fall to zero.

A *vertical* demand curve implies that an increase in price won't affect the quantity demanded. In this situation of completely *in*elastic ($E = 0$) demand, consumers are willing to pay *any* price to get the quantity q_1.

In reality, elasticities of demand for goods and services lie between these two extremes.

TABLE 20.1
Elasticity Estimates

Price elasticities vary greatly. When the price of gasoline increases, consumers reduce their consumption only slightly. When the price of fish increases, however, consumers cut back their consumption substantially. These differences reflect the availability of immediate substitutes, the prices of the goods, and the amount of time available for changing behavior.

Product	Price Elasticity
Relatively elastic (E > 1)	
Airline travel, long run	2.4
Restaurant meals	2.3
Fresh fish	2.2
New cars, short run	1.2–1.5
Unitary elastic (E = 1)	
Private education	1.1
Radios and televisions	1.2
Shoes	0.9
Movies	0.9
Relatively inelastic (E < 1)	
Cigarettes	0.4
Coffee	0.3
Gasoline, short run	0.2
Electricity (in homes)	0.1
Long-distance phone calls	0.1

Source: Compiled from Hendrick S. Houthakker and Lester D. Taylor, *Consumer Demand in the United States, 1929–1970* (Cambridge: Harvard University Press, 1966); F. W. Bell, "The Pope and Price of Fish," *American Economic Review*, December 1968; Herbert Scarf and John Shoven, *Applied General Equilibrium Analysis* (New York: Cambridge University Press, 1984); and Michael Ward, "Product Substitutability and Competition in Long-Distance Telecommunications," *Economic Inquiry*, October 1999.

Hence, higher cigarette prices can be an effective policy tool for curbing teen smoking. The drop in teen smoking after prices jumped in 1998 confirms this expectation.

According to Table 20.1, the demand for airline travel is even more price-elastic. Whenever a fare cut is announced, the airlines get swamped with telephone inquiries. If fares are discounted by 25 percent, the number of passengers may increase by as much as 60 percent. As Table 20.1 shows, the elasticity of airline demand is 2.4, meaning that the percentage change in quantity demanded (60 percent) will be 2.4 times larger than the price cut (25 percent).

IN THE NEWS

Dramatic Rise in Teenage Smoking

Smoking among youths in the United States rose precipitously starting in 1992 after declining for the previous 15 years. By 1997, the proportion of teenage smokers had risen by one-third from its 1991 trough.

A prominent explanation for the rise in youth smoking over the 1990s was a sharp decline in cigarette prices in the early 1990s, caused by a price war between the tobacco companies. Gruber and Zinman find that young people are very sensitive to the price of cigarettes in their smoking decisions. The authors estimate that for every 10 percent decline in the price, youth smoking rises by almost 7 percent, a much stronger price sensitivity than is typically found for adult smokers. As a result, the price decline of the early 1990s can explain about a quarter of the smoking rise from 1992 through 1997. Similarly, the significant decline in youth smoking observed in 1998 is at least partially explainable by the first steep rise in cigarette prices since the early 1990s. The authors also find that black youths and those with less educated parents are much more responsive to changes in cigarette prices than are white teens and those with more educated parents.

However, price does not appear to be an important determinant of smoking by younger teens. This may be because they are more experimental smokers.

Source: National Bureau of Economic Research, *NBER Digest*, October 2000. www.nber.org/digest

Analysis: The effectiveness of higher cigarette prices in curbing teen smoking depends on the price elasticity of demand.

Determinants of Elasticity

Why are consumers price-sensitive ($E > 1$) with some goods and not ($E < 1$) with others? To answer that, we must go back to the demand curve itself. The elasticity of demand is computed between points on a given demand curve. Hence, *the price elasticity of demand is influenced by all the determinants of demand.* Four factors are particularly worth noting.

Necessities vs. Luxuries. Some goods are so critical to our everyday life that we regard them as "necessities". A hair brush, toothpaste, and perhaps textbooks might fall into this category. Our "taste" for such goods is so strong that we can't imagine getting along without them. As a result, we don't change our consumption of "necessities" very much when the price increases; *demand for necessities is relatively inelastic.*

A "luxury" good, by contrast, is something we'd *like* to have but aren't likely to buy unless our income jumps or the price declines sharply, such as vacation travel, new cars, and HDTV sets. We want them but can get by without them. That is, *demand for luxury goods is relatively elastic.*

Availability of Substitutes. Our notion of which goods are necessities is also influenced by the availability of substitute goods. The high elasticity of demand for fish (Table 20.1) reflects the fact that consumers can always eat chicken, beef, or pork if fish prices rise. On the other hand, most coffee drinkers can't imagine any other product that could substitute for a cup of coffee. As a consequence, when coffee prices rise, consumers don't reduce their purchases very much at all. Likewise, the low elasticity of demand for gasoline reflects the fact that most cars can't run on alternative fuels. In general, *the greater the availability of substitutes, the higher the price elasticity of demand.* This is a principle that the Canadian government learned when it raised the price of cigarettes. As the World View explains, smugglers quickly supplied a substitute good and legal sales of cigarettes declined drastically.

Relative Price (to income). Another important determinant of elasticity is the price of the good in relation to a consumer's income. Airline travel and new cars are quite

WORLD VIEW

Cigarette Smuggling: A Lesson in Price Elasticity

Cigarette smuggling is flourishing again. In 2001, the state excise tax on cigarettes was only 2.5 cents per pack in Virginia and 3 cents in Kentucky. By contrast, the cigarette tax was $1.42 in Washington, $1.11 in New York, and $1 per pack in California, Alaska, and Hawaii. As a result, you could make money by buying cigarettes in low-tax states and reselling them in high-tax states. It's illegal but highly profitable to resell the cigarettes without paying all sales taxes. The U.S. Treasury estimates that hundreds of millions of cigarettes are smuggled across state lines.

Canada had the same problem. Between 1984 and 1993, the real price of Canadian cigarettes jumped from $2.64 to $5.65 per pack. The quantity legally demanded plummeted from 170 to 70 million cartons per year. But *consumption* didn't fall so much. Canadians evaded the tax hikes by exporting cigarettes to the United States (exports aren't taxed), then smuggling them back into Canada. Smugglers were reaping a profit of $500,000 per truckload.

In 1994, Canada cut cigarette taxes by $5 to $10 per carton. Shortly thereafter tax-free exports to the United States declined by 96 percent!

Source: The National Conference of State Legislatures publishes state excise tax rates @ www.ncsl.org/programs/health/cigarette.htm.

Analysis: If demand is price-elastic, a price increase will lead to a disproportionate drop in unit sales. In this case, the ready availability of substitutes (smuggled cigarettes) made demand highly price-elastic.

IN THE NEWS

Professor Becker Corrects President's Math

President Clinton has seized upon the cigarette excise tax as an expedient and politically correct means of increasing federal revenue. In 1994, the federal government took in $12 billion from the present 24-cents-per-pack tax. If the tax were quadrupled to $1 a pack, Clinton figures tax revenues would increase by more than $50 billion over three years. Those added revenues would help finance the health-care reforms the President so dearly wants.

Professor Gary Becker, a Nobel Prize–winning economist at the University of Chicago, says Clinton's math is wrong.

The White House assumed that cigarette sales would drop by 4 percent for every 10 percent increase in price. Professor Becker says that reflects only the first-year response to higher prices, not the full adjustment of smokers' behavior. Over a three-year period, cigarette consumption is likely to decline by 8 percent for every 10 percent increase in price—twice as much as Clinton assumed. As a result, the $1-a-pack tax will bring in much less revenue than President Clinton projected.

Source: *Business Week*, August 15, 1994. © 1994 The McGraw-Hill Companies, Inc. Reprinted with permission. www.businessweek.com

Analysis: It takes time for people to adjust their behavior to changed prices. Hence, the short-run price elasticity of demand is lower than the long-run elasticity.

---

expensive, so even a small percentage change in their prices can have a big impact on a consumer's budget (and consumption decisions). The demand for such "big-ticket" items tends to be elastic. By contrast, coffee is so cheap for most people that even a large *percentage* change in price doesn't affect consumer behavior very much.

Because the relative price of a good affects price elasticity, the value of E_1 *changes* along a given demand curve. At current prices the elasticity of demand for coffee is low. How would consumers behave, however, if coffee cost $5 a cup? Some people would still consume coffee. At such higher prices, however, the quantity demanded would be much more sensitive to price changes. Accordingly, when we observe, as in Table 20.1, that the demand for coffee is price-inelastic, that observation applies only to the current range of prices. Were coffee prices dramatically higher, the price elasticity of demand would be higher as well. As a rule, *the price elasticity of demand declines as price moves down the demand curve.*

Time. Finally, time affects the price elasticity of demand. Car owners can't switch to electric autos every time the price of gasoline goes up. In the short run, the elasticity of demand for gasoline is quite low. With more time to adjust, however, consumers can buy more fuel-efficient cars, relocate their homes or jobs, and even switch fuels. As a consequence, *the long-run price elasticity of demand is higher than the short-run elasticity.* Nobel Prize–winning economist Gary Becker used the distinction between long-run and short-run elasticities to explain why a proposed increase in cigarette excise taxes wouldn't generate nearly as much revenue as President Clinton expected (see News).

PRICE ELASTICITY AND TOTAL REVENUE

The concept of price elasticity refutes the popular misconception that producers charge the "highest price possible." Except in the very rare case of completely inelastic demand, this notion makes no sense. Indeed, higher prices may actually *lower* total sales revenue.

total revenue: The price of a product multiplied by the quantity sold in a given time period:

The **total revenue** of a seller is the amount of money received from product sales and is determined by the quantity of the product sold and the price at which it is sold:

$$\text{Total revenue} = \text{price} \times \text{quantity sold}$$

In the movie theater example, if the price of popcorn is 40 cents per ounce and only 4 ounces are sold, total revenue equals $1.60 per show. This revenue is illustrated by the shaded rectangle in Figure 20.5. (The area of a rectangle is equal to its height [p] times its width [q].)

Now consider what happens to total revenue when the price of popcorn is increased. From the law of demand, we know that an increase in price will lead to a decrease in quantity demanded. But what about total revenue? The change in total revenue depends on *how much* quantity demanded falls when price goes up.

Suppose we raise popcorn prices again, from 40 cents back to 45 cents. What happens to total revenue? At 40 cents per box, 4 ounces are sold (see Figure 20.5) and total revenue equals $1.60. If we increase the price to 45 cents, only 2 ounces are sold and total revenue drops to 90 cents. In this case, an increase in price leads to a *decrease* in total revenue. This new and smaller total revenue is illustrated by the dashed rectangle in Figure 20.5.

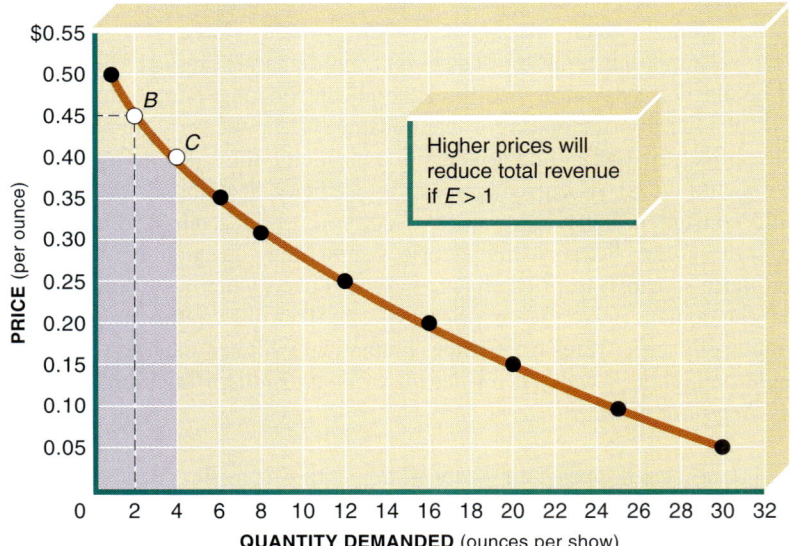

FIGURE 20.5
Elasticity and Total Revenue

Total revenue is equal to the price of the product times the quantity sold. It is illustrated by the area of the rectangle formed by $p \times q$. The shaded rectangle illustrates total revenue ($1.60) at a price of 40 cents and a quantity demanded of 4 ounces. When price is increased to 45 cents, the rectangle and total revenue shrink (see dashed lines) because demand is relatively elastic in that price range. Price hikes increase total revenue only if demand is inelastic.

	Price	×	Quantity Demanded	=	Total Revenue
A	50¢		1		$0.50
B	45		2		0.90
C	40		4		1.60
D	35		6		2.10
E	30		8		2.40
F	25		12		3.00
G	20		16		3.20
H	15		20		3.00
I	10		25		2.50
J	5		30		1.50

If Demand is	Effect on Total Revenue of	
	Price Increase	Price Reduction
Elastic ($E > 1$)	Decrease	Increase
Inelastic ($E < 1$)	Increase	Decrease
Unitary elastic ($E = 1$)	No change	No change

TABLE 20.2
Price Elasticity of Demand and Total Revenue
The impact of higher prices on total revenue depends on the price elasticity of demand. Higher prices result in higher total revenue only if demand is inelastic. If demand is elastic, *lower* prices result in *higher* revenues.

Price increases don't always lower total revenue. If consumer demand was relatively *inelastic* ($E < 1$), a price increase would lead to *higher* total revenue. Thus, we conclude that

- *A price hike increases total revenue only if demand is inelastic* **($E < 1$).**
- *A price hike reduces total revenue if demand is elastic* **($E > 1$).**
- *A price hike does not change total revenue if demand is unitary-elastic* **$E = 1$.**

Table 20.2 summarizes these and other responses to price changes.

Changing Value of E. Once we know the price elasticity of demand, we can predict how consumers will respond to changing prices. We can also predict what will happen to the total revenue of the seller when price is raised or reduced. Figure 20.6 shows how elasticity and total revenue change along a given demand curve. Demand for cigarettes is *elastic* ($E > 1$) at prices above $3 per pack but *inelastic* ($E < 1$) at lower prices.

The bottom half of Figure 20.6 shows how total revenue changes along the demand curve. At very high prices (e.g., $7 a pack), few cigarettes are sold and total revenue is low. As the price is reduced, however, the quantity demanded increases so much that total revenue *increases,* despite the lower price. With each price reduction from $7 down to $3 total revenue increases.

Price cuts below $3 a pack continue to increase the quantity demanded (the law of demand). The increase in unit sales is no longer large enough, however, to offset the price reductions. Total revenue starts falling after price drops below $3 per pack. The lesson to remember here is that *the impact of a price change on total revenue depends on the (changing) price elasticity of demand.*

OTHER ELASTICITIES

The price elasticity of demand tells us how consumers will respond to a change in the price of a good under the assumption of *ceteris paribus*. But other factors do change, and consumption behavior may respond to those changes as well.

We recognized this problem in Chapter 3 when we first distinguished *movements* along a demand curve from *shifts* of the demand curve. A movement along an unchanged demand curve represents consumer response to a change in the *price* of that specific good. The magnitude of that movement is expressed in the price elasticity of demand.

When the underlying determinants of demand change, the entire demand curve shifts. These shifts also alter consumer behavior. The *price* elasticity of demand is of no use in gauging these behavioral responses, since it refers to price changes (movements along a constant demand curve) for that good only.

Shifts vs. Movements

A change in any determinant of demand will shift the demand curve. Suppose consumer incomes were to increase. How would popcorn consumption be affected? Figure 20.7 provides an answer. Before the change in income, consumers demanded 12 ounces of popcorn at a price of 25 cents per ounce. With more income to spend, the new demand curve (D_2) suggests that consumers will now purchase a greater

Income Elasticity

FIGURE 20.6
Price Elasticity Changes along a Demand Curve

The concept of price elasticity can be used to determine whether people will spend more money on cigarettes when price rises. The answer to this question is yes and no, depending on how high the price goes.

Notice in the table and the graphs that total revenue rises when the price of cigarettes increases from $1 to $2 a pack and again to $3. At low prices, the demand for cigarettes appears relatively inelastic: Price and total revenue move in the same direction.

As the price of cigarettes continues to increase, however, total revenue starts to fall. As the price is increased from $3 to $4 a pack, total revenue drops. At higher prices, the demand for cigarettes is relatively elastic: Price and total revenue move in *opposite* directions. Hence, the price elasticity of demand depends on where one is on the demand curve.

(a) The demand curve

(b) Total revenue

Price of Cigarettes	×	Quantity Demanded	=	Total Revenue	
$1		100		$100 ⎫	Low elasticity
2		90		180 ⎬	(total revenue rising
3		70		210 ⎭	as price increases)
4		50		200 ⎫	High elasticity
5		25		125 ⎬	(total revenue falling
6		10		60 ⎪	as price increases)
7		6		42 ⎭	

shift in demand: A change in the quantity demanded at any (every) given price.

quantity of popcorn at every price. The increase in income has caused a rightward **shift in demand.** If popcorn continues to sell for 25 cents per ounce, consumers will now buy 16 ounces per show (point N) rather than only 12 ounces (point F).

It appears that changes in income have a substantial impact on consumer demand for popcorn. The graph in Figure 20.7 doesn't tell us, however, how large the change

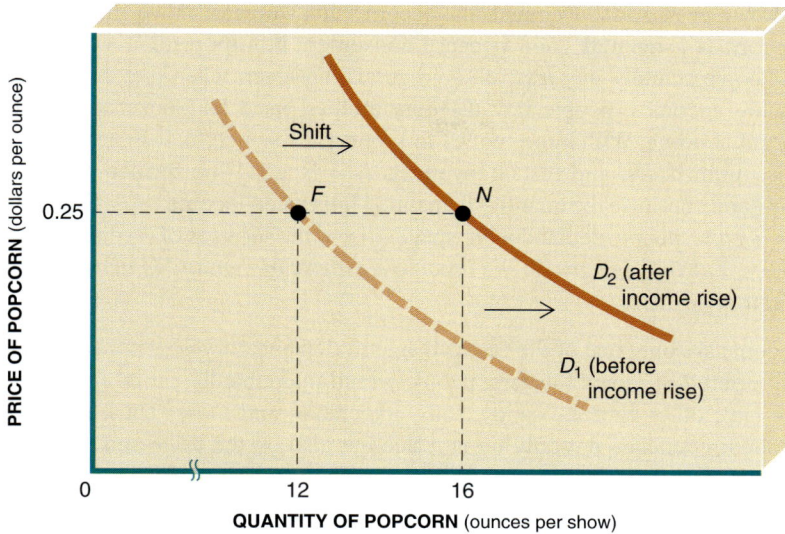

FIGURE 20.7
Income Elasticity

If income changes, the demand curve *shifts*. In this case, an increase in income enables consumers to buy more popcorn at every price. At a price of 25 cents, the quantity demanded increases from 12 ounces (point *F*) to 16 ounces (point *N*). The *income elasticity of demand* measures this response of demand to a change in income.

in income was. Will a *small* increase in income cause such a shift, or does popcorn demand increase only when moviegoers have a *lot* more money to spend?

Figure 20.7 doesn't answer these questions. But a little math will. Specifically, the **income elasticity of demand** relates the *percentage* change in quantity demanded to the *percentage* change in income—that is,

$$\text{Income elasticity of demand} = \frac{\%\text{ change in quantity demanded (at given price)}}{\%\text{ change in income}}$$

The similarity to the price elasticity of demand is apparent. In this case, however, the denominator is *income* (a determinant of demand), not *price*.

Computing Income Elasticity. As was the case with price elasticity, we compute income elasticity with *average* values for the changes in quantity and income. Suppose that the shift in popcorn demand illustrated in Figure 20.7 occurred when income increased from $110 per week to $120 per week. We would then compute

$$\text{Income elasticity} = \frac{\dfrac{\text{change in quantity demanded}}{\text{average quantity}}}{\dfrac{\text{change in income}}{\text{average income}}}$$

$$= \frac{\dfrac{16 \text{ ounces} - 12 \text{ ounces}}{14 \text{ ounces}}}{\dfrac{\$120 - \$110}{\$115}}$$

$$= \frac{4}{14} \div \frac{10}{115}$$

$$= \frac{0.286}{0.087} = 3.29$$

income elasticity of demand: Percentage change in quantity demanded divided by percentage change in income.

Popcorn purchases are very sensitive to changes in income. When incomes rise by 8.7 percent, popcorn sales increase by a whopping 28.6 percent (that is, 8.7% × 3.29). The computed elasticity of 3.29 summarizes this relationship.

normal good: Good for which demand increases when income rises.

inferior good: Good for which demand decreases when income rises.

Cross-Price Elasticity

substitute goods: Goods that substitute for each other; when the price of good X rises, the demand for good Y increases, *ceteris paribus*.

complementary goods: Goods frequently consumed in combination; when the price of good X rises, the demand for good Y falls, *ceteris paribus*.

Normal vs. Inferior Goods. Demand and income don't always move in the same direction. Popcorn is a **normal good** because consumers buy more of it when their incomes rise. People actually buy *less* of some goods, however, when they have more income. With low incomes, people buy discount clothes, used textbooks, and cheap beer, and they eat at home. With more money to spend, they switch to designer clothes, new books, premium beers, and restaurant meals (see News). The former items are called **inferior goods** because the quantity demanded falls when income rises. Similarly, when incomes *decline,* people demand *more* spaghetti and the services of credit agencies and pawnbrokers. *For inferior goods, the income elasticity of demand is negative; for normal goods, it is positive.*

Changes in income are only one of the forces that shift demand curves. If popcorn were the only snack offered in movie theaters, people would undoubtedly eat more of it. In reality, people have other choices: candy, soda, ice cream, and more. Thus, the decision to buy popcorn depends not only on its price but also on the price and availability of other goods.

Suppose for the moment that the prices of these other goods were to fall. Imagine that candy bars were put on sale for a quarter, rather than the usual dollar. Would this price reduction on candy affect the consumption of popcorn?

According to Figure 20.8, the demand for popcorn might *decrease* if the price of candy fell. The leftward shift of the demand curve from D_1 to D_2 tells us that consumers now demand less popcorn at every price. At 25 cents per ounce, consumers now demand only 8 ounces of popcorn (point R) rather than the previous 12 ounces (point F). In other words, a decline in the price of *candy* has caused a reduction in the demand for *popcorn.* We conclude that candy and popcorn are **substitute goods**—when the price of one declines, demand for the other falls.

Popcorn sales would follow a very different path if the price of soda fell. People like to wash down their popcorn with soda. When soda prices fall, moviegoers actually buy *more* popcorn. Here again, *a change in the price of one good affects the demand for another good.* In this case, however, we're dealing with **complementary goods,** since a decline in the price of one good causes an increase in the demand for the other good.

The distinction between substitute goods and complementary goods is illustrated in Figure 20.8. Note that *in the case of substitute goods the price of one good and the*

Stung by the Economy, Americans Lose Their Appetite for Dining Out

Restaurants' Sales Growth Slows as Consumers, Corporations Limit Nonessential Spending

Robin Gomes put her family on a budget last month, and that was bad news for restaurateurs.

Ms. Gomes, a 33-year-old home-loan coordinator in San Ramon, Calif., used to dine out with her husband and two children four times a week, dropping $50 to $60 a meal. Under the new budget, restaurant meals have been cut to once a week.

Far from being an isolated example, the Gomes family is part of a growing throng of stay-at-homes. As the shaky economy gives more consumers the jitters, the $258 billion restaurant and bar industry is grappling with its biggest slowdown in a decade. . . .

Growth in sales at restaurants and bars has declined steadily. For the 12 months ending this past Jan. 31, sales were 4.4 percent higher than the comparable year-earlier figure, according to figures from Technomic Inc., a Chicago food-consulting group, and the U.S. Census Bureau. But for the 12 months ending July 31, sales were only 2.4 percent above the prior 12-month period. Though sales are still above last year's, 2001 is shaping up to have the slowest growth since the 1991 recession, when sales dropped 1.2 percent. . . .

Upscale restaurants that thrived on corporate largesse are taking a big hit. Morton's Restaurant Group Inc., a chain of 61 steakhouses, saw same-store sales decline 9.6 percent in the second quarter.

—Shirley Leung

Source: *The Wall Street Journal,* August 22, 2001. Reprinted by permission of The Wall Street Journal. © 2001 Dow Jones & Company, Inc. All rights reserved worldwide. www.wsj.com

Analysis: Changes in income shift consumer demand curves. People buy fewer *normal* goods and more *inferior* goods when incomes decline.

FIGURE 20.8
Substitutes and Complements

The curve D_1 represents the initial demand for popcorn, given the prices of other goods. Other prices may change, however. If a reduction in the price of another good (candy) causes a *reduction* in the demand for this good (popcorn), the two goods are *substitutes*. Popcorn demand shifts to the left (to D_2) when the price of a substitute good falls.

If a reduction in the price of another good (e.g., Pepsi) leads to an *increase* in the demand for this good (popcorn), the two goods are *complements*. Popcorn demand shifts to the right (to D_3) when the price of a complementary good falls.

demand for the other move in the same direction. (A *decrease* in candy prices causes a *decrease* in popcorn demand.) Likewise, as the price of DVD players *declined*, the demand for digital videodisks (a complementary good) *increased* but the demand for videotapes and VCRs (substitute goods) *declined* (see News).

In the case of complementary goods (e.g., Pepsi and popcorn, cream and coffee), the price of one good and the demand for the other move in opposite directions. This helps explain why U.S. consumers bought more cars in 1998–99 when gasoline prices were falling and fewer cars in 2000 when gasoline prices were rising. The concept of complementary goods also explains why the demand for computer software increases when the price of computer hardware drops.

IN THE NEWS

DVD Sales Are Soaring As Prices Drop

Sales of digital video disks are soaring, fueled by dropping prices for the disks and players.

For the first eight months of the year, through Aug. 28, DVD sales had jumped to $127.7 million from $58.8 million a year earlier, research firm Alexander & Associates Inc. estimated. Studios are reissuing many old movies on DVD for as low as $10, and they sell disks of new movies within months of the films' theatrical release for as low as $20 each.

DVDs are so popular that Blockbuster Inc., the giant video-rental company, has been clearing shelves to make room. Blockbuster yesterday announced $450 million in charges against third- and fourth-quarter earnings partly for the cost of reducing its stock of older video tapes.

Catching On
Total number of DVD players sold to-date in the U.S. is 13.5 million. Annual sales of DVD players, in millions.

—Martin Peers

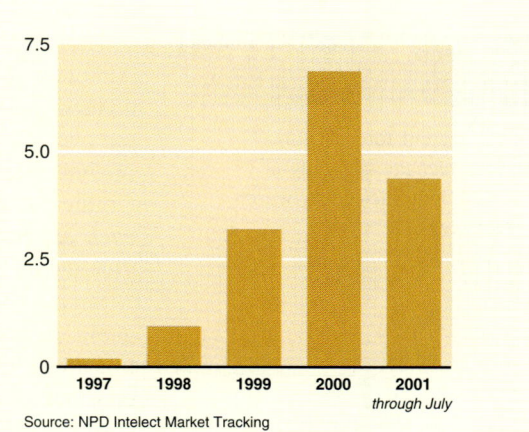

Source: NPD Intelect Market Tracking

Source: *The Wall Street Journal*, September 11 2001. Reprinted by permission of the Wall Street Journal. © 2001 Dow Jones & Company. All rights reserved worldwide. www.wsj.com

Analysis: DVD players and VCRs are *substitute goods*. As the price of DVDs falls, demand for VCRs will decline. Digital videodisks and DVD players are *complementary goods*.

cross-price elasticity of demand: Percentage change in the quantity demanded of X divided by percentage change in price of Y.

Calculating Cross-Price Elasticity. The mathmatical relationship between the price of one good and demand for another is summarized in yet another elasticity concept. The **cross-price elasticity of demand** is the *percentage* change in the quantity demanded on one good divided by the *percentage* change in the price of *another* good—that is,

$$\text{Income elasticity of demand} = \frac{\%\text{ change in quantity demanded of good X (at given price)}}{\%\text{ change in income}}$$

What has changed here is the denominator again. Now the denominator refers to a change in the price of *another* good rather than the *same* good.

The cross-price elasticity of demand makes it easy to distinguish substitute and complementary goods. If the cross-price elasticity is positive, the two goods are *substitutes;* if the cross-price elasticity is negative, the two goods are *complements*. Pepsi and popcorn are complements because a fall (−) in the price of one leads to an increase (+) in the demand for the other; in other words, the cross-price elasticity is negative.

CHOOSING AMONG PRODUCTS

Our analysis of demand thus far has focused on the decision to buy a single product, at varying prices. Actual consumer behavior is multidimensional, however, and therefore more complex. When we go shopping, our concern isn't limited to how much of one good to buy. Rather, we must decide *which* of many available goods to buy at their respective prices.

The presence of so many goods complicates consumption decisions. Our basic objective remains the same, however: We want to get as much satisfaction as possible from our available income. In striving for that objective, we have to recognize that the purchase of any single good means giving up the opportunity to buy more of other goods. In other words, consuming popcorn (or any other good) entails distinct **opportunity costs.**

opportunity cost: The most desired goods or services that are forgone in order to obtain something else.

Marginal Utility vs. Price

The economic explanation for consumer choice builds on the theory of marginal utility and the law of demand. Suppose you have a choice between buying a Coke and playing a video game. The first proposition of consumer choice simply states that if you think a Coke will be more satisfying than playing a video game, you'll prefer to buy the Coke. Hardly a revolutionary proposition.

The second postulate of consumer-choice theory takes into account market prices. Although you may *prefer* to drink a Coke rather than play a video game, one play of a video game is cheaper than a Coke. Under these circumstances, your budget may win out over your desires. There's nothing irrational about playing a video game instead of buying a more desirable Coke when you have a limited amount of income to spend. On the contrary, *rational behavior requires one to compare the anticipated utility of each expenditure with its price* and to choose those products which promise to provide the most pleasure for the amount of income available.

Find the current forecast for American teenage spending at www. demographics.com. Search for "teenagers."

Suppose your desire for a Coke is 1.5 times as great as your desire to play a video game. In economic terms, this means that the marginal utility of the first Coke is 1.5 times as high as the marginal utility of the first video game. Which one should you consume? Before reaching for the Coke, you'd better look at prices. What if a Coke cost 50 cents, while one play on a video game costs only 25 cents? In this case, you must pay *two* times as much for a Coke that gives only 1.5 times as much pleasure. This isn't a good deal. You could get more utility per dollar by playing video games.

The same kind of principle explains why some rich people drive around in a Ford rather than a shiny new Mercedes. The marginal utility (MU) of driving a Mercedes is substantially higher than the MU of driving a Ford. A nice Mercedes, however, costs about four times as much as a basic Ford. A rich person who drives a Ford must feel that driving a Mercedes is not four times as satisfying as driving a Ford. For such people, a Ford yields more *marginal utility per dollar spent*.

The key to utility maximization, then, isn't simply to buy the things you like best. Instead, you must compare goods on the basis of their marginal utility *and* price. ***To maximize utility, the consumer should choose that good which delivers the most marginal utility per dollar.***

This basic principle of consumer choice is easily illustrated. Suppose you have $1.50 to spend on a combination of Cokes and video games, the only consumer goods available. Your objective, as always, is to get the greatest satisfaction possible from this limited income. That is, you want to maximize the *total* utility attainable from the expenditure of your income. The question is how to do it. What combination of Cokes and games will maximize the utility you get from $1.50.?

We've already assumed that the marginal utility (MU) of the first Coke is 1.5 times as high as the MU of the first video game. This is reflected in the second row of Table 20.3. The MU of the first video game has been set arbitrarily at 10 utils (units of utility). We don't need to know whether 10 utils is a real thrill or just a bit of amusement. Indeed, the concept of "utils" has little meaning by itself; it's only a useful basis for comparison. In this case, we want to compare the MU of the first game with the MU of the first Coke. Hence, we set the MU of the first game at 10 utils and the MU of the first Coke at 15 utils. The first Coke is 1.5 times as satisfying as the first video game ($MU_{Coke} = 1.5\ MU_{game}$).

The remainder of Table 20.3 indicates how marginal utility diminishes with increasing consumption of a product. Look at what happens to the good taste of Coke. The marginal utility of the first Coke is 15; but the MU of the second Coke is only 8 utils. Once you've quenched your initial thirst, a second Coke still tastes good but isn't nearly so satisfying as the first one. A third Coke yields even less marginal utility, and a fourth one none at all (MU = 0). A fifth or sixth Coke would make your teeth rattle and cause other discomforts—its marginal utility is actually negative (−3 in Table 20.3).

Video games also conform to the law of diminishing marginal utility. However, marginal utility doesn't decline quite so rapidly in the consumption of video games. The second game is almost as much fun (MU = 9) as the first (MU = 10). Not until you've played several games do you begin to feel the tension and enjoy the game less. By the sixth game, marginal utility is fast approaching zero.

With these psychological insights to guide us, we can now determine how best to spend $1.50. What we're looking for is that combination of Cokes and video games which *maximizes* the total utility attainable from an expenditure of $1.50. We call this combination **optimal consumption**—that is, the mix of goods that yields the most utility for the available income.

We can start looking for the optimal mix of consumer purchases by assessing the utility of spending the entire $1.50 on video games. At 25 cents per play, we could buy 6 games. This would give us *total* utility of 35 utils (see Table 20.3).

Utility Maximization

optimal consumption: The mix of consumer purchases that maximizes the utility attainable from available income.

	Amount of Utility (in units of utility, or utils)			
	From Cokes		From Video Games	
Quantity Consumed	Total	Marginal	Total	Marginal
0	0	0	0	0
1	15	15	10	10
2	23	8	19	9
3	25	2	26	7
4	25	0	31	5
5	22	−3	34	3
6	12	−10	35	1

TABLE 20.3
Maximizing Utility
Q: How can you get the most satisfaction (utility) from $1.50 if you must choose between buying Cokes that cost 50 cents each and video games that cost 25 cents each?
A: By drinking one Coke and playing four video games. See text for explanation.

You could also spend all your income on Cokes. With $1.50 to spend, you could buy 3 Cokes. However, this would generate only 25 utils of total utility. Hence, if you were forced to choose between 3 Cokes and 6 games, you'd pick the games.

Fortunately, we don't have to make such extreme choices. In reality, we can buy a *combination* of Cokes and video games. This complicates our decision making (with more choices) but permits us to attain higher levels of total satisfaction.

To reach the peak of satisfaction, consider spending your $1.50 in three 50-cent increments. How should you spend the first 50 cents? If you spend it on 1 Coke, you'll get 15 utils of satisfaction. On the other hand, 50 cents will buy your first 2 video games. The first game has an MU of 10 and the second game adds another 9 utils to your happiness. Hence, by spending the first 50 cents on games, you reap 19 utils of total utility. This is superior to the pleasure of a first Coke and its therefore your first purchase.

Having played 2 video games, you now can spend the second 50 cents. How should it be spent? Your choice now is that first Coke or a third and fourth video game. That first unconsumed Coke still promises 15 utils of real pleasure. By contrast, the MU of a third video game is 7 utils and the MU of a fourth game only 5 utils. Together, then, the third and fourth games will increase your total utility by 12 utils, whereas a first Coke will give you 15 utils. You should spend the second 50 cents on a Coke.

The decision on how to spend the remaining half dollar is made the same way. The final choice is to purchase either a second Coke (MU = 8) or the third (MU = 7) and fourth (MU = 5) video games. The two games together offer more marginal utility and are thus the correct decision.

After working your way through these calculations, you'll end up drinking 1 Coke and playing 4 video games. Was it worth it? Do you end up with more total utility than you could have gotten from any other combination? The answer is yes. The *total* utility of 1 Coke (15 utils) and 4 games (31 utils) is 46 units of utility. This is significantly better than the alternatives of spending your $1.50 on Cokes alone (total utility = 25) or games alone (total utility = 35). In fact, the combination of 1 Coke and 4 games is the *best* one you can find. Because this combination maximizes the total utility of your income ($1.50), it represents *optimal consumption.*

Utility-Maximizing Rule

Optimal consumption refers to the mix of output that maximizes total utility for the limited amount of income you have to spend. The basic approach to utility maximization is to purchase that good next which delivers the most *marginal utility per dollar.* Marginal utility per dollar is simply the MU of the good divided by its price: MU ÷ P.

From Table 20.3 we know that a first Coke has an MU of 15 and a price of 50 cents. It thus delivers a marginal utility per dollar of

$$\frac{MU_{\text{first Coke}}}{P_{\text{Coke}}} = \frac{15}{0.50} = 30 \text{ utils per dollar}$$

On the other hand, the first video game has a marginal utility of 10 and a price of 25 cents. It offers a marginal utility per dollar of

$$\frac{MU_{\text{first game}}}{P_{\text{game}}} = \frac{10}{0.25} = 40 \text{ utils per dollar}$$

From this perspective, the first video game is a better deal than the first Coke and should be purchased.

Optimal consumption implies that the utility-maximizing combination of goods has been found. If this is true, you can't increase your total utility by trading one good for another. All goods included in the optimal consumption mix yield the *same* marginal utility per dollar. We know we've reached maximum utility when we've satisfied the following rule:

$$\text{Utility-maximizing rule:} \quad \frac{MU_x}{P_x} = \frac{MU_y}{P_y}$$

where *x* and *y* represent any two goods included in our consumption.

Rational consumer choice thus depends on comparisons of marginal utilities and prices. If a dollar spent on product *X* yields more marginal utility than a dollar spent on product *Y*, we should buy product *X*. To use this principle, of course, we have to know the amounts of utility obtainable from various goods and be able to perform a little arithmetic. By doing so, however, we can get the greatest satisfaction from our limited income.

Equilibrium Outcomes

All these graphs and equations make consumer choice look dull and mechanical. Economic theory seems to suggest that consumers walk through shopping malls with marginal-utility tables and hand-held computers. In reality, no one does this—not even your economics instructor. Yet, economic theory is pretty successful in predicting consumer decisions. Consumers don't always buy the optimal mix of goods and services with their limited income. But after some trial and error, consumers adjust their behavior. What economic theory predicts is that the final choices—the *equilibrium outcomes*—will be the predicted optimal ones.

THE ECONOMY TOMORROW

Caveat Emptor

Michael Jordan is paid over $40 million a year to help convince us to drink Gatorade, wear Nike shoes, put on Oakley sunglasses, and use MCI to call friends (see News). Do his sponsors know something economic theory doesn't? Economists *assume* consumers know what they want and will act rationally to get the most satisfaction they can. The companies that sponsor Michael Jordan don't accept that assumption. They think your tastes will follow Michael Jordan's lead.

Advertisers now spend over $200 *billion* per year to change our tastes. This spending works out to over $400 per consumer, one of the highest per capita advertising rates in the world (see World View on the next page). Some of this advertising (including

Marketers Jump with Jordan's Return

Michael Jordan's decision to return to the NBA has set off a flurry of soul-searching among corporate sponsors, who pay him an estimated $40 million a year to pitch their products.

Sponsors such as MCI are rolling out new ads to piggyback on the hype surrounding Jordan's return. . . .

- Jordan's newest sponsor, Palm, plans new print, online and arena ads, says Peter Klamka, president of PTN Media. Jordan's three-year deal calls for a minimum of $1.25 million a year, plus a cut of sales. The company had to submit its marketing plans to Jordan for approval.
- Nike is not planning any ads, even though the basketball superstar serves as part owner and chief designer of Nike's $300 million "Jordan" brand. . . .
- Ditto for Gatorade, which coined the ad slogan, "Be Like Mike." Gatorade created a TV commercial to celebrate

Jordan's return, but decided not to run it. "We want to let the story speak for itself," spokeswoman P.J. Sinopoli says.
- Hanes, the underwear company, says it will simply keep running a recent TV spot showing Jordan as the Pied Piper of the locker room.

While sponsors are reacting slowly, these campaigns are just the beginning, predicts Brandon Steiner of Steiner Sports Marketing.

Consumers should expect a wave of Jordan ads, jerseys, hats and T-shirts in coming months.

"I know I'll be wearing a Wizards hat," Steiner says. "Every day I'm in business, I could send Jordan a check. He drives the sports business."

—Michael McCarthy

Source: *USA Today*, September 26, 2001. © 2001 USA Today. Reprinted with permission. www.usatoday.com

Analysis: Companies pay huge amounts for celebrity endorsements, hoping to change consumer tastes (increase demand).

product labeling) is intended to provide information about existing products or to bring new products to our attention. A great deal of advertising, however, is also designed to exploit our senses and lack of knowledge. Recognizing that we're guilt-ridden, insecure, and sex-hungry, advertisers promise exoneration, recognition, and love; all we have to do is buy the right product.

A favorite target of advertisers is our sense of insecurity. Thousands of products are marketed in ways that appeal to our need for identity. Thousands of brand images are designed to help the consumer answer the nagging question, Who am I? The answers, of course, vary. *Playboy* magazine says, I'm a virile man of the world; Marlboro cigarettes say, I'm a rugged individualist who enjoys "man-sized flavor." Gatorade says, I'll be a winner if I drink the same sports drink Michael Jordan does. And I'll be able to jump 8 feet high if I wear Air Jordan shoes.

Are Wants Created?

Advertising can't be blamed for all of our foolish consumption. Even members of the most primitive tribes, uncontaminated by the seductions of advertising, adorned themselves with rings, bracelets, and pendants. Furthermore, advertising has grown to massive proportions only in the past four decades, but consumption spending has been increasing throughout recorded history. Finally, a lot of advertising simply fails to change buying decisions. Accordingly, it's a mistake to attribute the growth or content of consumption entirely to the persuasions of advertisers.

This isn't to say that advertising has necessarily made us happier. The objective of all advertising is to alter the choices we make. Just as product images are used to attract us to particular products, so are pictures of hungry, ill-clothed children used to persuade us to give money to charity. In the same way, public relations gimmicks are employed to sway our votes for public servants. In the case of consumer products, advertising seeks to increase tastes for particular goods and services and therewith our willingness to pay. *A successful advertising campaign is one that shifts the demand curve for a*

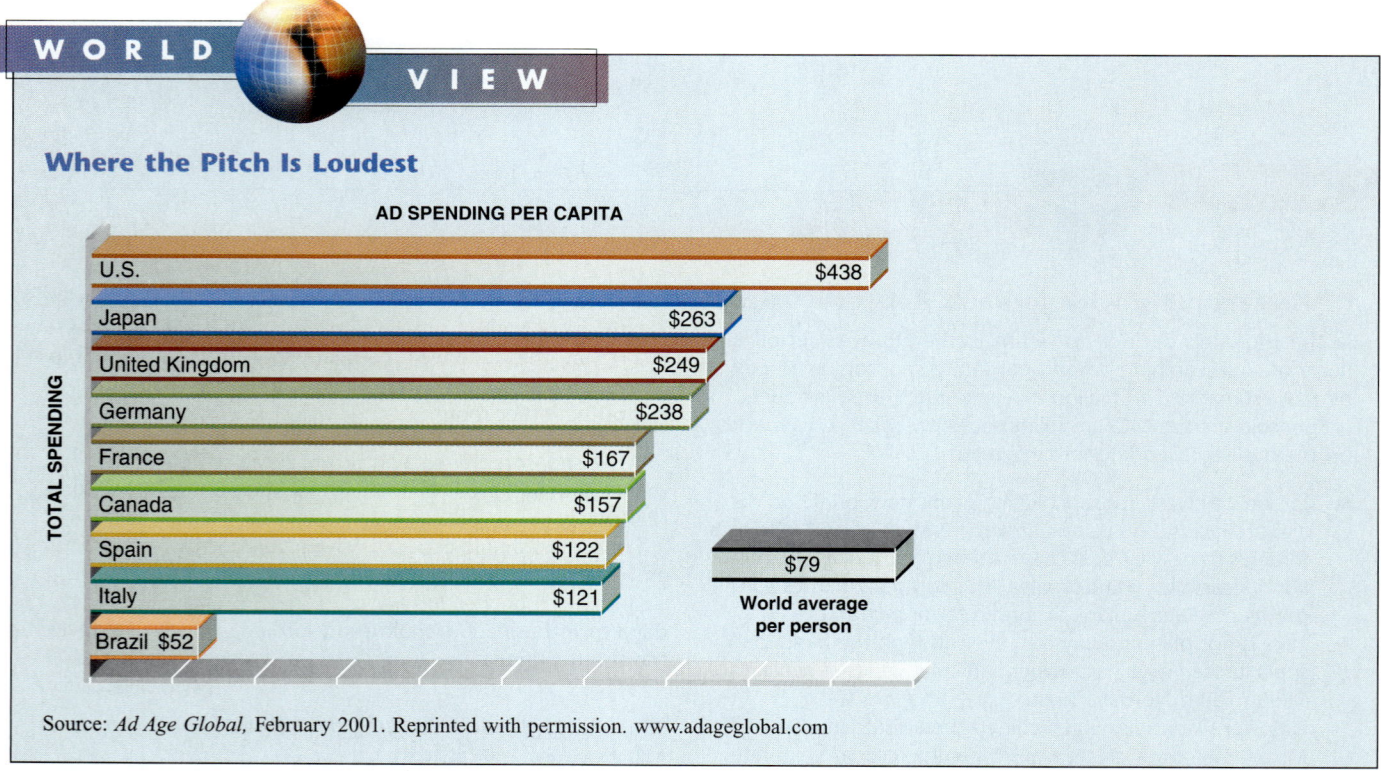

WORLD VIEW

Where the Pitch Is Loudest

AD SPENDING PER CAPITA

- U.S. $438
- Japan $263
- United Kingdom $249
- Germany $238
- France $167
- Canada $157
- Spain $122
- Italy $121
- Brazil $52

World average per person $79

Source: *Ad Age Global*, February 2001. Reprinted with permission. www.adageglobal.com

Analysis: Producers advertise to change consumer tastes (preferences). At higher levels of income, advertising is likely to play a greater role in consumption decisions.

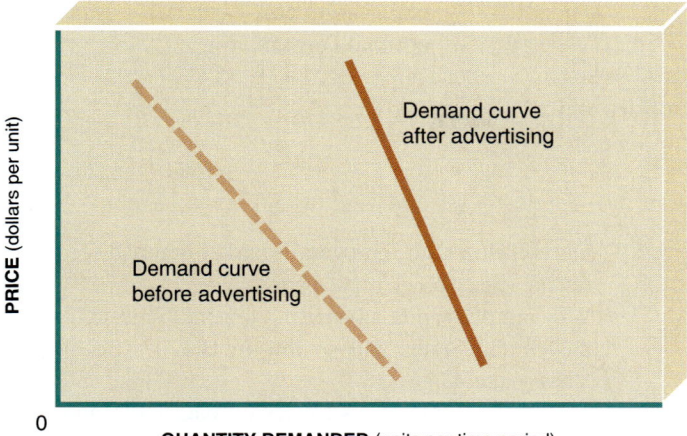

FIGURE 20.9
The Impact of Advertising on a Demand Curve

Advertising seeks to increase our taste for a particular product. If our taste (the product's perceived utility) increases, so will our willingness to buy. The resulting change in demand is reflected in a rightward shift of the demand curve, often accompanied by diminished elasticity.

specific product to the right, inducing consumers to increase their purchases of a product at every price (see Figure 20.9). Advertising may also increase brand loyalty, making the demand curve less elastic (reducing consumer responses to price increases). By influencing our choices in this way, advertising will affect the consumption choices we make in the economy tomorrow. Advertising alone is unlikely to affect the total *level* of consumption, however.

SUMMARY

- Our desires for goods and services originate in the structure of personality and social dynamics and aren't explained by economic theory. Economic theory focuses on *demand*—that is, our ability and willingness to buy specific quantities of a good at various prices.
- Marginal utility measures the additional satisfaction obtained from consuming one more unit of a good. The law of diminishing marginal utility says that the more of a product we consume, the smaller the increments of pleasure we tend to derive from additional units of it. This is a basis for the law of demand.
- The price elasticity of demand is a numerical measure of consumer response to a change in price, *ceteris paribus*. It equals the percentage change in quantity demanded divided by the percentage change in price. Elasticity depends on the relative price of a good, the availability of substitutes, and time.
- The effect of a price change on total revenue depends on price elasticity. Total revenue and price move in the same direction only if demand is price-inelastic ($E < 1$).
- The shape and position of any particular demand curve depend on a consumer's income, tastes, expectations, and the price and availability of other goods. Should any of these factors change, the assumption of *ceteris paribus* will no longer hold, and the demand curve will *shift*.
- The income elasticity of demand measures the response of demand to a change in income. If demand increases with income, the product being considered is a normal good. If the demand falls when income rises, it's an inferior good.
- Cross-price elasticity measures the response of demand for one good to a change in the price of another. The cross-price elasticity of demand is positive for substitute goods and negative for complementary goods.
- In choosing among alternative goods and services, a consumer compares the prices and anticipated satisfactions that they offer. To maximize utility with one's available income—to achieve an optimal mix of goods and services—one has to get the most utility for every dollar spent. To do so, one must compare the relative prices and pleasures and choose those goods which offer the most additional pleasure per dollar.
- Advertising seeks to change consumer tastes and thus the willingness to buy. If tastes do change, the demand curve will shift.

Key Terms

demand
utility
total utility
marginal utility
law of diminishing marginal utility
ceteris paribus
law of demand
demand curve
price elasticity of demand
total revenue

shift in demand
income elasticity of demand
normal good
inferior good
substitute goods
complementary goods
cross-price elasticity of demand
opportunity cost
optimal consumption

Questions for Discussion

1. What does the demand for enrollments in your college look like? What is on the axes? Is the demand price-elastic? Income-elastic? How could you find out?
2. If the marginal utility of pizza never diminished, how many pizzas would you eat?
3. How does total and marginal utility change as you spend more time surfing the net?
4. How would consumers adjust their behavior to a doubling of gasoline prices? How quickly would these adjustments be made?
5. Identify two goods each whose demand exhibits (*a*) high income elasticity, (*b*) low income elasticity, (*c*) high price elasticity, (*d*) low price elasticity. What accounts for the differences in elasticity?
6. Why is the demand for Canadian cigarettes so much more elastic than the overall market demand for cigarettes? (See World View, page 422.)
7. Why are per capita advertising expenditures so high in the United States and so low in Brazil? (See World View, page 434.)
8. According to the News stories on pages 421 and 423, how does the price elasticity of demand differ for teenagers and adults? Why?
9. If you owned a movie theater, would you want the demand for movies to be elastic or inelastic?
10. How has the Internet affected the price elasticity of demand for air travel?
11. What would happen to unit sales and total revenue for this textbook if the bookstore reduced its price?

Web Activities

1. Check the best interest rates in the nation on auto loans at www.bankrate.com/brm/rate/auto_home.asp. To access these rates click on "Check Latest Rate," access auto loans, and then search for rates in your state. Choose the metro area closest to your college or university.
   (*a*) What's the lowest interest rate available?
   (*b*) How many choices are there? Are there actually more choices than provided on this website? Explain.
   (*c*) Using the determinants of elasticity provided in the text, would you expect the price elasticity of demand for auto loans to be relatively elastic or relatively inelastic? Explain.
   (*d*) Has the Internet changed the price elasticity of demand for auto loans? Explain.
   (*e*) Does the interest rate on auto loans affect the price elasticity of demand for autos? Explain.
2. A Rand Corporation study of cocaine use estimated the price elasticity of demand for this illegal drug. Find the elasticity at http://www.Rand.org/publications/RB/RB6000/rb6000.html.
   (*a*) Given the price elasticity of demand estimate provided in this report, is the demand for cocaine considered to be relatively elastic or inelastic?
   (*b*) Using the list of determinants of elasticity found in the text, what is the most likely explanation for the elasticity value provided in the text of the Rand Corporation study?
   (*c*) Draw a demand curve for cocaine that demonstrates the elasticity estimate that you found for part *a*.
   (*d*) How does the level of elasticity affect the policies recommended in the report?
3. NPD INTELECT Market Tracking is a leading provider of sales tracking services for the consumer electronics, home appliance, information technology, and imaging industries. Log into its website at www.intelectmt.com/corp/intelectmt/press/press-ce/press_010924a.htm.
   (*a*) Assuming nothing else changed during the time period of the data except product price, use the data provided in the press release to calculate the price elasticity of demand for DVD players between 1998 and 2001.
   (*b*) Interpret the value that you calculated for part *a*.

 THE ACCOMPANYING STUDENT PROBLEM SET CONTAINS NUMERICAL AND GRAPHING PROBLEMS FOR THIS CHAPTER

APPENDIX

INDIFFERENCE CURVES

A consumer's demand for any specific product is an expression of many forces. As we've observed, the actual quantity of a product demanded by a consumer varies inversely with its price. The price-quantity relationship is determined by

- *Tastes* (desire for this and other goods).
- *Income* (of the consumer).
- *Expectations* (for income, prices, tastes).
- *Other goods* (their availability and price).

Economic theory attempts to show how each of these forces affects consumer demand. Thus far, we've used two-dimensional demand curves to illustrate the basic principles of demand. We saw that, in general, a change in the price of a good causes a movement along the demand curve, while a change in tastes, income, expectations, or other goods shifts the entire demand curve to a new position.

We haven't looked closely at the origins of demand curves, however. We assumed that a demand curve could be developed from observations of consumer behavior, such as the number of boxes of popcorn that were purchased at various prices (Figure 20.3). Likewise, we observed how the demand curve shifts in response to changes in tastes, income, expectations, or other goods (Figures 20.7 and 20.8).

It's possible, however, to derive a demand curve without actually observing consumer behavior. In theory we can identify consumer *preferences* (tastes), then use those preferences to construct a demand curve. In this case, the demand curve is developed explicitly from known preferences rather than on the basis of market observations. The end result—the demand curve—is the same, at least so long as consumers' behavior in product markets is consistent with their preferences.

Indifference curves are a mechanism for illustrating consumer tastes. We examine their construction and use in this appendix. As suggested above, indifference curves provide an explicit basis for constructing a demand curve. In addition, they are another way of viewing how consumption is affected by price, tastes, and income. Indifference curves are also a useful tool for illustrating explicitly consumer *choice*—that is, the decision to purchase one good rather than another.

Constructing an Indifference Curve

Recall the dilemma that arises when you want Coke and video games but don't have enough money to buy enough of each. The income constraint compels you to make hard decisions. You have to consider the **marginal utility** each additional Coke or video game will provide, compare their respective prices, then make a selection. With careful introspection and good arithmetic you can select the optimal mix of Cokes and video games—that is, the combination that yields the most satisfaction (utility) for the income available. This process of identifying your **optimal consumption** was illustrated in Table 20.3.

marginal utility: The change in total utility obtained by consuming one additional (marginal) unit of a good or service.

optimal consumption: The mix of consumer purchases that maximizes the utility attainable from available income.

Finding your optimal consumption is difficult because you must assess the marginal utility of each prospective purchase. In Table 20.3 we assumed that the marginal utility of the first Coke was 15 utils, while the first video game had a marginal utility of 10. Then we had to specify the marginal utility of every additional Coke and video game. Can we really be so specific about our tastes?

Indifference curves require a bit less arithmetic. ***Instead of trying to measure the marginal utility of each prospective purchase, we now look for combinations of goods that yield equal satisfaction.*** All we need do is determine that one particular combination of Cokes and video games is as satisfying as another. We don't have to say how many "units of pleasure" both combinations provide—it's sufficient that they're both equally satisfying.

TABLE 20A.1
Equally Satisfying Combinations

Different combinations of two goods may be equally satisfying. In this case we assume that the combinations A, B, and C all yield equal total utility. Hence, the consumer will be indifferent about which of the three combinations he or she receives.

Combination	Cokes	Video Games
A	1	8
B	2	5
C	3	4

The initial combination of 1 Coke and 8 video games is designated as a combination A in Table A.1. This combination of goods yields a certain, but unspecified, level of total utility. What we want to do now is to find another combination of Cokes and games that's just as satisfying as combination A. Finding other combinations of equal satisfaction isn't easy, but it's at least possible. After a lot of soul searching, we decide that 2 Cokes and 5 video games would be just as satisfying as 1 Coke and 8 games.[1] This combination is designated as B in Table A.1.

Table A.1 also depicts a third combination of Cokes and video games that's as satisfying as the first. Combination C includes 3 Cokes and 4 games, a mix of consumption assumed to yield the same total utility as 1 Coke and 8 games (combination A).

Notice that we haven't said anything about how much pleasure combinations A, B, and C provide. We're simply asserting that these three combinations are *equally* satisfying.

Figure A.1 illustrates the information about tastes that we've assembled. Points A, B, and C represent the three equally satisfying combinations of Cokes and video games we've identified. By connecting these points we create an **indifference curve.** The indifference curve illustrates all combinations of two goods that are equally satisfying. A consumer would be just as happy with any combination represented on the curve, so a choice among them would be a matter of indifference.

indifference curve: A curve depicting alternative combinations of goods that yield equal satisfaction.

An Indifference Map. Not all combinations of Cokes and video games are as satisfying as combination A, of course. Surely, 2 Cokes and 8 games would be preferred to only 1 Coke and 8 games. Indeed, *any combination that provided more of one good and no less of the other would be preferred.* Point D in Figure A.2 illustrates just one such combination. Combination D must yield more total utility than combination A because it includes one more Coke and no fewer games. A consumer wouldn't be indifferent to a choice between A and D; on the contrary, combination D would be preferred.

[1] The utility computations used here aren't based on Table 20.3; a different set of tastes is assumed.

FIGURE 20A.1
An Indifference Curve

An indifference curve illustrates the various combinations of two goods that would provide equal satisfaction. The consumer is assumed to be indifferent to a choice between combinations A, B, and C (and all other points on the curve), as they all yield the same total utility.

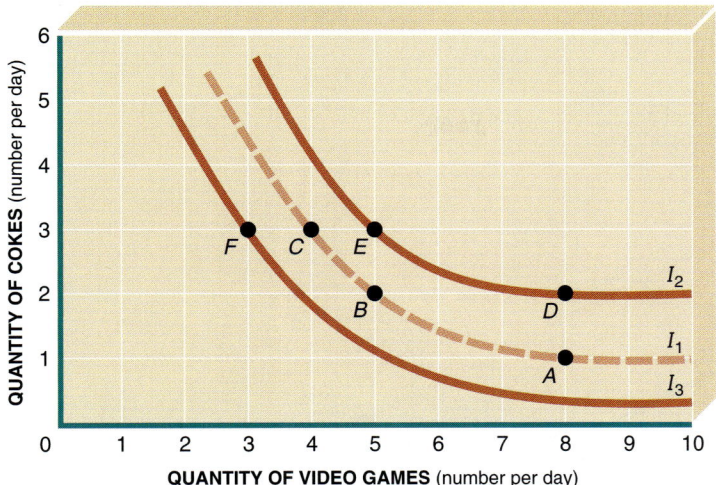

FIGURE 20A.2
An Indifference Map

All combinations of goods depicted on any given indifference curve (e.g., I_2) are equally satisfying. Other combinations are more or less satisfying, however, and thus lie on higher (I_2) or lower (I_3) indifference curves. An indifference map shows all possible levels of total utility (e.g., $I_1, I_2, I_3 \ldots I_n$) and their respective consumption combinations.

Combination D is also preferred to combinations B and C. How do we know? Recall that combinations A, B, and C are all equally satisfying. Hence, if combination D is better than A, it must also be better than B and C. Given a choice, a consumer would select combination D (2 Cokes, 8 games) in preference to *any* combination depicted on indifference curve I_1.

There are also combinations that are as satisfying as D, of course. These possibilities are illustrated on indifference curve I_2. All these combinations are equally satisfying and must therefore be preferred to any points on indifference curve I_1. In general, **the farther the indifference curve is from the origin, the more total utility it yields.**

The curve I_3 illustrates various combinations that are less satisfying. Combination F, for example, includes 3 Cokes and 3 games. This is 1 game less than the number available in combination C. Therefore, F yields less total utility than C and isn't preferred: A consumer would rather have combination C than F. By the same logic we used above, all points on indifference curve I_3 are less satisfying than combinations on curve I_2 or I_1.

Curves 1, 2, and 3 in Figure A.2 are the beginnings of an **indifference map.** An indifference map depicts all the combinations of goods that would yield various levels of satisfaction. A single indifference curve, in contrast, illustrates all combinations that provide a single (equal) level of total utility.

We assume that all consumers strive to maximize their utility. They want as much satisfaction as they can get. In the terminology of indifference curves, this means getting to the indifference curve that's farthest from the origin. The farther one is from the origin, the greater the total utility.

Although the goal of consumers is evident, the means of achieving it isn't so clear. Higher indifference curves aren't only more satisfying, they're also more expensive. We're confronted again with the basic conflict between preferences and prices. With a limited amount of income to spend, we can't attain infinite satisfaction (the farthest indifference curve). We have to settle for less (an indifference curve closer to the origin). The question is: How do we maximize the utility attainable with our limited income?

The Budget Constraint. For starters, we have to determine how much we have to spend. Suppose for the moment that we can spend $2 per day and that Cokes and video games are still the only objects of our consumption desires. The price of a Coke is 50 cents; the price of a game is 25 cents. Accordingly, the maximum number of Cokes we could buy is 4 per day if we didn't play any video games. On the other hand, we could play as many as 8 games if we were to forsake Coke.

indifference map: The set of indifference curves that depicts all possible levels of utility attainable from various combinations of goods.

Utility Maximization

FIGURE 20A.3
The Budget Constraint

Consumption possibilities are limited by available income. The budget constraint illustrates this limitation. The end points of the budget constraint are equal to income divided by the price of each good. All points on the budget constraint represent affordable combinations of goods.

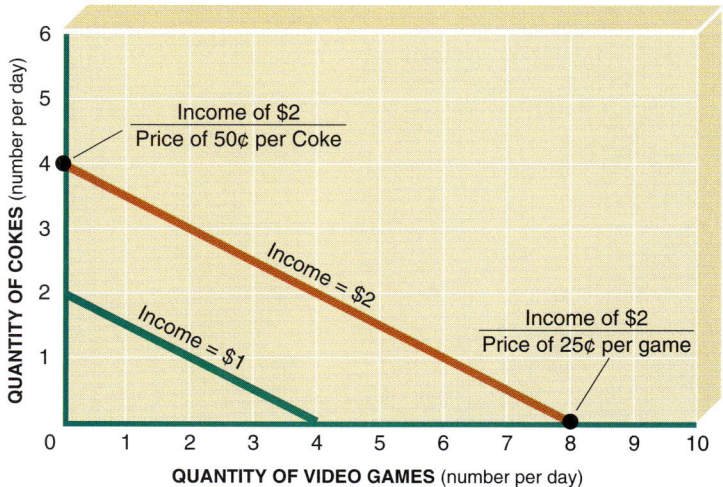

budget constraint: A line depicting all combinations of goods that are affordable with a given income and given prices.

Figure A.3 depicts the limitations placed on our consumption possibilities by a finite income. The **budget constraint** illustrates all combinations of goods affordable with a given income. In this case, the outermost budget line illustrates the combinations of Cokes and video games that can be purchased with $2.

The budget line is easily drawn. The end points of the budget constraint are found by dividing one's income by the price of the good on the corresponding axis. Thus, the outermost curve begins at 4 Cokes ($2 ÷ 50 cents) and ends at 8 games ($2 ÷ 25 cents). All the other points on the budget constraint represent other combinations of Cokes and video games that could be purchased with $2.

A smaller income is also illustrated in Figure A.3. If we had only $1 to spend, we could afford fewer Cokes and fewer games. Hence, a smaller income is represented by a budget constraint that lies closer to the origin.

Optimal Consumption. With a budget constraint looming before us, the limitation on utility maximization is evident. We want to reach the highest indifference curve possible. Our limited income, however, restricts our grasp. We can go only as far as our budget constraint allows. In this context, *the objective is to reach the highest indifference curve that is compatible with our budget constraint.*

Figure A.4 illustrates the process of achieving optimal consumption. We start with an indifference map depicting all utility levels and product combinations. Then we impose a budget line that reflects our income. In this case, we continue to assume that Coke costs 50 cents, video games cost 25 cents, and we have $2 to spend. Hence, *we can afford only those consumption combinations that are on or inside the budget line.*

Which particular combination of Cokes and video games maximizes the utility of our $2? It must be 2 Cokes and 4 video games, as reflected in point M. Notice that point M isn't only on the budget line but also touches indifference curve I_c. No other point on the budget line touches I_c or any higher indifference curve. Accordingly, I_c represents the most utility we can get for $2 and is attainable only if we consume 2 Cokes and 4 video games. Any other affordable combination yields less total utility—that is, falls on a lower indifference curve. Point G, for example, which offers 3 Cokes and 2 video games for $2, lies on the indifference curve I_b. Because I_b lies closer to the origin than I_c, point G must be less satisfying than point M. We conclude then, that *the point of tangency between the budget constraint and an indifference curve represents optimal consumption.* It's the combination we should buy if we want to maximize the utility of our limited income.

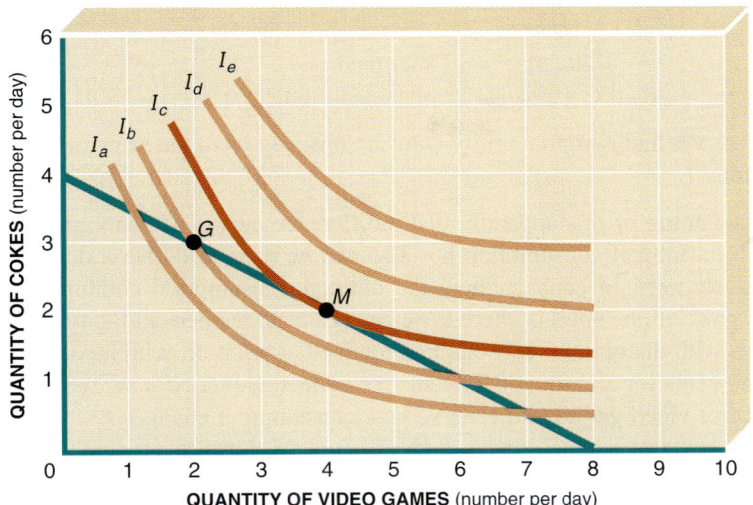

FIGURE 20A.4
Optimal Consumption

The optimal consumption combination—the one that maximizes the utility of spendable income—lies at the point where the budget line is tangent to (just touches) an indifference curve. In this case, point M represents the optimal mix of Cokes and video games, since no other affordable combination lies on a higher indifference curve than I_c.

Marginal Utility and Price: A Digression. We earlier illustrated the utility-maximizing rule, which required a comparison of the ratios of marginal utilities to prices. Specifically, optimal consumption was represented as that combination of Cokes and video games that yielded

$$\frac{\text{MU Coke}}{P \text{ Coke}} = \frac{\text{MU games}}{P \text{ games}}$$

Does point M in Figure A.4 conform to this rule?

To answer this question, first rearrange the preceding equation as follows:

$$\frac{\text{MU Coke}}{\text{MU games}} = \frac{P \text{ Coke}}{P \text{ games}}$$

In this form, the equation says that the relative marginal utilities of Cokes and video games should equal their relative prices when consumption is optimal. In other words, if a Coke costs twice as much as a video game, then it must yield twice as much marginal utility if the consumer is to be in an optimal state. Otherwise, some substitution of Cokes for video games, or vice versa, would be desirable.

With this foundation, we can show that point M conforms to our earlier rule. Consider first the slope of the budget constraint, which is determined by the relative prices of Cokes and video games. In fact, *the (absolute) slope of the budget constraint equals the relative price of the two goods.* In Figure A.4 the slope equals the price of video games divided by the price of Cokes (25 cents ÷ 50 cents = $\frac{1}{2}$). It tells us the rate at which video games can be exchanged for Cokes in the market. In this case, one video game is "worth" half a Coke.

The relative marginal utilities of the two goods are reflected in the slope of the indifference curve. Recall that the curve tells at what rate a consumer is willing to substitute one good for another, with no change in total utility. In fact, the slope of the indifference curve is called the **marginal rate of substitution.** It's equal to the relative marginal utilities of the two goods. Presumably one would be indifferent to a choice between 2 Cokes + 5 games and 3 Cokes + 4 games—as suggested in Table A.1—only if the third Coke were as satisfying as the fifth video game.

At the point of optimal consumption (M) in Figure A.4 the budget constraint is tangent to the indifference curve I_c, which means that the two curves must have the same slope at the point. In other words,

$$\frac{P \text{ games}}{P \text{ Cokes}} = \frac{\text{MU games}}{\text{MU Cokes}}$$

marginal rate of substitution: The rate at which a consumer is willing to exchange one good for another; the relative marginal utilities of two goods.

or alternatively,

$$\frac{\text{Rate of}}{\text{market exchange}} = \frac{\text{marginal rate}}{\text{of substitution}}$$

Both indifference curves and marginal utility comparisons lead us to the same optimal mix of consumption.

Deriving the Demand Curve

We noted at the beginning of this appendix that indifference curves not only give us an alternative path to optimal consumption but also can be used to derive a demand curve. To do this, we need to consider how the optimal consumption combination changes when the price of one good is altered. We can see what happens in Figure A.5.

Figure A.5 starts with the optimal consumption attained at point *M*, with income of $2 and prices of 50 cents for a Coke and 25 cents for a video game. Now we're going to change the price of video games and observe how consumption changes.

Suppose that the price of a video game doubles, from 25 cents to 50 cents. This change will shift the budget constraint inward: Our income of $2 now buys a maximum of 4 games rather than 8. Hence, the lower end point of the budget constraint moves from 8 games to 4 games. *Whenever the price of a good changes, the budget constraint shifts.*

Only one end of the budget constraint is changed in Figure A.5. The budget line still begins at 4 Cokes because the price of Coke is unchanged. If only one price is changed, then only one end of the budget constraint is shifted.

Because the budget constraint has shifted inward, the combination *M* is no longer attainable. Two Cokes (at 50 cents each) and 4 games (at 50 cents each) now cost more than $2. We're now forced to accept a lower level of total utility. According to Figure A.5, optimal consumption is now located at point *N*. This is the point of tangency between the new budget constraint and a lower indifference curve. At point *N* we consume 1 Coke and 3 video games.

Consider what has happened here. The price of video games has increased (from 25 cents to 50 cents), and the quantity of games demanded has decreased. This is the kind of relationship that demand curves describe. **Demand curves** indicate how the quantity demanded of a good changes in response to a change in its price, given a fixed income and all other things held constant. Not only does Figure A.5 provide the same information, it also conforms to the **law of demand:** As the price of games increases, the quantity demanded falls.

Suppose the price of video games were to fall rather than increase. Specifically, assume that the price of a game fell to 10 cents. This price reduction would shift the bud-

demand curve: A curve describing the quantities of a good a consumer is willing and able to buy at alternative prices in a given time period, *ceteris paribus*.

law of demand: The quantity of a good demanded in a given time period increases as its price falls, *ceteris paribus*.

FIGURE 20A.5
Changing Prices

When the price of a good changes, the budget constraint shifts, and a new consumption combination must be sought. In this case, the price of video games is changing. When the price of games increases from 25 cents to 50 cents, the budget constraint shifts inward and optimal consumption moves from point *M* to point *N*.

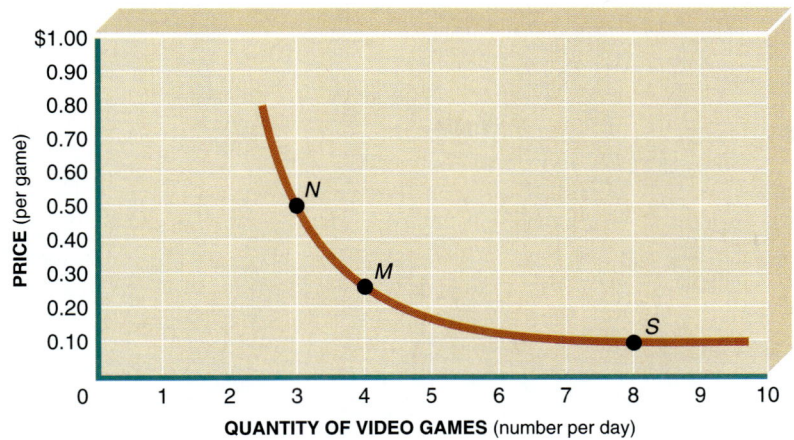

FIGURE 20A.6

The Demand for Video Games

Figure A.5 shows how optimal consumption is altered when the price of video games changes. From that figure we can determine the quantity of video games demanded at alternative prices, *ceteris paribus*. That information is summarized here in the demand schedule (below) and the demand curve (above).

Point	Price (per game)	Quantity Demanded (games per day)
N	50 cents	3
M	25 cents	4
S	10 cents	8

get constraint farther out on the horizontal axis, since as many as 20 games could then be purchased with $2. As a result of the price reduction, we can now buy more goods and thus attain a higher level of satisfaction.

Point S in Figure A.5 indicates the optimal combination of Cokes and video games at the new video game price. At these prices, we consume 8 video games and 2.4 Cokes (we may have to share with a friend). The law of demand is again evident: When the price of video games declines, the quantity demanded increases.

The Demand Schedule and Curve. Figure A.6 summarizes the information we've acquired about the demand for video games. The demand schedule depicts the price-quantity relationships prevailing at optimal consumption points N, M, and S (from Figure A.5). The demand curve generalizes these observations to encompass other prices. What we end up with is a demand curve explicitly derived from our (assumed) knowledge of consumer tastes.

CHAPTER 21

The Costs of Production

Last year U.S. consumers bought more than $1 *trillion* worth of imported goods, including Japanese cars, Italian shoes, and toys from China. As you might expect, this angers domestic producers, who frequently end up with unsold goods, half-empty factories, and unemployed workers. They rage against the "unfair" competition from abroad, asserting that producers in Korea, Brazil, and China can undersell U.S. producers because workers in these countries are paid dirt-poor wages.

But lower wages don't necessarily imply lower costs. You could pay me $2 per hour to type and still end up paying a lot for typing. Truth is, I type only about 10 words a minute, with lots of misteaks. The cost of producing goods depends not only on the price of inputs (e.g., labor) but also on how much they produce.

In this chapter we begin looking at the costs of producing the goods and services that market participants demand. We confront the following questions:

- How much output *can* a firm produce?
- How do the *costs* of production vary with the rate of output?
- Do larger firms have a cost advantage over smaller firms?

The answers to these questions are important not only to producers faced with foreign competition but to consumers as well. The costs of producing a good have a direct impact on the prices consumers pay.

THE PRODUCTION FUNCTION

No matter how large a business is or who owns it, all businesses confront one central fact: It costs something to produce goods. To produce corn, a farmer needs land, water, seed, equipment, and labor. To produce fillings, a dentist needs a chair, a drill, some space, and labor. Even the "production" of educational services such as this economics class requires the use of labor (your teacher), land (on which the school is built), and capital (the building, blackboard, computers). In short, unless you're producing unrefined, unpackaged air, you need **factors of production**—that is, resources that can be used to produce a good or service. The factors of production used in production provide the basic measure of economic cost. The costs of your economics class, for example, are measured by the amounts of land, labor, and capital it requires. These are *resource* costs of production.

To assess the costs of production, we must first determine how many resources are actually needed to produce a given product. You could use a lot of resources to produce a product or use just a few. What we really want to know is how *best* to produce. What's the *smallest* amount of resources needed to produce a specific product? Or we could ask the same question from a different perspective: What's the *maximum* amount of output attainable from a given quantity of resources.

The answers to these questions are reflected in the **production function,** which tells us the maximum amount of good *X* producible from various combinations of factor inputs. With one chair and one drill, a dentist can fill a *maximum* of 32 cavities per day. With two chairs, a drill, and an assistant, a dentist can fill up to 55 cavities per day.

A production function is a technological summary of our ability to produce a particular good.[1] Table 21.1 provides a partial glimpse of one such function. In this case, the output is designer jeans, as produced by Tight Jeans Corporation. The essential inputs in the production of jeans are land, labor (garment workers), and capital (a factory and sewing machines). With these inputs, Tight Jeans Corporation can produce and sell fancy jeans to status-conscious consumers.

factors of production: Resource inputs used to produce goods and services, such as land, labor, capital, entrepreneurship.

production function: A technological relationship expressing the maximum quantity of a good attainable from different combinations of factor inputs.

Varying Input Levels

As in all production endeavors, we want to know how much output we can produce with available resources. To make things easy, we'll assume that the factory is already built, with fixed space dimensions. The only inputs we can vary are labor (the number of garment workers per day) and additional capital (the number of sewing machines we lease per day).

In these circumstances, the quantity of jeans we can produce depends on the amount of labor and capital we employ. ***The purpose of a production function is to tell us just how much output we can produce with varying amounts of factor inputs.*** Table 21.1 provides such information for jeans production.

Consider the simplest option, that of employing no labor or capital (the upper-left corner in Table 21.1). An empty factory can't produce any jeans; maximum output is zero per day. Even though land, capital (an empty factory and idle machine), and even denim are available, some essential labor and capital inputs are missing, and jeans production is impossible.

[1] By contrast, the production possibilities curve discussed in Chapter 1 expresses our ability to produce various *combinations* of goods, given the use of *all* our resources. The production possibilities curve summarizes the output capacity of the entire economy. A production function describes the capacity of a single firm.

Capital Input (sewing machines per day)	Labor Input (workers per day)							
	0	1	2	3	4	5	6	7	8
	Jeans Output (pairs per day)							
0	0	0	0	0	0	0	0	0	0
1	0	15	34	44	48	50	51	51	47
2	0	20	46	64	72	78	81	82	80
3	0	21	50	73	83	92	99	103	103

TABLE 21.1
A Production Function
A production function tells us the maximum amount of output attainable from alternative combinations of factor inputs. This particular function tells us how many pairs of jeans we can produce in a day with a given factory and varying quantities of capital and labor. With one sewing machine, and one operator, we can produce a maximum of 15 pairs of jeans per day, as indicated in the second column of the second row. To produce more jeans, we need more labor or more capital.

Suppose now we employ some labor (a machine operator) but don't lease any sewing machines. Will output increase? Not according to the production function. The first row in Table 21.1 illustrates the consequences of employing labor without any capital equipment. Without sewing machines (or even needles, another form of capital), the operators can't make jeans. Maximum output remains at zero, no matter how much labor is employed in this case.

The dilemma of machine operators without sewing machines illustrates a general principle of production: *The* **productivity** *of any factor of production depends on the amount of other resources available to it.* Industrious, hardworking machine operators can't make designer jeans without sewing machines.

productivity: Output per unit of input, for example, output per labor-hour.

We can increase the productivity of garment workers by providing them with machines. The production function again tells us by *how much* jeans output could increase. Suppose we leased just one machine per day. Now the second row in Table 21.1 is the relevant one. It says jeans output will remain at zero if we lease one machine but employ no labor. If we employ one machine *and* one worker, however, the jeans will start rolling out the front door. Maximum output under these circumstances (row 2, column 2) is 15 pairs of jeans per day. Now we're in business!

The remaining columns in row 2 tell us how many additional jeans we can produce if we hire more workers, still leasing only one sewing machine. With one machine and two workers, maximum output rises to 34 pairs per day. If a third worker is hired, output could increase to 44 pairs.

Table 21.1 also indicates how production would increase with additional sewing machines (capital). By reading down any column of the table, you can see how more machines increase potential jeans output.

Efficiency

The production function summarized in Table 21.1 underscores the essential relationship between resource *inputs* and product *outputs*. It's also a basic introduction to economic costs. To produce 15 pairs of jeans per day, we need one sewing machine, an operator, a factory, and some denim. All these inputs comprise the *resource cost* of producing jeans.

Another feature of Table 21.1 is that it conveys the *maximum* output of jeans producible from particular input combinations. The standard garment worker and sewing machine, when brought together at Tight Jeans Corporation, can produce *at most* 15 pairs of jeans per day. They could also produce a lot less. Indeed, a careless cutter can waste a lot of denim. A lazy or inattentive one won't keep the sewing machines humming. As many a producer has learned, actual output can fall far short of the limits described in the production function. Indeed, jeans output will reach the levels in Table 21.1 only if the jeans factory operates with relative **efficiency.** This requires getting maximum output from the resources used in the production process. *The production function represents maximum technical efficiency—that is, the most output attainable from any given level of factor inputs.*

efficiency (technical): Maximum output of a good from the resources used in production.

We can always be inefficient, of course. This merely means getting less output than possible for the inputs we use. But this isn't a desirable situation. To a factory manager, it means less output for a given amount of input (cost). To society as a whole, inefficiency implies a waste of resources. If Tight Jeans isn't producing efficiently, we're being denied some potential output. It's not only a question of having fewer jeans. We could also use the labor and capital now employed by Tight Jeans to produce something else. Specifically, the **opportunity cost** of a product is measured by the most desired goods and services that could have been produced with the same resources. Hence, if jeans production isn't up to par, society is either (1) getting fewer jeans than it should for the resources devoted to jeans production or (2) giving up too many other goods and services in order to get a desired quantity of jeans.

opportunity cost: The most desired goods or services that are forgone in order to obtain something else.

Although we can always do worse than the production function suggests, we can't do better, at least in the short run. The production function represents the *best* we can do with our current technological know-how. For the moment, at least, there's no better way to produce a specific good. As our technological and managerial capabilities increase, however, we'll attain higher levels of future productivity. These advances in our productive capability will be represented by new production functions.

Let's step back from the threshold of scientific advance for a moment and return to Tight Jeans. Forget about possible technological breakthroughs in jeans production (e.g., electronic sewing machines or robot operators) and concentrate on the economic realities of our modest endeavor. For the present we're stuck with existing technology. In fact, all the output figures in Table 21.1 are based on the use of a specific factory. Once we've purchased or leased that factory, we've set a limit to current jeans production. When such commitments to fixed inputs (e.g., the factory) exist, we're dealing with a **short-run** production problem. If no land or capital were in place—if we could build or lease any-sized factory—we'd be dealing with a *long-run* decision.

Our short-run objective is to make the best possible use of the factory we've acquired. This entails selecting the right combination of labor and capital inputs to produce jeans. To simplify the decision, we'll limit the number of sewing machines in use. If we lease only one sewing machine, then the second row in Table 21.1 is the only one we have to consider. In this case, the single sewing machine (capital) becomes another short-run constraint on the production of jeans. With a given factory and one sewing machine, the short-run rate of output depends entirely on how many workers are hired.

Figure 21.1 illustrates the short-run production function applicable to the factory with one sewing machine. As noted before, a factory with a sewing machine but no machine operators produces no jeans. This was observed in Table 21.1 (row 1, column

Short-Run Constraints

short run: The period in which the quantity (and quality) of some inputs can't be changed.

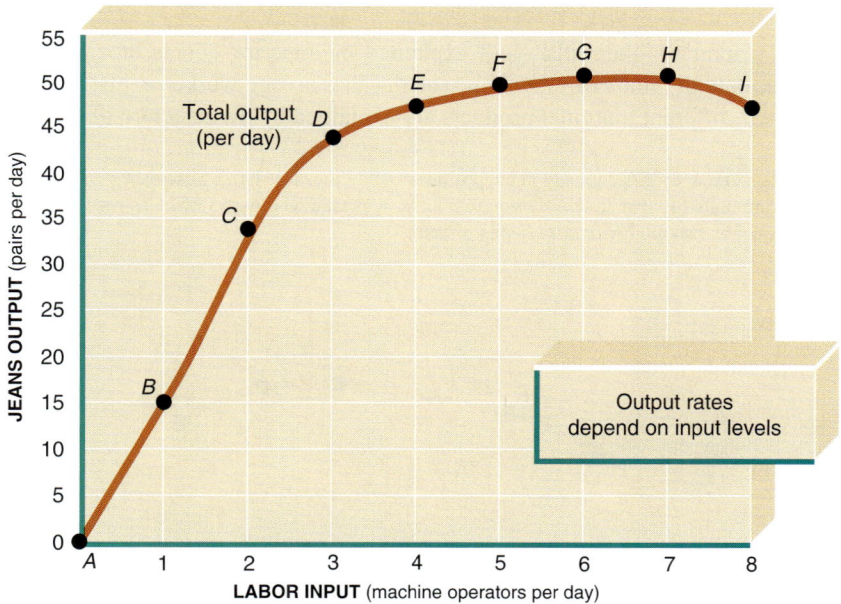

	A	B	C	D	E	F	G	H	I
Number of workers	0	1	2	3	4	5	6	7	8
Total output	0	15	34	44	48	50	51	51	47
Marginal physical product	—	15	19	10	4	2	1	0	−4

FIGURE 21.1
Short-Run Production Function

In the short run some inputs (e.g., land, capital) are fixed in quantity. Output then depends on how much of a variable input (e.g., labor) is used. The short-run production function shows how output changes when more labor is used. This figure and the table below are based on the second (one-machine) row in Table 21.1.

0) and is now illustrated by point *A* in Figure 21.1. To get any jeans output, we need to hire some labor. In this simplified example, *labor is the variable input that determines how much output we get from our fixed inputs (land and capital).* By placing one worker in the factory, we can produce 15 pairs of jeans per day. This possibility is represented by point *B*. The remainder of the production function shows how jeans output changes as we employ more workers in our single-machine factory.

MARGINAL PRODUCTIVITY

The short-run production function not only defines the *limit* to output but also shows how much each worker contributes to that limit. Notice again that jeans output increases from zero (point *A* in Figure 21.2) to 15 pairs (point *B*) when the first machine operator is hired. In other words, total output *increases* by 15 pairs when we employ the first worker. This increase is called the **marginal physical product (MPP)** of that first worker—that is, the *change* in total output that results from employment of one more unit of (labor) input, or

> **marginal physical product (MPP):** The change in total output associated with one additional unit of input.

$$\text{Marginal physical product (MPP)} = \frac{\text{change in total output}}{\text{change in input quantity}}$$

With zero workers, total output was zero. With the first worker, total output increases to 15 pairs of jeans per day. The MPP of the first worker is 15 pairs of jeans.

If we employ a second operator, jeans output more than doubles, to 34 pairs per day (point *C*). The 19-pair *increase* in output represents the marginal physical product of the *second* worker.

The higher MPP of the second worker raises a question about the first. Why was the first's MPP lower? Laziness? Is the second worker faster, less distracted, or harder working?

The second worker's higher MPP isn't explained by superior talents or effort. We assume, in fact, that all "units of labor" are equal—that is, one worker is just as good as another.[2] Their different marginal products are explained by the structure of the pro-

---

[2]In reality, garment workers do differ greatly in energy, talent, and diligence. These differences can be eliminated by measuring units of labor in *constant-quality* units. A person who works twice as hard as everyone else would count as two *quality-adjusted* units of labor.

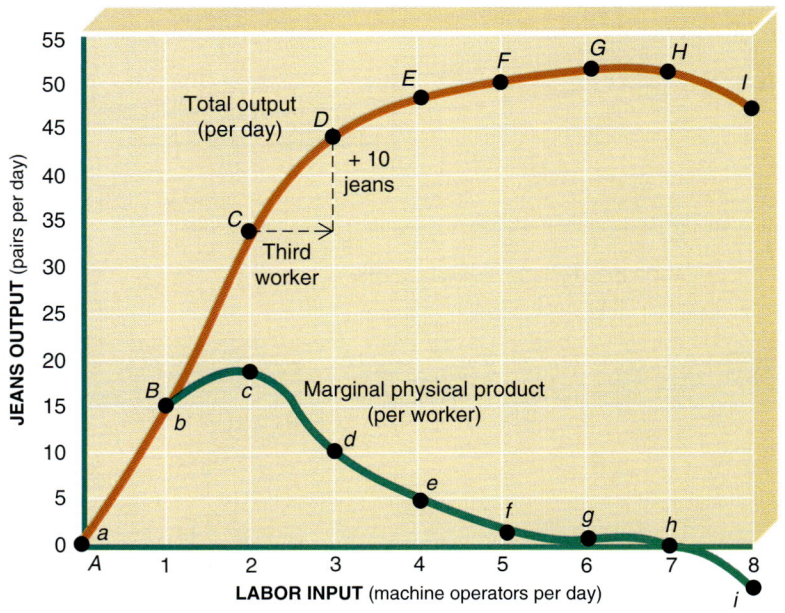

FIGURE 21.2
Marginal Physical Product (MPP)

Marginal physical product is the *change* in total output that results from employing one more unit of input. The *third* unit of labor, for example, increases *total output* from 34 (point *C*) to 44 (point *D*). Hence the *marginal* output of the third worker is 10 pairs of jeans (point *d*). What's the MPP of the fourth worker? What happens to *total* output when this worker is hired?

duction process, not by their respective abilities. The first garment worker not only had to sew jeans but also to unfold bolts of denim, measure the jeans, sketch out the patterns, and cut them to approximate size. A lot of time was spent going from one task to another. Despite the worker's best efforts, this person simply couldn't to everything at once.

A second worker alleviates this situation. With two workers, less time is spent running from one task to another. While one worker is measuring and cutting, the other can continue sewing. This improved *ratio* of labor to other factors of production results in the large jump in total output. The second worker's superior MPP isn't unique to this person: It would have occurred even if we'd hired the workers in the reverse order.

Diminishing Marginal Returns

Unfortunately, total output won't keep rising so sharply if still more workers are hired. Look what happens when a third worker is hired. Total jeans production continues to increase. But the increase from point *C* to point *D* in Figure 21.2 is only 10 pairs per day. Hence, the third worker's MPP (10 pairs) is *less* than that of the second (19 pairs). Marginal physical product is *diminishing*. This concept is illustrated by point *d* in Figure 21.2.

What accounts for this decline in MPP? The answer lies in the ratio of labor to other factors of production. A third worker begins to crowd our facilities. We still have only one sewing machine. Two people can't sew at the same time. As a result, some time is wasted as the operators wait for their turns at the machine. Even if they split up the various jobs, there will still be some "downtime," since measuring and cutting aren't as time-consuming as sewing. Consequently, we can't make full use of a third worker. The relative scarcity of other inputs (capital and land) constrains the third worker's marginal physical product.

Resource constraints are even more evident when a fourth worker is hired. Total output increases again, but the increase this time is very small. With three workers, we got 44 pairs of jeans per day (point *D*); with four workers, we get a maximum of 48 pairs (point *E*). Thus the fourth worker's MPP is only 4 pairs of jeans. There simply aren't enough machines to make productive use of so much labor.

If a seventh worker is hired, the operators get in one another's way, argue, and waste denim. Notice in Figure 21.1 that total output doesn't increase at all when a seventh worker is hired (point *H*). The MPP of the seventh worker is zero (point *h*). Were an eighth worker hired, total output would actually *decline,* from 51 pairs (point *H*) to 47 pairs (point *I*). The eighth worker has a *negative* MPP (point *i* in Figure 21.2).

Law of Diminishing Returns. The problems of crowded facilities apply to most production processes. In the short run, a production process is characterized by a fixed amount of available land and capital. Typically, the only factor that can be varied in the short run is labor. Yet, *as more labor is hired, each unit of labor has less capital and land to work with.* This is simple division: The available facilities are being shared by more and more workers. At some point, this constraint begins to pinch. When it does, marginal physical product declines. This situation is so common that it's the basis for the **law of diminishing returns,** which says that the marginal physical product of any factor of production such as labor, will diminish at some point, as more of it is used in a given production setting. Notice in Figure 21.2 how diminishing returns set in when the third worker was hired.

law of diminishing returns: The marginal physical product of a variable input declines as more of it is employed with a given quantity of other (fixed) inputs.

RESOURCE COSTS

A production function tells us how much output a firm *can* produce with its existing plant and equipment. It doesn't tell us how much the firm will *want* to produce. A firm *might* want to produce at capacity if the profit picture were bright enough. On the other hand, a firm might not produce *any* output if costs always exceeded sales revenue. The

450 PRODUCT MARKETS: THE BASICS

> **profit:** The difference between total revenue and total cost.

most desirable rate of output is the one that maximizes total **profit**—the difference between total revenue and total costs.

The production function therefore is just a starting point for supply decisions. To decide how much output to produce with that function, a firm must next examine the costs of production. How fast do costs rise when output increases?

The law of diminishing returns provides a clue to how fast costs rise. *The economic cost of a product is measured by the value of the resources needed to produce it.* What we've seen here is that those resource requirements eventually increase. Each additional sewing machine operator produces fewer and fewer jeans. In effect, then, each additional pair of jeans produced uses more and more labor.

Suppose we employ one sewing machine and one operator again, for a total output of 15 pairs of jeans per day; see point *b* in Figure 21.3*a*. Now look at production from another perspective, that of *costs*. How much labor cost are we using at point *b* to produce one pair of jeans? The answer is simple. Since one worker is producing 15 pairs of jeans, the labor input per pair of jeans must be one-fifteenth of a worker's day, that is, 0.067 unit of labor; see point 1/*b* in Figure 21.3*b*. All we're doing here is translating *output* data into related *input* (cost) data.

Marginal Resource Cost

The next question is, How do input costs change when output increases. As point *c* in Figure 21.3*a* reminds us, total output increases by 19 pairs when we hire a second worker. What's the implied labor cost of those *additional* 19 pairs? By dividing one worker by 19 pairs of jeans, we observe that the labor cost of that extra output is one-nineteenth, or 0.053 of a worker's day; see point 1/*c* in Figure 21.3*b*.

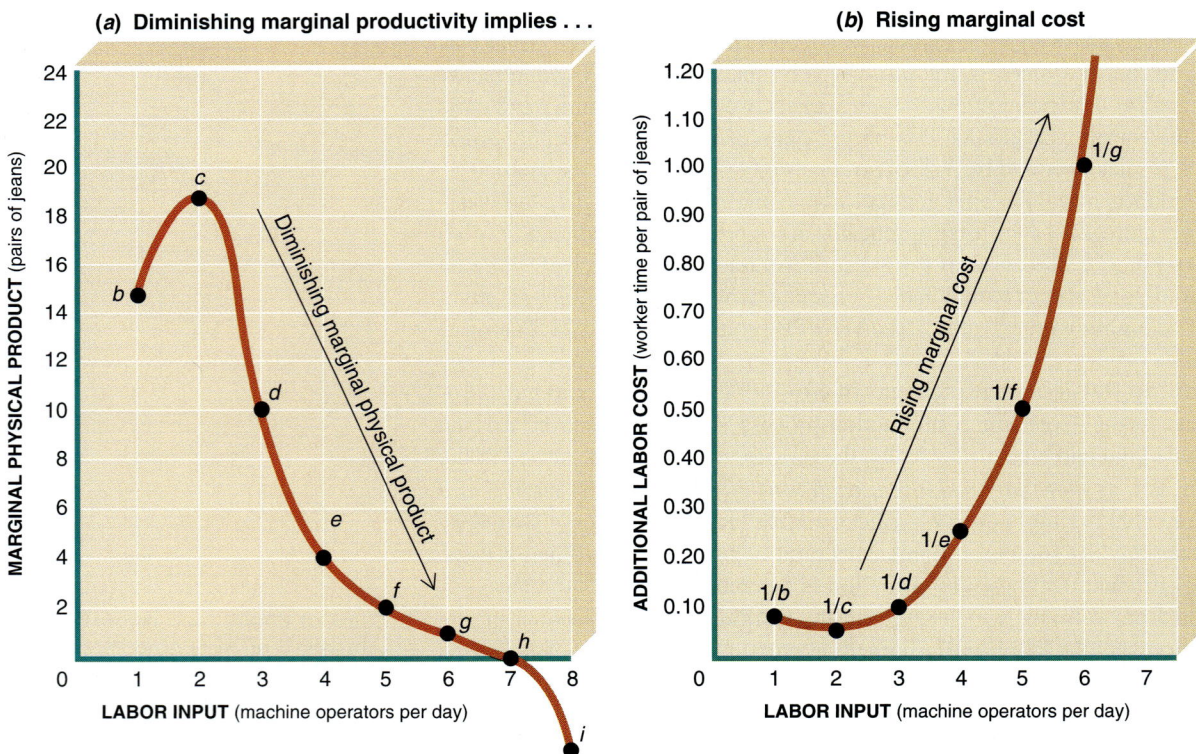

FIGURE 21.3
Falling MPP Implies Rising Marginal Cost

Marginal physical product (MPP) is the additional output obtained by employing one more unit of input. If MPP is falling, each additional unit of input is producing less additional output, which means that the input cost of each unit of output is rising.

The third worker's MPP is 10 pairs (point *d* in part *a*). Therefore, the labor cost of these additional jeans is approximately 1/10 unit of labor per pair (point 1/*d* in part *b*).

When we focus on the *additional* costs incurred from increasing production, we're talking about *marginal* costs. Specifically, **marginal cost (MC)** refers to the *increase* in total costs required to get one additional unit of output. More generally,

$$\frac{\text{Marginal}}{\text{cost (MC)}} = \frac{\text{change in total cost}}{\text{change in output}}$$

marginal cost (MC): The increase in total cost associated with a one-unit increase in production.

In our simple case where labor is the only variable input, the marginal cost of the added jeans is

$$\text{Marginal cost} = \frac{1 \text{ additional worker}}{19 \text{ additional pairs}}$$

$$= 0.053 \text{ workers per pair}$$

The amount 0.053 of labor represents the *change* in total resource cost when we produce one *additional* pair of jeans.

Notice in Figure 21.3*b* that the marginal labor cost of jeans production declines when the second worker is hired. Marginal cost falls from 0.067 unit of labor (plus denim) per pair (point 1/*b* in Figure 21.3*b*) to only 0.053 unit of labor per pair (point 1/*c*. It costs less labor *per pair* to use two workers rather than only one. This is a reflection of the second worker's increased MPP. ***Whenever MPP is increasing, the marginal cost of producing a good must be falling.*** This is illustrated in Figure 21.3 by the move from *b* to *c* in part *a* and the corresponding move from 1/*b* to 1/*c* in part *b*.

Unfortunately, marginal physical product typically declines at some point. As it does, the marginal costs of production rise. In this sense, each additional pair of jeans becomes more expensive—it uses more and more labor per pair. Figure 21.3 illustrates this inverse relationship between MPP and marginal cost. The third worker has an MPP of 10 pairs, as illustrated by point *d*. The marginal labor input of these extra 10 pairs is thus 1 ÷ 10, or 0.10 unit of labor. In other words, one-tenth of a third worker's daily effort goes into each pair of jeans. This additional labor cost *per unit* is illustrated by 1/*d* in part *b* of the figure.

Note in Figure 21.3 how marginal physical product declines after point *c* and how marginal costs rise after point 1/*c*. This is no accident. ***If marginal physical product declines, marginal cost increases.*** Thus, increasing marginal cost is as common as—and the direct result of—diminishing returns. These increasing marginal costs aren't the fault of any person or factor, simply a reflection of the resource constraints found in any established production setting (i.e., existing and limited plant and equipment). In the short run, the quantity and quality of land and capital are fixed, and we can vary only their intensity of use, such as with more or fewer workers. It's in this short-run context that we keep running into diminishing marginal returns and rising marginal costs.

DOLLAR COSTS

This entire discussion of diminishing returns and marginal costs may seem a bit alien. After all, we're interested in the costs of production, and costs are typically measured in *dollars,* not such technical notions as MPP. Jeans producers need to know how many dollars it costs to keep jeans flowing; they don't want a lecture on marginal physical product.

Jeans manufacturers don't have to study marginal physical products, or even the production function. They can confine their attention to dollar costs. The dollar costs observed, however, are directly related to the underlying production function. To understand *why* costs rise—and how they might be reduced—some understanding of the production function is necessary. In this section we translate production functions into dollar costs.

Total Cost

total cost: The market value of all resources used to produce a good or service.

The **total cost** of producing a product includes the market value of all the resources used in its production. To determine this cost we simply identify all the resources used in production, determine their value, and then add up everything.

In the production of jeans, these resources included land, labor, and capital. Table 21.2 identifies these resources, their unit values, and the total dollar cost associated with their use. This table is based on an assumed output of 15 pairs of jeans per day, with the use of one machine operator and one sewing machine (point *B* in Figure 21.2). The rent on the factory is $100 per day, a sewing machine rents for $20 per day, the wages of a garment worker are $80 per day. We'll assume Tight Jeans Corporation can purchase bolts of denim for $30 apiece, with each bolt providing enough denim for 10 pairs of jeans. In other words, one-tenth of a bolt ($3 worth of material) is required for one pair of jeans. We'll ignore any other potential expenses. With these assumptions, the total cost of producing 15 pairs of jeans per day amounts to $245, as shown in Table 21.2.

Fixed Costs. Total costs will change of course as we alter the rate of production. But not all costs increase. In the short run, some costs don't increase at all when output is increased. These are **fixed costs,** in the sense that they don't vary with the rate of output. The factory lease is an example. Once you lease a factory, you're obligated to pay for it, whether or not you use it. The person who owns the factory wants $100 per day. Even if you produce no jeans, you still have to pay that rent. That's the essence of fixed costs.

fixed costs: Costs of production that don't change when the rate of output is altered, for example, the cost of basic plant and equipment.

The leased sewing machine is another fixed cost. When you rent a sewing machine, you must pay the rental charge. It doesn't matter whether you use it for a few minutes or all day long—the rental charge is fixed at $20 per day.

Variable Costs. Labor costs are another story altogether. The amount of labor employed in jeans production can be varied easily. If we decide not to open the factory tomorrow, we can just tell our only worker to take the day off without pay. We'll still have to pay rent, but we can cut back on wages. On the other hand, if we want to increase daily output, we can also get additional workers easily and quickly. Labor is regarded as a **variable cost** in this line of work—that is, a cost that *varies* with the rate of output.

variable costs: Costs of production that change when the rate of output is altered, for example, labor and material costs.

The denim itself is another variable cost. Denim not used today can be saved for tomorrow. Hence, how much we "spend" on denim today is directly related to how many jeans we produce. In this sense, the cost of denim input varies with the rate of jeans output.

Figure 21.4 illustrates how these various costs are affected by the rate of production. On the vertical axis are the costs of production, in dollars per day. Notice that the total cost of producing 15 pairs per day is still $245, as indicated by point *B*. This cost figure consists of

Dollar Cost of Producing 15 Pairs

Fixed costs:		
Factory rent	$100	
Sewing machine rent	20	
Subtotal		$120
Variable costs:		
Wages to labor	$80	
Denim	45	
Subtotal		$125
Total costs		$245

If we increase the rate of output, total costs will rise. ***How fast total costs rise depends on variable costs only,*** however, since fixed costs remain at $120 per day. (Notice the horizontal fixed-cost curve in Figure 21.4.)

Resource Input	×	Unit Price	=	Total Cost
1 factory		$100 per day		$100
1 sewing machine		20 per day		20
1 operator		80 per day		80
1.5 bolts of denim		30 per bolt		45
Total cost				$245

TABLE 21.2

The Total Costs of Production (total cost of producing 15 pairs of jeans per day)

The total cost of producing a good equals the market value of all the resources used in its production. In this case, the production of 15 pairs of jeans per day requires resources worth $245.

With one sewing machine and one factory, there's an absolute limit to daily jeans production. According to the production function in Figure 21.1, the capacity of a factory with one machine is roughly 51 pairs of jeans per day. If we try to produce more jeans than this by hiring additional workers, our total costs will rise, but our output won't. Recall that the seventh worker had a *zero* marginal physical product (Figure 21.2). In fact, we could fill the factory with garment workers and drive total costs sky-high. But the limits of space and one sewing machine don't permit output in excess of 51 pairs per day. This limit to productive capacity is represented by point G on the total cost curve. Further expenditure on inputs will increase production *costs* but not *output*.

Although there's no upper limit to costs, there is a lower limit. If output is reduced to zero, total costs fall only to $120 per day, the level of fixed costs, as illustrated by point A in Figure 21.4. As before, **there's no way to avoid fixed costs in the short run.** Indeed, those fixed costs define the short run.

While Figure 21.4 illustrates *total* costs of production, other measures of cost are often desired. One of the most common measures of cost is average, or per-unit, cost. **Average total cost (ATC)** is simply total cost divided by the rate of output:

$$\frac{\text{Average total}}{\text{cost (ATC)}} = \frac{\text{total cost}}{\text{total output}}$$

At an output of 15 pairs of jeans per day, total costs are $245. The average cost of production is thus $16.33 per pair ($245 \div 15$) at this rate of output.

Average Costs

average total cost (ATC): Total cost divided by the quantity produced in a given time period.

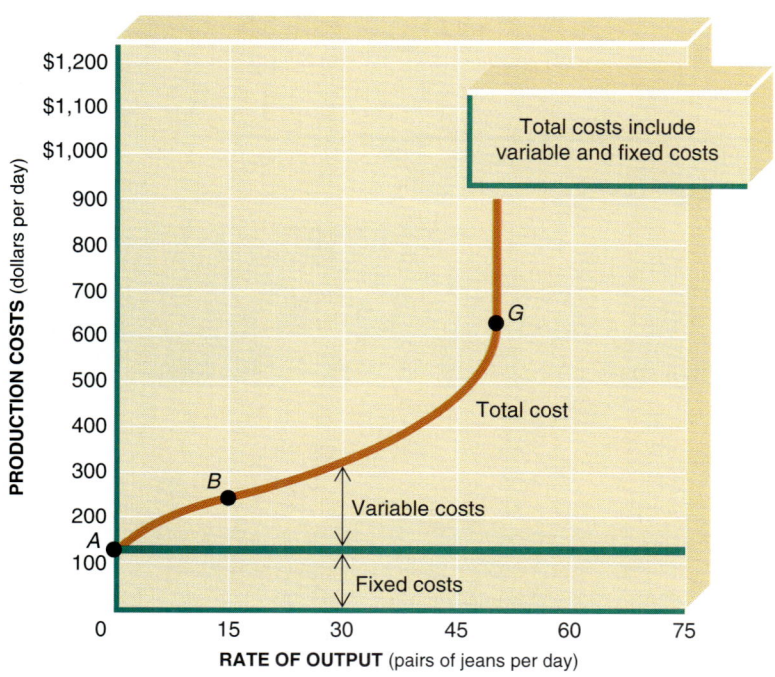

FIGURE 21.4

The Cost of Jeans Production

Total cost includes both fixed and variable costs. Fixed costs must be paid even if no output is produced (point A). Variable costs start at zero and increase with the rate of output. The total cost of producing 15 pairs of jeans (point B) includes $120 in fixed costs (rent on the factory and sewing machines) and $125 in variable costs (denim and wages). Total cost rises as output increases, because additional variable costs must be incurred.

In this example, the short-run capacity is equal to 51 pairs (point G). If still more inputs are employed, costs will rise but not total output.

Figure 21.5 shows how average costs change as the rate of output varies. Row *J* of the cost schedule, for example, again indicates the fixed, variable, and total costs of producing 15 pairs of jeans per day. Fixed costs are still $120; variable costs are $125. Thus the total cost of producing 15 pairs per day is $245, as we saw earlier.

The rest of row *J* shows the average costs of jeans production. These figures are obtained by dividing each dollar total (columns 2, 3, and 4) by the rate of physical output (column 1). At an output rate of 15 pairs per day, **average fixed cost (AFC)** is $8 per pair, **average variable cost (AVC)** is $8.33, and *average total cost (ATC)* is $16.33. ATC, then, is simply the sum of AFC and AVC:

$$ATC = AFC + AVC$$

Falling AFC. At this relatively low rate of output, fixed costs are a large portion of total costs. The rent paid for the factory and sewing machines works out to $8 per pair

> **average fixed cost (AFC):** Total fixed cost divided by the quantity produced in a given time period.

> **average variable cost (AVC):** Total variable cost divided by the quantity produced in a given time period.

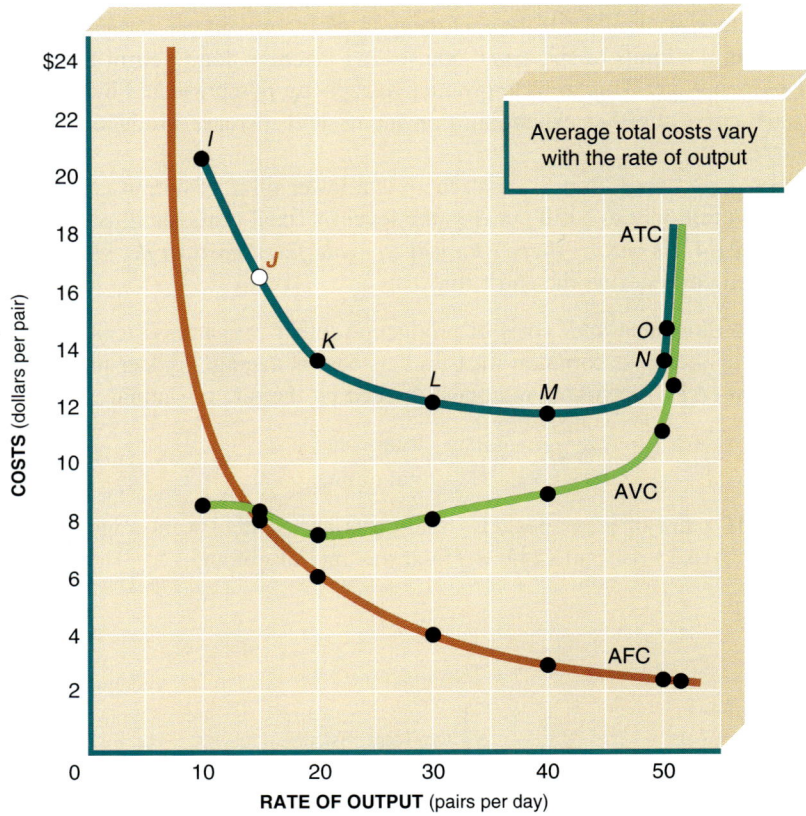

FIGURE 21.5
Average Costs

Average total cost (ATC) in column 7 equals total cost (column 4) divided by the rate of output (column 1). Since total cost includes both fixed (column 2) and variable (column 3) costs, ATC also equals AFC (column 5) plus AVC (column 6). This relationship is illustrated in the graph. The ATC of producing 15 pairs per day (point *J*) equals $16.33; the sum of AFC ($8) and AVC ($8.33).

	(1) Rate of Output	(2) Fixed Costs	+	(3) Variable Costs	=	(4) Total Cost	(5) Average Fixed Cost	+	(6) Average Variable Cost	=	(7) Average Total Cost
H	0	$120		$ 0		$120	—		—		—
I	10	120		85		205	$12.00		$ 8.50		$20.50
J	15	120		125		245	8.00		8.33		16.33
K	20	120		150		270	6.00		7.50		13.50
L	30	120		240		360	4.00		8.00		12.00
M	40	120		350		470	3.00		8.75		11.75
N	50	120		550		670	2.40		11.00		13.40
O	51	120		633		753	2.35		12.41		14.76

($120 ÷ 15). This high average fixed cost accounts for nearly one-half of total average costs. This suggests that it's quite expensive to lease a factory and sewing machine to produce only 15 pairs of jeans per day. To reduce average costs, we must make fuller use of our leased plant and equipment.

Notice what happens to average costs when the rate of output is increased to 20 pairs per day (row K in Figure 21.5). Average fixed costs go down, to only $6 per pair. This sharp decline in AFC results from the fact that total fixed costs ($120) are now spread over more output. Even though our rent hasn't dropped, the *average* fixed cost of producing jeans has.

If we produce more than 20 pairs of jeans per day, AFC will continue to fall. Recall that

$$\text{AFC} = \frac{\text{total fixed cost}}{\text{total output}}$$

The numerator is fixed (at $120 in this case). But the denominator increases as output expands. Hence, *any increase in output will lower average fixed cost.* This is reflected in Figure 21.5 by the constantly declining AFC curve.

As jeans output increases from 15 to 20 pairs per day, AVC falls as well. AVC includes the price of denim purchased and labor costs. The price of denim is unchanged, at $3 per pair ($30 per bolt). But per-unit *labor* costs have fallen, from $5.33 to $4.50 per pair. Thus, the reduction in AVC is completely due to the greater productivity of a second worker. To get 20 pairs of jeans, we had to employ a second worker part-time. In the process, the marginal physical product of labor rose and AVC fell.

With both AFC and AVC falling, ATC must decline as well. In this case, *average* total cost falls from $16.33 per pair to $13.50. This is reflected in row K in the table as well as in point K on the ATC curve in Figure 21.5.

Rising AVC. Although AFC continues to decline as output expands, AVC doesn't keep dropping. On the contrary, AVC tends to start rising quite early in the expansion process. Look at column 6 of the table in Figure 21.5. After an initial decline, AVC starts to increase. At an output of 20 pairs, AVC is $7.50. At 30 pairs, AVC is $8.00. By the time the rate of output reaches 51 pairs per day, AVC is $12.41.

Average variable cost rises because of diminishing returns in the production process. We discussed this concept before. As output expands, each unit of labor has less land and capital to work with. Marginal physical product falls. As it does, labor costs *per pair of jeans* rise, pushing up AVC.

U-Shaped ATC. The steady decline of AFC, when combined with the typical increase in AVC, results in a U-shaped pattern for average total costs. In the early stages of output expansion, the large declines in AFC outweigh any increases in AVC. As a result, ATC tends to fall. Notice that ATC declines from $20.50 to $11.75 as output increases from 10 to 40 pairs per day. This is also illustrated in Figure 21.5 with the downward move from point I to point M.

The battle between falling AFC and rising AVC takes an irreversible turn soon thereafter. When output is increased from 40 to 50 pairs of jeans per day, AFC continues to fall (row N in the table). But the decline in AFC (-60 cents) is overshadowed by the increase in AVC ($+$2.25$). Once rising AVC dominates, ATC starts to increase as well. ATC increases from $11.75 to $13.40 when jeans production expands from 40 to 50 pairs per day.

This and further increases in average total costs cause the ATC curve in Figure 21.5 to start rising. *The initial dominance of falling AFC, combined with the later resurgence of rising AVC, is what gives the ATC curve its characteristic U shape.*

Minimum Average Cost. It's easy to get lost in this thicket of intertwined graphs and jumble of equations. A couple of landmarks will help guide us out, however. One of those is located at the very bottom of the U-shaped average total cost curve. Point

M in Figure 21.5 represents *minimum* average total costs. By producing exactly 40 pairs per day, we minimize the amount of land, labor, and capital used per pair of jeans. For Tight Jeans Corporation, point *M* represents least-cost production—the lowest-cost jeans. For society as a whole, point *M* also represents the lowest possible opportunity cost: At point *M*, we're minimizing the amount of resources used to produce a pair of jeans and therefore maximizing the amount of resources left over for the production of other goods and services.

As attractive as point *M* is, you shouldn't conclude that it's everyone's dream. The primary objective of producers is to maximize *profits*. This is not necessarily the same thing as minimizing average *costs*.

Marginal Cost

One final cost concept is important. Indeed, this last concept is probably the most important one for production. It's *marginal cost*. We encountered this concept in our discussion of resource costs, where we noted that marginal cost refers to the value of the resources needed to produce one more unit of a good. To produce *one* more pair of jeans, we need the denim itself and a very small amount of additional labor. These are the extra or added costs of increasing output by one pair of jeans per day. To compute the *dollar* value of these marginal costs, we could determine the market price of denim and labor and then add them up. Table 21.3 provides an example. In this case, we calculate that the additional or *marginal* cost of producing a sixteenth pair of jeans is $7.24. This is how much *total* costs will increase if we decide to expand jeans output by only one pair per day (from 15 to 16).

Table 21.3 emphasizes the link between resource costs and dollar costs. However, there's a much easier way to compute marginal cost. **Marginal cost refers to the change in total costs associated with one more unit of output.** Accordingly, we can simply observe *total* dollar costs before and after the rate of output is increased. The difference between the two totals equals the *marginal cost* of increasing the rate of output. This technique is much easier for jeans manufacturers who don't know much about marginal resource utilization but have a sharp eye for dollar costs. It's also a lot easier for economics students, of course. But they have an obligation to understand the resource origins of marginal costs and what causes marginal costs to rise or fall. As we noted before, **diminishing returns in production cause marginal costs to increase as the rate of output is expanded.**

Figure 21.6 shows what the marginal costs of producing jeans looks like. At each output rate, marginal cost is computed as the *change* in total cost divided by the *change* in output. When output increases from 20 jeans to 30 jeans, total cost rises by $90. Dividing this change in costs by 10 (the change in output) gives us a marginal cost of $9, as illustrated by point *s*.

Notice in Figure 21.6 how the marginal cost curve slopes steeply up after twenty units of output have been produced. This rise in marginal costs reflects the law of di-

Resources Used to Produce 16th Pair of Jeans	Market Value	Marginal Cost
0.053 unit of labor	0.053 × $80 per unit of labor	$4.24
0.1 bolt of denim	0.1 × $30 per bolt	3.00
		$7.24

TABLE 21.3

Resource Computation of Marginal Cost
Marginal cost refers to the value of the additional inputs needed to produce one more unit of output. To increase daily jeans output from 15 to 16 pairs, we need 0.053 unit of labor and one-tenth of a bolt of denim. These extra inputs cost $7.24.

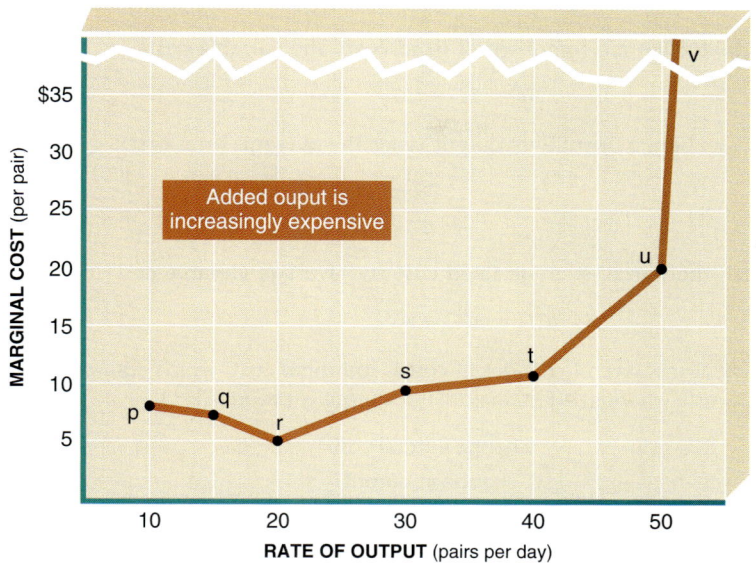

FIGURE 21.6
Marginal Costs

Marginal cost is the change in total cost that occurs when more output is produced. MC equals $\Delta TC/\Delta q$. When diminishing returns set in, MC begins rising, as it does here after the output rate of 20 pairs per day is exceeded.

	Rate of Output	Total Cost	$\dfrac{\Delta TC}{\Delta q}$ = MC
	0	$120	
p	10	205	$85/10 = $8.5
q	15	245	$40/5 = $8.0
r	20	270	$25/5 = $5.0
s	30	360	$90/10 = $9.0
t	40	470	$110/10 = $11.0
u	50	670	$200/10 = $20.0
v	51	753	$83/1 = $83.0

minishing returns. As increases in output become more difficult to achieve, they also become more expensive. Each additional pair of jeans beyond 20 requires a bit more labor than the preceding pair and thus entails rising marginal cost.

All these cost calculations can give you a real headache. They can also give you second thoughts about jumping into Tight Jeans or any other business. There are tough choices to be made. A given firm can produce many different rates of output, each of which entails a distinct level of costs. ***The output decision has to be based not only on the capacity to produce (the production function) but also on the costs of production (the cost functions).*** Only those who make the right decisions will succeed in business.

The decision-making process is made a bit easier with the glossary in Table 21.4 and the generalized cost curves in Figure 21.7. As before, we're concentrating on a short-run production process, with fixed quantities of land and capital. In this case, however, we've abandoned the Tight Jeans Corporation and provided hypothetical costs for an idealized production process. The purpose of these figures is to provide a more general view of how the various cost concepts relate to each other. Note that MC, ATC, AFC, and AVC can all be computed from total costs. All we need, then, are the first two columns of the table in Figure 21.7, and we can compute and graph all the rest of the cost figures.

The centerpiece of Figure 21.7 is the U-shaped ATC curve. Of special significance is its relationship to marginal costs. Notice that ***the MC curve intersects the ATC curve***

A Cost Summary

TABLE 21.4
A Guide to Costs
A quick reference to key measures of cost.

Total costs of production are comprised of **fixed costs** and **variable costs**:

$$TC = FC + VC$$

Dividing total costs by the quantity of output yields the **average total cost**:

$$ATC = \frac{TC}{q}$$

which also equals the sum of **average fixed cost** and **average variable cost**:

$$ATC = AFC + AVC$$

The most important measure of changes in cost is **marginal cost**, which equals the increase in total costs when an additional unit of output is produced:

$$MC = \frac{\text{change in total cost}}{\text{change in output}}$$

FIGURE 21.7
Basic Cost Curves

With total cost and the rate of output, all other cost concepts can be computed. The resulting cost curves have several distinct features. The AFC curve always slopes downward. The MC curve typically rises, sometimes after a brief decline. The ATC curve has a U shape. And the MC curve will always intersect both the ATC and AVC curves at their lowest points (m and n, respectively).

Rate of Output	TC	MC	ATC	AFC	AVC
0	$10.00	—	—	—	—
1	13.00	$ 3.00	$13.00	$10.00	$ 3.00
2	15.00	2.00	7.50	5.00	2.50
3	19.00	4.00	6.33	3.33	3.00
4	25.00	6.00	6.25	2.50	3.75
5	34.00	9.00	6.80	2.00	4.80
6	48.00	14.00	8.00	1.67	6.33
7	68.00	20.00	9.71	1.43	8.28
8	98.00	30.00	12.25	1.25	11.00

at its lowest point (point *m*). This will always be the case. So long as the marginal cost of producing one more unit is less than the previous average cost, average costs must fall. **Thus, average total costs decline as long as the marginal cost curve lies below the average cost curve,** as to the left of point *m* in Figure 21.7.

We already observed, however, that marginal costs rise as output expands, largely because additional workers reduce the amount of land and capital available to each worker (in the short run, the size of plant and equipment is fixed). Consequently, at some point (*m* in Figure 21.7) marginal costs will rise to the level of average costs.

As marginal costs continue to rise beyond point *m*, they begin to pull average costs up, giving the average cost curve its U shape. **Average total costs increase whenever marginal costs exceed average costs.** This is the case to the right of point *m*, since the marginal cost curve always lies above the average cost curve in that part of Figure 21.7.

To visualize the relationship between marginal cost and average cost, imagine computing the average height of people entering a room. If the first person who comes through the door is six feet tall, then the average height of people entering the room is six feet at that point. But what happens to average height if the second person entering the room is only three feet tall? *Average* height declines because the last (marginal) person entering the room is shorter than the previous average. Whenever the last entrant is shorter than the average, the average must fall.

The relationship between marginal costs and average costs is also similar to that between your grade in this course and your grade-point average. If your grade in economics is better (higher) than your other grades, then your overall grade-point average will rise. In other words, a high *marginal* grade will pull your *average* grade up. If you don't understand this, your grade-point average is likely to fall.

ECONOMIC VS. ACCOUNTING COSTS

The cost curves we observed here are based on *real* production relationships. The dollar costs we compute are a direct reflection of underlying resource costs: the land, labor, and capital used in the production process. Not everyone counts this way. On the contrary, accountants and businesspeople typically count dollar costs only and ignore any resource use that doesn't result in an explicit dollar cost.

Return to Tight Jeans for a moment to see the difference. When we computed the dollar cost of producing 15 pairs of jeans per day, we noted the following resource inputs:

INPUTS	COST PER DAY
1 factory rent	$100
1 machine rent	20
1 machine operator	80
1.5 bolts of denim	45
Total cost	$245

The total value of the resources used in the production of 15 pairs of jeans was thus $245 per day. But this figure needn't conform to *actual* dollar costs. Suppose the owners of Tight Jeans decided to sew jeans. Then they wouldn't have to hire a worker or pay $80 per day in wages. **Explicit costs**—the *dollar* payments—would drop to $165 per day. The producers and their accountant would consider this a remarkable achievement. They might assert that the cost of producing jeans had fallen.

An economist would draw no such conclusions. **The essential economic question is how many resources are used in production.** This hasn't changed. One unit of labor is still being employed at the factory; now it's simply the owner, not a hired worker. In either case, one unit of labor is not available for the production of other goods and ser-

explicit cost: A payment made for the use of a resource.

Economic Cost

460 PRODUCT MARKETS: THE BASICS

implicit cost: The value of resources used, even when no direct payment is made.

vices. Hence, society is still paying $245 for jeans, whether the owners of Tight Jeans write checks in that amount or not. The only difference is that we now have an **implicit cost** rather than an explicit one. We really don't care who sews jeans—the essential point is that someone (i.e., a unit of labor) does.

The same would be true if Tight Jeans owned its own factory rather than rented it. If the factory were owned rather than rented, the owners probably wouldn't write any rent checks. Hence, accounting costs would drop by $100 per day. But the factory would still be in use for jeans production and therefore unavailable for the production of other goods and services. The economic (resource) cost of producing 15 pairs of jeans would still be $245.

The distinction between an economic cost and an accounting cost is essentially one between resource and dollar costs. *Dollar cost* refers to the explicit dollar outlays made by a producer; it's the lifeblood of accountants. **Economic cost,** in contrast, refers to the *value* of *all* resources used in the production process; it's the lifeblood of economists. In other words, economists count costs as

economic cost: The value of all resources used to produce a good or service; opportunity cost.

Economic cost = explicit costs + implicit costs

As this formula suggests, *economic and accounting costs will diverge whenever any factor of production is not paid an explicit wage (or rent, etc.).*

The Cost of Homework. These distinctions between economic and accounting costs apply also to the "production" of homework. You can pay people to write term papers for you or buy them off the Internet. At large schools you can often buy lecture notes as well. But most students do their own homework so they'll learn something and not just turn in required assignments.

Doing homework is expensive, however, even if you don't pay someone to do it. The time you spend reading this chapter is valuable. You could be doing something else if you weren't reading right now. What would you be doing? The forgone activity—the best alternative use of your time—represents the economic cost of doing homework. Even if you don't pay yourself for reading this chapter, you'll still incur that *economic* cost.

LONG-RUN COSTS

We've confined our discussion thus far to short-run production costs. *The short run is characterized by fixed costs*—a commitment to specific plant and equipment. A factory, an office building, or some other plant and equipment have been leased or purchased: We're stuck with *fixed costs*. In the short run, our objective is to make the best use of those fixed costs by choosing the appropriate rate of production.

long run: A period of time long enough for all inputs to be varied (no fixed costs).

The long run opens up a whole new range of options. In the **long run,** we have no lease or purchase commitments. We're free to start all over again, with whatever scale of plant and equipment we desire and whatever technology is available. Quite simply, *there are no fixed costs in the long run.* Nor are there any commitments to existing technology. In 1998, General Motors and Isuzu could have built an engine plant of any size. But they decided to build one with a capacity of 200,000 engines (see News). In building the plant, the companies incurred a fixed cost. Once the plant is completed, the companies will focus on the short-run production decision of how many engines to manufacture.

Long-Run Average Costs

The opportunities available in the long run include building a plant of any desired size. Suppose we still wanted to go into the jeans business. In the long run, we could build or lease any size factory we wanted and could lease as many sewing machines as we desired. Figure 21.8 illustrates three choices: a small factory (ATC_1), a medium-sized factory (ATC_2), and a large factory (ATC_3). As we observed earlier, it's very expensive to produce lots of jeans with a small factory. The ATC curve for a small factory (ATC_1) starts to head straight up at relatively low rates of output. In the long run, we'd lease or build such a factory only if we anticipated a continuing low rate of output.

IN THE NEWS

GM, Isuzu Investing $320 Million to Build Advanced Diesel Engines for GM Pickups

DETROIT—General Motors Corp. and Isuzu Motors Ltd. of Japan are investing $320 million in a joint venture to build new-generation diesel engines for GM trucks at a new factory outside Dayton, Ohio.

In addition to broadening the relationship between the two companies, the venture gives GM a new source of advanced engines for pickup trucks, one of the most competitive sectors of the auto industry. . . .

Production at the new plant could begin as early as the third quarter of 2000, with full capacity of 200,000 units a year scheduled for 2004. Initial output would be around 100,000 units.

—Gregory L. White

Source: *The Wall Street Journal*, September 9, 1998. Reprinted by permission of *The Wall Street Journal*. © 1998 Dow Jones & Company, Inc. All rights reserved worldwide. www.wsj.com

Analysis: In the long run, a firm has no fixed costs and can select any desired plant size. Once a plant is built, leased, or purchased, a firm has fixed costs and focuses on short-run output decisions.

The ATC_2 curve illustrates how costs might fall if we leased or built a medium-sized factory. With a small-sized factory, ATC becomes prohibitive at an output of 50 to 60 pairs of jeans per day. A medium-sized factory can produce these quantities at lower cost. Moreover, ATC continues to drop as jeans production increases in the medium-sized factory—at least for a while. Even a medium-sized factory must contend with resource constraints and therefore rising average costs: Its ATC curve is U-shaped also.

If we expected to sell really large quantities of jeans, we'd want to build or lease a large factory. Beyond the rate of output b, the largest factory offers the lowest average total cost. There's a risk in leasing such a large factory, of course. If our sales don't live up to our high expectations, we'll end up with very high fixed costs and thus very expensive jeans. Look at the high average cost of producing only 60 pairs of jeans per day with the large factory (ATC_3).

In choosing an appropriate factory, then, we must decide how many jeans we expect to sell. Once we know our expected output, we can easily pick the right-sized factory. It will be the one that offers the lowest ATC for that rate of output. If we expect to sell fewer jeans than a, we'll choose the small factory in Figure 21.8. If we expect to sell

FIGURE 21.8
Long-Run Costs with Three Plant-Size Options

Long-run cost possibilities are determined by all possible short-run options. In this case, there are three options of varying size (ATC_1, ATC_2, and ATC_3). In the long run, we'd choose that plant which yielded the lowest average cost for any desired rate of output. The solid portion of the curves (LATC) represents these choices. The smallest factory (ATC_1) is best for output levels below a; the largest (ATC_3), output rates in excess of b.

FIGURE 21.9
Long-Run Costs with Unlimited Options

If plants of all sizes can be built, short-run options are infinite. In this case, the LATC curve becomes a smooth U-shaped curve. Each point on the curve represents lowest-cost production for a plant size best suited to one rate of output. The long-run ATC curve has its own MC curve.

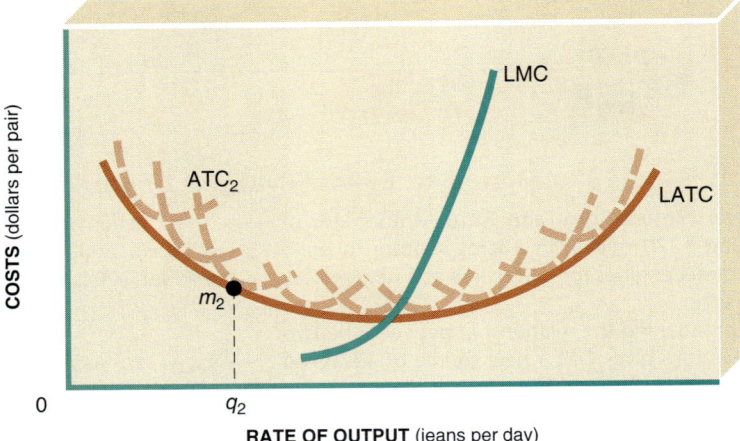

jeans at a rate between a and b, we'll select a medium-sized factory. Beyond rate b, we'll want the largest factory. These choices are reflected in the solid part of the three ATC curves. The composite "curve" created by these three segments constitutes our long-run cost possibilities. ***The long-run cost curve is just a summary of our best short-run cost possibilities, using existing technology and facilities.***

We might confront more than three choices, of course. There's really no reason we couldn't build a factory to any desired size. In the long run, we face an infinite number of scale choices, not just three. The effect of all these choices is to smooth out the long-run cost curve. Figure 21.9 depicts the long-run curve that results. Each rate of output is most efficiently produced by some size (scale) of plant. That sized plant indicates the minimum cost of producing a particular rate of output. Its corresponding short-run ATC curve provides one point on the long-run ATC curve.

Long-Run Marginal Costs

Like all average cost curves, the long-run (LATC) curve has its own marginal cost curve. The long-run marginal cost (LMC) curve isn't a composite of short-run marginal cost curves. Rather, it's computed on the basis of the costs reflected in the long-run ATC curve itself. We won't bother to compute those costs here. Note, however, that the long-run MC curve—like all MC curves—intersects its associated average cost curve at its lowest point.

ECONOMIES OF SCALE

Figure 21.8 seems to imply that a producer must choose either a small plant or a larger one. That isn't completely true. The choice is often between one large plant or *several* small ones. Suppose the desired level of output was relatively large, as at point c in Figure 21.8. A single small plant (ATC_1) is clearly not up to the task. But what about using several small plants rather than one large one (ATC_3)? How would costs be affected?

Notice what happens to *minimum ATC* in Figure 21.8 when the size (scale) of the factory changes. When a medium-sized factory (ATC_2) replaces a small factory (ATC_1), minimum average cost drops (the bottom of ATC_2 is below the bottom of ATC_1). This implies that a jeans producer who wants to minimize costs should build one medium-sized factory rather than try to produce the same quantity with two small ones. **Economies of scale** exist in this situation: Larger facilities reduce minimum average costs. Such economies of scale help explain why a single firm has come to dominate the funeral business (see News).

Larger production facilities don't always result in cost reductions. Suppose a firm has the choice of producing the quantity Q_m from several small factories or from one large, centralized facility. Centralization may have three different impacts on costs;

economies of scale: Reductions in minimum average costs that come about through increases in the size (scale) of plant and equipment.

IN THE NEWS

Funeral Giant Moves In on Small Rivals

Life's two certainties are death and taxes. Some day, it could be just as certain that Service Corp. International will handle your funeral.

The Houston-based company will handle one in 10 funeral services in the USA this year, or about 230,000. In just 32 years, the company has grown from a single funeral home into the world's biggest death-services provider with 2,631 funeral homes, 250 cemeteries and 137 crematoria in North America, Europe and Australia. . . .

SCI's sheer size provides big advantages over competitors. SCI is able to get cheaper prices on caskets and other products from suppliers.

Its funeral homes clustered in the same markets cut costs by sharing vehicles, personnel, services and supplies. That helps give SCI a profit of 31 cents on every dollar it takes in for a typical funeral, vs. 12 cents for the industry as a whole, SCI says.

Funeral directors "don't want to think of (death) as big business," says Betty Murray of the National Foundation of Funeral Directors. "But we're in the era of acquisitions and consolidations."

—Ron Trujillo

Source: *USA Today*, October 31, 1995. © 1995, USA Today. Reprinted with permission. www.usatoday.com

Analysis: As the size of a firm increases, it may be able to reduce the costs of doing business. Economies of scale give a large firm a competitive advantage over smaller firms.

---

these are illustrated in Figure 21.10. In each illustration, we see the average total cost (ATC) curve for a typical small firm or plant and the ATC curve for a much larger plant producing the same product.

Constant Returns. Figure 21.10a depicts a situation in which there's no economic advantage to centralization of manufacturing operations, because a large plant is no more efficient than a lot of small plants. The critical focus here is on the *minimum* average costs attainable for a given rate of output. Note that the lowest point on the smaller plant's ATC curve (point c) is no higher or lower than the lowest point on the larger firm's ATC curve (point m_1). Hence, it would be just as cheap to produce the quantity Q_m from a multitude of small plants as it would be to produce Q_m from one large plant.

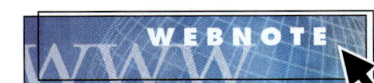

To learn more about the business of dying, go to www.sci-corp.com.

FIGURE 21.10
Economies of Scale

A lot of output (Q_m) can be produced from one large plant or many small ones. Here we contrast the average total costs associated with one small plant (ATC_s) and three large plants (ATC_1, ATC_2, and ATC_3). If a large plant attains the same minimum average costs (point m_1 in part a) as a smaller plant (point c), there's no advantage to large size (scale). Many small plants can produce the same output just as cheaply. However, either economies (part b) or diseconomies (part c) of scale may exist.

constant returns to scale: Increases in plant size do not affect minimum average cost: minimum per-unit costs are identical for small plants and large plants.

Thus increasing the size (or *scale*) of individual plants won't reduce minimum average costs: This is a situation of **constant returns to scale.**

Economies. Figure 21.10b illustrates the situation in which a larger plant can attain a lower minimum average cost than a smaller plant. That is, economies of scale (or *increasing returns to scale*) exist, which is evident from the fact that the larger firm's ATC curve falls *below* the dashed line in the graph (m_2 is less than c). The greater efficiency of the large factory might come from any of several sources. This is the situation of the funeral home depicted in the News feature. By centralizing core funeral services, Services Corp. International was able to reduce average costs per funeral. Larger organizations may also gain a cost advantage through specialization, by having each worker become expert in a particular skill. By contrast, a smaller establishment might have to use the same individual(s) to perform several functions, thereby reducing productivity at each task. Also, some kinds of machinery may be economical only if they're used to produce massive volumes,[3] an opportunity only very large factories have. Finally, a large plant might acquire a persistent cost advantage through the process of learning by doing. That is, its longer experience and greater volume of output may translate into improved organization and efficiency.

Diseconomies. Even though large plants may be able to achieve greater efficiencies than smaller plants, there's no assurance that they actually will. In fact, increasing the size (scale) of a plant may actually *reduce* operating efficiency, as depicted in Figure 21.10c. Workers may feel alienated in a plant of massive proportions and feel little commitment to productivity. Creativity may be stifled by rigid corporate structures and off-site management. A large plant may also foster a sense of anonymity that induces workers to underperform. When these things happen, *diseconomies of scale* result. Microsoft tries to avoid such diseconomies of scale by creating autonomous cells of no more than 35 employees ("small plants") within its larger corporate structure.

In evaluating long-run options, then, we must be careful to recognize that *efficiency and size don't necessarily go hand in hand.* Some firms and industries may be subject to economies of scale, but others may not. Bigger isn't always better.

THE ECONOMY TOMORROW

Global Competitiveness and B2B Cost Savings

From 1900 to 1970, the United States regularly exported more goods and services than it imported. Since then, America has had a trade deficit nearly every year. In 2000, U.S. imports exceeded exports by $369 billion. To many people, such trade deficits are a symptom that the United States can no longer compete effectively in world markets.

Global competitiveness ultimately depends on the costs of production. If international competitors can produce goods more cheaply, they'll be able to undersell U.S. goods in global markets.

Cheap Foreign Labor?

Cheap labor keeps costs down in many countries. The average wage in Mexico, for example, ranges from $2 to $3 an hour, compared to over $12 an hour in the United States. Low wages are *not*, however, a reliable measure of global competitiveness. To compete in global markets, one must produce more *output* for a given quantity of *inputs*. In other words, labor is "cheap" only if it produces a lot of output in return for the wages paid.

A worker's contribution to output is measured by *marginal physical product (MPP)*. What we saw in this chapter was that *a worker's productivity (MPP) depends on the quantity and quality of other resources in the production process.* In this regard, U.S. workers have a tremendous advantage: They work with vast quantities of capital and

---

[3]In other words, the machinery itself may be subject to economies of scale.

state-of-the-art technology. They also come to the workplace with more education. Their high wages reflect this greater productivity.

A true measure of global competitiveness must take into account both factor costs (e.g., wages) and productivity. One such measure is **unit labor costs,** which indicates the labor cost of producing one unit of output. It's computed as

$$\text{Unit labor cost} = \frac{\text{wage rate}}{\text{MPP}}$$

Unit Labor Costs

unit labor cost: Hourly wage rate divided by output per labor-hour.

Suppose the MPP of a U.S. worker is 6 units per hour and the wage is $12 an hour. The unit labor cost would be

$$\frac{\text{Unit labor cost}}{\text{(United States)}} = \frac{\$12/\text{hour}}{6 \text{ units/hour}} = \frac{\$2/\text{unit}}{\text{of output}}$$

By contrast, assume the average worker in Mexico has an MPP of 1 unit per hour and a wage of $3 an hour. In this case, the unit labor cost would be

$$\frac{\text{Unit labor cost}}{\text{(Mexico)}} = \frac{\$3}{1} = \frac{\$3/\text{unit}}{\text{of output}}$$

According to these hypothetical examples, "cheap" Mexican labor is no bargain. Mexican labor is actually *more* costly in production, despite the lower wage rate.

What these calculations illustrate is how important productivity is for global competitiveness. If we want the United States to stay competitive in global markets, U.S. productivity must increase as fast as that in other nations.

Productivity Advance

The production function introduced in this chapter helps illustrate the essence of global competitiveness in the economy tomorrow. Until now, we've regarded a firm's production function as a technological fact of life—the *best* we could do, given our state of technological and managerial knowledge. In the real world, however, the best is always getting better. Science and technology are continuously advancing. So is our knowledge of how to organize and manage our resources. These advances keep *shifting* production functions upward: More can be produced with any given quantity of inputs. In the process, the costs of production shift downward, as illustrated in Figure 21.11 by the downward shifts of the MC and ATC curves. These downward shifts imply that we can get more of the goods and services we desire with available resources. We can also compete more effectively in global markets.

For current data on unit labor costs and underlying wage and productivity trends, visit the U.S. Bureau of Labor Statistics at www.bls.gov.

B2B Solutions

The Internet has been an important source of productivity gains in the last 10 years. Although the Internet originated over 30 years ago, its commercial potential emerged with the creation of the World Wide Web around 1990. As recently as 1995 there were

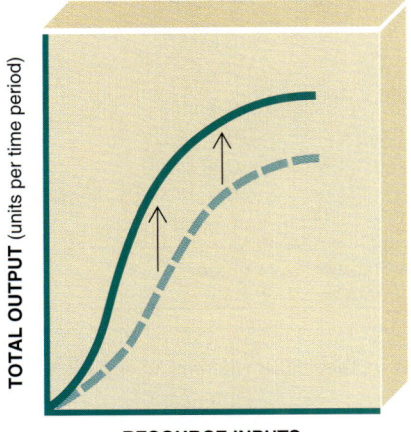

(a) When the production function shifts up

RESOURCE INPUTS
(units per time period)

(b) Cost curves shift down

RATE OF OUTPUT
(units per time period)

FIGURE 21.11

Improvements in Productivity Reduce Costs

Advances in technological or managerial knowledge increase our productive capability. This is reflected in upward shifts of the production function (part *a*) and downward shifts of production cost curves (part *b*).

WORLD VIEW

Number of Internet Sites Surges at End of Decade

Source: Federal Reserve Bank of Dallas, *Southwest Economy,* July–August 2001. www.dallasfed.gov

Analysis: The growth of B2B e-commerce has reduced information and transaction costs, thereby increasing productivity: "Smarter" workers produce more output.

WORLD VIEW

United States Gains Cost Advantage

In the 1970s, unit labor costs in the United States increased by 8 percent per year and by 2.6 percent in the 1980s. In the 1990s, however, productivity increased faster than wages; unit labor costs actually declined. This moderation of unit labor costs gave U.S. producers a cost advantage over most foreign producers, as the following figures reveal.

Country	Average Increase in Unit Labor Costs, 1990–2000 (percent per year)
Norway	3.5
Italy	2.2
Great Britain	1.9
Korea	1.2
Denmark	0.6
Canada	0.6
Taiwan	0.2
Belgium	−0.3
United States	−0.4
France	−0.9
Japan	−1.0

Source: U.S. Bureau of Labor Statistics. www.bls.gov

Analysis: Global competitiveness depends on unit labor costs. U.S. unit labor costs declined in the 1990s, increasing America's competitiveness in world markets.

only 10,000 websites. Now there are over 30 *million* sites (see World View). This vastly expanded spectrum of information has helped businesses cut costs in many ways. The cost of gathering information about markets and inputs has been reduced. With the reach of the Internet, firms can engage in greater specialization. Firms can also manage their inventories and supply chains much more efficiently. Transaction and communications costs are reduced as well. All of these productivity improvements are cutting U.S. production costs by $100–250 billion a year. These cost savings helped U.S. businesses *reduce* unit labor costs by 0.4 percent a year in the 1990s. As the accompanying World View confirms, those gains widened the United States' lead in the ongoing race for global competitiveness. To maintain that leading position in the economy tomorrow, U.S. productivity must continue to advance at a brisk pace.

SUMMARY

- A production function indicates the maximum amount of output that can be produced with different combinations of inputs. It's a technological relationship and changes (shifts) when new technology or management techniques are discovered.
- In the short run, some inputs (e.g., land and capital) are fixed in quantity. Increases in (short-run) output result from more use of variable inputs (e.g., labor).
- The contribution of a variable input to total output is measured by its marginal physical product (MPP). This is the amount by which *total* output increases when one more unit of the input is employed.
- The MPP of a factor tends to decline as more of it is used in a given production facility. Diminishing marginal returns result from crowding more of a variable input into a production process, reducing the amount of fixed inputs *per unit* of variable input.
- Marginal cost is the increase in total cost that results when output is increased by one unit. Marginal cost increases whenever marginal physical product diminishes.
- Not all costs go up when the rate of output is increased. Fixed costs such as space and equipment leases don't vary with the rate of output. Only variable costs such as labor and material go up when output is increased.
- Average total cost (ATC) equals total cost divided by the quantity of output produced. ATC declines whenever marginal cost (MC) is less than average cost and rises when MC exceeds it. The MC and ATC curves intersect at minimum ATC (the bottom of the U). That intersection represents least-cost production.
- The economic costs of production include the value of *all* resources used. Accounting costs typically include only those dollar costs actually paid (explicit costs).
- In the long run there are no fixed costs; the size (scale) of production can be varied. The long-run ATC curve indicates the lowest cost of producing output with facilities of appropriate size.
- Economies of scale refer to reductions in minimum average cost attained with larger plant size (scale). If minimum ATC rises with plant size, diseconomies of scale exist.
- Global competitiveness and domestic living standards depend on productivity advances. Improvements in productivity shift production functions up and push cost curves down.

Key Terms

factors of production
production function
productivity
efficiency
opportunity cost
short run
marginal physical product (MPP)
law of diminishing returns

profit
marginal cost (MC)
total cost
fixed costs
variable costs
average total cost (ATC)
average fixed cost (AFC)
average variable cost (AVC)

explicit cost
implicit cost
economic cost
long run
economies of scale
constant returns to scale
unit labor cost

Questions for Discussion

1. What are the production costs of your economics class? What are the fixed costs? The variable costs? What's the marginal cost of enrolling more students?
2. Suppose all your friends offered to help wash your car. Would marginal physical product decline as more friends helped? Why or why not?
3. How many engines *can* GM produce at its new factory? (See News, page 461.) How many engines will GM *want* to produce?
4. Owner/operators of small gas stations rarely pay themselves an hourly wage. How does this practice affect the economic cost of dispensing gasoline?
5. Corporate funeral giants have replaced small family-run funeral homes in many areas, in large part because of the lower costs they achieve (see News, page 463.) What kind of economies of scale exist in the funeral business? Why doesn't someone build one colossal funeral home and drive costs down further?
6. Are colleges subject to economies of scale or diseconomies?
7. Why don't more U.S. firms move to Mexico to take advantage of low wages there? Would an *identical* plant in Mexico be as productive as its U.S. counterpart?
8. How would your productivity in completing course work be measured? Has your productivity changed since you began college? What caused the productivity changes? How could you increase productivity further?

Web Activities

1. Log on to www.whitehouse.gov/fsbr/employment.html and click on the chart for productivity.
   (a) What has been the general trend for productivity in the United States since 1990?
   (b) What does this trend suggest has happened to production functions in the United States?
   (c) Assuming this change in productivity has happened to all firms, how will this change in productivity affect cost curves?
2. Log on to www.whitehouse.gov/fsbr/employment.html and click on the chart for the employment cost index.
   (a) Are hourly employment costs a fixed or variable cost?
   (b) How is the average total cost curve affected by these changes in costs? In the chart you found, what has been the trend in employment costs since 1996?
   (c) What is the likely implication of the trend in employment cost on profits?
3. Unit labor cost takes into account productivity and the cost of labor. Find the trend in unit labor cost for the United States at stats.bls.gov/news.release/prod2.toc.htm. Access Table 1 to find the unit labor cost index.
   (a) Record the values of the unit labor cost index for the most recent four quarters.
   (b) How did productivity and the cost of labor affect the unit labor cost for this time period?
   (c) *Ceteris paribus,* what will happen to the cost curves and economic profit as a result of these changes in labor cost?

ALERT! THE ACCOMPANYING STUDENT PROBLEM SET CONTAINS NUMERICAL AND GRAPHING PROBLEMS FOR THIS CHAPTER

PART 9

Market Structure

Although market demand and production functions set limits to output choices, not all firms respond the same way to these limits. The number and size of the firms in a market—industry structure—also affect production and pricing decisions. Chapters 22 through 26 examine how different market structures affect the supply of goods and services.

CHAPTER 22

The Competitive Firm

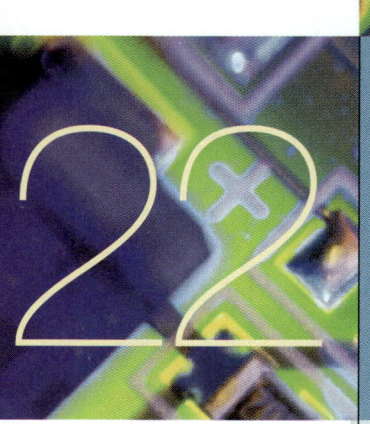

America Online would love to raise the price of accessing its archive of information and Internet services. It isn't likely to do so, however, because too many other firms also offer online services and Net access. If America Online raises its prices, customers might sign up with another company.

Your campus bookstore may be in a better position to raise prices. On most college campuses there's only one bookstore. If the campus store increases the price of books or supplies, most of its customers (you) will have little choice but to pay the higher tab.

As we discover in this and the next few chapters, the degree of competition in product markets is a major determinant of product prices, quality, and availability. Although all firms are in business to make a profit, their profit opportunities are limited by the amount of competition they face.

This chapter begins an examination of how businesses make price and production decisions. We first explore the nature of profits and how they're computed. We then observe how one type of firm—a perfectly competitive one—can *maximize* its profits by selecting the right rate of output. The following questions are at the center of this discussion:

- What are *profits?*
- What are the unique characteristics of competitive firms?
- How much output will a competitive firm produce?

The answers to these questions will shed more light on how the *supply* of goods and services is determined in a market economy.

THE PROFIT MOTIVE

The basic incentive for producing goods and services is the expectation of profit. *Owning* plant and equipment isn't enough. To generate a current flow of income, one must *use* that plant and equipment to produce and sell goods.

Profit is the difference between a firm's sales revenues and its total costs. It's the residual that the owners of a business receive. The recipient of the residual may be the sole owner of a corner grocery store, or it may be the group of stockholders who collectively own a large corporation. In either case, it's the quest for profit that motivates people to own and operate a business.

"You know what I think, folks? Improving technology isn't important. Increased profits aren't important. What's important is to be warm, decent human beings."

Analysis: The principal motivation for producing goods and services is to earn a profit. Although other goals may seem desirable, businesses that fail to earn a profit won't survive.

Other Motivations

Profit isn't the only thing that motivates producers. Like the rest of us, producers also worry about social status and crave recognition. People who need to feel important, to control others, or to demonstrate achievement are likely candidates for running a business. Many small businesses are maintained by people who gave up 40-hour weeks, $50,000 incomes, and a sense of alienation in exchange for 80-hour weeks, $45,000 incomes, and a sense of identity and control.

In large corporations, the profit motive may lie even deeper below the surface. Stockholders of large corporations rarely visit corporate headquarters. The people who manage the corporation's day-to-day business may have little or no stock in the company. Such nonowner-managers may be more interested in their own jobs, salaries, and self-preservation than in the profits that accrue to the stockholding owners. If profits suffer, however, the corporation may start looking for new managers. The accompanying cartoon notwithstanding, the "bottom line" for virtually all businesses is the level of profits.

profit: The difference between total revenue and total cost.

Is the Profit Motive Bad?

If it weren't possible to make a profit, few people would choose to supply goods and services. Yet the general public remains suspicious of the profit motive. As the News indicates, one out of four people think the profit motive is bad. An even higher percentage believes the profit motive results in *inferior* products at inflated prices.

As we'll see, the profit motive *can* induce business firms to pollute the environment, restrict competition, or maintain unsafe working conditions. However, **the profit motive also encourages businesses to produce the goods and services consumers desire, at prices they're willing to pay.** The profit motive, in fact, moves the "invisible hand" that Adam Smith said orchestrates market outcomes.

ECONOMIC VS. ACCOUNTING PROFITS

Although profits might be a necessary inducement for producers, most consumers feel that profits are too high. And that may be so in many cases. But most consumers have no idea how much profit U.S. businesses actually make. Public *perceptions* of profit are seven or eight times higher than actual profits. The typical consumer believes that

472 MARKET STRUCTURE

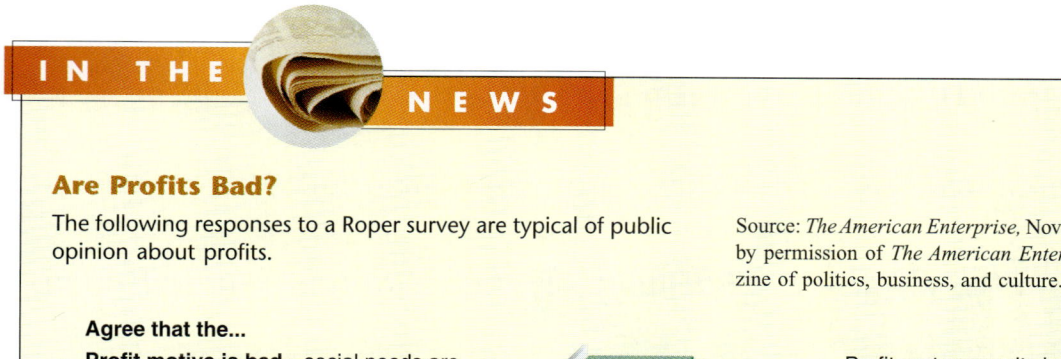

Are Profits Bad?
The following responses to a Roper survey are typical of public opinion about profits.

Source: *The American Enterprise,* November–December 1993. Reprinted by permission of *The American Enterprise,* a Washington-based magazine of politics, business, and culture. www.theamericanenterprise.org

Agree that the...
Profit motive is bad—social needs are ignored in pursuit of high profits 27%

Profit motive is good—it causes people to invest and provide monies to build plants, industries 42%

Both (vol.) 9%
Neither (vol.) 4%
Don't know 17%

Profit system results in better products at lower prices 39%

Profit system results in inferior products at inflated prices 29%

Both (vol.) 8%
Neither (vol.) 5%
Don't know 19%

Analysis: The profit motive is the primary incentive for supplying goods and services. Many consumers are distrustful of that motive, however.

---

35 cents of every sales dollar goes to profits. In reality, average profit per sales dollar is closer to 5 cents.

Faulty perceptions of profits aren't confined to the general public. As surprising as it might seem, most businesses also measure their profits incorrectly.

Economic Profits

economic cost: The value of all resources used to produce a good or service; opportunity cost.

explicit costs: A payment made for the use of a resource.

implicit cost: The value of resources used, even when no direct payment is made.

economic profit: The difference between total revenues and total economic costs.

Everyone agrees that profit represents the difference between total revenues and total costs. Where people part ways is over the decision of what to include in total costs. Recall from Chapter 21 how economists compute costs. **Economic cost** refers to the value of *all* resources used in production, whether or not they receive an explicit payment. By contrast, most businesses count only **explicit costs**—that is, those they actually write checks for. They typically don't take into account the **implicit costs** of the labor or land and buildings they might own. As a result, they understate costs.

If businesses (and their accountants) understate true costs, they'll overstate true profits. Part of the accounting "profit" will really be compensation to unpaid land, labor, or capital used in the production process. *Whenever economic costs exceed explicit costs, observed (accounting) profits will exceed true (economic) profits.* Indeed, what appears to be an accounting profit may actually disguise an economic loss, as illustrated by Mr. Fujishige's strawberry farm once located right next to Disneyland (see News). To determine the **economic profit** of a business, we must subtract all implicit factor costs from observed accounting profits:

$$\begin{aligned} \text{Economic profit} &= \text{total revenue} - \text{total economic cost} \\ &= \text{accounting profit} - \text{implicit costs} \end{aligned}$$

Suppose, for example, that Table 22.1 accurately summarizes the revenues and costs associated with a local drugstore. Monthly sales revenues amount to $27,000. Explicit costs paid by the owner-manager include the cost of merchandise bought from pro-

IN THE NEWS

Strawberry Fields Forever?

ANAHEIM, CALIFORNIA—Hiroshi Fujishige is a successful strawberry farmer. For over 40 years he has been earning a profit growing and selling strawberries and other produce from his 58-acre farm. Mr. Fujishige could make even more money if he stopped growing strawberries. His 58-acre strawberry patch is located across the street from Disneyland. The people from Disney have offered him $32 million just to *lease* the farm; developers have offered as much as $2 million per acre to *buy* the land. But Mr. Fujishige, who lives in a tiny house on the farm he bought 45 years ago (for $2500!) isn't selling. "I'm a farmer, and I've been farming since I got out of high school in 1941," he says. As long as he can make a profit from strawberries, he says, he'll keep growing them.

Source: *Washington Post*, March 9, 1994. © 1994, The Washington Post. Reprinted with permission. www.washingtonpost.com

Analysis: Accounting profits may overrate the profitability of an enterprise by failing to consider the opportunity cost of all resources used in production. If the opportunity cost of the land were deducted, this farm would show an economic loss. In August 1998 Mr. Fujishige sold all but 3.5 acres of his farm to Disneyland for its new California Adventure theme park.

---

ducers for resale to consumers ($17,000), wages to the employees of the drugstore, rent and utilities paid to the landlord, and local sales and business taxes. When all these explicit costs are subtracted from total revenue, we're left with an *accounting profit* of $6,000 per month.

The owner-manager of the drugstore may be quite pleased with an accounting profit of $6,000 per month. He's working hard for this income, however. To keep his store running, the owner-manager is working 10 hours per day, seven days a week. This adds up to 300 hours of labor per month. Were he to work this hard for someone else, his labor would be compensated explicitly—with a paycheck. Although he doesn't choose to pay himself this way, his labor still represents a real resource cost. To compute *economic* profit, we must subtract this implicit cost from the drugstore's accounting profits. Suppose the owner could earn $10 per hour in the best alternative job. Multiplying this wage rate ($10) by the number of hours he works in the drugstore (300), we see that the implicit cost of his labor is $3,000 per month.

The owner has also used his savings to purchase inventory for the store. He purchased the goods on his shelves for $120,000. If he had invested his savings in some other

Total (gross) revenues per month	$27,000
less explicit costs:	
Cost of merchandise sold	$17,000
Wages to cashier, stock, and delivery help	2,500
Rent and utilities	800
Taxes	700
Total explicit costs	$21,000
Accounting profit (revenue minus explicit costs)	$ 6,000
less implicit costs:	
Wages of owner-manager, 300 hours @ $10 per hour	$ 3,000
Return on inventory investment, 10% per year on $120,000	1,000
Total implicit costs	$ 4,000
Economic profit (revenue minus *all* costs)	$ 2,000

TABLE 22.1

The Computation of Economic Profit

To calculate economic profit, we must take account of *all* costs of production. The economic costs of production include the implicit (opportunity) costs of the labor and capital a producer contributes to the production process. The accounting profits of a business take into account only explicit costs paid by the owner. Reported (accounting) profits will exceed economic profits whenever implicit costs are ignored.

business, he could have earned a return of 10 percent per year. This forgone return represents a real cost. In this case, the implicit return (opportunity cost) on his capital investment amounts to $12,000 per year (10 percent × $120,000), or $1,000 per month.

To calculate the *economic* profit this drugstore generates, we count both explicit and implicit costs. Hence, we must subtract all implicit factor payments (costs) from reported profits. The residual in this case amounts to $2,000 per month. That's the drugstore's *economic* profit.

Note that when we compute the drugstore's economic profit, we deduct the opportunity cost of the owner's capital. Specifically, we assumed that his funds would have reaped a 10 percent return somewhere else. In effect, we've assumed that a "normal" rate of return is 10 percent. This **normal profit** (the opportunity cost of capital) is an economic cost. Rather than investing in a drugstore, the owner could have earned a 10 percent return on his funds by investing in a fast-food franchise, a music store, a steel plant, or some other production activity. By choosing to invest in a drugstore instead, the owner was seeking a *higher* return on his funds—more than he could have obtained elsewhere. In other words, *economic profits represent something over and above "normal profits."*

> **normal profit:** The opportunity cost of capital; zero economic profit.

Our treatment of "normal" returns as an economic cost leads to a startling conclusion: On average, economic profits are zero. Only firms that reap *above-average* returns can claim economic profits. This seemingly strange perspective on profits emphasizes the opportunity costs of all economic activities. *A productive activity reaps an economic profit only if it earns more than its opportunity cost.*

Entrepreneurship

Naturally, everyone in business wants to earn an economic profit. But relatively few people can stay ahead of the pack. To earn economic profits, a business must see opportunities that others have missed, discover new products, find new and better methods of production, or take above-average risks. In fact, economic profits are often regarded as a reward to entrepreneurship, the ability and willingness to take risks, to organize factors of production, and to produce something society desires.

Consider the local drugstore again. People in the neighborhood clearly want such a drugstore, as evidenced by its substantial sales revenue. But why should anyone go to the trouble and risk of starting and maintaining one? We noted that the owner-manager *could* earn $3,000 in wages by accepting a regular job plus $1,000 per month in returns on capital by investing in an "average" business. Why should he take on the added responsibilities and risk of owning and operating his own drugstore?

The inducement to take on the added responsibilities of owning and operating a business is the potential for profit, the extra income over and above normal factor payments. In the case of the drugstore owner, this extra income is the economic profit of $2,000 (Table 22.1). In the absence of such additional compensation, few people would want to make the extra effort required.

Risk

Don't forget, however, that the *potential* for profit is not a *guarantee* of profit. Quite the contrary. Substantial risks are attached to starting and operating a business. Tens of thousands of businesses fail every year, and still more suffer economic losses. From this perspective, profit also represents compensation for the risks incurred in owning or operating a business.

MARKET STRUCTURE

Not all businesses have an equal opportunity to earn an economic profit. The opportunity for profit may be limited by the *structure* of the industry in which the firm is engaged. One of the reasons Microsoft is such a profitable company is that it has long held a **monopoly** on computer operating systems. As the supplier of virtually all operating systems, Microsoft could raise software prices without losing many customers. T-shirt shops, by contrast, have to worry about all the other stores

> **monopoly:** A firm that produces the entire market supply of a particular good or service.

FIGURE 22.1
Market Structures

The number and relative size of firms producing a good vary across industries. Market structures range from perfect competition (a great many firms producing the same good) to monopoly (only one firm). Most real-world firms are along the continuum of *imperfect* competition. Included in that range are duopoly (two firms), oligopoly (a few firms), and monopolistic competition (many firms).

that sell similar products in the area (see News). Faced with so much competition, the owner of a T-shirt shop doesn't have the power to raise prices, or accumulate economic profits.

Figure 22.1 illustrates various **market structures.** At one extreme is the monopoly structure in which only one firm produces the entire supply of the good. At the other extreme is **perfect competition.** In perfect competition a great many firms supply the same good.

There are relatively few monopolies or perfectly competitive firms in the real world. Most of the 20 million businesses in the United States fall between these extremes. They're more accurately characterized by gradations of *imperfect* competition—markets in which competition exists, but individual firms still retain some discretionary power over prices. In a *duopoly,* two firms supply the entire market. In an *oligopoly,* like telephone service, a handful of firms (AT&T, WorldCom, Sprint) dominate. In *monopolistic competition,* like fast-food restaurants, there are enough firms to ensure some competition, but not so many as to preclude some limited monopoly-type power.

> **market structure:** The number and relative size of firms in an industry.
>
> **perfect competition:** A market in which no buyer or seller has market power.

IN THE NEWS

T-Shirt Shop Owner's Lament: Too Many T-Shirt Shops

The small Texas beach resort of South Padre Island boasts white sand, blue skies (much of the time), the buoyant waters of the Gulf of Mexico and, at last count, more than 40 T-shirt shops.

And that's a problem for Shy Oogav, who owns one of those shops. "Every day you have to compete with other shops," he says. "And if you invent something new, they will copy you."

Padre Island illustrates a common condition in the T-shirt industry—unbridled, ill-advised growth. Many people believe T-shirts are the ticket to a permanent vacation—far too many people. "In the past years, everything that closed opened up again as a T-shirt shop," says Maria C. Hall, executive director of the South Padre Island Chamber of Commerce.

Mr. Oogav, a 29-year-old immigrant from Israel, came to South Padre Island on vacation six years ago, thought he had found paradise and stayed on. He subsequently got a job with one of the town's T-shirt shops, which then numbered fewer than a dozen. Now that he owns his own shop, and the competition has quadrupled, his paradise is lost. "I don't sleep at night," he says, morosely.

—Mark Pawlosky

Source: *The Wall Street Journal,* July 31, 1995. Reprinted by permission of *The Wall Street Journal.* © 1995 Dow Jones & Company, Inc. All rights reserved worldwide. www.wsj.com

Analysis: The ability to earn a profit depends on how many other firms offer similar products. A perfectly competitive firm has difficulty maintaining prices or profits.

THE NATURE OF PERFECT COMPETITION

Structure

A perfectly competitive industry has several distinguishing characteristics, including

- *Many firms*—Lots of firms are competing for consumer purchases.
- *Identical products*—The products of the different firms are identical, or nearly so.
- *Low entry barriers*—It's relatively easy to get into the business.

The T-shirt business has all these traits, which is why storeowners have a hard time maintaining profits (see previous News).

Price Takers

Because they always have to contend with a lot of competition, T-shirt shops can't increase profits by raising T-shirt prices. More than 1 billion T-shirts are sold in the United States each year, by tens of thousands of retail outlets. In such a competitive industry the many individual firms that make up the industry are all *price takers:* They take the price the market sets. A competitive firm can sell all its output at the prevailing market price. If it boosts its price above that level, consumers will shop elsewhere. In this sense, a perfectly competitive firm has no **market power**—no ability to control the market price for the good it sells.

> **market power:** The ability to alter the market price of a good or service.

At first glance, it might appear that all firms have market power. After all, who's to stop a T-shirt shop from raising prices? The important concept here, however, is *market* price, that is, the price at which goods are actually sold. If one shop raises its price to $15 and 40 other shops sell the same T-shirts for $10, it won't sell many shirts, and maybe none at all.

You may confront the same problem if you try to sell this book at the end of the semester. You might want to resell this textbook for $50. But you'll discover that the bookstore won't buy it at that price. With many other students offering to sell their books, the bookstore knows it doesn't have to pay the $50 you're asking. Because you don't have any market power, you have to accept the going price if you want to sell this book.

The same kind of powerlessness is characteristic of the small wheat farmer. Like any producer, the lone wheat farmer can increase or reduce his rate of output by making alternative production decisions. But his decision won't affect the market price of wheat.

To get a sense of how much competition exists in wheat farming, check out www.econ.ag.gov/briefing/wheat.

Even the largest U.S. wheat farmers can't change the market price of wheat. The largest wheat farm produces nearly 100,000 bushels of wheat per year. But *2 billion* bushels of wheat are brought to market every year, so another 100,000 bushels simply won't be noticed. In other words, *the output of the lone farmer is so small relative to the market supply that it has no significant effect on the total quantity or price in the market.*

A distinguishing characteristic of *powerless* firms is that, individually, they can sell all the output they produce at the prevailing market price. We call all such producers **competitive firms;** they have no independent influence on market prices. *A perfectly competitive firm is one whose output is so small in relation to market volume that its output decisions have no perceptible impact on price.*

> **competitive firm:** A firm without market power, with no ability to alter the market price of the goods it produces.

Market Demand Curves vs. Firm Demand Curves

It's important to distinguish between the market demand curve and the demand curve confronting a particular firm. T-shirt shops don't contradict the law of demand. The quantity of T-shirts purchased in the market still depends on T-shirt prices. That is, the *market* demand curve for T-shirts is still downward-sloping. A single T-shirt shop faces a horizontal demand curve only because its share of the market is so small that changes in its output don't disturb market equilibrium.

Collectively, though, individual firms do count. If all 40 of the T-shirt shops on South Padre Island (see previous News) were to increase shirt production at the same time,

FIGURE 22.2
Market vs. Firm Demand

Consumer demand for any product is downward-sloping, as in the T-shirt market. The equilibrium price (p_e) of T-shirts is established by the intersection of *market* demand and *market* supply. This market-established price is the only one at which an individual shop can sell T-shirts. If the shop owner asks a higher price (e.g., p_i), no one will buy his shirts, since they can buy identical T-shirts from other shops at p_e. But he can sell all his shirts at the equilibrium price. The shop owner thus confronts a horizontal demand curve for his own output. (Notice the difference in market and individual shop quantities on the horizontal axes of the two graphs.)

the market equilibrium would be disturbed. That is, a competitive market composed of individually powerless producers still sees a lot of action. The power here resides in the collective action of all the producers, however, not in the individual action of any one. Were T-shirt production to increase so abruptly, the shirts could be sold only at lower prices, in accordance with the downward-sloping nature of the *market* demand curve. Figure 22.2 illustrates the distinction between the actions of a single producer and those of the market. Notice that

- *The market demand curve for a product is always downward-sloping.*
- *The demand curve confronting a perfectly competitive firm is horizontal.*

THE PRODUCTION DECISION

Since a competitive firm can sell all its output at the market price, it has only one decision to make: how much to produce. Choosing a rate of output is a firm's **production decision.** Should it produce all the output it can? Or should it produce at less than capacity?

In searching for the most desirable rate of output, be aware of the distinction between total *revenue* and total *profit*. **Total revenue** is simply the price of the good multiplied by the quantity sold:

Total revenue = price × quantity

Since a competitive firm can sell all its output at the market price (p_e), total revenue is a simple multiple of p_e. The total revenue of a T-shirt shop, for example, is the price of shirts (p_e) multiplied by the quantity sold. Figure 22.3 shows the total revenue curve that results from this multiplication. Note that ***the total revenue curve of a perfectly competitive firm is an upward-sloping straight line, with a slope equal to*** $\mathbf{p_e}$.

production decision: The selection of the short-run rate of output (with existing plant and equipment).

Output and Revenues

total revenue: The price of a product multiplied by the quantity sold in a given time period: $p \times q$.

478 MARKET STRUCTURE

FIGURE 22.3
Total Revenue

Because a competitive firm can sell all its output at the prevailing price, its revenue curve is linear. In this case, the market (equilibrium) price of T-shirts is assumed to be $8. Hence, a shop's total revenue is equal to $8 multiplied by quantity sold.

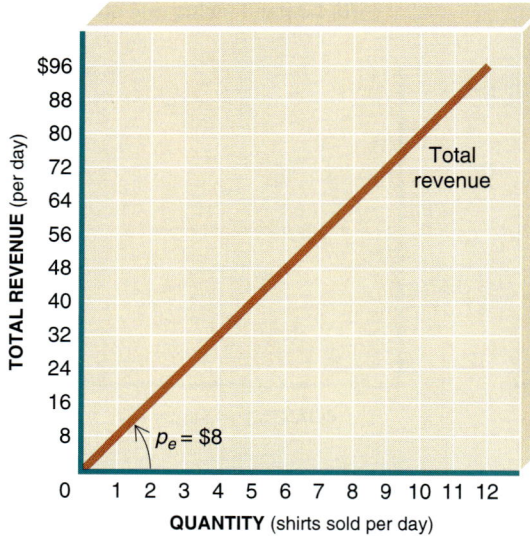

Price (per shirt)	×	Quantity (shirts per day)	=	Total revenue
$8		1		$ 8
8		2		16
8		3		24
8		4		32
8		5		40
8		6		48
8		7		56
8		8		64
8		9		72

If a competitive firm wanted to maximize its total *revenue,* its production decision would be simple: It would always produce at capacity. Life isn't that simple, however; **the objective is to maximize profits, not revenues.**

Output and Costs

To maximize profits, a firm must consider how increased production will affect *costs* as well as *revenues.* How do costs vary with the rate of output?

As we observed in Chapter 21, producers are saddled with certain costs in the **short run.** A T-shirt shop has to pay the rent every month no matter how few shirts it sells. The Tight Jeans Corporation in Chapter 21 had to pay the rent on its factory and lease payments on its sewing machine. These **fixed costs** are incurred even if no output is produced. Once a firm starts producing output in incurs **variable costs** as well.

Since profits depend on the *difference* between revenues and costs, the costs of added output will determine how much profit a producer can make. Figure 22.4 illustrates a typical total cost curve. Total costs increase as output expands. But the rate of cost increase varies. At first total costs rise slowly (notice the gradually declining slope until point z), then they increase more quickly (the rising slope after point z). This S-shaped curve reflects the *law of diminishing returns.* As we first observed in Chapter 21,

short run: The period in which the quantity (and quality) of some inputs can't be changed.

fixed costs: Costs of production that don't change when the rate of output is altered, e.g., the cost of basic plant and equipment.

variable costs: Costs of production that change when the rate of output is altered, e.g., labor and material costs.

FIGURE 22.4
Total Cost

Total cost increases with output. The rate of increase isn't steady, however. Typically, the rate of cost increase slows initially, then speeds up. After point z, diminishing returns (rising marginal costs) cause accelerating costs. These accelerating costs limit the profit potential of increased output.

FIGURE 22.5
Total Profit

Profit is the *difference* between total revenue and total cost. It is represented as the vertical distance between the total revenue curve and the total cost curve. At output *h*, profit equals *r* minus *s*. The objective is to find that rate of output that *maximizes* profit.

marginal costs (MC) often decline in the early stages of production and then increase as the available plant and equipment are used more intensively. These changes in marginal cost cause *total* costs to rise slowly at first, then to pick up speed as output increases.

You may suspect by now that the road to profits is not an easy one. It entails comparing ever-changing revenues with ever-changing costs. Figure 22.5 helps simplify the problem by bringing together typical total revenue and total cost curves. Notice how total costs exceed total revenues at high rates of output (beyond point *g*). As production capacity is approached, costs tend to skyrocket, offsetting any gain in sales revenue.

Total profit in Figure 22.5 is represented by the vertical distance between the two curves. Total costs in this case exceed total revenue at low rates of output as well as at very high rates. The firm is profitable only at output rates between *f* and *g*.

Although all rates of output between *f* and *g* are profitable, they aren't *equally* profitable. A quick glance at Figure 22.5 confirms that the vertical distance between total revenue and total cost varies considerably within that range. **The primary objective of the producer is to find that one particular rate of output that maximizes profits.** With a ruler, one could find it in Figure 22.5 by measuring the distance between the revenue and cost curves at all rates of output. In the real world, most producers need more practical guides to profit maximization.

marginal cost (MC): The increase in total costs associated with a one-unit increase in production.

PROFIT-MAXIMIZING RULE

The best single rule for maximizing profits in the short run is straightforward: Never produce a unit of output that costs more than it brings in. By following this simple rule, a producer is likely to make the right production decision. We see how this rule works by looking first at the revenue side of production ("what it brings in"), then at the cost side ("what it costs").

In searching for the most profitable rate of output, we need to know what an additional unit of output will bring in—that is, how much it adds to the total revenue of the firm. In general, the contribution to total revenue of an additional unit of output is called **marginal revenue (MR)**. Marginal revenue is the *change* in total revenue that occurs when output is increased by one unit; that is,

$$\text{Marginal revenue} = \frac{\text{change in total revenue}}{\text{change in output}}$$

Marginal Revenue = Price

marginal revenue (MR): The change in total revenue that results from a one-unit increase in the quantity sold.

Marginal Cost

To calculate marginal revenue, we compare the total revenues received before and after a one-unit increase in the rate of production; the *difference* between the two totals equals marginal revenue.

When the price of a product is constant, it's easy to compute marginal revenue. Suppose we're operating a catfish farm. Our product is catfish, sold at wholesale at the prevailing price of $13 per bushel. In this case, a one-unit increase in sales (one more bushel) increases total revenue by $13. As illustrated in Table 22.2, as long as the price of a product is constant, price and marginal revenue are one and the same thing. Hence, *for perfectly competitive firms, price equals marginal revenue.*

Keep in mind why we're breeding and selling catfish. It's not to maximize *revenues* but to maximize *profits*. To gauge profits, we need to know not only the price of fish but also how much each bushel costs to produce. As we saw in Chapter 21, the added cost of producing one more unit of a good is its *marginal cost*. Figure 22.6 summarizes the marginal costs associated with the production of catfish.

The production process for catfish farming is wonderfully simple. The factory is a pond; the rate of production is the number of fish harvested from the pond per day. A farmer can alter the rate of production at will, up to the breeding capacity of the pond.

Assume that the *fixed* cost of the pond is $10 per day. The fixed costs include the rental value of the pond and the cost of electricity for keeping the pond oxygenated so the fish can breathe. These fixed costs must be paid no matter how many fish the farmer harvests.

To harvest catfish from the pond, the farmer must incur additional costs. Labor is needed to net and sort the fish. The cost of labor is *variable,* depending on how much output the farmer decides to produce. If no fish are harvested, no variable costs are incurred.

The *marginal costs* of harvesting are the additional costs incurred to harvest *one* more basket of fish. Generally, we expect marginal costs to rise as the rate of production increases. The law of diminishing returns we encountered in Chapter 21 applies to catfish farming as well. As more labor is hired, each worker has less space (pond area) and capital (access to nets, sorting trays) to work with. Accordingly, it takes a little more labor time (marginal cost) to harvest each additional fish.

Figure 22.6 illustrates these marginal costs. Notice how the MC rises as the rate of output increases. At the output rate of 4 bushels per day (point *E*), marginal cost is $13. Hence, the fourth bushel increases total costs by $13. The fifth bushel is even more expensive, with a marginal cost of $17.

Profit-Maximizing Rate of Output

We're now in a position to make a production decision. The rule about never producing anything that adds more to cost than it brings in can now be stated in more technical terms. Since price equals marginal revenue for competitive firms, we can base the production decision on a comparison of *price* and marginal cost. We don't want to produce an additional unit of output if its MC exceeds its price. If MC exceeds price, we're spending more to produce that extra unit than we're getting back: total profits will decline if we produce it.

TABLE 22.2
Total and Marginal Revenue
Marginal revenue (MR) is the *change* in total revenue associated with the sale of one more unit of output. A third bushel increases total revenue from $26 to $39; MR equals $13. If the price is constant (at $13 here), marginal revenue equals price.

Quantity Sold (bushels per day)	×	Price (per bushel)	=	Total Revenue (per day)	Marginal Revenue (per bushel)
0	×	$13	=	$ 0 >	$13
1	×	13	=	13 >	$13
2	×	13	=	26 >	$13
3	×	13	=	39 >	$13
4	×	13	=	52 >	$13

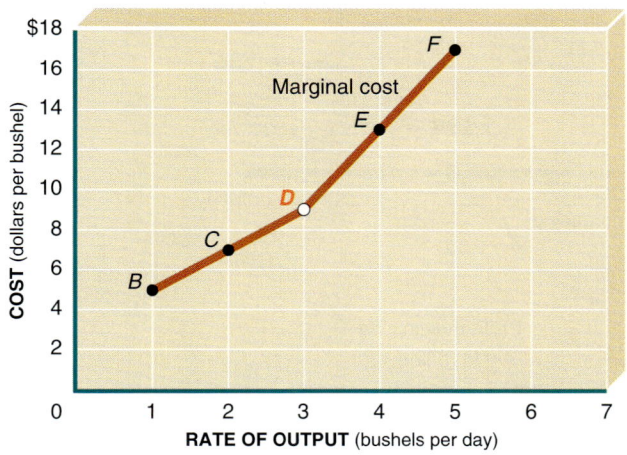

FIGURE 22.6
The Costs of Catfish Production

Marginal cost is the increase in total cost associated with a one-unit increase in production. When production expands from two to three units per day, total costs increase by $9 (from $22 to $31 per day). The marginal cost of the third bushel is therefore $9, as illustrated by point D in the graph.

	Rate of Output (bushels per day)	Total Cost (per day)	Marginal Cost (per unit)	Average Cost (per unit)
A	0	$10	—	—
B	1	15	$ 5	$15.00
C	2	22	7	11.00
D	3	31	9	10.33
E	4	44	13	11.00
F	5	61	17	12.20

The opposite is true when price exceeds MC. If an extra unit brings in more revenue than it costs to produce, it is adding to total profit. Total profits must increase in this case. Hence, a competitive firm wants to expand the rate of production whenever price exceeds MC.

Since we want to expand output when price exceeds MC and contract output if price is less than MC, the profit-maximizing rate of output is easily found. *For perfectly competitive firms, profits are maximized at the rate of output where price equals marginal cost.* The implications of this **profit-maximization rule** are summarized in Table 22.3.

Figure 22.7 illustrates the application of our profit-maximization rule in catfish farming. The prevailing wholesale price of catfish is $13 a bushel. At this price we can sell all the catfish we can produce, up to our short-run capacity. The catfish can't be sold

profit-maximization rule: Produce at that rate of output where marginal revenue equals marginal cost.

Price Level	Production Decision
price > MC	increase output
price = MC	maintain output (profits maximized)
price < MC	decrease output

TABLE 22.3
Short-Run Profit-Maximization Rules for Competitive Firm

The relationship between price and marginal cost dictates short-run production decisions. For competitive firms, profits are maximized at that rate of output where price = MC. (See Table 23.2 for long-run rules.)

FIGURE 22.7
Maximization of Profits for a Competitive Firm

A competitive firm maximizes total profit at the output rate where MC = p. If MC is less than price, the firm can increase profits by producing more. If MC exceeds price, the firm should reduce output. In this case, profit maximization occurs at an output of 4 bushels per day.

	(1) Number of Bushels (per day)	(2) Price	(3) Total Revenue	− (4) Total Cost	= (5) Total Profit	(6) Marginal Revenue	(7) Marginal Cost
A	0	—	—	$10	−$10	—	—
B	1	$13	$13	15	− 2	$13	$ 5
C	2	13	26	22	+ 4	13	7
D	3	13	39	31	+ 8	13	9
E	4	13	52	44	+ 8	13	13
F	5	13	65	61	+ 4	13	17

at a higher price because lots of farmers raise catfish and sell them for $13 (see News). If we try to charge a higher price, consumers will buy their fish from other vendors. Hence, we confront a horizontal demand curve at the price of $13.

The costs of producing catfish were examined in Figure 22.6. The key concept illustrated here is marginal cost. The MC curve slopes upward, in conventional fashion.

Figure 22.7 also depicts the total revenues, costs, and profits of alternative production rates. Study the table first. Notice that the firm loses $10 per day if it produces no fish (row *A*). At zero output, total revenue is zero ($p \times q = 0$). However, the firm must still contend with fixed costs of $10 per day. Total profit—total revenue minus total cost—is therefore *minus* $10; the firm incurs a loss.

Row *B* of the table shows how this loss is reduced when 1 bushel of fish is harvested per day. The production and sale of 1 bushel per day bring in $13 of total revenue (column 3). The total cost of producing 1 bushel per day is $15 (column 4). Hence, the total loss at an output rate of 1 bushel per day is $2 (column 5). This may not be what we hoped for, but it's certainly better than the $10 loss incurred at zero output.

The superiority of harvesting 1 bushel per day rather than none is also evident in columns 6 and 7 of row *B*. The first bushel produced has a *marginal revenue* of $13. Its *marginal cost* is only $5. Hence, it brings in more added revenue than it adds to costs. Under these circumstances—whenever price exceeds MC—output should definitely be expanded. That is one of the decision rules summarized in Table 22.3.

The excess of price over MC for the first unit of output is also illustrated by the graph in Figure 22.7. Point MR_B ($13) lies above MC_B ($5); the *difference* between these two points measures the contribution that the first bushel makes to the total prof-

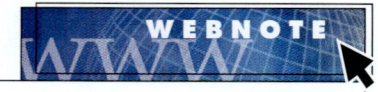

Check out the real world of catfish farming at www.aces.edu/ department/extcomm/publications/ anr/anr-273/anr-273.htm.

IN THE NEWS

Southern Farmers Hooked on New Cash Crop

Catfish are replacing crops and dairy farming as a cash industry in much of the South, particularly in Mississippi's Delta region, where 80 percent of farm-bred catfish are grown.

Production has skyrocketed in the USA from 16 million pounds in 1975 to an expected 340 million pounds this year.

The business is growing among farmers in Alabama, Arkansas and Louisiana.

Catfish farming is similar to other agriculture, experts say. One thing is the same: It takes money to get started.

"If you have a good row-crop farmer, you have a good catfish farmer," says James Hoffman of Farm Fresh Catfish Co. in Hollandale, Miss. "But you can't take a poor row-crop farmer and make him a good catfish farmer."

Greensboro, Ala., catfish farmer Steve Hollingsworth says he spends $18,000 a week on feed for the 1 million catfish in his ponds.

"Each of the ponds has about 100,000 fish," he says. "You get about 60 cents per fish, so that's about $60,000."

The investment can be lost very quickly "if something's wrong in that pond," like an inadequate oxygen level, Hollingsworth says.

"You can be 15 minutes too late getting here, and all your fish are gone," he says.

—Mark Mayfield

Source: *USA Today,* December 5, 1989. © 1989 USA Today. Reprinted with permission. www.usatoday.com

Analysis: People go into a competitive business like catfish farming to earn a profit. Once in business, they try to maximize total profits by equating price and marginal cost.

---

its of the firm. In this case, that contribution equals $13 − $5 = $8, and production losses are reduced by that amount when the rate of output is increased from zero to 1 bushel per day.

As long as price exceeds MC, further increases in the rate of output increase total profit. Notice what happens to profits when the rate of output is increased from 1 to 2 bushels per day (row *C*). The price (MR) of the second bushel is $13, its MC is $7. Therefore it *adds* $6 to total profits. Instead of losing $2 per day, the firm is now making a profit of $4 per day.

The firm can make even more profits by expanding the rate of output further. The marginal revenue of the third bushel is $13; its marginal cost is $9 (row *D* of the table). Therefore, the third bushel makes a $4 contribution to profits.

This firm will never make huge profits. For the fourth unit of output price and MC both equal $13. It doesn't contribute to total profits, and it doesn't subtract from them. The fourth unit of output represents the highest rate of output the firm desires. *At the rate of output where price = MC, total profits of the firm are maximized.*[1]

Notice what happens if we expand output beyond 4 bushels per day. The price of the fifth bushel is still $13; its MC is $17. The fifth bushel adds more to costs than to revenue. If we produce that fifth bushel, total profit will decline by $4. In Figure 22.7 the MC curve lies above the price line at all output levels in excess of 4. The lesson here is clear: *Output should not be increased if MC exceeds price.*

The correct production decision—the profit-maximizing decision—is shown in Figure 22.7 by the intersection of the price and MC curves. At this intersection, price equals MC and profits are maximized. If we produced less, we'd be giving up potential profits. If we produced more, total profits would also fall (review Table 22.3).

---

[1] In this case, profits are the same at output levels of three and four. Given the choice between the two levels, most firms will choose the higher level. By producing the extra unit of output, the firm increases its customer base. This not only denies rival firms an additional sale but also provides some additional cushion when the economy slumps. Also, corporate size may connote both prestige and power. In any case, the higher output level defines the limit to maximum-profit production.

Adding Up Profits

To reach the right production decision, we've relied on *marginal* revenues and costs. Having found the desired rate of output, however, we may want to take a closer look at the profits we are accumulating. Figure 22.8 provides pictures of our success.

Total profits are represented in Figure 22.8a by the vertical distance between the total revenue and total cost curves. This is a straightforward interpretation of our definition of total profits—that is,

$$\text{Total profits} = TR - TC$$

The vertical distance between the TR and TC curves is maximized at the output of 4 bushels per day.

Our success in catfish farming can also be illustrated by *average* revenue and costs. Total profit is equal to *average* profit per unit multiplied by the number of units produced. Profit *per unit,* in turn, is equal to price *minus* average total cost—that is,

$$\text{Profit per unit} = p - ATC$$

The price of catfish is illustrated in Figure 22.8b by the horizontal price line at $13. The average total cost of producing catfish is shown by the ATC curve. Like the ATC curve we encountered in Chapter 21, this one has a U shape. The *difference* between price and average cost—profit per unit—is illustrated by the vertical distance between the price and ATC curves. At 4 bushels per day, for example, profit per unit equals $13 - $11 = $2.

To compute *total* profits, we note that

$$\text{Total profits} = \text{profit per unit} \times \text{quantity}$$
$$= (p - ATC) \times q$$

In this case, the 4 bushels generate a profit of $2 each, for a *total* profit of $8 per day. *Total* profits are illustrated in Figure 22.8b by the shaded rectangle. (Recall that the area of a rectangle is equal to its height, the profit per unit, multiplied by its width, the quantity sold.)

Profit per unit is not only used to compute total profits but is often of interest in its own right. Businesspeople like to cite statistics on "markups," which are a crude index

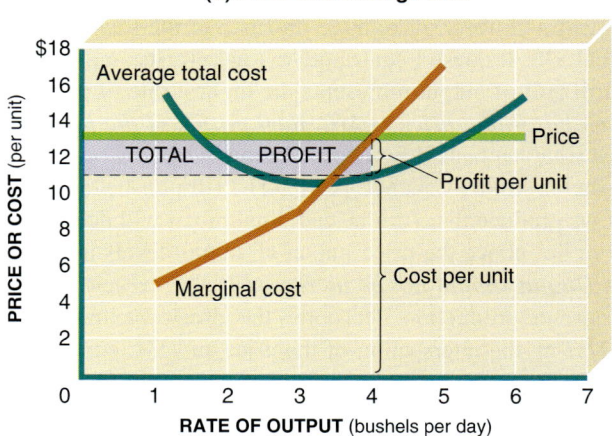

FIGURE 22.8
Alternative Views of Total Profit

Total profit can be computed as TR − TC, as in part *a*. Or it can be computed as profit *per unit* (*p* − ATC) multiplied by the quantity sold. This is illustrated in part *b* by the shaded rectangle. To find the profit-maximizing output, we could use either of these graphs or just the price and MC curves in Figure 22.7.

to per-unit profits. However, *the profit-maximizing producer never seeks to maximize per-unit profits. What counts is **total** profits, not the amount of profit per unit.* This is the old $4 ice cream problem again. You might be able to maximize profit per unit if you could sell 1 cone for $4, but you would make a lot more money if you sold 100 cones at a per-unit profit of only 50 cents each.

Similarly, *the profit-maximizing producer has no desire to produce at that rate of output where ATC is at a minimum.* Minimum ATC does represent least-cost production. But additional units of output, even though they raise average costs, will increase total profits. This is evident in Figure 22.8; price exceeds MC for some output to the right of minimum ATC (the bottom of the U). Therefore, total profits are increasing as we increase the rate of output beyond the point of minimum average costs.

THE SHUTDOWN DECISION

The rule established for short-run profit maximization doesn't guarantee any profits. By equating price and marginal cost, the competitive producer is only assured of achieving the *optimal* output. This is the best possible rate of output for the firm, given the existing market price and the (short-run) costs of production.

But what if the best possible rate of output generates a loss? What should the producer do in this case? Keep producing output? Or shut down the factory and find something else to do?

The first instinct may be to shut down the factory to stop the flow of red ink. But this isn't necessarily the wisest course of action. It may be smarter to keep operating a money-losing operation than to shut it down.

The rationale for this seemingly ill-advised course of action resides in the fixed costs of production. ***Fixed costs must be paid even if all output ceases.*** The firm must still pay rent on the factory and equipment even if it doesn't use these inputs. That's why we call such costs "fixed".

The persistence of fixed costs casts an entirely different light on the shutdown decision. Since fixed costs will have to be paid in any case, the question becomes: Which option creates greater losses? Does the firm lose more money by continuing to operate (and incurring a loss) or by shutting down (and incurring a loss equal to fixed costs)? In these terms, the answer becomes clear: ***A firm should shut down only if the losses from continuing production exceed fixed costs.*** This happens when total revenue is less than total *variable* cost.

Price vs. AVC

The shutdown decision can be made without explicit reference to fixed costs. Figure 22.9 shows how. The relationship to focus on is between the price of a good and its average *variable* cost.

The curves in Figure 22.9 represent the short-run costs and potential demand curves for catfish. As long as the price of catfish is $13 per bushel, the typical firm will produce 4 a day, as determined by the intersection of the MC and MR (= price) curves (point *X*, in part *a*). In this case, price ($13) exceeds average *total* cost ($11) and catfish farming is profitable.

The situation wouldn't look so good, however, if the market price of catfish fell to $9. Following the rule for profit maximization, the firm would be led to point *Y* in part *b*, where MC intersects the new demand (price) curve. At this intersection, the firm would produce three bushels per day. But total revenues would no longer cover total costs, as can be seen from the fact that the ATC curve now lies *above* the price line. The ATC of producing 3 bushels is $10.33 (Figure 22.6); price is $9. Hence, the firm is incurring a loss of $4 per day (3 bushels at a loss of $1.33 each).

Should the firm stay in business under the circumstances? The answer is yes. Recall that the catfish farmer has already dug the pond and installed equipment at a (fixed) cost of $10 per day. The producer will have to pay these fixed costs whether or not the machinery is used. Stopping production would result in a loss amounting to $10 per

486 MARKET STRUCTURE

FIGURE 22.9
The Firm's Shutdown Point

A firm should cease production only if total revenue is lower than total *variable* cost. The shutdown decision may be based on a comparison of price and AVC. If the price of catfish per bushel was $13, a firm would earn a profit at point X in part a. At a price of $9, (point Y in part b), the firm is losing money (p is less than ATC) but is more than covering all variable costs (p is greater than AVC). If the price falls to $4 per bushel, as in part c, output should cease (p is less than AVC).

The Shutdown Point

shutdown point: That rate of output where price equals minimum AVC.

day. Staying in business, even when catfish prices fall to $9 each, generates a loss of only $4 a day. In this case, *where price exceeds average variable cost but not average total cost, the profit-maximization rule minimizes losses.*

If the price of catfish falls far enough, the producer may be better off ceasing production altogether. Suppose the price of catfish fell to $4 per bushel (Figure 22.9c). A price this low doesn't even cover the variable cost of producing 1 bushel per day ($5). Continued production of even 1 bushel per day would imply a total loss of $11 per day ($10 of fixed costs plus $1 of variable costs). Higher rates of output would lead to still greater losses. Hence, the firm should shut down production, even though that action implies a loss of $10 per day. In all cases *where price doesn't cover average variable costs at any rate of output, production should cease.* Thus, the **shutdown point** occurs where price is equal to minimum average *variable* cost. Any lower price will result in losses larger than fixed costs. In Figure 22.9, the shutdown point occurs at a price of $5, where the MC and AVC curves intersect.

THE INVESTMENT DECISION

investment decision: The decision to build, buy, or lease plant and equipment; to enter or exit an industry.

long run: A period of time long enough for all inputs to be varied (no fixed costs).

When a firm shuts down, it doesn't necessarily leave (exit) the industry. General Motors still produces Cadillacs, for example, even though it idled one of its plants in 2001 (see News). *The shutdown decision is a **short-run** response.* It's based on the fixed costs of an established plant and the variable costs of operating it.

Ideally, a producer would never get into a money-losing business in the first place. Entry was based on an **investment decision** that the producer now regrets. *Investment decisions are **long-run** decisions,* however, and the firm now must pay for its bad luck or poor judgment. The investment decision entails the assumption of fixed costs (e.g., the lease of the factory); once the investment is made, the short-run production decision is designed to make the best possible use of those fixed inputs. The short-run profit-maximizing rule we've discussed applies only to this second decision; it assumes

IN THE NEWS

GM to Idle Cadillac Plant for Four Weeks

General Motors said Wednesday that it will idle the Lansing, Mich., Craft Center vehicle-assembly plant for four weeks beginning May 21 to cut inventories of unsold Cadillac Eldorado coupes. That will result in the temporary layoff of 300 workers, who will continue to receive 95 percent of their take-home pay.

Source: *USA Today*, February 22, 2001. © 2001 USA Today. Reprinted with permission. www.usatoday.com

EToys to Close Shop

Internet toy store eToys said it will file for bankruptcy protection in the next 5 to 10 days because it has been unable to find a buyer or more financing. EToys, which has never had a profit, will run out of cash by March 31 and is firing its remaining employees, the company said in a statement distributed by Business Wire. The retailer will close its Web site on March 8. EToys said its shares have no value and its stock will be delisted from the Nasdaq Stock Market.

Source: *Washington Post*, February 27, 2001. © 2001 The Washington Post. Reprinted with permission. www.washingtonpost.com

Analysis: GM's decision to idle a plant was a short-run *shutdown* decision; they are still in business. EToys, by contrast, made a long-run decision to cease operations and *exit* the industry.

that a production unit exists. The accompanying News shows the contrast between production and investment decisions.

The investment decision is of enormous importance to producers. The fixed costs that we've ignored in the production decision represent the producers' (or the stockholders') investment in the business. If they're going to avoid an economic loss, they have to generate at least enough revenue to recoup their investment—that is, the cost of (fixed) plant and equipment. Failure to do so will result in a net loss, despite allegiance to our profit-maximizing rule.

Whether or not fixed costs count, then, depends on the decision being made. For producers trying to decide how best to utilize the resources they've purchased or leased, fixed costs no longer enter the decision-making process. For producers deciding whether to enter business, sign a lease, or replace existing machinery and plant, fixed costs count very much. Businesspeople will proceed with an investment only if the *anticipated* profits are large enough to compensate for the effort and risk undertaken.

Long-Run Costs

When businesspeople make an investment decision, they confront not one set of cost figures but many. A plant not yet built can be designed for various rates of production and alternative technologies. In making long-run decisions, a producer isn't bound to one size of plant or to a particular mix of tools and machinery. In the long run, one can be flexible. In general, ***a producer will want to build, buy, or lease a plant that's the most efficient for the anticipated rate of output.*** This is the (dis)economy of scale phenomenon we discussed in the previous chapter. Once the right plant size is selected, the producer may proceed with the problem of short-run profit maximization. Once production is started, he can only hope that the investment decision was a good one and that a shutdown can be avoided.

DETERMINANTS OF SUPPLY

Whether the time frame is the short run or the long run, the one central force in production decisions is the quest for profits. Producers will go into production—incur fixed costs—only if they see the potential for economic profits. Once in business, they'll expand the rate of output so long as profits are increasing. They'll shut down—cease production—when revenues don't at least cover variable costs (loss exceeds fixed costs).

488 MARKET STRUCTURE

Nearly anyone could make money with these principles if given complete information on costs and revenues. What renders the road to fortune less congested is the general absence of such complete information. In the real world, production decisions involve considerably more risk. People often don't know how much profit or loss they'll incur until it's too late to alter production decisions. Consequently, businesspeople are compelled to make a reasoned guess about prices and costs, then proceed. By way of summary, we can identify the major influences that will shape their short- and long-run decisions on how much output to supply to the market.

Short-Run Determinants

A competitive firm's short-run production decisions are dominated by marginal costs. Hence, the quantity of a good supplied will be affected by all forces that alter MC. Specifically, ***the determinants of a firm's supply include***

- *The price of factor inputs.*
- *Technology* (the available production function).
- *Expectations* (for costs, sales, technology).
- *Taxes and subsidies.*

Each determinant affects a producer's ability and willingness to supply output at any particular price.

The price of factor inputs determines how much the producer must pay for resources used in production. Technology determines how much output the producer will get from each unit of input. Expectations are critical because they express producers' perceptions of what future costs, prices, sales, and profits are likely to be. And finally, taxes and subsidies may alter costs or the amount of profit a firm gets to keep.

The Short-Run Supply Curve. By using the familiar *ceteris paribus* assumption, we can isolate the effect of price on supply decisions. In other words, we can draw a short-run **supply curve** the same way we earlier constructed consumer demand curves. In this case, the forces we assume constant are input prices, technology, expectations, and taxes. The only variable we allow to change is the price of the product itself.

Figure 22.10 illustrates the response of quantity supplied to a change in price. Notice the critical role of marginal costs: ***The marginal cost curve is the short-run supply***

> **supply curve:** A curve describing the quantities of a good a producer is willing and able to sell (produce) at alternative prices in a given time period, *ceteris paribus*.

FIGURE 22.10
A Competitive Firm's Short-Run Supply Curve

For competitive firms, marginal cost defines the lowest price a firm will accept for a given quantity of output. In this sense, the marginal cost curve is the supply curve; it tells us how quantity supplied will respond to price. At $p = \$13$, the quantity supplied is 4; at $p = \$9$, the quantity supplied is 3.

Recall, however, that the firm will shut down if price falls below minimum average variable cost. The supply curve does not exist below minimum AVC ($5 in this case).

curve for a competitive firm. Recall our basic profit-maximization rule. A competitive producer wants to supply a good only if its price exceeds its marginal cost. Hence, marginal cost defines the lower limit for an "acceptable" price. A catfish farmer is willing and able to produce 4 bushels per day only if the price of a bushel is $13 (point X). If the price of catfish dropped to $9, the *quantity* supplied would fall to 3 (point Y). The marginal cost curve tells us what the quantity supplied would be at all other prices as well. As long as price exceeds minimum AVC (the shutdown point), the MC curve summarizes the response of a producer to price changes: It *is* the short-run supply curve of a perfectly competitive firm.

The shape of the marginal cost curve provides a basic foundation for the *law of supply*. Because marginal costs tend to rise as output expands, an increase in output makes sense only if the price of that output rises. If the price does rise, it's profitable to increase the quantity supplied.

Supply Shifts

All the forces that shape the short-run supply curve are subject to change. Factor prices change; technology changes; expectations change; and tax laws get revised. *If any determinant of supply changes, the supply curve shifts.*

A reduction in wage rates, for example, would reduce the marginal cost of producing catfish. This would shift the supply curve downward, making it possible for producers to supply larger quantities at any given price.

An improvement in technology would have the same effect. By increasing productivity, new technology would lower the marginal cost of producing a good. The supply curve would shift downward.

Tax Effects

Changes in taxes will also alter supply behavior. But not all taxes have the same effect; some alter short-run supply behavior, others affect only long-run supply decisions.

Property Taxes. Property taxes are levied by local governments on land and buildings. The tax rate is typically some small fraction (e.g., 1 percent) of total value. Hence, the owner of a $10 million factory might have to pay $100,000 per year in property taxes.

Property taxes have to be paid regardless of whether the factory is used. Hence, **property taxes are a fixed cost** for the firm. These additional fixed costs increase total costs and thus shift the average total cost (ATC) upward, as in Figure 22.11a.

Notice that the MC curve doesn't move when property taxes are imposed. Property taxes aren't based on the quantity of output produced. Accordingly, the production decision of the firm isn't affected by property taxes. The quantity q_1 in Figure 22.11a remains the optimal rate of output even after a property tax is introduced.

Although the optimal output remains at q_1, the profitability of the firm is reduced by the property tax. Profit per unit has been reduced by the upward shift of the ATC curve. If property taxes reduce profits too much, firms may move to a low-tax jurisdiction or another industry (investment decisions).

Payroll Taxes. Payroll taxes have very different effects on business decisions. Payroll taxes are levied on the wages paid by the firm. Employers must pay, for example, a 7.65 percent Social Security tax on the wages they pay (employees pay an identical amount). This tax is used to finance Social Security retirement benefits. Other payroll taxes are levied by federal and state governments to finance unemployment and disability benefits.

All payroll taxes add to the cost of hiring labor. In the absence of a tax, a worker might cost the firm $8 per hour. Once Social Security and other taxes are levied, the cost of labor increases to $8 plus the amount of tax. Hence, $8-per-hour labor might end up costing the firm $9 or more. In other words, *payroll taxes increase marginal costs.* This is illustrated in Figure 22.11b by the upward shift of the MC curve.

Notice how payroll taxes change the production decision. The new MC curve (MC_b) intersects the price line at a lower rate of output (q_b). Thus payroll taxes tend to reduce output and employment.

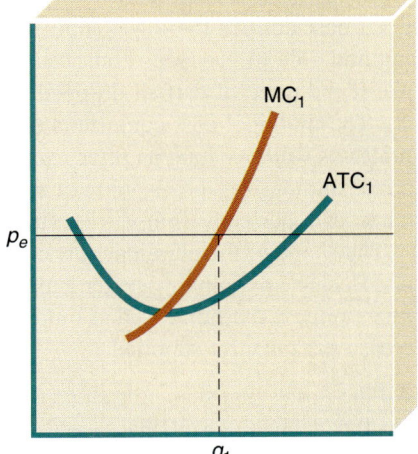

FIGURE 22.11
Impact of Taxes on Business Decisions

(a) Property taxes are a fixed cost for the firm. Since they don't affect marginal costs, they leave the optimal rate of output (q_1) unchanged. Property taxes raise average costs, however, and so reduce profits. Lower profits may alter investment decisions.

(b) Payroll taxes add directly to marginal costs and so reduce the optimal rate of output (to q_b). Payroll taxes also increase average costs and lower total and per-unit profits.

(c) Taxes on profits are neither a fixed cost nor a variable cost since they depend on the existence of profits. They don't affect marginal costs or price and so leave the optimal rate of output (q_1) unchanged. By reducing after-tax profits, however, such taxes lessen incentives to invest.

Profit Taxes. Taxes are also levied on the profits of a business. Such taxes are very different from either property or payroll taxes since profit taxes are paid only when profits are made. Thus they are neither a fixed cost nor a variable cost! As Figure 22.11c indicates, neither the MC nor the ATC curve moves when a profits tax is imposed. The only difference is that the firm now gets to keep less of its profits, instead "sharing" its profits with the government.

Although a profits tax has no direct effect on marginal or average costs, it does reduce the take-home (after-tax) profits of a business. This may reduce investments in new businesses. For this reason, many people urge the government to *reduce* corporate tax rates and so encourage increased investment.

THE ECONOMY TOMORROW

E-Commerce Increasing Competition

Ten years ago the T-shirt shop owners on South Padre Island (see News, page 475) had to worry only about the other 40 shops at that beach resort. They worried that other shops might offer T-shirts at lower prices, forcing all the shops to cut prices. Now the level of competition is way higher. Beachgoers can now buy T-shirts at virtual shops on the Internet. Indeed, consumers can click on the Internet to find out the price of almost anything. There are even electronic shopping services that will find the lowest price for a product. Want a better deal on a car? You don't have to visit a dozen dealerships. With a few clicks, you can find the lowest price for the car you want and get directions to the appropriate dealer. In fact, you don't have to go anywhere: More and more producers will sell you their products directly over the Internet.

E-commerce intensifies competition in many ways. By allowing a consumer to shop worldwide, the Net vastly increases the number of firms in a virtual market. Even your

If you want to shop for T-shirts at a cybermall, check out www.tshirtmall.com.

campus bookstore now has to worry about textbook prices available at Amazon.com, Barnes and Noble, and other online booksellers.

Electronic commerce also reduces transaction costs. Retailers don't need stores or catalogs to display their products, and they can greatly reduce inventories by producing to order. This is how Dell computer supplies the $12 million of computers it sells per day online.

Electronic retailers also get a tax break. Transactions on the Net aren't subject to sales taxes. Hence, electronic retailers can offer products at lower prices without cutting profit margins, especially in high-tax states.

The evident advantages of e-commerce have made it the virtual mall of choice for many consumers. In 2001, consumers spent over $60 billion on electronic purchases. That was less than 1 percent of total consumer spending. But the trend is what counts. With Net sales more than doubling every year, e-commerce is sure to intensify competition in the economy tomorrow.

SUMMARY

- Economic profit is the difference between total revenue and total cost. Total economic cost includes the value (opportunity cost) of *all* inputs used in the production, not just those inputs for which an explicit payment is made.
- Because it must contend with many competitors, a competitive firm has no control over the price of its output. If effectively confronts a horizontal demand for its output (even though the *market* demand for the product is downward-sloping).
- The short-run objective of a firm is to maximize profits from the operation of its existing facilities (fixed costs). For a competitive firm, the profit-maximizing output occurs at the point where marginal cost equals price (marginal revenue).
- A firm may incur a loss even at the optimal rate of output. It shouldn't shut down, however, so long as price exceeds average *variable* cost. If revenues at least cover variable costs, the firm's loss from production is less than fixed cost.
- In the long run a producer can be flexible. There are no fixed costs and the firm may choose any-sized plant it wants. The decision to incur fixed costs (i.e., build, buy, or lease a plant) or to enter or exit an industry is an investment decision.
- A competitive firm's supply curve is identical to its marginal cost curve (above the shutdown point at minimum average variable cost). In the short run, the quantity supplied will rise or fall with price.
- The determinants of supply include the price of inputs, technology, taxes, and expectations. Should any of these determinants change, the firm's supply curve will then shift.
- Business taxes alter business behavior. Property taxes raise fixed costs; payroll taxes increase marginal costs. Profit taxes raise neither fixed costs nor marginal costs but diminish the take-home (after-tax) profits of a business.
- The Internet has created virtual stores that intensify price competition.

Key Terms

profit
economic cost
explicit cost
implicit cost
economic profit
normal profit
monopoly
market structure
perfect competition

market power
competitive firm
production decision
total revenue
short run
fixed costs
variable costs

marginal cost (MC)
marginal revenue (MR)
profit-maximization rule
shutdown point
investment decision
long run
supply curve

Questions for Discussion

1. What economic costs will a large corporation likely overlook when computing its "profits"? How about the owner of a family-run business or farm?
2. How can the demand curve facing a firm be horizontal if the market demand curve is downward-sloping?
3. How many fish should a commercial fisherman try to catch in a day? Should he catch as many as possible or return to dock before filling the boat with fish? Under what economic circumstances should he not even take the boat out?
4. If a firm is incurring an economic loss, would society be better off if the firm shut down? Would the firm want to shut down? Explain.
5. Why wouldn't a profit-maximizing firm want to produce at the rate of output that minimizes average total cost?
6. What rate of output is appropriate for a "nonprofit" corporation (such as a hospital)?
7. Why did GM only temporarily shutdown its production facilities while eToys permanently got out of its business (see News, p. 487)? Explain in terms of fixed and variable costs.
8. What was the opportunity cost of Mr. Fujishige's farm? (See News, page 473.) Is society better off with a Disney parking lot? Explain.
9. Is America Online a perfectly competitive firm? Explain your answer.
10. If a perfectly competitive firm raises its price above the prevailing market rate, how much of its sales might it lose? Why? Can a competitive firm ever raise its prices? If so, when?

Web Activities

1. Go to www.jackinthebox.com/financial/pdfs/24.pdf to see Jack in the Box's statement of earnings.
   (a) What is the company's analysis of their market conditions?
   (b) What costs of production are listed? Which ones are likely to be fixed? variable?
   (c) Are there any opportunity costs listed?
   (d) How are the firm's profits calculated? Are these accounting or economic profits? Explain.

2. Log into www.census.gov. Follow this series of links: click on "economic census," then "construction reports," and click on the arrow for tables in your state.
   (a) How many construction establishments exist in your state?
   (b) Does this number constitute a competitive market? Explain.

THE ACCOMPANYING STUDENT PROBLEM SET CONTAINS NUMERICAL AND GRAPHING PROBLEMS FOR THIS CHAPTER

CHAPTER 23

Competitive Markets

Catfish farmers in the South are very upset. During the past two decades they've invested millions of dollars in converting cotton farms into breeding ponds for catfish. They now have over 150,000 acres of ponds and supply 90 percent of the nation's catfish. But unfortunately, catfish prices have been dropping. In 2001 alone catfish prices fell 15 percent, to a low of 62 cents per pound. With production costs averaging 65 cents a pound, most catfish farmers are now losing money. Indeed, many farmers in Arkansas, Mississippi and Louisiana have simply stopped feeding their fish. A lot of farmers are expected to refill their ponds with dirt and start planting cotton again.

It wasn't supposed to happen this way. Ten years ago, catfish looked like a sure thing. But so many Southern farmers got into the business that catfish prices started falling. Then Vietnam started exporting catfish to the United States, putting still further pressure on prices (see World View). Now even money-losing cranberry farmers in New England are converting their bogs to catfish ponds.

The dilemma the catfish farmers find themselves in is a familiar occurrence in competitive markets. When profits look good, everybody wants to get in on the act. As more and more firms start producing the good, prices and profits tumble. This helps explain why over 200,000 new firms are formed each year and why over 50,000 others fail.

This chapter focuses on the behavior of competitive markets. We have three principal questions:

- How are prices determined in competitive markets?
- How does competition affect the profits of a firm or industry?
- What does society gain from market competition?

The answers to these questions will reveal how markets work when all producers are relatively small and lack market power. In subsequent chapters we emphasize how market outcomes change when markets are less competitive.

THE MARKET SUPPLY CURVE

In the previous chapter we examined the supply behavior of a perfectly competitive firm. The perfectly competitive firm is a price taker. It *responds* to the market price by producing that rate of output where marginal cost equals price.

WORLD VIEW

Whiskered Catfish Stir a New Trade Controversy

LAKE VILLAGE, ARK.—Alleamer Tyler works in quality control at Farm Fresh Catfish, a processing plant in this small Delta town on the edge of the Mississippi River. Her days are sometimes slower than in the past, because she doesn't test as many fish as she once did.

"The imports have made a huge impact," says Ms. Tyler, one of Farm Fresh's 100 employees.

Because of Vietnamese fish imports, the US catfish production has plunged in the past year. At Farm Fresh, 95,000 pounds a day were processed last year. This year, it's down to 65,000.

Mississippi leads the nation in catfish production, followed by Arkansas and Louisiana. Most US catfish are raised in the Delta, one of the most poverty-stricken areas in the country. It's a place where the loss of even a few jobs that pay $8 an hour leaves a void in the local economy.

Catfish producers say imports from Vietnam have soared from 575,000 pounds in 1998 to as much as 20 million pounds this year.

—Suzi Parker

Source: *Christian Science Monitor*, October 3, 2001. Reprinted with permission. www.csmonitor.com

Analysis: When economic profits exist in an industry, more producers try to enter. As they do, prices and economic profits decline. When losses are incurred, firms begin to exit the industry.

---

equilibrium price: The price at which the quantity of a good demanded in a given time period equals the quantity supplied.

market supply: The total quantities of a good that sellers are willing and able to sell at alternative prices in a given time period, *ceteris paribus*.

But what about the *market* supply of catfish? We need a market supply curve to determine the **equilibrium price** the individual farmer will confront. In the previous chapter we simply drew a market supply curve arbitrarily, in order to establish a market price. Now, our objective is to find out where that **market supply** curve comes from.

Like the market supply curves we first encountered in Chapter 3, we can calculate the market supply of catfish by simple addition. All we have to do is add up the quantities each of America's 2,000 catfish farmers stands ready to supply at each price. Then we'll know the total quantity of fish to be supplied to the market at that price. Figure 23.1 illustrates this summation. Notice that *the market supply curve is the sum of the marginal cost curves of all the firms.* Hence, whatever determines the marginal

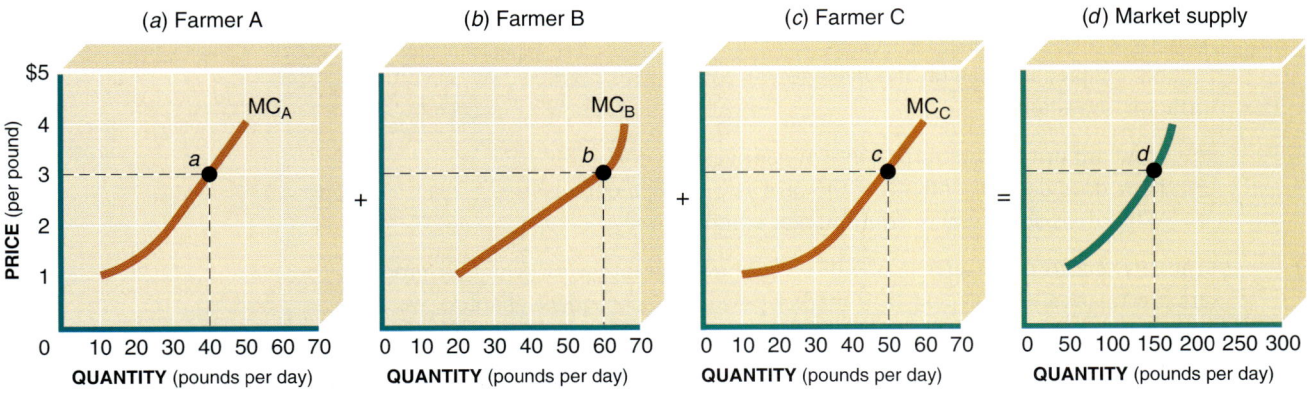

FIGURE 23.1
Competitive Market Supply

The portion of the MC curve that lies above AVC is a competitive firm's short-run supply curve. The curve MC_A tells us that Farmer A will produce 40 pounds of catfish per day if the market price is $3 per pound.

To determine the *market* supply, we add up the quantities supplied at each price by every farmer. The total quantity supplied to the market at the price of $3 is 150 pounds per day (a + b + c). Market supply depends on the number of firms and their respective marginal costs.

FIGURE 23.2
Market Entry

If economic profits exist in an industry, more firms will want to enter it. As they do, the market supply curve will shift to the right and cause the market price to drop from p_1 to p_2 (part a). The lower market price, in turn, will reduce the output and profits of the typical firm. In part b, the firm's output falls from q_1 to q_2.

cost of a typical firm will also affect industry supply. Specifically, *the market supply of a competitive industry is determined by*

- *The price of factor inputs.*
- *Technology.*
- *Expectations.*
- *Taxes and subsidies.*
- *The number of firms in the industry.*

If more firms enter an industry, the market supply curve will shift to the right. This is the problem confronting the catfish farmers in Mississippi (see News). It's fairly inexpensive to get into the catfish business: You can start with a pond, some breeding stock, and relatively little capital equipment. These **investment decisions** shift the market supply curve to the right and drive down catfish prices. This process is illustrated in Figure 23.2.

If prices fall too far, entry will cease and some catfish farmers will drain their ponds and plant cotton again. As they leave (exit) the industry, the market supply curve will shift to the left.

The profit motive drives these entry and exit decisions. Ten years ago catfish farming looked a whole lot more profitable than cotton farming. Farmers responded by flooding their cotton fields to create fish ponds.

The resulting shift of market supply caused the **economic profits** in catfish farming to disappear. Eventually the returns in catfish farming were no better than those in cotton farming. When that happened, cotton farmers stopped building fish ponds and resumed planting cotton. *When economic profits disappear, entry ceases, and the market stabilizes.* At that new equilibrium, catfish farmers earn only a normal (average) rate of return.

Catfish farmers would be happier, of course, if the price of catfish didn't decline to the point where economic profits disappear. But how are they going to prevent it? Alleamer Tyler evidently knows all about the laws of supply and demand (see the previous World View). She would dearly like to keep all those Vietnamese catfish out of

marginal cost (MC): The increase in total cost associated with a one-unit increase in production.

Entry and Exit

investment decision: The decision to build, buy, or lease plant and equipment; to enter or exit an industry.

Tendency toward Zero Profits

economic profit: The difference between total revenues and total economic costs.

competitive market: A market in which no buyer or seller has market power.

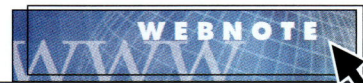

You can track catfish output and prices and even get recipes at the Catfish Institute's website: www.catfishinstitute.com.

Low Barriers to Entry

barriers to entry: Obstacles that make it difficult or impossible for would-be producers to enter a particular market, such as patents.

Market Characteristics of Perfect Competition

this country. She would also like to get other farmers to slow production a little before all the profits disappear. But Ms. Tyler is powerless to stop the forces of a **competitive market.** She can't afford to reduce her own catfish production. Even though she has 200 acres of ponds, nobody would notice the resulting drop in market supplies, and catfish prices would continue to slide. The only one affected would be Ms. Tyler, who'd be denying herself the opportunity to share in the (dwindling) fortunes of the catfish market while they lasted.

Ms. Tyler's dilemma goes a long way toward explaining why catfish farming isn't highly profitable. Whenever the profit picture looks good, everybody tries to get in on the action. This kind of pressure on prices and profits is a fundamental characteristic of competitive markets. *As long as it's easy for existing producers to expand production or for new firms to enter an industry, economic profits won't last long.*

New producers will be able to enter a profitable industry and help drive down prices and profits as long as they don't encounter significant barriers. Such **barriers to entry** may include patents, control of essential factors of production, control of distribution outlets, well-established brand loyalty, or even governmental regulation. All such barriers make it expensive, risky, or impossible for new firms to enter an industry. In the absence of such barriers, new firms can enter an industry more readily and at less risk. Not surprisingly, firms already entrenched in a profitable industry do their best to keep out newcomers by erecting barriers to entry. Unfortunately for Ms. Tyler, there are few barriers to entering the catfish business; all you need to get started is a pond and a few fish.

This brief review of catfish economics illustrates a few general observations about the structure, behavior, and outcomes of a competitive market:

- *Many firms.* A competitive market includes a great many firms, none of which has a significant share of total output.
- *Perfect information.* All buyers and sellers have complete information on available supply, demand, and prices.
- *Identical products.* Products are homogeneous. One firm's product is the same as any other firm's product.
- *MC = p.* All competitive firms will seek to expand output until marginal cost equals price, in as much as price and marginal revenue are identical for such firms.
- *Low barriers.* Barriers to enter the industry are low. If economic profits are available, more firms will enter the industry.
- *Zero economic profit.* The tendency of production and market supplies to expand when profit is high puts heavy pressures on prices and profits in competitive industries. Economic profit will approach zero in the long run as prices are driven down to the level of average production costs.

COMPETITION AT WORK: MICROCOMPUTERS

Few markets have all the characteristics listed above. That is, *few, if any, product markets are perfectly competitive.* However, many industries function much like the competitive model we sketched out. In addition to catfish farming, most other agricultural product markets are characterized by highly competitive market structures, with hundreds or even thousands of producers supplying the market. Other highly competitive, and hence not very profitable, businesses are T-shirt shops, retail food, printing, clothing manufacturing and retailing, dry-cleaning establishments, beauty salons, and furniture. Online stockbroker services have also become highly competitive. In these markets, prices and profits are always under the threat of expanded supplies brought to market by existing or new producers.

The electronics industry offers numerous examples of how competition reduces prices and profits. Between 1972 and 1983, the price of small, hand-held calculators fell from $200 to under $10. The price of digital watches fell even more dramatically, from roughly $2,000 in 1975 to under $7 in 1990. Videocassette recorders (VCRs) that sold for $2,000 in 1979 now sell for less than $90. DVD players that cost $1,500 in 1997 now sell for under $100. Cell phones that sold for $1,000 ten years ago are now given away. The same kind of competitive pressures have reduced the price of accessing the Web. New entrants keep bringing better Net products to market, making the price of surfing the Net ever cheaper (see News).

The driving force behind all these price reductions and quality improvements is *competition*. Do you really believe the price of accessing the Net would be falling if only one firm controlled access to the Internet? Do you think thousands of software writers would be toiling away right now if popular programs didn't generate enormous profits? Would America Online and Dell Computer keep rolling out new products and services if other companies weren't always snapping at their heels?

Market Evolution

To appreciate how the process of competition works, we will examine the development of the personal computer industry. *As in other industries, the market structure of the computer industry has evolved over time. It was never a monopoly, nor was it ever perfect competition.* In its first couple of years it was dominated by only a few companies (like Apple) that were enormously successful. The high profits the early microcomputer producers obtained attracted swarms of imitators. Over 250 firms entered the microcomputer industry between 1976 and 1983 in search of high profits. The entry of so many firms transformed the industry's market structure: The industry became *more* competitive, even though not *perfectly* competitive. The increased competition pushed prices downward and improved the product. When prices and profits tumbled, scores of companies went bankrupt. They left a legacy, however, of a vastly larger market, much improved computers, and sharply lower prices.

We'll use the early experiences of the microcomputer industry to illustrate the key behavioral features of a competitive market. As we'll see, many of these competitive features are still at work in the PC market and even more visible in the markets for Internet services and content software.

Initial Conditions: The Apple I

The microcomputer industry really got started in 1977. Prior to that time, microcomputers were essentially a hobby item for engineers and programmers, who bought

IN THE NEWS

Cost of Surfing the Internet Gets Cheaper As a Price War Flares

A new price war has broken out among companies that sell Internet access.

Last week, CompuServe, one of the Big Three online computer services, announced that it will sell three hours of Internet access for $4.95 a month by the end of the year. The new charge will be half the current minimum subscription price of each of the Big Three and a fraction of the $17 or more charged by smaller access providers for unlimited Internet use. . . .

Price cuts have become the hallmark of the online service business. CompuServe adjusted prices earlier this year for its total service package, resulting in a price cut for many users. Last year Prodigy and America Online dropped prices on the same day. The Big Three currently charge $9.95 a month for five hours of access to their services, including Internet access, and $2.95 for each additional hour. CompuServe will continue to charge those prices for services other than Internet access.

For many consumers, low-priced Internet access will provide the e-mail address they crave without the cost of services they don't use.

—William M. Bulkeley and Jared Sandberg

Source: *The Wall Street Journal,* October 13, 1995. Reprinted by permission of *The Wall Street Journal.* © 1995 Dow Jones & Company, Inc. All rights reserved worldwide. www.wsj.com

Analysis: Competitive pressures compel Internet service providers to keep improving service and reducing prices. The lure of profits encourages firms to enter this expanding market even as prices drop.

circuits, keyboards, monitors, and tape recorders and then assembled their own basic computers. Steve Jobs, then working at Atari, and Steven Wozniak, then working at Hewlett-Packard, were among these early computer enthusiasts. They spent their days working on large systems and their nights and weekends trying to put together small computers from mail-order parts.

Eventually, Jobs and Wozniak decided they had the capability to build commercially attractive small computers. They ordered the parts necessary for building 100 computers and set up shop in the garage of Jobs' parents. Their finished product—the Apple I (see photo)—was nothing more than a circuit board with a simple, built-in operating system. This first microcomputer was packaged in a wooden box. Despite primitive characteristics, the first 100 Apple I computers sold out immediately. This quick success convinced Jobs and Wozniak to package their computers more fully—which they did by enclosing them in plastic housing—and to offer more of them for sale. Shortly thereafter, in January 1977, the Apple Computer Corporation was established.

Apple revolutionized the market by offering a preassembled desktop computer with attractive features and an accessible price. The impact on the marketplace was much like that of Henry Ford's early Model T: Suddenly a newfangled piece of technology came into reach of the average U.S. household, and everybody, it seemed, wanted one. The first mass-produced Apple computer—called the Apple II—was just a basic keyboard with an operating system that permitted users to write their own programs. The computer had no disk drive, no monitor, and only 4K of random access memory (RAM). Consumers had to use their TV sets as screens and audiocassettes for data storage. This primitive Apple II was priced at just under $1,300 when it debuted in June 1977. The Apple Corporation was producing computers at the rate of 500 per month.

Apple didn't engineer or manufacture chips or semiconductor components. Instead, it simply packaged existing components purchased from outside suppliers. Hence, it was easy for other companies to follow Apple's lead. Within a very brief time, other firms, such as Tandy (Radio Shack), also started to assemble computers. By the middle of 1978, the basic small computer was selling for $1,000, and industry sales were about 20,000 a month. Figure 23.3 depicts the initial (1978) equilibrium in the computer market and the approximate costs of production for the typical computer manufacturer at that time.

Apple Computer's website details the development of their computer, including photos. Visit Apple at www.apple-history.com.

The Production Decision

The short-run goal of every producer is to find the rate of output that maximizes profits. Finding this rate entails making the best possible **production decision.** In this short-

The Apple I launched the personal computer industry in 1976. Hundreds of firms entered the industry to improve on this first preassembled microcomputer.

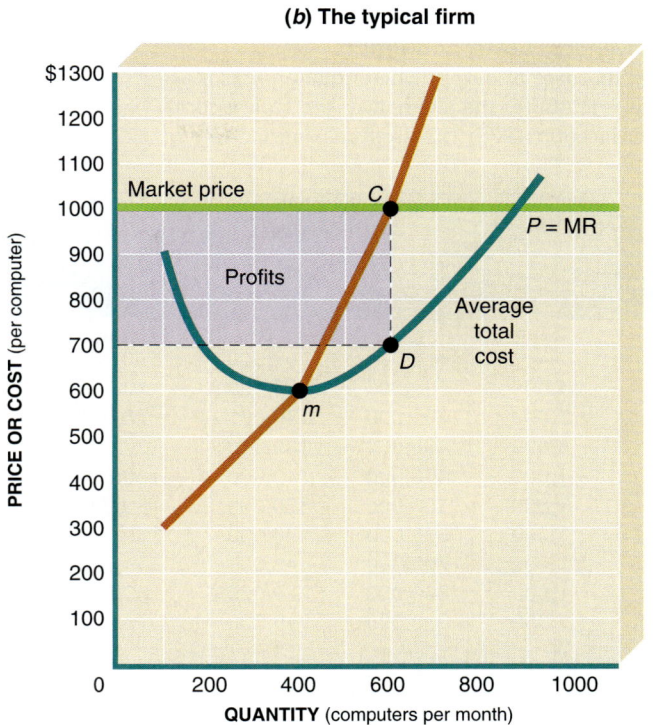

FIGURE 23.3
Initial Equilibrium in the Computer Market

(a) The Industry In 1978, the market price of microcomputers was $1000. This price was established by the intersection of the market supply and demand curves.

(b) A Firm Each competitive producer in the market sought to produce computers at that rate (600 per month) where marginal cost equaled price (point C). Profit per computer was equal to price (point C) minus average total cost (point D). Total profits for the typical firm are indicated by the shaded rectangle.

run context, *each competitive firm seeks the rate of output at which marginal cost equals price.*

Figure 23.3b illustrates the cost and price curves the typical computer producer confronted in 1978. As in most lines of production, the marginal costs of computer production increased with the rate of output. Marginal costs rose in part because output could be increased in the short run (with existing plant and equipment) only by crowding additional workers onto the assembly line. In 1978, Apple had only 10,000 square feet of manufacturing space. As more workers were hired, each worker had less capital and land to work with, and marginal physical product fell. The law of diminishing returns pushed marginal costs up.

The upward-sloping marginal cost curve intersected the price line at an output level of 600 computers per month (point C in Figure 23.3b).[1] That was the profit-maximizing rate of output (MC = p) for the typical manufacturer. To manufacture any more than 600 computers per month would raise marginal costs over price and reduce total profits. To manufacture any less would be to pass up an opportunity to make another buck.

production decision: The selection of the short-run rate of output (with existing plant and equipment).

Table 23.1 shows how much *profit* a typical computer manufacturer was making in 1978. As the profit column indicates, the typical computer manufacturer could make a real killing in the computer market, reaping a monthly profit of $180,000 by producing and selling 600 microcomputers.

Profit Calculations

---

[1]The marginal cost curves depicted here rise more steeply than they did in reality, but the general shape of the curves is our primary concern at this point.

TABLE 23.1
Computer Revenues, Costs, and Profits

Producers seek that rate of output where total profit is maximized. This table illustrates the alternatives the typical computer producer faced in 1978. The profit-maximizing rate of output occurred at 600 computers per month. At that rate of output, marginal cost was equal to price ($1,000), and profits were $180,000 per month.

Output per Month	Price	Total Revenue	Total Cost	Total Profit	Marginal Revenue*	Marginal Cost*	Average Total Cost	Profit per Unit (price minus average cost)
0	—	—	$ 60,000	−$60,000	—	—	—	—
100	$1,000	$100,000	90,000	10,000	$1,000	$ 300	$ 900	$100
200	1,000	200,000	130,000	70,000	1,000	400	650	350
300	1,000	300,000	180,000	120,000	1,000	500	600	400
400	1,000	400,000	240,000	160,000	1,000	600	600	400
500	1,000	500,000	320,000	180,000	1,000	800	640	360
600	1,000	600,000	420,000	180,000	1,000	1,000	700	300
700	1,000	700,000	546,000	154,000	1,000	1,260	780	220
800	1,000	800,000	720,000	80,000	1,000	1,740	900	100
900	1,000	900,000	919,800	−19,800	1,000	1,998	1,022	−22

*Note that output levels are calibrated in hundreds in this example; that's why we must have divided the *change* in total costs and revenues from one output level to another by 100 to calculate marginal revenue and marginal cost. Very few manufacturers deal in units of 1.

We could also calculate the computer manufacturers' profits by asking how much the manufacturers make on *each* computer and then multiplying that figure by total output since

$$\text{Total profit} = \text{profit per unit} \times \text{quantity sold}$$

average total cost (ATC): Total cost divided by the quantity produced in a given time period.

profit per unit: Total profit divided by the quantity produced in a given time period; price minus average total cost.

We can compute these profits by studying the first and last columns in Table 23.1 or by using a little geometry in Figure 23.3b. In the figure, average costs (total costs divided by the rate of output) are portrayed by the **average total cost (ATC)** curve. At the output rate of 600 (the row in white in Table 23.1), the distance between the price line ($1,000 at point *C*) and the ATC curve ($700 at point *D*) is $300, which represents the average **profit per unit.** Multiplying this figure by the number of units sold (600 per month) will give us *total* profit per month. Total profits are represented by the shaded rectangle in Figure 23.3b and are equal to our earlier profit figure of $180,000 per month.

The Lure of Profits

While gaping at the computer manufacturer's enormous profits, we should remind ourselves that those profits might not last long. Indeed, the more quick-witted among us already will have seen and heard enough to know they've discovered a good thing. And in fact, the kind of profits the early microcomputer manufacturers attained attracted a lot of entrepreneurial interest. *In competitive markets, economic profits attract new entrants.* This is what happened in the catfish industry and also in the computer industry. Within a very short time, a whole crowd of profit maximizers entered the microcomputer industry in hot pursuit of its fabulous profits. By the end of 1980, Apple had a lot of competition, including new entrants from IBM, Xerox, Digital Equipment, Casio, Sharp, and others.

Low Entry Barriers

A critical feature of the microcomputer market was its lack of entry barriers. A microcomputer is little more than a box containing a microprocessor "brain," which connects to a keyboard (to enter data), a memory (to store data), and a screen (to display data). Although the microprocessors that guide the computer are extremely sophisticated, they can be purchased on the open market. Thus, to enter the computer industry, all one needs is some space, some money to buy components, and some dexterity in putting parts together. Such *low entry barriers permit new firms to enter competitive markets.* According to Table 23.1, the typical producer needed only $60,000 of plant and equipment (fixed costs) to get started in the microcomputer market. Jobs and Wozniak had even less when they started making Apples.

A Shift of Market Supply

Figure 23.4 shows what happened to the computer market and the profits of the typical firm once the word got out. As more and more entrepreneurs heard how profitable computer manufacturing could be, they quickly got hold of a book on electronic circuitry, rushed to the bank, got a little financing, and set up shop. Before many months had passed, scores of new firms had started producing small computers. *The entry of new firms shifts the market supply curve to the right.* In Figure 23.4a, the supply curve shifted from S_1 to S_2. Almost as fast as a computer can calculate a profit (loss) statement, the willingness to supply increased abruptly.

But the new computer companies were in for a bit of disappointment. With so many new firms hawking microcomputers, it became increasingly difficult to make a fast buck. The downward-sloping market demand curve confirms that a greater quantity of microcomputers could be sold only if the price of computers dropped. And drop it did. The price slide began as computer manufacturers found their inventories growing and so offered price discounts to maintain sales volume. The price fell rapidly, from $1,000 in mid-1978 to $800 in early 1980.

The sliding market price squeezed the profits of each firm, causing the profit rectangle to shrink (compare Figure 23.3b to Figure 23.4b). The lower price also changed the production decision of the typical firm. The new price ($800) intersected the unchanged MC curve at the output rate of 500 computers per month. With average pro-

FIGURE 23.4
The Competitive Price and Profit Squeeze

(a) The Industry The economic profits in the computer industry encouraged new firms to enter the industry. As they did, the market supply curve shifted from S_1 to S_2. This rightward shift of the supply curve lowered the equilibrium price of computers.

(b) A Firm The lower market price, in turn, forced the typical producer to reduce output to the point where MC and price were equal again (point G). At this reduced rate of output, the typical firm earned less total profit than it had earned before.

duction costs of $640 (Table 23.1), the firm's total profits in 1980 were only $80,000 per month $[(P - ATC) \times 500]$. Not a paltry sum, to be sure, but nothing like the fantastic fortunes pocketed earlier.

As long as an economic profit is available, it will continue to attract new entrants. Those entrepreneurs who were a little slow in absorbing the implications of Figure 23.3 eventually woke up to what was going on and tried to get in on the action, too. Even though they were a little late, they didn't want to miss the chance to cash in on the $80,000 in monthly profits still available to the typical firm. Hence, the market supply curve continued to shift, and computer prices slid further, as in Figure 23.5. This process squeezed the profits of the typical firm still more, further shrinking the profit rectangle.

short-run competitive equilibrium: $p = MC$.

So long as economic profits exist in **short-run competitive equilibrium**, that equilibrium won't last. If the rate of profit obtainable in computer production is higher than that available in other industries, new firms will enter the industry. Conversely, if the short-run equilibrium is unprofitable, firms will exit the industry. Profit-maximizing entrepreneurs have a special place in their hearts for economic profits, not computers.

Price and profit declines will cease when the price of computers equals the minimum average cost of production. At that price (point m in Figure 23.5b), there's no more economic profit to be squeezed out. Firms no longer have an incentive to enter the industry, and the supply curve stops shifting. This situation represents the **long-run competitive equilibrium** for the firm and for the industry. *In long-run equilibrium, entry and exit cease, and zero economic profit (that is, normal profit) prevails* (see Figure 23.6). Table 23.2 summarizes the profit-maximizing rules that bring about this long-run equilibrium.

long-run competitive equilibrium: $p = MC = $ minimum ATC.

Once a long-run equilibrium is established, it will continue until market demand shifts or technological progress reduces the cost of computer production. In fact, that's just what happened in the computer market.

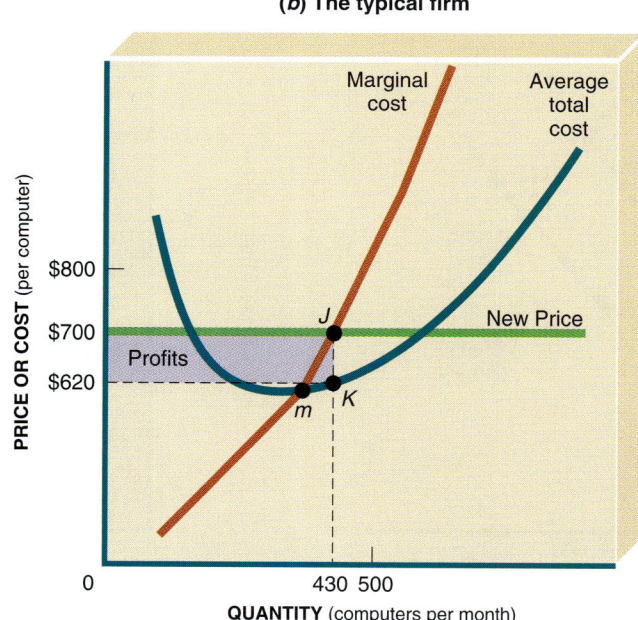

FIGURE 23.5
The Competitive Squeeze Approaching Its Limit

(*a*) **The Industry** Even at a price of $800 per computer, economic profits attracted still more entrepreneurs, shifting the market supply curve further (S_3). The next short-term equilibrium occurred at a price of $700 per computer.

(*b*) **A Firm** At this reduced market price, the typical manufacturer wanted to supply only 430 computers per month (point *J*). Total profits were much lower than they had been earlier, with fewer producers and higher prices.

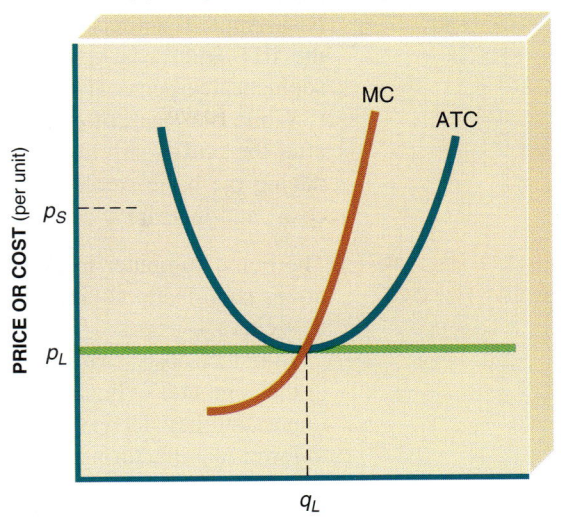

FIGURE 23.6
Short- vs. Long-run Equilibrium for the Competitive Firm

(a) Short-Run Competitive firms strive for the rate of output at which marginal cost (MC) equals price. When they achieve that rate of output, they are in *short-run equilibrium*. They have no incentive to alter the rate of output produced with existing (fixed) plant and equipment.

(b) Long-Run If the short-run equilibrium is profitable ($p >$ ATC), other firms will want to enter the industry. As they do, market price will fall until it reaches the level of minimum ATC. In this *long-run equilibrium*, economic profits are zero and nobody wants to enter or exit the industry.

As profit margins narrowed to the levels shown in Figure 23.5, quick-thinking entrepreneurs realized that future profits would have to come from product improvements or cost reductions. By adding features to the basic microcomputer, firms could expect to increase the demand for microcomputers and fetch higher prices. On the other hand, cost reductions would permit firms to widen their profit margins at existing prices or to reduce prices and increase sales. This second strategy wouldn't require assembling more complex computers or risking consumer rejection of an upgraded product.

In late 1979 and early 1980, both product-development strategies were pursued. In the process, two distinct markets were created. Microcomputers upgraded with new features came to be known as *personal* computers, or PCs. The basic unadorned computer first introduced by Apple came to be known as a *home* computer. The limited capabilities of that basic home computer greatly restricted its usefulness to simple household record keeping, games, and elementary programming.

Apple chose the personal computer route. It started enlarging the memory of the Apple II in late 1978 (from 4K to as much as 48K). It offered a monitor (produced by

Home Computers vs. Personal Computers

Price Level	Result for a Typical Firm	Market Response
$p >$ ATC	Profits	Enter industry (or expand capacity)
$p <$ ATC	Loss	Exit industry (or reduce capacity)
$p =$ ATC	Break even	Maintain existing capacity (no entry or exit)

TABLE 23.2
Long-Run Rules for Entry and Exit
Firms will enter an industry if economic profits exist ($p >$ ATC). They will exit if economic losses prevail ($p <$ ATC). Entry and exit cease in long-run equilibrium ($p =$ ATC). (See Table 22.4 for short-run profit-maximization rules.)

Sanyo) for the first time in May 1979. Shortly thereafter, Apple ceased making the basic Apple II and instead produced only upgraded versions (the Apple IIe, the IIc, and the III). Hundreds of other companies followed Apple's lead, touting increasingly sophisticated personal computers.

While one pack of entrepreneurs was chasing PC profits, another pack was going after the profits still available in home computers. This group chose to continue producing the basic Apple II look-alike, hoping to profit from greater efficiency, lower costs, and increasing sales.

Price Competition in Home Computers

The home computer market confronted the fiercest form of price competition. With prices continually sliding, the only way to make an extra buck was to push down the cost curve.

To reduce costs, firms sought to reduce the number of microprocessor chips installed in the computer's "brain." Fewer chips not only reduce direct materials costs, but more important, they decrease the amount of labor required for computer assembly. The key to lower manufacturing costs was more powerful chips. More powerful chips appeared when Intel, Motorola, and Texas Instruments developed 16-bit chips, doubling the computer's "brain" capabilities.

Further Supply Shifts

The impact of the improved chips on computer production costs and profits is illustrated in Figure 23.7, which takes over where Figure 23.5 left off. Recall that the market price of computers had been driven down to $700 by the beginning of 1980. At this price the typical firm maximized profits by producing 430 computers per month, as determined by the intersection of the prevailing price and MC curves (point J in Figure 23.7).

The only way for the firm to improve profitability at this point was to reduce costs. The new chips made such cost reductions easy. Such *technological improvements are illustrated by a downward shift of the ATC and MC curves.* Notice, for example, that the new technology permits 430 home computers to be produced for a lower marginal cost (about $500) than previously (point J).

The lower cost structure increases the profitability of computer production and stimulates a further increase in production. Note in particular that the "new MC" curve intersects the price ($700) line at an output of 600 computers per month (point N). By

Find information on U.S. business failures compiled by Dun and Bradstreet at www.loc.gov/rr/business/duns/duns9.htm.

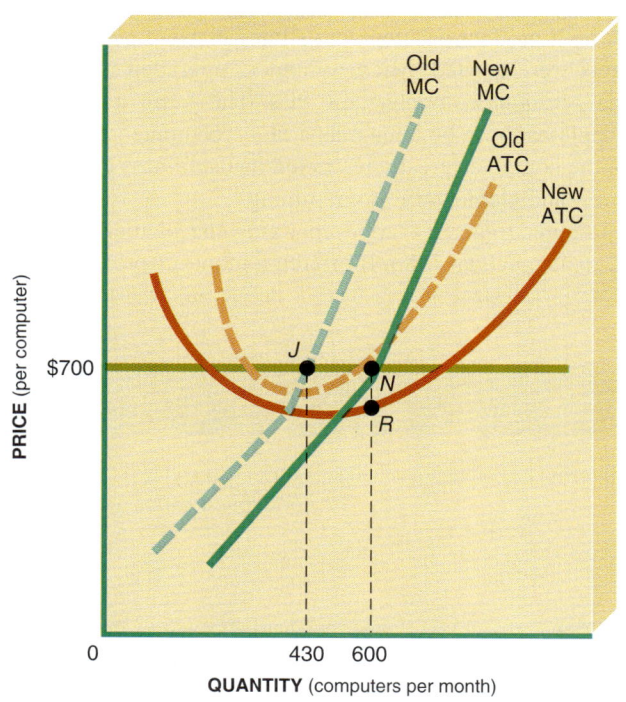

FIGURE 23.7
A Downward Shift of Costs Improves Profits and Stimulates Output

The quest for profits encouraged producers to discover cheaper ways to manufacture computers. The resulting improvements lowered costs and encouraged further increases in the rate of output. The typical computer producer increased output from point J (where p = old MC) to point N (where p = new MC).

contrast, the old, higher MC curve dictated a production rate of only 430 computers per month for the typical firm (point *J*) at that price. Thus, existing producers suddenly had an incentive to *expand* production, and new firms had a greater incentive to *enter* the industry. The great rush into computer production was on again.

The market implications of another entrepreneurial stampede should now be obvious. As more and more firms tried to get in on the action, the market supply curve again shifted to the right. As output increased, computer prices slid further down the market demand curve.

Table 23.3 illustrates how steeply home computer prices fell after 1980. Texas Instruments (TI) was one of the largest firms producing home computers in 1980. The lower costs made possible by improved microprocessors enabled TI to sell its basic home computer for $650 in 1980. Despite modest improvements in the TI machine, TI had to reduce its price to $525 in early 1981 in order to maintain unit sales. Shortly thereafter, the additional output of new entrants and existing companies pushed market prices down still further, to around $400.

Even at $400, TI and other home computer manufacturers were making handsome profits. In the fourth quarter of 1981, total industry sales were in excess of 200,000 per month—10 times the volume sold just three years earlier. Profits were good, too. Just one company, Atari, recorded total profits of $137 million in the fourth quarter of 1981, far more profit than Apple Computer had made during its first five *years* of production. The profits of the home computer market appeared boundless.

The remainder of Table 23.3 shows the consequences of the continued competition for those "boundless" profits. Between December 1981 and January 1983, the retail price of home computers fell from $400 to $149. Profit margins became razor-thin. Fourth-quarter profits at Atari, for example, fell from $137 million in 1981 to only $1.2 million in 1983.

Shutdowns

That didn't stop the competitive process, however. At Texas Instruments, minimum *variable* costs were roughly $100 per computer, so TI and other manufacturers could afford to keep producing even at lower prices. And they had little choice but to do so, since if they didn't, other companies would quickly take up the slack. Industry output kept increasing, pushing computer prices ever lower.

By the time computer prices reached $99, TI was losing $300 million per year. In September 1983, the company recognized that the price would no longer even cover average variable costs. ***Once a firm is no longer able to cover variable costs, it should shut down production.*** When the price of home computers dipped below minimum average variable costs, TI had reached the **shutdown point,** and the company ceased production. At the time TI made the shutdown decision, the company had an inventory of nearly 500,000 unsold computers. To unload them, TI reduced its price to $49, forcing lower prices and losses on other computer firms.

shutdown point: The rate of output where price equals minimum AVC.

Date		Price of Texas Instruments Model 99/4A
December	1979	$950
February	1980	700
June	1980	650
April	1981	525
December	1981	400
April	1982	249
September	1982	199
January	1983	149
September	1983	99
November	1983	49

TABLE 23.3
Plummeting Prices
Improved technology and fierce competition forced home computer prices down. In the span of only a few years, the price of a basic home computer fell from just under $1,000 to only $49. In the process, price fell below average variable cost, and many firms were forced to shut down.

IN THE NEWS

IBM to Halt PCjr Output Next Month
Computer's Sales Dried Up After Steep Price Cuts Ended Earlier This Year

NEW YORK—International Business Machines Corp. ended its up-and-down struggle to revive its PCjr home computer by announcing it would stop making the product next month.

The surprise move marks IBM's most visible product failure since its enormously successful entry into the personal-computer business four years ago. IBM announced the PCjr in late 1983 and began selling it early last year with an advertising campaign believed to exceed $40 million. IBM's efforts to make junior a hit ranged from technical changes to steep price cuts. But while aggressive IBM price cuts before Christmas increased PCjr sales substantially, sales dried up after the promotions ended in January. . . .

At the time of its introduction, the PCjr had a list of $699 or $1,269, depending on the model. The prices later were cut to $599 and $999, and the more powerful model's price dropped below the $800 level during the Christmas promotion.

—Dennis Kneale

Source: *The Wall Street Journal,* March 20, 1985. Reprinted by permission of *The Wall Street Journal.* © 1985 Dow Jones & Company, Inc. All rights reserved worldwide. www.wsj.com

Analysis: Competition forces firms to improve products and reduce prices. Those firms that can't keep up are forced to shut down and perhaps exit the industry.

Exits

Shortly after Texas Instruments shut down its production, it got out of the home computer business altogether. Mattel, Atari, and scores of smaller companies also withdrew from the home computer market. The exit rate between 1983 and 1985 matched the entry rate of the period 1979 to 1982.

The Personal Computer Market

The same kind of price competition that characterized the home computer market eventually hit the personal computer market too. As noted earlier, the microcomputer industry split into two segments around 1980, with most firms pursuing the upgraded personal computer market.

At first, competition in the PC market was largely confined to product improvements. Firms added more memory, faster microprocessors, better monitors, expanded operating systems, new applications software, and other features. New entrants into the market—Compaq in 1982; then Dell, AST, Gateway, and more—were the source of most product innovations.

The stampede of new firms and products into the PC market soon led to outright price competition too. As firms discovered that they couldn't sell all the PCs they were producing at prevailing prices, they were forced to offer price discounts. These discounts soon spread, and the slide down the demand curve accelerated.

Firms that couldn't keep up with the dual pace of improving technology and falling prices soon fell by the wayside. Scores of firms ceased production and withdrew from the industry once price fell below minimum average variable cost. Even Apple Computer, which had taken the "high road" to avoid price competition in home computers, was slowed by price competition. And IBM, which had entered the industry late, was forced to shut down its PC division after realizing that steep price cuts would be required to sell its small PCs (the "PCjr") to household users (News).

WEBNOTE

For a history of computer features, visit the Computer History Association of California at www.chac.org/chac.

THE COMPETITIVE PROCESS

That consumers reaped substantial benefit from competition in the computer market is by now evident. Over 300 million home and personal computers have been sold. Along the way, technology has made personal computers 100 times faster than the first Apple IIs, with 100 times more memory. The iMac computer introduced by Apple in 1998 makes the Apple I of 1976 look prehistoric (see Table 23.4). A lot of consumers have

The 1998 iMac evolved from the Apple I because of intense competition. (Photo courtesy of Apple Computer, Inc.)

Basic Features	Apple I (1976)	iMac (1998)
Microprocessor	MOS Technology 6502, 1.023 MHz	Power PC G3, 233 MHz
Internal RAM (random access memory)	4K (expandable to 8K)	32 MB (expandable to 128 MB)
Interfaces	Keyboard; cassette board connector; 44 pin edge connector	Two 12-Mbps universal serial bus port connectors; infrared technology port; 10/100 BASE-T Ethernet port; internal 56-Kbps modem
Video	No monitor; interfaces with TV or other video monitor	Supports millions of colors at 800 × 600 resolutions
Multimedia capabilities	None	Accelerated 2- and 3-dimension graphics chip; built-in stereo speakers with SRS surround sound; built-in microphone; two front headphone jacks; 16-bit stereo in/output jacks; 44.1-kHz sampling rate
Data storage	Via cassette interface (sold separately)	Internal 4GB hard disk drive; internal 24x-speed CD ROM
Price	$666.66 ($1,943 in 1998 dollars)	$1,299.00

Source: The Computer Museum History Center, Boston, www.computerhistory.org.

Analysis: Competition in the computer industry spurred product innovations and new technology that revolutionized computers. Today's iMac bears little resemblance to the Apple I. Despite its far superior capabilities, the iMac's inflation-adjusted price is much less than that of the Apple I.

TABLE 23.4
Apple I vs. iMac

found that computers are great for doing accounting chores, keeping records, writing papers, playing games, and accessing the Internet. Perhaps it's true that an abundance of inexpensive computers would have been produced in other market (or nonmarket) situations as well. But we can't ignore the fact that *competitive market pressures were a driving force in the spectacular growth of the computer industry.* And they still are, as the accompanying News confirms.

Allocative Efficiency: The Right Output Mix

The squeeze on prices and profits that we've observed in the computer market is a fundamental characteristic of the competitive process. Indeed, the **market mechanism** works best under such circumstances. The existence of economic profits is an indication that consumers place a high value on a particular product and are willing to pay a comparatively high price to get it. The high price and profits signal this information to profit-hungry entrepreneurs, who come forward to satisfy consumer demands. Thus, *high profits in a particular industry indicate that consumers want a different mix of output* (more of that industry's goods). The competitive squeeze on those same profits indicates that resources are being reallocated to produce that desired mix. In a competitive market, consumers get more of the goods they desire—and at a lower price.

market mechanism: The use of market prices and sales to signal desired outputs (or resource allocations).

The ability of competitive markets to allocate resources efficiently across industries originates in the way competitive prices are set. To attain the optimal mix of output, we must know the **opportunity cost** of producing different goods. A competitive market gives us the information necessary for making such choices. Why? Because competitive firms always strive to produce at the rate of output at which price equals marginal cost. Hence, *the price signal the consumer gets in a competitive market is an accurate reflection of opportunity cost.* As such, it offers a reliable basis for making choices

opportunity cost: The most desired goods or services that are forgone in order to obtain something else.

FIGURE 23.8
Summary of Competitive Process

All competitive firms seek to produce at that output where MC = p. Hence, a competitive *industry* will produce at that rate of output where *industry* MC (the sum of all firms' MC curves) intersects market demand (point *a*).

If economic profits exist in the industry (as they do here), more firms will enter the industry. As they do, the *industry* MC (supply) curve will shift to the right. The shifting MC curve will pull the *industry* ATC curve along with it. As the *industry* MC curve continues to shift rightward, the intersection of MC and ATC (point *b*) eventually will reach the demand curve at point *c*. At point *c*, MC still equals price, but no economic profits exist and entry (shifts) will cease. Point *c* will be the *long-term* equilibrium of the industry.

If competitive pressures reduce costs (i.e., improve technology), the supply (MC) curve will shift further to the right and *down*, reducing long-term prices even more.

Note that MC = p in both short- and long-run equilibrium. Notice also that equilibrium must occur on the market demand curve.

IN THE NEWS

Price War Squeezes PC Makers

Cuts Make Companies Bleed As Profits, Sales Decline; Some Predict a Shakeout

It's getting ugly in the personal-computer market.

Just last summer computer makers were boosting already-strong sales by hawking sleek new hardware designs and faster processors. Today, the PC business is showing all the signs of a brutal price war: rapid price cuts, rebates and lots of freebies. Dell Computer Corp., which launched the current price battle at the end of last year, now is tossing in free delivery, a free printer and free Internet access to customers who buy a PC through its website.

That's a good thing for customers. But computer makers are reeling as the stiffening competition slices into profits. Compaq Computer Corp., the world's largest PC maker, said earlier this month it will consolidate operations and cut more than 7,000 workers to help compensate for new price reductions. Other major players also are axing jobs and warning investors of lower sales.

In the past, computer prices have fallen steadily as they became cheaper to make, yet that simply fueled higher demand. But recent price cuts have been much steeper than anything seen before, and, combined with a slowdown in demand, could result in a first-ever decline in PC revenue in the U.S.

If prices continue to fall at the current pace, the resulting squeeze also could trigger a wave of consolidation among the biggest PC makers, analysts say, as the companies try to cope either by selling businesses or seeking more market clout by acquiring competitors.

"The earnings risk from price pressure on all these PC hardware companies is increasing rapidly," warns UBS Warburg analyst Don Young. "At some point, either this industry says enough is enough, or . . . everybody loses."

—Gary McWilliams

Source: *The Wall Street Journal*, March 26, 2001, p. B1. Reprinted by permission of The Wall Street Journal. © 2001 Dow Jones & Company, Inc. All rights reserved worldwide. www.wsj.com

Analysis: Competitive pressures force companies to continually improve products and cut prices.

---

about the mix of output and attendant allocation of resources. In this sense, the **marginal cost pricing** characteristic of competitive markets permits society to answer the WHAT-to-produce question efficiently. The amount consumers are willing to pay for a good (its price) equals its opportunity cost (marginal cost).

When the competitive pressure on prices is carried to the limit, we also get the right answer to the HOW-to-produce question. Competition drives costs down to their bare minimum—the hallmark of economic **efficiency.** This was illustrated by the tendency of computer prices to be driven down to the level of *minimum* average costs. Figure 23.8 summarizes this competitive process, showing how the industry moves from short-run to long-run equilibrium. Once the long-run equilibrium has been established, society is getting the most it can from its available (scarce) resources.

Competitive pressures also affect the FOR WHOM question. At the limit of long-run equilibrium, all economic profit is eliminated. This doesn't mean that producers are left empty-handed, however. First, the zero-profit limit is rarely, if ever, reached, because new products are continually being introduced, consumer demands change, and more efficient production processes are discovered. In fact, the competitive process creates strong pressures to pursue product and technological innovation. In a competitive market, the adage about the early bird getting the worm is particularly apt. As we observed in the computer market, the first ones to perceive and respond to the potential profitability of computer production were the ones who made the greatest profits.

The sequence of events common to competitive markets evolves as follows:

- High prices and profits signal consumers' demand for more output.
- Economic profit attracts new suppliers.
- The market supply curve shifts to the right.

marginal cost pricing: The offer (supply) of goods at prices equal to their marginal cost.

Production Efficiency: Minimum Average Cost

efficiency: Maximum output of a good from the resources used in production.

Zero Economic Profit

Relentless Profit Squeeze

- Prices slide down the market demand curve.
- A new equilibrium is reached at which increased quantities of the desired product are produced and its price is lower. Average costs of production are at or near a minimum, much more of the product is supplied and consumed, and economic profit approaches zero.
- Throughout the process, producers experience great pressure to keep ahead of the profit squeeze by reducing costs, a pressure that frequently results in product and technological innovation.

What is essential to remember about the competitive process is that the ***potential threat of other firms expanding production or of new firms entering the industry keeps existing firms on their toes.*** Even the most successful firm can't rest on its laurels for long. To stay in the game, competitive firms must continually update technology, improve their product, and reduce costs. It is the same lesson a lot of entrepreneurs learned in the unusually fast rise and quick death of "dot.com" companies (1998–2001), (as the accompanying News relates).

THE ECONOMY TOMORROW

HDTV for $500?

The first high-definition television (HDTV) sets appeared on the American market in 1993. But they weren't supplied in commercial quantities until 1998—and they were expensive. The 56-inch Panasonic HDTV went on sale for a base price of $5,500 in August 1998. Despite its high price, the Federal Communications Commission (FCC) established HDTV as the standard for the economy tomorrow. The FCC required television stations to start trans-

IN THE NEWS

Death Valley

The Bay Area Is Coming to Terms with the End of an Era.

Earlier this year, not long before the Net "correction," which became a "slump" and ended up as a "crash," a San Francisco company called Esurance threw a party at one of the city's newest, sparkliest restaurants. Esurance clearly subscribed to the theory that if you have a dull business—selling insurance over the Web—you should at least throw a really fun party. Having raised $34 million in its latest round of financing, Esurance certainly had the money to do it. The restaurant was in a converted theater with a huge heated garden. Trays of scrumptions beef tips circulated about the room in acrobatic flights.

In late October, I called Esurance to ask how things were going. I glanced at the company's website to double-check the name of Esurance's head honcho: Jean-Bernard Duler, founder and chief executive officer. I picked up the phone and asked for "Jean-Bernard." The receptionist said he was no longer with the company. I asked if there was a new chief executive. The receptionist said she thought there was, and she gave me a name. I left a message. An hour later I got a call from Esurance's press officer. I asked him where I could reach Jean-Bernard. "I hope," the press officer said, "he's sailing off Baja California. He's been planning to do that for a long time." In other words, gone fishing.

Just a few months ago, no business was too big, too small, too weird, or too difficult to get the dot.com treatment. Got an idea? What about online restaurant reservations? Sold! A Web store for asthmatics? Sure! A network for five-minute films made by rank amateurs? Why not?

Robert Noyce, the late founder of Intel, once famously said that in Silicon Valley, "the money doesn't seem real. It's just a way of keeping score." A trenchant observation—as long as everybody's making money. But in March, the game was up: Barron's ran a cover story pointing out that Net companies that lost millions of dollars every quarter would eventually run out of money. Net stocks started falling out of the sky. And the money suddenly seemed awfully real.

—Mark Gimein

Source: Business 2.0 online, December 2000. Reprinted with permission. www.business2.com

Analysis: The specter of boundless profits lured hundreds of companies into the dot.com business. Before long, however, entrepreneurs discovered that profits weren't readily available and started exiting the industry.

IN THE NEWS

The Future of HDTV

August 1998 Debuting in San Diego, the 56" HDTVs quickly sell out. Price: $5,499.

November 1998 CBS, NBC, Fox and ABC are scheduled to show HDTV programs in the top 10 TV markets (map).

November 1999 Prices for less-expensive digital TV's may drop below $2,000.

2000 Cable companies resolve technical and business issues and go digital. Maybe.

2002 All commercial TV stations are required to be digital. Prices for cheaper sets could drop as low as $500.

2003 Public TV stations must go digital.

2006 If consumers embrace HDTV, all analog broadcasting ends.

Top 10 TV markets: Boston, New York, Detroit, Chicago, Philadelphia, Washington, D.C., San Francisco, Los Angeles, Dallas-Ft. Worth, Atlanta

Source: *Newsweek*, September 28, 1998. Reprinted with permission. www.newsweek.com

Analysis: HDTV prices are declining rapidly. Whether they fall to $500 will depend on how much competition exists.

---

mitting HDTV signals in 1998 and has ordered them to stop transmitting standard (analog) television signals in the year 2006 (see News).

The FCC order was a remarkable testimonial to the power of competitive markets. Back in 1998, the price of an HDTV was way too high for the average U.S. household. Only 10,000 HDTVs were bought that year, at the price of $5,500. That same year, Americans bought 23 *million* analog TV sets, at prices closer to $300. Yet the FCC was essentially consigning analog sets to the junkyard.

Why did the FCC think HDTVs would become affordable in such a short amount of time? For starters, they knew what had happened to prices in the computer industry. A price decline from $5,500 to $500 in four years would in fact be less dramatic than the price plunge in home computers (from $950 to $49 in four years; see Table 23.3). Moreover, by the time the FCC report was published, the competitive process was already underway in the HDTV market. Shortly after Panasonic brought its HDTV to market, a dozen other firms announced that they were launching similar sets. Sony, Sharp, Hitachi, Zenith, RCA, Samsung, Sanyo, and other companies promised better and cheaper HDTVs.

No one knows for sure how cheap HDTVs will get. By late 2001, the price of a standard HDTV was already below $1,000, and 2 million sets had been sold. HDTVs were also getting better, with an increasing array of viewing and recording features. If entry barriers to the HDTV industry stay low, everyone will be able to afford high-definition TV in the economy tomorrow.

Price and Competition

SUMMARY

- A perfectly competitive firm has no power to alter the market price of the product it sells. The perfectly competitive firm confronts a horizontal demand curve for its own output even though the relevant *market* demand curve is negatively sloped.

- Profit maximization induces the competitive firm to produce at that rate of output where marginal costs equals price. This represents the short-run equilibrium of the firm.

- If short-run profits exist in a competitive industry, new firms will enter the market. The resulting shift of supply

will drive market prices down the market demand curve. As prices fall, the profit of the industry and its constituent firms will be squeezed.
- The limit to the competitive price and profit squeeze is reached when price is driven down to the level of minimum average total cost. At this point (long-run equilibrium) additional output and profit will be attained only if technology is improved (lowering costs) or if demand increases.
- Firms will shut down production if price falls below average variable cost. Firms will exit the industry if they foresee continued economic losses.
- The most distinctive thing about competitive markets is the persistent pressure they exert on prices and profits. The threat of competition is a tremendous incentive for producers to respond quickly to consumer demands and to seek more efficient means of production. In this sense, competitive markets do best what markets are supposed to do—efficiently allocate resources.

Key Terms

equilibrium price
market supply
marginal cost (MC)
investment decision
economic profit
competitive market
barriers to entry

production decision
average total cost (ATC)
profit per unit
short-run competitive equilibrium
long-run competitive equilibrium

shutdown point
market mechanism
opportunity cost
marginal cost pricing
efficiency

Questions for Discussion

1. Why would anyone want to enter a profitable industry knowing that profits would eventually be eliminated by competition?
2. Why wouldn't producers necessarily want to produce output at the lowest average cost? Under what conditions would they end up doing so?
3. What industries do you regard as being highly competitive? Can you identify any barriers to entry in those industries?
4. At what point will the "enough is enough" statement in the News on the PC price war (page 509) be located?
5. What might cause catfish prices to rise far enough to eliminate losses in the industry? (See News, page 494.)
6. As the price of computers fell, what happened to their quality? How is this possible?
7. Why is the price of "surfing the Net" declining? (See News, page 497.)
8. Is "long-run" equilibrium permanent? What forces might dislodge it?
9. What might stop HDTV prices from falling as fast as the FCC anticipated? (See Economy Tomorrow.) Might they fall even faster?
10. Identify two products that have either (a) fallen sharply in price or (b) gotten significantly better without price increases. How did these changes come about?

Web Activities

1. Log on to www.cnn.com or www.msnbc.com, and complete a word search using "beef market."
   (a) Explain why the market for beef in the United States is a competitive market.
   (b) In the article you found, what determinant of supply or demand in the market for beef is changing?
   (c) How will this change affect the short-run equilibrium price? The long-run equilibrium price?
2. Log on to www.ce.org/market_overview/uceit_99/video.cfm, and read the industry analysis for HDTV and its future.
   (a) What do you predict will happen to the profits of existing manufacturers of HDTVs in the coming years? Explain.
   (b) Based on this prediction, what is likely to happen to the number of manufacturers? Explain.
   (c) What long-run implications does this have for the price of HDTVs? Explain.
3. Log on to www.census.gov/econ/www, click on "retail," and then access "national statistics."
   (a) How many gas stations exist in the United States?
   (b) Does this mean that the gas market in your town or city constitutes a competitive market? Explain.

ALERT! THE ACCOMPANYING STUDENT PROBLEM SET CONTAINS NUMERICAL AND GRAPHING PROBLEMS FOR THIS CHAPTER

CHAPTER 24

Monopoly

In 1908 Ford produced the Model T, the car "designed for the common man." It was cheap, reliable, and as easy to drive as the horse and buggy it was replacing. Ford sold 10,000 Model Ts in its first full year of production (1909). After that, sales more than doubled every year. In 1913, nearly 200,000 Model Ts were sold; and Ford was fast changing U.S. patterns of consumption, travel, and living standards.

During this early development of the U.S. auto industry, Henry Ford dominated the field. There were other producers, but the Ford Motor Company was the only producer of an inexpensive "motorcar for the multitudes." In this situation, Henry Ford could dictate the price and the features of his cars. When he opened his new assembly line factory at Highland Park, he abruptly raised the Model Ts price by $100—an increase of 12 percent—to help pay for the new plant. Then he decided to paint all Model Ts black. When told of consumer complaints about the lack of colors, Ford advised one of his executives in 1913: "Give them any color they want so long as it's black."[1]

Henry Ford had **market power.** He could dictate what color car Americans would buy. And he could raise the price of Model Ts without fear of losing all his customers. Such power is alien to competitive firms. Competitive firms are always under pressure to reduce costs, improve quality, and cater to consumer preferences.

In this chapter we examine how market structure influences market outcomes. Specifically, we examine how a market controlled by a single producer—a monopoly—behaves. We're particularly interested in the following questions:

* What price will a monopolist charge?
* How much output will the monopolist produce?
* Are consumers better or worse off when only one firm controls an entire market?

MARKET POWER

The essence of market power is the ability to alter the price of a product. The catfish farmers in Chapter 23 had no such power. Because 2,000 farms were producing and selling the same good, each catfish producer had to act as a *price*

[1] Charles E. Sorensen, *My Forty Years with Ford* (New York: W. W. Norton & Co., 1956), p. 127.

The Downward-Sloping Demand Curve

market power: The ability to alter the market price of a good or service.

taker. Each producer could sell all it wanted at the prevailing price but would lose all its customers if it tried to charge a higher price.

Firms that have market power *can* alter the price of their output without losing all their customers. Sales volume may drop when price is increased, but the quantity demanded won't drop to zero. In other words, *firms with market power confront downward-sloping demand curves for their own output.*

The distinction between perfectly competitive (powerless) and imperfectly competitive (powerful) firms is illustrated again in Figure 24.1. Figure 24.1a re-creates the market situation that confronts a single catfish farmer. In Chapter 22, we assumed that the prevailing price of catfish was $13 a bushel and that a small, competitive firm could sell its entire output at this price. Hence, each individual firm effectively confronted a horizontal demand curve.

We also noted earlier that catfish don't violate the law of demand. As good as catfish taste, people aren't willing to buy unlimited quantities of them at $13 a bushel. To induce consumers to buy more catfish, the market price of catfish must be reduced.

This seeming contradiction between the law of demand and the situation of the competitive firm is resolved in Figure 24.1. There are *two* relevant demand curves. The one on the left, which appears to contradict the law of demand, refers to a single competitive producer. The one on the right refers to the entire *industry,* of which the competitive producer is one very tiny part. The industry or market demand curve *does* slope downward, even though individual competitive firms are able to sell their own output at the going price.

Monopoly

monopoly: A firm that produces the entire market supply of a particular good or service.

An industry needn't be composed of many small firms. The entire output of catfish could be produced by a single large producer. Such a firm would be a **monopoly**—a single firm that produces the entire market supply of a good.

The emergence of a monopoly obliterates the distinction between industry demand and the demand curve facing the firm. A monopolistic firm *is* the industry. Hence, there's only *one* demand curve to worry about, and that's the market (industry) demand curve, as illustrated in Figure 24.1b. This simplifies things: *In monopoly situations, the demand curve facing the firm is identical to the market demand curve for the product.*

Price and Marginal Revenue

profit-maximization rule: Produce at that rate of output where marginal revenue equals marginal cost.

Although monopolies simplify the geometry, they complicate the arithmetic of **profit maximization.** The basic rule for maximizing profits is unchanged—that is, produce the rate of output where marginal revenue equals marginal cost. This rule applies to *all* firms. In a competitive industry, however, this general rule was simplified. For competitive firms, marginal revenue is equal to price. Hence, a competitive firm can maximize profits by producing at that rate of output where marginal cost equals *price.*

FIGURE 24.1
Firm vs. Industry Demand

A competitive firm can sell its entire output at the prevailing market price. In this sense, the firm confronts a horizontal demand curve, as in part *a*. Nevertheless, market demand for the product still slopes downward. The demand curve confronting the industry is illustrated in part *b*. Note the difference in the units of measurement (single bushels vs. thousands).

This special adaptation of the profit-maximizing rule doesn't work for a monopolist. The demand curve facing a monopolist is downward-sloping. Because of this, *marginal revenue isn't equal to price for a monopolist.* On the contrary, marginal revenue is always *less* than price in a monopoly, which makes it just a bit more difficult to find the profit-maximizing rate of output.

Figure 24.2 is a simple illustration of the relationship between price and marginal revenue. The monopolist can sell 1 bushel of fish per day at a price of $13. If he wants to sell a larger quantity of fish, however, he has to reduce his price. According to the demand curve shown here, the price must be lowered to $12 to sell 2 bushels per day. This reduction in price is shown by a movement along the demand curve from point *A* to point *B*.

How much additional revenue does the second bushel bring in? It's tempting to say that it brings in $12, since that's its price. **Marginal revenue (MR)**, however, refers to the *change* in *total* revenue that results from a one-unit increase in output. More generally, we use the formula

$$\frac{\text{Marginal}}{\text{revenue}} = \frac{\text{change in total revenue}}{\text{change in quantity sold}} = \frac{\Delta TR}{\Delta q}$$

marginal revenue (MR): The change in total revenue that results from a one-unit increase in the quantity sold.

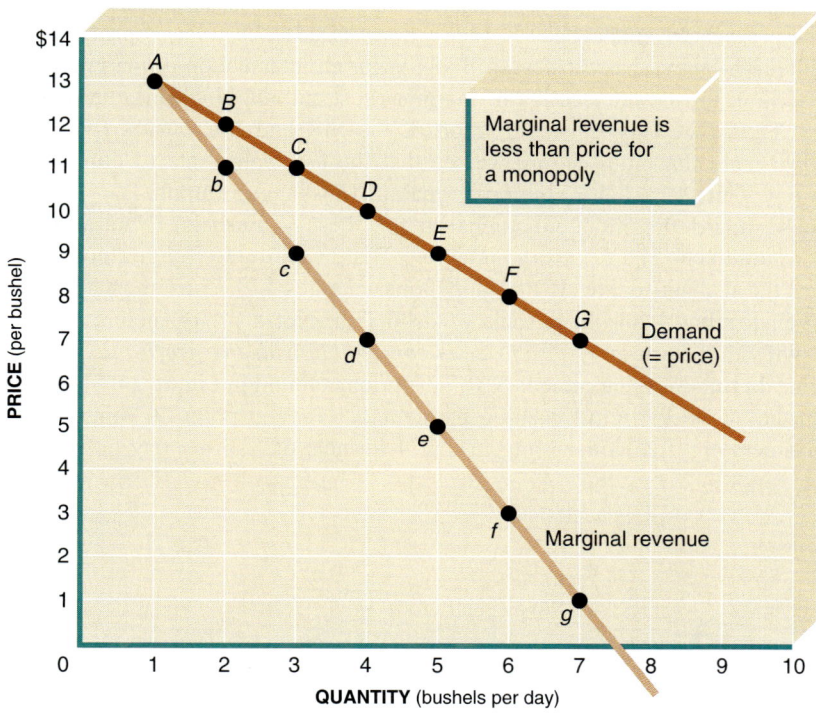

	(1) Quantity	×	(2) Price	=	(3) Total Revenue	(4) Marginal Revenue (= ΔTR ÷ Δq)
A	1		$13		$13	
B	2		12		24	$11
C	3		11		33	9
D	4		10		40	7
E	5		9		45	5

FIGURE 24.2
Price Exceeds Marginal Revenue in Monopoly

If a firm must lower its price to sell additional output, marginal revenue is less than price. If this firm wants to increase its sales from 1 to 2 bushels per day, for example, price must be reduced from $13 to $12. The marginal revenue of the second bushel is therefore only $11. This is indicated in row B of the table and by point *b* on the graph.

where the delta symbol (Δ) denotes "change in." According to this formula, the marginal revenue of the second bushel is only $11, not the $12 price for which it was sold.

Figure 24.2 summarizes the calculations necessary for computing MR. Row *A* of the table indicates that the total revenue resulting from one sale per day is $13. To increase sales, price must be reduced. Row *B* indicates that total revenue rises to $24 per day when fish sales double. The *increase* in total revenue resulting from the added sales is thus $11. This concept is illustrated in the last column of the table and by point *b* on the marginal revenue curve.

Notice that the MR of the second bushel ($11) is *less* than its price ($12) because both bushels are being sold for $12 apiece. In effect, the firm is giving up the opportunity to sell only 1 bushel per day at $13 in order to sell a larger quantity at a lower price. In this sense, the firm is sacrificing $1 of potential revenue on the first bushel in order to increase *total* revenue. Marginal revenue measures the change in total revenue that results.

So long as the demand curve is downward-sloping, MR will always be less than price. Compare columns 2 and 4 of the table in Figure 24.2. At each rate of output in excess of 1 bushel, marginal revenue is less than price. This is also evident in the graph: ***The MR curve lies below the demand (price) curve at every point but the first.***

Profit Maximization

Although the presence of market power adds a new wrinkle, the rules of profit maximization remain the same. Now instead of looking for an intersection of marginal cost and price, we look for the intersection of marginal cost and marginal revenue. This is illustrated in Figure 24.3 by the intersection of the MR and MC curves (point *d*). Looking down from that intersection, we see that the associated rate of output is 4 bushels per day. Thus 4 bushels is the profit-maximizing rate of output.

How much should the monopolist charge for these 4 bushels? Naturally, the monopolist would like to charge a very high price. But the ability to charge a high price is limited by the demand curve. If the monopolist charges $13, consumers will buy only 1 bushel, leaving 3 unsold bushels of dead fish. Not a pretty picture. As the monopolist will soon learn, ***only one price is compatible with the profit-maximizing rate of output.*** In this case, the price is $10. This price is found in Figure 24.3 by moving up from the quantity 4 until reaching the demand curve at point *D*. Point *D* tells us that consumers are able and willing to buy 4 bushels of fish per day only at the

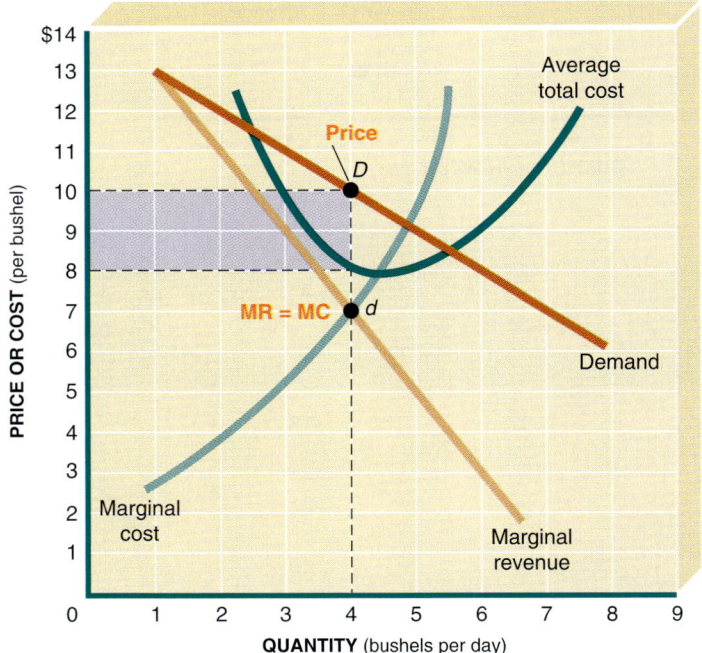

FIGURE 24.3
Profit Maximization

The most profitable rate of output is indicated by the intersection of marginal revenue and marginal cost (point *d*). This intersection (MC = MR) establishes 4 bushels as the profit maximizing rate of output. Point *D* indicates that consumers will pay $10 per bushel for this much output. Total profits equal price ($10) minus average total cost ($8), multiplied by the quantity sold (4).

price of $10 each. A monopolist who tries to charge more than $10 won't be able to sell all 4 bushels.

Figure 24.3 also illustrates the total profits of the catfish monopoly. To compute total profits we can first calculate profit per unit, that is, price minus *average* total cost. In this case, profit per unit is $2. Multiplying profit per unit by the quantity sold (4) gives us total profits of $8 per day, as illustrated by the shaded rectangle.

MARKET POWER AT WORK: THE COMPUTER MARKET REVISITED

To develop a keener appreciation for the nature of market power, we can return to the computer market of Chapter 23. This time we make some different assumptions about market structure. In particular, assume that a single firm, Universal Electronics, acquires an exclusive patent on the production of the microprocessors that function as the computer's "brain." This one firm is now in a position to deny potential competitors access to the basic ingredient of computers. The patent thus functions as a **barrier to entry**, to be erected or set aside at the will of Universal Electronics.

Universal's management is familiar enough with the principles of economics (including W.C. Fields's advice about never giving a sucker an even break) to know when it's onto a good thing. It's not about to let every would-be Horatio Alger have a slice of the profit pie. Even the Russians understood this strategy during the heyday of communism. They made sure no one else could produce sable furs that could compete with their monopoly (see World View). Let's assume that Universal Electronics is equally protective of its turf and will refuse to sell or give away any rights to its patent or the chips it produces. That is, Universal Electronics sets itself up as a computer monopoly.

Let's also assume that Universal has a multitude of manufacturing plants, each of which is identical to the typical competitive firm in Chapter 23. This is an unlikely situation because a monopolist would probably achieve **economies of scale** by closing at least a few plants and consolidating production in larger plants. Universal would

barriers to entry: Obstacles that make it difficult or impossible for would-be producers to enter a particular market, such as patents.

economies of scale: Reductions in minimum average costs that come about through increases in the size (scale) of plant and equipment.

WORLD VIEW

Foxy Soviets Pelt the West

Sable Monopoly Traps Hard Currency, Coats Capitalists

LENINGRAD—Crown sable from the eastern Siberian region of Barguzin, star of the Soviet fur collection, went on sale just as a deep freeze gripped this former imperial city. . . .

Fur is one of the Soviet Union's best known consumer goods exports. It is also bait for a country eager to trap hard currency: last year, the Soviet Union earned $100 million in fur sales.

In the case of sable, the Soviet Union has something no one else has—in capitalist lingo, a monopoly.

Ivan the Terrible is said to have made the sale of live sables abroad a crime punishable by death. Peter the Great on his travels in the West is said to have carried along trunks of sable skins to use as currency.

In the best-selling novel *Gorky Park*, popular among fur traders, it was the Soviet sable monopoly that was the key to the tangled tale of murderous intrigue.

There is another story, origin and veracity unknown, that an American once traded a rare North American species to the Soviets in exchange for two live Russian sables—only to find when he got home that they had been sterilized.

—Celestine Bohlen

Source: *Washington Post*, February 5, 1985. © 1985 The Washington Post. Reprinted with permission. www.washingtonpost.com

Analysis: To ward off potential competition, a monopoly must erect barriers to entry. By not letting live sables leave the country, Russia maintained a monopoly on sable furs.

maintain a multitude of small plants only if constant returns to scale or actual diseconomies of scale were rampant. Nevertheless, by assuming that multiple plants are maintained, we can compare monopoly behavior with competitive behavior on the basis of identical cost structures. In particular, if Universal continues to operate the many plants that once comprised the competitive home computer industry, it will confront the same short-run marginal and average cost curves already encountered in Chapter 23. Later in this chapter we relax this assumption of multiplant operations to determine whether, in the long run, a monopolist may actually lower production costs below those of a competitive industry.

Figure 24.4a re-creates the marginal costs the typical competitive firm faced in the early stages of the microcomputer boom (from Figure 23.3 and Table 23.1). We now assume that this MC curve also expresses the costs of operating one of Universal's many (identical) plants. Thus, the extension of monopoly control is assumed to have no immediate effect on production costs.

The market demand for computers is also assumed to be unchanged. There's no reason why people should be less willing to buy computers now than they were when the market was competitive. Most consumers have no notion of how many firms produce a product. Even if they knew, there's no reason why their demand for the product would change. Thus, Figure 24.4b expresses an unchanged demand for computers.

Our immediate concern is to determine how Universal Electronics, as a monopolist, will respond to these unchanged demand and cost curves. Will it produce exactly as many computers as the competitive industry did? Will it sell the computers at the same price that the competitive industry did? Will it improve the product as much or as fast?

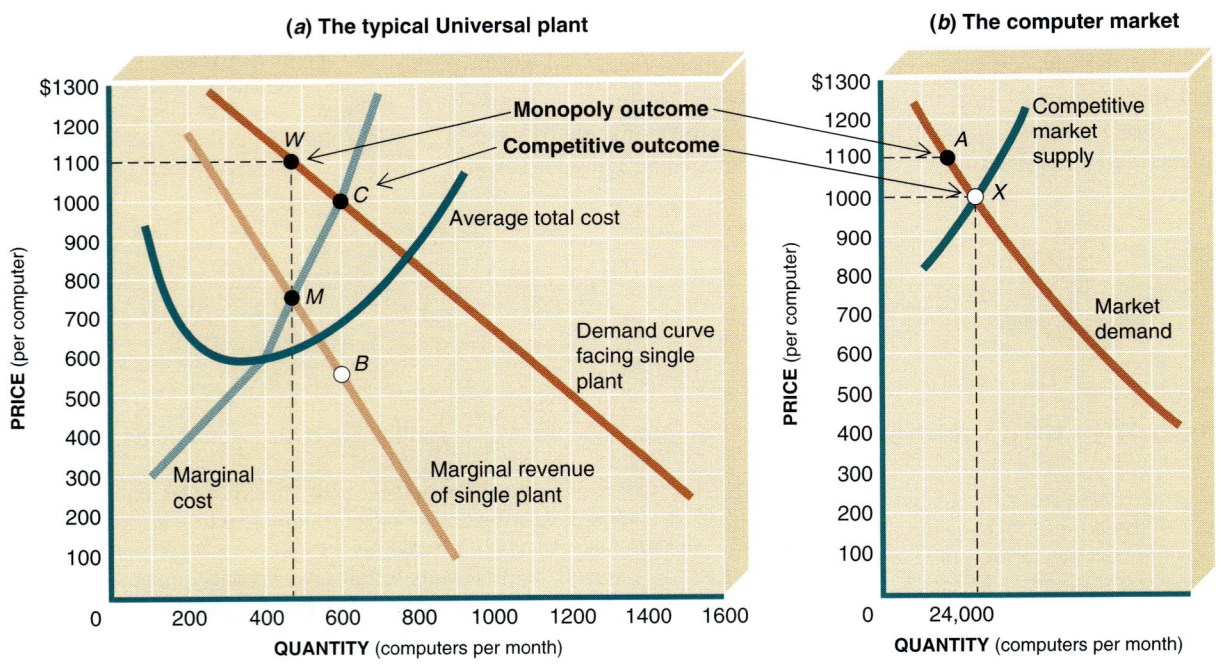

FIGURE 24.4
Initial Conditions in the Monopolized Computer Market

We assume that a monopoly firm (Universal Electronics) would confront the same costs (MC and ATC) and demand as would the competitive industry in Chapter 23. In the initial short-run equilibrium, the competitive price was $1,000 (point C). However, the monopolist isn't bound by the competitive market price. Instead, the monopolist must contend with downward-sloping demand and marginal revenue curves. If each monopoly plant produced where MC = $1,000 (point C in part a), marginal cost (point C) would exceed marginal revenue (point B). To maximize profits, the monopolist must find that rate of output where MC = MR (point M in part a). That rate of output can be sold at the monopoly price of $1,100 (point W in part a). Part b illustrates the market implications of the monopolist's production decision: A reduced quantity is sold at a higher price (point A).

Like any producer, Universal Electronics will strive to produce its output at the rate that maximizes total profits. But unlike competitive firms, Universal will explicitly take account of the fact that an increase in output will put downward pressure on computer prices. This may threaten corporate profits.

The implications of Universal's market position for the **production decision** of its many plants can be seen in the new price and marginal revenue curves imposed on each of its manufacturing plants. Universal can't afford to let each of its plants compete with the others, expanding output and driving down prices; that's the kind of folly reserved for truly competitive firms. Instead, Universal will seek to *coordinate* the production decisions of its plants, instructing all plant managers to expand or contract output simultaneously, to achieve the corporate goal of profit maximization.

A simultaneous reduction of output by each Universal plant will lead to a significant reduction in the quantity of computers supplied to the market. This reduced supply will cause a move up the market demand curve to higher prices. By the same token, an expansion of output by all Universal plants will lead to an increase in the quantity supplied to the market and a slide down the market demand curve. As a consequence, each of the monopolist's plants effectively confronts a downward-sloping demand curve. These downward-sloping demand curves are illustrated in Figure 24.4a.[2]

Notice that in Figure 24.4b the *market* demand for computers is unchanged; only the demand curve confronting each plant (firm) has changed. A competitive *industry*, like a monopoly, must obey the law of demand. But the individual firms that comprise a competitive industry all act independently, *as if* they could sell unlimited quantities at the prevailing price. That is, they all act as if they confronted a horizontal demand curve at the market price of $1,000. A competitive firm that doesn't behave in this fashion will simply lose sales to other firms. In contrast, a monopolist not only foresees the impact of increased production on market price but can also prevent such production increases by its separate plants.

The Production Decision

production decision: The selection of the short-run rate of output (with existing plant and equipment).

Marginal Revenue. The downward-sloping demand curve now confronting each Universal plant implies that marginal revenue no longer equals price. Notice that the marginal revenue curve in Figure 24.4a lies *below* the demand curve at every rate of output. Because marginal revenue is less than price for a monopoly, Universal's plants would no longer wish to produce up to the point where marginal cost equals price. ***Only firms that confront a horizontal demand curve (perfect competitors) equate marginal cost and price.*** Universal's plants must stick to the generic profit-maximizing rule about equating marginal revenue and marginal cost. Should the individual plant managers forget this rule, Universal's central management will fire them.

The output and price implications of Universal's monopoly position become apparent as we examine the new revenue and cost relationships. Recall that the equilibrium price of computers in the early stages of the home computer boom was $1,000. This equilibrium price is indicated in Figure 24.4b by the intersection of the competitive market supply curve with the market demand curve (point *X*). Each competitive *firm* produced up to the point where marginal cost (MC) equaled that price (point *C* in Figure 24.4a). At that point, each competitive firm was producing 600 computers a month.

Reduced Output. The emergence of Universal as a monopolist alters these production decisions. Now each Universal plant *does* have an impact on market price because its behavior is imitated simultaneously by all Universal plants. In fact, the marginal revenue associated with the 600th computer is only $575, as indicated by point *B* in Figure 24.4a. At this rate of output, the typical Universal plant would be operating with

---

[2]The demand and marginal revenue curves in Figure 24.4a are illustrative; they're not derived from earlier tables. As discussed above, we're assuming that the central management of Universal determines the profit-maximizing rate of output and then instructs all individual plants to produce equal shares of that output.

marginal costs ($1,000) far in excess of marginal revenues ($575). Such behavior is inconsistent with profit maximization.

The enlightened Universal plant manager will soon discover that the profit-maximizing rate of output is less than 600 computers per month. In Figure 24.4a we see that the marginal revenue and marginal cost curves intersect at point M. This MR = MC intersection occurs at an output level of only 475 computers per month. Accordingly, the typical Universal plant will want to produce *fewer* computers than were produced by the typical competitive firm in the early stages of the home computer boom. Recall that individual competitive firms had no incentive to engage in such production cutbacks. They couldn't alter the market supply curve or price on their own and weren't coordinated by a central management. Thus, the first consequence of Universal's monopoly position is a reduction in the rate of industry output.

The Monopoly Price

The reduction in output at each Universal plant translates automatically into a decrease in the *quantity supplied* to the market. As consumers compete for this reduced market supply, they'll bid computer prices up. We can observe the increased prices in Figure 24.4 by looking at either the typical Universal plant or the computer market. Notice that in Figure 24.4a the price is determined by moving directly up from point M to the demand curve confronting the typical Universal plant. The demand curve always tells how much consumers are willing to pay for any given quantity. Hence, once we've determined the quantity that's going to be supplied (475 computers per month), we can look at the demand curve to determine the price ($1,100 at point W) that consumers will pay for these computers. That is,

- ***The intersection of the marginal revenue and marginal cost curves establishes the profit-maximizing rate of output.***
- ***The demand curve tells us how much consumers are willing to pay for that specific quantity of output.***

Figure 24.4a shows how Universal's monopoly position results in both reduced output and increased prices. This result is also evident in Figure 24.4b, where we see that a smaller quantity supplied to the market will force a move up the demand curve to the higher price of $1,100 per computer (point A).

Monopoly Profits

Universal's objective was and remains the maximization of profits. That it has succeeded in its effort can be confirmed by scrutinizing Figure 24.5. As you can see, the typical

FIGURE 24.5
Monopoly Profits: The Typical Universal Plant

The profit-maximizing rate of output occurs where the marginal cost and marginal revenue curves intersect (point M). The demand curve indicates the price (point W) that consumers will pay for this output. Total profit equals price (W) minus average total cost (K) multiplied by the quantity sold (475). Total profits are represented by the shaded rectangle.

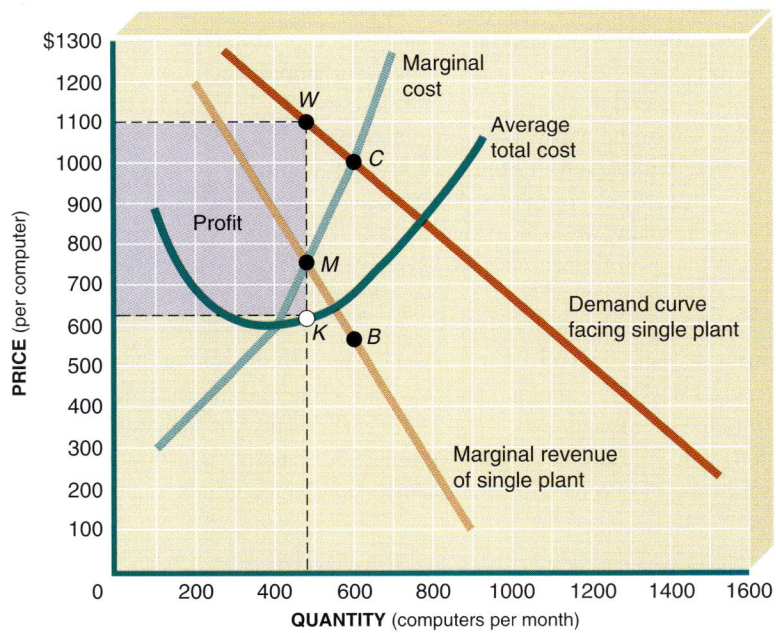

Universal plant ends up selling 475 computers a month at a price of $1,100 each (point W). The **average total cost (ATC)** of production at this rate of output is only $630 (point K), as was detailed in Table 23.1.

As always, we can compute total profit as

Total profit = profit per unit × quantity sold

In this case, we see that

$$\text{Total profit} = (\$1{,}100 - \$630) \times 475$$
$$= \$223{,}250$$

This figure may be compared with the monthly profit of $180,000 earned by the typical competitive firm in the early stages of the computer boom (see Table 23.1).

It's apparent from these profit figures that Universal management has learned its economic principles well. By reducing the output of each plant and raising prices a little, it has managed to enlarge the size of the profit pie while keeping it all to itself, of course. This can be seen again in Figure 24.6, which is an enlarged illustration of the *market* situation for the home computer industry. The figure translates the economics of our single-plant and competitive-firm comparison into the dimensions of the whole industry.

Figure 24.6 reaffirms that the competitive industry in Chapter 23 initially produces the quantity q_c and sells it at a price of $1,000 each. Its profits are denoted by the rectangle formed by the points R, X, U, T. The monopolist, on the other hand, produces the smaller q_m and charges a higher price, $1,100. The monopoly firm's profits are indicated by the larger profit rectangle shaded in the figure. We see that *a monopoly receives larger profits than a comparable competitive industry by reducing the quantity supplied and pushing prices up.* The larger profits make Universal very happy and make consumers a little sadder and wiser. Consumers are now paying more and getting less.

The higher profits Universal Electronics attained as a result of its monopoly position aren't the end of the story. The existence of economic profit tends to bring profit-hungry entrepreneurs swarming like locusts. In the competitive home computer

average total cost (ATC): Total cost divided by the quantity produced in a given time period.

Barriers to Entry

FIGURE 24.6

Monopoly Profit: The Entire Company

Total profits of the monopolist (including all plants) are illustrated by the shaded rectangle. The monopolist's total output q_m is determined by the intersection of the (industry) MR and MC curves. The price of this output is determined by the market demand curve (point A). In contrast, a competitive industry would produce q_c computers in the short run and sell them at a lower price (X) and profit per unit (X − U). Those profits would attract new entrants until long-run equilibrium (point V) was reached. (See Figure 23.8 for a summary of competitive market equilibrium.)

IN THE NEWS

Concerts Becoming a Pricier Affair; Music Industry Consolidation Has Brought Higher Ticket Fees. Some Cry Foul.

Members of the popular heavy-rock band Godsmack say they want to make tickets affordable for their current U.S. tour. But the economics of the concert industry may jar fans harder than the mosh pit at the band's show.

The face value of a general admission ticket to Godsmack's concert Wednesday at Verizon Wireless Amphitheater is $20. But no one attending the band's performance gets to pay that amount.

Instead, fans who purchase tickets on the phone or online are socked with a series of surcharges that boost the price to $35.60. These added costs, tacked on by distribution giant Ticketmaster and concert promotion conglomerate Clear Channel Entertainment, include a convenience fee, a facility fee and a handling charge.

Moreover, a hidden $3.50 parking fee is buried in the price of each ticket by Clear Channel, owner of the Verizon Amphitheater in Irvine. All told, the fees add a 116% markup to the cost of a $16.50 ticket. . . .

In recent years, Clear Channel has emerged as the dominant force in the $1.6-billion concert industry. . . .

"They can pretty much dictate the costs, ad rates and ticket prices," said Jon Stoll, president of Fantasma Productions, a competing promoter in West Palm Beach, Fla. "If one company controls the live-music industry, there's nobody that can really bring ticket prices down."

—Jeff Leeds

Source: *Los Angeles Times,* July 17, 2001. Reprinted with permission. www.latimes.com

Analysis: Control of concert sites and ticket distribution allow Clear Channel and Ticketmaster to charge monopoly prices for live concerts.

industry in Chapter 23, the lure of high profits brought about an enormous expansion of home computer output and a steep decline in home computer prices. In Figure 24.6 the long-run equilibrium of a competitive industry is indicated by point V. What then can we expect to happen in the home computer market now that Universal has a monopoly position and is enjoying huge profits?

Remember that Universal is now assumed to have an exclusive patent on microprocessor chips and can use this patent as an impassable barrier to entry. Consequently, would-be competitors can swarm around Universal's profits until their wings drop off; Universal isn't about to let them in on the spoils. By locking out the potential competition, Universal can prevent the surge in computer output that pushed prices down the market demand curve. As long as Universal is able to keep out the competition, only the more affluent consumers will be able to use computers. The same phenomenom explains why ticket prices for live concerts are so high. Because Clear Channel controls most concert venues and Ticketmaster is the exclusive ticket distributor, fans have to pay monopoly prices to see Godsmack, Bare Naked Ladies, Pearl Jam or other live concerts (see News). A monopoly has no incentive to move from point A in Figure 24.6, and there's no competitive pressure to force such a move. Universal may discover ways to reduce the costs of production and thus lower prices, but there's no *pressure* on it to do so, as there was in the competitive situation.

A COMPARATIVE PERSPECTIVE OF MARKET POWER

The different outcomes of the computer industry under competitive and monopoly conditions illustrate basic features of market structures. We may summarize the sequence of events that occurs in each type of market structure as follows:

COMPETITIVE INDUSTRY

- High prices and profits signal consumers' demand for more output.
- The high profits attract new suppliers.
- Production and supplies expand.
- Prices slide down the market demand curve.
- A new equilibrium is established wherein more of the desired product is produced, its price falls, average costs of production approach their minimum, and economic profits approach zero.
- Price equals marginal cost throughout the process.
- Throughout the process, there's great pressure to keep ahead of the profit squeeze by reducing costs or improving product quality.

MONOPOLY INDUSTRY

- High prices and profits signal consumers' demand for more output.
- Barriers to entry are erected to exclude potential competition.
- Production and supplies are constrained.
- Prices don't move down the market demand curve.
- No new equilibrium is established; average costs aren't necessarily at or near a minimum, and economic profits are at a maximum.
- Price exceeds marginal cost at all times.
- There's no squeeze on profits and thus no pressure to reduce costs or improve product quality.

In our discussion, we assumed that the competitive industry and the monopoly both started from the same position—an initial equilibrium in which the price of computers is $1,000. In reality, an industry may manifest concentrations of market power *before* such an equilibrium is established. That is, the sequence of events we've depicted may be altered (with step 3 occurring first, for example). Nevertheless, the basic distinctions between competitive and monopolistic behavior are evident.

Productivity Advances. To the extent that monopolies behave as we've discussed, they affect not just the price and output of a specific product but broader economic outcomes as well. Remember that competitive industries tend, in the long run, to produce at minimum average costs. Competitive industries also pursue cost reductions and product improvements relentlessly. These pressures tend to expand our production possibilities. No such forces are at work in the monopoly we've discussed here. Hence, there's a basic tendency for monopolies to inhibit productivity advances and economic growth.

The Mix of Output. Another important feature of competitive markets is their observed tendency toward **marginal cost pricing.** Marginal cost pricing is important to consumers because it permits rational choices among alternative goods and services. In particular, it informs consumers of the true opportunity costs of various goods, thereby allowing them to choose the mix of output that delivers the most utility with available resources. In our monopoly example, however, consumers end up getting fewer computers than they'd like, while the economy continues to produce other, less desired goods. Thus, the mix of output shifted away from computers when Universal took over the industry.

The power to influence prices and product flows may have far-reaching consequences for our economic welfare. Changes in prices and product flows directly influence the level and composition of output, employment and resource allocation, the level and distribution of income, and of course, the level and structure of prices. Hence, firms that wield significant market power affect all dimensions of economic welfare.

> **marginal cost pricing:** The offer (supply) of goods at prices equal to their marginal cost.

Political Power. Market power isn't the only kind of power wielded in society, of course. Political power, for example, is a different kind of power and important in its own right. Indeed, the power to influence an election or to sway a Senate committee vote may ultimately be more important than the power to increase the price of laundry soap. Nevertheless, market power is a force that influences the way we live, the incomes we earn, and our relationships with other countries. Moreover, market power may be the basis for political power: The individual or firm with considerable market power is likely to have the necessary resources to influence an election or sway a vote on a congressional committee.

The Limits to Power

Even though market power enables a producer to manipulate market outcomes, there's a clear limit to the exercise of power. Even a monopolist can't get everything it wants. Universal, for example, would really like to sell q_m computers at a price of $1,500 each because that kind of price would bring it even greater profits. Yet, despite its monopoly position, Universal is constrained to sell that quantity of computers at the lower price of $1,100 each. Even monopolists have their little disappointments.

The ultimate limit to a monopolist's power is evident in Figure 24.6. Universal's attainment of a monopoly position allows it only one prerogative: the ability to alter the quantity of output *supplied* to the market. This is no small prerogative, but it's far from absolute power. Universal, and every other monopolist, must still contend with the market *demand* curve. Note again that the new equilibrium in Figure 24.6 occurs at a point on the *unchanged* demand curve. In effect, a monopolist has the opportunity to pick any point on the market demand curve and designate it as the new market equilibrium. The point it selects will depend on its own perceptions of effort, profit, and risk (in this case point *A*, determined by the intersection of marginal revenue and marginal cost).

The ultimate constraint on the exercise of market power, then, resides in the market demand curve. How great a constraint the demand curve imposes depends largely on the **price elasticity of demand.** The greater the price elasticity of demand, the more a monopolist will be frustrated in attempts to establish both high prices and high volume. Consumers will simply reduce their purchases if price is increased. If, however, consumer demand is highly inelastic—if consumers need or want that product badly and few viable substitutes are available—the monopolist can reap tremendous profits from market power.

price elasticity of demand: The percentage change in quantity demanded divided by the percentage change in price.

Price Discrimination

Even in situations where the *market* demand is relatively elastic, a monopolist may be able to extract high prices. A monopolist has the power not only to raise the market price of a good (by reducing the quantity supplied) but also to charge various prices for the same good. Recall that the market demand curve reflects the combined willingness of many individuals to buy. Some of those individuals are willing to buy the good at prices higher than the market price, just as other individuals will buy only at lower prices. A monopolist may be able to increase total profits by selling each unit of the good separately, at a price each *individual* consumer is willing to pay. This practice is called **price discrimination.**

price discrimination: The sale of an identical good at different prices to different consumers by a single seller.

The airline industry has practiced price discrimination for many years. Basically, there are two distinct groups of travelers: business and nonbusiness travelers. Business executives must fly from one city to another on a certain day and at a particular time. They typically make flight arrangements on short notice and may have no other way to get to their destination. Nonbusiness travelers, such as people on vacation and students going home during semester break, usually have more flexible schedules. They may plan their trips weeks or months in advance and often have the option of traveling by car, bus, or train.

The different travel needs of business and vacation travelers are reflected in their respective demand curves. Business demand for air travel tends to be less price-elastic than the demand of nonbusiness travelers. Few business executives would stop flying if airfares increased. Higher airfares would, however, discourage air travel by nonbusiness travelers.

What should airlines do in this case? Should they *raise* airfares to take advantage of the relative price inelasticity of business demand, or should they *lower* airfares to attract more nonbusiness travelers?

They should do both. In fact, they *have* done both. The airlines offer a full-fare ride, available at any time, and a discount-fare ride, available only by purchasing a ticket in advance and agreeing to some restrictions on time of departure. The advance purchase and other restrictions on discount fares effectively exclude most business travelers, who end up paying full fare. The higher full fare doesn't, however, discourage most nonbusiness travelers, who can fly at a discount. Consequently, the airlines are able to sell essentially identical units of the same good (an airplane ride) at substantially different prices to different customers. Indeed, by experimenting with various discount fares and travel restrictions, airlines can discriminate even more thoroughly among passengers, thereby reaping the highest possible *average* price for the quantity supplied. Doctors, lawyers, and car dealers commonly practice the same type of price discrimination. In all these cases, the seller may "adjust" the price to the income and taste of each individual consumer. In effect, the seller is able to "divide and conquer" the individual consumers who are positioned along the length of the market demand curve. A monopolist is best positioned to engage in price discrimination, since consumers have no competitive alternatives.

Entry Barriers

It's the lack of competitors that gives monopolists such pricing power. Accordingly, the preservation of monopoly power depends on keeping potential competitors out of the market. A monopolist doesn't want anyone else to produce an *identical* product or even a *close substitute*. To do that, a monopoly must erect and maintain barriers to market entry. Some common entry barriers are now discussed.

Patents. This was the critical barrier in the mythical Universal Electronics case. A government-awarded patent gives a producer 20 years of exclusive rights to produce a particular product. The Polaroid Corporation used its patents to keep Eastman Kodak and other potential rivals out of the market for instant development cameras.

Monopoly Franchises. The government also creates and maintains monopolies by giving a single firm the exclusive right to supply a particular good or service, even though other firms can produce it. Local cable TV stations and telephone companies are examples. Congress also bestows monopoly privileges to baseball teams and the U.S. Postal Service. Your campus bookstore may have exclusive rights to sell textbooks on campus.

Control of Key Inputs. A company may lock out competition by securing exclusive access to key inputs. Airlines need landing rights and terminal gates in order to compete. Oil and gas producers need pipelines to supply their product. Utility companies need transmission networks to supply consumers with electricity. Pepsi says it needs access to Coke-dominated restaurants (see News on the next page). Software vendors need to know the features of computer operating systems. If a single company controls these critical inputs, it can lock out potential competition. That's alleged to be a prime source of Microsoft's monopoly power (see The Economy Tomorrow).

Lawsuits. In the event that competitors actually surmount other entry barriers, a monopoly may sue it out of existence. Typically, start-up firms are rich in ideas but cash poor. They need to get their products to the market quickly to generate some cash. A timely lawsuit alleging patent or copyright infringement can derail such a company by absorbing critical management, cash, and time. Long before the merits of the lawsuit are adjudicated, the company may be forced to withdraw from the market.

IN THE NEWS

Pepsi Takes Coke to Court
Rival Presses for Monopoly of Fountain Sales, Suit Says

NEW YORK, May 7—Pepsi accused Coke today of monopolizing the sales of fountain soft drinks at restaurant chains and movie theaters by threatening to take away Coke from distributors that carried Pepsi as well.

The lawsuit filed in U.S. District Court did not pertain to sales of bottles or cans of the soft drinks, only to fountain-dispensed drinks handled by large food service distributors who control deliveries to chains of restaurants and theaters.

The lawsuit, filed by Pepsi-Cola's parent, PepsiCo Inc., asked the court to restrain Coca-Cola from entering into agreements with its distributors to exclude Pepsi and to award Pepsi undetermined damages.

"Coca-Cola's message to food service distributors is clear: If a distributor carries Pepsi at a customer's request, the distributor will be terminated by Coke," the lawsuit said.

Source: *Washington Post*, May 8, 1998. © 1998 The Washington Post. Reprinted with permission. www.washingtonpost.com

Analysis: A firm can acquire a monopoly by attaining exclusive access to key inputs or distribution systems.

Acquisition. When all else fails, a monopolist may simply purchase a potential competitor. As the accompanying cartoon suggests, mergers tend to raise consumer prices.

Economies of Scale. Last but far from least, a monopoly may persist because of economies of scale. If large firms have a substantial cost advantage over smaller firms, the smaller firms may not be able to compete. We look at this entry barrier again in a moment.

PROS AND CONS OF MARKET POWER

Despite the strong case against market power, it's conceivable that monopolies could also benefit society. One argument made for concentrations of market power is that monopolies have greater ability to pursue research and development. Another argument

Analysis: Mergers and acquisitions reduce competition in an industry. The increased industry concentration may lead to higher prices.

is that the lure of market power creates a tremendous incentive for invention and innovation. A third argument in defense of monopoly is that large companies can produce goods more efficiently than smaller firms. Finally, it's argued that even monopolies have to worry about *potential* competition and will behave accordingly.

Research and Development

In principle, monopolies are well positioned to undertake valuable research and development. First, such firms are sheltered from the constant pressure of competition. Second, they have the resources (monopoly profits) with which to carry out expensive R&D functions. The manager of a perfectly competitive firm, by contrast, has to worry about day-to-day production decisions and profit margins. As a result, she is unable to take the longer view necessary for significant research and development and couldn't afford to purchase such a view even if she could see it.

The basic problem with the R&D argument is that it says nothing about *incentives*. Although monopolists have a clear financial advantage in pursuing research and development activities, they have no clear incentive to do so. Research and development aren't necessarily required for profitable survival. In fact, research and development that make existing plant and equipment technologically obsolete run counter to a monopolist's vested interest and so may actually be suppressed (see News). In contrast, a perfectly competitive firm can't continue to make significant profits unless it stays ahead of the competition. This pressure constitutes a significant incentive to discover new products or new and cheaper ways of producing existing products.

Entrepreneurial Incentives

The second defense of market power uses a novel incentive argument. Every business is out to make a buck, and it's the quest for profits that keeps industries running. Thus, it's argued, even greater profit prizes will stimulate more entrepreneurial activity. Little Horatio Algers will work harder and longer if they can dream of one day possessing a whole monopoly.

The incentive argument for market power is enticing but not entirely convincing. After all, an innovator can make substantial profits in a competitive market before the competition catches up. Recall that the early birds did get the worm in the competitive com-

IN THE NEWS

Jury Rules Magnetek Unit Is Liable for Keeping Technology off Market

SAN FRANCISCO—Is a company liable if it deliberately keeps a technology off the market? Apparently so, judging from an unusual ruling by a California jury.

A county superior court jury in Oakland ordered a unit of Magnetek Inc. to pay $25.8 million to two California entrepreneurs and their companies. They charged that the unit had failed to bring the pair's energy-saving fluorescent-light technology to market in a profitable manner, suppressing it in favor of an outmoded technology.

The lawsuit reads like familiar legends of big business quashing inventions that threaten its interests. . . .

In 1984, the two entrepreneurs, C. R. Stevens and William R. Alling, charged that Universal Manufacturing Corp., now a unit of Los Angeles–based Magnetek, buried a technology through which fluorescent lights use 70 percent less energy. The two said they sold Universal the technology, called a solid-state ballast, in 1981 after the company promised to market it aggressively.

Instead, they charged, Universal suppressed the technology to protect its less-efficient existing ballast models. "They told us they were going to be first on the market with our tech, yet they planned otherwise," said Mr. Alling.

—Stephen Kreider Yoder

Source: *The Wall Street Journal*, January 10, 1990. Reprinted by permission of *The Wall Street Journal*. © 1990 Dow Jones & Company, Inc. All rights reserved worldwide. www.wsj.com

Analysis: A monopoly has little incentive (no competitive pressure) to pursue R&D. In fact, R&D that threatens established products or processes may be suppressed.

puter industry (see Chapter 23), even though profit margins were later squeezed. It's not evident that the profit incentives available in a competitive industry are at all inadequate.

We must also recall the arguments about research and development efforts. A monopolist has little incentive to pursue R&D. Furthermore, entrepreneurs who might pursue product innovation or technological improvements may be dissuaded by their inability to penetrate a monopolized market. The barriers to entry that surround market power may not only keep out potential competitors but also lock out promising ideas.

Economies of Scale

A third defense of market power is the most convincing. A large firm, it's argued, can produce goods at a lower unit (average) cost than a small firm. If such *economies of scale* exist, we could attain greater efficiency (higher productivity) by permitting firms to grow to market-dominating size.

We sidestepped this argument in our story about the Universal Electronics monopoly. We explicitly assumed that Universal confronted the same production costs as the competitive industry. We simply converted each typical competitive firm into a separate plant owned and operated by Universal. Universal wasn't able to produce computers any more cheaply than the competitive counterpart, and we concerned ourselves only with the different production decisions made by competitive and monopolistic firms.

A monopoly *could*, however, attain greater cost savings. By centralizing various functions it might be able to eliminate some duplicative efforts. It might also shut down some plants and concentrate production in fewer facilities. If these kinds of efficiencies are attained, a monopoly would offer attractive resource savings.

There's no guarantee, however, of such economies of scale. As we observed in Chapter 21, increasing the size (scale) of a plant may actually *reduce* operating efficiency (see Figure 21.10). In evaluating the economies-of-scale argument for market power, then, we must recognize that *efficiency and size don't necessarily go hand in hand. Some firms and industries may be subject to economies of scale, but others won't.*

Even when economies of scale are present there is no guarantee that consumers will benefit. This is why the Pentagon opposed the merger of the nation's only two nuclear-ship builders (see News). Even though there were substantial short-run economies of scale in eliminating duplicate facilities, the Navy concluded that even a little competition (two firms) was better than none (a monopoly) in the long run.

Natural Monopolies. Industries that exhibit economies of scale over the entire range of market output are called **natural monopolies.** In these cases, one single firm can produce the entire market supply more efficiently than any large number of (smaller) firms. As the size (scale) of the one firm increases, its minimum average costs continue to fall. These economies of scale give the one large producer a decided advantage over would-be rivals. Hence, *economies of scale act as a "natural" barrier to entry.*

natural monopoly: An industry in which one firm can achieve economies of scale over the entire range of market supply.

Local telephone and utility services are classic examples of natural monopoly. A single telephone or utility company can supply the market more efficiently than a large number of competing firms.

Although natural monopolies are economically desirable, they may be abused. We must ask whether and to what extent consumers are reaping some benefit from the efficiency a natural monopoly makes possible. Do consumers end up with lower prices, expanded output, and better service? Or does the monopoly keep most of the benefits for itself, in the form of higher prices and profits? Multiplex movie theaters, for example, achieve economies of scale by sharing operating and concession facilities among as many as 30 screens. But do moviegoers get lower prices for movies or popcorn? Not often. Because megamultiplex theaters tend to drive out competition, they don't have to reduce prices when costs drop. Under such circumstances, we may need government "trustbusters" to ensure that the benefits of increased efficiency are shared with consumers. (The potential and pitfalls of government regulation are examined in Chapter 27.)

Pentagon Opposes Ship Monopoly

The Pentagon yesterday approved Northrop Grumman Corp.'s bid to purchase Newport News Shipbuilding Inc., and antitrust regulators sued to block a competing offer from General Dynamics, citing concern about consolidating the nation's construction of nuclear ships into one company.

Allowing General Dynamics to buy Newport News would have united the only two U.S. builders of nuclear submarines, creating a "merger-to-monopoly" that "would reduce innovation and, ultimately, the quality of the products supplied to the military, while raising prices to the U.S. military and to U.S. taxpayers," Justice Department antitrust chief Charles A. James said in a news release....

Navy officials hoped that Falls Church-based General Dynamics, which builds nuclear submarines at its Electric Boat shipyard in Connecticut, could cut costs at Newport News by eliminating overlap between the two similar businesses.

But Northrop Grumman argued that allowing General Dynamics to make the purchase would have increased costs over time by eliminating competition for nuclear-ship contracts.

"In the end you could argue that the competition angle outweighed the cost savings. That's a message that will resonate throughout the rest of the defense industry," said Byron Callan, an industry analyst with Merrill Lynch in New York.

—Greg Schneider

Source: *Washington Post*, October 24, 2001. © 2001 The Washington Post. Reprinted with permission. www.washingtonpost.com

Analysis: Monopolies may enjoy economies of scale. In the long run, however, consumers may benefit more from competitive pressures to reduce costs, improve product quality, and lower prices.

Governmental regulators aren't necessarily the only force keeping monopolists in line. Even though a firm may produce the entire supply of a particular product at present, it may face *potential* competition from other firms. Potential rivals may be sitting on the sidelines, watching how well the monopoly fares. If it does too well, these rivals may enter the industry, undermining the monopoly structure and profits. In such **contestable markets,** monopoly behavior may be restrained by potential competition.

How "contestable" a market is depends not so much on its structure as on entry barriers. If entry barriers are insurmountable, would-be competitors are locked out of the market. But if entry barriers are modest, they'll be surmounted when the lure of monopoly profits is irresistible. When CNN's profits reached irresistible proportions, both domestic and foreign companies decided to invade CNN's monopoly market (see World View). Since then, CNN hasn't been nearly as profitable.

Structure vs. Behavior. From the perspective of contestable markets, the whole case against monopoly is misconceived. Market *structure* per se isn't a problem; what counts is market *behavior*. If potential rivals force a monopolist to behave like a competitive firm, then monopoly imposes no cost on consumers or on society at large.

The experience with the Model T Ford illustrates the basic notion of contestable markets. At the time Henry Ford decided to increase the price of the Model T and paint them all black, the Ford Motor Company enjoyed a virtual monopoly on mass-produced cars. But potential rivals saw the profitability of offering additional colors and features such as a self-starter and left-hand drive. When rivals began producing cars in volume, Ford's market power was greatly reduced. In 1926, the Ford Motor Company tried to regain its dominant position by again supplying cars in colors other than black. By that time, however, consumers had more choices. Ford ceased production of the Model T in May 1927.

The experience with the Model T suggests that potential competition can force a monopoly to change its ways. Critics point out, however, that even contestable markets don't force a monopolist to act *exactly* like a competitive firm. There will always be a

Contestable Markets

contestable market: An imperfectly competitive industry subject to potential entry if prices or profits increase.

Information on Federal Communications Commission regulation and deregulation can be found at www.fcc.gov.

WORLD VIEW

New Competition May Mean Bad News for CNN

A growing crowd of media giants wants to make sure that most people don't get their news from Cable News Network. They're all gunning for the lucrative, Turner Broadcasting System unit with a host of rival 24-hour news networks, spurred by new technologies for delivering TV programs and shifting alliances in the cable business. . . .

Last year, with the market to itself, CNN and its related news businesses, including a Headline News channel, generated about $227 million in operating profit for Turner Broadcasting System Inc.

But CNN may not keep its monopoly for long. If the proposed services can overcome huge distribution hurdles caused by lack of space on crowded cable systems, their strong brand names and well-known correspondents and anchors may be enough to lure viewers away from CNN.

Capital Cities/ABC Inc., for example, said yesterday that it will launch a 24-hour news service in the U.S. in 1997, using ABC News's star talent and rerunning some of its popular shows. . . .

Other companies have similar ideas. General Electric Co.'s NBC for the past year has been putting together a detailed plan for launching its own national news network with a strong local component. . . .

Meanwhile, Britain's BBC is also trying to start a global news channel. And News Corp. Chairman Rupert Murdoch, whose British BSkyB service already offers a 24-hour news channel, said last week that he wants to launch a U.S. competitor to CNN. . . .

Behind all the expansion plans is a straightforward economic calculation: Companies already in the news business think they can squeeze out more profits with relatively little new cost by expanding to 24 hours of TV news.

—Elizabeth Jensen and John Lippman

Source: *The Wall Street Journal,* December 6, 1995. Reprinted by permission of *The Wall Street Journal.* © 1995 Dow Jones & Company, Inc. All rights reserved worldwide. www.wsj.com

Analysis: As a monopolist's profits grow, would-be competitors will try to overcome barriers to entry. If entry is possible, a monopolized market may be contestable.

---

gap between competitive outcomes and those monopoly outcomes likely to entice new entry. That gap can cost consumers a lot. The absence of *existing* rivals is also likely to inhibit product and productivity improvements. From 1913 to 1926, all Model Ts were black, and consumers had few alternatives. Ford changed its behavior only after *potential* competition became *actual* competition. Even after 1927, when the Ford Motor Company could no longer act like a monopolist, it still didn't price its cars at marginal cost.

THE ECONOMY TOMORROW

Microsoft: Bully or Genius?

Ford Motor Company's experience is a useful reminder that monopolies rarely last forever. Potential competitors will always look for ways to enter a profitable market. Eventually they'll surmount entry barriers or develop substitute goods that supplant a monopolist's products.

Consumer advocates assert that we shouldn't have to wait for the invisible hand to dismantle a monopoly. They say the government should intervene to dismantle a monopoly or at least force it to change its behavior. Then consumers would get lower prices and better products a whole lot sooner.

Microsoft's dominant position in the computer industry highlights this issue. Microsoft produces the operating system (Windows) that powers 9 out of 10 personal computers. It also produces a huge share of applications software, including Internet browsers. Critics fear that this kind of monopoly power is a threat to consumers. They say Microsoft charges too much for its systems software, suppresses substitute technologies, and pushes potential competitors around. In short, Microsoft is a bully. In April 2000, a federal court accepted this argument (see News). To weaken Microsoft's

> **IN THE NEWS**
>
> ### Judge Says Microsoft Broke Antitrust Law
>
> A federal judge yesterday found Microsoft Corp. guilty of violating antitrust law by waging a campaign to crush threats to its Windows monopoly, a severe verdict that opens the door for the government to seek a breakup of one of the most successful companies in history.
>
> Saying that Microsoft put an "oppressive thumb on the scale of competitive fortune," U.S. District Judge Thomas Penfield Jackson gave the Justice Department and 19 states near-total victory in their lawsuit. His ruling puts a black mark on the reputation of a software giant that has been the starter engine of the "new economy."
>
> "Microsoft mounted a deliberate assault upon entrepreneurial efforts that, left to rise or fall on their own merits, could well have enabled the introduction of competition into the market for Intelcompatible PC operating systems," Jackson said.
>
> The sweeping guilty verdict—coming two days after out-of-court settlement talks collapsed—harkens back to the monumental monopolization cases against Standard Oil and AT&T and validates the government's power to enforce antitrust law in the information age. It comes at a time when Microsoft faces substantial business obstacles to expanding its software dominance from the desktop to the Internet.
>
> In blunt language, Jackson depicted a powerful and predatory company that employed a wide array of tactics to destroy any innovation that posed a danger to the dominance of Windows. Among the victims were corporate stars of the multibillion-dollar computer industry: Intel Corp., Apple Computer Inc., International Business Machines Corp. and RealNetworks Inc.
>
> To crush the competitive threat posed by the Internet browser, Jackson ruled, Microsoft integrated its own Internet browser into its Windows operating system "to quell incipient competition," bullied computer makers into carrying Microsoft's browser by threatening to withhold price discounts and demanded that computer makers not feature rival Netscape's browser in the PC desktop as a condition of licensing the Windows operating system.
>
> Only when the separate categories of conduct are viewed, as they should be, as a single, well-coordinated course of action does the full extent of the violence that Microsoft has done to the competitive process reveal itself," Jackson wrote in the 43-page ruling.
>
> —James V. Grimaldi
>
> Source: *Washington Post*, April 4, 2000. © 2000 The Washington Post. Reprinted with permission. www.washingtonpost.com

Analysis: A federal court concluded that Microsoft followed the textbook script of monopoly: erecting entry barriers, suppressing innovation, and charging high prices.

grip on the computer market, the court considered forcing changes in both Microsoft's behavior and structure.

The federal government's authority to mend Microsoft's ways originates in the Sherman, the Clayton, and the Federal Trade Commission Acts. As noted in Table 24.1, these acts give the government broad **antitrust** authority to break up monopolies or compel them to change their behavior. The government used this authority in 1984 to dismantle American Telephone and Telegraph's (AT&T's) phone monopoly. AT&T then supplied 96 percent of all long-distance service and over 80 percent of local telephone service. AT&T kept long-distance charges high and compelled consumers to purchase hardware from its own subsidiary (Western Electric). Potential competitors claimed they could supply better and cheaper services if the government ended the AT&T monopoly. After four years of antitrust litigation, AT&T agreed to (1) separate its long-distance and local services and (2) turn over the local transmission networks to new "Baby Bell" companies. Since then there has been a competitive revolution in telephone hardware, services, and pricing.

The U.S. Department of Justice filed a similar antitrust action against Microsoft. The first accusation leveled against Microsoft was that it thwarted competitors in operating systems by erecting entry barriers such as exclusive purchase agreements with computer manufacturers. These agreements either forbade manufacturers from installing a rival operating system or made it prohibitively expensive. The second accusation against Microsoft was that it used its monopoly position in *operating* systems

The AT&T Case

antitrust: Government intervention to alter market structure of prevent abuse of market power.

The Microsoft Case

TABLE 24.1
Antitrust Laws
The legal foundations for antitrust intervention are contained in three landmark antitrust laws.

- **The Sherman Act (1890).** The Sherman Act prohibits "conspiracies in restraint of trade," including mergers, contracts, or acquisitions that threaten to monopolize an industry. Firms that violate the Sherman Act are subject to fines of up to $1 million, and their executives may be subject to imprisonment. In addition, consumers who are damaged—for example, via high prices—by a "conspiracy in restraint of trade" may recover treble damages. With this act as its principal "trustbusting" weapon, the U.S. Department of Justice has blocked attempted mergers and acquisitions, forced changes in price or output behavior, required large companies to sell some of their assets, and even sent corporate executives to jail for "conspiracies in restraint of trade."
- The Clayton Act (1914). The Clayton Act of 1914 was passed to outlaw specific antitrust behavior not covered by the Sherman Act. The principal aim of the act was to prevent the development of monopolies. To this end, the Clayton Act prohibited price discrimination, exclusive dealing agreements, certain types of mergers, and interlocking boards of directors among competing firms.
- **The Federal Trade Commission Act (1914).** The increased antitrust responsibilities of the federal government created the need for an agency that could study industry structures and behavior so as to identify anticompetitive practices. The Federal Trade Commission was created for this purpose in 1914.

Although the Sherman, Clayton, and FTC Acts create a legal basis for government antitrust activity, they leave some basic implementation issues unanswered. What, for example, constitutes a "monopoly" in the real world? Must a company produce 100 percent of a particular good to be a threat to consumer welfare? How about 99 percent? Or even 75 percent?

And what specific monopolistic practices should be prohibited? Should we be looking for specific evidence of price gouging? Or should we focus on barriers to entry and unfair market practices?

These kinds of questions determine how and when antitrust laws will be enforced. The first question relates to the *structure* of markets, the second to their *behavior*.

---

to gain an unfair advantage in the *applications* market. It did this by not disclosing operating features that make applications run more efficiently or by bundling software, thereby forcing consumers to accept Microsoft applications along with the operating system. When the latter occurs, consumers have little incentive to buy a competing product. Microsoft also prohibited computer manufacturers from displaying rival product icons on the Windows desktop. Finally, Microsoft was accused of thwarting competition by simply buying out promising rivals (see cartoon).

Microsoft's Defense Bill Gates, Microsoft's chairman, scoffed at the government's charges. He contends that Microsoft dominates the computer industry only because it continues to produce the best products at attractive prices. Microsoft doesn't need to lock out potential competitors, he argues, because it can and does beat the competition with superior products. Furthermore, Gates argues, the software industry is a highly *contestable* market even if not a perfectly competitive one. So Microsoft has to behave like a competitive firm even though it supplies most of the industry's output. In short, Microsoft is a genius, not a bully. Therefore, the government should leave Microsoft alone and let the market decide who best serves consumers.

The Verdict After nine years of litigation, a federal court determined that Microsoft was more of a bully than a genius. The court concluded that Microsoft not only held a monopoly position in operating systems but that it had abused that position in a variety of anticompetitive ways. As a result, consumers were harmed. The real economic issue, the court asserted, was not whether Microsoft was improving its products (it was) or reducing prices (it was) but instead how much *faster* products would have improved and prices fallen in a more competitive market. By limiting consumer choices and stifling competition, Microsoft had denied consumers better and cheaper information technology.

DOONESBURY

Analysis: By acquiring promising new competitors, a monopoly can preserve its dominant market position. Such acquisitions may slow innovation, however.

The trial judge suggested that Microsoft might have to be broken into two companies—an operating software company and an applications software company—to ensure enough competition. Such a *structural* remedy would have resembled the court-ordered breakup of AT&T. In November 2001, however, the U.S. Department of Justice decided to seek *behavioral* remedies only. With Windows XP about to be launched, the Justice Department only required Microsoft to lower entry barriers for competing software applications (e.g. disclose middleware specifications, refrain from exclusive contracts, open desktops to competition). Although Microsoft reluctantly agreed to change its conduct in many ways, rivals still complain that they don't have a fair chance of competing against the Microsoft monopoly. Market *structure*, they say, is still the critical factor in determining market outcomes.

The Remedy

You can track the antitrust case against Microsoft on several websites. See www.antitrust.org, a source for news and research, and usdoj.gov/atr/index.html for DOJ documents.

SUMMARY

- Market power is the ability to influence the market price of goods and services. The extreme case of market power is monopoly, a situation in which only one firm produces the entire supply of a particular product.
- The distinguishing feature of any firm with market power is the fact that the demand curve it faces is downward-sloping. In the case of monopoly, the demand curve facing the firm and the market demand curve are identical.
- The downward-sloping demand curve facing a monopolist creates a divergence between marginal revenue and price. To sell larger quantities of output, the monopolist must lower product prices. A firm without market power has no such problem.
- Like other producers, a monopolist will produce at the rate of output at which marginal revenue equals marginal cost. Because marginal revenue is always less than price in monopoly, the monopolist will produce less output than a competitive industry confronting the same market demand and costs. That reduced rate of output will be sold at higher prices, in accordance with the (downward-sloping) market demand curve.
- A monopoly will attain a higher level of profit than a competitive industry because of its ability to equate industry (that is, its own) marginal revenues and costs. By contrast, a competitive industry ends up equating marginal costs and price, because its individual firms have no control over market supply.
- Because the higher profits attained by a monopoly will attract envious entrepreneurs, barriers to entry are needed to prohibit other firms from expanding market supplies. Patents are one such barrier to entry.
- The defense of market power rests on (1) the alleged ability of large firms to pursue long-term research and development, (2) the incentives implicit in the chance to attain market power, (3) the efficiency that larger firms may attain, and (4) the contestability of even monopolized markets. The first two arguments are weakened by the fact that competitive firms are under much greater

pressure to innovate and can stay ahead of the profit game only if they do so. The contestability defense at best concedes some amount of monopoly exploitation.
- A natural monopoly exists when one firm can produce the output of the entire industry more efficiently than can a number of small firms. This advantage is attained from economies of scale. Large firms aren't necessarily more efficient, however, because either constant returns to scale or diseconomies of scale may prevail.
- Antitrust laws restrain the acquisition and abuse of monopoly power. Where barriers to entry aren't insurmountable, market forces may ultimately overcome a monopoly as well.

Key Terms

market power
monopoly
profit maximization rule
marginal revenue (MR)
barriers to entry

economies of scale
production decision
average total cost (ATC)
marginal cost pricing
price elasticity of demand

price discrimination
natural monopoly
contestable market
antitrust

Questions for Discussion

1. The objective in the game of Monopoly is to get all the property and then raise the rents. Can this power be explained with market supply and demand curves?
2. Is single ownership of a whole industry necessary to exercise monopoly power? How might an industry with many firms achieve the same result? Can you think of any examples?
3. Why don't monopolists try to establish "the highest price possible," as many people allege? What would happen to sales? To profits?
4. In 1990, a federal court decided that Eastman Kodak had infringed on Polaroid's patent when it produced similar instant-photo cameras. The court then had to award Polaroid compensation for damages. What was the nature of the damages to Polaroid? How could you compute them? (The court awarded Polaroid a record $900 million!)
5. What entry barriers helped protect the following?
    (a) The Russian sable monopoly (see World View, page 517).
    (b) The Ticketmaster monopoly (see News, page 522).
    (c) The CNN monopoly (see World View, page 530).
6. What similarities exist between the AT&T and Microsoft antitrust cases? What should the government do?
7. Do price reductions and quality enhancements on Microsoft products prove that Microsoft is a perfectly competitive firm? What should be the test of competitiveness?

Web Activities

1. Log on to www.usdoj.gov, and complete a search using the word "monopoly." List two current activities the Department of Justice is involved in against monopolies. Explain briefly why each action is being taken.
2. Find the website for the natural gas utility in your area at www.aga.org/AboutAGA/AboutAGAMembers/MemberWebsiteLinks. What makes this utility a monopoly? What are the controls on this monopoly? What type of potential competition exists for this monopoly?
3. Log on to www.antitrust.org and pick two articles that discuss potential violations of antitrust law. Which antitrust law(s) is being violated? Explain.

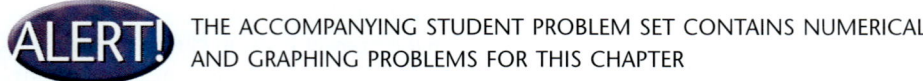

THE ACCOMPANYING STUDENT PROBLEM SET CONTAINS NUMERICAL AND GRAPHING PROBLEMS FOR THIS CHAPTER

CHAPTER 25

Oligopoly

> People of the same trade seldom meet together, but the conversation ends in a conspiracy against the public, or in some diversion to raise prices.
> —Adam Smith, *The Wealth of Nations*, 1776

Although it's convenient to think of the economy as composed of the powerful and the powerless, market realities don't always provide such clear distinctions. There are very few perfectly competitive markets in the world, and few monopolies. Market power is an important phenomenon nonetheless; it's just that it's typically shared by several firms rather than monopolized by one. In the soft drink industry, for example, Coca-Cola and Pepsi share tremendous market power, even though neither company qualifies as a pure monopoly. The same kind of power is shared by Kellogg, General Mills, and General Foods in the breakfast cereals market, and by Sony, Nintendo, and Microsoft in the video game market.

These market structures fall between the extremes of perfect competition and pure monopoly; they represent *imperfect competition*. They contain some elements of competitive rivalry but also exhibit traces of monopoly. In many cases, imperfect competitors behave much like a monopoly, restricting output, charging higher prices, and reaping greater profits than firms in a competitive market. But behavior in imperfectly competitive markets is more complicated than in a monopoly because it involves a number of decision makers (firms) rather than only one.

This chapter focuses on one form of imperfect competition: *oligopoly*. We examine the nature of decision making in this market structure and the likely impacts on prices, production, and profits. What we want to know is:

- What determines how much market power a firm has?
- How do firms in an oligopoly set prices and output?
- What problems does an oligopoly have in maintaining price and profit?

MARKET STRUCTURE

As we saw in Chapter 24, Microsoft is virtually the sole supplier of computer operating systems; as a monopoly, it has tremendous market power. The corner

536 MARKET STRUCTURE

grocery store, on the other hand, must compete with other stores and has less control over prices. But even the corner grocery isn't completely powerless. If it's the only grocery within walking distance, or the only one open on Sunday—it too exerts *some* influence on prices and product flows. The amount of power it possesses depends on the availability of *substitute goods,* that is, the proximity and convenience of alternative retail outlets.

Degrees of Power

market structure: The number and relative size of firms in an industry.

Between the extremes of monopoly and perfect competition are many gradations of market power (see Figure 22.1). To sort them out, we classify firms into five specific **market structures,** based on the number and relative size of firms in an industry.

Table 25.1 summarizes the characteristics of the five major market structures. At one extreme is the structure of *perfect competition,* the subject of Chapters 22 and 23. At the other extreme of the power spectrum is perfect *monopoly.* A perfect monopoly exists when only one firm is the exclusive supplier of a particular product. Our illustration of Universal Electronics (the imaginary computer monopolist in Chapter 24) exemplifies such a firm.

Between the two extremes of perfect competition and perfect monopoly lies most of the real world, which we call *imperfectly competitive.* **In imperfect competition, individual firms have some power in a particular product market.** Oligopoly refers to one of these imperfectly competitive market structures. **Oligopoly** is a situation in which only a *few* firms have a great deal of power in a product market. An oligopoly may exist because only a few firms produce a particular product or because a few firms account for most, although not all, of a product's output.

oligopoly: A market in which a few firms produce all or most of the market supply of a particular good or service.

Determinants of Market Power

The number of firms in an industry is a key characteristic of market structure. The amount of market power the firms possess, however, depends on several factors. **The determinants of market power include**

* *Number of producers.*
* *Size of each firm.*
* *Barriers to entry.*
* *Availability of substitute goods.*

When only one or a few producers or suppliers exist, market power is automatically conferred. In addition to the number of producers, however, the size of each firm is also important. Over 800 firms supply long-distance telephone service in the United States. But just three of those firms (ATT, WorldCom, Sprint) account for 74 percent of all calls. Hence, it wouldn't make sense to categorize that industry on the basis of only the number of firms; relative size is also important.

TABLE 25.1
Characteristics of Market Structures
Market structure varies, depending on the number of producers, their size, barriers to entry, and the availability of substitute goods. An oligopoly is an imperfectly competitive structure in which a few firms dominate the market.

	Market Structure				
Characteristic	Perfect Competition	Monopolistic Competition	Oligopoly	Duopoly	Monopoly
Number of firms	Very large number	Many	Few	Two	One
Barriers to entry	None	Low	High	High	High
Market power (control over price)	None	Some	Substantial	Substantial	Substantial
Type of product	Standardized	Differentiated	Standardized or differentiated	Standardized or differentiated	Unique

A third and critical determinant of market power is the extent of barriers to entry. A highly successful monopoly or oligopoly arouses the envy of other profit maximizers. If it's a **contestable market,** potential rivals will seek to enter the market and share in the spoils. Should they succeed, the power of the former monopolist or oligopolists would be reduced. Accordingly, ease of entry into an industry limits the ability of a powerful firm to dictate prices and product flows. In Chapter 24 we saw how monopolies erect barriers to entry (e.g., patents) to maintain their power.

A fourth determinant of market power is the availability of substitute goods. If a monopolist or other power baron sets the price of a product too high, consumers may decide to switch to close substitutes. Thus, the price of Coors is kept in check by the price of Coke, and the price of sirloin steak is restrained by the price of chicken and pork. By the same token, a lack of available substitute products keeps the prices of insulin and AZT high.

contestable market: An imperfectly competitive industry subject to potential entry if prices or profits increase.

Although there are many determinants of market power, most observers use just one yardstick to measure the extent of power in an industry.

Measuring Market Power

Concentration Ratio. The standard measure of market power is the **concentration ratio.** This ratio tells the share of output (or combined market share) accounted for by the largest firms in an industry. Using this ratio, one can readily distinguish between an industry composed of hundreds of small, relatively powerless firms and another industry also composed of hundreds of firms but dominated by a few that are large and powerful. Thus, *the concentration ratio is a measure of market power that relates the size of firms to the size of the product market.*

concentration ratio: The proportion of total industry output produced by the largest firms (usually the four largest).

Table 25.2 gives the concentration ratios for selected products in the United States. The standard measure used here depicts the proportion of domestic production accounted for by the largest firms, usually the four largest. As is apparent from the table, the supply side of these product markets can be described as *oligopolies,* since most of the industry's output is produced by just three or four firms. Indeed, in some markets, one single firm is so large that an outright monopoly is nearly attained. For example, 70 percent of all canned soup is produced by Campbell. Eastman Kodak supplies two-thirds of all still cameras and film. Procter & Gamble makes 62 percent of this country's disposable diapers. All firms that have a market share of at least 40 percent are denoted by **boldface** type in Table 25.2.

The Federal Trade Commission publishes data on *industry,* not product concentration; check www.ftc.gov

Firm Size. We noted before that market power isn't necessarily associated with firm size—in other words, a small firm could possess a lot of power in a relatively small market. Table 25.2, however, should be convincing testimony that we're not talking about small product markets here. Every one of the products listed enjoys a broad-based market. Even the chewing gum market rings up annual sales of $2 billion. Sales of autos exceed $500 billion per year. Accordingly, for most of the firms listed in the table, market power and firm size go hand in hand. Indeed, the largest firms enjoy sales volumes that exceed the entire output of most of the *countries* in the world (see World View).

Measurement Problems

A high concentration ratio or large firm size isn't the only way to achieve market power. The supply and price of a product can be altered by many firms acting in unison. Even 1,000 small producers can band together to change the quantity supplied to the market, thus exercising market power. Recall how our mythical Universal Electronics (Chapter 24) exercised market power by coordinating the production decisions of its many separate plants. Those plants could have attempted such coordination on their own even if they hadn't all been owned by the same corporation. Lawyers and doctors exercise this kind of power by maintaining uniform fee schedules for members of the American Bar Association (ABA) and the American Medical Association (AMA).[1]

---

[1] The courts have ruled that uniform fee schedules are illegal and that individual lawyers and doctors have the right to advertise their prices (fees). Nevertheless, a combination of inertia and self-interest has effectively maintained high fee schedules and inhibited advertising.

TABLE 25.2
Power in U.S. Product Markets

The domestic production of many familiar products is concentrated among a few firms. These firms have substantial control over the quantity supplied to the market and thus over market price. The concentration ratio measures the share of total output produced by the largest producers in a given market.

Product	Largest Firms	Concentration Ratio (percent)
Baby food	**Gerber Products**, Heinz, Beech-Nut	100
Instant breakfast	**Carnation**, Pillsbury, Dean Foods	100
Laser eye surgery	**VISX**, Summit Technology	100
Tennis balls	**Gen Corp (Penn)**, PepsiCo **(Wilson)**, Dunlop, Spalding	100
Credit cards	**Visa**, MasterCard, American Express, Discover	99
Disposable diapers	**Procter & Gamble**, Kimberly-Clark, Curity, Romar Tissue Mills	99
Video game players	**Sony**, Nintendo, Microsoft	99
Razor blades	**Gillette**, Warner-Lambert (Schick; Wilkinson), Bic, American Safety Razor	98
Sports drinks	**PepsiCo** (Gatorade), Coca-Cola (PowerAde), Monarch (All Sport)	98
Baseball cards	Topps, Upper Deck, Fleer, Leaf Inc. (Donruss)	96
Cigarettes	**Philip Morris**, RJ Reynolds, Brown & Williamson, Lorillard	96
Electric razors	**Norelco**, Remington, Warner-Lambert, Sunbeam	96
Sanitary napkins	**Johnson & Johnson**, Kimberly-Clark, Procter & Gamble	96
Batteries	**Duracell**, Eveready, Ray-O-Vac, Kodak	94
Camera, film	**Eastman Kodak**, Fuji, Polaroid	94
Chewing gum	**Wm. Wrigley**, Pfizer, Hershey	94
Soft drinks	**Coca-Cola**, Pepsico, Cadbury Schweppes (7-Up, Dr. Pepper, A&W), Royal Crown	93
Beer	**Anheuser-Busch**, Philip Morris (Miller), Coors, Stroh	92
Breakfast cereals	General Mills, Kelloggs, Philip Morris (Kraft Foods), PepsiCo (Quaker Oats).	92
Toothpaste	**Procter & Gamble**, Colgate-Palmolive, Lever Bros., Beecham	91
Detergents	**Procter & Gamble**, Lever Bros., Dial, Colgate-Palmolive	90
Soap	Lever Bros., Procter & Gamble, Dial, Colgate-Palmolive	89
Greeting cards	**Hallmark**, American Greetings, Gibson	88
Coffee	General Foods, Procter & Gamble, Nestlé, Philip Morris	86
Contact lens care	Bausch & Lomb, Allergan Optical, Alcon, Coopervision	86
Canned soup	**Campbell**, Progresso	85
Chocolate candy	Hershey, Mars, Nestlé, Brach	85
Tires and tubes	Goodyear, Firestone, Uniroyal, B.F. Goodrich	85
Cable TV (for-pay)	Time Warner (HBO), Viacom (Showtime), Cinemax, Movie Channel	83
Canned tuna	**Heinz** (Starkist), Unicord (Bumble Bee), Van Camp (Chicken of the Sea)	82
Spaghetti sauce	Unilever (Ragu), Campbell Soup (Prego), Hunt-Wesson (Healthy Choice)	80
Car rentals	Hertz, Enterprise, Avis, National	76
Athletic shoes	**Nike**, Reebok, Adidas, Fila	74
Telephone service (long distance)	**AT&T**, WorldCom(MCI), Sprint	74
Automobiles	General Motors, Ford, Toyota, Honda	70

Sources: Data from Federal Trade Commission, *The Wall Street Journal, Advertising Age, Financial World, Standard & Poor's, Fortune,* and industry sources.

Note: Individual corporations with a market share of at least 40 percent are designated in **boldface**. Market shares based on selected years, 1998–2001.

Similarly, dairy farmers act jointly through three large cooperatives (the American Milk Producers, Mid-America Dairies, and Dairymen, Inc.), which together control 50 percent of all milk production.

Finally, all the figures and corporations cited here refer to *national* markets. They don't convey the extent to which market power may be concentrated in a *local* market.

WORLD VIEW

Putting Size in Global Perspective

The largest firms in the United States are also the dominant forces in global markets. They export products to foreign markets and produce goods abroad for sale there or to import back into the United States. In terms of size alone, these business giants rival most of the world's nations. GM's gross sales, for example, would make it the twenty-fifth largest "country" in terms of national GDP.

American corporations aren't the only giants in the global markets. Toyota (Japan) and Royal Dutch Shell (Netherlands) are among the foreign giants that contest global markets.

Rank	Country or Corporation	Sales or GDP	Rank	Country or Corporation	Sales or GDP
1	United States	$9,883	21	**ExxonMobil**	$210
2	Japan	4,677	22	Turkey	200
3	Germany	1,870	23	**Wal-Mart Stores**	193
4	United Kingdom	1,413	24	Austria	191
5	France	1,286	25	**General Motors**	185
6	China	1,080	26	**Ford Motor**	181
7	Italy	1,068	27	Hong Kong	163
8	Canada	690	28	Denmark	161
9	Brazil	588	29	Poland	159
10	Mexico	575	30	Indonesia	153
11	Spain	555	31	**Daimler/Chrysler**	150
12	India	479	32	Norway	149
13	South Korea	457	33	**Royal Dutch/Shell**	149
14	Australia	394	34	**British Petroleum**	148
15	The Netherlands	365	35	Saudi Arabia	139
16	Argentina	285	36	**General Electric**	130
17	Russia	251	37	Mitsubishi	127
18	Switzerland	240	38	South Africa	126
19	Belgium	231	39	Thailand	122
20	Sweden	227	40	**Toyota**	121

Sources: World Bank and *Fortune* magazine (2000 data in billions).

Analysis: Firm size is a determinant of market power. The size of the largest firms, as measured by total revenue, exceeds the value of total output in most of the world's 200-plus countries.

In fact, many industries with low concentration ratios nationally are represented by just one or a few firms locally. Prime examples include milk, newspapers, and transportation (both public and private). For example, fewer than 60 cities in the United States have two or more independently owned daily newspapers, and nearly all those newspapers rely on only two news services (Associated Press and United Press International). Perhaps you've also noticed that most college campuses have only one bookstore. It may not be a *national* powerhouse, but it does have the power to influence what goods are available on campus and how much they cost.

OLIGOPOLY BEHAVIOR

With so much market power concentrated in so few hands, it's unrealistic to expect market outcomes to resemble those of perfect competition. As we observed in Chapter 24, ***market structure affects market behavior and outcomes.*** In that chapter we focused on the contrast between monopoly and perfect competition. Now we focus on the behavior of a more common market structure: oligopoly.

To isolate the unique character of oligopoly, we'll return to the computer market. In Chapter 23 we observed that the computer market was highly competitive in its early stages, when entry barriers were low and hundreds of firms were producing similar products. In Chapter 24 we created an impassable barrier to entry (a patent on the electronic brain of the computer) that transformed the computer industry into a monopoly of Universal Electronics. Now we'll transform the industry again. This time we'll create an oligopoly by assuming that three separate firms (Universal, World, and International) all possess patent rights. The patent rights permit each firm to produce and sell all the computers it wants and to exclude all other would-be producers from the market. With these assumptions, we create three **oligopolists,** the firms that share an *oligopoly.* Our objective is to see how market outcomes would change in such a market structure.

oligopolist: One of the dominant firms in an oligopoly.

The Initial Equilibrium

As before, we'll assume that the initial conditions in the computer market are represented by a market price of $1,000 and market sales of 20,000 computers per month, as illustrated in Figure 25.1.

market share: The percentage of total market output produced by a single firm.

We'll also assume that the **market share** of each producer is accurately depicted in Table 25.3. Thus, Universal Electronics is assumed to be producing 8,000 computers per month, or 40 percent of total market supply. World Computers has a market share of 32.5 percent, while International Semiconductor has only a 27.5 percent share.

The Battle for Market Shares

The first thing to note about the computer oligopoly is that it's likely to exhibit great internal tension. Neither World Computers nor International Semiconductor is really happy playing second or third fiddle to Universal Electronics. Each company would like to be number one in this market. On the other hand, Universal too would like a larger market share, particularly in view of the huge profits being made on computers. As we observed in Chapter 23, the initial equilibrium in the computer industry yielded an *average* profit of $300 per computer, and total *industry* profits of $6 million per month (20,000 × $300). Universal would love to acquire the market shares of its rivals, thereby grabbing all this industry profit for itself.

But how does an oligopolist acquire a larger market share? In a truly competitive market, a single producer could expand production at will, with no discernible impact on market supply. But *in an oligopoly, increased sales on the part of one firm will be noticed immediately by the other firms.*

How do we know that increased sales will be noticed so quickly? Because increased sales by one firm will have to take place either at the existing market price ($1,000) or at a lower price. Either of these two events will ring an alarm at the corporate headquarters of the other two firms.

FIGURE 25.1
Initial Conditions in the Computer Market

As in Chapters 23 and 24, we assume that the initial equilibrium in the home computer market occurs at a price of $1,000 and a quantity of 20,000 per month. How will an oligopoly alter these outcomes?

TABLE 25.3
Initial Market Shares of Microcomputer Producers
The market share of a firm is the percentage of total market output it produces. These are hypothetical market shares of three fictional oligopolists.

Producer	Output (computers per month)	Market Share (percent)
Universal Electronics	8,000	40.0
World Computers	6,500	32.5
International Semiconductor	5,500	27.5
Total industry output	20,000	100.0

Increased Sales at the Prevailing Market Price. Consider first the possibility of Universal Electronics increasing its sales at the going price of $1,000 per computer. We know from the demand curve in Figure 25.1 that consumers are willing to buy *only* 20,000 microcomputers per month at that price. Hence, any increase in computer sales by Universal must be immediately reflected in *lower* sales by World or International. That is, ***increases in the market share of one oligopolist necessarily reduce the shares of the remaining oligopolists.*** If Universal were to increase its sales from 8,000 to 9,000 computers per month, the combined monthly sales of World and International would have to fall from 12,000 to 11,000 (see Table 25.3). The *quantity demanded* at $1,000 remains 20,000 computers per month (see Figure 25.1). Thus, any increased sales at that price by Universal must be offset by reduced sales by its rivals.

This interaction among the market shares of the three oligopolists ensures that Universal's sales success will be noticed. It won't be necessary for World Computers or International Semiconductor to engage in industrial espionage. These firms can quickly figure out what Universal is doing simply by looking at their own (declining) sales figures.

Increased Sales at Reduced Prices. Universal could pursue a different strategy. Specifically, Universal could attempt to increase its sales by lowering the price of its computers. Reduced prices would expand total market sales, possibly enabling Universal to increase its sales without directly reducing the sales of either World or International.

But this outcome is most unlikely. If Universal lowered its price from $1,000 to, say, $900, consumers would flock to Universal Computers, and the sales of World and International would plummet. After all, we've always assumed that consumers are rational enough to want to pay the lowest possible price for any particular good. It's unlikely that consumers would continue to pay $1,000 for a World or International machine when they could get basically the same computer from Universal for only $900. If there were no difference, either perceived or real, among the computers of the three firms, a *pure* oligopoly would exist. In that case, Universal would capture the *entire* market if it lowered its price below that of its rivals.

More often, consumers perceive differences in the products of rival oligopolists, even when the products are essentially identical. These perceptions (or any real differences that may exist) create a *differentiated* oligopoly. In this case, Universal would gain many but not all customers if it reduced the price of its computers. That's the outcome we'll assume here. In either case, there simply isn't any way that Universal can increase its sales at reduced prices without causing all the alarms to go off at World and International.

Retaliation

So what if all the alarms do go off at World Computers and International Semiconductor? As long as Universal Electronics is able to enlarge its share of the market and grab more profits, why should it care if World and International find out? Indeed, Universal might even get some added satisfaction knowing that World and International are upset by its marketing success.

Universal *does* have something to worry about, though. World and International may not be content to stand by and watch their market shares and profits diminish. On the contrary, World and International are likely to take some action of their own once they discover what's going on.

There are two things World and International can do once they decide to act. In the first case, where Universal is expanding its market share at prevailing prices ($1,000), World and International can retaliate by

- Stepping up their own marketing efforts.
- Cutting prices on their computers.

To step up their marketing efforts, World and International might increase their advertising expenditures, repackage their computers, put more sales representatives on the street, or sponsor a college homecoming week. This is the kind of behavior RC Cola used to gain market share from Coke and Pepsi (see News). Such attempts at **product differentiation** are designed to make one firm's products appear different and superior to those produced by other firms. If successful, such marketing efforts will increase RC Cola sales and market share or at least stop its rivals from grabbing larger shares.

An even quicker way to stop Universal from enlarging its market share is for World and International to lower the price of *their* computers. Such price reductions will destroy Universal's hopes of increasing its market share at the old price. In fact, this is the other side of a story we've already told. If the price of World and International computers drops to, say, $900, it's preposterous to assume that Universal will be able to expand its market share at a price of $1,000. Universal's market share will shrink if

> **product differentiation:** Features that make one product appear different from competing products in the same market.

IN THE NEWS

Pop Culture: RC Goes for the Youth Market

RC Cola, like the Brady Bunch and push-up bras, is attempting a '90s comeback. . . .

To that end, the company is spending $15 million on a new advertising campaign—the largest in RC's history—designed to cast the blue-collar drink of the Midwest and South as the hip alternative to "corporate colas," as it refers to market leaders Coke and Pepsi. Accompanying the ad blitz are new products, including a sour-tasting, Windex-colored Nehi and a long-neck brew called RC Draft, formulated specifically for younger palates.

"This company spent no money on advertising during the 1980s, and we lost an entire generation of cola drinkers who grew up in that decade," said John Carson, Royal Crown's chief executive. . . .

"Anybody in the soft drink business trying to compete with Pepsi and Coke has an uphill battle—they have huge amounts of marketing muscle, financial resources, experience and bottling agreements," said John Sicher, co-editor of Beverage Digest, an industry publication. "But RC's new tactics are smart. They are tossing out a bunch of beverages targeted toward younger drinkers. Against Coke and Pepsi, guerrilla warfare is the only thing that might work."

—Anthony Faiola

The U.S. Soda Market

Market share of soft drink makers, 2001.

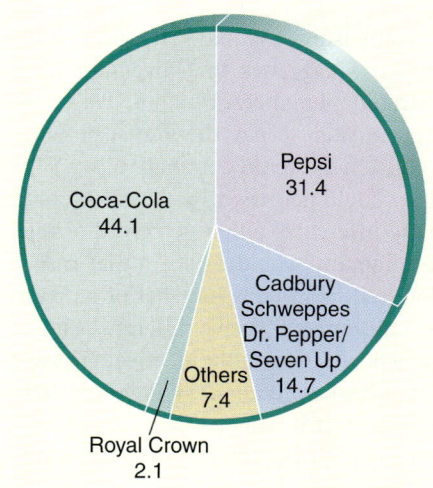

Source: *Washington Post*, February 17, 1995. © 1995 The Washington Post. Reprinted with permission. www.washingtonpost.com

Analysis: Because price competition is typically self-defeating in an oligopoly, rival firms in an oligopoly rely on advertising and product differentiation (nonprice competition) to gain market share.

FIGURE 25.2
Rivalry for Market Shares Threatens an Oligopoly

If oligopolists start cutting prices to capture larger market shares, they'll be behaving much like truly competitive firms. The result will be a slide down the market demand curve to lower prices, increased output, and smaller profits. In this case, the market price and quantity would move from point F to point G if rival oligopolists cut prices to gain market shares.

it maintains a price of $1,000 per computer after World and International drop their prices to $900. Hence, the threat to Universal's market share grab is that the other two oligopolists will retaliate by reducing *their* prices. Should they carry out this threat, Universal would be forced to cut computer prices too, or accept a greatly reduced market share.

The same kind of threat exists in the second case, where we assumed that Universal Electronics expands its sales by initiating a price reduction. World and International aren't going to just sit by and applaud Universal's marketing success. They'll have to respond with price cuts of their own. Universal would then have the highest price on the market, and computer buyers would flock to cheaper substitutes. Accordingly, it's safe to conclude that **an attempt by one oligopolist to increase its market share by cutting prices will lead to a general reduction in the market price.** The three oligopolists will end up using price reductions as weapons in the battle for market shares, the kind of behavior normally associated with competitive firms. Should this behavior continue, not only will oligopoly become less fun, but it will also become less profitable as prices slide down the market demand curve (Figure 25.2). This is why **oligopolists avoid price competition and instead pursue nonprice competition** (e.g., advertising, production differentiation).

THE KINKED DEMAND CURVE

The close interdependence of oligopolists—and the limitations it imposes on individual price and output decisions—is the principal moral of this story about Universal Electronics, World Computers, and International Semiconductor. We can summarize this story with the aid of the kinked demand curve in Figure 25.3.

Recall that at the beginning of this oligopoly story Universal Electronics had a market share of 40 percent and was selling 8,000 computers per month at a price of $1,000 each. This output is represented by point A in Figure 25.3. The rest of the demand curve illustrates what would happen to Universal's unit sales if it changed its selling price. What we have to figure out is why this particular demand curve has such a strange "kinked" shape.

Consider first what would happen to Universal's sales if it lowered the price of its computers to $900. In general, we expect a price reduction to increase sales. However, **the degree to which an oligopolist's sales increase when its price is reduced depends on the response of rival oligopolists.** Suppose World and International didn't match Universal's price reduction. In this case, Universal would have the only low-priced

Rivals' Response to Price Reductions

FIGURE 25.3
The Kinked Demand Curve Confronting an Oligopolist

The shape of the demand curve facing an oligopolist depends on the responses of its rivals to its price and output decisions. If rival oligopolists match price reductions but not price increases, the demand curve will be kinked.

Initially, the oligopolist is at point *A*. If it raises its price to $1,100 and its rivals don't raise their prices, it will be driven to point *B*. If its rivals match a price reduction (to $900), the oligopolist will end up at point *C*.

computer in the market. Consumers would flock to Universal, and sales would increase dramatically, to point *D*. But point *D* is little more than a dream, as we've observed. World and International are sure to cut their prices to $900 too, in order to maintain their market shares. As a consequence, Universal's sales will expand only slightly, to point *C* rather than to point *D*. Universal's increased sales at point *C* reflect the fact that the total quantity demanded in the market has risen as the market price has fallen to $900 (see Figure 25.2). Thus, although Universal's *market share* may not have increased, its monthly sales have.

The section of the demand curve that runs from point *A* to point *D* is unlikely to exist in an oligopolistic market. Instead, **we expect rival oligopolists to match any price reductions** that Universal initiates, forcing Universal to accept the demand curve that runs from point *A* through point *C*. The News illustrates such behavior in the airline industry, where rivals were forced to match price cuts introduced by Delta.

Rivals' Response to Price Increases

What about price increases? How will World and International respond if Universal raises the price of its computers to $1,100?

Recall that the demand for computers is assumed to be price-elastic in the neighborhood of $1,000 and that all computers are basically similar. Accordingly, if Universal raises its price and neither World nor International follows suit, Universal will be out there alone with a higher price and reduced sales. **Rival oligopolists may not match price increases.** In terms of Figure 25.3, a price increase that isn't matched by rival oligopolists will drive Universal from point *A* to point *B*. At point *B*, Universal is selling very few computers at its price of $1,100 each.[2]

Is this a likely outcome? Suffice it to say that World Computers and International Semiconductor wouldn't be unhappy about enlarging their own market shares. Unless they see the desirability of an industrywide price increase, they're not likely to come to Universal's rescue with price increases of their own. This is why Northwest Airlines decided not to match the fare hikes announced by its rivals (see News).

Anything is possible, however, and World and International might match Universal's price increase. In this case, the *market price* would rise to $1,100 and the total quantity of computers demanded would diminish. Under such circumstances Universal's sales would diminish, too, in accordance with its (constant) share of a smaller market. This would lead us to point *M* in Figure 25.3.

---

[2]Notice again that we're assuming that Universal is able to sell some computers at a higher price (point *B*) than its rivals. The kinked demand curve applies primarily to differentiated oligopolies. As we'll discuss later, such differentiation may result from slight product variations, advertising, customer habits, location, friendly service, or any number of other factors. Most oligopolies exhibit some differentiation.

IN THE NEWS

Airlines Roll Back Fare Hike

Major airlines rolled back fare increases they put in place over the weekend, but airfare experts say another attempt to raise prices may come as soon as this weekend.

America West, American, Continental, Delta, TWA, United and US Airways rescinded a 5 percent increase in business and leisure fares this week after Northwest did not follow.

—Salina Khan

Source: *USA Today*, May 23, 2001. © 2001 USA Today. Reprinted with permission. www.usatoday.com

Delta Cuts Fares 25 Percent; Rival Lines Follow Suit

Major airlines slashed fares about 25 percent yesterday in the hope that leisure summer passengers will make up for the sharp decline in business travel that has pushed airline revenue down dramatically.

Delta Air Lines cut fares in the United States, Latin America and Asia. Other airlines such as United, American, Continental, Northwest and US Airways immediately said they would match Delta's 25 percent fare reductions in markets where they compete.

—Keith L. Alexander

Source: *Washington Post*, June 26, 2001. © 2001 The Washington Post. Reprinted with permission. www.washingtonpost.com

Analysis: If rivals match price cuts but not price increases, the demand curve confronting an oligopolist will be kinked. Prices will increase only when all firms agree to raise them at the same time.

We may draw two conclusions from Figure 25.3:

- *The shape of the demand curve an oligopolist faces depends on the responses of its rivals to a change in the price of its own output.*
- *That demand curve will be kinked if rival oligopolists match price reductions but not price increases.*

GAME THEORY

One implication of the kinked demand curve is that oligopolists can't make truly independent price or output decisions. Because only a few producers participate in the market, **each oligopolist has to consider the potential responses of rivals when formulating price or output strategies.** This *strategic interaction* is the inevitable consequence of their oligopolistic position.

What makes oligopoly particularly interesting is the *uncertainty* of rivals' behavior. For example, Universal *would* want to lower its prices *if* it thought its rivals wouldn't retaliate with similar price cuts. But it can't be sure of that response. Universal must instead consider the odds of its rivals not matching a price cut. If the odds are low, Universal might decide *not* to initiate a price cut. Or maybe Universal might offer price discounts to just a few select customers, hoping World and International might not notice or react to small changes in market share.

The Payoff Matrix. Table 25.4 summarizes the strategic options each oligopolist confronts. In this case, let's assume that Universal is contemplating a price cut. The "payoff matrix" in the table summarizes the various profit consequences of such a move. One thing should be immediately clear: **The payoff to an oligopolist's price cut depends on how its rivals respond.** Indeed, the only scenario that increases Universal's profit is one in which Universal reduces its price and its rivals don't. We visualized this outcome earlier as a move from point *A* to point *D* in Figure 25.3. Note again that this scenario implies losses for Universal's two rival oligopolists.

The remaining cells in the payoff matrix show how profits change with other action/response scenarios. One thing is evident: If Universal *doesn't* reduce prices, it

TABLE 25.4
Oligopoly Payoff Matrix

The payoff to an oligopolist's price cut depends on its rivals' responses. Each oligopolist must assess the risks and rewards of each scenario before initiating a price change. Which option would you choose?

	Rivals' Actions	
Universal's Options	Reduce Price	Don't Reduce Price
Reduce price	Small loss for everyone	Huge gain for Universal; rivals lose
Don't reduce price	Huge loss for Universal; rivals gain	No change

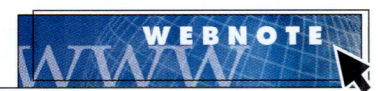

The "Prisoner's Dilemma" (who should confess) is a classic game theory problem. Try solving this and other games at www.cmu.edu/comlabgames.

can't increase profits. In fact, it might end up as the Big Loser if its rivals reduce *their* prices while Universal stands pat.

The option of reducing price doesn't guarantee a profit, but at least it won't decimate Universal's market share or profits. If rivals match a Universal price cut, all three oligopolists will suffer small losses.

So what should Universal do? The *collective* interests of the oligopoly are protected if no one cuts the market price. But an individual oligopolist could lose big time if it holds the line on price when rivals reduce price. Hence each oligopolist might decide to play it safe by *initiating* a price cut.

The decision to initiate a price cut boils down to an assessment of *risk*. If you thought the risk of a "first strike" was high, you'd be more inclined to reduce price. This kind of risk assessment is the foundation of game theory. In this sense, oligopolistic behavior isn't unlike the kind of Cold War games that the world's great powers played. Neither

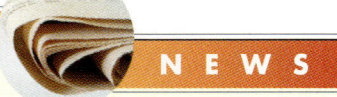

Coke and Pepsi May Call Off Pricing Battle

ATLANTA—A brief but bitter pricing war within the soft-drink industry might be drawing to a close—all because no one wants to be blamed for having fired the first shot.

Coca-Cola Enterprises Inc., Coca-Cola Co.'s biggest bottler, said in a recent memorandum to executives that it will "attempt to increase prices" after July 4 amid concern that heavy price discounting in most of the industry is squeezing profit margins.

The memo is a response to statements made to analysts last week by top PepsiCo Inc. executives. Pepsi, of Purchase, N.Y., said "irrational" pricing in much of the soft-drink industry might temporarily squeeze domestic profits, and it laid the blame for the price cuts at Coke's door.

That clearly incensed executives at Coca-Cola and Coca-Cola Enterprises, which had no desire to be criticized for threatening profit margins for the entire industry. Indeed, industry analysts in the wake of Pepsi's statements expressed concern that profit margins for Pepsi and Coke bottlers may erode as a result of cutthroat pricing. . . .

In the June 5 memo, Summerfield K. Johnston Jr. and Henry A. Schimberg, the chief executive and the president of Coca-Cola Enterprises, respectively, said the bottler's plan is to "succeed based on superior marketing programs and execution rather than the short-term approach of buying share through price discounting. . . . We have absolutely no motivation to decrease prices except in response to a competitive initiative."

—Nikhil Deogun

Source: *The Wall Street Journal,* June 12, 1997. Reprinted by permission of *The Wall Street Journal.* © 1998 Dow Jones & Company, Inc. All rights reserved worldwide. www.wsj.com

Analysis: Price discounting can destroy oligopoly profits. When it occurs, rival oligopolists seek to end it as quickly as possible.

side was certain of the enemy's next move but knew it could bring total destruction. As a consequence, the United States and the former Soviet Union continually probed each other's responses but were quick to retreat from the brink whenever all-out retaliation was threatened. Oligopolists play the same kind of game on a much smaller scale, using price discounts and advertising rather than nuclear warheads as their principal weapons. The reward they receive for coexistence is the oligopoly profits that they continue to share. This reward, together with the threat of mutual destruction, leads oligopolists to limit their price rivalry. This explains why Coke and Pepsi quickly ended their brief 1997 price war (see News). After finger-pointing about who started the war, the companies pulled back from the brink of mutual profit destruction.

This isn't to say oligopolists won't ever cut prices or use other means to gain market share. They might, given the right circumstances and certain expectations of how rivals will behave. Indeed, there are a host of different price, output, and marketing strategies an oligopolist might want to pursue. The field of **game theory** is dedicated to the study of how decisions are made when such strategic interaction exists, for example, when the outcome of a business strategy depends on the decisions rival firms make. Just as there are dozens of different moves and countermoves in a chess game, so too are there numerous strategies oligopolists might use to gain market share.

game theory: The study of decision making in situations where strategic interaction (moves and countermoves) between rivals occurs.

OLIGOPOLY VS. COMPETITION

While contemplating alternative strategies for maximizing their *individual* profits, oligopolists are also mindful of their common interest in maximizing *joint* (industry) profits. They want to avoid behavior that destroys the very profits that they're vying for. Indeed, they might want to coordinate their behavior in a way that maximizes *industry* profits. If they do, how will market outcomes be affected?

Price and Output

Thus far we've focused on a single oligopolist's decision about whether to *change* the price of its output. But how was the initial (market) price determined? In this example, we assumed that the initial price was $1,000 per computer, the price that prevailed initially in a *competitive* market. But the market is no longer competitive. As we saw in the previous chapter, a change in industry structure will affect market outcomes. A monopolist, for example, would try to maximize *industry* profits, all of which it would keep. To do this, it would select that one rate of output where marginal revenue equals marginal cost, and it would charge whatever price consumers were willing and able to pay for that rate of output (see Figure 25.4).

FIGURE 25.4
Maximizing Oligopoly Profits

An oligopoly strives to behave like a monopoly. Industry profits are maximized at the rate of output at which the industry's marginal cost equals the marginal revenue (point J). In a monopoly, this profit all goes to one firm; in an oligopoly, it must be shared among a few firms.

In an oligopoly, the MC and ATC curves represent the combined production capabilities of several firms, rather than only one. The industry MC curve is derived by horizontally summing the MC curves of the individual firms.

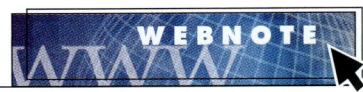

To assess the effects of OPEC's 2001 agreement, check the trend of oil prices at www.eia.doe.gov.

An oligopoly would seek similar profits. An oligopoly is really just a *shared* monopoly. Hence, **an oligopoly will want to behave like a monopoly, choosing a rate of industry output that maximizes total industry profit.**

The challenge for an oligopoly is to replicate monopoly outcomes. To do so, the firms in an oligopoly must find the monopoly price and maintain it. This is what the members of OPEC are trying to do when they meet to establish a common price for the oil they sell (see World View). To reach agreement requires a common view of the industry demand curve, satisfaction with respective market shares, and precise coordination.

Competitive industries would also like to reap monopoly-like profits. But competitive industries experience relentless pressure on profits, as individual firms expand output, reduce costs, and lower prices. To maximize industry profits, competitive firms would have to band together and agree to restrict output and raise prices. If they did, though, the industry would no longer be competitive. The potential for maximizing industry profits is clearly greater in an oligopoly because fewer firms are involved and each is aware of its dependence on the behavior of the others.

Sticky Prices

An oligopoly may not be coordinated enough to set the price that maximizes industry profits. Whatever price is established, however, will tend to be stable. This price stability is partly a reflection of the strategic interdependence that characterizes oligopoly. If rival oligopolists trust one another, they won't initiate price changes. Instead, they'll act in unison to maintain the most profitable industry price.

Price stability is also facilitated by the "cost cushion" that surrounds an oligopolist's production decision. Like all producers, an oligopolist wants to produce where MR = MC. This **profit-maximization rule** implies that a *change* in marginal cost will alter the production decision. This isn't necessarily the case for an oligopolist, however. An oligopolist has a gap in its MR curve that serves as a cushion against small changes in MC. This cushion results from the kink in the oligopolist's demand curve.

The kinked demand curve is really a composite of two separate demand curves (Figure 25.5). One curve is predicated on the assumption that rival oligopolists don't respond to price increases (d_1). The other curve is predicated on the assumption that

profit-maximization rule: Produce at that rate of output where marginal revenue equals marginal cost.

WORLD VIEW

OPEC to Cut Oil Output by 1 Million Barrels

BRUSSELS, July 25—Fearing the impact of falling energy consumption in a global economic slowdown, the Organization of Petroleum Exporting Countries decided today to cut oil production by 1 million barrels a day in a bid to drive crude prices back to $25 a barrel.

The decision by the cartel's 11 members marked the third time this year that they have cut output in the face of sharply eroding demand from their principal customers in the United States, Europe and Japan.

The new quota will reduce OPEC's production to 23.2 million barrels a day, the lowest level since April 1999. The cartel has trimmed output by 3.5 million barrels a day since the start of the year.

Analysts said the success of OPEC's strategy may depend on whether non-cartel members that produce large amounts of oil, such as Mexico, Norway and Russia, follow suit in curbing production. OPEC is responsible for producing about 40 percent of the world's oil.

If other countries do not curb output, OPEC members may be tempted to cheat on the new quotas.

The International Energy Agency said that OPEC members have secretly been pumping about 1 million barrels in excess of their target.

—William Drozdiak

Source: *Washington Post*, July 26, 2001. © 2001 The Washington Post. Reprinted with permission. www.washingtonpost.com

Analysis: An oligopoly tries to act like a shared monopoly. To maximize industry profit, the firms in an oligopoly must concur on what the monopoly price is and agree to maintain it by limiting and allocating market shares.

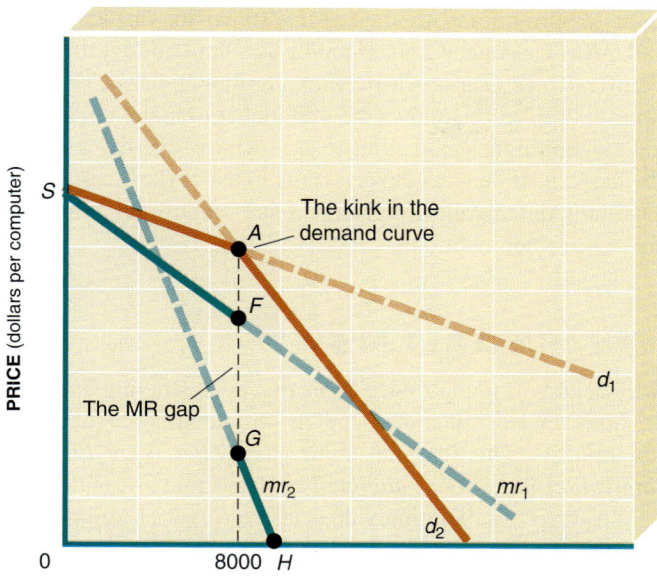

FIGURE 25.5
An Oligopolist's Marginal Revenue Curve

A kinked demand curve incorporates portions of two different demand curves (d_1 and d_2). Hence a kinked demand curve also has portions of two distinct marginal revenue curves (mr_1 and mr_2). Below the kink in the demand curve (point A), a gap exists between the two marginal revenue curves. The segment SF comes from marginal revenue curve mr_1; the segment GH comes from mr_2.

rivals do respond to price cuts (d_2). Each demand curve has its own marginal revenue curve, as shown in Figure 25.5. The demand curve d_1 has **marginal revenue (MR)** curve mr_1, for example, while demand curve d_2 has marginal revenue curve mr_2.

If the kinked demand curve dictates an oligopolist's behavior, each firm confronts the possibility of starting down the demand curve d_1 and switching to d_2 at point A. Hence, from point S to point A the curve mr_1 depicts the relevant marginal revenues. At point A (the quantity of 8,000 computers per month), however, we suddenly switch demand curves (to d_2). Hence, we must seek out a new marginal revenue curve corresponding to d_2. To the right of point A, the marginal revenue curve mr_2 is operational.

The oligopolist's marginal revenue curve thus contains two distinct segments. In Figure 25.5, the first segment runs from point S to point F. The second segment runs from point G down to point H (below the horizontal axis MR is negative and so of no interest here).

Between points F and G *there's a gap in the oligopolist's marginal revenue curve.* Notice that *this gap occurs just below the kink in the demand curve.* This gap creates a cost cushion. Look at the marginal cost curves in Figure 25.6. If the marginal cost curve passes through the gap in the marginal revenue curve, *modest shifts of the cost curve will have no impact on the production decision of an oligopolist.* That is, an

marginal revenue (MR): The change in total revenue that results from a one-unit increase in the quantity sold.

FIGURE 25.6
The Cost Cushion

The gap in an oligopolist's marginal revenue curve creates a "cost cushion." If marginal cost rises (MC_2) or falls (MC_3) within that gap ($F - G$), the profit-maximizing rate of output (MC = MR) is unchanged.

oligopolist need not reduce its rate of output when costs rise somewhat or increase its rate of output when costs fall. As a consequence, an oligopolist's output doesn't fluctuate as much as either a competitive firm's or a profit-maximizing monopolist's. The cost cushion implied by the gap in its MR curve allows the oligopolist to maintain a given price for longer periods and to incur higher marketing costs (such as advertising) if the need arises. In other words, the kinked demand curve results in "sticky" prices. Given the uncertain consequences of any unilateral price change, this cost cushion reinforces the aversion of oligopolists to price competition.

COORDINATION PROBLEMS

A successful oligopoly will achieve monopoly-level profits by restricting industry output. As we've observed, however, this outcome depends on mutual agreement and coordination among the oligopolists. This may not come easy. ***There's an inherent conflict in the joint and individual interests of oligopolists.*** Their joint, or collective, interest is in maximizing industry profit. The individual interest of each oligopolist, however, is to maximize its own share of sales and profit. This conflict creates great internal tension within an oligopoly. Recall that each firm wants as large a market share as possible, at prevailing prices. But encroachments in the market shares of rival oligopolists threaten to bring retaliation, price reductions, and reduced industry profits. To avoid such self-destructive behavior, oligopolists must coordinate their production decisions so that

- *Industry* output and price are maintained at profit-maximizing levels.
- Each oligopolistic *firm* is content with its market share.

Price-Fixing

To bring about this happy outcome, rival oligopolists could discuss their common interests and attempt to iron out an agreement on both issues. Identifying the profit-maximizing rate of industry output would be comparatively simple, as Figure 25.4 illustrated. Once the optimal rate of output was found the associated profit-maximizing price would be evident. The only remaining issue would be the division of industry output among the oligopolists, that is, the assignment of market shares.

The most explicit form of coordination among oligopolists is called **price-fixing**. In this case, the firms in an oligopoly explicitly agree to charge a uniform (monopoly) price. This is what OPEC members do when they get together to set oil prices. This is also what Ivy League schools did when they met to establish uniform scholarship and tuition rates (see News). Some other examples of price-fixing include the following:

price-fixing: Explicit agreements among producers regarding the price(s) at which a good is to be sold.

Electric Generators. In 1961, General Electric and Westinghouse were convicted of fixing prices on $2 billion worth of electrical generators that they'd been selling to the Tennessee Valley Authority and commercial customers. Among the corporate executives, 7 went to prison and 23 others were put on probation. In addition, the companies were fined a total of $1.8 million and compelled to pay triple damages in excess of $500 million to their victimized customers. Nevertheless, another suit was filed against General Electric and Westinghouse in 1972, charging these same companies—still the only two U.S. manufacturers of turbine generators—with continued price-fixing.

School Milk. Between 1988 and 1991, the U.S. Justice Department filed charges against 50 companies for fixing the price of milk sold to public schools in 16 states. Dairy companies paid over $20 million in fines. In 1993, Borden Inc. paid $8 million in fines for fixing bids on milk sold to Texas Tech University, public schools, and hospitals.

Vitamins. Seven firms from four nations were accused of fixing global prices on bulk vitamins from 1990 to 1998. They also allocated market shares for vitamins A, B2, C, and E. In 1999, the companies paid a record $1.05 billion fine.

IN THE NEWS

Charitable Conspiracy

A Judge Finds M.I.T. and the Ivy League Guilty of Price-Fixing

For more than 30 years the eight Ivy League colleges and M.I.T., as well as dozens of other private institutions, mostly in the Northeast, agreed that they would not try to outbid one another for talented students who needed financial assistance. Each spring this so-called Overlap Group, led by M.I.T. and the Ivies (Brown, Columbia, Cornell, Dartmouth, Harvard, Pennsylvania, Princeton, and Yale), would share information about needy students accepted by more than one of the member schools, working out a standard financial-aid package. Last year the Justice Department charged that this practice violated U.S. antitrust laws by suppressing competition among the schools.

Said Charles James, the Justice Department's lawyer: "Students and their families are entitled to the full benefits of price competition when they pick a college." But M.I.T. President Charles Vest warned that the decision would make it harder for colleges to admit students without regard to financial need and "effectively erode the freedom of opportunity to get a college education, regardless of income."

Source: *Time*, September 14, 1992. © 1992 Time Inc. Reprinted by permission. www.time.com

Analysis: Agreements to limit scholarship assistance effectively fix the price of college tuition. Ivy League schools routinely engaged in such price-fixing practices until the U.S. Justice Department intervened.

Baby Formula. Two makers of baby formula (Bristol-Myers Squibb and American Home Products) agreed to pay $5 million in 1992 to settle Florida charges that they had fixed prices on baby formula. Three companies control 95 percent of this $1.3 billion national market.

Cola. The Coca-Cola Bottling Co. of North Carolina agreed to pay a fine and give consumers discount coupons to settle charges of conspiring to fix soft drink prices from 1982 to 1985. Similar charges in Virginia led to fines and prison sentences for local executives of Coca-Cola and PepsiCo.

Auction Commissions. Sotheby's and Christie's, who together control 90 percent of the world's art auction business, admitted in 2000 to fixing commission rates throughout the 1990s. They paid a $512 million fine when they got caught.

Music CDs. In 2001, the Federal Trade Commission charged AOL–TimeWarner and Universal Music with fixing prices on the best-selling "Three Tenors" CD. The FTC also forced TimeWarner, Sony, Bertelsman, and EMI to end prohibitions on the advertising of discounted CD prices.

Laser Eye Surgery. The FTC charged the two companies that sell the lasers used for corrective eye surgery (VISX and Summit Technology) with price-fixing that inflated the retail price of surgery by $500 per eye.

Price Leadership

Although price-fixing agreements are still a reality in many product markets, oligopolies have discovered that they don't need *explicit* agreements to arrive at uniform prices; they can achieve the same outcome in more subtle ways. **Price leadership** rather than price-fixing will suffice. If all oligopolists in a particular product market follow the lead of one firm in raising prices, the result is the same as if they had all agreed to raise prices simultaneously. Instead of conspiring in motel rooms (as in the electrical products and soft drink cases), the firms can achieve their objective simply by reading *The Wall Street Journal* or industry publications and responding appropriately. This is apparently how Coke and Pepsi communicated their desire to end their 1997 price war (see News earlier in the chapter).

price leadership: An oligopolistic pricing pattern that allows one firm to establish the (market) price for all firms in the industry.

According to the U.S. Department of Justice, the major airlines developed a highly sophisticated form of price leadership. They used their shared computer reservation systems to signal *intended* price hikes (see the following News). Rival oligopolists then responded with their own *intended* price changes. Only after it was clear that all the airlines would match a planned price increase was the price hike announced. The Justice Department argued that this "electronic dialogue" was equivalent to a price-fixing conspiracy that cost consumers $1.9 billion in excessive fares. In 1994, the major airlines agreed to stop using the reservations system to communicate *planned* fare hikes.

Allocation of Market Shares

Whenever oligopolists successfully raise the price of a product, the law of demand tells us that unit sales will decline. Even in markets with highly inelastic demand (such as those for school milk and generic drugs), *some* decrease in sales always accompanies an increase in price. When this happens in a monopolistic industry, the monopolist simply cuts back his rate of output. In an oligopoly, however, no single firm will wish to incur the whole weight of that cutback. Some form of accommodation is required by all the oligopolists.

The adjustment to the reduced sales volume can take many forms. Members of OPEC, for example, assign explicit quotas for the oil output of each member country (see World View, page 548). Such open and explicit production-sharing agreements transform an oligopoly into a **cartel.**

cartel: A group of firms with an explicit, formal agreement to fix prices and output shares in a particular market.

Because cartels openly violate U.S. antitrust laws, American oligopolies have to be more circumspect in divvying up shared markets. A particularly novel method of allocating market shares occurred in the price-fixing case involving General Electric and Westinghouse. Agreeing to establish high prices on electric generators wasn't particularly difficult. But how would the companies decide who was to get the restricted

IN THE NEWS

Behind the Screens

The Justice Department says airlines can illegally fix fares by electronically posting future fare changes or restrictions, watching rivals' responses and adjusting the fares until all airlines agree. Here's a hypothetical example:

MONDAY	TUESDAY	WEDNESDAY	THURSDAY	FRIDAY
D.C. to Orlando: $200 Jan. 15 – Feb. 15	D.C. to Orlando: $250 Feb. 1 – Feb. 15 D.C. to Denver: $300 Jan. 15 – March 1	D.C. to Orlando: $250 Feb. 1 – Feb. 15 D.C. to Denver: $350 Jan. 15 – March 1	D.C. to Orlando: $250 Feb. 1 – Feb. 15 D.C. to Denver: $350 Jan. 15 – March 1	D.C. to Orlando: $250 Feb. 1 – Feb. 15 D.C. to Denver: $350 Jan. 15 – March 1
Airline A: Posts $200 fare to Orlando, a cut from $300.	*Airline B:* Posts a smaller, later fare cut to Orlando, a profitable route, and posts a $300 fare, down from $400, to Denver, a big route for Airline A.	*Airline A:* Changes its Orlando fare to match Airline B's, but posts a smaller fare cut on Denver route.	*Airline B:* Matches the higher Denver fare because Airline A matched its higher Orlando fare. At this point the fares take effect.	Travel agents and consumers learn of the fare cuts, but never know of the even deeper cuts initially proposed by both airlines.

Source: *Washington Post,* December 23, 1992. © 1992 The Washington Post. Reprinted with permission. www.washingtonpost.com

Analysis: Before changing prices, an oligopolist must know how its rivals will respond. The U.S. Department of Justice has accused major airlines of using their common computer reservation systems to test rivals' responses and set common prices.

sales? Their solution was to designate one firm as the "low" bidder for a particular phase of the moon. The "low" bidder would charge the previously agreed-upon (high) price, with the other firms offering their products at even higher prices. The "low" bidder would naturally get the sale. Each time the moon entered a new phase, the order of "low" and "high" bidders changed. Each firm got a share of the business, and the price-fixing scheme hid behind a facade of "competitive" bidding.

Such intricate systems for allocating market shares are more the exception than the rule. More often the oligopolists let the sales and output reduction be divided up according to consumer demands, intervening only when market shares are thrown markedly out of balance. At such times an oligopolist may take drastic action, such as **predatory pricing.** Predatory price cuts are temporary price reductions intended to drive out new competition or reestablish market shares. The sophisticated use of price cutting can also function as a significant barrier to entry, inhibiting potential competitors from trying to gain a foothold in the price cutter's market. The following News feature describes how three major airlines were accused in 1999 of using this technique to reduce competition on their routes.

predatory pricing: Temporary price reductions designed to alter market shares or drive out competition.

BARRIERS TO ENTRY

If oligopolies succeed in establishing monopoly prices and profits, they'll attract the envy of would-be entrants. To keep potential competitors out of their industry, oligopolists must maintain **barriers to entry.** *Above-normal profits can't be maintained over the long run unless barriers to entry exist.* The entry barriers erected include those monopolists use (Chapter 24).

barriers to entry: Obstacles that make it difficult or impossible for would-be producers to enter a particular market, such as patents.

Patents

Patents are a very effective barrier to entry. Potential competitors can't set up shop until they either develop an alternative method for producing a product or receive permission from the patent holder to use the patented process. Such permission, when given, costs something, of course.

Distribution Control

Another way of controlling the supply of a product is to take control of distribution outlets. If a firm can persuade retail outlets not to peddle anyone else's competitive wares, it will increase its market power. This control of distribution outlets can be accomplished through selective discounts, long-term supply contracts, or expensive

---

IN THE NEWS

New Airline Accuses Rivals of Predatory Pricing Tactics

AccessAir, the nation's newest airline, accused three major competitors of using artificially low fares in an effort to drive it out of business just as airline competition and passenger rights have begun to emerge as part of the national political debate.

The Des Moines–based airline asked Transportation Secretary Rodney E. Slater to investigate charges that Trans World Airlines, Delta Air Lines and Northwest Airlines are offering fares so far below their costs that it amounts to illegal predatory pricing.

"Unfortunately, the expected bear hug by the major airlines has begun," AccessAir President D. Roger Ferguson wrote to Slater on Monday. "Three of the [major airlines] are now offering fares in AccessAir markets that are one-third below our fares—and far below both their normal fares and their costs. If continued, these fares will force us out of business."

—Frank Swoboda

Source: *Washington Post*, March 17, 1999. © 1999 The Washington Post. Reprinted with permission. www.washingtonpost.com

Analysis: Predatory pricing entails the use of temporary price cuts to weaken the financial condition of rival companies. It can be used to enforce higher prices or otherwise reduce competition.

gifts at Christmas. Recall from Chapter 24 (see News, page 522) how Clear Channel and Ticketmaster locked up concert arenas. According to the U.S. Justice Department, Visa and MasterCard prevent banks that issue their credit cards from offering rival cards. Frito-Lay elbows out competing snack companies by paying high fees to "rent" shelf space in grocery stores (see the News below). Such up-front costs create an entry barrier for potential rivals. Even if a potential rival can come up with the up-front money, the owner of an arena or grocery store chain may not wish to anger the firm that dominates the market.

New car warranties also serve as an entry barrier. The warranties typically require regular maintenance at authorized dealerships and the exclusive use of authorized parts. These provisions limit the ability of would-be competitors to provide cheaper auto parts and service.

Mergers and Acquisition

Large and powerful firms can also limit competition by outright *acquisition*. A *merger* between two firms amounts to the same thing, although mergers often entail the creation of new corporate identities.

Perhaps the single most dramatic case of acquisition for this purpose occurred in the breakfast cereals industry. In 1946, General Foods acquired the cereal manufacturing facilities of Campbell Cereal Company, a substantial competitor. Following this acquisition, General Foods dismantled the production facilities of Campbell Cereal and shipped them off to South Africa!

Vanderbilt University has an Antitrust Policy site that tracks news on mergers, price-fixing, and related issues. Visit www.Antitrust.org.

Although the General Foods acquisition was more dramatic than most, acquisitions have been the most popular route to increased market power. General Motors attained a dominant share of the auto market largely by its success in merging with and acquiring two dozen independent manufacturers. In the cigarette industry, the American Tobacco Company attained monopoly powers by absorbing 250 independent companies. Later antitrust action (1911) split up the resultant tobacco monopoly into an oligopoly

IN THE NEWS

Frito-Lay Devours Snack-Food Business

Once again, Frito-Lay is chewing up the competition.

The announcement Wednesday that Anheuser-Busch Cos. is selling off its Eagle Snacks business highlights the danger of trying to compete against Frito-Lay in the salty-snacks game. The company owns half of the $15 billion salty-snacks market.

"Frito's a fortress," says Michael Branca, an analyst at NatWest Securities. "And it continues to expand its realm. I'd tell anyone else trying to get into the business, don't try to expand, don't try to impinge on Frito's territory or you'll get crushed."

In fact, competitors say that it is Frito-Lay's tactics with retailers that make it an invincible foe. Because many retailers are charging more and more for shelf space—$40,000 a foot annually in some instances—many regional companies say Frito-Lay is paying retailers to squeeze out competing brands.

"Frito can afford it," says a regional snack company executive. "But we can't. It's become a real-estate business."

Frito-Lay can also afford to out-promote its competitors. In 1993, the company spent more than $60 million on advertising, while Eagle spent less than $2 million.

—Robert Frank

Snack-Food Giant

Frito-Lay's market share in various snack-food categories.

	Salty Snacks		Potato Chips		Tortilla Chips	
	1990	1995	1990	1995	1990	1995
Market share	43%	52%	45%	52%	63%	72%

Source: *The Wall Street Journal*, October 27, 1995. Reprinted by permission of *The Wall Street Journal*. © 1995 Dow Jones & Company, Inc. All rights reserved worldwide. www.wsj.com

Analysis: Barriers to entry such as self-space rental and advertising enable a firm to maintain market dominance. Acquisitions also reduce competition.

consisting of four companies, which continue to dominate the cigarette market. Other companies that came to dominate their product markets through mergers and acquisitions include U.S. Steel, U.S. Rubber, General Electric, United Fruit, National Biscuit Company, International Salt, and Ticketmaster. Frito-Lay's 1995 acquisitions of Eagle Snacks (see News) extended its already dominant control of the chip, pretzel, and nuts markets.

The government often helps companies acquire and maintain control of market supply. Patents are issued by and enforced by the federal government and so represent one form of supply-restricting regulation. Barriers to international trade are another government-imposed barrier to entry. By limiting imports of everything from Chinese mushrooms to Japanese cars (see Chapter 35), the federal government reduces potential competition in U.S. product markets. Government regulation also limits *domestic* competition in many industries. From 1984 to 1990, the Federal Communications Commission (FCC) allowed only one company (GTE Corporation) to provide telephone service on airlines. When the FCC ended the monopoly in 1990, phone charges declined sharply.

Government Regulation

New York City also limits competition—in this case, the number of taxicabs on the streets. The maximum number of cabs was set at 11,787 in 1937 and stayed at that ceiling until 1996. The city's Taxi and Limousine Commission raised the ceiling by a scant 400 cabs in 1996. That didn't do much to eliminate New York's perennial taxi shortage, much less reduce fares. As a result, license holders continue to reap monopoly-like profits. A good measure of those profits is the price of the medallions that the city sells as taxi licenses. The market price of a New York City taxi medallion—and thus the price of entry into the industry—was $185,000 in 2001. By contrast, a Washington, D.C., taxi license costs only $35, and fares are about half those in New York.

Producers who control market supply can enhance their power even further by establishing some influence over market demand. The primary mechanism of control is *advertising*. To the extent that a firm can convince you that its product is essential to your well-being and happiness, it has effectively shifted your demand curve. ***Advertising not only strengthens brand loyalty but also makes it expensive for new producers to enter the market.*** A new entrant must buy both production facilities and advertising outlets.

Nonprice Competition

The cigarette industry is a classic case of high concentration and product differentiation. As Table 25.2 shows, the top four cigarette companies produce 96 percent of all domestic output; two more firms produce the rest. Yet you would never guess that such high concentration exists in the industry if you glanced at the cigarette shelves at the local supermarket. Together, the six cigarette companies produce well over 100 brands. To solidify brand loyalties, the cigarette industry spent over $8 billion on advertising and promotions in 2001.

Another highly concentrated industry that advertises heavily is the $10 billion per year breakfast cereals industry. Although the Federal Trade Commission has suggested that "a corn flake is a corn flake no matter who makes it," the four firms (Kellogg, General Mills, Philip Morris, and Quaker Oats) that supply more than 90 percent of all ready-to-eat breakfast cereals spend over $400 million a year—about $1 per box!—to convince consumers otherwise. During the last 20 years, more than 200 brands of cereal have been marketed by these companies. As the FTC has documented, the four companies "produce basically similar RTE [ready-to-eat] cereals, and then emphasize and exaggerate trivial variations such as color and shape. . . . [They] employ trademarks to conceal such basic similarities and to differentiate cereal brands."[3]

In today's technology-driven markets, early market entry can create an important barrier to later competition. Customers of computer hardware and software, for example,

Training

---

[3]Complaint, *Kellogg Company et al.,* FTC Dkt. 8883 (1972).

often become familiar with a particular system or computer package. To switch to a new product may entail significant cost, including the retraining of user staff. As a consequence, would-be competitors will find it difficult to sell their products even if they offer better quality and lower prices.

The popular Lotus 1-2-3 spreadsheet program illustrates this market barrier. Lotus Development Corporation introduced Lotus 1-2-3 in 1982 as one of the first spreadsheets for the IBM personal computer. By 1988, Lotus had 3.5 million copies of its program in use—82 percent of all spreadsheet sales. Although other software firms offered comparable (and even better) products at much lower prices, users were reluctant to try new software that would require retraining. (IBM bought Lotus in 1995, further raising the entry barrier.) Microsoft gained a similar advantage by bundling Net-access and applications software with Windows. Once consumers become accustomed to Microsoft features, they're less inclined to purchase potential substitutes.

Network Economies

The widespread use of a particular product may also heighten its value to consumers, thereby making potential substitutes less viable. The utility of instant messaging—or even a telephone—depends on how many of your friends have computers or telephones. If no one else had a phone or computer, there'd be no reason to own one. In other words, the larger the network of users, the greater the value of the product. Such network economies help explain why software developers prefer to write Windows-based programs than programs for rival operating systems. Network economics also explains why Microsoft doesn't want computer manufacturers to display icons for rival instant-messaging services on the Windows XP desktop. Whichever instant-messaging service expands the quickest may achieve a network entry barrier.

THE ECONOMY TOMORROW

Antitrust Guidelines

Examples of market power at work in U.S. product markets could be extended to the closing pages of this book. The few cases cited here, however, are testimony enough to the fact that market power has some influence on our lives. Market power *does* exist; market power *is* used. Although market power may result in economies of scale, the potential for abuse is evident. Market power contributes to **market failure** when it leads to resource misallocation (restricted output) or greater inequity (monopoly profits; higher prices).

What should we do about these abuses? Should we leave it to market forces to find ways of changing industry structure and behavior? Or should the government step in to curb noncompetitive practices?

market failure: An imperfection in the market mechanism that prevents optimal outcomes.

Industry Behavior

Our primary concern is the *behavior* of market participants. What ultimately counts is the quantity of goods supplied to the market, their quality, and their price. Few consumers care about the underlying *structure* of markets; what we seek are good market *outcomes*.

In principle, the government could change industry behavior without changing industry structure. We could, for example, explicitly outlaw collusive agreements and cast a wary eye on industries that regularly exhibit price leadership. We could also dismantle barriers to entry and thereby promote contestable markets. We might also prohibit oligopolists from extending their market power via such mechanisms as acquisitions, excessive or deceptive advertising, and, alas, the financing of political campaigns. In fact, the existing **antitrust** laws—the Sherman Act, the Clayton Act, and the Federal Trade Commission Act (see Table 24.1)—explicitly forbid most of these practices.

antitrust: Government intervention to alter market structure or prevent abuse of market power.

There are several problems with this behavioral approach. The first limitation is scarce resources. Policing markets and penalizing noncompetitive conduct require more resources than the public sector can muster. Indeed, the firms being investigated often have more resources than the public watchdogs. The advertising expenditures of just one oligopolist, Procter & Gamble, are more than 10 times as large as the *combined* budgets of both the Justice Department's Antitrust Division and the Federal Trade Commission. As Ralph Nader has suggested, "The posture of two agencies with a combined budget of $20 million and 550 lawyers and economists trying to deal with anticompetitive abuses in a trillion-dollar economy, not to mention an economy where the 200 largest corporations control two-thirds of all manufacturing assets, is truly a charade."[4]

The paucity of antitrust resources is partly a reflection of public apathy. Consumers generally are unaware of the relationship between market structure and their own economic welfare. They (and you) rarely think about the connection between market power and the price of the goods they buy, the wages they receive, or the way they live. As Ralph Nader discovered, "Antitrust violations are part of a phenomenon which, to the public is too complex, too abstract, and supremely dull."[5] As a result, there's little political pressure to regulate market behavior.

The behavioral approach also suffers from the "burden-of-proof" requirement. How often will "trustbusters" catch colluding executives in the act? More often than not, the case for collusion rests on such circumstantial evidence as simultaneous price hikes, identical bids, or other market outcomes. The charge of explicit collusion is hard to prove. Even in the absence of explicit collusion, however, consumers suffer. If an oligopoly price is higher than what a competitive industry would charge, consumers get stuck with the bill whether or not the price was "rigged" by explicit collusions. The U.S. Supreme Court recognized that consumers may suffer from *tacit* collusion, even where no *explicit* collusion occurs.

Industry Structure

The concept of tacit collusion directs attention to the *structure* of an industry. It essentially says that oligopolists and monopolists will act in their own best interest. As former Supreme Court Chief Justice Earl Warren observed, "An industry which does not have a competitive structure will not have competitive behavior."[6] To expect an oligopolist to disavow profit opportunities or to ignore its interdependence with fellow oligopolists is naive. It also violates the basic motivations imputed to a market economy. As long as markets are highly concentrated, we must expect to observe oligopolistic behavior.

Judge Learned Hand used these arguments to dismantle the Aluminum Company of America (Alcoa) in 1945. Alcoa wasn't charged with any illegal *behavior*. Nevertheless, the company controlled over 90 percent of the aluminum supplied to the market. This monopoly structure, the Supreme Court concluded, was itself a threat to the public interest.

Public efforts to alter market structure have been less frequent than efforts to alter market behavior. With the exception of the AT&T case (Chapter 24) and Alcoa, the few really concerted efforts to break up market concentration occurred at the beginning of the century, when Standard Oil and the Tobacco Trust were partially dismantled. In 2001, the Justice Department withdrew a proposal to break up Microsoft into separate systems and applications companies. The prevalent feeling today, even among antitrust practitioners, is that the powerful firms are too big and too entrenched to make deconcentration a viable policy alternative.

Objections to Antitrust

Some people think *less* antitrust activity is actually a wise policy. The companies challenged by the public "trustbusters" protest that they're being penalized for their success. Alcoa, for example, attained a monopoly by investing heavily in a new product before anyone else recognized its value. Other firms too have captured dominant market shares by being first, best, or most efficient. Having "won" the game fairly, why should they have to give up their prize? They contend that noncompetitive *behavior,* not industry *structure,* should be the only concern of antitrust.

---

[4]Mark J. Green et al., *The Closed Enterprise System: The Report on Antitrust Enforcement* (New York: Grossman, 1972), p. x.
[5]Ibid, p. ix.
[6]Ibid., p. 7.

Essentially the same argument is made for proposed mergers and acquisitions. The firms involved claim that the increased concentration will enhance productive efficiency (e.g., via economies of scale). Antitrust critics also argue that big firms are needed to maintain America's competitive position in international markets (which are themselves often dominated by foreign monopolies and oligopolies). Those same global markets, they contend, ensure that even highly concentrated domestic markets will be contested by international rivals.

Finally, critics of antitrust suggest that market forces themselves will ensure competitive behavior. Foreign firms and domestic entrepreneurs will stalk a monopolist's preserve. People will always be looking for ways to enter a profitable market. Monopoly or oligopoly power may slow entry but is unlikely to stop it forever. Eventually, competitive forces will prevail.

Structural Guidelines: The Herfindahl-Hirshman Index

There are no easy answers. In theory, competition is valuable, but some mergers and acquisitions undoubtedly increase efficiency. Moreover, some international markets may require a minimum firm size not consistent with perfect competition. Finally, our regulatory resources are limited; not every acquisition or merger is worthy of public scrutiny.

Where would we draw the line? Can a firm hold a 22 percent market share, but not 30 percent? Are five firms too few, but six firms in an industry enough? Someone has to make those decisions. That is, **the broad mandates of the antitrust laws must be transformed into specific guidelines for government intervention.**

In 1982, the Antitrust Division of the U.S. Department of Justice adopted specific guidelines for intervention based on industry *structure* alone. They're based on an index that takes into account the market share of *each* firm rather than just the *combined* market share of the top four firms. Specifically, the **Herfindahl-Hirshman Index (HHI)** of market concentration is calculated as

Herfindahl-Hirsham Index (HHI): Measure of industry concentration that accounts for number of firms and size of each.

$$\text{HHI} = \sum_{i=1}^{n} = \left(\begin{array}{c}\text{share of}\\ \text{firm 1}\end{array}\right)^2 + \left(\begin{array}{c}\text{Share of}\\ \text{firm 2}\end{array}\right)^2 + \cdots \left(\begin{array}{c}\text{share of}\\ \text{firm } n\end{array}\right)^2$$

Thus, a three-firm oligopoly like that described in Table 25.3 would have an HHI value of

$$\text{HHI} = (40.0)^2 + (32.5)^2 + (27.5)^2 = 3{,}412.5$$

where the numbers in parentheses indicate the market shares of the three fictional computer companies. The calculation yields an HHI value of 3,412.5.

For policy purposes, the Justice Department decided it would draw the line at 1,800. Any merger that creates an HHI value over 1,800 will be challenged by the Justice Department. If an industry has an HHI value between 1,000 and 1,800, the Justice Department will challenge any merger that *increases* the HHI by 100 points or more. Mergers and acquisitions in industries with an HHI value of less than 1,000 won't be challenged.

The HHI is an arbitrary but workable tool for deciding when the government should intervene to challenge mergers and acquisitions. The Justice Department reviews about 2,500 mergers a year but challenges less than 50.

For concentration ratios and HHIs in U.S. industries, go to www.census.gov/epcd and www/concentration.html.

Contestability

Even when intervention is signaled, however, there are still decisions to make. Should a challenged merger be allowed? The same old questions arise. Will the proposed merger enhance efficiency in domestic and global markets? Or will it tend to constrain competitive forces, keeping consumer prices high?

In 1992, the Justice Department broadened its antitrust focus. Rather than just look at the *existing* market structure, the department decided to examine entry barriers as well. If entry barriers were low enough, even a highly concentrated industry might be compelled to behave more competitively. In other words, *contestability* as well as *structure* now motivates antitrust decisions.

Behavioral Guidelines: Cost Savings

In 1996, the Federal Trade Commission (FTC) moved even further away from strict *structural* (market share) criteria by deciding to take potential cost savings into account. Previously, the FTC and Justice Department had declined to consider greater efficiencies that might result from a merger. The focus was strictly on the structural threat to competition. Since 1996, the focus has shifted from the concept of "unfair competition" to an emphasis on consumer welfare. If companies can show how a merger or acquisition will result in greater efficiency and lower costs, they will get the green light from the trustbusters. In December 2000, the Federal Trade Commission flashed the green light for AOL's acquisition of Time Warner. As a condition of approval, however, Time Warner had to open its cable lines to Internet rivals, thereby lowering entry barriers to Internet services. In 2001, United Airlines got the red light when it attempted to create the world's largest airline by acquiring USAirways. The Justice Department said the deal would reduce competition and raise airfares for millions of passengers. As we observed in the previous chapter, Microsoft was also prosecuted for the abuses that limited consumer choice and raised software prices.

SUMMARY

- Imperfect competition refers to markets in which individual suppliers (firms) have some independent influence on the price at which their output is sold. Examples of imperfectly competitive market structures are duopoly, oligopoly, and monopolistic competition.
- The extent of market power (control over price) depends on the number of firms in an industry, their size, barriers to entry, and the availability of substitutes.
- The concentration ratio is a measure of market power in a particular product market. It equals the share of total industry output accounted for by the largest firms, usually the top four.
- An oligopoly is a market structure in which a few firms produce all or most of a particular good or service; it's essentially a shared monopoly.
- Because oligopolies involve several firms rather than only one, each firm must consider the effect of its price and output decisions on the behavior of rivals. Such firms are highly interdependent.
- Game theory attempts to identify different strategies a firm might use, taking into account the consequences of rivals' moves and countermoves.
- The kinked demand curve illustrates a pattern of strategic interaction in which rivals match a price cut but not a price hike. Such behavior reinforces the oligopolistic aversion to price competition.
- A basic conflict exists between the desire of each individual oligopolist to expand its market share and the *mutual* interest of all the oligopolists in restricting total output so as to maximize industry profits. This conflict must be resolved in some way, via either collusion or some less explicit form of agreement (such as price leadership).
- Oligopolists may use price-fixing agreements or price leadership to establish the market price. To maintain that price, the oligopolists must also agree on their respective market shares.
- To maintain economic profits, an oligopoly must erect barriers to entry. Patents are one form of barrier. Other barriers include predatory price cutting (price wars), control of distribution outlets, government regulations, advertising (product differentiation), training, and network economies. Outright acquisition and merger may also eliminate competition.
- Market power may cause market failure. The symptoms of that failure include increased prices, reduced output, and a transfer of income from the consuming public to a relatively few powerful corporations and the people who own them.
- Government intervention may focus on either market structure or market behavior. In either case, difficult decisions must be made about when and how to intervene.
- The Herfindahl-Hirshman Index is a measure of industry concentration that takes into account the number of firms and the size of each. It is used as a structural guideline to identify cases worthy of antitrust concern.

Key Terms

market structure
oligopoly
contestable market
concentration ratio
oligopolist
market share
product differentiation

game theory
profit maximization rule
marginal revenue (MR)
price-fixing
price leadership
cartel
predatory pricing

barriers to entry
market failure
antitrust
Herfindahl-Hirshman Index (HHI)

Questions for Discussion

1. How many bookstores are on or near your campus? If there were more bookstores, how would the price of new and used books be affected?
2. What entry barriers exist in (*a*) the fast-food industry, (*b*) cable television, (*c*) the auto industry, (*d*) illegal drug trade, (*e*) beauty parlors?
3. Why does RC Cola depend on advertising to gain market share? (See News, page 542.) Why not offer cheaper sodas than Coke or Pepsi?
4. Why would OPEC members have a difficult time setting and maintaining a monopoly price? (See World View, page 548.)
5. If an oligopolist knows rivals will match a price cut, would he ever reduce his price?
6. How might the high concentration ratio in the credit card industry (Table 25.2) affect the annual fees and interest charges on credit card services?
7. Identify three products you purchase that aren't listed in Table 25.2. What's the structure of those three markets?
8. What reasons might Northwest Airlines have for *not* matching its rivals' fare increases? (See News, page 545.)
9. The Ivy League schools defended their price-fixing arrangement (see News, page 551) by arguing that their coordination assured a fair distribution of scholarship aid. Who was hurt or helped by this arrangement?
10. Using the payoff matrix in Table 25.4, decide whether Universal should cut its price. What factors will influence the decision?
11. Dominos and Pizza Hut hold 66 percent of the delivered-pizza market. Should antitrust action be taken?

Web Activities

1. Examine the charges of price-fixing in the international vitamin industry at www.usdoj.gov/atr/public/press_releases/1999/2266.htm.
    (*a*) What is price-fixing, and why is it against the law?
    (*b*) What antitrust legislation is being violated?
    (*c*) Who were the defendants in the suit, and what were the charges against them?
    (*d*) Was the alleged price-fixing at the retail or wholesale level? What was the fine?
2. A recent merger antitrust case involved the fountain pen industry. Find a summary of this case—*U.S.* v. *The Gillette Company and Parker Pen Holdings, Ltd.*—at www.antitrust.org/cases/mergers.htm#pencase. What was the decision in the case (see the "Conclusion")? How did the definition of the market affect the relevant market shares in this case?
3. Log on to www.census.gov/epcd/www/concentration.html. Click on "Arts, Entertainment, and Recreation." Using the information you find in the chart, calculate the concentration ratio for the entire sports industry. How does this compare to the concentration ratio for football and baseball?

THE ACCOMPANYING STUDENT PROBLEM SET CONTAINS NUMERICAL AND GRAPHING PROBLEMS FOR THIS CHAPTER

CHAPTER 26

Monopolistic Competition

Starbucks is already the biggest coffee bar chain in the country, with roughly 4,500 locations on three continents. And the company is determined to keep growing by setting up coffee bars in airports, department stores, and just about anywhere consumers congregate. Even if Starbucks achieves such meteoric growth, however, it will never have great market power. There are more than 8,000 coffee bars in the United States, not to mention a million or so other places you can buy a cup of coffee. With so many other close substitutes, the best Starbucks can hope for is a little brand loyalty. If enough consumers think of Starbucks when they get the caffeine urge, Starbucks will at least be able to charge more for coffee than a perfectly competitive firm. It won't enjoy *monopoly* profits, or even share the kind of monopoly profits *oligopolies* sometimes achieve. It may, however, be able to maintain an economic profit for many years.

Starbucks is an example of yet another market structure—*monopolistic competition*. In this chapter we focus on how such firms make price and output decisions and the market outcomes that result. Our objective is to determine

- The unique features of monopolistic competition.
- How market outcomes are affected by this market structure.
- The long-run consequences of different market structures.

In this chapter we'll also see why we can't escape the relentless advertising that bombards us from every angle.

STRUCTURE

As we first noted in Table 25.1, the distinguishing structural characteristic of **monopolistic competition** is that there are *many* firms in an industry. "Many" isn't an exact specification, of course. It's best understood as lying somewhere between the few that characterize oligopoly and the hordes that characterize perfect competition.

Another way to distinguish monopolistic competition is to examine **concentration ratios**. Oligopolies have very high four-firm concentration ratios. As we saw in Chapter 25 (Table 25.2), concentration ratios of 70 to 100 percent are common

Low Concentration

monopolistic competition: A market in which many firms produce similar goods or services but each maintains some independent control of its own price.

concentration ratio: The proportion of total industry output produced by the largest firms (usually the four largest).

Market Power

market power: The ability to alter the market price of a good or service.

in oligopolies. By contrast, there's much less concentration in monopolistic competition. A few firms may stand above the rest, but the combined market share of the top four firms will typically be in the range of 20 to 40 percent. Hence, *low concentration ratios are common in monopolistic competition.*

Starbucks has less than 15 percent of the coffee bar business and a mere 5 percent of all coffee sales. The top four coffee bar outlets (Starbucks, Second Cup, The Coffee Beanery, and Barnie's) have a concentration ratio of only 28 percent (see Table 26.1). Other examples of monopolistic competition include banks, radio stations, health spas, apparel stores, convenience stores, and law firms. Notice in Table 26.1 that the personal computer market now has a monopolistically competitive structure as well. Even as large a firm as McDonald's might be regarded as a monopolistic competitor. Although "Mickey D's" has a huge share (40 percent) of the quickie *hamburger* market, its share of the much larger *fast-food* market is significantly smaller. The 12,000+ McDonald's outlets in the United States compete with over 200,000 fast-food outlets. If consumers regard pizzas, Chinese carry-outs, and delis as close substitutes for hamburgers, then the broader fast-food market is the appropriate basis for measuring market power and concentration.

Although concentration rates are low in monopolistic competition, the individual firms aren't powerless. There is a *monopoly* aspect to monopolistic competition. Each producer in monopolistic competition is large enough to have some **market power.** If a perfectly competitive firm increases the price of its product, it will lose all its customers. Recall that a perfectly competitive firm confronts a horizontal demand curve for its output. Competition is less intense in monopolistic competition. *A monopolis-*

TABLE 26.1
Monopolistic Competition
Monopolistically competitive industries are characterized by modest concentration ratios and low entry barriers. Contrast these four-firm concentration ratios with those of oligopoly (see Table 25.2).

Product	Largest Firms (market share)	Concentration Ratio
Movie studios	Paramount (15.8%), Disney (15.7%), 20th Century Fox (10.8%), Sony (10.6%)	53%
Personal computers	Dell (15%), Compaq (11%), Hewlett-Packard (7%), IBM (7%)	40%
Auto tires (replacement)	Goodyear (16%), Michelin (8%), Firestone (7.5%), General (5%)	36%
Bottled water	PepsiCo (Aquafina 15.8%), Coca-Cola (Dasani 8.7%), Perrier (Poland Spring, 6.4%), Dannon (5.3%)	36%
Toys	Hasbro (15%), Mattel (11%), Tyco (5%), Fisher-Price (4%)	35%
Coffee bars	Starbucks (15%), Second Cup (9%), Coffee Beanery (3%), Barnie's (1.5%)	28%
Drugs	Glaxo-Wellcome (5.8%), Hoechst-Marion Merrell Dow (4.4%), Merck (4.4%), American Home Products (3.8%)	18%

Source: Industry sources and business publications (1998–2001 data).

tically competitive firm confronts a downward-sloping demand curve for its output. When Starbucks increases the price of coffee, it loses some customers, but nowhere close to all its customers. Hence, Starbucks, like other monopolistically competitive firms, has some control over the price of its output. This is the *monopoly* dimension of monopolistic competition.

In an oligopoly, a firm that increased its price would have to worry about how rivals might respond. In monopolistic competition, however, there are many more firms. As a result, **modest changes in the output or price of any single firm will have no perceptible influence on the sales of any other firm.** This relative independence results from the fact that the effects of any one firm's behavior will be spread over many other firms (rather than only two or three other firms, as in an oligopoly).

The relative independence of monopolistic competitors means that they don't have to worry about retaliatory responses to every price or output change. As a result, they confront more traditional demand curves, with no kinks. The kink in the oligopolist's curve results from the likelihood that rival oligopolists would match any price reduction (to preserve market shares) but not necessarily any price increase (to increase their shares). In monopolistic competition, the market shares of rival firms aren't perceptibly altered by one firm's price changes.

Another characteristic of monopolistic competition is the presence of *low* **barriers to entry**—it's relatively easy to get in and out of the industry. To become a coffee vendor, all you need is boiling water, some fresh beans, and cups. You can save on rent by using a pushcart to dispense the brew. These unusually low entry barriers keep Starbucks and other coffee bars on their toes. Low entry barriers also tend to push economic profits toward zero. This is the *competitive* dimension of monopolistic competition.

BEHAVIOR

Given the unique structural characteristics of monopolistic competition we should anticipate some distinctive behavior.

One of the most notable features of monopolistically competitive behavior is **product differentiation.** A monopolistically competitive firm is distinguished from a purely competitive firm by its downward-sloping demand curve. Individual firms in a perfectly competitive market confront horizontal demand curves because consumers view their respective products as interchangeable (homogeneous). As a result, an attempt by one firm to raise its price will drive its customers to other firms.

Brand Image. In monopolistic competition, each firm has a distinct identity—a *brand image*. Its output is perceived by consumers as being somewhat different from the output of all other firms in the industry. Nowhere is this more evident than in the fast growing bottled water industry. Pepsi and Coke have become the leaders in the the bottled water market as a result of effective marketing (see News on the next page). Although Aquafina (Pepsi) and Dasani (Coke) are just filtered municipal water, clever advertising campaigns have convinced consumers that these branded waters are different—and better—than hundreds of other bottled waters. As a result of such product differentiation, Pepsi and Coke can raise the price of their bottled waters without losing all their customers to rival firms.

At first blush, the demand curve facing a monopolistically competitive firm looks like the demand curve confronting a monopolist. There's a profound difference, however. In a monopoly, there are no other firms. In monopolistic competition, **each firm has a monopoly only on its brand image; it still competes with other firms offering close substitutes.** This implies that the extent of power a monopolistically competitive firm has depends on how successfully it can differentiate its product from that of other firms.

Independent Production Decisions

Low Entry Barriers

barriers to entry: Obstacles that make it difficult or impossible for would-be producers to enter a particular market, such as patents.

Product Differentiation

product differentiation: Features that make one product appear different from competing products in the same market.

Brand Loyalty

IN THE NEWS

Water, Water Everywhere; Coke, Pepsi Unleash Flood of Ad Muscle

Water is water, at least until the marketers get hold of it.

Then a humble commodity that literally falls from the sky becomes something else. Something with "personality."

Not long ago, it would have been silly to think about branding water. But the big beverage companies are doing just that, and this summer marks the biggest-ever ad barrage for Dasani, Coke's water brand, and Aquafina, bottled by Pepsi-Cola Co.

Branding is an important issue in a category where sales grew by nearly 26 percent in 2000, to 807 million cases — the highest growth rate in the beverage industry. The challenge is getting attention in a highly fragmented market.

There are hundreds of different water brands, and some are so small that they serve just a few towns.

"Consumers are trading up. They're willing to search for a brand, " said Kellam Graitcer, Dasani brand manager at Coca-Cola. "We're trying to inject a little bit of personality into the category."

The two companies are likely to spend about $20 million each this year on ads.

—Scott Leith

Source: *Atlanta Journal–Constitution*, July 12, 2001. Reprinted with permission. www.accessatlanta.com/ajc

Analysis: By differentiating their products, monopolistic competitors establish brand loyalty. Brand loyalty gives producers greater control over the price of their products.

IN THE NEWS

Who Can Be Loyal to a Trash Bag?

When generic products were coming on strong a few years ago, J. Walter Thompson, the New York–based ad agency, gauged consumers' loyalty to brands in 80 product categories. It found that the leader in market share was not necessarily the brand-loyalty leader. At that time, Bayer aspirin was the market share leader among headache remedies, but Tylenol had the most loyal following.

Thompson measured the degree of loyalty by asking people whether they'd switch for a 50 percent discount. Cigarette smokers most often said no, making them the most brand-loyal of consumers (see table). Film is the only one of the top five products that the user doesn't put in his mouth—so why such loyalty? According to Edith Gilson, Thompson's senior vice president of research, 35-mm film is used by photography buffs, who are not your average snapshooter: "It's for long-lasting emotionally valued pictures, taken by someone who has invested a lot of money in his camera." Plenty of shoppers will try a different cola for 50 percent off, and most consumers think one plastic garbage bag or facial tissue is much like another.

—Anne B. Fisher

Source: *Fortune*, August 5, 1985. © 1985 by Time Inc. All rights reserved. www.fortune.com

High-Loyalty Products	Medium-Loyalty Products	Low-Loyalty Products
Cigarettes	Cola drinks	Paper towels
Laxatives	Margarine	Crackers
Cold remedies	Shampoo	Scouring powder
35-mm film	Hand lotion	Plastic trash bags
Toothpaste	Furniture polish	Facial tissue

Brand names matter more in some products than in others, researchers find.

Analysis: Brand loyalty implies that consumers shun substitute goods even when they are cheaper. This renders the demand curve less price-elastic.

The more brand loyalty a firm can establish, the less likely consumers are to switch brands when price is increased. In other words, *brand loyalty makes the demand curve facing the firm less price-elastic.*

Brand loyalty exists even when products are virtually identical. Gasoline of a given octane rating is a very standardized product. Nevertheless, most consumers regularly buy one particular brand. Because of that brand loyalty, Texaco can raise the price of its gasoline by a penny or two a gallon without losing its customers to competing companies. According to the accompanying News feature, brand loyalty is particularly high for cigarettes, toothpaste, and even laxatives. Brand loyalty is less strong for paper towels and virtually nonexistent for tomatoes.

In the computer industry, product differentiation has been used to establish brand loyalty. Although virtually all computers use identical microprocessor "brains" and operating platforms, the particular mix of functions performed on any computer can be varied, as can its appearance (packaging). Effective advertising can convince consumers that one computer is "smarter," more efficient, or more versatile than another. Also, a single firm may differentiate itself by providing faster or more courteous customer service. If successful in any of these efforts, *each monopolistically competitive firm will establish some consumer loyalty.* With such loyalty a firm can alter its own price somewhat, without fear of great changes in unit sales (quantity demanded). In other words, the demand curve facing each firm will slope downward, as in Figure 26.1*a*.

One symptom of brand loyalty is consumers' tendency to repurchase the same brand. Nearly 9 out of 10 Apple Macintosh users stick with Apple products when they upgrade or replace computer components. Repurchase rates are 74 percent for Dell, 72 percent for Hewlett-Packard, and 66 percent for Gateway.

Another symptom of brand loyalty is the price differences between computer brands. As the News on the next page indicates, consumers are willing to pay more for an IBM-branded computer than a no-name computer with identical features. For the same reason, consumers are willing to pay more for Starbuck's coffee or ice cream, even when identical products are available at lower prices.

Short-Run Price and Output

The monopolistically competitive firm's **production decision** is similar to that of a monopolist. Both types of firms confront downward-sloping demand and marginal

FIGURE 26.1
Equilibrium in Monopolistic Competition

(*a*) Short run In the short run, a monopolistically competitive firm equates marginal revenue and marginal cost (point *K*). In this case, the firm sells the resulting output at a price (point *F*) above marginal cost. Total profits are represented by the shaded rectangle.

(*b*) Long run In the long run, more firms enter the industry. As they do so, the demand curve facing each firm *shifts* to the left, as all market shares decline. Firms still equate MR and MC. Ultimately, however, the demand curve will be tangent to the ATC curve (point *G*), at which point price equals average total cost and no economic profits exist.

566 MARKET STRUCTURE

production decision: The selection of the short-run rate of output (with existing plant and equipment).

revenue curves. To maximize profits, both seek the rate of output at which marginal revenue equals marginal cost. This short-run profit-maximizing outcome is illustrated by point K in Figure 26.1a. That MC = MR intersection establishes q_a as the profit-maximizing rate of output. The demand curve indicates (point F) that q_a of output can be sold at the price of p_a. Hence q_a, p_a illustrates the short-run equilibrium of the monopolistically competitive firm.

Entry and Exit

economic profit: The difference between total revenues and total economic costs.

Figure 26.1a indicates that this monopolistically competitive firm is earning an **economic profit:** Price (p_a) exceeds average total cost (c_a) at the short-run rate of output. These profits are of course a welcome discovery for the firm. They also portend increased competition, however.

If firms in monopolistic competition are earning an economic profit, other firms will flock to the industry. Remember that *entry barriers are low so that new entrants can't be kept out of the market.* If they get wind of the short-run profits depicted in Figure 26.1a, they'll come running.

As new firms enter the industry, supply increases and prices will be pushed down the market demand curve, just as in competitive markets. Figure 26.2a illustrates these market changes. The impact of entry on the firms already in the market will be different than it was in competitive markets, however. As new firms enter a monopolistically competitive industry, existing firms will lose customers. This is illustrated by the leftward shift of the demand curve facing each firm, as in Figure 26.2b. Accordingly, we conclude that *when firms enter a monopolistically competitive industry,*

- *The market supply curve shifts to the right* (Figure 26.2a).
- *The demand curves facing individual firms shift to the left* (Figure 26.2b).

IN THE NEWS

Computers: They're No Commodity

Despite all the talk of the commoditization of the personal computer industry, a new survey of business users suggests that PC buyers pay attention to the brand name on the front of the machine.

McKinsey & Co. and Intelliquest Inc., an Austin, Tex., research firm, asked 300 computer buyers, "What is the incremental dollar value you would be willing to pay over the average computer brand?" At the top: International Business Machines Corp., Compaq Computer Corp., Apple Computer Inc. and Digital Equipment Corp. Lower-tier vendors like Zeos International Ltd. and Packard-Bell Electronics Inc. actually produced negative numbers, meaning that consumers will buy those brands only if they're discounted.

The results also show that a computer's brand name ranks second, behind performance, in the list of what's most important when considering the purchase of a PC. Price—the subject of so much recent attention—ranks fifth.

Analysts say this means more trouble for the industry's smaller players. With price a less important factor, the battle will increasingly focus on image and on what people at Intelliquest call "brand equity."

—Kyle Pope

What They'll Pay

Brands for which PC buyers say they'll pay a premium, and brands they say they'll only buy at a discount.

Premium	
IBM	$295
Compaq	232
Apple	195
Digital	129
AST Computer	107
Dell	92
Hewlett-Packard	76

Discount	
Zeos	−$15
NEC	−44
Everex	−47
Packard Bell	−69

Source: *The Wall Street Journal,* October 15, 1993. Reprinted by permission of *The Wall Street Journal.* © Dow, Jones & Company, Inc. All rights reserved worldwide. www.wsj.com

Analysis: Brand loyalty enables a company to raise its price without losing all its customers. Monopolistically competitive firms can charge different prices for essentially identical products.

FIGURE 26.2
Market vs. Firm Effects of Entry

Barriers to entry are low in monopolistic competition. Hence, new firms will enter if economic profits are available.

(a) The Market The entry of new firms will shift the *market* supply curve to the right, as in part *a*. This pushes the average price down the *market* demand curve.

(b) The Firm The entry of new firms also affects the demand curve facing the typical firm. The *firm's* demand curve shifts to the left and becomes more elastic because more close substitutes (other firms) are available.

As the demand curve it faces shifts leftward, the monopolistically competitive firm will have to make a new production decision. It need not charge the same price as its rivals, however, or coordinate its output with theirs. Each monopolistically competitive firm has some independent power over its (shrinking numbers of) captive customers.

Although each firm has some control over its own pricing decisions, continued leftward shifts of its demand curve will ultimately eliminate economic profits.

No Long-Run Profits

Long-run Equilibrium. Notice in Figure 26.1*b* where the firm eventually ends up. In long-run equilibrium, marginal cost is again equal to marginal revenue. At that rate of output (q_g), however, there are no economic profits. At that output, price (p_g) is exactly equal to average total cost. The profit-maximizing equilibrium (point G) occurs where the demand curve is tangent to the ATC curve. If the demand curve shifted any farther left, price would always be less than ATC and the firm would incur losses. If the demand curve were positioned farther to the right, price would exceed ATC at some rates of output. When the demand curve is *tangent* to the ATC curve, the firm's best possible outcome is to breakeven. At point G in Figure 26.1*b*, price equals ATC and economic profit is zero.

Will a monopolistically competitive firm end up at point G? As long as other firms can enter the industry, the disappearance of economic profits is inevitable. Firms will enter as long as the demand (price) line lies above ATC at some point. Firms will exit when the demand facing the firm lies to the left and below the ATC curve. Entry and exit cease when the firm's demand curve is *tangent* to the ATC curve. Once entry and exit cease, the long-run equilibrium has been established. ***In the long run, there are no economic profits in monopolistic competition.***

Inefficiency

The zero-profit equilibrium of firms in monopolistic competition, as illustrated in Figure 26.1*b*, differs from the perfectly competitive equilibrium. In the long run, a competitive industry produces at the *lowest* point on the ATC curve and thus maximizes efficiency. In monopolistic competition, however, the demand curve facing each firm slopes downward. Hence, it can't be tangent to the ATC curve at its lowest point (the bottom of the U), as in perfect competition. Instead, the demand curve of a monopolistically competitive firm must touch the ATC curve on the *left* side of the U. Note in Figure 26.1*b* how point *G* lies above and to the left of the bottom of the ATC curve. This long-run equilibrium occurs at an output rate that is less than the minimum-cost rate of production. In long-run equilibrium, the monopolistically competitive industry isn't producing at minimum average cost. As a consequence, ***monopolistic competition tends to be less efficient in the long run than a perfectly competitive industry.***

Excess Capacity. One symptom of the inefficiencies associated with monopolistic competition is industrywide excess capacity. Each firm tries to gain market share by building more outlets and advertising heavily. In equilibrium, however, the typical firm is producing at a rate of output that's less than its minimum-ATC output rate. This implies that the *same* level of *industry* output could be produced at lower cost with fewer firms. If that happened, the resources used to develop that excess capacity could be used for more desired purposes.

Flawed Price Signals. The misallocation of resources that occurs in monopolistic competition is a by-product of the flawed price signal that is transmitted in imperfectly competitive markets. Because the demand curve facing a firm in monopolistic competition slopes downward, such a firm will violate the principle of **marginal cost pricing.** Specifically, it will always price its output above the level of marginal costs, just like firms in an oligopoly or monopoly. Notice in Figure 26.1 that price lies above marginal cost in both the short- and long-run equilibrium. As a consequence, price always exceeds the opportunity cost. Consumers respond to these flawed signals by demanding fewer goods from monopolistically competitive industries than they would otherwise. We end up with the wrong (suboptimal) mix of output and misallocated resources.

Thus, ***monopolistic competition results in both production inefficiency (above-minimum average cost) and allocative inefficiency (wrong mix of output).*** This contrasts with the model of perfect competition, which delivers both minimum average total cost and efficient (MC-based) price signals.

> **marginal cost pricing:** The offer (supply) of goods at prices equal to their marginal cost.

THE ECONOMY TOMORROW

No Cease-Fire in Advertising Wars

Models of oligopoly and monopolistic competition show how industry structure affects market behavior. Of particular interest is the way different kinds of firms "compete" for sales and profits. ***In truly (perfectly) competitive industries, firms compete on the basis of price.*** Competitive firms win by achieving greater efficiency and offering their products at the lowest possible price.

Firms in imperfectly competitive markets don't "compete" in the same way. In oligopolies, the kink commonly found in the demand curve facing each firm inhibits price reductions. In monopolistic competition, there's also a reluctance to engage in price competition. Because each firm has its own captive market—consumers who prefer its particular brand over competing brands—price reductions by one firm won't induce many consumers to switch brands. Thus, price reductions aren't a very effective way to increase sales or market share in monopolistic competition.

If imperfectly competitive firms don't compete on the basis of price, do they really compete at all? The answer is evident to anyone who listens to the radio, watches television, reads magazines or newspapers, or drives on the highway: ***Imperfectly competitive firms engage in nonprice competition.***

IN THE NEWS

The Cola Wars: It's Not All Taste

American consumers gulp nearly 40 million soft drinks per day. The Coca-Cola Company produces about 40 percent of those soft drinks, while Pepsi-Cola produces about 30 percent of the market supply. With nearly 70 percent of the market between them, Pepsi and Coke wage fierce battles for market share.

The major weapon in these "cola wars" is advertising. Coke spends over $900 million a year to convince consumers that its products are superior. Pepsi spends almost as much to win the hearts and taste buds of American consumers. The advertisements not only tout the superior taste of their respective products but also try to create a particular image for each cola.

The advertising apparently works. Half of all soft drink consumers profess loyalty to either Coke or Pepsi. In their view, there's only one "real" cola, and that's the one they'll buy every time. Few of these loyalists can be persuaded to switch cola brands, even when offered lower prices for the "other" cola.

Ironically, few people can identify their favorite cola in blind taste tests. Seventy percent of the people who swore loyalty to either Coke or Pepsi picked the wrong cola in a taste test.

The moral of the story? That in imperfectly competitive markets, product *image* and *perceptions* may be as important as product quality and price in winning market shares.

Analysis: Advertising is intended to create brand loyalty. Loyal consumers are likely to buy the same brand all the time, even if competitors offer nearly identical products.

The most prominent form of *nonprice competition* is advertising. An imperfectly competitive firm typically uses advertising to enhance its own product's image, thereby increasing the size of its captive market (consumers who identify with a particular brand). The Coca-Cola Company hires rock stars to create the image that Coke is superior to other soft drinks (see News), thereby creating brand loyalty. In 2000, oligopolies and monopolistic competitive firms spent over $300 *billion* on advertising for such purposes. Procter & Gamble alone spent $2.4 billion (see Table 26.2). P&G hopes that these expenditures shift the demand for its products (e.g., Ivory Soap, Pampers, Jif peanut butter, Crest, Tide) to the right, while perhaps making it less price-elastic as well. America Online, Yahoo!, and Amazon.com spent hundred of millions of dollars in the 1990s to establish brand loyalty in crowded dot.com markets. By contrast, perfectly competitive firms have no incentive to advertise because they can individually sell their entire output at the current market price.

Company	Ad Spending in 2000
General Motors	$3.9 billion
Philip Morris	2.6 billion
Procter & Gamble	2.4 billion
Ford Motor	2.3 billion
Pfizer	2.3 billion
PepsiCo	2.1 billion
Daimler-Chrysler	2.0 billion
AOL Time Warner	1.8 billion
Disney	1.8 billion
Verizon Communications	1.6 billion

Source: *Advertising Age*, September 28, 2001. Reprinted by permission. www.adage.com

TABLE 26.2
Top 10 Advertisers
Firms with market power attempt to preserve and extend that power through advertising. A successful advertising campaign alters the demand curve facing the firm, thus increasing potential profits. Shown here are the advertising outlays of the biggest advertisers in 2000.

WORLD VIEW

The Best Global Brands

A belief in the power of brands and brand management has spread far beyond the traditional consumer-goods marketers who invented the discipline. For companies in almost every industry, brands are important in a way they never were before. Why? For one thing, customers for everything from soda pop to software now have a staggering number of choices. And the Net can bring the full array to any computer screen with a click of the mouse. Without trusted brand names as touchstones, shopping for almost anything would be overwhelming. Meanwhile, in a global economy, corporations must reach customers in markets far from their home base. A strong brand acts as an ambassador when companies enter new markets or offer new products.

That's why companies that once measured their worth strictly in terms of tangibles such as factories, inventory, and cash have realized that a vibrant brand, with its implicit promise of quality, is an equally important asset. A brand has the power to command a premium price among customers and a premium stock price among investors. It can boost earnings and cushion cyclical downturns—and now, a brand's value can be measured.

The World's 10 Most Valuable Brands

Rank	Brand	2001 Brand Value ($billions)
1	Coca-Cola	68.9
2	Microsoft	65.1
3	IBM	52.8
4	GE	42.4
5	Nokia	35.0
6	Intel	34.7
7	Disney	32.6
8	Ford	30.1
9	McDonald's	25.3
10	AT&T	22.8

Data: Interbrand, Citigroup.
Source: *BusinessWeek*, August 6, 2001. © 2001 The McGraw Hill Companies, Inc. Reprinted with permission. www.businessweek.com

Analysis: Brand names are valuable economic assets and assist a firm in maintaining a base of loyal customers. These brands have worldwide recognition as a result of heavy advertising.

Forecasts of advertising spending can be found at www.myersreport.com.

A company that runs a successful advertising campaign can create enormous *goodwill* value. That value is reflected in stronger brand loyalty—as expressed in greater demand and smaller price elasticity. Often a successful brand image can be used to sell related products as well. According to the World View, the most valuable brand name in the world is Coca-Cola, whose worldwide name recognition is worth nearly $70 *billion*.

Advertising isn't the only form of nonprice competition. Before the airline industry was deregulated (1978), individual airlines were compelled to charge the same price for any given trip; hence, price competition was prohibited. But airlines did compete—not only by advertising, but also by offering "special" meals, movies, more frequent or convenient departures, and faster ticketing and baggage services.

Is there anything wrong with nonprice competition? Surely airline passengers enjoyed their "special" meals, "extra" services, and "more convenient" departure times. But these services weren't free. As always, there were opportunity costs. From an air traveler's perspective, the "special" services stimulated by nonprice competition substituted for cheaper fares. With more price competition, customers could have chosen travel more cheaply *or* in greater comfort. From society's perspective, the resources used in advertising and other forms of nonprice competition could be used instead to produce larger quantities of desired goods and services (including airplane trips). Unless consumers are given the chance to *choose* between "more" service and lower prices, there's a presumption that nonprice competition leads to an undesirable use of our scarce resources. Notice in the following News how much marketing costs add to the price of breakfast cereal. As a result of such behavior, consumers end up with more advertis-

IN THE NEWS

A Closer Look at Prices

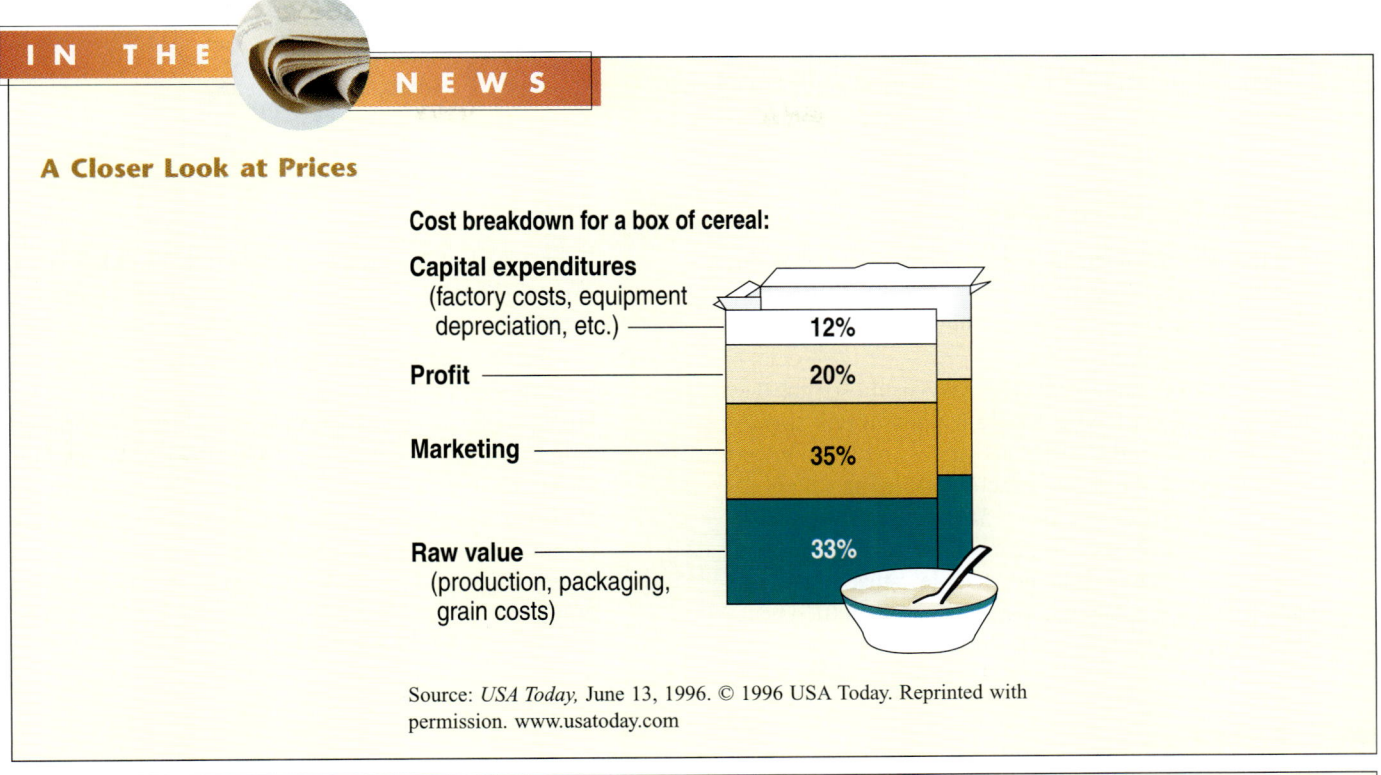

Cost breakdown for a box of cereal:
- **Capital expenditures** (factory costs, equipment depreciation, etc.) — 12%
- **Profit** — 20%
- **Marketing** — 35%
- **Raw value** (production, packaging, grain costs) — 33%

Source: *USA Today,* June 13, 1996. © 1996 USA Today. Reprinted with permission. www.usatoday.com

Analysis: Advertising uses scarce resources that could be used to produce other goods and services. Marketing also pushes consumer prices up.

---

ing but less cereal than they would otherwise. They could, of course, save money by buying store brand or generic cereals. But they've never seen athletes or cartoon characters endorse such products. So consumers pay the higher price for branded cereals.

Models of imperfect competition imply that advertising wars between powerful corporations won't end anytime soon. As long as markets have the *structure* of oligopoly or monopolistic competition, we expect the *behavior* of nonprice competition. Advertising jingles will be as pervasive in the economy tomorrow as they are today.

SUMMARY

- There are many (rather than few) firms in monopolistic competition. The concentration ratio in such industries tends to be low (20–40 percent).
- Each monopolistically competitive firm enjoys some brand loyalty. This brand loyalty, together with its relatively small market share, gives each firm a high degree of independence in price and output decisions.
- The amount of market share and power a monopolistically competitive firm possesses depends on how successfully it differentiates its product from similar products. Accordingly, monopolistically competitive firms tend to devote more resources to advertising.
- Low entry barriers permit new firms to enter a monopolistically competitive industry whenever economic profits exist. Such entry eliminates long-run economic profit and reduces (shifts leftward) the demand for the output of existing firms.
- Monopolistic competition results in resource misallocations (due to flawed price signals) and inefficiency (above-minimum average cost).
- Monopolistic competition encourages nonprice competition instead of price competition. Because the resources used in nonprice competition (advertising, packaging, service, etc.) may have more desirable uses, these industry structures lead to resource misallocation.

Key Terms

monopolistic competition
concentration ratio
market power

barriers to entry
product differentiation
production decision

economic profit
marginal cost pricing

Questions for Discussion

1. If Starbucks doubled its coffee prices, would anyone buy its coffee? Why or why not?
2. What are the entry barriers to the pizza business? Are they relatively high or low?
3. If auto firms eliminated their advertising, could they reduce car prices? What would happen to unit sales?
4. If one gas station reduces its prices, must other gas stations match the price reduction? Why or why not?
5. The News article on page 569 suggests that most consumers can't identify their favorite cola in blind taste tests. Why then do people stick with one brand? What accounts for brand loyalty in bottled water (News, p. 564)?
6. What kinds of resources are used in a TV advertising campaign? How else might those resources be used?
7. Why is the mix of output produced in competitive markets more desirable than that in monopolistically competitive markets?
8. How would our consumption of cereal change if cereal manufacturers stopped advertising? Would we be better or worse off?
9. Why are people willing to pay more for Dreyer's ice cream when it has a Starbucks brand on it?
10. According to the World View on page 570, what gives brand names their value?

Web Activities

1. Find three examples of monopolistic competition (four-firm concentration ratios of 20 to 40 percent) at www.census.gov/epcd/www/concentration.html. Which characteristics of monopolistic competition described in the text are true for each example?
2. Log on to www.knowledgecrossing.com/branding.html, and read this company's views on why product branding is economically important to a company. What are the steps it recommends for product branding? How does branding help maintain market share for a company?
3. Go to www.starbucks.com. List at least two ways Starbucks is trying to increase brand loyalty to its product. Explain how these activities help Starbucks maintain its market share.

THE ACCOMPANYING STUDENT PROBLEM SET CONTAINS NUMERICAL AND GRAPHING PROBLEMS FOR THIS CHAPTER

PART 10

Regulatory Issues

Microeconomic theory provides insights into how prices and product flows are determined in unregulated markets. Sometimes those market outcomes are not optimal and the government intervenes to improve them. In this section we examine government regulation of natural monopolies (Chapter 27), environmental protection (Chapter 28), and farm output and prices (Chapter 29). The goal is to determine whether and how government regulation might improve market outcomes or worsen them.

CHAPTER 27

(De)Regulation of Business

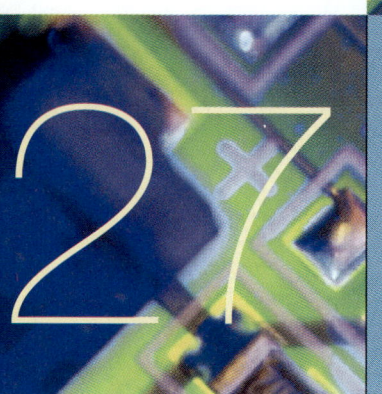

The lights went out in California in 2001—not just once but repeatedly. Offices went dark, air conditioners shut down, assembly lines stopped, and TV screens went blank. The state governor blamed power-company "profiteers" for the rolling blackouts. He charged the companies with curtailing power supplies and hiking prices. He wanted *more* regulation of the power industry. Industry representatives responded that government regulation was itself responsible for throwing California into a new Dark Age. *Less* regulation, not more, would keep the lights on, they claimed.

The battle over government regulation of the power industry quickly spread to other states. Some states that were deregulating power companies suspended the process. Other states also put (de)regulation plans on hold until they could better assess what went wrong in California.

Everyone agrees that markets sometime fail—that unregulated markets may produce the wrong mix of output, undesirable methods of production, or an unfair distribution of income. But government intervention can fail as well. Hence, we need to ask,

- When is government regulation necessary?
- What form should that regulation take?
- When is it appropriate to deregulate an industry?

In answering these questions we draw on economic principles as well as recent experience. This will permit us to contrast the theory of (de)regulation with reality.

ANTITRUST VS. REGULATION

A perfectly competitive market provides a model for economic efficiency. As we first observed in Chapter 3, the market mechanism can answer the basic economic questions of WHAT to produce, HOW to produce it, and FOR WHOM. Under ideal conditions, the market's answers may also be optimal—that is, they may represent the best possible mix of output. To achieve this **laissez-faire** ideal, all producers must be perfect competitors; people must have full information about tastes, costs and prices; all costs and benefits must be reflected in market prices; and pervasive economies of scale must be absent.

In reality, these conditions are rarely if ever fully attained. Markets may be dominated by large and powerful producers. In wielding their power, these producers may restrict output, raise prices, stifle competition, and inhibit innovation.

In other words, market power may cause **market failure,** leaving us with suboptimal market outcomes.

As we observed in Chapter 25, the government has two options for intervention where market power prevails. It may focus on the *structure* of an industry or on its *behavior.* **Antitrust** laws cover both options: They prohibit mergers and acquisitions that reduce potential competition (structures) and forbid market practices (behavior) that are anticompetitive.

Government **regulation** has a different focus. Instead of worrying about industry structure, regulation focuses almost exclusively on *behavior.* In general, regulation seeks to change market outcomes directly, by imposing specific limitations on price, output, or investment decisions.

NATURAL MONOPOLY

When a natural monopoly exists, the choice between structural remedies and behavioral remedies is simplified. A **natural monopoly** is a *desirable* market structure, because it generates pervasive economies of scale. Because of these scale economies, a natural monopoly can produce the products consumers want at the lowest possible price. A single cable company is more efficient than a horde of cable firms developing a maze of cable networks. The same is true of local telephone service and many utilities. In all of these cases, a single company can deliver products at lower cost than a bunch of smaller firms. Dismantling such a natural monopoly would destroy that cost advantage. Hence, *regulation,* not antitrust, is the more sensible intervention.

Do we need to regulate natural monopolies? Even though a natural monopoly might enjoy economies of scale, it might not pass those savings along to consumers. In that case, the economies of scale don't do consumers any good, and the government might have to regulate the firm's behavior.

To determine whether regulation is desirable, we first have to determine how an *unregulated* natural monopoly will behave.

Figure 27.1 illustrates the unique characteristics of a natural monopoly. *The distinctive characteristic of a natural monopoly is its downward-sloping average total cost (ATC) curve.* Because unit costs keep falling as the rate of production increases, a single large firm can underprice any smaller firm. Ultimately, it can produce all the market supply at the lowest attainable cost. In an unregulated market, such a firm will "naturally" come to dominate the industry.

The force that pulls down the ATC curve in a natural monopoly is low marginal cost. Notice in Figure 27.1 that *the marginal cost (MC) curve lies below the ATC curve at all rates of output for a natural monopoly.* The ATC curve never rises into its conventional U shape because marginal costs never exceed average costs.

Subway systems, local telephone and utility companies, and cable TV operators are examples of natural monopoly. In all these cases, huge fixed costs are required to establish production facilities (such as subway tunnels and transmission cables). The marginal cost of producing another rider, call, or program is negligible, however. As a result, average total costs start high but continuously decline until capacity is reached.

The declining costs of a natural monopoly are of potential benefit to society. The **economies of scale** offered by a natural monopoly imply that no other market structure can supply the good as cheaply. Hence, *natural monopoly is a desirable market structure.* A competitive market structure—with many smaller firms—would have higher average cost.

Although the structure of a natural monopoly may be beneficial, its behavior may leave something to be desired. Natural monopolists have the same profit-maximizing motivations as other producers. Moreover, they have the monopoly power to achieve and maintain economic profits. Hence, there's no guarantee that consumers will reap

Behavioral Focus

laissez faire: The doctrine of "leave it alone," or nonintervention by government in the market mechanism.

market failure: An imperfection in the market mechanism that prevents optimal outcomes.

antitrust: Government intervention to alter market structure or prevent abuse of market power.

regulation: Government intervention to alter the behavior of firms, for example, in pricing, output, or advertising.

natural monopoly: An industry in which one firm can achieve economies of scale over the entire range of market supply.

Declining ATC Curve

economies of scale: Reductions in minimum average costs that come about through increases in the size (scale) of plant and equipment.

Unregulated Behavior

FIGURE 27.1
Natural Monopoly: Price Regulation

A natural monopoly confronts a downward-sloping ATC curve; MC is always less than ATC. If unregulated, a natural monopoly will produce q_A and charge p_A, as determined by the intersection of the marginal cost and marginal revenue curves (point A).

Regulation designed to achieve efficient prices will seek point B, where $p = MC$. Still lower average costs (production efficiency) are attainable at higher rates of output, however. On the other hand, a zero-profit, zero-subsidy outcome exists only at point C.

Which price-output combination should be sought?

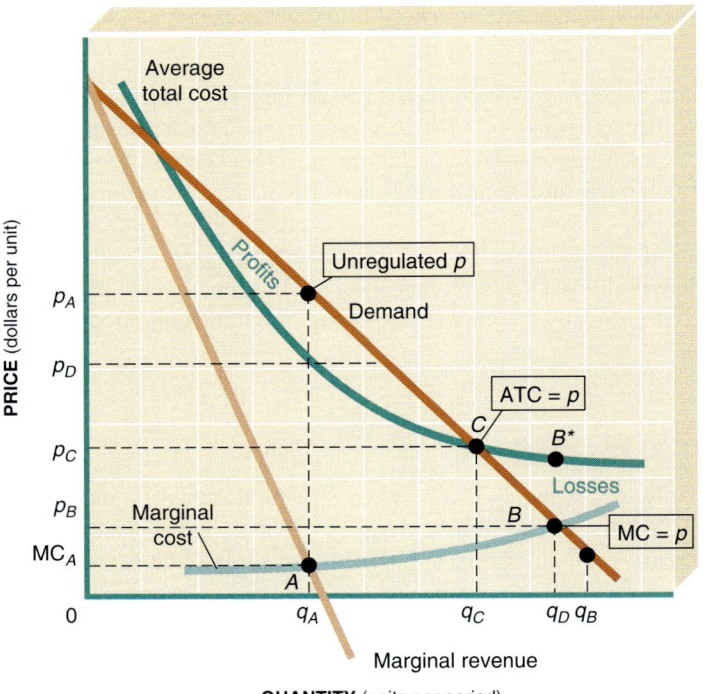

marginal cost pricing: The offer (supply) of goods at prices equal to their marginal cost.

opportunity cost: The most desired goods or services that are forgone in order to obtain something else.

economic profit: The difference between total revenues and total economic costs.

the benefits of a natural monopoly. Critics charge that the monopolist tends to keep most of the benefits. This has been a recurrent criticism of cable TV operators: Consumers have complained about high prices, poor service, and a lack of programming choices from local cable monopolies.

Figure 27.1 illustrates the unregulated behavior of a natural monopolist. Like all other producers, the natural monopolist will maximize profits by producing at that rate of output where marginal revenue equals marginal cost. Point A in Figure 27.1 indicates that an unregulated monopoly will end up producing the quantity q_A and charging the price p_A.

The natural monopolist's preferred outcome isn't the most desirable one for society. This price-output combination violates the competitive principle of **marginal cost pricing**. The monopoly price p_A greatly exceeds the marginal cost of producing q_A of output, as represented by MC_A in Figure 27.1. As a result of this gap, consumers aren't getting accurate information about the **opportunity cost** of this product. This flawed price signal is the cause of market failure. We end up consuming less of this product (and more of other goods) than we would if charged its true opportunity cost. A suboptimal mix of output results.

The natural monopolist's profit-maximizing output (q_A) also fails to minimize average total cost. In a competitive industry, ATC is driven down to its minimum by relentless competition. In this case, however, reductions in ATC cease when the monopolist achieves the profit-maximizing rate of output (q_A). Were output to increase further, average total costs would fall.

Finally, notice that the higher price (p_A) associated with the monopolist's preferred output (q_A) ensures a fat profit. The **economic profit** may violate our visions of equity. In 2001, millions of Californians were convinced that this kind of "profiteering" was the root of their electricity woes.

REGULATORY OPTIONS

The suboptimal outcomes likely to emerge from a free-swinging natural monopoly send up a loud cry for government intervention. The market alone can't overcome the natural advantage of pervasive economies of scale. But the government could compel different outcomes. The question is, Which outcomes do we want? And how will we get them?

For starters, we might consider price regulation. The natural monopolist's preferred price (p_A) is, after all, a basic cause of market failure. By regulating the firm, the government can compel a lower price . The California legislature did this in 1996 when it set a maximum retail price for electricity.

As is apparent from Figure 27.1 that there are lots of choices in setting a regulated price. We start with the conviction that the unregulated price p_A is too high. But where on the demand curve below p_A do we want to be?

Price Regulation

Price Efficiency. One possibility is to set the price at a level consistent with opportunity costs. As we saw earlier, a monopolist's unregulated price sends out a flawed price signal. By charging a price in excess of marginal cost, the monopolist causes a suboptimal allocation of resources. We could improve market outcomes, therefore, by compelling the monopolist to set the price equal to marginal cost. Such an efficient price would lead us to point B in Figure 27.1, where the demand curve and the marginal cost curve intersect. At that price (p_B), consumers would get optimal use of the good or service produced.

Subsidy. Although the price p_B will ensure allocative efficiency, it will also bankrupt the producer. In a natural monopoly, MC is always less than ATC. Hence, *marginal cost pricing by a natural monopolist implies a loss on every unit of output produced.* In this case, the loss per unit is equal to $B^* - B$. If confronted with the price p_B, the firm will ultimately shut down and exit from the market. This was one of the many problems that plagued California. Unable to charge a price high enough to cover their costs, some of the state's utility companies were forced into bankruptcy.

If we want to require efficient pricing, we must provide a subsidy to the natural monopoly. In Figure 27.1 the amount of the subsidy would have to equal the anticipated loss at q_B, that is, the quantity q_B multiplied by the per-unit loss ($B^* - B$). Such subsidies are provided to subway systems. With subsidies, local subway systems can charge fees below *average* cost and closer to *marginal* cost. These subsidized fares increase ridership, thus ensuring greater use of very expensive transportation systems.

Despite the advantages of this subsidized pricing strategy, taxpayers always complain about the cost of such subsidies. Taxpayers are particularly loath to provide them for private companies. Hence, political considerations typically preclude efficient (marginal cost) pricing, despite the economic benefits of this regulatory strategy.

Production Efficiency. Even if it were possible to impose marginal cost pricing, we still wouldn't achieve production efficiency. Production efficiency is attained at the lowest possible average total cost. At q_B we're producing a lot of output but still have some unused capacity. Since ATC falls continuously, we could achieve still lower average costs if we increased output beyond q_B. In a natural monopoly, production efficiency is achieved at capacity production, where ATC is at a minimum.

Increasing output beyond q_B raises the same problems we encountered at that rate of output. At production rates in excess of q_B, ATC is always higher than price. Even MC is higher than price to the right of point B. Thus, *no regulated price can induce the monopolist to achieve minimum average cost. A subsidy would be required to offset the market losses.*

Instead of price regulation, we could try profit regulation. If we choose not to subsidize a natural monopolist, we must permit it to charge a price high enough to cover all its costs, including a normal profit. We can achieve the result by mandating a price equal to average total cost. In Figure 27.1 this regulatory objective is achieved at point C. In this case, the rate of output is q_C and the regulated price is p_C.

Profit Regulation

Profit regulation looks appealing for two reasons. First, it eliminates the need to subsidize the monopolist. Second, it allows us to focus on profits only, thus removing the need to develop demand and cost curves. In theory, all we have to do is check the firm's annual profit-and-loss statement to confirm that it's earning a normal (average) profit. If its profits are too high, we can force the firm to reduce its price; if profits are too low, we may permit a price increase.

Bloated Costs. In practice, profit regulation can lead to bloated costs and dynamic inefficiency. *If a firm is permitted a specific profit rate (or rate of return), it has no incentive to limit costs.* On the contrary, higher costs imply higher profits. If permitted to charge 10 percent over unit costs, a monopolist may be better off with average costs of $6 rather than only $5. The higher costs translate into 60 cents of profit per unit rather than only 50 cents. Hence, there's an incentive to "pad costs." If those costs actually represent improvements in wages and salaries, fringe benefits, or the work environment, then cost increases are doubly attractive to the firm and its employees. Cost efficiency is as welcome as the plague under such circumstances.

Profit regulation can also motivate a firm to inflate its costs by paying above-market prices for products purchased from an unregulated subsidiary. This was the strategy AT&T used to increase its *regulated* cost base while ringing up high profits at Western Electric, its *unregulated* subsidiary (see Chapter 24). The FCC accused Nynex (the "Baby Bell" that provides phone service in New York and New England) of using the same strategy to pad its profits (see News).

Output Regulation

Given the difficulties in regulating prices and profits, regulators may choose to regulate output instead. The natural monopolist's preferred output rate is q_A, as illustrated in Figure 27.2. We could compel this monopolist to provide a minimum level of service in excess of q_A. This regulated minimum is designated q_D in Figure 27.2. At q_D consumers get the benefit not only of more output but also of a lower price (p_D). At q_D total monopoly profit must also be less than at q_A, since q_A was the profit-maximizing rate of output.

It appears, then, that compelling any rate of output in excess of q_A can only benefit consumers. Moreover, output regulation is an easy rule to enforce.

Quality Deterioration. Unfortunately, minimum-service regulation can also cause problems. If forced to produce at the rate of q_D, the monopolist may seek to increase profits by cutting cost corners. This can be accomplished by deferring plant and equipment maintenance, reducing quality control, or otherwise lowering the quality of ser-

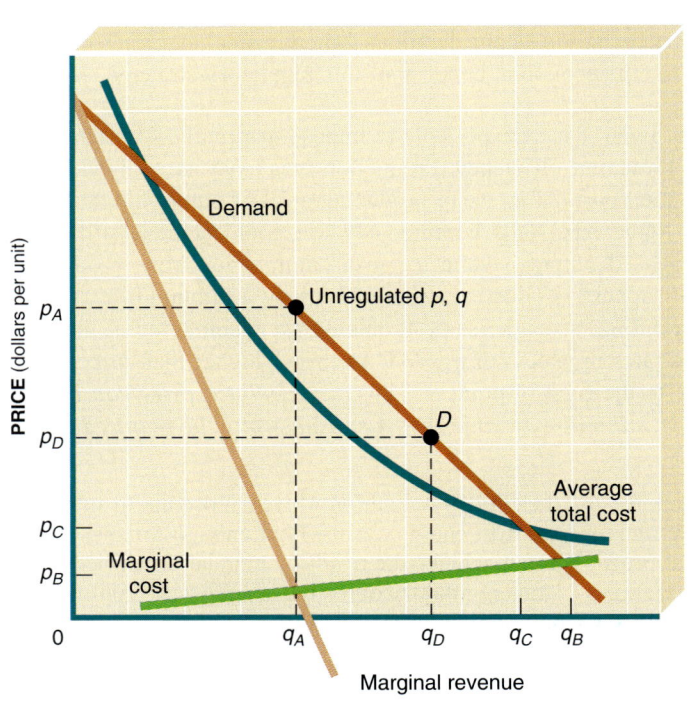

FIGURE 27.2
Minimum Service Regulation

Regulation may seek to ensure some minimal level of service. In this case, the required rate of output is arbitrarily set at q_D. Consumers are willing to pay p_D per unit for that output.

Regulated output q_D is preferable to the unregulated outcome (q_A, p_A) but may induce a decline in quality. Cost cutting is the only way to increase profits when the rate of output is fixed and price is on the demand curve.

IN THE NEWS

FCC: Nynex Padded Millions in Profits
Commission Urges Refunds, $1.4 Million Fine

Regional phone company Nynex Corp. overcharged its customers by tens of millions of dollars over a four-year period so that the company could pad its profits illegally, the Federal Communications Commission said yesterday.

The commission proposed refunds as well as a $1.4 million fine that would be the largest it has ever imposed.

Nynex, which provides phone service in New York and New England, denied wrongdoing, saying that the commission was applying newly passed rules retroactively. "There was no intent to overcharge," said Nynex Chairman William C. Ferguson. Under FCC rules, Nynex has 30 days in which to respond to the charges and seek dismissal of them.

The commission found that Nynex violated complex rules of accounting that are designed to keep telephone companies from subsidizing unregulated subsidiaries with money that they collect from customers of their monopoly phone service. This resulted, the FCC said, in a transfer of profits to a subsidiary whose bottom line is not regulated, boosting the overall profits of Nynex.

—John Burgess

Source: *Washington Post*, February 8, 1990. © 1990 The Washington Post. Reprinted with permission. www.washingtonpost.com

Source: Environmental Protection Agency (www.epa.gov), American Lung Association (www.lungusa.org).

Analysis: Profit regulation creates incentives for a regulated firm to inflate ("pad") its costs. One way to accomplish that is to pay high prices for products purchased from unregulated subsidiaries.

---

vice. *Regulation of the quantity produced may induce a decline in quality.* Since a monopolist has no direct competition, consumers pretty much have to accept whatever quality the monopolist offers. This structural reality may explain why consumers complain so much about the services of local cable monopolies.

In addition to encouraging quality deterioration, output regulation at q_D also violates the principle of marginal cost pricing. Because an economic profit exists at q_D, equity goals may be jeopardized as well. Hence, minimum service (output) regulation isn't a panacea for the regulatory dilemma. In fact, there is no panacea: *Goal conflicts are inescapable, and any regulatory rule may induce undesired producer responses.*

Imperfect Answers

The call for public regulation of natural monopolies is based on the recognition that the profit motive doesn't generate optimal outcomes in any monopoly environment. If unregulated, a natural monopolist will charge too much and produce too little. The regulatory remedy for these market failures isn't evident, however. Regulators can compel efficient prices or least-cost production only by offering a subsidy. Profit regulation is likely to induce cost-inflating responses. Output regulation is an incentive for quality deterioration. No matter which way we turn, regulatory problems result.

There's not much hope for transforming unregulated market failure into perfect regulated outcomes. In reality, regulators must choose a strategy that balances competing objectives (e.g., price efficiency and equity). A realistic goal for regulation is to *improve* market outcomes, not to *perfect* them. In the real world, **the choice isn't between imperfect markets and flawless government intervention but rather between imperfect markets and imperfect intervention.**

The argument for *deregulation* rests on the observation that government regulation sometimes worsens market outcomes. In some cases, **government failure** may be worse than market failure. Specifically, regulation may lead to price, cost, or production outcomes that are inferior to those of an unregulated market.

> **government failure:** Government intervention that fails to improve economic outcomes.

THE COSTS OF REGULATION

Improving outcomes in a particular market isn't adequate proof of regulatory success. We also have to consider the *costs* incurred to change market outcomes.

Administrative Costs

The Center for the Study of American Business at Washington University tracks and analyzes regulation: csab.wustl.edu.

As we've observed, industry regulation entails various options and a host of trade-offs. Someone must sit down and assess these trade-offs. To make a sound decision, a regulatory administration must have access to lots of information. At a minimum, the regulator must have some clue as to the actual shape and position of the demand and cost curves depicted in Figures 27.1 and 27.2. Crude illustrations won't suffice when decisions about the prices, output, or costs of a multibillion-dollar industry are being made. The regulatory commission needs volumes of details about actual costs and demand and a platoon of experts to collect and analyze the needed data. When Congress passed the 1992 Cable Act, for example, the Federal Communications Commission (FCC) had to develop and enforce new regulations of cable TV operators. To do this, the FCC asked Congress for $16 million to hire 240 more lawyers, accountants, engineers, and other staff (see News). All this labor represents a real cost to society,

---

IN THE NEWS

FCC Seeking More Money to Enforce New Cable Rules

In an effort to bring down cable TV prices, the Federal Communications Commission is proposing to raise them.

With a tidal wave of rate hearings, consumer complaints and other bureaucratic duties looming, the FCC wants to charge the nation's cable TV operators $16 million to carry out provisions of the new cable price law. Without the money, interim FCC Chairman James C. Quello warned yesterday, the agency won't have enough staff to enforce regulations projected to save cable subscribers as much as $1.5 billion a year.

"Either we get the people or we won't be able to implement" it, Quello said in an interview. "This is essential.". . .

Even if he gets the additional funds, Quello said he would be pressed to find work space for new employees. The FCC's downtown headquarters are already at capacity.

—Paul Farhi

Source: *Washington Post*, May 14, 1993. © 1993 The Washington Post. Reprinted with permission. www.washingtonpost.com

Analysis: Regulation entails the use of scarce resources to write and enforce industry rules. Regulated firms also incur real costs in complying with regulatory rules.

since the commission's lawyers, accountants, and economists could be employed elsewhere. The staff of the FCC is only the tip of a much larger bureaucratic iceberg. As Table 27.1 illustrates, 131,861 people are employed in regulatory agencies of the federal government. Thousands more have regulatory responsibilities in smaller agencies and the major executive departments. In addition to these federal workers, tens of thousands more people are employed by state and local regulatory agencies. All of these regulators are part of our limited labor resources. By using them to regulate private industry, we are forgoing their use in the production of desired goods and services. This is a significant economic cost.

The administrative costs of regulation focus on resources used in the public sector. By its very nature, however, regulation also changes resource use in the private sector. Regulated industries must expend resources to educate themselves about the regulations, to change their production behavior, and often to file reports with the regulatory authorities. The human and capital resources used for these purposes represent the *compliance* cost of regulation.

Compliance Costs

TABLE 27.1
Employment in Federal Regulatory Agencies

The human and capital resources the bureaucracy employs represent a real opportunity cost. The 131,861 people employed in 53 federal agencies—and tens of thousands more employed in state and local bureaucracies—could be producing other goods and services. These and other costs must be compared to the benefits of regulation.

Agency	Number of Employees	Agency	Number of Employees
Social Regulation		**Economic Regulation**	
Consumer Safety and Health		*General Business*	
Consumer Product Safety Commission	480	Patent and Trademark Office	7,449
Animal and Plant Health Inspection	6,900	Dept. of Justice Antitrust Division	809
Food Safety and Inspection Service	9,645	Federal Trade Commission	1,055
Food and Drug Administration	9,150	Library of Congress: Copyright Office	530
Coast Guard	17,868	Securities and Exchange Commission	3,038
Federal Aviation Administration	6,270	Subtotal—General Business	14,369
Federal Highway Administration	636	*Finance and Banking*	
Bureau of Alcohol, Tobacco, Firearms	4,745	Comptroller of the Currency	2,897
Subtotal—Consumer Safety and Health	62,067	Federal Deposit Insurance Corporation	5,173
		Federal Reserve Banks	3,050
Job Safety and Working Conditions		Subtotal—Finance and Banking	12,717
Employment Standards Administration	2,349	*Industry-Specific Regulation*	
Mine Safety and Health Administration	2,357	Commodity Futures Trading Commission	567
Occupational Safety and Health Adm.	2,386	Federal Communications Commission	1,967
Equal Employment Opportunity Com.	3,055	Federal Energy Regulatory Commission	1,200
National Labor Relations Board	2,002	Federal Maritime Commission	131
Subtotal—Job Safety and Working Conditions	13,101	Subtotal—Industry-Specific Regulation	3,865
Environment and Energy			
Army Corps of Engineers	1,400		
Fish and Wildlife Service	1,890	**Totals**	
Environmental Protection Agency	17,714	Social regulation	100,910
Nuclear Regulatory Commission	2,730	Economic regulation	30,951
Subtotal—Environment and Energy	25,742		
		Grand total	**131,861**

Source: Melinda Warren, Weidenbaum Center on the Economy, Government, and Public Policy, Washington University, 2001.

Efficiency Costs

Finally, we have to consider the potential costs of changes in output. Most regulation alters the mix of output, either directly or indirectly. Ideally, regulation will always improve the mix of output. But it's possible that bad decisions, incomplete information, or faulty implementation may actually *worsen* the mix of output. If this occurs, then the loss of utility associated with an inferior mix of output imposes a further cost on society, over and above administrative and compliance costs.

Efficiency costs may increase significantly over time. Over time, consumer tastes change, demand and marginal revenue curves shift, costs change, and new technologies emerge. Can regulatory commissions respond to these changes as fast as the market mechanism does? If not, even optimal regulations may soon become obsolete and counterproductive. Worse still, the regulatory process itself may impede new technology, new marketing approaches, or improved production processes. These losses may be the most important. As Robert Hahn of the American Enterprise Institute observed:

> The measurable costs of regulation pale against the distortions that sap the economy's dynamism. The public never sees the factories that weren't built, the new products that didn't appear, or the entrepreneurial idea that drowned in a cumbersome regulatory process.[1]

These kinds of dynamic efficiency losses are a drag on economic growth, limiting outward shifts of the production possibilities curve while perpetuating an increasingly undesired mix of output.

Balancing Benefits and Costs

The economic costs of regulation are a reminder of the "no free lunch" maxim. Although regulatory intervention may improve market outcomes, that intervention isn't without cost. The real resources used in the regulatory process could be used for other purposes. Hence, even if we could achieve perfect outcomes with enough regulation, the cost of achieving perfection might outweigh the benefits. ***Regulatory intervention must balance the anticipated improvements in market outcomes against the economic cost of regulation.*** In principle, the marginal benefit of regulation must exceed its marginal cost. If this isn't the case, then additional regulation isn't desirable, even if it would improve short-run market outcomes.

DEREGULATION IN PRACTICE

The push to *de*regulate was prompted by two concerns. The first concern focused on the dynamic inefficiencies that regulation imposes. It appeared that these inefficiencies had accumulated over time, rendering regulated industries less productive than desired. The other push for deregulation came from advancing technology, which destroyed the basis for natural monopoly in some industries. A brief review of the resulting deregulation illustrates the impact of these forces.

Railroads

The railroad industry was the federal government's first broad regulatory target. Railroads are an example of natural monopoly, with high fixed costs and negligible marginal costs. Furthermore, there were no airports or interstate highways to compete with the railroads in 1887, when Congress created the Interstate Commerce Commission (ICC). The ICC was established to limit monopolistic exploitation of this situation while assuring a fair profit to railroad owners. The ICC established rates and routes for the railroads while limiting both entry to and exit from the industry.

With the advent of buses, trucks, subways, airplanes, and pipelines as alternative modes of transportation, railroad regulation became increasingly obsolete. Regulated cargoes, routes, and prices prevented railroads from adapting their prices or services to meet changing consumer demands. With regulation-protected routes, they also had little incentive to invest in new technologies or equipment. As a result, railroad traffic and profits declined while other transportation industries flourished.

---

[1]Cited in *Fortune,* October 19, 1992, p. 94.

FIGURE 27.3

Railroad Traffic, before and after Deregulation

Deregulation enabled railroads to offer more competitive prices and services. When fruit and vegetable freight rates were deregulated in 1979, railroads reduced their prices and reversed a serious decline in traffic.

The Railroad Revitalization and Regulatory Reform Act of 1976 was a response to this crisis. Its major goal was to reduce the scope of government regulation. Reinforced by the Staggers Rail Act of 1980, railroads were granted much greater freedom to adapt their prices and service to market demands.

Railroad companies used that flexibility to increase their share of total freight traffic. Fresh fruits and vegetables, for example, were exempted from ICC rate regulation in 1979. Railroads responded by *reducing* their rates and improving service. In the first year of deregulated rates, fruits and vegetable shipments increased over 30 percent. As Figure 27.3 shows, this was a dramatic reversal of earlier trends. Deregulation of coal traffic (in 1980) and piggyback (trucks on railroad flatcars) traffic (in 1982) prompted similar turnarounds. The railroads prospered by reconfiguring routes and services, cutting operating costs, and offering lower rates. Between 1986 and 1993, the average cost of moving freight by rail dropped by 69 percent.

Not all rates have fallen. Indeed, one worrisome effect of deregulation is the increased concentration in the rail industry. After a series of mergers and acquisitions, the top four railroads moved nearly 90 percent of all rail freight (ton-miles) during 1998 and 1999. Moreover, these same firms held monopoly positions on specific routes. Shippers in these captive markets were paying rates 20 to 30 percent higher than in nonmonopoly routes.

Telephone Service

The telephone industry has long been the classic example of natural monopoly. Although enormous fixed costs are necessary to establish a telephone network, the marginal cost of an additional telephone call approaches zero. Hence, it made economic sense to have a single network of telephone lines and switches rather than a maze of competing ones. Recognizing these economies of scale, Congress permitted AT&T to maintain a monopoly on both long-distance and most local telephone service. To assure that consumers would benefit from this natural monopoly, the Federal Communications Commission (FCC) regulated phone services and prices.

Once again, technology outpaced regulation. Communications satellites made it much easier and less costly for new firms to provide long-distance telephone service. Moreover, the rate structure that AT&T and the Federal Communications Commission had established made long-distance service highly profitable. Accordingly, start-up firms clamored to get into the industry, and consumers petitioned for lower rates.

Long Distance. In 1982, the courts put an end to AT&T's monopoly, transforming long-distance telecommunications into a more competitive industry with more firms and less regulation. Since then, over 800 firms have entered the industry, and long-distance telephone rates have dropped sharply. Between 1983 and 1990, long-distance telephone rates fell more than 40 percent. The quality of service also improved with fiber-optic cable, advanced switching systems, cell phones, and myriad new phone-line services such as fax transmissions, remote access, and Internet access. All these changes have contributed to a tripling of long-distance telephone use in the United States. The same kinds of changes have occurred around the world as other telephone monopolies have crumbled (see World View).

Local Service. The deregulation of long-distance services was so spectacularly successful that observers wondered whether local telephone service might be deregulated as well. As competition in *long-distance* services increased, the monopoly nature of *local* rates became painfully apparent: Local rates kept increasing after 1983 while long-distance rates were tumbling.

The Baby Bells that held monopolies on local service defended their high rates based on the high costs of building and maintaining transmission networks. But new technologies permitted wireless companies to offer local service if they could gain access to the monopoly networks. Congress responded in 1996. The Telecommunications Act of 1996 required the Baby Bells to grant rivals access to their transmission networks. Rivals are supposed to be able to lease excess capacity from the Baby Bells, then resell services directly to consumers. Potential rivals accuse the Baby Bells of foot dragging, however. They say the Baby Bells charge excessive access fees, impose overly complex access codes, require unnecessary capital equipment, and raise other entry barriers. Five years after the mandate for "open access," the Baby Bells still held near monopoly positions in local phone service, and local phone charges were still rising (see News on the next page).

Find out what has happened to the Telecommunications Act of 1996 at www.fcc.gov/telecom.html.

Airlines

The Civil Aeronautics Board (CAB) was created in 1938 to regulate airline routes and fares. From its inception, the primary concern of the CAB was to ensure a viable sys-

WORLD VIEW

Demise of Telephone Monopolies

The breakup of AT&T was spurred by new technology that undercut the basis for natural monopoly. The same technological advances have transformed the telecommunications industry around the world:

- **Canada:** In 1994, the 10 regional phone companies were required to provide equal access to their transmission networks. Over 200 new companies entered the industry, and telephone rates fell by 40 percent.
- **Japan:** In 1984, the Japanese government ended the monopoly long held by Nippon Telegraph & Telephone (NTT). More than 500 companies have now entered the industry, chipping away at NTT's market share.
- **Great Britain:** The British government has privatized British Telecommunications and licensed another company to build a second, competing network.
- **France:** The French government has retained a single, state-owned network but opened the door to competition in equipment and services.
- **Germany:** The former state-owned monopoly was privatized in 1996. Competitive entry began in 1998.
- **Chile:** The long-established monopoly (Entel) was deregulated in 1994, and entry barriers dropped. Rates plunged and volume doubled. Within two years Entel's market share fell from 100 to 40 percent.
- **Brazil:** The state-owned monopoly (Telebras) was opened to competition in 1998.
- **Mexico:** In 1997, Mexico opened its telecommunications market to competition. New domestic and international fiber-optic networks have been built, and phone rates have dropped dramatically.
- **European Union:** At the beginning of 1998, all local and long-distance markets were opened to competition.
- **China:** At the end of 2001, China split its fixed-line monopoly into two regional companies.

Analysis: The deregulation of telephone industries has spurred price competition and innovation, while greatly increasing the volume of telephone service.

IN THE NEWS

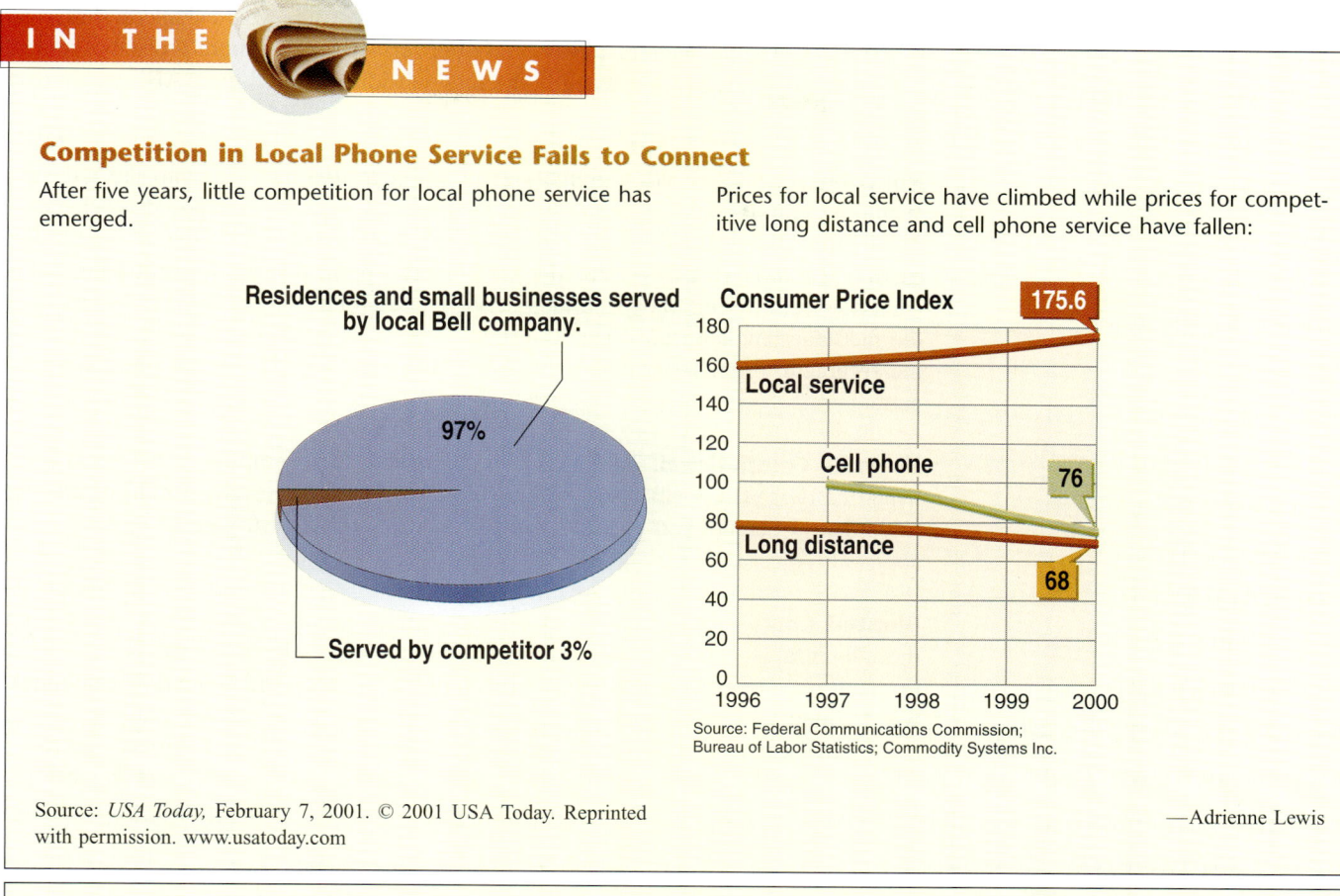

Competition in Local Phone Service Fails to Connect

After five years, little competition for local phone service has emerged.

Prices for local service have climbed while prices for competitive long distance and cell phone service have fallen:

Source: *USA Today*, February 7, 2001. © 2001 USA Today. Reprinted with permission. www.usatoday.com

—Adrienne Lewis

Analysis: The widening gap between deregulated long-distance telephone rates and monopolized local telephone rates affirmed the power of competitive forces. Local phone monopolies are now the focus of regulatory policy.

---

tem of air transportation for both large and small communities. Such a system would be ensured, the CAB believed, only if a fair level of profits was maintained by entry and price regulations. Thus, the focus of the CAB was on *profit* regulation.

Price Regulation. Initially, the CAB set airline fares at roughly the levels of Pullman rates for train travel. This implied that airfares would be proportional to distance, as they were for train travel. In the late 1930s, this fare structure wasn't unreasonable, as most flights were relatively short and planes were small.

As the airline industry grew, the CAB abandoned fare comparisons with trains but maintained the basic distance-based fare structure. To ensure fair profits, the CAB set fares in accordance with airline costs. This required the CAB to undertake intensive cost studies, based on accounting data provided by the airlines. Once the average cost of service and capital equipment was established, the CAB then set an average price that would ensure a fair rate of return (profit) (see Figure 27.1).

A secondary objective of the CAB was to ensure air service to smaller, less traveled communities. Short hauls entail higher average costs and therefore justify higher fares. To avoid high fares on such routes, the CAB permitted airlines to charge prices well in excess of average costs on longer, more efficient routes as long as they maintained service on shorter, unprofitable routes. This **cross-subsidization** was similar to that of the telephone industry, in which long-distance profits helped keep local telephone charges low.

cross-subsidization: Use of high prices and profits on one product to subsidize low prices on another product.

To maintain this price and profit structure, the CAB had to regulate routes and limit entry into the airline industry. Otherwise, established carriers would abandon short, unprofitable routes, and new carriers would offer service only on more profitable routes. Unregulated entry thus threatened both cross-subsidization and the CAB's vision of a fair profit.

No Entry. The CAB was extremely effective in restricting entry into the industry. Would-be entrants had to demonstrate to the CAB that their proposed service was required by "public convenience and necessity" and was superior to that of established carriers. Established carriers could oppose a new application by demonstrating sufficient service, offering to expand their service, or claiming superior service. In view of the fact that new applicants had no airline experience, established carriers easily won the argument. From 1938 until 1977, the CAB *never* awarded a major route to a new entrant.

No Price Competition. The CAB also eliminated price competition between established carriers. The CAB fixed airfares on all routes. Airlines could reduce fares no more than 5 percent and couldn't increase them more than 10 percent without CAB approval.

Bloated Costs. Ironically, the established airlines failed to reap much profit from these high fares. Unable to compete on the basis of price, the established carriers had to engage in nonprice competition. The most costly form of nonprice competition was frequency of service. Once the CAB authorized service between any two cities, a regulated carrier could provide as many flights as desired. This enticed the regulated carriers to purchase huge fleets of planes and provide frequent departures. In the process, load factors (the percentage of seats filled with passengers) fell and average costs rose.

The regulated carriers also pursued **product differentiation** by offering special meals, first-run movies, free drinks, better service, and wider seats. This nonprice competition further inflated average costs and reduced profits.

> **product differentiation:** Features that make one product appear different from competing products in the same market.

Profit regulation ultimately came to be regarded as a failure. The regulated airline industry was not as profitable as anticipated. And consumers weren't being offered very many price-service combinations.

New Entrants. The Airline Deregulation Act of 1978 changed the structure and behavior of the airline industry. Entry regulation was effectively abandoned. With the elimination of this **barrier to entry,** the number of carriers increased greatly. Between 1978 and 1985, the number of airline companies increased from 37 to 174! The new entrants intensified competition on nearly all routes. The share of domestic markets with four or more carriers grew from 13 percent in May 1978 to 73 percent in May 1981.

> **barriers to entry:** Obstacles that make it difficult or impossible for would-be producers to enter a particular market, such as patents.

The new entrants into the airline industry brought not only more service possibilities but also sharply lower costs. In the era of regulation, airlines had little incentive to control costs. Wages and salaries had increased continually, while productivity had declined. By contrast, new entrants were able to offer lower wages and experiment with new management systems, greatly reducing the average cost of providing service. In 1995, for example, Southwest Airlines had average costs of 6.3 cents per available seat-mile, while United Airlines had an average cost of 10.6 cents and Delta had 9.1 cents. This cost advantage enabled the new entrants to offer significantly lower fares. The resulting price competition reduced average fares as much as 40 percent below regulated levels (see Table 27.2).

The CAB's authority over airfares ended January 1, 1983. Since then, airlines have been able to adapt their fares to market supply and demand. The CAB itself was eliminated at the end of 1984. Its remaining responsibilities—for foreign travel, mail

Market Distance	Percentage Change in Airfare by Market Density (passengers per day)			
	10–50	51–200	201–500	500+
1–400 miles	+14	+12	−5	−29
401–1,500 miles	+10	−3	−13	−20
1,501+ miles	N/A	−25	−35	−40

Source: Civil Aeronautics Board, *Implementation of the Provisions of the Airline Deregulation Act of 1978,* January 1984.

TABLE 27.2
Airfare Reductions after Deregulation (deregulated fares as percentage of regulated levels)
Airfares have risen since 1978. But the fare increases have been much smaller than they would have been under the CAB's previous pricing formula. Five years after being deregulated, fares on heavily used long-distance routes were 40 percent lower than those dictated by the CAB's pricing formula. Rates on previously subsidized short hauls were higher, however.

service, mergers, and operating authority—were transferred to the U.S. Department of Transportation.

Deregulation of the airline industry greatly increased market entry and price competition. According to a 1988 study by the Federal Trade Commission, deregulation saved consumers $100 billion in airfares and enabled millions of Americans who otherwise couldn't afford it to fly. The massive increase in airline use even had an unforseen externality. As air traffic increased from 250 million to 455 million trips per year, highways became less congested. According to Richard McKenzie, airline deregulation resulted in 600,000 fewer *auto* accidents a year and reduced traffic fatalities by nearly 1,700 per year. At the same time, *air* traffic safety also improved, as evidenced by a decline in the rate of air accidents and fatalities.

Increasing Concentration. Although airline deregulation is hailed as one of the greatest policy achievements of the 1980s, airline industry structure and behavior remain imperfect. Of particular concern has been the sharp increase in the industry's concentration ratio in the last 10 years. In the competitive fray spawned by deregulation, lots of new entrants and even some established airlines went broke. Unable to match lower fares and increased service, scores of airline companies exited the industry in the period 1985–95. In the process, a handful of major carriers increased their market share. The combined market share of the three largest carriers (American, United, Delta) increased from 35 percent in 1985 to 60 percent in 2001. In many cases, firms gained near-monopoly power in specific hub airports; for example, USAir provides 86 percent of the flights departing Pittsburgh; and 90 percent of the traffic in Charlotte, Northwest has 78 percent of the Minneapolis market and 80 percent of Detroit's. Southwest services 86 percent of the flights from Love Field in Dallas; Delta has 92 percent of Cincinnati; American has 70 percent of St. Louis, and United, 70 percent of Denver. Not surprisingly, a study by the U.S. General Accounting Office found that ticket prices are 45 to 85 percent higher on monopolized routes than on routes where at least two airlines compete. In 2001, USAir charged $206 to fly its monopoly route between Pittsburgh and Washington, D.C. Yet the fare for Las Vegas to Los Angeles trips—approximately the same distance but with several carriers—was as low as $61.

For a sense of how competition affects airfares, check the number of carriers serving each of the following routes and the cheapest available fare *per mile:* (*a*) Detroit–Boston, (*b*) Pittsburgh–Washington, (*c*) Minneapolis–Milwaukee, (*d*) Denver–Colorado Springs, (*e*) Charlotte–Atlanta, (*f*) Las Vegas–Los Angeles. For information on carriers and fares, check expedia.com or visit www.thetrip.com and set up a free user's account.

Entry Barriers. To exploit their hub dominance, major carriers must keep out rivals. One of the most effective entry barriers is their ownership of landing slots. Air traffic is limited by the number of these slots, or authorized landing permits. In 1998, United Airlines controlled 82 percent of the slots at Chicago's O'Hare, up from 66 percent in 1986. Delta controls 83 percent of the slots at New York's Kennedy Airport. Smaller airlines complain that they can't get access to these slots, even when the slots aren't being used. In 1998, the U.S. Department of Transportation began studying how such slot concentration affects competition and airfares.

Defenders of deregulation are quick to point out that despite increasing *industry* concentration, there's more competition in most airline markets. In 1979, about 22 percent of all traffic was in monopoly markets, where a single carrier supplied at least 90 percent of all traffic. By 1989, only 11 percent of all traffic was in such monopoly markets. Furthermore, entry is still easier today than it was before deregulation, as a flock of new entrants attests (see News). Hence, the airline industry is more of a **contestable market,** even if not a perfectly competitive one. If entry barriers (including slot access) are lowered, consumers will continue to enjoy the low fares deregulation made possible.

contestable market: An imperfectly competitive industry subject to potential entry if prices or profits increase.

Airline Security. Since the September 11, 2001, terrorist attacks that used commercial airliners as weapons, consumers have worried more about airline security than lower airfares. Individual airlines, of course, want safe flights as well. However, security at airports is a **public good;** all travelers benefit from increased security regardless of who pays for it. Moreover, firms or travelers who don't pay for increased airport security can't easily be excluded from its benefits. This creates a classic "free-rider" problem, wherein everyone waits for someone else to pay for tighter security. Hence, unregulated airlines are likely to minimize expenditures on airport security. Government intervention is required to assure that enough of the public good is produced, even in an otherwise unregulated industry.

public good: A good or service whose consumption by one person does not exclude consumption by others.

IN THE NEWS

Flock of New Low-Fare Carriers Means Savings for Consumers

A new flock of low-fare airlines is helping to save consumers a hefty $4 billion a year—or $46 to $54 per one-way flight, a new government study calculates. . . .

Hoping to duplicate the success of low cost, low-fare specialist Southwest Airlines, 14 new passenger carriers have begun flying in the past three years. Nine more are awaiting government approval, and the Transportation Department is fielding more applications to fly than it has in a decade.

New entrants are having a "dramatic effect" on the U.S. airline industry from the bottom up, said Patrick Murphy, the Transportation Department's deputy assistant secretary for aviation and international affairs.

As discount carriers have underpriced major carriers on hundreds of short-haul routes, major airlines have been forced to cut fares and become more efficient. . . .

For now, though, consumers are benefiting. The Transportation Department estimates passengers are saving $54 on one-way trips involving at least one airport dominated by a major carrier; and $46 per trip between nonhub airports. The savings could grow if low-fare entrants keep cropping up, department analysts said. . . .

Low-fare airlines now compete on routes that account for 37 percent of U.S. passenger traffic.

—Bryan Gruley and Scott McCartney

Source: *The Wall Street Journal,* November 2, 1995. Reprinted by permission of *The Wall Street Journal.* © 1995 Dow Jones & Company, Inc. All rights reserved worldwide. www.wsj.com

Analysis: If entry barriers are low enough, new entrants will contest a market, keeping pressure on prices and service.

The cable TV industry offers examples of both deregulation and *re*regulation. Up until 1986, city and county governments had the authority to franchise (approve) local cable TV operators and regulate their rates. In almost all cases, local governments franchised only one operator, thus establishing local monopolies. The monopoly structure was justified by pervasive economies of scale and the desire to avoid the cost and disruption of laying multiple cable systems. The rationale behind local regulation of cable prices (rates) was to ensure that consumers shared in the benefits of natural monopoly.

Cable TV

Deregulation. By 1984, Congress was convinced that broadcast TV and emerging technologies (such as microwave transmissions and direct satellite broadcasts) offered sufficient competition to ensure consumers fair prices and quality service. The Cable Communications Policy Act of 1984 *de*regulated cable TV by stripping local governments of the authority to regulate prices. From 1986 to 1992, cable TV was essentially unregulated.

Soon after price regulation ended, cable companies began increasing their rates sharply. As Figure 27.4 shows, the rate of price acceleration nearly doubled after the cable industry was deregulated. Consumers also complained that local cable companies offered poor service. They demanded that Congress *re*regulate the industry.

Reregulation. In 1992, Congress responded with the Cable Television Consumer Protection and Competition Act. That act gave the Federal Communications Commission authority to reregulate cable TV rates. The FCC required cable operators to *reduce* prices by nearly 17 percent in 1993–94. It then issued 450 pages of new rules that would limit future price increases. As Figure 27.4 illustrates, these interventions had a dramatic effect on cable prices.

While consumers applauded the new price rules, cable operators warned of unwelcome long-term effects. The rate cuts reduced cable-industry revenues by nearly $4 billion between 1993 and 1995. The cable companies say they would have used that revenue to invest in improved networks and services. The cable companies also argued that increased competition from satellite transmissions and the Internet made government regulation of (wired) cable TV increasingly unnecessary.

Deregulation. Congress responded to these industry complaints by *de*regulating the cable industry again. The Telecommunications Act of 1996 mandated that rate regulation be phased out and ended completely by March 1999. Almost immediately, cable prices soared again, as Figure 27.4 shows. Critics asserted that alternative technologies were still not viable competitors to local cable monopolies.

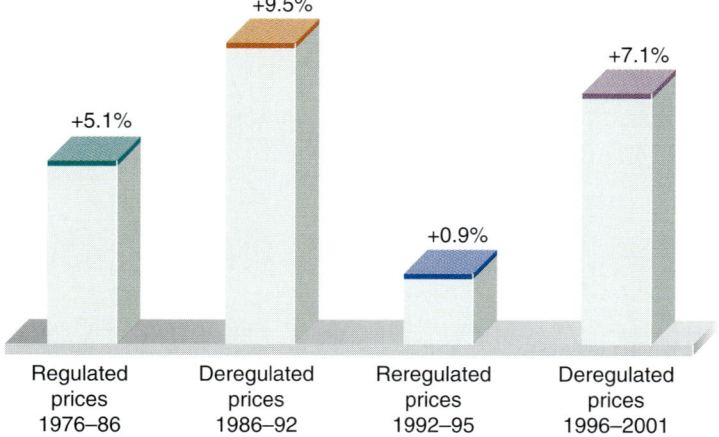

FIGURE 27.4
Annual Increase in Price of Basic Cable Service

After cable TV prices were deregulated in 1986, monthly charges moved up sharply. In 1992 Congress *re*regulated cable TV and prices stabilized. The Telecommunications Act of 1996 again deregulated prices and they surged.

Source: Industry publications.

590 REGULATORY ISSUES

Electricity

The electric utility industry is the latest target for deregulation. Here again, the industry has long been regarded as a natural monopoly. The enormous fixed costs of a power plant and transmission network, combined with negligible marginal costs for delivering another kilowatt of electricity, gave electric utilities a downward-sloping average total cost curve. The focus of government intervention was therefore on rate regulation (behavior) rather than promoting competition (structure).

Bloated Costs, High Prices. Critics of local utility monopolies complained that local rate regulation wasn't working well enough. In order to get higher (retail) prices, the utility companies allowed costs to rise. They also had no incentive to pursue new technologies that would reduce the costs of power generation or distribution. Big power users like steel companies complained that high electricity prices were crippling their competitive position. The only viable option for consumers was to move from a state with a high-cost power monopoly to a state with low-cost power monopoly.

Demise of Power Plant Monopolies. Advances in transmission technology gave consumers a new choice. High-voltage transmission lines can carry power thousands of miles with negligible power loss. Utility companies used these lines to link their power grids, thereby creating backup power sources in the event of regional blackouts. In doing so, however, they created a new entry point for potential competition. Now a Kentucky power plant with surplus capacity can supply electricity to consumers in California. There's no longer any need to rely on a regional utility monopoly. At the wholesale level, utility companies have been trading electricity across state lines since 1992. In 1998, California's power companies had to make their transmission networks available to rival companies, wherever located (see News).

Local Distribution Monopolies. Although technology destroyed the basis for natural monopolies in power *production,* local monopolies in power *distribution* remain. Electricity reaches consumers through the wires attached to every house and business. As with TV cables, there is a natural monopoly in electricity distribution; competing wire grids would be costly and inefficient.

IN THE NEWS

California Consumers Can Choose Power Company

LOS ANGELES—Starting today, California becomes the largest state to let consumers pick their own electric company.

The $20 billion experiment in the nation's biggest market for electricity will be closely watched as other states prepare for deregulation.

"California is providing the lead for the nation," Energy Secretary Federico Peña said Monday in a telephone interview from Moscow.

Customers of California's three giant investor-owned utilities—about 70 percent of homes and businesses—will be able to pick from about 50 different electricity providers. . . .

To win business, power companies are trying to segment the market. For instance, former San Francisco 49ers coach Bill Walsh pitches for Friendly Power and Gas, "the friendly power company,"

Green Mountain Energy Resources promises to buy electricity only from environmentally friendly sources. It offers electricity produced from water, wind or other renewable sources. It costs customers more, but deregulation "isn't just about price," says Vice President Kevin Hartley.

—Chris Woodyard

Source: *USA Today,* March 31, 1998. © 1998 USA Today. Reprinted with permission. www.usatoday.com

---

Analysis: Retail competition in electricity has been created by forcing local utility monopolies to grant rival power companies access to their transmission networks. This is the same approach that's transforming local telephone service.

To deliver the benefits of competition in power *production,* rival producers must be able to access these local distribution grids. This is the same problem that has plagued competition in local telephone service. The local power companies that own the local distribution grids aren't anxious to open the wires to new competition. The central problem for electricity deregulation has been to assure wider access to local distribution grids.

California's Mistakes. The California legislature decided to resolve this problem by stripping local utility monopolies of their production capacity. By forcing utility companies to sell their power plants, California transformed its utilities into pure power *distributors*. This seemed to resolve the conflict between ownership and access to the distribution system. However, it also made California's utility companies totally dependent on third-party power producers, many of which were then out of state.

California also put a ceiling on the *retail* price its utilities could charge. But the state had no power to control the *wholesale* price of electricity in interstate markets. When wholesale prices rose sharply in 2000 (see News), California's utilities were trapped between rising costs and a fixed price ceiling. Fearful of a political backlash, the governor refused to raise the retail price ceiling. As a result, some of the utility companies were forced into bankruptcy and power supplies were interrupted. The state itself entered the utility business by buying power plants and more out-of-state power supplies. In the end, Californians ended up with very expensive electricity.

Better Strategies. Other states and countries have demonstrated how deregulation can generate much better results. Norway deregulated its electric industry in 1991, and prices soon declined by 20 percent. After the European Union started deregulating its electric industries in 1999, prices fell as well. In the United States, the 50 states are at various stages of deregulation (see News on the next page), amassing lots of evidence on how best to use competition to reduce electricity costs and prices.

Visit the Center for the Advancement of Energy Markets at www.caem.org to see how states differ in the extent of electricity deregulation and price changes.

IN THE NEWS

Financial Woes Heating Up

Pacific Gas and Electric is in financial trouble because the cost of power it purchases on the wholesale market is soaring higher than the fixed rate it charges its customers:

—Suzy Parker

Source: Pacific Gas and Electric

Source: *USA Today*, January 10, 2001. © 2001 USA Today. Reprinted with permission. www.usatoday.com

Analysis: When wholesale prices for electricity rose above the retail price ceiling established by the California legislature, the state's utility companies lost money on every kilowatt supplied. It was a recipe for financial disaster.

IN THE NEWS

Power Check
Where the States Stand on Deregulation of Electricity Markets

States that have deregulated retail markets, including residential customers:

- Arizona
- Connecticut
- Delaware
- District of Columbia
- Maine
- Maryland*
- Massachusetts
- New Hampshire
- New Jersey
- New York
- Ohio
- Pennsylvania
- Rhode Island

States that have deregulated retail markets, excluding residential customers:

- Illinois†
- Montana
- Oregon

States that have moved to revise or delay restructuring rules in reaction to California's problems:

- Arkansas
- California
- Montana
- Nevada
- New Mexico
- Oklahoma
- Oregon

States moving ahead with plans for full retail access in 2002:

- Michigan
- Texas
- Virginia

States that are continuing to study restructuring issues:

- Florida
- Georgia
- Kentucky
- Louisiana
- Minnesota
- Mississippi
- Missouri
- Nebraska
- North Carolina
- North Dakota
- Tennessee
- Vermont
- Washington
- West Virginia

States that have rejected retail electric competition; no current activity in legislature or by regulators:

- Alabama
- Alaska
- Colorado
- Hawaii
- Idaho
- Indiana
- Iowa
- Kansas
- South Carolina
- South Dakota
- Utah
- Wisconsin
- Wyoming

*Maryland plans to add the final third of its market by July 2002.
†Illinois plans to add residential customers by May 2002.
Source: National Regulatory Research Institute, as reported in *The Wall Street Journal*, September 17, 2001. Reprinted by permission of The Wall Street Journal. © 2001 Dow Jones & Company, Inc. All rights reserved worldwide. www.wsj.com

Analysis: Competition in the electricity industry depends on rival power producers having access to local distribution grids. The various states are pursuing different (de)regulation strategies for accomplishing this goal.

THE ECONOMY TOMORROW

Deregulate Everything?

Deregulation of the railroad, telephone, airline, and electricity industries has yielded substantial benefits: more competition, lower prices and improved services. Such experiences bolster the case for laissez faire. Nevertheless, we shouldn't jump to the conclusion that all regulation of business should be dismantled. All we know from experience is that the regulation of certain industries has become outmoded. Changing consumer demands, new technologies, and substitute goods had simply made existing regulations obsolete, even counterproductive. A combination of economic and political forces doomed them to extinction.

But were these regulations ever necessary? In the 1880s there were no viable alternatives to railroads for overland transportation. The forces of natural monopoly could easily have exploited consumers and retarded economic growth. The same was largely true for long-distance telephone service prior to the launching of communications satellites. Even the limitations on competition in trucking and banking made some sense in the depths of the Great Depression. One shouldn't conclude that regulatory intervention never made sense just because the regulations themselves later became obsolete.

Even today, most people recognize the need for regulation of many industries. The transmission networks for local telephone service and electricity delivery are still natural monopolies. The government can force owners to permit greater access. But an unregulated network owner could still extract monopoly profits through excessive prices. Hence, even a deregulated industry may still require some regulation at critical entry or supply junctures. Existing regulations may not be optimal, but they probably generate better outcomes than totally unregulated monopolies.

Likewise, few people seriously propose relying on competition and the good judgment of consumers to determine the variety or quality of drugs on the market. Regulations imposed by the Food and Drug Administration restrain competition in the drug industry, raise production costs, and inhibit new technology. But they also make drugs safer. Here, as in other industries, there's a trade-off between the virtues of competition and those of regulation. The basic policy issue, as always, is whether the benefits of regulation exceed their administrative, compliance, and efficiency costs. The persistent challenge for public policy is to adapt regulations—or to discard them (that is, deregulate)—as market conditions, consumer demands, or technology changes.

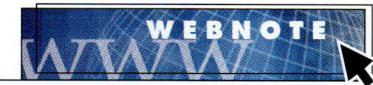

The Brookings Institution and the American Enterprise Institute have a joint project to analyze regulatory programs at www.aei.brookings.org.

SUMMARY

- Government intervention is justified when the market fails to generate the optimal (best possible) mix of output or distribution of income.
- Antitrust and regulation are alternative options for dealing with market power. Antitrust focuses on market structure and anticompetitive practices. Regulation stipulates specific market behavior.
- Natural monopolies offer pervasive economies of scale. Because of this potential efficiency, antitrust may be inappropriate.
- Regulation of natural monopoly can focus on price, profit, or output. Price regulation may require subsidies; profit regulation may induce cost escalation; and output regulation may lead to quality deterioration. These problems compel compromises and acceptance of second-best solutions.
- The demand for deregulation rests on the argument that the costs of regulation exceed the benefits. These costs include the opportunity costs associated with regulatory administration and compliance as well as the (dynamic) efficiency losses that result from inflexible pricing and production rules.
- Deregulation of the railroad, telephone, and airline industries has been a success. In all these industries, regulation has been outmoded by changing consumer demands, products, and technology. As regulation was relaxed, these industries became more competitive, output increased, and prices fell.
- Recent experiences with deregulation don't imply that all regulation should end. Regulation is appropriate if market failure exists *and* if the benefits of regulation exceed the costs. As benefits and costs change, decisions about what and how to regulate must be reevaluated.

Key Terms

laissez faire
market failure
antitrust
regulation
natural monopoly

economies of scale
marginal cost pricing
opportunity cost
economic profit
government failure

cross-subsidization
product differentiation
barriers to entry
contestable market
public good

Questions for Discussion

1. Given the inevitable limit on airplane landings, how should available slots be allocated? How would market outcomes be altered?
2. Should the airline industry be reregulated?
3. Prior to 1982, AT&T kept local phone rates low by subsidizing them from long-distance profits. Was such cross-subsidization in the public interest? Explain.
4. In most cities local taxi fares are regulated. Should such regulation end? Who would gain or lose?
5. The News story on page 579 describes how Nynex inflated its regulated costs. What advantage did Nynex gain from this practice? How else might a regulated company pad its costs?
6. How could a local phone or cable company reduce service quality if forced to accept price ceilings?
7. If cable TV were completely deregulated, would local monopolies ever confront effective competition? Does profit regulation inhibit or accelerate would-be competition?
8. Why is there resistance to (*a*) local phone companies providing video and data services and (*b*) mergers of local cable and telephone companies?
9. Will reregulation of cable TV prices slow or hasten competition from alternative technologies?
10. What should California have done to get better results from electricity deregulation?

Web Activities

1. Does the U.S. Food and Drug Administration successfully regulate business? For two positions, see the Center for Food Safety at www.foodsafetynow.org and the Cato Institute, a group that advocates policies based on limited government, at www.ncpa.org/pd/regulat/pd042500f.html. What is the strongest argument given? What is the weakest argument?
2. Log on to www.fda.gov, and find two product categories that the FDA regulates that you believe should not be regulated. What are the reasons given by the FDA for regulating these products? What impact does this regulation have on a firm's cost of production? On consumer prices?
3. Log on to csab.wustl.edu/atissue.html. What does the Weidenbaum Center conclude about the regulation of children's environmental health?
4. Log on to www.fcc.gov/dtv, and find the Review of the Federal Communications Commission's rules and policies affecting the conversion to digital television. What are the benefits of this regulation for the nation? Are the benefits worth the costs?

THE ACCOMPANYING STUDENT PROBLEM SET CONTAINS NUMERICAL AND GRAPHING PROBLEMS FOR THIS CHAPTER

CHAPTER 28
Environmental Protection

> Progress in environmental problems is impossible without a clear understanding of how the economic system works in the environment and what alternatives are available to take away the many roadblocks to environmental quality.
> —Council on Environmental Quality, First Annual Report

> What good is a clean river if you've got no jobs?
> —Steelworkers Union Official in Youngstown, Ohio

A hole in the ozone layer is allowing increased ultraviolet radiation to reach the earth's surface. The hole is the result of excessive release of chlorine gases (chlorofluorocarbons, or CFCs) from air conditioners, plastic-foam manufacture, industrial solvents, and aerosol spray cans such as deodorants and insecticides. The resulting damage to the stratosphere is causing skin cancer, cataracts, and immune-system disorders.

Skin cancer may turn out to be one of our less serious problems. As carbon dioxide is building up in the atmosphere, it is creating a gaseous blanket around the earth that is trapping radiation and heating the atmosphere. Scientists predict that this greenhouse effect will melt the polar ice caps, raise sea levels, flood coastal areas, and turn rich croplands into deserts within 60 years.

Everyone wants a cleaner and safer environment. So why don't we stop polluting the environment with CFCs, carbon dioxide, toxic chemicals, and other waste? If we don't do it ourselves, why doesn't the government force people to stop polluting?

Economics is part of the answer. To reduce pollution, we have to change our patterns of production and consumption. This entails economic costs, in terms of restricted consumption choices, more expensive ways of producing goods, and higher prices. Thus, we have to weigh the benefits of a cleaner, safer environment against the costs of environmental protection.

Instinctively, most people don't like the idea of measuring the value of a cleaner environment in dollars and cents. But most people might also agree that spending $2 trillion to avoid a few cataracts is awfully expensive. There has to be *some* balance between the benefits of a cleaner environment and the cost of cleaning it up.

This chapter assesses our environmental problems from this economic perspective, considering three primary concerns:

- How do (unregulated) markets encourage pollution?
- What are the costs of greater environmental protection?
- How can government policy best ensure an *optimal* environment?

To answer these questions, we first survey the major types and sources of pollution. Then we examine the benefits and costs of environmental protection, highlighting the economic incentives that shape market behavior.

THE ENVIRONMENTAL THREAT

The hole in the ozone layer and the earth's rising temperature are at the top of the list of environmental concerns. The list is much longer, however, and very old as well. As early as A.D. 61, the statesman and philosopher Seneca was complaining about the smoky air emitted from household chimneys in Rome. Lead emissions from ancient Greek and Roman silver refineries poisoned the air in Europe and the remote Arctic. And historians are quick to remind us that open sewers running down the street were once the principal mode of urban waste disposal. Typhoid epidemics were a recurrent penalty for water pollution. So we can't say that environmental damage is a new phenomenon or that it's now worse than ever before.

But we do know more about the sources of environmental damage than our ancestors did, and we can better afford to do something about it. Our understanding of the economics of pollution has increased as well. We've come to recognize that pollution impairs health, reduces life expectancy, and thus reduces labor-force activity and output. Pollution also destroys capital (such as the effects of air pollution on steel structures) and diverts resources to undesired activities (like car washes, laundry, and cleaning). Not least of all, pollution directly reduces our social welfare by denying us access to clean air, water, and beaches.

Air Pollution

Air pollution is as familiar as a smoggy horizon. But smog is only one form of air pollution.

Acid Rain. Sulfur dioxide (SO_2) is an acrid, corrosive, and poisonous gas that's created by burning high-sulfur fuels such as coal. As a contributor to acid rain, it destroys vegetation and forests. Electric utilities and industrial plants that burn high-sulfur coal or fuel oil are the prime sources of SO_2. Coal burning alone accounts for about 60 percent of all emissions of sulfur oxides. Canada claims that the acid rain destroying its forests and lakes comes from coal-burning power plants in the American Midwest.

Smog. Nitrogen oxides (NO_x), another ingredient in the formation of acid rain, are also a principal ingredient in the formation of smog. Smog not only irritates the eyes and spoils the view, it also damages plants, trees, and human lungs. Automobile emissions account for 40 percent of urban smog. Bakeries, dry cleaners, and production of other consumer goods account for an equal amount of smog. The rest comes from electric power plants and industrial boilers.

The Greenhouse Effect. The prime villain in the greenhouse effect is the otherwise harmless carbon dioxide (CO_2) that we exhale. Unfortunately, we and nature now release so much CO_2 that the earth's oceans and vegetation can no longer absorb it all. The excess CO_2 is creating a gaseous blanket around the earth that may warm the earth to disastrous levels. The burning of fossil fuels is a significant source of CO_2 buildup. The destruction of rain forests, which absorb CO_2, also contributes to the greenhouse effect.

IN THE NEWS

Dirty Air Can Shorten Your Life

The largest study ever conducted on the health effects of airborne particles from traffic and smokestacks has found that people in the nation's most polluted cities are 15 to 17 percent more likely to die prematurely than those in cities with the cleanest air.

This form of pollution is killing citizens even in areas that meet Environmental Protection Agency air quality standards, said study coauthor Douglas Dockery of the Harvard School of Public Health, who said "the impact on life and health is more pervasive than previously thought."

In Washington, where levels of airborne particles fall in the low middle range for U.S. cities, the average long-term resident loses approximately one year of life expectancy compared to the average for such relatively pristine places as Topeka, Kan., or Madison, Wis., Dockery said. In highly polluted places like Los Angeles or Salt Lake City, the toll is much greater: Compared to people in the cleanest metropolitan areas, those exposed to the highest concentrations of particles run a risk of premature death about one-sixth as great as if they had been smoking for 25 years.

—Curt Suplee

Source: *Washington Post*, March 10, 1995. © 1995 The Washington Post. Reprinted with permission. www.washingtonpost.com

LARGE PARTICLES: Ash, dust, soot, drops

Sources: Agriculture, construction, industry

Effects: Throat, eye irritation, but most do not reach the lungs

GASES: Ozone, nitrogen oxides, sulfur dioxide, carbon monoxide, hydrocarbons

Sources: Automobile exhaust, industry, utilities

Effects: Eye irritation, lung irritation

FINE PARTICLES: Solids and liquid droplets

Sources: Power plants, automobile exhaust, industry, wood burning, mining, and construction

Effects: Possibly carcinogenic, can aggravate asthma, bronchitis, emphysema, and heart disease

Analysis: Pollution entails real costs, as measured by impaired health, reduced life spans, and other damages.

Water Pollution

Water pollution is another environmental threat. Its effects are apparent in the contamination of drinking water, restrictions on swimming and boating, foul-smelling waterways, swarms of dead fish, and floating debris.

Organic Pollution. The most common form of water pollution occurs in the disposal of organic wastes from toilets and garbage disposals. The wastes that originate there are collected in sewer systems and ultimately discharged into the nearest waterway. The key question is whether the wastes are treated (separated and decomposed) before ultimate discharge. Sophisticated waste-treatment plants can reduce organic pollution up to 99 percent. Unfortunately, only 70 percent of the U.S. population is served by a system of sewers and adequate (secondary) treatment plants. Inadequate treatment systems often result in the closure of waterways and beaches (see News).

In addition to household wastes, our waterways must also contend with industrial wastes. Over half the volume of industrial discharge comes from just a few industries—principally paper, organic chemicals, petroleum, and steel. Finally, there are all those farm animals: The 7.5 billion chickens and 161 million cows and hogs raised each year generate 1.4 billion tons of manure (whew!). If improperly managed, that organic waste will contaminate water supplies and trigger algae blooms that can choke waterways and kill fish. Animal wastes don't cause too great a problem in Boston or New York City, but they can wreak havoc on the water supplies of towns in California, Texas, Kansas, and Iowa.

Find out about pollution in your zip code area from the Environmental Defense Fund's Chemical Scoreboard at www.scorecard.org.

Thermal Pollution. *Thermal pollution* is an increase in the temperature of waterways brought about by the discharge of steam or heated water. Heat discharges can kill fish, upset marine reproductive cycles, and accelerate biological and chemical processes in water, thereby reducing its ability to retain oxygen. Electric power plants account for over 80 percent of all thermal discharges, with primary metal, chemical, and petroleum-refining plants accounting for nearly all the rest.

Solid-Waste Pollution

Solid waste is yet another environmental threat. Solid-waste pollution is apparent everywhere, from the garbage can to litter on the streets and beaches, to debris in the water, to open dumps. According to EPA estimates, we generate over 5 billion tons of solid waste each year. This figure includes more than 30 billion bottles, 60 billion cans, 100 million tires, and millions of discarded automobiles and major appliances. Where do you think all this refuse goes?

Most solid wastes originate in agriculture (slaughter wastes, orchard prunings, harvest residues) and mining (slag heaps, mill tailings). The much smaller amount of solid waste originating in residential and commercial use is considered more dangerous, however, simply because it accumulates where people live. New York City alone generates 24,000 tons of trash a day. Because it has neither the land area nor the incinerators needed for disposal, it must ship its garbage to other states. Seattle ships its trash to Oregon; Los Angeles transports its trash to the Mojave Desert; New York City sludge is dumped in west Texas; and Philadelphia ships its garbage all the way to Panama.

IN THE NEWS

Beach Closings Linked to Pollution on Rise

Beach closings and advisories caused by high bacteria levels are increasing nationwide, according to a report released Thursday. The report awards high praise for pollution control to only five beach areas. The nationwide survey by the Natural Resources Defense Council singles out four states—Louisiana, Oregon, Texas and Washington—as "beach burns" for failing to regularly monitor their coastlines. There were 6,160 beach closings and advisories nationwide in 1999, up almost 50 percent from 1997. About 70 percent were due to bacteria associated with sewage or polluted runoff, according to the council's 10th annual report. The "beach buddies" were East Haven Town Beach in Connecticut; North Beach and Oceanside at the Assateague Island National Seashore in Maryland; and Revere Beach and Short Beach in Massachusetts.

Source: *USA Today*, August 4, 2000. © 2000 USA Today. Reprinted with permission. www.usatoday.com

Analysis: The pollution that closes beaches can be avoided with better sewage treatment facilities. Who should bear that cost?

POLLUTION DAMAGES

Shipping garbage to Panama is an expensive answer to our waste disposal problem. But even those costs are a small fraction of the total cost of environmental damage. Much greater costs are associated with the damage to our health (labor), buildings (capital), and land. Even the little things count, like being able to enjoy a clear sunset or take a deep breath.

Although many people don't like to put a price on the environment, some monetary measure of environmental damage is important in decision making. Unless we value the environment above everything else, we have to establish some method of ranking the importance of environmental damage. Although it's tempting to say that clean air is priceless, **we won't get clean air unless we spend resources to get it.** This economic reality suggests that we begin by determining how much cleaner air is worth to us.

Assigning Prices

In some cases, it's fairly easy to put a price on environmental damage. Scientists can measure the increase in cancer, heart attacks, and other disorders attributable to air pollution, as the EPA does for air toxins (see News, page 597). Engineers can also measure the rate at which buildings decay or forests and lakes die. Economists can then estimate the dollar value of this damage by assessing the economic value of lives, forests, lakes, and other resources. For example, if people are willing to pay $5,000 for a cataract operation, then we could assert that the avoidance of such eye damage is worth at least $5,000. Saving a tree is worth whatever the marketplace is willing to pay for the products of that tree. Using such computations, the EPA estimates that air pollution alone inflicts health, property, and vegetation damage in excess of $50 billion a year.

The job of pricing environmental damage is much more difficult with intangible losses like sunsets. Nevertheless, when governmental agencies and courts are asked to assess the damages of oil spills and other accidents, they must try to inventory *all* costs, including polluted sunsets, reduced wildlife, and lost recreation opportunities. The science of computing such environmental damage is very inexact. Nevertheless, crude but reasonable procedures generate damage estimates measured in hundreds of billions of dollars per year.

Cleanup Possibilities

One of the most frustrating things about all this environmental damage is that it can be avoided. The EPA estimates that *95 percent of current air and water pollution could be eliminated by known and available technology.* Nothing very exotic is needed: just simple things like auto-emission controls, smokestack cleaners, improved sewage and waste treatment facilities, and cooling towers for electric power plants. Even solid-waste pollution could be reduced by comparable proportions if we used less packaging, recycled more materials, or transformed our garbage into a useful (relatively low-polluting) energy source. The critical question here is, Why we don't do these things? Why do we continue to pollute so much?

MARKET INCENTIVES

Previous chapters emphasized how market incentives influence the behavior of individual consumers, firms, and government agencies. Incentives in the form of price reductions can be used to change consumer buying habits. Incentives in the form of high profit margins encourage production of desired goods and services. And market incentives in the form of cost differentials help allocate resources efficiently. Accordingly, we shouldn't be too surprised to learn that **market incentives play a major role in pollution behavior.**

The Production Decision

Imagine that you're the majority stockholder and manager of an electric power plant. Such plants are responsible for a significant amount of air pollution (especially sulfur dioxide and particulates) and nearly all thermal water pollution. Hence, your position

production decision: The selection of the short-run rate of output (with existing plant and equipment).

immediately puts you on the most-wanted list of pollution offenders. But suppose you bear society no grudges and would truly like to help eliminate pollution. Let's consider the alternatives.

As the owner-manager of an electric power plant, you'll strive to make a profit-maximizing **production decision.** That is, you'll seek the rate of output at which marginal revenue equals marginal cost. Let's assume that the electric power industry is still regulated by the state power commission so that the price of electricity is fixed, at least in the short run. The effect of this assumption is to render marginal revenue equal to price, thus giving us a horizontal price line, as in Figure 28.1a.

Figure 28.1a also depicts the marginal and average total costs (MC and ATC) associated with the production of electricity. By equating marginal cost (MC) to price (marginal revenue, MR), we observe (point A) that profit maximization occurs at an output of 1,000 kilowatt-hours per day. Total profits are illustrated by the shaded rectangle between the price line and the average total cost (ATC) curve.

The Efficiency Decision

efficiency decision: The choice of a production process for any given rate of output.

The profits illustrated in Figure 28.1a are achieved in part by use of the cheapest available fuel under the boilers (which create the steam that rotates the generators). Recall that the construction of a marginal cost curve presumes some knowledge of alternative production processes. Recall too that the **efficiency decision** requires a producer to choose that production process (and its associated cost curve) that minimizes costs for any particular rate of output.

Costs of Pollution Abatement. Unfortunately, the efficiency decision in this case leads to the use of high-sulfur coal, the prime villain in SO_2 and particulate pollution. Other fuels, such as low-sulfur coal, fuel oil, and nuclear energy, cost considerably more. Were you to switch to one of them, the ATC and MC curves would both shift upward, as in Figure 28.1b. Under these conditions, the most profitable rate of output would be lower than before (point B), and total profits would decline (note the smaller profit rectangle in Figure 28.1b). Thus, *pollution abatement can be achieved, but only at significant cost to the plant.*

The same kind of cost considerations lead the plant to engage in thermal pollution. Cool water must be run through an electric utility plant to keep the turbines from overheating. Once the water has run through the plant, it's too hot to recirculate. It must be

FIGURE 28.1
Profit Maximization in Electric Power Production

Production processes that control pollution may be more expensive than those that don't. If they are, the MC and ATC curves will shift upward (to MC_2 and ATC_2). At the new profit-maximizing rate of output (point B), output and total profit shrink. Hence, a producer has an incentive to continue polluting, using cheaper technology.

either dumped back into the adjacent river or cooled off by being circulated through cooling towers. As you might expect, it's cheaper to simply dump the hot water in the river. The fish don't like it, but they don't have to pay the construction costs associated with cooling towers.

The big question here is whether you and your fellow stockholders would be willing to incur higher costs in order to cut down on pollution. Eliminating either the air pollution or the water pollution emanating from the electric plant will cost a lot of money. And to whose benefit? To the people who live downstream and downwind? We don't expect profit-maximizing producers to take such concerns into account. *The behavior of profit maximizers is guided by comparisons of revenues and costs, not by philanthropy, aesthetic concerns, or the welfare of fish.*

MARKET FAILURE: EXTERNAL COSTS

The moral of this story—and the critical factor in pollution behavior—is that **people tend to maximize their personal welfare, balancing private benefits against private costs.** For the electric power plant, this means making production decisions on the basis of revenues received and costs incurred. The fact that the power plant imposes costs on others, in the form of air and water pollution, is irrelevant to its profit-maximizing decisions. Those costs are *external* to the firm and don't appear on its profit-and-loss statement. Those **external costs**—or *externalities*—are no less real, but they're incurred by society at large rather than by the firm.

Whenever external costs exist, a private firm won't allocate its resources and operate its plant in such a way as to maximize social welfare. In effect, society permits the power plant the free use of valued resources—clean air and clean water. The power plant has a tremendous incentive to substitute those resources for others (such as high-priced fuel or cooling towers) in the production process. The inefficiency of such an arrangement is obvious when we recall that the function of markets is to allocate scarce resources in accordance with the consumer's expressed demands. Yet here we are, proclaiming a high value for clean air and clean water and encouraging the power plant to use up both resources by offering them at zero cost to the firm.

external cost: Cost of a market activity borne by a third party; the difference between the social and private costs of a market activity.

Externalities in Production

"Where there's smoke, there's money."

Analysis: If a firm can substitute external costs for private (internal) costs, its profits may increase.

social costs: The full resource costs of an economic activity, including externalities.

private costs: The costs of an economic activity directly borne by the immediate producer or consumer (excluding externalities).

market failure: An imperfection in the market mechanism that prevents optimal outcomes.

The inefficiency of this market arrangement can be expressed in terms of a distinction between social costs and private costs. **Social costs** are the total costs of all the resources used in a particular production activity. On the other hand, **private costs** are the resource costs incurred by the specific producer.

Ideally, a producer's private costs will encompass all the attendant social costs, and production decision will be consistent with our social welfare. Unfortunately, this happy identity doesn't always exist, as our experience with the power plant illustrates. *When social costs differ from private costs, external costs exist. In fact, external costs are equal to the difference between the social and private costs*—that is,

External costs = social costs − private costs

When external costs are present, the market mechanism won't allocate resources efficiently. This is a case of **market failure.** The price signal confronting producers is flawed. By not conveying the full (social) cost of scarce resources, the market encourages excessive pollution. We end up with a suboptimal mix of output (too much electricity, too little clean air) and the wrong production processes.

The consequences of this market failure are illustrated in Figure 28.2, which again depicts the cost situation confronting the electric power plant. Notice that we use two different marginal cost curves this time. The lower one, the *private* MC curve, reflects the private costs incurred by the power plant when it operates on a profit-maximization basis, using high-sulfur coal and no cooling towers. It's identical to the MC curve in Figure 28.1a. We now know, however, that such operations impose external costs on others in the form of air and water pollution. These external costs must be added on to private marginal costs. When this is done, we get a *social* marginal cost curve that lies above the private MC curve.

To maximize profits, private firms seek the rate of output that equates private MC to MR(price). *To maximize social welfare, we need to equate social marginal cost to marginal revenue (price).* This social optimum occurs at point A in Figure 28.2 and results in output of q_s. By contrast, the firm's private profit maximization occurs at point B, where q_p is produced. Hence, the private firm ends up producing more output than socially desired, while earning more profit and causing more pollution. As a general rule, *if pollution costs are external, firms will produce too much of a polluting good.*

Externalities in Consumption

A divergence between private and social costs can also be observed in consumption. A consumer, like a producer, tends to maximize personal welfare. We buy and use more of those goods and services that yield the highest satisfaction (marginal utility) per dol-

FIGURE 28.2
Market Failure

Social costs exceed private costs by the amount of external costs. Production decisions based on private costs alone will lead us to point B, where private MC = MR. At point B, the rate of output is q_p.

To maximize social welfare, we equate *social* MC and MR, as at point A. Only q_s of output is socially desirable. The failure of the market to convey the full costs of production keeps us from attaining this outcome.

lar expended. By implication (and the law of demand), we tend to use more of a product if we can get it at a discount—that is, pay less than the full price. Unfortunately, the "discount" often takes the form of an external cost imposed on neighbors and friends.

Automobile driving illustrates the problem. The amount of driving one does is influenced by the price of a car and the marginal costs of driving it. People buy smaller cars and drive less when the attendant marginal costs (for instance, gasoline prices) increase substantially. But automobile use involves not only *private costs* but *external costs* as well. Auto emissions (carbon monoxide, hydrocarbons, and nitrogen oxides) are a principal cause of air pollution. In effect, automobile drivers have been able to use a valued resource, clean air, at no cost to themselves. Few motorists see any personal benefit in installing exhaust control devices because the quality of the air they breathe would be little affected by their efforts. Hence, low private costs lead to excessive pollution when high social costs are dictating cleaner air.

A divergence between social and private costs can be observed even in the simplest of consumer activities, such as throwing an empty soda can out the window of your car. To hang onto the can and later dispose of it in a trash barrel involves personal effort and thus private marginal costs. To throw it out the window not only is more exciting but effectively transfers the burden of disposal costs to someone else. The resulting externality ends up as roadside litter.

The same kind of divergence between private and social costs helps explain why people abandon old cars in the street rather than haul them to scrapyards. It also explains why people use vacant lots as open dumps. In all these cases, **the polluter benefits by substituting external costs for private costs.** In other words, market incentives encourage environmental damage.

REGULATORY OPTIONS

The failure of the market to include external costs in production and consumption decisions creates a basis for government intervention. As always, however, we confront a variety of policy options. We may define these options in terms of **two general strategies for environmental protection:**

- *Alter market incentives* in such a way that they discourage pollution.
- *Bypass market incentives* with some form of regulatory intervention.

Insofar as market incentives are concerned, the key to environmental protection is to eliminate the divergence between private costs and social costs. The opportunity to shift some costs onto others lies at the heart of the pollution problem. If we could somehow compel producers to *internalize* all costs—pay for both private and previously external costs—the divergence would disappear, along with the incentive to pollute.

Market-Based Options

Emission Charges. One possibility is to establish a system of **emission charges,** direct costs attached to the act of polluting. Suppose that we let you keep your power plant and permit you to operate it according to profit-maximizing principles. The only difference is that we no longer agree to supply you with clean air and cool water at zero cost. From now on, we'll charge you for these scarce resources. We might, say, charge you 2 cents for every gram of noxious emission you discharge into the air. In addition we might charge you 3 cents for every gallon of water you use, heat, and discharge back into the river.

Confronted with such emission charges, you'd have to alter your production decision. **An emission charge increases private marginal cost and encourages lower output and cleaner technology.** Figure 28.3 illustrates this effect.

Once an emission fee is in place, a producer may also reevaluate the efficiency decision. Consider again the choice of fuels to be used in our fictional power plant.

> **emission charge:** A fee imposed on polluters, based on the quantity of pollution.

FIGURE 28.3
Emission Fees

Emission charges can be used to close the gap between marginal social costs and marginal private costs. Faced with an emission charge of t, a private producer will reduce output from q_0 to q_1. Emission charges may also induce different investment and efficiency decisions.

We earlier chose high-sulfur coal, for the very good reason that it was the cheapest fuel available. Now, however, there's an additional cost attached to burning such fuel, in the form of an emission charge. This added cost may encourage the firm to switch to cleaner sources of energy, which would increase private marginal costs but reduce emission fees.

An emission charge might also persuade a firm to incur higher fixed costs. Rather than pay emission charges, it might be more economical to install scrubbers and other smokestack controls that reduce the volume of emissions from the burning of high-sulfur coal. This would entail additional capital outlays for the necessary abatement equipment but might not alter marginal costs. In this case, the fee-induced change in fixed costs might reduce pollution without any reduction in output.

The actual response of producers will depend on the relative costs involved. If emission charges are too low, it may be more profitable to continue burning and polluting with high-sulfur coal and simply pay a nominal fee. This is a simple pricing problem. We could set the emission price higher, prompting the behavioral responses we desire.

The same kind of relative cost considerations would apply to the thermal pollution associated with the power plant. The choice heretofore has been between building expensive cooling towers (and not polluting) or not incurring such capital costs (and simply discharging the heated water into the river). The profit-maximizing choice was fairly obvious. Now, however, the choice is between building cooling towers or paying out a steady flow of emission charges. The profit-maximizing decision is no longer evident. The decisive factor will be how high we set the emission charges. If the emission charges are set high enough, the producer will find it unprofitable to pollute.

Economic incentives can also change consumer behavior. At one time beverage producers imposed deposits to encourage consumers to bring the bottle back so it could be used again. But producers discovered that such deposits discouraged sales and yielded very little cost savings. Today, returnable bottles are rarely used. One result is the inclusion of over 30 billion bottles and 60 billion cans in our solid-waste disposal problem. We could reverse this trend by imposing a deposit on all beverage containers. Many states do this, at least for certain cans and bottles. Such deposits internalize pollution costs for the consumer and render the throwing of a soda can out the window equivalent to throwing away money.

Some communities have also tried to reduce solid-waste processing by charging a fee for each container of garbage collected. In Charlotte, Virginia, a fee of 80 cents per 32-gallon bag of garbage had a noticeable impact on consumer behavior. Economists Don Fullerton and Thomas Kinnaman observed that households reduced the weight of their garbage by 14 percent and the volume by 37 percent. As they noted,

"Households somehow stomped their garbage to get more in a container and trim their garbage bill."

Recycling Materials. An important bonus that emission charges offer is an increased incentive for the recycling of materials. The glass and metal in used bottles and cans can be recycled to produce new bottles and cans. Such recycling not only eliminates a lot of unsightly litter but also diminishes the need to mine new resources from the earth, a process that often involves its own environmental problems. The critical issues are once again relative costs and market incentives. *A container producer has no incentive to use recycled materials unless they offer superior cost efficiency and thus greater profits.* The largest component in the costs of recycled materials is usually the associated costs of collection and transportation. In this regard, an emission charge such as the 5-cent container deposit lowers collection costs because it motivates consumers to return all their bottles and cans to a central location.

Trends in recycling are posted by the U.S. Environmental Protection Agency (EPA) at www.epa.gov/epaoswer/non-hw/recycle.htm.

Higher User Fees. Another market alternative is to raise the price consumers pay for scarce resources. If people used less water, we wouldn't have to build so many sewage treatment plants. In most communities, however, the price of water is so low that people use it indiscriminately. Higher water fees would encourage water conservation.

A similar logic applies to auto pollution. The cheapest way to cut down on auto pollution is to drive less. Higher gasoline prices would encourage people to use alternative transportation and drive more fuel-efficient cars.

"Green" Taxes. Automakers don't want gasoline prices to go up; neither do consumers. So the government may have to impose *green taxes* to get the desired response. A green tax on gasoline, for example, raises the price of gasoline. The taxes not only curb auto emissions (less driving) but also create a revenue source for other pollution-abatement efforts. As the World View on the next page indicates, other nations impose far more green taxes than does the United States. Because public opinion polls show that a plurality of American consumers oppose such taxes, this disparity isn't likely to disappear.

Pollution Fines. Not far removed from the concept of emission and user charges is the imposition of fines or liability for cleanup costs. In some situations, such as an oil spill, the pollution is so sudden and concentrated that society has little choice but to clean it up quickly. The costs for such cleanup can be imposed on the polluter, however, through appropriate fines. Such fines place the cost burden where it belongs. In addition, they serve as an incentive for greater safety, for such things as double-hulled oil tankers and more efficient safety mechanisms on offshore oil wells. When Royal Caribbean Cruises was fined $9 million in 1998 for dumping garbage and oil from its cruise ships, the firm decided to monitor waste disposal practices more closely. In the absence of such fines, firms have little incentive to invest in environmental protection.

The EPA acquired still greater authority to control oil and chemical spills with passage of the Comprehensive Environmental Response, Compensation, and Liability Act of 1980. The act established a tax on crude oil and an assortment of chemical products. The resulting revenues created a superfund used to monitor and clean up hazardous oil and chemical spills. The act also allows the EPA to recoup *treble* damages from a firm that causes a spill but fails to help clean it up.

Tradable Pollution Permits

Another environmental policy option makes even greater use of market incentives. Rather than penalize firms that have already polluted, let firms *purchase* the right to continue polluting. As crazy as this policy might sound, it can be highly effective in limiting environmental damage.

The key to the success of pollution permits is that they're bought and sold among private firms. The system starts with a government-set standard for pollution reduc-

WORLD VIEW

Guess Who Taxes Pollution Least?
Making a Mess Costs Less in the U.S.

Economists have long argued that an efficient way to control pollution is to make those who cause it bear some of the costs via environmentally related or "green" taxes. These can run the gamut from retail taxes on gasoline to landfill charges on waste disposal.

By dint of its economic heft, the U.S. is commonly regarded as the world's biggest polluter. Yet the Organization for Economic Cooperation & Development reports that it imposes the lowest green taxes as a percent of gross domestic product of any industrial nation. While the average for OECD countries in 1998 was 2.7 percent of GDP, for example, the U.S. level was estimated at less than 1 percent.

Between 1994 and 1998, a majority of OECD members boosted their green-tax ratios, with Denmark's and Turkey's both rising by a full percentage point to 5 percent and 3 percent respectively. By contrast, the U.S., Germany, and France actually reduced their green-tax levels over the four-year period.

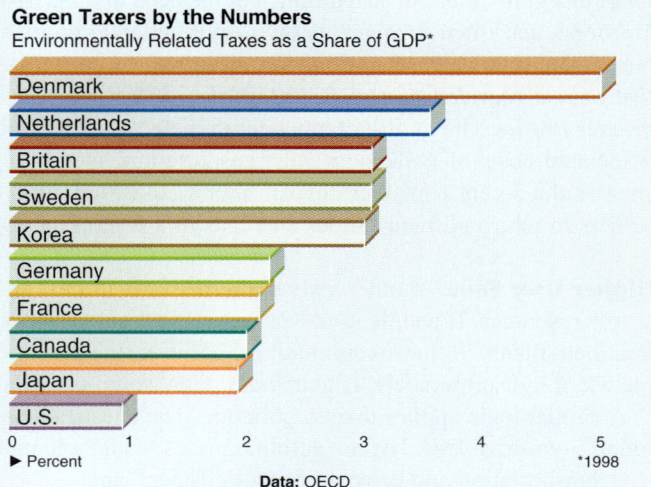

Green Taxers by the Numbers
Environmentally Related Taxes as a Share of GDP*

*1998

Source: *Business Week*, September 17, 2001. © 2001 The McGraw-Hill Companies, Inc. Reprinted with permission. www.businessweek.com

Analysis: "Green" taxes can be used to reduce the level of polluting consumption or production activities. They are not popular in the United States, however.

---

tion. Firms that reduce pollution by more than the standard earn pollution credits. They may then sell these credits to other firms, who are thereby relieved of cleanup chores. **The principal advantage of pollution permits is their incentive to minimize the cost of pollution control.**

To see how the permits work, suppose the policy objective is to reduce sulfur dioxide emissions by 2 tons. There are only two major polluters in the community: a copper smelter and an electric utility. Should each company be required to reduce its SO_2 emissions by 1 ton? Or can the same SO_2 reduction be achieved more cheaply with marketable pollution rights?

Table 28.1 depicts the assumed cost of pollution abatement at each plant. The copper smelter would have to spend $200 to achieve a 1-ton reduction in SO_2 emissions. The utility can do it for only $100. Table 28.1 also indicates that the utility can attain a *second* ton of SO_2 abatement for $150. Even though its marginal cost of pollution control is increasing, the utility still has lower abatement costs than the smelter. This cost advantage creates an interesting economic opportunity.

TABLE 28.1
Pricing Pollution Permits
If both firms reduce emissions by 1 ton each, the cost is $300. If the utility instead reduces emissions by 2 tons, the cost is only $250. A permit system allows the smelter to pay the utility for assuming the abatement responsibility.

	Marginal Cost of Pollution Abatement	
Reduction in Emissions (in tons)	Copper Smelter	Electric Utility
1	$200	$100
2	250	150
3	300	200

Recall that the policy goal is to reduce emissions by 2 tons. The copper smelter would have to spend $200 to achieve its share. But the utility can abate that second ton for $150. Accordingly, the smelter would save money by *paying* the utility for additional pollution abatement.

How much would the smelter have to pay? The utility would want at least $150 to cover its own costs. The smelter would benefit at any price below $200. Accordingly, the price of this transaction would be somewhere between $150 (the utility's cost) and $200 (the smelter's cost). The smelter would continue to pollute, but total SO_2 emissions would still drop by 2 tons. Both firms and society would be better off.

At the first real auction of pollution credits the average price paid was $156 (see News). For this price a firm could pay someone else to reduce SO_2 emissions by 1 ton rather than curb its own emissions. The Carolina Power and Light Company spent $11.5 *million* buying such permits.

Since they first became available in 1992, tradable pollution permits ("allowances") have become a popular mechanism for pollution control. Millions of allowances are now traded in the open market every year. Moreover, the permit market has gotten increasingly efficient, with visible bid and ask prices, broker specialists, and low transaction costs. In 2000, 12.7 *million* sulfur dioxide allowances were traded, each covering one ton of emission reduction. The price of a permit has also steadily declined, indicating that companies are discovering cheaper methods of pollution control. Entrepreneurs now have an incentive to discover cheaper methods for pollution abatement. They don't have to own a smelter or utility; they can now *sell* their pollution control expertise to the highest bidder. As the market for permits has expanded, the profit opportunities for environmental engineering firms have increased. This has accelerated productivity and reduced the cost of pollution abatement by 25 to 34 percent.

Public policy needn't rely on tradable permits or other market incentives to achieve desired pollution abatement. The government could instead simply *require* firms to reduce pollutants by specific amounts and even specify which abatement technology must be used. This approach is often referred to as the "command-and-control" option. The government *commands* firms to reduce pollution and then *controls* the process for doing so.

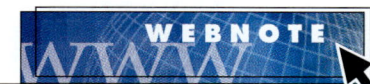

The Environmental Protection Agency has a website (www.epa.gov/airmarkets/acidrain) that explains the sulfur dioxide allowance trading system. The site also provides information on trading volume and prices. A private brokerage firm also offers a succinct explanation of permit trading and more timely prices; see www.cantor.com/ebs.

Command-and-Control Options

IN THE NEWS

Auction: $156 to Emit a Ton of Pollutants

CHICAGO—The right to spew a ton of sulfur dioxide into the air in 1995 costs about $156. That was the average sale price Tuesday at the first auction of pollution credits.

Total sold: 150,010 permits for $21.4 million. Permits sold for the year 2000 were cheaper, an average $136.

Price range: $122 to $450.

The auction of credits, at the Chicago Board of Trade, is key to the Environmental Protection Agency's efforts to halve acid rain pollutants by 2010. . . .

Who sells credits? Utilities that have less pollution than allowed under EPA rules. Who buys? Utilities with pollution problems, or speculators.

Top buyer: Carolina Power & Light Co. spent $11.5 million. . . .

Consumers could gain: The program could halve the cost of anti-pollution rules for utilities, which could lower bills.

—Kevin Johnson

Source: *USA Today*, March 31, 1993. © 1993, USA Today. Reprinted with permission. www.usatoday.com. For current price on pollution credits see www.epa.gov/airmarkets/trading/SO2 market.

Analysis: Marketable pollution permits encourage firms with more efficient pollution control technologies to overachieve, thereby earning pollution permits that can be sold to firms with more expensive pollution control technologies. Such trades reduce the *average* cost of pollution control.

The potential inefficiency of the command-and-control strategy was outlined earlier in Table 28.1. Had the government required *each* firm to reduce pollution by 1 ton, the total cost would have been $300. By allowing firms to use tradable permits, the cost of obtaining the same level of pollution abatement was only $250. The cost saving of $50 represents valuable resources that could be used to produce other desired goods and services.

Despite the superior efficiency of market-based environmental policies, the government often relies on the command-and-control approach. The Clean Air Acts of 1970 and 1990, for example, mandated not only fewer auto emissions but also specific processes such as catalytic converters and lead-free gasoline for attaining them. Specific processes and technologies are also required for toxic waste disposal and water treatment. Laws requiring the sorting and recycling of trash (see News) are other examples of process regulation.

Although such command-and-control regulation can be effective, this policy option also entails risks. By requiring all market participants to follow specific rules, the regulations may impose excessive costs on some activities and too low a constraint on others. Some communities may not need the level of sewage treatment the federal government prescribes. Individual households may not generate enough trash to make sorting and separate pickups economically sound. Some producers may have better or cheaper ways of attaining environmental standards. ***Excessive process regulation may raise the costs of environmental protection*** and discourage cost-saving innovation. There's also the risk of regulated processes becoming entrenched long after they are obsolete. When that happens we may end up with worse outcomes than a less regulated market would have generated—that is, **government failure.**

government failure: Government intervention that fails to improve economic outcomes.

Central Planning

Some of the worst government failure occurs in the most regulated economies. Prior to 1990, Eastern Europe relied on central planning to make production and investment decisions. There was no *market* incentive to pollute since there was no opportunity for private profit. On the other hand, the central planners had to set priorities. Their choice was to maximize production. Environmental concerns had lower priority. This set of priorities created an environmental catastrophe: polluted air and water, dying forests, poisoned food, and deteriorating human health. Poland, for example, produced six times more air pollution per unit of output than did Western Europe. Europe's largest coal-burning power plant, located in Belchatow, burns soft brown coal, covering the countryside with sulfur and soot. The world's largest single source of air pollution is the

IN THE NEWS

Los Angeles Requires Recycling, Trash Separation

LOS ANGELES—The City Council has unanimously approved mandatory trash separation and recycling in a $160 million program to halve the amount of garbage deposited in the city's rapidly filling landfills.

While about 1,000 U.S. cities, including Washington, D.C., have some kind of recycling program, the Los Angeles effort will be among the nation's largest, along with those in New York City and statewide in New Jersey.

The plan will require all 720,000 single-family households in the city to separate glass and plastic bottles, aluminum cans and newspaper into different containers for collection. The city eventually will sell reusable materials to recyclers.

—Frederick M. Muir

Source: *Los Angeles Times,* December 21, 1989. © 1989 Los Angeles Times. Reprinted by permission. www.latimes.com

Analysis: The government may require specific processes for reducing pollution. Such a command-and-control approach runs the risk of increasing costs more than necessary.

complex of ore smelters in Norilsk (central Siberia), which emits 2 *million* tons of sulfur a day. Cars made in Russia and Eastern Europe still burn leaded gas. The Volga River has been crippled by factory waste, untreated sewage, and hydroelectric dams, while the Black Sea has virtually been destroyed. The polluted environments of Eastern Europe and the former Soviet republics amply document that government-directed production isn't necessarily more environment-friendly than market-directed production.

BALANCING BENEFITS AND COSTS

Protecting the environment entails costs as well as benefits. Installing smokestack scrubbers on factory chimneys and catalytic converters on cars requires the use of scarce resources. Taking the lead out of gasoline wears out engines faster and requires expensive changes in technology. Switching to clean fuels requires enormous investments in technology, plant, and equipment. The EPA estimates that a 10-year program to achieve national air and water standards would cost more than $1 trillion. Restoring the ozone layer, removing hazardous wastes, and cleaning up the rest of the environment would cost trillions more.

Whatever the exact costs of environmental protection, it's apparent that we're talking about an enormous reallocation of productive resources. Although cleaning up the environment is a universally acknowledged goal, we must remind ourselves that those resources could be used to fulfill other goals as well. The multitrillion-dollar tab would buy a lot of subways and parks or build decent homes for the poor. If we choose to devote those resources instead to pollution-abatement efforts, we'll have to forgo some other goods and services. This isn't to say that environmental goals don't deserve that kind of priority but simply to remind us that any use of our scarce resources involves an **opportunity cost**.

Opportunity Costs

opportunity cost: The most desired goods or services that are forgone in order to obtain something else.

Fortunately, the amount of additional resources required to clean up the environment is relatively modest in comparison to our productive capacity. Over a 10-year period we'll produce well over $100 trillion of goods and services (GDP). On this basis, the environmental expenditures contemplated by present environmental policies and goals represent only 1 to 3 percent of total output.

The Optimal Rate of Pollution

Whether a small percentage of GDP is too much or too little to spend on environmental protection depends on the value we assign to other goods and services and to a cleaner environment. That is, the **optimal rate of pollution** occurs at the point at which the opportunity costs of further pollution control equal the benefits of further reductions in pollution. To determine the optimal rate of pollution, we need to compare the marginal social benefits of additional pollution abatement with the marginal social costs of additional pollution control expenditure. The optimal rate of pollution is achieved when we've satisfied the following equality:

optimal rate of pollution: The rate of pollution that occurs when the marginal social benefit of pollution control equals its marginal social cost.

$$\begin{array}{c} \text{Optimal} \\ \text{rate of} \\ \text{pollution} \end{array} : \begin{array}{c} \text{marginal benefit} \\ \text{of pollution} \\ \text{abatement} \end{array} = \begin{array}{c} \text{marginal cost} \\ \text{of pollution} \\ \text{abatement} \end{array}$$

This formulation is analogous to the utility-maximizing rule in consumption. If another dollar spent on pollution control yields less than a dollar of social benefits, then additional pollution control expenditure isn't desirable. In such a situation, the goods and services that would be forsaken for additional pollution control are more valued than the environmental improvements that would result. The News on the next page suggests that we may already have crossed that threshold in combating air pollution.

The formula for the optimal rate of pollution implies that ***a totally clean environment isn't economically desirable.*** The marginal benefit of achieving zero pollution is infinitesimally small. But the marginal cost of eliminating that last particle of pollution will be very high. As we weigh the marginal benefits and costs, we'll conclude that *some* pollution is cost-effective.

Cost-Benefit Analysis

Although marginal analysis tells us that a zero-pollution goal isn't economically desirable, it doesn't really pinpoint the optimal level of pollution. To apply those guidelines we need to identify and evaluate the marginal benefits of any intervention and its marginal costs. Sometimes such calculations yield extraordinarily high cost-benefit ratios. According to researchers at the Harvard Center for Risk Analysis, the *median* cost per life-year saved by EPA regulations is $7.6 million. One of the highest cost-benefit ratios is attached to chloroform emission controls at pulp mills: The cost per life-year saved exceeds $99 billion (see Table 28.2). A human life may in fact be too precious to value in dollars and cents. But in a world of limited resources, the opportunity costs of every intervention need to be assessed. How many lives would be saved if we spent $99 billion on cancer or AIDS research?

Who Will Pay?

The costs of pollution control aren't distributed equally. A relatively small number of economic activities account for the bulk of emissions and effluents. These activities will have to bear a disproportionate share of the cleanup burden.

Find out how economists measure the costs and benefits of environmental programs at www.epa.gov. Click on "Programs," then "Research," then "Office of Research and Development."

To ascertain how the burden of environmental protection will be distributed, consider first the electric power plant discussed earlier. As we observed (Figure 28.2), the plant's output will decrease if production decisions are based on social rather than private marginal costs—that is, if environmental consequences are considered. If the plant itself is compelled to pay full social costs, in the form of either compulsory investment or emission charges, its profits will be reduced. Were no other changes to take place, the burden of environmental improvements would be borne primarily by the producer.

Such a scenario is unlikely, however. Rather than absorb all the costs of pollution controls themselves, producers will seek to pass on some of this burden to their customers in the form of higher prices. Their ability to do so will depend on the extent of competition in their industry, their relative cost position in it, and the price elasticity of consumer demand. In reality, the electric power industry isn't very competitive as yet, and its prices are still subject to government regulation. In addition, consumer de-

---

IN THE NEWS

Two Economists Question Benefit of Cleaning Up a Major Air Pollutant

The health benefits of cleaning up a widespread urban air pollutant, ground-level ozone, may not be worth the price, two economists argue in a new study.

The economists at Resources for the Future, a respected nonadvocacy research institute in Washington, compared the costs of plans for Los Angeles and the nation as a whole to meet national air quality standards for ground-level ozone with their potential health benefits. In both cases, the most optimistic estimate of the costs fell far short of the most optimistic measure of the health benefits.

They chose to look at ground-level ozone because it is one of the most difficult air pollution problems to solve. They also said they believed they could effectively apply cost-benefit analysis to it.

According to cost estimates based on 1989 government data, they found the cost for the nation to meet the standards would be $8.8 billion to $12.8 billion through 2004 while health benefits would be $250 million to $1 billion. They estimated that the cost of a more ambitious 1989 Los Angeles plan would be $13 billion through 2010 but that it would yield only $3 billion in health benefits.

Basis of Conclusions The economists, Alan J. Krupnick and Paul R. Portney, concluded that air should be cleaned up in the most polluted areas but that investing billions of dollars to get people to quit smoking, control radon gas and provide better prenatal and neonatal care might contribute much more. . . .

"I don't expect people to like the conclusion," Mr. Portney said, "But this is not a justification for not cleaning up the air. It just says maybe we could get more health benefits for our money if we spent it someplace else."

Source: *New York Times,* April 30, 1991. © 1991 The New York Times Company. Reprinted by permission. www.nytimes.com

Analysis: The costs of environmental protection are substantial and must be compared to the benefits. The *optimal* amount of pollution balances marginal benefits and costs.

TABLE 28.2
High-Cost, Low-Benefit Regulations
Environmental protection may have an excessive cost-benefit ratio if (*a*) the benefits of pollution control are miniscule (for example, if there's little difference in life expectancy) or (*b*) the costs of intervention are very high. The scarcity of resources implies that interventions with low-cost, high-benefit ratios are more efficient.

Regulation	Cost per Life-Year
Radionuclide emission control at coal-fired utility boilers	$ 2,395,161,000
Benzene emission control at rubber tire manufacturing plants	19,865,323,000
Radionuclide emission control at uranium fuel cycle facilities	33,750,000,000
Chloroform private well emission standard at 48 pulp mills	99,351,684,000

Source: "Five Hundred Lifesaving Interventions and Their Cost-Effectiveness," Tommy O. Tengs, Sc.D., et al., Harvard Center for Risk Analysis 1994.

mand is relatively price-inelastic. Accordingly, the profit-maximizing producer will appeal to the state or local power commission for an increase in electricity prices based on the costs of pollution control. Electric power consumers are likely to end up footing part or all of the environmental bill. The increased prices will more fully reflect the social costs associated with electricity use.

In addition to the electric power industry, the automobile, paper, steel, and chemical industries will be adversely affected by pollution controls. In all these cases, the prices of the related products will increase, in some instances by significant percentages. These price increases will help reduce pollution in two ways. First, they'll help pay for pollution control equipment. Second, they'll encourage consumers to change their expenditure patterns in the direction of less polluting goods.

THE ECONOMY TOMORROW

Forget about littered beaches, smelly landfills, eye-stinging smog, and contaminated water. The really scary problem for the economy tomorrow is much more serious: Some scientists say that the carbon emissions we're now spewing into the air are warming the earth's atmosphere. If the earth's temperature rises only a few degrees, they contend, polar caps will melt, continents will flood, and weather patterns will go haywire (see World View on the next page). If things get bad enough, there may not be any economy tomorrow.

The Greenhouse Threat

The earth's climate is driven by solar radiation. The energy the sun absorbs must be balanced by outgoing radiation from the earth and the atmosphere. Scientists fear that a flow imbalance is developing. Of particular concern is a buildup of carbon dioxide (CO_2) that might trap heat in the earth's atmosphere, warming the planet.

The natural release of CO_2 dwarfs the emissions from human activities. But there's a concern that the steady increase in man-made CO_2 emissions—principally from burning fossil fuels like gasoline and coal—is tipping the balance.

The Greenhouse Effect

Other scientists are skeptical about both the temperature change and its causes. A 1988 National Oceanic and Atmospheric Administration study concluded that there's been no ocean warming in this past century. Furthermore, they say, the amount of CO_2 emitted into the atmosphere by human activity (about 7 billion tons per year) is only a tiny fraction of natural emissions from volcanoes, fires, and lightning (200 billion tons per year). Skeptics also point out that the same computer models predicting global warming in the next generation predicted a much larger increase in temperature for the previous century than actually occurred.

The Skeptics

In mid-2001, the National Academy of Sciences resolved at least one of those issues. The Academy confirmed that the earth is warming, largely due to the increased buildup of greenhouse gas concentrations. But the Academy wasn't able to identify whether the problem originates in human behavior or natural climate variability.

Global Externalities

The uncertainty about the causes of the greenhouse effect makes policy decisions difficult. One thing is certain, however: **CO_2 emissions are a global externality** of industrial production and fuel consumption. Without some form of government intervention, there's little likelihood that market participants will voluntarily reduce CO_2 emissions.

Kyoto Treaty. In December 1997, most of the world's industrialized nations pledged to reduce CO_2 emissions. The Kyoto treaty they initiated in 1997 expressed an international commitment to reduce greenhouse emissions during the period 2008–12. The world's industrialized nations promised to cut their emissions by 5.2 percent below 1990 levels. That would require some industries (e.g., autos, steel, paper, electric power) to substantially alter production methods and, possibly, output. For their part, the developing nations of the world promised to curb their *growth* of emissions.

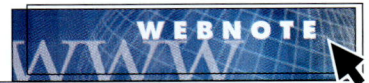

The United Nations provides information on climate change and emissions data for individual nations at www.unfccc.de.

After four years of design and debate, 178 nations signed the Kyoto treaty at a June 2001 United Nations convention. The United States, however, refused to sign. The Bush administration argued that the implied costs of pollution abatement were far too high, especially in view of the uncertain payoff. Bush also argued that the treaty put the United States and other industrialized nations at a competitive disadvantage, since only they (not developing nations) had to absorb the higher pollution-abatement costs.

With neither universal support nor enforcement mechanisms, the Kyoto treaty will not achieve the target levels of pollution abatement. However, the treaty has increased public awareness of global environmental externalities and encouraged more efforts to control them. As with domestic policy, the challenge for the economy tomorrow is to find a policy mix that will generate the optimal level of global pollution.

WORLD VIEW

Scientists Issue Dire Prediction on Warming
Faster Climate Shift Portends Global Calamity This Century

BEIJING, Jan. 22—In the most forceful warning yet on the threat of global warming, an international panel of hundreds of scientists issued a report today predicting brutal droughts, floods and violent storms across the planet over the next century because air pollution is causing surface temperatures to rise faster than anticipated.

The report, approved unanimously at a U.N. conference in Shanghai and described as the most comprehensive study on the subject to date, says that Earth's average temperature could rise by as much as 10.4 degrees over the next 100 years—the most rapid change in 10 millennia and more than 60 percent higher than the same group predicted less than six years ago.

If new scientific models are accurate, rising temperatures will melt polar ice caps and raise sea levels by as much as 34 inches, causing floods that could displace tens of millions of people in low-lying areas—such as China's Pearl River Delta, much of Bangladesh and the most densely populated area of Egypt. Droughts will parch farmlands and aggravate world hunger. Storms triggered by such climatic extremes as El Niño will become more frequent. Diseases such as malaria and dengue fever will spread. . . .

The report cited "new and stronger evidence that most of the observed warming of the last 50 years is attributable to human activities," primarily the burning of oil, gasoline and coal, which produces carbon dioxide and other gases that trap heat in Earth's atmosphere. . . .

The global warming issue has proved highly contentious among environmental scientists, with many respected figures arguing that Earth undergoes periodic climatic changes with or without contributions from mankind.

—Philip P. Pan

Source: *Washington Post*, January 23, 2001. © 2001 The Washington Post. Reprinted with permission. www.washingtonpost.com

---

Analysis: The external costs of consumption and production activities contribute to global environmental problems. What should be done to curb these global external costs?

SUMMARY

- Air, water, and solid-waste pollution impose social and economic costs. The costs of pollution include the direct damages inflicted on our health and resources, the expense of cleaning up, and the general aesthetic deterioration of the environment.
- Pollution is an external cost, a cost of a market activity imposed on someone (a third party) other than the immediate producer or consumer.
- Producers and consumers generally operate on the basis of private benefits and costs. Accordingly, a private producer or consumer has an incentive to minimize his own costs by transforming private costs into external costs. One way of making such a substitution is to pollute — to use "free" air and water rather than install pollution control equipment, or to leave the job of waste disposal to others.
- Social costs are the total amount of resources used in a production or consumption process. When social costs are greater than private costs, the market's price signals are flawed. This market failure will induce people to harm the environment by using suboptimal processes and products.
- One way to correct the market inefficiency created by externalities is to compel producers and consumers to internalize all (social) costs. This can be done by imposing emission charges and higher user fees. Such charges create an incentive to invest in pollution abatement equipment, recycle reusable materials, and conserve scarce elements of the environment.
- Tradable pollution permits help minimize the cost of pollution control by (*a*) promoting low-cost controls to substitute for high-cost controls and (*b*) encouraging innovation in pollution control technology.
- An alternative approach to cleaning up the environment is to require specific pollution controls or to prohibit specific kinds of activities. Direct regulation runs the risk of higher cost and discouraging innovations in environmental protection.
- The opportunity costs of pollution abatement are the most desired goods and services given up when factors of production are used to control pollution. The optimal rate of pollution is reached when the marginal social benefits of further pollution control equal associated marginal social costs.
- In addition to diverting resources, pollution control efforts alter relative prices, change the mix of output, and redistribute incomes. These outcomes cause losses for particular groups and may thus require special economic or political attention.
- The greenhouse effect represents a global externality. Reducing global emissions requires consensus on optimal pollution levels (i.e., the optimal balance of pollution-abatement costs and benefits).

Key Terms

production decision
efficiency decision
external cost
social costs
private costs
market failure
emission charge
government failure
opportunity cost
optimal rate of pollution

Questions for Discussion

1. What are the *economic* costs of the externalities caused by air toxins? Or beach closings? (See News, page 598.) How would you measure their value?
2. Should we try to eliminate *all* pollution? What economic considerations might favor permitting some pollution?
3. Why would auto manufacturers resist exhaust control devices? How would their costs, sales, and profits be affected?
4. Does anyone have an incentive to maintain auto-exhaust control devices in good working order? How can we ensure that they will be maintained?
5. Suppose we established a $10,000 fine for water pollution. Would some companies still find that polluting was economical? Under what conditions?
6. What economic costs are imposed by mandatory sorting of trash?
7. The issuance of a pollution permit is just a license to destroy the environment. Do you agree? Explain.
8. What opportunity costs of combating ozone pollution are identified in the News article on page 610?
9. If a high per-bag fee were charged for garbage collection, would illegal dumping increase?
10. Should the United States have signed the Kyoto Treaty? What are the arguments for and against U.S. participation?

Web Activities

1. Is the U.S. Environmental Protection Agency (EPA) going too far or not far enough? Read the executive summary at www.heartland.org/studies/gli-sum.htm. Does the author of this study believe that appropriate economic decisions have been made in the EPA's Great Lakes initiative? What errors does the author believe the EPA has made in the study?
2. Log on to www.scorecard.org, and enter your zip code. What is the most likely form of pollution for your area? Does this rank higher or lower than the national average? If this pollution problem is resolved in your area, how will employment in your area be affected? Is the socially optimal level of output by this organization higher or lower than current production levels? Explain.
3. Log on to yosemite1.epa.gov/ee/epa/eed.nsf/pages/incentives, and read a summary of the EPA's report on economic incentives for pollution control. Have the incentives been successful?

 THE ACCOMPANYING STUDENT PROBLEM SET CONTAINS NUMERICAL AND GRAPHING PROBLEMS FOR THIS CHAPTER

CHAPTER

The Farm Problem

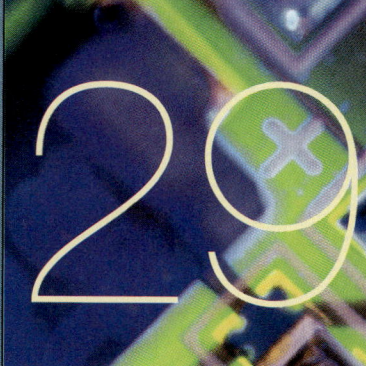

In 1996, the U.S. Congress charted a new future for U.S. farmers. No longer would they look to Washington, D.C., for decisions on what crops to plant or how much farmland to leave fallow. The Freedom to Farm Act would get the government out of the farm business and let "laissez faire" dictate farm outcomes. Farmers would lose their federal subsidies but could earn as much as they wanted in the marketplace. Taxpayers loved the idea. So did most farmers, who were enjoying high prices and bumper profits in 1996.

The Asian crisis that began in mid-1997 dealt farmers a severe blow. U.S. farms export 25–50 percent of all the wheat, corn, soybeans, and cotton they grow. When Asia's economies plunged into recession, those export sales plummeted. With sales, prices, and profits all declining, farmers lost their enthusiasm for the "freedom to farm"; they wanted Uncle Sam to jump back into the farm business with price and income guarantees. The U.S. Congress obliged with a series of emergency appropriations that restored price and income guarantees. Then the U.S. House of Representatives passed the Farm Security Act of 2001 that would make those subsidies permanent. Between 2002 and 2012, taxpayers will pay U.S. farmers $176 billion in subsidies.

This chapter examines the rationale for continuing farm subsidies and their effects on farm production, prices, and exports. In particular, we confront these questions:

- Why do farmers need any subsidies?
- How do government subsidies affect farm production, prices, and incomes?
- Who pays for farm subsidies?

DESTABILIZING FORCES

The agriculture industry is one of the most competitive of all U.S. industries. First, there are 2 million farms in the United States. Although some of these farms are immense—with tens of thousands of acres—no single farm has the power to affect the market supply or price of farm products. That is, individual farmers have no **market power**.

Competition in agriculture is maintained by low **barriers to entry**. Although farmers need large acreages, expensive farm equipment, substantial credit, hard work, and hired labor, all these resources become affordable when farming is

Competition in Agriculture

market power: The ability to alter the market price of a good or service.

barriers to entry: Obstacles that make it difficult or impossible for would-be producers to enter a particular market, such as patents.

economic profit: The difference between total revenues and total economic costs.

generating **economic profits.** When farming is profitable, existing farmers expand their farms, farmers' children are able to start new farms, and new farmers can obtain enough credit to start farming on a large enough scale to survive. It would be much harder to enter the automobile industry, the airline business, or even the farm machinery market than it would be to enter farming. Because of these low barriers to entry, economic profits don't last long in agriculture.

Given the competitive structure of U.S. agriculture, *individual farmers tend to behave like perfect competitors.* Individual farmers seek to expand their rate of output until marginal cost equals price. By following this rule, each farmer makes as much profit as possible from existing resources, prices, and technology.

Like other competitive firms, U.S. farmers can maintain economic profits only if they achieve continuing cost reductions. Above-normal profits obtained from current production techniques and prices aren't likely to last. Such economic profits will entice more people into agriculture and will stimulate greater output from existing farmers. That is exactly the kind of dilemma that confronted the early producers of microcomputers. To stay ahead, individual firms (farms) must continue to improve their productivity.

Technological Advance

The rate of technological advance in agriculture has, in fact, been spectacular. Since 1929, the farm labor force has shrunk by two-thirds, yet farm output has increased by 60 percent. Between the early 1950s and today,

- Annual egg production has jumped from 183 to 257 eggs per laying chicken.
- Milk output has increased from 5,400 to 17,772 pounds per cow annually.
- Wheat output has increased from 17.3 to 41.9 bushels per acre.
- Corn output has jumped from 39.4 to 105 bushels per acre.

Farm output per labor hour has grown even faster, having increased nearly 10 times over in the same period. Such spectacular rates of productivity advance rival those of our most high-tech industries. These technological advances resulted from the development of higher-yielding seeds (the "green revolution"), advanced machinery (mechanical feeders and milkers), improved animal breeding (crossbreeding), improved plants (rust-resistant wheat), better land-use practices (crop rotation and fertilizers), and computer-based management systems.

Inelastic Demand

In most industries, continuous increases in technology and output would be most welcome. The agricultural industry, however, confronts a long-term problem. Simply put, there's a limit to the amount of food people want to eat.

This constraint on the demand for agricultural output is reflected in the relatively inelastic demand for food. Consumers don't increase their food purchases very much when farm prices fall. The **price elasticity** of food demand is low. As a consequence, when harvests are good, farmers must reduce prices a lot to induce a substantial increase in the quantity of food demanded. Even if the price elasticity of demand were as high as 0.2, the percentage change in price would have to be five times as large as the percentage change in quantity produced. Hence, prices would have to fall 25 percent in order to sell a bumper crop that was 5 percent larger than normal, that is,

price elasticity of demand: The percentage change in quantity demanded divided by the percentage change in price.

$$\text{Required percentage change in price} = \frac{\text{percentage change in quantity(harvest)}}{\text{price elasticity of demand}}$$

so,

$$\% \Delta p = \frac{0.05}{0.20} = 0.25$$

In 1998, the *corn* crop was 6 percent larger than the year before. In 1999, the corn crop decreased by 3.5 percent. As Figure 29.1 illustrates, *with low price elasticity of demand, abrupt changes in farm output have a magnified effect on market prices.*

The **income elasticity** of food demand is also low. The income elasticity of demand for food refers to the responsiveness of food demand to changes in income. Specifically,

$$\text{Income elasticity of demand} = \frac{\text{\% change in quantity demanded (at constant price)}}{\text{\% change in income}}$$

income elasticity of demand: Percentage change in quantity demanded divided by percentage change in income.

Since 1929, per capita income has nearly tripled. But per capita food consumption has increased only 85 percent. Hence, neither lower prices nor higher incomes significantly increase the quantity of food demanded.

In the long run, then, the increasing ability of U.S. agriculture to produce food must be reconciled with very slow growth of U.S. demand for food. Over time, this implies that farm prices will fall, relative to nonfarm prices. And they have. Between the years 1910–14 and 2001, the ratio of farm prices to nonfarm prices fell 60 percent. In the absence of government price-support programs and foreign demand for U.S. farm products, farm prices would have fallen still further.

The long-term downtrend in (relative) farm prices is only one of the major problems confronting U.S. agriculture. The second major problem is short run in nature. Prices of farm products are subject to abrupt short-term swings. If the weather is good, harvests are abundant. As we saw in Figure 29.1, abundant harvests imply a severe drop in prices, however, particularly when food demand is relatively price-inelastic. On the other hand, a late or early freeze, a drought, or an infestation by disease or insect pests can reduce harvests substantially and push prices sharply higher.

Abrupt Shifts of Supply

Response Lags. Natural forces aren't the only cause of short-term price instability. Time lags between the production decision and the resultant harvest also contribute to price instability. If prices are high one year, farmers have an incentive to increase their rate of output. In this sense, prices serve the same signaling function in agriculture as they do in nonfarm industries. What distinguishes the farmers' response is the lack of inventories and the fixed duration of the production process. In the computer industry, a larger quantity of output can be supplied to the market fairly quickly by drawing down inventories or stepping up the rate of production. In farming, supply can't respond so quickly. In the short run, the farmer can only till more land, plant additional seed, or breed more livestock. No additional food supplies will be available until a new crop or herd grows. Hence, the agricultural supply response to a change in prices is always one harvest (or breeding period) later.

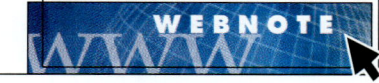

Annual prices for farm products are compiled by the National Agricultural Statistics Service at the U.S. Department of Agriculture. Visit usda.mannlib.cornell.edu/reports/nassr/price/zap-bb.

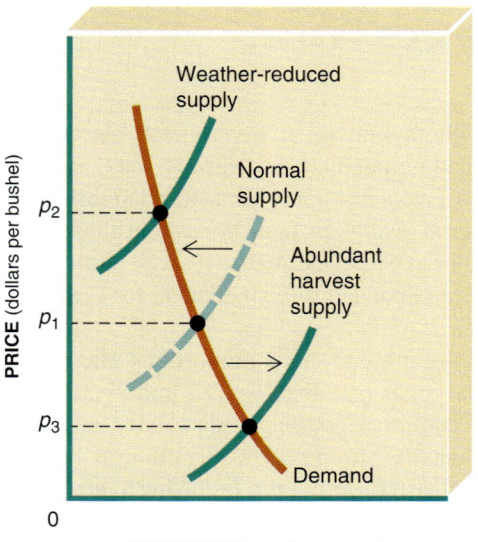

FIGURE 29.1
Short-Term Instability

Changes in weather cause abrupt shifts of the food supply curve. When combined with the relatively inelastic demand for food, these supply shifts result in wide price swings. Notice how the price of grain jumps from p_1 to p_2 when bad weather reduces the harvest. If good weather follows, prices may fall to p_3.

FIGURE 29.2
Unstable Corn Prices

Most agricultural prices are subject to abrupt short-term changes. Notice how corn prices rose dramatically during World Wars I and II, then fell sharply. Poor harvests in the rest of the world increased demand for U.S. food in 1973–74. Since then prices have moved sharply in both directions.

Source: U.S. Department of Agriculture.

The natural lag in responses of agricultural supplies intensifies short-term price swings. Suppose corn prices are exceptionally high at the end of a year, because of a reduced harvest. High prices will make corn farming appear unusually profitable. Farmers will want to expand their rate of output—plant more corn acreage—to share in these high profits. But the corn won't appear on the market until the following year. By that time, there's likely to be an abundance of corn on the market, as a result of both better weather and increased corn acreage. Hence, corn prices are likely to plummet (look again at Figure 29.1).

No single farmer can avoid the boom-or-bust movement of prices. Even a corn farmer who has mastered the principles of economics has little choice but to plant more corn when prices are high. If he doesn't plant additional corn, prices will fall anyway, because his own production decisions don't affect market prices. By not planting additional corn, he only denies himself a share of corn market sales. ***In a highly competitive market, each producer acts independently.***

Figure 29.2 demonstrates the historical instability of corn prices. Notice how corn prices repeatedly rise, then abruptly fall. This kind of price swing is particularly evident in 1915–20, 1935–37, 1946–48, 1973–76, 1980–84, and 1997–2000.

THE FIRST FARM DEPRESSION, 1920–1940

The U.S. agricultural industry operated without substantial government intervention until the 1930s. In earlier decades, an expanding population, recurrent wars, and less advanced technology had helped maintain a favorable supply-demand relationship for farm products. There were frequent short-term swings in farm prices, but these were absorbed by a generally healthy farm sector. The period 1910–19 was particularly prosperous for farmers, largely because of the expanded foreign demand for U.S. farm products by countries engaged in World War I.

The two basic problems of U.S. agriculture grew to crisis proportions after 1920. In 1919, most farm prices were at historical highs (see Figures 29.2 and 29.3). After World War I ended, however, European countries no longer demanded as much American food. U.S. exports of farm products fell from nearly $4 billion in 1919 to $1.9 billion in 1921. Farm exports were further reduced in the following years by increasing restrictions on international trade. At home, the end of the war implied an increased availability of factors of production and continuing improvement in farm technology.

FIGURE 29.3

Farm Prices, 1910–1940 (1910–1914 = 100)

Farm prices are less stable than nonfarm prices. During the 1930s, relative farm prices fell 50 percent. This experience was the catalyst for government price supports and other agricultural assistance programs.

The impact of reduced demand and increasing supply is evident in Figure 29.3. In 1919 farm prices were more than double their levels of the period 1910–14. Prices then fell abruptly. In 1921 alone, farm prices fell nearly 40 percent.

Farm prices stabilized in the mid-1920s but resumed a steep decline in 1930. In 1932 average farm prices were 75 percent lower than they had been in 1919. At the same time, the average income per farmer from farming fell from $2,651 in 1919 to $855 in 1932.

The Great Depression hit small farmers particularly hard. They had fewer resources to withstand consecutive years of declining prices and income. Even in good times, small farmers must continually expand output and reduce costs just to maintain their incomes. Hence, the Great Depression accelerated an exodus of small farmers from agriculture, a trend that continues today.

Table 29.1 shows that the number of small farms has declined dramatically. In 1910, there were 3.7 million farmers under 100 acres in size. Today, there are fewer than 800,000 small farms. During the same period, the number of large farms (500 acres or more) has more than doubled. This loss of small farmers, together with the increased mechanization of larger farms, has reduced the farm population by 23 million people since 1910.

U.S. FARM POLICY

The U.S. Congress has responded to these agricultural problems with a variety of programs. Most seek to raise and stabilize the price of farm products. Other programs seek to reduce the costs of production. When all else fails, the federal government also provides direct income support to farmers.

Size of Farm	Number, 1910	Percent	Number, 1997	Percent
Under 100 acres	3,691,611	58.0	746,767	39.4
100–499 acres	2,494,461	39.2	815,152	42.2
500–999 acres	125,295	2.0	176,974	9.2
1000 acres and over	50,135	0.8	176,207	9.2
Total	6,361,502	100.0	1,915,100	100.0

Source: U.S. Department of Agriculture.

TABLE 29.1

Size Distribution of U.S. Farms, 1910 and 1997

Inelastic food demand, combined with increasing agricultural productivity, implies a declining number of farmers. Small farmers are particularly vulnerable because they don't have the resources to maintain a high rate of technological improvement. As a result, the number of small farms has declined dramatically, while the number of large farms has grown.

Price Supports

market surplus: The amount by which the quantity supplied exceeds the quantity demanded at a given price; excess supply.

Price supports have always been the primary focus of U.S. farm policy. As early as 1926, Congress decreed that farm products should sell at a fair price. By "fair," Congress meant a price higher than the market equilibrium. The consequences of this policy are evident in Figure 29.4: *A price floor creates a* **market surplus.**

Once it set an above-equilibrium price for food, Congress had to find some way of disposing of the resultant food surplus. Initially, Congress proposed to get rid of this surplus by selling it abroad at world market prices. President Calvin Coolidge, a staunch opponent of government intervention, vetoed this legislation both times Congress passed it.

parity: The relative price of farm products in the period 1910–14.

The notion of fair prices resurfaced in the Agricultural Adjustment Act of 1933. During the Great Depression farmers were going bankrupt in droves. To help them, Congress sought to restore the purchasing power of farm products to the 1909–14 level. The farm-nonfarm price relationships of 1909–14 were regarded by Congress as fair and came to be known as **parity** prices. If parity prices could be restored, Congress reasoned, farm incomes would improve.

Supply Restrictions

The goal of parity pricing couldn't be attained without altering market supply and demand in some way.

Set-Asides. The easiest way to increase farm prices without creating a surplus is to reduce the production of food. Congress does this by paying farmers for voluntary reductions in crop acreage. These **acreage set-asides** shift the food supply curve to the left. In 1995, roughly 50 *million* acres of farmland—nearly one-fifth of the nation's wheat, corn, sorghum, rice, and cotton acreage—was idled by government set-asides. If farmers didn't agree to these set-asides, they couldn't participate in the price support programs.

acreage set-aside: Land withdrawn from production as part of policy to increase crop prices.

Dairy Termination Program. To prop up dairy prices, the federal government also started a Dairy Termination Program in 1985. This is analogous to a set-aside program. In this case, however, the government pays dairy farmers to slaughter or export dairy cattle. Between 1995 and 1987, the government paid dairy farmers over $1 billion to "terminate" 1.6 million cows. The reduction in dairy herds boosted prices for milk and other dairy products.

Marketing Orders. The federal government also permits industry groups to limit the quantity of output brought to market. By themselves, individual farmers can't raise the

FIGURE 29.4
Fair Prices and Market Surplus

The interaction of market supply and demand establishes an equilibrium price (p_e) for any product, including food. If a higher price (p_f) is set, the quantity of food supplied (q_s) will be larger than the quantity demanded (q_d). Hence, attempts to establish a "fair" (higher) price for farm products must cope with resultant market surpluses.

market price by withholding output. If they act collectively, however, they can. If a quantity greater than authorized is actually grown, the "surplus" is disposed of by individual farmers. In the 1980s, these *marketing orders* forced farmers to waste each year roughly 500 million lemons, 1 billion(!) oranges, 70 million pounds of raisins, 70 million pounds of almonds, and millions of plums, nectarines, and other fruits. This wholesale destruction of crops gave growers market power and kept farm prices artificially high.

Import Quotas. The market supply of farm products is also limited by import restrictions. Imports of sugar, dairy products, cotton, and peanuts are severely limited by import quotas. Imports of beef are limited by "voluntary" export limits in foreign countries. Import taxes (duties) limit the foreign supply of other farm products.

While trying to limit the *supply* of farm products, the government also inflates the *demand* for selected farm products.

Demand Distortions

Government Stockpiles. An executive order signed by President Franklin Roosevelt in 1933 altered the demand for farm products. The Commodity Credit Corporation (CCC) created at that time is effectively a buyer of last resort for selected farm products.

The CCC becomes a buyer of last resort through its loan programs. Farmers can borrow money from the CCC at **loan rates** set by Congress (see Table 29.2). In 2001, for example, a wheat farmer could borrow $2.53 in cash for every bushel of wheat he relinquished to the CCC. If the market price of wheat went above $2.53, the farmer could sell the wheat, repay the CCC, and pocket the difference. If, instead, the price fell below the loan rate, the farmer could simply let the CCC keep the wheat and repay nothing. Hence, ***whenever market prices are below CCC loan rates, the government ends up buying surplus crops.***

loan rate: The implicit price paid by the government for surplus crops taken as collateral for loans to farmers.

Figure 29.5 illustrates the effect of CCC price supports on individual farmers and the agricultural market. In the absence of price supports, competitive farmers would confront a horizontal demand curve at price p_e, itself determined by the intersection of market supply and demand (in part *b*). The CCC's offer to buy ("loan") unlimited quantities at a higher price shifts the demand curve facing each farmer upward, to the guaranteed price p_2. This higher price induces individual farmers to increase their rate of output, from q_1 to q_2.

As farmers respond to price supports, the agriculture market is pushed out of equilibrium. At the support level p_2, more output is supplied than demanded. The market surplus created by government price supports creates an additional policy dilemma. ***The market surplus induced by price supports must be eliminated in one of three ways:***

Commodity	Loan Rate
Corn	$1.94 per bushel
Sorghum	1.71
Barley	1.62
Oats	1.16
Wheat	2.53
Soybeans	5.38
Cotton (upland)	0.5192 per pound
Rice	6.50 per hundredweight

Source: U.S. Department of Agriculture.

TABLE 29.2
2001 Loan Rates
The Commodity Credit Corporation lends money to farmers at fixed "loan rates" that are implicit price floors. If the market price falls below the CCC loan rate, the government keeps the crop as full payment of the loan.

FIGURE 29.5
The Impact of Price Supports

In the absence of price supports, the price of farm products would be determined by the intersection of market supply and demand. In this case, the equilibrium price would be p_e, as shown in part b. All individual farmers would confront this price and produce up to the point where MC = p_e, as in part a.

Government price supports raise the price to p_2. By offering to buy (or "loan") unlimited quantities at this price, the government shifts the demand curve facing each farmer upward. Individual farmers respond by increasing their output from q_1 to q_2. As farmers increase their output, a market surplus develops (part b).

- *Government purchases* and stockpiling of surplus food.
- *Export sales.*
- *Restrictions on supply.*

Government purchases of surplus crops have led to massive stockpiles of wheat, cotton, corn, and dairy products. At one time, the excess wheat was stored in old ammunition bunkers in Nebraska and scrubbed-out oil tanks in Texas. Surplus nonfat dry milk was stored in caverns near Kansas City, and surplus cotton filled warehouses in the South. Even today about one fourth of U.S. farm output is destroyed or stored.

Because farm prices are artificially high in the United States, export sales are sometimes difficult. As a result, the federal government must give away lots of food to poor nations and even subsidize exports to developed nations. The United States isn't alone in this regard: The European Union maintains even higher prices and subsidies (see World View).

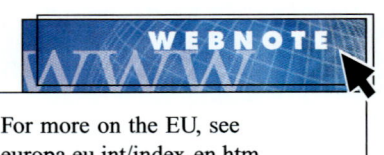

For more on the EU, see europa.eu.int/index-en.htm.

Cost Subsidies

The market surplus induced by price supports is exacerbated by cost subsidies. Irrigation water, for example, is delivered to many farmers by federally funded reclamation projects. The price farmers pay for the water is substantially below the cost of delivering it; the difference amounts to a subsidy. In 1986, this water subsidy cost taxpayers over $500 million. The Department of Agriculture has distributed an additional $150 million to $200 million a year to farmers to help defray the costs of fertilizer, drainage, and other production costs.

The federal government has also provided basic research, insurance, marketing, grading, and inspection services to farmers at subsidized prices. All these subsidies serve to lower fixed or variable costs. Their net impact is to stimulate additional output, as illustrated in Figure 29.6.

Direct Income Support

Price supports, cost subsidies, and supply restrictions are designed to stabilize agricultural markets and assure farmers an adequate income. As we've seen, however, they en-

EU Farm Subsidies

In Europe, believe it or not, the subsidy for every cow is greater than the personal income of half the people in the world.
—Former British Prime Minister Margaret Thatcher

United States farm policy isn't unique. Most industrialized countries go to even greater lengths to protect domestic agriculture. For example, France, Germany, and Switzerland all shield their farmers from international competition while subsidizing their exports. Japan protects its inefficient rice producers, while the Netherlands subsidizes greenhouse vegetable farmers.

The motivations for farm subsidies are pretty much the same in every country in the world. Every country wants a secure source of food in the event of war. Most nations also want to maintain a viable farm sector, which is viewed as a source of social stability. Finally, politicians in every country must be responsive to a well-established and vocal political constituency.

The European Union (EU) imposes high tariffs on imported food, keeping domestic prices high. The member governments also agree to purchase any surplus production. To get rid of the surplus, the governments then subsidize exports. In 2000, direct EU farm subsidies exceeded $45 billion, triple the size of U.S. farm subsidies. All this protection costs the average EU consumer over $200 a year.

Analysis: Farm subsidies are common around the world. Such subsidies alter not only domestic output decisions but international trade patterns as well.

---

tail significant distortions of market outcomes. The Congressional Budget Office estimates that the milk price supports alone have increased retail dairy prices 3 to 6 percent, reduced consumption 1 to 5 percent, and encouraged excessive dairy production. Because of such distortions, direct income supports were authorized by the Agriculture and Consumer Protection Act of 1973. *The advantage of direct income supports is that they achieve the goal of income security without distortions of market prices and output.*

The principal form of direct income support is so-called **deficiency payments.** Congress identifies specific "target prices" for selected crops. In 1995, the target price for wheat was $4 a bushel (see Table 29.3). If market prices fell below these targets, the government made up the difference. Target prices are another form of price floor. Unlike the case of CCC loan rates, however, target prices don't trigger government purchases of surplus crops. The target price is only used to compute the amount of the deficiency payment paid directly to farmers.

In principle, direct income payments are a more efficient mechanism for subsidizing farm incomes. But farmers don't like them. Five thousand angry farmers drove their tractors to Washington, D.C., in February 1979 to protest this policy approach. Their rallying cry was "parity, not charity." They wanted higher price supports (an indirect subsidy) rather than more deficiency payments (a direct subsidy).

deficiency payment: Income transfer paid to farmers for difference between target and market prices.

FIGURE 29.6
The Impact of Cost Subsidies

Cost subsidies lower the marginal cost of producing at any given rate of output, thereby shifting the marginal cost curve downward. The lower marginal costs make higher rates of output more profitable and thus increase output. At price p_2, lower marginal costs increase the farmer's profit-maximizing rate of output from q_2 to q_3.

TABLE 29.3
1995 Target Prices
Congress sets target prices for selected commodities. If the market price falls below the target price, a *deficiency payment* is made directly to the farmer.

Commodity	Target Price
Corn	$ 2.75 per bushel
Sorghum	2.61
Barley	2.38
Oats	1.45
Wheat	4.00
Cotton (upland)	0.729 per pound
Rice	10.71 per hundredweight

Source: U.S. Department of Agriculture.

THE SECOND FARM DEPRESSION, 1980–1986

With so many price supports, supply restrictions, cost subsidies, and income transfers, one would think that farming is a riskless and profitable business. But this hasn't been the case. Incomes remain low and unstable, especially for small farmers. In fact, the entire agricultural sector experienced another setback in the 1980s. In 1980, the net income of U.S. farmers fell 42 percent. As Figure 29.7 shows, farm incomes recovered somewhat in 1981 but then resumed their steep decline in 1982. In 1983, farmers' net income was only one-third the level of 1979. This income loss was steeper than that of the Great Depression. Real farm income was actually lower in 1983 than in 1933. This second depression of farm incomes accelerated the exodus of small farmers from agriculture, severely weakened rural economies, and bankrupted many farm banks and manufacturers of farm equipment and supplies.

The Cost Squeeze

This second depression of farm incomes was not caused by abrupt price declines. Prices for farm products increased slightly between 1979 and 1983, but production costs rose much faster. Average farm production costs rose 30 percent between 1979 and 1983 while the average price of farm products increased only 1.5 percent. As a result, the **profit** (net income) of farmers fell abruptly.

profit: The difference between total revenue and total cost.

Fuel Costs. The cost squeeze on farm incomes started with an abrupt increase in fuel prices. In 1979, the OPEC nations raised crude oil prices 50 percent. This action pushed up the price of gasoline and related fuels 37 percent in 1980 alone, making it more expensive to operate farm equipment.

FIGURE 29.7
Net Farm Income, 1977–2000

Between 1979 and 1983 net farm income fell 64 percent. This decline was steeper than the income slide that occurred during the Great Depression (when net farm income fell 45 percent between 1929 and 1933). Farm incomes rose sharply from 1983 to 1989 but were unstable throughout the 1990s.

Source: *Economic Report of the President, 2001.*

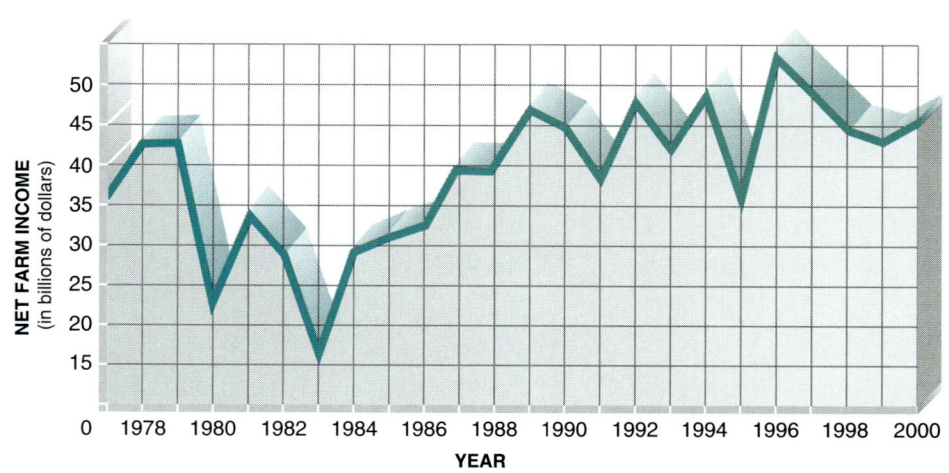

Fertilizer Costs. The increase in crude oil prices also pushed up the price of fertilizer. Most fertilizers are manufactured from a petroleum base. As a consequence, fertilizer prices rose in tandem with fuel prices, increasing 24 percent in 1980 and another 7 percent in 1981.

Interest Rates. The third, and perhaps most devastating, source of the farmers' cost squeeze was an increase in interest rates. Farming is extremely land- and capital-intensive. The value of U.S. farmers' assets is roughly $1 trillion. Many of these assets (such as land and machinery) are purchased with borrowed funds, often at variable interest rates. Farmers also borrow money for planting and harvesting. All this debt renders farmers vulnerable to abrupt changes in interest rates. When interest rates skyrocketed—the prime rate rose from 9 percent in 1978 to over 20 percent in 1980—the debt burden of farmers mounted.

Declining Land Values. High interest rates and declining incomes also reduced the value of farmers' most important asset—their land. The value of land reflects its present and future income-generating potential. The cost squeeze reduced potential income, and high interest rates made future income less valuable. These twin forces sent land values into a tailspin, which made it more difficult and more expensive for farmers to get needed credit.

Declining Exports. The farmers' plight was worsened still further by declining export sales. In 1980, in response to the Soviet invasion of Afghanistan, President Jimmy Carter imposed an embargo on grain sales to the Soviet Union. This directly reduced wheat sales by 15,000 to 20,000 tons per year and indirectly encouraged foreign competition.

Export sales were reduced even further by the strong value of the U.S. dollar. Between 1980 and 1984, the international value of the dollar rose a staggering 50 percent. This made it much more expensive for global consumers to buy U.S. farm output. As a result, the quantity of exports declined.

THE ECONOMY TOMORROW

Farmers on the Dole

To a large extent, the farm crisis of the 1980s had nothing to do with federal farm policy. The increase in oil prices was initiated by OPEC. Higher interest rates were a reflection of macroeconomic conditions. Likewise, the high value of the dollar was a response to U.S. interest rates and the economic recovery, and its effects weren't confined to the farm sector. All these adverse forces were reversed in the mid-1980s, and farm incomes rose sharply from their 1983 lows (see Figure 29.7).

Steps toward Deregulation

The post-1983 recovery of the farm sector created an opportunity to redesign farm policy. With production, prices, exports, and incomes all rising, the timing was perfect for the deregulation of the farm sector.

1985 Farm Act. The Farm Security Act of 1985 took a few steps in that direction. The core feature of the act was a gradual reduction in government support prices. For example, the support price ("loan rate") for wheat was reduced from $3.30 per bushel in 1986 to $1.95 in 1990. By reducing the support price, the government hoped to discourage overproduction and recurrent market surpluses.

Another feature of the 1985 act was to limit the government purchase of market surpluses. Rather than buying surpluses at the guaranteed loan rate, the government encouraged farmers to sell their surpluses at market prices. The government then reimbursed the farmers for the difference between the guaranteed (support) price and the market price.

The 1985 act also capped deficiency payments at $50,000 per farm. The intent of this cap was to reduce subsidy payments to huge corporate farms and to lessen their incentive for overproduction. In practice, however, large farms have been subdivided into many smaller farms, allowing individual farmers to collect multiple deficiency payments.

The 1990 Act. By the time the authority of the 1985 act expired (in 1990), crop prices, farm incomes, and the price of farmland had all risen significantly. These improvements had little to do with government farm policy, however. Rather they reflected the continued expansion of the U.S. economy, declining oil and fertilizer costs, and strong foreign demand for U.S. farm products.

Despite the increased prosperity of farming during the 1985–90 period, the basic structure of farm subsidies was continued in the 1990 Farm Act. Indeed, loan rates were *increased,* effectively raising the price floor for farm products. At the same time, however, Congress reduced the amount of set-aside acreage by 15 percent. It also gave farmers more discretion to farm on unsubsidized acreage. Target prices were reduced and frozen for five years.

The net effect of the 1990 legislation was to move farming another small step closer to market realities. A bit more acreage was freed from government regulation, target prices were set closer to market prices, and more market surpluses were sold rather than stored in government warehouses.

The 1996 Freedom to Farm Act. In 1996, Congress moved farmers considerably further down the road toward deregulation with two radical changes in farm policy. The first change was the phaseout of deficiency payments. Target prices (Table 29.3) and their associated deficiency payments were terminated. In their place, farmers were offered "market transition payments." The size of the transition payments wasn't dependent on commodity prices but instead was fixed by Congress for a period of seven years. In this way, Congress focused on stabilizing farm *incomes* rather than farm *prices*. In 2002, all such income support was scheduled to end, leaving farmers the "freedom to farm" (off the dole).

The 1996 act also eliminated many restrictions on acreage set-asides. Up to 36.4 million acres were still eligible for "production flexibility contract payments" (set-asides). But farmers no longer had to keep set-aside acreage completely idle or to grow only specific commodities. Markets, not politicians, would decide what to grow.

Back from the Brink

At first, farmers loved the 1996 policy reforms. In the 1996–97 crop year, commodity prices were up and farm incomes were at an all-time high (Figure 29.7). Yet farmers were still getting billions of dollars in taxpayer subsidies. What a great deal!

The Asian Crisis. Then the farm economy turned sour again. The Asian crisis that began in July 1997 was the principal cause. When the currencies of Thailand, Korea, Indonesia and Malaysia, and other Asian nations tumbled, the foreign price of U.S. farm output soared. When the economies of these Asian nations stumbled into recession, their ability to buy American farm products was further diminished. As a result, U.S. farm exports fell sharply during 1997 and 1998.

The decline in export demand weakened farm prices. Abundant harvests in the United States, China, Europe, and elsewhere also depressed farm prices. Between October 1997 and October 1998, grain prices tumbled 40 to 60 percent (see News). These price declines rivaled those of 1929–32 and 1980–85.

Renewed Subsidies. When farm prices and incomes plunged, farmers again demanded federal aid. Just prior to the November 1998 elections, Congress increased

The U.S. Department of Agriculture makes available a broad array of statistics on the U.S. farm sector at www.usda.gov.

IN THE NEWS

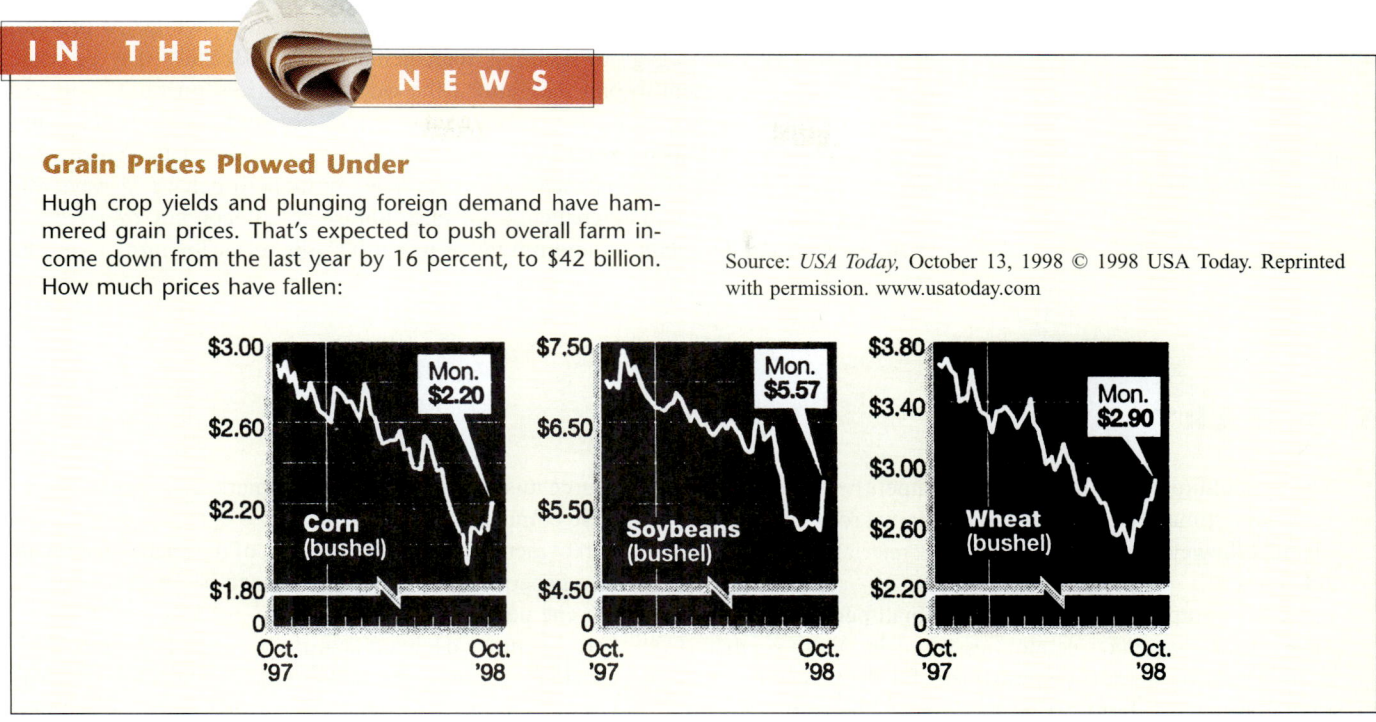

Grain Prices Plowed Under

Hugh crop yields and plunging foreign demand have hammered grain prices. That's expected to push overall farm income down from the last year by 16 percent, to $42 billion. How much prices have fallen:

Source: *USA Today*, October 13, 1998 © 1998 USA Today. Reprinted with permission. www.usatoday.com

Analysis: The 1997–98 Asian crisis reduced the demand for U.S. farm products while good weather increased supply. The resultant price plunge created another farm crisis that reversed the process of deregulation.

---

market transition payments by 50 percent. Congress also authorized the early payment of $5 billion in farm aid not due until 1999. Finally, Congress approved $500 million in "disaster payments"—a new form of aid—to offset falling prices and exports. Congress continued "emergency" funding of the farm sector for several years.

The 2001 Farm Act. The intent of the 1996 Farm Act ostensibly was to wean farmers off the dole, making them more reliant on market forces. "Freedom to farm" implied a deregulation of farm prices and production decisions. That isn't how it worked out, however. Farmers only *promised* to forsake price supports in exchange for temporary (seven-year) income support. By 1998, however, it was clear that *farmers were prepared to rely only on good markets, not bad ones.* When the market for farm products went bad, they expected more federal aid, not more freedom to farm.

Farmers got more permanent aid in 2001. Even before the 1996 Freedom to Farm Act had expired, farm lobbyists petitioned Congress not only to continue deficiency payments (based on target prices) but also to increase loan rates. With the U.S. and global economies sliding into recession, the farmers' appeal was well timed. The September 11, 2001, terrorist attacks also enhanced the chances of congressional approval. In explaining the October 5, 2001, House of Representatives vote to approve the Farm Security Act of 2001, a congressional aide noted that "you can't be going to war and beating up on farmers at the same time." Congress responded by increasing farm subsidies and creating new ones for sugar growers, plant farmers, hog operators, and even horse breeders.

Moral Hazard. The Farm Act of 2001 assures that U.S. farmers will remain on the government dole in the economy tomorrow. Even while on the dole, however, farmers could do more to manage the inevitable risks of the weather, price changes, and global

See the latest U.S. House of Representatives Agriculture Committee at www.house.gov/agriculture.

moral hazard: An incentive to engage in undesirable behavior.

competition. Farmers can buy crop insurance to mitigate the effects of the weather. They can also use forward contracts to eliminate the risks of price swings. At present, however, few farmers engage in such risk management. Why? Because they've come to expect the government to bail them out if the weather or prices turn out badly. So they've no incentive to pay insurance premiums or sign forward contracts that limit their profit potential. This is the kind of **moral hazard** that government assistance often creates. The very offer of government aid encourages farmers to behave in ways that worsen market outcomes. The challenge for farm policy in the economy tomorrow is to maximize market incentives and minimize moral hazards, even for farmers on the dole.

SUMMARY

- The agricultural sector has a highly competitive structure, with approximately 2 million farms. Many crops are regulated, however, by government restrictions and subsidies.
- Most farm output is produced by the small percentage of large farms that enjoy economies of scale. Most small farmers rely on nonfarm employment for their income.
- In a free market, farm prices tend to decline over time because of increasing productivity and low income elasticity of demand. Variations in harvests, combined with a low price elasticity of demand, make farm prices unstable.
- Most of today's farm policies originated during the Great Depression, in response to low farm prices and incomes.
- The government uses price supports and cost subsidies to raise farm prices and profits. These policies cause resource misallocations and create market surpluses of specific commodities.
- Direct income support in the form of deficiency payments also generates excess supply, but can be targeted more to income needs.
- Farm incomes declined sharply between 1979 and 1983, causing a second depression in the farm sector. The drop was caused by sharp increases in fuel, fertilizer, and interest costs. The Asian crisis that began in 1997 caused another farm crisis.
- The 1996 Farm Act called for a phaseout of farm subsidies. Falling prices and incomes during 1997–2001 stalled and eventually reversed that process.
- Government regulation not only risks design flaws but creates moral hazards that may reduce efficiency.

Key Terms

market power
barriers to entry
economic profit
price elasticity of demand
income elasticity of demand
market surplus
parity
acreage set-aside
loan rate
deficiency payment
profit
moral hazard

Questions for Discussion

1. Would the U.S. economy be better off without government intervention in agriculture? Who would benefit? Who would lose?
2. Are large price movements inevitable in agricultural markets? What other mechanisms might be used to limit such movement?
3. Why doesn't the United States just give its crop surpluses to poor countries? What problems might such an approach create?
4. Farmers can eliminate the uncertainties of fluctuating crop prices by selling their crops in futures markets (agreeing to a fixed price for crops to be delivered in the future). Who gains or loses from this practice?
5. Why do farmers prefer price supports to deficiency payments?
6. If two-thirds of all U.S. farms fail to earn a profit, why do they stay in business?
7. You need a government permit (allotment) to grow peanuts or tobacco. Who gains or loses from such regulation?

Web Activities

1. How are agricultural groups using the Internet to promote their business? Check out one of the following: wine growers (www.winezone.com), peach growers (www.calpeach.com), dairy farmers (dfamilk.com), or almond growers (www.almondsarein.com). What is the target audience for this site? What is the purpose of this site?
2. Should the government help farmers by setting minimum prices for their products? See both sides of the debate on price supports at www.nfo.org/PressReleases/ PR032801.pdf (pro position) and www.cato.org/pubs/briefs/bp-070es.html (con position). Identify the economic arguments used on each side in the debate. Which is more persuasive? Why?
3. Log on to www.ers.usda.gov/briefing/FarmPolicy, and access the "U.S. commodity loan program." Summarize how the farm commodity loan program works. What does this do to production in each farm sector eligible for the loan program? How does this affect the market price?

 THE ACCOMPANYING STUDENT PROBLEM SET CONTAINS NUMERICAL AND GRAPHING PROBLEMS FOR THIS CHAPTER

PART 11

Factor Markets: Basic Theory

Factor markets operate like product markets, with supply and demand interacting to determine prices and quantities. In factor markets, however, resource inputs rather than products are exchanged. Those exchanges determine the wages paid to workers and the rent, interest, and profits paid to other inputs. The micro theories presented in Chapters 30 through 32 explain how those factor payments are determined.

CHAPTER 30

The Labor Market

In 2002, the CEO of Walt Disney Company was midway through a 10-year contract that could end up paying him $771 million for his services. Tiger Woods was in the third year of a Nike endorsement contract worth at least $70 million. Yet the president of the United States was paid only $400,000. And the secretary who typed the manuscript of this book was paid just $19,000. What accounts for these tremendous disparities in earnings?

Why does the average college graduate earns over $40,000 while the average high school graduate earns just $25,000? Are such disparities simply a reward for enduring four years of college, or do they reflect real differences in talent?

Surely we can't hope to explain these earnings disparities on the basis of the willingness to work. After all, my secretary would be more than willing to work day and night for $77 million per year. For that matter, so would I. Accordingly, the earnings disparities can't be attributed to differences in the quantity of labor supplied. If we're going to explain why some people earn a great deal of income while others earn very little, we must consider both the *supply* and the *demand* for labor. In this regard, the following questions arise:

- How do people decide how much time to spend working?
- What determines the wage rate an employer is willing to pay?
- Why are some workers paid so much and others so little?

To answer these questions, we must examine the behavior of labor *markets*.

LABOR SUPPLY

The following two ads recently appeared in the campus newspaper of a well-known university:

Will do ANYTHING for money: able-bodied liberal-minded male needs money, will work to get it. Have car. Call Tom 765-3210.

Web architect. Experienced website designer. Looking for part-time or consulting position on or off campus. Please call Margaret, ext. 0872, 9–5.

Although placed by individuals of very different talents, the ads clearly expressed Tom's and Margaret's willingness to work. Although we don't know how much money they were asking for their respective talents, or whether they ever found jobs, we can be sure that they were prepared to take a job at some wage rate.

Otherwise, they wouldn't have paid for the ads in the "Jobs Wanted" column of their campus newspaper.

The advertised willingness to work expressed by both Tom and Margaret represents a **supply of labor.** They're offering to sell their time and talents to anyone who's willing to pay the right price. Their explicit offers are similar to those of anyone who looks for a job. Job seekers who check the current job openings at the student employment office or send résumés to potential employers are demonstrating a willingness to accept employment—that is, to *supply* labor. The 25,000 Muscovites who applied for jobs at Russia's first McDonald's were also offering to supply labor (see World View).

Our first concern in this chapter is to explain these labor supply decisions. How do people decide how many hours to supply at any given wage rate? Do people try to maximize their total wages? If they did, we'd all be holding three jobs and sleeping on the commuter bus. Since most of us don't behave this way, other motives must be present. What are these other motivations, and how do they affect the quantity of labor supplied at various wage rates?

labor supply: The willingness and ability to work specific amounts of time at alternative wage rates in a given time period, *ceteris paribus.*

Income vs. Leisure

The reward for working comes in two forms: (1) the intrinsic satisfaction of working and (2) a paycheck. MBA grads say they care more about the intrinsic satisfaction than the pay (see News on the next page). They also get huge paychecks, however. Those big paychecks are explained in part by the quantity of labor supplied: MBA grads often end up working 60 or more hours a week. The reason people are willing to work so many hours is that they want more income.

Not working obviously has some value, too. In part, we need some nonwork time just to recuperate from working. We also want some time to watch television, go to a soccer game, or enjoy other goods and services we've purchased.

Our conflicting desires for income and leisure create a dilemma: The more time we spend working, the more income we have but also less time to enjoy it. Working, like all activities, involves an opportunity cost. Generally, we say that *the opportunity cost of working is the amount of leisure time that must be given up in the process.*

The inevitable trade-off between labor and leisure explains the shape of individual labor supply curves. As we work more hours, our leisure time becomes more scarce—and thus more valuable. Hence, **higher wage rates are required to compensate for the**

WORLD VIEW

In Moscow, 25,000 Apply for 630 Jobs at McDonald's

More than 25,000 Muscovites have dreams of flipping burgers beneath the golden arches as a member of the worldwide Big Mac and French fry brigade, eager to share in the West's most greasy right of passage.

The flood of job seekers started almost immediately after a Moscow newspaper advertisement was published last month. More than 1,000 applications for the 630 available crew spots came the first day, said George Cohon, deputy chairman of Moscow McDonald's. More than 3,100 interviews have been conducted, seven days a week. . . .

Many job seekers are housewives and students from the prestigious Moscow University, and more than 20 percent speak two languages. . . .

The Pushkin Square outlet, the biggest McDonald's in the world, will serve 15,000 diners a day, with 700 seats inside and 200 outside. . . .

Part-time Soviet workers make about $1^1/_2$ rubles per hour, said Cohon, which is $2.50 at the commercial rate. But workers will also be rewarded every few months for productivity.

—Kara Swisher

Source: *Washington Post,* December 14, 1989. © 1989 The Washington Post. Reprinted with permission. www.washingtonpost.com

Analysis: The quantity of labor supplied at any given wage rate depends on the value of leisure and the desire for income. Even a seemingly low wage offer attracted a huge quantity of labor in Moscow.

IN THE NEWS

MBA Grads Seek Challenge at Work, Not Just Big Bucks

Cynics might argue, but money apparently isn't what drives most graduate business students, *Inc.* magazine says. . . .

Inc. talked to 907 graduating MBA students at 10 schools this spring. Just 12 percent of those questioned said they went into graduate school primarily because of big salaries down the road. Only 24 percent rated a high salary as one of the most important considerations in choosing their next job.

Those answers don't surprise Teresa Miles, 23, who just earned her MBA at Duke University's Fuqua School of Business. "There are definitely some students who fit that greedy mold," says Miles, a native of Greenwich, Conn. "But it's such a stereotype I have to laugh at it."

Miles, who starts work June 15 at the Bank of New York's commercial lending department, will earn about $60,000 annually. But it was "a challenging experience and something that will do something for me" that led her to accept the bank's offer.

Most students think along those lines, says Associate Dean Dennis Weidenear at Purdue University's Krannert School of Management. "I don't think you should discount the pay they'll be getting because it is important," he says. "But they're not willing to walk over their grandmothers just to get a better salary."

Other poll results:

Challenging work was rated a "most important" job characteristic by 75 percent of the students; 44 percent ranked atmosphere first; 40 percent, location. . . .

—Mark Memmott

What MBAs at Some Top Schools Earn

School	Starting Salaries in 2000
Harvard	$99,274
Stanford	97,876
MIT	92,343
Northwestern	92,101
Dartmouth	91,223
Chicago	88,707
Virginia	85,116
Michigan	85,081

Source: *U.S. News and World Report,* April 9, 2001. Reprinted with permission. www.usnews.com

Source: *USA Today,* May 28, 1987. © 1987 USA Today. Reprinted with permission (updated in 2001 by author). www.usatoday.com

Analysis: The quantity of labor supplied depends on the intrinsic satisfaction of working and the wages paid. MBA grads apparently work long hours for both high wages and job satisfaction.

Cornell University tracks the salaries of its MBA graduates at www.gsm.cornell.edu/newideas/pressreleases/mba_jobs.dg.html.

increasing opportunity cost of labor. We'll supply a larger quantity of labor only if offered a higher wage rate. This is reflected in the labor supply curve in Figure 30.1.

The upward slope of the labor supply curve may be reinforced with the changing value of income. Those first few dollars earned on the job are really precious, especially if you have bills to pay. As you work and earn more, however, your most urgent needs will be satisfied. You may still want more things, but the urgency of your consumption desires is likely to be diminished. In other words, *the marginal utility of income may decline as you earn more.* If this happens, the wages offered for more work lose some of their allure. You may not be willing to work more hours unless offered a higher wage rate.

The upward slope of an individual's labor supply curve is thus a reflection of two potential phenomena:

- The increasing opportunity cost of labor as leisure time declines.
- The decreasing marginal utility of income as a person works more hours.

Money isn't necessarily the only thing that motivates people to work. People *do* turn down higher-paying jobs in favor of lower-wage jobs that they like. Many parents forgo high-wage "career" jobs in order to have more flexible hours and time at home. Volunteers offer their services just for the sense of contributing to their communities; they don't need a paycheck. Even MBA graduates say they're motivated more by the challenge of high-paying jobs than the money (see News). But money almost always makes a difference: People *do* supply more labor when offered higher wages.

FIGURE 30.1
The Supply of Labor

The quantity of any good or service offered for sale typically increases as its price rises. Labor supply responds in the same way. At the wage rate w_1, the quantity of labor supplied is q_1 (point A). At the higher wage w_2, workers are willing to work more hours per week, that is, to supply a larger quantity of labor (q_2).

The force that drives people up the labor supply curve is the lust for more income. Higher wages enable people to buy more goods and services. The quest for higher levels of consumption induces people to *substitute* labor for leisure.

At some point, however, additional goods and services will lose their allure. Individuals with extremely high incomes already have a multitude of goods and services to enjoy. If they are offered a higher wage rate, the **substitution effect of wages** may not be persuasive. Rather than supplying *more* labor, they might even *reduce* the number of hours they work, thereby maintaining a high income *and* increasing their leisure. While you might do cartwheels for $25 an hour, Bill Gates or Brad Pitt might not lift a finger for such a paltry sum. Muhammad Ali once announced that he wouldn't spend an hour in the ring for less than $1 million and would box *less,* not more, as the pay for his fights exceeded $3 million. For him, the added income obtainable from one championship fight was so great that he felt he didn't have to fight more to satisfy his income and consumption desires.

A low-wage worker might also respond to higher wage rates by working *less,* not more. People receiving very low wages (such as migrant workers, household help, and babysitters) have to work long hours just to pay the rent. The increased income made possible by higher wage rates might permit them to work *fewer* hours. These *negative* labor supply responses to increased wage rates are referred to as the **income effect** of a wage increase.

A Backward Bend?

substitution effect of wages: An increased wage rate encourages people to work more hours (to substitute labor for leisure).

income effect of wages: An increased wage rate allows a person to reduce hours worked without losing income.

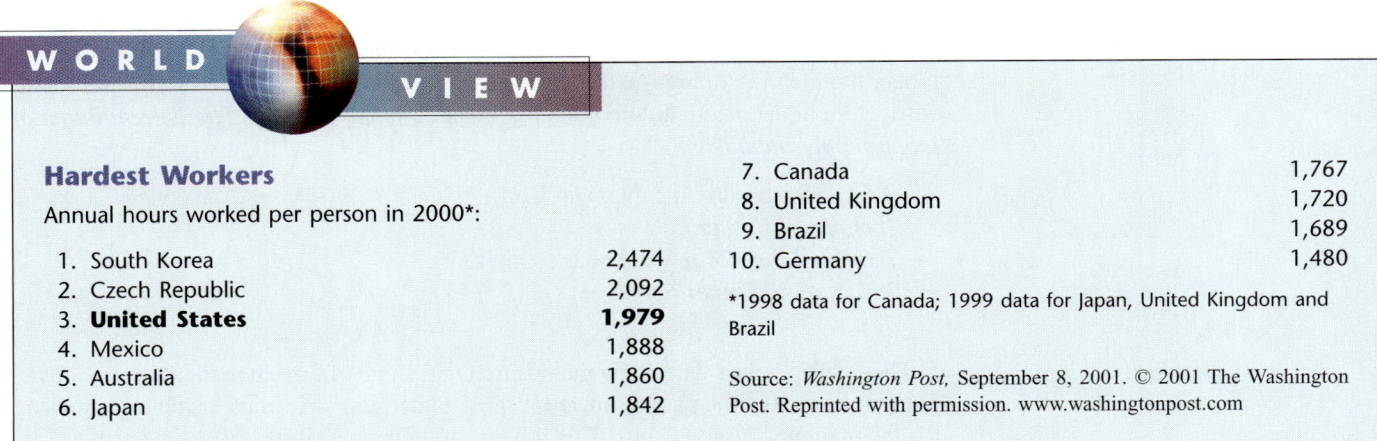

WORLD VIEW

Hardest Workers
Annual hours worked per person in 2000*:

1. South Korea	2,474
2. Czech Republic	2,092
3. United States	**1,979**
4. Mexico	1,888
5. Australia	1,860
6. Japan	1,842
7. Canada	1,767
8. United Kingdom	1,720
9. Brazil	1,689
10. Germany	1,480

*1998 data for Canada; 1999 data for Japan, United Kingdom and Brazil

Source: *Washington Post,* September 8, 2001. © 2001 The Washington Post. Reprinted with permission. www.washingtonpost.com

Analysis: Despite their high standard of living, Americans continue to work long hours. This suggests that substitution effects still outweigh income effects.

FIGURE 30.2
The Backward-Bending Supply Curve

Increases in wage rates make additional hours of work more valuable, but also less necessary. Higher wage rates increase the quantity of labor supplied as long as substitution effects outweigh income effects. At the point where income effects begin to outweigh substitution effects, the labor supply curve starts to bend backward.

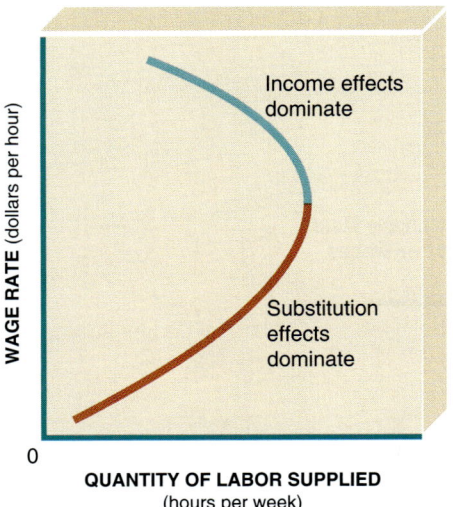

A utility-maximizing individual will respond to these income and substitution effects by offering different quantities of labor at alternative wage rates. The *substitution effect* of high wages encourages people to work more hours. The *income effect,* on the other hand, allows them to reduce work hours without losing income. If substitution effects dominate, the labor supply curve will be upward-sloping. ***If income effects outweigh substitution effects, an individual will supply*** less ***labor at higher wages.*** This kind of reaction is illustrated by the backward-bending portion of the supply curve in Figure 30.2.

Backward-bending labor supply curves are more the exception than the rule. Most Americans do want more leisure. But given the choice between more leisure or more income, people are more likely to choose added income. In other words, substitution effects outweigh income effects. This explains why Americans work such long hours (see the previous World View) despite their comparatively high incomes.

MARKET SUPPLY

The **market supply of labor** represents the sum of all individual labor supply decisions. Although it's true that some individuals have backward-bending supply curves, these negative responses to higher wages are swamped by positive responses from the 140 million individuals who participate in the U.S. labor market. As a result, the *market supply curve is upward-sloping.*

The upward slope of the labor supply curve doesn't imply that we'll all be working longer hours in the future. As time passes, the labor supply curve can *shift.* And it will whenever one of the underlying determinants of supply change. ***The determinants of labor supply include***

- *Tastes* (for leisure, income, and work).
- ***Income and wealth.***
- ***Expectations*** (for income or consumption).
- ***Prices*** of consumer goods.
- ***Taxes.***

These shift factors determine the position and slope of the labor supply curve at any point in time. As time passes, however, these underlying determinants change, causing the labor supply curve to shift. This has evidently happened. In 1890, the average U.S. worker was employed 60 hours a week at a wage rate of 20 cents an hour. In 2001, the average worker worked less than 35 hours per week at a wage rate of $14 an hour. Contributing to this long-run leftward shift has been (1) the spectacular rise in living

market supply of labor: The total quantity of labor that workers are willing and able to supply at alternative wage rates in a given time period, *ceteris paribus.*

standards (a change in income and wealth), (2) the growth of income transfer programs that provide economic security when one isn't working (a change in income and expectations), and (3) the increased diversity and attractiveness of leisure activities (a change in tastes and other goods).

Despite the evident long-run shifts of the labor supply curve, workers still respond positively to higher wage rates in the short run. To measure the resulting movements along the labor supply curve, we use the concept of elasticity. Specifically, **elasticity of labor supply** is the percentage change in the quantity of labor supplied divided by the percentage change in the wage rate—that is,

$$\text{Elasticity of labor supply} = \frac{\%\text{ change in quantity of labor supplied}}{\%\text{ change in wage rate}}$$

Elasticity of Labor Supply

elasticity of labor supply: The percentage change in the quantity of labor supplied divided by the percentage change in wage rate.

The elasticity of labor tells us how much more labor will be available if a higher wage is offered. If the elasticity of labor is 0.2, a 10 percent increase in wage rates will induce a 2 percent increase in the quantity of labor supplied.

The actual responsiveness of workers to a change in wage rates depends on the determinants of labor supply. Time is also important for labor supply elasticity, as individuals can't adjust their schedules or change jobs instantaneously.

Institutional Constraints

The labor supply curve and its related elasticities tell us how much time people would like to allocate to work. We must recognize, however, that people seldom have the opportunity to adjust their hours of employment at will. True, a Bill Gates or a Britney Spears can easily choose to work more or fewer hours. Most workers, however, face more rigid choices. They must usually choose to work at a regular job for eight hours a day, five days a week, or not to work at all. Very few firms are flexible enough to accommodate a desire to work only between the hours of 11 A.M. and 3 P.M. on alternate Thursdays. Adjustments in work hours are more commonly confined to choices about overtime work or secondary jobs (moonlighting) and vacation and retirement. Families may also alter the labor supply by varying the number of family members sent into the labor force at any given time. Students, too, can often adjust their work hours. The flow of immigrants into the U.S. labor market also increases when U.S. wages rise.

LABOR DEMAND

Regardless of how many people are *willing* to work, it's up to employers to decide how many people will *actually* work. That is, there must be a **demand for labor.** What determines the number of workers employers are willing to hire at various wage rates?

In earlier chapters we emphasized that employers are profit maximizers. In their quest for maximum profits, firms seek the rate of output at which marginal revenue equals marginal cost. Once they've identified the profit-maximizing rate of output, firms enter factor markets to purchase the required amounts of labor, equipment, and other resources. Thus, *the quantity of resources purchased by a business depends on the firm's expected sales and output.* In this sense, the demand for factors of production, including labor, is a **derived demand;** it's derived from the demand for goods and services.

Consider the plight of strawberry pickers. Strawberry pickers are paid very low wages and are employed only part of the year. But their plight can't be blamed on the greed of the strawberry growers. Strawberry growers, like most producers, would love to sell more strawberries at higher prices. If they did, the growers would hire more pickers and might even pay them higher wages. But the growers must contend with the market demand for strawberries: Consumers aren't willing to buy more strawberries at higher prices. As a consequence, the growers can't afford to hire more pickers or pay

Derived Demand

demand for labor: The quantities of labor employers are willing and able to hire at alternative wage rates in a given time period, *ceteris paribus*.

derived demand: The demand for labor and other factors of production results from (depends on) the demand for final goods and services produced by these factors.

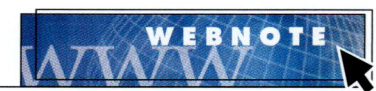

Average earnings by occupation can be obtained from the U.S. Bureau of Labor Statistics at stats.bls.gov. Under "Wages, Earnings, and Benefits" choose "Wages by Area and Occupation."

The Labor Demand Curve

them higher wages. In contrast, information-technology (IT) firms are always looking for more workers and offer very high wages to get them. This helps explain why college students who major in engineering, math, or computer science get paid a lot more than philosophy majors (see News). IT specialists benefit from the growing demand for Internet services, while philosophy majors suffer because the search for meaning in life is not a growth industry.

The principle of derived demand suggests that if consumers really want to improve the lot of strawberry pickers, they should eat more strawberries. An increase in the demand for strawberries will motivate growers to plant more berries and hire more labor to pick them. Until then, the plight of the pickers isn't likely to improve.

The number of strawberry pickers hired by the growers isn't completely determined by the demand for strawberries. The number of pickers hired will also depend on the wage rate. That is, *the quantity of labor demanded depends on its price (the wage rate).* In general, we expect that strawberry growers will be *willing to hire* more pickers at low wages than at higher wages. Hence, the demand for labor look very much like the demand for any good or service (see Figure 30.3).

Majoring in Money

Unfortunately, wisdom apparently is its own reward, as the job market for professional philosophers—or at least philosophy majors—continues to be weak, according to the latest Monthly Labor Review.

Daniel Hecker, an economist for the federal Bureau of Labor Statistics, computed the annual earnings of everyone who had graduated from college before 1991 and had a full-time job in 1993.

The least lucrative majors for both men and women: philosophy, religion and theology, probably because many of the paying gigs for these students are in church, where the rewards presumably come in the next lifetime and not in the pay envelope.

Among mid-career men between the ages of 35 and 44, Hecker found that those who had majored in engineering and math as undergraduates earned the most. For similarly aged women, an economics degree was golden.

—Richard Morin

Source: *Washington Post,* March 24, 1996. © 1996 The Washington Post. Reprinted with permission. www.washingtonpost.com

Annual Earnings by College Undergraduate Major Men and Women Ages 35–44

Men		Women	
Top Five Majors		**Top Five Majors**	
1. Engineering	$53,286	1. Economics	$49,170
2. Mathematics	51,584	2. Engineering	49,070
3. Computer science	50,509	3. Pharmacy	48,427
4. Pharmacy	50,480	4. Architecture	46,353
5. Physics	50,128	5. Computer science	43,757
Bottom Five Majors		**Bottom Five Majors**	
1. Philosophy/religion	$31,848	1. Philosophy/religion	$25,788
2. Social work	32,171	2. Education	27,988
3. Visual and performing arts	32,972	3. Home economics	28,275
4. Foreign language/linguistics	33,780	4. Social work	28,594
5. Education	34,470	5. Agriculture	28,751

Source: Bureau of Labor Statistics.

Analysis: The earnings of college graduates depends in part on what major they chose. Graduates who can produce goods and services in great demand get the highest pay.

FIGURE 30.3
The Demand for Labor

The higher the wage rate, the smaller the quantity of labor demanded (ceteris paribus). At the wage rate W_1, only L_1 of labor is demanded. If the wage rate falls to W_2, a larger quantity of labor (L_2) will be demanded. The labor demand curve obeys the law of demand.

The fact that the demand curve for labor slopes downward doesn't tell us what quantity of labor will be hired. Nor does it tell us what wage rate will be paid. To answer such questions, we need to know what determines the particular shape and position of the labor demand curve.

A strawberry grower will be willing to hire another picker only if that picker contributes more to output than he or she costs. Growers, as rational businesspeople, recognize that *every* sale, *every* expenditure has some impact on total profits. Hence, the truly profit-maximizing grower will evaluate each picker's job application in terms of the applicant's potential contribution to profits.

Fortunately, a strawberry picker's contribution to output is easy to measure; it's the number of boxes of strawberries he or she picks. Suppose for the moment that Marvin, a college dropout with three summers of experience as a canoe instructor, is able to pick 5 boxes per hour. These 5 boxes represent Marvin's **marginal physical product (MPP)**. In other words, the *addition* to total output that occurs when the grower hires Marvin for an hour; that is,

Marginal Physical Product

marginal physical product (MPP): The change in total output associated with one additional unit of input.

$$\frac{\text{Marginal}}{\text{physical product}} = \frac{\text{change in total output}}{\text{change in quantity of labor}}$$

Marginal physical product establishes an *upper* limit to the grower's willingness to pay. Clearly the grower can't afford to pay Marvin more than 5 boxes of strawberries for an hour's work; the grower won't pay Marvin more than he produces.

Most strawberry pickers don't want to be paid in strawberries. At the end of a day in the fields, the last thing a picker wants to see is another strawberry. Marvin, like the rest of the pickers, wants to be paid in cash. To find out how much cash he might be paid, we need to know what a box of strawberries is worth. This is easy to determine. The market value of a box of strawberries is simply the price at which the grower can sell it. Thus, Marvin's contribution to output can be measured in either marginal physical product (5 boxes per hour) or the dollar value of that product.

The dollar value of a worker's contribution to output is called **marginal revenue product (MRP)**. Marginal revenue product is the change in total revenue that occurs when more labor is hired—that is,

Marginal Revenue Product

marginal revenue product (MRP): The change in total revenue associated with one additional unit of input.

$$\frac{\text{Marginal}}{\text{revenue product}} = \frac{\text{change in total revenue}}{\text{change in quantity of labor}}$$

In Marvin's case, the "change in quantity of labor" is one extra hour of picking strawberries. The "change in total revenue" is the *value* of the extra 5 boxes of berries Marvin picks in that hour. If the grower can sell strawberries for $2 a box, Marvin's marginal revenue product is simply 5 boxes per hour × $2 per box, or $10 per hour.

	(per hour)	(boxes per hour)	(boxes per hour)
A	1 (Marvin)	5	5
B	2 (George)	10	5
C	3	14	4
D	4	17	3
E	5	19	2
F	6	20	1
G	7	20	0
H	8	18	−2
I	9	15	−3

to fall as additional workers are hired in any given production process. This decline occurs because each worker has increasingly less of other factors (e.g., land) with which to work.

When the second worker (George) is hired, total output increases from 5 to 10 boxes per hour. Hence, the second worker's MPP equals 5 boxes per hour. Thereafter, capital and land constraints diminish marginal physical product.

We could have come to the same conclusion by multiplying marginal *physical* product times *price*, that is

$$MRP = MPP \times p$$

or

$$\$10 = 5 \text{ boxes} \times \$2 \text{ per box}$$

We calculate MRP to determine how much Marvin should be paid. In compliance with the rule about not paying anybody more than he or she contributes, the profit-maximizing grower should be willing to pay Marvin up to $10 an hour. Thus, *marginal revenue product sets an upper limit to the wage rate an employer will pay.*

---

the last worker hired is less able than the others. Accordingly, the "fifth" picker can't be identified as any particular individual. Once 5 pickers are hired, Marvin's MRP is no higher than any other picker's. **Each (identical) worker is worth no more than the marginal revenue product of the last worker hired, and all workers are paid the same wage rate.**

The principles of marginal revenue product apply to football coaches as well as strawberry pickers. The University of Florida's football coach earned more than $2 million in 2001–02. Why was he paid nine times more than the university's president? It's because his winning football team brought in 70,000 paying fans per game and got lots of media exposure for the school (see News). The university thinks his MRP justifies the high salary.

Whatever the explanation for the disparity between the incomes of football coaches and strawberry pickers, the enormous gap between them seems awfully unfair. An obvious question then arises. Can't the number of pickers or their wages be increased?

Changes in Wage Rates

Suppose the government were to set a minimum wage for strawberry pickers at $6 an hour. At first glance this action would appear to boost the wages of pickers, who have been earning only $4 an hour. This isn't all good news for the strawberry pickers, however. **There's a trade-off between wage rates and the number of workers demanded.** If wage rates go up, growers will hire fewer pickers.

Figure 30.6 illustrates this trade-off. The grower's earlier decision to hire 5 pickers was based on a wage of $4 an hour (point *C*). If the wage jumps to $6 an hour, it no longer makes economic sense to keep 5 pickers employed. The MRP of the fifth worker

IN THE NEWS

Top Dollars, Top Coaches

Count it out. Two million dollars. Guaranteed.

What Bob Stoops will make as the University of Oklahoma football coach this season is more than the average American wage earner will see in a lifetime. It's roughly 25 times what the average college professor will pull down in the coming school year.

The figure is so sizable it disgusts some in higher education—an example, they say, of how far many colleges and universities have strayed from their basic mission, from teaching and research to the pursuit of athletic reputation and the purveyance of entertainment.

One of the anticipated returns on Oklahoma's dollar is now evident. Stoops and the defending national champion Sooners are projected among the front-runners for this year's title. They're No. 3 in the preseason USA Today/ESPN Coaches' Poll.

Voted No. 1: Florida, which is paying Steve Spurrier, entering his 12th season as coach, $2.1 million.

Beneath them are at least another 20 schools—including 13 of the top 14 in the poll and 17 of the top 25—that have struck million-dollar deals with their football coaches.

—Steve Wieberg

Source: *USA Today*, August 3, 2001. © 2001 USA Today. Reprinted with permission. www.usatoday.com

Millionaires Row

22 college football and 17 basketball head coaches who have annual deals worth at least $1 million:

Football

$2.1 million	Steve Spurrier	Florida
$2 million	Bob Stoops	Oklahoma
$1.5 million	Bobby Bowden	Florida State
$1.45 million	Mack Brown	Texas
$1.3 million	Barry Alvarez	Wisconsin
$1.3 million	Phillip Fulmer	Tennessee
$1.3 million	Glen Mason	Minnesota

Basketball

$2.2 million	Rick Pitino	Louisville
$1.6 million	Mike Krzyzewski	Duke
$1.5 million	Tubby Smith	Kentucky
$1.2 million	Billy Donovan	Florida
$1.2 million	Matt Doherty	North Carolina
$1.2 million	Bob Huggins	Cincinnati

Analysis: Colleges are willing to pay 25 times more for football coaches than for professors. Successful coaches bring in much more revenue.

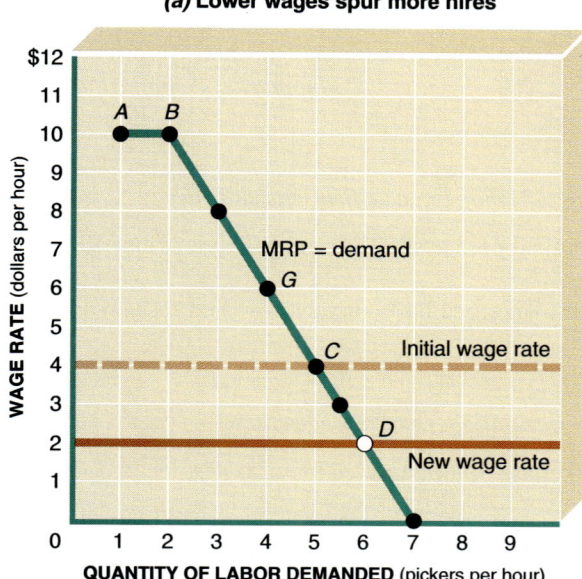

FIGURE 30.6
Incentives to Hire

(*a*) **Lower wage** If the wage rate drops, an employer will be willing to hire more workers, *ceteris paribus*. At $4 an hour, only 5 pickers per hour would be demanded (point C). If the wage rate dropped to $2 an hour, 6 pickers per hour would be demanded (point D).

(*b*) **Higher productivity** If the marginal revenue product of labor improves, the employer will hire a greater quantity of labor at any given wage rate. The labor demand curve will shift up (from D_1 to D_2). In this case, an increase in MRP leads the employer to hire 6 workers (point E) rather than only 5 workers (point C) at $4 per hour.

is only $4 an hour. The grower will respond to higher wage rates by moving up the labor demand curve to point G. At point G, only 4 pickers are hired and MRP again equals the wage rate. If more workers are to be hired, the wage rate must drop.

The downward slope of the labor demand curve doesn't doom strawberry pickers to low wages. It does emphasize, however, the inevitable link between workers' productivity and wages. *To get higher wages without sacrificing jobs, productivity (MRP) must increase.*

Changes in Productivity

Suppose Marvin and his friends all enroll in a local agricultural extension course and learn new methods of strawberry picking. With these new methods, the marginal physical product of each picker increases by 1 box per hour. With the price of strawberries still at $2 a box, this productivity improvement implies an increase in marginal *revenue* product of $2 per worker. This change causes an upward *shift* of the labor demand (MRP) curve, as in Figure 30.6*b*.

Notice how the improvement in productivity has altered the value of strawberry pickers. The MRP of the fifth picker is now $6 an hour (point F) rather than $4 (point C). Hence, the grower can now afford to pay higher wages. Or the grower could employ more pickers than before, moving from point C to point E. *Increased productivity implies that workers can get higher wages without sacrificing jobs or more employment without lowering wages.* Historically, increased productivity has been the most important source of rising wages and living standards.

Changes in Price

An increase in the price of strawberries would also help the pickers. Marginal revenue product reflects the interaction of productivity and product prices. If strawberry prices were to double, strawberry pickers would become twice as valuable, even without an increase in physical productivity. Such a change in product prices depends, however, on changes in the market supply and demand for strawberries.

MARKET EQUILIBRIUM

The principles that guide the hiring decisions of a single strawberry grower can be extended to the entire labor market. This suggests that *the market demand for labor depends on*

- *The number of employers.*
- *The marginal revenue product of labor in each firm and industry.*

Increases in either the demand for final products or the productivity of labor will tend to increase the demand for labor.

On the supply side of the labor market we have already observed that *the market supply of labor depends on*

- *The number of available workers.*
- *Each worker's willingness to work at alternative wage rates.*

The supply decisions of each worker are in turn a reflection of tastes, income, wealth, expectations, other prices, and taxes.

Equilibrium Wage

Figure 30.7 brings these market forces together. *The intersection of the market supply and demand curves establishes the **equilibrium wage**.* This is the only wage rate at which the quantity of labor supplied equals the quantity of labor demanded. Everyone who's willing and able to work for this wage will find a job.

equilibrium wage: The wage rate at which the quantity of labor supplied in a given time period equals the quantity of labor demanded.

If the labor market is perfectly competitive, all employers will be able to hire as many workers as they want at the equilibrium wage. Like our strawberry grower, every competitive firm is assumed to have no discernible effect on market wages. *Competitive employers act like price takers with respect to wages as well as prices.* This phenomenon is also portrayed in Figure 30.7.

Minimum Wages

Some people will be unhappy with the equilibrium wage. Employers may grumble that wages are too high. Workers may complain that wages are too low. They may seek government intervention to change market outcomes. This is the goal of Congress when it seeks to increase the federal minimum wage (see Table 30.2).

FIGURE 30.7
Equilibrium Wage

The intersection of *market* supply and demand determines the equilibrium wage in a competitive labor market. All the firms in the industry can then hire as much labor as they want at that equilibrium wage. In this case, the firm can hire all the workers it wants at the equilibrium wage, w_e. It chooses to hire q_0 workers, as determined by their marginal revenue product within the firm.

TABLE 30.2
Minimum Wage History

The federal minimum wage has been increased periodically since first set in 1938. In 2002 Congress was considering another increase, to $6.65 by 2004.

Oct. '38	$0.25	Jan. '75	$2.10
Oct. '39	0.30	Jan. '76	2.30
Oct. '45	0.40	Jan. '78	2.65
Jan. '50	0.75	Jan. '79	2.90
Mar. '56	1.00	Jan. '80	3.10
Sept. '61	1.15	Jan. '81	3.35
Sept. '63	1.25	Apr. '90	3.80
Feb. '67	1.40	Apr. '91	4.25
Feb. '68	1.60	Oct. '96	4.75
May '74	2.00	Sept. '97	5.15

Figure 30.8 illustrates the effects of such government intervention. The equilibrium wage is W_e, and q_e workers are employed. A minimum wage of W_M is then set, above the market equilibrium. The wage W_M encourages more low-skilled workers to seek employment; the quantity supplied increases from q_e to q_s. At the same time, however, the number of available jobs declines from q_e to q_d. This leaves a market surplus at the wage W_M. As a result of the increased wage, some workers have lost jobs ($q_e - q_d$) and some new entrants fail to find employment ($q_s - q_e$). Only those workers who remain employed (q_d) benefit from the higher wage.

Government-imposed wage floors thus have two distinct effects: *A minimum wage*

- *Reduces the quantity of labor demanded.*
- *Increases the quantity of labor supplied.*
- *Creates a market surplus.*

The extent of job loss resulting from a minimum wage hike is hotly debated. How many jobs are lost obviously depends on how far the minimum wage is raised. The elasticity of labor demand is also important. Democrats argue that labor demand is inelastic, so few jobs will be lost. Republicans assert that labor demand is elastic, so more jobs will be lost. In the early 1980s, the elasticity of labor demand was found to be 0.10. Hence, a 10 percent increase in the minimum wage would cause a 1 percent reduction in employment. Between 1981 and 1990, however, the minimum was stuck at $3.35 an hour while average wages increased 30 percent. By 1989, the federal minimum may have actually been below the equilibrium wage for low-skilled labor. When the minimum wage is below the equilibrium wage, an increase in the minimum may have little or no adverse employment effects. This appeared to be the case again in 1996. Because the federal minimum hadn't been raised for five years (see Table 30.2), the 50 cents per hour hike in October 1996 caused few job losses. According to Federal

WEBNOTE

For pros and cons of raising the minimum wage, see the Electronic Policy Network (pro) at www.epn.org/issues/minimumwage.html and Employment Policies Institute (con) at www.epionline.org. Click on "Minimum Wage."

FIGURE 30.8
Minimum Wage Effects

If the minimum wage exceeds the equilibrium wage, a labor surplus will result: More workers will be willing to work at that wage rate than employers will be willing to hire. Some workers will end up with higher wages, but others will end up unemployed.

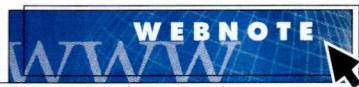

WEBNOTE

For historical data on the federal minimum wage, in real and nominal terms, visit the U.S. Department of Labor at www.dol.gov/dol/esa/public/minwage/main.htm.

Reserve estimates, the 1997 wage hike may have reduced employment growth by only 100,000 to 200,000 jobs. However, ***the further the minimum wage rises above the market's equilibrium wage, the greater the job loss.*** This is why Congress rejected President Clinton's 1998 proposal for another wage hike. Three years later, the implied job loss was smaller, and Congress contemplated another hike (to $6.65) in the minimum wage (see News).

CHOOSING AMONG INPUTS

One of the options employers have when wage rates rise is to utilize more machinery in place of labor. In most production processes there are possibilities for substituting capital inputs for labor inputs. In the long run, there are still more possibilities for redesigning the whole production process. Given these options, how should the choice of inputs be made?

Suppose a mechanical strawberry picker can pick berries twice as fast as Marvin. Who will the grower hire, Marvin or the mechanical picker? At first it would seem that the grower would choose the mechanical picker. But the choice isn't so obvious. So far, all we know is that the mechanical picker's MPP is twice as large as Marvin's. But we haven't said anything about the *cost* of the mechanical picker.

Cost Efficiency

Suppose that a mechanical picker can be rented for $10 an hour, while Marvin is still willing to work for $4 an hour. Will this difference in hourly cost change the grower's input choice?

To determine the relative desirability of hiring Marvin or renting the mechanical picker, the grower must compare the ratio of their marginal physical products to their cost. This ratio of marginal product to cost expresses the **cost efficiency** of an input—that is,

cost efficiency: The amount of output associated with an additional dollar spent on input; the MPP of an input divided by its price (cost).

$$\text{Cost efficiency} = \frac{\text{marginal physical product of an input}}{\text{cost of an input}}$$

IN THE NEWS

Wage Bill May Have Tax Breaks for Businesses

Calling a minimum-wage increase "a matter of elementary justice," Democrats are denouncing the GOP tax tradeoff.

If Congress votes to increase the minimum wage to $6.65 an hour, Doron Jensen figures it will cost an additional $21,000 a year to pay the 15 servers who work for him at Jensen's Supper Club in Eagan, Minn.

For Jensen, that's too much. He fears he might have to respond by raising meal prices or cutting health insurance benefits for his employees. If the wage increase is passed, Jensen wouldn't mind if Congress in turn approved a higher tax deduction for business meals, which could increase sales at his restaurant.

"I mean, help me out a little bit here," said Jensen, adding that business owners who provide jobs shouldn't have to "completely foot the bill."

The federal minimum wage hasn't changed since 1997, when it rose from $4.75 to $5.15 an hour. Last year, Congress considered raising the minimum wage by $1 an hour, but the plan fizzled.

This time around, Rep. Gil Gutknecht, R-Minn., said the minimum wage will be increased, but he added that "there will be some accommodations for the businesspeople who will have to pay for it."

Armey said Republicans are showing "general resolve" to help businesses. If Congress approves an increase in the minimum wage, businesses should be compensated for the "adverse employment effects," he said.

—Rob Hotakainen; Craig Gustafson

Source: *Minneapolis Star Tribune,* May 21, 2001. Reprinted with permission. www.startribune.com

Analysis: A higher minimum wage encourages firms to hire fewer workers. Too alleviate the higher labor costs, businesses may seek tax breaks that increase demand for output or reduce other costs.

Marvin's MPP is 5 boxes of strawberries per hour and his cost (wage) is $4. Thus, the return on each dollar of wages paid to Marvin is

$$\text{Cost efficiency of labor} = \frac{\text{MPP}_{\text{labor}}}{\text{cost}_{\text{labor}}} = \frac{5 \text{ boxes}}{\$4} = 1.25 \text{ boxes per } \$1 \text{ of cost}$$

By contrast, the mechanical picker has an MPP of 10 boxes per hour and costs $10 per hour; thus

$$\text{Cost efficiency of mechanical picker} = \frac{\text{MPP of mechanical picker}}{\text{cost of mechanical picker}} = \frac{10 \text{ boxes}}{\$10} = 1 \text{ box per } \$1 \text{ of cost}$$

These calculations indicate that Marvin is more cost-effective than the mechanical picker. From this perspective, the grower is better off hiring Marvin than renting a mechanical picker.

From the perspective of cost efficiency, the cheapness of a productive input is measured not by its price but by the amount of output it delivers for that price. Thus, *the most cost-efficient factor of production is the one that produces the most output per dollar.*

The concept of cost efficiency helps explain why American firms don't move en masse to Haiti, where peasants are willing to work for as little as 80 cents an hour. Although this wage rate is far below the minimum wage in the United States, the marginal physical product of Haitian peasants is even further below American standards. American workers remain more cost-efficient than the "cheap" labor available in Haiti and other less developed countries, as long as they deliver more output per dollar of wages.

Alternative Production Processes

Typically a producer doesn't choose between individual inputs but rather between alternative production processes. General Motors, for example, can't afford to compare the cost efficiency of each job applicant with the cost efficiency of mechanical tire mounters. Instead, GM compares the relative desirability of a **production process** that is labor-intensive (uses a lot of labor) with others that are less labor-intensive. GM ignores individual differences in marginal revenue product. Nevertheless, the same principles of cost efficiency guide the decision.

production process: A specific combination of resources used to produce a good or service.

The Efficiency Decision

Let's return to the strawberry patch to see how the choice of an entire production process is made. We again assume that strawberries can be picked by either human or mechanical hands. Now, however, we assume that one ton of strawberries can be produced by only one of the three production processes described in Table 30.3. Process *A* is most *labor-intensive*; it uses the most labor and thus keeps more human pickers employed. By contrast, process *C* is *capital-intensive*; it uses the most mechanical pickers and provides the least employment to human pickers. Process *B* falls between these two extremes.

Which of these three production processes should the grower use? If he used labor-intensive process *A*, he'd be doing the pickers a real favor. But his goal is to maximize

	Alternative Processes for Producing One Ton of Strawberries		
Input	Process A	Process B	Process C
Labor (hours)	400	270	220
Machinery (hours)	13	15	18
Land (acres)	1	1	1

TABLE 30.3
Alternative Production Processes
One ton of strawberries can be produced with varying input combinations. Which process is most efficient? What information is missing?

TABLE 30.4
The Least-Cost Combination

A producer wants to produce a given rate of output for the least cost. Choosing the least expensive production process is the efficiency decision. In this case, process C represents the most cost-efficient production process for producing one ton of strawberries.

Input	Cost Calculation	
Process A		
Labor	400 hours at $4 per hour =	$1,600
Machinery	13 hours at $10 per hour =	130
Land	1 acre at $500 =	500
	Total cost	$2,230
Process B		
Labor	270 hours at $4 per hour =	$1,080
Machinery	15 hours at $10 per hour =	150
Land	1 acre at $500 =	500
	Total cost	$1,730
Process C		
Labor	220 hours at $4 per hour =	$ 880
Machinery	18 hours at $10 per hour =	180
Land	1 acre at $500 =	500
	Total cost	$1,560

profits, so we assume he'll choose the production process that best serves this objective. That is, he'll choose the *least-cost* process to produce one ton of strawberries.

But which of the production processes in Table 30.3 is least expensive? We really can't tell on the basis of the information provided. To determine the relative cost of each process—and thus to understand the producer's choice—we must know something more about input costs. In particular, we have to know how much an hour of mechanical picking costs and how much an hour of human picking (labor) costs. Then we can determine which combination of inputs is least expensive in producing one ton of strawberries—that is, which is most *cost-efficient*. Note that we don't have to know how much the land costs, because the same amount of land is used in all three production processes. Thus, land costs won't affect our efficiency decision.

Suppose that strawberry pickers are still paid $4 an hour and that mechanical pickers can be rented for $10 an hour. The acre of land rents for $500 per year. With this information we can now calculate the total dollar cost of each production process and quickly determine the most cost-efficient. Table 30.4 summarizes the required calculations.

The calculations performed in Table 30.4 clearly identify process *C* as the least expensive way of producing one ton of strawberries. Process *A* entails a total cost of $2,230, whereas the capital-intensive process *C* costs only $1,560 to produce the same quantity of output. As a profit maximizer, the grower will choose process *C*, even though it implies less employment for strawberry pickers.

The choice of an appropriate production process—the decision about *how* to produce—is called the **efficiency decision.** As we've seen, a producer seeks to use the combination of resources that produces a given rate of output for the least cost. The efficiency decision requires the producer to find that particular least-cost combination.

efficiency decision: The choice of a production process for any given rate of output.

THE ECONOMY TOMORROW

Capping CEO Pay

At the beginning of this chapter we noted that Michael Eisner, the CEO of Walt Disney Company, signed a 10-year contract that could pay him an astronomical $771 million. When challenged to defend his pay, Disney's CEO asserted he had earned every penny of it by enhancing the value of the company's stock.

Critics of CEO pay don't accept this explanation. They make three points. First, the rise in the price of Disney's *stock* is not a measure of marginal revenue product. Only part of the increase in share prices was due to the company's performance; the rest was caused by a general upswing in the stock market. Second, the revenues of the Walt Disney Company probably wouldn't be $771 million lower in the absence of Eisner. Hence, his marginal revenue product is less than $771 million. Finally, Eisner probably would have worked just as hard for, say, just $400 million or so. Therefore, his actual pay was more than required to elicit the desired supply response.

Critics conclude that many CEO paychecks are out of line with realities of supply and demand (see cartoon). They want corporations to reduce CEO pay and revise the process used for setting CEO pay levels.

Motivated by money? Check out the highest-paying occupations at www.acinet.org/acinet.

Unmeasured MRP

One of the difficulties in determining the appropriate level of CEO pay is the elusiveness of marginal revenue product. It's easy to measure the MRP of a strawberry picker or even a salesclerk who sells Disney toys. But a corporate CEO's contributions are less well defined. A CEO is supposed to provide strategic leadership and a sense of mission. These are critical to a corporation's success but hard to quantify.

Congress confronts the same problem in setting the president's pay. We noted earlier that the president of the United States is paid $400,000 a year. Can we argue that this salary represents the president's marginal revenue product? The accompanying News suggests that the president's pay would be in the range of $38–58 million if he was paid on performance (MRP). The wage we actually pay a president is less a reflection of contribution to total output than a matter of custom. The salary also reflects the price voters believe is required to induce competent individuals to forsake private-sector jobs and assume the responsibilities of the presidency. In this sense, the wage paid to the president and other public officials is set by their **opportunity wage**—that is, the wage they could earn in private industry.

opportunity wage: The highest wage an individual would earn in his or her best alternative job.

The same kinds of considerations influence the wages of college professors. The marginal revenue product of a college professor isn't easy to measure. Is it the number of students she teaches, the amount of knowledge conveyed, or something else? Confronted with such problems, most universities tend to pay college professors according to their opportunity wage—that is, the amount the professors could earn elsewhere.

Opportunity wages also help explain the difference between the wage of the CEO of Disney and the workers who peddle its products. The lower wage of salesclerks reflects not only their marginal revenue product at Disney stores but also the fact that

Find out what top CEOs make at the AFL-CIO website:
http://www.aflcio.org/cgi-bin/aflcio.pl

"O.K. guys, now lets go and *earn* that four hundred times our workers' salaries."

Analysis: The wages of top corporate officers may not be fully justified by their marginal revenue product.

IN THE NEWS

What's a President Worth?

So what if the president were paid like a CEO? Based on performance, a president would be worth up to $58 million a year—if he meets certain goals, compensation experts say. What those goals might be are shown below.

If the nation's president and chief executive were running a major corporation, he probably would find a proposed pay raise to $400,000 laughable.

Compared with what Jack Welch makes at General Electric and Lou Gerstner makes at IBM, that's pocket change.

In the private sector, a CEO running a huge corporation would earn $34 million to $58 million a year, much of it from incentive bonuses and stock options, says compensation expert Graef Crystal of the on-line newsletter crystal-report.com.

At $200,000 a year, the president makes more than 99 percent of all workers. But he oversees a budget of $1.8 trillion, 11 times the annual revenue of the nation's largest company, General Motors. He's boss of 4.2 million employees, both civilian and military, six times as many as the largest private employer, Wal-Mart.

Yet he would have to work 2,878 years to bring home the $576 million that Walt Disney CEO Michael Eisner made last year, largely from exercising stock options he was granted as incentives.

In 1980, *Fortune* 500 CEOs averaged $625,000 a year, a little more than three times what President Carter was making. By 1990, the average CEO was making 10 times more than President Bush. And last year, in the wake of generous stock options awarded in a booming market, the CEO-to-president ratio swelled to 53-to-1.

—Del Jones and Gary Strauss

Source: *USA Today*, May 27, 1999. © 1999 USA Today. Reprinted with permission. www.usatoday.com

Analysis: If the nation's president were paid on the basis of his marginal revenue product, his salary would be a lot higher than $400,000.

they're not trained for many other jobs. That is, their opportunity wages are low. By contrast, Disney's CEO has impressive managerial skills that are in demand by many corporations; his opportunity wages are high.

Opportunity wages help explain CEO pay but don't fully justify such high pay levels. If Disney's CEO pay is justified by opportunity wages, that means that another company would be willing to pay him that much. But what would justify such high pay at another company? Would his MRP be any easier to measure? Maybe *all* CEO paychecks have been inflated.

Critics of CEO pay conclude that the process of setting CEO pay levels should be changed. All too often, executive pay scales are set by self-serving committees composed of executives of the same or similar corporations. Critics want a more independent assessment of pay scales, with nonaffiliated experts and stockholder representatives. Some critics want to go a step further and set mandatory "caps" on CEO pay. President Clinton rejected legislated caps but convinced Congress to limit the tax deductibility of CEO pay. Any "unjustified" CEO pay in excess of $1 million a year can't be treated as a business expense but instead must be paid out of after-tax profits. This change puts more pressure on corporations to examine the rationale for multimillion-dollar paychecks.

If markets work efficiently, such government intervention shouldn't be necessary. Corporations that pay their CEOs excessively will end up with smaller profits than companies who pay market-based wages. Over time, "lean" companies will be more competitive than "fat" companies, and excessive pay packages will be eliminated. Legislated CEO pay caps imply that CEO labor markets aren't efficient or that the adjustment process is too slow. To forestall more government intervention in pay decisions, companies may tie executive pay more explicitly to performance (marginal revenue product) in the economy tomorrow.

SUMMARY

- The motivation to work arises from social, psychological, and economic forces. People need income to pay their bills, but they also need a sense of achievement. As a consequence, people are willing to work—to supply labor.
- There's an opportunity cost involved in working—namely, the amount of leisure time one sacrifices. By the same token, the opportunity cost of not working (leisure) is the income and related consumption possibilities thereby forgone. Thus each person confronts a trade-off between leisure and income.
- Increases in wage rates induce people to work more—that is, to substitute labor for leisure. But this substitution effect may be offset by an income effect. Higher wages also enable a person to work fewer hours with no loss of income. When income effects outweigh substitution effects, the labor supply curve bends backward.
- A firm's demand for labor reflects labor's marginal revenue product. A profit-maximizing employer won't pay a worker more than the worker produces.
- The marginal revenue product of labor diminishes as additional workers are employed on a particular job (the law of diminishing returns). This decline occurs because additional workers have to share existing land and capital, leaving each worker with less land and capital to work with.
- A producer seeks to get the most output for every dollar spent on inputs. This means getting the highest ratio of marginal product to input price. A profit-maximizing producer will choose the most cost-efficient input (not necessarily the one with the cheapest price).
- The efficiency decision involves the choice of the least-cost productive process and is also made on the basis of cost efficiency. A producer seeks the least expensive process to produce a given rate of output.
- Differences in marginal revenue product are an important explanation of wage inequalities. But the difficulty of measuring MRP in many instances leaves many wage rates to be determined by opportunity wages or other mechanisms.

Key Terms

labor supply
substitution effect of wages
income effect of wages
market supply of labor
elasticity of labor supply
demand for labor
derived demand
marginal physical product (MPP)
marginal revenue product (MRP)
law of diminishing returns
equilibrium wage
cost efficiency
production process
efficiency decision
opportunity wage

Questions for Discussion

1. Why are you doing this homework? What are you giving up? What utility do you expect to gain?
2. Would you continue to work after winning a lottery prize of $50,000 a year for life? Would you change schools, jobs, or career objectives? What factors besides income influence work decisions?
3. The News on page 638 implies that students sacrifice a lot of potential income when they major in philosophy, education, or other social work. Is such behavior rational?
4. What's the justification for the merit pay plan discussed in the News on page 640? How could you compute marginal revenue product for priests?
5. Is this course increasing your marginal productivity? If so, in what way?
6. How might you measure the marginal revenue product of (*a*) a quarterback and (*b*) the team's coach?
7. Who is hurt and who is helped by an increase in the legal minimum wage? Under what circumstances might a higher minimum *not* reduce employment?
8. Explain why marginal physical product would diminish as
   (*a*) More secretaries are hired in an office.
   (*b*) More professors are hired in the economics department.
   (*c*) More construction workers are hired to build a school.
9. Is it possible that the president of the United States is overpaid? How should his MRP be measured?
10. What kind of tax breaks might help a restaurant absorb the cost of a higher minimum wage (see News, p. 648).

Web Activities

1. Log on to www.aflcio.org/women/equalpay.htm. On average, how much are women paid compared to men? Confirm whether this statistic is accurate at www.dol.gov/dol/wb/public/wb_pubs/wagegap2000.htm. What acounts for the difference? Should there be government intervention in the market to assure equal pay?
2. Log on to www.dol.gov/dol/esa/public/minwage/main.htm. What is the current minimum wage? Why was the minimum wage law first enacted? Has this pur-pose been fulfilled? What are the arguments for and against raising the minimum wage? Go to speakout.com/activism/opinions/5371-1.html to see a Fed economist's opinion of the minimum wage. Summarize his views.
3. Log on to us.ilo.org/news/prsrls/20010831_kilm.html, and read the article from which the World View "Hardest Workers" (page 635) was taken. How many more hours is the average American working now compared to in 1990? Is this a movement along the labor supply curve or a shift of the entire curve? *Ceteris paribus,* how does this affect the average wage rate? How does this affect the relative U.S. competitiveness in the global market?

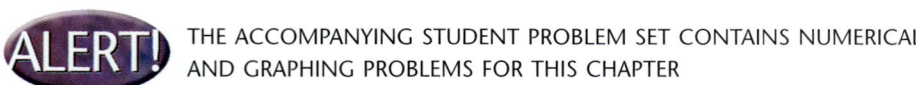

THE ACCOMPANYING STUDENT PROBLEM SET CONTAINS NUMERICAL AND GRAPHING PROBLEMS FOR THIS CHAPTER

CHAPTER 31

Labor Unions

The United Auto Workers Union (UAW) launched a strike against Caterpillar, Inc., in November 1991. The union wanted the manufacturer of construction machinery to increase pay, benefits, and job security. *Four years* later, Caterpillar hadn't budged; it continued to operate with replacement workers, management crews, and union members who crossed the picket line. The union finally capitulated in December 1995, sending its 8,700 members back to work with neither higher pay nor even a new contract. The union struck again in 1996 but relented after 17 months. Seven years after their first strike, the Caterpillar workers still had no contract.

To many observers, the failed UAW strike at Caterpillar climaxed a steady decline in the power of labor unions. But, the union movement is far from dead—as the 1998 UAW strike at General Motors and the 1999 pilots' "sickout" at American Airlines demonstrated. Labor unions are even expanding in some sectors (especially government employment). Many unions still have **market power**—the ability to alter market outcomes. This chapter focuses on how power in the labor market affects wages, employment, and other economic outcomes. We address the following questions:

- How do large and powerful employers affect market wages?
- How do labor unions alter wages and employment?
- What outcomes are possible from collective bargaining between management and unions?

In the process of answering these questions, we look at the nation's most powerful unions and their actual behavior.

THE LABOR MARKET

To gauge the impact of labor market power, we must first observe how a competitive labor market sets wages and employment. On the supply side, we have all those individuals who are willing to work—to supply labor—at various wage rates. By counting the number of individuals willing to work at each and every wage rate, we can construct a *market* **labor supply** curve, as in Figure 31.1.

FIGURE 31.1
Competitive Equilibrium in the Labor Market

The market labor supply curve includes all persons willing to work at various wage rates. The labor demand curve tells us how many workers employers are willing to hire. In a competitive market, the intersection of the labor supply and labor demand curves (point C) determines the equilibrium wage (w_e) and employment (q_e) levels.

market power: The ability to alter the market price of a good or service.

labor supply: The willingness and ability to work specific amounts of time at alternative wage rates in a given time period, *ceteris paribus*.

demand for labor: The quantities of labor employers are willing and able to hire at alternative wages in a given time period, *ceteris paribus*.

Competitive Equilibrium

equilibrium wage: The wage rate at which the quantity of labor supplied in a given time period equals the quantity of labor demanded.

Local Labor Markets

The willingness of producers (firms) to hire labor is reflected in the market labor demand curve. The curve itself is constructed by counting the number of workers each firm says it is willing and able to hire at each and every wage rate. The curve illustrates the market **demand for labor.**

The intersection of the labor supply and labor demand curves (point C in Figure 31.1) reveals the **equilibrium wage** rate (w_e): the wage rate at which the quantity of labor supplied equals the quantity demanded. At this wage rate, every job seeker who's willing and able to work for the wage w_e is employed. In addition, firms are able to acquire all the labor they're willing and able to hire at that wage.

Not everyone is employed in equilibrium. Workers who demand wages in excess of w_e are unable to find jobs. By the same token, employers who refuse to pay a wage as high as w_e are unable to attract workers.

Figure 31.1 appears to suggest that there's only *one* labor market and thus only one equilibrium wage. This is a gross oversimplification. If you were looking for a job in Tulsa, you'd have little interest in employment prospects or power configurations in New York City. You'd be more concerned about the available jobs and wages in Tulsa — that is, the condition of the *local* labor market.

Even within a particular geographical area, interest usually focuses on particular occupations and workers rather than on all the people supplying or demanding labor. If you were looking for work as a dancer, you'd have little interest in the employment situation for carpenters or dentists. Rather, you'd want to know how many nightclubs or dance troupes had job vacancies, and what wages and working conditions they offered.

The distinction among various geographical, occupational, and industrial labor markets provides a more meaningful basis for analyzing labor market power. The tremendous size of the national labor market, with over 140 million workers, precludes anyone from acquiring control of the entire market. The largest employer in the United States (Wal-Mart) employs less than 0.8 percent of the labor force. General Motors employs fewer than that, and the top 500 industrial corporations employ less than 20 percent of all workers. The situation on the supply side is similar. The largest labor union (the Teamsters) represents less than 1 percent of all workers in the country. All unions together represent less than one-seventh of the labor force. This doesn't mean that particular employers or unions have no influence on our economic welfare. It does suggest, however, that *power in labor markets is likely to be more effective in specific areas, occupations, and industries.*

LABOR UNIONS

Types of Unions

The immediate objective of labor unions is to alter the equilibrium wage and employment conditions in specific labor markets. ***To be successful, unions must be able to exert control over the market supply curve.*** That's why workers have organized themselves along either industry or occupational craft lines. *Industrial unions* include workers in a particular industry (the United Auto Workers, for example). *Craft unions* represent workers with a particular skill (like the International Brotherhood of Electrical Workers), regardless of the industry in which they work.

The purpose of both types of labor unions is to coordinate the actions of thousands of individual workers, thereby achieving control of market supply. If a union is able to control the supply of workers in a particular industry or occupation, the union acquires a *monopoly* in that market. Like most monopolies, unions attempt to use their market power to increase their incomes.

Union Objectives

A primary objective of unions is to raise the wages of union members. In the 1998 dispute between pro basketball team owners and players, money was the sole issue. The players, who were already getting an average paycheck of $2.6 million per season, were resisting a salary cap that would restrain wages. The team owners wanted to limit total player salaries to 51.8 percent of league revenues.

An exclusive focus on wages is somewhat unusual. Union objectives also include improved working conditions, job security, and other nonwage forms of compensation, such as retirement (pension) benefits, vacation time, and health insurance. The Players Association and the National Football League have bargained about the use of artificial turf, early retirement, player fines, television revenues, game rules, and the use of team doctors, drug tests, pensions, and the number of players permitted on a team. In 1998, the foremost concern of the United Auto Workers was job security. Cutbacks and plant closings had eliminated more than 400,000 auto industry jobs in the 1980s. When General Motors announced plans to buy more parts from outside suppliers, the UAW feared still more job losses. To protest proposed new work rules and more threatened job losses, the union struck GM's Flint, Michigan, parts plant in June 1998. The resulting parts shortage shut down virtually all GM operations within a matter of weeks.

For an overview and update on UAW activity, visit the organization's website at www.uaw.org.

Although union objectives tend to be as broad as the concerns of union members, we focus here on just one objective, wage rates. This isn't too great a simplification, because most nonwage issues can be translated into their effective impact on wage rates. In 1999, for example, the UAW and GM agreed to nearly two dozen different job provisions, ranging from job security to child care (see News on the next page). It was possible, however, to figure out the cost of these many provisions (just under $7,500 per worker per year). Hence, the "bottom line" of the compensation package could be expressed in terms of wage costs. What we seek to determine is whether and how unions can raise effective wage rates in a specific labor market by altering the competitive equilibrium depicted in Figure 31.1.

THE POTENTIAL USE OF POWER

In a competitive labor market, each worker makes a labor supply decision on the basis of his or her own perceptions of the relative values of labor and leisure (Chapter 30). Whatever decision is made won't alter the market wage. One worker simply isn't that significant in a market composed of thousands. Once a market is unionized, however, these conditions no longer hold. A ***union evaluates job offers on the basis of the collective interests of its members.*** In particular, it must be concerned with the effects of increased employment on the wage rate paid to its members.

IN THE NEWS

What Autoworkers Won

After two months of negotiations, the UAW and GM signed a new four-year contract in October 1999. The contract included these provisions.

- **Wages** $1,350 lump-sum payment, plus 3 percent increase in each year.
- **Cola** Cost of living adjustment raised to 1 cent for each 0.25 change in CPI-W (up from 0.36)
- **Holidays** Increased to 67 days with addition of National Election Days and Fridays before Memorial Day and Labor Day.
- **Pensions** Increased to $7.45 per month for each year of service.
- **Job security** Requires new employees to be hired as attrition replacements.
- **Tuition assistance** Increased from $3,800 to $4,200 per year; children eligible for $1,250 (up from $1,000).
- **Dental services** Benefit increased from $1,400 to $1,500 per year.
- **Supplemental unemployment benefits** GM to add $755 million to benefit reserves.
- **Relocation allowance** Increased from $22,000 to $23,500.
- **Personal saving plan** 21 new investment fund options.
- **Life insurance** Maximum benefit increased to $71,500.
- **Child care** New tax-free spending account established.

Analysis: Labor unions bargain with management over a variety of employment conditions. Most issues, however, can be expressed in terms of their impact on wage costs.

The Marginal Wage

Like all monopolists, unions have to worry about the downward slope of the demand curve. In the case of labor markets, a larger quantity of labor can be "sold" only at lower wage rates. Suppose the workers in a particular labor market confront the market labor demand schedule depicted in Figure 31.2. This schedule tells us that employers aren't willing to hire any workers at a wage rate of $6 per hour (row S) but will hire 1 worker per hour if the wage rate is $5 (row T). At still lower rates, the quantity of labor demanded increases; 5 workers per hour are demanded at a wage of $1 per hour.

An individual worker offered a wage of $1 an hour would have to decide whether such wages merited the sacrifice of an hour's leisure. But a union would evaluate the offer differently. A union must consider how the hiring of one more worker will affect the wages of all the workers.

Total Wages Paid. Notice that when 4 workers are hired at a wage rate of $2 an hour (row W), total wages are $8 per hour. In order for a fifth worker to be employed, the wage rate must drop to $1 an hour (row X). At wages of $1 per hour, the *total* wages paid to the 5 workers amount to only $5 per hour. Thus, total wages paid to the workers actually *fall* when a fifth worker is employed. Collectively the workers would be better off sending only 4 people to work at the higher wage of $2 an hour and paying the fifth worker $1 an hour to stay home!

The basic mandate of a labor union is to evaluate wage and employment offers from this *collective* perspective. To do so, *a union must distinguish the marginal wage from the market wage.* The market wage is simply the current wage rate paid by the employer; it's the wage received by individual workers. The **marginal wage**, on the other hand, is the change in *total* wages paid (to all workers) when an additional worker is hired—that is,

marginal wage: The change in total wages paid associated with a one-unit increase in the quantity of labor employed.

$$\frac{\text{Marginal}}{\text{wage}} = \frac{\text{change in total wages paid}}{\text{change in quantity of labor employed}}$$

The distinction between marginal wages and market wages arises from the downward slope of the labor demand curve. It's analogous to the distinction we made between

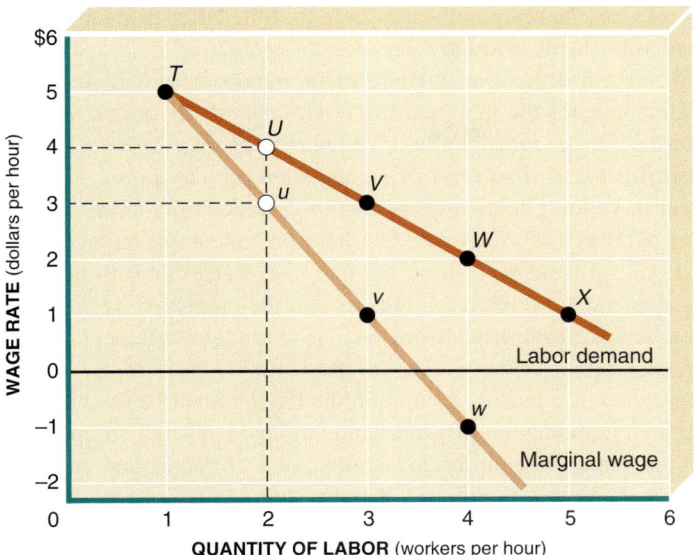

FIGURE 31.2
The Marginal Wage

The *marginal wage* is the change in *total wages* (paid to all workers) associated with the employment of an additional worker. If the wage rate is $4 per hour, only 2 workers will be hired. The wage rate must fall to $3 per hour if 3 workers are to be hired. In the process, *total* wages paid rise from $8 ($4 × 2 workers) to $9 ($3 × 3 workers). The *marginal* wage of the third worker is only $1.

The graph illustrates the relationship of the marginal wage to labor demand. The marginal wage curve lies below the labor demand curve, because the marginal wage is less than the nominal wage. Compare the marginal wage (point *v*) and the nominal wage (point *V*) of the third worker.

	Wage Rate (per hour)	×	Number of Workers Demanded (per hour)	=	Total Wages Paid (per hour)	Marginal Wage (per labor hour)
S	$6		0		$0	$0
T	5		1		5	5
U	4		2		8	3
V	3		3		9	1
W	2		4		8	−1
X	1		5		5	−3

marginal revenue and price for monopolists in product markets. The distinction simply reflects the law of demand: As wages fall, the number of workers hired increases.

The impact of increased employment on marginal wages is also illustrated in Figure 31.2. According to the labor demand curve, 1 worker will be hired at a wage rate of $5 an hour (point *T*); 2 workers will be hired only if the market wage falls to $4 an hour (point *U*), at which point the first and second workers will each be getting $4 an hour. Thus, the increased wages of the second worker (from zero to $4) will be partially offset by the reduction in the wage rate paid to the first worker (from $5 to $4). *Total* wages paid will increase by only $3; this is the *marginal* wage (point *u*). The marginal wage actually becomes negative at some point, when the implied wage loss to workers already on the job begins to exceed the wage of a new hired worker.

A union never wants to accept a negative marginal wage, of course. At such a point, union members would be better off paying someone to stay home. The question, then, is what level of (positive) marginal wage the union should accept.

We can answer this question by looking at the labor supply curve. The labor supply curve tells us how much labor workers are *willing to supply* at various wage rates. Hence, the labor supply curve defines the lowest wage *individual* union members would accept. If the union adopts a *collective* perspective on the welfare of its members, however, it will view the wage offer differently. From their collective perspective, the wage that union members are getting for additional labor is the *marginal* wage, not the

The Union Wage Goal

nominal (market) wage. Hence, the marginal wage curve, not the labor demand curve, is decisive in the union's assessment of wage offers.

If the union wants to maximize the *total* welfare of its members, it will seek that level of employment which equates the marginal wage with the supply preferences of union members. In Figure 31.3, **the intersection of the marginal wage curve with the labor supply curve identifies the desired level of employment for the union.** This intersection occurs at point u, yielding total employment of 2 workers per hour.

The marginal wage at point u is $3. However, the union members will get a higher actual wage than that. Look up from point u on the marginal wage curve to point U on the employer's labor demand curve. Point U tells us that the employer is *willing to pay* a wage rate of $4 an hour to employ two workers. The union knows it can demand and get $4 an hour if it supplies only two workers to the firm.

What the union is doing here is choosing a point on the labor demand curve that the union regards as the optimal combination of wages and employment. In a competitive market, point C would represent the equilibrium combination of wages and employment. But the union forces employers to point U, thereby attaining a higher wage rate and reducing employment.

Exclusion

The union's ability to maintain a wage rate of $4 an hour depends on its ability to exclude some workers from the market. Figure 31.3 suggests that three workers are willing and able to work at the union wage of $4 an hour (point N), whereas only two are hired (point U). If the additional worker were to offer his services, the wage rate would be pushed down the labor demand curve (to $3 per hour). Hence, **to maintain a noncompetitive wage, the union must be able to exercise some control over the labor supply decisions of individual workers.** The essential force here is union solidarity. Once unionized, the individual workers in an industry or occupation must agree not to compete among themselves by offering their labor at nonunion wage rates. Instead, the workers must agree to withhold labor—to strike, if necessary—if wage rates are too low, and to supply labor only if a specified wage rate is offered.

Unions can solidify their control of the labor supply by establishing **union shops,** workplaces where workers must join the union within 30 days after being employed. In this way, the unions gain control of all the workers employed in a particular company or industry, thereby reducing the number of replacement workers available for employment during a strike. Stiff penalties (such as loss of seniority or pension rights) and general union solidarity ensure that only nonunion workers will "fink" or "scab"— take the job of a worker on strike.

union shop: An employment setting in which all workers must join the union within 30 days after being employed.

FIGURE 31.3
The Union Wage Objective

The intersection of the marginal wage and labor supply curves (point u) determines the union's desired employment. Employers are willing to pay a wage rate of $4 per hour for that many workers, as revealed by point U on the labor demand curve.

More workers (N) are willing to work at $4 per hour than employers demand (U). To maintain that wage rate, the union must exclude some workers from the market. In the absence of such power, wages would fall to the competitive equilibrium (point C).

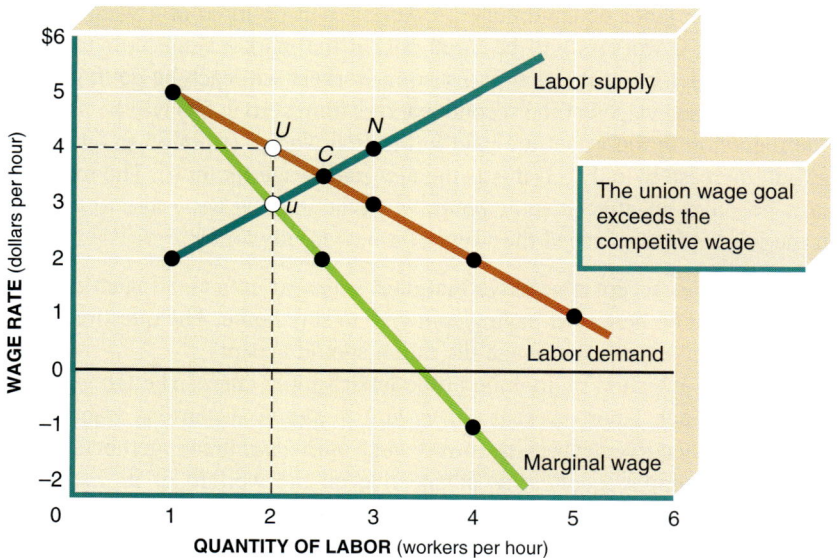

Replacement Workers. Even union shops, however, are subject to potential competition from substitute labor. When the UAW struck Caterpillar in 1991, the company advertised nationally for replacement workers and set up a toll-free phone line for applicants. In the midst of a recession the company got a huge response. The resulting flow of replacement workers crippled the UAW strike. Professional baseball players faced the same problem in 1995. When the continued strike threatened a second consecutive season, the team owners started hiring new players to replace the regulars. The huge supply of aspiring ball players forced the strikers to reconsider.

Replacement workers are even more abundant in agriculture. The United Farm Workers has been trying for decades to organize California's 20,000 strawberry pickers. But the workers know that thousands of additional workers will flock to California from Mexico if they protest wages and working conditions.

THE EXTENT OF UNION POWER

Early Growth

The first labor unions in America were organized in the 1780s, and the first worker protests as early as 1636. Union power wasn't a significant force in labor markets, however, until the 1900s, when heavily populated commercial centers and large-scale manufacturing became common. Only then did large numbers of workers begin to view their employment situations from a common perspective.

The period 1916–20 was one of particularly fast growth for labor unions, largely because of the high demand for labor resulting from World War I. All these membership gains were lost, however, when the Great Depression threw millions of people out of work. By 1933, union membership had dwindled to the levels of 1915.

As the depression lingered on, public attitudes and government policy changed. Too many people had learned the meaning of layoffs, wage cuts, and prolonged unemployment. In 1933, the National Industrial Recovery Act (NIRA) established the right of employees to bargain collectively with their employers. When the NIRA was declared unconstitutional by the Supreme Court in 1935, its labor provisions were incorporated into a new law, the Wagner Act. With this legislative encouragement, union membership doubled between 1933 and 1937. Unions continued to gain in strength as the production needs of World War II increased the demand for labor. Figure 31.4 reflects the tremendous spurt of union activity between the depths of the depression and the height of World War II.

Union Power Today

Union membership stopped increasing in the 1950s, even though the labor force kept growing. As a result, the unionized percentage of the labor force—the **unionization rate**—has been in steady decline for more than 40 years. The current unionization rate of 13.5 percent is less than half of its post–World War II peak and far below unionization rates in other industrialized nations (see World View on the next page).

unionization ratio: The percentage of the labor force belonging to a union.

Private vs. Public-Sector Trends. The decline in the *national* unionization rate conceals two very different trends. Union representation of *private*-sector workers has

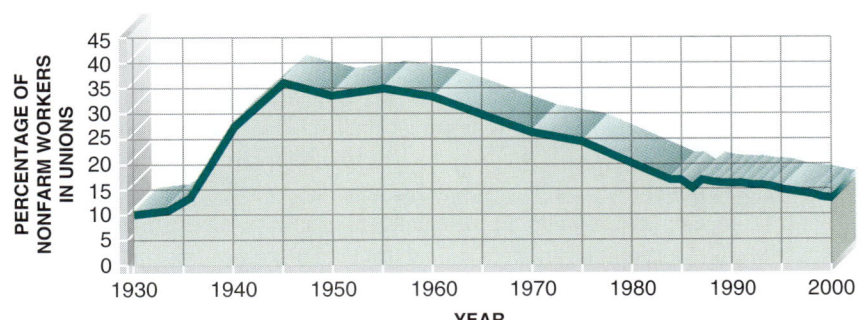

FIGURE 31.4
Changing Unionization Rates

Unions grew most rapidly during the decade 1935–45. Since that time, the growth of unions hasn't kept pace with the growth of the U.S. labor force. Most employment growth has occurred in service industries that have traditionally been nonunion.

Source: U.S. Department of Labor.

WORLD VIEW

Union Membership

Union membership in the United States is far below that of other industrialized countries. Moreover, while unionization rates have been declining in the United States, they've been rising in many other countries. In Sweden and Denmark nearly all workers belong to a union.

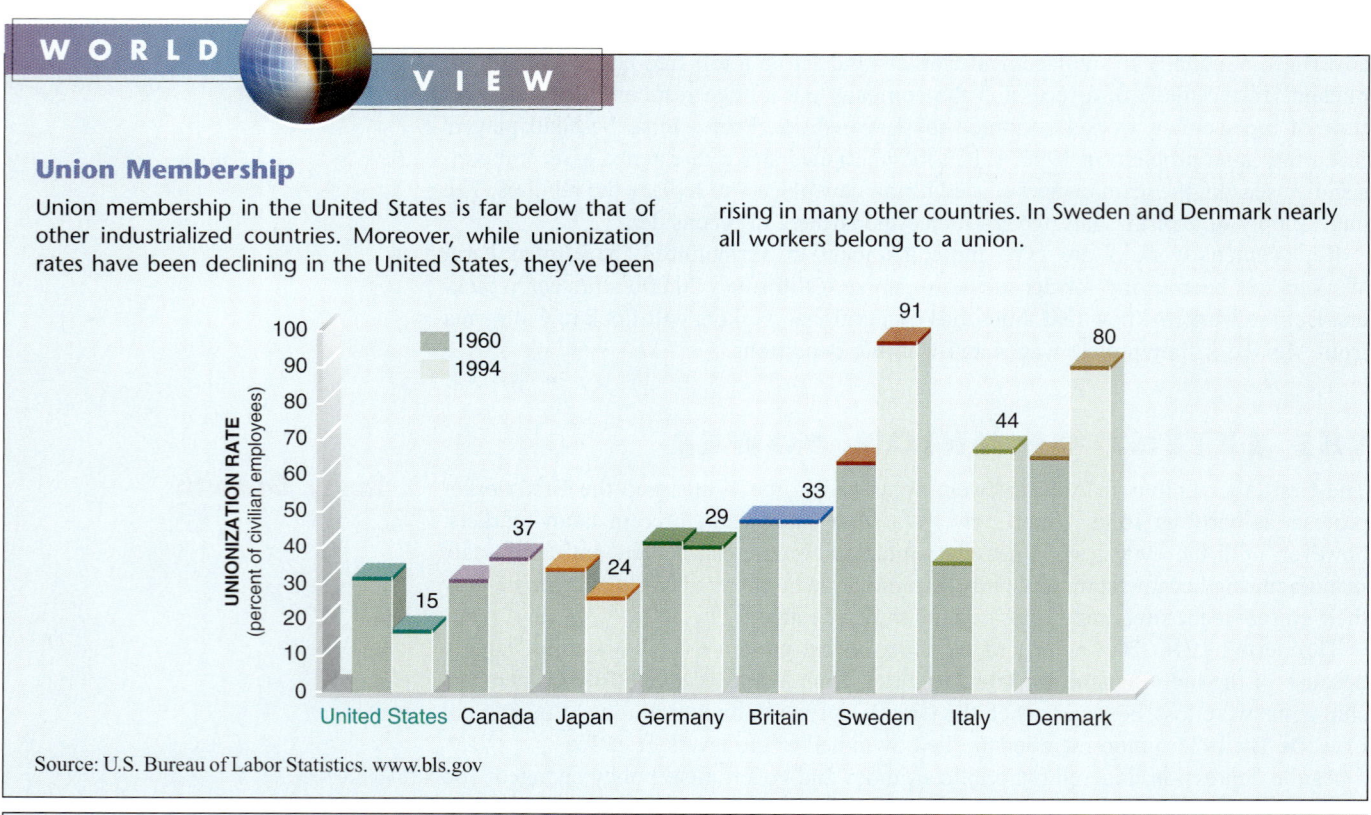

Source: U.S. Bureau of Labor Statistics. www.bls.gov

Analysis: Unionization rates are comparatively low in the United States and declining. Unionization rates are still increasing in many other nations.

plunged even more sharply than Figure 31.4 suggests. In the last 10 years, the unionization rate in the private sector has fallen from 11.5 percent to only 8.5 percent. At the same time, union membership has increased sharply among teachers, government workers, and nonprofit employees. As of 2001, over 37 percent of workers on government payrolls were union members. *The old industrial unions are being supplanted by unions of service workers, especially those employed in the public sector.*

Although industrial unions have been in general decline, they still possess significant pockets of market power. The Teamsters, the UAW, the United Mine Workers, the Union of Needletrades and Textile Employees, and the Food Workers all have substantial representation in their respective markets. Their strength in those specific markets, not national averages, determines their ability to alter market outcomes.

The AFL-CIO. One labor organization with a decidedly national focus is the AFL-CIO (the American Federation of Labor–Congress of Industrial Organizations). The AFL-CIO is not a separate union but a representational body of 120 national unions. It doesn't represent or negotiate for any particular group of workers but focuses instead on issues of general labor interest. The AFL-CIO acts as an advocate for the labor movement and represents labor's interest in legislative areas. It's the primary vehicle for political action. In addition, the AFL-CIO may render economic assistance to member unions or to groups of workers who wish to organize.

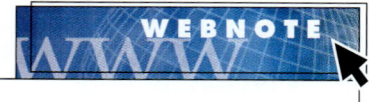

The AFL-CIO's website offers a brief mission statement and a map of affiliated unions; visit www.aflcio.org.

EMPLOYER POWER

The power possessed by labor unions in various occupations and industries seldom exists in a power vacuum. Power exists on the demand side of labor markets, too. The United Auto Workers confront GM, Ford, and Chrysler; the Steelworkers confront U.S. Steel, Bethlehem, and LTV; the Teamsters confront the Truckers' Association; the Communications Workers confront AT&T; and so on. An imbalance of power often exists on one side of the market or the other (as with, say, the Carpenters versus individual construction contractors). Labor markets with significant power on both sides, however, are common. To understand how wage rates and employment are determined in such markets, we have to assess the market power possessed by employers.

Power on the demand side of a market belongs to a *buyer* who is able to influence the market price of a good. With respect to labor markets, market power on the demand side implies the ability of a single employer to alter the market wage rate. The extreme case of such power is a **monopsony,** a situation in which one employer is the only buyer in a particular market. The classic example of a monopsony is a company town—that is, a town that depends for its livelihood on the decisions of a single employer.

Graduate teaching assistants have complained that the universities that employ them are much like company towns. Once they've started taking graduate classes at one university, it's difficult to transfer to another. As they see it, there is only one local labor market for graduate students. They complain that their monopsony employer compels them to work long hours at low wages. In 1998, University of California graduate students went out on strike to protest those conditions. In 1999, over 10,000 of those graduate students affiliated with the United Auto Workers to gain more power. In November 2000, the National Labor Relations Board decreed that graduate research and teaching assistants are employees with the right to organize and strike (see News).

Before 1976, professional sports teams also had monopsony power. As the News on the next page relates, sports contracts prohibited pro players from moving from one team (employer) to another without permission. This gave team owners a lot of power to set wages and working conditions.

Monopsony

monopsony: A market in which there's only one buyer.

IN THE NEWS

A Win for the Graduate(s)
Finally, Teaching Assistants Can Unionize

For years, New York University and other private institutions have argued successfully that graduate students who work as research and teaching assistants shouldn't be treated as employees under federal labor law. The money that grad students earn is financial aid, not compensation, universities say. And while critics complain that grad students are exploited as cheap labor, administrators respond that aspiring Ph.D.'s gain vital career training by teaching undergraduate discussion sections and conducting research.

Last week, however, in a case involving NYU graduate assistants, the National Labor Relations Board gave a decisive thumbs down to these claims. Overturning nearly a quarter century of precedent, the federal panel said that graduate research and teaching assistants at private universities are employees who have the right to form unions and bargain collectively. "We will not deprive workers . . . of their fundamental statutory rights to organize and bargain with their employer, simply because they also are students," the ruling said, upholding a decision issued last spring by a regional NLRB director. Grad student unions have already been recognized at a growing number of public universities, which are governed by state labor laws.

—Ben Wildavsky

Source: *U.S. News & World Report.* November 13, 2000. Reprinted with permission. www.usnews.com

Analysis: Universities have monopsony power in setting wage and workloads for graduate assistants. To counterbalance that power, grad assistants may organize and bargain collectively.

There are many degrees of market power, and they can be defined in terms of *buyer concentration*. When buyers are many and of limited market power, the demand for resources is likely to be competitive. When only one buyer has access to a particular resource market, a monopsony exists. Between the two extremes lie the various degrees of imperfect competition, including the awkward-sounding but empirically important case of *oligopsony*. In an oligopsony (e.g. the auto industry), only a few firms account for most of the industry's employment.

The Potential Use of Power

Firms with power in labor markets generally have the same objective as all other firms—to maximize profits. What distinguishes them from competitive (powerless) firms is their ability to attain and keep economic profits. In labor markets, this means using fewer workers and paying them lower wages.

The distinguishing characteristic of labor market monopsonies is that their hiring decisions influence the market wage rate. In a competitive labor market, no single employer has any direct influence on the market wage rate; each firm can hire as much labor as it needs at the prevailing wage. But a monopsonist confronts the *market* labor supply curve. As a result, any increase in the quantity of labor demanded will force the monopsonist to climb up the labor supply curve in search of additional workers. In other words, *a monopsonist can hire additional workers only if it offers a higher wage rate.*

Marginal Factor Cost. Any time the price of a resource (or product) changes as a result of a firm's purchases, a distinction between marginal cost and price (average cost) must be made. Making this distinction is one of the little headaches—and potential sources of profit—of a monopsonist. For labor, we distinguish between the **marginal factor cost (MFC)** of labor and its wage rate.

marginal factor cost (MFC): The change in total costs that results from a one-unit increase in the quantity of a factor employed.

Suppose that Figure 31.5 accurately described the labor supply schedule confronting a monopsonist. It's evident that the monopsonist will have to pay a wage of at least $2 an hour if it wants any labor. But even at that wage rate (row F of the supply sched-

IN THE NEWS

Free Agents in Sports: A Threat to Monopsony

Before 1976, the owners of professional baseball, football, and basketball teams enjoyed monopsonistic power. This power was bestowed by the "reserve clause" included in player contracts. Individual players were permitted to negotiate with only one team. Once signed, they couldn't move to another team without their owner's permission. The player's only option was to "take it or leave"—that is, to accept his team's wage offer or quit playing altogether for at least one season. Team owners used the reserve clause to hold down player salaries far below their marginal revenue product.

The reserve clause began to unravel in 1975, when an arbitration panel ruled it was too restrictive. In 1976, baseball players won the right to become free agents—to negotiate and play for any team—after six years of major-league experience. In 1977, pro football players also won the right to become free agents, but under more restrictive conditions (the team losing a free agent had to be "compensated" with draft choices). Pro basketball players first won limited mobility rights in 1976 and became true free agents in 1980.

The weakening of monopsonistic power led to dramatically higher player salaries. The average baseball salary soared from about $51,000 in 1976 to $900,000 in 1992. Pro basketball players enjoyed the same kind of wage gain, attaining an *average* salary of over $750,000 in 1990. Only pro football players lagged behind. Their more limited free-agent rights kept a lid on average football salaries. Football players went out on strike in 1982 and again in 1987 but failed to achieve free-agent status. In 1992, however, a federal court ruled that reserve clauses were anticompetitive. This decision prompted football owners to offer greater free agency and higher salaries.

Analysis: Because "reserve clauses" limit competing wage offers, they confer monopsony power on team owners. This kept athletes' wages below competitive equilibrium. Free agency changed that.

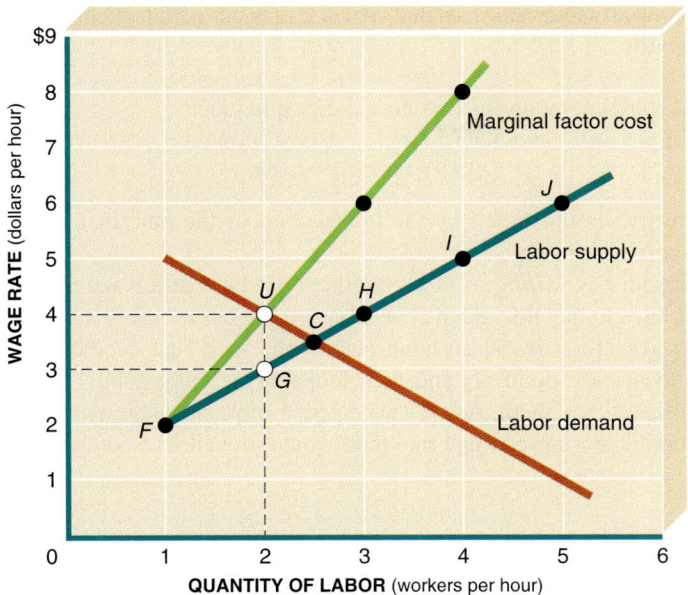

FIGURE 31.5
Marginal Factor Cost

More workers can be attracted only if the wage rate is increased. As it rises, all workers must be paid the higher wage. Consequently, the change in *total* wage costs exceeds the actual wage paid to the last worker. In the table, notice that in row *I*, for example, the marginal factor cost of the fourth worker ($8) exceeds the wage actually paid to that worker ($5). Thus, the marginal factor cost curve lies above the labor supply curve.

In the graph, the intersection of the marginal factor cost and labor demand curves (point *U*) indicates the quantity of labor a monopsonist will want to hire. The labor supply curve (at point *G*) indicates the wage rate that must be paid to attract the desired number of workers. This is the monopsonist's desired wage ($3). In the absence of market power, an employer would end up at point *C* (the competitive equilibrium), paying a higher wage and employing more workers.

	Wage Rate (per hour)	×	Quantity of Labor Supplied (workers per hour)	=	Total Wage Cost (per hour)	Marginal Factor Cost (per labor-hour)
D	$0		0		$0	$0
E	1		0		0	0
F	2		1		2	2
G	3		2		6	4
H	4		3		12	6
I	5		4		20	8
J	6		5		30	10

ule), only 1 worker will be willing to work. If the firm wants more labor, it will have to offer higher wages.

Two things happen when the firm raises its wage offer to $3 an hour (row *G*). First, the quantity of labor supplied increases (to 2 workers per hour). Second, the total wages paid rise by $4. This high *marginal* cost of labor is attributable to the fact that the first worker's wages rise when the wage rate is increased to attract additional workers. If all the workers perform the same job, the first worker will demand to be paid the new (higher) wage rate. Thus, *the marginal factor cost exceeds the wage rate, because additional workers can be hired only if the wage rate for all workers is increased.*

The Monopsony Firm's Goal. The marginal factor cost curve confronting this monopsonist is shown in the upper half of Figure 31.5. It starts at the bottom of the labor supply curve and rises above it. The monopsonist must now decide how many workers to hire, given the impact of its hiring decision on the market wage rate.

Remember from Chapter 30 that the labor demand curve is a reflection of labor's **marginal revenue product,** that is, the increase in total revenue attributable to the employment of one additional worker.

As we've emphasized, the profit-maximizing producer always seeks to equalize marginal revenue and marginal cost. Accordingly, the monopsonistic employer will seek

marginal revenue product (MRP): The change in total revenue associated with one additional unit of input.

to hire the amount of labor at which the marginal revenue product of labor equals its marginal factor cost—that is,

$$\begin{array}{c} \text{Profit-maximizing} \\ \text{level of input use} \end{array} : \begin{array}{c} \text{marginal revenue} \\ \text{product of input} \\ \text{(MRP)} \end{array} = \begin{array}{c} \text{marginal factor} \\ \text{cost of input} \\ \text{(MFC)} \end{array}$$

In Figure 31.5, this objective is illustrated by the intersection of the marginal factor cost and labor demand curves at point U.

At point U the monopsonist is *willing to hire* 2 workers per hour at a wage rate of $4. But the firm doesn't have to pay this much. The labor supply curve informs us that 2 workers are *willing to work* for only $3 an hour. Hence, the firm first decides how many workers it wants to hire (at point U) and then looks at the labor supply curve (point G) to see what it has to pay them. As we suspected, a monopsonistic employer ends up hiring fewer workers at a lower wage rate than would prevail in a competitive market (point C).

COLLECTIVE BARGAINING

The potential for conflict between a powerful employer and a labor union should be evident:

- *The objective of a labor union is to establish a wage rate that's **higher** than the competitive wage (Figure 31.3).*
- *A monopsonist employer seeks to establish a wage rate that's **lower** than competitive standards (Figure 31.5).*

The resultant clash generates intense bargaining that often spills over into politics, the courts, and open conflict.

The confrontation of power on both sides of the labor market is a situation referred to as **bilateral monopoly.** In such a market, wages and employment aren't determined simply by supply and demand. Rather, economic outcomes must be determined by **collective bargaining**—that is, direct negotiations between employers and labor unions for the purpose of determining wages, employment, working conditions, and related issues.

bilateral monopoly: A market with only one buyer (a monopsonist) and one seller (a monopolist).

collective bargaining: Direct negotiations between employers and unions to determine labor market outcomes.

Possible Agreements

In a typical labor-business confrontation, the two sides begin by stating their preferences for equilibrium wages and employment. The *demands* laid down by the union are likely to revolve around point U in Figure 31.6; the *offer* enunciated by management is likely to

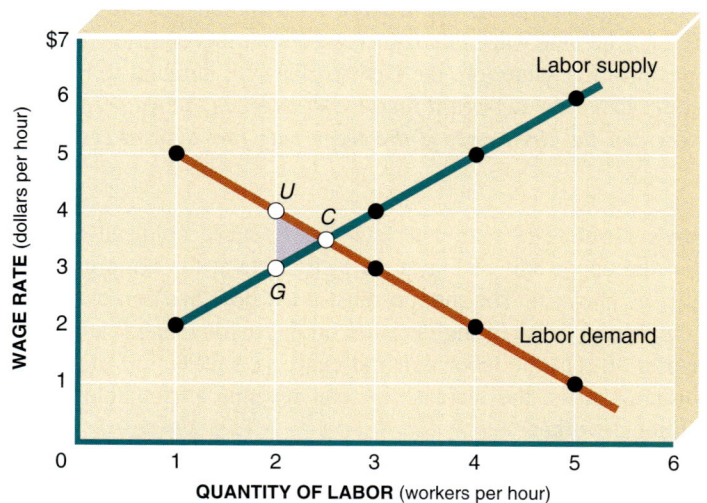

FIGURE 31.6

The Boundaries of Collective Bargaining

Firms with power in the labor market seek to establish wages and employment levels corresponding to point G (from Figure 31.5). Unions, on the other hand, seek to establish an equilibrium at point U (from Figure 31.3). The competitive equilibrium is at point C. The function of collective bargaining is to identify a compromise between these points—that is, to locate an equilibrium somewhere in the shaded area.

IN THE NEWS

Caterpillar vs. the UAW

	What Separates the Two Sides	
	Company Proposal	**Union Proposal**
Wages	One 3% wage hike for 12,800 of Cat's 16,500 union workers	One 3% wage hike for all workers, plus two one-time payments of 3% each
	Lower pay for new hires at parts-distribution centers	Same wage scales for all union workers
Benefits	Medical co-payments and a preferred-provider plan	A traditional plan with no co-payments
Job security	Employment levels can fall by attrition	Guaranteed number of union jobs

Source: *Business Week*, March 23, 1992. Reprinted by permission. © 1992 by The McGraw-Hill Companies, Inc. www.businessweek.com

Analysis: Collective bargaining begins with a set of union demands and management offers. The outcome depends on the relative strength and tactics of the two parties.

---

be at point G.[1] Thus the boundaries of a potential settlement—a negotiated final equilibrium—are usually established at the outset of collective bargaining. The accompanying News summarizes the points of contention in the 1991–98 dispute between Caterpillar and the UAW.

The interesting part of collective bargaining isn't the initial bargaining positions but the negotiation of the final settlement. The speed with which a settlement is reached and the nature of the compromise it embodies depend on the patience, tactics, and resources of the negotiating parties. ***The fundamental source of negotiating power for either side is its ability to withhold labor or jobs.*** The union can threaten to strike, thereby cutting off the flow of union labor to the employer. The employer can impose a lockout, thereby cutting off jobs and paychecks. The effectiveness of those threats depends on the availability of substitute workers or jobs.

Labor and management both suffer from either a strike or a lockout, no matter who initiates the work stoppage. The strike benefits paid to workers are rarely comparable to wages they would otherwise have received, and the payment of those benefits depletes the union treasury. By the same token, the reduction in labor costs and other expenses rarely compensates the employer for lost profits.

When the UAW was unable to attain its bargaining goals with Caterpillar, it instructed its 12,600 workers to go out on strike. The Caterpillar company however, held a strong bargaining position. As a result of the 1990–91 recession, it had a huge inventory of unsold farm equipment and was in no hurry to settle. When inventories got low, Caterpillar found a willing supply of replacement workers. This substitute labor put all the pressure on the union to settle. In 1994, the company actually attained record profits, despite the continuing strike.

In 1996, a strike by UAW workers at a GM brake plant caused shutdowns at all of GM's 29 U.S. assembly plants. More than 175,000 workers were idled. GM's 1,600

The Pressure of Settle

---

[1] Even though points U and G may not be identical to the initial bargaining positions, they represent the positions of maximum attainable benefit for both sides. Points outside the demand or supply curve will be rejected out of hand by one side or the other.

parts suppliers also had to lay off workers. With heavy inventories of unsold cars, GM had a relatively strong bargaining position. The UAW caved in quickly (17 days later). In 1998, the balance of power was different. Car sales were brisk and inventories were lean. So when the UAW struck a key parts plant in June 1998, GM was under greater pressure to settle. Rather than continuing to lose over $100 million a day, GM relented after 54 days, accepting little more than a UAW promise not to strike again for a year and a half. Ironically, the decline in GM profits due to the UAW strike cost GM autoworkers more that $6,000 apiece in *profit-sharing* bonuses that year.

Because potential income losses are usually high, both labor and management try to avoid a strike or lockout if they can. In fact, over 90 percent of all collective bargaining agreements are concluded without recourse to a strike and often without even the explicit threat of one.

The Final Settlement

The built-in pressures for settlement help resolve collective bargaining. They don't tell us, however, what the dimensions of that final settlement will be. All we know is that the settlement will be located within the boundaries established in Figure 31.6. The relative pressures on each side will determine whether the final equilibrium is closer to the union or the management position.

In the 1987 National Football League strike, the pressures to settle were very one-sided. The average pro football player was losing $14,375 per missed game. But the team owners were actually making *more* profit during the strike than before it. Although their revenues from ticket sales, parking, and food concessions fell, weekly TV revenues of $1 million per team continued to pour in. Those revenues, together with the sharply lower costs of replacement teams, led to higher profits. It didn't take long for the striking players to capitulate and accept the team owners' offer.

The 1998–99 pro basketball lockout wasn't so one-sided. When the season startup was canceled in November, the players started missing paychecks (an average of $2.6 million per season). But the team owners were also losing ticket revenue and concession sales, and they stood to lose another $465 million in TV revenues if the season didn't start by January. As that deadline approached, the owners decided to compromise with the players and commence a shortened basketball season.

The final settlement almost always necessitates hard choices on both sides. The union usually has to choose between an increase in job security or higher pay. A union must also consider how management will react in the long run to higher wages, perhaps by introducing new technology that reduces its dependence on labor. The employer has to worry whether productivity will suffer if workers are dissatisfied with their pay package.

For information about recent union contracts and strikes, see the U.S. Bureau of Labor Statistics at www.bls.gov. Click on "Collective Bargaining."

THE IMPACT OF UNIONS

Stepping back from the negotiations that take place between individual unions and companies, we may ask whether the presence of unions has altered broader economic outcomes. We know that unions tend to raise wage rates in individual companies, industries, and occupations. But can we be equally sure that unions have raised wages in general? If the UAW is successful in raising wages in the automobile industry, what, if anything, happens to car prices when autoworkers' wages go up? If car prices rise in step with UAW wage rates, labor and management in the auto industry will get proportionally larger slices of the economic pie. At the same time, workers in other industries will be burdened with higher car prices.

Relative Wages

One measure of union impact is *relative* wages—the wages of union members in comparison with those of nonunion workers. As we've noted, unions seek to control the supply of labor in a particular industry or occupation and thereby increase union wages. In their efforts to control labor supply, they restrict the number of people who can compete for available jobs, forcing those workers who are excluded to seek work elsewhere. As a result of this labor supply imbalance, wages tend to be higher in unionized industries than in nonunionized industries. Figure 31.7 illustrates this effect.

Although the theoretical impact of union exclusionism on relative wages is clear, empirical estimates of that impact are fairly rare. We do know that union wages in general are significantly higher than nonunion wages ($696 versus $542 per week in 2000). But part of this differential is due to the fact that unions are more common in industries that have always been more capital-intensive and paid relatively high wages. When comparisons are made within particular industries or sectors, the differential narrows considerably. Nevertheless, there's a general consensus that unions have managed to increase their relative wages from 15 to 20 percent.

Labor's Share of Total Income

Even though unions have been successful in redistributing some income from nonunion to union workers, the question still remains as to whether they've increased labor's share of *total* income. The *labor share* of total income is the proportion of income received by all workers, in contrast to the share of income received by owners of capital (the *capital share*). The labor share of total income will rise only if the gains to union workers exceed the losses to the (excluded) nonunion workers.

Evidence of unions' impact on labor's share is almost as difficult to assemble as evidence on relative wages, and for much the same reasons. Labor's share has risen dramatically, from only 56 percent in 1919 to 76 percent in 2001. But there have been tremendous changes in the mix of output during that same period. The proportion of output composed of personal services (accountants, teachers, electricians) is much larger now than it was in 1919. The labor share of income derived from personal services is and always was close to 100 percent. Accordingly, *most of the rise in labor's share of total income is due to changes in the structure of the economy rather than to unionization.*

Prices

One way firms can protect their profits in the face of rising union wages is to raise product prices. If firms raise prices along with union wages, then consumers end up footing the bill. In that case, profits and the capital share of total income might not be reduced.

The ability of firms to pass along increased union wages depends on the structure of product markets as well as labor markets. If a firm has power in both markets, it's

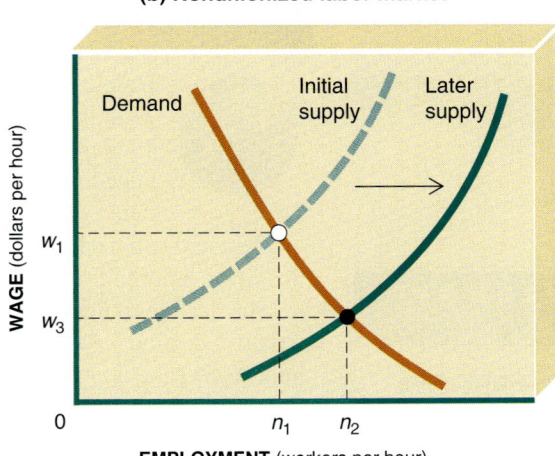

FIGURE 31.7
The Effect of Unions on Relative Wages

In the absence of unions, the average wage rate would be equal to w_1. As unions take control of the market, however, they seek to raise wage rates to w_2, in the process reducing the amount of employment in that market from l_1 to l_2. The workers displaced from the unionized market will seek work in the nonunionized market, thereby shifting the nonunion supply curve to the right. The result will be a reduction of wage rates (to w_3) in the nonunionized market. Thus, union wages end up higher than nonunion wages.

better able to protect itself in this way. There's little evidence, however, that unions have contributed significantly to general cost-push inflation.

Productivity

productivity: Output per unit of input, such as output per labor-hour.

Unions also affect prices indirectly, via changes in **productivity.** Unions bargain not only for wages but also for work rules that specify how goods should be produced. Work rules may limit the pace of production, restrict the type of jobs a particular individual can perform, or require a minimum number of workers to accomplish a certain task. A factory carpenter, for example, may not be permitted to change a lightbulb that burns out in his shop area. And the electrician who is summoned may be required to have an apprentice on all work assignments. Such restrictive work rules would make it very costly to change a burned-out lightbulb.

Not all work rules are so restrictive. In general, however, work rules are designed to protect jobs and maximize the level of employment at any given rate of output. From this perspective, work rules directly restrain productivity and thus inflate costs and prices.

Work rules may also have some beneficial effects. The added job security provided by work rules and seniority provisions tends to reduce labor turnover (quitting) and thus saves recruitment and training costs. Protective rules may also make workers more willing to learn new tasks and to train others in specific skills. Richard Freeman of Harvard concluded that unions have actually accelerated advances in productivity and economic growth.

Political Impact

Perhaps more important than any of these specific union effects is the general impact the union movement has had on our economic, social, and political institutions. Unions are a major political force in the United States. They've not only provided critical electoral and financial support for selected political candidates, but they've also fought hard for important legislation. Unions have succeeded in establishing minimum wage laws, work and safety rules, and retirement benefits. They've also actively lobbied for such things as civil rights legislation and health and education programs. Whatever one may think of any particular union or specific union action, it's clear that our institutions and national welfare would be very different in their absence.

THE ECONOMY TOMORROW

Merging to Survive

Unions have been in retreat for nearly a generation. As shown in Figure 31.4, the unionized share of the labor force has fallen from 35 percent in 1950 to less than 14 percent today. Even that modest share has been maintained only by the spread of unionism among public school teachers and other government employees. In the private sector, the unionization rate is closer to 9 percent and still declining. The Teamsters, the Auto Workers, and the Steelworkers have lost over 1 million members in the last 15 years.

The decline in unionization is explained by three phenomena. Most important is the relative decline in manufacturing, coupled with rapid growth in high-tech service industries (like computer software, accounting, and medical technology). The second force is the downsizing of major corporations and the relatively faster growth of smaller companies. These structural changes have combined to shrink the traditional employment base of labor unions.

The third cause of shrinking unionization is increased global competition. The decline of worldwide trade and investment barriers has made it easier for firms to import products from low-wage nations and even to relocate production plants. With more options, firms can more easily resist noncompetitive wage demands.

The labor-union movement is fully aware of these forces and determined to resist them. To increase their power, unions are merging across craft and industry lines. In 1995, the Rubber Workers merged with the Steelworkers, the two major textile unions

For trends in union membership, see www.aflcio.org/uniondifference/uniondiff11.htm.

combined forces, and the Food Workers and Retail Clerks formed a new union. In 1999, the Grain Millers merged with the Paperworkers Union. By merging, the unions hope to increase representation, gain financial strength, and enhance their political clout. They're also seeking to broaden their appeal by organizing low-wage workers in the service industries. These efforts, together with their political strength, will help unions to play a continuing role in the economy tomorrow, even if their share of total employment continues to shrink.

SUMMARY

- Power in labor markets is the ability to alter market wage rates. Such power is most evident in local labor markets defined by geographical, occupational, or industrial boundaries.
- Power on the supply side of labor markets is manifested by unions, organized along industry or craft lines. The basic function of a union is to evaluate employment offers in terms of the *collective* interest of its members.
- The downward slope of the labor demand curve creates a distinction between the marginal wage and the market wage. The marginal wage is the change in *total* wages occasioned by employment of one additional worker and is less than the market wage.
- Unions seek to establish that rate of employment at which the marginal wage curve intersects the labor supply curve. The desired union wage is then found on the labor demand curve at that level of employment.
- Power on the demand side of labor market is manifested in buyer concentrations such as monopsony and oligopsony. Such power is usually found among the same firms that exercise market power in product markets.
- By definition, power on the demand side implies some direct influence on market wage rates; additional hiring by a monopsonist will force up the market wage rate. Hence, a monopsonist must recognize a distinction between the marginal factor cost of labor and its (lower) market wage rate.
- The goal of a monopsonistic employer is to hire the number of workers indicated by the point at which the marginal factor cost of labor equals its marginal revenue product. The employer then looks at the labor supply curve to determine the wage rate that must be paid for that number of workers.
- The desire of unions to establish a wage rate that's higher than competitive wages directly opposes the desire of powerful employers to establish lower wage rates. In bilateral monopolies, in which power exists on both sides of the labor market, unions and employers engage in collective bargaining to negotiate a final settlement.
- The impact of unions on the economy is difficult to measure. It appears, however, that they've increased their own relative wages and contributed to rising prices. They've also had substantial political impact.

Key Terms

market power
labor supply
demand for labor
equilibrium wage
marginal wage
union shop
unionization ratio
monopsony
marginal factor cost
 (MFC)
marginal revenue product
 (MRP)
bilateral monopoly
collective bargaining
productivity

Questions for Discussion

1. Collective bargaining sessions often start with unreasonable demands and categorical rejections. Why do unions and employers tend to begin bargaining from extreme positions?
2. Does a strike for a raise of 5 cents an hour make any sense? What kinds of long-term benefits might a union gain from such a strike?
3. Are large and powerful firms easier targets for union organization than small firms? Why or why not?
4. Nonunionized firms tend to offer wage rates that are close to rates paid by unionized firms in the same industry. How do you explain this?
5. Why are farm workers much less successful than airplane machinists in securing higher wages?

6. In 1998, teaching assistants at the University of California struck for higher wages and union recognition, something they had sought for 14 years. How did the availability of replacement workers affect their power?
7. A key issue in the 1998 GM strike involved "peg rates" that allow workers to go home or get paid overtime wages once production reaches a specified level. How do peg rates affect productivity and costs?
8. How will union mergers affect the market power of unions?

Web Activities

1. Are unions a good idea? Evaluate the claim by the AFL-CIO (www.aflcio.org/uniondifference/index.htm) that "union membership helps raise workers' pay and narrow the income gap that disadvantages minorities and women."
2. Do union workers really earn higher wages? Log on to stats.bls.gov/opub/cwc/2000/Spring/brief2.htm#D to find out. What is the average wage differential for union vs. nonunion members in private industry?
3. Does your state have much union employment? Check it out at www.bls.gov/news.release/union2.05.htm. What percentage of your state's labor force belongs to a union?

THE ACCOMPANYING STUDENT PROBLEM SET CONTAINS NUMERICAL AND GRAPHING PROBLEMS FOR THIS CHAPTER

CHAPTER 32

Financial Markets

Christopher Columbus had a crazy entrepreneurial idea: He was certain he could find a new route to the Indies by sailing not east from Europe but west—around the world. Such a route, he surmised, would give Europe quicker access to the riches of the East Indies. Whoever discovered that western route could become very, very rich.

To find that route, Columbus needed ships, sailors, and tons of provisions. He couldn't afford to supply these resources himself. He needed financial backers who would put up the money. For several years he tried to convince King Ferdinand of Spain to provide the necessary funds. But the king didn't want to risk so much wealth on a single venture. Twice he'd turned Columbus down.

Fortunately, Genoese merchant bankers in Seville came to Columbus' rescue. Convinced that Columbus' "enterprise of the Indies" might bring back "pearls, precious stones, gold, silver, spiceries," and other valuable merchandise, they guaranteed repayment of any funds lent to Columbus. With that guarantee in hand, the Duke of Medina Sidonia, in April 1492, offered to lend 1,000 maravedis (about $5,000 in today's dollars) to Queen Isabella for the purpose of funding Columbus' expedition. With no personal financial risk, King Ferdinand then granted Columbus the funds and authority for a royal expedition.

Columbus' experience in raising funds for his expedition illustrates a critical function of financial markets, namely, the management of *risk*. This chapter examines how financial markets facilitate economic activities (like Columbus' expedition) by managing the risks of failure. Three central questions guide the discussion:

- What is traded in financial markets?
- How do the financial markets affect the economic outcomes of WHO, WHAT, and FOR WHOM?
- Why do financial markets fluctuate so much?

THE ROLE OF FINANCIAL MARKETS

A central question for every economy is WHAT to produce. In 1492, all available resources were employed in farming, fishing, food distribution, metalworking, and other basic services. For Columbus to pursue his quest, he needed some of

Financial Intermediaries

these resources. To get them, he needed money to bid scarce resources from other pursuits and employ them on his expedition.

Entrepreneurs who don't have great personal wealth must get start-up funds from other people. There are two possibilities: either *borrow* the money, or invite other people to *invest* in the new venture.

How might you pursue these options? You could ask your relatives for a loan or go door-to-door in your neighborhood seeking investors. But such direct fund-raising is costly, inefficient, and often unproductive. Columbus went hat in hand to the Spanish royal court twice, but each time he came back empty-handed.

The task of raising start-up funds is made much easier by the existence of **financial intermediaries**—institutions that steer the flow of savings to cash-strapped entrepreneurs and other investors. Funds flow into banks, pension funds, bond markets, stock markets, and other financial intermediaries from businesses, households, and government entities that have some unspent income. This pool of national savings is then passed on to entrepreneurs, expanding businesses, and other borrowers by these same institutions (see Figure 32.1).

> **financial intermediary:** Institution (e.g., bank or the stock market) that makes savings available to dissavers (e.g., investors).

Financial intermediaries provide several important services: They greatly reduce the cost of locating loanable funds. Their pool of savings offers a clear economy of scale compared to the alternative of door-to-door solicitations. They also reduce the cost to savers of finding suitable lending or investment opportunities. Few individuals have the time, resources, or interest to do the searching on their own. With huge pools of amassed savings, however, financial intermediaries have the incentive to acquire and analyze information about lending and investment opportunities. Hence, *financial intermediaries reduce search and information costs* in the financial markets. In so doing, they make the allocation of resources more efficient.

Although financial intermediaries make the job of acquiring start-up funds a lot easier, there's no guarantee that the funds needed will be acquired. First, there must be an adequate supply of funds available. Second, financial intermediaries must be convinced that they should allocate some of those funds to a project.

The Supply of Loanable Funds

As noted, the supply of loanable funds originates in the decisions of market participants to not spend all their current income. Those saving decisions are influenced by time preferences and interest rates.

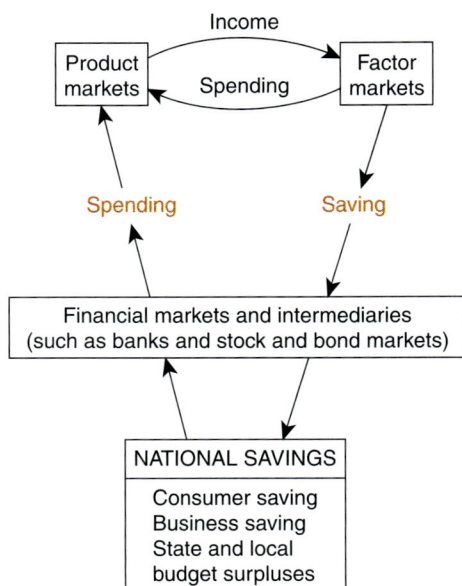

FIGURE 32.1
Mobilizing Savings

The central economic function of financial markets is to channel the national savings into new investment and other desired expenditure. Financial intermediaries such as banks, insurance companies, and stockbrokers help transfer purchasing power from savers to spenders.

Time Preferences. In deciding to *save* rather than *spend,* people effectively reallocate their spending over time. That is, people save *now* in order to spend more *later.* How much to save, then, depends partly on *time preference.* If a person doesn't give any thought to the future, she's likely to save little. If, by contrast, a person wants to buy a car, a vacation, or a house in the future, he's more inclined to save some income now.

Interest Rates. Interest rates also affect saving decisions. If interest rates are high, the future payoff to every dollar saved is greater. A higher return on savings translates into more future income for every dollar of current income saved. Hence, ***higher interest rates increase the quantity of available savings (loanable funds).***

Risk. In the early 1990s, banks in Russia were offering interest rates on savings accounts of nearly 100 percent a year. In Latin America, banks have offered even higher interest rates on occasion. Yet few people rushed to deposit their savings in these banks. People worried that the banks might fail, wiping out their savings in the process. In other words, there was a high *risk* attached to those high interest rates.

Anyone who contemplated lending funds to Columbus confronted a similar risk. That was the dilemma King Ferdinand confronted. He had enough funds to finance Columbus' expedition, but he didn't want to risk losing so much on a single venture.

Risk Management. This is why the Genoese bankers were so critical: These financial intermediaries could spread the risk of failure among many individuals. Each investor could put up just a fraction of the needed funds. No one had to put all his eggs in one basket. Once the consortium of bankers agreed to share the risks of Columbus' expedition, the venture had wings. The Genoese merchant bankers could afford to take portions of the expedition's risks because they also financed many less risky projects. By diversifying their portfolios, they could select any degree of average risk they preferred. That is the essence of risk management.

Risk Premiums. Even though diversification permits greater risk management, lenders will want to be compensated for any above-average risks they take. Money lent to local merchants must have seemed a lot less risky than lending funds to Columbus. Thus no one would have stepped forward to finance Columbus if he hadn't been promised an *above-average* return upon the expedition's success. The difference between the rates of return on a safe (certain) investment and a risky (uncertain) one is called the **risk premium.** Risk premiums compensate people who finance risky ventures that succeed. Because these ventures are risky, however, investors often lose their money in such ventures too.

Risk premiums help explain why blue-chip corporations such as Microsoft can borrow money from a bank at the low "prime" rate while ordinary consumers have to pay much higher interest rates on personal loans. Corporate loans are less risky because corporations typically have plenty of revenue and assets to cover their debts. Consumers often get overextended, however, and can't pay all their bills. As a result, there's a greater risk that consumers loans won't be paid back. It may also be more expensive to collect payments from consumers who fall behind. Banks charge higher interest rates on consumer loans to compensate for this risk.

risk premium: The difference in rates of return on risky (uncertain) and safe (certain) investments.

THE PRESENT VALUE OF FUTURE PROFITS

In deciding whether to assume the *risk* of supplying funds to a new venture, financial intermediaries assess the potential *rewards.* People who are *demanding* funds must also have some sense of what the payoff to their venture will be. In Columbus' case, the rewards were the fabled treasures of the East Indies. Even if he found those treasures, however, the rewards would only come long after the expedition was financed. When

Columbus proposed his East Indies expedition, he envisioned a round trip that would last at least six months. Were he successful in finding the fabled treasures of the East, he planned subsequent trips to acquire and transport his precious cargoes back home. Although King Ferdinand granted Columbus only one-tenth of any profits from the first expedition, Columbus had a claim on one-eighth of the profits of any subsequent voyages. Hence, even if Columbus succeeded in finding a shortcut to the East, he wouldn't generate any substantial profit for perhaps two years or more.

Suppose for the moment that Columbus expected no profit from the first expedition but a profit of $1,000 at the end of two years from a second voyage. How much was that future profit worth to Columbus?

Time Value of Money

To assess the value of *future* receipts, we have to consider the *time value* of money. A dollar received today is worth more than a dollar received two years from today. Why? Because a dollar received today can earn *interest*. If you have a dollar today and put it in an interest-bearing account, in two years you'll have your original dollar *plus* accumulated interest.[1] **As long as interest-earning opportunities exist, present dollars are worth more than future dollars.**

In 1492, there were plenty of opportunities to earn interest. Indeed, the Genoese bankers were charging high interest rates on their loans and guarantees. If Columbus had had the cash, he too could have lent money to others and earned interest on his funds.

To calculate the present value of future dollars, this forgone interest must be taken into account. This computation is essentially interest accrual in reverse. **We "discount" future dollars by the opportunity cost of money**—that is, the market rate of interest.

Suppose the market rate of interest in 1492 was 10 percent. To compute the **present discounted value (PDV)** of future payment, we discount as follows:

present discounted value (PDV): The value today of future payments, adjusted for interest accrual.

$$\text{PDV value} = \frac{\text{future payment}_N}{(1 + \text{interest rate})^N}$$

where N refers to the number of years into the future when a payment is to be made. If the future payment is to be made in 1 year, the N in the equation equals 1, and we have

$$\text{PDV} = \frac{\$1,000}{1.10}$$

$$= \$909.09$$

Hence, the present discounted value of $1,000 to be paid one year from today is $909.09. If $909.09 were received today, it could earn interest. In a year's time, the $909.09 would grow to $1,000 with interest accrued at the rate of 10 percent per year.

Suppose it would have taken Columbus two years to complete his expeditions and collect his profits. In that case, the present value of the $1,000 payment would be lower. The N in the formula would be 2 and the present value would be

$$\text{PDV} = \frac{\$1,000}{(1.10)^2} = \frac{\$1,000}{1.21} = \$826.45$$

Hence, **the longer one has to wait for a future payment, the less present value it has.**

Lottery winners often have to choose between present and future values. In August 2001, for example, four people split a $295 million Powerball lottery. The $295 million was payable in 25 annual installments of $11.8 million. If the lucky winners wanted to get their prize sooner, they could accept an immediate but smaller payout rather than 25 future installments.

Table 32.1 shows how the lottery officials figured the present value of the $294.8 prize. The first installment of $11.8 million would be paid immediately. The winners would have had to wait one year for the second check, however. At the then-prevailing inter-

---

[1] Part of that interest payment will compensate for anticipated inflation; the remainder will compensate for the pure time value of money (postponed spending). Real (inflation-adjusted) interest rates express the time value of money.

TABLE 32.1
Computing Present Value

Years in the Future	Future Payment (in millions of dollars)	Present Value (in millions of dollars)
0	$ 11.8	$ 11.80
1	11.8	11.25
2	11.8	10.73
3	11.8	10.23
4	11.8	9.76
5	11.8	9.30
*	*	*
*	*	*
*	*	*
24	11.8	3.77
	$294.8	$165.6

Note: The general formula for computing present values is $PDV = \sum \frac{\text{payment in year } N}{(1 + r)^N}$, where r is the prevailing rate.

The present value of a future payment declines the longer one must wait for a payment. At an interest rate of 4.87 percent, $11.8 million payable in 1 year is worth only $11.25 million today. A payout of $11.8 million 24 years from now has a present value of only $3.77 million. A string of $11.8 million payments spread out over 24 years has a present value of $165.6 million (at 4.87 percent interest).

est rate of 4.87 percent, the *present* value of that second $11.8 million check was only $11.25 million. The *last* payoff check had even less value since it wasn't due to be paid for 24 years. With so much time for interest to accrue, that final $11.8 million payment had a present value of only $3.77 million. The calculations in Table 32.1 convinced lottery officials to offer the winners an immediate payout of only $165.6 million on their $295 million win. The winners were a bit disappointed but took the cash anyway.

Interest Rate Effects

The winners would have received even less money had interest rates been higher. At the time they won the lottery, the interest rate on bonds was 4.87 percent. Had the rate been higher, the discount for immediate payment would have been higher as well. Table 32.2 indicates that the powerball winners would have received only $107 million had the prevailing interest rate been 10 percent. What Tables 32.1 and 32.2 illustrate, then, is that *the present discounted value of a future payment declines with*

- *Higher interest rates.*
- *Longer delays in future payment.*

Uncertainty

The valuation of future payments must also consider the possibility of *non*payment. State governments are virtually certain to make promised lottery payouts, so there's little risk in accepting a promised payout of 25 annual installments. But what about the booty from Columbus' expeditions? There was great uncertainty that Columbus would ever return from his expeditions, much less bring back the "pearls, precious stones, gold, silver, spiceries" that people coveted. Investing in those expeditions was far riskier than deferring a lottery payment.

Interest Rate	Present Discounted Value of $295 Million Lottery Prize (in millions of dollars)
5.0%	$166.3
6.0	150.8
7.0	137.5
8.0	126.0
9.0	115.9
10.0	107.1

TABLE 32.2
Higher Interest Rates Reduce Present Values

Higher interest rates raise the *future* value of current dollars. The rates therefore reduce the *present* value of future payments. Shown here is the present value of the August 2001 Powerball lottery prize of $295 million at different interest rates.

Expected Value. Whenever an anticipated future payment is uncertain, a risk factor should be included in present-value computations. This is done by calculating the **expected value** of a future payment. Suppose there was only a 50:50 chance that Columbus would bring back the bacon. In that event, the expected payoff would be

$$\text{Expected value} = (1 - \text{risk factor}) \times \text{present discounted value}$$

expected value: The probable value of a future payment, including the risk of nonpayment.

With a 50:50 chance of failure, the expected value of Columbus' first-year profits would have been

$$\text{Expected value} = (1 - 0.5) \times \$909.09$$
$$= \$454.55$$

Expected values also explain why people buy more lottery tickets when the prize is larger. The odds of winning the multistate Powerball lottery are 80 *million*:1. That's about the same odds as getting struck by lightning *14 times* in the same year. So it makes almost no sense to buy a ticket. With a $16 million prize, the *undiscounted* expected value of a $1 lottery ticket is only 20 cents. When the lottery prize increases, however, the expected value of a ticket grows as well (there are still only 80 million possible combinations of numbers). When the grand prize reached $250 million in July 1998, the undiscounted expected value of a lone winning ticket jumped to over $3. Millions of people decided that the expected value was high enough to justify playing the lottery. People took off from work, skipped classes, and drove across state lines to queue up for lottery tickets. So many people bought tickets on the last day that the lottery grand prize swelled to $295 million. (13 machinists from Ohio had the winning ticket and chose the present discounted value of $165.6 million.) When the prize is only $10 million, far fewer people buy tickets.

The Demand for Loanable Funds

People rarely borrow money to buy lottery tickets. But entrepreneurs and other market participants often use other people's funds to finance their ventures. *How much loanable funds are demanded depends on*

- *the expected rate of return.*
- *the cost of funds.*

The higher the expected return, or the lower the cost of funds, the greater will be the amount of loanable funds demanded.

Figure 32.2 offers a general view of the loanable funds market that emerges from these considerations. From the entrepreneur's perspective, the prevailing interest rate represents the cost of funds. From the perspective of savers, the interest rate represents

FIGURE 32.2
The Loanable Funds Market

The market rate of interest (r_e) is determined by the intersection of the curves representing supply of and demand for loanable funds. The rate of interest represents the price paid for the use of money.

the payoff to savings. When interest rates rise, the quantity of funds supplied goes up and the quantity demanded goes down. The prevailing (equilibrium) interest rate is set by the intersection of these supply and demand curves.

THE STOCK MARKET

The concept of a loanable funds market sounds a bit alien. But the same principles of supply, demand, and risk management go a long way in explaining the action in stock markets. Suppose you had $1,000 to invest. Should you invest it all in lottery tickets that offer a multimillion dollar payoff? Put it in a savings account that pays next to nothing? Or how about the stock market? The stock market can reward you handsomely; or it can wipe out your savings if the stocks you own tumble. Hence, stocks offer a higher average return than bank accounts but also entail greater average risk. People who bought Amazon.com stock in May 1997 got a 1,000 percent profit on their stock in only two years. But people who bought Amazon.com stock in December 1999 lost 90 percent of their investment in even less time.

Corporate Stock

When people buy a share of stock, they're buying partial ownership of a corporation. The three legal forms of business entities are

- Corporations
- Partnerships
- Proprietorships

Limited Liability. Proprietorships are businesses owned by a single individual. The owner-proprietor is responsible for all the business, including repayment of any debts. Members of a partnership are typically liable for all business debts and activities as well. By contrast, a **corporation** is a limited liability form of business. The corporation itself, not its individual shareholders, is responsible for all business activity and debts. As a result of this limited liability, you can own a piece of a corporation without worrying about being sued for business mishaps (like environmental damage) or nonpayment of debt. This feature significantly reduces the risk of owning corporate stock.

corporation: A business organization having a continuous existence independent of its members (owners) and power and liabilities distinct from those of its members.

Shared Ownership. The ownership of a corporation is defined in terms of stock shares. Each share of **corporate stock** represents partial ownership of the business. Chipmaker Intel, for example, has nearly 7 *billion* shares of stock outstanding (that is, shares held by the public). Hence, each share of Intel stock represents less than one seventh of one-billionth ownership of the corporation. Potentially, this means that as many as 7 billion people could own the Intel Corporation. In reality, however, many individuals own hundreds of shares, and institutions may own thousands. Indeed, some of the largest pension funds in the United States own over a million shares of Intel.

corporate stock: Shares of ownership in a corporation.

In principle, the owners of corporate stock collectively run the business. In practice, the shareholders select a board of directors to monitor corporate activity and protect their interests. The day-to-day business of running a corporation is the job of managers who report to the board of directors.

Stock Returns

If shareholders don't have any direct role in running a corporation, why would they want to own a piece of it? Essentially, for the same reason that the Genoese bankers agreed to finance Columbus' expedition: profits. Owners (shareholders) of a corporation hope to share in the profits the corporation earns.

Dividends. Shareholders rarely receive their full share of the company's profits in cash. Corporations typically use some of the profits for investment in new plants or equipment. They may also want to retain some of the profits for operational needs or unforeseen contingencies. ***Corporations may choose to retain earnings or pay them***

dividend: Amount of corporate profits paid out for each share of stock.

retained earnings: Amount of corporate profits not paid out in dividends.

capital gain: An increase in the market value of an asset.

out to shareholders as **dividends.** Any profits not paid to shareholders are referred to as **retained earnings.** Thus,

Dividends = corporate profits − retained earnings

In 2000, Intel paid quarterly dividends amounting to 8 cents per share for the year. But the company earned profits equal to 44 cents per share. Thus, shareholders received less than 20 percent of their accrued profits in dividend checks; Intel retained the remaining 36 cents per-share profit earned in 2000 for future investments.

Capital Gains. If Intel invests its retained earnings wisely, the corporation may reap even larger profits in the future. As a company grows and prospers, each share of ownership may become more valuable. This increase in value would be reflected in higher market prices for shares of Intel stock. Any increase in the value of a stock represents a **capital gain** for shareholders. Capital gains directly increase shareholder wealth.

Total Return. People who own stocks can thus get two distinct payoffs: dividends and capital gains. Together, these payoffs represent the total return on stock investments. Hence, *the higher the expected total return (future dividends and capital gains), the greater the desire to buy and hold stocks.* If a stock paid no dividends and had no prospects for price appreciation (capital gain, for example) you'd probably hold your savings in a different form (such as another stock or maybe an interest-earning bank account).

Initial Public Offering

initial public offering (IPO): The first issuance (sale) to the general public of stock in a corporation.

When a corporation is formed, its future sales and profits are uncertain. When shares are first offered to the public, the seller of stock is the company itself. By *going public,* the corporation seeks to raise funds for investment and growth. A true *start-up* company may have nothing more than a good idea, a couple of dedicated employees, and Big Plans. To fund these plans, it sells shares of itself in an **initial public offering (IPO).** People who buy the newly issued stock are putting their savings directly into the corporation's accounts.[2] As new owners, they stand to profit from the corporation's business or take their lumps if the corporation fails.

In 1997, Amazon.com Inc. was still a relatively new company. Although the company had been in operation since 1994, its capacity to sell books on the Internet was limited. To expand, it needed more warehouse space, more computers, and additional staff. To finance this expansion, Amazon needed more money. The company could have *borrowed* money from a bank or other financial institution, but that would have saddled the company with debt and forced it to make a regular interest payments. Lenders might have even wanted the officers of the company to guarantee repayment of the loan, burdening them with personal liability.

Rather than borrow money, Amazon's directors elected to sell ownership shares in the company. In May 1997, the company raised $54 million in cash by selling 3 million shares for $18 per share in its initial public offering.

Secondary Trading

Why were people eager to buy shares in Amazon.com Inc.? They certainly weren't buying the stock with expectations of high dividends. The company hadn't earned any profit in its first three years and didn't expect to earn a profit for at least another three years.

What might those future profits be worth? Suppose the company expected to earn profits of $1 per share in four years. What current value might those future profits have? In 1997, the prevailing long-term interest rate was close to 6 percent. Thus, the present discounted value of those future profits was

$$\text{PDV} = \frac{\$1}{(1 + 0.06)^4} = \frac{\$1}{1.262} = \$0.79$$

[2]In reality, some of the initial proceeds will go to stockbrokers and investment bankers as compensation for their services as financial intermediaries. The entrepreneur who starts the company, other company employees, and any venture capitalists who help fund the company before the public offering may also get some of the IPO receipts by selling shares they acquired before the company went public.

If you paid $18 for a share of stock that earned only 79 cents, you'd be paying a reasonable price for a share of company profits. This can be seen by computing the **price/earnings (P/E) ratio:**

$$\text{P/E ratio} = \frac{\text{price of stock share}}{\text{earnings (profit) per share}}$$

price/earnings (P/E) ratio: The price of a stock share divided by earnings (profit) per share.

For Amazon.com in 1997,

$$\text{P/E ratio} = \frac{\$18}{0.79} = 22.8$$

In other words, investors were paying $22.80 for every $1 of discounted future profits. That implies a rate of return of $1 \div \$22.80$, or 4.4 percent. Compared to the interest rates banks were paying on deposit balances, Amazon.com shares looked like a good buy.

Risk Factors. The stock didn't look quite as cheap, however, when the risks of failure were considered. The 79 cents of discounted future profits were far from certain; they were merely a projection. In reality, the road to riches on the Internet is riddled with risks. Other companies (e.g., Barnes and Noble or Borders) also sell books in cyberspace. Still more companies might enter the market if the outlook for profits improves. Technological advances might make Amazon.com's setup obsolete. Marketing and production costs may escalate. Any of these problems could jeopardize Amazon.com's future profits.

In view of these many risks, any projections of future profits must be adjusted for their uncertainty. If there's a 25 percent chance that Amazon.com will fail to hit the profit target, the *expected* value of future profits is

$$\text{Expected value of profit} = (1 - \text{risk factor}) \times \text{PDV}$$
$$= (1 - 0.25) \times 0.79$$
$$= 0.59$$

From this perspective, the IPO price of Amazon.com wasn't quite so cheap. The expected rate of return was

$$\frac{\text{Expected rate}}{\text{of return}} = \frac{\text{expected value of profit}}{\text{purchase price of stock}}$$
$$= \frac{\$0.59}{\$18.00} = 3.2\%$$

This was still better than most bank accounts but hardly exciting.

What *was* exciting about Amazon.com's IPO was the upside potential for growth. If e-commerce really took off, Amazon.com might generate exceptional profits, not a mere dollar or two. As people saw this potential unfold, they would surely want to buy shares of the company. As they did, the share price would increase, generating capital gains for those who bought earlier.

The prospect of such capital gains enticed a lot of stock buyers. On the first day of trading, the price of Amazon.com shares rose from the IPO price of $18 to as high as $30. Within a year the stock was selling for nearly $100. Within two year's time, the stock rose to $200 a share. This meteoric rise in the price of Amazon's stock represented a huge *capital gain* for its shareholders. The people who paid $200 a share were hoping for still higher share prices.

That post-IPO rise in Amazon's stock price had no direct effect on the company. A corporation reaps the proceeds of stock sales only when it sells shares to the public (the initial public offering). After the IPO, the company's stock is traded among individuals in the "after market." Virtually, all the trading activity on major stock

FIGURE 32.3
Changing Expectations

The supply and demand for stocks is fueled in part by expectations of future profits. When investors concluded that Amazon.com's future profit potential wasn't so great (see News), demand for the stock decreased, supply increased, and the share price fell.

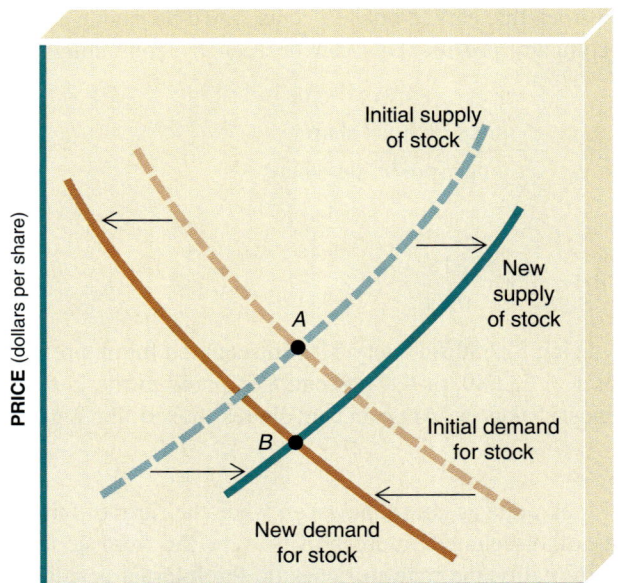

exchanges consists of such after-market sales. Mr. Dow sells his Amazon share to Ms. Jones, who may later sell them to Destiny's Child. Such *secondary* trades may take place at the New York Stock Exchange (NYSE) on Wall Street or in the computerized over-the-counter market.

Market Fluctuations

The price of a stock at any moment is the outcome of supply-and-demand interactions. I wouldn't mind owning a piece of Amazon.com. But since I think the current share price is too high, I'll buy the stock only if the price falls substantially. Even though I'm not buying any Amazon stock now, I'm part of the *market demand*. That is, all the people who are willing and able to buy Amazon.com stock at *some* price are included in the demand curve in Figure 32.3. The cheaper the stock, the more people will want to buy it, *ceteris paribus*. The opposite is true on the supply side of the market: Ever-higher prices are necessary to induce more shareholders to part with their shares.

Changing Expectations. In 2000–01, investors reevaluated the profit prospects for Amazon.com and other "dot.com" companies. Several years of experience had shown that earning profits in e-commerce wasn't so easy. Projections of sales growth and future profits were sharply reduced. When Amazon.com failed to meet even those reduced expectations (see News), its stock fell 20 percent in a single day. Figure 32.3

IN THE NEWS

Amazon.com's stock price fell 20 percent after the company reported third-quarter sales that fell short of forecasts and reduced its fourth-quarter estimate. Amazon shares declined $1.91, to $7.64.

Source: *Washington Post*, October 25, 2001. © 2001 The Washington Post. Reprinted with permission. www.washingtonpost.com

Analysis: A change in expectations will shift the demand and supply of a stock (see Figure 32.3).

TABLE 32.3
Reading Stock Quotes

The financial pages of the daily newspaper summarize the trading activity in corporate stocks. The following quotation summarizes trading in AT&T and Amazon.com shares on October 24, 2001.

52 Weeks Hi	52 Weeks Lo	Stock	Sym	Div	Yld%	P/E	Vol 100s	Hi	Lo	Close	Net Chg
25.15	14.75	ATT	T	.15	0.8	dd	142327	17.92	17.51	17.75	−.15
27.63	5.51	Amazon	AMZN	—	—	dd	66976	7.67	7.15	7.64	−1.91

The information provided by this quotation includes:
52-Weeks Hi and Lo: The highest and lowest prices paid for a share of stock in the previous year.
Stock: The name of the corporation whose shares are being traded.
Sym: The symbol used as a shorthand description for the stock.
Div: A dividend is the amount of profit paid out by the corporation in the preceding year for each share of stock.
Yld%: The yield is the dividend paid per share divided by the price of a share.
P/E: The price of the stock (P) divided by the earnings (profit) per share (E). This indicates how much a purchaser is effectively paying for each dollar of profits. Because Amazon.com had a loss in 1998, the P/E ratio is not computed.
Vol 100s: The number of shares traded in hundreds.
Hi: The highest price paid for a share of stock on the previous day.
Lo: The lowest price paid for a share of stock on the previous day.
Close: The price paid in the last trade of the day as the market was closing.
Net Chg: The change in the closing price yesterday vs. the previous day's closing price.

Source: *The Wall Street Journal,* October 25, 2001.

illustrates how this happened. The bad news reduced the demand for Amazon.com stock and increased the willingness of existing shareholders to sell. Such **changes in expectations imply shifts in supply and demand for a company's stock.** As Figure 32.3 illustrates, these combined shifts sent Amazon.com stock plummeting.

As Table 32.3 shows, the share price was $7.64 when the market closed on October 24, 2001. On that day, over 6 million shares of Amazon.com stock were traded. Along the path to the equilibrium closing price—the last trade of the day—the stock price fluctuated between a low ("Lo") of $7.15 and a high ("Hi") of $7.67. The price of Amazon.com stock fluctuated much more than that during the previous 52 weeks. As Table 32.3 documents, the stock traded as high as $40.88 and as low as $5.51 during the year. What accounts for these dramatic price fluctuations?

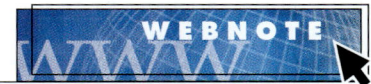
How is *your* stock doing? Find current and past stock prices at www.finweb.com.

The Value of Information. The abrupt rise and later plunge in the price of Amazon.com stock highlights a critical dimension of financial markets, namely, the value of information. People who bought Amazon.com shares on the way up were poorly informed about the prospects for e-commerce sales and profits. Had they known profits would be so hard to make, they wouldn't have paid so much for the stock.

The evident value of information raises a question of access. Do some people have better information than others? Do they get their information fairly? Or do they have "inside" sources (such as company technicians, managers, directors) who give them preferential access to information? If so, these insiders would have an unfair advantage in the marketplace and could alter the distribution of income and wealth in their favor.

The value of information also explains the demand for information services. People pay hundreds and even thousands of dollars for newsletters, wire services, and online

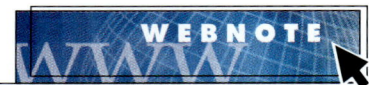

You can retrieve the latest news about a company and its stock from various online brokerage and investment-advice services, including cnnfin.com. You can also retrieve charts showing how a stock price has fluctuated during the day or over longer periods. Free charts on individual stocks are available at www.bigcharts.com.

computer services that provide up-to-date information on companies and markets. They also pay for the services of investment bankers, advisers, and brokers to help keep them informed. These services help disseminate information quickly, thereby helping financial markets operate efficiently (that is, they provide the best possible signal of changing resource values).

Booms and Busts. If stock markets are so efficient at computing the present value of future profits, why does the entire market make abrupt moves every so often? Fundamentally, the same factors that determine the price of a single stock influence the broader stock market averages as well. An increase in interest rates, for example, raises the opportunity cost of holding stocks. Hence, higher interest rates should cause stock prices to fall, *ceteris paribus*. Stocks might decline even further if higher interest rates are expected to curtail investment and consumption, thus reducing future sales and profits. Such a double whammy could cause the whole stock market to tumble.

Other factors also affect the relative desirability of holding stock. Congressional budget and deficit decisions, monetary policy, consumer confidence, business investment plans, international trade patterns, and new inventions are just a few of the factors that may alter present and future profits. These *broad changes in the economic outlook tend to push all stock prices up or down at the same time.*

Broad changes in the economic outlook, however, seldom occur overnight. Moreover, these changes are rarely of a magnitude that could precipitate a stock market boom or bust. In reality, the stock market often changes more abruptly than the economic outlook. These exaggerated movements in the stock market are caused by sudden and widespread changes in expectations. Keep in mind that the value of the stock depends on anticipated *future* profits and expectations for interest rates and the economic outlook. No elements of the future are certain. Instead, people use present clues to try to discern the likely course of future events. In other words, *all information must be filtered through people's expectations.*

Think you can make a profit in the stock market? Try the Stock Market Game, an electronic simulation of Wall Street trading, at www.smg2000.org.

The central role of expectations implies that the economy can change more gradually than the stock market. If, for example, interest rates rise, market participants may regard the increase as temporary or inconsequential: Their expectations for the future may not change. If interest rates keep rising, however, investors may have greater doubts.

IN THE NEWS

Market Battered, but Intact

The Dow Jones industrial average suffered its worst one-day point loss ever on Monday as the stock market was swamped with selling on the first day of trading since last week's terrorist attacks.

Forecasts for today's trading were hard to find. In contrast, the market's first-day sell-off was widely expected in the aftermath of terrorists crashing hijacked airliners into the World Trade Center in New York and the Pentagon near Washington.

A sense that "everything had changed" pervaded Wall Street over the four days last week that the market was closed following the Sept. 11 attack. That was the longest market closing since World War I. Monday's session was a technical victory, given the damage to phone lines, computers and other equipment that had to be repaired. By day's end, the system handled a record 2.37 billion New York Stock Exchange shares.

The Dow's plunge of 684.81 points to 8,920.70 in Monday's trading eclipsed its previous one-day record loss of 617.78 points on April 14, 2000, at the beginning of the current bear market. But the percentage loss was not among the 10 worst of all time.

—Tom Walker

Source: *Atlanta Journal-Constitution*, September 18, 2001. Reprinted with permission. www.accessatlanta.com/ajc

Analysis: A sudden change in expectations can cause severe fluctuations in stock market values. The September 11 terrorist attacks created new uncertainties and reduced profit expectations.

Just a normal day at the nation's most important financial institution...

At some point, the market participants may revise their expectations. Stock prices may falter, triggering an adjustment in expectations. A herding instinct may surface, sending expectations in stock prices abruptly lower (see cartoon).

Shocks. The September 11, 2001, terrorist attacks on the World Trade Center and the Pentagon illustrated how much faster expectations can change than does the real economy. The attacks paralyzed the U.S. economy for several days and made people fearful for both their physical and economic security. People wanted to withdraw from the marketplace, taking their assets with them. When the U.S. stock exchanges opened several days after the attacks, stocks tumbled (see News). The Dow Jones industrial average (see Table 32.4) fell 685 points, its biggest loss ever. The NASDAQ Composite (Table 32.4) also plunged by more than 7 percent in one day. Within 10 days, the value of U.S. stocks had declined by more than $1 *trillion*.

The economy didn't fare nearly as bad as the stock market. Although the attacks were tragic in human terms, they made only a tiny dent in the economy's productive capacity. Quick responses by the government in defending the financial markets also dispelled fears of a financial meltdown. As people's worst fears subsided, the demand for stocks picked up again. Within a month's time, the stock markets had fully recovered their post-attack losses. Along the way, however, changing expectations caused wild gyrations in stock prices.

Although it's fascinating and sometimes fun to watch stock market gyrations, we shouldn't lost sight of the *economic* role of financial markets. Columbus needed *real* resources—ships, men, equipment—for his expeditions. Five centuries later, Amazon.com also needed real resources—computers, labor, warehouse space—to get under way. To find the necessary economic resources, both Columbus and Amazon.com had to convince society to reallocate resources from other activities to their new ventures.

Resource Allocations

TABLE 32.4
Stock Market Averages

> Over 1,600 stocks are listed (traded) on the New York Stock Exchange, and many times that number are traded in other stock markets. To gauge changes in so many stocks, people refer to various indices, such as the Dow Jones industrial average. The Dow and similar indexes help us keep track of the market's ups and downs. Some of the most frequently quoted indexes are
>
> **Dow Jones**
>   **Industrial average:** An arithmetic average of the prices of 30 blue-chip industrial stocks traded on the New York Stock Exchange (NYSE) and by computers of the National Association of Securities Dealers (NASD).
>   **Transportation average:** An average of 20 transportation stocks traded on the NYSE.
>   **Utilities average:** An average of 15 utility stocks traded on the NYSE.
> **S&P 500:** An index compiled by Standard and Poor of 500 stocks drawn from major stock exchanges as well as over the-counter-stocks. The S&P 500 is made up of 400 industrial companies, 40 utilities, 20 transportation companies, and 40 financial institutions.
> **NASDAQ Composite:** Index of stocks traded in the over-the-counter market among securities dealers.
> **New York Stock Exchange composite index:** The "Big Board" index, which includes all 1,600-plus stocks traded on the NYSE.
> **Nikkei index:** An index of 225 stocks traded on the Tokyo stock market.

Financial markets facilitate resource reallocations. In Columbus' case, the Genoese bankers lent the funds that Columbus used to buy scarce resources. The funds obtained from Amazon.com's 1997 initial public offering served the same purpose. In both cases, the funds obtained in the financial markets helped change the mix of output. If the financial markets hadn't supplied the necessary funding, neither Columbus nor Amazon.com would have been able to get under way. The available resources would have been used to produce other goods.

THE BOND MARKET

The bond market is another mechanism for transferring the pool of national savings into the hands of would-be spenders. It operates much like the stock market. The major difference is the kind of paper traded. *In the stock market, people buy and sell shares of corporate ownership. In the bond market, people buy and sell promissory notes (IOUs).* A **bond** is simply an IOU, a written promise to repay a loan. The bond itself specifies the terms of repayment, noting both the amount of interest to be paid each year and the maturity date (the date on which the borrower is to repay the entire debt). The borrower may be a corporation (corporate bonds), local governments (municipal bonds), the federal government (Treasury bonds), or other institutions.

bond: A certificate acknowledging a debt and the amount of interest to be paid each year until repayment; an IOU.

Bond Issuance

A bond is first issued when an institution wants to borrow money. Recall the situation Amazon.com faced in 1997. The company needed additional funds to expand its Internet operations. Rather than sell equity shares in itself, Amazon.com could have *borrowed* funds. The advantage of borrowing funds rather than issuing stock is that the owners can keep control of their company. *Lenders aren't owners, but shareholders are.* The disadvantage of borrowing funds is that the company gets saddled with a repayment schedule. Lenders want to be paid back—with interest. For a new company like Amazon.com, the burden of interest payments may be too great.

Ignoring these problems momentarily, let's assume that Amazon.com decided in 1997 to borrow funds rather than sell stock in itself. To do so, it would have *issued* bonds. This, simply means that it would have printed formal IOUs called bonds. Typically, each bond certificate would have a **par value** (face value) of $1,000. The bond certificate would also specify the rate of interest to be paid and the promised date of repayment. An Amazon.com bond issued in 1997, for example, might specify repayment in 10 years, with annual interest payments of $100. The individual who bought the bond from Amazon.com would lend $1,000 for 10 years and receive annual interest payments of $100. Thus, ***the initial bond purchaser lends funds directly to the bond issuer.*** The borrower (such as Amazon.com, General Motors, or the U.S. Treasury) can then use those funds to acquire real resources. Thus, the bond market also functions as a financial intermediary, transferring available savings (wealth) to those who want to acquire more resources (invest).

As in the case of IPOs of stock, the critical issue here is the *price* of the bond. How many people are willing and able to lend funds to the company? What rate of interest will they charge?

As we observed in Figure 32.2, the quantity of loanable funds supplied depends on the interest rate. At low interest rates no one is willing to lend funds to the company. Why lend your savings to a risky venture like Amazon.com when more secure bonds and even banks pay higher interest rates? Amazon.com might not sell enough books and may later **default** (not pay) on its obligations. Potential lenders would want to be compensated for this extra risk with above-average interest rates, that is, a risk premium. Remember that lenders don't share in any profits Amazon.com might earn. Hence, they'd want a hefty premium to compensate them for the risk of default.

Suppose that market participants will lend the desired amount of money to Amazon.com only at 16 percent interest. In this case, Amazon.com may agree to pay an interest rate—the so-called **coupon rate**—of 16 percent to secure start-up funding of $50 million. That means Amazon.com agrees to pay $160 of interest each year for every $1,000 borrowed and to repay the entire $50 million at the end of 10 years.

Once a bond has been issued, the initial lenders don't have to wait 10 years to get their money back. They can't go back to the company and demand early repayment, but they can sell their bonds to someone else. This **liquidity** is an important consideration for prospective bondholders. If a person had no choice but to wait 10 years for repayment, he or she might be less willing to buy a bond (lend funds). ***By facilitating resales, the bond market increases the availability of funds to new ventures and other borrowers.*** As is the case with stocks, most of the action in the bond markets consists of such after-market trades, that is, the buying and selling of bonds issued at some earlier time. The company that first issued the bonds doesn't participate in these trades.

The portfolio decision in the bond market is motivated by the same factors that influence stock purchases. The *opportunity cost* of buying and selling bonds is the best alternative rate of return—for example, the interest rate on other bonds or money market mutual funds. *Expectations* also play a role, in gauging both likely changes in opportunity costs and the ability of the borrower to redeem (pay off) the bond when it's due. ***Changes in expectations or opportunity costs shift the bond supply and demand curves,*** thereby altering market interest rates.

We've assumed that Amazon.com would have had to offer 16 percent interest to induce enough people to lend the company (buy bonds worth) $50 million. This was far higher than the 6 percent the U.S. Treasury was paying on its bonds (borrowed funds) because lenders feared that Amazon.com might not be able to convert its great ideas into actual

par value: The face value of a bond; the amount to be repaid when the bond is due.

default: Failure to make scheduled payments of interest or principal on a bond.

coupon rate: Interest rate set for a bond at time of issuance.

Bond Trading

liquidity: The ability of an asset to be converted into cash.

Current Yields

FIGURE 32.4
Shifts in Funds Supply

If lenders decide that a company's future is less risky, they will be more willing to lend it money or hold its bonds. This will raise the market price of existing bonds and lower current yields.

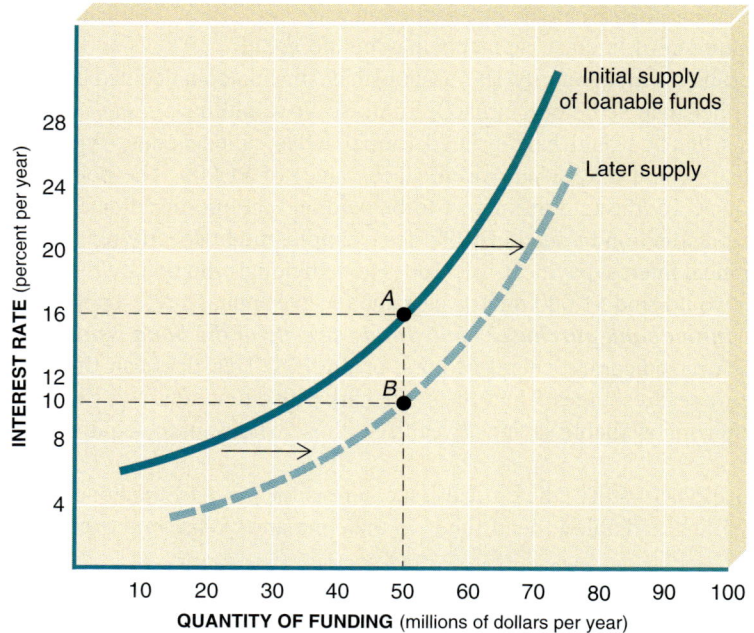

sales in a timely and profitable manner. In lending their funds to Amazon.com, they incur a risk of never getting their wealth back.

Suppose that Amazon.com actually got off to a good start and began selling books on the Web. The risk of a bond default would diminish, and people would be more willing to lend it funds. This change in the availability of loanable funds is illustrated in the rightward shift of the supply curve in Figure 32.4.

According to the new supply curve in Figure 32.4, Amazon.com could now borrow $50 million at 10 percent interest (point *B*) rather than paying 16 percent (point *A*). Unfortunately, Amazon.com already borrowed the funds and is obliged to continue paying $160 per year in interest on each bond. Hence, the company doesn't benefit directly from the supply shift.

The change in the equilibrium value of Amazon.com bonds must show up somewhere, however. People who hold Amazon.com bonds continue to get $160 per year in interest (16 percent of $1,000). Now there are lots of people who would be willing to lend funds to Amazon.com at that rate. These people want to hold Amazon.com bonds themselves. To get them, they'll have to buy the bonds in the market from existing bondholders. Thus, the *increased willingness to lend funds is reflected in an increased demand for bonds.* This increased demand will push up the price of Amazon.com bonds. As bond prices rise, their implied effective interest rate (**current yield**) falls. Table 32.5 illustrates this relationship.

Changing bond prices and yields are important market signals for resource allocation. In our example, the rising price of Amazon.com's bonds reflects increased optimism for the company's sales prospects. The collective assessment of the marketplace is that e-commerce will be a profitable venture. The increase in the price of Amazon.com bonds will make it easier and less costly for the company to borrow additional funds. The reverse scenario unfolded in 2000–01. When investors concluded that e-commerce wasn't going to generate fast profits, the supply of funds to dot.coms dried up. That supply shift made it more difficult for firms to survive, much less expand e-commerce capacity.

current yield: The rate of return on a bond; the annual interest payment divided by the bond's price.

TABLE 32.5
Bond Price and Yields Move in Opposite Directions

Price of Bond	Annual Interest Payment	Current Yield
$ 600	$150	25.0%
800	150	18.8
1,000	150	15.0
1,200	150	12.5

The annual interest payments on a bond are fixed at the time of issuance. Accordingly, only the market (resale) prices of the bond can change. An increase in the price of the bond lowers its *effective* interest rate, or yield. The formula for computing the current yield on a bond is

$$\text{Current yield} = \frac{\text{annual interest payment}}{\text{market (resale) price of bond}}$$

Thus, higher bond prices imply lower yields (effective interest rates), as confirmed in the table above. Bond prices and yields vary with changes in expectations and opportunity costs.

The newspaper quotation below shows how changing bond prices and yields are reported. This AT&T bond was issued with a coupon rate (nominal interest rate) of $6\frac{1}{2}$ percent. Hence, AT&T promised to pay $65 in interest each year until it redeemed (paid off) the $1,000 bond in the year 2029 (29). In October 2001, however, the market price of the bond was $905 ($90\frac{1}{2}$). This created a yield of 7.2 percent.

Bond	Current Yield	Volume	Close	Net Change
ATT $6\frac{1}{2}$ 29	7.2	37	$90\frac{1}{2}$	$+\frac{1}{4}$

THE ECONOMY TOMORROW

Venture Capitalists—Financing Tomorrow's Products

One of the proven paths to high incomes and wealth is entrepreneurship. Most of the great American fortunes originated in entrepreneurial ventures, for example, building railroads, mass-producing automobiles, introducing new computers, or perfecting mass-merchandising techniques. These successful ventures all required more than just a great idea. To convert the original idea into actual output requires the investment of real resources.

Recall that Apple Computer started in a garage, with a minimum of resources (Chapter 23). The idea of packaging a personal computer was novel, and few resources were required to demonstrate that it could be done. But Steven Jobs couldn't have become a multimillionaire by building just a few dozen computers a month. To reap huge economic profits from his idea, he needed much greater production capacity. He also needed resources for marketing the new Apples to a broader customer base. In other words, Steven Jobs needed lots of economic resources—land, labor, and capital—to convert his entrepreneurial dream into a profit-making reality.

Steven Jobs and his partner, Steve Wozniak, had few resources of their own. In fact, they'd sold Jobs's Volkswagen and Wozniak's scientific calculator to raise the finances for the first computer. To go any further, they needed financial support from others. Loans were hard to obtain since the company had no assets, no financial history, and no certainty of success. Jobs needed people who were willing to share the *risks* associated with a new venture. He found one such person in A. C. Markkula, who put up

IN THE NEWS

Venture Capital Falls 72 Percent from Last Year

SAN FRANCISCO—Venture capitalists, hunkered down because of the dot-com collapse, are tightening the financing spigot even more in the post-terrorist-attack economy.

"What's happened is so significant as to put . . . business on hold," says venture capitalist Richard Kramlich of New Enterprise Associates in Menlo Park.

Third-quarter venture investments totaled $6.7 billion, down 72 percent from the same quarter a year ago, says industry newsletter *VentureWire*. The number of private companies receiving venture capital dropped to 540, down 67 percent from a year earlier and down 39 percent from the second quarter.

—Jim Hopkins

Source: *USA Today*, October 8, 2001. © 2001 USA Today. Reprinted with permission. www.usatoday.com

Venture capital blues

The Sept. 11 attacks may further dampen investing by the nation's nearly 800 venture capital firms.

Quarter	Amount
3rd qtr 2000	$28.6
4th qtr 2000	$21.0
1st qtr 2001	$12.1
2nd qtr 2001	$10.6
3rd qtr 2001	$6.7

(in billions)

Sources: National Venture Capital Association, Venture Economics, *VentureWire*.

Analysis: Venture capital is a critical ingredient in entrepreneurship. When the flow of venture capital slows, so does the pace of technology and innovation.

$250,000 and became a partner in the new venture. Shortly thereafter, other venture capitalists provided additional financing. With this start-up financing, Jobs was able to acquire more resources and make the Apple Computer Company a reality.

This is a classic case study in venture capitalism. Venture capitalists provide initial funding for entrepreneurial ventures. In return for their financial backing, the venture capitalists are entitled to a share of any profits that result. If the venture fails, however, they get nothing. Thus, **venture capitalists provide financial support for entrepreneurial ideas and share in the risks and rewards.** Even Christopher Columbus needed venture capitalists to fund his risky expeditions to the New World.

Venture capital is as important to the economy tomorrow as it was to Columbus. In the immediate aftermath of the September 11, 2001, terrorist attacks, venture capitalists briefly withdrew their checkbooks (see News). This slowed the pace of entrepreneurship, innovation, and economic growth. For technology and entrepreneurship to continue growing, market conditions must be amenable to venture capitalists.

SUMMARY

- The primary economic function of financial markets is to help allocate scarce resources to desired uses. They do this by providing access to the pool of national savings for entrepreneurs, investors, and other would-be spenders.
- Financial markets enable individuals to manage risk by holding different kinds of assets. Financial intermediaries also reduce the costs of information and search, thereby increasing market efficiency.
- Future returns on investments must be discounted to present value. The present discounted value (PDV) of a future payment adjusts for forgone interest accrual.
- Future returns are also uncertain. The *expected* value of future payments must also reflect the risk of nonpayment.
- Shares of stock represent ownership in a corporation. The shares are initially issued to raise funds and are then traded on the stock exchanges.

- Changes in the value of a corporation's stock reflect changing expectations and opportunity costs. Share price changes, in turn, act as market signals to direct more or fewer resources to a company.
- Bonds are IOUs issued when a company (or government agency) borrows funds. After issuance, bonds are traded in the after (secondary) market.
- The interest (coupon) rate on a bond is fixed at the time of issuance. The price of the bond itself, however, varies with changes in expectations (perceived risk) and opportunity cost. Yields vary inversely with bond prices.

Key Terms

financial intermediary
risk premium
present discounted value (PDV)
expected value
corporation
corporate stock

dividend
retained earnings
capital gain
initial public offering (IPO)
price/earnings (P/E) ratio
bond

par value
default
coupon rate
liquidity
current yield

Questions for Discussion

1. If there were no organized financial markets, how would an entrepreneur acquire resources to develop and produce a new product?
2. Why would anyone buy shares of a corporation that had no profits and paid no dividends? What's the highest price a person would pay for such a stock?
3. Why would anyone sell a bond for less than its par value?
4. If you could finance a new venture with either a stock issue or bonds, which option would you choose? What are their respective (dis)advantages?
5. Why is it considered riskier to own stock in a software company than to hold U.S. Treasury savings bonds? Which asset will generate a higher return?
6. How does a successful IPO affect WHAT, HOW, and FOR WHOM the economy produces?
7. What considerations might have created the difference between the coupon rate and current yield on ATT bonds (Table 32.5)?

Web Activities

1. Log on to bigcharts.marketwatch.com, and read a "market pulse" report about a major company. Summarize the report about the company. Are the company's profits increasing or decreasing? Has this caused the value of the company's stocks to increase or decrease? Explain.
2. Is it better to invest in stocks or in bonds? Read about investing in bonds at the Bond Marketing Association site, www.investinginbonds.com/info/bondbasics/what.htm. Identify two advantages of bond investments compared to stock investments. Identify two disadvantages of bond investments compared to stock investments.
3. Log on to ea.grolier.com/ea-online/wsja/text/ch05/tables/mi002-a.htm, and identify what major events caused uncertainty in the economy as reflected by changes in the Dow Jones industrial average.

 THE ACCOMPANYING STUDENT PROBLEM SET CONTAINS NUMERICAL AND GRAPHING PROBLEMS FOR THIS CHAPTER

PART 12

Distributional Issues

Efficiency and equity are central concerns of every society. Collectively, we seek to get as much output as possible from the resources we use. But we also care about how that output is distributed. We want some sort of fairness in the distribution of goods and services; that is to say, we want both *efficiency* in the production of goods and *equity* in the distribution of goods. Unfortunately, these goals may conflict. If we use taxes to redistribute incomes, incentives to produce may be impaired. Similarly, if we provide income support for the poor, people may choose to work less. Chapters 33 and 34 examine these issues.

CHAPTER 33

Taxes: Equity vs. Efficiency

> Insistence on carving the pie into equal slices would shrink the size of the pie. That fact poses the trade-off between economic equality and economic efficiency.
> —Arthur M. Okun

Steve Jobs, chairman of Apple Computer, got a $90 million private jet as a pay bonus in 2001. That would have been enough income to lift nearly 50,000 poor persons out of poverty. But Jobs didn't share his good fortune with those people, and they remained poor.

The market mechanism generated both Steve Jobs' extraordinary income and that of so many poor families. Is this the way we want the basic FOR WHOM question to be settled? Should some people own vast fortunes while others seek shelter in abandoned cars? Or do the inequalities that emerge in product and factor markets violate our notions of equity? If the market's answer to the FOR WHOM question isn't right, some form of government intervention to redistribute incomes may be desired.

The tax system is the government's primary lever for redistributing income. But taxing Peter to pay Paul may affect more than just income shares. If taxed too heavily, Peter may stop producing so much. Paul, too, may work less if assured of government support. The end result may be *less* total income to share. In other words: ***Taxes affect production as well as distribution. This creates a potential trade-off between the goal of equity and the goal of efficiency.***

This chapter examines this equity-efficiency trade-off, with the following questions as a guide:

- How are incomes distributed in the United States?
- How do taxes alter that distribution?
- How do taxes affect the rate and mix of output?

After addressing these questions, we examine the allure of a "flat tax."

WHAT IS INCOME?

Before examining the distribution of income in the United States, let's decide what to count as *income*. There are several possibilities. The most obvious choice is **personal income (PI)**—the flow of annual income received by households before payment of personal income taxes. Personal income includes wages and salaries, corporate dividends, rent, interest, Social Security benefits, welfare payments, and any other form of money income.

Personal income isn't a complete measure of income, however. Many goods and services are distributed directly as **in-kind income** rather than through market purchases. Many poor people, for example, live in public housing and pay little or no rent. As a consequence, they receive a larger share of total output than their money incomes imply. People with low incomes also receive food stamps that allow them to purchase more food than their money incomes would allow. In this sense, food stamp recipients are better off than the distribution of personal income (which omits food stamps) implies.

In-kind benefits aren't limited to low-income households. Students who attend public schools and colleges consume more goods and services than they directly pay for; public education is subsidized by all taxpayers. People over age 65 also get medical services through Medicare that they don't directly pay for. And middle-class workers get noncash fringe benefits (like health insurance, paid vacations, pension contributions) that don't show up in their paychecks.

So long as some goods and services needn't be purchased in the marketplace, *the distribution of money income isn't synonymous with the distribution of goods and services.* This measurement problem is particularly important when comparisons are made over time. For example, the federal government officially classifies people as "poor" if their money income is below a certain threshold. By this standard, we've made no progress against poverty. The Census Bureau counted 31 million Americans as "poor" in 2000, nearly the same number it counted in 1965. In both years the Census Bureau counted only money incomes. In 1965 that approach was acceptable, since little income was transferred in kind. In 2000, however, the federal government spent over $23 billion on Food Stamps, $20 billion on housing subsidies, and $190 billion on Medicaid. Had all this in-kind income been counted, 7 million fewer Americans would have been counted poor in 2000. Although that would still leave a lot of people in poverty, at least more progress in eliminating poverty would be evident.

If our ultimate concern is access to goods and services, the distribution of wealth is also important. **Wealth** refers to the market value of assets (such as houses and bank accounts) people own. Hence, *wealth represents a stock of potential purchasing power; income statistics tell us only how this year's flow of purchasing power (income) is being distributed.* Accordingly, to provide a complete answer to the FOR WHOM question, we have to know how wealth, as well as income, is distributed. In general, wealth tends to be distributed much less equally than income. The Internal Revenue Service estimates that 3 percent of the adult population owns 30 percent of all personal wealth in the United States but gets less than 20 percent of total income.

THE SIZE DISTRIBUTION OF INCOME

Although incomes aren't a perfect measure of access to goods and services (much less happiness), they're the best single indicator of the FOR WHOM outcomes. The **size distribution of income** tells us how large a share of total personal income is received by various households, grouped by income class. Imagine for the moment that the entire population is lined up in order of income, with lowest-income recipients in front and highest-income recipients at the end of the line. We want to know how much income the people in front get in comparison with those at the back.

Personal Income

personal income (PI): Income received by households before payment of personal taxes.

in-kind income: Goods and services received directly, without payment, in a market transaction.

The Census Bureau compiles data on poverty from each year's March household survey. For the most recent data, visit www.census.gov/hhes/www/income.

Wealth

wealth: The market value of assets.

size distribution of income: The way total personal income is divided up among households or income classes.

income share: The proportion of total income received by a particular group.

We first examined the size distribution of income in Chapter 2. Table 2.1 showed that households in the lowest quintile received less than $18,000 apiece in 2000. As a group, this class received only 3.6 percent of total income, despite the fact that it included 20 percent of all households (the lowest fifth). Thus, the **income share** of the people in the lowest group (3.6 percent) was much smaller than their proportion in the total population (20 percent).

Moving back to the end of the line, we observed that a household needed $82,000 to make it into the highest income class in 2000. Many families in that class made much more than $82,000—some even millions of dollars. But $82,000 was at least enough to get into the top fifth (quintile).

The top quintile ended up with almost half of total U.S. income and, by implication, that much of total output.

The Lorenz Curve

Lorenz curve: A graphic illustration of the cumulative size distribution of income; contrasts complete equality with the actual distribution of income.

The size distribution of income provides the kind of information we need to determine how total income (and output) is distributed. The **Lorenz curve** is a convenient summary of that information; it is a graphical illustration of the size distribution.

Figure 33.1 is a Lorenz curve for the United States. Our lineup of individuals is on the horizontal axis, with the lowest income earners on the left. On the vertical axis we depict the cumulative share of income received by people in our income line. Consider the lowest quintile of the distribution again. They're represented on the horizontal axis at 20 percent. If their share of income was identical to their share of population, they'd get 20 percent of total income. This would be represented by point *C* in the figure. In fact, the lowest quintile gets only 3.6 percent, as indicated by point *A*. Point *B* tells us that the *cumulative* share of income received by the lowest *three*-fifths of the population was 27.3 percent.

The really handy feature of the Lorenz curve is the way it contrasts the actual distribution of income with an absolutely equal one. If incomes were distributed equally, the first 20 percent of the people in line would be getting exactly 20 percent of all income. In that case, the Lorenz curve would run through point *C*. Indeed, the Lorenz "curve" would be a straight line along the diagonal. The actual Lorenz curve lies below the diagonal because our national income isn't distributed equally. In fact, the area between the diagonal and the actual Lorenz curve (the shaded area in Figure 33.1) is a convenient measure of the degree of inequality. *The greater the area between the Lorenz curve and the diagonal, the more inequality exists.*

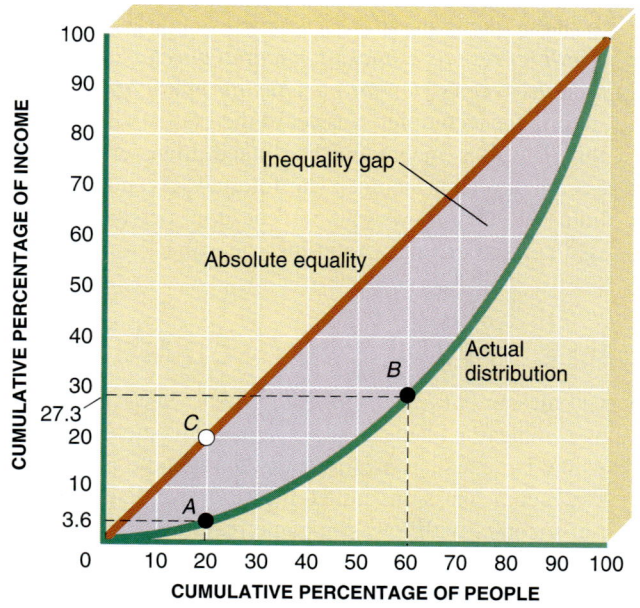

FIGURE 33.1
The Lorenz Curve

The Lorenz curve illustrates the extent of income inequality. If all incomes were equal, each fifth of the population would receive one-fifth of total income. In this case, the diagonal line through point *C* would represent the cumulative size distribution of income. In reality, incomes aren't distributed equally. Point *A*, for example, indicates that the 20 percent of the population with the lowest income receives only 3.6 percent of total income.

Source: Table 2.1.

Analysis: An increase in the size of the economic pie doesn't ensure everyone a larger slice. A goal of the tax system is to attain a fairer distribution of the economic pie.

The visual summary of inequality the Lorenz curve provides is also expressed in a mathematical relationship. The ratio of the shaded area in Figure 33.1 to the area of the triangle formed by the diagonal is called the **Gini coefficient.** The higher the Gini coefficient, the greater the degree of inequality. Between 1980 and 2000, the Gini coefficient rose from 0.403 to 0.460. In other words, the shaded area in Figure 33.1 expanded by about 14 percent, indicating *increased* inequality. Although the size of the economic pie (real GDP) nearly doubled between 1980 and 2000, some people's slices got a lot bigger while other people saw little improvement, or even less (see cartoon).

To many people, large and increasing inequality represents a form of **market failure:** The market is generating a suboptimal (unfair) answer to the FOR WHOM question. As in other instances of market failure, the government is called on to intervene. The policy lever in this case is taxes. By levying higher taxes on the rich and providing more generous transfer payments to the poor, the government could promote greater equality.

Gini coefficient: A mathematical summary of inequality based on the Lorenz curve.

The Call for Intervention

market failure: An imperfection in the market mechanism that prevents optimal outcomes.

THE FEDERAL INCOME TAX

The federal income tax is designed for this redistributional purpose. Specifically, the federal income tax is designed to be **progressive**—that is, to impose higher tax *rates* on high incomes than on low ones. Progressivity is achieved by imposing increasing **marginal tax rates** on higher incomes. The *marginal* tax rate refers to the tax rate imposed on the last (marginal) dollar of income.

In 2000, the tax code specified the five tax brackets shown in Table 33.1. For an individual with less than $26,250 of income, the tax rate was 15 percent. Any income in excess of $26,250 was taxed at a *higher* rate of 28 percent. If an individual's income rose above $63,550, the amount between $63,550 and $132,600 was taxed at 31 percent. Any income greater than $288,350 was taxed at 39.6 percent.

progressive tax: A tax system in which tax rates rise as incomes rise.

marginal tax rate: The tax rate imposed on the last (marginal) dollar of income.

TABLE 33.1
Progressive Taxes

The federal income tax is progressive because it levies higher tax rates on higher incomes. The 2000 marginal tax rate started out at 15 percent and rose to 39.6 percent.

Tax Bracket, $	Marginal Tax Rate, %
0–26,250	15
26,250–63,550	28
63,550–132,600	31
132,600–288,350	36
Over 288,350	39.6

Note: Marginal tax *rates* go up as income rises. This is the hallmark of a progressive tax system.
Source: Internal Revenue Service.

To understand the efficiency and equity effects of taxes, we must distinguish between the *marginal* tax rate and the *average* tax rate. A person who earned $300,000 in 2000 paid the 39.6 percent tax only on the income in excess of $288,350, that is, the last (marginal) $11,650. The first $26,250 was taxed at a marginal rate of only 15 percent. Hence this individual's tax bill was

Marginal Tax Rate	Income		Tax
15% of	$ 26,250	=	$ 3,937.50
28% of	37,300	=	10,444.00
31% of	69,050	=	21,405.50
36% of	155,750	=	56,070.00
39.6% of	11,650	=	4,613.40
	$300,000		$96,470.40

Current tax rate schedules are available from the Internal Revenue Service at www.irs.gov. Click on "Tax Info For You," then "Tax Tables."

The total tax of $96,470 represented only 32.2 percent of this individual's income. Hence, this person had a

- Marginal tax rate of 39.6 percent.
- Average tax rate of 32.2 percent.

The rationale behind this progressive system is to tax ever-larger percentages of rising incomes, thereby restraining inequalities.

Efficiency Concerns

Although the redistributive intent of a progressive tax system is evident, it raises concerns about efficiency. As noted in the chapter-opening quote, attempts to reslice the pie may end up reducing the size of the pie. The central issue here is incentives. Chapter 30 emphasized that the supply of labor is motivated by the pursuit of income. If Uncle Sam takes away ever-larger chunks of income, won't that dampen the desire to work? If so, **the incentive to work more, produce more, or invest more is reduced by higher marginal tax rates.** This suggests that as marginal tax rates increase, total output shrinks, creating a basic conflict between the goals of equity (more progressive taxes) and efficiency (more output).

Tax Elasticity. How great the conflict is between the equity and efficiency depends on how responsive market participants are to higher tax rates. The Rolling Stones left Great Britain off their 1998–99 world tour because the British marginal tax rate was so high (see World View). Many other businesses relocate to low-tax nations for the same reason. For the typical household, however, the response to higher tax rates is limited to reducing hours worked. In all cases we can summarize the response with **the tax elasticity of supply;** that is,

$$\text{Tax elasticity of supply} = \frac{\% \text{ change in quantity supplied}}{\% \text{ change in tax rate}}$$

tax elasticity of supply: The percentage change in quantity supplied divided by the percentage change in tax rates.

WORLD VIEW

Stones Keep England off '98 Tour to Avoid Tax

MUNICH, Germany, June 11—Mick Jagger said today that the Rolling Stones were disappointed they would not be playing in England this year, but the band looked forward to coming home for a series of concerts in 1999.

Lambasted by the British press for calling off a four-date tour at home because of a new tax law, members of the Stones said they opted out because the band stood to lose $19.6 million in taxes.

Under the previous tax code, Britons who lived and worked abroad for more than a year were exempt from British taxes on their earnings so long as they did not spend more than 62 days on native soil.

But the Labor government elected a year ago has scrapped that arrangement for everyone except some 10,000 seafarers. Now any citizen who works in Britain at all must pay tax on his or her entire year's earnings.

More than 300,000 tickets had been sold for the four British dates, which have been rescheduled for June 1999.

—Dorothee Stoewahse

Source: *Washington Post*, June 12, 1998. © 1998 The Washington Post. Reprinted with permission. www.washingtonpost.com

Analysis: High tax rates deter people from supplying resources—in this case, staging a concert.

If the tax elasticity of supply were zero, there'd be no conflict between equity and efficiency. But a zero tax elasticity would also imply that people would continue to work, produce, and invest even if Uncle Sam took *all* their income in taxes. In today's range of taxes, the average household's elasticity of labor supply is between 0.15 and 0.30. Hence, if tax rates go up by 20 percent, the quantity of labor supplied would decline by 3 to 6 percent. Figure 33.2 confirms that the top marginal tax rate has changed by more than that in the past.

Equity Concerns

As if the concern about efficiency weren't enough, critics also raise questions about how well the federal income tax promotes equity. What appears to be a fairly progres-

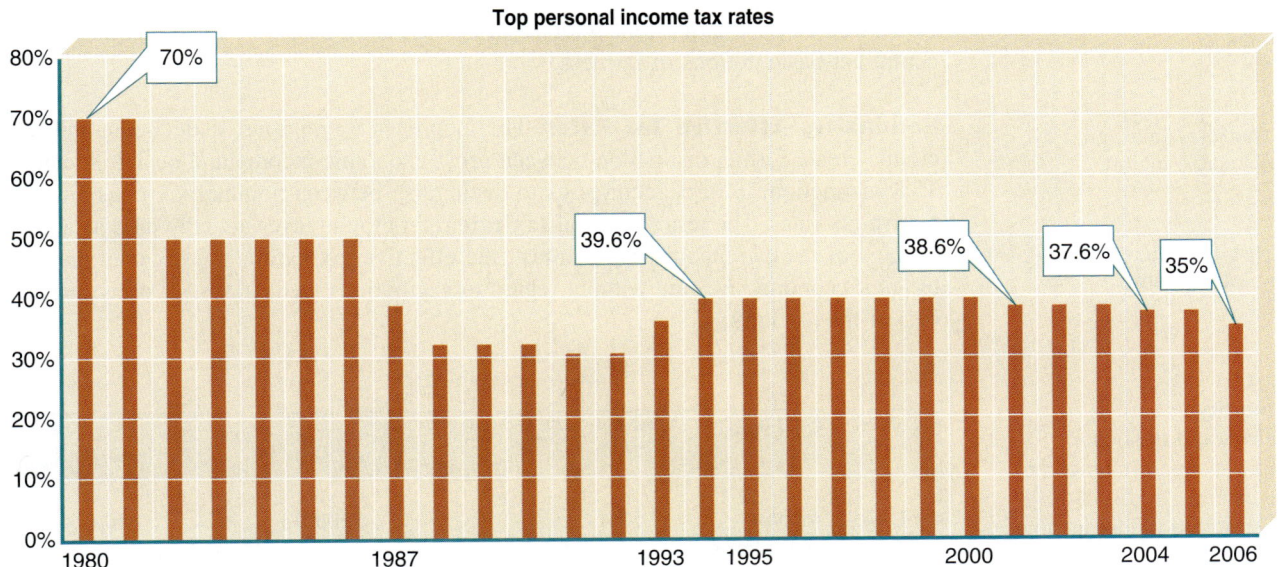

FIGURE 33.2
Changes in Marginal Tax Rates

During the past 20 years, Congress revised the federal income tax system many times. The top marginal tax rates were steadily reduced until 1993, then raised again. The Bush tax cuts of 2001 reduce marginal tax rates again.

Source: Internal Revenue Service.

sive tax in theory turns out to be a lot less progressive in practice. Hundreds of people with $1 million incomes pay no taxes. They aren't necessarily breaking any laws, just taking advantage of loopholes in the tax system.

Loopholes. The progressive *tax rates described in the tax code apply to "taxable" income, not to all income.* The so-called loopholes in the system arise from the way Congress defines taxable income. The tax laws permit one to subtract certain exemptions and deductions from gross income in computing taxable income; that is,

$$\frac{\text{Taxable}}{\text{income}} = \frac{\text{gross}}{\text{income}} - \text{exemptions and deductions}$$

Exemptions are permitted for dependent children, spouses, old age, and disabilities. Prior to the 1986 law, deductions were permitted for home mortgage interest, work-related expenses, child care, depreciation of investments, oil exploration, interest payments, union dues, medical expenses, and many other items.

The purpose of these many *itemized deductions* was to encourage specific economic activities and reduce potential hardship. The deduction for mortgage interest payments, for example, encourages people to buy their own homes. The deduction for medical expenses helps relieve the financial burden of illness.

Whatever the merits of specific exemptions and deductions, they create potential inequities. People with high incomes can avoid high taxes by claiming large exemptions and deductions. Each year the Internal Revenue Service discovers individuals earning $1 million incomes and paying little or no taxes. They aren't doing anything illegal, just taking advantage of the many deductions Congress permits. Nevertheless, this means that some people with high incomes could end up paying *less* tax than people with lower incomes. This would violate the principle of **vertical equity,** the progressive intent of taxing people on the basis of their ability to pay.

Table 33.2 illustrates vertical *in*equity. Mr. Jones has an income three times larger than Ms. Smith's. However, Mr. Jones also has huge deductions that reduce his *taxable* income dramatically. In fact, Mr. Jones ends up with less *taxable* income than Ms. Smith. As a result, he also ends up paying lower taxes.

The deductions that create the vertical inequity between Mr. Jones and Ms. Smith could also violate the principle of **horizontal equity**—as people with the *same* incomes end up paying different amounts of income tax. These horizontal *in*equities also contradict basic notions of fairness.

Nominal vs. Effective Tax Rates. The loopholes exemptions, deductions, and tax credits create form a distinction between gross economic income and taxable income. That distinction, in turn, requires us to distinguish between nominal tax rates and effective tax rates. The term **nominal tax rate** refers to the taxes actually paid as a percentage of *taxable* income. By contrast, the **effective tax rate** is the tax paid divided by *total* economic income without regard to exemptions, deductions, or other intricacies of the tax laws.

vertical equity: Principle that people with higher incomes should pay more taxes.

horizontal equity: Principle that people with equal incomes should pay equal taxes.

nominal tax rate: Taxes paid divided by taxable income.

effective tax rate: Taxes paid divided by total income.

TABLE 33.2
Vertical Inequity
Tax exemptions and deductions create a gap between total income and *taxable* income. In this case, Mr. Jones has both a higher income and extensive deductions. He ends up with less taxable income than Ms. Smith and so pays less taxes. This vertical inequity is reflected in the lower effective tax rate paid by Mr. Jones.

	Mr. Jones	Ms. Smith
1. Total income	$90,000	$30,000
2. Less exemptions and deductions	−$70,000	−$ 5,000
3. Taxable income	$20,000	$25,000
4. Tax	$ 4,000	$ 5,500
5. Nominal tax rate (= row 4 ÷ row 3)	20%	22%
6. Effective tax rate (= row 4 ÷ row 1)	4.4%	18.3%

As Table 33.2 illustrates, a single individual with a gross income of $90,000 might end up with a very low *taxable* income, thanks to the benefits of various tax deductions and exemptions. Mr. Jones ended up with a taxable income of only $20,000 and a tax bill of merely $4,000. We could then characterize Mr. Jones' tax burden in two ways:

$$\text{Nominal tax rate} = \frac{\text{tax paid}}{\text{taxable income}}$$

$$= \frac{\$4,000}{\$20,000} = 20 \text{ percent}$$

or, alternatively,

$$\text{Effective tax rate} = \frac{\text{tax paid}}{\text{total economic income}}$$

$$= \frac{\$4,000}{\$90,000} = 4.4 \text{ percent}$$

This huge gap between the nominal tax rate (20 percent) and the effective tax rate (4.4 percent) is a reflection of loopholes in the tax code. It's also the source of the vertical and horizontal inequities discussed earlier. Notice that Ms. Smith, with much less income, ends up with an effective tax rate (18.3 percent) that's more than four times higher than Mr. Jones' (4.4 percent).

Tax-Induced Misallocations. Tax loopholes not only foster inequity but encourage inefficiency as well. The optimal mix of output is the one that balances consumer preferences and opportunity costs. Tax loopholes, however, encourage a different mix of output. By offering preferential treatment for some activities, the tax code reduces their relative accounting cost. In so doing, ***tax preferences induce resource shifts into tax-preferred activities.***

These resource allocations are a principal objective of tax preferences. By 1986, however, the accumulation of exemptions, deductions, and credits had become so unwieldy and complex that tax considerations were overwhelming economic considerations in many investment and consumption decisions. The resulting mix of output, many observers felt, was decidedly inferior to a *pure* market outcome. From this viewpoint, the federal income tax was promoting both inequity and inefficiency.

A Shrinking Tax Base. Loopholes in the tax code create yet another problem. As the **tax base** gets smaller and smaller, it becomes increasingly difficult to sustain, much less increase, tax revenues. The tax arithmetic is simple:

$$\text{Tax revenue} = \frac{\text{average}}{\text{tax rate}} \times \frac{\text{tax}}{\text{base}}$$

As deductions, exemptions, and credits accumulate, the tax base (taxable income) keeps shrinking. To keep tax rates low—or to reduce them further—Congress had to stop this erosion of the tax base.

tax base: The amount of income or property directly subject to nominal tax rates.

Rising discontent with a shrinking tax base, horizontal and vertical inequities, and tax-distorted resource allocations led to a major reform of federal taxes in 1986. The basic features of the Tax Reform Act (TRA) of 1986 included

The 1986 Tax Reform Act

- *Loophole closing.* Major loopholes were closed or reduced.
- *Reductions in marginal tax rates.* The top marginal tax rate was reduced from 50 to 28 percent.
- *Fewer tax brackets.* The number of tax brackets dropped from 16 to 2.
- *Tax relief for the poor.* Increases in the personal exemption and standard deduction removed nearly 5 million poor people from the tax rolls.

- **Shift from personal to corporate taxes.** The direct tax burden on individuals was reduced while the corporate tax burden was increased.

Base Broadening. The elimination or reduction of scores of tax preferences increased the tax base almost 25 percent. By broadening the tax base to encompass more economic income, the TRA eliminated the source of many horizontal and vertical inequities. This loophole closing also made the tax system more progressive, since tax preferences disproportionately benefited higher-income families.

To view tax returns of U.S. presidents and to review the history of tax features, visit http://www.tax.org/THP/Presidential/default.htm

Rate Reductions. By broadening the tax base, the TRA made it possible to reduce tax rates. This was of particular concern to those who feared that high marginal tax rates were inhibiting labor supply, investment, and production. The cut in the top marginal tax rate from 50 to 28 percent was intended to stimulate a greater supply of labor and capital and thus promote efficiency.

1990 and 1993 Tax Increases

Although the 1986 reforms increased the progressivity of the tax system, some critics claimed that the reforms were a "giveaway" to the rich. In 1990, Congress responded to this sentiment by raising top marginal tax rate from 28 to 31 percent. President Clinton pushed Congress to raise taxes even further in 1993. Two more tax brackets were added, with marginal tax rates of 36 and 39.6 percent. Although these higher marginal tax rates increased progressivity, remaining loopholes left a lot of variation in *effective* tax rates. The News shows how then-Governor George W. Bush used some of these same loopholes to reduce his effective tax rate to 27 percent in 2000, despite receiving nearly $900,000 of income.

The Bush Tax Cuts (2001–2010)

After he was elected, President Bush made tax cuts his top priority. He wanted to reduce marginal tax rates, thereby encouraging more production. And he wanted to encourage more education, saving, and family development with an expanded array of tax exemptions, deductions, and credits.

Reduced Marginal Rates. President Bush wanted the top marginal tax rate of 39.6 percent reduced to 33 percent. Compromises with Congress achieved a smaller rate

IN THE NEWS

The President's Taxes

President and Mrs. Bush received about $900,000 of income in 2000, while still governor of Texas. Taxable income was reduced by deductions, however. Their $240,342 tax bill represented 32 percent of *taxable* income (the *nominal* tax rate) but only 27 percent of *total* income (the *effective* rate).

Income			
Wages	$ 70,954		
Interest	549,236	Deductions	
Dividends	61,346	Charitable contributions	143,300
Business income	314	Other deductions	6,898
Capital gains	138,358	Total deductions	$150,198
Partnership loss	−128	Taxable income	$744,682
Book royalties	75,000	Tax	$240,342
Adjusted gross income	$894,880	Source: The White House. www.whitehouse.gov	

Analysis: Taxes are levied on *taxable* income, not total income. Various deductions and exemptions reduce taxable income and *effective* tax rates.

reduction, however, phased in over several years. As Figure 33.2 illustrated, the 2001 Tax Relief Act reduces the highest marginal tax rate in three steps, to 35 percent in 2006. The new law also reduces the marginal tax rate for the *lowest* income class to only 10 percent (from 15 percent). The goal of this rate cut was to increase the disposable income of low-wage workers (equity) while giving them more incentive to work (efficiency).

Education Incentives. Aside from encouraging more *work*, President Bush also sought to encourage more *education*. The biggest incentive was a tuition tax deduction of $3,000 per year. This allows students, or their parents, to reduce their taxable income by the amount of tuition payments. In effect, Uncle Sam ends up paying part of the first $3,000 in tuition. In addition, the 2001 legislation allows people to save more money for college in tax-free accounts.

As welcome as these "loopholes" are to college students, they raise the same kind of efficiency and equity concerns as other tax preferences. If most of the students who take the tax deduction would have gone to college anyway, the deduction isn't very efficient in promoting education. Furthermore, most of the deductions go to middle-class families who itemize deductions. Hence, the tuition deduction introduces new vertical inequities. Few students have protested this particular loophole, however.

Check out the lastest tax deductions for college expenses at http://www.irs.gov. Under "Contents" click "Individuals" then "Students."

Family Incentives. President Bush also sought to use the tax code to promote "family values." To encourage marital stability, the "marriage penalty" of the standard deduction was phased out (allowing a married couple to have twice the standard deduction of a single person). To defray the cost of raising children, the child tax credit was increased.

Saving Incentives. The Tax Relief Act of 2001 also encouraged people to save more by raising the ceiling on deductions for retirement savings accounts (IRA, 401(k) plans). The estate tax was also targeted for phase-out.

The creation of these and other tax preferences raises all the same issues about equity and efficiency. As we noted above, the tuition deduction favors the middle class over the poor. The same can be said of the saving incentives. Although the Bush tax cuts also gave specific tax breaks to the poor, critics said the whole package was tilted toward the rich. Critics also questioned whether the various tax preferences would achieve their efficiency purposes, that is, promoting more college enrollments, more marriages and children, and greater saving.

Just as the first phase of the Bush tax cuts were being implemented, terrorists attacked the World Trade Center and the Pentagon. In response to those attacks, Congress passed a $40 billion package of grants, loans, and tax preferences. Congress also debated a much larger set of tax preferences to help stimulate more investment activity. The business community got virtually no new breaks in the Bush tax-cut package; the May 2001 legislation focused on *personal* taxes. So when Congress decided to stimulate the economy after the September 11 attacks, business interests were at the front of the line.

The Post-Terrorist Stimulus Package

Senate Democats objected to the business tax breaks on the grounds of both equity and efficiency. Critics complained that corporate tax breaks always favor the rich. They also doubted whether the new tax preferences would really stimulate new investment or rather just subsidize investments that would have occurred anyway.

PAYROLL, STATE, AND LOCAL TAXES

The federal income tax is only one of many taxes the average taxpayer must pay. For many families, in fact, the federal income tax is the smallest of many tax bills. Other tax bills come from the Social Security Administration and from state and local governments. These taxes also affect both efficiency and equity.

Sales and Property Taxes

regressive tax: A tax system in which tax rates fall as incomes rise.

Sales taxes are the major source of revenue for state governments. Many local governments also impose sales taxes, but most cities rely on *property taxes* for the bulk of their tax receipts. Both taxes are **regressive:** They impose higher tax rates on lower incomes.

At first glance, a 5 percent sales tax doesn't look very regressive. After all, the same 5 percent tax is imposed on virtually all goods. But we're interested in *people,* not goods and services, so **we gauge tax burdens in relation to people's incomes.** A tax is regressive if it imposes a proportionally *larger* burden on *lower* incomes.

This is exactly what a uniform sales tax does. To understand this concept, we have to look not only at how much tax is levied on each dollar of consumption but also at *what percentage of income* is spent on consumer goods.

Low-income families spend everything they've got (and sometimes more) on basic consumption. As a result, most of their income ends up subject to sales tax. By contrast, higher-income families save more. As a result, a smaller proportion of their income is subject to a sales tax. Table 33.3 illustrates this regressive feature of a sales tax. Notice that the low-income family ends up paying a larger fraction of its income (4.7 percent) than does the high income family (3 percent).

Property taxes are regressive also and for the same reason. Low-income families spend a higher percentage of their incomes for shelter. A uniform property tax thus ends up taking a larger fraction of their income than it does of the incomes of high-income families.

Tax Incidence. It may sound strange to suggest that low-income families bear the brunt of property taxes. After all, the tax is imposed on the landlords who *own* property, not on people who *rent* apartments and houses. However, here again we have to distinguish between the nominal payee and the individual whose income is actually reduced by the tax. **Tax incidence** refers to the actual burden of a tax—that is, who really ends up paying it.

tax incidence: Distribution of the real burden of a tax.

In general, people who rent apartments pay higher rents as a result of property taxes. In other words, landlords tend to pass along to tenants any property taxes they must pay. Thus, to a large extent **the burden of property taxes is reflected in higher rents.** Tenants pay property taxes *indirectly* via these higher rents. The incidence of the property tax thus falls on renters, in the form of higher rents, rather than on the landlords who write checks to the local tax authority.

Payroll Taxes

Payroll taxes also impose effective tax burdens quite different from their nominal appearance. Consider, for example, the Social Security payroll tax, the second largest source of federal tax revenue (see Figure 4.6). Every worker sees a Social Security (FICA) tax taken out of his or her paycheck. The nominal tax rate on workers is 7.65 percent. But there's a catch: Only wages below a legislated ceiling are taxable. In 2002, the taxable wage ceiling was $84,900. Hence, a worker earning $200,000 paid no more tax than a worker earning $84,900. As a result, the tax *rate* (tax paid ÷ total wages) is lower for high-income workers than low- and middle-income workers. That's a *regressive* tax.

There is another problem in gauging the impact of the Social Security payroll tax. Nominally, the Social Security payroll tax consists of two parts: half paid by employ-

TABLE 33.3
The Regressivity of Sales Taxes
A sales tax is imposed on consumer purchases. Although the sales tax itself is uniform (here at 5 percent), the taxes paid represent different proportions of high and low incomes. In this case, the low-income family's *sales tax* bill equals 4.7 percent of its *income*. The high-income family has a sales tax bill equal to only 3 percent of its income.

	High-Income Family	Low-Income Family
Income	$50,000	$15,000
Consumption	$30,000	$14,000
Saving	$20,000	$ 1,000
Sales tax paid (5% of consumption)	$ 1,500	$ 700
Effective tax rate (sales tax ÷ income)	3.0%	4.7%

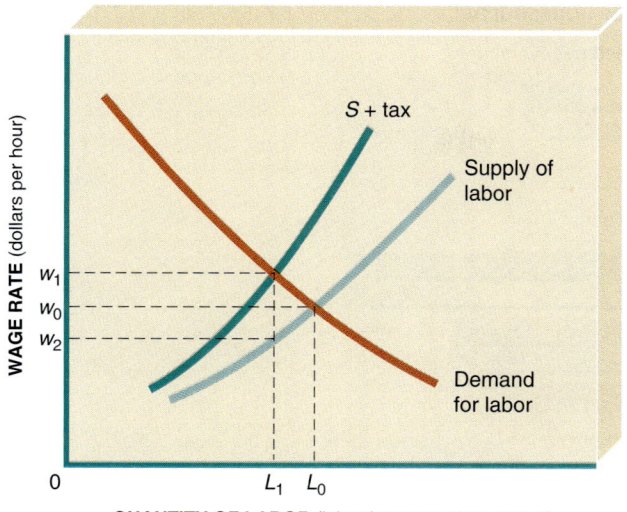

FIGURE 33.3
The Incidence of a Payroll Tax

Some portion of a payroll tax imposed on employers may actually be borne by workers. The tax raises the cost of labor and so shifts the supply curve upward (to $S + $ tax). The intersection of this tax-burdened supply curve with the labor demand curve determines a new equilibrium of employment (L_1). At that level, employers pay w_1 in wages and taxes, but workers get only w_2 in wages. The wage reduction from w_0 to w_2 is a real burden of the payroll tax, and it is borne by workers.

ees and half by employers. But do employers really pay their half? Or do they end up paying lower wages to compensate for their tax share? If so, employees end up paying *both* halves of the Social Security payroll tax.

Figure 33.3 illustrates how the tax incidence of the payroll tax is distributed. The supply of labor reflects the ability and willingness of people to work for various wage rates. Labor demand reflects the **marginal revenue product (MRP)** of labor; it sets a *limit* to the wage an employer is willing to pay.

The employer's half of the payroll tax increases the nominal cost of labor. Thus, the $S + $ tax curve lies above the labor supply curve. It incorporates the wages that must be paid to workers *plus* the payroll tax that must be paid to the Social Security Administration. This total labor cost is the one that will determine how many workers are hired. Specifically, the intersection of the $S + $ tax curve and the labor demand curve determines the equilibrium level of employment (L_1). The employer will pay the amount w_1 for this much labor. But part of that outlay ($w_1 - w_2$) will go to the public treasury in the form of payroll taxes. Workers will receive only w_2 in wages. This is less than they'd get in the absence of the payroll tax (compare w_0 and w_2). Thus, *fewer workers are employed, and the net wage is reduced when a payroll tax is imposed.*

These reflections on tax incidence don't imply that payroll taxes are necessarily bad. They do emphasize, however, that the apparent taxpayer isn't necessarily the individual who bears the real burden of a tax.

marginal revenue product (MRP): The change in total revenue associated with one additional unit of input.

TAXES AND INEQUALITY

The regressivity of the Social Security payroll tax and of many state and local taxes offsets most of the progressivity of the federal income tax (see Figure 33.4). The top 1 percent of income recipients gets 13 percent of total income and pays 26 percent of federal income tax. Hence, the federal income tax is highly progressive. Other federal taxes (Social Security, excise), however, reduce the tax share of the rich to only 18 percent. State and local tax incidence reduces their tax share still further. The final result is that *the tax system as a whole ends up being nearly proportional.* High-income families end up paying roughly the same percentage of their income in taxes as do low-income families. The tax system does reduce inequality somewhat, but the redistributive impact is quite small.

A Proportional System

The tax system tells only half the redistribution story. It tells whose income was taken away. Equally important is who gets the income the government collects. The government completes the redistribution process by *transferring* income to consumers. The

The Impact of Transfers

FIGURE 33.4
Taxes on the Rich

The progressivity of the federal income tax is offset by other federal, state, and local taxes. The net tax burden is only slightly progressive—the tax share of the rich (16 percent) is just a bit larger than their income share (13 percent).

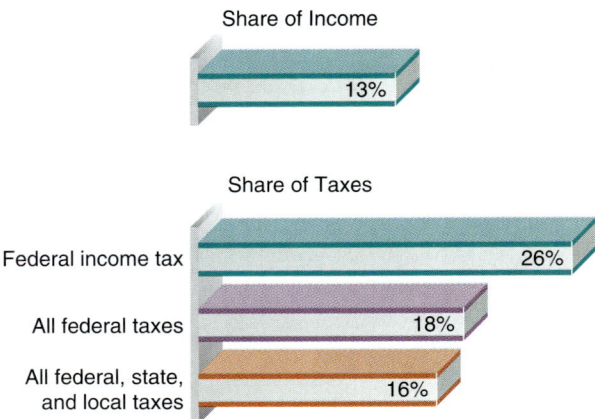

income transfers: Payments to individuals for which no current goods or services are exchanged, for example, Social Security, welfare, unemployment benefits.

income transfers may be explicit, as in the case of welfare benefits, Social Security payments, and unemployment insurance. Or the transfers may be indirect, as in the case of public schools, farm subsidies, and student loans. The direct transfers are more likely to be progressive, that is, to increase the income share of lower-income households. This progressivity results from the fact that low-income status is often a requirement for a direct income transfer. By contrast, most indirect transfers are ostensibly designed to fulfill other purposes, such as education and agricultural stability. As a consequence, they're less likely to be progressive and may even be regressive in some cases. One study of *social welfare* expenditures (including all direct transfers, housing, and education) attempted to assess the share of such transfers going to the poor. It found that only half of federal transfers and even a smaller proportion (30 percent) of state and local transfers go to the poor. We'll look more closely at income transfers in the next chapter.

WHAT IS FAIR?

government failure: Government intervention that fails to improve economic outcomes.

To many people, the apparent ineffectiveness of the tax system in redistributing income is a mark of **government failure.** They want a much more decisive reslicing of the pie—one in which the top quintile gets a *lot* less than half the pie and the poor get more than 4 percent (Figure 2.6). But how much redistribution should we attempt? Rich people can rattle off as many good reasons for preserving income inequalities as poor people can recite for eliminating them.

Economists aren't uniquely qualified to overcome self-interest, much less to divine what a fair distribution of income might look like. But economists can assess some of the costs and benefits of altering the distribution of income.

The Costs of Greater Equality

The greatest potential cost of a move toward greater equality is the reduced incentives it might leave in its wake. People *are* motivated by income. In factor markets, higher wages call forth more workers and may induce them to work longer hours. In fields where earnings are very high, as in the medical and legal professions, people are willing to spend many years and thousands of dollars acquiring the skills such earnings require. Could we really expect people to make such sacrifices in a market that paid everyone the same wage?

The same problem exists in product markets. The willingness of producers to supply goods and services depends on their expectation of profits. Why should they work hard and take risks to produce goods and services if their efforts won't make them any better off? If incomes were in fact distributed equally, producers might just as well sit back and enjoy the fruits of someone else's labor.

The essential economic problem absolute income equality poses is that it breaks the market link between effort and reward. If all incomes were equal, it would no

"I suppose one could say it favors the rich, but, on the other hand it's a great incentive for everyone to make two hundred grand a year."

Analysis: Inequalities are an incentive for individuals to work and invest more.

longer pay to make an above-average effort. If people stopped making such efforts, total output would decline, and we'd have less income to share (a smaller pie). Not that all high incomes are attributable to great skill or effort. Such factors as luck, market power, and family connections also influence incomes. It remains true, however, that the promise of higher income encourages work effort. Absolute income equality threatens those conditions.

The argument for preserving income inequalities is thus anchored in a concern for productivity. From this perspective, income inequalities are the driving force behind much of our production. By preserving inequalities, we not only enrich the fortunate few, but also provide incentives to take risks, invest more, and work harder. In so doing, we enlarge the economic pie, including the slices available to lower-income groups. Thus, everyone is potentially better off, even if only a few end up rich. This is the rationale that keeps the top marginal tax rate in the United States below that in most other countries (see World View on the next page).

Although the potential benefits of inequality are impressive, ***there's a trade-off between efficiency and equality.*** Moreover, many people are convinced that the terms of the trade-off are exaggerated and the benefits of greater equality are ignored. These rebuttals take the form of economic and noneconomic arguments.

The Benefits of Greater Equality

The economic arguments for greater equality also focus on incentives. The first argument is that the present degree of inequality is more than necessary to maintain work incentives. Upper-class incomes needn't be 13 times as large as those of the lowest-income classes; perhaps 5 times as large would do as well.

The second argument is that low-income earners might actually work harder if incomes were distributed more fairly. As matters now stand, the low-income worker sees little chance of making it big. Extremely low income can also inhibit workers' ability to work by subjecting them to poor health, malnutrition, or inadequate educational opportunities. Accordingly, some redistribution of income to the poor might improve the productivity of low-income workers and compensate for reduced productivity among the rich.

Finally, we noted that the maze of loopholes that preserves inequality also distorts economic incentives. Labor and investment decisions are influenced by tax considerations, not just economic benefits and costs. If greater equality were achieved via tax simplification, a more efficient allocation of resources might result.

WORLD VIEW

TOP TAX RATES
Highest Marginal Tax Rate (1999)

Country	Rate
Netherlands	60%
Dominican Republic	59%
Iran	54%
Germany	53%
Australia	47%
Venezuela	45%
UNITED STATES	39.6%
Canada	29%
Singapore	28%
Hong Kong	17%
Bolivia	13%

Source: World Bank, *World Development Indicators*, 2001.

Analysis: The highest marginal tax rate in the United States is lower than in most nations, but still a lot higher than in some countries.

THE ECONOMY TOMORROW

A Flat Tax?

flat tax: A single-rate tax system.

Widespread dissatisfaction with the present tax system has spawned numerous reform proposals. One of the most debated proposals is to replace the current federal income tax with a **flat tax.** First proposed by Nobel Prize winner Milton Friedman in the early 1960s, the flat tax was championed in Congress by former majority leader (and former economics professor) Dick Armey. In the 2000 election campaign, Malcomb Forbes trumpeted the idea.

The key features of a flat tax include

- Replacing the current system of multiple tax brackets and rates with a single (flat) tax rate that would apply to all taxable income.
- Eliminating all deductions, credits, and most exemptions.

Simplicity

A major attraction of the flat tax is its simplicity. The current 1,400-page tax code that details all the provisions of the present system would be scrapped. The 437 different IRS tax forms now in use would be replaced by a single, postcard-sized form.

Fairness

Flat-tax advocates also emphasize its fairness. They point to the rampant vertical and horizontal inequities created by the current tangle of tax loopholes. By scrapping all those deductions, the flat tax would treat everyone equally.

Some progressivity could also be preserved with a flat tax. In the version proposed by Dick Armey, the flat tax rate would be 17 percent, but one personal exemption would be maintained. Every adult would get a personal exemption of $13,100 and each child an exemption of $5,300. Accordingly, a family of four would have personal exemptions of $36,800. Hence, a family earning less than that amount would pay no income tax. *Effective* tax rates would increase along with rising incomes above that threshold.

Proponents of a flat tax claim it enhances efficiency as well as equity. Taxpayers now spend over a billion hours a year preparing tax returns. Legions of lobbyists, accountants, and lawyers devote their energy to tax analysis and avoidance. With a simplified flat tax, all those labor resources could be put to more productive use.

Efficiency

A flat tax would also change the mix of output. Consumption and investment decisions would be made on the basis of economic considerations, not tax consequences.

As alluring as a flat tax appears, it has aroused substantial opposition. As proposed by Dick Armey, the flat tax would not apply to all income. Income on savings and investments (such as interest and dividends, capital gains) wouldn't be taxed. The purpose of that exemption would be to encourage greater saving, investment, and economic growth. At the same time, however, such a broad exemption creates a whole new set of horizontal and vertical inequities. Someone receiving $1 million in interest and dividends could escape all income taxes, while a family earning $50,000 would have to pay.

The Critique

Critics also object to the wholesale elimination of all deductions and credits. Many of those loopholes are expressly designed to encourage desired economic activity. The Bush tax cuts were explicitly designed to encourage education, family stability, and savings. By discarding all tax preferences, the flat tax significantly reduces the government's ability to alter the mix of output. Even if the current maze of loopholes

IN THE NEWS

Americans Like the Principle of a Flat Tax . . .

Do you favor or oppose changing the federal income tax system to a flat tax system?	Favor	Oppose
	48%	42%

. . . But Not the Details

Do you favor or oppose a flat tax system if the new system:	Favor	Oppose
Taxed all Americans at a flat rate of 17%	41%	48%
Eliminated all tax deductions for state and local taxes	35	55
Taxed wages, but not profits from the sale of stocks and real estate	34	57
Eliminated the tax deduction for charitable contributions	31	64
Eliminated all tax deductions for home mortgages	29	60
Increased the size of the federal budget deficit	11	82

Source: *Time*, January 29, 1996. © 1996 Time Warner, Inc. Reprinted by permission. www.time.com

Analysis: Although taxpayers grumble about the many loopholes in the federal income tax, they don't want to give up the tax deductions that they currently use. A true flat tax would eliminate all deductions.

exceeds the threshold of government failure, complete reliance on the market mechanism isn't necessarily appropriate. A careful pruning of the tax code rather than a complete uprooting might yield better results.

Finally, critics point out that the transition to a flat tax would entail a wholesale reshuffling of wealth and income. Home values would fall precipitously if the tax preference for homeownership were eliminated. That would hit the middle class particularly hard. State and local governments would have greater difficulty raising their own revenues if the federal deduction for state and local taxes were eliminated. Millionaires might benefit by sharply reduced tax burdens. Confronted with such adjustments, many people begin to have second thoughts about the desirability of adopting a flat tax in the economy tomorrow. As the previous News documents, taxpayers seem to like the principle of a flat tax more than its actual provisions.

SUMMARY

- The distribution of income is a vital economic issue because incomes largely determine access to the goods and services we produce. Wealth distribution is important for the same reason.
- The size distribution of income tells us how incomes are divided up among individuals. The Lorenz curve is a graphic summary of the cumulative size distribution of income. The Gini coefficient is a mathematical summary.
- Personal incomes are distributed quite unevenly in the United States. At present, the highest quintile (the top 20 percent) gets nearly half of all cash income, and the bottom quintile gets only 4 percent.
- The trade-off between equity and efficiency is rooted in supply disincentives. The tax elasticity of supply measures how the quantity of resources (labor and capital) declines when tax rates rise.
- The progressivity of the federal income tax is weakened by various loopholes (exemptions, deductions, and credits), which create a distinction between nominal and effective tax rates and cause vertical and horizontal inequities.
- The Tax Reform Act of 1986 broadened the tax base (by eliminating many deductions), reduced tax rates, and shifted more of the tax burden onto corporations. The reforms made federal taxes a bit more progressive.
- Tax rates and brackets were increased in 1990 and 1993, reversing earlier trends.
- The 2001 Bush tax cuts reduced marginal tax rates and created new tax preferences for education, marriage, and saving.
- Mildly progressive federal income taxes are offset by regressive payroll, state, and local taxes. Overall, the tax system redistributes little income; most redistribution occurs through transfer payments.
- Tax incidence refers to the real burden of a tax. In many cases, reductions in wages, increases in rent, or other real income changes represent the true burden of a tax.
- There is a trade-off between efficiency and equality. If all incomes are equal, there's no economic reward for superior productivity. On the other hand, a more equal distribution of incomes might increase the productivity of lower income groups and serve important noneconomic goals as well.
- A flat tax is a nominally proportional tax system. A personal exemption and the exclusion of capital income can render a flat tax progressive or regressive, however. A flat tax reduces the government's role in resource allocation.

Key Terms

personal income (PI)
in-kind income
wealth
size distribution of income
income share
Lorenz curve
Gini coefficient

market failure
progressive tax
marginal tax rate
tax elasticity of supply
vertical equity
horizontal equity
nominal tax rate
effective tax rate

tax base
regressive tax
tax incidence
marginal revenue product (MRP)
income transfers
government failure
flat tax

Questions for Discussion

1. What goods or services do you and your family receive without directly paying for them? How do these goods affect the distribution of economic welfare?
2. Why are incomes distributed so unevenly? Identify and explain three major causes of inequality.
3. Do inequalities stimulate productivity? In what ways? Provide two specific examples.
4. What loopholes reduced the president's tax bill (see News, page 702)? What's the purpose of those loopholes? How else might those purposes be achieved?
5. How might a flat tax affect efficiency? Fairness?
6. If a new tax system encouraged more output but also created greater inequality, would it be desirable?
7. If the tax elasticity of supply were zero, how high could the tax rate go before people reduced their work effort? How do families vary the quantity of labor supplied when tax rates change?
8. Is the new tax deduction for tuition (page 703) likely to increase college enrollments? How will it affect horizontal and vertical equities?
9. If tax breaks for the rich really stimulated investment and growth, wouldn't everyone benefit from them? Why would anyone oppose them?

Web Activities

1. Go to www.taxhistory.org and compute the nominal and effective tax rates for President Bush's most recent tax return.
2. How have the income shares of the richest and poorest quintiles changed in the last few years? Log on to www.census.gov/hhes/www/income.html. Access the report "Money income in the United States" for the most recent year. Then access the PDF file for " Money Income in the United States" and find Table C. Look under "Percent Share of Household Income by Quintile" for your answer. Is income equitably distributed? Explain!
3. Log on to www.irs.ustreas.gov/prod/ind_info/tax_tables/tax_sched.html. Using the information provided in the table, determine whether the U.S. income tax code is progressive. Explain.

THE ACCOMPANYING STUDENT PROBLEM SET CONTAINS NUMERICAL AND GRAPHING PROBLEMS FOR THIS CHAPTER

CHAPTER 34

Transfer Payments: Welfare and Social Security

Americans are compassionate. Public opinion polls reveal that an overwhelming majority of the public wants to "help the needy." Most Americans say they're even willing to pay more taxes to help fund aid to the poor. But their compassion is tempered by caution: Taxpayers don't want to be ripped off. They want to be sure their money is helping the "truly needy," not being squandered by deadbeats, drug addicts, shirkers, and "welfare queens."

The conflict between compassion and resentment affects not only welfare programs for the poor but also Social Security for the aged, unemployment insurance benefits for the jobless, and even disability benefits for injured workers. In every one of these programs, people are getting money without working. **Transfer payments** are payments to individuals for which no current goods or services are exchanged. In effect, they're a "free ride." The risk of providing a free ride is that some of the people who take it could have gotten by without it. As the humorist Dave Barry observed, if the government offers $1 million to people with six toes, a lot of people will try to grow a sixth toe or claim they have one. Income transfers create similar incentives: They encourage people to change their behavior in order to get a free ride.

This chapter focuses on how income transfer programs alter work incentives and behavior. Central questions include

- What are the goals of income transfer programs?
- How are transfer benefits computed?
- How do transfer payments alter market behavior?

MAJOR TRANSFER PROGRAMS

Roughly 50 cents out of every federal tax dollar now is devoted to income transfers (see Figure 4.4). That amounts to *$1 trillion* a year in transfer payments. Who gets all this money?

The easy answer to this question is that almost every household gets some of the transfer money. There are over 100 federal income transfer programs. Students get tuition grants and subsidized loans. Farmers get crop assistance. Homeowners get disaster relief when their homes are destroyed. Veterans get benefit checks and subsidized health care. People over age 65 get Social Security benefits and subsidized health care. And poor people get welfare checks, food stamps, and subsidized housing.

Although income transfers are widely distributed, not everyone shares equally in the tax-paid bounty. As Figure 34.1 shows, just three of the myriad transfer programs account for nearly 80 percent of total outlays. Social Security, the largest program, alone accounts for 44 percent of the transfer budget. Medicare and Medicaid benefits absorb another 35 percent. By contrast, welfare checks account for only 5 percent of all income transfers.

Income transfer doesn't always entail cash payments. The Medicare program, for example, is a health insurance subsidy program that pays hospital and doctor bills for people over age 65. The 40 million people who receive Medicare benefits don't get checks from Uncle Sam; instead, Uncle Sam pays the bills for the medical *services* they receive. The same is true for the 42 million people who get Medicaid. Poor people get free health care from the Medicaid program; their benefits are paid *in-kind*, not in cash. Such programs provide **in-kind transfers,** that is, direct transfers of goods and services rather than cash. Food stamps, rent subsidies, legal aid, and subsidized school lunches are all in-kind programs. By contrast, Social Security is a **cash transfer** because it mails benefit checks, not services, to recipients.

The provision of in-kind benefits rather than cash is intended to promote specific objectives. Few taxpayers object to feeding the hungry. But they bristle at the thought that welfare recipients might spend the income they receive on something potentially harmful like liquor or drugs or on nonessentials like cars or fancy clothes. To minimize that risk, taxpayers offer coupons, not cash, thereby limiting the recipient's consumption choices. This helps reassure taxpayers that their assistance is being well spent.[1]

Similar considerations shape the Medicare program. Taxpayers could "cash out" Medicare by simply mailing older people the $215 billion now spent on the program. But then some healthy older Americans would get cash they didn't need. Some sick people might choose to spend their new-found income on something other than health care. Such outcomes would conflict with the goal of the program, which is to improve health care for the aged. The end result would be a smaller health care gain than in-kind transfers attain.

Cash vs. In-Kind Benefits

transfer payments: Payments to individuals for which no current goods or services are exchanged, like Social Security, welfare, unemployment benefits.

in-kind transfers: Direct transfers of goods and services rather than cash; examples include food stamps, Medicaid benefits, and housing subsidies.

cash transfers: Income transfers that entail direct cash payments to recipients, for example, Social Security, welfare, and unemployment benefits.

[1] In reality, a black market in food stamps allows recipients to convert coupons into cash, albeit at a discounted price.

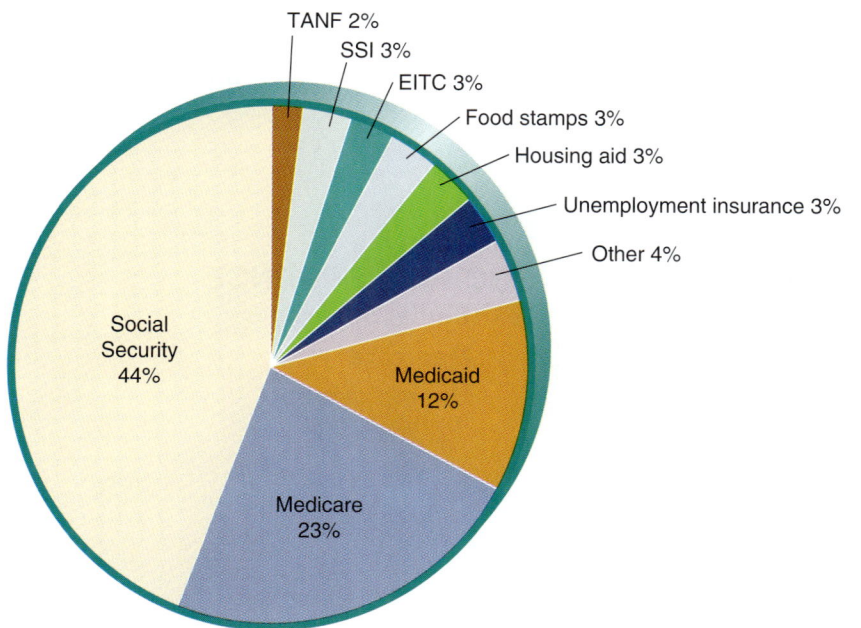

FIGURE 34.1
Income Transfer Program

There are nearly 100 different federal income transfer programs. However, just three programs—Social Security, Medicare and Medicaid—account for nearly 80 percent of all transfers. Cash welfare benefits (TANF, SSI) absorb only 5 percent of all income transfers.

Source: U.S. Office of Management and Budget (FY 2001 data).

target efficiency: The percentage of income transfers that go to the intended recipients and purposes.

The **target efficiency** of a transfer program refers to how well the transfers attain their intended purpose. In-kind medical transfers are more target-efficient than cash transfers because recipients would use equivalent cash transfers for other purposes. Food stamps are more target-efficient than cash in reducing hunger for the same reasons. If given cash rather than coupons, recipients would spend less than 70 cents of each dollar on food.

Social Insurance vs. Welfare

You may have noted by now that not all income transfers go to the poor. A lot of student loans go to middle-class college students. And disaster relief helps rebuild both mansions and trailer parks. Such income transfers are triggered by specific *events,* not the recipient's income. By contrast, welfare checks are *means-tested:* They go only to families with little income and fewer assets.

welfare programs: Means-tested income transfer programs, for example, welfare and food stamps.

Welfare programs always entail some kind of income eligibility test. To receive welfare payments, a family must prove that it has too little income to fend for itself. Medicaid is an in-kind **welfare program** because only poor people are eligible for the health care benefits of that program. To get food stamps, another in-kind welfare program, a family must also pass an income test.

social insurance programs: Event conditioned income transfers intended to reduce the costs of specific problems, for example, Social Security and unemployment insurance.

Social Security and Medicare aren't *welfare* programs because recipients don't have to be poor. To get Social Security or Medicare benefits you just have to be old enough. The *event* of reaching age 63 makes some people eligible for Social Security retirement benefits. At age 65 everyone—whether rich or poor—gets Medicare benefits. These event-conditioned benefits are the hallmark of **social insurance programs:** They insure people against the costs of old age, illness, disability, unemployment, and other specific problems. As Figure 34.2 illustrates, *most income transfers are for social insurance programs, not welfare.*

Transfer Goals

Because there are so many income transfer programs, it's hard to keep track of their many purposes. In general, however, all transfer programs aim to alter the distribution of income in some way.

Market Failure. If the market sliced up the economic pie in a manner that society deemed fair, there would be no need for government-provided income transfers. Hence, the existence of such programs implies a **market failure**—an unfair market-generated distribution of income. When the market alone slices up the pie, some people get too much and others get too little. To redress this inequity, we ask the government to play Robin Hood—taking income from the rich and giving it to the poor. Thus, *the basic goal of income transfer programs is to reduce income inequalities.* Oftentimes, the goal is even more specific, like reducing poverty. If successful, the post-transfer answer to the FOR WHOM question will differ from the pre-transfer (market) answer.

market failure: An imperfection in the market mechanism that prevents optimal outcomes.

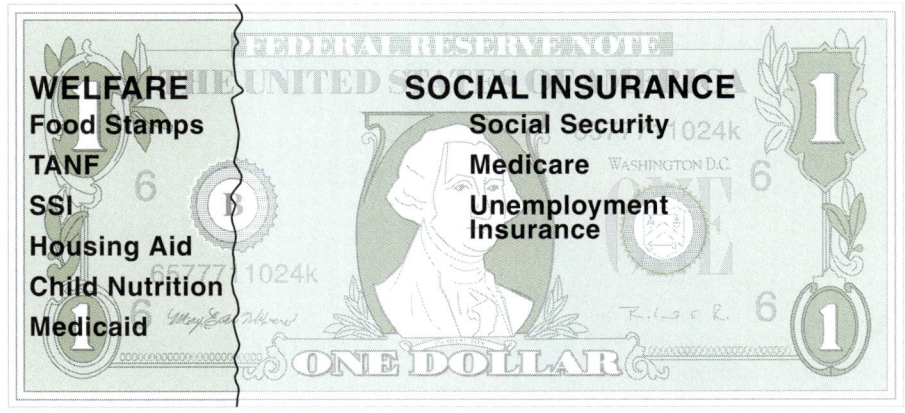

FIGURE 34.2
Social Insurance vs. Welfare

Social insurance programs provide *event*-based transfers—for example, upon reaching age 65 or becoming unemployed or disabled. Welfare programs offer benefits only to those in need; they're *means-tested.* Social insurance transfers greatly outnumber welfare transfers.

Source: U.S. Office of Management and Budget.

FIGURE 34.3
Reduced Labor Supply and Output

Transfer payments may induce people to supply less labor at any market wage rate. If this happens, the supply of labor shifts to the left and the economy's production possibilities shrink. We end up with less total output.

WHAT to Produce. In the process of redistributing incomes, income transfers also change the mix of output. The goal of food stamps, for example, is to increase food consumption by the poor. The strategy isn't to take food off rich people's plates, however. Instead, it is expected that the additional food purchases of the poor will encourage more food *production,* thereby changing the mix of output. Housing subsidies and free health care have similar effects on the mix of output. So do student loans: If more students end up going to college, the mix of output changes in favor of educational services.

While redistributing incomes and altering the mix of output we have to confront the Law of Unintended Consequences: Income transfer programs may change market behavior in unintended ways.

Unintended Consequences

Reduced Output. First, the provision of transfer payments may dull work incentives. If you can get paid for *not* working (via a transfer payment), why would you go to work? Why endure 40 hours of toil for a paycheck when you can stay home and collect a welfare check, an unemployment check, or Social Security? If the income transfers are large enough, I'll stay home too. When people reduce their **labor supply** in response to income transfers, total output will shrink. Figure 34.3 shows that *attempts to redistribute income may reduce total income.* In other words, the pie shrinks when we try to reslice it.

labor supply: The willingness and ability to work specific amounts of time at alternative wage rates in a given time period, *ceteris paribus.*

Undesirable Behavior. A reduction in labor supply isn't the only unintended consequence of income transfer programs. People may also change their *nonwork* behavior. Welfare benefits give women a (small) incentive to have more children and teen moms to establish their own households. Medicare and Medicaid encourage people to overuse health care services and neglect the associated costs. Unemployment benefits encourage workers to stay jobless longer. And, as Dave Berry noted at the beginning of the chapter, disability payments encourage people to grow a sixth toe. Although the actual response to these incentives is hotly debated, the existence of the undesired incentives is unambiguous.

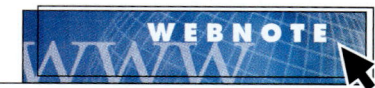

Compare federal welfare programs before and after the major 1996 reform at aspe.os.dhhs.gov/hsp/isp/reform.htm.

WELFARE PROGRAMS

To understand how income transfer programs change market behavior and outcomes, let's look closer at how welfare programs operate. The largest federal cash welfare program is called Temporary Aid to Needy Families (TANF). The TANF program was created by congressional welfare reforms in 1996 and replaced an earlier program (AFDC) that had operated since 1935. The new program offers states much discretion to decide who gets welfare, under what conditions, and for how long. States can also supplement their federal TANF block grants with their own tax revenues and even establish supplementary programs. However, all such programs confront a central dilemma: how to help the poor without encouraging undesired market behavior.

Benefit Determination

The first task of the TANF program is to identify potential recipients. In principle, this task is easy: Find out who is poor. To do this, the federal government has established a poverty line that specifies how much cash income families of different sizes need just to buy basic necessities. In 2001, the federal government estimated that a family of four was poor if its income was less than $17,900. Table 34.1 shows how this poverty threshold varies by family size.

According to Table 34.1, a four-person family with $15,000 of income in 2001 would have been considered poor. In their case, the **poverty gap**—the shortfall between actual income and the poverty threshold—was $2,900. The Jones family needed at least that much additional income to purchase what the government deems a "minimally adequate" standard of living.

poverty gap: The shortfall between actual income and the poverty threshold.

So how much welfare should the government give this family? Should it give $2,900 to this family, thereby closing its poverty gap? As simple as that proposition sounds, it creates some unintended problems.

The Work Incentive Problem

Suppose we guaranteed all families enough income to reach their respective poverty line. Any family earning less than the poverty line would receive a welfare check in the amount of their poverty gap. In that case, poor people would get enough welfare to escape poverty. No one would be poor.

There are two potential problems with such a welfare policy. First, people who *weren't* poor would have a strong incentive to become poor. Why try to support a family of four with a paycheck of $18,000 when you can quit and get $17,900 in welfare checks? Recall from Chapter 30 that the decision to work is largely a response to both the financial and psychological rewards associated with employment. People in dull, dirty, low-paying jobs get little of either. By quitting their jobs, declaring themselves poor, and accepting a guaranteed income transfer, they would gain much more leisure at little financial or psychological cost. In the process, total output would shrink (Figure 34.3).

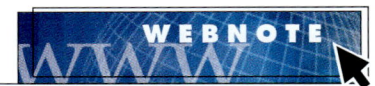

Current statistics on poverty are available from the U.S. Census Bureau at www.census.gov/hhes/www/poverty.html.

The second potential problem affects the work behavior of people who were poor to begin with. We assumed that the Jones family was earning $15,000 before they got a welfare check. The question now is whether the welfare check will change their work behavior.

Number of Family Members	Family Income
1	$ 9,200
2	11,800
3	14,200
4	17,900
5	21,100
6	23,600
7	27,400
8	30,000

Source: U.S. Department of Commerce, Bureau of the Census (rounded to 100s).

TABLE 34.1
Poverty Lines
The official definition of poverty relates current income to the minimal needs of a family. Poverty thresholds vary with family size. In 2001, a family of four was considered poor if it had less than $17,900 of income.

Suppose that family gets an opportunity to earn an extra $1,000 a year by working overtime. Should they seize that opportunity? Consider the effect of the higher *wages* on the family's *income*. Before working overtime, the Jones family earned

INCOME WITHOUT OVERTIME WAGES
Wages	$15,000
Welfare benefits	2,900
Total income	$17,900

If they now work overtime, their income is

INCOME WITH OVERTIME WAGES
Wages	$16,000
Welfare benefits	1,900
Total income	$17,900

Something is wrong here: Although *wages* have gone up, the family's *income* hasn't.

Marginal Tax Rates. The failure of income to rise with wages is the by-product of how welfare benefits were computed. *If welfare benefits are set equal to the poverty gap, every additional dollar of wages reduces welfare benefits by the same amount.* In effect, the Jones family confronts a **marginal tax rate** of 100 percent: Every dollar of wages results in a lost dollar of benefits. Uncle Sam isn't literally raising the family's taxes by a dollar. By reducing benefits dollar for dollar, however, the end result is the same.

marginal tax rate: The tax rate imposed on the last (marginal) dollar of income.

With a 100 percent marginal tax rate, a family can't improve its income by working more. In fact, this family might as well work *less*. As wages decline, welfare benefits increase by the same amount. Thus, we end up with a conflict between compassion and work incentives. By guaranteeing a poverty-level income, we destroy the economic incentive of low-income workers to support themselves. This creates a **moral hazard** for welfare recipients; that is, we encourage undesirable behavior. The moral hazard here is the temptation not to support oneself by working—choosing welfare checks instead.

moral hazard: An incentive to engage in undesirable behavior.

To reduce this moral hazard, Congress and the states changed the way benefits are computed. First, they set a much lower ceiling on welfare benefits. States don't offer to close the poverty gap; instead, they set a maximum benefit far below the poverty line. Hence, we have the benefit formula:

Less Compassion

$$\frac{\text{Welfare}}{\text{benefit}} = \frac{\text{maximum}}{\text{benefit}} - \text{wages}$$

In 2001, the typical state set a maximum benefit of about $8,000 for a family of four. Hence, a family without any other income couldn't get enough money from welfare to stay out of poverty. As a result, *a family totally dependent on welfare is unquestionably poor.* Although the lower benefit ceiling is less compassionate, it reduces the risk of climbing on the welfare wagon for a free ride.

To encourage welfare recipients to lift their own incomes above the poverty line, welfare departments made another change in the benefit formula. As we saw above, *the rate at which benefits are reduced as income increases is the marginal tax rate.* The dollar-for-dollar benefit cuts illustrated above destroyed the financial incentive to work. To give recipients more incentive to work, the marginal tax rate was cut from 100 to 67 percent. So we now have a new benefit formula:

More Incentives

$$\frac{\text{Welfare}}{\text{benefit}} = \frac{\text{maximum}}{\text{benefit}} - \frac{2}{3}[\text{wages}]$$

Figure 34.4 illustrates how a lower marginal tax rate alters the relationship of total income to wages. The black line in the figure shows the total wages Mrs. Jones could

FIGURE 34.4
Work (Dis)Incentives

If welfare benefits are reduced dollar for dollar as wages increase, the implied marginal tax rate is 100 percent. In that case, total income remains at the benefit limit of $8,000 (point A) as work effort increases from 0 to 1,000 hours (point B). There is no incentive to work in this range. When the marginal tax rate is reduced to 67 percent, total income starts increasing as soon as the welfare recipient starts working. At 1,000 hours of work, total income is $10,226 (point G).

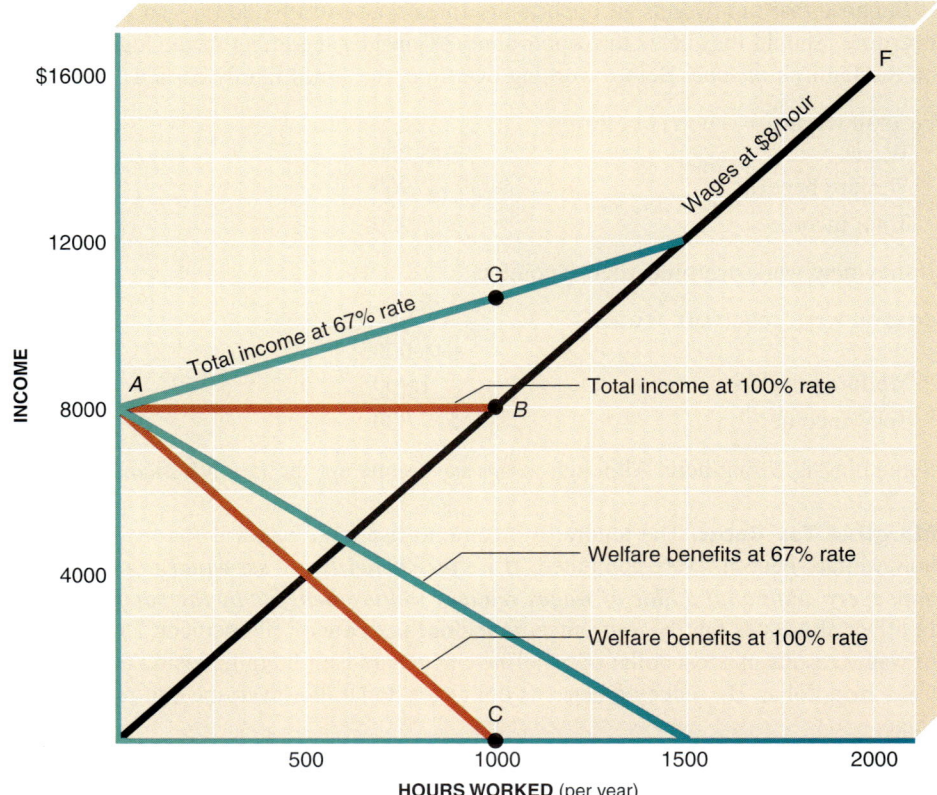

earn at $8 per hour. She could earn nothing by not working or as much as $16,000 per year by working full time (point F in the figure).

The red lines in the figure show what happens to her welfare benefits and total income when a 100 percent marginal tax rate is imposed. At point A she gets $8,000 in welfare benefits and total income because she's not working at all.

Now consider what happens to the family's total income if Mrs. Jones goes to work. If she works 1,000 hours per year (essentially half-time), she could earn $8,000 (point B). But what would happen to her income? If the welfare department cuts her benefit by $1 for every dollar she earns, her benefit check slides down the red "welfare benefits" line to point C, where she gets nothing from welfare. By working 1,000 hours per year, all Mrs. Jones has done is replace her welfare check with a paycheck. That might make taxpayers smile, but Mrs. Jones will wonder why she bothered to go to work. With a 100 percent tax rate, her total income doesn't rise above $8,000 until she works more than 1,000 hours.

The green lines in Figure 34.4 show how work incentives improve with a lower marginal tax rate. Now welfare benefits are reduced by only 67 cents for every $1 of wages earned. As a result, total income starts rising as soon as Mrs. Jones goes to work. If she works 1,000 hours, her total income will include

Wages	$ 8,000
Welfare benefit	2,667 = $8,000 − 2/3 ($8,000)
Total income	$10,667

Point G on the graph illustrates this outcome.

Incentives vs. Costs

It may be comforting to know that the Jones family can now increase its income to $10,667 by working 1,000 hours per year. But they still face a higher marginal tax rate (67 percent) than rich people (the top marginal tax rate on federal income taxes is less than 39 percent). Why not lower their marginal tax rate even further, thus increasing both their work incentives and their total income?

Unfortunately, a reduction in the marginal tax rate would also increase welfare costs. Suppose we eliminated the marginal tax rate altogether. Then, the Jones family could earn $8,000 *and* keep welfare benefits of $8,000. That would boost their total income to $16,000. Sounds great, doesn't it? But should we still be providing $8,000 in welfare payments to someone who earns $8,000 on her own? How about someone earning $20,000 or $30,000? Where should we draw the line? Clearly, *if we don't impose a marginal tax rate at some point, everyone will be eligible for welfare benefits.*

The thought of giving everyone a welfare check might sound like a great idea, but it would turn out to be incredibly expensive. In the end, we'd have to take those checks back, in the form of increased taxes, in order to pay for the vastly expanded program. We must recognize, then, a basic dilemma:

- *Low marginal tax rates encourage more work effort but make more people eligible for welfare.*
- *High marginal tax rates discourage work effort but make fewer people eligible for welfare.*

The conflict between work incentives and the desire to limit welfare costs and eligibility can be summarized in this simple equation:

$$\text{Breakeven level of income} = \frac{\text{basic benefits}}{\text{marginal tax rate}}$$

The **breakeven level of income** is the amount of income a person can earn before losing all welfare benefits. In the Jones case, the basic welfare benefit was $8,000 per year and the benefit-reduction (marginal tax) rate was 0.67. Hence, the family could earn as much as

$$\text{Breakeven level of income} = \frac{\$8,000}{0.67} \text{ per year}$$

$$= \$12,000$$

breakeven level of income: The income level at which welfare eligibility ceases.

before losing all welfare benefits. Thus, *low marginal tax rates encourage work but make it hard to get completely off welfare.*

If the marginal tax rate were 100 percent, as under the old welfare system, the breakeven point would be 8,000 divided by 1.00. In that case, people who earned $8,000 on their own would get no assistance from welfare. Fewer people would be eligible for welfare, but those who drew benefits would have no incentive to work. If the marginal tax rate were lowered to 0, the breakeven point would rise to infinity ($8,000 divided by 0)—and we'd all be on welfare.

As this arithmetic shows, *there's a basic conflict between work incentives (low marginal tax rates) and welfare containment (smaller welfare rolls and outlays).* We can achieve a lower breakeven level of income (less welfare eligibility) only by sacrificing low marginal tax rates or higher income floors (basic benefits). Hence, welfare costs can be minimized only if we sacrifice income provision or work incentives.

Tax Elasticity of Labor Supply. The terms of the trade-off between more welfare and less work depend on how responsive people are to marginal tax rates. As we first noted in Chapter 33, the **tax elasticity of labor supply** measures the response to changes in tax rates; that is,

$$\text{Tax elasticity of labor supply} = \frac{\text{\% change in quantity of labor supplied}}{\text{\% change in tax rate}}$$

tax elasticity of labor supply: The percentage change in quantity of labor supplied divided by the percentage change in tax rates.

If the tax elasticity of labor supply were zero, it wouldn't matter how high the marginal tax rate was: People would work for nothing (100 percent tax rate). In reality, the tax elasticity of labor supply is more in the range of 0.2 to 0.4, so marginal tax rates *do* affect work effort.

Time Limits. The 1996 welfare reforms sidestepped this dilemma by setting time limits on welfare eligibility. TANF recipients must engage in some sort of employment-related activity (e.g., a job, job search, or training) within two years of first receiving benefits. There is also a five-year lifetime limit on welfare eligibility. If fully enforced, these time limits will render moot the marginal work-welfare incentive computation for thousands of welfare recipients.

SOCIAL SECURITY

Like welfare programs, the Social Security program was developed to redistribute incomes. In the case of Social Security, however, *age*, not low income, is the primary determinant of eligibility. The program seeks to provide a financial prop under retirement incomes. Here again, however, we have to confront policy conflicts between the goals of compassion, work incentives, and program costs.

Program Features

The Social Security program is actually a mix of three separate income transfers. The main program is for retired workers, the second for survivors of deceased workers, and the third for disabled workers. Created in 1935, this combined Old Age Survivors and Disability Insurance (OASDI) program is now so large that it accounts for over 40 percent of all federal income transfers. The monthly benefit checks distributed to 45 million recipients are financed with a payroll tax on workers and employees.

Retirement Age. As Figure 34.5 confirms, the retirement program is by far the largest component of OASDI. Individuals become eligible for Social Security retirement benefits when they reach certain ages. People can choose either "early" retirement (at age 62 to 64) or "normal" retirement (at age 65 to 67). Those who choose early retirement receive a smaller monthly benefit because they're expected to live longer in retirement.

For people born after 1940, the age threshold for "normal" retirement is increasing each year. By the year 2022, the age threshold for normal retirement will be age 67. This delay in benefit eligibility is intended to keep aging baby boomers working longer, thereby curtailing a surge in benefit outlays.

Progressive Benefits. Retirement benefits are based on an individual's wages. In 2002, the median Social Security retirement benefit for an individual was about $12,000. But high-wage workers could get nearly $20,000 and low-wage workers as little as $6,000 a year.

Where Tax Revenue Comes From

Payroll taxes
  7.65% paid by workers
  7.65% paid by employers

Where Transfer Payments Go

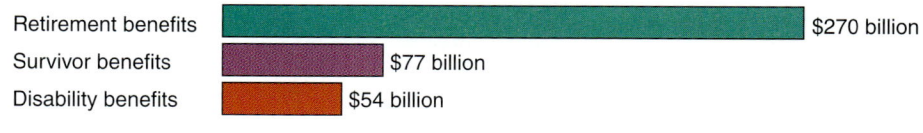

Retirement benefits — $270 billion
Survivor benefits — $77 billion
Disability benefits — $54 billion

Annual Retirement Benefit

Minimum — $80
Median — $12,000
Maximum — $20,000

FIGURE 34.5
Social Security Finances

The Social Security retirement, survivor, and disability programs are financed with payroll taxes. Most benefits go to retired workers, who get a median transfer of $12,000 per year.

Source: U.S. Social Security Administration (2000 data).

Although high-wage workers receive larger benefit checks than low-wage workers, the *ratio* of benefits to prior wages isn't constant. Instead, the **Social Security benefits formula is progressive** because the ratio of benefits to prior wages declines as wages increase. Social Security replaces 90 percent of the first $561 of prior average monthly earnings but only 15 percent of monthly wages above $3,381 (see Table 34.2). The declining **wage-replacement rate** ensures that low-wage workers receive *proportionately* greater benefits. Thus, retirement benefits end up more equally distributed than wages.

wage replacement rate: The percentage of base wages paid out in benefits.

In reality, a worker doesn't have to retire in order to receive Social Security benefits. But the government imposes an *earnings test* to determine how much retirement benefits an older person can collect while still working. The earnings test is very similar to the formula used to compute welfare benefits. The formula establishes a maximum benefit amount and a marginal tax rate that reduces benefits as wages increase:

The Earnings Test

$$\frac{\text{Benefit}}{\text{amount}} = \frac{\text{maximum}}{\text{award}} - 0.5 \,(\text{wages in excess of ceiling})$$

Consider the case of Leonard, a 62-year-old worker contemplating retirement. Suppose Leonard's wage history entitles him to a maximum award of $12,000 per year. But he wants to keep working to supplement Social Security benefits with wages. What happens to his benefits if he continues to work?

In 2001, the wage "ceiling" for workers 62 to 64 was $10,680. Hence, the benefit formula was

$$\frac{\text{Benefit}}{\text{amount}} = \$12{,}000 - 0.5 \,(\text{wage} > \$10{,}680)$$

As a result, a person could earn as much as $10,680 and still get maximum retirement benefits ($12,000), putting the total income at $22,680.

Suppose Leonard wants a bit more income than that. Can he increase his total income by working more? Yes, but not by much. He faces the same kind of work incentives the Jones family had when on welfare. The formula says benefits will drop by 50 cents for every $1 of wages earned over $10,680. Hence, the implicit marginal tax rate is 50 percent. Uncle Sam is effectively getting half of any wages Leonard earns in excess of $10,680 per year.

The Work Disincentive

In reality, the marginal tax rate on Leonard's wages is even higher. If he works, Leonard will have to pay the Social Security payroll tax (7.65 percent) as well as federal, state, and local income taxes (say, another 10 percent). Hence, the full burden of taxes and benefit losses includes

ITEM	MARGINAL TAX RATE
Society Security benefit loss	50.00%
Payroll tax	7.65
Income taxes	10.00
Total	67.65%

Wage Replacement Rate %	For Average Monthly Wages of
90	$1–561
32	561–3,381
15	over $3,381

Source: U.S. Social Security Administration

TABLE 34.2
Progressive Benefits
Social Security redistributes income progressively by replacing a larger share of low wages than high wages. Shown here are the wage-replacement rates for 2001.

FIGURE 34.6
THE SOCIAL SECURITY WORK TEST

A worker aged 62–64 can earn up to $10,680 (point A) without losing any Social Security benefits. If wages increase beyond $10,680 however, Social Security benefits decline by 50 cents for every $1 earned. After point C, income rises only half as fast as wages. At the breakeven point D, earnings and income are $33,600, and there are no Social Security benefits (point B).

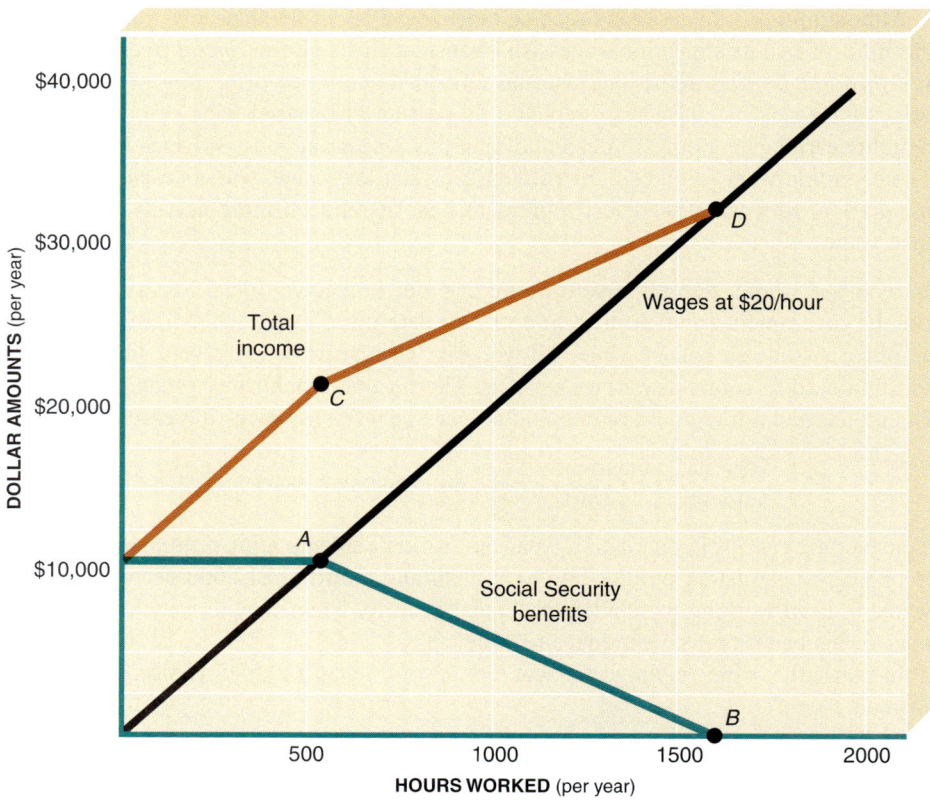

As a consequence, Leonard's income goes up by only 32.35 cents with every $1 he earns. Figure 34.6 illustrates this sorry state of affairs.

Declining Labor Supply

labor-force participation rate: The percentage of the working-age population working or seeking employment.

Like welfare recipients, older people are quick to realize that work no longer pays. Not surprisingly, they've exited the labor market in droves. The **labor-force participation rate** measures the percentage of the population that is either employed or actively seeking a job (unemployed). Figure 34.7 shows how precipitously the labor-force participation rate has declined among older Americans. As the World View illustrates, this problem isn't unique to the United States. The relative size of the over-65 population is growing everywhere, and more older people are retiring earlier.

Prior to the creation of the Social Security system, most older people had to continue working until advanced age. Many "died with their boots on" because they had

FIGURE 34.7
Declining Labor-Force Participation

In the 1960s and 1970s, the eligibility age for Social Security was lowered for men and benefits were increased. This convinced an increased percentage of older men to leave the labor force and retire. In a single generation the labor-force participation rate of men over age 65 was halved.

Source: U.S. Bureau of Labor Statistics.

WORLD VIEW

An Aging World
Richer Countries Aging Fastest
The whole world is aging, but the trend is most pronounced in developed countries, where elders will outnumber youths next year.

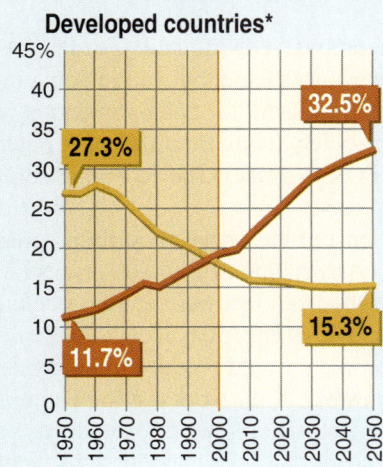

*(Includes North America, Japan, Europe, Australia, New Zealand)

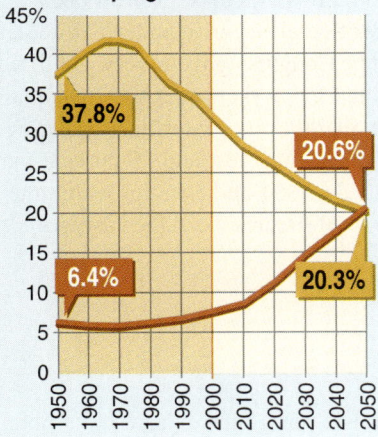

Source: *U.S. News & World Report,* March 1, 1999. Reprinted with permission. www.usnews.com

Workers have been retiring earlier . . .
Average age of retirement for men in industrialized countries

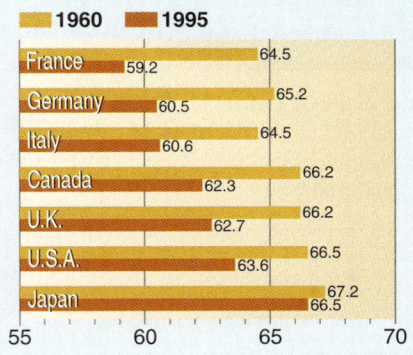

. . . but fewer workers will be supporting retirees in the future . . .
Average number of contributors per retiree in public pension systems

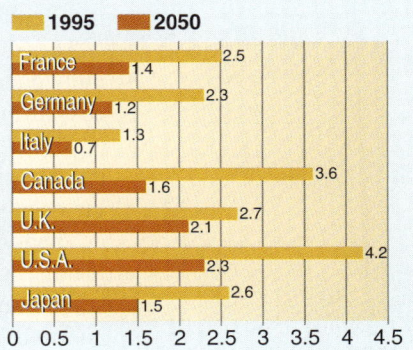

. . . which could lead to higher taxes
Projected payroll tax rates needed to cover all retirees

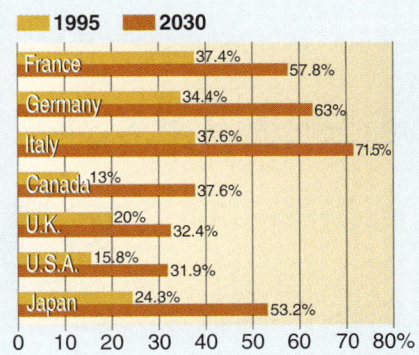

Analysis: The aging of the world's population implies an increasing income transfer burden. As older workers choose to retire earlier, the burden increases still further.

Compassion, Incentives, and Cost

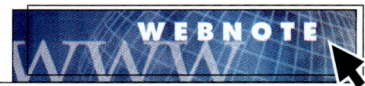

Read about the future of Social Security `as analyzed by the Social Security Administration at www.ssa.gov/pubs/10055.htm.

no other means of support. Just a generation ago, over 75 percent of men 62 to 64 were working. Today, less than 50 percent of that group is working.

The primary economic cost of the Social Security program isn't the benefits it pays but the reduction in total output that occurs when workers retire early. In the absence of Social Security benefits, millions of older workers would still be on the job, contributing to the output of goods and services. When they instead retire—or simply work less—total output shrinks.

The economic cost of Social Security is increased further by a labor supply reduction among *younger* workers. Recall how all those retirement benefits are *financed* (Figure 34.5). The payroll taxes levied on employees and employers increase the cost of labor and discourage people from working more, which further reduces total output. As the behavior of both older and younger workers changes, *the economic pie shrinks as we try to redistribute it from younger to older workers.*

Trade-Offs. Just because the intergenerational redistribution is expensive doesn't mean we shouldn't do it. Going to college is expensive too, but you're doing it. The real economic issue is benefits versus costs. Compassion for older workers is what motivates Social Security transfers. Presumably, society gains from the more equitable distribution of income that results (a revised FOR WHOM). The economic concern is that we *balance* this gain against the implied costs.

One way of reducing the economic cost of the Social Security program would be to eliminate the work test. The American Association of Retired Persons (AARP) has advocated this option for many years. If the work test were eliminated, the marginal tax rate on the wages of older workers would drop from 50 percent to 0. In a flash, the work disincentive would vanish, and older workers would produce more goods and services.

There's a downside to this reform, however. If the work test were eliminated, all older individuals would get their full retirement benefit, which would raise the budgetary cost of the program substantially. To cover that cost, payroll taxes would have to increase. Higher payroll taxes would in turn reduce supply and demand for *younger* workers. Hence, the financial burden of eliminating the work test might actually *increase* the economic cost of Social Security.

There's also an equity issue here. Should we increase payroll taxes on younger low-income workers in order to give higher Social Security benefits to older workers who still command higher salaries? In 2000, Congress gave a very qualified "yes" to this question. The earnings test was eliminated for workers over age 70 and raised to $30,000 in 2002 for workers aged 65–69. The marginal tax rate for workers aged 65–69 was also reduced to 33.3 percent. The lower earnings test and 50 percent marginal tax rate were left intact, however, for people aged 62–64, the ones for whom the retirement decision is most pressing. The *budget* cost of greater work incentives for "early retirees" was regarded as too high.

THE ECONOMY TOMORROW

Privatize Social Security?

As we saw, all income transfer programs entail a redistribution of income. In the case of Social Security, the redistribution is largely intergenerational: Payroll taxes levied on younger workers finance retirement benefits for older workers. The system is financed on a pay-as-you-go basis; future benefits depend on future taxes. This is very different from private pension plans, whereby you salt away some wages while working to finance your own eventual benefits. Such private plans are advance-*funded.*

Many people say we should run the Social Security system the same way. They want to "privatize" Social Security by permitting workers to establish their own retirement plans. Instead of paying payroll taxes to fund someone else's benefits, you'd make a contribution to your own pension fund.

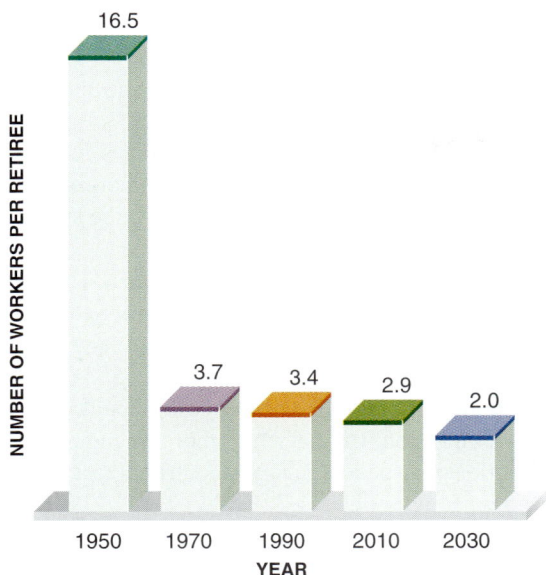

FIGURE 34.8
A Declining Tax Base

Because Social Security benefits are financed by payroll taxes, the ratio of workers to retirees is a basic measure of the program's fiscal health. That ratio has declined dramatically, and it will decline even more when the baby boomers start retiring.

Source: U.S. Social Security Administration.

The case for privatizing Social Security is based on both efficiency and equity. The efficiency argument reflects the core laissez-faire argument that markets know best. In a privatized system, individuals would have the freedom to tailor their consumption and saving choices. The elimination of mandatory payroll taxes and the work test would also lessen work disincentives.

Advocates of privatization also note how inequitable the existing program is for younger workers. The people now retired are getting a great deal: They paid relatively low payroll taxes when young and now receive substantial benefits. In part this high payoff is due to demographics. Thirty years ago there were four workers for every retired person. By the time the post–World War II baby boomers retire, the ratio of workers to retirees will be a lot lower. By the year 2030, there will be only two workers for every retiree (see Figure 34.8). As a result, the tax burden on tomorrow's workers will have to be a lot higher, or the baby boomers will have to accept much lower Social Security benefits. Either way, some generation of workers will get a lot less than everyone else. If Social Security is privatized, tomorrow's workers won't have to bear such a demographic tax burden.

As alluring as these suggestions sound, the privatization of Social Security would foster other inequities. The primary goal of Social Security is to fend off poverty among the aged. Social Security does this in two ways: by (1) transferring income from workers to retirees and (2) redistributing income from high-wage workers to low-wage workers in retirement with progressive wage-replacement rates. In these ways the program changes market outcomes. By contrast, a privatized system would let the market alone determine FOR WHOM goods are produced. Low-income workers and other people who saved little while working would end up poor in their golden years. In a privatized system, even some high earners and savers might end up poor if their investments turned sour. Would we turn our collective backs on these people? If not, then the government would have to intervene with *some* kind of transfer program. The real issue, therefore, may not be whether a privatized Social Security system would work but what kind of *public* transfer program we'd have to create to supplement it. Then the choice would be either (1) Social Security or (2) a privatized retirement system plus a public welfare program for the aged poor. Framed in this context, the choice for the economy tomorrow is a lot more complex. In early 2001, President Bush appointed a commission to develop privatization options that would preserve the commitment to retirement income security.

SUMMARY

- Income transfers are all payments for which no current goods or services are exchanged. They include both cash payments such as welfare checks and in-kind transfers such as food stamps and Medicare.
- Most transfer payments come from social insurance programs that cushion the income effects of specific events, for example, aging, illness, or unemployment. Welfare programs are means-tested; they pay benefits only to the poor.
- The basic goal of transfer programs is to alter the market's FOR WHOM outcome. Attempts to redistribute income may, however, have the unintended effect of reducing total income.
- Welfare programs reduce work incentives in two ways. They offer some income to people who don't work at all, and they also tax the wages of recipients who do work via offsetting benefit reductions.
- The benefit reduction that occurs when wages increase is an implicit marginal tax. The higher the marginal tax rate, (1) the less the incentive to work but (2) the smaller the welfare caseload.
- The Social Security retirement program creates similar work disincentives. It provides an income floor for people who don't work and imposes a high marginal tax rate on workers aged 62–64.
- The core policy dilemma is to find an optimal balance between compassion (transferring more income) and incentives (keeping people at work contributing to total output).

Key Terms

transfer payment	social insurance programs	moral hazard
in-kind transfers	market failure	breakeven level of income
cash transfers	labor supply	tax elasticity of labor supply
target efficiency	poverty gap	wage-replacement rate
welfare programs	marginal tax rate	labor-force participation rate

Questions for Discussion

1. If we have to choose between compassion and incentives, which should we choose? Do the terms of the trade-off matter?
2. What's so hard about guaranteeing everyone a minimal level of income support? What problems arise?
3. If poor people don't want to work, should they get welfare? What about their children?
4. Once someone has received TANF welfare benefits for a total of five years, they are permanently ineligible for more TANF benefits. Should they receive any further assistance? How will work incentives be affected?
5. In what ways do younger workers pay for Social Security benefits received by retired workers?
6. Should the Social Security earnings test be eliminated? What are the benefits and costs of doing so?
7. How would the distribution of income change if Social Security were privatized?

Web Activities

1. How much will you collect in social security when you retire? Log into www.ssa.gov/OACT/ANYPIA to calculate the answer. Assume a current income of $40,000 and do not adjust for inflation.
2. Should the Social Security system be privatized? Make your own decision after reading www.mysocialsecurity.org/index.html, www.socialsecurity.org, and www.urban.org/periodcl/prr25_3h.htm.
3. Are there poor people in the United States, the wealthiest nation in the world? Go to www.census.gov/hhes/www/poverty.html for a definition and statistics on poverty. How is *poverty* defined in the United States? What percentage of the U.S. population is defined to be poor? What programs exist to alleviate this situation?

THE ACCOMPANYING STUDENT PROBLEM SET CONTAINS NUMERICAL AND GRAPHING PROBLEMS FOR THIS CHAPTER

PART 13

International Economics

Our interactions with the rest of the world have a profound impact on the mix of output (WHAT), the methods of production (HOW), and the distribution of income (FOR WHOM). Trade and global money flows can also affect the stability of the macro economy. Chapters 35 and 36 explore the motives, the nature, and the effects of international trade and finance.

CHAPTER 35

International Trade

The 2001 World Series between the New York Yankees and the Arizona Diamondbacks was played with Japanese gloves, baseballs made in Costa Rica, and Mexican bats. Most of the players were wearing shoes made in Korea or China. And during the regular season, many of the games throughout the league were played on artificial grass made in Taiwan. Baseball, it seems, has become something less than the "all-American" game.

Imported goods have made inroads into other activities as well. All DVDs, VCRs and video-game machines are imported, as are most televisions, fax machines, personal computers, and cell phones. Most of these imported goods could have been produced in the United States. Why did we purchase them from other countries? For that matter, why does the rest of the world buy computers, tractors, chemicals, airplanes, and wheat from us rather than produce such products for themselves? Wouldn't we all be better off relying on ourselves for the goods we consume (and the jobs we need) rather than buying and selling products in international markets? Or is there some advantage to be gained from international trade?

This chapter begins with a survey of international trade patterns—what goods and services we trade, and with whom. Then we address basic issues related to such trade:

- What benefit, if any, do we get from international trade?
- How much harm do imports cause, and to whom?
- Should we protect ourselves from "unfair" trade by limiting imports?

After examining the arguments for and against international trade, we draw some general conclusions about trade policy. As we'll see, international trade tends to increase *average* incomes, although it may diminish the job and income opportunities for specific industries and workers.

U.S. TRADE PATTERNS

The United States is by far the largest player in global product and resource markets. In 2000, we purchased 20 percent of the world's exports and sold 15 percent of the same total.

In dollar terms, our imports in 2000 exceeded $1.4 trillion. These **imports** included the consumer items mentioned earlier as well as capital equipment, raw materials, and food. Table 35.1 is a sampler of the goods and services we purchase from foreign suppliers.

Although imports represent only 14 percent of total GDP, they account for larger shares of specific product markets. Coffee is a familiar example. Since virtually all coffee is imported (except for a tiny amount produced in Hawaii), Americans would have a harder time staying awake without imports. Likewise, there'd be no aluminum if we didn't import bauxite, no chrome bumpers if we didn't import chromium, no tin cans without imported tin, and a lot fewer computers without imported components. We couldn't even play the all-American game of baseball without imports, since baseballs are no longer made in the United States.

We import *services* as well as *goods*. If you fly to Europe on British Airways you're importing transportation services. If you stay in a London hotel, you're importing lodging services. When you go to Barclay's Bank to cash traveler's checks, you're importing foreign financial services. These and other services now account for one-sixth of U.S. imports.

While we're buying goods (merchandise) and services from the rest of the world, global consumers are buying our **exports**. In 2000, we exported $773 billion of *goods*, including farm products (wheat, corn, soybeans), tobacco, machinery (computers), aircraft, automobiles and auto parts, raw materials (lumber, iron ore), and chemicals (see

Imports

imports: Goods and services purchased from international sources.

Exports

exports: Goods and services sold to foreign buyers.

Country	Imports from	Exports to
Australia	Beef Alumina Autos	Airplanes Computers Auto parts
Belgium	Jewelry Cars Optical glass	Cigarettes Airplanes Diamonds
Canada	Cars Trucks Paper	Auto parts Cars Computers
China	Toys Shoes Clothes	Fertilizer Airplanes Cotton
Germany	Cars Engines Auto parts	Airplanes Computers Cars
Japan	Cars Computers Telephones	Airplanes Computers Timber
Russia	Oil Platinum Artworks	Corn Wheat Oil seeds
South Korea	Shoes Cars Computers	Airplanes Leather Iron ingots and oxides

Source: U.S. Department of Commerce.

TABLE 35.1
A U.S. Trade Sampler
The United States imports and exports a staggering array of goods and services. Shown here are the top exports and imports with various countries. Notice that we export many of the same goods we import (such as cars and computers). What's the purpose of trading goods we produce ourselves?

Table 35.1 for a sample of U.S. merchandise exports). We also exported $296 billion of services (movies, software licenses, tourism, engineering, financial services, etc.).

Although the United States is the world's largest exporter of goods and services, exports represent a relatively modest fraction of our total output. As the World View illustrates, other nations export much larger proportions of their GDP. Ireland is one of the most export-oriented countries, with tourist services pushing its export ratio to 88 percent. By contrast, Myanmar (Burma) is basically a closed economy, with few exports (other than opium and other drugs traded in the black market).

The low U.S. export ratio disguises our heavy dependence on exports in specific industries. We export 25 to 50 percent of our rice, corn, and wheat production each year, and still more of our soybeans. Clearly, a decision by international consumers to stop eating U.S. agricultural products could devastate a lot of American farmers. Such companies as Boeing (planes), Caterpillar Tractor (construction and farm machinery), Weyerhaeuser (logs, lumber), Eastman Kodak (film), Dow (chemicals), and Sun Microsystems (computer workstations) sell over one-fourth of their output in foreign markets. McDonald's sells hamburgers in 121 countries around the world; to do so, the company exports management and marketing services from the United States. The Walt Disney Company produces the most popular TV shows in Russia and Germany, publishes Italy's best-selling weekly magazine, and has the most popular tourist attraction in Japan (Tokyo Disneyland). The 500,000 foreign students attending U.S. universities are purchasing $5 billion of American educational services. All these activities are part of America's service exports.

WEBNOTE
Find the most recent trends in trade statistics at www.whitehouse.gov/fsbr/international.html.

Trade Balances

Although we export a lot of products, we often have an imbalance in our trade flows. The trade balance is the difference between the value of exports and imports; that is,

$$\text{Trade balance} = \text{exports} - \text{imports}$$

WORLD VIEW

Export Ratios

Very poor countries often have little to export and thus low export ratios. Saudi Arabia, by contrast, depends heavily on its oil exports. Fast-developing countries in Asia also rely on exports to enlarge their markets and raise incomes. The U.S. export ratio is low by international standards.

Source: World Bank, *World Development Indicators 2002*. www.worldbank.org

Country	Exports (% of GDP)
Myanmar	1
Japan	10
Brazil	11
United States	11
Haiti	12
India	12
Egypt	16
Great Britain	26
Germany	29
Saudi Arabia	40
Korea (South)	42
Canada	44
Sweden	44
Ireland	88

Analysis: The relatively low U.S. export ratio reflects the vast size of our domestic market and our relative self-sufficiency in food and resources. European nations are smaller and highly interdependent.

Product Category	Exports (in billions of dollars)	Imports (in billions of dollars)	Surplus (Deficit) (in billions of dollars)
Merchandise	773	1,223	(450)
Services	296	215	81
Total trade	1,069	1,438	(369)

Source: U.S. Department of Commerce.

TABLE 35.2
Trade Balances
Both merchandise (goods) and services are traded between countries. The United States typically has a merchandise deficit and a services surplus. When combined, an overall trade deficit remained in 2000.

During 2000, we imported much more than we exported and so had a negative trade balance. A negative trade balance is called a **trade deficit**.

Although the overall trade balance includes both goods and services, these flows are usually reported separately, with the *merchandise* trade balance distinguished from the *services* trade balance. As Table 35.2 shows, the United States had a merchandise (goods) trade deficit of $450 billion in 2000 and a *services* trade *surplus* of $81 billion, leaving the overall trade balance in the red.

When the United States has a trade deficit with the rest of the world, other countries must have an offsetting **trade surplus**. On a global scale, imports must equal exports, since every good exported by one country must be imported by another. Hence, any imbalance in America's trade must be offset by reverse imbalances elsewhere.

Whatever the overall balance in our trade accounts, bilateral balances vary greatly. Table 35.3 shows, for example, that our 2000 aggregate trade deficit ($369 billion) incorporated huge bilateral trade deficits with Japan and China. In the same year, however, we had trade surpluses with the Netherlands, Belgium, Australia, Hong Kong, and Egypt.

trade deficit: The amount by which the value of imports exceeds the value of exports in a given time period.

trade surplus: The amount by which the value of exports exceeds the value of imports in a given time period.

MOTIVATION TO TRADE

Many people wonder why we trade so much, particularly since (1) we import many of the things we also export (like computers, airplanes, clothes), (2) we *could* produce many of the other things we import, and (3) we worry so much about trade imbalances.

Country	Exports to ($ billions)	Imports from ($ billions)	Trade Balance ($ billions)
Top Deficit Countries			
China	16.2	100.0	−83.8
Japan	64.9	146.5	−81.6
Canada	178.9	230.8	−51.9
Germany	29.4	58.5	−29.1
Mexico	111.3	135.9	−24.6
Top Surplus Countries			
Netherlands	21.8	9.6	+12.2
Australia	12.5	6.5	+6.0
Belgium	13.9	9.9	+4.0
Hong Kong	14.6	11.5	+3.1
Egypt	3.3	0.9	+2.4

Source: U.S. Census Bureau, Foreign Trade Division.

TABLE 35.3
Bilateral Trade Balances
The U.S. trade deficit is the net result of bilateral deficits and surpluses. We had huge trade deficits with Japan and China in 2000, for example, but small trade surpluses with the Netherlands, Belgium, Australia, and Hong Kong. International trade is multinational, with surpluses in some countries being offset by trade deficits elsewhere.

Specialization

Why not just import those few things that we can't produce ourselves, and export just enough to balance that trade?

Although it might seem strange to be importing goods we could produce ourselves, such trade is entirely rational. Our decision to trade with other countries arises from the same considerations that motivate individuals to specialize in production: satisfying their remaining needs in the marketplace. Why don't you become self-sufficient, growing all your own food, building your own shelter, recording your own songs? Presumably because you've found that you can enjoy a much higher standard of living (and better music) by working at just one job then buying other goods in the marketplace. When you do so, you're no longer self-sufficient. Instead, you are *specializing* in production, relying on others to produce the array of goods and services you want. When countries trade goods and services, they are doing the same thing—*specializing* in production, then *trading* for other desired goods. Why do they do this? Because *specialization increases total output.*

To see how nations benefit from trade, we'll examine the production possibilities of two countries. We want to demonstrate that two countries that trade can together produce more output than they could in the absence of trade. If they can, *the gain from trade is increased world output and a higher standard of living in all trading countries.* This is the essential message of the *theory of comparative advantage.*

Production and Consumption without Trade

Consider the production and consumption possibilities of just two countries—say, the United States and France. For the sake of illustration, assume that both countries produce only two goods: bread and wine. Let's also set aside worries about the law of diminishing returns and the substitutability of resources, thus transforming the familiar **production possibilities** curve into a straight line, as in Figure 35.1.

The "curves" in Figure 35.1 suggest that the United States is capable of producing much more bread than France. With our greater abundance of labor, land, and other resources, we assume that the United States is capable of producing up to 100 zillion loaves of bread per year. To do so, we'd have to devote all our resources to that purpose. This capability is indicated by point *A* in Figure 35.1*a* and in row *A* of the accompanying production possibilities schedule. France (Figure 35.1*b*), on the other hand, confronts a *maximum* bread production of only 15 zillion loaves per year (point *G*) because it has little available land, less fuel, and fewer potential workers.

The capacities of the two countries for wine production are 50 zillion barrels for us (point *F*) and 60 zillion for France (point *L*), largely reflecting France's greater experience in tending vines. Both countries are also capable of producing alternative *combinations* of bread and wine, as evidenced by their respective production possibilities curves (points *A–F* for the United States and *G–L* for France).

In the absence of contact with the outside world, the production possibilities curve for each country would also define its **consumption possibilities**. Without imports, a country cannot consume more than it produces. Thus, the only immediate issue in a closed economy is which mix of output to choose—*what* to produce and consume— out of the domestic choices available.

Assume that Americans choose point *D* on their production possibilities curve, producing and consuming 40 zillion loaves of bread and 30 zillion barrels of wine. The French, on the other hand, prefer the mix of output represented by point *I* on their production possibilities curve. At that point they produce and consume 9 zillion loaves of bread and 24 zillion barrels of wine.

To assess the potential gain from trade, we must focus the *combined* output of the United States and France. In this case, total world output (points *D* and *I*) comes to 49 zillion loaves of bread and 54 zillion barrels of wine. What we want to know is whether world output would increase if France and the United States abandoned their isolation and started trading. Could either country, or both, consume more output by engaging in a little trade?

---

production possibilities: The alternative combinations of final goods and services that could be produced in a given time period with all available resources and technology.

consumption possibilities: The alternative combinations of goods and services that a country could consume in a given time period.

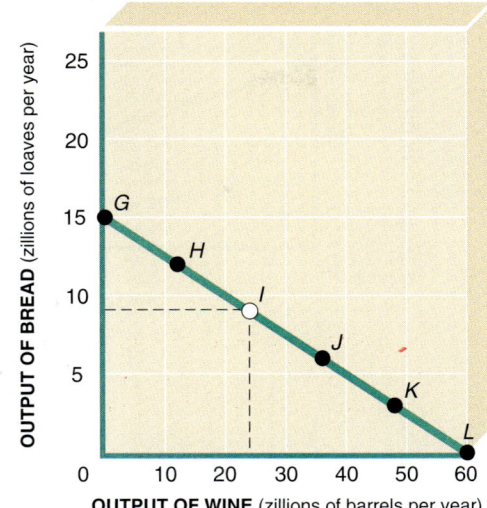

U.S. Production Possibilities				French Production Possibilities			
	Bread (zillions of loaves)	+	Wine (zillions of barrels)		Bread (zillions of loaves)	+	Wine (zillions of barrels)
A	100	+	0	G	15	+	0
B	80	+	10	H	12	+	12
C	60	+	20	I	9	+	24
D	40	+	30	J	6	+	36
E	20	+	40	K	3	+	48
F	0	+	50	L	0	+	60

FIGURE 35.1
Consumption Possibilities without Trade

In the absence of trade, a country's consumption possibilities are identical to its production possibilities. The assumed production possibilities of the United States and France are illustrated in the graphs and the corresponding schedules. Before entering into trade, the United States chose to produce and consume at point D, with 40 zillion loaves of bread and 30 zillion barrels of wine. France chose point I on its own production possibilities curve. By trading, each country hopes to increase its consumption beyond these levels.

Production and Consumption with Trade

Because both countries are saddled with limited production possibilities, trying to eke out a little extra wine and bread from this situation might not appear very promising. Such a conclusion is unwarranted, however. Take another look at the production possibilities confronting the United States, as reproduced in Figure 35.2. Suppose the United States were to produce at point C rather than point D. At point C we could produce 60 zillion loaves of bread and 20 zillion barrels of wine. That combination is clearly possible, since it lies on the production possibilities curve. We didn't choose that point earlier because we assumed the mix of output at point D was preferable. The mix of output at point C could be produced, however.

We could also change the mix of output in France. Assume that France moved from point I to point K, producing 48 zillion barrels of wine and only 3 zillion loaves of bread.

FIGURE 35.2
Consumption Possibilities with Trade

A country can increase its consumption possibilities through international trade. Each country alters its mix of domestic output to produce more of the good it produces best. As it does so, total world output increases, and each country enjoys more consumption. In this case, trade allows U.S. consumption to move from point D to point N. France moves from point I to point M.

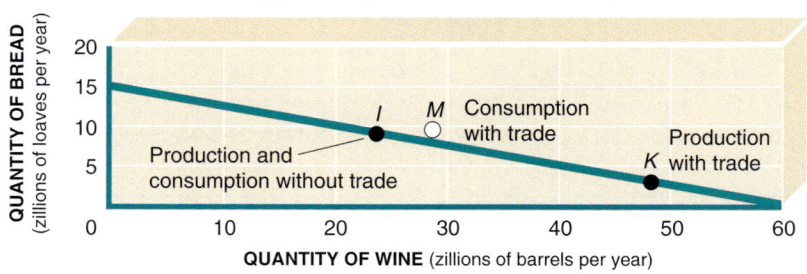

Two observations are now called for. The first is simply that output mixes have changed in each country. The second, and more interesting, is that total world output has increased. When the United States and France were at points D and I, their *combined* output consisted of

	Bread (zillions of loaves)	Wine (zillions of barrels)
United States (at point D)	40	30
France (at point I)	9	24
Total pretrade output	49	54

After moving along their respective production possibilities curves to points C and K, the combined world output becomes

	Bread (zillions of loaves)	Wine (zillions of barrels)
United States (at point C)	60	20
France (at point K)	3	48
Total output with trade	63	68

Total world output has increased by 14 zillion loaves of bread and 14 zillion barrels of wine. *Just by changing the mix of output in each country, we've increased total world output.* This additional output creates the potential for making both countries better off than they were in the absence of trade.

The United States and France weren't producing at points C and K before because they simply didn't want to *consume* those particular output combinations. Nevertheless, our discovery that points C and K allow us to produce *more* output suggests that everybody can consume more goods and services if we change the mix of output in each country. This is our first clue as to how specialization and trade can benefit an economy.

Suppose we're the first to discover the potential benefits from trade. Using Figure 35.2 as our guide, we suggest to the French that they move their mix of output from point *I* to point *K*. As an incentive for making such a move, we promise to give them 6 zillion loaves of bread in exchange for 20 zillion barrels of wine. This would leave them at point *M*, with as much bread to consume as they used to have, plus an extra 4 zillion barrels of wine. At point *I* they had 9 zillion loaves of bread and 24 zillion barrels of wine. At point *M* they can have 9 zillion loaves of bread and 28 zillion barrels of wine. Thus, by altering their mix of output (from point *I* to point *K*) and then trading (point *K* to point *M*), the French end up with more goods and services than they had in the beginning. Notice in particular that this new consumption possibility (point *M*) lies *outside* France's domestic production possibilities curve.

The French will be quite pleased with the extra output they get from trading. But where does this leave us? Does France's gain imply a loss for us? Or do we gain from trade as well?

As it turns out, *both* the United States and France gain by trading. The United States, too, ends up consuming a mix of output that lies outside our production possibilities curve.

Mutual Gains

Note that at point *C* we produce 60 zillion loaves of bread per year and 20 zillion barrels of wine. We then export 6 zillion loaves to France. This leaves us with 54 zillion loaves of bread to consume. In return for our exported bread, the French give us 20 zillion barrels of wine. These imports, plus our domestic production, permit us to *consume* 40 zillion barrels of wine. Hence, we end up consuming at point *N*, enjoying 54 zillion loaves of bread and 40 zillion barrels of wine. Thus, by first changing our mix of output (from point *D* to point *C*), then trading (point *C* to point *N*), we end up with 14 zillion more loaves of bread and 10 zillion more barrels of wine than we started with. International trade has made us better off, too.

Table 35.4 recaps the gains from trade for both countries. Notice that U.S. imports match French exports and vice versa. Also notice how the trade-facilitated consumption in each country exceeds no-trade levels.

There's no sleight of hand going on here; the gains from trade are due to specialization in production. When each country goes it alone, it's a prisoner of its own production possibilities curve; it must make production decisions on the basis of its own consumption desires. When international trade is permitted, however, each country can concentrate on the exploitation of its production capabilities. *Each country produces those goods it makes best and then trades with other countries to acquire the goods it desires to consume.*

TABLE 35.4
Gains from Trade

When nations specialize in production, they can export one good and import another and end up with more goods to consume than they had without trade. In this case, the United States specializes in bread production.

		Production and Consumption with Trade							Production and Consumption with No Trade
	Production	+	Imports	−	Exports	=	Consumption	
United States at...	Point C						Point N		Point D
Bread	60	+	0	−	6	=	54		40
Wine	20	+	20	−	0	=	40		30
France at...	Point K						Point M		Point I
Bread	3	+	6	−	0	=	9		9
Wine	48	+	0	−	20	=	28		24

The resultant specialization increases total world output. In the process, each country is able to escape the confines of its own production possibilities curve, to reach beyond it for a larger basket of consumption goods. *When a country engages in international trade, its consumption possibilities always exceed its production possibilities.* These enhanced consumption possibilities are emphasized by the positions of points N and M outside the production possibilities curves (Figure 35.2). If it weren't possible for countries to increase their consumption by trading, there'd be no incentive for trading, and thus no trade.

PURSUIT OF COMPARATIVE ADVANTAGE

Although international trade can make everyone better off, it's not so obvious which goods should be traded, or on what terms. In our previous illustration, the United States ended up trading bread for wine in terms that were decidedly favorable to us. Why did we export bread rather than wine, and how did we end up getting such a good deal?

Opportunity Costs

comparative advantage: The ability of a country to produce a specific good at a lower opportunity cost than its trading partners.

opportunity cost: The most desired goods or services that are forgone in order to obtain something else.

The decision to export bread is based on **comparative advantage**, that is, the *relative cost of producing different goods*. Recall that we can produce a maximum of 100 zillion loaves of bread per year or 50 zillion barrels of wine. Thus, the domestic **opportunity cost** of producing 100 zillion loaves of bread is the 50 zillion barrels of wine we forsake in order to devote our resources to bread production. In fact, at every point on the U.S. production possibilities curve (Figure 35.2a), the opportunity cost of a loaf of bread is $\frac{1}{2}$ barrel of wine. We're effectively paying half a barrel of wine to get a loaf of bread.

Although the cost of bread production in the United States might appear outrageous, even higher opportunity costs prevail in France. According to Figure 35.2b, the opportunity cost of producing a loaf of bread in France is a staggering 4 barrels of wine. To produce a loaf of bread, the French must use factors of production that could otherwise be used to produce 4 barrels of wine.

Comparative Advantage. A comparison of the opportunity costs prevailing in each country exposes the nature of comparative advantage. The United States has a comparative advantage in bread production because less wine has to be given up to produce bread in the United States than in France. In other words, the opportunity costs of bread production are lower in the United States than in France. *Comparative advantage refers to the relative (opportunity) costs of producing particular goods.*

A country should specialize in what it's *relatively* efficient at producing, that is, goods for which it has the lowest opportunity costs. In this case, the United States should produce bread because its opportunity cost ($\frac{1}{2}$ barrel of wine) is less than France's (4 barrels of wine). Were you the production manager for the whole world, you'd certainly want each country to exploit its relative abilities, thus maximizing world output. Each country can arrive at that same decision itself by comparing its own opportunity costs to those prevailing elsewhere. *World output, and thus the potential gains from trade, will be maximized when each country pursues its comparative advantage.* Each country does so by exporting goods that entail relatively low domestic opportunity costs and importing goods that involve relatively high domestic opportunity costs. That's the kind of situation depicted in Table 35.4.

Absolute Costs Don't Count

In assessing the nature of comparative advantage, notice that we needn't know anything about the actual costs involved in production. Have you seen any data suggesting how much labor, land, or capital is required to produce a loaf of bread in either France or the United States? For all you and I know, the French may be able to produce both a loaf of bread and a barrel of wine with fewer resources than we're using. Such an **absolute advantage** in production might exist because of their much longer experience in cultivating both grapes and wheat or simply because they have more talent.

We can envy such productivity, and even try to emulate it, but it shouldn't alter our production or trade decisions. All we really care about are *opportunity costs*—what we have to give up in order to get more of a desired good. If we can get a barrel of wine for less bread in trade than in production, we have a comparative advantage in producing bread. As long as we have a *comparative* advantage in bread production we should exploit it. It doesn't matter to us whether France could produce either good with fewer resources. For that matter, even if France had an absolute advantage in *both* goods, we'd still have a comparative advantage in bread production, as we've already confirmed. The absolute costs of production were omitted from the previous illustration because they were irrelevant.

To clarify the distinction between absolute advantage and comparative advantage, consider this example. When Charlie Osgood joined the Willamette Warriors football team, he was the fastest runner ever to play football in Willamette. He could also throw the ball farther than most people could see. In other words, he had an *absolute advantage* in both throwing and running. Charlie would have made the greatest quarterback or the greatest end ever to play football. *Would have*. The problem was that he could play only one position at a time. Thus, the Willamette coach had to play Charlie either as a quarterback or as an end. He reasoned that Charlie could throw only a bit farther than some of the other top quarterbacks but could far outdistance all the other ends. In other words, Charlie had a *comparative advantage* in running and was assigned to play as an end.

absolute advantage: The ability of a country to produce a specific good with fewer resources (per unit of output) than other countries.

TERMS OF TRADE

It definitely pays to pursue one's comparative advantage by specializing in production. It may not yet be clear, however, how we got such a good deal with France. We're clever traders, but beyond that, is there any way to determine the terms of trade, the quantity of good *A* that must be given up in exchange for good *B*? In our previous illustration, the terms of trade were very favorable to us; we exchanged only 6 zillion loaves of bread for 20 zillion barrels of wine (Table 35.4). The terms of trade were thus 6 loaves = 20 barrels.

The terms of trade with France were determined by our offer and France's ready acceptance. But why did France accept those terms? France was willing to accept our offer because the terms of trade permitted France to increase its wine consumption without giving up any bread consumption. Our offer of 6 loaves for 20 barrels was an improvement over France's domestic opportunity costs. France's domestic possibilities required it to give up 24 barrels of wine in order to produce 6 loaves of bread (see Figure 35.2b). Getting bread via trade was simply cheaper for France than producing bread at home. France ended up with an extra 4 zillion barrels of wine (Table 35.4).

Our first clue to the terms of trade, then, lies in each country's domestic opportunity costs. A country won't trade unless the terms of trade are superior to domestic opportunities. In our example, the opportunity cost of 1 barrel of wine in the United States is 2 loaves of bread. Accordingly, we won't export bread unless we get at least 1 barrel of wine in exchange for every 2 loaves of bread we ship overseas.

All countries want to gain from trade. Hence, we can predict that the terms of trade between any two countries will lie somewhere between their respective opportunity costs in production. That is, a loaf of bread in international trade will be worth at least $\frac{1}{2}$ barrel of wine (the U.S. opportunity cost) but no more than 4 barrels (the French opportunity cost). In our example, the terms of trade ended up at 1 loaf = 3.33 barrels (that is, at 6 loaves = 20 barrels). This represented a very large gain for the United States and a small gain for France. Figure 35.3 illustrates this outcome and several other possibilities.

Relatively little trade is subject to such direct negotiations between countries. More often than not, the decision to import or export a particular good is left up to the market decisions of individual consumers and producers.

terms of trade: The rate at which goods are exchanged; the amount of good *A* given up for good *B* in trade.

Limits to the Terms of Trade

The Role of Markets and Prices

FIGURE 35.3
Searching for the Terms of Trade

Assume the United States can produce 100 zillion loaves of bread per year (point A). If we reduce output to only 85 zillion loaves, we could move to point X. At point X we have 7.5 zillion barrels of wine and 85 zillion loaves of bread.

Trade increases consumption possibilities. If we continued to produce 100 zillion loaves of bread, we could trade 15 zillion loaves to France in exchange for as much as 60 zillion barrels of wine. This would leave us *producing* at point A but *consuming* at point Y. At point Y we have more wine and no less bread than we had at point X.

A country will end up on its consumption possibilities curve only if it gets *all* the gains from trade. It will remain on its production possibilities curve only if it gets *none* of the gains from trade. The terms of trade determine how the gains from trade are distributed, and thus at what point in the shaded area each country ends up.

Note: The kink in the consumption possibilities curve at point Y occurs because France is unable to produce more than 60 zillion barrels of wine.

Find out more from the International Trade Commission at dataweb.usitc.gov.

Individual consumers and producers aren't much impressed by such abstractions as comparative advantage. Market participants tend to focus on prices, always trying to allocate their resources in order to maximize profits or personal satisfaction. Consumers tend to buy the products that deliver the most utility per dollar of expenditure, while producers try to get the most output per dollar of cost. Everybody's looking for a bargain.

So what does this have to do with international trade? Well, suppose that Henri, an enterprising Frenchman, visited the United States before the advent of international trade. He observed that bread was relatively cheap while wine was relatively expensive—the opposite of the price relationship prevailing in France. These price comparisons brought to his mind the opportunity for making a fast franc. All he had to do was bring over some French wine and trade it in the United States for a large quantity of bread. Then he could return to France and exchange the bread for a greater quantity of wine. *Alors!* Were he to do this a few times, he'd amass substantial profits.

Henri's entrepreneurial exploits will not only enrich him but will also move each country toward its comparative advantage. The United States ends up exporting bread to France, and France ends up exporting wine to the United States, exactly as the theory of comparative advantage suggests. The activating agent isn't the Ministry of Trade and its 620 trained economists but simply one enterprising French trader. He's aided and encouraged, of course, by consumers and producers in each country. American consumers are happy to trade their bread for his wines. They thereby end up paying less for wine (in terms of bread) than they'd otherwise have to. In other words, the terms of trade Henri offers are more attractive than the prevailing (domestic) relative prices. On the other side of the Atlantic, Henri's welcome is equally warm. French consumers are able to get a better deal by trading their wine for his imported bread than by trading with the local bakers.

Even some producers are happy. The wheat farmers and bakers in the United States are eager to deal with Henri. He's willing to buy a lot of bread and even to pay a premium price for it. Indeed, bread production has become so profitable in the United States that a lot of people who used to grow and mash grapes are now growing wheat and kneading dough. This alters the mix of U.S. output in the direction of more bread, exactly as suggested in Figure 35.2a.

In France, the opposite kind of production shift is taking place. French wheat farmers are planting more grape vines so they can take advantage of Henri's generous purchases. Thus, Henri is able to lead each country in the direction of its comparative advantage while raking in a substantial profit for himself along the way.

Where the terms of trade and the volume of exports and imports end up depends partly on how good a trader Henri is. It will also depend on the behavior of the thousands of individual consumers and producers who participate in the market exchanges. In other words, trade flows depend on both the supply and the demand for bread and wine in each country. *The terms of trade, like the price of any good, depend on the willingness of market participants to buy or sell at various prices.* All we know for sure is that the terms of trade will end up somewhere between the limits set by each country's opportunity costs.

PROTECTIONIST PRESSURES

Although the potential gains from world trade are impressive, not everyone will smile at the Franco-American trade celebration. On the contrary, some people will be upset about the trade routes that Henri has established. They'll not only boycott the celebration but actively seek to discourage us from continuing to trade with France.

Consider, for example, the winegrowers in western New York. Do you think they're going to be happy about Henri's entrepreneurship? Americans can now buy wine more cheaply from France than they can from New York. Before long we may hear talk about unfair foreign competition or about the greater nutritional value of American grapes (see News). The New York winegrowers may also emphasize the importance of

Microeconomic Pressures

IN THE NEWS

Whining over Wine

A new type of wine bar has sprung up on Capitol Hill, and it's not likely to tickle the palate of a dedicated oenophile. California wine makers are hawking a bill that could slap higher tariffs on imported wine, and Congress shows some sign of becoming intoxicated with what the wine makers have to offer. First introduced last summer, the Wine Equity Act, as the measure is called, is already sponsored by 345 Congressmen and 60 Senators.

The wine makers aren't putting all their grapes into one bottle. Behind the scenes they have been making common cause with the American Grape Growers Alliance for Fair Trade, a group that represents many of the farmer cooperatives that supply domestic wineries. In a suit they filed with the Commerce Department and International Trade Commission in January, the growers complained that the Europeans, and particularly the Italians, are unfairly subsidizing the wine producers. If their suit is upheld, the ITC could impose stiff duties on the imports. The importers say there is no good evidence of substantial government subsidies.

Source: *Fortune*, February 20, 1984. © 1984 Time Inc. All rights reserved. www.fortune.com

Analysis: Although trade increases consumption possibilities, imports typically compete with a domestic industry. The affected industries will try to restrict imports in order to preserve their own jobs and incomes.

maintaining an adequate grape supply and a strong wine industry at home, just in case of terrorist attacks.

Import-Competing Industries. Joining with the growers will be the farm workers and the other producers and merchants whose livelihood depends on the New York wine industry. If they're clever enough, the growers will also get the governor of the state to join their demonstration. After all, the governor must recognize the needs of his people, and his people definitely don't include the wheat farmers in Kansas who are making a bundle from international trade. New York consumers are of course benefiting from lower wine prices, but they're unlikely to demonstrate over a few cents a bottle. On the other hand, those few extra pennies translate into millions of dollars for domestic wine producers.

The wheat farmers in France are no happier about international trade than are the winegrowers in the United States. They'd dearly love to sink all those boats bringing wheat from America, thereby protecting their own market position.

If we're to make sense of trade policies, then, we must recognize one central fact of life: Some producers have a vested interest in restricting international trade. In particular, workers and producers who compete with imported products—who work in import-competing industries—have an economic interest in restricting trade. This helps explain why GM, Ford, and Chrysler are unhappy about auto imports and why workers in Massachusetts want to end the importation of Italian shoes. It also explains why textile producers in South Carolina think China is behaving irresponsibly when it sells cotton shirts and dresses in the United States.

Export Industries. Although imports typically mean fewer jobs and less income for some domestic industries, exports represent increased jobs and income for other industries. Producers and workers in export industries gain from trade. Thus, on a microeconomic level there are identifiable gainers and losers from international trade. Trade not only alters the mix of output but also redistributes income from import-competing industries to export industries. This potential redistribution is the source of political and economic friction.

We must be careful to note, however, that the microeconomic gains from trade are greater than the microeconomic losses. It's not simply a question of robbing Peter to enrich Paul. We must remind ourselves that consumers in general enjoy a higher standard of living as a result of international trade. As we saw earlier, trade increases world efficiency and total output. Accordingly, we end up slicing up a larger pie rather than just reslicing the same old smaller pie.

The gains from trade will mean nothing to workers who end up with a smaller slice of the (larger) pie. It's important to remember, however, that the gains from trade are large enough to make everybody better off. Whether we actually choose to distribute the gains from trade in this way is a separate question, to which we shall return shortly. Note here, however, that trade restrictions designed to protect specific microeconomic interests reduce the total gains from trade. Trade restrictions leave us with a smaller pie to split up.

Additional Pressures

Import-competing industries are the principal obstacle to expanded international trade. Selfish micro interests aren't the only source of trade restrictions, however. Other arguments are also used to restrict trade.

National Security. The national security argument for trade restrictions is twofold. We can't depend on foreign suppliers to provide us with essential defense-related goods, it is said, because that would leave us vulnerable in time of war. The machine tool industry used this argument to protect itself from imports. In 1991, the Pentagon again sided with the toolmakers, citing the need for the United States to "gear up military production quickly in case of war," a contingency that couldn't be assured if weapons manufacturers relied on imported lathes, milling machines, and other tools. After the September 11, 2001, terrorist attacks on the World Trade Center and Pentagon, U.S. farmers convinced Congress to safeguard the nation's food supply with additional subsidies (see Chapter 29). The steel industry emphasized the importance of not depending on foreign suppliers.

Dumping. Another argument against free trade arises from the practice of **dumping**. Foreign producers "dump" their goods when they sell them in the United States at prices lower than those prevailing in their own country, perhaps even below the costs of production.

> **dumping:** The sale of goods in export markets at prices below domestic prices.

Dumping may be unfair to import-competing producers, but it isn't necessarily unwelcome to the rest of us. As long as foreign producers continue dumping, we're getting foreign products at low prices. How bad can that be? There's a legitimate worry, however. Foreign producers might hold prices down only until domestic producers are driven out of business. Then we might be compelled to pay the foreign producers higher prices for their products. In that case, dumping could consolidate market power and lead to monopoly-type pricing. The fear of dumping, then, is analogous to the fear of predatory pricing.

The potential costs of dumping are serious. It's not always easy to determine when dumping occurs, however. Those who compete with imports have an uncanny ability to associate any and all low prices with predatory dumping. Low import prices may also reflect greater productivity and lower costs. Lower import prices may also result from a drop in the value of the exporting country's currency. Thus, responsible policymakers must take special care to confirm that dumping has occurred before attempting to restrict trade. If it has, taxes or penalties can be imposed on the foreign producer. This is what Russia did when it concluded that Ukraine producers were dumping steel (see World View).

Infant Industries. Dumping threatens to damage already established domestic industries. Even normal import prices, however, may make it difficult or impossible for a new domestic industry to develop. Infant industries are often burdened with abnormally high startup costs. These high costs may arise from the need to train a whole workforce and the expenses of establishing new marketing channels. With time to grow, however, an infant industry might experience substantial cost reductions and establish

WORLD VIEW

Ukraine Faces Wide Range of Steel Dumping Probes

KIEV. A sharp increase in Ukraine's exports of steel over the past year is being threatened by a number of anti-dumping investigations opened recently in several of its main foreign markets.

Ukraine's competitors in Russia, Europe and North America say Ukraine's metals industry is selling below market cost in order to expand market share. Ukrainian officials are protesting, saying the suits threaten the fragile economic growth achieved last year for the first time since independence in 1991. Ukraine's non-precious metals exports, roughly 40 per cent of total exports, have increased from Dollars 2.1bn (Pounds 1.45bn) in the first half of 1999 to Dollars 3bn in the first half of 2000, the latest period for which there is data.

—Charles Clover

Source: *Financial Times* (London), March 29, 2001. Reprinted with permission. www.ft.com

Analysis: *Dumping* means that a foreign producer is selling exports at prices below cost or below prices in the home market. Dumping puts import-competing industries at a competitive disadvantage.

a comparative advantage. When this is the case, trade restrictions might help nurture an industry in its infancy. Trade restrictions are justified, however, only if there's tangible evidence that the industry can develop a comparative advantage reasonably quickly.

Improving the Terms of Trade. A final argument for restricting trade rests on how the gains from trade are distributed. As we observed, the distribution of the gains from trade depends on the terms of trade. If we were to buy fewer imports, foreign producers might lower their prices. If that happened, the terms of trade would move in our favor, and we'd end up with a larger share of the gains from trade.

One way to bring about this sequence of events is to put restrictions on imports, making it more difficult or expensive for Americans to buy foreign products. Such restrictions will reduce the volume of imports, thereby inducing foreign producers to lower their prices. Unfortunately, this strategy can easily backfire. Retaliatory restrictions on imports, each designed to improve the terms of trade, will ultimately eliminate all trade and therewith all the gains people were competing for in the first place.

BARRIERS TO TRADE

The microeconomic losses associated with imports give rise to a constant clamor for trade restrictions. People whose jobs and incomes are threatened by international trade tend to organize quickly and air their grievances. The News depicts the efforts of farmers in Montana and North Dakota to limit imports of Canadian wheat and livestock. They hope to convince Congress to impose restrictions on imports. More often than not, Congress grants the wishes of these well-organized and well-financed special interests.

Embargoes

embargo: A prohibition on exports or imports.

The surefire way to restrict trade is simply to eliminate it. To do so, a country need only impose an embargo on exports or imports, or both. An **embargo** is nothing more than a prohibition against trading particular goods.

In 1951, Senator Joseph McCarthy convinced the U.S. Senate to impose an embargo on Soviet mink, fox, and five other furs. He argued that such imports helped finance world communism. Senator McCarthy also represented the state of Wisconsin, where most U.S. minks are raised. The Reagan administration tried to end the fur embargo in 1987 but met with stiff congressional opposition. By then, U.S. mink ranchers had developed a $120 million per year industry.

IN THE NEWS

Farmers Stage Protests over Import of Products

Farmers claiming that imports of Canadian grain and other agricultural products are depressing U.S. prices threatened on Tuesday more blockades at border crossings unless the U.S. government acts to slow the flow of goods.

Farmers also want Canadian wheat and livestock tested for diseases and additives that are banned here.

Blockades and other protests have appeared at various border crossings in North Dakota and Montana for several days. In Montana, 20 long-haul truckers were ticketed Monday, the first day of a state crackdown on border inspections. And farmers in North Dakota dumped grain on U.S. Highway 281, stopping truck traffic for eight hours.

"We've got an oversupply of wheat, hogs and cattle already," said Curt Trulson, a farmer in Ross, N.D. "We don't need any more foreign commodities."

Source: *USA Today*, September 23, 1998. © 1998, USA Today. Reprinted with permission. www.usatoday.com

Analysis: Import-competing industries cite lots of reasons for restricting trade. Their primary concern, however, is to protect their own jobs and profits.

The United States has also maintained an embargo on Cuban goods since 1959, when Fidel Castro took power there. This embargo severely damaged Cuba's sugar industry and deprived American smokers of the famed Havana cigars. It also fostered the development of U.S. sugar beet and tobacco farmers, who now have a vested interest in maintaining the embargo.

A more frequent trade restriction is a **tariff,** a special tax imposed on imported goods. Tariffs, also called *customs duties,* were once the principal source of revenue for governments. In the eighteenth century, tariffs on tea, glass, wine, lead, and paper were imposed on the American colonies to provide extra revenue for the British government. The tariff on tea led to the Boston Tea Party in 1773 and gave added momentum to the American independence movement. In modern times, tariffs have been used primarily as a means to protect specific industries from import competition. The current U.S. tariff code specifies tariffs on over 10,000 different products—nearly 50 percent of all U.S. imports. Although the average tariff is only 5 percent, individual tariffs vary widely. The tariff on cars, for example, is only 2.5 percent, while cotton sweaters confront a 17.8 percent tariff.

The attraction of tariffs to import-competing industries should be obvious. *A tariff on imported goods makes them more expensive to domestic consumers and thus less competitive with domestically produced goods.* Among familiar tariffs in effect in 2001 were $0.50 per gallon on Scotch whiskey and 76 cents per gallon on imported champagne. These tariffs made American-produced spirits look relatively cheap and thus contributed to higher sales and profits for domestic distillers and grape growers. In the same manner, imported baby clothes are taxed at 12.5 percent, maple sugar at 9.4 percent, golf shoes at 8.5 percent, and imported sailboats at 1.5 percent. In each case, domestic producers in import-competing industries gain. The losers are domestic consumers, who end up paying higher prices. The tariff on orange juice, for example, raises the price of drinking orange juice by $525 million a year. Tariffs also hurt foreign producers, who lose business, and world efficiency, as trade is reduced.

"Beggar Thy Neighbor." Microeconomic interests aren't the only source of pressure for tariff protection. Imports represent leakage from the domestic circular flow and a potential loss of jobs at home. From this perspective, the curtailment of imports looks like an easy solution to the problem of domestic unemployment. Just get people to "buy American" instead of buying imported products, so the argument goes, and domestic output and employment will surely expand. Congressman Willis Hawley used this argument in 1930. He assured his colleagues that higher tariffs would "bring about the growth and development in this country that has followed every other tariff bill, bringing as it does a new prosperity in which all people, in all sections, will increase their comforts, their enjoyment, and their happiness."[1] Congress responded by passing the Smoot-Hawley Tariff Act of 1930, which raised tariffs to an average of nearly 60 percent, effectively cutting off most imports.

Tariffs designed to expand domestic employment are more likely to fail than to succeed. If a tariff wall does stem the flow of imports, it effectively transfers the unemployment problem to other countries, a phenomenon often referred to as "beggar thy neighbor." The resultant loss of business in other countries leaves them less able to purchase our exports. The imported unemployment also creates intense political pressures for retaliatory action. That's exactly what happened in the 1930s. Other countries erected trade barriers to compensate for the effects of the Smoot-Hawley tariff. World trade subsequently fell from $60 billion in 1928 to a mere $25 billion in 1938. This trade contraction increased the severity of the Great Depression (see World View).

Tariffs reduce the flow of imports by raising import prices. The same outcome can be attained more directly by imposing import **quotas,** numerical restrictions on the

Tariffs

tariff: A tax (duty) imposed on imported goods.

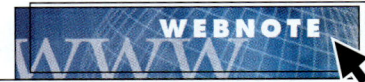

The tariff schedule for imported products is available online from the U.S. Customs Service. Go to www.customs.ustreas.gov, and click on "Importing and Exporting," then "Rulings & Regulations."

Quotas

---
[1]*New York Times,* June 15, 1930, p. 25.

WORLD VIEW

"Beggar-Thy-Neighbor" Policies in the 1930s

President Herbert Hoover, ignoring the pleas of 1,028 economists to veto it, signed the Smoot-Hawley Tariff Act on June 17, 1930. It was a hollow celebration. The day before, anticipating the signing, the stock market suffered its worst collapse since November 1929, and the law quickly helped push the Great Depression deeper.

The new tariffs, which by 1932 rose to an all-time high of 59 percent of the average value of imports (today it's 5 percent), were designed to save American jobs by restricting foreign competition. Economists warned that angry nations would retaliate, and they did.

- Spain passed the Wais tariff in July in reaction to U.S. tariffs on grapes, oranges, cork, and onions.
- Switzerland, objecting to new U.S. tariffs on watches, embroideries, and shoes, boycotted American exports.
- Italy retaliated against tariffs on hats and olive oil with high tariffs on U.S. and French automobiles in June 1930.
- Canada reacted to high duties on many food products, logs, and timber by raising tariffs threefold in August 1932.
- Australia, Cuba, France, Mexico, and New Zealand also joined in the tariff wars.

From 1930 to 1931 U.S. imports dropped 29 percent, but U.S. exports fell even more, 33 percent, and continued their collapse to a modern-day low of $2.4 billion in 1933. World trade contracted by similar proportions, spreading unemployment around the globe.

In 1934 the U.S. Congress passed the Reciprocal Trade Agreements Act to empower the president to reduce tariffs by half the 1930 rates in return for like cuts in foreign duties on U.S. goods. The "beggar-thy-neighbor" policy was dead. Since then, the nations of the world have been reducing tariffs and other trade barriers.

Source: World Bank, *World Development Report 1987;* and *The Wall Street Journal,* April 28, 1989. www.worldbank.org; www.wsj.com

Analysis: Tariffs inflict harm on foreign producers. If foreign countries retaliate with tariffs of their own, world trade will shrink and unemployment will increase in all countries.

---

quota: A limit on the quantity of a good that may be imported in a given time period.

quantity of a particular good that may be imported. The United States limits the quantity of ice cream imported from Jamaica to 950 gallons a year. Only 1.4 million kilograms of Australian cheddar cheese and no more than 7,730 tons of Haitian sugar can be imported. Textile quotas are imposed on every country that wants to ship textiles to the U.S. market. According to the U.S. Department of State, approximately 12 percent of our imports are subject to import quotas.

Comparative Effects

Quotas, like all barriers to trade, reduce world efficiency and invite retaliatory action. Moreover, their impact can be even more damaging than tariffs. To see this, we may compare market outcomes in four different contexts: no trade, free trade, tariff-restricted trade, and quota-restricted trade.

No-Trade Equilibrium. Figure 35.4a depicts the supply-and-demand relationships that would prevail in an economy that imposed a trade *embargo* on foreign textiles. In this situation, the equilibrium price of textiles is completely determined by domestic demand and supply curves. The no-trade equilibrium price is p_1, and the quantity of textiles consumed is q_1.

equilibrium price: The price at which the quantity of a good demanded in a given time period equals the quantity supplied.

Free-Trade Equilibrium. Suppose now that the embargo is lifted. The immediate effect of this decision will be a rightward shift of the market supply curve, as foreign supplies are added to domestic supplies (Figure 35.4b). If an unlimited quantity of textiles can be bought in world markets at a price of p_2, the new supply curve will look like S_2 (infinitely elastic at p_2). The new supply curve (S_2) intersects the old demand curve (D_1) at a new equilibrium price of p_2 and an expanded consumption of q_2. At this new equilibrium, domestic producers are supplying the quantity q_d while foreign producers are supplying the rest ($q_2 - q_d$). Comparing the new equilibrium to the old one, we see that *free trade results in reduced prices and increased consumption.*

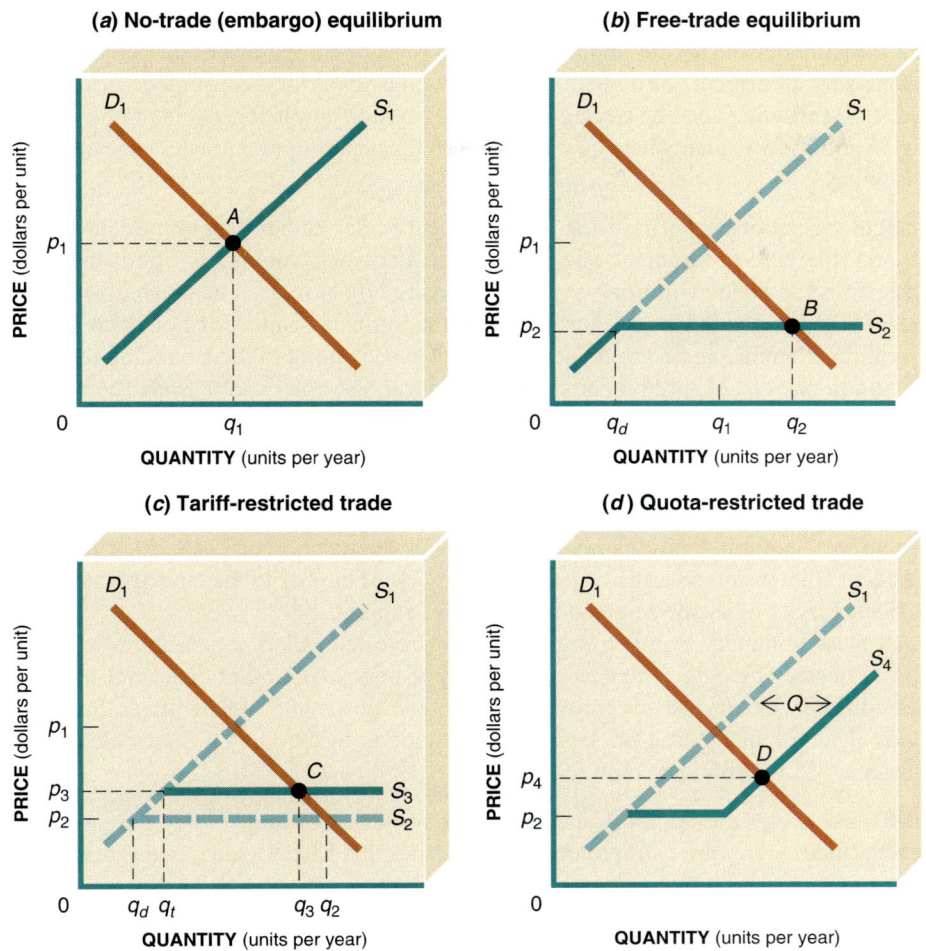

FIGURE 35.4
The Impact of Trade Restrictions
In the *absence of trade*, the domestic price and sales of a good will be determined by domestic supply and demand curves (point A in part a). Once trade is permitted, the market supply curve will be altered by the availability of imports. With *free trade* and unlimited availability of imports at price p_2, a new market equilibrium will be established at world prices (point B).

Tariffs raise domestic prices and reduce the quantity sold (point C). *Quotas* put an absolute limit on imported sales and thus give domestic producers a great opportunity to raise the market price (point D).

Domestic textile producers are unhappy, of course, with their foreign competition. In the absence of trade, the domestic producers would sell more output (q_1) and get higher prices (p_1). Once trade is opened up, the willingness of foreign producers to sell unlimited quantities of textiles at the price p_2 puts a lid on domestic prices.

Tariff-Restricted Trade. Figure 35.4c illustrates what would happen to prices and sales if the United Textile Producers were successful in persuading the government to impose a tariff. Assume that the tariff raises imported textile prices from p_2 to p_3, making it more difficult for foreign producers to undersell domestic producers. Domestic production expands from q_d to q_1, imports are reduced from $q_2 - q_d$ to $q_3 - q_t$, and the market price of textiles rises. Domestic textile producers are clearly better off, whereas consumers and foreign producers are worse off. In addition, the U.S. Treasury will collect increased tariff revenues.

Quota-Restricted Trade. Now consider the impact of a textile *quota*. Suppose we eliminate tariffs but decree that imports can't exceed the quantity Q. Because the quantity of imports can never exceed Q, the supply curve is effectively shifted to the right by that amount. The new curve S_4 (Figure 35.4d) indicates that no imports will occur below the world price p_2 and above that price the quantity Q will be imported. Thus, the *domestic* demand curve determines subsequent prices. Foreign producers are precluded from selling greater quantities as prices rise further. This outcome is in marked contrast to that of tariff-restricted trade (Figure 35.4c), which at least permits foreign producers to respond to rising prices. Accordingly, *quotas are a greater threat to* *competition than tariffs, because quotas preclude additional imports at any price.* The actual quotas on textile imports raise the prices of shirts, towels, and other textile products by 58 percent. As a result, a $10 shirt ends up costing consumers $15.80. All told, U.S. consumers end up paying an extra $25 billion a year for textile products. The next World View explains how quotas also prop up sugar prices and who benefits from that policy.

Voluntary Restraint Agreements

voluntary restraint agreement (VRA): An agreement to reduce the volume of trade in a specific good; a voluntary quota.

A slight variant of quotas has been used in recent years. Rather than impose quotas on imports, the U.S. government asks foreign producers to "voluntarily" limit their exports. These so-called **voluntary restraint agreements** have been negotiated with producers in Japan, South Korea, Taiwan, China, the European Union, and other countries. Korea, for example, agreed to reduce its annual shoe exports to the United States from 44 million pairs to 33 million pairs. Taiwan reduced its shoe exports from 156 million pairs to 122 million pairs per year. In 1989, China agreed to slow its exports of clothing, limiting its sales growth to 3 percent a year. For their part, the Japanese agreed to reduce sales of color TV sets in the United States from 2.8 million to 1.75 million per year. In 1989, President George H. Bush extended voluntary restraint agreements on foreign steel exports, limiting imported steel to 18.4 percent of total U.S. sales. In 1996, President Clinton forced Canada to limit its exports of lumber to the United States, and in 1999, Russia reluctantly agreed to limit steel exports.

All these voluntary export restraints, as they're often called, represent an informal type of quota. The only difference is that they're negotiated rather than imposed. But these differences are lost on consumers, who end up paying higher prices for these goods. The voluntary limit on Japanese auto exports to the United States alone cost consumers $15.7 billion in only four years.

Nontariff Barriers

Tariffs and quotas are the most visible barriers to trade, but they're only the tip of the iceberg. Indeed, the variety of protectionist measures that have been devised is testimony

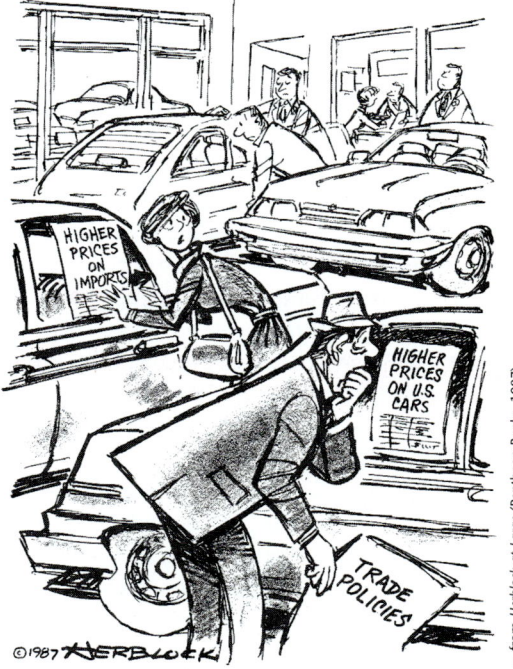

Analysis: Trade restrictions that protect import-competing industries also raise consumer prices.

WORLD VIEW

Sugar Quota a Sour Deal

Very little sugar cane is grown in the United States. Most domestically produced sugar comes from beet sugar. The rest of our sugar is imported from tropical countries.

The 12,000 domestic beet sugar growers have convinced Congress to protect their industry to ensure a secure supply of sugar in the event of a war. The U.S. Department of Agriculture guarantees the beet sugar growers a minimum of 18 cents per pound for their output. To keep prices at that level, the U.S. Congress limits sugar imports to 1.6 million tons a year. As a result, domestic sugar prices are typically twice as high as world sugar prices. In 2001, the price of sugar in U.S. markets was 22 cents per pound, versus only 10 cents in world markets. This price difference cost American consumers nearly $2 billion in 2001 alone. Foreign producers and workers who were excluded from the U.S. market also lost out. Between 1983 and 1990, over 400,000 workers in Caribbean nations lost their jobs as a result of shrinking U.S. sugar quotas.

Who benefits from these sugar quotas? The list includes

- The 12,000 American beet sugar farmers who produce over nine tons of sugar per year.
- Producers of sugar substitutes (such as corn syrups).
- Those nations and producers that get a share of the U.S. quota.
- Former and current members of Congress who receive millions of dollars in campaign contributions for perpetuating the sugar quota system.

Analysis: Import quotas preclude increased foreign competition when domestic prices rise. Protected domestic producers enjoy higher prices and profits while consumers pay higher prices.

---

to the ingenuity of the human mind. At the turn of the century, the Germans were committed to a most-favored-nation policy, a policy of extending equal treatment to all trading partners. The Germans, however, wanted to lower the tariff on cattle imports from Denmark without extending the same break to Switzerland. Such a preferential tariff would have violated the most-favored-nation policy. Accordingly, the Germans created a new and higher tariff on "brown and dappled cows reared at a level of at least 300 meters above sea level and passing at least one month in every summer at an altitude of at least 800 meters." The new tariff was, of course, applied equally to all countries. But Danish cows never climb that high, so they weren't burdened with the new tariff.

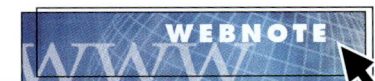

WEBNOTE

Differing views on the cost of sugar quotas are offered by the Sugar Alliance at www.sugar-alliance.org and the Coalition for Sugar Reform at www.sugar-reform.org.

WORLD VIEW

House Acts to Block Mexican Trucks

Move Is Setback for Bush's Trade Plans

The House voted last night to bar Mexican trucks from operating in the United States, rejecting President Bush's efforts to increase unfettered U.S.-Mexican trade by opening the country to Mexican carriers.

The surprisingly lopsided vote of 285 to 143, which came as the House approved a $59.1 billion transportation spending bill, would block the administration from going ahead with plans to allow Mexican trucks to ship goods to and from any point in the United States.

The truck access, which was part of the 1993 North American Free Trade Agreement, has been stalled for years. But the Bush administration, reflecting the president's emphasis on improving U.S.-Mexican relations, issued rules in May governing the circumstances under which Mexican trucks would be allowed onto U.S. roads, beginning next January.

The amendment to block the department from going ahead with the plan was backed by a coalition of Democrats and Republicans allied with organized labor. The Teamsters had lobbied aggressively in favor of the amendment.

—Juliet Eilperin

Source: *Washington Post*, June 27, 2001. © 2001 The Washington Post. Reprinted with permission. www.washingtonpost.com

Analysis: Nontariff barriers like extraordinary safety requirements on Mexican trucks limit import competition.

With the decline in tariffs over the last 20 years, nontariff barriers have increased. The United States uses product standards, licensing restrictions, restrictive procurement practices, and other nontariff barriers to restrict roughly 15 percent of imports. In 1999–2000, the European Union banned imports of U.S. beef, arguing that the use of hormones on U.S. ranches created a health hazard for European consumers. Although both the U.S. government and the World Trade Organization disputed that claim, the ban was a highly effective nontariff trade barrier. The United States responded by slapping 100 percent tariffs on dozens of European products. In 2001, the U.S. Congress blocked Mexican trucks from open access to U.S. highways (see the previous World View). Although the safety of Mexican trucks was spotlighted, the underlying motive was to limit competition in the multibillion-dollar U.S. transport services market.

THE ECONOMY TOMORROW

An Increasingly Global Market

Proponents of free trade and representatives of special interests that profit from trade protection are in constant conflict. But most of the time the trade-policy deck seems stacked in favor of the special interests. Because the interests of import-competing firms and workers are highly concentrated, they're quick to mobilize politically. By contrast, the benefits of freer trade are less direct and spread over millions of consumers. As a consequence, the beneficiaries of freer trade are less likely to monitor trade policy—much less lobby actively to change it. Hence, the political odds favor the spread of trade barriers.

Multilateral Trade Pacts

Despite these odds, the long-term trend is toward *lowering* trade barriers, thereby increasing global competition. Two forces encourage this trend. The principal barrier to protectionist policies is worldwide recognition of the gains from freer trade. Since world nations now understand that trade barriers are ultimately self-defeating, they're more willing to rise above the din of protectionist cries and dismantle trade barriers. They diffuse political opposition by creating across-the-board trade pacts that seem to spread the pain (and gain) from freer trade across a broad swath of industries. Such pacts also incorporate multiyear timetables that give affected industries time to adjust.

The opposition of import-competing industries to these multilateral, multiyear trade pacts is countered by a second force: the interests of *export*-oriented industries and other multilateral firms. Barriers to auto imports from Japan may keep out cars produced by General Motors in that country. Tariffs on imported steel raise product costs for U.S.-based auto producers. Foreign retaliation to our trade barriers may hurt our own exports. Increasing awareness of such damage has created a political climate for freer trade.

Global Pacts: GATT and WTO

The granddaddy of the multilateral, multiyear free-trade pacts was the 1947 *General Agreement on Tariffs and Trade (GATT)*. Twenty-three nations pledged to reduce trade barriers and give all GATT nations equal access to their domestic markets.

Since the first GATT pact, seven more "rounds" of negotiations have expanded the scope of GATT: 117 nations signed the 1994 pact. As a result of these GATT pacts, average tariff rates in developed countries have fallen from 40 percent in 1948 to less than 4 percent today.

WTO. The 1994 GATT pact also created the *World Trade Organization (WTO)* to enforce free-trade rules. If a nation feels its exports are being unfairly excluded from another country's market, it can file a complaint with the WTO. This is exactly what the United States did when the European Union (EU) banned U.S. beef imports. The WTO ruled in favor of the United States. When the EU failed to lift its import ban, the WTO authorized the United States to impose retaliatory tariffs on European exports.

In effect, the WTO is now the world's trade police force. It is empowered to cite nations that violate trade agreements and even to impose remedial action when violations persist. Why do sovereign nations give the WTO such power? Because they are all convinced that free trade is the surest route to GDP growth.

WTO Protests. Although freer trade clearly boosts economic growth, some people say that it does more harm than good. Environmentalists question the very desirability of continued economic growth. They worry about the depletion of resources, congestion and pollution, and the social friction that growth often promotes. Labor organizations worry that global competition will depress wages and working conditions. And many Third World nations are concerned about playing by trade rules that always seem to benefit rich nations (e.g., copyright protection, import protection).

These varied concerns hit the streets when the WTO initiated the latest round of trade negotiations in November 1999. Thousands of protestors showed up in Seattle to demand that the WTO pay more attention to social goals other than GDP growth. As the multyear Millennium Round continues, negotiators are trying to find ways to continue dismantling trade barriers while paying more heed to broader social concerns.

Regional Pacts: NAFTA and EU

Groups of nations have moved even faster toward open markets by developing regional trade pacts. In December 1992, the United States, Canada, and Mexico signed the *North American Free Trade Agreement (NAFTA)*, a 1,000-page document covering more than 9,000 products. The ultimate goal of NAFTA is to eliminate all trade barriers between these three countries. At the time of signing, intraregional tariffs averaged 11 percent in Mexico, 5 percent in Canada, and 4 percent in the United States. NAFTA requires that all tariffs between the three countries be eliminated by 2007. The pact also requires the elimination of specific nontariff barriers.

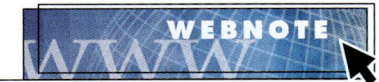

To see how detailed a trade pact can be, access the NAFTA pact at www.nafta-sec-alena.org.

The NAFTA-initiated reduction in trade barriers substantially increased trade flows between Mexico, Canada, and the United States. It also prompted a wave of foreign investment in Mexico, where both cheap labor and NAFTA access were available. Overall, NAFTA accelerated economic growth and reduced inflationary pressures in

IN THE NEWS

NAFTA Reallocates Labor: Comparative Advantage at Work

More Jobs in These Industries		but . . .	Few Jobs in These Industries	
Agriculture	+10,600		Construction	−12,800
Metal products	+6,100		Medicine	−6,000
Electrical appliances	+5,200		Apparel	−5,900
Business services	+5,000		Lumber	−1,200
Motor vehicles	+5,000		Furniture	−400

Source: Congressional Budget Office.

The lowering of trade barriers between Mexico and the United States is changing the mix of output in both countries. New export opportunities create jobs in some industries while increased imports eliminate jobs in other industries. (Estimated gains and losses are during the first five years of NAFTA.)

Analysis: The specialization encouraged by free trade creates new jobs in export but reduces employment in import-competing industries. In the process, total world output increases.

all three nations. Some industries (like construction and apparel) suffered from the freer trade, but others (like trucking, farming, and finance) reaped huge gains (see News).

The *European Union* is another regional pact, but one that virtually eliminates national boundaries between 15 countries. The EU not only eliminates trade barriers but also enhances full intercountry mobility of workers and capital. In 1999, 12 of the EU nations also created a new currency (the euro) that has replaced the German mark, the French franc, and other national currencies. In effect, Europe has become one large, unified market. As trade barriers continue to fall around the world, the global marketplace is likely to become more like an open bazaar as well. The resulting increase in competition should spur efficiency and growth in the economy tomorrow.

SUMMARY

- International trade permits each country to specialize in areas of relative efficiency, increasing world output. For each country, the gains from trade are reflected in consumption possibilities that exceed production possibilities.
- One way to determine where comparative advantage lies is to compare the quantity of good A that must be given up in order to get a given quantity of good B from domestic production. If the same quantity of B can be obtained for less A by engaging in world trade, we have a comparative advantage in the production of good A. Comparative advantage rests on a comparison of relative opportunity costs.
- The terms of trade—the rate at which goods are exchanged—are subject to the forces of international supply and demand. The terms of trade will lie somewhere between the opportunity costs of the trading partners. The terms of trade determine how the gains from trade are shared.
- Resistance to trade emanates from workers and firms that must compete with imports. Even though the country as a whole stands to benefit from trade, these individuals and companies may lose jobs and incomes in the process.
- Trade barriers take many forms. Embargoes are outright prohibitions against import or export of particular goods. Quotas limit the quantity of a good imported or exported. Tariffs discourage imports by making them more expensive. Other nontariff barriers make trade too costly or time-consuming.
- The World Trade Organization (WTO) seeks to reduce worldwide trade barriers and enforce trade rules. Regional accords such as the European Union (EU) and North American Free Trade Agreement (NAFTA) pursue similar objectives among fewer countries.

Key Terms

imports
exports
trade deficit
trade surplus
production possibilities
consumption possibilities

comparative advantage
opportunity cost
absolute advantage
terms of trade
dumping
embargo

tariff
quota
equilibrium price
voluntary restraint
   agreement (VRA)

Questions for Discussion

1. Suppose a lawyer can type faster than any secretary. Should the lawyer do her own typing? Can you demonstrate the validity of your answer?
2. What would be the effects of a law requiring bilateral trade balances?
3. If a nation exported much of its output but imported little, would it be better or worse off? How about the reverse, that is, exporting little but importing a lot?
4. How does international trade restrain the price behavior of domestic firms?
5. Suppose we refused to sell goods to any country that reduced or halted its exports to us. Who would benefit and who would lose from such retaliation? Can you suggest alternative ways to ensure import supplies?
6. Domestic producers often base their claim for import protection on the fact that workers in country X are

paid substandard wages. Is this a valid argument for protection?
7. Based on the News on page 749, how do U.S. furniture manufacturers feel about NAFTA? How about farmers?
8. Who would gain or lose from the proposed Wine Equity Act? (See the News, page 739.)
9. What are the benefits of sugar quotas and auto VRAs? (See World View, page 747.) Could these goals be achieved more efficiently in other ways?
10. Who gains and who loses from restrictions on the access of Mexican trucks to U.S. markets? (See World View, page 747.)

Web Activities

1. Log on to www.wto.org/english/res_e/statis_e/chp_1_e.pdf, and find the table that lists the leading exporters and importers of world trade. List the top 10 exporters and importers in world merchandise trade, including the value and share of world trade, for the most recent year reported.
2. Log on to www.census.gov/indicator/www/ustrade.html. What is the current balance of trade for the United States? Has this balance been increasing or decreasing?
3. Does a tariff exist on the clothing you buy? Log on to dataweb.usitc.gov/scripts/tariff2001.asp to find out. Type "clothing" as the category search word. Then access "worn clothing" and "other worn apparel." What is the value of the ad valorem tariff for nations that have most-favored-nation status with the U.S.? What is the rate for nations without NTR status? In the United States, who gains and who loses from these tariffs? Explain.

THE ACCOMPANYING STUDENT PROBLEM SET CONTAINS NUMERICAL AND GRAPHING PROBLEMS FOR THIS CHAPTER

CHAPTER 36

International Finance

A sudden change in the value of the baht sparked an "Asian crisis" that sent shock waves all the way to Iowa hog farms. But many people there didn't even know what a baht was!

The Thai currency set off a global crisis in 1997–98 that threw millions of people out of work, deprived millions more of basic necessities, sent world stock markets plunging, and destabilized governments. It also sent hog prices to a 40-year low, devastating farmers in the American Midwest. Besides not knowing that the baht is the national currency of Thailand, most people affected by the 1997–98 crisis didn't have a clue as to how a change in the value of another currency could possibly affect midwestern hog prices.

This chapter examines why and how changes in the value of national currencies can have such debilitating effects worldwide. In so doing, we focus on the following questions:

- What determines the value of one country's money as compared to the value of another's?
- What causes the international value of currencies to change?
- Should governments intervene to limit currency fluctuations?

EXCHANGE RATES: THE GLOBAL LINK

As we saw in Chapter 35, the United States exports and imports a staggering volume of goods and services. Although we trade with nearly 200 nations around the world, we seldom give much thought to where imports come from and much less to how we acquire them. Most of the time, all we want to know is which products are available and at what price.

Suppose you want to buy a Magnavox DVD player. You don't have to know that Magnavox players are produced by the Dutch company Philips Electronics. And you certainly don't have to fly to the Netherlands to pick it up. All you have to do is drive to the nearest electronics store; or you can just "click and buy" at the Internet's virtual mall.

But you may wonder how the purchase of an imported product was so simple. Dutch companies sell their products in euros, the new currency of Europe. But you purchase the DVD player in dollars. How is such an exchange possible?

There's a chain of distributions between your dollar purchase in the United States and the euro-denominated sale in the Netherlands. Somewhere along that chain someone has to convert your dollars into euros. The critical question for everybody concerned is how many euros we can get for our dollars—that is, what the **exchange rate** is. If we can get two euros for every dollar, the exchange rate is 2 euros = 1 dollar. Alternatively, we could note that the price of a euro is 50 U.S. cents when the exchange rate is 2 to 1. Thus, *an exchange rate is the price of one currency in terms of another.*

> **exchange rate:** The price of one country's currency expressed in terms of another's; the domestic price of a foreign currency.

FOREIGN-EXCHANGE MARKETS

Most exchange rates are determined in foreign-exchange markets. Stop thinking of money as some sort of magical substance, and instead view it as a useful commodity that can facilitate market exchanges. From that perspective, an exchange rate—the price of money—is subject to the same influences that determine all market prices: demand and supply.

The Demand for Dollars

When Daimler-Benz bought Chrysler in 1998, it paid $36 billion. When the Sony Corporation bought Columbia Pictures, it also needed dollars—over 3 billion of them! In both cases, the objective of the foreign investor was to acquire an American business. To attain their objectives, however, the buyers first had to buy *dollars*. The German and Japanese buyers had to exchange their own currency for American dollars.

Canadian tourists also need American dollars. Few American restaurants or hotels will accept Canadian currency as payment for goods and services; they want to be paid in U.S. dollars. Accordingly, Canadian tourists must buy American dollars if they want to see the United States.

Europeans love iMac computers. The Apple Corporation, however, wants to be paid in U.S. dollars. Hence, European consumers must exchange their currencies for U.S. dollars if they want an iMac. Individual consumers can spend euros at their local computer store. When they do so, however, they're initiating a series of market transactions that will end when Apple Corporation gets paid in U.S. dollars. In this case, some intermediary exchanges the European currency for American dollars.

Some foreign investors also buy U.S. dollars for speculative purposes. When the ruble collapsed, Russians feared that the value of the ruble would drop further and preferred to hold U.S. dollars. Barclay's Bank also speculates in dollars on occasions when it fears that the value of the British pound will drop.

All these motivations give rise to a demand for U.S. dollars. Specifically, *the market demand for U.S. dollars originates in*

- *Foreign demand for American exports.*
- *Foreign demand for American investments.*
- *Speculation.*

Governments may also create a demand for dollars through currency *swaps* and other activities.

The Supply of Dollars

The *supply* of dollars arises from similar sources. On the supply side, however, it's Americans who initiate most of the exchanges. Suppose you take a trip to Mexico. You'll need to buy Mexican pesos at some point. When you do, you'll be offering to *buy* pesos by offering to *sell* dollars. In other words, *the demand for foreign currency represents a supply of U.S. dollars.*

When Americans buy BMW cars, they also supply U.S. dollars. American consumers pay for their BMWs in dollars. Somewhere down the road, however, those dollars will be exchanged for European euros. At that exchange, dollars are being *supplied* and euros *demanded*.

American corporations demand foreign exchange too. General Motors builds cars in Germany, Coca-Cola produces Coke in China, Exxon produces and refines oil all over the world. In nearly every such case, the U.S. firm must first build or buy some plant and equipment, using another country's factors of production. This activity requires foreign currency and thus becomes another component of our demand for foreign currency.

We may summarize these market activities by noting that *the supply of dollars originates in*

- *American demand for imports.*
- *American investments in foreign countries.*
- *Speculation.*

As on the demand side, government intervention can also contribute to the supply of dollars.

The Value of the Dollar

Whether American consumers will choose to buy a BMW depends partly on what the car costs. The price tag isn't always apparent in international transactions. Remember that the BMW producer and workers want to be paid in their own currency. Hence, the *dollar* price of a BMW depends on two factors: (1) the German price of a BMW and (2) the *exchange rate* between U.S. dollars and euros. Specifically, the U.S. price of a BMW is

$$\text{Dollar price of BMW} = \text{euro price of BMW} \times \text{dollar price of euro}$$

Suppose the BMW company is prepared to sell a BMW for 100,000 euros and that the current exchange rate is 2 euros = $1. At these rates, a BMW will cost you

$$\text{Dollar price of BMW} = 100{,}000 \text{ euros} \times \frac{\$1}{2 \text{ euros}}$$

$$= \$50{,}000$$

If you're willing to pay this much for a shiny new BMW, you may do so at current exchange rates.

Now suppose the exchange rate changes from 2 euros = $1 to 1 euro = $1. *A higher dollar price for euros will raise the dollar costs of European goods.* In this case, the dollar price of a euro increases from $0.50 to $1. At this new exchange rate, the BMW company is still willing to sell BMWs at 100,000 euros apiece. And German consumers continue to buy BMWs at that price. But this constant euro price now translates into a higher *dollar* price. Thus a BMW now costs you $100,000.

As the dollar price of a BMW rises, the number of BMWs sold in the United States will decline. As BMW sales decline, the quantity of euros demanded may decline as well. Thus, the quantity of foreign currency demanded declines when the exchange rate rises because foreign goods become more expensive and imports decline.[1] When the dollar price of European currencies actually increased in 1992, BMW decided to start producing cars in South Carolina. A year later Mercedes-Benz decided to produce cars in the United States as well. Sales of American-made BMWs and Mercedes don't depend on the exchange rate of the U.S. dollars.

The Supply Curve. These market responses suggest that the supply of dollars is upward-sloping. If the value of the dollar rises, Americans will be able to buy more euros. As a result, the dollar price of imported BMWs will decline. American consumers will respond by demanding more imports, thereby supplying a larger quantity of dollars. The supply curve in Figure 36.1 shows how the quantity of dollars supplied rises as the value of the dollar increases.

The Demand Curve. The demand for dollars can be explained in similar terms. Remember that the demand for dollars arises from the foreign demand for U.S. exports

What's a euro? Read more about the new European currency at www.europe-euro.com.

---

[1] The extent to which imports decline as the cost of foreign currency rises depends on the *price elasticity of demand*.

FIGURE 36.1

The Foreign-Exchange Market

The foreign-exchange market operates like other markets. In this case, the "good" bought and sold is dollars (foreign exchange). The price and quantity of dollars actually exchanged are determined by the intersection of market supply and demand.

and investments. If the exchange rate moves from 2 euros = $1 to 1 euro = $1, the euro price of dollars will fall. As dollars become cheaper for Germans, all American exports effectively fall in price. Germans will buy more American products (including trips to Disney World) and therefore demand a greater quantity of dollars. In addition, foreign investors will perceive in a cheaper dollar the opportunity to buy U.S. stocks, businesses, and property at fire-sale prices. Accordingly, they join foreign consumers in demanding more dollars. Not all these behavioral responses will occur overnight, but they're reasonably predictable over a brief period of time.

Given market demand and supply curves, we can predict the **equilibrium price** of any commodity, that is, the price at which the quantity demanded will equal the quantity supplied. This occurs in Figure 36.1 where the two curves cross. At that equilibrium, the value of the dollar (the exchange rate) is established. In this case, the euro price of the dollar turns out to be 0.90, the price prevailing in October 2001.

The value of the dollar can also be expressed in terms of other currencies. The World View on the next page displays a sampling of dollar exchange rates in October 2001. (Notice how many Indonesian rupiah you could buy for $1.) The *average* value of the dollar is a weighted mean of the exchange rates between the U.S. dollar and all these currencies. The value of the dollar is "high" when its foreign-exchange price is above recent levels, "low" when it is below recent averages.

The equilibrium depicted in Figure 36.1 determines not only the *price* of the dollar but also a specific *quantity* of international transactions. Those transactions include the exports, imports, international investments, and other sources of dollar supply and demand. A summary of all those international money flows is contained in the **balance of payments**—an accounting statement of all international money flows in a given period of time.

Trade Balance. Table 36.1 depicts the U.S. balance of payments for 2000. Notice first how the millions of separate transactions are classified into a few summary measures. The trade balance is the difference between exports and imports of goods (merchandise) and services. In 2000, the United States imported over $1.4 trillion of goods and services but exported less than $1.1 trillion. This created a **trade deficit** of $369 billion. That trade deficit represents a net outflow of dollars to the rest of the world.

Trade balance = exports − imports

The excess supply of dollars created by the trade gap widened further by other net outflows. Profits from U.S. overseas investments ($345 billion) were less than the

Equilibrium

equilibrium price: The price at which the quantity of a good demanded in a given time period equals the quantity supplied.

The Balance of Payments

balance of payments: A summary record of a country's international economic transactions in a given period of time.

trade deficit: The amount by which the value of imports exceeds the value of exports in a given time period.

WORLD VIEW

Foreign-Exchange Rates

Friday, October 19, 2001—The New York foreign exchange selling rates below apply to trading among banks in amounts of $1 million and more, as quoted at 4 P.M. Eastern time by Reuters and other sources. Retail transactions provide fewer units of foreign currency per dollar.

Country	U.S. Dollar per Unit (dollar price of foreign currency)	Currency per U.S. Dollar (foreign price of U.S. dollar)
Brazil (real)	0.3659	2.7330
Britain (pound)	1.4333	0.6977
Canada (dollar)	0.6348	1.5753
China (renminbi)	0.1208	8.2768
Indonesia (rupiah)	0.0001	10,090.00
Japan (yen)	0.0083	121.20
Mexico (peso)	0.1084	9.2270
Russia (ruble)	0.0338	29.565
Euroland (euro)	0.8984	1.1131

Source: *The Wall Street Journal*, October 22, 2001. Reprinted by permission of *The Wall Street Journal*, © 2001 Dow Jones & Company, Inc. All rights reserved worldwide. www.wsj.com

Analysis: The exchange rates between currencies are determined by supply and demand in foreign-exchange markets. The rates reported here represent the equilibrium exchange rates on a particular day.

---

outgoing profits to foreign investors ($359 billion). The $14 billion difference in repatriated profits contributed to the net *supply* of dollars.

Current-Account Balance. The current-account balance is a subtotal in Table 36.1. It includes the merchandise, services, and investment balances as well as government grants and private transfers such as wages sent home by foreign citizens working in the United States.

$$\text{Current-account balance} = \text{trade balance} + \text{unilateral transfers}$$

The current-account balance is the most comprehensive summary of our trade relations. As indicated in Table 36.1, the United States had a current-account deficit of $436 billion in 2000.

Capital-Account Balance. The current-account deficit is offset by the capital-account surplus. The capital-account balance takes into consideration assets bought and sold across international borders; that is,

$$\text{Capital-account balance} = \text{foreign purchases of U.S. assets} - \text{U.S. purchases of foreign assets}$$

As Table 36.1 shows, foreign consumers demanded $917 billion worth of dollars in 2000 to buy farms and factories as well as U.S. bonds, stocks, and other investments (item 9). This exceeded the flow of U.S. dollars going overseas to purchase foreign as-

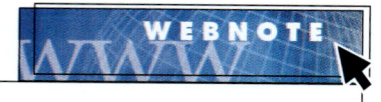

The latest statistics on the balance of payments are available from the Bureau of Economic Analysis at www.bea.doc.gov/bea/di1.htm.

TABLE 36.1
The U.S. Balance of Payments

The balance of payments is a summary statement of a country's international transactions. The major components of that activity are the trade balance (merchandise exports minus merchandise imports), the current-account balance (trade, services, and transfers), and the capital-account balance. The net total of these balances must equal zero, since the quantity of dollars paid must equal the quantity received.

Item	Amount (in billions)
1. Merchandise exports	$773
2. Merchandise imports	(1,223)
3. Service exports	296
4. Service imports	(215)
Trade balance (items 1–4)	**−369**
5. Income from U.S. overseas investments	345
6. Income outflow for foreign-owned U.S. investments	(359)
7. Net U.S. government grants	(21)
8. Net private transfers and pensions	(32)
Current-account balance (items 1–8)	**−436**
9. U.S. capital inflow	917
10. U.S. capital outflow	(552)
11. Increase in U.S. official reserves	(1)
12. Increase in foreign official assets in U.S.	35
Capital-account balance (items 9–12)	**399**
13. Statistical discrepancy	37
Net balance (items 1–13)	**0**

Source: U.S. Department of Commerce (2000 data).

sets (item 10). In addition, the United States and foreign governments bought and sold dollars, creating an additional outflow of dollars (items 11 and 12).

The net capital inflows were essential in financing the U.S. trade deficit (negative trade balance). As in any market, the number of dollars demanded must equal the number of dollars supplied. Thus, **the capital-account surplus must equal the current-account deficit.** In other words, there can't be any dollars left lying around unaccounted for. Item 13 in Table 36.1 reminds us that our accounting system isn't perfect—that we can't identify every transaction. Nevertheless, all the accounts must eventually "balance out":

$$\frac{\text{Net balance}}{\text{of payments}} = \frac{\text{current-account}}{\text{balance}} + \frac{\text{capital-account}}{\text{balance}} = 0$$

That's the character of a market *equilibrium:* The quantity of dollars demanded equals the quantity of dollars supplied.

MARKET DYNAMICS

The interesting thing about markets isn't their character in equilibrium but the fact that prices and quantities are always changing in response to shifts in demand and supply. The U.S. demand for BMWs shifted overnight when Japan introduced a new line of sleek, competitively priced cars. The reduced demand for BMWs shifted the supply of dollars leftward. That supply shift raised the value of the dollar vis-á-vis the euro, as illustrated in Figure 36.2. (It also increased the demand for Japanese yen, causing the yen value of the dollar to *fall.*)

Exchange-rate changes have their own terminology. **Depreciation** of a currency refers to the fact that one currency has become cheaper in terms of another currency. In our earlier discussion of exchange rates, for example, we assumed that the exchange rate between euros and dollars changed from 2 euros = $1 to 1 euro = $1, making the euro price of a dollar cheaper. In this case, the dollar depreciated with respect to the euro.

Depreciation and Appreciation

depreciation (currency): A fall in the price of one currency relative to another.

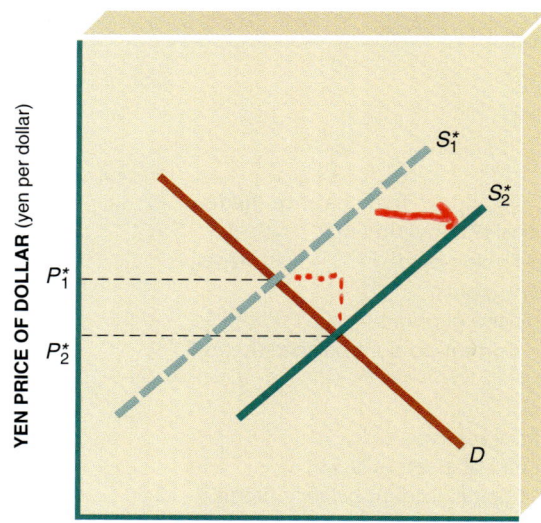

FIGURE 36.2
Shifts in Foreign-Exchange Markets

When the Japanese introduced luxury autos into the United States, the American demand for German cars fell. As a consequence, the supply of dollars in the dollar-euro market (part a) shifted to the left and the euro value of the dollar rose. At the same time, the increased American demand for Japanese cars shifted the dollar supply curve in the yen market (part b) to the right, reducing the yen price of the dollar.

appreciation: A rise in the price of one currency relative to another.

The other side of depreciation is **appreciation,** an increase in value of one currency as expressed in another country's currency. *Whenever one currency depreciates, another currency must appreciate.* When the exchange rate changed from 2 euros = \$1 to 1 euro = \$1, not only did the euro price of a dollar fall, the dollar price of a euro rose. Hence, the euro appreciated as the dollar depreciated.

Figure 36.3 illustrates actual changes in the exchange rate of the U.S. dollar since 1973. The trade-adjusted value of the U.S. dollar is the (weighted) average of all exchange rates for the dollar. In general, the dollar lost value in the late 1970s but recovered in the early 1980s. Between 1980 and 1985, the U.S. dollar appreciated over 80 percent. This appreciation greatly reduced the price of imports and thus increased their quantity. At the same time, the dollar appreciation raised the foreign price of U.S. exports and so reduced their volume. U.S. farmers, aircraft manufacturers, and tourist services suffered huge sales losses. The trade deficit ballooned.

How much are 100 Japanese yen worth in U.S. dollars? Find out at the currency converter at www.oanda.com/site/cc_index.shtml.

The value of the dollar reversed course after 1985. This brief dollar depreciation set in motion forces that reduced the trade deficit in the late 1980s. Then the dollar started appreciating again, slowing export growth and increasing imports throughout the 1990s.

Market Forces

Exchange rates change for the same reasons that any market price changes: The underlying supply or demand (or both) has shifted. Among the more important sources of such shifts are

- *Relative income changes.* If incomes are increasing faster in country *A* than in country *B*, consumers in *A* will tend to spend more, thus increasing the demand for *B*'s exports and currency. *B*'s currency will appreciate.
- *Relative price changes.* If domestic prices are rising rapidly in country *A*, consumers will seek out lower-priced imports. The demand for *B*'s exports and currency will increase. *B*'s currency will appreciate.
- *Changes in product availability.* If country *A* experiences a disastrous wheat crop failure, it will have to increase its food imports. *B*'s currency will appreciate.

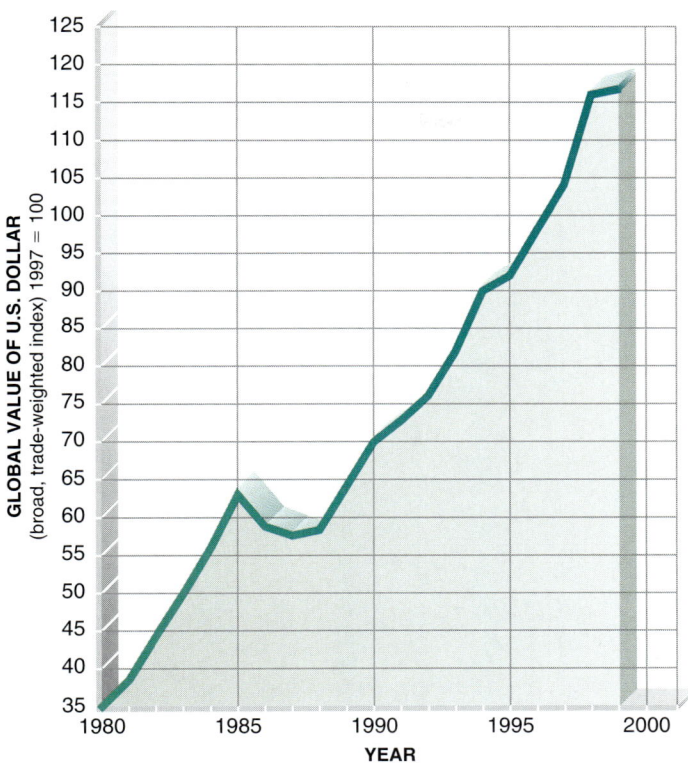

FIGURE 36.3

Changing Values of U.S. Dollar

Since 1973, exchange rates have been flexible. As a result, the value of the U.S. dollar has fluctuated with international differences in inflation, interest rates, and economic growth. U.S. economic stability has given the U.S. dollar increasing value over time.

- **Relative interest rate changes.** If interest rates rise in country A, people in country B will want to move their deposits to A. Demand for A's currency will rise and it will appreciate.
- **Speculation.** If speculators anticipate an increase in the price of A's currency, for the preceding reasons or any other, they'll begin buying it, thus pushing its price up. A's currency will appreciate.

All these various changes are taking place every minute of every day, thus keeping **foreign-exchange markets** active. On an average day, over *$1 trillion* of foreign exchange is bought and sold in the market. Significant changes occur in currency values, however, only when several of these forces move in the same direction at the same time. This is what caused the Asian crisis of 1997–98.

In July 1997, the Thai government decided the baht was overvalued and let market forces find a new equilibrium. Within days, the dollar prices of the baht plunged 25 percent. This sharp decline in the value of the Thai baht simultaneously increased the Thai price of the U.S. dollar. As a consequence, Thais could no longer afford to buy as many American products.

The devaluation of the baht had a domino effect on other Asian currencies. The plunge in the baht shook confidence in the Malaysian ringget, the Indonesian rupiah, and even the Korean won. People wanted to hold "hard" currencies like the U.S. dollar. As people rushed to buy U.S. dollars with their local currencies, the value of those currencies plunged. At one point the Indonesian rupiah had lost 80 percent of its dollar value, making U.S. exports five times more expensive for Indonesians. As a result, Indonesians could no longer afford to buy imported rice, machinery, cars, or pork. Indonesian students attending U.S. colleges could no longer afford to pay tuition (see World View). The sudden surge in prices and scarcity of goods led to street demonstrations and a change in government. Similar problems erupted throughout Southeast Asia.

The "Asian contagion" unfortunately wasn't confined to that area of the world. Hog farmers in the United States saw foreign demand for their pork evaporate. Koreans

foreign-exchange markets: Places where foreign currencies are bought and sold.

The Asian Crisis of 1997–1998

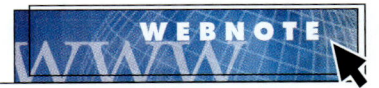

Check out the latest exchange rates for the euro and the rupiah at the Chicago Fed site: www.chicagofed.org. Click on "Economic Research and Data," then "Economic and Financial Data," then see "Foreign Exchange Rates."

WORLD VIEW

Money Crisis Pulling Asian Students Home

The financial tsunami that swamped Asian economies in the last few months is sloshing back across the Pacific toward American colleges and universities, where thousands of Asian students are suddenly short of dollars.

Since last July, the Indonesian currency, the rupiah, has lost 80 percent of its value as measured against the U.S. dollar. A half-dozen Asian currencies have lost about half their value against the dollar.

That means, for example, that what would have been $20,000 in Korean money (the won) a year ago is now worth only $10,000. Consequently, Korean and Indonesian students—plus Malaysians, Thais, Singaporeans and Japanese—are struggling to pay their tuition bills. Some can't—so they're going home.

There are about 458,000 foreign students in the USA—about 3 percent of total higher education enrollment, according to the Institute of International Education, a nonprofit cultural exchange organization that conducts an annual census of foreign students. About 57 percent of the students are Asians.

Source: *USA Today*, February 18, 1998. © 1998 USA Today. Reprinted with permission. www.usatoday.com

Analysis: When the foreign price of the U.S. dollar rises (dollar appreciation), American exports (including educational services) become more expensive, which causes a decline in enrollments (quantity demanded).

---

stopped taking vacations in Hawaii. Thai Airways canceled orders for Boeing jets. And Japanese consumers bought fewer Washington state apples and California oranges. This loss of export markets slowed economic growth in the United States, Europe, Japan, and other nations.

RESISTANCE TO EXCHANGE-RATE CHANGES

Given the scope and depth of the Asian crisis of 1997–98, it's easy to understand why people crave *stable* exchange rates. The resistance to exchange-rate fluctuations originates in various micro and macro economic interests.

Micro Interests

The microeconomic resistance to changes in the value of the dollar arises from two concerns. First, people who trade or invest in world markets want a solid basis for forecasting future costs, prices, and profits. Forecasts are always uncertain, but they're even less dependable when the value of money is subject to change. An American firm that invests $2 million in a ski factory in Sweden expects not only to make a profit on the production there but also to return that profit to the United States. If the Swedish krona depreciates sharply in the interim, however, the profits amassed in Sweden may dwindle to a mere trickle, or even a loss, when the kronor are exchanged back into dollars. Even the Nobel Prize loses a bit of its luster when the krona depreciates (see World View on the next page). From this view, the uncertainty associated with fluctuating exchange rates is an unwanted burden.

Even when the direction of an exchange rate move is certain, those who stand to lose from the change are prone to resist. *A change in the price of a country's money automatically alters the price of all its exports and imports.* When the Russian ruble and Japanese yen depreciated in 2000–01, for example, the dollar price of Russian and Japanese steel declined as well. This prompted U.S. steelmakers to accuse Russia and Japan of "dumping" steel (see News). Steel companies and unions appealed to Washington to protect their sales and jobs.

Even in the country whose currency becomes cheaper, there'll be opposition to exchange-rate movements. When the U.S. dollar appreciates, Americans buy more for-

WORLD VIEW

Nobel Prize Was Nobler in October

STOCKHOLM—Winners of the four Nobel science awards said yesterday that the honor is more important than the money, so it does not matter much that each award has lost $242,000 in value since October.

"If we had been more intelligent, we would have done some hedging," said Gary S. Becker, 61, a University of Chicago professor and a Nobel economics laureate. Sweden's decision last month to let the krona float caused the prizes' value to drop from $1.2 million each when announced in October to $958,000 when King Carl XVI Gustaf presents them Thursday.

The recipients are Becker; American Rudolph A. Marcus, the chemistry laureate; Frenchman Georges Charpak, the physics laureate; and medicine prize winners Edmond Fischer and Edwin Krebs of the University of Washington in Seattle.

—Associated Press

Source: *Boston Globe*, December 8, 1992. Reprinted by permission of the Associated Press. www.ap.org.

Analysis: Currency depreciation reduces the external value of domestic income and assets. The dollar value of the Nobel Prize fell when the Swedish krona depreciated.

---

eign products. This increased U.S. demand for imports may drive up prices in other countries. In addition, foreign firms may take advantage of the reduced American competition by raising their prices. In either case, some inflation will result. The consumer's insistence that the government "do something" about rising prices may turn into a political force for "correcting" foreign-exchange rates.

Any microeconomic problem that becomes widespread enough can turn into a macroeconomic problem. The huge U.S. trade deficits of the 1980s effectively exported jobs to foreign nations. Although the U.S. economy expanded rapidly in 1983–85, the unemployment rate stayed high, partly because American consumers were spending more of their income on imports. Yet fear of renewed inflation precluded more stimulative fiscal and monetary policies.

Macro Interests

The U.S. trade deficits of the 1980s were offset by huge capital-account surpluses. Foreign investors sought to participate in the U.S. economic expansion by buying land,

IN THE NEWS

Bush to Seek Protection for U.S. Steel Firms
President Yields to Industry Pressure

The Bush administration unveiled an ambitious initiative yesterday to protect battered U.S. steel companies from a worldwide glut, bowing to pressure from an industry that has suffered mounting bankruptcies and job losses in recent months.

President Bush announced that the White House will file a trade case aimed at curbing steel imports, and he said his administration will seek to reach a longer-term agreement with other countries aimed at reducing "inefficient excess capacity" in global steel production. . . .

The announcement capped several years of intense lobbying in Washington by large steelmakers and their unions, who were hit hard when financial crises in Asia, Russia and Brazil in the late 1990s led foreign steel producers to unload much of their production in the United States. Prices for some steel products have fallen to their lowest levels in two decades, and with about one-quarter of the industry already in bankruptcy proceedings, analysts predict that the number could rise to 40 percent by the end of this year.

—Paul Blustein

Source: *Washington Post*, June 6, 2001. © 2001 The Washington Post. Reprinted with permission. www.washingtonpost.com

Analysis: Import-competing industries suffer when currency depreciations make imports cheaper. They want to be protected from "unfair" competition.

plant, and equipment and by lending money in U.S. financial markets. These capital inflows complicated monetary policy, however, and greatly increased U.S. foreign debt and interest costs.

U.S. a Net Debtor

The inflow of foreign investment also raised anxieties about "selling off" America. As Japanese and other foreign investors increased their purchases of farmland, factories, and real estate (e.g., Rockefeller Center), many Americans worried that foreign investors were taking control of the U.S. economy. A Gallup poll in 1989 revealed that Americans were much more worried about foreign economic domination than foreign military threats.

Fueling these fears was the dramatic change in America's international financial position. From 1914 to 1984, the United States had been a net creditor in the world economy. We owned more assets abroad than foreign investors owned in the United States. Our financial position changed in 1985. Continuing trade deficits and offsetting capital inflows transformed the United States into a net debtor in that year. Since then, foreigners have owned more U.S. assets than Americans own of foreign assets.

America's new debtor status can complicate domestic policy. A sudden flight from U.S. assets could severely weaken the dollar and disrupt the domestic economy. To prevent that from occurring, policymakers must consider the impact of their decisions on foreign investors. This may necessitate difficult policy choices.

There's a silver lining to this cloud, however. The inflow of foreign investment is a reflection of confidence in the U.S. economy. Foreign investors want to share in our growth and profitability. In the process, their investments (like BMW's auto plant) expand America's production possibilities and stimulate still more economic growth.

Foreign investors actually assume substantial risk when they invest in the United States. If the dollar falls, the foreign value of their U.S. investments will decline. Hence, foreigners who've already invested in the United States have no incentive to start a flight from the dollar. On the contrary, a strong dollar protects the value of their U.S. holdings.

EXCHANGE-RATE INTERVENTION

Given the potential opposition to exchange-rate movements, governments often feel compelled to intervene in foreign-exchange markets. The intervention is usually intended to achieve greater exchange-rate stability. But such stability may itself give rise to undesirable micro- and macroeconomic effects.

Fixed Exchange Rates

One way to eliminate fluctuations in exchange rates is to fix the rate's value. To fix exchange rates, each country may simply proclaim that its currency is worth so much in relation to that of other countries. The easiest way to do this is for each country to define the worth of its currency in terms of some common standard. Under a **gold standard,** each country determines that its currency is worth so much gold. In so doing, it implicitly defines the worth of its currency in terms of all other currencies, which also have a fixed gold value. In 1944, the major trading nations met at Bretton Woods, New Hampshire, and agreed that each currency was worth so much gold. The value of the U.S. dollar was defined as being equal to 0.0294 ounce of gold, while the British pound was defined as being worth 0.0823 ounce of gold. Thus, the exchange rate between British pounds and U.S. dollars was effectively fixed at $1 = 0.357 pound, or 1 pound = $2.80 (or $2.80/0.0823 = $1/0.0294).

> **gold standard:** An agreement by countries to fix the price of their currencies in terms of gold; a mechanism for fixing exchange rates.

Balance-of-Payments Problems. It's one thing to proclaim the worth of a country's currency; it's quite another to *maintain* the fixed rate of exchange. As we've observed, foreign-exchange rates are subject to continual and often unpredictable changes in supply and demand. Hence, two countries that seek to stabilize their exchange rate at some fixed value are going to find it necessary to compensate for such foreign-exchange market pressures.

Suppose the exchange rate officially established by the United States and Great Britain is equal to e_1, as illustrated in Figure 36.4. As is apparent, that particular exchange rate is consistent with the then-prevailing demand and supply conditions in the foreign-exchange market (as indicated by curves D_1 and S_1).

Now suppose that Americans suddenly acquire a greater taste for British cars and start spending more income on Jaguars and the like. Although Ford Motor owns Jaguar, the cars are still produced in Great Britain. Hence, as U.S. purchases of British goods increase, the demand for British currency will *shift* from D_1 to D_2 in Figure 36.4. Were exchange rates allowed to respond to market influences, the dollar price of a British pound would rise, in this case to the rate e_2. But government intervention has fixed the exchange rate at e_1. Unfortunately, at e_1, American consumers want to buy more pounds (q_D) than the British are willing to supply (q_S). The difference between the quantity demanded and the quantity supplied in the market at the rate e_1 represents a **market shortage** of British pounds.

The excess demand for pounds implies a **balance-of-payments deficit** for the United States: More dollars are flowing out of the country than into it. The same disequilibrium represents a **balance-of-payments surplus** for Britain, because its outward flow of pounds is less than its incoming flow.

Basically, there are only two solutions to balance-of-payments problems brought about by the attempt to fix exchange rates:

- Allow exchange rates to rise to e_2 (Figure 36.4), thereby eliminating the excess demand for pounds.
- Alter market supply or demand so that they intersect at the fixed rate e_1.

Since fixed exchange rates were the initial objective of policy, only the second alternative is of immediate interest.

The Need for Reserves. One way to alter market conditions would be for someone simply to supply British pounds to American consumers. The U.S. Treasury could have accumulated a reserve of foreign exchange in earlier periods. By selling some of those **foreign-exchange reserves** now, the Treasury could help to stabilize market conditions at the officially established exchange rate. The rightward shift of the pound supply curve in Figure 36.5 illustrates the sale of accumulated British pounds—and related purchase of U.S. dollars—by the U.S. Treasury. (In 2000, the U.S. Treasury reduced foreign-exchange reserves by $1 billion; see item 12 in Table 36.1.)

Although foreign-exchange reserves can be used to fix exchange rates, such reserves may not be adequate. Indeed, Figure 36.6 should be testimony enough to the fact that today's deficit isn't always offset by tomorrow's surplus. A principal reason that fixed exchange rates didn't live up to their expectations is that the United States had

market shortage: The amount by which the quantity demanded exceeds the quantity supplied at a given price; excess demand.

balance-of-payments deficit: An excess demand for foreign currency at current exchange rates.

balance-of-payments surplus: An excess demand for domestic currency at current exchange rates.

foreign-exchange reserves: Holdings of foreign exchange by official government agencies, usually the central bank or treasury.

FIGURE 36.4

Fixed Rates and Market Imbalance

If exchange rates are fixed, they can't adjust to changes in market supply and demand. Suppose the exchange rate is initially fixed at e_1. When the demand for British pounds increases (shifts to the right), an excess demand for pounds emerges. More pounds are demanded (q_D) at the rate e_1 than are supplied (q_S). This causes a balance-of-payments deficit for the United States.

FIGURE 36.5
The Impact of Monetary Intervention

If the U.S. Treasury holds reserves of British pounds, it can use them to buy U.S. dollars in foreign-exchange markets. As it does so, the supply of pounds will shift to the right, to S_2, thereby maintaining the desired exchange rate, e_1. The Bank of England could bring about the same result by offering to buy U.S. dollars with pounds.

balance-of-payments deficits for 22 consecutive years. This long-term deficit overwhelmed our stock of foreign-exchange reserves.

The Role of Gold. Gold reserves are a potential substitute for foreign-exchange reserves. As long as each country's money has a value defined in terms of gold, we can use gold to buy British pounds, thereby restocking our foreign-exchange reserves. Or we can simply use the gold to purchase U.S. dollars in foreign-exchange markets. In either case, the exchange value of the dollar will tend to rise. However, we must have **gold reserves** available for this purpose. Unfortunately, the continuing U.S. balance-of-payments deficits recorded in Figure 36.6 exceeded even the hoards of gold buried under Fort Knox. As a consequence, our gold reserves lost their credibility as a potential guarantee of fixed exchange rates.

gold reserves: Stocks of gold held by a government to purchase foreign exchange.

Domestic Adjustments. The supply and demand for foreign exchange can also be shifted by changes in basic fiscal, monetary, or trade policies. With respect to trade policy, *trade protection can be used to prop up fixed exchange rates.* We could eliminate the excess demand for pounds (Figure 36.4), for example, by imposing quotas

FIGURE 36.6
The U.S. Balance of Payments, 1950–1973

The United States had a balance-of-payments deficit for 22 consecutive years. During this period, the foreign-exchange reserves of the U.S. Treasury were sharply reduced. Fixed exchange rates were maintained by the willingness of foreign countries to accumulate large reserves of U.S. dollars. However, neither the Treasury's reserves nor the willingness of foreigners to accumulate dollars was unlimited. In 1973, fixed exchange rates were abandoned.

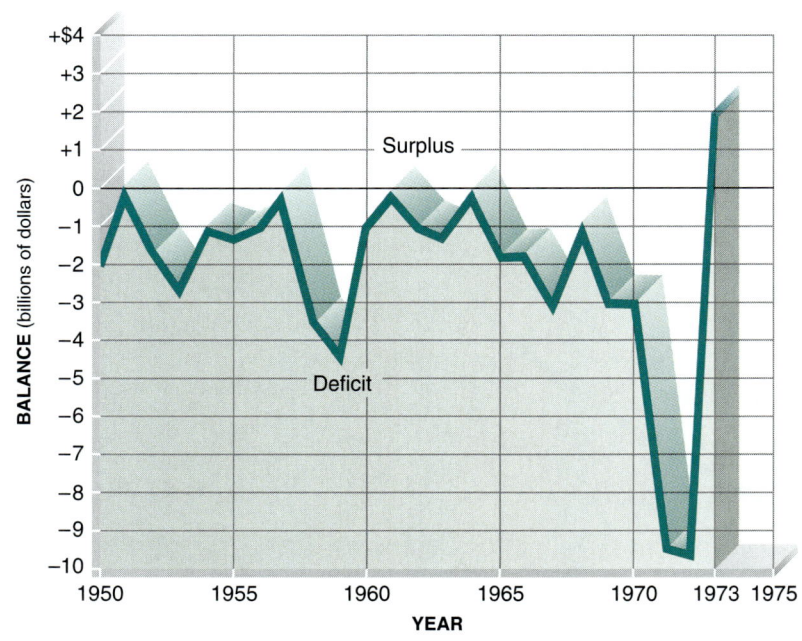

and tariffs on British goods. Such trade restrictions would reduce British imports to the United States and thus the demand for British pounds. In August 1971, President Nixon imposed an emergency 10 percent surcharge on all imported goods to help reduce the payments deficit that fixed exchange rates had spawned. Such restrictions on international trade, however, violate the principle of comparative advantage and thus reduce total world output. Trade protection also invites retaliatory trade restrictions.

Fiscal policy is another way out of the imbalance. An increase in U.S. income tax rates will reduce disposable income and have a negative effect on the demand for all goods, including imports. A reduction in government spending will have similar effects. In general, ***deflationary (or restrictive) policies help correct a balance-of-payments deficit by lowering domestic incomes and thus the demand for imports.***

Monetary policies in a deficit country could follow the same restrictive course. A reduction in the money supply will tend to raise interest rates. The balance of payments will benefit in two ways. The resultant slowdown in spending will reduce import demand. In addition, higher interest rates may induce international investors to move some of their funds into the deficit country. Such moves will provide immediate relief to the payments imbalance.[2] Russia tried this strategy in 1998, tripling key interest rates (to as much as 150 percent). But even that wasn't enough to restore confidence in the ruble, which kept depreciating. Within three months of the monetary policy tightening, the ruble lost half its value.

A surplus country could help solve the balance-of-payments problem. By pursuing expansionary—even inflationary—fiscal and monetary policies, a surplus country could stimulate the demand for imports. Moreover, any inflation at home will reduce the competitiveness of exports, thereby helping to restrain the inflow of foreign demand. Taken together, such efforts would help reverse an international payments imbalance. The U.S. government has tried repeatedly to persuade Japan to pursue such expansionary policies.

Even under the best of circumstances, domestic economic adjustments entail significant costs. In effect, ***domestic adjustments to payments imbalances require a deficit country to forsake full employment and a surplus country to forsake price stability.*** These are sacrifices few countries are willing to make, as Argentina demonstrated in 2002. Austerity measures designed to maintain the value of Argentina's currency caused a recession, high unemployment, and political upheaval. There's no easy way out of this impasse. Market imbalances caused by fixed exchange rates can be corrected only with abundant supplies of foreign-exchange reserves or deliberate changes in fiscal, monetary, or trade policies.

The Euro Fix. As noted earlier in the chapter, the 12 nations of the European Monetary Union (EMU) did fix their exchange rates in 1999. They went far beyond the kind of exchange-rate fix we're discussing here. Members of the EMU *eliminated* their national currencies, making the euro the common currency of Euroland. They don't have to worry about reserve balances or domestic adjustments. However, they do have to reconcile their varied national interests to a single monetary authority, which may prove to be difficult politically in times of economic stress.

Balance-of-payments problems wouldn't arise in the first place if exchange rates were allowed to respond to market forces. Under a system of **flexible exchange rates** (often called floating exchange rates), the exchange rate moves up or down to choke off any excess supply of or demand for foreign exchange. Notice again in Figure 36.4 that

Flexible Exchange Rates

flexible exchange rates: A system in which exchange rates are permitted to vary with market supply-and-demand conditions; floating exchange rates.

---

[2]Before 1930, not only were foreign-exchange rates fixed, but domestic monetary supplies were tied to gold stocks as well. Countries experiencing a balance-of-payments deficit were thus forced to contract their money supply, and countries experiencing a payments surplus were forced to expand their money supply by a set amount. Monetary authorities were powerless to control domestic money supplies except by erecting barriers to trade. The system was abandoned when the world economy collapsed into the Great Depression.

"Damn it! How *can* I relax, knowing that out there, somewhere, somehow, someone's attacking the dollar?"

Analysis: A "weak" dollar reduces the buying power of American tourists.

the exchange-rate move from e_1 to e_2 prevents any excess demand from emerging. **With flexible exchange rates, the quantity of foreign exchange demanded always equals the quantity supplied,** and there's no imbalance. For the same reason, there's no need for foreign-exchange reserves.

Although flexible exchange rates eliminate balance-of-payments and foreign-exchange reserves problems, they don't solve all of a country's international trade problems. *Exchange-rate movements associated with flexible rates alter relative prices and may disrupt import and export flows.* As noted before, depreciation of the dollar raises the price of all imported goods. The price increases may contribute to domestic cost-push inflation. Also, domestic businesses that sell imported goods or use them as production inputs may suffer sales losses. On the other hand, appreciation of the dollar raises the foreign price of U.S. goods and reduces the sales of American exporters. Hence, *someone is always hurt, and others are helped, by exchange-rate movements.* The resistance to flexible exchange rates originates in these potential losses. Such resistance creates pressure for official intervention in foreign-exchange markets or increased trade barriers.

The United States and its major trading partners abandoned fixed exchange rates in 1973. Although exchange rates are now able to fluctuate freely, it shouldn't be assumed that they necessarily undergo wild gyrations. On the contrary, experience with flexible rates since 1973 suggests that some semblance of stability is possible even when exchange rates are free to change in response to market forces.

Speculation. One force that often helps maintain stability in a flexible exchange-rate system is speculation. Speculators often counteract short-term changes in foreign-exchange supply and demand. If an exchange rate temporarily rises above its long-term equilibrium, speculators will move in to sell foreign exchange. By selling at high prices and later buying at lower prices, speculators hope to make a profit. In the process, they also help stabilize foreign-exchange rates.

Speculation isn't always stabilizing, however. Speculators may not correctly gauge the long-term equilibrium. Instead, they may move "with the market" and help push exchange rates far out of kilter. This kind of destabilizing speculation sharply lowered the international value of the U.S. dollar in 1987, forcing the Reagan administration to intervene in foreign-exchange markets, borrowing foreign currencies to buy U.S. dollars. In 1997, the Clinton administration intervened for the opposite purpose: stemming the rise in the U.S. dollar. the Bush administration has been more willing to stay on the sidelines, letting global markets set the exchange rates for the U.S. dollar.

Managed Exchange Rates. Governments can intervene in foreign-exchange markets without completely fixing exchange rates. That is, they may buy and sell foreign exchange for the purpose of *narrowing* rather than *eliminating* exchange-rate movements. Such limited intervention in foreign-exchange markets is often referred to as **managed exchange rates,** or, popularly, "dirty floats."

The basic objective of exchange-rate management is to provide a stabilizing force. The U.S. Treasury, for example, may use its foreign-exchange reserves to buy dollars when they're depreciating too much. Or it will buy foreign exchange if the dollar is rising too fast. From this perspective, exchange-rate management appears as a fail-safe system for the private market. Unfortunately, the motivation for official intervention is sometimes suspect. Private speculators buy and sell foreign exchange for the sole purpose of making a profit. But government sales and purchases may be motivated by other considerations. A falling exchange rate increases the competitive advantage of a country's exports. A rising exchange rate makes international investment less expensive. Hence, a country's efforts to manage exchange-rate movements may arouse suspicion and outright hostility in its trading partners.

Although managed exchange rates would seem to be an ideal compromise between fixed rates and flexible rates, they can work only when some acceptable "rules of the game" and mutual trust have been established. As Sherman Maisel, a former governor of the Federal Reserve Board, put it, "Monetary systems are based on credit and faith: If these are lacking, a . . . crisis occurs."[3]

managed exchange rates: A system in which governments intervene in foreign-exchange markets to limit but not eliminate exchange-rate fluctuations; "dirty floats."

THE ECONOMY TOMORROW

Currency Bailouts

 The world has witnessed a string of currency crises, including the one in Asia during 1997–98, the Brazilian crisis of 1999, the Argentine crisis of 2001–02, recurrent ruble crises in Russia, and periodic panics in Mexico and South America. In every instance, the country in trouble pleads for external help. In most cases, a currency "bailout" is arranged, whereby global monetary authorities lend the troubled nation enough reserves (such as U.S. dollars) to defend its currency. Typically, the International Monetary Fund (IMF) heads the rescue party, joined by the central banks of the strongest economies.

The Case for Bailouts

The argument for currency bailouts typically rests on the domino theory. Weakness in one currency can undermine another. This seemed to be the case during the 1997–98 Asian crisis. After the **devaluation** of the Thai baht, global investors began worrying about currency values in other Asian nations. Choosing to be safe rather than sorry, they moved funds out of Korea, Malaysia, and the Philippines and invested in U.S. and European markets (notice in Figure 36.3 the 1997–98 appecication of the U.S. dollar).

devaluation: An abrupt depreciation of a currency whose value was fixed or managed by the government.

The initial baht devaluation also weakened the competitive trade position of these same economies. Thai exports became cheaper, diverting export demand from other Asian nations. To prevent loss of export markets, Thailand's neighbors felt they had to devalue as well. Speculators who foresaw these effects accelerated the domino effect by selling the region's currencies.

When Brazil devalued its currency (the *real*) in January 1999, global investors worried that a "samba effect" might sweep across Latin American (see World View). The domino effect could reach across the ocean and damage U.S. and European exports as well. Hence, the industrial countries often offer a currency bailout as a form of self-defense.

---

[3]Sherman Maisel, *Managing the Dollar* (New York: W. W. Norton, 1973), p. 196.

WORLD VIEW

Brazil's Ills Distress Continent
Money Crisis Shakes Investors' Confidence

BUENOS AIRES—Fallout from the continuing currency crisis in Brazil has sparked the most serious financial turmoil in Latin America since the Mexican peso crisis of four years ago, scaring away foreign investors and undermining growth after years of rapid gains.

In the days since Brazil, Latin America's largest nation, devalued its currency on January 12, a number of leading economists have scaled back their forecasts for Latin American growth, predicting it will be flat or negative for the first half of 1999.

The "samba effect," as Brazil's impact on its neighbors is called, is exacerbating regional unemployment rates and sending already high interest rates climbing. Even more significantly, perhaps, it is eroding foreign investment and confidence in the region amid fears that Brazil may default on its foreign debt despite government promises to the contrary.

To encourage investors to keep their money in Brazil, the central bank raised interest rates to stratospheric levels, with dire consequences for Brazilian borrowers. Economists predict that the world's eighth-largest economy will contract by 6 percent this year.

With the Brazilian real's value having fallen sharply, Brazil's neighbors, especially Argentina, are now discovering that one of their biggest markets has been closed off—essentially because of the weaker real, which has raised the price of imported goods in the nation of 165 million people.

—Anthony Faiola

Source: *Washington Post*, February 1, 1999. © 1999 The Washington Post. Reprinted with permission. www.washingtonpost.com

Analysis: When a nation devalues its currency, its imports become more expensive and its exports cheaper. These price changes disrupt trade flows of other nations. Devaluations also shake the confidence of global investors.

The Case against Bailouts

Critics of bailouts argue that such interventions are ultimately self-defeating. They say that once a country knows for sure that currency bailouts are in the wings, it doesn't have to pursue the domestic policy adjustments that might stabilize its currency. A nation can avoid politically unpopular options such as high interest rates, tax hikes, or cutbacks in government spending. It can also turn a blind eye to trade barriers, monopoly power, lax lending policies, and other constraints on productive growth. Hence, the expectation of readily available bailouts may foster the very conditions that cause currency crises.

Future Bailouts?

The decision to bail out a depreciating currency isn't as simple as it appears. To minimize the ill effects of bailouts, the IMF and other institutions typically require the crisis nation to pledge more prudent monetary, fiscal, and trade policies. Usually there's a lot of debate about what kinds of adjustments will be made—and how soon. As long as the crisis nation is confident of an eventual bailout, however, it has a lot of bargaining power to resist policy changes. Only after the IMF finally said "No" to further bailouts in 2001, did Argentina devalue its currency and pursue more domestic reforms.

SUMMARY

- Money serves the same purposes in international trade as it does in the domestic economy, namely, to facilitate productive specialization and market exchanges. The basic challenge of international finance is to create acceptable standards of value from the various currencies maintained by separate countries.
- Exchange rates are the basic mechanism for translating the value of one national currency into the equivalent value of another. An exchange rate of $1 = 2 euros means that one dollar is worth two euros in foreign-exchange markets.
- Foreign currencies have value because they can be used to acquire goods and resources from other countries. Accordingly, the supply of and demand for foreign currency reflect the demands for imports and exports, for international investment, and for overseas activities of governments.

- The balance of payments summarizes a country's international transactions. Its components are the trade balance, the current-account balance, and the capital-account balance. The current and capital accounts must offset each other.
- The equilibrium exchange rate is subject to any and all shifts of supply and demand for foreign exchange. If relative incomes, prices, or interest rates change, the demand for foreign exchange will be affected. A depreciation is a change in market exchange rates that makes one country's currency cheaper in terms of another currency. An appreciation is the opposite kind of change.
- Changes in exchange rates are often resisted. Producers of export goods don't want their currencies to rise in value (appreciate); importers and people who travel dislike it when their currencies fall in value (depreciate).
- Under a system of fixed exchange rates, changes in the supply and demand for foreign exchange can't be expressed in exchange-rate movements. Instead, such shifts will be reflected in excess demand for or excess supply of foreign exchange. Such market imbalances are referred to as balance-of-payments deficits or surpluses.
- To maintain fixed exchange rates, monetary authorities must enter the market to buy and sell foreign exchange. In order to do so, deficit countries must have foreign-exchange reserves. In the absence of sufficient reserves, a country can maintain fixed exchange rates only if it's willing to alter basic fiscal, monetary, or trade policies.
- Flexible exchange rates eliminate balance-of-payments problems and the crises that accompany them. But complete flexibility can lead to excessive changes. To avoid this contingency, many countries prefer to adopt managed exchange rates, that is, rates determined by the market but subject to government intervention.

Key Terms

exchange rate
equilibrium price
balance of payments
trade deficit
depreciation (currency)
appreciation
foreign-exchange markets
gold standard
market shortage
balance-of-payments deficit
balance-of-payments surplus
foreign-exchange reserves
gold reserves
flexible exchange rates
managed exchange rates
devaluation

Questions for Discussion

1. Why would a decline in the value of the dollar prompt foreign manufacturers such as BMW to build production plants in the United States?
2. How do changes in the foreign value of the U.S. dollar affect foreign enrollments at U.S. colleges? (See World View, page 760.)
3. How would rapid inflation in Canada alter our demand for travel to Canada and for Canadian imports? Does it make any difference whether the exchange rate between Canadian and U.S. dollars is fixed or flexible?
4. Under what conditions would a country welcome a balance-of-payments deficit? When would it *not* want a deficit?
5. In what sense do fixed exchange rates permit a country to "export its inflation"?
6. Why did the Mexican government have to restrain the economy after the peso devaluation?
7. If a nation's currency depreciates, are the reduced export prices that result "unfair"?
8. How would each of these events affect the supply or demand for Japanese yen?
   (a) Stronger U.S. economic growth.
   (b) A decline in Japanese interest rates.
   (c) Higher inflation in the USA.
9. Is a stronger dollar good or bad for America? Explain.
10. Could government-induced currency depreciations act as barriers to trade? Should nations pursue such a policy?

Web Activities

1. What is the currrent exchange rate with the European euro? To find out, log on to moneycentral.msn.com/investor/market/rates.asp. Track the change over a three-day period. What happens to the U.S. $ price of an imported item worth 3,000 euros during that three-day period?
2. Find out possible benefits of the euro for European consumers at www.europe-euro.com. What are the possible problems?
3. What was the value of the U.S. current-account balance in the most recently reported period? Find out at www.whitehouse.gov/fsbr/international.html. What does this balance represent? If the value of the U.S. $ were to increase, would the current account balance likely increase or decrease? Explain.

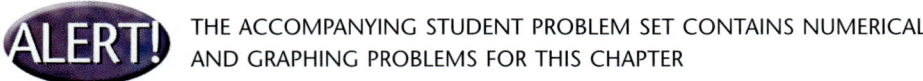

THE ACCOMPANYING STUDENT PROBLEM SET CONTAINS NUMERICAL AND GRAPHING PROBLEMS FOR THIS CHAPTER

GLOSSARY

Note: Numbers in parentheses indicate the chapters in which the definitions appear.

absolute advantage: The ability of a country to produce a specific good with fewer resources (per unit of output) than other countries. (35)

acreage set-aside: Land withdrawn from production as part of policy to increase crop prices. (29)

AD excess: The amount by which aggregate demand must be reduced to achieve full-employment equilibrium after allowing for price-level changes. (11)

AD shortfall: The amount of additional aggregate demand needed to achieve full employment after allowing for price-level changes. (11)

adjustable-rate mortgage (ARM): A mortgage (home loan) that adjusts the nominal interest rate to changing rates of inflation. (7)

aggregate demand (AD): The total quantity of output (real GDP) demanded at alternative price levels in a given time period, *ceteris paribus*. (8)(9)(10)(11)(13)(15)

aggregate expenditure: The rate of total expenditure desired at alternative levels of income, *ceteris paribus*. (9)

aggregate supply (AS): The total quantity of output (real GDP) producers are willing and able to supply at alternative price levels in a given time period, *ceteris paribus*. (8)(9)(10)(11)(16)

antitrust: Government intervention to alter market structure or prevent abuse of market power. (4)(24)(25)(27)

appreciation: A rise in the price of one currency relative to another. (36)

arithmetic growth: An increase in quantity by a constant amount each year. (17)

asset: Anything having exchange value in the marketplace; wealth. (12)

automatic stabilizer: Federal expenditure or revenue item that automatically responds countercyclically to changes in national income, like unemployment benefits, income taxes. (12)(19)

average fixed cost (AFC): Total fixed cost divided by the quantity produced in a given time period. (21)

average propensity to consume (APC): Total consumption in a given period divided by total disposable income. (9)

average total cost (ATC): Total cost divided by the quantity produced in a given time period. (21)(23)(24)

average variable cost (AVC): Total variable cost divided by the quantity produced in a given time period. (21)

balance of payments: A summary record of a country's international economic transactions in a given period of time. (36)

balance-of-payments deficit: An excess demand for foreign currency at current exchange rates. (36)

balance-of-payments surplus: An excess demand for domestic currency at current exchange rates. (36)

bank reserves: Assets held by a bank to fulfill its deposit obligations. (13)

barriers to entry: Obstacles that make it difficult or impossible for would-be producers to enter a particular market, such as patents. (23)(24)(25)(26)(27)(28)(29)

barter: The direct exchange of one good for another, without the use of money. (13)

base period: The time period used for comparative analysis; the basis for indexing, e.g., of price changes. (5)(7)(17)

bilateral monopoly: A market with only one buyer (a monopsonist) and one seller (a monopolist). (31)

bond: A certificate acknowledging a debt and the amount of interest to be paid each year until repayment; an IOU. (14)(32)

bracket creep: The movement of taxpayers into higher tax brackets (rates) as nominal incomes grow. (7)

breakeven level of income: The income level at which welfare eligibility ceases. (34)

budget constraint: A line depicting all combinations of goods that are affordable with a given income and given prices. (20)

budget deficit: Amount by which government spending exceeds government revenue in a given time period. (12)

budget surplus: An excess of government revenues over government expenditures in a given time period. (12)

business cycle: Alternating periods of economic growth and contraction. (8)(9)(19)

capital: Final goods produced for use in the production of other goods, e.g., equipment, structures. (1)

capital deficit: The amount by which the capital outflow exceeds the capital inflow in a given time period. (18)

capital gain: An increase in the market value of an asset. (32)

capital-intensive: Production processes that use a high ratio of capital to labor inputs. (2)

capital surplus: The amount by which the capital inflow exceeds the capital outflow in a given time period. (18)

cartel: A group of firms with an explicit, formal agreement to fix prices and output shares in a particular market. (25)

cash transfers: Income transfers that entail direct cash payments to recipients, e.g., Social Security, welfare, and unemployment benefits. (34)

categorical grants: Federal grants to state and local governments for specific expenditure purposes. (4)

ceteris paribus: The assumption of nothing else changing. (1)(3)(20)

collective bargaining: Direct negotiations between employers and unions to determine labor market outcomes. (31)

comparative advantage: The ability of a country to produce a specific good at a lower opportunity cost than its trading partners. (2)(18)(35)

competitive firm: A firm without market power, with no ability to alter the market price of the goods it produces. (22)

competitive market: A market in which no buyer or seller has market power. (23)

complementary goods: Goods frequently consumed in combination; when the price of good x rises, the demand for good y falls, *ceteris paribus*. (3)(20)

concentration ratio: The proportion of total industry output produced by the largest firms (usually the four largest). (25)(26)

constant returns to scale: Increases in plant size do not affect minimum average cost; minimum per-unit costs are identical for small plants and large plants. (21)

Consumer Price Index (CPI): A measure (index) of changes in the average price of consumer goods and services. (7)

consumption: Expenditure by consumers on final goods and services. (9)

consumption function: A mathematical relationship indicating the rate of desired consumer spending at various income levels. (9)

consumption possibilities: The alternative combinations of goods and services that a country could consume in a given time period. (35)

contestable market: An imperfectly competitive industry subject to potential entry if prices or profits increase. (24)(25)(27)

corporate stock: Shares of ownership in a corporation. (32)

corporation: A business organization having a continuous existence independent of its members (owners) and power and liabilities distinct from those of its members. (32)

cost efficiency: The amount of output associated with an additional dollar spent on input; the MPP of an input divided by its price (cost). (30)

cost-of-living adjustment (COLA): Automatic adjustments of nominal income to the rate of inflation. (7)

coupon rate: Interest rate set for a bond at time of issuance. (32)

cross-price elasticity of demand: Percentage change in the quantity demanded of X divided by percentage change in price of Y. (20)

cross-subsidization: Use of high prices and profits on one product to subsidize low prices on another product. (27)

crowding in: An increase in private-sector borrowing (and spending) caused by decreased government borrowing. (12)(17)

crowding out: A reduction in private-sector borrowing (and spending) caused by increased government borrowing. (11)(12)(15)(17)(18)

current yield: The rate of return on a bond; the annual interest payment divided by the bond's price. (32)

cyclical deficit: That portion of the budget deficit attributable to unemployment or inflation. (12)

cyclical unemployment: Unemployment attributable to a lack of job vacancies, that is, to inadequate aggregate demand. (6)(9)(10)

debt ceiling: An explicit, legislated limit on the amount of outstanding national debt. (12)

debt service: The interest required to be paid each year on outstanding debt. (12)

default: Failure to make scheduled payments of interest or principal on a bond. (32)

deficiency payment: Income transfer paid to farmers for difference between target and support prices. (29)

deficit ceiling: An explicit, legislated limitation on the size of the budget deficit. (12)

deficit spending: The use of borrowed funds to finance government expenditures that exceed tax revenues. (12)

deflation: A decrease in the average level of prices of goods and services. (7)

demand: The willingness and ability to buy specific quantities of a good at alternative prices in a given time period, *ceteris paribus*. (3)(20)

demand curve: A curve describing the quantities of a good a consumer is willing and able to buy at alternative prices in a given time period, *ceteris paribus*. (3)(20)

demand for labor: The quantities of labor employers are willing and able to hire at alternative wage rates in a given time period, *ceteris paribus*. (30)(31)

demand for money: The quantities of money people are willing and able to hold at alternative interest rates, *ceteris paribus*. (15)

demand-pull inflation: An increase in the price level initiated by excessive aggregate demand. (9)(10)

demand schedule: A table showing the quantities of a good a consumer is willing and able to buy at alternative prices in a given time period, *ceteris paribus*. (3)

deposit creation: The creation of transactions deposits by bank lending. (13)

depreciation: The consumption of capital in the production process; the wearing out of plant and equipment. (5)

depreciation (currency): A fall in the price of one currency relative to another. (36)

derived demand: The demand for labor and other factors of production results from (depends on) the demand for final goods and services produced by these factors. (30)

devaluation: An abrupt depreciation of a currency whose value was fixed or managed by the government. (36)

discount rate: The rate of interest the Federal Reserve charges for lending reserves to private banks. (14)

discounting: Federal Reserve lending of reserves to private banks. (14)

discouraged worker: An individual who isn't actively seeking employment but would look for or accept a job if one were available. (6)

discretionary fiscal spending: Those elements of the federal budget not determined by past legislative or executive commitments. (12)

disposable income (DI): After-tax income of households; personal income less personal taxes. (5)(9)(11)

dissaving: Consumption expenditure in excess of disposable income; a negative saving flow. (9)

dividend: Amount of corporate profits paid out for each share of stock. (32)

dumping: The sale of goods in export markets at prices below domestic prices. (35)

economic cost: The value of all resources used to produce a good or service; opportunity cost. (21)(22)

economic growth: An increase in output (real GDP); an expansion of production possibilities. (1)(2)(6)(17)

economic profit: The difference between total revenues and total economic costs. (22)(23)(26)(27)(29)

economics: The study of how best to allocate scarce resources among competing uses. (1)

economies of scale: Reductions in minimum average costs that come about through increases in the size (scale) of plant and equipment. (21)(24)(27)

effective tax rate: Taxes paid divided by total income. (33)

efficiency: Maximum output of a good from the resources used in production. (1)(21)(23)

efficiency decision: The choice of a production process for any given rate of output. (28)(30)

elasticity of labor supply: The percentage change in the quantity of labor supplied divided by the percentage change in wage rate. (30)

embargo: A prohibition on exports or imports. (35)

emission charge: A fee imposed on polluters, based on the quantity of pollution. (28)

employment rate: The percentage of the adult population that is employed. (17)

entrepreneurship: The assembling of resources to produce new or improved products and technologies. (1)

equation of exchange: Money supply (M) times velocity of circulation (V) equals level of aggregate spending ($P \times Q$). (15)(16)

equilibrium (macro): The combination of price level and real output that is compatible with both aggregate demand and aggregate supply. (8)(9)(11)

equilibrium GDP: The value of total output at (real GDP) produced at macro equilibrium (AS-AD)(9)

equilibrium price: The price at which the quantity of a good demanded in a given time period equals the quantity supplied. (3)(23)(35)(36)

equilibrium rate of interest: The interest rate at which the quantity of money demanded in a given time period equals the quantity of money supplied. (15)

equilibrium wage: The wage rate at which the quantity of labor supplied in a given time period equals the quantity of labor demanded. (30)(31)

excess reserves: Bank reserves in excess of required reserves. (13)(14)

exchange rate: The price of one country's currency expressed in terms of another's; the domestic price of a foreign currency. (18)(36)

expected value: The probable value of a future payment, including the risk of nonpayment. (32)

expenditure equilibrium: The rate of output at which desired spending equals the value of output. (9)

explicit costs: A payment made for the use of a resource (21)(22)

exports: Goods and services sold to foreign buyers. (2)(5)(18)(35)

external costs: Costs of a market activity borne by a third party; the difference between the social and private costs of a market activity. (28)

external debt: U.S. government debt (Treasury bonds) held by foreign households and institutions. (12)

externalities: Costs (or benefits) of a market activity borne by a third party; the difference between the social and private costs (benefits) of a market activity. (2)(4)(28)

factor market: Any place where factors of production (e.g., land, labor, capital) are bought and sold. (3)

factors of production: Resource inputs used to produce goods and services, e.g., land, labor, capital, entrepreneurship. (1)(2)(21)

federal funds rate: The interest rate for interbank reserve loans. (14)(15)

financial intermediary: Institution (e.g., a bank or the stock market) that makes savings available to dissavers (e.g., investors). (32)

fine-tuning: Adjustments in economic policy designed to counteract small changes in economic outcomes; continuous responses to changing economic conditions. (19)

fiscal policy: The use of government taxes and spending to alter macroeconomic outcomes. (8)(11)(12)(19)

fiscal restraint: Tax hikes or spending cuts intended to reduce (shift) aggregate demand. (11)(12)(19)

fiscal stimulus: Tax cuts or spending hikes intended to increase (shift) aggregate demand. (11)(19)

fiscal year (FY): The 12-month period used for accounting purposes; begins October 1 for the federal government. (12)

fixed costs: Costs of production that don't change when the rate of output is altered, e.g., the cost of basic plant and equipment. (21)(22)

flat tax: A single-rate tax system. (33)

flexible exchange rates: A system in which exchange rates are permitted to vary with market supply-and-demand conditions; floating exchange rates. (36)

foreign-exchange markets: Places where foreign currencies are bought and sold. (36)

foreign-exchange reserves: Holdings of foreign exchange by official government agencies, usually the central bank or treasury. (36)

free rider: An individual who reaps direct benefits from someone else's purchase (consumption) of a public good. (4)

frictional unemployment: Brief periods of unemployment experienced by people moving between jobs or into the labor market. (6)

full employment: The lowest rate of unemployment compatible with price stability; variously estimated at between 4 and 6 percent unemployment. (6)(10)

full-employment GDP: The value of total market output (real GDP) produced at full employment. (8)(9)(10)

game theory: The study of decision making in situations where strategic interaction (moves and countermoves) occurs between rivals. (25)

GDP deflator: A price index that refers to all goods and services included in GDP. (7)

GDP gap (real): The difference between full-employment GDP and equilibrium GDP. (10)(11)(19)

GDP per capita: Total GDP divided by total population; average GDP. (5)(17)

geometric growth: An increase in quantity by a constant proportion each year. (17)

Gini coefficient: A mathematical summary of inequality based on the Lorenz curve. (33)

gold reserves: Stocks of gold held by a government to purchase foreign exchange. (36)

gold standard: An agreement by countries to fix the price of their currencies in terms of gold; a mechanism for fixing exchange rates. (36)

government failure: Government intervention that fails to improve economic outcomes. (1)(4)(27)(28)(33)

gross business saving: Depreciation allowances and retained earnings. (10)

gross domestic product (GDP): The total market value of all final goods and services produced within a nation's borders in a given time period. (2)(5)

gross investment: Total investment expenditure in a given time period. (5)

growth rate: Percentage change in real output from one period to another. (17)

growth recession: A period during which real GDP grows but at a rate below the long-term trend of 3 percent. (8)(19)

Herfindahl-Hirshman Index (HHI): Measure of industry concentration that accounts for number of firms and size of each. (25)

horizontal equity: Principle that people with equal incomes should pay equal taxes. (33)

human capital: The knowledge and skills possessed by the workforce. (2)(16)(17)

hyperinflation: Inflation rate in excess of 200 percent, lasting at least one year. (7)

implicit cost: The value of resources used, even when no direct payment is made. (21)(22)

imports: Goods and services purchased from international sources. (2)(5)(18)(35)

income effect of wages: An increased wage rate allows a person to reduce hours worked without losing income. (30)

income elasticity of demand: Percentage change in quantity demanded divided by percentage change in income. (20)(29)

income quintile: One-fifth of the population, rank-ordered by income (e.g., top fifth). (2)

income share: The proportion of total income received by a particular group. (33)

income transfers: Payments to individuals for which no current goods or services are exchanged, e.g., Social Security, welfare, unemployment benefits. (2)(11)(12)(33)

income velocity of money (V): The number of times per year, on average, a dollar is used to purchase final goods and services; $PQ \div M$. (15)

indifference curve: A curve depicting alternative combinations of goods that yield equal satisfaction. (20)

indifference map: The set of indifference curves that depicts all possible levels of utility attainable from various combinations of goods. (20)

inferior good: Good for which demand decreases when income rises. (20)

inflation: An increase in the average level of prices of goods and services. (4)(5)(7)(8)

inflation rate: The annual percentage rate of increase in the average price level. (7)

inflationary GDP gap: The amount by which equilibrium GDP exceeds full employment GDP. (9)(10)(19)

infrastructure: The transportation, communications, education, judicial, and other institutional systems that facilitate market exchanges. (16)

initial public offering (IPO): The first issuance (sale) to the general public of stock in a corporation. (32)

injection: An addition of spending to the circular flow of income. (10)

in-kind income: Goods and services received directly, without payment, in a market transaction. (33)

in-kind transfers: Direct transfers of goods and services rather than cash; examples include food stamps, Medicaid benefits, and housing subsidies. (34)

interest rate: The price paid for the use of money. (15)

intermediate goods: Goods or services purchased for use as input in the production of final goods or in services. (5)

internal debt: U.S. government debt (Treasury bonds) held by U.S. households and institutions. (12)

investment: Expenditures on (production of) new plant, equipment, and structures (capital) in a given time period, plus changes in business inventories. (2)(5)(9)(16)

investment decision: The decision to build, buy, or lease plant and equipment; to enter or exit an industry. (22)(23)

item weight: The percentage of total expenditure spent on a specific product; used to compute inflation indexes. (7)

labor force: All persons over age 16 who are either working for pay or actively seeking paid employment. (6)(17)

labor-force participation rate: The percentage of the working-age population working or seeking employment. (6)(34)

labor productivity: Amount of output produced by a worker in a given period of time; output per hour (or day, etc.). (16)

labor supply: The willingness and ability to work specific amounts of time at alternative wage rates in a given time period, *ceteris paribus*. (30)(31)(34)

laissez faire: The doctrine of "leave it alone," of nonintervention by government in the market mechanism. (l)(8)(27)

law of demand: The quantity of a good demanded in a given time period increases as its price falls, *ceteris paribus*. (3)(8)(20)

law of diminishing marginal utility: The marginal utility of a good declines as more of it is consumed in a given time period. (20)

law of diminishing returns: The marginal physical product of a variable input declines as more of it is employed with a given quantity of other (fixed) inputs. (21)(30)

law of supply: The quantity of a good supplied in a given time period increases as its price increases, *ceteris paribus*. (3)

leakage: Income not spent directly on domestic output but instead diverted from the circular flow, e.g., saving, imports, taxes. (10)(18)

liability: An obligation to make future payment; debt. (12)

liquidity: The ability of an asset to be converted into cash. (32)

liquidity trap: The portion of the money demand curve that is horizontal; people are willing to hold unlimited amounts of money at some (low) interest rate. (15)

loan rate: The implicit price paid by the government for surplus crops taken as collateral for loans to farmers. (29)

long run: A period of time long enough for all inputs to be varied (no fixed costs). (21)(22)

long-run competitive equilibrium: $p = MC = $ minimum ATC. (23)

Lorenz curve: A graphic illustration of the cumulative size distribution of income; contrasts complete equality with the actual distribution of income. (33)

macroeconomics: The study of aggregate economic behavior, of the economy as a whole. (1)(8)

managed exchange rates: A system in which governments intervene in foreign-exchange markets to limit but not eliminate exchange-rate fluctuations; "dirty floats." (36)

marginal cost (MC): The increase in total cost associated with a one-unit increase in production. (21)(22)(23)

marginal cost pricing: The offer (supply) of goods at prices equal to their marginal cost. (23)(24)(26)(27)

marginal factor cost (MFC): The change in total costs that results from a one-unit increase in the quantity of a factor employed. (31)

marginal physical product (MPP): The change in total output associated with one additional unit of input. (21)(30)

marginal propensity to consume (MPC): The fraction of each additional (marginal) dollar of disposable income spent on consumption; the change in consumption divided by the change in disposable income. (9)(10)(11)

marginal propensity to import (MPM): The fraction of each additional (marginal) dollar of disposable income spent on imports. (18)

marginal propensity to save (MPS): The fraction of each additional (marginal) dollar of disposable income not spent on consumption; $1 - $ MPC. (9)(18)

marginal rate of substitution: The rate at which a consumer is willing to exchange one good for another; the relative marginal utilities of two goods. (20)

marginal revenue (MR): The change in total revenue that results from a one-unit increase in the quantity sold. (22)(24)(25)

marginal revenue product (MRP): The change in total revenue associated with one additional unit of input. (30)(31)(33)

marginal tax rate: The tax rate imposed on the last (marginal) dollar of income. (16)(33)(34)

marginal utility: The change in total utility obtained by consuming one additional (marginal) unit of a good or service. (20)

marginal wage: The change in total wages paid associated with a one-unit increase in the quantity of labor employed. (31)

market demand: The total quantities of a good or service people are willing and able to buy at alternative prices in a given time period; the sum of individual demands. (3)

market failure: An imperfection in the market mechanism that prevents optimal outcomes. (1)(4)(25)(27)(28)(33)(34)

market mechanism: The use of market prices and sales to signal desired outputs (or resource allocations). (1)(3)(4)(23)(32)

market power: The ability to alter the market price of a good or service. (4)(22)(24)(26)(29)(31)

market share: The percentage of total market output produced by a single firm. (25)

market shortage: The amount by which the quantity demanded exceeds the quantity supplied at a given price; excess demand. (3)(36)

market structure: The number and relative size of firms in an industry. (22)(25)

market supply: The total quantities of a good that sellers are willing and able to sell at alternative prices in a given time period, *ceteris paribus*. (3)(23)

market supply of labor: The total quantity of labor that workers are willing and able to supply at alternative wage rates in a given time period, *ceteris paribus*. (30)

market surplus: The amount by which the quantity supplied exceeds the quantity demanded at a given price; excess supply. (3)(29)

merit good: A good or service society deems everyone is entitled to some minimal quantity of. (4)

microeconomics: The study of individual behavior in the economy, of the components of the larger economy. (1)

mixed economy: An economy that uses both market signals and government directives to allocate goods and resources. (1)

monetary policy: The use of money and credit controls to influence macroeconomic outcomes. (8)(14)(15)(19)

money: Anything generally accepted as a medium of exchange. (13)

money illusion: The use of nominal dollars rather than real dollars to gauge changes in one's income or wealth. (7)

money multiplier: The number of deposit (loan) dollars that the banking system can create from $1 of excess reserves; equal to $1 \div$ required reserve ratio. (13)(14)

money supply (M1): Currency held by the public, plus balances in transactions accounts. (13)(14)(15)

money supply (M2): M1 plus balances in most savings accounts and money market funds. (13)(14)(15)

monopolistic competition: A market in which many firms produce similar goods or services but each maintains some independent control of its own price. (26)

monopoly: A firm that produces the entire market supply of a particular good or service. (2)(4)(22)(24)

monopsony: A market in which there's only one buyer. (31)

moral hazard: An incentive to engage in undesirable behavior. (29)(34)

multiplier: The multiple by which an initial change in aggregate spending will alter total expenditure after an infinite number of spending cycles; $1/(1 - $ MPC). (10)(11)(18)(19)

national debt: Accumulated debt of the federal government. (12)

Injections, 199, **201**
   exports as, 375
   financing, 277
   and macro stability, 212
In-kind income, 695
In-kind transfers, 77, **713**
Innovation, 186
Inputs
   alternative production processes, 649
   control of, 525
   cost efficiency, 648–649
   efficiency decision, 649–650
   least-cost combination, 650
   varying levels of, 445–446
Instability, 153, 164, 197
   empirical, 187–188
   short-run, 166–168
Institutional constraints, 114–115
Insurance companies, 295
Intangibles, 108
Intel Corporation, 1, 2, 504, 679–680
Interest, on national debt, 252
Interest-rate effect, 160–161, 677
Interest rates, 299
   and agriculture, 625
   changing, 301–302
   equilibrium, 301
   in Europe, 293
   and exchange rates, 759
   Federal Reserve regulation, 19
   flexible, 201
   hierarchy of, 302
   higher, 303–304
   and investment, 186, 302
   in Latin America, 145
   and liquidity trap, 305–306
   monetarist view, 311
   monetary stimulus, 302–303
   and money supply changes, 293, 294
   and mortgage rates, 304
   real, 145
   real versus nominal, 312–314
   and savings, 675
   short- versus long-term, 304, 314
   and spending, 302–304
   time value of money, 676–677
Intergenerational redistribution, 724
Intermediate goods, 96–97
Internal debt, 250
Internal Revenue Service, 700
   on underground economy, 96, 97
International Brotherhood of Electrical Workers, 657
International capital flows, 380
International Energy Agency, 548
International finance
   Asian crisis, 759–760, 767
   balance of payments, 755–757
   Brazilian crisis, 767–768
   capital account balance, 757
   capital inflows/outflows, 378
   currency bailouts, 767–768
   current account balance, 757
   demand/supply of dollars, 753–754
   exchange rate intervention, 762–767
   exchange rates, 752–753
   fixed exchange rates, 762–765
   flexible exchange rates, 765–767
   foreign exchange markets, 753–754
   market forces, 758–759
   resistance to exchange rate changes, 760–762
   value of the dollar, 754–755
International Institute for Strategic Studies, 8
International Monetary Fund, 382
   bailouts, 767–768
International Paper, 381
International trade; *see also* Protectionist measures; Trade barriers
   absolute advantage, 736–737

   balance of payments, 755–757
   comparative advantage, 736
   and competitiveness, 381–382
   exchange rate changes, 760–762
   exchange rates, 752–753
   exports, 729–731
   exports as injections, 375
   and flexible exchange rates, 766
   GATT, 748
   in global market, 748–750
   imbalances, 375–377
   impact of restrictions, 744–746
   imports, 729
   imports as leakage, 371–374
   motivation to trade, 731–736
   multilateral pacts, 748
   mutual gains, 735–736
   net exports, 32–33
   opportunity costs, 736
   production and consumption with, 733–735
   production and consumption without, 732–733
   protests against, 749
   regional pacts, 749–750
   role of prices and markets, 737–739
   and specialization, 380–381, 732
   terms of trade, 737–739
   trade balances, 730–731
   U. S. trade patterns, 728–731
   U. S. trading partners, 729
   voluntary restraint agreements, 746
   World Trade Organization, 748–749
International Trade Commission, 739
Internet, 497
Internet sites, 466
Internet stock collapse, 510
Interstate Commerce Commission, 343, 582–583
Inventory, undesired, 203
Inventory depletion, 212
Inventory investment, 185
Investment, 31, 101, 186, 336
   actual versus desired, 203
   by businesses, 201–202
   crowded out, 232
   decline in, 203–204
   determinants of, 185–186
   for economic growth, 41
   and expectations, 186, 306–308
   expected value, 678
   fixed, 185
   foreign, 359
   impact of deficit spending, 253
   incentives, 339–340, 361
   interest rate effect, 677
   and interest rates, 186, 302
   inventory, 185
   and macro instability, 187–188
   in physical capital, 361–362
   risk premium, 675
   and savings, 358
   shifts in, 186–188
   and taxes, 226–228
   and technology/innovation, 186
Investment decision, 486–487, **495**
Investment demand curve, 307
Investment goods, 31–32, 102
Investment spending, 187
   and aggregate demand, 202
   consequences of, 211–212
   by small business, 203
Investment tax credit, 339
Invisible hand, 12–13, 58–59, 64
IOEC, 164–165
Ip, Greg, 308
Isuzu Motors Ltd, 460, 461
Itemized deductions, 700
Item weight, 140
Ivy League Colleges, 551
Iwata, Edward, 50, 208

J. Walter Thompson, 564
Jackson, Thomas Penfield, 531
James, Charles A., 529, 551
Japan
   economic crisis, 307
   GDP growth in 2001, 167
   liquidity trap, 307
   soy sauce index, 402
   thrift, 213
   voluntary restraint agreements, 746
Jensen, Elizabeth, 530
Jevons, W. Stanley, 367
Jobs, Steve, 498, 689–690, 694
Johnson, Kevin, 607
Johnson, Lyndon B., 227, 395, 404
Johnston, Summerfield K., 546
Jones, Del, 652
Jordan, Mary, 402

Kapital (Marx), 13
Karl, Kurt, 230
Keller, Larry, 165
Kelman, Steven, 87
Kennedy, John F., 227
Kennedy, Paul, 364
Kessler, Glenn, 338
Keynes, John Maynard, 13
   adjustment process, 208
   aggregate expenditure, 194–195
   aggregate supply curve, 327, 328
   autonomous consumption, 179
   average propensity to consume, 177, 178
   budget deficits, 238
   business cycles, 212
   business investments, 201–202
   on consumption, 176–177
   consumption function, 179–185
   consumption shortfall, 195
   critics of, 234
   cure for recession, 315
   demand side of market, 174
   expectations, 306–308
   fiscal policy, 171, 220–221, 238, 241
   full-employment GDP, 190
   government intervention, 218
   government spending, 233
   higher interest rates, 314
   inflationary GDP gap, 190, 191
   on leakages and injections, 199
   liquidity trap, 306
   on long run, 170
   on macro equilibrium, 189
   macro failure, 175, 191–192
   macro instability, 197
   macro stability, 212
   marginal propensity to consume, 177–178
   market economy, 198
   model of the economy, 157–158
   monetary policy, 317–321
   monetary stimulus, 308–309
   money supply changes, 309
   money supply targets, 319–321
   multiplier process, 201–208
   nominal interest rate, 315
   nonconsumer spending, 195–196
   paradox of thrift, 213
   policy levers, 316, 391
   recessionary GDP gap, 190, 191
   response to Great Depression, 152–153
   on short-run instability, 166–167
   tax cuts, 334, 335
   unstable equilibrium, 190–191
   velocity of money, 316–317
Keynesian cross, 194–107, 196
Keynesian macro model, 398
Keynesian revolution, 152–153
Keynesians, 407

I-10 INDEX

Khan, Salina, 545
Kinked demand curve, 543–545, 548–550
Kinnaman, Thomas, 604–605
Klamka, Peter, 433
Klingenberg, Diether, 371
Knowledge, advances in, 359–360
Knox, Kevin, 50
Kramlich, Richard, 690
Krebs, Edwin, 761
Krueger, Alan B., 361
Krupnick, Alan J., 610
Ku, Neha, 167
Kuznets, Simon, 91
Kyoto Treaty, 612

Labor, 4
    marginal factor cost, 664–665
    marginal revenue product, 665–666
    share of total income, 669
Labor costs, 464–465
Labor demand
    derived demand, 637–638
    employer power, 663–666
    hiring decision, 643–645
    law of diminishing returns, 640–642
    marginal physical product, 639
    marginal revenue product, 639–640, 705
    and minimum wage, 647–648
Labor demand curve, 638–639, 643–644
Labor force, 113–115, **355**
    expansion, 122–123
    growth, 114–115
    participants, 113–114
Labor-force participation rate, 114, 722–724
Labor-intensive production, 34
Labor legislation, 37–38
Labor-leisure trade-off, 633–634
Labor market, 655–657
    and affirmative action, 341
    bilateral monopoly, 666
    choosing among inputs, 648–650
    competitive equilibrium, 656
    efficiency decision, 649–650
    equilibrium wage, 646, 656
    hiring decision, 643–645
    and immigration policy, 345
    income effect of wages, 635–636
    income versus leisure, 633–634
    labor demand, 637–642
    labor supply, 632–636
    local, 656–657
    market supply, 636–637
    minimum wage, 646–648
    monopsony, 664
    national comparisons, 635
    and NAFTA, 749
    skills gap, 340–341
    substitution effect of wages, 635–636
    union exclusion principle, 660
    union versus nonunion, 669
Labor productivity, 341
Labor supply, 335, 632–636, **633**, **655**–**656, 715**
    declining, 722–724
    determinants, 636–637, 646
    elasticity of, 637
    of firms, 643
    and income transfers, 715
    institutional constraints, 637
    and minimum wage, 647–648
    tax elasticity of, 719–720
    and wage rate, 659–660
Labor supply curve, 634–636
Labor unions
    AFL-CIO, 662
    changing unionization rates, 661
    collective bargaining, 666–668

    early growth, 661
    effect on prices, 669–670
    employer power, 663–666
    exclusion policy, 660–661
    extent of power, 661–662
    impact of, 668–670
    labor contract, 658
    marginal wage, 658–659
    membership trends, 661–662, 670
    merging to survive, 670–671
    and monopsony, 663–666
    objectives, 657
    political impact, 670
    productivity and, 670
    relative wages, 668–669
    replacement workers, 661
    and share of total income, 669
    teaching assistants, 663
    types of, 657
    use of power, 657–661
    wage goal, 659–660
    work rules, 670
La Connivence restaurant, Paris, 63
Laffer, Arthur, 338
Laissez-faire, 13, 151, 574–**575**
Land, 4
Land values, 625
Law of demand, 50, 152, 417, 442
Law of diminishing marginal utility, 415
Law of diminishing returns, 149, 478–479, 640–642
Law of increasing opportunity costs, 8
Law of supply, 56
Lawsuits, 525
Lazarus, David, 66
Leading economic indicators, 192–193
Leading indicators, 399
Leakage, 198–202, **199, 373**
    and aggregate demand, 200
    business saving, 200–201
    consumer saving, 199–201, 277
    and disposable income, 200
    from government surpluses, 246
    imports, 371–374, 743
    imports and taxes, 200
    and macro stability, 212
Least-cost production process, 650
Leeds, Jeff, 522
Legal fees, 537n
Legal framework, 36–37
Leisure, 633–634
Leith, Scott, 564
Lenin, Vladimir, 298
Leung, Shirley, 428
Liabilities, 249–**250,** 271
Liagre, Christina de, 63
Limited liability, 679
Linear curves, 24
Lippman, John, 530
Lippman, Thomas W., 9
Liquidity, 687
Liquidity trap, 305–**306, 317**
    in Japan, 307
Living standards, 350, 732
L money supply, 266
Loanable funds
    current yield, 688
    demand for, 678–679
    and interest rate, 687
    supply of, 674–675
Loan rate, 621
Local distribution monopolies, 590–591
Local labor market, 656–657
Local markets, 538–539
Local telephone rates, 584
Lockouts, 667
Long-distance telephone rates, 583–584
Long-run, 460, 486–487

Long-run aggregate supply curve, 311
Long-run average costs, 460–461
Long-run competitive equilibrium, 502–503
Long-run marginal costs, 462
Long-run production costs, 487
Long-run profit, 567
Long-run self-adjustment, 169–170
Long-term interest rates, 305–305, 314
Loopholes, 700
Lorenz curve, 696–**697**
Los Angeles City Council, 608
Lott, Trent, 405
Lotteries, 83
Lotus Development Corporation, 556
Low-income countries, 30
Lucent Technologies, 207
Luxuries versus necessities, 422

Macro disturbances, 164–165
Macroeconomics, 16–17, **151**
    classical view, 151–152
    focus of, 91
Macroeconomic theory, 386
Macro economy, 157–166
Macro equilibrium, 162–163, 174–175, **175,** 208–211, **220**
Macro failure, 152–153, 163–165, 189–192, 197
Macro instability, 77, 185, 197
Macro intervention, 19–20
Macro models, 398–399
Macro outcomes, 393–395
Macro policy options, 170–172
Macro stability, 201, 212
Macro success, 189
Maddox, John, 365n
Madigan, Kathleen, 374
Maglev trains, 347
Magnetek Inc., 527
Maisel, Sherman, 767
Malthus, Thomas R., 1, 362–363
Malthusian formula, 362–364
Managed exchange rates, 767
Management-labor relations, 359
Management training, 359
Mandatory Benefits Act, 342
Manufacturing
    decline in, 30–31, 125
    slump in 2001, 187
Marcus, Rudolph A., 761
Marginal cost, 450–**451,** 456–**457,** 458, 479, 480, 489, 494–**495,** 575
Marginal cost curve, 494–495
Marginal cost pricing, 509, 523, 568, 576, 577
Marginal factor cost, 664–**665**
Marginal physical product, 448–449, **451,** 464, **639**
    diminishing, 640–642
Marginal productivity, 448–449
Marginal propensity to consume, 177–178, **204**–205, **222**
    equal to consumption function, 182
Marginal propensity to import, 373
Marginal propensity to save, 178, 373
Marginal rate of substitution, 441–442
Marginal resource cost, 450–451
Marginal revenue, 479–480, **515,** 549–550
    of monopoly, 519–520
Marginal revenue product, 665–666, **639**–640, **705**
    changes in, 645
    diminishing, 642
    as labor demand, 643–644
Marginal tax rate, 334–340, **697**–**698, 717**
    changes in, 699
    national comparisons, 708
    reductions, 702–703
    in United Kingdom, 699
    and welfare payments, 717–719

Marginal utility, 415, 437–438
　and price, 441–442
　versus price, 430–431
Marginal utility of income, 634
Marginal wage, 658–660
Market-based environmental options, 603–607
Market-basket of goods, 138–139
Market clearing, 58–59
Market demand, 53, 682
　determinants of, 51
　for dollars, 753
　for labor, 646
Market demand curve, 53–55, 476–477
　construction of, 54
Market economy
　inherently unstable, 153
　invisible hand, 12–13
　Keynes distrust of, 198
Market entry/exit; *see* Entry; Exit
Market failure, 15, 38, 70, 70–77, **556,** 575, 602, 697, 714
　causes of, 70–71
　consumption externalities, 602–603
　externalities, 73–75
　income distribution, 697
　and income transfers, 714–715
　and macro instability, 77
　and market power, 76–77
　private costs, 602
　production externalities, 601–602
　and public goods, 71–73
　social costs, 602
Market forces, 158, 758–759
Market freedom, 36
Market incentives, 599–601
Marketing orders, 620–621
Market labor supply curve, 656
Market mechanism, 12–13, **59,** 64, 70, **508**
　in public goods, 71–72
　versus voting mechanism, 86
Market outcomes, 62–64
Market participants
　factor markets, 46
　maximizing behavior, 45
　product markets, 46–47
　specialization and exchange, 45
Market power, 76, 476, 513–517, **514, 562**–563, **616,** 656
　in agriculture, 615–616
　comparative perspective, 522–526
　concentration ratio, 537, 538
　contestable market, 537
　defense of, 526–530
　degrees of, 536
　demand curve, 514
　determinants of, 536–537
　firm size, 537, 539
　inequity in, 76–77
　measurement problems, 537–539
　monopolistic competition, 562–563
　monopsony, 663–666
　oligopoly behavior, 539–543
　and political power, 524
　profit maximization, 514–517
　restricted supply, 76
　of unions, 655
Market price, 476, 544
Markets, 47
　adequacy or inadequacy, 69
　equilibrium, 57–62
　overproduction, 73
Market share, 540–541, 552–553
Market shortage, 60, 61–62, **763**
　of electricity, 66
Market signals, 14–15
　and environmental destruction, 41
　and future inequality, 42

　and government failure, 15
　versus government intervention, 44
　and income stagnation, 41
　and interest rates, 19
　and market failure, 15
　and Microsoft case, 19
Market structure, 474–476, **536**
　and antitrust, 511
　barriers to entry, 496
　characteristics, 536
　comparative perspective, 522–526
　degrees of power, 536
　monopolistic competition, 561–571
　monopoly, 513–533
　natural monopoly, 575
　oligopoly, 535–559
　perfect competition, 476–491, 493–511
Market supply, 55, 494–495
　determinants of, 55
Market supply curve, 493–496, 501–503
　construction of, 56–57
Market supply of labor, 636–637
Market surplus, 59–60, **620**
Market transactions, 47
Market wage, 658–659
Markkula, A. C., 689–690
Marriage penalty, 703
Marx, Karl, 13, 39, 365
Marxists, 407
Mattel, 506
Maximizing behavior, 45
Maximizing utility, 431–432
Mayfield, Mark, 483
MBA graduates, 634
McCain, John, 404
McCarthy, Joseph R., 742
McCarthy, Michael, 433
McCartney, Scott, 588
McDonald's, 562, 633
McFadden, Daniel, 44
McGraw-Hill, 76
McKenzie, Richard, 587
McKinnon, John D., 234
McKinsey and Company, 566
McWilliams, Gary, 509
Meadows, Dennis, L., 364n
Means-tested welfare programs, 714
Measures of output, 93–101
Mechanisms of choice
　command economies, 13
　continuing debate over, 13–14
　and government failure, 15
　government intervention, 13
　invisible hand, 12–13
　and market failure, 15
　mixed economy, 14–15
Medicaid, 713
Medicare, 713, 714
Medium of exchange, 263
Mellon, Andrew, 152
Meltzer, Allan H., 311
Memmott, Mark, 634
Merchandise trade, 731
Mergers and acquisitions, 554–555
Merit goods, 77
Merit pay, 640
Merrill Lynch, 152
Merva, Mary, 121
Metropolitan Statistical Areas, 142
Mexican War, 247
Mexico
　inflation in, 135
　peso crisis, 370
　trucking industry, 345
　U. S. truck ban, 747
Microcomputer industry, 496–506
　competitive process, 506–508
　entry and exit rules, 503

　exits, 506
　home versus personal computers, 503–504
　initial conditions, 497–498
　low barriers to entry, 500–501
　lure of profit, 500
　market evolution, 497
　and market power, 517–522
　personal computer market, 506
　price competition, 504
　price decline, 505
　price war, 509
　production decision, 498–499
　profit calculation, 499–500
　shift in market supply, 501–503
　shutdowns, 505
　supply shifts, 504–505
Microeconomics, 16–17
Micro intervention, 19
Microsoft Corporation, 464, 474, 535, 556
　antitrust case, 19, 76, 525, 530–533, 557, 559
Midway Airlines, 205
Military buildup, 253
Military spending, 5, 18
　cuts in, 88
Milk price supports, 623
Minimum average cost, 455–456
Minimum service regulation, 578
Minimum wage, 342, 646–648
Mischer, Michael, 44
Misery index, 330, 333
Mixed economy, 14–15
M1 money supply, 265–266, **299,** 320–321
M2 money supply, 266, 266, 299, 320–321
Models, 17
Model T Ford, 513, 529–530
Mogi, Yuzaburo, 402
Monetarists, 388–389
　aggregate supply curve, 327, 328
　equation of exchange, 309–310
　fighting inflation, 312
　fighting unemployment, 315
　focus on money supply, 310–311
　hands-off policy, 406–407
　on monetary policy, 317–321
　money supply targets, 319–321
　natural rate of unemployment, 311–312
　nominal interest rate, 315
　policy levers, 316, 391
　real output, 313
　real versus nominal rates, 312–314
　rejection of interest rate focus, 311
　short- versus long-term rates, 314
　velocity of money, 309–310
Monetarist theory, 167–168, 169–170
Monetary policy, 171, 281, 298, **299,** 383, **388–389**
　content of GDP, 315
　effect of capital imbalances, 378–379
　effect on exchange rates, 379–380
　Fed eclecticism, 319–321
　and fixed exchange rates, 765
　and income redistribution, 315
　interest rates and spending, 302–304
　Keynesian versus monetarist, 317–321
　milestones, 389
　and mix of output, 315
　monetarist view, 309
　monetary restraint, 303–304
　monetary stimulus, 302–303
　and money market, 299–302
　money supply targets, 319–321
　policy constraints, 304–309
　quantitative impact, 303
Monetary restraint, 303–304
　limits on, 307–308
Monetary stimulus, 302–303, 327
　failure in Japan, 307

Monetary tools
    to decrease money supply, 294
    discount rate, 285–287
    to increase money supply, 291–293
    open market operations, 287–291
    reserve requirement, 283–285
Money, 262–263, **264**
    common currency, 383–384
    concepts of, 264–265
    creation of, 267–273
    demand for, 299–300
    global sources, 308
    international finance, 377–378
    price of, 299
    real value of, 160
    time value of, 676–677
    types of, 263–267
Money demand curve, 300
Money illusion, 136
Money laundering, 295
Money market, 299–302
Money market equilibrium, 300–301
Money market mutual funds, 266, 294–295
Money multiplier, 272–276, **274**, **284**–285
Money supply, 263–267, **265**, **283**, 299
    changes in, 272
    composition of, 265
    decreasing, 294
    extent of Fed control, 294–296
    Fed control of, 283–291
    versus federal funds rate, 295–296
    focus of monetarists, 310–311
    impact of cuts in, 378–379
    increasing, 291–293
    L, 266
    M1, 265
    M2, 266
    M3, 266
    rate of growth, 294
Money supply targets, 319–321
Money trail, 295
Monopolistic competition, 475, **561**–**562**, 563–571
    advertising, 568–571
    barriers to entry, 563
    behavior, 563–568
    brand image, 563
    brand loyalty, 563–565
    characteristics, 536
    concentration ratio, 561–562
    entry and exit, 566–567
    excess capacity, 568
    flawed price signals, 568
    inefficiency, 567–568
    largest firms, 562
    long-run profits, 567
    marginal cost pricing, 568
    market power, 562–563
    product differentiation, 563
    production decision, 563, 565–566
Monopoly, 37, 76, 474, 513–533, **514**; *see also* Natural monopoly
    and antitrust, 530–533
    barriers to entry, 517, 521–522, 525–526
    characteristics, 536
    comparative perspective, 522–526
    computer market, 517–522
    contestable market, 529–530
    demand curve, 514
    economies of scale, 517–518, 528
    electric power plants, 590
    entrepreneurial incentives, 527–528
    marginal revenue, 519–520
    and market power, 513–517
    Microsoft case, 19
    price, 520
    price discrimination, 524–525
    price elasticity of demand, 524
    production decision, 519–520
    profit, 520–521, 561
    profit maximization, 514–517
    pros and cons of, 526–530
    reduced output, 519–520
    research and development, 527
    unions as, 658
Monopoly bank, 268–271
Monopoly franchising, 525
Monopsony, 663–666
Moral hazard, 627–**628**, **717**
    welfare, 717
Morin, Richard, 638
Mortgage loans, 144–146
Mortgage rates, 304
Morton's Restaurant Group, 428
Motorola, 504
Movement along a demand curve, 52–53, 425
MPP; *see* Marginal physical product
MRP; *see* Marginal revenue product
Muir, Frederick M., 608
Multibank world, 271–273
Multilateral trade pacts, 748
Multiplier, 205–208, **207**, **222**, 371–**372**, **390**
    balanced budget, 227
    cross-border effect, 208
    tax cut, 225–226
Multiplier cycles, 206
Multiplier effect, 201–208, 209
    of budget cuts, 230–231
    and consumer confidence, 213–214
    falling output prices, 204
    of fiscal stimulus, 222–223
    household incomes, 204
    of imports, 371–374
    income-dependent consumption, 204–205
    in inflationary GDP gap, 211–212
    inflation-unemployment trade-off, 209–211
    price and output effects, 209
    shift in aggregate demand curve, 208–209
    steps in, 206
Murdoch, Rupert, 530
Murray, Betty, 463
Mutual savings banks, 268

Nader, Ralph, 557
Naive Keynesian model, 220–221
Napster, 72
NASDAQ, 185, 487
NASDAQ Composite Index, 685–686
National Academy of Sciences, 611
National Association for Business Economics, 400
National Banking Act of 1863, 246
National Bureau of Economic Research, 142, 397
National Conference of State Legislatures, 86
National Council of Senior Citizens, 396
National debt, 246–**247**
    history of, 249
National Economic Council, 401–402
National Federation of Independent Business, 203
National Football League, 657
National Football League strike, 668
National Foundation of Funeral Directors, 463
National income, 104–**105**
National income accounting, 91–110, **92**–**93**
    chain-weighted price index, 101–102
    flow of income, 106–107
    measurement problems, 95–96
    measures of output, 93–101
    measures of income, 103–106
    national income, 104–105
    net domestic product, 101
    nominal versus real GDP, 97–101
    personal income, 105–106
    purpose, 91
    uses of output, 102–103
    value added, 96–97
National Industrial Recovery Act, 661
National Labor Relations Board, 663
National markets, 538–539
National Monetary Commission, 281–282
National Oceanic and Atmospheric Administration, 611
National Resources Defense Council, 598
National security argument, 740–741
Natural disasters, 331, 332
Natural monopoly, 76, 528, 575
    ATC curve, 575
    economies of scale, 575
    ended in phone service, 584
    minimum service regulation, 578
    output regulation, 578–579
    price regulation, 576, 577
    profit regulation, 577–578
    railroads, 582
    regulatory options, 576–580
    telephone service, 583
    unregulated behavior, 575–576
Natural rate of output, 169
Natural rate of unemployment, 124, 311–312, **388**
Natural unemployment, 211
NBC, 530
NDCHealth, 63
Necessities versus luxuries, 422
Nelson, Scott Bernard, 295
Neo-Keynesians, 407
Net domestic product, 101
Net exports, 32, 102–103, **375**
    in aggregate demand, 188–189
    crowding out, 376
Net foreign factor income, 105
Net investment, 101, 358
Netscape Communications, 531
Network economies, 556
Neusner, Noam, 381
New classical economics, 171, 406–407
New Deal, 14, 87
New Economy, 352–353
New equilibrium, 212
New growth theory, 359–360
Newport News Shipbuilding Company, 529
New products, 141
News Corporation, 530
New York City Taxi and Limousine Commission, 555
New York Mercantile Exchange, 68
New York Stock Exchange, 151, 682
New York Stock Exchange composite index, 686
Nike, Inc., 33
Nikkei Index, 686
Nintendo, 535
Nitrogen oxides, 596
Nixon, Richard M., 129, 365, 765
Nobel Prize, 761
Nominal GDP, 97–101, **98**, **140**, 352
Nominal income, 131–133
Nominal interest rate, 312–314
Nominal tax rate, 700–701
Nominal wages and prices, 134
Nonconsumer spending, 195–196
Nonlinear curves, 24
Nonmarket activities, 95–96
Nonmilitary government downsizing, 88–89
Nonprice competition, 555
    advertising, 568–571
Nontariff trade barriers, 746–748
Normal goods, 428
Normal profit, 474
Nortel Networks, 308
North American Free Trade Agreement, 344–345, 370, 747, 749–750
North Korea, 8–9, 13
Northrup Grumman Corporation, 529
Northwest Airlines, 205

No-trade equilibrium, 744
Noyce, Robert, 510
Nynex, 578, 579

Occupational Safety and Health Administration, 342–343
O'Donnell, Carey, 203
Office of Management and Budget, 81, 401
Office of Thrift Supervision, 278
Oil prices, 144, 164–165, 548
Oil price shocks, 377
Okun, Arthur M., 115, 135, 330, 694
Okun's law, 115
Old Age, Survivors, and Disability Insurance, 720
Oligopolist, 540
Oligopoly, 475, 535–559, **536**
　allocation of market share, 552–553
　antitrust guidelines, 556–559
　barriers to entry, 553–556
　battle for market share, 540–541
　behavior of, 539–543
　characteristics, 536
　versus competition, 547–550
　concentration ratio, 561–562
　coordination problems, 550–553
　game theory, 545–547
　initial equilibrium, 540
　kinked demand curve, 543–545, 548–550
　marginal revenue curve, 549–550
　network economies, 556
　payoff matrix, 545–546
　predatory pricing, 553
　price and output, 547–548
　price fixing, 550–551
　price leadership, 551–552
　price reduction, 542–543
　product differentiation, 542
　in product market, 537, 538
　profit maximization, 547–548
　response to price increase, 544–545
　response to price reduction, 543–544
　retaliation, 541–543
　sales tactics, 541
　sticky prices, 548–550
Oligopsony, 664
O'Neill, Paul, 44, 381, 383
Open economy, 372–373
Open market operations, 287–291, **289**–291, 292–293
Open market purchases, 290
Open market sales, 290–291
Opportunity cost, 5–6, **48**, **430**, **446**, **508**, **576**, **609**, **736**
　absolute advantage, 737
　bonds, 687
　in competitive market, 508–509
　of debt service, 252–253
　and demand, 48
　environmental protection, 609
　of government spending, 245
　of government failure, 84–85
　of government purchases, 252
　of government spending, 80
　of holding money, 299
　in international trade, 736
　of national debt, 253
　in North Korea, 8–9
　and product choice, 430
　and production possibilities, 6–8
　of products, 446–447
　of transfer payments, 252–253
　of working, 633–634
Opportunity wage, 651
Optimal consumption, 431–432, 440–441
Optimal mix of output, 70, 254
Optimal outcomes, 64

Optimal rate of pollution, 609
Organic pollution, 597–598
Organization for Economic Cooperation and Development, 146, 606
Organization of Petroleum Exporting Countries, 144, 331–333, 377, 548, 614
O'Sullivan, Jim, 230
Output
　actual versus potential, 10
　and costs, 478–479
　decline in, 187
　decline in Great Depression, 158
　equal to income, 103–104
　falling, 204
　gains from trade, 735–736
　growth in U.S. 1900-2000, 29
　and income transfers, 715
　inflation-adjusted value, 140
　limits to, 4, 5
　and marginal revenue, 479–480
　measures of, 93–101
　monetarist view, 313
　monopolistic competition, 565–566
　of monopoly, 519–520
　in multiplier process, 209
　national comparisons, 27
　natural rate of, 169
　of oligopoly, 547–548
　optimal mix, 70, 254
　in perfect competition, 476
　and production possibilities curve, 7–8
　profit-maximizing rate, 480–483
　and revenue, 477–478
　and specialization, 732
　with trade, 733–735
　uses of, 102–103
　without trade, 732–733
Output decision, 457
Output mix, 508–509, 523
Output regulation, 578–579
Ozone layer, 595, 596

Pacific Gas and Electric, 591
Pan, Philip P., 612
Panasonic, 510–511
Paradox of thrift, 213
Parity, 620
Parker, Suzi, 494, 591
Par value, 687
Patents, 76, 525, 553
Pawlosky, Mark, 475
Payoff matrix, 545–546
Payroll taxes, 489, 704–705
Peablstein, Steven, 398–399
Peace dividend, 5
Peers, Martin, 429
Peña, Federico, 590
Pension funds, 295
Pentagon, 5, 165, 183, 412, 529, 684–685
Pentium 4 processor, 1
PepsiCo, 525, 526, 535, 542, 546, 551, 564, 569
Per capita Gross Domestic Product; *see* Gross Domestic Product per capita
Perfect competition, 475, 493–511
　barriers to entry, 496
　characteristics, 536
　compared to monopoly, 522–526
　competitive process, 506–510
　demand curves, 476–477
　determinants of supply, 487–490
　E-commerce, 490–491
　economic profit, 500
　entry and exit, 495
　in HDTV market, 510–511
　investment decision, 486–487, 495
　marginal cost pricing, 523

　market characteristics, 496
　market supply curve, 493–496
　microcomputers, 496–506
　output mix, 523
　price = marginal revenue, 480
　price takers, 476
　production decision, 477–479, 480–483
　productivity advances, 523
　profit-maximization rule, 479–485
　short-run supply curve, 488
　shutdown decision, 485–486
　structure, 476
　total profit, 484–485
　total revenue curve, 477–478
Personal computer, 503–504, 509
　industry, 566
　market, 506
　price decline, 50
Personal income, 105–106, **695**
Personal Responsibility and Work Opportunity Act, 341
Phantom unemployed, 118
Phillips, Alban W., 329n
Phillips, Michael M., 383
Phillips curve, 329–330
　shifts, 330–331
Physical capital investment, 357–359, 361–362
Pianin, Eric, 396
Piotrowski, John, 278
Pitt, Brad, 635
Plant and equipment, 101
Plant size options, 461–462
Players Association, 657
Play-or-pay concept, 341
Point elasticity of demand, 419n
Policy-induced business cycle, 404
Policy levers, 158; *see also* Government regulation
　crystal balls, 399
　design problems, 401
　economic record, 393–395
　fine-tuning, 393
　fiscal policy, 387–388
　and forecasts, 399–400
　goal conflicts, 396–397
　hands-off view, 406–407
　hands-on view, 408
　ideological uses, 390–393
　implementation problems, 401–402
　for inflation, 391
　leading indicators, 399
　measurement problems, 397–401
　modest expectations from, 408
　monetary policy, 388–389
　obstacles to success, 395–406
　and politics, 404–406
　for recession, 392–393
　schools of economists, 407
　for stagflation, 392–393
　supply-side policy, 389
　time lags, 402–404
Politics; *see also* Government *entries*
　of fiscal stimulus, 404–405
　of market power, 524
　of policy levers, 404–406
　pork barrel, 233
　role in economics, 17–18
　of tax cuts, 234
Pollution, 364–365; *see also* Environmental threat
Pollution abatement costs, 600–601
Pollution fines, 605
Pollution permits, 605–607
Poor nations
　education in, 34
　GDP, 29
　income shares, 40
Pope, Kyle, 566
Population growth, 1, 363–364, 366
　in U.S. 1900-2000, 29

Pork barrel politics, 233
Portfolio decision, 287–288, **299**
Portney, Paul R., 610
Poses, Fred, 400
Potential output, 10
Poverty, 695
Poverty gap, 716
Poverty lines, 716
Power plant monopolies, 590
Prakken, Joel, 398
Precautionary demand for money, 299
Predatory pricing, 553
Present discounted value, 676
Present value
   computing, 676–677
   interest rate effect, 677
   and uncertainty, 677–678
President of U. S., 652
Price(s)
   average, 130
   breakdown of costs, 571
   changes in, 645
   and competition, 511
   cross-subsidization, 585
   in deflation, 137–138
   disequilibrium, 65–66
   effect of unions, 669–670
   of environmental damage, 599
   equilibrium, 755
   falling, 204
   flexible, 152, 202
   and inflation, 77
   marginal revenue, 479–480
   and marginal utility, 430-431, 441–442
   market-clearing, 58–59
   with market power, 513–517
   monopolistic competition, 565–566
   monopoly, 520
   in multiplier process, 209
   of oligopoly, 547–548
   parity, 620
   and quantity, 416–417
   relative, 130
   relative to income, 422–423
   self-adjusting, 60–61
   and terms of trade, 737–739
   and total revenue, 424
Price, Elizabeth, 187
Price ceilings, 65
   shortage caused by, 65–66
Price changes
   in 2000, 133
   chain-weighted, 101–102
   in computing GDP, 98–101
   and demand curve, 51
   for energy, 64
   for personal computers, 50
   and supply curve, 56
   two centuries of, 142
   visible in inflation, 131–133
Price competition, 504, 586
Price controls, 129
Price discrimination, 524–525
Price-earnings ratio, 681
Price effect of inflation, 131–133
Price efficiency, 577
Price elasticity of demand, 417–419, **524, 616**
   computing, 419–421
   determinants, 422–423
   elastic versus inelastic, 420–421
   estimates, 421
   for food, 616
   and market power, 524
   time factor, 423
   and total revenue, 423–425
Price fixing, 550–551
Price increase, 544–545

Price index, chain-weighted, 101
Price leadership, 551–552
Price level
   aggregate supply, 161–162
   in base period, 138–139
   determinant of consumption, 179
   and inflation or deflation, 160
   target of fiscal stimulus, 221
Priceline.com, 52–53
Price of money, 299
Price-quantity relationship, 437
Price reduction, 542–543, 543–544
Price regulation, 585–586
Price signals, 12–13, 70, 508–509; *see also* Market signals
   flawed, 568
Price stability, 140–**141,** 548–550
   historical record, 142–144
   and new products, 141
   numerical goal, 141
   potential, 146–147
   and quality changes, 141
   unemployment concerns, 141
Price supports, 620, 621–622
Price takers, 476, 513–514
Price targets, 623–624
Price uncertainties, 136
Price wars, 509, 546
Priest, Dana, 9
Prisoner's dilemma, 546
Private charity, 77
Private costs, 602, 603
Private goods, 71
   overproduction of, 73
Private-sector unions, 661–662
Privatization of Social Security, 724–725
Procter and Gamble, 537, 556–557, 569
Prodigy, 497
Producer price indexes, 140
Product choice
   advertising expenditures, 433–434
   equilibrium outcomes, 433
   marginal utility versus price, 430–431
   opportunity costs, 430
   optimal consumption, 431–432
   utility-maximizing rule, 432–433
   utility maximization, 431–432
Product differentiation, 542, 563, 586
Production, 649
   capital-intensive, 34
   decline in 2001, 187
   externalities from, 37
   externalities in, 75
   labor-intensive, 34
   national comparisons, 27
   in U. S., 26–33
   with trade, 733–735
   without trade, 732–733
Production decision, 477–479, 480–483, **499, 519, 565**–**566, 600**
   computer industry, 498–499
   and environment, 599–600
   monopolistic competition, 563, 565–566
   by monopoly, 519–520
Production efficiency, 509, 577
Production externalities, 601–602
Production function, 444–**445**
   efficiency, 446–447
   and global competitiveness, 464–467
   and profit, 449–450
   short-run constraints, 447–448
   varying input levels, 445–446
Production inefficiency, 568
Production possibilities, 6–**11, 101, 114**–**115, 351, 732**–**733,** 736
Production possibilities curve, 7–8, 115
   basic decisions, 11–12
   and economic growth, 11, 114

   and efficiency, 9–10
   essential principles, 8
   increasing opportunity costs, 8
   and inefficiency, 10
   and international trade, 732–733
   and investment goods, 31–32
   and macro instability, 77
   and unemployment, 11
Production possibilities schedule, 7
Production stages, 97–98
Productivity, 33, 146, 356, 380–**381, 670**
   effect of unions, 670
   and global competitiveness, 464–467
   impact of income redistribution, 706–707
   of United States, 33–34
Productivity advances, 523
Productivity changes, 645
Productivity gains, 356, 357
Productivity turnaround, 356–357
Product market, 46–**47**
   monopolistic competition, 562
   oligopolies, 537, 538
   regulation of, 343–344
   and trade barriers, 344–345
Profit, 450, 470–**471, 479, 624**
   accounting versus economic, 471–475
   long-run, 567
   and market structure, 474–476
   monopoly, 520–521, 561
   normal, 474
   padded, 579
   and production function, 449–450
Profit effect, 161
Profit maximization, 514
   and market power, 514–517
   in oligopoly, 547–548
Profit-maximization rule, 479–**485, 481, 548**
Profit-maximizing rate of output, 520
Profit motive, 470–471, 495–496
Profit per unit, 500
Profit regulation, 577–578, 585–586
Profit-sharing bonuses, 668
Profit squeeze, 509–510
Profit taxes, 490
Progressive tax, 80, 137, 697–698
   loopholes, 700
Property tax, 489, 704, 823
Proportional tax, 81, 705
Protectionist measures; *see also* Trade barriers
   and dumping, 741
   export industries, 740
   for fixed exchange rates, 764–765
   import-competing industries, 740
   improving terms of trade, 742
   infant industry argument, 741–742
   microeconomic pressures, 739–740
   national security argument, 740–741
   for steel industry, 761
Public choice theory, 87
Public good, 71, 588
   free-rider dilemma, 71–72
   nonexcludability, 71
   underproduction of, 72–73
Public sector; *see also* Government *entries*
   balanced with private sector, 234
   government failure, 84–87
   government growth, 77–80
   and market failure, 70–77
   maximizing behavior, 45
   and public choice theory, 87
   spending, 78–80, 102
   taxation, 80–83
Public sector unions, 662
Purchasing power, 267

Quality deterioration, 578–579
Quality improvements, 141

Quality of life, 108–109
Quello, James C., 580
Quick, Rebecca, 383
Quintile distribution of personal income, 696
Quota-restricted trade, 745–746
Quotas, 621, 743–**744**
    compared to tariffs, 745–746
    on sugar imports, 747
    voluntary restraint agreements, 746

Race and unemployment, 116–117
Radio Shack, 498
Railroad Revitalization and Regulatory Reform Act, 583
Railroads, 582–583
Rational expectations, 407
Ratner, Sidney, 312
RC Draft, 542
Reagan, Ronald W., 14, 88, 172, 227, 249, 282, 336, 338
Reagan administration, 123, 171, 330, 742, 766
Real-balances effect, 160
Real GDP, 98, 140, 352
    in business cycles, 154–156
    changes in growth, 242
    decline in recessions, 156–157
Real income, 131–**133**
Real interest rate, 145, 312–314, **313**
Real versus **nominal GDP,** 97–101
Rebuild America program, 390
Recession, 156, 345–346
    costs of, 121
    and deregulation, 342–344
    easing trade barriers, 344–345
    in East Asia, 208
    effectiveness of monetary stimulus, 308–309
    Fed policies for, 319–321
    global, 400
    human capital investment, 340–342
    and investment demand, 306–307
    job loss in 1990-1991, 112
    and oil prices, 377
    policy levers, 390–391
    post-World War II, 156–157
    spillover effect, 188
    tax incentives, 334–340
    in 2001, 183, 374
Recessionary gap, 197
Recessionary GDP gap, 190, 191, **209,** 210, **220, 390**
Reciprocal Trade Agreements, 744
Recycling, 605, 608
Redistribution effect of inflation, 135
Refinancing, 251
Regressive tax, 81, 82, 704
Regulation, 575; see also Government regulation
Relative prices, 130, 422–423
Relative wages, 668–669
Replacement workers, 661
Required reserves, 270–271, **283**–**284**
Research and development, 359–360, 527
Reserve clause, 664
Reserve ratio, 270, 284–285
Reserve requirement, 283–285
    lowering, 292
    raising, 294
Resolution Trust Corporation, 279
Resource allocation, 685–686
Resource constraints, 364
Resource costs, 444, 446, 449–451
Resources for the Future, 610
Response lags, 617–618
Restaurant sales growth, 428
Restricted supply, 76
Retained earnings, 105, **680**
Retaliation, 541–543
Retirement age, 720
    national comparisons, 723

Revenue
    and output, 477–478
    production decision, 477–479
Revenue sharing, 83
Revolutionary War, 246–247, 312
Rhoads, Christopher, 371
Rich nations
    education in, 34
    income shares, 40
Ricks, Thomas E., 18
Riesman, David, 413
Risk, 474, 675, 681–682
Risk management, 675
Risk premium, 675
Robinson, Joan, 233, 315n
Rolling Stones, 698, 699
Romer, Christine, 403
Romer, Paul, 359, 403
Roosevelt, Franklin D., 14, 87, 140, 151, 171–172, 234, 244, 395, 621
Rosen, Harvey, 336
Roy, Stuart D., 343
Royal Caribbean Cruises, 605
Royal Crown, 542
Rule of 72, 355
Rumsfeld, Donald H., 18
Russia, 14
    barter economy, 263
    hyperinflation, 137
    military spending, 9
    Moscow McDonald's, 633
    sable monopoly, 517

Sales tactics, 541
Sales tax, 704, 823
Samba effect, 768
Samsung Electronics Company, 400
Samuelson, Paul A., 320, 329
Sanchez, Rene, 44n
Sandberg, Jared, 497
Saphir, Ann, 167
Sarmiento, Sergio, 135
Saving, 106, 176, 177, **338**
    average propensity, 178
    by businesses, 359
    and consumption, 176–177
    crisis in Japan, 213
    effect of tax cuts, 225
    and financial markets, 674
    by households, 359
    impact of tax increases, 231
    incentives, 338–339, 361
    interest rate, 675
    and investment rate, 358
    as leakage, 199–201, 277
    marginal propensity, **178**
    risk, 675
    tax incentives, 703
    time preferences, 675
Saving rate, 41
Savings accounts, 266
Savings and loan associations, 268
Savings and loan crisis, 278
Savings Association Insurance Fund, 279
Say, Jean-Baptiste, 152
Say's Law, 152, 153
Scarcity, 4–6
    and limits to growth, 5
    and opportunity costs, 5–6
    and production possibilities curve, 8
Scarf, Herbert, 421
Schacht, Henry, 207
Schimberg, Henry A., Jr., 546
Schlesinger, Jacob M., 213, 392
Schneider, Greg, 529
School vouchers, 341
Schroeder, William, 295

Schumpeter, Joseph, 5
Sears, 295
Seasonal unemployment, 120
Seattle protests of 1999, 749
Secondary deposits, 270
Secondary trading, 681–682
Second crisis of economic theory, 233–234
Second-hand smoke, 74
Self-adjustment, 198–215
    and aggregate demand, 191–192
    by business investment, 201–202
    and fiscal policy, 171
    by flexible prices, 202
    to inflationary GDP gap, 211–212
    Keynesian, 198, 208
    in long run, 169–170
    multiplier process, 201–208
Self-adjusting prices, 60–61
Self-regulating economy, 152
Sellers, number of, 55–56
Sequential aggregate demand shifts, 208–209
Service Corporation International, 463, 464
Service economy, 30–31
Service exports, 730
Service jobs, 125–126
Services, 29–30
Service trade, 731
Set-asides, 620
Shadow Open Market Committee, 311
Shannon, David A., 152n
Shared ownership, 679
Shareholders, 679–680
Sherman Antitrust Act, 531, 532, 556
Shift in demand, 51–53, 61, 425, **426**–**427**
    versus movements in demand, 52–53
Shift in supply, 56–57, 61–62
Shifts, 23–24
Shifts in aggregate demand, 183–185
Shifts in consumption function, 182–185
Shifts of investment, 186–188
Shortages, 59–60
    caused by price ceilings, 65–66
Short run, 447, 460, **478, 486**
Short-run competitive equilibrium, 502–**503**
Short-run instability
    demand-side theories, 166–167
    eclectic explanations, 168
    monetarist theory, 167–168
    supply-side theories, 168
Short-run production function, 447–448
Short-run supply curve, 488–489
Short-term interest rates, 305–305, 314
Shoven, John, 421
Shutdown decision, 485–486, 505
Shutdown point, 486, 505
Sicher, John, 542
Silk, Leonard, 108n
Simon, Julian, 364, 365, 367
Sims, G. Thomas, 293, 371
Sinai, Allen, 398
Singapore, 13
Sinopoli, P. J., 433
Sixteenth Amendment, 80, 218
Size distribution of income, 695–697
Skilled workers, 361
Skills gap, 125–**127,** 340–341
Slater, Rodney E., 553
Sloan, Allan, 304
Slopes, 23
Small business, 203
Smart cars, 347
Smith, Adam, 12, 14, 19, 58–59, 535
Smith, Elliot Blair, 165
Smog, 596
Smoking, 421
Smoot-Hawley Tariff Act, 743, 744
Snack food industry, 554
Social costs, 602

Social demand curve, 74–75
Social insurance programs, 714
Social regulation, 581
Social Security, 714
    adjusted for inflation, 241
    aging population, 723
    declining labor supply, 722–724
    declining tax base, 725
    deficits, 257–258
    earnings test, 721, 724
    economic costs, 724
    finances of, 720
    indexing benefits, 144
    intergenerational redistribution, 724
    privatization proposal, 724–725
    progressive benefits, 720–721
    program features, 720–721
    retirement age, 720
    wage replacement rate, 721
    work disincentive, 721–722
    work test, 721–722, 724
Social Security taxes, 81, 105–106, 489, 704–705
Social Security Trust Fund, 257–258
Social tensions, 135–136
Social welfare, 108–109
Sociopsychiatric explanation of demand, 413
Sorensen, Charles E., 513n
Soft drink market, 542, 569
Sohn, Sung Won, 400
Solid-waste pollution, 598–599
Solow, Robert M., 329, 365
Soltow, James H., 312
Sony Corporation, 535, 753
Sophocles, 262
Sotheby's, 551
Southwest Airlines, 586, 588
Soviet Union, 517
Soy sauce index, 402
Spanish-American War, 248
Spears, Britney, 637
Specialization, 380–381, 732
    and exchange, 45
Speculation, 137, 759, 766–767
Speculative demand for money, 299–300
Spending
    aggregate demand shifts in, 207–208
    by consumers, 213–214
    at full-employment output, 196–197
Spillover effect, 188
Spurrier, Steve, 644
Stagflation, 326–327, 392
    policy levers, 392–393
Staggers Rail Act, 583
Stalin, Josef, 155
Standard and Poor's 500 Index, 686
Standard of value, 264
Standard Oil case, 531, 557
Starbuck's, 561, 562
Start-up company, 680
Starwood Hotels and Resorts, 205
State and local government
    growth, 79–80
    purchases, 78
    revenues, 82–83
    services, 32
State and local taxes, 703–704
Steel exports, 741
Steel industry, 761–762
Steiner, Brandon, 433
Stern, Laurence, 151
Stevens, C. R., 527
Sticky prices, 548–550
Stock market
    booms and busts, 684
    changing expectations, 682–683
    corporate stock, 679–680
    crash of 1929, 150, 151
    crash of 1987, 381

    decline in 2001, 185
    dividends, 679–680
    fluctuations in, 682–686
    initial public offering, 680
    resource allocation, 685–686
    secondary trading, 681–682
    shocks to, 685
    stock quotes, 683
    stock returns, 679–680
    value of information, 683–684
Stock market indexes, 686
Stock quotes, 683
Stock returns, 679–680
Stoewahse, Dorothee, 699
Stoll, John, 522
Stoops, Bob, 644
Store of value, 263
Strauss, Gary, /652
Strikes, 655, 661, 667
Structural deficits, 243–244, 388
Structural unemployment, 121–122, 340
    changes in, 123
    skills gap, 126–127
Subsidies, 577, 626–627
    and market supply, 55–56
Substitute goods, 51, 428–429, 536
    availability of, 422
Substitution effect of wages, 635–636
Sugar import quotas, 747
Sulfur dioxide emissions, 596
Sullivan, Kevin, 9, 402
Sun Microsystems, 185
Superior Bank failure, 278
Suplee, Curt, 597
Supply, 47, 55–57
    abrupt shifts in, 617–618
    decreased, 65
    determinants of, 487–490
    of dollars, 753–754
    restricted by market power, 76
    restrictions, 620–621
    shift in, 56–57, 61–62, 504–505
    tax effects, 489–490
    tax elasticity of, 337–338
    tax-induced shifts in, 489
Supply and demand
    causes of inflation, 144
    equilibrium, 57–62
    and market failure, 70
    market outcomes, 62–64
    prospects for energy, 64–66
    Say's Law, 152
Supply curve, 56, 488–489, 754
    shifts in, 56–57
Supply-side economists, 407
Supply-side policy, 171, 389-390
    aggregate supply, 326–334
    deregulation, 342–344
    easing trade barriers, 344–345
    and expectations, 346
    human capital investment, 340–342
    infrastructure development, 345–346
    milestones, 390
    short-run options, 336–348
    tax incentives, 334–340
Supply-side shocks, 331–333
Supply-side theories, 168
Surplus, 59–60
Swisher, Kara, 633
Swissair, 205
Swoboda, Frank, 533
Sylla, Richard, 312

T-account, 271
Taiwan, 208
Tandy Corporation, 498
Tannenbaum, Carl, 400

Target efficiency, 714
Target prices, 623–624
Tariff, 743
    compared to quotas, 745–746
Tariff-restricted trade, 745
Taste, 51
Taxable income, 700–701
Taxation
    bracket creep, 137
    corporate taxes, 105
    costs/benefits of greater equality, 706–707
    determinant of consumption, 179
    effect on consumption, 224–226
    efficiency concerns, 698–699
    equity concerns, 699–701
    fairness issue, 706–707
    federal income tax, 80-82, 697–703
    flat tax, 708–710
    and government spending, 218–220
    horizontal equity principle, 700
    impact of transfer payments, 705–706
    indirect business, 104
    and inequality, 705–706
    and investment, 226–228
    investment tax credit, 339
    as leakage, 200
    marginal tax rate, 334–340, 697-698
    and market supply, 55–56
    payroll taxes, 489, 704-705
    primary purpose, 80
    profit taxes, 490
    progressive tax, 80, 697–698
    property tax, 489, 704
    proportional, 81, 705
    regressive, 81, 704
    sales tax, 704
    state and local, 82, 703–704
    tax cuts of 2001, 702–703
    tax elasticity, 698–699
    tax-induced misallocations, 701
    for transfer payments, 77, 712–713
    in United Kingdom, 699
    vertical equity principle, 700
    worsening economic outcomes, 15
Tax base, 701
    declining, 725
Tax breaks, 41
Tax cut multiplier, 225–226
Tax cuts, 171, 223–226, 247, 338
    in recession of 2001, 234
Tax elasticity of labor supply, 719
Tax elasticity of supply, 337–338, 698–699
Tax Equity and Fiscal Responsibility Act of 1982, 231
Tax incentives, 334–340
Tax incidence, 704
Tax-induced misallocations, 701
Tax-induced supply shifts, 489–490
Taxpayer Relief Act of 1997, 389–390
Tax rebates, 336
Tax Reform Act of 1986, 701–702
Tax Relief Act of 2001, 703
Taylor, Lester D., 421
Teachers Insurance and Annuity Association, 295
Teaching assistants, 663
Teamsters Union, 656
Technological advance, 36, 616
Technology
    and investment decisions, 186
    market supply and costs of, 55–56
Technomic Inc., 428
Teenagers
    affluent, 414
    increased unemployment, 123
    smokers, 421
    unemployment, 122
Telecommunications Act of 1996, 584, 589
Telecommunications industry, 584
Telephone industry, 536, 583–584

Temple-Easton, Dina, 185
Temporary Assistance to Needy Families, 715–716, 720
Tengs, Tommy O., 611
Terms of trade, 737
    improving, 742
    limits to, 737
    role of prices and markets, 737–739
Terrorist attack of 2001, 5, 165, 183, 187, 198, 212, 223, 238, 306–307, 333, 370–371, 387, 400–401, 412
    and airline security, 588
    economic aftermath, 205
    and farm subsidies, 741
    response to, 89
    and stock market, 684–685
    tax stimulus package, 703
Terrorists, war against, 295
Texas Instruments, 504, 505, 506
Textron, 205
Thatcher, Margaret, 623
Theory versus reality, 17
Thermal pollution, 598
Thompson, Tommy, 63
3Com, 207
Time, and price elasticity, 423
Time horizon
    with deflation, 137–138
    shortened, 137
Time lags, 232–233, 402–404
Time preferences, 675
Time value of money, 676–677
Tobacco Trust, 557
Total cost, 452–453, 458, 479
Total profit, 484–485
Total revenue, 423–425, 424, 477–478, 479
Total utility, 415
Total wages paid, 658–659
Tradable pollution permits, 605–607
Trade balances, 730–731
Trade barriers, 344–345, 743–748
    comparative effects, 744–746
    embargoes, 742–743
    versus free-trade pacts, 748–750
    nontariff, 746–748
    protectionist measures, 739–742
    quotas, 743–744
    tariffs, 743
    voluntary restraint agreements, 746
Trade deficit, 375–376, **731**, 755–757, 761–762
Trade imbalances, 375–376
Trade policy, 171
Trade surplus, 375, 376, **731**
Training, 555–556
Transaction account, 265–266
Transactions demand for money, 299
Transfer payments, 32, 77, 341, **712**, 712–725
    cash versus in-kind, 713
    doubtful merits of, 86
    goals, 714–715
    impact on taxes, 705–706
    major programs, 712–715
    and market failure, 714–715
    means-tested, 714
    opportunity cost, 252–253
    reduced, 231–232
    social insurance versus welfare, 714
    Social Security, 720–724
    target efficiency of, 714
    and unemployment, 123, 341–342
    unintended consequences, 715
    welfare programs, 714–720
    and WHAT to produce, 715
    worsening economic outcomes, 15
Transfer payments increasing, 228
Transportation costs, 343
Transportation Equity Act of 2000, 347, 390
Transportation system, 347
Trash separation, 608
Trastour, Jean-Paul, 63

Treasury bonds, 247
    held by government agencies, 250
Treasury Department, Financial Crimes Enforcement Network, 295
Trujillo, Ron, 463
Tuition increases, 132
Turner Broadcasting System, 530
Tyler, Alleamer, 494, 495

Ukraine, 741
Uncertainty, 136, 677–678
Underemployment, 117–118
Underground economy, 96, 97
Undesired equilibrium, 163–164, 189–190
Undesired inventory, 203
Unemployment, 11, **77, 115.** see also Inflation-unemployment trade-off; Natural rate of unemployment; Phillips curve
    aftermath of terrorist attacks, 205
    Congressional targets, 124
    cyclical, 122–123, 190
    discouraged workers, 117
    displaced workers, 126
    duration of, 117
    easing trade barriers, 344–345
    frictional, 120–121
    health hazard, 120
    human cost, 118–120, 121
    with inadequate aggregate demand, 166–167
    and inflation, 153
    layoffs in recession of 2001, 207
    measures of, 115–118
    misery index, 330, 333
    monetarist policy, 315
    natural, 211
    natural rate of, 124
    Okun's law, 115
    phantom unemployed, 118
    Phillips curve, 329–330
    and price stability, 141
    race, gender, and education factors, 116–117
    reasons for, 117
    in recession of 1990-1991, 112
    skills gap, 125–127
    and stagflation, 326–327
    structural, 121–122, 123, 126–127, 340
    and underemployment, 117–118
Unemployment benefits, 119
Unemployment-inflation trade-off, 209–211
Unemployment insurance, 241
Unemployment rate, 116–117
    in Europe, 119
    historical record, 125
    increase in late 2000, 125
    natural, 311–312
    record 1900-2000, 122
    seasonal variations, 120n
Unionization rate, 661–662, 670
Union shop, 660
United Airlines, 559, 586
United Auto Workers, 655, 657, 661, 667, 668
United Farm Workers, 661
United Nations Human Development Index, 109, 111
United States, 3–4
    balance of payments 1950-1973, 764
    business cycles 1930-2000, 154, 155
    capital stock, 34
    comparative advantage, 32–33
    consumer goods and services, 31
    consumption and income, 176–177
    decline of social health, 109
    economy of, 26–42
    export ratios, 730
    exports and imports, 33
    factor mobility, 35–36
    farmer protests, 742
    farm policy, 619–624

    first farm depression, 618–619
    future prospects, 64–67
    government services, 32
    GDP, 26–27, 28-29, 167
    human capital, 3–35
    impact on Asian economies, 208
    income distribution, 38–40
    inflation in, 129
    investment goods and services, 31–32
    labor force in 2000, 112
    market freedom, 36
    mix of output, 29–32
    and NAFTA, 749
    net debtor, 762
    net exports, 32
    output and population growth, 29
    per capital GDP, 27–28
    price stability, 142–144
    production in, 26–33
    production patterns, 30–31
    productivity, 33–34
    prospects for, 41
    role of government, 36–38
    second farm depression, 624–625
    small employers, 203
    sugar quotas, 747
    technology advances, 36
    trade patterns, 728–731
    trade policies in 1930s, 744
    trading partners, 729
    voluntary restraint agreements, 746
United States Congress, 233
United States Constitution
    Article 1, 218
    Sixteenth Amendment, 218
United States Textile Producers, 745
Unit labor costs, 465, 466, 467
Universal Manufacturing Corporation, 527
Unreported income, 96
Unstable equilibrium, 190–191
USAirways, 205, 559, 587
User charges, 83
User fees, 605
Utility, 415
Utility maximization, 45, 431–432, 439–442
Utility-maximizing rule, 432–433
Utility theory, 415–416
U2 concert tickets, 60, 61

Value added, 96–97
Variable costs, 452–453, 458, **478–479**
Variables, 21
Velge, Baodouin, 371
Velocity of money, 309–310, 316–317, 318, **391**
Venture capitalists, 689–690
VentureWire, 690
Vertical equity, 700
Vest, Charles, 551
Vietnam War, 402–403
Virgin Atlantic, 205
Volatile investment spending, 187
Volcker, Paul, 319–320, 408
Voluntary restraint agreement, 746
Voting mechanism, 86

Wage rate, 638, 639, 640, 644–645
    equilibrium, 646, 656
    flexible, 152
    income effect, 635–636
    during inflation, 134
    and labor supply, 635
    and labor supply curve, 659–660
    marginal, 658–659
    marginal factor cost, 664–665
    market, 658–659
    minimum wage, 646–648

Wage rate (*cont.*)
   and payroll taxes, 705
   relative, 668–669
   substitution effect, 635–636
   union objective, 657
Wage replacement rate, 721
Wagner Act, 661
Walker, Tom, 684
Wal-Mart, 656
Walsh, Bill, 590
Walt Disney Company, 308, 632, 650–653
Wants, 434–435
War against terrorism, 89
Ward, Michael, 421
Warner, Lloyd, 413
War of 1912, 247
War on Poverty, 87–88
Warren, Earl, 557
Warshaw, Steven, 332
Washington, George, 312
Waste treatment plants, 598
Water pollution, 597–598
Water Quality Act, 365
Wealth, 695
   determinant of consumption, 179
Wealth effect, 134, **179–180,** 184, 185
Wealth of Nations (Smith), 12
Weidenbaum, Murray, 392
Weisman, Jonathan, 247
Welch, Jack, 652
Welch, William M., 405
Welfare benefits, 241

Welfare programs, 695, **714**
   benefit determination, 716
   benefit formula, 717–718
   breakeven level of income, 719
   incentives versus costs, 718–720
   and marginal tax rate, 717, 718–720
   means-tested, 714
   moral hazard, 717
   reforms of 1996, 720
   Temporary Assistance to Needy Families, 715–716, 720
   time limits, 720
   work (dis)incentives, 715, 716–717, 717–718
Welfare reform, 341
Wells Fargo Bank, 208
Wessel, David, 285
Western Power Trading Forum, 66
Westinghouse, 550
WHAT to produce, 11–12
   core issue, 3, 11–12
   impact of deficit financing, 253
   marginal cost pricing, 509
   market outcomes, 62–64
   mechanisms of choice, 12–23
   and transfer payments, 715
   in U. S. economy, 26–33
When to produce, 11–12
White, Alan, 308
White Gregory L., 461
Wieberg, Steve, 644
Wildavsky, Ben, 663
Wilson, Woodrow, 282

Wine Equity Act, 739
Women, increased unemployment, 123
Wonacott, Peter, 224
Woods, Tiger, 632
Woodyard, Chris, 590
Work disincentive, 721–722
Worker-retiree ratio, 257
Worker training, 340–341
Work incentive problem, 715, 716–717
Workplace safety, 342–343
Work rules, 670
Work test, 721–722
WorldCom, 475
World Trade Center, 5, 165, 183, 370, 412, 684–685
World Trade Organization, 344, 748–749
World War I, 248
World War II, 155, 248
Wozniak, Steve, 498, 689

Yanus, Chuck, 185
Yield, 289
Yield to maturity, 290
Yoder, Stephen Kreider, 527
Young, Don, 509

Zarnowitz, Victor, 408
Zero-coupon bonds, 290
Zero economic profit, 502, 509
Zero percent inflation goal, 129
Zero-profit equilibrium, 567–568
Zero profits, 495–496

CONSUMER PRICE INDEX, 1925–2000 (1982–84 = 100)

Year	Index (all items)	Percent Change
1925	17.5	3.5
1926	17.7	−1.1
1927	17.4	−2.3
1928	17.1	−1.2
1929	17.1	0.6
1930	16.7	−6.4
1931	15.2	−9.3
1932	13.7	−10.3
1933	13.0	0.8
1934	13.4	1.5
1935	13.7	3.0
1936	13.9	1.4
1937	14.4	2.9
1938	14.1	−2.8
1939	13.9	0.0
1940	14.0	0.7
1941	14.7	9.9
1942	16.3	9.0
1943	17.3	3.0
1944	17.6	2.3
1945	18.0	2.2
1946	19.5	18.1
1947	22.3	8.8
1948	24.1	3.0
1949	23.8	−2.1
1950	24.1	5.9
1951	26.0	6.0
1952	26.5	0.8
1953	26.7	0.7
1954	26.9	−0.7
1955	26.8	0.4
1956	27.2	3.0
1957	28.1	2.9
1958	28.9	1.8
1959	29.1	1.7
1960	29.6	1.4
1961	29.9	0.7
1962	30.2	1.3
1963	30.6	1.6
1964	31.0	1.0
1965	31.5	1.9
1966	32.4	3.5
1967	33.4	3.0
1968	34.8	4.7
1969	36.7	6.2
1970	38.8	5.6
1971	40.5	3.3
1972	41.8	3.4
1973	44.4	8.7
1974	49.3	12.3
1975	53.8	6.9
1976	56.9	4.9
1977	60.6	6.7
1978	65.2	9.0
1979	72.6	13.3
1980	82.4	12.5
1981	90.9	8.9
1982	96.5	3.8
1983	99.6	3.8
1984	103.9	3.9
1985	107.6	3.8
1986	109.6	1.1
1987	113.6	4.4
1988	118.3	4.6
1989	124.0	4.6
1990	130.7	6.1
1991	136.2	3.1
1992	140.3	2.9
1993	144.5	2.7

CONSUMER PRICE INDEX, 1925–2000 (continued)

Year	Index (all items)	Percent Change
1994	148.2	2.7
1995	152.4	2.5
1996	156.9	3.3
1997	160.5	1.7
1998	163.0	1.6
1999	166.6	2.7
2000	172.8	3.4

Note: Data beginning 1978 are for all urban consumers; earlier data are for urban wage earners and clerical workers.

Source: U.S. Department of Labor, Bureau of Statistics.

CHAIN-WEIGHTED PRICE DEFLATORS FOR GROSS DOMESTIC PRODUCT, 1959–2000 (1996 = 100)

Year	Index (all items)	Percent Change
1959	21.9	1.1
1960	22.2	1.4
1961	22.4	1.1
1962	22.7	1.4
1963	23.0	1.1
1964	23.3	1.5
1965	23.8	1.9
1966	24.4	2.8
1967	25.2	3.1
1968	26.3	4.3
1969	27.6	4.9
1970	29.1	5.3
1971	30.5	5.0
1972	31.8	4.2
1973	33.6	5.6
1974	36.6	9.0
1975	40.0	9.4
1976	42.3	5.7
1977	45.0	6.4
1978	48.2	7.1
1979	52.2	8.3
1980	57.1	9.2
1981	62.4	9.3
1982	66.3	6.2
1983	68.9	3.9
1984	71.4	3.7
1985	73.7	3.2
1986	75.3	2.2
1987	77.6	3.0
1988	80.2	3.4
1989	83.3	3.8
1990	86.5	3.9
1991	89.7	3.6
1992	91.9	2.4
1993	94.0	2.4
1994	96.0	2.1
1995	98.1	2.2
1996	100.0	1.9
1997	101.9	1.9
1998	163.2	1.3
1999	104.8	1.5
2000	107.0	2.1

Source: U.S. Department of Commerce, Bureau of Economic Analysis.

INTEREST RATES, 1929–2000 (percent per annum)

Year	Prime Rate Charged by Banks	Discount Rate, Federal Reserve Bank of New York
1929	5.50–6.00	5.16
1933	1.50–4.00	2.56
1939	1.50	1.00
1940	1.50	1.00
1941	1.50	1.00
1942	1.50	1.00
1943	1.50	1.00
1944	1.50	1.00
1945	1.50	1.00
1946	1.50	1.00
1947	1.50–1.75	1.00
1948	1.75–2.00	1.34
1949	2.00	1.50
1950	2.07	1.59
1951	2.56	1.75
1952	3.00	1.75
1953	3.17	1.99
1954	3.05	1.60
1955	3.16	1.89
1956	3.77	2.77
1957	4.20	3.12
1958	3.83	2.15
1959	4.48	3.36
1960	4.82	3.53
1961	4.50	3.00
1962	4.50	3.00
1963	4.50	3.23
1964	4.50	3.55
1965	4.54	4.04
1966	5.63	4.50
1967	5.61	4.19
1968	6.30	5.16
1969	7.96	5.87
1970	7.91	5.95
1971	5.72	4.88
1972	5.25	4.50
1973	8.03	6.44
1974	10.81	7.83
1975	7.86	6.25
1976	6.84	5.50
1977	6.83	5.46
1978	9.06	7.46
1979	12.67	10.28
1980	15.27	11.77
1981	18.87	13.42
1982	14.86	11.02
1983	10.79	8.50
1984	12.04	8.80
1985	9.93	7.69
1986	8.83	6.33
1987	8.21	5.66
1988	9.32	6.20
1989	10.87	6.93
1990	10.01	6.98
1991	8.46	5.45
1992	6.25	3.25
1993	6.00	3.00
1994	7.15	3.60
1995	8.83	5.21
1996	8.27	5.02
1997	8.44	5.00
1998	8.35	4.92
1999	8.00	4.62
2000	9.23	5.73

Source: Board of Governors of the Federal Reserve System.